Strategic Marketing

Tenth Edition

David W. Cravens
M.J. Neeley School of Business
Texas Christian University

Nigel F. Piercy
Warwick Business School
The University of Warwick

McGraw Hill Education

STRATEGIC MARKETING, TENTH EDITION
International Edition 2013

10 09 08 07 06 05 04
20 15 14
CTP SLP

When ordering this title, use ISBN 978-007-132623-0 or MHID 007-132623-5

Printed in Singapore

www.mhhe.com

To Sue and Karen

DWC

To the memory of Helena G. Piercy
(1911–2001)

NFP

Preface

Executives in companies around the world are confronted with unprecedented strategic marketing challenges and exciting opportunities as we advance into the second decade of the 21st century. Driven by demanding customers with complex value requirements, aggressive global competition, turbulent markets, rapid emergence of disruptive new technologies, and global expansion initiatives, strategic marketing has become an enterprise-spanning responsibility with major bottom-line implications. Central to the opportunities generated by these challenges is a critical need to improve executives' understanding of markets and competitive space, customer value delivery, ethical behavior and social imperatives, innovation culture and processes, and effective organizational design and processes.

Strategic marketing's demanding role in business performance is demonstrated in the market-driven strategies of successful organizations competing in a wide array of market and competitive situations. Superior customer value, leveraging distinctive capabilities, responding rapidly to diversity and change in the marketplace, developing innovation cultures, and recognizing global business challenges are demanding initiatives which require effective marketing strategies for gaining and sustaining a competitive edge. *Strategic Marketing* examines the underlying logic and processes for designing and implementing market-driven strategies.

Market-Driven Strategy

Delivering superior value to customers is the core objective of market-driven strategy. Several initiatives are necessary in achieving this objective.

- Marketing strategy provides the guidelines for action that are essential in providing superior customer value.

- Marketing is a major stakeholder in the essential organizational core processes—new product development, customer relationship management, value/supply-chain management, and business strategy implementation.

- Essential relationship initiatives place new priorities on collaborating with customers, suppliers, value-chain members, and even competitors.

- Understanding customers, competitors, and the market environment requires the active involvement of the entire organization to gain and manage market knowledge decisively.

- Developing methods that enable the organization to continually learn from customers, competitors, and other relevant sources is vital to sustaining a competitive edge.

- The powerful technologies provided by the Internet, corporate intranets, and advanced communication and collaboration systems for customer and supplier relationship management underpin effective strategy processes.

- The environmental, ethical, and corporate responsibility aspects of business practice are critical concerns for individual executives as well as their companies, requiring management direction and active involvement by the entire organization.

Customer diversity and new forms of competition create impressive growth and performance opportunities for organizations that successfully apply strategic marketing concepts and analyses in business strategy development and implementation. The challenge to become market-driven is apparent in a wide array of industries around the world. Analyzing market behavior and matching strategies to changing conditions require a hands-on approach to marketing strategy development and implementation. Penetrating financial analysis is an important strategic marketing requirement.

Strategic Marketing examines marketing strategy using a combination of concepts, application processes, and cases to develop managers' and professionals' decision making processes and apply them to business situations. The book is intended for use in undergraduate capstone marketing strategy courses and the MBA marketing core and advanced strategy courses.

New and Expanded Scope

Regardless of business size and scope, competing in any market today demands a global perspective. The tenth edition accentuates this global perspective. The author team provides an extensive range of global involvement. The shrinking time-and-access boundaries of global markets establish new competitive requirements. The global dimensions of marketing strategy are integrated throughout the chapters of the book and also considered in several cases. The rapid emergence of powerful new competitive forces throughout the world, often facilitated by new business models, mandates an international viewpoint for executives in most organizations.

Strategic customer management coverage is significantly expanded to address customer relationship management (CRM) systems, ethics, and social responsibility, recognizing the escalating importance of these topics in business firms and their essential role in guiding marketing strategy. Customer equity and customer lifetime value are examined along with other relevant aspects of CRM. Ethical standards and corporate social responsibility initiatives are closely tied to customer relationships. Strategic social responsibility initiatives can have important impact on customer value and effective relationships. This important coverage is new to the tenth edition.

Innovation and new-product planning and strategic brand management have received expanded coverage in this edition. Enhancing brand equity has become a top priority challenge in companies around the world.

Internet initiatives comprise a rapidly expanding vital part of the marketing strategies of all companies. Internet strategies are rapidly increasing on a global basis. Because of the nature and scope of the various uses of the Internet, we have integrated this important topic into several chapters rather than developing a separate chapter. Internet Applications are included in all chapters.

Expanded attention and emphasis are given to marketing metrics throughout the book. Improving the measurement of marketing effectiveness is a high priority issue in a wide range of companies around the world.

New applications of business marketing initiatives are included in every chapter. These examples from marketing practice examine strategy, innovations, relationships, global ethics and corporate responsibility, Internet, and metrics aspects of business operations.

Teaching and Learning Process

Strategic Marketing employs a decision-making process to examine the key concepts and application issues involved in analyzing and selecting strategies. It is apparent that many instructors want to examine marketing strategy beyond the traditional emphasis on marketing functions. Marketing strategy is considered from a total business perspective. The length and design of the book offer flexibility in the use of the text material and cases. The applications included in each chapter can be used for class discussion and assignments.

The book is designed around the marketing strategy process with a clear emphasis on analysis, planning, and implementation. Part I provides an overview of market-driven strategy and business and marketing strategies. Part II considers markets, segments, customer relationships, and market sensing and learning processes. Part III provides the foundation for designing market-driven strategies. Part IV considers market-driven program development. Finally, Part V examines organization design and implementing and managing market-driven strategies. Decision process guidelines and applications are provided throughout the book to assist the reader in applying the analysis and strategy development approaches discussed in the text.

The Cases

There are 10 new cases out of a total of 20. Many are well-known companies that students should find both interesting and challenging. These cases are useful in applying the concepts and methods discussed in the chapters, and they can be used for class discussion, hand-in assignments, and/or class presentations. The cases consider a wide variety of business environments, both domestic and international. They include goods and services; organizations at different value-chain levels; and small, medium, and large enterprises. The Applications in every chapter provide additional illustrations and material for consideration and discussion.

Most of the cases examine the marketing and business strategies of well-known companies. Many of the cases are very timely, offering an interesting and challenging look at contemporary business practice. Certain cases with earlier dates are included because they involve important applications. Obtaining a set of cases covering a relevant range of applications all with current dates is not feasible. Many of the companies have available extensive financial, product, and corporate information on the Internet, which expands analysis opportunities.

The comprehensive cases offer students a variety of opportunities to apply marketing strategy concepts. Each case considers several important strategy issues. The cases represent different competitive situations for consumer and business goods and services as well as domestic and international markets.

Changes in the Tenth Edition

Reaching the tenth edition of the book is an important milestone, and the authors are delighted to have reached this point in the evolution of the book. In this new edition, we have endeavored throughout to provide provocative new examples and applications to stimulate readers, while at the same retaining the underlying structure of the book. Accordingly, the tenth edition of *Strategic Marketing* follows the basic design of previous editions. Nevertheless, the revision incorporates many significant changes, topic additions, and updated examples. Every chapter includes new material and expanded treatment of important topics.

Each chapter has been revised to incorporate new concepts and examples, improve readability and flow, and encourage reader interest and involvement. Topical coverage has been expanded (or reduced) where appropriate, to better position the book for teaching and learning in today's rapidly changing business environment. An expanded set of applications is included at the end of each chapter. Marketing planning guidelines are provided in the Chapter 1 Appendix, financial analysis suggestions are included in the Chapter 2 Appendix, and marketing metrics proposals are given in the Chapter 15 Appendix. The short case vignettes in each chapter, which were titled Features in the last edition have been called Applications in the new edition to emphasize their relevance to the reader. Specific and detailed changes for the new tenth edition compared to the last edition are summarized below.

Chapter 1: New Challenges for Market-Driven Strategy—The introductory chapter has been updated throughout and we emphasize new influences on marketing thought development. We have updated applications on Tesco International, Blackberry, emerging market competition, and new applications concerning cloud computing and one focused on marketing in the network organization. The supporting examples and literature have been updated, while the underlying structure of the chapter remains constant.

Chapter 2: Markets and Competitive Space—This chapter has been updated in its supporting literature and examples. We have added a new application concerning the Flip video camera, and the e-Bay application has been extensively updated, and updates have been added to other applications. We have added new examples and commentary to recognize the impact of disruptive innovation in the music business, strategic transformation in the steel industry, and the impact of economic recession on marketing strategy. The underlying structure of the chapter remains the same as the last edition.

Chapter 3: Strategic Market Segmentation—Here we introduce new material on market granularity and micro-trends to support the conventional logic for market segmentation, and we update the supporting examples and literature throughout the chapter. We introduce new applications concerning new lifestyle segments for luxury hotels, the core customer focus at Wal-Mart, and one examining the Web strategy for the Harry Potter books. The BMW Mini application has been updated, along with the ethics application related to targeting children with marketing efforts. Overall, the chapter structure remains close to that in the last edition.

Chapter 4: Strategic Customer Management: Systems, Ethics, and Corporate Social Responsibility—In this chapter, we have updated our coverage of strategic customer relationship management. The major change from the last edition is the addition of a substantial new section concerned with ethics and corporate social responsibility (CSR). These topics are linked to corporate reputation and customer value. We examine ethical imperatives and their impact on customer relationships. We have expanded coverage of corporate social responsibility, encompassing the drivers of CSR, and company defensive and strategic moves toward creating shared value. These topics are very topical and relevant to strategic marketing decisions. We include here new applications examining CSR at Unilever, and new environmentally responsible business models in the transportation sector. The new material is supported by new company examples and literature.

Chapter 5: Capabilities for Learning About Customers and Markets—In addition to updating the examples and supporting literature throughout this chapter, we have added new material here emphasizing strategic agility and the interpretation of information in building learning capabilities. There is new material added on Internet-based marketing research and an extended application concerning Internet-based information resources. We have added a new applications concerning Black Swan logic, the search for market insights, and one examining cultural anthropology and customer understanding. There is also a new application added concerning customer feedback through social media. The application concerning customer knowledge at Best Buy has been extensively updated. The figures on research agencies have been updated. While there has been a considerable amount of new material and examples/applications added to this chapter, we have retained the overall chapter structure from the last edition.

Chapter 6: Market Targeting and Strategic Positioning—In this chapter, we have added a new strategy application concerning Numis Network, replacing the Intel feature in the last edition, as well as revising the application concerning Levi Strauss. In addition, we have included new applications concerning Zappos.com, and Reebok's changing positioning in the U.S. market. Applications concerning Harry Potter books and Hennes & Mauritz have been updated. We have placed an application concerning ArcelorMittal Steel in this chapter to replace the Harley-Davidson feature from the last edition. While the material has been updated and modifications made to the examples and applications, the underlying structure of the chapter remains intact.

Chapter 7: Strategic Relationships—We start this chapter with additional support from the literature for collaboration between companies in going to market. A new strategy application has been added describing the relationship between Microsoft and Nokia, while a new innovation application examines the development of "apps" around Apple's iPhone. Another new application assesses BP's experiences with strategic alliances in Russia. A new Internet application looks at P&G's move into online business. Another new application has been added to examine the Boeing Dreamliner issues in managing supplier relationships. Additional material has been added on the topic of outsourcing and its impact on strategic marketing, and material on strategic account management. New coverage has been added concerning reputational risk in intercompany relationships. Additional commentary is provided on the topics of alliances in emerging markets and the challenges of competing with state-owned enterprises. This material is supported by a new application describing the De Beers strategy in the changing diamond business. Examples and literature support throughout this chapter have been supplemented and updated.

Chapter 8: Innovation and New-Product Strategy—This chapter has additional coverage of additive manufacturing in innovation and product concept test formats, and innovation through collaboration. As well as updating the supporting examples and literature throughout the chapter, there is a new global application concerning emerging markets and reverse innovation, and a new ethics application relating to social responsibility initiatives and new-product innovation. Another addition is an innovation application describing Nestlé's BabyNes new product.

Chapter 9: Strategic Brand Management—The supporting literature and examples have been updated throughout this chapter. A new technology application has been added relating to IBM. Additional coverage of the link between corporate social responsibility and branding has been introduced together with a new ethics application describing Product Red. A new innovation application examines brand engagement and social media. New sections have been added examining corporate brands in the postrecession environment, the role of fighter brands, and the dilemma of orphan brands. A new global application looks at emerging market brands.

Chapter 10: Value-Chain Strategy—This chapter introduces new coverage of value chain redesign strategies and examples. A new strategy application looks at Forever 21 in the fashion business and a new innovation application examines virtual networks in the cell phone area. A new section has been added examining value chain innovation and new channels. A new ethics application assesses moral imperatives in value chains, and a new global application looks at Nestlé's innovative value chain in Brazil. We have extended the coverage relating to distribution channels in emerging markets. The supporting literature and examples have been updated throughout.

Chapter 11: Pricing Strategy—The coverage of price as an indicator of quality and the contrast with low price strategies has been extended. The role of price in postrecession markets is also expanded and features throughout the chapter. A new innovation application examines reinventing price strategy, and a new strategy application looks at recession price influences for P&G. A new innovation application assesses the challenges faced by Apple in pricing the iPhone. An additional ethics application considers Amazon and sales taxes. We have added a new section to the chapter addressing global pricing issues, featuring pricing regulation and restriction issues in global markets, the impact of emerging markets, and global competition from emerging market multinationals. This section includes a new global application concerning the Tata Nano automobile in India. Examples have been streamlined and updated and new literature references added throughout the chapter.

Chapter 12: Promotion, Advertising, and Sales Promotion Strategies—New data on global advertising expenditure have been added and include mobile advertising spend for the first time. Examples and supporting literature have been updated throughout the chapter.

Chapter 13: Sales, Digital, and Direct Marketing Strategies—The structure of this chapter has been amended to incorporate recognition of the impact of social media, with examples and coverage throughout, and to introduce new coverage of the phenomenon of the strategic sales organization and to expand our commentary on salesforce strategy. We add a new exhibit detailing customer demands for new types of sales relationships. We have also added coverage of the use of third-party sales organizations. We have expanded coverage of what is now titled Digital Strategy rather than Internet Strategy, to include additional commentary on Internet and social media impact on audiences and communications, creating a new communications landscape and influencing the role of traditional advertising agencies. A new innovation application looks at social media statistics, while a new Internet application examines Dell's social media touchpoints. We add comments on the development of new business models and provide a new innovation application examining Groupon. We have added commentary on mobile communications to the material on direct marketing strategies and added an innovation application on placecasting. A new strategy application considers Victoria's Secret catalog strategy. Literature references and supporting examples have been updated throughout.

Chapter 14: Designing Market-Driven Organizations—In addition to updating examples and literature throughout the chapter, a new innovation application is provided concerned with the future of work and organizations. Additional commentary on organizational design shifts is supported by a new strategy application looking at organizational change at Shell. Additional commentary is provided on organizational agility and a new strategy application on change imperatives in Hollywood is added. An extended and revised relationship application looks at the Millennial Generation as employees. Our commentary links organizational change to corporate social responsibility and includes a new ethics application on organizational priorities at Siemens. In adding new coverage of organizational realignment, we provide a new strategy application concerning organizational strategy differences at BP and ExxonMobil. We also add a new global application concerning global organization at P&G.

Chapter 15: Strategic Marketing Implementation and Control—A new section has been added to this chapter concerning the strategic role of the chief marketing officer, examining capabilities, tasks, and accountability. A new strategy application looks at Google and Motorola, while a new ethics application examines green product ratings. Supporting literature and examples have been updated throughout the chapter.

Cases—In the Comprehensive Cases in Part VI of the book, we have added 10 new case studies concerning: Facebook, Wentworth Industrial Cleaning Supplies Samsung Electronics, Tesco, Wal-Mart, British Airports Authority, California Credit Life Insurance Group, International Business Machines, Rover Automobile, and Hong Kong Disneyland. These topical and relevant cases replace or update material in the ninth edition. Ten cases are retained from the last edition. The result is a total of 20 comprehensive case studies, compared to 25 in the last edition.

In addition, we have removed the end-of-part cases in the new edition. User feedback suggested this material was not heavily used and that reducing the length of the book would be a welcome option for users. Nonetheless, for instructors who wish to continue using the end-of-part cases from the last edition, these are now available on the book's website (www.mhhe.com/cravens10e), along with the associated teaching notes, and the material can be accessed from that source.

Teaching / Learning Resources

A complete and expanded teaching-learning portfolio is available on the Online Learning Center at www.mhhe.com/cravens10e. It includes an Instructor's Manual with course-planning suggestions, answers to end-of-chapter questions, Application guidelines, and extensive instructor's notes for each of the 20 cases. A multiple-choice question test bank and a PowerPoint® presentation for each chapter are also included. The PowerPoints provide an organized coverage of the chapter topics and application examples.

This edition of the manual has been substantially revised and expanded to improve its effectiveness in supporting course planning, case discussion, and examination preparation. Detailed instructor's notes concerning the use of the cases are provided, including epilogues when available. The text, cases, and Instructor's Manual offer considerable flexibility in course design, depending on the instructor's objectives and the course for which the book is used.

Acknowledgments

The tenth edition has benefited from the contributions and experiences of many people and organizations. Business executives and colleagues at universities in many countries have influenced the development of *Strategic Marketing*. While space does not permit thanking each person, a sincere note of appreciation is extended to all. We shall identify several individuals whose assistance was particularly important.

A special thank you is extended to the reviewers of this and prior editions and to many colleagues that have offered numerous suggestions and ideas. Throughout the development of the tenth edition, several individuals made important suggestions for improving the book.

We are also indebted to the case authors who gave us permission to use their cases. We appreciate the opportunity to include them in the book. Each author or authors are specifically identified with each case.

A special note of thanks is due to the management and professional team of McGraw-Hill/Irwin for their support and encouragement on this and prior editions of *Strategic Marketing;* Paul Ducham, as publisher, has provided an important editorial leadership role; Editors Laura Spell and Sponsoring Editor for Business and Economics Daryl Bruflodt have been a constant source of valuable assistance and encouragement; Colleen Havens provided important marketing direction for the project; Lisa Bruflodt guided the book through the various stages of production, while Margarite Reynolds polished the design.

Students have provided various kinds of support that were essential to completing the revision. We also acknowledge the helpful comments and suggestions of many students in our classes.

We appreciate the support and encouragement provided by Dan Short and Homer Erekson, Deans of the TCU Neeley School of Business and Mark Taylor, Dean of Warwick Business School. Special thanks are due to Connie Clark at TCU and Sheila Frost at Warwick University for their help on the manuscript and for their assistance in other aspects of the project.

David W. Cravens

Nigel F. Piercy

About the Authors

David W. Cravens

David W. Cravens is Emeritus Professor of Marketing in the M.J. Neeley School of Business at Texas Christian University. He previously held the Eunice and James L. West Chair of American Enterprise Studies and was Professor of Marketing. Formerly, he was the Alcoa Foundation Professor at the University of Tennessee, where he chaired the Department of Marketing and Transportation and the Management Science Program. He has a Doctorate in Business Administration and MBA from Indiana University. He holds a Bachelor of Science in Civil Engineering from Massachusetts Institute of Technology. Before becoming an educator, Dave held various industry and government management positions. He is internationally recognized for his research on marketing strategy and sales management and has contributed over 150 articles and 25 books. Dave is a former editor of the *Journal of Academy of Marketing Science*. He has held various positions in the American Marketing Association and the Academy of Marketing Science. He received the Lifetime Achievement Award from the American Marketing Association in 2002 and was selected as the 1996 Outstanding Marketing Educator by the Academy of Marketing Science. He serves on the editorial boards of several academic journals. He has been a visiting scholar at universities in Austria, Australia, Chile, Czech Republic, England, Ireland, Italy, Germany, Mexico, The Netherlands, New Zealand, Singapore, Switzerland, and Wales. He has conducted management seminars and executive briefings in many countries in Asia, Europe, and South America. He is a frequent speaker at management development seminars and industry conferences.

Nigel F. Piercy

Nigel F. Piercy is Professor of Marketing and Strategic Management at Warwick Business School, in the University of Warwick, United Kingdom, where he also leads the Sales and Account Management Strategy research unit. He was previously Professor of Strategic Marketing and Head of the Marketing Group at Cranfield School of Management, and for a number of years was the Sir Julian Hodge Chair in Marketing and Strategy at Cardiff University. He has been a visiting scholar at Texas Christian University; University of California, Berkeley; Fuqua School of Business, Duke University; Columbia Business School; Athens Laboratory of Business Administration; and Vienna University of Business and Economics. He has extensive experience in executive education and as a management workshop speaker. He has worked with managers and business students in the United States, Europe, the Far East, South Africa, and Zimbabwe. He holds a PhD from the University of Wales, an MA from Durham University Business School, and a BA from Heriot-Watt University, Edinburgh, Scotland. He has been awarded the distinction of a higher doctorate (Doctor of Letters) from Heriot-Watt University for his published research work. Prior to academic life, Nigel was in retail management and latterly in strategic market planning with Nycomed Amersham plc. His research is in the areas of marketing strategy and implementation, and sales management. He has published some 200 articles and chapters and 16 books. He is editor of the *Journal of Strategic Marketing* and serves on the editorial boards of several scholarly journals.

Brief Contents

Preface   iv

About the Authors   xi

PART ONE
Strategic Marketing   1

1 New Challenges for Market-Driven Strategy   2

PART TWO
Markets, Segments, and Customer Value   33

2 Markets and Competitive Space   34

3 Strategic Market Segmentation   71

4 Strategic Customer Management: Systems, Ethics, and Social Responsibility   104

5 Capabilities for Learning About Customers and Markets   132

PART THREE
Designing Market-Driven Strategies   161

6 Market Targeting and Strategic Positioning   162

7 Strategic Relationships   186

8 Innovation and New-Product Strategy   218

PART FOUR
Market-Driven Program Development   253

9 Strategic Brand Management   254

10 Value-Chain Strategy   284

11 Pricing Strategy   317

12 Promotion, Advertising, and Sales Promotion Strategies   349

13 Sales, Digital, and Direct Marketing Strategies   373

PART FIVE
Implementing and Managing Market-Driven Strategies   403

14 Designing Market-Driven Organizations   404

15 Strategic Marketing Implementation and Control   437

PART SIX
Comprehensive Cases   471

INDEXES

Name Index   639

Subject Index   647

Table of Contents

Preface   iv
About the Authors   xi

PART ONE
STRATEGIC MARKETING   1

Chapter One
New Challenges for Market-Driven Strategy   2

Market-Driven Strategy   4
  Characteristics of Market-Driven Strategies   4
  Classifying Capabilities   8
  Creating Value for Customers   9
  Becoming Customer Driven   9
Corporate, Business, and Marketing Strategy   10
  Corporate, Business, and Marketing Strategy   12
  Components of Corporate Strategy   12
  Corporate Strategy Framework   12
  Business and Marketing Strategy   14
  The Marketing Strategy Process   16
Challenges of a New Era for
Strategic Marketing   20
  Escalating Globalization   20
  Technology Diversity and Uncertainty   21
  Internet Dynamics   22
  *Ethical Behavior and Corporate Social
  Responsiveness   23*
Summary   27
Appendix 1A
Strategic Marketing Planning   29

PART TWO
MARKETS, SEGMENTS,
AND CUSTOMER VALUE   33

Chapter Two
Markets and Competitive Space   34

Markets and Strategies   35
  Markets and Strategies are Interlinked   35
  An Array of Challenges   37
Matching Needs with Product Benefits   39

Defining and Analyzing Product-Markets   40
  *Determining Product-Market Boundaries
  and Structure   40*
  Forming Product-Markets   42
  Illustrative Product-Market Structure   44
Describing and Analyzing End-Users   45
  Identifying and Describing Buyers   45
  How Buyers Make Choices   46
  Environmental Influences   46
  Building Customer Profiles   48
Analyzing Competition   48
  Defining the Competitive Arena   48
  Key Competitor Analysis   51
  Anticipating Competitors' Actions   53
Market Size Estimation   54
  Market Potential   54
  Sales Forecast   55
  Market Share   56
  Evaluating Market Opportunity   56
Developing a Strategic Vision About
the Future   58
  Phases of Competition   58
  Anticipating the Future   58
Summary   59
Appendix 2A   62
**Financial Analysis for Marketing Planning
and Control   62**

Chapter Three
Strategic Market Segmentation   71

Levels and Types of Market Segmentation   73
Market-Driven Strategy and Segmentation   74
  *Market Segmentation, Value Opportunities
  and New Market Space   75*
  Market Targeting and Strategic Positioning   75
Activities and Decisions in Market
Segmentation   77
Defining the Market to Be Segmented   78
Identifying Market Segments   79
  Segmentation Variables   79
  Characteristics of People and Organizations   79
  Product Use Situation Segmentation   80
  Buyers' Needs and Preferences   82
  Purchase Behavior   83
Forming Market Segments   85
  Requirements for Segmentation   85

xiii

Approaches to Segment Identification   88
Customer Group Identification   89
Forming Groups Based on Response
Differences   93
Finer Segmentation Strategies   95
Logic of Finer Segments   96
Finer Segmentation Strategies   96
Selecting the Segmentation Strategy   97
Deciding How to Segment   98
Strategic Analysis of Market Segments   98
Summary   102

Chapter Four
Strategic Customer Management:
Systems, Ethics, and Social
Responsibility   104

Pivotal Role of Customer Relationship
Management   105
CRM in Perspective   105
CRM and Database Marketing   106
Customer Lifetime Value   107
Developing a CRM Strategy   108
CRM Levels   108
CRM Strategy Development   109
CRM Implementation   110
Value Creation Process   112
Customer Value   113
Value Received by the Organization   113
CRM and Value Chain Strategy   114
CRM and Strategic Marketing   115
Implementation   115
Performance Metrics   116
Short-Term Versus Long-Term Value   116
Competitive Differentiation   116
Ethics and Social Responsibility in Strategic
Marketing   118
Corporate Reputation   118
Customer Value and Competitive Positioning   127
Summary   130

Chapter Five
Capabilities for Learning About
Customers and Markets   132

Market-Driven Strategy, Market Sensing,
and Learning Processes   134
Market-Sensing Processes   135
Learning Organizations   135

Marketing Information and Knowledge
Resources   140
Scanning Processes   140
Specific Marketing Research Studies   143
Internal and External Marketing Information
Resources   143
Existing Marketing Information Sources   147
Creating New Marketing Information   148
Marketing and Management Information Systems   151
Marketing Intelligence and Knowledge
Management   153
Marketing Intelligence   153
Knowledge Management   154
Role of the Chief Knowledge Officer   154
Leveraging Customer Knowledge   154
Ethical Issues in Collecting and Using
Information   155
Invasion of Customer Privacy   155
Information and Ethics   156
Summary   157

PART THREE
DESIGNING MARKET-DRIVEN
STRATEGIES   161

Chapter Six
Market Targeting and Strategic
Positioning   162

Market Targeting Strategy   163
Targeting Alternatives   163
Factors Influencing Targeting Decisions   165
Targeting in Different Market Environments   165
Emerging Markets   166
Growth Markets   167
Mature Markets   168
Global Markets   170
Positioning Strategy   172
Selecting the Positioning Concept   175
Developing the Positioning Strategy   176
Scope of Positioning Strategy   176
Marketing Program Decisions   177
Determining Positioning Effectiveness   180
Customer and Competitor Research   181
Test Marketing   181
Analytical Positioning Techniques   182
Determining Positioning Effectiveness   182
Positioning and Targeting Strategies   183
Summary   183

Chapter Seven
Strategic Relationships   186

The Rationale for Interorganizational Relationships   187
  Opportunities to Enhance Value   187
  Environmental Complexity   189
  Competitive Strategy   190
  Skills and Resource Gaps   190
  Evaluating the Potential for Collaboration   193
Forms of Organizational Relationships   196
  Supplier Relationships   197
  Intermediate Customer Relationships   199
  End-User Customer Relationships   199
  Strategic Customers   200
  Strategic Alliances   202
  Joint Ventures   203
  Internal Partnering   204
  Managing Interorganizational Relationships   205
  Objective of the Relationship   205
  Relationship Management   206
  Partnering Capabilities   208
  Control and Evaluation   208
  Exiting from Alliance   209
Global Relationships Among Organizations   210
  The Global Integrated Enterprise   210
  Inter-Nation Collaborations   211
  The Strategic Role of Government   211
Summary   215

Chapter Eight
Innovation and New-Product Strategy   218

Innovation as a Customer-Driven Process   219
  Types of Innovations   219
  Finding Customer Value Opportunities   220
  Finding New-Product Opportunities   221
  Initiatives of Successful Innovators   223
  Innovation Through Collaboration   225
  Recognizing the Realities of Product Cannibalization   226
New-Product Planning   226
  Developing a Culture and Strategy for Innovation   227
  Developing Effective New-Product-Planning Processes   229
  Responsibility for New-Product Planning   230
Idea Generation   231
  Sources of Ideas   231
  Methods of Generating Ideas   234

Screening, Evaluating, and Business Analysis   235
  Screening   235
  Concept Evaluation   237
  Business Analysis   238
Product and Process Development   240
  Product Development Process   240
Marketing Strategy and Market Testing   243
  Marketing Strategy Decisions   243
  Market Testing   244
Commercialization   247
  The Marketing Plan   247
  Monitoring and Control   247
Variations in the Generic New-Product-Planning Process   248
Summary   250

PART FOUR
MARKET-DRIVEN PROGRAM DEVELOPMENT   253

Chapter Nine
Strategic Brand Management   254

Strategic Brand Management   255
  The Strategic Role of Brands   255
  Brand Management Challenges   257
  Brand Management Responsibility   258
  Strategic Brand Management   260
Strategic Brand Analysis   262
  Tracking Brand Performance   262
  Product Life-Cycle Analysis   264
  Product Performance Analysis   264
  Brand Positioning Analysis   265
Brand Equity Measurement and Management   265
  Measuring Brand Equity   265
  Brand Health Reports   265
Brand Identity Strategy   266
  Alternatives for Brand Identification   266
  Brand Focus   267
  Identity Implementation   268
Managing Brand Strategy   268
  Strategies for Improving Product Performance   270
Managing the Brand Portfolio   271
  Determining Roles of Brands   272
  Strategies for Brand Strength   272
  Strategic Brand Vulnerabilities   274
Brand Leveraging Strategy   275
  Line Extension   275
  Stretching the Brand Vertically   276

Brand Extension   276
Co-Branding   277
Licensing   277
Global Branding   277
Internet Brands   279
Brand Theft   280
Summary   281

Chapter Ten
Value-Chain Strategy   284

Strategic Role of Value Chain   285
Distribution Functions   286
Channels for Services   288
Direct Distribution by Manufacturers   288
Channel Strategy   290
Types of Channels   292
Distribution Intensity   296
Channel Configuration   297
Channel Maps   298
Selecting the Channel Strategy   298
Changing Channel Strategy   300
Managing the Channel   303
Channel Leadership   303
Management Structure and Systems   303
Physical Distribution Management   303
Channel Relationships   305
Channel Globalization   306
Multichanneling   306
Conflict Resolution   307
Channel Performance   308
Legal and Ethical Considerations   308
International Channels   310
Examining International Distribution
Patterns   311
Factors Affecting Global Channel Selection   314
Global Issues Regarding Multichannel
Strategies   314
Summary   314

Chapter Eleven
Pricing Strategy   317

Strategic Role of Price   318
Price in the Positioning Strategy   320
Pricing Situations   322
Roles of Pricing   322
Pricing Strategy   323
Pricing Objectives   324

Analyzing the Pricing Situation   326
Customer Price Sensitivity   326
Cost Analysis   329
Competitor Analysis   331
Pricing Objectives   332
Selecting the Pricing Strategy   333
How Much Flexibility Exists?   333
Price Positioning and Visibility   334
Illustrative Pricing Strategies   336
Legal and Ethical Considerations   337
Determining Specific Prices and Policies   338
Determining Specific Prices   339
Establishing Pricing Policy and Structure   341
Pricing Management   341
Global Issues in Pricing   343
Pricing Regulation and Restriction in Global
Markets   343
The Impact of Emerging Markets   343
Global Competition from Emerging Market
Multinationals   345
Summary   346

Chapter Twelve
Promotion, Advertising, and Sales
Promotion Strategies   349

Promotion Strategy   350
The Composition of Promotion Strategy   350
Designing Promotion Strategy   353
Communication Objectives   354
Deciding the Role of the Promotion
Components   356
Determining the Promotion Budget   356
Promotion Component Strategies   358
Integrating and Implementing the Promotion
Strategy   358
Effectiveness of Promotion Strategy   359
Advertising Strategy   359
Setting Advertising Objectives and Budgeting   360
Creative Strategy   362
Media/Scheduling Decisions   363
Role of the Advertising Agency   363
Implementing the Advertising Strategy
and Measuring Its Effectiveness   365
Sales Promotion Strategy   366
Nature and Scope of Sales Promotion   367
Sales Promotion Activities   368
Advantages and Limitations of Sales Promotion   370
Sales Promotion Strategy   371
Summary   371

Chapter Thirteen
Sales, Digital, and Direct Marketing Strategies   373

Salesforce Strategy   374
  Strategic Sales Perspective   374
  Salesforce Strategy   376
  The Role of Selling in Promotion Strategy   377
  Types of Sales Jobs   378
  Defining the Selling Process   380
  Sales Channels   381
  Designing the Sales Organization   382
  Salesforce Evaluation and Control   387
Digital Strategy   389
  Strategy Development   391
  Deciding Internet Objectives   393
  Digital Strategy   394
  Value Opportunities and Risks   395
  Measuring Internet Effectiveness   395
Direct Marketing Strategies   396
  Reasons for Using Direct Marketing   396
  Direct Marketing Methods   397
  Advantages of Direct Marketing   400
  Direct Marketing Strategy   401
Summary   401

PART FIVE
IMPLEMENTING AND MANAGING MARKET-DRIVEN STRATEGIES   403

Chapter Fourteen
Designing Market-Driven Organizations   404

Trends in Organization Strategy   405
  The New Organization   406
  Managing Organizational Process   410
  Organizational Agility and Flexibility   411
  Employee Motivation   413
Organizing for Market-Driven Strategy   414
  Strategic Marketing and Organization Structure   414
  Aligning the Organization With the Market   414
  Marketing Functions Versus Marketing Processes   416
  Marketing as Cross-Functional Process   416
Marketing Departments   418
  Centralization Versus Decentralization   420

  Integration or Diffusion   420
  Contingencies for Organizing   421
  Evaluating Organization Designs   423
Structuring Marketing Resources   423
  Structuring Issues   423
  Functional Organizational Design   424
  Product-Focused Design   424
  Market-Focused Design   425
  Matrix Design   426
  New Marketing Roles   427
Organizing for Global Marketing and Global Customers   430
  Organizing for Global Marketing Strategies   431
  Organizing for Global Customers   433
Summary   435

Chapter Fifteen
Strategic Marketing Implementation and Control   437

The Strategic Role of the Chief Marketing Officer   438
  Strategic CMO Capabilities   438
  Core CMO Tasks   439
  Planning, Implementation, and Accountability   439
The Strategic Marketing Planning Process   439
  Marketing Plans Guide Implementation   439
  Contents of the Marketing Plan   440
  Managing the Planning Process   440
Implementing the Strategic Marketing Plan   443
  Implementation Process   443
  Building Implementation Effectiveness   443
  Internal Marketing   446
  A Comprehensive Approach to Improving Implementation   448
  Internal Strategy-Organization Fit   449
Strategic Marketing Evaluation and Control   450
  Customer Relationship Management   450
  Overview of Control and Evaluation Activities   451
  The Strategic Marketing Audit   451
Marketing Performance Measurement   454
  The Importance of Marketing Metrics   455
  The Use of Marketing Metrics   455
  Types of Marketing Metrics   456
  Selecting Relevant Metrics   456
  Designing a Marketing Management Dashboard   458
  Interpreting Performance Measurement Results   459

Global Issues for Planning, Implementation,
and Control   463
  Global Marketing Planning   464
  Implementation Globally   464
  Performance Measurement and Control
  Globally   464
Summary   466
Appendix 15A
Marketing Metrics   468

PART SIX
COMPREHENSIVE CASES

Cases for Part Six   471
Case 6-1 Facebook   471
Case 6-2 Wentworth Industrial Cleaning
Supplies   475
Case 6-3 General Electric Appliances   486
Case 6-4 China and India: Opportunities and
Challenges   496
Case 6-5 Toyota   505

Case 6-6 Samsung Electronics Co.   511
Case 6-7 Keurig Inc.   519
Case 6-8 Tesco   532
Case 6-9 Supply Chain Management at
Wal-Mart   538
Case 6-10 British Airports Authority   547
Case 6-11 California Credit Life Insurance
Group   555
Case 6-12 Home Depot Inc.   563
Case 6-13 International Business Machines   569
Case 6-14 Rover Automobile   576
Case 6-15 ESPN   581
Case 6-16 Cowgirl Chocolates   588
Case 6-17 Procter & Gamble Co.   600
Case 6-18 Amazon.com Inc.   608
Case 6-19 Nanophase Technologies Corporation   613
Case 6-20 Hong Kong Disneyland   627

Indexes

Name Index   639
Subject Index   647

Strategic Marketing

Chapter

1

New Challenges for Market-Driven Strategy

Radical market changes, new demands for superior performance, and intense competition are rapidly escalating and pose great challenges to executives around the world. Market and industry boundaries are no longer easy to define because of the entry of new and disruptive forms of competition. Customers' demands for superior value from the goods and services (products) they purchase are unprecedented, as they become yet more knowledgeable and more perceptive in the judgments they make.

Marketing thought leaders Lusch and Webster argue convincingly that marketing is entering an important new stage of development involving a complex network mechanism that interrelates customer value and the value of the organization for all of its stakeholders.[1] The infrastructure for this system involves the microprocessor, the capture and use of the electromagnetic spectrum, and the emergence of the Internet, which fostered the communications and computation revolution. "As the focus of marketplace control has shifted from individual firms to consumers and resellers, traditional hierarchical bureaucratic organizational forms, guided by command and control systems, have become obsolete."[2]

External influences from diverse pressure groups and lobbyists have escalated dramatically in country after country. The level of searching scrutiny of the ethical standards and corporate responsibility initiatives has never been so high and exerts compelling influence on decision makers in companies.

Correspondingly, marketing guru Philip Kotler looks at Marketing 3.0 as the new marketing discipline that reflects values that amount to caring about the state of the world. He points to companies like General Electric aiming to prosper by doing good and solving societal problems in the energy field, and IBM looking to make the world a "smarter planet." Kotler's message is that increasingly customers prefer companies that stand for positive societal change and collaborate to serve all their stakeholders.[3]

Moreover, it is increasingly clear that significant enhancements in customer value provide a primary route to delivering superior shareholder value:[4] "To compete in this

---

[1]Robert F. Lusch and Frederick E. Webster, "Marketing's Responsibility for the Value of Enterprise," *Marketing Science Institute Working Paper Series,* Report No. 10–111, 2011.
[2]Ibid, 3.
[3]Philip Kotler, Hermawan Kartajaya, and Iwan Setiawan, *Marketing 3.0: From Products to Customers to the Human Spirit,* New York: Wiley, 2010. Michael Krauss, "Evolution of an Academic: Kotler on Marketing 3.0," *Marketing News,* January 30, 2011, 12.
[4]Peter Doyle, *Value-Based Marketing-Marketing Strategies for Corporate Growth and Shareholder Value* (Chichester: John Wiley, 2000).

Marketing Strategy Application

Market-Driven Strategy at Tesco International

Tesco is the leading British supermarket retailer. The company has impressive international growth achievements, particularly in Asia and Eastern Europe. International developments are carefully tailored to local customer preferences and shopping behavior.

The United States is a difficult market for European retailers and many have failed to adapt to the demands of the American consumer or meet the intense competition.

Tesco entered the U.S. market with Fresh & Easy, a new neighborhood store chain, focused on selling fresh food. Initial store openings were in Los Angeles, Las Vegas, Phoenix, and San Diego, and early plans were for a chain of 10,000 stores.

In planning the new venture, a Tesco team spent thousands of hours trying to discover what the American consumer wants:

- For two weeks 50 senior Tesco directors and managers lived the "American dream"—shopping and eating with U.S. families on the West Coast, even sharing their leisure activities.

- Hiring researchers to probe the refrigerator contents and lifestyles of 60 American families—checking what time they get up, what they eat for breakfast, when they shop, and preparing meals for them to try.

- A prototype store was built in secrecy in Los Angeles—the cover story was that they were making a movie, and executives used plastic bags of cash rather than corporate charge cards to buy things for the mock store, rather than tip off rivals to what they were doing. Consumers were flown in to test new ideas and products. More than 200 focus groups toured the store and gave feedback.

The goal was not to transfer the Tesco format from Britain to America, but to design an American store for American consumers. The vision was a U.S. convenience chain led by fresh, mainstream food.

While most Tesco U.S. stores will be located in prosperous suburbs surrounding Los Angeles, Phoenix, San Diego, and Las Vegas, others will be situated in poor, inner-city areas to address the "grocery gap"—the lack of supermarkets in inner-city areas like South Central Los Angeles. Wal-Mart has been unable to establish inner-city store because of union opposition, but the new Tesco small retail formats do not need the environmental and planning approvals that have provided trade unions with the opportunity to block Wal-Mart's expansion.

Fresh & Easy was launched in the United States in 2007. Difficulties were encountered from the beginning due, in part, to the global financial crisis. Nevertheless, top management decided in 2010 to continue the U.S. venture, but to focus primarily on California. Store openings were planned and 13 stores closed with plans to reopen them in 4 or 5 years after improvement in the economy. By 2011 annual losses were running at $280 million, but with sales growth. U.S. profitability was expected by 2013.

In early 2011 Tesco Plc was experiencing strong competition in the U.K. Customers may have been switching to lower priced chains including Wal-Mart Stores Inc.'s, Asda and William Morrison Supermarkets Plc. The bottom line was below performance by Tesco.

Sources: Kerry Capell, "Tesco: California Dreaming?" *BusinessWeek*, February 27, 2006, 38. Richard Fletcher and John Harlow, "Tesco's Leahy is Wild About the West," *Sunday Times*, September 3, 2006, 3–7. Jenny Davey, "Tesco Drives into America, *Sunday Times*, June 10, 2007, 3–1. Jonathan Birchall, "Tesco Aims to Fill 'Grocery Gap'," *Financial Times*, Thursday, June 28, 2007, 20. Paul Sonne, "Tesco Signals It Will Push Ahead in U.S.," *Wall Street Journal*, Wednesday, October 6, 2010, B9. Clementine Fletcher, "Tesco Sales Growth Trails Rivals as Non-Food Drags," *BusinessWeek*, 1/13/2011 as reported by www.businessweek.com/news. Jonathan Guthrie, "Case Strengthens for Tesco to Ditch Fresh & Easy," *Financial Times*, April 20, 2011, 18.

aggressively interactive environment, companies must shift their focus from driving transactions to maximizing customer lifetime value."[5]

Nonetheless, while it is important to recognize that the challenges are extreme, there is huge scope for achieving business success. The risks and uncertainties have escalated, and in many ways so have the rewards for developing strategies that deliver superior value. Innovative Web-based businesses like Google and eBay may be prototypes, but in more conventional industries a company like Tesco, the British retailer, is illustrative. Tesco's Global Challenges are described in accompanying MARKETING STRATEGY APPLICATION.

This chapter examines three important market-driven strategy topics:

- *First,* we develop the theme of market-driven strategy and its pivotal role in designing and implementing effective business and marketing strategies. To achieve this, we review the characteristics of market-oriented organizations, the development of distinctive capabilities, and the creation of value for customers.

- *Second,* we look at the links between business and marketing strategy and corporate strategy to clarify the scope of strategy and the marketing strategy process. The Appendix discusses Strategic Marketing Planning.

- *Lastly,* to emphasize the turbulent context in which executives make strategic choices, we explore some of the most important challenges in the dynamic and challenging marketplace—escalating globalization, technological change, growth of on-time-tracking, escalating consumer scrutiny of the provenance of the products they buy, and the imperatives of ethical behavior and corporate social responsibility.

Market-Driven Strategy

The underlying logic of market-driven strategy is that the customers that form the market should be the starting point in business strategy. Importantly, market-driven strategy provides a company-wide perspective, which mandates more effective integration of activities and processes that impact customer value. The development of a market-driven strategy is not a short-term endeavor. A considerable amount of effort is necessary to build a market-driven organizational culture and processes. Also, the methods of measuring progress extend beyond short-term financial performance measures. Certainly, it is important that we recognize that single-minded pursuit of short-term cost savings and profit enhancements may undermine the achievement of strategic goals and the building of superior customer value. Even in tough economic times of downturn and depression, strong companies have protected and maintained their investment in enhancing customer value.[6] Exhibit 1.1 summarizes the characteristics of market-driven strategies.

Characteristics of Market-Driven Strategies

Becoming Market Oriented

Market orientation is a business perspective that makes the customer the focal point of a company's total operations. "A business is market-oriented when its culture is systematically and entirely committed to the continuous creation of superior customer value."[7] Importantly, achieving a market orientation involves the use of superior organizational

---

[5]Roland T. Rust, Christine Moorman, and Gaukav Bhalla, "Rethinking Marketing," *Harvard Business Review,* January–February 2010, 96.

[6]Nigel F. Piercy, David W. Cravens, and Nikala Lane, "Marketing Out of Recession: Recovery is Coming, But Things Will Never Be the Same Again," *The Marketing Review,* 10(1), 2010, 3–23.

[7]Stanley F. Slater and John C. Narver, "Market Orientation, Customer Value, and Superior Performance," *Business Horizons,* March–April 1994, 22–27.

EXHIBIT 1.1
Characteristics of Market-Driven Strategies

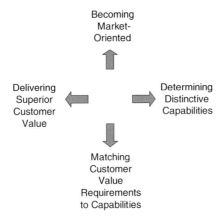

skills in understanding and satisfying customers.[8] Becoming market oriented requires the involvement and support of the entire workforce. The organization must monitor rapidly changing customer needs and wants, determine the impact of these changes on customer behavior, increase the rate of product/service innovation, and implement strategies that build the organization's competitive advantage.

A market-oriented organization continuously gathers information about customers, competitors, and markets; views the information from a total business perspective; decides how to deliver superior customer value; and takes actions to provide value to customers.[9] Importantly, these initiatives involve cross-functional participation. Market orientation requires participation by everyone in the organization. An organization that is market oriented has both a culture committed to providing superior customer value and processes for creating value for buyers. Market orientation requires a customer focus, competitor intelligence, and cross-functional cooperation and involvement. This initiative extends beyond the marketing function in an organization.

Customer Focus

The marketing concept has proposed customer focus for half a century, yet until the 1990s this emphasis had limited impact on managers as a basis for managing a business.[10] There are many similarities between the marketing concept and market orientation, although the former implies a functional (marketing) emphasis. The important difference is that market orientation is more than a philosophy since it consists of a process for delivering customer value. The market-oriented organization understands customers' preferences and requirements and effectively deploys the skills and resources of the entire organization to satisfy customers. Becoming customer oriented requires finding out what values buyers want to help them satisfy their purchasing objectives.

Competitor Intelligence

A market-oriented organization recognizes the importance of understanding its competition as well as the customer:

> The key questions are which competitors, and what technologies, and whether target customers perceive them as alternate satisfiers. Superior value requires that the seller identify and understand the principal competitors' short-term strengths and weaknesses and long-term capabilities and strategies.[11]

---

[8]George S. Day, *Market-Driven Strategy: Processes for Creating Value* (New York: Free Press, 1990).
[9]Slater and Narver, "Market Orientation," 23.
[10]George S. Day, "The Capabilities of Market-Driven Organizations," *Journal of Marketing,* October 1994, 37.
[11]Slater and Narver, "Market Orientation," 23.

Failure to identify and respond to competitive threats can create serious consequences for a company. For example, Polaroid's management did not define its competitive area as all forms of photography, concentrating instead on its instant photo monopoly position, and eventually the company was outflanked by digital photography. Had Polaroid been market oriented its management might have better understood the changes taking place, recognized the competitive threat, and developed strategies to counter the threat. Instead, the company filed for bankruptcy. In 2011 Eastman Kodak was experiencing similar problems with its photography business. Its digital business was experiencing sales declines and the narrow profit margins were impacting bottom line performance.

Cross-Functional Coordination

Market-oriented companies are effective in getting all business functions working together to provide superior customer value. These organizations are successful in removing the walls between business functions—marketing talks with research and development and finance. Cross-functional teamwork guides the entire organization toward providing superior customer value.

Performance Implications

Companies that are market oriented begin strategic analysis with a penetrating view of the market and competition. Moreover, an expanding body of research findings points to a positive relationship between market orientation and superior performance.[12] Companies that are market oriented display favorable organizational performance, compared to companies that are not market oriented. The positive market orientation/performance relationship has been found in several U.S., European, and Asian studies.[13]

Determining Distinctive Capabilities

Identifying an organization's distinctive capabilities (competencies) is a vital part of market-driven strategy. "Capabilities are complex bundles of skills and accumu-

lated knowledge, exercised through organizational processes, that enables firms to coordinate activities and make use of their assets."[14] The major components of distinctive capabilities are shown in Exhibit 1.2, using Southwest Airlines' business model to illustrate each component. The airline's growth and financial performance are impressive. In 2010, Southwest reported its 76th straight quarter of profitability, a record unmatched in the airline sector. The U.S. airline is the largest in the world by passengers carried. The pioneer of "no frills" flying, the airline now carries more domestic passengers than any other U.S. airline.

---

[12]Rohit Deshpandé and John V. Farley, "Organizational Culture, Market Orientation, Innovativeness, and Firm Performance: An International Research Odyssey," *International Journal of Research in Marketing,* 21, 2004, 3–22.

[13]D. A. Colton, M. S. Roth, and W. O. Bearden, "Drivers of International E-tail Performance: The Complexities of Orientations and Resources," *Journal of International Marketing,* 18(1), 2010, 1–22.

[14]Day, "The Capabilities of Market-Driven Organizations," 38.

EXHIBIT 1.2
Distinctive Capabilities at Southwest Airlines

Sources: Wendy Zellner, "Dressed to Kill," *Business-Week,* February 21, 2005, 58–59. Doug Cameron, "Southwest Seeks New Sources of Passenger Revenue," *Financial Times,* Friday, April 20, 2007, 24. "Smile and Free Peanuts," *The Economist,* June 4, 2011, 76.

Organizational Processes

Southwest pioneered a point-to-point route system contrasting with the hub-and-spoke design used by many conventional airlines.

The value proposition consists of low fares and limited services (e.g., no in-flight meals).

Major emphasis throughout the organization is on building a loyal customer base. Southwest was rated by *Consumer Reports* in 2011 as the favorite airline in the United States.

Operating costs are kept low by using a single aircraft type, minimizing the time between a plane landing and taking off, no assigned seating, and developing strong customer loyalty (lower selling costs).

The business model is characterized by "keeping it simple."

Skills and Accumulated Knowledge

Southwest has developed impressive skills in operating its business model at very low cost.

Accumulated knowledge has guided management in improving its business design over time.

The business model is being leveraged to drive more non-flying revenue, such as hotel booking from its website and charging for a broader array of services.

Additional directions identified include carrying more cargo, international flights and alliances with other carriers, and in-flight Internet services.

Coordination of Activities

Coordination of activities is facilitated by the point-to-point business model.

High aircraft utilization, simplification of functions, and limited passenger services enable management efficiency, and the provision of on-time, point-to-point services offered on a frequent basis.

Assets

Very low operating costs.

Loyal customer base. Southwest was America's largest low-cost carrier in 2011.

High employee esprit de corps.

An organization's capabilities are not a particular business function, asset, or individual, and instead, consist of core processes of the organization. Michael Porter indicates that "the essence of strategy is in the activities—choosing to perform activities differently or to perform different activities than rivals."[15] His concept of activity networks is consistent with viewing distinctive capabilities as groupings of skills and accumulated knowledge, applied through organizational processes. Tesco's carefully tailored service to local customer preferences is illustrative.

Organizational capabilities and organizational processes are closely related:

> . . . it is the capability that enables the activities in a business process to be carried out. The business will have as many processes as are necessary to carry out the natural business activities defined by the stage in the value chain and the key success factors in the market.[16]

---

[15]Michael Porter, "What is Strategy?" *Harvard Business Review,* November–December 1996, 64.
[16]Day, "The Capabilities of Market-Driven Organizations," 38.

EXHIBIT 1.3
**Classifying
Capabilities**

Source: Chart from George S.
Day, "The Capabilities of
Market-Driven Organizations,"
Journal of Marketing, October
1994, 41. Reprinted with
permission of the American
Marketing Association.

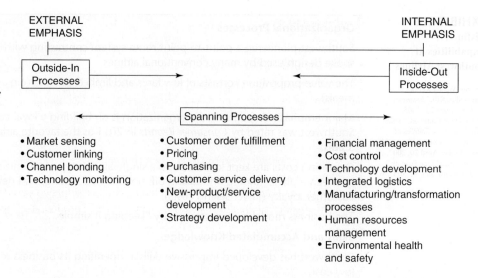

EXTERNAL
EMPHASIS

INTERNAL
EMPHASIS

Outside-In
Processes

Inside-Out
Processes

Spanning Processes

- Market sensing
- Customer linking
- Channel bonding
- Technology monitoring

- Customer order fulfillment
- Pricing
- Purchasing
- Customer service delivery
- New-product/service
  development
- Strategy development

- Financial management
- Cost control
- Technology development
- Integrated logistics
- Manufacturing/transformation
  processes
- Human resources
  management
- Environmental health
  and safety

Classifying the organization's capabilities is useful in identifying distinctive capabilities. As shown in Exhibit 1.3, one way of classification is to determine whether processes operate from outside the business to inside, inside out, or spanning processes. The processes shown are illustrative rather than a complete enumeration of processes. Moreover, since a company may have unique capabilities, the intent is not to identify a generic inventory of processes.

Classifying Capabilities

The process capabilities shown in Exhibit 1.3 differ in purpose and focus.[17] The outside-in processes connect the organization to the external environment, providing market feedback and forging external relationships. The inside-out processes are the activities necessary to satisfy customer value requirements (e.g., manufacturing/operations). The outside-in processes play a key role in offering direction for the spanning and inside-out capabilities, which respond to the customer needs and requirements identified by the outside-in processes. Market sensing, customer linking, channel bonding (e.g., producer/retailer relationships), and technology monitoring provide vital information for new product opportunities, service requirements, and competitive threats.

The organizational process view of distinctive capabilities requires shifting away from the traditional specialization of business functions (e.g., operations, marketing, research and development) toward a cross-functional process perspective.[18]

Capabilities and Customer Value

Value for buyers consists of the benefits and costs resulting from the purchase and use of products. Value is perceived by the buyer. Superior value occurs when there are positive net benefits. A company needs to pursue value opportunities that match its distinctive capabilities. A market-oriented company uses its market-sensing processes, shared diagnosis, and cross-functional decision making to identify and take advantage of superior value opportunities. Management must determine where and how it can offer superior value, directing these

---

[17]Ibid., 40–43.

[18]Frederick E. Webster, Jr., "The Future Role of Marketing in the Organization," *Reflections on the Futures of Marketing,"* Donald R. Lehmann and Katherine E. Jocz, eds. (Cambridge, MA: Marketing Science Institute), 1997, 39–66.

capabilities to customer groups (market segments) that result in a favorable competency/value match.

Creating Value for Customers

Intense global competition and the increasing demands of ever-more sophisticated customers make the creation of customer value an important challenge for managers. We take a closer look at the concept of customer value, and consider how value is generated.

Customer Value

Offering superior customer value is at the core of business design at companies as diverse as Google, and Southwest Airlines. Customer lifetime value (CLV) provides a long-term measure of the future profits generated by a customer, adjusted based on the time value of money.[19] Customer satisfaction indicates how well the product use experience compares to the buyer's value expectations. Superior customer value results from a very favorable use experience compared to expectations and the value offerings of competitors.

Providing Value to Customers

As discussed earlier, the organization's distinctive capabilities are used to deliver value by differentiating the product/service offer, offering lower prices relative to competing brands, or a combination of lower cost and differentiation.[20] Deciding which avenue to follow requires matching capabilities to the best value opportunities. Kodak's approach to pricing the ink cartridges for its latest printers challenges industry conventions. Competitors price printers low, but charge high prices for ink cartridges (in some cases, as much for the cartridge as the printer it fits). Kodak EasyShare printers cost more, but the ink cartridges are substantially cheaper than competitors'. Kodak's gamble is to attract high-volume users by offering them better value, leaving low-volume users to the competition.[21]

Nonetheless, there is an important distinction between value and innovation. An *Economist Intelligence Unit Report* included interviews with executives from many leading companies throughout the world: "What counts, conclude the participants, is value innovation. This is defined as creating new value propositions . . . that lead to increased customer satisfaction, loyalty, and—ultimately—sustainable, profitable growth. Market leaders are just that—pioneers."[22]

Becoming Customer Driven

The discussion so far points to the importance of becoming market oriented, leveraging distinctive capabilities, and finding a good match between customers' value requirements and the organization's capabilities. The supporting logic for these actions is that they are expected to lead to superior customer value and organizational performance. Research evidence indicates that these characteristics are present in customer-driven organizations, which display higher performance than their counterparts that are not customer driven. A customer-driven organization must identify which capabilities to develop and which investment commitments to make. Market orientation research and evolving business strategy paradigms point to the importance of market sensing and customer linking capabilities in achieving successful customer-driven strategies.[23]

---

[19]Rust, Moorman, and Rhalla, "Rethinking Marketing," 101.

[20]George S. Day and Robin Wensley, "Assessing Advantage: A Framework for Diagnosing Competitive Superiority," *Journal of Marketing*, April 1998, 1–20.

[21]Paul Taylor, "The Wicked Price of Print," *Financial Times*, June 1, 2007, 18.

[22]Laura Mazur, "Wrong Sort of Innovation," *Marketing Business*, June 1999, 49.

[23]Ibid., 43–45.

Market Sensing Capabilities

Market-driven companies have effective processes for learning about their customers and markets. Sensing involves more than collecting information. It must be shared across functions and interpreted to determine what actions need to be initiated. Tesco's market sensing links managers and generates valuable information for diagnosis and action to improve performance. Developing an effective market-sensing capability is not a simple task. Various information sources must be identified and processes developed to collect and analyze the information. Information technology plays a vital role in market sensing activities. Different business functions have access to useful information and need to be involved in market sensing activities.

Customer Linking Capabilities

There is substantial evidence that creating and maintaining close relationships with customers is important in market-driven strategies.[24] These relationships offer advantages to both buyer and seller through information sharing and collaboration. Customer linking also reduces the possibility of a customer shifting to another supplier. Customers are valuable assets.

Quintiles Transnational has very effective customer linking capabilities.[25] Its drug testing and sales services are available in more than 50 countries. The company has extensive experience in clinical trials and marketing. Quintiles' customers are drug companies located in many countries around the world. Ongoing collaborative relationships are essential to Quintiles' success. It offers specialized expertise, assisting drug producers to reduce the time necessary in developing and testing new drugs. Quintiles helped develop or commercialize every one of the world's top 30 best-selling drugs.

Aligning Structure and Processes

Becoming market driven may require changing the design of the organization, placing more emphasis on cross-functional processes. Market orientation and process capabilities require cross-functional coordination and involvement. Many companies have made changes in organization structures and processes as a part of their customer value initiatives. The changes include improving existing processes as well as redesigning processes. Primary targets for reengineering are sales and marketing, customer relationship management, order fulfillment, and distribution. The objectives of the business process changes are to improve the overall level of product quality, reduce costs, and improve service delivery. Underpinning such changes and initiatives is the importance of what has been called "implementation capabilities," or the ability of an organization to execute and sustain market-driven strategy, and do so on a global basis.[26] In addition to formulating the strategies essential to delivering superior customer value, it is vital to adopt a thorough and detailed approach to strategy implementation.

Corporate, Business, and Marketing Strategy

Business and marketing strategies are being renewed by executives in a wide range of companies in their efforts to survive and prosper in an increasingly complex and demanding global business environment. The tough postrecession conditions faced in many sectors

---

[24]Ibid.

[25]David W. Cravens, Gordon Greenley, Nigel F. Piercy, and Stanley Slater, "Mapping the Path to Market Leadership: The Market-Driven Strategy Imperative," *Marketing Management,* Fall 1998.

[26]Nigel F. Piercy, "Marketing Implementation: The Implications of Marketing Paradigm Weakness for the Strategy Execution Process," *Journal of the Academy of Marketing Science,* 26 (3), 1998, 222–236.

The firm must be understood as a complex network mechanism linking customer value and the value of the firm for all of its stakeholders. Marketing can be more effectively researched and managed in the context of its intra-firm and its networked organizational relationships, not just customer relationships external to the firm . . .

A central feature of the network economy and the transformed organizational environment is the ascendance of information technology and the emphasis on knowledge (not land and labor) as the prime resource for competitive advantage. . . . The microprocessor, capture and capitalization of the electromagnetic spectrum, and the emergence of the internet fostered a communications and computation revolution that provided the essential infrastructure for a network economy.

Source: Robert F. Lusch and Frederick E. Webster, Jr., "Marketing's Responsibility for the Value of the Enterprise," Report No. 10-111, Marketing Science Institute, 2010, 16–17.

and many countries underline the priority for effective strategies. Choosing high performance strategies in this environment of constant change requires vision, sound strategic logic, and commitment. Market-driven organizations develop closely coordinated business and marketing strategies. Executives in many companies are reinventing their business models with the objective of improving their competitive advantage. These changes include altering market focus, expanding product scope, forming relationships with other organizations, outsourcing manufacturing, and modifying internal structure. The capacity for continuous reconstruction requires innovation with respect to the organizational values, processes, and behaviors that systematically favor perpetuating the past rather than innovation for renewal.[27]

Lusch and Webster propose that marketing is entering a new era as management practice in new organizational forms that are significantly different from the traditional, bureaucratic, functional, self-contained corporate types.[28] These organizational forms are described in the MARKETING STRATEGY APPLICATION.

Conventionally, we distinguish between corporate, business, and marketing strategy as shown in Exhibit 1.4. Corporate strategy consists of deciding the scope and purpose of the business, its objectives, and the initiatives and resources necessary to achieve the

EXHIBIT 1.4
Corporate, Business, and Marketing Strategy

---

[27]Gary Hamel and Liisa Välikangas, "The Quest for Resilience," *Harvard Business Review,* September 2003, 52–63.

[28]Lusch and Webster, Jr., "Marketing's Responsibility for the Value of Enterprise," 1–48.

EXHIBIT 1.5
Components of Corporate Strategy

Scope, Mission, and Strategic Intent → Corporate Objectives → Strategy → Resource Allocation → Synergies

objectives. Business and marketing strategy is guided by the decisions top management makes about how, when, and where to compete. This should be a two-way relationship—while corporate strategy defines strategic direction, allocates resources, and defines constraints on what cannot be done, executives responsible for marketing strategy have a responsibility to inform corporate strategists about external change in the market that identifies opportunities and threats. We will examine each level or approach to strategy in turn, before describing and illustrating the marketing strategy process in more detail.

Corporate, Business, and Marketing Strategy

Corporate strategy consists of the decisions made by top management and the resulting actions taken to achieve the objectives set for the business. The major corporate strategy components are shown in Exhibit 1.5. *Scope* is concerned with resolving questions about the business the firm should be in, where it should focus, and its enduring strategic purpose. *Corporate objectives* indicate the dimensions of performance upon which to focus and the levels of achievement required. *Corporate strategies* are concerned with how the company can achieve its growth objectives in current or new business areas. *Resource allocation* addresses the division of limited resources across businesses and opportunities. *Synergies* highlight competencies, resources, and capabilities that drive efficiency and effectiveness in the business. Essential to corporate success is matching the capabilities of the organization with opportunities to provide long-term superior customer value (customer lifetime value).

Components of Corporate Strategy

It is apparent that in the 21st century marketing environments, companies are drastically altering their business and marketing strategies to get closer to their customers, counter competitive threats, and strengthen competitive advantages. Challenges to management include escalating international competition, new types and sources of competition, political and economic upheaval, dominance of the customer, and increasing marketing complexity. These challenges create imperatives for organizational change, which may sometimes be radical.

Corporate Strategy Framework

A useful basis for examining corporate strategy consists of (1) management's long-term vision for the corporation; (2) objectives that serve as milestones toward the vision; (3) resources; (4) businesses in which the corporation competes; (5) structure, systems, and processes; and (6) gaining corporate advantage through multimarket activity.[29]

Deciding Corporate Vision

Management's vision defines what the corporation is and what it does and provides important guidelines for managing and improving the corporation. Strategic choices about where the firm is going in the future—choices that take into account company capabilities,

---

[29]David J. Collis and Cynthia A. Montgomery, *Corporate Strategy,* 2nd ed. (Burr Ridge IL: McGraw-Hill/Irwin, 2005), 10–16.

resources, opportunities, and problems—establish the vision of the enterprise. Developing strategies for sustainable competitive advantage, implementing them, and adjusting the strategies to respond to new environmental requirements is a continuing process. Managers monitor the market and competitive environment. Early in the strategy-development process management needs to define the vision of the corporation. It is reviewed and updated as shifts in the strategic direction of the enterprise occur over time.

Top management vision may be radical and sometimes involves risks. While Amazon.com initially promised to revolutionize retailing with its online operations, founder Jeff Bezos wants to transform Amazon into a digital utility—running customers' business logistics and processes using the same state-of-the-art technologies and operations that power Amazon's own online retailing. Amazon is renting out resources it uses to run its own business and has even allowed outside programmers access to its pricing and product data.[30]

Objectives

Objectives need to be set so that the performance of the enterprise can be gauged. Corporate objectives may be established in the following areas: *marketing, innovation, resources, productivity, social responsibility,* and *finance.*[31] Examples include growth and market-share expectations, product quality improvement, employee training and development, new-product targets, return on invested capital, earnings growth rates, debt limits, energy reduction objectives, and pollution standards. Objectives are set at several levels in an organization beginning with those indicating the enterprise's overall objectives. The time frame necessary for strategic change often goes beyond short-term financial reporting requirements. Companies are using more than financial measures to evaluate longer-term strategic objectives, and nonfinancial measures for short-term budgets.

Resources

It is important to place a company's strategic focus on its resources—assets, skills, and capabilities.[32] These resources may offer the organization the potential to compete in different markets, provide significant value to end-user customers, and create barriers to competitor duplication. We know that distinctive capabilities are important in shaping the organization's strategy. A key strategy issue is matching capabilities to market opportunities. Capabilities that can be leveraged into different markets and applications are particularly valuable. For example, the GoreTex high-performance fabric is used in many applications from apparel to dental floss.

Business Composition

Defining the composition of the business provides direction for both corporate and marketing strategy design. In single-product firms that serve one market, it is easy to determine the composition of the business. In many other firms it is necessary to separate the business into parts to facilitate strategic analyses and planning. When firms are serving multiple markets with different products, grouping similar business areas together aids decision making.

Business segment, group, or division designations are used to identify the major areas of business of a diversified corporation. Each segment, group, or division often contains a mix of related products (or services), though a single product can be assigned such a

---

[30]Robert D. Hof, "Jeff Bezos' Risky Bet," *BusinessWeek,* November 12, 2006, 52–58.
[31]Peter F. Drucker, *Management* (New York: Harper & Row, 1974), 100.
[32]Collis and Montgomery, *Corporate Strategy,* 13.

designation. Some firms may establish subgroups of related products within a business segment that are targeted to different customer groups.

A business segment, group, or division is often too large in terms of product and market composition to use in strategic analysis and planning, so it is divided into more specific strategic units. A popular name for these units is the *strategic business unit* (SBU). Typically SBUs display product and customer group similarities. A strategic business unit is a single product or brand, a line of products, or a mix of related products that meets a common market need or a group of related needs, and the unit's management is responsible for all (or most) of the basic business functions. Typically, the SBU has a specific strategy rather than a shared strategy with another business area. It is a cohesive organizational unit that is separately managed and produces sales and profit results.

For example, part of the remarkable strategic turnaround at Hewlett-Packard involved restructuring choices made in 2005 by incoming CEO Mark Hurd. He reversed his predecessor's merge of the computer and printer divisions, on the grounds that smaller, more focused business units would perform better than larger, more diffused alternatives, and separated the computer and printer units.[33]

In a business that has two or more strategic business units, decisions must be made at two levels. Corporate management must first decide what business areas to pursue and set priorities for allocating resources to each SBU. The decision makers for each SBU must select the strategies for implementing the corporate strategy and producing the results that corporate management expects. Corporate-level management is often involved in assisting SBUs to achieve their objectives.

Structure, Systems, and Processes

This aspect of strategy considers how the organization controls and coordinates the activities of its various business units and staff functions.[34] Structure determines the composition of the corporation. Systems are the formal policies and procedures that enable the organization to operate. Processes consider the informal aspects of the organization's activities. Strategic choices provide the logic for different structure, systems, and process configurations.

The logic of how the business is designed is receiving considerable attention. "A business design is the totality of how a company selects its customers, defines and differentiates its offerings, defines the tasks it will perform itself and those it will outsource, configures its resources, goes to market, creates utility for customers, and captures profit."[35] The business design (or business model) provides a focus on more than the product and/or technology, instead looking at the processes and relationships that comprise the design.

Business and Marketing Strategy

Many strategy guidelines are offered by consultants, executives, and academics to guide business strategy formulation. These strategy paradigms propose a range of actions including re-engineering the corporation, total quality management, building distinctive competencies, reinventing the organization, supply chain strategy, and strategic partnering. It is not feasible to review the various strategy concepts and methods that are available in many books, seminars, and consulting services. The corporate strategy framework presented here offers a basis for incorporating relevant strategy perspectives and guidelines.

An important issue is whether selecting a successful strategy has a favorable impact on results. Does the uncontrollable environment largely determine business performance or

---

[33]Simon London, "The Whole Can Be Less Than the Sum of Its Parts," *Financial Times,* Monday, July 4, 2005, 10.
[34]Collis and Montgomery, Corporate Strategy, 14–15.
[35]Adrian J. Slywotzky, *Value Migration* (Boston: Harvard Business School Press, 1996), 4.

instead, will the organization's strategy have a major impact on its performance? The evidence suggests that strategic choices matter.[36] While environmental factors such as market demand, intensity of competition, government, and social change influence corporate performance, the strategic choices made by specific companies also have a significant impact on their performance. Importantly, the impact may be positive or negative. For example, Kmart held the leading market position over Wal-Mart in 1980, yet Wal-Mart overtook Kmart by investing heavily in information systems and distribution to develop a powerful market-driven, low-cost retail network. Kmart declared bankruptcy in early 2002, and was sold for less than $1 billion.

Business and Marketing Strategy Relationships

An understanding of business purpose, scope, objectives, resources, and strategy is essential in designing and implementing marketing strategies that are consistent with the corporate and business unit plan of action. The chief marketing executive's business strategy responsibilities include (1) participating in strategy formulation and (2) developing marketing strategies that are consistent with business strategy priorities and integrated with other functional strategies. Since these two responsibilities are closely interrelated, it is important to examine marketing's role and functions in both areas to gain more insight into marketing's responsibilities and contributions. Peter F. Drucker described this role:

> Marketing is so basic that it cannot be considered a separate function (i.e., a separate skill or work) within the business, on a par with others such as manufacturing or personnel. Marketing requires separate work and a distinct group of activities. But it is, first, a central dimension of the entire business. It is the whole business seen from the point of view of its final result, that is, from the customer's point of view.[37]

According to Lusch and Webster "marketing management is the leadership function in the organization that designs and guides organizational processes for sensing, resourcing, realizing, and learning from the changing market environment, supplementing the traditional bureaucratic view of management as analysis, planning, implementation, and control."[38]

Strategic Marketing

Marketing strategy consists of the analysis, strategy development, and implementation of activities in developing a vision about the market(s) of interest to the organization, selecting market target strategies, setting objectives, and developing, implementing, and managing the marketing program positioning strategies designed to meet the value requirements of the customers in each market target.

Strategic marketing is a market-driven process of strategy development, taking into account a constantly changing business environment and the need to deliver superior customer value. The focus of strategic marketing is on organizational performance rather than a primary concern about increasing sales. Marketing strategy seeks to deliver superior customer value by combining the customer-influencing strategies of the business into a coordinated set of market-driven actions. Strategic marketing links the organization with the environment and views marketing as a responsibility of the entire business rather than a specialized function.

[36]Shelby D. Hunt and Robert M. Morgan, "The Comparative Advantage Theory of Competition," *Journal of Marketing,* April 1995, 1–15.
[37]Peter F. Drucker, *Management: Tasks, Responsibilities, Practices* (New York: Harper & Row, 1974), 63.
[38]Lusch and Webster, "Marketing's Responsibility for the Value of the Enterprise," 21.

EXHIBIT 1.6
Marketing Strategy Process

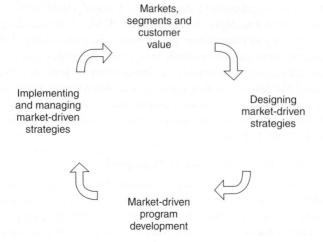

The Marketing Strategy Process diagram showing a cycle: Markets, segments and customer value → Designing market-driven strategies → Market-driven program development → Implementing and managing market-driven strategies.

The Marketing Strategy Process

The marketing strategy analysis, planning, implementation, and management process that we follow is described in Exhibit 1.6. The strategy stages shown are examined and applied through the later parts of this book. *Markets, segments, and customer value* consider market and competitor analysis, market segmentation, strategic customer relationship management, and continuous learning about markets. *Designing market-driven strategy* examines customer targeting and positioning strategies, marketing relationship strategies, and innovation and new product strategy. *Market-driven program development* consists of brand, value-chain, pricing, and promotion and selling strategies designed and implemented to meet the value requirements of targeted buyers. *Implementing and managing market-driven strategy* considers organizational design and marketing strategy implementation and control.

Markets, Segments, and Customer Value

Marketing management identifies and evaluates markets, segments, and customers to guide the design of a new strategy or to change an existing strategy. Analysis is conducted on a regular basis after the strategy is underway to evaluate strategy performance and identify needed strategy changes. Activities include:

- **Markets and Competitive Space.** Markets need to be defined so that buyers and competition can be analyzed. A product-market consists of a specific product (or line of related products) that can satisfy a set of needs and wants for the people (or organizations) willing and able to purchase it. The objective is to identify and describe the buyers, understand their preferences for products, estimate the size and rate of growth of the market, and find out what companies and products are competing in the market. Evaluation of competitors' strategies, strengths, limitations, and plans is a key aspect of this analysis.

- **Strategic Market Segmentation.** Market segmentation offers an opportunity for an organization to focus its business capabilities on the requirements of one or more groups of buyers. The objective of segmentation is to examine differences in needs and wants and to identify the segments (subgroups) within the product-market of interest. The segments are described using the various characteristics of people, the reasons that they buy or use certain products, and their preferences for certain brands of products. Likewise, segments of industrial product-markets may be formed according to the type of industry, the uses for the product, frequency of product purchase, and various other factors. The similarities of buyers' needs within a segment enable better targeting of the organization's capabilities to buyers with corresponding value requirements.

- **Strategic Customer Relationship Management.** A strategic perspective on customer relationship management (CRM) emphasizes delivering superior customer value by personalizing the interaction between the customer and the company and achieving the coordination of complex organizational capabilities around the customer. CRM aims to increase the value of a company's customer base by developing better relationships with customers and retaining their business. CRM can play a vital role in market targeting and positioning strategies. Since CRM is an enterprise-spanning initiative, it needs to be carefully integrated with marketing strategy.

- **Capabilities for Continuous Learning About Markets.** Understanding markets and competition has become a necessity in modern business. Sensing what is happening and is likely to occur in the future is complicated by competitive threats that may exist beyond traditional industry boundaries. Managers and professionals in market-driven firms are able to sense what is happening in their markets, develop business and marketing strategies to seize opportunities and counter threats, and anticipate what the market will be like in the future. Several market sensing methods are available to guide the collection and analysis of information.

Designing Market-Driven Strategies

Evaluating markets, segments, and customer value drivers at the outset of the marketing strategy process identifies market opportunities, defines market segments, evaluates competition, and assesses the organization's strengths and weaknesses. Market sensing information plays a key role in designing marketing strategy, which includes market targeting and positioning strategies, building marketing relationships, and developing and introducing new products (goods and services).

- **Market Targeting and Strategic Positioning.** A core issue is deciding how, when, and where to compete, given a firm's market and competitive environment. The purpose of *market targeting strategy* is to select the people (or organizations) that management wishes to serve in the product-market. When buyers' needs and wants vary, the market target is usually one or more segments of the product-market. Once the segments are identified and their relative importance to the firm determined, the targeting strategy is selected. The objective is to find the best match between the value requirements of each segment and the organization's distinctive capabilities. The targeting decision is the focal point of marketing strategy since targeting guides the setting of objectives and developing the corporate positioning strategy. Examples of market target objectives are desired levels of sales, market share, customer retention, profit contribution, and customer lifetime value. *Positioning strategy* is the combination of the product, value chain, price, and promotion strategies a firm uses to position itself against its key competitors in meeting the needs and wants of the buyers in the market target. The strategies and tactics used to gain a favorable position are called the marketing mix or the marketing program. The positioning strategy seeks to position the brand in the eyes and mind of the buyer and distinguish the product from the competition. The product, distribution, price, and promotion strategy components make up a bundle of actions that are used to influence buyers' positioning of a brand.

- **Strategic Relationships.** Marketing relationship partners may include end-user customers, marketing channel members, suppliers, competitor alliances, and internal teams. The driving force underlying these relationships is that a company may enhance

The Canadian company, Research in Motion Ltd. (RIM), achieved remarkable success with the BlackBerry product range—cell phones with wireless e-mail capabilities. It took RIM from 1997 to early 2004 to sign up the first million users, but by 2007 BlackBerry had 12 million users worldwide. However, the potential market is estimated at 400–800 million users. Growing competition from Apple's iPhone and touchscreen devices using Google's Android software is impacting on BlackBerry's global smartphone market share.

The design and functionality of BlackBerry made RIM the market leader in personal digital assistants (PDAs), overtaking more established players like Palm, Hewlett-Packard, and Dell.

RIM achieved an important first-mover advantage with BlackBerry. The brand became an icon—with its own nickname "The CrackBerry" because of its addictive nature, and its own malady "BlackBerry Thumb" referring to the penalty for over-use of the small keyboard.

The challenge is to stay ahead of aggressive competitors from across the tech industry, including Apple, Dell, Hewlett-Packard, Good Technology, and Microsoft. There is a danger that e-mail may become standard on all cell phones. However, one unique BlackBerry capability is BlackBerry Messenger (or BBM), an instant messaging application available only on BlackBerry, which provides a service similar to text messaging, which is both faster and cheaper. In building a stronger position in the consumer market BBM is attracting many younger users. In some markets, BBM is a serious threat to other operators' text messaging revenues.

RIM's strategy has been to accept that the vast majority of handhelds for e-mail and other services will be made by competitors, and to stake out leadership in software and services:

- Licensing software to phone and handheld manufacturers
- Working with the carriers to push its devices and others using its software
- Offering software and services to allow companies to offer their own services or software applications on a BlackBerry device.

In early 2011, RIM was shifting from corporate-work-horse devices toward the production of media-savvy products to compete with Apple Inc. iPhone and iPads: The new PlayBook was intended to demonstrate the firm's product innovation strategy. Unexpectedly, RIMs chief marketing officer resigned in early 2011, giving top management a major challenge in building the firm's marketing capabilities.

By mid-2011 the competition had intensified. RIM's stock had lost nearly half of the market value so far in the year. Management planned to "streamline operations." The company had not released a new model for nearly a year. The product line sales in the North American market declined to 16.5% at the end of the first quarter in 2011 compared to 41.3% for a year earlier.

Sources: Heather Green and Cliff Edwards, "The Squeeze on BlackBerry," *BusinessWeek,* December 6, 2004, 74–75. Paul Taylor and Bernard Simon, "RIM Sees Fine BlackBerry Harvest," *Financial Times,* April 12, 2005, 11. Ben Hunt and Stephen Pritchard, "BlackBerries Are Not the Only Fruit," *Financial Times IT Report,* Wednesday June 29, 2005, 1. Jessica E. Vascellaro, "Research in Motion Net, Revenue More Than Double," *Wall Street Journal,* October 5, 2007, B3. Phred Dvorak and Stuart Weinberg, "RIM Loses Marketing Chief," *Wall Street Journal,* March 5, 2011, B3. Phred Dvorak and Stuart Weinberg, "RIM Warns of More BlackBerry Blues," *Wall Street Journal,* June 17, 2011, B1. Tim Bradshaw, "Messenger Delivers BlackBerry with a Loyal Following," *Financial Times,* April 25, 2011, 22.

its ability to satisfy customers and cope with a rapidly changing business environment through collaboration of the parties involved. Building long-term relationships with customers and value chain partners offers companies a way to deliver superior customer value. Strategic partnering has become an important strategic initiative for many well-known companies and brands. Many firms outsource the manufacturing of their products. Strong relationships with outsourcing partners are vital to the success of these powerful brands.

- **Innovation and New Product Strategy.** New products are needed to replace old products when sales and profit growth decline. Closely coordinated new product planning is essential to satisfy customer requirements and produce products with high quality at competitive prices. New product decisions include finding and evaluating ideas, selecting the most promising for development, designing the products, developing marketing programs, market testing the products, and introducing them to the market. The differences between existing product attributes and those desired by customers offer opportunities for new and improved products. Successful innovation is a major business challenge. An interesting example of a new product achieving remarkable results is the Blackberry handheld device, as described in the INNOVATION APPLICATION.

Market-Driven Program Development

Market targeting and positioning strategies for new and existing products guide the choice of strategies for the marketing program components. Product, value chain (distribution), price, and promotion strategies are combined to form the positioning strategy selected for each market target. The marketing program (mix) strategies implement the positioning strategy.

- **Strategic Brand Management.** Products (goods and services) often are the focal point of positioning strategy, particularly when companies or business units adopt organizational approaches emphasizing product or brand management. Product strategy includes: (1) developing plans for new products; (2) managing programs for successful products; and (3) deciding what to do about problem products (e.g., reduce costs or improve the product). Strategic brand management consists of building brand value (equity) and managing the organization's system of brands for overall performance.

- **Value-Chain Strategy.** Market target buyers may be contacted on a direct basis using the firm's salesforce or by direct marketing contact (e.g., Internet), or, instead, through a value-added chain (distribution channel) of marketing intermediaries (e.g., wholesalers, retailers, or dealers). Distribution channels are often used in linking producers with end-user household and business markets. Decisions that need to be made include the type of channel organizations to use, the extent of channel management performed by the firm, and the intensity of distribution appropriate for the good or service.

- **Pricing Strategy.** Price also plays an important role in positioning a product or service. Customer reaction to alternative prices, the cost of the product, the prices of the competition, and various legal and ethical factors establish the extent of flexibility management has in setting prices. Pricing strategy involves choosing the role of price in the positioning strategy, including the desired positioning of the product or brand as well as the margins necessary to satisfy and motivate distribution channel participants.

- **Promotion Strategy.** Advertising, sales promotion, the salesforce, direct marketing, and public relations help the organization to communicate with its customers, value-chain partners, the public, and other target audiences. These activities make up the promotion strategy, which performs an essential role in communicating the positioning strategy to buyers and other relevant influences. Promotion informs, reminds, and persuades buyers and others who influence the purchasing process.

Implementing and Managing Market-Driven Strategy

Selecting the customers to target and the positioning strategy for each target moves marketing strategy development to the action stage (see Exhibit 1.6). This stage considers designing the marketing organization and implementing and managing the strategy.

- **Designing Market-Driven Organizations.** An effective organization design matches people and work responsibilities in a way that is best for accomplishing the firm's marketing strategy. Deciding how to assemble people into organizational units and assign responsibility to the various mix components that make up the marketing strategy are important influences on performance. Organizational structures and processes must be matched to the business and marketing strategies that are developed and implemented. Organizational design needs to be evaluated on a regular basis to assess its adequacy and to identify necessary changes. Restructuring and reengineering of organizations has led to many changes in the structures of marketing units.

- **Marketing Strategy Implementation and Control.** Marketing strategy implementation and control consists of: (1) preparing the marketing plan and budget; (2) implementing the plan; and (3) using the plan in managing and controlling the strategy on an ongoing basis. The marketing plan includes details concerning targeting, positioning, and marketing mix activities. The plan spells out what is going to happen over the planning period, who is responsible, how much it will cost, and the expected results (e.g., sales forecasts). The preparation of the marketing plan is discussed in the Appendix to this chapter.

Marketing strategy is an ongoing process of making decisions, implementing them, and tracking their effectiveness over time. In time requirements, strategic evaluation is far more demanding than planning. Evaluation and control are concerned with tracking performance and, when necessary, altering plans to keep performance on track. Evaluation also includes looking for new opportunities and potential threats in the future. It is the connecting link in the strategic marketing planning process shown in Exhibit 1.6. By serving as both the last stage and the first stage (evaluation before taking action) in the planning process, strategic evaluation ensures that strategy is an ongoing activity.

Challenges of a New Era for Strategic Marketing

Moving into the second decade of the 21st century, it is apparent that executives face unprecedented challenges in strategic marketing to cope with global changes, turbulent markets, competitive revolution, and escalating customer demands for value superiority. In this chapter we describe the rationale for market-driven strategy and its components, as a business approach relevant to the new challenges of the present and future. Importantly, the personal demands for incisiveness and ingenuity in creating and implementing innovative and robust marketing strategies should not be ignored. In addition to the technical skills of analysis and planning required to implement market-driven strategy, capabilities for understanding new market and competitor phenomena will be at a premium. Societal and global change and unrest also mandate high levels of personal integrity in managers and leaders, and the reflection of these qualities in the social responsiveness of organizations.

Escalating Globalization

The internationalization of business is well-recognized in terms of the importance of export/import trade and the growth of international corporations, particularly in the Triad, comprising North America, Europe, and Japan. However, for strategic marketing in the

21st century, such a view of the international marketing issue may be short-sighted. The most intriguing and surprising challenges are likely to come from outside the mature Triad economies. It is important to understand the degree and extent of difference between the developed economies and the new world beyond. The effects may be dramatic.

The ability of competitors in emerging countries like China and Korea to produce goods at very low costs and prices was well-documented in the 1990s and early 2000s, and many markets like apparel have been severely affected. It is clear that some major customers may source from countries with massive cost advantages in labor costs. In 2004, Wal-Mart was the world's largest purchaser of Chinese goods, spending $15 billion in China in 2003, making the company China's fifth largest trading partner, ahead of countries like Russia and Britain. Indeed, U.S. consumers are reacting to price differences for medical treatments by traveling abroad. While a heart bypass may cost $25,000–35,000 in the United States, the operation is available in Thailand and India for $8,000–$15,000.[39]

The corollary is that emerging markets offer huge opportunities for exporters because of the population size and growing wealth. For example, one of the driving forces in the huge merger of consumer products companies Procter and Gamble and Gillette was to pool expertise in emerging markets—the goal of the combined enterprise is to serve the world's six billion consumers, not just the one billion most affluent. The focus is on the "lower income consumer" in markets like India and China, through the development of affordable products.[40]

Furthermore, the most important exports from countries like India and China may not just be goods and services but new business models, which will impact established ways of doing business in the developed world. The GLOBAL APPLICATION describes the aggressive expansion and acquisition strategies of companies in several emerging markets.

It is clear that the new breed of multinational company will be from developing nations, like Brazil, China, India, Russia, and South Africa. They are mostly companies that have prevailed in brutally competitive home markets, against local competitors and Western multinationals. They have business models that can generate profits from extremely low prices and survive in very tough environments.[41]

The global marketplace is dynamic and changing in complex ways with fundamental effects on the competitiveness and viability of companies in many sectors. Those who underestimate the rate of change and important shifts in international relationships run the risk of being outmaneuvered.

Technology Diversity and Uncertainty

The skills and vision required to decide which radical innovation opportunities can be successfully commercialized will be extremely demanding, and the risks of failure will be high. Innovations have the potential to revolutionize a range of different industries. They demand a strategic perspective that accepts the potential for revolution but balances this with commercial imperatives. The danger is that conventional approaches and short-sighted management may miss out on the most important opportunities.

Much innovation will reflect increased globalization. Chinese innovators are on the cutting edge in fields as diverse as autos, energy, semiconductors, and telecommunications.[42] China manufactures the bulk of the world's DVD players, cell phones, shoes, and

[39]"Over the Sea, Then Under the Knife," *BusinessWeek,* February 16, 2004, 20–22.
[40]Jeremy Grant, "Mr Daley's Mission: To Reach Six Billion Shoppers and Make Money," *Financial Times,* Friday, July 15, 2005, 32.
[41]Pete Engardio, "Emerging Giants," *BusinessWeek,* July 31, 2006, 39–49.
[42]Bruce Einhorn, "A Dragon in R&D," *BusinessWeek,* November 6, 2006, 44–50.

India. In 2006, for the first time, the value of India's acquisitions of overseas companies ($22.4 billion) exceeded the value of foreign companies buying into the country ($11.3 billion). The attraction is gaining access to lucrative developed country markets while maintaining the high productivity of the low-cost base in India. High-profile deals include:

- Suzlon Energy, manufacturer of wind turbines, pays $521 million for Hansen Transmissions, a gearbox producer in Belgium.
- Tata Steel pays $13.1 billion for Corus, the Anglo-Dutch steelmaker.
- Ranbaxy Laboratories makes acquisitions in Europe and the United States, and targets Germany's Merck in pharmaceuticals.

China. In 2007, a survey by the Economist Intelligence Unit showed record numbers of Chinese companies are looking to make overseas acquisitions, targeting Asia, Europe, and the United States. The highest profile deal is the acquisition by Lenovo of IBM's personal computer business. China is also an important market for products from other countries. In late 2010 Adidas AG, the German sporting-goods company, was making a major expansion in China. The firm planned to open 2500 new stores by 2015. Distribution will be expanded to 1400 cities from the present 500. In 2011 China was the second largest world economy.

Russia. The value of Russian overseas merger and acquisition deals in 2006 reached $13 billion, compared to $1 billion in 2002. Russia is cash rich on the basis of its exports of oil, gas, and metals. Many large Russian companies see expansion into international markets as essential. Energy and metals groups want to move beyond raw materials into higher profit areas such as refining and manufacturing. In 2006, $50 billion of Russian international deals failed. Gas giant Gazprom's interest in Centrica in Britain was rejected for political reasons. Steelmaker Exraz is rumored to be looking at Ipsco Inc, a pipemaker in Illinois. The success rate of international deals is expected to grow rapidly.

Sources: Dan Roberts, Richard McGregor and Stephanie Kirchgaessner, "A New Asian Invasion: China's Champions Bid High for American Brands and Resources," *Financial Times,* Friday, June 24, 2005, 17. Joe Leahy, "Unleashed: Why Indian Companies Are Setting Their Sights on Western Rivals," *Financial Times,* Wednesday, February 7, 2007, 13. Jason Bush, "Rubles Across the Sea," *BusinessWeek,* April 30, 2007, 43. Sundeep Tucker, "Reluctant Player Prepares to Step On to World Stage," *Financial Times,* May 31, 2007, 7. Laurie Burkitt, "Adidas Makes Big China Push," *Wall Street Journal,* November 17, 2010, B5.

certain other products. In the past these products have been designed elsewhere and produced in China. Now, some of the most innovative designs are developed in China, for both Chinese and foreign companies.[43] Major organizations like Microsoft and IBM are investing in worldwide innovation networks spanning countries like India, China, Russia, Israel, Singapore, Taiwan, and South Korea to speed development cycles and bring new technologies to market sooner.[44]

Internet Dynamics

As the impact of the Web on business became apparent in the 1990s, some authorities argued that the Internet would make conventional strategies obsolete. However, this phase of Internet business (Web 1.0) led to the failure of many Web-based businesses in the early

---

[43]David Rocks, "China Design," *Business Week,* November 21, 2005, 66–73.
[44]Pete Engardio, "Scouring the Planet for Brainiacs," *BusinessWeek,* October 11, 2004, 62–66.

2000s. A more compelling logic is that the Internet is a powerful complement to traditional business and marketing strategies.[45] Nonetheless, competitive boundaries are likely to be altered and competition will become more intense.

A current example of the power of Internet dynamics is the emergence of cloud computing as described in the INTERNET APPLICATION. This emerging development has potentially huge disruptive impacts on businesses as diverse as data storage, software applications, computer games, and music.

However, discussions of Web 2.0 dominated by emerging phenomena like social networking sites, such as MySpace—purchased for $580 million by News Corporation in 2005—and video-sharing sites, such as YouTube—purchased by Google for $1.65 billion in 2006. While such sites are highly popular among users—particularly younger consumers—the commercial implications are becoming apparent. It is possible, for example, that a social networking site like MySpace may be a highly effective advertising medium because it can achieve high engagement between individual brands and consumers, displacing traditional advertising spending from some advertisers' budgets.[46] Nonetheless, turbulent competition saw Facebook and Twitter displace MySpace in social net dominance, and by 2011 Facebook was looking at slowing growth and loss of members in many markets.

Internet tracking has experienced dynamic growth since 2000 enabling analysts to obtain extensive information about the online activities of people.[47] Not surprisingly, aggressive and widespread tracking has stimulated the development of privacy services by large technology firms and start-ups. Moreover, the size and scope of the tracking industry have generated regulatory concerns of trackers.

More generally, file-sharing, blogs, and social networking services have spawned many new services, including the online encyclopedia, Wikipedia, and the free Internet telephone network, Skype. The Web is providing a collaboration mechanism allowing companies to tap into the collective intelligence of employees, customers, and outsiders to solve problems and identify new opportunities. Outcomes range from the new retail marketplace found at eBay to consumer-generated content for advertising.[48] Internet strategy is considered throughout the book as an integral part of thinking about strategic marketing, not as a separate topic.

Ethical Behavior and Corporate Social Responsiveness

The demand on individuals to display high levels of personal integrity will likely increase in the future. Increasing levels of transparency mandate that manager behavior should meet the highest standards. The penalties for failing to meet the highest standards are likely to be severe. Growing emphasis is placed on corporate citizenship and the establishment and protection of secure corporate reputation as an asset with a financial return associated.[49]

While in the past corporate ethics and social responsibility may not have been center-stage in corporate and business strategy, this situation has changed dramatically. Major concerns about fairness and justice, and the impact of business activities on the physical environment are high on the management agenda. Indeed, even concerns about corporate social responsibility are being overtaken by the pressure on companies and communities to create shared value, focusing on the connection between societal and economic progress.

---

[45]Michael E. Porter, "Strategy and the Internet," *Harvard Business Review,* March 2001, 63–78.

[46]Matthew Garahan, "A Hunt for Revenue in the Ecosystem," *Financial Times,* Monday, April 30, 2007, 24.

[47]Julia Angwin and Emily Steel, "Web's Hot New Commodity: Privacy," *Wall Street Journal,* February 28, 2011, A1 and A16.

[48]Robert D. Hof, "The Power of Us," *BusinessWeek,* June 20, 2005, 47–56.

[49]Roger L. Martin, "The Virtue Matrix: Calculating the Return on Corporate Responsibility," *Harvard Business Review,* March, 2002, 69–75.

Internet Application

Market Impact of Cloud Computing

Pioneered by Google, cloud computing uses a global-spanning network of computers and data centers to create a computing system that outperforms the efficiency, speed, and flexibility of any company's computing system. Other innovating cloud operators were salesforce.com and Amazon—the first to sell cloud computing as a service (Amazon Web Services). A move toward cloud computing is a fundamental change in how information is handled across the world. It is the computing equivalent of the evolution in electricity supply from a hundred years ago when farms and businesses closed down their own power generators and brought power instead from efficient industrial utilities. Most consumers have been using cloud computing for years without realizing it—in the form of services like Google's Gmail and social networking sites like Facebook.

In fact, cloud computing is a major disruption for the conventional data storage industry, and for software producers (why buy software when it can be "rented" on the cloud?), and computer manufacturers (the computing power is on the cloud and can be accessed with smaller, cheaper computers).

In 2011, in a competitive move against Amazon and Google, Steve Jobs at Apple launched the iCloud with an online music service called iTunes Match, allowing customers to access music stored at data centers rather than on their independent devices. iTunes Match promises users access to as many as 20,000 pieces of music for around $25 a year. This is part of a broader online storage service letting Apple customers share documents, contacts, and pictures between devices. The potential impact is to move consumers of music away from the tradition of "owning" their music (on CDs or as downloads) toward a subscription model allowing cheap access to more music than could ever be "owned" by an individual. Sites like Spotify already allow unlimited access to a cloud-based library of millions of tracks in return for a subscription payment. This is a major disruption to conventional business models in the hard-pressed music business.

Sources: Menn, Joseph and Richard Waters, "Apple Looks to New Horizon as it Sets Out iCloud Service," *Financial Times,* June 7, 2011. Smith, Ethan and Yukari Iwatani Kane, "Apple Puts iTunes in Cloud," *Wall Street Journal,* June 7, 2011, p. 19. Waters, Richard and Chris Nuttall, "CloudThreatens to End PC's Reign," *Financial Times,* June 11/12, 2011, p. 17.

The pressure is underlined by the logic that societal needs, not just economic need, defines markets, and social harms create internal costs for companies.[50] For example, a research study by McKinsey suggests that as many as 70 percent of company managers believe there is room for improvement in the way large companies anticipate social pressure and respond to it. Managers see risks for their businesses in some social challenges—such as, climate change, data privacy, and healthcare—but opportunities in other challenges—such as the growing demand for more ethical, healthier, and safer products.[51]

Further indications of the importance of ethical and social responsibility issues are shown in studies of the perceptions of business school students—who will provide the next generations of managers. Business students appear to believe that companies should work more aggressively toward the betterment of society and want to find socially responsible employment in their careers.[52]

---

[50]Michael E. Porter and Mark R. Kramer, "Creating Shared Value," *Harvard Business Review,* January–February 2011, 62–77.

[51]Alison Maitland, "The Frustrated Will to Act for Public Good," *Financial Times,* Wednesday, January 25, 2006, 15.

[52]Rebecca Knight, "Business Students Portrayed as Ethically Minded in Study," *Financial Times,* Wednesday, October 25, 2006, 9.

However, concern for corporate social responsibility (CSR) extends beyond altruism or corporate philanthropy to a shift in the way that firms develop their business models. Customer pressures on suppliers to evidence higher standards of corporate behavior are considerable. In business-to-business marketing, suppliers unable or unwilling to meet the social responsibilities defined by major customers stand the considerable risk of losing those customers.[53]

In consumer marketing, a recent five-country survey, conducted by market research group GfK NOP, suggests that consumers in five of the world's leading economies believe that business ethics have worsened in the past five years, and they are turning to "ethical consumerism" to make companies more accountable.[54] Respondents believe that brands with "ethical" claims—of environmental policies or treatment of staff or suppliers—would make business more answerable to the public, and that companies should "promote ethical credentials more strongly."[55] The impact of "ethical consumerism" is of escalating significance.

However, while compliance with social demands for more ethical and responsible behavior is an important issue in strategic marketing, exciting new opportunities are being identified by companies in combining social initiatives with their business models and value propositions, to seek new types of competitive advantage. Porter and Kramer have argued that many prevailing approaches to CSR are fragmented and disconnected from business and strategy, while in fact the real challenge is for companies to analyze their social responsibility prospects using the same frameworks that guide their core business choices. The goal is to establish CSR not simply as corporate altruism, but as a source of opportunity, innovation, and competitive advantage.[56] The most strategic CSR adds a dimension to a company's value proposition, so that social impact is central to strategy. They note that the number of industries and companies whose competitive advantage can involve social value propositions is rapidly growing:

> Organizations that make the right choices and build focused, proactive, and integrated social initiatives in concert with their core strategies will increasingly distance themselves from the pack. Perceiving social responsibility as building shared value rather than as damage control or as a PR campaign will require dramatically different thinking in business. We are convinced, however, that CSR will become increasingly important to competitive success.[57]

Prototypes for the pursuit of social initiatives as a key part of the business model and to achieve competitive strength are illustrated in the ETHICS APPLICATION, describing the One Laptop Per Child program and recent high-profile developments at Dell Inc. and Microsoft.

Indeed, environmental initiatives that make business sense are not restricted to high-technology business. Remanufacturing at Caterpillar Inc. is one of the company's fastest growing divisions, with sales in excess of $1 billion a year—remanufacturing takes used diesel engines and uses the reclaimed parts to produce "like new" engines that sell for half the cost of a new engine. Similarly, at Xerox reclaimed photocopier parts go straight onto the new-build assembly line.[58] A major interest in the financial services field is the creation of new sustainable financial products, which enable companies like banks to achieve competitive differentiation.[59]

---

[53] Andrew Taylor, "Microsoft Drops Supplier over Diversity Policy," *Financial Times,* March 24–March 25, 2007, 5.

[54] Carlos Grande, "Businesses Behaving Badly, Say Consumers," *Financial Times,* Tuesday, February 20, 2007, 24.

[55] Carlo Grande, "Ethical Consumption Makes Mark on Branding," *Financial Times,* Tuesday, February 20, 2007, 24.

[56] Michael E. Porter and Mark R Kramer, "Strategy and Society: The Link Between Competitive Advantage and Corporate Social Responsibility," *Harvard Business Review,* December, 2006, 78–92.

[57] Ibid., 91–92.

[58] Brian Hindo, "Everything Old Is New Again," *BusinessWeek,* September 25, 2006, 63–70.

[59] John Willman, "New Way of Gaining Competitive Edge," *Financial Times Special Report: Sustainable Banking,* Thursday, June 7, 2007, 1.

One Laptop Per Child. In 2004 an MIT team said they were going to overcome the digital divide between the rich and poor by making a $100 laptop for the poor children of the world—the One Laptop Per Child (OLPC) project. Initially dismissed as a charitable project, the MIT team's vision has underlined to the commercial IT sector the market power of the poor. The effects on hardware and software companies have been dramatic: Intel has developed low-cost computers aimed at students in third-world countries; AMD has pledged to get half the world's population online by 2015 with its Personal Internet Communicator; Microsoft is supporting the establishment of computer kiosks in villages in developing countries to allow shared online access; Quanta Computer, the world's largest contract manufacturer of notebook computers, is making OLPC laptops selling for $200. The OLPC project underlines the social benefits and the commercial opportunities of a cheap laptop, which was relatively easy to make using newer technologies, open source software, by stripping out unneeded functions.

Dell Inc. Leading computer supplier, Dell Inc, is leveraging its distinctive competitive competences in initiatives with both business and social benefits—using the strengths of its direct business model to generate collective efforts to reduce energy consumption and protect the environment. The initiative centers on improving the efficiency of IT products, reducing the harmful materials used in them, and cooperating with customers to dispose of old products. Michael Dell's environmental strategy focuses on three areas: (1) creating easy, low-cost ways for businesses to do better in protecting the environment—providing, for example, global recycling and product recovery programs for customers, with participation requiring little effort on their part; (2) taking creative approaches to lessen the environmental impact of products from design to disposal—helping customers to take full advantage of new, energy-saving technology and processes, and advising on upgrades of legacy systems to reduce electricity usage; and (3) looking to partnership with governments to promote environmental stewardship PC. The link between this CSR initiative and the company's business model and value proposition is clear.

Microsoft. In 2007 Microsoft was partnering with governments in less developed countries to offer Microsoft Windows and Office software packages for $3 to governments that subsidize the cost of computers for schoolchildren. The potential business benefit for Microsoft is to double the number of PC users worldwide, and reinforce the company's market growth. The social benefit is the greater investment in technology in some of the poorest countries in the world, with the goal of improving living standards and reducing global inequality.

Sources: Michael Dell, "Everyone Has a Choice," *Financial Times Digital Business—Special Report,* Wednesday, April 18, 2007, 1. "Footing the Bill: Gates Offers $3 Software to Poor," *Financial Times,* Friday April 20, 2007, 1.

The challenges to executives to develop and implement business models which achieve the goals of both business and society are considerable and span all sectors of industry. While these forces of change portray a challenging yet exciting environment for strategic marketing, across the world marketing professionals are finding new and better ways to respond to the new realities, to deliver superior customer value to their markets, and to enhance shareholder value. Underpinning processes of reinvention and radical innovation are principles of robust marketing strategy. The goal of this book is to identify and illustrate these principles, and provide processes for responding to the challenges.

Summary

The challenges facing business executives are framed by turbulence in the business and competitive environment challenging the resilience of companies to prosper. This chapter aims, first, to examine the nature of market-driven strategy and the market-oriented company; second, to explain the links between corporate strategy and business and marketing strategy; and, third, to underline some of the major challenges of the current marketing era, including customer, technology change, and ethics and corporate social responsibility.

A customer-driven strategy requires that the market and customers should be the starting point in business strategy formulation. Market orientation provides the appropriate business perspective that makes the customer the focal point of the company's operations. A company's distinctive capabilities provide the skills and knowledge that are deployed to create value for customers. Becoming customer-driven relies on market-sensing and customer-linking capabilities, and the alignment of structure and process with market-driven priorities.

Corporate strategy involves management in deciding the long-term vision for the company, setting objectives, focusing on capabilities, choosing the businesses in which the corporation competes, and defining the business design and how it will create value. Business strategy focuses on the strategic plan for each unit. The marketing strategy process involves evaluating markets, segments, and value drivers, designing customer-driven strategies, developing market-driven programs, and implementing and managing strategies.

The modern era for customer-driven strategy involves many complex and challenging issues for executives. We underline the importance of escalating globalization, emerging Web phenomena, technology diversity and uncertainty, and strategic mandates for ethical behavior and corporate social responsibility initiatives linked not simply to compliance but to new sources of competitive advantage.

Questions for Review and Discussion

1. Top management of companies probably devotes more time to reviewing (and sometimes changing) their corporate vision (mission) now than in the past. Discuss the major reasons for this increased concern with the vision for the corporation.

2. Discuss the role of organizational capabilities in corporate strategy.

3. What is the relationship between the corporate strategy and the strategies for the businesses that comprise the corporate portfolio?

4. Discuss the major issues that top management should consider when deciding whether or not to expand business operations into new business areas.

5. Develop an outline of how you would explain the marketing strategy process to an inventor who is forming a new business to develop, produce, and market a new product.

6. Discuss the role of market targeting and positioning in an organization's marketing strategy.

7. Explain the logic of pursuing a market-driven strategy.

8. Examine the relevance of market orientation as a guiding philosophy for a social service organization, giving particular attention to user needs and wants.

9. How do the organization's distinctive capabilities contribute to developing market-driven strategy?

10. How would you explain the concept of superior customer value to a new finance manager?

11. Suppose you have been appointed to the top marketing post of a corporation and the president has asked you to explain market-driven strategy to the board of directors. What will you include in your presentation?

12. Develop a list of the personal challenges confronting the marketing executive, and consider the qualities and capabilities which may be most relevant to meeting these challenges.

Internet Applications

A. Visit the websites of fashion clothing companies Zara (*www.zara.com*) and H&M (*www .hm.com*). What do these sites tell you about the targeting and positioning strategies being pursued by these companies?

B. What does Google's website (*www.Google.com*) tell us about the company's ability to collect information about individuals and businesses? What privacy issues arise, and how can they be resolved?

C. Review the McKinsey & Co. website. Are there indications that the consulting company is market oriented?

Applications

A. Read the ETHICS APPLICATION—Corporate Social Responsibility for Competitive Advantage. Summarize the reasons why companies are adopting corporate social responsibility initiatives. What arguments support the pursuit of social initiatives by business organizations, and what arguments suggest that the role of business is primarily to make profits?

B. Review the MARKETING STRATEGY APPLICATION. What are the challenges created by relationships in Network Organizations? How can these challenges be overcome? What role does marketing play in these relationships?

Appendix **1A**

Strategic Marketing Planning

Developing the Strategic Plan for Each Business

Strategic analysis is conducted to: (1) diagnose business units' strengths and limitations, and (2) select strategies for maintaining or improving performance. Management decides what priority to place on each business regarding resource allocation and implements a strategy to meet the objectives for the SBU. The strategic plan indicates the action agenda for the business.

The strategic analysis guides establishing the SBU's mission, setting objectives, and determining the strategy to use to meet these objectives. The SBU's strategy indicates market target priorities, available resources, financial constraints, and other strategic guidelines needed to develop marketing plans. Depending on the size and diversity of the SBU, marketing plans may either be included in the SBU plan or developed separately. If combined, the marketing portion of the business plan will represent half or more of the business plan. In a small business (e.g., retail store, restaurant, etc.), the marketing portion of the plan may account for most of the plan. Plans may be developed to obtain financial support for a new venture, or to spell out internal business and marketing strategies.

Preparing the Marketing Plan

Marketing plans vary widely in scope and detail. Nevertheless, all plans need to be based on analyses of the product-market and segments, industry and competitive structure, and the organization's value proposition. We look at several important planning issues that provide a checklist for plan preparation.

Planning Relationships and Frequency

Marketing plans are developed, implemented, evaluated, and adjusted to keep the strategy on target. Since the marketing strategy normally extends beyond one year, it is useful to develop a 3-year strategic plan and an annual plan to manage marketing activities during the year. Budgets for marketing activities (e.g., advertising) are set annually. Planning is really a series of annual plans guided by the marketing strategic plan.

The frequency of planning activities varies by company and marketing activity. Market targeting and positioning strategies are not changed significantly during the year. Tactical changes in product, distribution, price, and promotion strategies may be included in the annual plan. For example, the aggressive response of competitors to Healthy Choice's successful market entry required changes in ConAgra's pricing and promotion tactics for the frozen food line.

Planning Considerations

Suppose that you need to develop a plan for a new product to be introduced into the national market next year. The plan for the introduction should include the expected results (objectives), market targets, actions, responsibilities, schedules, and dates. The plan indicates details and deadlines, product plans, a market introduction program, advertising and sales promotion actions, employee training, and other information necessary to launching the product. The plan needs to answer a series of questions—what, when, where, who, how, and why—for each action targeted for completion during the planning period.

Responsibility for Preparing Plans

A marketing executive or team is responsible for preparing the marketing plan. Some companies combine the business plan and the marketing plan into a single planning activity. Regardless of the format used, the marketing plan is developed in close coordination with the strategic plan for the business. There is also much greater emphasis today to involve all business functions in the marketing planning process. A product or marketing manager may draft the formal plan for his or her area of responsibility, coordinating and receiving inputs from advertising, marketing research, sales, and other marketing specialists. Coordination and involvement with other business functions (R&D, finance, operations) is also essential.

Planning Unit

The choice of the planning unit may vary due to the product-market portfolio of the organization. Some firms plan and manage by individual market targets or target. Others work with product lines, markets, or specific customers. The planning unit may reflect how marketing activities and responsibilities are organized. The market target is a useful focus for planning regardless of how the plan is aggregated.

Using the target as the basis for planning helps to place the customer in the center of the planning process and keeps the positioning strategy linked to the market target.

Preparing the Marketing Plan

Format and content depend on the size of the organization, managerial responsibility for planning, product and market scope, and other situational factors. An outline for a typical marketing plan is shown in Exhibit 1A-1. We take a brief look at the major parts of the planning outline to illustrate the nature and scope of the planning process. In this discussion the market target serves as the planning unit.

Outline for Preparing an Annual Marketing Plan

The Situation Summary

This part of the plan describes the market and its important characteristics, size estimates, and growth projections. Market segment analysis indicates the segments to be targeted and their relative importance. The competitor analysis indicates the key competitors (actual and potential), their strengths and weaknesses, probable future actions, and the organization's competitive advantage(s) in each segment of interest. The summary should be very brief. Supporting detailed information for the summary can be placed in an appendix or in a separate analysis.

EXHIBIT 1A-1 Outline for Preparing an Annual Marketing Plan

Strategic Situation Summary

A summary of the strategic situation for the planning unit (business unit, market segment, product line, etc.).

Market Target(s) Description

Define and describe each market target, including customer profiles, customer preferences and buying habits, size and growth estimates, distribution channels, analysis of key competitors, and guidelines for positioning strategy.

Objectives for the Market Target(s)

Set objectives for the market target (such as market position, sales, and profits). Also state objectives for each component of the marketing program. Indicate how each objective will be measured.

Marketing Program Positioning Strategy

State how management wants the firm to be positioned relative to the competition in the eyes and mind of the buyer.

A. *Product Strategy*

   Set strategy for new products, product improvements, and product deletions.

B. *Distribution Strategy*

   Indicate the strategy to be used for each distribution channel, including the role of channel members, assistance and support provided, and specific activities planned.

C. *Price Strategy*

   Specify the role of price in the marketing strategy and the planned actions regarding price.

D. *Promotion Strategy*

   Indicate the planned strategy and actions for advertising, publicity, Internet, personal selling, and sales promotion.

E. *Marketing Research*

   Identify information needs and planned projects, objectives, estimated costs, and timetable.

F. *Coordination with Other Business Functions*

   Specify the responsibilities and activities of other departments that have an important influence on the planned marketing strategy.

Forecasts and Budgets

Forecast sales and profit for the marketing plan and prepare the budget for accomplishing the forecast.

Describe the Market Target

A description of each market target, size and growth rate, end-users' characteristics, positioning strategy guidelines, and other available information useful in planning and implementation are essential parts of the plan. When two or more targets are involved, it is helpful to indicate priorities for guiding resource allocation.

Objectives for the Market Target(s)

Here we spell out what the marketing strategy is expected to accomplish during the planning period. Objectives are needed for each market target, indicating financial performance, sales, market position, customer satisfaction, and other desired results. Objectives are also usually included for each marketing program component.

Marketing Program Positioning Strategy

The positioning statement indicates how management wants the targeted customers and prospects to perceive the brand. Specific strategies and tactics for product, distribution, price, and promotion are explained in this part of the plan. Actions to be taken, responsibilities, time schedules, and other implementation information are included at this point in the plan.

Planning and implementation responsibilities often involve more than one person or department. One approach is to assign a planning team the responsibility for each market target and marketing mix component. Product and geographical responsibilities are sometimes allocated to individuals or teams. The responsibilities and coordination requirements need to be indicated for marketing units and other business functions. Importantly, the planning process should encourage participation from all of the areas responsible for implementing the plan. Contingency plans may be included in the plan. The contingencies consider possible actions if the anticipated planning environment is different from what actually occurs.

Forecasting and Budgeting

Financial planning includes forecasting revenues and profits and estimating the costs necessary to carry out the marketing plan (see the Appendix to Chapter 2 for financial analysis details). The people responsible for market target, product, geographical area, or other units should prepare the forecasts and budgets. Comparative data on sales, profits, and expenses for prior years is useful to link the plan to previous results.

Markets, Segments, and Customer Value

Part

2

Chapter

2

Markets and Competitive Space

Markets are increasingly complex, turbulent, and interrelated, creating challenges for managers in understanding market structure and identifying opportunities for growth. The traditional view assumes that the market and competitive space are stable and changes are predictable. Importantly, this perspective may be misleading and even dangerous when market boundaries reconfigure because of new technologies and competition and the emergence of new business designs (such as Google, Inc., the world's leading Internet search business). Sustaining and building competitive advantage increasingly requires altered strategic thinking about market boundaries and structure. Rapid technological change, market convergence, Internet access, global competition, and the diversity of buyers' preferences in many markets require continuous monitoring to identify promising business opportunities, assess the shifting requirements of buyers, and evaluate changes in competitive positioning, and they guide managers' decisions about which buyers to target and how to position brands to appeal to targeted buyers. A complete view of the market is important, even when management's interest centers on one or a few market segments within a particular market. Understanding the scope and structure of the entire market is necessary to develop strategy and anticipate market changes and competitive threats. Understanding markets and how they are likely to change in the future are vital inputs to market-driven strategies.

Illustrative of the challenges and struggles created by rapid changes in markets and competitive space are Eastman Kodak's delayed responses to the potential disruptive impact of digital photography on traditional film and camera markets. The pervasive impact of digital imaging technology demanded a rapid change in Kodak's business design and understanding of the market.[1] Kodak's revenues from its traditional products and services declined from $10 billion in 2001 to $5 billion in 2007, when total revenues were $10.3 billion. The consequences of Kodak's delayed responses to the changing markets include major financial losses, extensive layoffs, expensive plant closures, and escalating debt. Kodak's prior management (new CEO in June 2005) had significantly underestimated the speed and rate of

---

[1]This illustration is based on William M. Bulkeley, "Kodak's Loss Widens as Revenue Declines 8.8%," *Wall Street Journal,* August 2, 2006, B10; "A Tense Kodak Moment," *BusinessWeek,* October 17, 2005, 84–85; "Another Kodak Moment," *The Economist,* May 14, 2005, 69. Dana Mattioli, "At Kodak, Patents Hold the Key to the Future," *Wall Street Journal,* April 20, 2010, B8. *The Value Line Investment Survey,* Part 3 Ratings & Reports, Issue 1, February 25, 2011, 119.

decline of purchases in film markets around the world. Interestingly, Kodak invented the digital camera in the mid-1970s, but responded very slowly to commercialization opportunities. Management has been successful in obtaining income from intellectual-property patents. While Kodak holds a strong position in the U.S. digital camera market, adding to the firm's financial problems are the very small margins on digital cameras. Kodak continues to struggle. Sales were an estimated $6.4 billion in 2012, earnings were negative from 2008 through 2011, and the stock price declined from a high of $41 in 2003 to below $4 in 2011.

Kodak's competitive threats are not unique. Many companies and industries are experiencing major changes in their core markets. Strategic thinking in changing markets confronts executives with complex challenges but also exciting opportunities. These new challenges are driven by demanding customers with changing value requirements, aggressive global competition, market turbulence, rapid emergence of new and increasingly turbulent technologies, and the escalating globalization initiatives of many companies.

The Kodak illustration highlights several important issues concerning markets and competitive space. The changes described show how competitive threats may develop from new competition (electronics firms). Importantly, the rapid growth of digital photography points to the importance of market sensing and strategic vision in assessing the nature and scope of new competitive threats and guiding strategic initiatives to counter the threats.

The chapter begins with a discussion of how markets and strategies are interrelated, followed by an approach to determining product-market scope and structure. Next, we look at how buyers are described and analyzed, and examine the important process of competitor analysis. Guidelines follow for developing a strategic vision about the scope and composition of markets in the future. Finally, we consider how to estimate market size. Financial analysis guidelines are included in the Appendix.

Markets and Strategies

Knowledge about markets and competitive space is essential in guiding business and marketing strategies. First, we look at how markets impact strategy and discuss the importance of thinking outside the competitive box. Next, we examine several forces that are creating changes in market boundaries and structure, and consider the need to define markets in terms of buyers' needs and product benefits.

Markets and Strategies are Interlinked

Market changes often require altering business and marketing strategies. The Kodak example is illustrative. Managers who do not understand their markets and how they will change in the future may find their strategies inadequate as buyers' value requirements change and new products become available that better satisfy buyers' requirements. Many forces are causing the transformation of industries and are changing the structure of markets and nature of competition. These influences create both market opportunities and threats by altering the nature and scope of products, markets, and competitive space. Market-driven companies proactively alter their strategies to deliver superior value to existing and new customers. For example, PepsiCo shows impressive performance in understanding and catering to changing tastes in the beverage and snacks market, rather than trying to change them.[2] The company faces the facts about market change and adapts products to them. To capitalize on the growing market for New Age herbally enhanced beverages, PepsiCo acquired SoBe Beverages in 2001, and extended the brand into an energy drink for the

---

[2]Diane Brady, "A Thousand and One Noshes," *BusinessWeek,* June 14, 2004, 44.

school age market—SoBe No Fear—and SoBe Fuerte, aimed at the Hispanic market. Sabritas chips were brought in from PepsiCo's Mexican subsidiary targeting the foreign-born segment of the large and escalating U.S. Hispanic market. PepsiCo defines its mission as serving the consumer, not protecting its existing brands.

Thinking Outside the Competitive Box[3]

Not surprisingly there is a tendency for executives to think in terms of a stable "competitive box" around their businesses—defined by technology, geography, competitors, and the existing customer base. This frame of reference enables analytical tools to be successfully applied, research to be carried out, and plans to be made. This traditional perspective is logical in stable markets but fails to address the reality that the real threats as well as exciting opportunities may be present outside the conventional competitive box shown in Exhibit 2.1. Increasingly, new markets, new types of competition, and new business designs are emerging that fuel market growth and cannibalize the existing customer base of incumbents' markets. Importantly, effective processes for understanding markets and competitive space and guiding the strategic initiatives appropriate for the markets require strategic thinking outside the competitive box.

The revolution in the global recorded music business is illustrative. The drivers of market change have not been conventional music recording companies but instead, artists delivering music direct to consumers through the Internet; high-quality digital downloading of music from sites like Apple's iTunes; the rapid spread of high-quality digital music players like the iPod, and more recently cell phones; and the growing availability of subscription services allowing consumers access to huge quantities of music without the need to ever buy a CD. The challenge to the traditional music companies is locating opportunities to make profit in a wholly reconfigured market space.

EXHIBIT 2.1
Opportunities Outside the Competitive Box

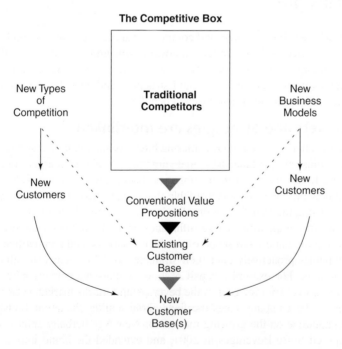

[3]This discussion is based on David W. Cravens, Nigel F. Piercy, and Artur Baldauf, "Management Framework for Guiding Strategic Thinking in Rapidly Changing Markets," *Journal of Marketing Management,* 25(1–2), 2009.

The Flip video camera was an immediate success but ended its life cycle in 4 years. Developed by start-up entrepreneurs, it was introduced in 2007 and achieved impressive sales of 2 million units in 2 years. The entrepreneurs sold the product to Cisco Systems Inc. in 2009 for $590 million! The easy-to-use cameras were very popular with consumers until impacted by disruptive technology.

The Flip video camera illustrates what happens to an existing product when competitive new technology enters the market. The Flip video camera experienced a fast life cycle. In April 2011 Cisco announced it was closing the Flip camera division. The rapid innovation of smart phones signaled the demise of the Flip camera. The array of features of the smart phone not only ended the very short life cycle of the single-function camera, GPS devices, point-and-shoot cameras, and many other consumer devices experienced significant sales declines.

The Flip video camera provides a dramatic illustration of the disruptive impact of new technology and the effects of an extremely short life cycle. The negative impact on Cisco was 550 job reductions and a quarterly negative charge of $300 million. The acquisition points to the critical importance of market and competitive analysis in the rapidly changing business and market environment.

Sources: Roger Cheng and Don Clark, "Cisco Flips Consumer Strategy," *Wall Street Journal,* April 13, 2011, B3; Sam Grobart and Evelyn M. Rusli, "For Flip Video Camera, Four Years From Hot Start-Up to Obsolete," *New York Times,* April 13, 2011, B1 and B8.

An Array of Challenges

Changes in markets are drastically altering opportunities and competitive space and increasing the importance of strategic thinking in these changing markets. Disruptive innovation, commoditization of product designs, creation of new market space, and fast-changing markets are challenges that underline the need to identify changes in the market(s) and diagnose the strategic implications of the changes.

Disruptive Innovation

These innovations provide simpler and less costly ways to match the value requirements offered by the products (goods and services) of incumbent firms serving the market.[4] Examples of disruptive innovations and new business models are illustrated by the impact of Amazon.com on traditional bookstores, digital photography on cameras and film, and steel mini-mills on integrated mills. The opportunity for market access by disruptive innovations is created by the products of incumbent firms in the market which are exceeding the value requirements of buyers. Disruptive innovations may meet the needs of new segments or entire markets.

Disruptive innovations may impact various technologies and industries. Indications of these new threats to existing firms can often be identified through perceptive market sensing outside the competitive box. Complacency and management's hesitancy to consider options beyond the core business focus are potential problems. When indications are found that markets are changing, strategic thinking initiatives need to be pursued. The strategic development of the smart phone is illustrative of the disruptive changes that can be created by an able competitor. This is described in the STRATEGY APPLICATION.

---

[4]Clayton M. Christensen and Michael E. Raynor, *The Innovator's Solution* (Boston: Harvard Business School Press, 2003), Chapter 1.

Commoditization Threats

When modularization (products comprised of standardized components) occurs products become commodities, making it difficult to earn anything more than subsistence returns.[5] For example, when the personal computer (PC) market became commoditized, the opportunity for profits shifted to microprocessors (Intel) and operating system software (Microsoft). Commoditization was a key factor for IBM's management in deciding to move out of the PC market. The business was sold to Lenovo, the leading Chinese PC company.

The potential effect of commoditization in markets highlights the importance of developing a vision about how the market is likely to change in the future, and deciding what business strategy initiatives to pursue. Strategies to overcome commoditization threats may involve competing at a different stage in the value chain or moving into a different product category that provides attractive growth and profit opportunities.

Creating New Market Space

Kim and Mauborgne offer an interesting and relevant perspective on how companies can create new market space.[6] These actions require finding and pursuing opportunities to offer potential buyers value in markets and segments that are not being served. The purpose is to target new opportunities where buyers' value requirements are not being satisfied by existing products. For example, unit sales of camera phones were estimated to exceed 400 million units in 2006, over four times digital camera sales.[7] Cell phone users have access to digital photography because the camera is subsidized by wireless carriers. This creates new market space and new uses by digital camera users. Creating new market space requires changing management's traditional strategic perspective of looking for market opportunities inside the competitive box.

The goals of Tesco's U.S. grocery retailing venture, Fresh & Easy, considered in Chapter 1 are illustrative of a strategy aiming to create a new market space. Fresh & Easy is trying to develop the space between existing specialist food retailers like Trader Joes and Bristol Farms and general market discounters like Wal-Mart. The strategic intent is to persuade some consumers to trade up from discount retailers by offering fresher food and ready-meals, and others to trade down from expensive specialist retailers by offering fresh food at lower prices.

Fast-Changing Markets

Increasingly, fewer markets are stable, and instead, many are changing rapidly. Fast-changing markets require modifications in management's strategic thinking. Indications of changes are signaled by shifting customer value requirements, new technologies, changes in competitive space, and new business models. Fast-changing markets may sometimes be difficult to predict and strategy initiatives may necessitate trial-and-error adjustments guided by market responses. Not acknowledging or responding to the threats and requirements of fast-changing markets is the real danger. Importantly, even in markets assumed to be comparatively stable, innovation can quickly alter market space.

For example, the global steel business has been transformed by Lakshmi Mittal's strategy at Arcelor Mittal. While existing companies focused on tonnages of steel produced,

[5]Ibid., Chapter 6.
[6]W. C. Kim and R. Mauborgne, *Blue Ocean Strategy* (Boston: Harvard Business School Press, 2005).
[7]Pui-Wing Tam, "Entreaty to Camera-Phone Photographers: Please Print," *Wall Street Journal,* December 28, 2004, B1 and B3.

not profits, and regional supply chains, not global, Mittal's strategy was based on global consolidation, continuous improvement, knowledge sharing, and competitive strength through superior customer value. A slow-moving sector has been transformed into a fast-changing market by one company's strategy.[8]

Matching Needs with Product Benefits

The term *product-market* recognizes that a market exists only when there are buyers with needs who have the ability to purchase goods and services and products are available to satisfy the needs. There is a compelling logic that competitive strength comes from putting customer needs at the center of a company's operations; that this perspective should guide strategic thinking for markets. For example, Progressive Insurance shows remarkable sales growth and shareholder value creation by its focus on the most important needs of its customers. The INNOVATION APPLICATION describes how the company has adapted its operations to effectively meet customer needs.

Markets are comprised of groups of people who have the *ability* and *willingness* to buy something because they have a need (value requirement) for it. The ability to buy and willingness to buy indicate that there is demand for a particular product. People with needs and wants buy the benefits provided by a good or service to satisfy either a household or organizational use situation. A product-market matches people with needs—needs that lead to a demand for a good or service—to the product benefits that satisfy those needs. Thus, a product-market combines the benefits of a product with the needs that motivate people to express a demand for that product.

Accordingly, markets are defined in terms of needs substitutability among different products and brands and by the different ways in which people choose to satisfy their needs. "A product-market is the set of products judged to be substitutes within those usage situations in which similar patterns of benefits are sought by groups of customers."[9] The influence of competing brands becomes stronger the closer the substitutability and the more direct the competition. The Ford Taurus competes directly with the Toyota Camry, whereas in a less direct yet relevant way, other major purchases (e.g., vacation travel) compete with automobile expenditures due to the buyer's budget constraints.

As an example, a financial services product-market for short-term investments may include money market accounts, mutual funds, U.S. Treasury bills, bank certificates of deposit, and other short-term investment alternatives. If one type of product is a substitute for another, then both should be included in the product-market.

By determining how a firm's specific product or brand is positioned within the product-market, management can monitor and evaluate changes in the product-market to decide whether alternate targeting and positioning strategies and product offerings are needed. When defining a product-market, it is essential to establish boundaries that are broad enough to contain all of the relevant product categories which are competing for the same buyer needs.

---

[8]Stanley Reed, "Mittal & Son," *BusinessWeek,* April 16, 2007, 44–50. Reed, Stanley, "The Raja of Steel," *BusinessWeek,* December 20, 2004, 18–22.

[9]Rajendra K. Srivastava, Mark I. Alpert, and Allan D. Shocker, "A Customer-Oriented Approach for Determining Market Structures," *Journal of Marketing,* Spring 1984, 32.

- In the period 1994 to 2010, Progressive Insurance increased net premiums earned from $1.3 billion to $14.3 billion, and ranks high in the *BusinessWeek* Top 50 U.S. companies for shareholder value creation.

- The company invents new ways of providing services to save customers time, money, and irritation, while often lowering costs at the same time.
- Loss adjusters are sent to the road accidents rather than working at the head office, and they have the power to write checks on the spot.
- Progressive reduced the time needed to see a damaged automobile from seven days to nine hours.
- Policyholders' cars are repaired quicker, and the focus on this central customer need has won much auto insurance business for Progressive.
- These initiatives also enable Progressive to reduce its own costs—the cost of storing a damaged automobile for a day is $28, about the same as the profit from a six-month policy.

Sources: *Value Line Investment Survey,* Ratings & Reports, Issue 4, March 18, 2011, 771. Adapted from Adrian Mitchell, "Heart of the Matter," *The Marketer,* June 12, 2004, 14.

Defining and Analyzing Product-Markets

In the remainder of the chapter we discuss the activities involved in defining and analyzing product-markets. The steps are shown in Exhibit 2.2, beginning with determining product-market boundaries and structure.

Determining Product-Market Boundaries and Structure

Product-market boundaries and structure provide managers with important information for developing business and marketing strategies, and alert management to new competition. Considering only a company's brands and the direct competitors may mask potential competitive threats or opportunities.

Product-Market Structure

A company's brand competes with other companies' brands in generic, product-type, and product-variant product-markets. The *generic product-market* includes a broad group of products that satisfy a general, yet similar, need. For example, several classes or types of products can be combined to form the generic product-market for kitchen appliances. The starting point in determining product-market boundaries is to identify the particular need or want that a group of products satisfies, such as performing kitchen functions. Since people with a similar need may not satisfy the need in the same manner, generic product-markets are often heterogeneous, containing different end-user groups and several types of related products (e.g., kitchen appliances).

The *product-type product-market* includes all brands of a particular product type, such as ovens for use in food preparation by consumers. The product type is a product category or product classification that offers a specific set of benefits intended to satisfy a customer's

EXHIBIT 2.2
Defining and
Analyzing
Product-Markets

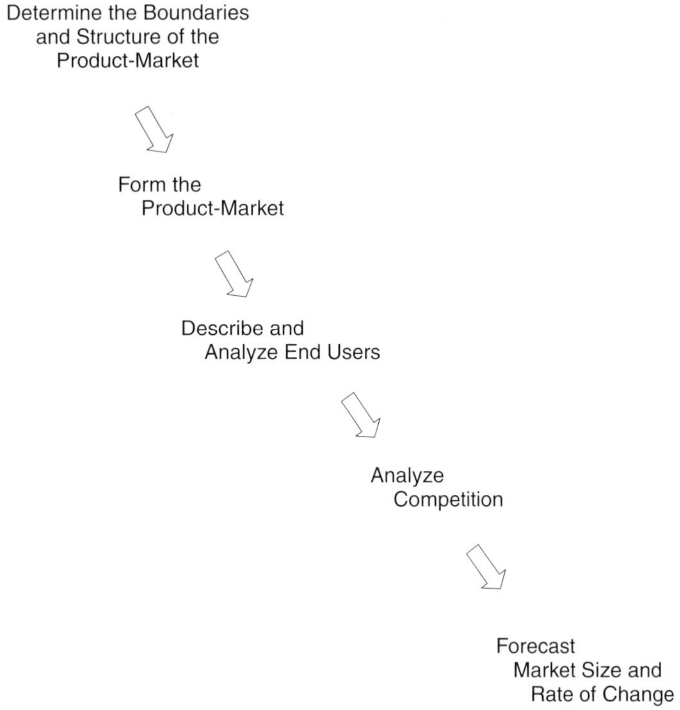

Determine the Boundaries
and Structure of the
Product-Market

⬇

Form the
Product-Market

⬇

Describe and
Analyze End Users

⬇

Analyze
Competition

⬇

Forecast
Market Size and
Rate of Change

need or want in a specific way. Differences in the products within a product-type product-market may exist, creating *product-variants.*[10] For example, electric, gas, and microwave ovens all provide heating functions but employ different technologies.

Guidelines for Definition

In defining the product-market, it is helpful to indicate (1) the basis for identifying buyers in the product-market of interest (geographical area, consumer/business, etc.); (2) the market size and characteristics; and (3) the brand and/or product categories competing for the needs and wants of the buyers included in the product-market.

The composition of a product-market can be determined by following the steps shown in Exhibit 2.3. We illustrate how this process can be used to determine the composition of the kitchen appliance product-market. Suppose top management of a kitchen appliance firm is considering expanding its mix of products. The company's present line of laundry and dishwashing products meets a generic need for the kitchen functions of cleaning. Other kitchen use situations include heating and cooling of foods. In this example the generic need is performing various kitchen functions. The products that provide kitchen functions are ways of satisfying the generic need. The break out of products into specific product-markets (e.g., A, B, C, and D) would include equipment for washing and drying clothing, appliances for cooling food, cooking appliances, and dishwashers. The buyers in various specific product-markets and the different brands competing in these product-markets can be identified and analyzed. The process of mapping the product-market structure begins by identifying the generic need (function) satisfied by the product of interest to management. Need identification is the basis for selecting the products that fit into the product market.

---

[10]George S. Day, *Strategic Marketing Planning: The Pursuit of Competitive Advantage* (St. Paul, MN: West Publishing, 1984), 72.

EXHIBIT 2.3
**Determining the
Composition of a
Product-Market**

Start with the generic need satisfied by
the product category of interest to
management

Identify the product categories (types)
that can satisfy the generic need

Identify the specific product-markets
within the generic product-market

A   B   C   D

An example of the product-market structure to meet people's needs for food is shown in Exhibit 2.4. A fast-food restaurant chain such as McDonald's should consider more than its regular customers and direct competitors in its market opportunity analysis. The consumption need being satisfied is fast and convenient preparation of food. The buyer has several ways of meeting the need such as purchasing fast foods, preparing food in the microwave in the home, patronizing supermarket delis, buying prepared foods in convenience stores, home delivery of meals, and ordering take outs from traditional restaurants. The relevant competitive space includes all of these fast-food sources. It is essential to analyze market behavior and trends in the product-markets shown in Exhibit 2.4, since competition may come from any of the alternative services.

Forming Product-Markets

The factors that influence how product-market boundaries should be determined include the purpose for analyzing the product-market, the rate of changes in market composition over time, and the extent of market complexity.

Purpose of Analysis

If management is deciding whether or not to exit from a business, primary emphasis may be on financial performance and competitive position. Detailed analysis of the product-market may not be necessary. In contrast, if the objective is finding one or more attractive market segments to target in the product-market, a much more penetrating analysis is

EXHIBIT 2.4
**Illustrative Fast-Food
Product-Market
Structure**

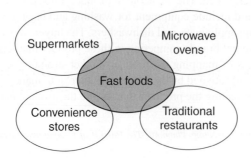

necessary. When different products satisfy the same need, the product-market boundaries should contain all relevant products and brands. For example, the photography product-market should include digital cameras, related equipment and services, smart phones, and services. Product-market boundaries should be determined in a manner that will facilitate strategic analysis and thinking, enabling management to capitalize on existing and potential opportunities and to avoid possible threats.

Changing Composition of Markets

As discussed earlier product-markets may change as new technologies become available and new competition emerges. New technologies offer buyers different ways of meeting their needs. For example, Internet technology gave people in need of rapid delivery an alternative way to transmit the information. The entry into the market by new competitors also alters competitive space.

Industry classifications often do not clearly define product-market boundaries. For example, people may meet their needs for food with products from several industries as shown in Exhibit 2.4. Industry-based definitions do not consider alternative ways of meeting needs. Industry classifications typically have a product supply rather than a customer demand orientation. Of course, since industry associations, trade publications, and government agencies generate a lot of information about products and markets, information from these sources should be examined in market analysis. However, market analysis activities should not be constrained by industry boundaries.

Extent of Market Complexity

Three characteristics of markets capture a large portion of the variation in their complexity: (1) the *functions* or uses of the product needed by the customer, (2) the *technology* used in the product to provide the desired function, and (3) the different *customer segments* using the product to perform a particular function.[11]

Customer function considers the role or purpose of the good or service. It is the value provided to the customer. Thus, the function provides the capability to satisfy the value requirements of the customer. In the case of the personal computer, the function performed may be entertainment for the household, information search, Internet purchasing, or the performance of various business functions.

Different *technologies* may satisfy the use situation of the customer. Steel and aluminum materials meet a similar need in various use situations. The technology consists of the materials and designs incorporated into products. In the case of a service, technology relates to how the service is rendered. For example, voice calls can be sent via the Internet, traditional phone lines, and wireless phones.

Customer segment recognizes the diversity of the needs of customers in a particular product-market such as automobiles. A specific brand and model won't satisfy all buyers' needs and wants. Two broad market segments for automobile use are households and organizations. These classifications can be further divided into more specific customer segments, such as preferences for European-style luxury sedans, sport utility vehicles, and sports cars.

It is important to focus on the consumer (or organizational) end-user of the product when defining the market, since the end-user drives demand for the product. When the end-users' needs and wants change, the market changes. Even though a producer considers the distributor to which its products are sold to be the customer, the market is

---

[11]Derek F. Abell, *Defining the Business: The Starting Point of Strategic Planning* (Englewood Cliffs, NY: Prentice Hall, 1980).

really defined by the consumer and organizational end-users who purchase the product for consumption.

Illustrative Product-Market Structure

Suppose you are a brand manager for a cereal producer. You know that brands like Life, Product 19, and Special K compete for sales to people that want nutritional benefits from cereal. Nonetheless, our earlier discussion highlights the value of considering a more complete picture of how competing brands like Life, Product 19, and Special K also may experience competition from other ways of meeting the needs satisfied by these brands. For example, a person may decide to eat a Kellogg's Nutri-Grain cereal bar instead of a bowl of cereal, and the consumer may want to vary the type of cereal, eating a natural or regular type of cereal. Because of the different product types and variants competing for the same needs and wants, the cereal brand manager should develop a picture of the product-market structure within which her/his brand is positioned. Exhibit 2.5 provides an illustrative product-market structure for cereals. The diagram can be expanded to portray other relevant product types (e.g., breakfast bars) in the generic product-market for food and beverages.

EXHIBIT 2.5
Illustrative Product-Market Structure

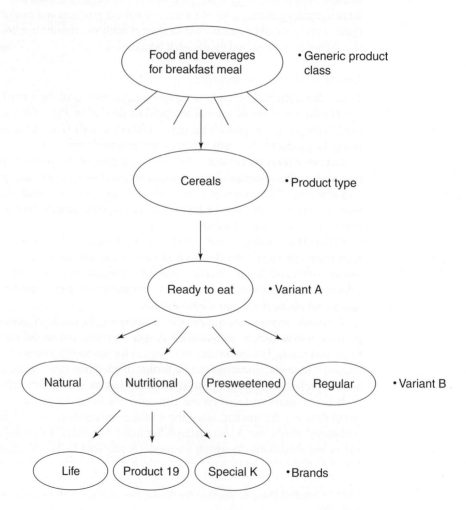

RICH CHINA, POOR CHINA
Incomes vary hugely across the mainland

- URBAN PER CAPITA INCOME, 2003
- RURAL PER CAPITA INCOME, 2003
  IN U.S. DOLLARS

	Urban	Rural
BEIJING	$691	$1,714
LIAONING	$362	$894
JIANGSU	$523	$1,144
SHANGHAI	$821	$1,835
HUBEI	$317	$904
SICHUAN	$275	$869
YUNNAN	$210	$944
GUANGDONG	$501	$1,528

HEILONGJIANG, JILIN, XINJIANG, INNER MONGOLIA, TIANJIN, HEBEI, SHANXI, SHANDONG, QINGHAI, NINGXIA, GANSU, SHAANXI, HENAN, ANHUI, ZHEJIANG, TIBET, HUNAN, JIANGXI, FUJIAN, GUIZHOU, GUANGXI, HONG KONG

Data: National Bureau of Statistics, China

Source: "Let a Thousand Brands Bloom," *BusinessWeek,* October, 17, 2005, 58.

Describing and Analyzing End-Users

After determining the product-market structure it is useful to develop profiles of end-user buyers for the generic, product-type, and product-variant levels of the product-market (see Exhibit 2.2). Buyers are identified and described, value requirements are indicated, and environmental influences (e.g., interest rate trends) are determined. Analysis of the buyers in the market segments within a product-market is considered in Chapter 3.

Identifying and Describing Buyers

Characteristics such as family size, age, income, geographical location, sex, and occupation are often useful in identifying buyers in consumer markets. Illustrative factors used to identify end-users in organizational markets include type of industry, company size, location, and types of products. Many published sources of information are available for use in identifying and describing customers. Examples include U.S. Census data, trade association publications, and studies by advertising media (TV, radio, magazines). When experience and existing information are not adequate in determining buyers, research studies may be necessary to identify and describe customers and prospects.

An interesting profile of per capita income variations across China is shown in the GLOBAL APPLICATION.[12] Note the huge differences between rural and urban income. Recognizing these income variations, Haier, the leading appliance producer in China, designs its larger washing machines for Chinese cities, but offers a very small model at $37 for poorer areas. The Chinese population information is useful in identifying and describing buyers where income is a relevant predictor of purchases of goods and services such as automobiles and kitchen appliances.

How Buyers Make Choices

Often, simply describing buyers does not provide enough information to guide market targeting and positioning decisions. We also need to try to find out *why* people buy products and specific product brands. In considering how customers decide what to buy, it is useful to analyze how they move through the sequence of steps leading to a decision to purchase a particular brand. Buyers normally follow a decision process. They begin by recognizing a need (problem recognition); next, they seek information; then, they identify and evaluate alternative products; and finally, they purchase a brand. Of course, the length and complexity of this process varies by product and purchasing situation. Decisions for frequently purchased products with which a buyer has past experience tend to be routine. One part of studying buyer decision processes is finding out what criteria people use in making decisions. For example, how important is the brand name of a product in the purchase decision?

Illustrations of the buying decision process stages for a consumer purchase and an organizational purchase are shown in Exhibit 2.6. The consumer purchase involves a portable CD player purchased by a student, whereas the organizational purchase is for a portable CD player component from an outside supplier. Both processes move through the major stages in the buying decision process, but the issues and activities are quite different.

Environmental Influences

The final step in building customer profiles is to identify the external environmental factors that influence buyers and thus impact the size and composition of the market over time. These influences include government actions (e.g., tax cuts), social change, economic shifts, technology, and other factors that may alter buyers' needs and wants. For example, the economic downturn and recession in the late 2000s and early 2010s has led many governments across the world to develop severe austerity packages, impacting negatively on consumer spending power and public sector purchasing plans. Typically, these factors are not controlled by the buyer or the firms that market the product, and substantial changes in environmental influences can have a major impact on customers' purchasing activities. Therefore, it is important to identify the relevant external influences on a product-market and to estimate their future impact. During the past decade various changes in market opportunities occurred as a result of uncontrollable environmental factors. Illustrations include the shifts in population age-group composition, changes in tax laws affecting investments, and variations in interest rates. Consider, for example, the population trends for the 50 states in the United States from 1995 to 2025. Note that some states (see Exhibit 2.7) display high growth rates while others are declining in size. Residential construction rates and various other product-markets will be impacted by differences in population growth across regions and states in the United States.

---

[12]"Let a Thousand Brands Bloom," *BusinessWeek,* October 17, 2005, 58 and 60.

EXHIBIT 2.6 **Comparing the Stages in Consumer and Organizational Purchases**

Source: Adopted from Roger A. Kerin, Steve W. Hartley, and William Rudelius, *Marketing* 9th ed. (Burr Ridge, IL: McGraw-Hill/Irwin, 2009), 155.

STAGE IN THE BUYING DECISION PROCESS	CONSUMER PURCHASE: MEDIA PLAYER FOR A STUDENT	ORGANIZATIONAL PURCHASE: EARPHONES FOR A MEDIA PLAYER
Problem recognition	Student doesn't like the features of the media player now owned and desires a new one.	Marketing research and sales departments observe that competitors are improving the earphones on their media player. The firm decides to improve the earphones on its own new models, which will be purchased from an outside supplier.
Information search	Student uses past experience, that of friends, ads, the Internet, and *Consumer Reports* to collect information and uncover alternatives.	Design and production engineers draft specifications for earphones. The purchasing department identifies suppliers of media player earphones.
Alternative evaluation	Alternative media players are evaluated on the basis of important attributes desired in a player, and several stores are visited.	Purchasing and engineering personnel visit with suppliers and assess (1) facilities, (2) capacity, (3) quality control, and (4) financial status. They drop any suppliers not satisfactory on these factors.
Purchase decision	A specific brand of media player is selected, the price is paid, and the student leaves the store.	They use (1) quality, (2) price, (3) delivery, and (4) technical capability as key buying criteria to select a supplier. Then they negotiate terms and award a contract.
Postpurchase behavior	Student reevaluates the purchase decision, may return the player to the store if it is unsatisfactory.	They evaluate suppliers using a formal vendor rating system and notify a supplier if earphones do not meet their quality standard. If the problem is not corrected, they drop the firm as a future supplier.

EXHIBIT 2.7
Population Trends for the 50 States in the United States: 1995 to 2025

Source: U.S. Bureau of the Census, Population Division, PPL-47.

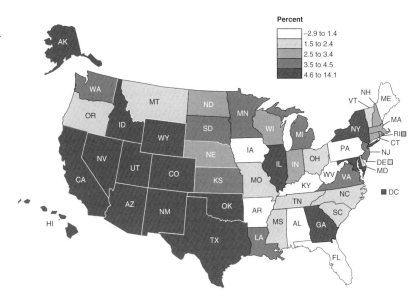

Percent
- −2.9 to 1.4
- 1.5 to 2.4
- 2.5 to 3.4
- 3.5 to 4.5
- 4.6 to 14.1

Building Customer Profiles

Describing customers begins with the generic product-market. At this level customer profiles are likely to describe the size and general composition of the customer base. For example, the commercial air travel customer profile for a specified geographical area (e.g., South America) would include market size, growth rates, mix of business and pleasure travelers, and other general characteristics. The product-type and variant profiles are more specific about customer characteristics such as needs and wants, use situations, activities and interests, opinions, purchase processes and choice criteria, and environmental influences on buying decisions. Normally, product-type analysis considers the organization's product and closely related product types.

In developing marketing strategy, management is concerned with deciding which buyers to target within the product-market of interest and how to position to each target. The customer profiles help to guide these decisions. The profile information is also useful in deciding how to segment the market. More comprehensive customer analyses are necessary in market segmentation analysis, which we discuss in Chapter 3.

Analyzing Competition

Competitor analysis considers the companies and brands that compete in the product-market of interest. Analyzing the competition follows the five steps shown in Exhibit 2.8. In step 1 we determine the competitive arena in which an organization competes and describe the characteristics of the competitive space. Steps 2 and 3 identify, describe, and evaluate the organization's key competitors. Steps 4 and 5 anticipate competitors' future actions and identify potential competitors that may enter the market.

Defining the Competitive Arena

Competition often includes more than the firms that are direct competitors, like Coke and Pepsi. For example, the different levels of competition for diet colas are shown in Exhibit 2.9. The product variant is the most direct type of competition. Nevertheless, other product categories of soft drinks also compete for buyers, as do other beverages. A complete understanding of the competitive arena helps to guide strategy design and implementation. Since competition often occurs within specific industries, study of the industry structure is useful in defining the competitive arena, recognizing that more than one industry may be competing in the same product-market, depending on the complexity of the

EXHIBIT 2.8
Analyzing the Competition

1 > Define the competitive arena for the generic, specific, and variant product-markets.

2 > Identify key competitors.

3 > Evaluate key competitors.

4 > Anticipate actions by competitors.

5 > Identify and evaluate potential competitors.

EXHIBIT 2.9
Examples of Levels of Competition

Source: Donald R. Lehmann and Russell S. Winer, *Analysis for Marketing Planning,* 7th ed. (Burr Ridge, IL: Richard D. Irwin, 2008), 34. Copyright © The McGraw-Hill Companies. Used with permission.

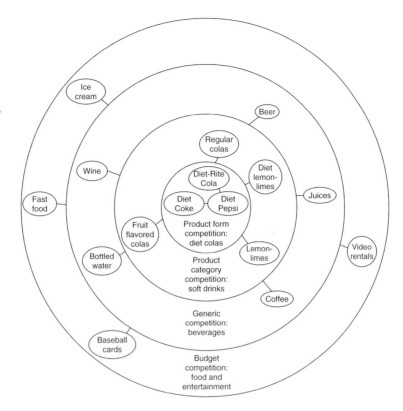

product-market structure. For example, the digital photography product-market includes traditional camera and film competitors and electronics industry competitors.

Industry Analysis

Competitor analysis is conducted from the point of view of a particular firm. For example, a soft drink firm such as Coca-Cola should include other beverage brands in its industry analysis. Two kinds of information are needed: (1) a descriptive profile of the industry; and (2) an analysis of the value chain (distribution) channels that link together the various organizations in the value-added system from suppliers to end-users. Thus, the industry analysis is horizontal and covers similar types of firms (e.g., soft drink producers), whereas the value chain analysis considers the vertical network of firms that supply materials and/or parts, produce products (and services), and distribute the products to end-users.

The industry analysis includes (1) industry characteristics and trends, such as sales, number of firms, and growth rates; and (2) operating practices of the firms in the industry, including product mix, service provided, barriers to entry, and geographical scope. Many industries provide information in publications and websites that is useful in the analysis. Industry associations also publish research reports, which typically include growth forecasts.

First, we need to identify the companies that comprise the industry and develop descriptive information on the industry and its members. It is important to examine industry structure beyond domestic market boundaries, since international industry developments often affect regional, national, and international markets. It is also necessary to include all relevant industries in the analysis. For example, as shown in Exhibit 2.10, including only

EXHIBIT 2.10 The Shifting Telecom Landscape

Source: "The Shifting Telecom Landscape," *BusinessWeek*, February 28, 2005, 36.

	Revenue in Billions						
	2003	**2004**	**2005**	**2006**	**2007**	**2008**	**Compound Annual Growth Rate**
• Video	$ 0.2	$ 0.3	$ 0.5	$ 1.0	$ 1.6	$ 2.5	**65.7%**
• Consumer broadband	2.8	3.5	4.0	4.2	4.6	4.8	**11.4**
• Consumer long-distance	20.7	18.2	16.0	13.6	11.3	9.2	**−15.0**
• Business local	26.3	26.7	26.4	26.1	25.8	25.5	**−0.6**
• Business long-distance	26.1	24.5	23.0	21.3	19.7	18.2	**−7.0**
• Business data*	44.8	45.6	46.6	47.1	46.8	45.4	**0.3**
• Consumer local	46.9	42.2	39.0	36.2	34.0	32.3	**−7.25**
• Wireless	91.5	108.7	119.2	132.8	144.5	153.6	**10.9**
Total	**$260.7**	**$271.5**	**$277.0**	**$285.0**	**$291.3**	**$294.9**	**2.5%**

*Includes Internet access, private data lines, ATM traffic, and frame relay data: In-Stat/MDR

the firms providing traditional long-distance phone services would provide an incomplete assessment of the industries and firms that provide services. The traditional boundaries between phone companies, cable providers, and other tech firms are changing rapidly. Note the large differences in revenue growth.

The industry identification is based on product similarity, location at the same level in the value chain (e.g., manufacturer, distributor, retailer) and geographical scope. The industry analysis considers

- Industry size, growth, and composition.
- Typical marketing practices.
- Industry changes that are anticipated (e.g., consolidation trends).
- Industry strengths and weaknesses.
- Strategic alliances and potential mergers/acquisitions among competitors.

Analysis of the Value-Added Chain

The study of supplier and distribution channels is important in understanding and serving product-markets. While some producers may go directly to their end-users, many work with other organizations through distribution channels. The extent of vertical integration by competitor backward (supply) and forward toward end-users is also useful information. The types of relationships (collaborative or transactional) in the distribution channel should be identified and evaluated. The extent of outsourcing activities in the value chain is also of interest. Different channels that access end-user customers should be included in the channel analysis. By looking at the distribution approaches of industry members, we can identify important patterns and trends in serving end-users. Value chain analysis may also uncover new market opportunities that are not served by present channels of distribution. Finally, information from various value chain levels can help in forecasting end-user sales.

The use of outsourcing manufacturing and other business functions expanded rapidly in the United States and Europe during the last decade. By outsourcing an organization may gain strategic advantage by focusing on its core competencies, while outsourcing other necessary business functions to independent partners. Thus, analysis of outsourcing activities may be an important aspect of competitor analysis.

Competitive Forces

Different competitive forces are present in the value-added chain. The traditional view of competition is expanded by recognizing Michael Porter's five competitive forces that impact industry performance:

1. Rivalry among existing firms.
2. Threat of new entrants.
3. Threat of substitute products.
4. Bargaining power of suppliers.
5. Bargaining power of buyers.[13]

The first force recognizes that active competition among industry members helps determine industry performance, and it is the most direct and intense form of competition. The aggressive competition between General Motors and Toyota is illustrative. Rivalry may occur within a market segment or across an entire product-market. The nature and scope of competition may vary according to the maturity of the industry.

The second force highlights the possibility of new competitors entering the market. Existing firms may try to discourage new competition by aggressive expansion and other types of market entry barriers. The entry of Wal-Mart into the supermarket business has substantially expanded and intensified the competitive arena in this market.

The third force considers the potential impact of substitutes. New technologies that satisfy the same customer value requirement are important sources of competition. Including alternative technologies (e.g., disruptive innovations) in the definition of product-market structure identifies substitute forms of competition. The impact of the smart phone on Flip video camera sales is illustrative.

The fourth force is the power that suppliers may be able to exert on the producers in an industry. For example, the high costs of labor exert major pressures on the commercial airline industry. Coke and Pepsi exert important influences on their independent bottlers and encourage collaboration. Companies may pursue vertical integration strategies to reduce the bargaining power of suppliers. Collaborative relationships are useful to respond to the needs of both partners.

Finally, buyers may use their purchasing power to influence their suppliers. Wal-Mart, for example, has a strong influence on the suppliers of its many products. Understanding which organizations have power and influence in the value chain provides important insights into the structure of competition.

Key Competitor Analysis

Competitor analysis is conducted for the firms directly competing with each other (e.g., Nike and Reebok) and other companies that management may consider important in strategy analysis (for example, potential market entrants). The rapid expansion of competitor intelligence activities by many companies in the last decade highlights the high priority executives place on monitoring competitors' activities. Many companies around the world

---

[13]Michael E. Porter, *Competitive Advantage* (New York: Free Press, 1985), 5.

have developed very effective intelligence units. Nonetheless, there are important ethical and legal issues to consider in competitive intelligence gathering. These issues are illustrated in the ETHICS APPLICATION.

We now look at two major aspects of competitor analysis: (1) preparing a descriptive profile for each competitor; and (2) evaluating the competitor's strengths and weaknesses (steps 2 and 3 of Exhibit 2.8).

Describing and Evaluating the Competitor

A *key competitor* is any organization going after the same market target as the firm conducting the analysis. American and Southwest Airlines are key competitors on many U.S. routes. Key competitors are brands that compete in the same product-market or segment(s) within the market (Motorola, Nokia, and Samsung cell phones). Different product types that satisfy the same need or want may also actively compete against each other. Thus, microwave dinners may compete with fast-food operators.

Information that is typically included in the competitor profile is shown in Exhibit 2.11. Sources of information include annual reports, industry studies by government and private organizations, business magazines and newspapers, industry trade publications and websites, reports by financial analysts (e.g., *Value Line Investment Survey*), government reports, standardized data services (e.g., Information Resources, Inc., and Nielsen), databases, suppliers, customers, company personnel, and salespeople. Direct contact with the research directors of trade publications is often a useful source of information about the industry and key competitors.

It is important to gain as much knowledge as possible about the background, experience, qualifications, and tenure of key executives for each major competitor. This information includes the executives' performance records, their particular areas of expertise, and the firms where they were previously employed. These analyses may suggest the future strategic initiatives of a key competitor.

Market targets and customer base analyses center on the market segments targeted by the competitor and the competitor's actual and relative market-share position. Relative market position is measured by comparing the share of the firm against the competitor with the highest market share in the segment. All segments in the product-market that could be targeted by the firm should be included in the competitor evaluation.

The competitor's past performance offers a useful basis for comparing competitors. The customer value proposition offered by the competitor for each segment is important information. This may indicate competitive opportunities as well as a possible threat. The competitor's distinctive capabilities need to be identified and evaluated.

An analysis of each competitor's past sales and financial performance indicates how well the competitor has performed on a historical basis. Competitor ratings are also useful in the comparisons (e.g., *Consumer Reports*). A typical period of analysis is 3 to 5 years or longer, depending on the rate of change in the market. Performance information

EXHIBIT 2.11
Describing and Evaluating Key Competitors

- Business scope and objectives
- Management experience, capabilities, and weaknesses
- Market position and trends
- Market target(s) and customer base
- Positioning strategy for each target
- Distinctive capabilities
- Financial performance (current and historical)

Competitor Intelligence Gathering

Most competitive intelligence gathering relies on publicly available information and the views of distributors and customers. However, there are important limits to the behavior of intelligence gatherers. The Society of Competitive Intelligence Professionals outlaws misrepresentation by intelligence gatherers in its code of ethics. Nonetheless, there are gray areas, which raise serious ethical dilemmas:

- What if intelligence researchers pose as something else—conference organizers, headhunters, students, or journalists to tease information out of intelligence targets?
- Is it acceptable if competitor staff members are interviewed for phantom jobs that do not exist, to see what they reveal when questioned?
- Is it reasonable for researchers to pose as customers to collect competitor information?

Unethical intelligence-gathering practices carry substantial risks if discovered, and are completely unacceptable to reputable companies. Many organizations now operate ethics compliance systems, and report corporate citizenship actions to stakeholders.

Direct contact with competitors to gather intelligence may be interpreted as "inappropriate conversations" associated with anticompetitive behavior, and attract investigation and punishment by regulatory bodies.

Source: Stephen Overell, "Agents Who Shed Light on Hidden Corporate Life," *Financial Times,* Monday, March 19, 2001, p. 14; Joseph Weber, "The New Ethics Enforcers," *BusinessWeek,* February 13, 2006, 76–77.

may include sales, market share, net profit, net profit margin, cash flow, and debt. Additionally, for specific types of businesses other performance information may be useful. For example, sales-per-square-foot is often used to compare the performance of retail stores. Operating cost per passenger mile is a relevant measure for airline performance comparisons.

Assessing how well competitors meet customer value requirements requires finding out what criteria buyers use to rate each supplier. Customer-focused assessments are more useful than relying only on management judgments of value delivery. Measurement methods include customer comparisons of value attributes of the firm versus its competitors, customer surveys, loyalty measures, and the relative market share of end-use segments.[14] Customer value assessment is further considered in Chapter 4.

Using the competitor information, we can develop an overall evaluation of the key competitor's current strengths and weaknesses. Additionally, the summary assessment of distinctive capabilities includes information on the competitor's management capabilities and limitations, technical and operating advantages and weaknesses, marketing strategy, and other key strengths and limitations. Since competitors often display different capabilities, it is important to highlight these differences.

Anticipating Competitors' Actions

Steps 4 and 5 in competitor analysis (see Exhibit 2.8) consider what each key competitor may do in the future and identify potential new competitors. The information obtained in the previous steps of the analysis should be helpful in estimating future trends, although possible strategy shifts by competitors may occur.

---

[14]George S. Day and Robin Wensley, "Assessing Advantage: A Framework for Diagnosing Competitive Superiority," *Journal of Marketing,* April, 1988, 12–16.

Estimating Competitors' Future Strategies

Competitors' future strategies may continue the directions that they have established in the past, particularly if no major external influences require changing their strategies. Nevertheless, assuming an existing strategy will continue is not wise. Competitors' current actions may signal probable strategy shifts that may create future threats.

An interesting development in the telecommunication market is the growth in the use of Internet calling. First introduced in 1995, voice-over Internet protocol (VOIP) experienced start-up problems but by 2003, the technology was a rapidly growing share of home and business markets.[15] Industry authorities expect the technology to become a significant competitive threat. VOIP subscribers are estimated to increase to over five times the 2003 level by 2006.

Relatedly, the acquisition strategy at eBay is a strong indicator of the company's goal to move from being an online auction site to an e-commerce engine that sells Web tools to small businesses. Current developments at eBay are illustrated in the INTERNET APPLICATION, and are indicative of the areas in which eBay will be a competitor in the future.

Identifying New Competitors

New competitors may come from four major sources: (1) companies competing in a related product-market; (2) companies with related technologies; (3) companies already targeting similar customer groups with other products; and/or (4) companies competing in other geographical regions with similar products. Market entry by a new competitor is likely under one or more of these conditions:

- High profit margins are being achieved by market incumbents.
- Future growth opportunities in the market are attractive.
- No major market-entry barriers are present.
- Competition is limited to one or a few competitors.
- Gaining an equivalent (or better) competitive advantage over the existing firm(s) serving the market is feasible.

If one or more of these conditions are present in a competitive situation, new competition will probably appear.

Market Size Estimation

An important part of market opportunity analysis is estimating the present and potential size of the market. Market size is usually measured by dollar sales and/or unit sales for a defined product-market and specified time period. Other size measures include the number of buyers, average purchase quantity, and frequency of purchase. Three key measures of market size are *market potential, sales forecast,* and *market share.*

Market Potential

Market potential is the maximum amount of product sales that can be obtained from a defined product-market during a specified time period. It includes the total opportunity for sales by all firms serving the product-market. Market potential is the upper limit of sales that can be achieved by all firms for a specified product-market over an indicated

---

[15]Peter Grant and Almar Latour, "Circuit Breaker," *Wall Street Journal,* October 9, 2003, A1 and A9; "Net Phones Start Ringing Up Customers," *BusinessWeek,* December 29, 2003, 45–46.

The online auction site eBay.com has become one of the Web's most successful businesses, with around 73 million monthly visitors to the site (running neck to neck with Amazon's site). The impact on many areas of conventional retailing has been substantial.

eBay executives believe future growth depends on evolving the company beyond a destination site into a provider of tools and services that power e-commerce across the Web. eBay has taken an early lead in the growing market for mobile shopping using smart phones and pads. The company is making considerable efforts to break out of its current business model. Key acquisitions include:

- PayPal—payment processor for eBay and other websites—$1.5 billion (July 2002).
- Rent.com provides property rental and roommate search services—$415 million (December 2004).
- Kurant/Pro—helps sellers set up online storefronts separate from eBay (January 2005).
- Shopping.com runs a comparison-shopping website—$620 million (June 2005).
- Skype—its Internet telephone service can connect sellers with shoppers—$2.5 billion (September 2005). (Subsequently sold by the new eBay chief executive to private equity investors for $2.75 billion in 2009, and purchased by Microsoft in 2011.)
- Stubhub—a ticket reselling site that is promoted on eBay—$310 million (January 2007).
- Stumbleupon—recommends websites based on user interests—$75 million (May 2007).
- Bill Me Later—instant consumer credit company—$945 million (October 2008).
- Dba.dk—Danish classified advertising site—$390 million (October 2008).
- GSI Commerce—interactive marketing company for major brands and large retailers—$2.4 billion (March 2011).

Sources: Catherine Holahan, "Going, Going . . . Everywhere," *BusinessWeek,* June 18, 2007, 62–64. Douglas MacMillian and Joseph Galante, "As Mobile Shopping Takes Off, eBay is an Early Winner," *BusinessWeek,* June 29–July 4, 2010, 27–28.

time period. Often, actual industry sales in a specified year fall somewhat below market potential because the production and distribution systems are unable to completely meet the needs of all buyers who are both *willing* and *able* to purchase the product during the period of interest.

Useful information for considering market potential and growth rates for various product categories in Russia is shown in Exhibit 2.12. The share of household ownership percentages and share increases provide an indication of where the market potential appears promising. Not surprisingly, cell phone and computer penetration is expanding rapidly. Household income is increasing fast and 70 percent of all income is disposable in Russia compared to 40 percent in Western countries.[16] Market potential is exploding for many product categories including tourism and financial services.

Sales Forecast

The sales forecast indicates the expected sales for a defined product-market during a specified time period. The industry sales forecast is the total volume of sales expected by all firms serving the product market. The sales forecast can be no greater than market potential

---

[16]Jason Bush, "Shoppers Gone Wild," *BusinessWeek,* February 20, 2006, 46.

EXHIBIT 2.12
Market Penetration and Growth Rates for Selected Consumer Product Categories in Russia

Source: Jason Bush, "Shoppers Gone Wild," *BusinessWeek*, February 20, 2006, 46.

Ownership by Share of Households		
	2001	2005
Mobile phone	6%	50%
Computer	5	20
Washing machine	16	35
Stereo	15	31
Video recorder	39	50
Car	25	31
Imported TV	58	71
Apartment or house	71	82
August 2001 vs. August 2005		Data: GfK Rus.

and typically falls short of potential as discussed above. A forecast can be made for total sales at any product-market level (generic, product type, variant) and for specific subsets of the product-market (e.g., market segments). A company sales forecast can also be made for sales expected by a particular firm.

Several sales forecasting methods are described in Exhibit 2.13. The advantages of each technique are indicated. Time-series analysis is popular for projecting future sales but is very dependent on the stability of historical trends.

Market Share

Company sales divided by the total sales of all firms for a specified product-market determines the market share of a particular firm. Market share may be calculated on the basis of actual sales or forecasted sales. Market share can be used to forecast future company sales and to compare actual market position among competing brands of a product. Market share may vary depending on the use of dollar sales or unit sales due to price differences across competitors.

It is essential in preparing forecasts to specify exactly what is being forecast (defined product-market), the time period involved, and the geographical area. Otherwise, comparisons of sales and market share with those of competing firms will not be meaningful.

Evaluating Market Opportunity

Since a company's sales depend, in part, on its marketing plans, management's forecasts and marketing strategy are closely interrelated. Forecasting involves "what if" analyses. Alternative positioning strategies (product, distribution, price, and promotion) need to be evaluated for their estimated effects on sales. Because of the marketing effort/sales relationship, it is important to consider both market potential (opportunity) and planned marketing expenditures in determining the forecast. The impact of different sales forecasts must be evaluated from a total business perspective, since these forecasts affect production planning, human resource needs, and financial requirements.

Sales forecasts of target markets are needed so that management can estimate the financial attractiveness of both new and existing market opportunities. The market potential and growth estimates gauge the overall attractiveness of the market. The sales forecast for the company's brand in combination with cost estimates provide a basis for profit projections. The decision to enter a new market or to exit from an existing market depends heavily on financial analyses and projections. Alternate market targets under consideration can be compared using sales and profit projections. Similar projections of key competitors are also useful in evaluating market opportunities.

EXHIBIT 2.13 **Summary of Advantages and Disadvantages of Various Sales Forecasting Techniques**

Source: Mark W. Johnston and Greg W. Marshall, *Sales Force Management,* 9th ed. (New York: McGraw-Hill/Irwin, 2009), 141.

Sales Forecasting Method	Advantages	Disadvantages
User expectations	1. Forecast estimates obtained directly from buyers 2. Projected product usage information can be highly detailed 3. Insightful method aids planning marketing strategy 4. Useful for new product forecasting	1. Potential customers must be few and well defined 2. Does not work well for consumer goods 3. Depends on the accuracy of user's estimates 4. Expensive, time-consuming, labor-intensive
Sales force composite	1. Involves the people (sales personnel) who will be held responsible for the results 2. Is fairly accurate 3. Aids in controlling and directing sales effort 4. Forecast is available for individual sales territories	1. Estimators (sales personnel) have a vested interest and therefore may be biased 2. Elaborate schemes sometimes are necessary to counteract bias 3. If estimates are biased, process to correct the data can be expensive
Jury of executive opinion	1. Easily done, very quick 2. Does not require elaborate statistics 3. Utilizes "collected wisdom" of the top people 4. Useful for new or innovative products	1. Produces aggregate forecasts 2. Expensive 3. Disperses responsibility for the forecast 4. Group dynamics operate
Delphi technique	1. Minimizes effects of group dynamics	1. Can be expensive and time-consuming
Market test	1. Provides ultimate test of consumers' reactions to the product 2. Allows assessment of the effectiveness of the total marketing program 3. Useful for new and innovative products	1. Lets competitors know what firm is doing 2. Invites competitive reaction 3. Expensive and time-consuming to set up 4. Often takes a long time to accurately assess level of initial and repeat demand
Time-series analysis	1. Utilizes historical data 2. Objective, inexpensive	1. Not useful for new or innovative products 2. Factors for trend, cyclical, seasonal, or product life-cycle phase must be accurately assessed and included 3. Technical skill and good judgment required
Statistical demand analysis	1. Great intuitive appeal 2. Requires quantification of assumptions underlying the estimates 3. Allows management to check results 4. Uncovers hidden factors affecting sales 5. Method is objective	1. Factors affecting sales must remain constant and be identified accurately to produce an accurate estimate 2. Requires technical skill and expertise 3. Some managers reluctant to use method due to the sophistication

Developing a Strategic Vision About the Future

Market development and competitive space may not follow clearly defined and predictable paths. Nonetheless, signals can be identified that are useful in pointing to possible market changes. Answers to the questions shown in Exhibit 2.14 are needed in developing a strategic vision concerning the firm's market(s). These issues need to be addressed for each product-market.

Phases of Competition

It is useful to distinguish between different phases in the development of competition. In the initial stage, companies compete in identifying product concepts, technology choices, and building competencies.[17] This phase involves experimentation with ideas, and the path to market leadership is not clearly defined. Phase 2 may involve partnering of companies with the objective of controlling industry standards, though these firms eventually become competitors. Finally, as the market becomes clearly defined and the competitive space established, the competitors concentrate on market share for end products and profits.

Anticipating the Future

Increasingly, we find that change and turbulence, rather than stability, characterize many product-markets. Moreover, as discussed above, it is often possible to determine the forces underway that will alter product-market structure. Though these influences are not easily identified and analyzed, the organizations that choose to invest substantial time and effort in anticipating the future create an opportunity for competitive advantage. Fuji appears to have done a better job of anticipating the future of digital photography than did Kodak. Executives in market-driven companies recognize the importance of developing these capabilities.

Hamel and Prahalad offer a compelling blueprint for analyzing the forces of change. While the details of their process cannot be captured in a few pages of discussion, the following questions are examples of the information needed to anticipate the future:[18]

EXHIBIT 2.14
Developing a Strategic Vision

- Are product-market boundaries and composition of the product-market undergoing transformation?
- How and to what extent is the end-user customer base changing?
- Are the scope and structure of competitor space changing due to market and industry transformation and entry/exit of competitors?
- Are there potential threats from disruptive technologies and/or commoditization?
- Are the composition and structure of the value chain(s) serving the end-user market(s) changing?
- Do other influences operating in the product-market have the potential to significantly transform the product?
- At what life-cycle stage is the product-market (new, growth, maturity, decline), and how fast is the life cycle advancing?

[17]C. K. Prahalad, "Weak Signals Versus Strong Paradigms," *Journal of Marketing Research,* August 1995, iii–vi.
[18]Gary Hamel and C. K. Prahalad, *Competing for the Future* (Boston: Harvard Business School Press, 1994), 101.

- What are the influences (discontinuities) present in the product-market that have the potential to profoundly transform market/competitor structure?
- Investigate each discontinuity in substantial depth.
- How will the trend impact customers?
- What is the likely economic impact?
- How fast is the trend developing?
- Who is exploiting this trend?
- Who has the most to gain/lose?
- What new product opportunities will be created by this discontinuity?
- How can we learn more about this trend?

Following the blueprint requires looking in depth at the relevant forces of change in a product-market and other markets that are interrelated. Anticipating the future requires searching beyond the existing competitive arena for influences that promise to impact product-market boundaries. The process requires the involvement of the entire organization and it demands a substantial amount of time. A company with a market orientation and cross-functional processes should be able to utilize these processes for anticipating the future. Importantly, developing a vision about the future needs to be an ongoing process.

Summary

Analyzing markets and competition is essential to making sound business and marketing decisions. The uses of product-market analyses are many and varied. An important aspect of market definition and analysis is moving beyond a product or industry focus by incorporating market needs into the analysts' viewpoint.

Business strategies and markets are interrelated and companies that do not understand their markets and how they are likely to change in the future are at a competitive disadvantage. Effective market sensing is essential in guiding business and marketing strategies. Disruptive innovation, the process of customers shifting their purchases to new products that better meet their needs, should be anticipated and counterstrategies developed. An essential part of becoming market oriented is identifying future directions of market change.

This chapter examines the nature and scope of defining and analyzing product-market structure. By using different levels of aggregation (generic, product-type, and product-variant), products and brands are positioned within more aggregate categories, thus helping to better understand customers, product interrelationships, industry structure, distribution approaches, and key competitors. This approach to product-market analysis offers a consistent guide to needed information, regardless of the type of product-market being analyzed. Analyzing market opportunity includes (1) determining product-market boundaries and structure; (2) forming the product-market; (3) describing and analyzing end-users; (4) analyzing competition; and (5) estimating market size and growth rates.

After determining the product-market boundaries and structure, information on various aspects of the market is collected and examined. First, it is useful to study the people or organizations who are the end-users in the product-market at each level (generic, product type, and variant). These market profiles of customers help us to evaluate opportunities and guide market targeting and positioning strategies. Next, we identify and analyze the firms that market products and services at each product-market level to aid strategy development. Industry and key competitor analysis considers the firms that compete with the company performing the market opportunity analysis. Thus, industry analysis for a personal computer producer would include the producers that make up the industry. The analysis should also include firms operating at all stages (levels) in the value-added chain, such as suppliers, manufacturers, distributors, and retailers.

The next step is a comprehensive assessment of the major competitors. The competitor analysis should include both actual and potential competitors that management considers important. Competitor analysis includes (1) describing the company; (2) evaluating the competitor; and (3) anticipating the future actions of competitors. It is also important to identify possible new competitors. Competitor analysis is an ongoing activity and requires coordinated information collection and analysis.

An important part of product-market analysis is estimating potential and forecasting sales. The forecasts often used in product-market analysis include estimates of market potential, sales forecasts of total sales by firms competing in the product-market, and the sales forecast for the firm of interest. This information is needed for various purposes and is prepared for different units of analysis, such as product category, brands, and geographical areas. The forecasting approach and techniques should be matched to the organization's needs.

The mounting evidence about markets points to the critical importance of understanding and anticipating changes in markets by developing a strategic vision about the future. In gaining these insights, it is useful to view competition as a three-stage process of experimentation, partnering to set industry standards, and then pursuing market share and profits. Analyzing the forces of change provides a basis for anticipating how product-markets will change in the future.

Questions for Review and Discussion

1. Discuss the important issues that should be considered in defining the product-market for a totally new product.

2. Under what product and market conditions is the end-user customer more likely to make an important contribution to product-market definition?

3. What recommendations can you make to the management of a company competing in a rapid growth market to help it identify new competitive threats early enough so that counterstrategies can be developed?

4. There are some dangers in concentrating product-market analysis only on a firm's specific brand and those brands that compete directly with a firm's brand. Discuss.

5. Using the approach to product-market definition and analysis discussed in the chapter, select a brand and describe the generic, product type, and brand product-markets of which the brand is a part.

6. For the brand you selected in Question 5, indicate the kinds of information needed to conduct a complete product-market analysis. Also suggest sources for obtaining each type of information.

7. Select an industry and describe its characteristics, participants, and structure.

8. A competitor analysis of the 7UP soft drink brand is being conducted. Management plans to position the brand against its key competitors. Should the competitors consist of only other non-cola drinks?

9. Outline an approach to competitor evaluation, assuming you are preparing the analysis for a regional bank holding company.

10. Discuss how a small company (less than $1 million in sales) should analyze its competition.

11. Many popular forecasting techniques draw from past experience and historical data. Discuss some of the more important problems that may occur in using these methods.

12. What are the relevant issues a cross-functional team should consider in developing a strategic vision about the future for the organization's product-market(s)?

Internet Applications

A. Visit the website of Project 2000 (www2000.ogsm.Vanderbilt.edu), founded at the Owen Graduate School of Vanderbilt University to determine if the Web provides useful information for market and competitor analysis. Describe the various types of market information available on the Web.

B. Visit Hoover's website (www.hoovers.com). Investigate the different options for competitive and market analysis provided. How can these online tools best be utilized? What limitations apply?

C. Johnson & Johnson is currently competitive in the surgical stent market (a device inserted surgically in an artery to enable blood flow). Perform an Internet analysis of the stent market indicating past and current unit sales levels and forecasts for 2006–2010.

D. Samsung Electronics is one of the top producers of cell phones. Draw from Internet sources to prepare an analysis of the global cell phone market.

Applications

A. Select a product-market where new types of competition and/or new business models are developing. Discuss how and to what extent "opportunities outside the competitive box are developing."

B. Review the GLOBAL APPLICATION concerning China's geographical income distributions. Discuss how this information could be useful to a company planning to enter the Chinese market with water purification treatment units for use in residences.

APPENDIX **2A**

Financial Analysis for Marketing Planning and Control

Several kinds of financial analyses are needed for marketing analysis, planning, and control activities. Such analyses represent an important part of case preparation activities. In some instances it will be necessary to review and interpret the financial information provided in the cases. In other instances analyses may be prepared to support specific recommendations. The methods covered in this appendix represent a group of tools and techniques for use in marketing financial analysis. Throughout the discussion, it is assumed that accounting and finance fundamentals are understood.

Unit of Financial Analysis

Various units of analysis that can be used in marketing financial analysis are shown in Exhibit 2A.1. Two factors often influence the choice of a unit of analysis: (1) the purpose of the analysis and (2) the costs and availability of the information needed to perform the analysis.

Financial Situation Analysis

Financial measures can be used to help assess the present situation. One of the most common and best ways to quantify the financial situation of a firm is through ratio analysis. These ratios should be analyzed over a period of at least 3 years to discern trends.

Key Financial Ratios

Financial information will be more useful to management if it is prepared so that comparisons can be made. James Van Horne comments upon this need.

To evaluate a firm's financial condition and performance, the financial analyst needs certain yardsticks. The yardstick frequently used is a ratio or index, relating two pieces of financial data to each other. Analysis and interpretation of various ratios should give an experienced and skilled analyst a better understanding of the financial condition and performance of the firm than he would obtain from analysis of the financial data alone.[1]

As we examine the financial analysis model in the next section, note how the ratio or index provides a useful frame of reference. Typically, ratios are used to compare historical and/or future trends within the firm or to compare a firm or business unit with an industry or other firms.

Several financial ratios often used to measure business performance are shown in Exhibit 2A.2. Note that these ratios are primarily useful as a means of comparing:

1. Ratio values for several time periods for a particular business.
2. A firm to its key competitors.
3. A firm to an industry or business standard.

There are several sources of ratio data. These include data services such as Dun & Bradstreet, *The Value Line Investment Survey,* industry and trade associations, government agencies, and investment advisory services.

Other ways to gauge the productivity of marketing activities include sales per square feet of retail floor space, occupancy rates of hotels and office buildings, and sales per salesperson.

[1]James C. Van Horne, *Fundamentals of Financial Management,* 4th ed. (Englewood Cliffs, NJ: Prentice-Hall, 1980), 103–4.

EXHIBIT 2A.1
Alternative Units for Financial Analysis

Market	Product/Service	Organization
Market	Industry	Company
Market niche(s)	Product mix	Segment/division/unit
Geographic area(s)	Product line	Marketing department
Customer groups	Specific product	Sales unit:
Individual customers	Brand	Region
	Model	District branch
		Office/store

EXHIBIT 2A.2 Summary of Key Financial Ratios

Source: Adapted from Arthur A. Thompson, Jr., and A. J. Strickland III, *Strategy and Policy*, 4th ed. (Homewood, IL: Richard D. Irwin, 1987), 270–1.

Ratio	How Calculated	What It Shows
Profitability ratios:		
1. Gross profit margin	$$\frac{\text{Sales} - \text{Cost of goods sold}}{\text{Sales}}$$	An indication of the total margin available to cover operating expenses and yield a profit.
2. Operating profit margin	$$\frac{\text{Profit before taxes and before interest}}{\text{Sales}}$$	An indication of the firm's profitability from current operations without regard to the interest charges accruing from the capital structure.
3. Net profit margin (or return on sales)	$$\frac{\text{Profit after taxes}}{\text{Sales}}$$	Shows after-tax profits per dollar of sales. Subpar profit margins indicate that the firm's relatively low, its costs are relatively high, or both.
4. Return on total assets	$$\frac{\text{Profits after taxes}}{\text{Total assets}}$$ or $$\frac{\text{Profit after taxes} + \text{Interest}}{\text{Total assets}}$$	A measure of the return on total investment in the enterprise. It is sometimes desirable to add interest to after-tax profits to form the numerator of the ratio, since total assets are financed by creditors as well as by stockholders; hence, it is accurate to measure the productivity of assets by the returns provided to both classes of investors.
5. Return on stockholders' equity (or return on net worth)	$$\frac{\text{Profits after taxes}}{\text{Total stockholders' equity}}$$	A measure of the rate on stockholders' investment in the enterprise.
6. Return on common equity	$$\frac{\text{Profits after taxes} - \text{Preferred stock dividends}}{\text{Total stockholders' equity} - \text{Par value of preferred stock}}$$	A measure of the rate of return on the investment that the owners of common stock have made in the enterprise.
7. Earnings per share	$$\frac{\text{Profits after taxes} - \text{Preferred stock dividends}}{\text{Number of shares of common stock outstanding}}$$	Shows the earnings available to the owners of common stock.
Liquidity ratios:		
1. Current ratio	$$\frac{\text{Current assets}}{\text{Current liabilities}}$$	Indicates the extent to which the claims of short-term creditors are covered by assets that are expected to be converted to cash in a period roughly corresponding to the maturity of the liabilities.
2. Quick ratio (or acid-test ratio)	$$\frac{\text{Current assets} - \text{Inventory}}{\text{Current liabilities}}$$	A measure of the firm's ability to pay off short-term obligations without relying on the sale of its inventories.
3. Cash ratio	$$\frac{\text{Cash \& Marketable securities}}{\text{Current liabilities}}$$	An indicator of how long the company can go without further inflow of funds.

(continued)

EXHIBIT 2A.2—(*concluded*)

Ratio	Formula	Description
4. Inventory to net working capital	$\dfrac{\text{Inventory}}{\text{Current assets} - \text{Current liabilities}}$	A measure of the extent to which the firm's working capital is tied up in inventory.
Leverage ratios:		
1. Debt to assets ratio	$\dfrac{\text{Total debt}}{\text{Total assets}}$	Measures the extent to which borrowed funds have been used to finance the firm's operations.
2. Debt to equity ratio	$\dfrac{\text{Total debt}}{\text{Total stockholders' equity}}$	Provides another measure of the funds provided the creditors versus the funds provided by owners.
3. Long-term debt to equity ratio	$\dfrac{\text{Long-term debt}}{\text{Total stockholders' equity}}$	A widely used measure of the balance between debt and equity in the firm's overall capital structure.
4. Times-interest-earned (or coverage ratios)	$\dfrac{\text{Profits before interest and taxes}}{\text{Total interest charges}}$	Measures the extent to which earnings can decline without the firm becoming unable to meet its annual interest costs.
5. Fixed-charge coverage	$\dfrac{\text{Profit before taxes and interest} + \text{Lease obligations}}{\text{Total interest charges} + \text{Lease obligations}}$	A more inclusive indication of the firm's ability to meet all of its fixed-charge obligations.
Activity ratios:		
1. Inventory turnover	$\dfrac{\text{Cost of goods sold}}{\text{Inventory}}$	When compared to industry averages, it provides an indication of whether a company has excessive inventory or perhaps inadequate inventory.
2. Fixed-assets turnover*	$\dfrac{\text{Sales}}{\text{Fixed assets}}$	A measure of the sales productivity and utilization of plant and equipment.
3. Total-assets turnover	$\dfrac{\text{Sales}}{\text{Total assets}}$	A measure of the utilization of all the firm's assets; a ratio below the industry average indicates the company is not generating a sufficient volume of business given the size of its asset investment.
4. Accounts receivable turnover	$\dfrac{\text{Annual credit sales}}{\text{Accounts receivable}}$	A measure of the average length of time it takes the firm to collect on the sales made on credit.
5. Average collection period	$\dfrac{\text{Accounts receivable}}{\text{Total sales} \div 365}$ or $\dfrac{\text{Accounts receivable}}{\text{Average daily sales}}$	Indicates the average length of time the firm must wait after making a sale before it receives payment.

*The manager should also keep in mind the fixed charges associated with noncapitalized lease obligations.

EXHIBIT 2A.3   **Illustrative Contribution Margin Analysis for Product X ($000)**

Sales	$300
Less: Variable manufacturing costs	100
Other variable costs traceable to product X	50
Equals: Contribution margin	150
Less: Fixed costs directly traceable to product X	100
Equals: Product net income	$ 50

Contribution Analysis

When the performance of products, market segments, and other marketing units is being analyzed, management should examine the unit's profit contribution. Contribution margin is equal to sales (revenue) less variable costs. Thus, contribution margin represents the amount of money available to cover fixed costs, and contribution margin less fixed costs is net income. An illustration of contribution margin analysis is given in Exhibit 2A.3. In this example, product X is generating a positive contribution margin. If product X were eliminated, $50,000 of product net income would be lost, and the remaining products would have to cover fixed costs not directly traceable to them. If the product is retained, the $50,000 can be used to contribute to other fixed costs and/or net income.

Financial Analysis Model

The model shown in Exhibit 2A.4 provides a useful guide for examining financial performance and identifying possible problem areas. The model combines several important financial ratios into one equation. Let's examine the model, moving from left to right. Profit margin multiplied by asset turnover yields return on assets. Moreover, assuming that the performance target is return on net worth (or return on equity), the product of return on assets and financial leverage determines performance. Increasing either ratio will increase net worth. The values of these ratios will vary considerably

from one industry to another. For example, in grocery wholesaling, profit margins are typically very low, whereas asset turnover is very high. Through efficient management and high turnover, a wholesaler can stack up impressive returns on net worth. Furthermore, space productivity measures are obtained for individual departments in retail stores that offer more than one line, such as department stores. The measures selected depend on the particular characteristics of the business.

Evaluating Alternatives

As we move through the discussion of financial analysis, it is important to recognize the type of costs being used in the analysis. Using accounting terminology, costs can be designated as fixed or variable. A cost is *fixed* if it remains constant over the observation period, even though the volume of activity varies. In contrast, a *variable* cost is an expense that varies with sales over the observation period. Costs are designated as mixed or semi-variable in instances when they contain both fixed and variable components.

Break-Even Analysis

This technique is used to examine the relationship between sales and costs. An illustration is given in Exhibit 2A.5. Using sales and cost information, it is easy to determine from a break-even analysis how many units of a product must be sold in order to break even, or cover total costs. In this example 65,000 units at sales of $120,000 are equal to total costs of $120,000. Any additional units sold will produce a profit. The break-even point can be calculated in this manner:

$$\text{Break-even units} = \frac{\text{Fixed costs}}{\text{Price per unit} - \text{Variable cost per unit}}$$

Price in the illustration shown in Exhibit 2A.5 is $1.846 per unit, and variable cost is $0.769 per unit. With fixed costs of $70,000, this results in the break-even calculation:

EXHIBIT 2A.4
Financial Analysis Model

Profit margin		Asset turnover		Return on assets		Financial leverage		Return on net worth
↓		↓		↓		↓		↓
Net profits (after taxes) Net sales	×	Net sales Total assets	→	Net profits (after taxes) Total assets	×	Total assets Net worth	=	Net profits (after taxes) Net worth

$$\text{BE units} = \frac{\$70,000}{\$1.846 - \$0.769} = 65,000 \text{ units}$$

To determine how many units must be sold to achieve a target profit (expressed in before-tax dollars), the formula is amended as follows:

$$\text{Target profit units} = \frac{\text{Fixed costs} + \text{Target profit (before tax)}}{\text{Price per unit} - \text{Variable cost per unit}}$$

Using the same illustration as above and including a target before-tax profit of $37,700, the target profit calculation becomes:

$$\text{Target profit units} = \frac{\$70,000 + \$37,700}{\$1.846 - \$0.769}$$
$$= 100,000 \text{ units}$$

Break-even analysis is not a forecast. It indicates how many units of a product at a given price and cost must be sold in order to break even or achieve a target profit. Some important assumptions that underlie the above break-even analysis include the use of constant fixed and variable costs, a constant price, and a single product.

In addition to break-even analysis, several other financial tools are used to evaluate alternatives. Net present value of cash flow analysis and return on investment are among the most useful. For example, assume

there are two projects with the cash flows shown in Exhibit 2A.6.

Though return on investment is widely used, it is limited by its inability to consider the time value of money. This is shown in Exhibit 2A.7. Return on investment for *both* projects X and Y is 10 percent. However, a dollar today is worth more than a dollar given in 3 years. Therefore, in assessing cash flows of a project or investment, future cash flows must be discounted back to the present at a rate comparable to the risk of the project.

Discounting cash flows is a simple process. Assume that the firm is considering projects X and Y and that its cost of capital is 12 percent. Additionally, assume that both projects carry risk comparable to the normal business risk. Under these circumstances, the analyst should discount the cash flows back to the present at the cost of capital, 12 percent. Present value factors can

EXHIBIT 2A.6   **Cash Flow Comparison ($000s)**

	Project X	Project Y
Start-Up-Costs	<1,000>	<1,000>
Year 1	500	300
Year 2	500	400
Year 3	300	600

EXHIBIT 2A.5
Illustrative Break-Even Analysis

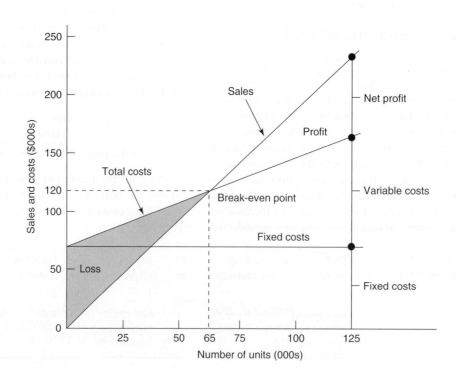

EXHIBIT 2A.7
Present Value
of Cash Flow

	Time	Cash Flow	PV Factor	NPV of Cash Flow
Project X				
	0	<1,000>	$1/(1 + .12^{\circ}) = 1$	<1,000>
	1	500	$1/(1 + .12)^1 = 0.8929$	=446.45
	2	500	$1/(1 + .12)^2 = 0.7972$	=398.60
	3	300	$1/(1 + .12)^3 = 0.7118$	=213.54
			Present value	+ 58.59
Project Y				
	0	<1,000>	$1/(1 + .12)^0 = 1$	<1,000>
	1	300	$1/(1 + .12)^1 = 0.8929$	=267.87
	2	400	$1/(1 + .12)^2 = 0.7972$	=318.88
	3	600	$1/(1 + .12)^3 = 0.7118$	=427.08
			Net present value	+ 13.83

be looked up or computed using the formula $1/(1 + i)^n$, where i equals our discounting rate per time period and n equals the number of compounding periods. In this example, the present value of cash flows would be as shown in Exhibit 2A.7.

Because both projects have a positive net present value, both are good. However, if they are mutually exclusive, the project with the highest net present value should be selected.

Financial Planning

Financial planning involves two major activities: (1) forecasting revenues and (2) budgeting (estimating future expenses). The actual financial analyses and forecasts included in the strategic marketing plan vary considerably from firm to firm. In addition, internal financial reporting and budgeting procedures vary widely among companies. Therefore, consider this approach as one example rather than the norm.

The choice of the financial information to be used for marketing planning and control will depend on its relationship with the corporate or business unit strategic plan. Another important consideration is the selection of performance measures to be used in gauging marketing performance. The objective is to indicate the range of possibilities and suggest some of the more frequently used financial analysis.

Pro forma income statements can be very useful when one is projecting performance and budgeting. Usually, this is done on a spreadsheet so that assumptions can be altered rapidly. Usually, only a few

assumptions need be made. For example, sales growth rates can be projected from past trends and adjusted for new information. From this starting point, cost of goods can be determined as a percentage of sales. Operating expenses can also be determined as a percentage of sales based on past relationships, and the effective tax rate as a percentage of earnings before taxes. However, past relationships may not hold in the future. It may be necessary to analyze possible divergence from past relationships.

In addition, pro forma income statements can be used to generate pro forma cash flow statements. It is then possible to compare alternative courses of action by employing a uniformly comparable standard cash flow.

Supplemental Financial Analyses

The preceding sections of this appendix detailed the various forms of traditional financial analysis useful in marketing decision making. There are supplemental forms of analysis that can also be helpful in different types of marketing decisions. These supplemental techniques draw mainly from the management accounting discipline and rely on data that are available only to internal decision makers. Many of the financial analyses in the earlier sections employed data from published financial statements.

Only recently have marketing decision makers been able to look to management accounting to provide an additional set of quantitative tools to aid in the decision process.[2] These tools may be referred to collectively as strategic management accounting practices. Simmonds is generally credited with originating the term *strategic management accounting,* which he defines as "the provision and analysis of management accounting data about a business and its competitors for use in developing and monitoring the business strategy."[3] Although academic researchers may disagree about the specific techniques that constitute strategic management accounting, a wide selection of management accounting practices available for use in marketing decision making. These practices are described in Exhibit 2A.8 and include activity-based costing, attribute costing, benchmarking, brand valuation budgeting and monitoring, competitor cost assessment, competitive position monitoring, competitor performance appraisal, integrated performance

measurement, life-cycle costing, quality costing, strategic costing, strategic pricing, target costing, and value-chain costing.[4]

Exhibit 2A.8 also provides a description of the various marketing applications of strategic management accounting practices in terms of specific decision-making situations. Most of these practices require the marketing decision maker to gather information additional to that normally used for the preparation of external financial statements. In most cases, this information is already available in the accounting information system of the firm. However, it may be necessary to compile data from outside the firm in a more formalized manner to perform analysis using some of these strategic management accounting practices.

---

[2]George Foster and Mahendra Gupta, "Marketing, Cost Management and Management Accounting," *Journal of Management Accounting Research,* 6, 1994, 43–77.

[3]K. Simmonds, "Strategic Management Accounting," *Management Accounting* (UK), 59(4), 1981, 26–29.

[4]For a comprehensive description of strategic management accounting techniques and differences in attitudes toward the use of these techniques between accounting and marketing managers, see Karen S. Cravens and Chris Guilding, "An Empirical Study of the Application of Strategic Management Accounting Techniques," *Advances in Management Accounting* 10, 2001, 95–124.

EXHIBIT 2A.8 Supplemental Financial Analyses Using Management Accounting Practices

Strategic Management Accounting Practice	Description of the Practice	Description of Marketing Application
Activity-based costing	Indirect costs are assigned to a product or service in relation to the activities used to produce the product or provide the service. Decision making focuses on the collection of activities necessary to produce the product or service rather than the costs in a specific category.	This technique is particularly useful in determining the costs of customization or the provision of additional services to customers. Since the activities are the central focus for costing, decision makers can evaluate customers and markets in terms of the activities required to serve their needs.
Attribute costing	Products or services are costed in terms of attributes that appeal to customers. Thus, the cost object is not the entire product but a collection of features that respond to customer needs.	The nature of the cost object can be modified to support different strategic decision-making situations. As customers modify their preferences, decision makers can consider how particular product attributes satisfy their needs relative to marketing positioning strategies.
Benchmarking	Benchmarking is improving existing processes by looking to an ideal standard. The standard may be established from an external source such as a competitor, a partner, or an unrelated industry or company or by another area of the same firm.	Benchmarking provides an opportunity to assess processes for improvement and strategic advantage in terms of operational effectiveness. Critical lapses in customer service or customer contact situations can be remedied.
Brand valuation—budgeting and monitoring	Brand valuation assesses the current and future potential of a brand in quantitative terms. A "capitalized" value for internally developed brands can be created even though in the United States this value may not be included on a balance sheet.	Current spending on brand promotion activities can be evaluated in terms of future benefits. This can assist with budgeting decisions relative to a portfolio of brands or products and in monitoring the mix and potential of existing products.
Competitive position monitoring	This type of analysis is used in evaluating the market strategy of a competitor. Overall competitor positions in the market and industry are assessed, including sales and trend information, along with market share and cost estimates.	Since this technique requires an external focus, it allows decision makers to assess the position of a product in terms of existing and future strategy relative to competitors. Situations allowing a firm to improve competitive position can be identified and acted upon.
Competitor performance appraisal	This form of analysis is a detailed part of competitive position monitoring and focuses on preparing a quantitative analysis of the competitor's external financial statements.	Decision makers can identify the key areas of a competitor's market advantage and relate areas of advantage to strategic decisions.

(continued)

EXHIBIT 2A.8—(concluded)

Integrated performance measurement	This form of analysis uses performance appraisal based on measures that are developed in terms of a customer focus. Integrated measures may be linked to customer satisfaction and may include nonfinancial measures monitored at the individual and departmental levels.	Measures focusing on the customer can be linked to overall strategic objectives throughout the organization. Decision makers can get a clear picture of how their decisions (and performance) affect overall corporate performance.
Life-cycle costing	A product or service is costed based on stages in the life of a product rather than financial reporting periods.	Decision makers can adopt a longer-term perspective to evaluate the performance of a product without the constraints of annual reporting periods.
Quality costing	Accounting measures support determining the cost of quality and the cost of a quality failure.	Decision makers can evaluate the impact on customers and market position when choices are made regarding quality issues.
Strategic costing	Strategic costing involves recognizing that the ultimate objective of expenditures related to a product or service may be more long-term in perspective. Thus, cost minimization is not the prime objective. Choices involving costs are evaluated in terms of long-term issues and the future potential of strategies.	Long-term strategy and strategic objectives considering product positioning and market penetration can be evaluated more completely. The long-term implications of a decision receive precedence over the short-term effect.
Strategic pricing	Strategic pricing adopts a more long-term and demand-focused approach to pricing rather than considering a cost-based and historical foundation.	Pricing decisions can be evaluated more in terms of competitive and market choices.
Target costing	A market-based approach is used to determine the target cost for a future product. The target cost is the remainder after a desired profit margin is subtracted from the estimated market price of a new product.	Since the product is designed to meet the target cost, decision makers know that the product will be able to enter the market at a price that allows an adequate level of profits. External rather than internal factors determine the price.
Value-chain costing	The cost of a product is evaluated over the entire value chain of production from research and development to customer service. This value chain may include multiple functional areas within the organization and cover different financial accounting reporting periods.	Operational efficiencies and competitive positioning can be evaluated at all stages of the value chain, not merely from the costs incurred during production. Links to suppliers, customers, and competitors can be considered at all points of the value chain.

3

Strategic Market Segmentation

Segmenting markets is a foundation for superior performance. Understanding how buyers' needs and wants vary is essential to designing effective marketing strategies. Effective approaches to segmenting markets may be one of the most critical factors in developing and implementing market-driven strategy. The need to improve an organization's understanding of buyers is escalating because of buyers' demands for uniqueness and the growing array of technology available to generate products to satisfy these demands. Companies are responding to the opportunities to provide unique customer value with products ranging from customized phone pagers for business users to self-designed, individualized greeting cards for consumers.

Indeed, McKinsey research underlines the weakness of thinking about markets only in general terms—talking of market trends, growth markets, mass markets, declining markets, and so on—and collecting information that describes only broad trends, where differences within markets are averaged-out. They point to the identification of opportunities from a deeper understanding of markets at a "granular" level. Market fragmentation and increasing granularity characterize a growing number of markets. The compelling logic of market granularity is that effective strategy can emerge only from a much finer understanding of market segments, their needs, and the capabilities required to serve them.[1]

Best Buy provides an interesting illustration of strategic market segmentation. Best Buy is the world's largest electronics retailer with sales revenue of $50 billion. In 2003 Best Buy piloted its "customer-centricity" strategy, radically shifting the company's strategic emphasis from products and technology to customers. The goal was to focus on the most attractive customers based on the important differences between them in their purchasing and preferences in consumer electronics. The customer base has been segmented into several basic lifestyle groups. High-priority target groups are described as:

- **Jill**—the "soccer mom," who is the main shopper for the family, but often avoids electronics stores, well-educated and confident, wants to enrich her children's lives with technology, yet intimidated by technology and jargon
- **Barry**—the wealthy professional man, who demands the latest technology and best service

---

[1]Patrick Vigerie, Sven Smit and Mehrdad Baghai, *The Granularity of Growth: Making Choices That Drive Enduring Company Performance* (New York: Cyan/Marshall Cavendish), 2007.

- **Buzz**—the young "tech enthusiast," who wants technology and entertainment
- **Ray**—the family man, who wants technology that improves his and his family's life
- **Mr. Storefront**—the small business customer who can use Best Buy's product solutions and services.

Other interesting segments are the **Carries's** (young, single females) and the **Helen and Charlie's** (older couples whose children have left home). Stores have been adapted to serve at least one dominant customer segment shopping at the store—though Jill and Barry stores are a frequent combination of segments in the same store. At the store level, employees are trained to recognize and focus on the needs and preferences of the target segments for that store. Indications are that stores converted to focus on the target segments perform substantially better than other stores.[2]

Best Buy's understanding of the granularity of its consumer markets is further underlined by encouraging local stores to identify and target market niches specific to their areas—eastern European workers from cargo ships or oil tankers docked at Baytown in Houston, Texas, looking for iPods and Apple laptops; Polish-language CDs in Chicago, in an area where 25 percent of residents are Polish speakers; North Carolina retiree clubs; newly returned soldiers in Georgia. Local ingenuity and insight is linked to profiting from market granularity.[3]

In most markets buyers vary in how they use products, the needs and preferences that the products satisfy, and their consumption patterns. These differences create market segments. Market segmentation is the process of identifying and analyzing subgroups of buyers in a product-market with similar response characteristics (e.g., frequency of purchase). Recognizing differences between market segments, and how they change, better and faster than competitors is an increasingly important source of competitive advantage.

In fact, for companies producing consumer products, the concept of a "one-size-fits-all mass market" is increasingly less relevant. Many consumer markets show signs of fragmentation into "microsegments" driven by diverse product preferences and media usage and demanding "right for me" in products purchased.[4] This is why Nike offers more than 300 varieties of sport shoe, not just one.

The most specific form of market segmentation is to consider each buyer as a market segment. This is the basis for "one-to-one marketing."[5] Such fine-tuned segmentation is possible for an expanding array of products due to mass customization techniques (the use of flexible computer-aided manufacturing systems to produce custom output, which combines the low unit costs of mass production processes with the flexibility of individual customization[6]). It offers an exciting new approach to serving the unique needs and wants of individual buyers. Custom-designed products satisfy individual buyer's needs and wants at prices comparable to mass-produced products. The growing adoption of customer relationship management systems that integrate all information about each individual customer into a single location provides unprecedented opportunities to learn about customer needs from their actual behavior. This is discussed in Chapter 4.

---

[2]This illustration is based on Ariana Eunjung Cha, "In Retail, Profiling for Profit," *Washington Post,* Wednesday, August 17, 2005, A01; Matthew Boyle, "Best Buy's Giant Gamble," *Fortune,* April 3, 2006.

[3]Jena McGregor, "At Best Buy, Marketing Goes Micro," *BusinessWeek,* May 26, 2008, 52–54.

[4]Anthony Bianco, "The Vanishing Mass Market," *BusinessWeek,* July 12, 2004, 62–68.

[5]Don Peppers and Martha Rogers, *Enterprise One-to-One* (New York: Doubleday), 1997.

[6]Richard B Chase, Robert F. Jacobs, and Nicholas J. Aquilano, *Operations Management for Competitive Advantage,* 11th ed. (New York: McGraw-Hill/Irwin, 2006).

For example, globally the apparel industry is adopting mass-customization technologies to allow clothing to be designed and produced for the individual consumer. Pioneered by Levi Strauss & Co with Personal Pair jeans (later Original Spin), stores as diverse as Brooks Brothers, Harrods in London, Bon Marché in Paris, and other retailers use body scanning to measure dimensions and produce clothes customized for the individual consumer. For Levi's the goal is to reduce the traditional struggle to locate jeans that fit well, into a 10-second shopping experience—when the consumer steps out of the "measure me up" kiosk, personal stylists are available to help choose the best styles. At Harrods, customized apparel by designers like Vivienne Westwood and Nick Holland produced based on body scanning information. Internet-based companies offer mass-customized clothing, including IC3D (Interactive Custom Clothes Company Designs), American Fit, and Beyond Fleece.[7]

We begin the chapter with a discussion of the different purposes that segmentation models can fulfil and the role of market segmentation in marketing strategy, followed by a discussion of the variables used to identify segments. Next, we look at the methods for forming segments followed by a review of high-variety strategies. Finally, we consider the issues and guidelines involved in selecting the segmentation strategy and in its implementation.

Levels and Types of Market Segmentation

Segmentation is an important tool in strategic marketing, which is linked to choosing market targets and positioning against alternatives to build competitive advantage. Importantly, segmentation may serve several purposes at levels which range from the strategic to the operational. The Best Buy analysis of its customer base and realignment of its stores and employee behaviors around segments illustrates an interesting approach to strategic market segmentation. Many traditional views emphasize segmentation as an operational tool—for example, to aim advertising effectively at different types of customers.

However, segmentation models appropriate to developing advertising programs may be quite different to those used to develop marketing strategy. While advertising-oriented segmentation aims to identify targets that differ in their responses to a given message, strategic segmentation has the goal of identifying market segments that differ in their purchasing power, goals, aspirations and behavior, in ways relevant to identifying new product and value opportunities.[8]

It is useful to examine segmentation as operating at several decision-making levels in the way suggested by see Exhibit 3.1. Strategic segmentation links to the management vision and strategic intent of corporate strategy, and emphasizes product benefits that different types of buyers seek. Managerial segmentation is concerned with allocating resources around segment targets, including them in marketing plans, and aligning organizational processes around them. Operational segmentation issues are concerned with the marketing program changes needed to reach segment targets with advertising and promotions, and with distribution systems. The Best Buy example illustrates these levels of segmentation approach. The strategic issues are concerned with consumer lifestyles and the benefits that different types of consumers seek in choosing and purchasing consumer electronics. The managerial issues are concerned with identifying target segment members, redesigning stores to serve chosen segments, and providing employees with the training and power to

[7]Hadley Freeman, "Nothing In Your Size? Stores Seek to Measure Up," *The Guardian,* September 6, 2006; "Levi's Extends Its 10 Second Fitting Kiosk Market Tour," *TheWiseMarketer.com,* September 6, 2006.
[8]Daniel Yankelovich and David Meer, "Rediscovering Market Segmentation," *Harvard Business Review,* February 2006, 122–131.

EXHIBIT 3.1
**Levels of Market
Segmentation**

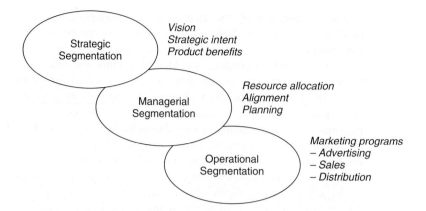

focus on the segment targets. Operational segmentation issues are concerned with delivering relevant messages to targets, and supporting the segmentation strategy at store level.

In considering the role of segmentation, the deepest decisions are whether to revise the business model in response to how social forces are changing the lives of different types of customer, how to position a brand, which segments to pursue, and whether to make fundamental changes to the product or to develop and entirely new product. The shallowest decisions are concerned with issues like whether to make small improvements in existing products, how to select targets of a media campaign, or whether to adjust prices.[9]

It is important to effective market-driven strategy that these different aspects of segmentation should be aligned and integrated. The goal of strategic marketing segmentation is to support processes whereby products are designed and developed around the needs of different types of purchaser to offer superior customer value, and then to identify the mechanisms by which that value can be delivered. This requires segmenting markets in ways that reflect how customers actually live their lives and the jobs that they need to get done.[10]

Market-Driven Strategy and Segmentation

Market segmentation needs to be considered early in the development of market-driven strategy. Segments are identified, customer value opportunities and new market spaces are explored in each segment, organizational capabilities are matched to promising segment opportunities, market target(s) are selected from the segment(s) of interest, and a positioning strategy is developed and implemented for each market target (see Exhibit 3.2). We examine each of these activities to indicate the role of segmentation in the marketing strategy process.

EXHIBIT 3.2
**Segmentation in
the Market-Driven
Strategy Process**

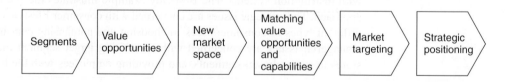

---

[9]Daniel Yankelovich and David Meer, "Rediscovering Market Segmentation," *Harvard Business Review,* February 2006, 122–131.
[10]Clayton M. Christensen, Scott Cook, and Taddy Hall, "Marketing Malpractice: The Cause and the Cure," *Harvard Business Review,* December 2005, 74–83.

Market Segmentation, Value Opportunities and New Market Space

Market segmentation is the process of placing the buyers in a product-market into sub-groups so that the members of each segment display similar responsiveness to a particular positioning strategy. Buyer similarities are indicated by the amount and frequency of purchase, loyalty to a particular brand, how the product is used, and other measures of responsiveness. So, segmentation is an identification process aimed at finding subgroups of buyers within a total market. The opportunity for segmentation occurs when differences in buyers' demand (response) functions allow market demand to be divided into segments, each with a distinct demand function.[11] For example, auto manufacturer Subaru has established a fiercely loyal body of consumers in its market niche, with a focus on "experience seekers" and particular success in locations that have hills and snow.[12] On the other hand, office products distributor Staples has introduced its "M by Staples" products to tempt the market niche comprising stationery "addicts," with more expensive, better-designed alternatives to standard stationery products.[13]

The term "market niche" is sometimes used to refer to a market segment that represents a relatively small portion of the buyers in the total market. We consider a niche and a segment to be the same.

Segmentation identifies customer groups within a product-market, each containing buyers with similar value requirements concerning specific product/brand attributes. A segment is a possible market target for an organization competing in the market. Segmentation offers a company an opportunity to better match its products and capabilities to buyers' value requirements. Customer satisfaction can be improved by providing a value offering that matches the value proposition considered most important by the buyer in a segment.

Importantly, market analysis may identify segments not recognized or served effectively by competitors. There may be opportunities to tap into new areas of value and create a unique space in the market. For example, while the luxury hotel business is highly competitive and has been hard-hit by economic recession, several companies have been able to develop profitable opportunities. Interestingly, the newest hotel formats are boutique or lifestyle hotels, where sales growth is considerably higher than in the mainstream hotel business. This development is described in the INNOVATION APPLICATION.

While broad competitive comparisons can be made for an entire product-market, more penetrating insights about competitive advantage and market opportunity result from market segment analyses. Examining specific market segments helps to identify how to (1) attain a closer match between buyers' value preferences and the organization's capabilities, and (2) compare the organization's strengths (and weaknesses) to the key competitors in each segment.

Market Targeting and Strategic Positioning

Market targeting consists of evaluating and selecting one or more segments whose value requirements provide a good match with the organization's capabilities. Companies typically appeal to only a portion of the people or organizations in a product-market, regardless of how many segments are targeted. Management may decide to target one, a few, or several segments to gain the strength and advantage of specialization. Alternatively, while

[11]Peter R. Dickson and James L. Ginter, "Market Segmentation, Product Differentiation, and Marketing Strategy," *Journal of Marketing,* April 1987, 1–10.
[12]Bernard Simon, "On the Trail of Experience-Seekers On and Off the Road," *Financial Times,* July 17, 2009, 12.
[13]Aaron Pressman, "Upwardly Mobile Stationery," *BusinessWeek,* March 17, 2008, 60–61.

Luxury hotels have recognized that different people want different things from upmarket accommodation—the customer staying at a convention hotel has different needs than the senior executive traveling on business or the leisure traveler. Rivals have developed quirkier and more individualistic lifestyle hotel formats to reflect this evolving segmentation in their market, where some travelers find traditional hotels too staid and uniform. These new formats tap into several areas of above-average growth prospects and unmet customer needs.

- Marriott, whose "one-size-fits-all" hotel chain is sometimes called "the McDonalds of lodging" is partnering with Ian Schroder, king of the design hotel, to create the Edition boutique hotels aimed at younger, wealthier, more fashionable travellers, to gain entry to the fastest-growing sector of the market-boutique hotel growth is running at 11 percent a year in the United States, one-third above the industry norm.

- Chicago-based Hyatt Hotels and Resorts has launched its first boutique hotel in the form of the Andaz (an Urdu word meaning "personal style"), with minimalist design concepts.

- InterContinental Hotels has its Indigo boutique hotel format.

- Starwood has won plaudits for its stylish W chain and is expanding its new Aloft concept.

- In addition, Hyatt Hotels and Resorts recognized that the Internet was a surefire way to reach the gay, lesbian, bisexual, and transgender (GLBT) market, and launched its own GLBT website, winning PlanetOut's "Best Hotel Collection" award for its commitment, sensitivity, and appeal to lesbian, gay, bisexual, and transgender travelers.

Sources: Deborah L. Vence, "Divide and Conquer," *Marketing News*, July 15, 2007, 15–18. John Arlidge, "Marriott Goes for Boutique Hotels," *Sunday Times*, November 11, 2007, S3, 7. Matthew Goodman, "Hyatt Checks In with Its First Boutique Hotel," *Sunday Times*, November 18, 2007, S3, 10.

a specific segment strategy is not used, the marketing program selected by management is likely to appeal to a particular subgroup of buyers within the market. Segment identification and targeting are obviously preferred. Finding a segment by chance does not give management the opportunity of evaluating different segments in terms of the financial and competitive advantage implications of each segment. When segmentation is employed, it should be by design, and the underlying analyses should lead to the selection of one or more promising segments to target.

Recall the Chapter 1 description of positioning strategy as the combination of the actions management takes to meet the needs and wants of each market target. The strategy consists of product(s) and supporting services, distribution, pricing, and promotion components. Management's choices about how to influence target buyers to favorably position the product in their eyes and minds help in designing the positioning strategy.

The GLOBAL APPLICATION describes the positioning strategy chosen by BMW for the new Mini, as a lifestyle vehicle, and the innovative marketing program choices that fit with buyer characteristics in this niche of the automobile market.

Market segmentation lays the groundwork for market targeting and positioning strategies. The skills and insights used in segmenting a product-market may give a company important competitive advantages by identifying buyer groups that will respond favorably to the firm's marketing efforts. The previous Best Buy example is illustrative. Faulty segmentation reduces the effectiveness of targeting and positioning decisions. For example, when apparel retailer Talbots attempted to attract new, younger consumers to their stores, they risked alienating shoppers who were already loyal fans. The result of trying to entice "thirtysomethings" with cocktail dresses and frilly tank tops was to leave the pearl-wearing

- Notwithstanding depressed car markets in the United States and Europe, BMW's remake of the 1959 classic is one of the most successful model overhauls ever. The Oxford, England, factory is running at full capacity, producing 300,000 vehicles a year. In 2007, the plant produced the millionth Mini. Following an electric powered version and a four-wheel driver, 2011 saw the announcement of the Mini Rocketman, smaller and even closer in design to the 1959 original.

  - The new Mini look is a cute snout and bull-dog-like stance, offering an appealing contrast to boxy sports utility vehicles. While based on the original Mini, this is a premium priced vehicle, packed with technology. The car is positioned to be "quintessentially cool"—its biggest selling point is its individualistic appeal.
  - Budget for the U.S. launch was only $13 million, so BMW used event-focused "guerrilla tactics," unconventional stunts, and irreverent humor to spark an infectious buzz. One of the first Mini-sightings in the United States was a Mini strapped to the roof of a sports utility vehicle with the sign "What are you doing for fun this weekend?" The Mini also appeared seated in football stadiums like a fan watching the game.
  - The cool status of the Mini was cemented in place when it was used in the 2003 remake of the movie *The Italian Job*. The 2006 launch of the Mini-Cooper used an Internet-only campaign in homage to *The Matrix*.
  - When the Mini convertible came to the U.S. and European market in 2004, the cars was delivered with the top down and a seal to be broken when the roof was raised for the first time. Buyers were asked to sign a mock contract committing them to keep the roof down as long as they could—to stay true to the Mini convertible's open-minded spirit.
  - BMW nurtured Mini mania by keeping supply just short of demand. More than half of buyers custom-order the mini and wait three months for delivery. Prospective Mini purchasers are "net savvy"—the Mini Cooper launch in 2007 was led by an Internet-only teaser produced by a digital ad agency, not conventional TV and cinema advertising.

Source: Gail Edmondson and Michael Eidam, "The Mini Just Keeps Getting Mightier," *BusinessWeek*, April 5, 2004, 26. John Reed, "Millionth Mini Marks Milestone for BMW," *Financial Times*, April 16, 2007, 4. John Arlidge, "BMW Creates a Mini Monster," *Sunday Times*, September 26, 2010, S3, 1.

career woman feeling neglected. Talbots has suffered badly from faulty segmentation reflected in sales losses and lower stock price.[14]

Activities and Decisions in Market Segmentation

The process of segmenting a market involves several interrelated activities and decisions beginning with defining the market to be segmented (see Exhibit 3.3). It is necessary to decide how to segment the market and identifying segments, which involves selecting the

---

[14]Ashley Lutz, "How Talbots Got the Girl and Lost the Woman," *BusinessWeek,* June 20–25, 2011, 25–26.

EXHIBIT 3.3
Activities and Decisions in Market Segmentation

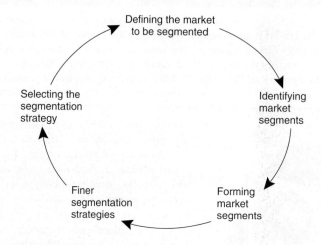

variable(s) to use as the basis for identifying segments. For example, frequency of use of a product (e.g., frequent, moderate, and occasional) may be a possible basis for segmentation. Next, the method of forming market segments is decided. This may consist of managers using judgment and experience to divide the market into segments. Alternatively, segments may be formed using statistical analysis. The availability of customer purchase behavior information in CRM systems, for example, provides a growing base for this analysis. Part of forming segments is deciding whether finer (smaller) segments should be used. Finally, strategic analysis is conducted on each segment to assist management in deciding which segment(s) to target.

Defining the Market to Be Segmented

Market segmentation may occur at any of the product-market levels shown in see Exhibit 3.4. Generic-level segmentation is illustrated by segmenting supermarket buyers based on shopper types (e.g., on the basis of available shopping time). Product-type segmentation is shown by the differences in price, quality, and features of shaving equipment. Product variant–segmentation considers the segments within a category such as electric razors.

An important consideration in defining the market to be segmented is estimating the variation in buyers' needs and requirements at the different product-market levels and identifying the types of buyers included in the market. The boutique hotel format discussed in the earlier INNOVATION APPLICATION illustrates a strategy focused on a specific segment. Nonetheless, in contemporary markets, boundaries and definitions can

EXHIBIT 3.4
Market Segmentation in the Health and Beauty Supplies Market

Level of Competition	Product Definition	Illustrative Competitors	Need/Want Satisfied
Generic	Health and beauty aids	Consumer products companies	Enhancement of health and beauty
Product type	Shaving equipment	Gillette, Remington, Bic	Shaving
Product variant	Electric razors	Braun, Norelco, Remington, Panasonic	Electric shaving

change rapidly, underlining the strategic importance of market definition and selection, and the need for frequent re-evaluation.

Identifying Market Segments

After the market to be segmented is defined, one or more variables are selected to identify segments. For example, the U.S. Automobile Association (USAA) segments by type of employment. Although unknown to many people, USAA has built a successful business serving the financial services needs of U.S. military personnel located throughout the world. USAA has close relationships with its 6.8 million members using powerful information technology. The USAA service representative has immediate access to the client's consolidated file, and the one-to-one service encounter is highly personalized, and USAA achieves a 98 percent retention rate in its market chosen segment.[15] In 2007, USAA was "#1 Customer Service Champ" in Bloomberg BusinessWeek's survey, and retained number 1 or 2 position for four years running.[16] In 2011, USAA was recognized by J.D. Powers for a decade of outstanding customer satisfaction.[17]

First, we discuss segmentation variables, followed by a review of the variables that are used in segmentation analyses.

Segmentation Variables

One or more variables (e.g., frequency of use) may be used to divide the product-market into segments. *Demographic* and *psychographic* (lifestyle and personality) characteristics of buyers are of interest, since this information is available from the U.S. Census reports and many other sources including electronic databases. The *use situation* variables consider how the buyer uses the product, such as purchasing a meal away from home for the purpose of entertainment. Variables measuring buyers' *needs* and *preferences* include attitudes, brand awareness, and brand preference. *Purchase-behavior* variables describe brand-use and consumption (e.g., size and frequency of purchase). We examine these variables to highlight their uses, features, and other considerations important in segmenting markets.

Characteristics of People and Organizations

Consumer Markets

The characteristics of people fall into two major categories: (1) geographic and demographic and (2) psychographic (lifestyle and personality). Demographics are often more useful to describe consumer segments after they have been formed rather than to identify them. Nonetheless, these variables are popular because available data often relate demographics to the other segmentation variables. Geographic location may be useful for segmenting product-markets. For example, more than 20 years since the fall of the Berlin wall, underlying values expressed in brand preferences still differ between eastern German consumers and western Germans. Detergent Persil was a top seller in the west but not the east—Persil was seen in the east as an elite product for the rich people portrayed in the TV advertising. The appeal of the brand in the east only increased in response to a more

---

[15]Leonard L. Berry, "Relationship Marketing of Services—Growing Interest, Emerging Perspectives," *Journal of the Academy of Marketing Science,* Fall 1995, 238–240.

[16]Jena McGregor, "Customer Service Champs," *BusinessWeek,* February 18, 2010, www.businessweek.com, accessed July 12, 2011.

[17]www.usaa.com/.../about_usaa_corporate_overview_awards_and_rankings, accessed June 24 2011.

emotional and ironic appeal. Other western brands have encountered similar barriers in the unified German state.[18]

Demographic variables describe buyers according to their age, income, education, occupation, and many other characteristics. Demographic information helps to describe groups of buyers such as heavy users of a product or brand. Demographics used in combination with buyer behavior information are useful in segmenting markets, selecting distribution channels, designing promotion strategies, and other decisions on marketing strategy.

Lifestyle variables indicate what people do (activities), their interests, their opinions, and their buying behavior. Lifestyle characteristics extend beyond demographics and offer a more penetrating description of the consumer.[19] Profiles can be developed using lifestyle characteristics. This information is used to segment markets, help position products, and guide the design of advertising messages.

For example, consumer goods companies in many personal care and beauty product areas are looking for sales growth with male purchasers, rather than females. The male shopper is conventionally not well understood by companies in these product fields. Lifestyle and product choice differences between different types of males are shown in the STRATEGY APPLICATION. While crude, this model provides an initial basis for examining product development opportunities for different segments of the male personal care product market.

Organizational Markets

Several characteristics help in segmenting business markets. The type of industry (sometimes called a vertical market) is related to purchase behavior for certain types of products. For example, automobile producers purchase steel, paint, and other raw materials. Since automobile firms' needs may vary from companies in other industries, this form of segmentation enables suppliers to specialize their efforts and satisfy customer needs. Other variables for segmenting organizational markets include size of the company, the stage of industry development, and the stage of the value-added system (e.g., producer, distribution, retailer). Organizational segmentation is aided by first examining (1) the extent of market concentration, and (2) the degree of product customization.[20] Concentration considers the number of customers and their relative buying power. Product customization determines the extent to which the supplier must tailor the product to each organizational buyer. If one or both of these factors indicate quite a bit of diversity, segmentation opportunities may exist.

For example, Boeing caters to the specific needs of each air carrier purchasing commercial aircraft, adapting designs to meet customer priorities. Nonetheless, the costs of customization are high and Boeing has had to evaluate the value/cost relationships of its attempts to satisfy the needs of single airline segments.

Product Use Situation Segmentation

Markets can be segmented based on how the product is used. As an illustration, Nikon, the Japanese camera and precision instruments company, offers a line of high-performance sunglasses designed for activities and light conditions when skiing, snowboarding, skating, and driving. Nikon competes in the premium portion of the market with prices somewhat higher than Ray-Ban, the market leader. Timex uses a similar basis of segmentation for its watches.

[18]Hugh Williamson, "Advertisers Try to Bridge Germany's Consumer Divide," *Financial Times,* July 27, 2007, 12.
[19]Henry Assael, *Consumer Behavior and Marketing Action,* 2nd ed. (Boston: PWS-Kent Publishing, 1984), 225.
[20]Jay L. Laughlin and Charles R. Taylor, "An Approach to Industrial Market Segmentation," *Industrial Marketing Management,* 20 1991, 127–136.

Consumer products companies in fields like personal care and cosmetics are focusing more attention on the male consumer. They are having to re-think the characteristics of the male purchaser. Male shopper stereotypes or segments include:

The Metrosexual

- The affluent, urban sophisticate, who adds deeper meaning, quality, and beauty to consumption. Thinks of loafers as objets d'art.
- P&G, Beiersdorf, and Polo Ralph Lauren do good business with the metro.

The Maturiteen

- More savvy, responsible, mature, and pragmatic than previous cohorts, with poise attributed to baby boomer parents who treat kids as equals.
- A technology master, adept at online research, often acting as an inhouse shopping consultant. Never knew a time without the Web, and its interactivity has nurtured in them a radical view of brands—they own them.
- Adidas, Sony, and Unilever are skillful at playing along with them.

The Modern Man

- Neither retro nor metro, he's something in the middle. A sophisticated consumer in his 20s and 30s—a bigger shopper than his dad, but still a sports fan
- Comfortable with women but doesn't like shopping with them. Moisturizer and hair gel are perfectly ordinary to him.
- Philips Norelco used locker-room humor to get the modern man comfortable with the below-the-neck shaver, Bodygroom.

The Dad

- Largely ignored, but in their peak earning years
- Smart companies like Dyson and Patek Philippe are reaching out to them.

The Retrosexual

- If the metrosexual champions the female ethos with a "go Girl," the retrosexual is screaming "Stop!" Has lived through the same cultural turmoil and consumerism, but rejects feminism and happily wallows in traditional male behavior. Nostalgic for the good old days before moisturizers for men.
- Burger King and P&G's Old Spice have this dude nailed.

Source: Nanette Byrnes, "Secrets of the Male Shopper," *BusinessWeek*, September 4, 2006, 45–54.

Needs and preferences vary according to different use situations. Consider, for example, segmenting the market for prescription drugs. Astra/Merck identifies the following segments based on the type of physician/patient drug use situation:

- **Health care as a business**—customers such as managed care administrators who consider economic factors of drug use foremost.
- **Traditional**—physicians with standard patient needs centered around the treatment of disease.
- **Cost sensitive**—physicians for whom cost is paramount, such as those with a sizable number of indigent patients.
- **Medical thought leaders**—people on the leading edge, often at teaching hospitals, who champion the newest therapies.[21]

---

[21]Daniel S. Levine, "Justice Served," *Sales & Marketing Management,* May, 1995, 53–61.

A sales representative provides the medical thought leader with cutting-edge clinical studies, whereas the cost-sensitive doctor is provided information related to costs of treatments.

Mass customization offers a promising means of responding to different use situations at competitive prices. Recall the earlier clothing industry examples.

Buyers' Needs and Preferences

Needs and preferences that are specific to products and brands can be used as segmentation bases and segment descriptors. Examples include brand loyalty status, benefits sought, and proneness to make a deal. Buyers may be attracted to different brands because of the benefits they offer. For example, the "fairtrade" branding of products as diverse as coffee and clothing, with goals of benefiting producers in developing countries, has shown remarkable growth. The segment consists of consumers who are prepared to pay a higher price for staple products, if their actions benefit people in poorer countries. This is an example of "ethical branding" aimed at a new and growing segment of ethically-motivated consumers.[22]

Consumer Needs

Needs motivate people to act. Understanding how buyers satisfy their needs provides guidelines for marketing actions. Consumers attempt to match their needs with the products that satisfy their needs. People have a variety of needs, including basic physiological needs (food, rest, and sex); the need for safety; the need for relationships with other people (friendship); and personal satisfaction needs.[23] Understanding the nature and intensity of these needs is important in (1) determining how well a particular brand may satisfy the need, and/or (2) indicating what change(s) in the brand may be necessary to provide a better solution to the buyer's needs.

Attitudes

Buyer's attitudes toward brands are important because experience and research findings indicate that attitudes influence behavior. Attitudes are enduring systems of favorable or unfavorable evaluations about brands.[24] They reflect the buyer's overall liking or preference for a brand. Attitudes may develop from personal experience, interactions with other buyers, or by marketing efforts, such as advertising and personal selling.

Attitude information is useful in marketing strategy development. A strategy may be designed either to respond to established attitudes or, instead, to attempt to change an attitude. In a given situation, relevant attitudes should be identified and measured to indicate how brands compare. If important attitude influences on buyer behavior are identified and a firm's brand is measured against these attitudes, management may be able to improve the brand's position by using this information. Attitudes are often difficult to change, but firms may be able to do so if buyers' perceptions about the brand are incorrect. For example, if the trade-in value of an automobile is important to buyers in a targeted segment and a company learns through market research that its brand (which actually has a high trade-in value) is perceived as having a low trade-in value, advertising can communicate this information to buyers.

---

[22]Meg Carter, "Big Business Pitches Itself on Fair Trade Territory," *Financial Times,* October 25, 2005, 13.
[23]A. H. Maslow, "Theory of Human Motivation," *Psychology Review,* July 1943, 43–45.
[24]Assael, *Consumer Behavior and Marketing Action,* 650.

EXHIBIT 3.5
Television Viewers
Watch Fewer Ads

Source: Survey of the 15 largest
U.S. television markets in 2003
by CNW Marketing Research
Inc. reported in Anthony
Bianco, "The Vanishing Mass
Market," *BusinessWeek,*
July 12, 2004, 65.

	Ads Actively Ignored on Television	Ads Skipped Using Personal Video Recorder
Beer	4.8%	31.9%
Movie trailers	11.6	44.1
Soft drinks	21.6	82.7
Drug	32.3	45.6
Specialty clothing	33.4	62.4
Home products	41.6	90.3
Fast food	45.1	95.7
Cars (national)	52.8	68.8
Pet-related	55.5	81.5
Credit cards	62.7	94.2
Mortgage financing	74.1	94.7
Upcoming program	75.3	94.4
Unweighted average	43.1	71.6

Perceptions

Perception is defined as "the process by which an individual selects, organizes, and interprets information inputs to create a meaningful picture of the world."[25] Perceptions are how buyers select, organize, and interpret marketing stimuli, such as advertising, personal selling, price, and the product. Perceptions form attitudes. Buyers are selective in the information they process. As an illustration of selective perception, some advertising messages may not be received by viewers because of the large number of messages vying for their attention. For example, see Exhibit 3.5 lists products where substantial proportions of TV advertisements are actively ignored or skipped using a personal video recorder. Negative attitudes and perception may be a major barrier to communicating with consumers. Or, more simply, for example, a salesperson's conversation may be misunderstood or not understood because the buyer is trying to decide if the purchase is necessary while the salesperson is talking.

People often perceive things differently. Business executives are interested in how their products, salespeople, stores, and companies are perceived. Perception is important strategically in helping management to evaluate the current positioning strategy and in making changes in this positioning strategy. Perception mapping is a useful research technique for showing how brands are perceived by buyers according to various criteria. We discuss how preference mapping is used to form segments later in the chapter.

Purchase Behavior

Consumption variables such as the size and frequency of a purchase are useful in segmenting consumer and business markets. Marketers of industrial products often classify customers and prospects into categories on the basis of the volume of the purchase. For example, a specialty chemical producer concentrates its marketing efforts on chemical users that purchase at least $100,000 of chemicals each year. The firm further segments the market on the basis of how the customer uses the chemical.

The development of CRM systems offers fast access to records of actual customer purchase behavior and characteristics. CRM and loyalty programs are generating insights into

---

[25]Bernard Berelson and Gary A. Steiner, *Human Behavior: An Inventory of Scientific Findings* (New York: Harcourt Brace Jovanovich, 1964), 88.

customer behavior and segment differences, and providing the ability to respond more precisely to the needs of customers in different segments. We discuss the impact of CRM on analyzing customer characteristics in Chapter 4.

Interestingly, level of product use may not necessarily identify the best value opportunities. While casino companies call their best customers (gamblers) "whales" (and give them free hotel rooms and special tables with high limits), yet in the cell phone business the top 1 percent of wireless data customers who provide 30 percent of the traffic are stigmatized as "gluttons" or "bandwidth hogs" (and operators want to penalize them with higher prices).[26]

Since buying decisions vary in importance and complexity, it is useful to classify them to better understand their characteristics, the products to which they apply, and the marketing strategy implications of each type of purchase behavior. Buyer decisions can be classified according to the extent to which the buyer is involved in the decision.[27] A high-involvement decision may be an expensive purchase, have important personal consequences, and impact the consumer's ego and social needs. The decision situation may consist of extended problem solving (high involvement), limited problem solving, or routine problem solving (low involvement). The characteristics of these situations are illustrated in see Exhibit 3.6.

These categories are very broad since the range of involvement covers various buying situations. Even so, the classifications provide a useful way to compare and contrast buying situations. Also, involvement may vary from individual to individual. For example, a high-involvement purchase for one person may not be such for another person, since perceptions of expense, personal consequences, and social impact may vary across individuals. See Exhibit 3.7 summarizes the various segmentation variables and shows examples of segmentation bases and descriptors for consumer and organizational markets. As we examine the methods used to form segments, the role of these variables in segment determination and analysis is illustrated.

For example, a brand perspective is sometimes represented by a single "golden question" posed to consumers. One manufacturer of an expensive, upmarket, premium cat food in Europe identified prospective members of the high-maintenance cat-pampering segment with the question "Do you buy your cat a birthday present?" (a positive response was a good indicator of a consumer likely to pay over the odds for a premium cat food).

EXHIBIT 3.6
Consumer Involvement in Purchase Decisions

Source: Eric N. Berkowitz, Roger A. Kerin, Steven W. Hartley, and William Rudelius, *Marketing,* 5th ed. (Chicago: Richard D. Irwin, 1997), 156. Copyright © The McGraw-Hill Companies. Used with permission.

	Consumer Involvement		
	High		**Low**
Characteristics of Purchase Decision Process	**Extended Problem Solving**	**Limited Problem Solving**	**Routine Problem Solving**
Number of brands examined	Many	Several	One
Number of sellers considered	Many	Several	Few
Number of product attributes evaluated	Many	Moderate	One
Number of external information sources used	Many	Few	None
Time spent searching	Considerable	Little	Minimal

[26]Brendan Greeley, "Who Are You Calling a Data Hog?" *Bloomberg BusinessWeek,* February 14–20, 2011, 31–32.
[27]Eric N. Berkowitz, Steven W. Hartley, William Rudelius, and Roger A. Kerin, *Marketing,* 7th ed. (Burr Ridge, IL: McGraw-Hill/Irwin), 2003.

EXHIBIT 3.7
Illustrative
Segmentation
Variables

Source: Eric N. Berkowitz,
Steven W. Hartley, William
Rudelius, and Roger A. Kerin,
Marketing, 7th ed. (Burr Ridge,
IL: McGraw-Hill/Irwin, 2003).

	Consumer Markets	Industrial/Organizational Markets
Characteristics of people/ organizations	Age, gender, race Income Family size Lifecycle stage Geographic location Lifestyle	Type of industry Size Geographic location Corporate culture Stage of development Producer/intermediary
Use situation	Occasion Importance of purchase Prior experience with product User status	Application Purchasing procedure New task, modified rebuy, straight rebuy
Buyers' needs/ preferences	Brand loyalty status Brand preference Benefits sought Quality Proneness to make a deal	Performance requirements Brand preferences Desired features Service requirements
Purchase behavior	Size of purchase Frequency of purchase	Volume Frequency of purchase

The question was later refined to "Do you spend more on your cat's birthday or Christmas present?" (any thought given to the issue suggested a member of the target segment).

Forming Market Segments

Turning round the performance of Miller Brewing's business was in part based on developing new strategic segment targets for Miller's beer brands. Targets for some of the biggest brands are:

- **Miller Genuine Draft**—aiming at "mainstream sophisticates," males aged 25–35 attracted by the tag line "Beer. Grown Up."
- **Milwaukee's Best Light**—targeting "hardworking men" with a beer to be picked up after a long day at work, sponsors the World Series of Poker on ESPN to get the attention of these poker-playing consumers
- **Pilsner Urquell**—for "beer aficionados," or more discerning drinkers. Select salespeople—"beer merchants"—educate bar staff and retailers on the special character of the Czech beer, the original golden pilsner
- **Miller Icehouse**—for "drinking buddies," hanging out, playing Xbox, or getting ready to go out, targeting the modern young male.[28]

The requirements for segmentation are discussed first, and then the methods of segment formation are described and illustrated.

Requirements for Segmentation

An important question is deciding if it is worthwhile to segment a product-market. For example, for many years Gillette successfully adopted a "one product for all" strategy in the razor market. While in many instances segmentation is a sound strategy, its feasibility

[28]Adrienne Carter, "It's Norman Time," *BusinessWeek,* May 29, 2006, 64–68.

The attractiveness of market segments is influenced by the ability to reach targets with marketing communications. The Internet is rapidly changing the ability to reach both narrow and broad target segments.

J.K. Rowling, author of the books about the boy wizard Harry Potter, announced in 2011 that the Potter books would be available for the first time as e-books, but through an exclusive interactive website offering users access to her "world of wizardry"—on a site named Pottermore—and excluding online stores run by Amazon and Apple.

Potter fans can join one of the Hogwarts wizardry school's houses and travel virtually though the first Harry Potter book, accessing new material from the author, giving fans much-desired insider information into the riddles in the book.

The Potter books have broken publishing records, with sales of 450 million copies worldwide, and adaptations have become a highly bankable movie franchise for Time Warner. The goal of Pottermore is to generate new sales and readership for the mature book properties.

The Pottermore site is a mixture of social networking, gaming, and online literary content, which is free to use, apart from the downloading of e-books. The site has a monopoly over Harry Potter audiobooks and e-books, and Rowling retains control over pricing.

The website provides Rowling with direct access to her young fan base as well as control over the Potter material that reaches them.

Sources: Paul Sonne and Jeffrey A. Trachtenberg, "Rowling Conjures E-Books," *Wall Street Journal*, June 24–26, 2011, 19, 23. Helen Warrell and Andrew Edgecliffe-Johnson, "J.K. Rowling to Work Potter Magic Online," *Financial Times*, June 24, 2011, 1. Andrew Edgecliffe-Johnson and Helen Warrell, "Rowling Casts Spell on Digital Publishing," *Financial Times*, June 24, 2011, 3.

and value need to be evaluated. Nonetheless, the growing fragmentation of mature mass-markets into segments with different needs and responsiveness to marketing actions may mandate an effective segmentation strategy. Correspondingly, the growth of narrowcast media—cable television and radio; specialized magazines; cell-phone and personal digital assistant screens; and the Internet—has made major changes to the costs of reaching market segments. Segment targets that could not traditionally be reached with communications and product variants to match their needs at reasonable costs to the seller may now be accessible targets.[29] Indeed, vast databases of people's online behavior are continuously created through tracking technology and cross—referenced with personal data to provide a foundation for predicting interests and future behavior, as well as targeting them very precisely with direct communications and new products.[30]

For example, the INTERNET APPLICATION illustrates how author J.K. Rowling is using the Web to directly access her Harry Potter readership (market segment) and importantly to reach them more precisely with targeted communications, which she controls.

It is important to decide if it is worthwhile to segment a product market. Five criteria are useful for evaluating a potential segmentation strategy.

Response Differences

Determining differences in the responsiveness of the buyers in the product-market to positioning strategies is a key segment identification requirement. Suppose the customers in a product-market are placed into four groups, each a potential segment, using a variable such

---

[29]Anthony Bianco, "The Vanishing Mass Market," *BusinessWeek*, July 12, 2004, 62–68.
[30]Emily Steel and Julia Angwin, "On the Web's Cutting Edge, Anonymity is in Name Only," *Wall Street Journal*, August 5, 2010, 14–15.

as income (affluent, high, medium, and low). If each group responds (e.g., amount of purchase) in the same way as all other groups to a marketing mix strategy, then the four groups are not market segments. If segments actually exist in this illustration, there must be differences in the responsiveness of the groups to marketing actions, such as pricing, product features, and promotion. The presence of real segments requires actual response differences. Simply finding differences in buyers' characteristics such as income is not enough.

For example, income is useful in finding response differences in emerging markets. Average incomes in the "BRIC" countries are low. In gross domestic product per capita in 2010 the U.S. statistic was $47,200, while in the BRIC countries income was Brazil ($10,800), Russia ($15,700), India ($3,500), and China ($7,600).[31] Nonetheless, emerging market incomes are growing far faster than in the developed countries. In addition, income concentration is typically much higher—in spite of low average incomes, BRIC country billionaires outnumber those in Europe. Sheer population numbers make these markets attractive prospects for food companies like McDonalds and retailers like Tesco and Wal-Mart. However, simultaneously, the rise of an affluent middle class provides an attractive target for luxury goods brands like Mercedes-Benz, Cartier, and Christian Dior. Fast economic growth and globalization place high priority on understanding emerging market income level and dispersion.[32]

Identifiable Segments

It must be possible to identify the customer groups that exhibit response differences, and sometimes finding the correct groups may be difficult. For example, even though variations in the amount of purchase by customers occur in a market, it may not be possible to identify which people correspond to the different response groups in the market. While it is usually feasible to find descriptive differences among the buyers in a product-market, these variations must be matched to response differences. The impact of the Internet is important to identifying segments.

Actionable Segments

A business must be able to aim a marketing program strategy at each segment selected as a market target. Ideally, marketing efforts should focus on the segment of interest and not be wasted on non-segment buyers. Cable television, magazine, and radio media are able to provide coverage of narrowly defined market segments. The Internet offers great potential for direct marketing channels to reach specialized segments. Similarly, databases offer very focused access to buyers.

Cost/Benefits of Segmentation

Segmentation must be financially attractive in terms of revenues generated and costs incurred. It is important to evaluate the benefits of segmentation. While segmentation may cost more in terms of research and added marketing expenses, it should also generate more sales and higher margins. The objective is to use a segmentation approach that offers a favorable revenue and cost combination. Interestingly, Bain & Co research suggests that in their studies over a 5-year period, companies that successfully tailor product and service offerings to desirable customer segments show annual profit growth of around 15 percent—compared to only 5 percent annual growth in other companies in their sectors.[33]

---

[31]www.cia.gov/library/publications/the-world-factbook, accessed July 12, 2011.

[32]Neil Buckley, "From Shock Therapy to Retail Therapy: Russia's Middle Class Starts Spending," *Financial Times,* October 31, 2006, 17. Jason Bush, "Russia: Shoppers Gone Wild," *BusinessWeek,* February 20, 2006, 46–47.

[33]Rob Markey, John Ott, and Gerard du Toit, "Winning New Customers Using Loyalty-Based Segmentation," *Strategy and Leadership,* 35(3), 2007, 32–37.

Stability over Time

Finally, the segments must show adequate stability over time so that the firm's marketing efforts will have enough time to produce favorable results. If buyers' needs change too fast, a group with similar response patterns at one point may display quite different patterns several months later. The time period may be too short to justify using a segmentation strategy. However, this question is also one where the impact of narrowcast media and advanced production technology may drastically reduce the time over which a segment targets needs to be stable for it to be an attractive target.

Product Differentiation and Market Segmentation

The distinction between product differentiation and market segmentation is not always clear. *Product differentiation* occurs when a product offering is perceived by the buyer as different from the competition on any physical or nonphysical product characteristic, including price.[34] Using a product differentiation strategy, a firm may target an entire market or one (or more) segments. Competing firms may differentiate their product offerings in trying to gain competitive advantage with the same group of targeted buyers. Market targeting using a differentiation strategy is considered further in Chapter 6.

Approaches to Segment Identification

Segments are formed by (A) grouping customers using descriptive characteristics and then comparing response differences across the groups or (B) forming groups based on response differences (e.g., frequency of purchase) and determining if the groups can be identified based on differences in their characteristics. see Exhibit 3.8 illustrates the two approaches. Approach A uses a characteristic such as income or family size believed to be related to buyer response. After forming the groups, they are examined to see if response varies across groups. Approach B places buyers with similar response patterns into groups and then develops buyer profiles using buyer characteristics. We describe each approach to show how it is used to identify segments.

EXHIBIT 3.8
Approaches
to Segment
Identification

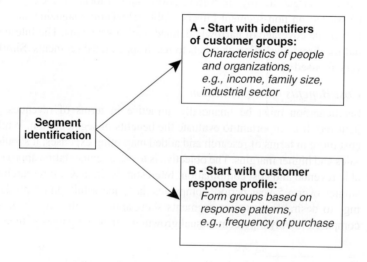

[34]Peter R. Dickson and James L. Ginter, "Market Segmentation, Product Differentiation, and Marketing Strategy," *Journal of Marketing,* April 1987, 1–10.

Customer Group Identification

After the product-market of interest is defined, promising segments may be identified, using management judgment in combination with analysis of available information and/or marketing research studies. Consider, for example, hotel lodging services. See Exhibit 3.9 illustrates ways to segment the hotel lodging product-market. An additional breakdown can be made according to business and leisure travelers. These categories may be further refined by individual customer and group customer segments. Groups may include conventions, corporate meetings, and tour groups. Several possible segments can be distinguished. Consider, for example, Marriott's Courtyard hotel chain. These hotels fall into the midpriced category and are targeted primarily to frequent business travelers who fly to destinations, are in the 40-plus age range, and have relatively high incomes.

When using the customer group identification approach, it is necessary to select one or more of the characteristics of people or organizations as the basis of segmentation. Using these variables, segments are formed by (1) management judgment and experience or (2) supporting statistical analyses. The objective is to find differences in responsiveness among the customer groups. We look at some of the customer-grouping methods to show how segments are formed.

Management Insight and Available Information

Management's knowledge of customer needs is often a useful guide to segmentation. For example, both experience and analysis of published information are often helpful in segmenting business markets. Business segment variables include type of industry, size of purchase, and product application. Company records often contain information for analyzing the existing customer base. This is a particularly important contribution of the customer relationship management technology discussed in Chapter 4. Published data such as industry mailing lists can be used to identify potential market segments. These groups are then analyzed to determine if they display different levels of response. Effec-

EXHIBIT 3.9
Product-Market Segmentation Dimensions for Hotel Lodging Services

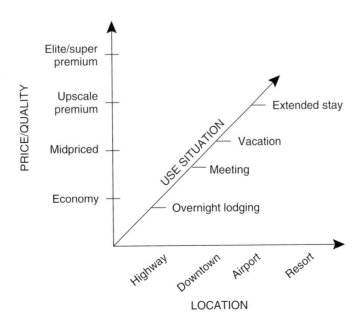

A new Wal-Mart CEO was appointed in February of 2009. He moved aggressively to appeal to higher income shoppers attracted by low prices during the 2009–2010 recession. A core objective was to move Wal-Mart upscale.

By 2011, the retailer had experienced two years of declining domestic same-store sales. Walmart neglected its core customers (households earning less than $70,000 a year), in seeking to appeal to higher income customers. Management raised prices on some offerings and offered special promotions on others.

Management recognized its error in early 2011 and altered its targeting strategy and offerings. The new CEO left the company in 2009. The focus was shifted to the core customer segment. The challenge is appealing to the U.S. core customer. Wal-Mart was performing well at Sam's Club and its booming international operation.

Sources: Miguel Bostillo, "With Sales Flabby, Wal-mart Turns to It's Core," *Wall Street Journal,* March 21, 2011, B1, B8. Miguel Bostillo, "Wal-Mart Tries to Recapture Mr. Sam's Winning Formula," *Wall Street Journal,* February 22, 2011, A1, A12. Matthew Boyle, "Wal-Mart's Magic Moment," *Bloomberg BusinessWeek,* June 15, 2009, 51–53.

tive segmentation may sometimes be achieved through insight and creativity, but it is important to avoid stereotyped thinking based on industry norms. A distinctive segmentation strategy which does not mirror those of competitors may be an important source of advantage.

Segmenting using management judgment and experience underpins the success of Coach in serving both fashion-conscious consumers and factory outlet customers. The luxury positioning of the Coach brand places it on a par with Gucci, Versace, and Dior, although Coach prices are much lower. Flagship Coach stores are located on Beverley Hills' Rodeo Drive and New York's Madison Avenue. Nonetheless, the fastest-growing part of Coach's business is the factory outlets where the previous season's products are sold at discounted prices. Although an unconventional approach to segmentation in the luxury goods market, Coach carefully manages its brand position with upscale shoppers, but also builds sales with older, bargain-hunters in factory outlets.[35]

Nonetheless, management judgment may be flawed with serious consequences for performance. Wal-Mart's U.S. performance with its core customer segment is illustrative and is discussed in the STRATEGY APPLICATION.

Cross Classification Analyses

Another method of forming segments is to identify customer groups using descriptive characteristics and compare response rates (e.g., sales) by placing the information in a table. Customer groups form the rows and response categories from the columns. Review of industry publications and other published information may identify ways to break up a product-market into segments. Standardized information services such as Information Resources Inc. collect and publish consumer panel data on a regular basis. These data provide a wide range of consumer characteristics, advertising media usage, and other information, which are analyzed by product and brand sales and market share. The data are

---

[35]Diane Brady, "Coach's Split Personality," *BusinessWeek,* November 7, 2005, 36.

obtained from a large sample of households throughout the United States. Similar statistical data are available in many overseas countries.

Information is available for use in forming population subgroups within product-markets. The analyst can use many sources, as well as management's insights and hunches regarding the market. The essential concern is whether a segmentation scheme identifies customer groups that display different product and brand responsiveness. The more evidence of meaningful differences, the better chance that useful segments exist. Cross-classification has some real advantages in terms of cost and ease of use. There may be a strong basis for choosing a segmenting scheme that uses this approach. This occurs more often in business and organizational markets, where management has a good knowledge of user needs, because there are fewer users than there are in consumer product-markets. Alternatively, this approach may be a first step leading to a more comprehensive type of analysis.

Data Mining for Segmentation

The availability of computerized databases offers a wide range of segmentation analysis capabilities. This type of analysis is particularly useful in consumer market segmentation. Databases are organized by geography and buyers' descriptive characteristics. Databases can be used to identify customer groups, design effective marketing programs, and improve the effectiveness of existing programs. The number of available databases is rapidly expanding, the costs are declining, and the information systems are becoming user-friendly. Several marketing research and direct mail firms offer database services. Further discussion on data mining is provided in Chapter 4.

By identifying customer groups using descriptive characteristics and comparing them to a measure of customer responsiveness to a marketing mix such as product usage rate (e.g., number of printer ink cartridges per year), potential segments can be identified. If the response rates are similar within a segment, and differences in response exist between segments, then promising segments are identified. Segments do not always emerge from these analyses, because in some product-markets distinct segments may not exist, or the segment interrelationships may be so complex that an analysis of these predetermined groupings will not identify useful segments. Product differentiation strategies may be used in these situations.

Segmentation Illustrations

A now-classic study for Mobil (now ExxonMobil) examines buyers in the gasoline market to identify segments. The findings, including information obtained from over 2,000 motorists, are summarized in see Exhibit 3.10. The research identified five primary purchasing groups.[36] Interestingly, the study found that the Price Shopper spent an average of $700 annually, compared to $1,200 for the Road Warriors and True Blues. Mobil's marketing strategy was to offer gasoline buyers a quality buying experience, including upgraded facilities, more lighting for safety, responsive attendants, and quality convenience products. The target segments are Road Warriors and Generation F3, involving a major effort on convenience stores and reduced time at the gas pump based on the Mobil *Speed Pass*. The test results from the new strategy raised revenues by 25 percent over previous sales for the same retail sites.

As shown by the profiles described in see Exhibit 3.10, needs and preferences can vary considerably within a market. Trying to satisfy all of the buyers in the market with the

---

[36]Allanna Sullivan, "Mobil Bets Drivers Pick Cappuccino Over Low Prices," *Wall Street Journal*, January 30, 1995, B1 and B4.

EXHIBIT 3.10 **Gasoline Buyer Segmentation Model**

Source: Alanna Sullivan, "Mobil Bets Drivers Pick Cappuccino over Low Prices," *The Wall Street Journal*, January 30, 1995, Bl. Wall Street Journal. Central Edition [Staff Produced Copy Only] by Alanna Sullivan. Copyright 1995 by Dow Jones & Co Inc. Reproduced with permission of Dow Jones & Co Inc. in the format Textbook via Copyright Clearance Center.

Road Warriors:	True Blues:	Generation F3:	Homebodies:	Price Shoppers:
Generally higher-income, middle-aged men, who drive 25,000 to 50,000 miles a year . . . buy premium with a credit card . . . purchase sandwiches and drinks from the convenience store . . . will some-times wash their cars at the carwash.	Usually men and women with moderate to high incomes who are loyal to a brand and sometimes to a particular station . . . frequently buy premium gasoline and pay in cash.	(for fuel, food, and fast): Upwardly mobile men and women—half under 25 years of age—who are constantly on the go . . . drive a lot and snack heavily from the conven-ience store.	Usually house-wives who shuttle their children around during the day and use whatever gasoline station is based in town or along their route of travel.	Generally aren't loyal to either brand or a particular station; and rarely buy the premium line . . . frequently on tight budgets . . . efforts to woo them have been the basis of marketing strategies for years.
16% of buyers	**16% of buyers**	**27% of buyers**	**21% of buyers**	**20% of buyers**

same marketing approach is difficult. Analyzing both the customer and the competition is important. Specific competitors may be better (or worse) at meeting the needs of specific customer groups (e.g., Mobil's Road Warriors). Finding gaps between buyers' needs and competitors' offerings provides opportunities for improving customer satisfaction. Also, companies study competitors' products to identify ways to improve their own.

In a completely different sector, one European bank employed a psychologist to exam-ine customers' monthly statements to search for clues to lifestyle and personality profiles. The study identified three customer groups:

• **Hedonistic Grazers**—impulsive and spontaneous people, with a tendency to live for the moment; Bridget Jones characters who are instant pleasure seekers and do not like to postpone fun and extravagance any longer than is absolutely necessary

• **Material Martyrs**—masters of time management and efficiency; control freaks who plan their weekly meals in advance and prefer to buy furniture than to go out; intro-verted and home loving; careful and frugal

• **Steady Builders**—mature, settled, stable people, with a strong sense of responsibility, who debate a big expense rather than spend spontaneously.[37]

Understanding lifestyle differences is critical to providing financial services tailored to the differences between these groups, since there is a link between lifestyle and the needs for financial services, as well as responsiveness to different offers.

At a broader level, in an era of increased globalization it is also important to recog-nize that segmentation has an international dimension in many markets. At the simplest level, country differences may dictate the need for variations in the sizes of products like apparel and household furniture based on ethnic identity in overseas countries. However, a strategic approach to segmentation internationally requires deeper analysis. For example, Global brands may be judged on quality, global, and social responsibility characteristics by

---

[37]"Bank Asks Lying Expert to Study Accounts," *The Sunday Times*, November 19, 2000, 1.

consumers. An international research study suggests segments relating to how consumer relate to global brands are:

- **Global Citizens** (55 percent)—rely on the global success of a company to indicate quality and innovation, but concerned about social responsibility issues. The United States and the UK have relatively few global citizens, but they are more common on Brazil, China, and Indonesia.
- **Global Dreamers** (23 percent)—less discerning about and more fervent in their admiration of transnational companies. They see global brands as quality products and accept the cultural symbols they provide, and are less concerned with social responsibility issues.
- **Antiglobals** (13 percent)—skeptical that transnational companies deliver higher quality goods, and dislike brands that preach American values. Do not trust global companies to behave responsibly, and their brand preferences indicate they try to avoid doing business with transnational firms.
- **Global Agnostics** (9 percent)—do not base purchase decisions on a brand's global attributes, and judge them on the same criteria they use for local brands. Higher numbers in the United States, but lower in Japan, Indonesia, and China.[38]

Nonetheless, it is also important to recognize that one impact of globalization is to reduce some international differences. In some situations, a powerful global segmentation approach may be less about tailoring products to fit the tastes of local consumers in different countries, and more about recognizing the commonality of "global tribes"— subcultures of customers who share very similar outlooks, styles and aspirations despite their different nationalities and languages. For example, teenagers from every continent socialize on the Internet and share tastes in fashion and music. Working women trying to juggle careers and families share challenges and needs which span cultures. Baby boomers are aging and many need hearing aids, but as a group spanning continents they reject products associated with aging, which provides a global challenge for manufacturers of such products.[39]

Forming Groups Based on Response Differences

The alternative to selecting customer groups based on descriptive characteristics is to identify groups of buyers by using response differences to form the segments. A look at a segmentation analysis for the packaging division of Signode Corporation illustrates how this method is used.[40] The products consist of steel strappings for various packaging applications. An analysis of the customer base identified the following segments: programmed buyers (limited service needs), relationship buyers, transaction buyers, and bargain hunters (low price, high service). Statistical (cluster) analysis formed the segments using 12 variables concerning price and service trade offs and buying power. The study included 161 of Signode's national accounts. Measures of the variables were obtained from sales records, sales managers, and sales representatives. The segments vary in responsiveness based on relative price and relative service.

---

[38]Douglas B. Holt, John A. Quelch, and Earl L. Taylor, "How Global Brands Compete," *Harvard Business Review,* September 2004, 68–75.

[39]Carol Hymowitz, "Fitted for Global 'Tribes' Instead of Nationalities," *Wall Street Journal,* December 11, 2007, 33.

[40]V. Kasturi Ranga, Rowland T. Moriarity, and Gordon S. Swartz, "Segmenting Customers in Mature Industrial Markets," *Journal of Marketing,* October 1992, 72–82.

The widespread adoption of CRM systems offers greater opportunity for timely and detailed analysis of response differences between customers. The "data warehouse" by integrating transactional data around customer types, makes possible complex analyses to understand differences in the behavior of different customers groups, to observe customer life-cycles, and to predict behavior.[41] We discuss CRM in Chapter 4.

Response difference approaches draw more extensively from buyer behavior information than the customer group identification methods discussed earlier. Note, for example, the information on Signode's customer responsiveness to price and service. We now look at additional applications to more fully explore the potential of the customer response approaches.

Cluster Analysis

Cluster analysis (a statistical technique) groups people according to the similarity of their answers to questions such as brand preferences or product attributes. This method was useful to form segments for Signode Corporation. The objective of cluster analysis is to identify groupings in which the similarity within a group is high and the variation among groups is as great as possible. Each cluster is a potential segment.

Perceptual Maps

Another segmentation method uses consumer research data to construct perceptual maps of buyers' perceptions of products and brands. The information helps select market-target strategies and decide how to position a product for a market target.

While the end result of perceptual mapping is simple to understand, its execution is demanding in terms of research skills. Although there are variations in approach, the following steps are illustrative:

1. Select the product-market area to be segmented.
2. Decide which brands compete in the product-market.
3. Collect buyers' perceptions about attributes for the available brands (and an ideal brand) obtained from a sample of people.
4. Analyze the data to form one, two, or more composite attribute dimensions, each independent of the other.
5. Prepare a map (two-dimensional X and Y grid) of attributes on which are positioned consumer perceptions of competing brands.
6. Plot consumers with similar ideal preferences to see if subgroups (potential segments) will form.
7. Evaluate how well the solution corresponds to the data that are analyzed.
8. Interpret the results as to market-target and product-positioning strategies.

An example of a perception map is shown in see Exhibit 3.11. Each Group (I–V) contains people from a survey sample with similar preferences concerning expensiveness and quality for the product category. The Brands (A–E) are positioned using the preference data obtained from the survey participants. Assuming you are product manager for Brand C, what does the information indicate concerning possible targeting? Group V is a logical market target and Group III may represent a secondary market target. To appeal most effectively to Group V, we will probably need to change somewhat Group V consumers' price perceptions of Brand C. Offering a second brand less expensive than C to appeal to Group IV

---

[41]*Financial Times, Understanding Customer Relationship Management* (London: *Financial Times*), Spring 2000.

EXHIBIT 3.11
Consumer Perception
Mapping Illustration

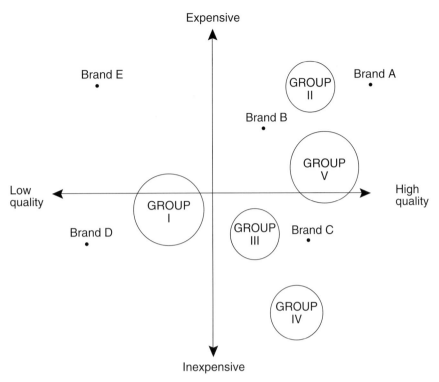

is another possible action. Of course, it is necessary to study the research results in much greater depth than this brief examination of see Exhibit 3.11. Our intent is to illustrate the method of segmenting and show how the results might be used.

Perceptual mapping, like many of the research methods used for segment identification, is time-consuming and represents a technical challenge. When used and interpreted properly, these methods are useful tools for analyzing product-market structure to identify possible market targets and positioning concepts. Of course, there are many issues to be considered in specific applications such as choosing the attributes, identifying relevant products and brands, selecting the sample, and evaluating the strength of results.

Finer Segmentation Strategies

A combination of factors may help a company utilize finer segmentation strategies. Technology may be available to produce customized product offerings. Furthermore, highly sophisticated databases for accessing buyers can be used, and buyers' escalating preferences for unique products encourage consideration of increasingly smaller segments. In some situations, an individual buyer may comprise a market segment. Thus, an important segmentation issue is deciding how small segments should be. For example, Los Angeles company Drybar is part of a new market niche for specialist hair drying services (no cutting, shampooing, or other services) for females who are very focused on their appearance and willing to regularly outsource their blow-drying needs.[42]

---

[42]Neel Shah, "Some Like It Hot… and Dry," *Bloomberg BusinessWeek,* March 21–27, 2011, 94–95.

Growing market granularity encourages strategists to consider finer segments. Penn and Zalesne's "microtrends" research suggests growing niches in the U.S. market: growing numbers of home knitters (knitting has become "cool"); decline of baseball fans; increasing population of vegan children, rise of women archers, surge in employees in the not-for-profit sector; trend toward "do-it-yourself doctors" in health care.[43] For example, Penn predicts the prospect of chains of hygienic, upmarket tattoo parlors, as small shifts in tastes and behavior create new possibilities.[44] We consider the logic of finer segments followed by a discussion of the available finer segmentation strategies.

Logic of Finer Segments

Several factors working together point to the benefits of considering very small segments in some cases, segments of one. These include (1) the capabilities of companies to offer cost effective, customized offerings; (2) the desires of buyers for highly customized products; and (3) the organizational advantages of close customer relationships.

Customized Offerings

The capabilities of organizations to offer customized products is feasible because of extensive information flow and comprehensive data bases, computerized manufacturing systems, and integrated value chains.[45] Database knowledge, computer-aided product design and manufacturing, and distribution technology (e.g., just-in-time inventory) offer promising opportunities for serving the needs and preferences of very small market segments. This technology combined with the Internet has led to the emergence of "sliver" companies or "micromultinationals"—small, flexible organizations selling highly specialized products across the world. For example, with products that can be digitized and delivered online—for example, computer software, music collections, financial services like travel and auto insurance, e-books—there is already capacity for almost infinite customization.

Diverse Customer Base

The requirements of an increasingly diverse customer base for many products are apparent. For example, the international automobile industry is facing the challenge of the Three Day Car Program—allowing the buyer to specify the detail and design choices of a vehicle online, the order stimulates production, with delivery 3 days later. This program has been designed because of the diversity in customer preferences in autos, and the sheer number of variants included in modern vehicles.

Close Customer Relationships

Companies recognize the benefits of close relationships with their customers. By identifying customer value opportunities and developing cost-effective customized offerings, relationships can be profitable and effective in creating competitive barriers.

Finer Segmentation Strategies

We examine three approaches for finer segmentation opportunities: microsegmentation, mass customization, and variety seeking.[46] (Mass customization is discussed further in Chapter 8.)

---

[43]Mark J. Penn and E. Kinney Zalesne, *Microtrends: The Small Forces Behind Tomorrow's Big Changes* (New York: Hachette), 2008.

[44]Sarah Baxter, "Microtrends Are Taking Over the World," *Sunday Times,* August 26, 2007, S1, 24.

[45]Ali Kara and Erdener Kaynak, "Markets of a Single Customer: Exploiting Conceptual Developments in Market Segmentation," *European Journal of Marketing,* No. 11/12, 1997, 873–895.

[46]Barbara E. Kahn, "Dynamic Relationships with Customers: High-Variety Strategies," *Journal of the Academy of Marketing Science,* Winter 1998, 45–53.

Microsegmentation

This form of segmentation seeks to identify narrowly defined segments using one or more of the previously discussed segmentation variables (see Exhibit 3.7). It differs from more aggregate segment formation in that microsegmentation results in a large number of very small segments. Each segment of interest to the organization receives a marketing mix designed to meet the value requirements of the segment.

Mass Customization

Providing customized products at prices not much higher than mass-produced items is feasible using mass customization concepts and methods. Achieving mass customization objectives is possible through computer-aided design and manufacturing software, flexible manufacturing techniques, and flexible supply systems.

Variety-Seeking Strategy

This product strategy is intended to offer buyers opportunities to vary their choices in contrast to making unique choices.[47] The logic is that buyers who are offered alternatives may increase their total purchases of a brand. Mass customization methods also enable companies to offer an extensive variety at relatively low prices, thus gaining the advantages of customized and variety offerings.

Finer Segmentation Issues

While the benefits of customization are apparent, there are several issues that need to be examined when considering finer segmentation strategies:[48]

1. How much variety should be offered to buyers? What attributes are important in buyers choices and to what extent do they need to be varied?
2. Will too much variety have negative effects on buyers? It is possible that buyers will become confused and frustrated when offered too many choices?
3. Is it possible to increase buyers' desire for variety, creating a competitive advantage?
4. What processes should be used to learn about customer preferences? This may involve indirect methods (e.g., database analysis), or involving buyers in the process.

High-variety strategies, properly conceived and executed, offer powerful opportunities for competitive advantage by providing superior value to customers. As highlighted by the above issues, pursuing these finer segmentation strategies involves major decisions including which strategy to pursue and how to implement the strategy. Important in deciding how fine the segmentation should be is estimating the value and cost tradeoffs of the relevant alternatives.

Selecting the Segmentation Strategy

We have considered several approaches to market segmentation, ranging from forming segments via experience and judgment to finer segmentation strategies. We now discuss deciding how to segment the market, and strategic analysis of the segments that have been identified.

---

[47]Kahn, "Dynamic Relationships."
[48]Kahn, "Dynamic Relationships."

Deciding How to Segment

The choice of a segmentation method depends on such factors as the maturity of market, the competitive structure, and the organization's experience in the market. The more comprehensive the segmentation process, the higher the costs of segment identification will be, reaching the highest level when field research studies are involved and finer segmentation strategies are considered. It is important to maximize the available knowledge about the product-market. An essential first step in segmentation is analyzing the existing customer base to identify groups of buyers with different response behavior (e.g., frequent purchase versus occasional purchase). Developing a view of how to segment the market by managers may be helpful. In some instances this information will provide a sufficient basis for segment formation. If not, experience and existing information are often helpful in guiding the design of customer research studies.

The five segmentation criteria discussed earlier help to evaluate potential segments. Deciding if the criteria are satisfied rests with management after examining response differences among the segments. The segmentation plan should satisfy the responsiveness criterion plus the other criteria (end-users are identifiable, they are accessible via marketing program, the segment(s) is economically viable, and the segment is stable over time). The latter criterion may be less of an issue with mass customization since changes can be accommodated. Segmentation strategy should not be static. The competitive advantage gained by finding (or developing) a new market segment can be very important.

Strategic Analysis of Market Segments

Each market segment of interest needs to be studied to determine its potential attractiveness as a market target. The major areas of analysis include customers, competitors, positioning strategy, and financial and market attractiveness.

Customer Analysis

When forming segments, it is useful to find out as much as possible about the customers in each segment. Variables such as those used in dividing product-markets into segments are also helpful in describing the people in the same segments. The objective is to find descriptive characteristics that are highly correlated to the variables used to form the segments. Standardized information services are available for some product-markets including foods, health and beauty aids, and pharmaceuticals. Large markets involving many competitors make it profitable for research firms to collect and analyze data that are useful to the firms serving the market. We discuss marketing information resources in Chapter 5.

An essential part of customer analysis is determining how well the buyers in the segment are satisfied. Customer satisfaction depends on the perceived performance of a product and supporting services and the standards that customers use to evaluate that performance.[49] The customer's standards complicate the relationship between organizational product specifications (e.g., product attribute tolerances) and satisfaction. Standards may involve something other than prepurchase expectations such as the perceived performance of competing products. Importantly, the standards are likely to vary across market segments.

---

[49]The following discussion of customer satisfaction is based on discussions with Robert B. Woodruff, The University of Tennessee, Knoxville.

Competitor Analysis

Market segment analysis considers the set of key competitors currently active in the market in which the segment is located plus any potential segment entrants. In complex market structures, mapping the competitive arena requires detailed analysis. The competing firms are described and evaluated to highlight their strengths and weaknesses. Information useful in the competitor analysis includes business scope and objectives; market position; market target(s) and customer base; positioning strategy; financial, technical, and operating strengths; management experience and capabilities, and special competitive advantages (e.g., patents). It is also important to anticipate the future strategies of key competitors.

Value chain analysis can be used to examine competitive advantage at the segment level. A complete assessment of the nature and intensity of competition in the segment is important in determining whether to enter (or exit from) the segment and how to compete in the segment. Competitor and value chain analysis are discussed in Chapter 2.

Positioning Analysis

We consider positioning strategy in Chapter 6. Segment analysis involves some preliminary choices about positioning strategy. One objective of segment analysis is to obtain guidelines for developing a positioning strategy. Flexibility exists in selecting how to position the firm (or brand) with its customers and against its competition in a segment. Positioning analysis shows how to combine product, distribution, pricing, and promotion strategies to favorably position the brand with buyers in the segment. Information from positioning maps like see Exhibit 3.11 is useful in guiding positioning strategy. The positioning strategy should meet the needs and requirements of the targeted buyers at a cost that yields a profitable margin for the organization.

Estimating Segment Attractiveness

The financial and market attractiveness of each segment needs to be evaluated. Included are specific estimates of revenue, cost, and segment profit contribution over the planning horizon. Market attractiveness can be measured by market growth rate projections and attractiveness assessments made by management.

Financial analysis obtains sales, cost, and profit contribution estimates for each segment of interest. Since accurate forecasting is difficult if the projections are too far into the future, detailed projections typically extend 2 to 5 years ahead. Both the segment's competitive position evaluation and the financial forecasts are used in comparing segments. In all instances the risks and returns associated with serving a particular segment need to be considered. Flows of revenues and costs can be weighted to take into account risks and the time value of revenues and expenditures.

It should be recognized that as information availability grows, for example through the data warehouses associated with CRM systems, the evaluation of segment attractiveness also has the potential for identifying unattractive market segments and even individual customers, which may be candidates for deletion. There may also be ethical considerations which limit the attractiveness of certain segments. The ETHICS APPLICATION describes some of the issues surrounding targeting children (or some groups of children), and some of the undesirable practices that have emerged. The potential for damage to brand and corporate reputation in such situations is considerable.

Segmentation studies for many markets identify children as a high-value opportunity. Disney, with its Club Penguin, and Viacom have invested heavily to capture the audience of children on the Web. Disney has extended "princess mania" to outfits for 3- to 6-year-old girls. Confectionery, fast food, music, and toys are also illustrative. Another example is Sweet & Sassy, based in Southlake, Texas, which provides spas offering manicures and facials for five to twelve year old children.

It is well-known that children exhibit great "pester power" influencing their own consumption and that of the family.

Parents and health advisors across the world warn of the dangers of childhood obesity. For food firms, an ethical dilemma or targeting this segment concerns the impact of their marketing actions on the young.

If accepted as proper market targets, ethical questions surround the ways in which advertisers reach young consumers with promotional messages, in ways which get around parental controls and conventional media:

- Reports in Europe suggest some advertising agencies use Internet chat rooms to place commercial messages to reach young consumers, getting around strict rules concerning advertising to children.
- Food companies have been accused of using text messaging (SMS), websites, and viral marketing campaigns to sell products to children.
- Some advertising agencies run focus group research with consumers as young as 3 years old, to establish ways to channel "pester power" onto family purchasing.
- Aggressive and invasive promotion stands accused of creating child "shopaholics" operating as undercover sales agents for brands.

Sources: Glen Owen, "Scandal of the Advertisers Who Pose As Young Girls on Internet Chatrooms," *Daily Mail*, April 2, 2006, 27. Jenny Wiggins, "Food Industry Criticised Over Tactics to Tempt Children," *Financial Times*, January 31, 2006, 5. Louise Lee "What Next, Bubblegum Botox?" *BusinessWeek*, July 2, 2007, 18. Rushe, Dominic, "Hooking the Kids with the Internet," *Sunday Times*, November 18 2007, S3, 7. Merissa Marr, "Disney Extends Princess Mania to the Crib," *Wall Street Journal*, November 22, 2007, 27. Ed May and Agnes Nairn, Consumer Kids: How Big Business Is Grooming Our Children for Profit (London: Constable), 2009.

Segment "Fit" and Implementation

One important aspect of evaluating segment attractiveness is how well the segments match company capabilities and the ability to implement marketing strategies around those segments.[50] There are many organizational barriers to the effective use of segmentation strategies. New segment targets that do not fit into conventional information reporting, planning processes, and budget systems in the company may be ignored or not adequately resourced. Innovative models of customer segments and market opportunities may be rejected by managers or the culture of the organization.

There are dangers that managers may prefer to retain traditional views of the market and structure information in that way, or that segmentation strategy will be driven by existing organizational structures and competitive norms.[51] It is important to be realistic in balancing the attractiveness of segments against the ability of the organization to implement appropriate marketing strategies to take advantage of the opportunities identified. Building

---

[50]Nigel F. Piercy and Neil A. Morgan, "Strategic and Operational Segmentation," *Journal of Strategic Marketing,* 1(2), 1993, 123–140.

[51]Noel Capon and James M. Hulbert, *Marketing Management in the 21st Century* (New Jersey: Prentice-Hall, 2001), 185–186.

effective marketing strategy around market segmentation mandates an emphasis on action-ability as well as technique and analysis.[52]

Many of the issues we consider in later chapters impact on the operational capabilities of a company to implement segmentation strategies, for example, strength in cross-functional relationships may be a prerequisite to deliver value to new segments; the ability to work with partners may be needed to develop new products to build a strong position in a key market segment. The existence of these capabilities, or the ability to develop them should be considered in making segmentation decisions.

Example of Segment Attractiveness Analysis

An illustrative market segment analysis is shown in see Exhibit 3.12. A 2-year period is used for estimating sales, costs, contribution margin, and market share. Depending on the forecasting difficulty, estimates for a longer time period can be used. When appropriate, estimates can be expressed as present values of future revenues and costs. Business strength in see Exhibit 3.12 refers to the present position of the firm relative to the competition in the segment. Alternatively, it can be expressed as the present position and an estimated future position, based upon plans for increasing business strength. Attractiveness is typically evaluated for some future time period. In the illustration a 5-year projection is used.

The example shows how segment opportunities are ranked according to their overall attractiveness. The analysis can be expanded to include additional information such as profiles of key competitors. The rankings are admittedly subjective since decision makers will vary in their weighing of estimated financial position, business strength, and segment attractiveness. Place yourself in the role of a manager evaluating the segments. Using the information in see Exhibit 3.12, rank segments X, Y, and Z as to their overall importance as market targets. Unless management is ready to allocate a major portion of resources to segment Z to build business strength, it is a candidate for the last-place position. Yet Z has some attractive characteristics. The segment has the most favorable market attractiveness of the three, and its estimated total sales are nearly equal to Y's for the next 2 years. The big problem with Z is its business strength. The key question is whether Z's market share can be increased. If not, X looks like a good prospect for top rating, followed by Y, and by Z. Of course, management may decide to go after all three segments.

EXHIBIT 3.12
Segment Attractiveness Analysis

Estimated ($ millions)	Segment		
	X	Y	Z
Sales*	10	16	5
Variable costs*	4	9	3
Contribution margin*	6	7	2
Market share[†]	60%	30%	10%
Total segment sales	17	53	50
Segment position:			
Business strength	High	Medium	Low
Attractiveness[‡]	Medium	Low	High

*For a two-year period.
[†]Percent of total sales in the segment.
[‡]Based on a five-year projection.

[52]D. Young, "The Politics Behind Market Segmentation," *Marketing News,* October 21, 1996, 17.

Summary

Because buyers differ in their preferences for products, finding out what these preferences are and grouping buyers with similar needs is an essential part of business and marketing strategy development. Market fragmentation and granularity characterize many mature markets. Effective segmentation is key to market-driven strategy, linking strategic issues with the management of resources and operations around segment targets. Segmentation links value opportunities in the market and new market spaces to a company's capabilities to achieve a strong strategic positioning.

Segmentation demands close attention to market definition, identifying market segments and forming segment targets, which are described, analyzed and evaluated. Segmentation of a product-market requires that response differences exist between segments, and that the segments are identifiable and stable over time. Also, the benefits of segmentation should exceed the costs. The variables useful as bases for forming and describing segments include the characteristics of people and organizations, use situation, buyers' needs and preferences, and purchase behavior.

Segments can be formed by identifying customer groups using the characteristics of people or organizations. The groups are analyzed to determine if the response profiles are different across the candidate segments. Alternatively, customer response information can be used to form customer groupings and then the descriptive characteristics of the groups analyzed to find out if segments can be identified. Several examples of segment formation are discussed to illustrate the methods that are available for this purpose.

Finer segmenting strategies present attractive options for moving toward small segments and responding to buyers' unique value requirements. Technology, buyer diversity, and relationship opportunities are the drivers of finer segmentation strategies. These strategies include microsegmentation, mass customization, and variety seeking. While potentially attractive finer segmentation strategies are more complex than other forms of segmentation and require comprehensive benefit and cost evaluations.

Segment analysis and evaluation consider the strengths and limitations of each segment as a potential market target for the organization. Segment analysis includes customer descriptions and satisfaction analysis, evaluating existing and potential competitors and competitive advantage, marketing program positioning analysis, and financial and market attractiveness. Segment analysis is important in evaluating customer satisfaction, finding new-product opportunities, selecting market targets, and designing positioning strategies. Nonetheless, it is also important to understand the organizational barriers to implementing segmentation strategy which may exist in a company, and to evaluate the "fit" of segmentation with company capabilities. Effectively implemented, a good segmentation strategy creates an important competitive edge for an organization.

Questions for Review and Discussion

1. Competing in the single European market raises some interesting market segment questions. Discuss the segmentation issues regarding this multiple-country market.

2. Why are there marketing strategy advantages in using demographic characteristics to break out product-markets into segments?

3. The real test of a segment formation scheme occurs after it has been tried and the results evaluated. Are there ways to evaluate alternative segmenting schemes without actually trying them?

4. Suggest ways of obtaining the information needed to conduct a market segment analysis.

5. Why may it become necessary for companies to change their market segmentation identification over time?

6. Is considering segments of one buyer a reality or a myth? Discuss.

7. Is it necessary to use a unique positioning strategy for each market segment targeted by an organization?

8. Under what circumstances may it not be possible to break up a product-market into segments? What are the dangers of using an incorrect segment formation scheme?

9. What are some of the advantages in using mass customization technology to satisfy the needs of buyers?

10. Does the use of mass customization eliminate the need to segment a market?

Internet Applications

A. Explore several of the following websites

www.adquest.com

www.americanet.com

www.autosite.com

www.mlm2000.com

www.sidewalk.com

www.monster.com

www.realtor.com

How does the information from these sites affect our traditional concept of market segmentation? How is the segmentation process altered by such Internet providers?

B. Evaluate the following site for additional ideas and material concerned with market segmentation and the types of support that can be provided for companies:

www.marketsegmentation.co.uk

Applications

A. Review the material in the INNOVATION APPLICATION "New Lifestyle Segments for Luxury Hotels." Do these new ventures represent a robust segmentation strategy? What other segment opportunities can be identified in the luxury hotel business? How could these be exploited?

B. Review the BMW Mini case in the GLOBAL APPLICATION "The BMW Mini." Do you believe that BMW has built a robust niche or segment strategy, or is the car a fashion item with limited lasting appeal to car buyers, like other "retro" attempts?

Chapter 4

Strategic Customer Management: Systems, Ethics, and Social Responsibility

Building effective customer relationships is widely recognized by executives as a high priority business initiative.[1] A study of 960 international executives rated customer relationship management (CRM) and strategic planning highest among 10 priority strategic initiatives for improving organizational performance.[2] CRM is a cross-functional core business process concerned with achieving improved shareholder value through the development of effective relationships with key customers and customer segments.[3]

Forming and sustaining valuable customer relationships is the most prized strategic outcome of correctly visualized and implemented CRM programs.[4] A Mercer consultant survey of top executives found developing and sustaining customer relationships to be the most important source of competitive advantage in the 21st century. One of the primary conclusions of research concerning CRM failures is that achieving desired customer outcomes requires the alignment of the entire organization, while avoiding the narrow and incomplete perspective of viewing CRM as a technology initiative. Moreover, a fragmented or functional focus is not sufficient.

Successful CRM initiatives are guided by a carefully formulated and implemented organizational strategy. CRM offers sellers the opportunity to gather customer information rapidly, identify the most valuable customers over the relevant time horizon, and increase

[1]Sridhar N. Ramaswami, Mukesh Bhargava, and Rajendra Srivastava, "Market-based Assets and Capabilities, Business Process, and Financial Performance," MSI Working Paper Series, No. 04–001, 2004.
[2]"The Cart Pulling the Horse," *The Economist,* April 9, 2005.
[3]Adrian Payne and Pennie Frow, "A Strategic Framework for Customer Relationship Management," *Journal of Marketing,* 69, October 2005, 167–176.
[4]Sudhir Kale, "CRM Failure and the Seven Deadly Sins," *Marketing Management,* 13, April 2004, 42–46.

customer loyalty by providing customized products and services. This is described as "tying in an asset" when the asset is the customer. CRM supports a customer-responsive strategy, which gains competitive advantage when it:

- Delivers superior customer value by personalizing the interaction between the customer and the company.
- Demonstrates the company's trustworthiness and reliability to the customer.
- Tightens connections with the customer.
- Achieves the coordination of complex organizational capabilities around the customer.[5]

CRM encourages a focus on customer loyalty and retention, with the goal of winning a larger share of the total lifetime value of each profitable customer.

Ethical standards and corporate social responsibility initiatives are closely linked to customer relationships. Increasingly, companies that proactively pursue ethical behavior throughout the organization and accomplish favorable ethical standards should benefit from enhanced corporate reputation and competitive strength. In many situations social responsibility initiatives, in such areas as sustainability, environmental concerns, and energy conservation, aim to combine social benefits with business goals. Strategic social responsibility actions can have significant impact on customer value and the ability of a seller to establish and maintain effective customer relationships.

We begin by taking a more detailed look at CRM and its pivotal role in contributing to bottom-line enterprise performance. Next, developing a CRM strategy and building customer lifetime value are examined. We discuss the value creation process and consider the relationship between CRM and market segmentation, targeting, and strategic positioning. Finally, we examine the issues surrounding ethical standards and social responsibility issues as they impact customer value and customer relationships.

Pivotal Role of Customer Relationship Management

The term CRM means very different things in different circumstances, a consequence of the rapid evolution and development of this approach to managing customer relationships. CRM may be used to identify an array of initiatives including automated customer contact systems, salesforce productivity, customer service and automated call centers, and enterprise-wide systems designed to integrate information about customers into a single access point.

CRM in Perspective

CRM may refer to little more than building relationships with customers to match a company's product and service offer better with customer needs. Others see CRM as developing a unified and cohesive view of the customer, without regard to how the customer chooses to communicate with the organization (in person, by mail, Internet, or telephone). Emphasis is placed on enhanced customer service and the use of call centers to provide consistency in how the company interacts with customers. Alternatively, CRM may focus only on the creation and use of a customer database to support decision makers.

---

[5]George Day, "Tying on an Asset," in *Understanding CRM* (London: *Financial Times,* 2000).

It is important to shift attention from the technology and hardware of CRM to the continuing process of "making managerial decisions with the end goal of increasing the value of the customer base through better relationships with customers, usually on an individual basis."[6] The emphasis on strategy built around profitable customers as the primary concern of CRM is emphasized by Bain & Co. whose view is that CRM must combine business processes with customer strategies to develop customer loyalty and enhance financial performance.[7]

Importantly, CRM systems are providing new predictive analytics, for example, tracking signs of dissatisfaction and defection. For example, in the cell phone industry where problems of customer churn are major, an early warning sign is when the customer starts forwarding calls to a different number, which may trigger action to identify and overcome the customer's problems. Cablecom, Switzerland's largest operator, discovered unhappy customers were most likely to quit after nine months, so began a feedback campaign targeting people who had been customers for seven months.[8]

Another useful viewpoint suggests that CRM consists of three main elements:

- Identifying, satisfying, retaining, and maximizing the value of a firm's best customers.
- Wrapping the firm around the customer to ensure that each contact with the customer is appropriate and based upon extensive knowledge of both the customer's needs and profitability.
- Creating a full picture of the customer.[9]

Advances in technology are highly supportive to the implementation of CRM at all levels of the business. One interesting development is described in the INNOVATION APPLICATION.

CRM and Database Marketing

Information technology has enabled companies to develop extensive databases concerning existing and potential customers. This information is useful in segmentation, account management, and many other marketing applications. Technology can be used by companies to interact with the customer and develop flexible customer-level responses. Databases are an important part of CRM. However, firms spend far more on integration, back-up, and management of CRM compared to software expenditures.[10]

A database created through CRM technology should contain information about the following:

- *Transactions*—should include a complete purchase history for each customer with accompanying details (date, price paid, products purchased).
- *Customer Contacts*—with multiple channels of distribution and communication the database should record all customer contacts with the company and its distributors, including sales calls, service requests, complaints, inquiries, and loyalty program participation.

---

[6]Don Peppers and Martha Rogers, *Managing Customer Relationships* (Hobroken, NJ: Wiley, 2004), 33.

[7]Darrell K. Rigby, Frederick F. Reichheld, and Phil Schafter, "Avoid the Four Perils of CRM," *Harvard Business Review,* February 2002, 101–109.

[8]Geoff Nairn, "System Gives Warning of Unhappiness," *Financial Times,* September 17, 2009, 29.

[9]Lynette Ryals, Simon D. Knox, and Stan Maklan, *Customer Relationship Management: The Business Case for CRM,* Financial Times Report (London: Prentice Hall, 2000).

[10]Gary K. Hunter, Chapter 16, "Sales Technology," in David W. Cravens, Kenneth LeMenunier-Fitzhugh, and Nigel F. Piercy, *The Oxford Handbook of Strategic Sales and Sales Management* (Oxford: Oxford University Press, 2011), 438.

Pay by Touch is a rapidly growing company operating a biometric network. To pay, customers press a finger on a scanner and enter a personal number to have the goods charged to a credit card or bank account. From a pilot scheme at Piggly Wiggly supermarkets in South Carolina, Pay By Touch has expanded to more than 3,000 locations in the U.S. Supervalu, the second largest traditional U.S. grocer, is the largest user. Aside from payment efficiency, purchases can be tied to the biometric identity of the customer.

Beyond simplifying payments, Pay By Touch can use its SmartShop technology to direct weekly incentives and special price cuts to an individual customer based on shopping habits and preferences. For retailers, this system offers a way to direct offers effectively to their most loyal customers, rather than supporting the "cherry picking" on bargains by customers who only buy the offers.

Source: Adapted from Jonathan Birchall, "Pay By Touch Puts Its Finger on Loyalty," *Financial Times,* Friday, June 22, 2007, 19.

- *Descriptive Information*—for each individual customer, relevant descriptive data that provide the basis for market segmentation and targeted marketing communications.
- *Response to Marketing Stimuli*—whether the customer responded to specific advertising, a price offer, a direct marketing initiative, or a sales call, or any other direct contact.[11]

Increasingly sophisticated software is available to undertake data mining and model data from the CRM database.

Customer Lifetime Value

While traditional approaches to market segmentation identify groups of customers by their purchase behavior and/or descriptive data, CRM offers the opportunity to examine individual customers or narrowly defined groups, and to calculate what each customer offers the company in profits. The metric *customer lifetime value* (CLV) calculates past profit produced by the customer for the firm—the sum of all the margins of all the products purchased over time, *less* the cost of reaching that customer. To this is added a forecast of margins on future purchases (under different assumptions for different customers), discounted back to their present value. This process provides an estimate of the profitability of a customer during the time span of the relationship. The CLV calculation is a powerful tool for focusing marketing and promotional efforts where they will be most productive.

Thus, CLV provides the estimated profitability of a customer (business or consumer) during the time span of the relationship. A study conducted by Deloitte Consulting found that companies which recognize the importance of understanding CLV are 60 percent more profitable than firms that do not consider CLV.[12] The familiar Pareto Rule suggests that 20 percent of customers yield 80 percent of the profits, so it is very important to find the high value customers, which are typically a small part of the total customer base.

For example, online retailers have been quick to deploy the insights they gain from monitoring customer browsing and purchase behavior—as shown by Amazon's recommendations of products to users. Through its iTunes App Store and iBooks retail platforms Apple

[11]Russell S. Winer, "A Framework for Customer Relationship Management," *California Management Review* 43(4), Summer 2001, 89–105, 92.

[12]Kale, "CRM Failure and the Seven Deadly Sins."

In 1998, Joe Simpson, a British mountain climber, wrote a book called *Touching the Void,* an account of his near-death climbing experience in the Andes. It sold only modestly. Ten years later, Jon Krakauer wrote *Into Thin Air,* another book about a mountain climbing tragedy, which became a best seller. Suddenly, *Touching the Void* began to sell again. Random House rushed out a new edition to meet demand. Booksellers promoted *Touching the Void* in their *Into Thin Air* displays. A paperback of the older book spent 14 weeks on the New York Times best-seller list. *Touching the Void* now outsells *Into Thin Air* more than two to one. The decisive factor was Amazon.com recommendations, suggesting that readers who liked *Into Thin Air* would also like *Touching the Void.*

The theory of "The Long Tail" reflects Internet economics. Selling products like music or film downloads can be done with extremely low inventory and distribution costs, which means that a company can capture the entire market, including the long tail of non-hits, which is often where the real value is. The biggest money may be in the smallest sales. The basis of a long tail strategy is to make everything available and to assist buyers in the search.

Non-hits may be a bigger market than hits. In 2004 in the U.S. books selling more than 250,000 copies sold 53 million copies in total. Books selling under 1,000 copies totaled 84 million. Hits are only what appeals to the largest available middle ground of the population. Music companies and publishers are actively repackaging products from their back catalogs to exploit the "long tail."

"Long Tail" strategies have become attractive because of enhanced customer knowledge and insight into the existence of very small niches in markets, driven by CRM and Internet technology.

Sources: Chris Anderson, *The Long Tail: How Endless Choice Is Creating Unlimited Demand* (London: Random House Business Books, 2007). Dominic Rushe, "Retailers Start to Climb the Long Tail Tail," *The Sunday Times,* October 29, 2006, 3–13. Tony Jackson, "The Freedom in Selection," *Financial Times,* Wednesday, July 12, 2006, 11.

has 200 million customers with Apple ID accounts, linked to credit cards and one-click purchase access. Increasingly, data from CRM systems are being linked to information from social networks like Facebook and Twitter for further insights.[13]

The power of CRM to enhance a company's depth of customer knowledge and to allow access to individuals and small groups of customers is having profound effects on strategic thinking. The STRATEGY APPLICATION discusses the "Long Tail" issue as an example of new strategies being driven by the combination of CRM and Internet technology.

Developing a CRM Strategy

We discuss alternative levels of an organization's focus toward CRM, followed by strategy development guidelines and the CRM implementation process.

CRM Levels

CRM can be viewed from company-wide, customer-facing, and functional levels.[14] Each level has important but different implications for strategic marketing. All three perspectives are important, although the company-wide or strategic level provides the most complete view of CRM. The functional perspective considers the processes that are needed to fulfill required marketing functions. The customer-facing level offers a single view of

---

[13]Philip Delves Broughton, "The Value of Information," *Financial Times,* March 8, 2011, 8.
[14]The following discussion is based on Kumar and Reinartz, *Customer Relationship Management,* 33–47.

the customer across all of the organization's access channels to the customer. This level of CRM is concerned with coordinating information across all contact channels on a continuing basis.

The company-wide level provides a strategic focus for CRM.[15] It considers the implications of knowledge about customers and their preferences across the entire company. The intent is to guide the interactions between the organization and its customers in seeking to maximize the lifetime value of customers for the firm. Importantly, the strategic perspective acknowledges that (1) customers vary in their economic value to the company and (2) customers differ in their expectations toward the firm.

The strategic use of CRM resources reflects the shift in focus by marketing executives to the customer who delivers long-term profits, that is, an emphasis on customer retention rather than acquisition. Well-known metrics suggest that as little as a 5 percent increase in customer retention can have an impact as high as 95 percent on the net present value delivered by the customer.[16] Other studies by McKinsey consultants find that repeat customers generate over twice as much gross income as new customers.[17] CRM emphasizes that executives should focus the organization's strategy on customer profitability and the gains from reducing customer "churn."

Interestingly, as CRM evolves and offers executives deeper insights into their customer base, the new information may challenge strategic assumptions in important ways. For example, the points made above suggest a powerful linkage between enhanced customer loyalty and higher customer profitability. However, companies are discovering through CRM database analysis that this is not always true. Some groups of customers may not justify the costs required to retain them, because the real fit between their needs and the company's products is weak. Just because a group of customers was profitable in the past, it may be dangerous to assume this will always be true. For example, many non-loyal customers are initially profitable, causing the company to chase them for further profits— but once these customers have ceased buying they become increasingly unprofitable if the company continues to invest in them. CRM data provides executives with a unique basis to address such issues as loyalty and profitability on the basis of fact instead of assumption, and to focus on individual customers, rather than groups containing many dissimilar buyers.[18]

CRM Strategy Development

The major steps in developing a CRM strategy are shown in Exhibit 4.1. We provide an overview of each step.

Organizational Commitment to CRM

Everyone in the firm needs to be supportive of the CRM initiative, beginning with top management. This commitment is consistent with the characteristics of a market-oriented organizational culture. All functions in the firm are likely to have an involvement with certain of the CRM processes and activities. These parts of the business need to be involved at the beginning of strategy development. Ongoing cooperation and acceptance are essential to success. The customer is the unifying basis for employee and functional involvement.

---

[15]Ibid.

[16]Frederick F. Reichheld, *The Loyalty Effect* (Cambridge, MA: Harvard Business School Press, 1996).

[17]Winer, "A Framework for Customer Relationship Management."

[18]Werner Reinartz and V. Kumar, "The Mismanagement of Customer Loyalty," *Harvard Business Review,* July 2002, 86–94.

EXHIBIT 4.1
The Steps in Developing a CRM Strategy

Source: V. Kumar and Werner J. Reinartz, *Customer Relationship Management* (Hoboken, NJ: John Wiley & Sons, Inc.), 2006, 39.

1. Gain an organization-wide commitment to CRM strategy.
2. Form a cross-functional CRM project team for decision analysis and actions.
3. Conduct a business needs analysis concerning customer relationships.
4. Develop and define the CRM strategy to guide management process.

The Project Team

The cross-functional team is the center of decision analysis and action for the CRM process. The team will need to become familiar with the CRM process before pursuing analysis and action initiatives. All relevant functions and departments should be involved. Initially, external consulting capabilities may be needed. Major financial commitments will be required as well as management and professional time commitments. Value chain representation may also be needed depending on the firm's position in the value chain (supplier, producer, or marketing intermediary). For example, a CRM strategy by PepsiCo would need to include independent bottler representation.

Business Needs Analysis

Each company's requirements concerning customer relationships need to be examined. These analyses are critical in providing direction to CRM initiatives, which must be integrated into the business strategy. The departments and individuals utilizing the CRM system (e.g., managers from sales, marketing, customer service, and the value chain) should clearly indicate what is needed from the strategy and agreement must be reached concerning CRM expectations and performance metrics.

The CRM Strategy

The components of the CRM strategy are shown in Exhibit 4.2.[19] The value proposition spells out what the organization must provide in order to satisfy customer expectations. Understanding customers' value requirements is essential. The business case is an assessment that indicates the shareholder value and financial return of delivery of the required customer value. CRM initiatives require substantial resources and the return needs to be carefully evaluated. The customer strategy indicates how different customer segments will be formed and managed. In business-to-business markets, firms may need to target individual customers. The enterprise transformation plan indicates the necessary initiatives to launch the CRM strategy—the changes which are required throughout the enterprise. Finally, all relevant stakeholders must be familiar with the plan, to ensure that the necessary value propositions are determined and provided to the targeted customer segments.

CRM Implementation

The evidence of the performance of CRM systems has been disappointing for many companies. A Bain & Co. 2001 survey of management tools ranked CRM at the bottom for satisfaction—indeed, one in five users in the Bain survey reported their CRM initiatives had not only failed to deliver profitable growth, but had also damaged long-term customer relationships.[20]

---

[19]V. Kumar and Werner J. Reinartz, *Customer Relationship Management* (Hobroken, NJ: John Wiley & Sons, Inc. 2006).
[20]Rigby, Reichheld, and Schafter, "Avoid the Four Perils of CRM."

EXHIBIT 4.2
**Develop and Define
the CRM Strategy
to Guide the
Management Process**

Source: V. Kumar and Werner J.
Reinartz, *Customer Relationship Management* (Hoboken,
NJ: John Wiley & Sons, Inc.,
2006), 42.

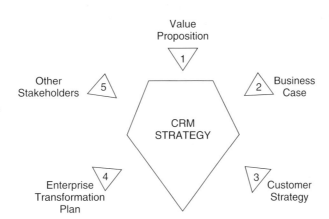

Successful Implementation

One recommendation proposes that the major components of the successful implementation of CRM are:

- A front office that integrates sales, marketing, and service functions across all media (call centers, people, retail outlets, value chain members, Internet).

- A data warehouse that stores customer information and the appropriate analytical tools with which to analyze that data and learn about customer behavior.

- Business rules developed from the data analysis to ensure the front office benefits from the firm's learning about its customers.

- Measures of performance that enable customer relationships to continually improve.

- Integration into the firm's operational support (or "back office") systems, ensuring the front office's promises are delivered.[21]

Causes of Failure

There have been several suggestions that high failure rates associated with CRM are caused by managers underestimating the necessary organizational changes required for effective implementation that obtains the benefits of CRM. While the front end of CRM systems is concerned with building databases, integrating customer data, providing better customer service, and establishing systems like automated call centers for enhanced responsiveness, achieving the full potential of CRM requires change in company-wide processes, organization structure, and corporate culture.

Some of the early lessons learned about CRM implementation relate to the call centers and surrounding technology. The call center may be the most important point of contact with the customer. The GLOBAL APPLICATION examines the challenges of operating international call centers, which have caused some controversy.

Bain & Co. research suggests that there are four significant pitfalls to avoid in CRM initiatives:

1. Implementing CRM before creating a customer strategy—success relies on making strategic customer and positioning choices, and this outweighs the importance of the computer systems, software, call centers, and other technologies.

---

[21]Simon Knox, Stan Maklan, Adrian Payne, Joe Peppard, and Lynette Ryals, *Customer Relationship Management: Perspectives from the Marketplace* (Oxford: Butterworth-Heinemann, 2003).

Call centers provide support and service to customers, though some sell as well. They are used predominantly in mass-market consumer industries. The centers exist to improve the quality of customer service.

There are many attractions in outsourcing call center operations to low-pay countries like India and Taiwan—an in-house call center agent in the United States is likely to be paid around $29,000, while the agent in India receives $2,667. The majority of call centers in India use college-educated employees. The better Indian call center operators train staff in the accent and dialect of their customers' regions, and staff adapt sleeping patterns to align with working hours in the customers' country. The intent is that consumers contacting the call center will not even be aware that they are speaking to someone in a foreign country.

Nonetheless, some major companies are pulling back from overseas call center operations for several reasons:

- Customer complaints about service received and language difficulties.
- Survey data suggest 60 percent of Americans say they are less likely to do business with a company after a bad call center experience, and 62 percent say their most recent experience with an overseas call center was disappointing. The dissatisfaction level is twice that shown by calls to centers that they believe are in the United States.
- Technology difficulties leave call center agents with no information about customers, giving the impression they do not know what the customer is talking about.
- Media coverage has become increasingly critical of companies off-shoring call center jobs.

While sometimes attractive economically, there is a risk that overseas call centers may undermine the quality of customer relationships and pose a threat to corporate and brand reputation for those who employ them.

Sources: Kerry Miller, "Hello India? Er, Des Moines," *BusinessWeek,* June 25, 2007, 14. Pete Encardio, "Making Bangalore Sound Like Boston," *BusinessWeek,* April 10, 2006, 48.

2. Putting CRM in place before changing the organization to match—CRM affects more than customer-facing processes: it impacts internal structures and systems that may have to change.

3. Assuming that more CRM technology is necessarily better, rather than matching the technology to the customer strategy.

4. Investing in building relationships with disinterested customers, instead of those customers who value them.[22]

Websites giving additional information on various aspects of CRM are shown in Exhibit 4.3. There is also extensive literature on the topic and several recent books have been published.

Value Creation Process

Payne and Frow define the value creation process in CRM as (1) the value the customer receives; and (2) the value the organization receives.[23] Successfully managing the value exchange between the customer and the firm is essential in achieving effective CRM.

---

[22]Rigby, Reichheld, and Schafter, "Avoid the Four Perils of CRM."

[23]Payne and Frow, "A Strategic Framework for Customer Relationship Management," 170–172.

EXHIBIT 4.3
Useful Websites for
Additional CRM
Material

www.dbmarketing.com

The website of the Database Marketing Institute, with a number of articles and speeches concerning recent developments in database marketing, available to be downloaded.

www.thearling.com

A site with extensive information about developments in data mining, and articles and papers on this topic for download.

www.1to1.com

The website of the Peppers & Rogers Group features the work and consultancy of Don Peppers and Martha Rogers. White Papers are available for download. A free subscription to the inside 1 to 1 newsletter is also available.

www.teradata.com

The website of the Teradata Division of NCR. It contains an interesting technical library on data warehousing and data mining as well as customer case studies.

www.crmdaily.com

This website provides new headline material on a daily basis concerning various CRM applications and management issues on a free subscription basis.

Customer Value

The benefits the customer receives are expressed by the value proposition. The objective of the organization is to provide a superior customer experience. The value proposition "explains the relationship among the performance of the product, the fulfillment of the customer's needs, and the total cost to the customer over the customer relationship life cycle."[24]

Assessing whether a superior customer experience is accomplished requires determining the relative importance placed by customers on different attributes of the product. Market segmentation may be useful in analyses to find the extent of correspondence between customer value requirements and value provided by the firm. Conjoint analysis and other techniques can be used in these assessments. An interesting approach to measuring customers' experience used by General Electric Co. is described in the METRICS APPLICATION.

Value Received by the Organization

Determining value received from CRM requires the following information:

> First, it is necessary to determine how existing and potential customer profitability varies across different customers and customer segments. Second, the economics of customer acquisition and customer retention and opportunity for selling, up-selling, and building customer advocacy must be understood.[25]

As discussed earlier a key concept associated with the value received by the organization via CRM is customer lifetime value (CLV). CLV is the expected profitability of a customer over the time-span of the relationship with the customer. The sum of CLV for all of a firm's customers is termed customer equity. CLV provides useful information in selecting valuable customers for targeting.

---

[24]Ibid., 172.
[25]Ibid., 172.

HAPPY (AND NOT-SO-HAPPY) CUSTOMERS

General Electric is a big user of the "Net Promoter" concept of customer satisfaction, popularized by Fred Reichheld of Bain & Co. Below are questions similar to those on which GE's Capital Solutions unit asks customers to rate the unit's performance on a 0–10 scale.

- How willing are you to recommend us to a friend or associate?
- How would you rate our ability to meet your needs?
- How would you rate our people?
- How would you rate our processes?
- What is your impression of our market reputation?
- How would you rate the cost of doing business with us?
- How would you rate the overall value of our product or service as being worth what you paid?

Source: Kathryn Kranhold, "Client-Satisfaction Tool Takes Root," *Wall Street Journal,* July 10, 2006, B3.

Value received by the customer is also relevant. It is important to recognize the potential negative impact of issues regarding consumer trust on CRM activities.[26] If buyers believe that the information collected by their suppliers may be used to exploit them, their trust in the relationship may be jeopardized. Accordingly, executives need to recognize trust and privacy implications of CRM initiatives.

CRM approaches may also be valuable in identifying less attractive customers and developing effective ways to handle this issue.[27] For example, the INTERNET APPLICATION describes an approach adopted by retailers to manage the problem of excessive product returns by some customers.

Managing customer profitability begins by analyzing the alternative.[28] The options include customer profitability, customer lifetime value, and customer equity. Based on this assessment the objective is to manage the customer-portfolio for profit. Finally, the organization needs to work toward acquiring more profitable customers. The key to the whole process is understanding the profitability of the firm's customers.

Importantly, analyzing CRM data identifies customers who are unprofitable or marginally profitable—this may be as high as twenty percent for some companies while it is estimated that in the 1990s 60 percent of household accounts were loss making for U.S. banks. Some businesses have even "fired" their weakest customers. American Express, for example, invited a group of high-risk credit card holders to pay off their balance and close their accounts in return for a payment of $300.[29]

CRM and Value Chain Strategy

It is important that CRM be integrated with the different channels that access end-user customers. "The multi-channel integration process is arguably one of the most important processes in CRM because it takes the outputs of the business strategy and value creation

---

[26]Larry Selden and G. Colvin, *Angel Customers and Demon Customers: Discover Which Is Which and Turbo-Charge Your Stock* (Knoxville, TN: Portfolio Hardcover, 2003).

[27]Lynette Ryals, "Managing Customers Profitability," *Management Focus,* 26, Spring 2009, 20–22.

[28]Payne and Frow, "A Strategic Framework for Customer Relationship Management," 172.

[29]Geoff Nairn, "System Gives Warning of Unhappiness," *Financial Times,* September 17, 2009, 29.

Some consumers cost retailers a lot of money because of such practices as: "wardrobing"—buying expensive clothes, wearing them once, and then returning them; "pack attacks"—damaging a package on display to buy it later at a discount; and excessive returning. Excessive or fraudulent returning is estimated to cost U.S. retailers $16 billion annually. Some consumers buy hundreds of items and return them all (or all but one).

The Return Exchange is a California-based data warehouse that can analyze customers return behavior from retail companies. When products are returned to stores, customer ID and product details are sent to The Return Exchange. If analysis suggests the individual is an excessive returner, the customer's pattern of returns—the number, frequency, and value—are displayed at the store when returns are made. The retailer can decide whether the customer should be given a warning or refused a return.

Source: Adapted from Paul Rubens, "How to Get Rid of 'Devil Customers,'" ft.com, accessed June 13, 2007.

EXHIBIT 4.4
**The Perfect
Customer Experience**

Source: Adrian Payne and
Pennie Frow, "A Strategic
Framework for Customer
Relationship Management,"
Journal of Marketing (October
2005), 173.

"The perfect customer experience," which must be affordable for the company in the context of the segments in which it operates and its competition, is a relatively new concept. This concept is now being embraced in industry by companies such as TNT, Toyota's Lexus, Oce, and Guinness Breweries. Therefore, multichannel integration is a critical process in CRM because it represents the point of cocreation of customer value. However, a company's ability to execute multichannel integration successfully is heavily dependent on the organization's ability to gather and deploy customer information from all channels and to integrate it with other relevant information.

processes and translates them into value-adding activities with customers."[30] Many companies interact with customers using multiple channels including salespeople, value chain partners, email and Internet, telephoning, and direct marketing. The concept of the "perfect customer experience," an example of integrated channel management, is described in Exhibit 4.4.

CRM and Strategic Marketing

From the perspective of strategic marketing, there are several reasons why CRM is important and why there should be extensive marketing involvement in decisions about CRM. Importantly, an organizational perspective is needed in guiding the firm's CRM strategy.

Implementation

It is critical that the adoption and implementation of CRM be seen as more than technology focused on efficiency. There are significant implications for the strategic positioning of a company and its customer relationships, where the voice of marketing should be heard. Our earlier discussion of CRM implementation highlights several relevant issues.

Operationally it is important not to assume that the drivers of value for all customers are the same, or that CRM is the key to all important customer relationships. For example, there are signs that many customers are weary of call centers and automated responses.

---

[30]Winer, "A Framework for Customer Relationship Management," 92.

Performance Metrics

The availability of CRM data provides the opportunity to update the measures used by managers to assess the success of their brands in the marketplace. Traditional financial and market-based indicators like sales, profitability, and market share will continue to be important. However, CRM allows the development of measures that are customer-centric and more insightful concerning marketing strategy effectiveness. CRM-based measures of performance (both online and offline) may include: customer acquisition cost, conversion rates (from lookers to buyers), retention/churn rates, same customer sales rates, loyalty measures, and customer "share of wallet."[31]

Short-Term Versus Long-Term Value

It is important that when decisions are made about a company's customer priorities using historical customer profitability, long-term issues should be considered. Customers who are currently unprofitable may be attractive long-term prospects for suppliers who maintain loyalty through the hard times until the customers become profitable, and customers who are currently profitable may not be the best prospects for the future. The simple availability of CRM information should not be allowed to override strategic choices of customers to be retained where a long-term relationship may be highly attractive. This is why the active participation of marketing executives in CRM initiatives is important.

Customer lifetime value is an attractive measure to use to examine long-term customer attractiveness. For example, in many countries retail banks aggressively recruit young people as customers when they are undergraduate and graduate students (and likely to be unprofitable to the bank) with the goal of retaining the customer with a better than average chance of becoming a high-net-worth individual (and offering profitable opportunities to the bank).

Competitive Differentiation

If certain customers are unprofitable, then rather than "firing" the customer, the competitive issue may be how to change the route to market to make them profitable to the company. For example, when British Airways made the decision to focus only on its profitable business-class passengers at the expense of economy travelers, Virgin Airways gained the economy-class passengers by offering a better value proposition than BA. CRM data may provide one of the most powerful tools for identifying different customers on the basis of their behavior and other characteristics, to locate those whose needs have good fit with a company's capabilities. As one-to-one marketing expert Don Peppers has noted: "For every credit card company that wants to concentrate on higher income customers, there's another credit card company that wants to concentrate on lower income customers, and they do it by streamlining their service and making it more cost-efficient."[32] It is important that decisions about customer choices reflect strategic priorities.

There are issues of social responsibility and ethics which surround the ways in which CRM technology can be used to differentiate between attractive and less attractive customers. If handled insensitively this differentiation may be damaging to corporate and brand reputation. The ETHICS APPLICATION highlights some of these dilemmas.

Lack of Competitive Advantage

Investment in CRM to build competitive advantage may be an illusion if a company focuses only on automated call centers and customer complaint systems. The level of expenditure on CRM suggests that most competitors in most markets will have similar resources, and

---

[31]Kathryn Kranhold, "Client-Satisfaction Tool Takes Root," *Wall Street Journal,* July 10, 2006, B3.

[32]Richard Tomkins, "Goodbye to Small Spenders," *Financial Times,* February 4, 2000, 13.

The logic of CRM as a source of customer knowledge suggests that some customers will be more attractive than others—they are more profitable, they buy more, or they are better prospects. In retailing, the "devil customers" who cost retailers money may be as much as 20 percent of the customer base. The dilemma is the stance to take with less profitable customers.

With unattractive customers we can . . .

Stop doing business with them, or do less business with them . . .
- Turn their business away.
- Less attractive customers can be charged for services that are free to others.
- More attractive customers are offered better deals if they threaten to defect, but these offers are not available to less attractive customers.

Offer them a lower level of service or added value . . .
- Call center technology can "recognize" customers and direct calls to different sales and service teams, based on the prospects with that customer. The most attractive prospects can be dealt with quicker and offered special deals and discounts.
- More attractive customers can be offered special deals through loyalty or frequent user programs.

Work to make them more attractive and profitable . . .
- Focus on factors that can make the less profitable customer more attractive—a higher share of their spending spent, cross-selling, promoting higher margin products.

However, there may be a moral dilemma regarding the fairness of treating some customers differently than others. When Express clothing stores stopped accepting returns from "serial returners" and Filene's Basement banned a few customers from its stores because of excessive returns and complaints, both received much adverse publicity. European banks that have tried to restrict access of poorer customers to bank branches and services have been similarly criticized. The logic of favoring some customers over others may be weakened by potential damage to the brand. The key is developing a logical and fair process for shedding high-maintenance and delinquent clients.

Sources: Ariana Eunjung Cha, "In Retail, Profiling for Profit," *Washington Post,* August 17, 2005, A01. Paul Rubens, "How to Get Rid of 'Devil Customers,'" ft.com, June 13, 2007. Raymund Flandez, "It Just Isn't Working? Some File for Customer Divorce," *Wall Street Journal,* November 10, 2009, B7.

may be quicker to get to the real competitive strengths in aligning resources and capabilities around customers. Competitive advantage requires more than just investment in CRM technology, particularly if it is poorly implemented. Our earlier discussion indicated the danger of allowing technology to drive the CRM strategy. Similar CRM technology is available to most companies in most markets, and the issue for competitive advantage enhancement is not having the technology but how it is used.

Information-Based Competitive Advantage

One of the most important aspects of CRM from a strategic marketing perspective is the creation of a major new source of knowledge about customers. Used appropriately the databases and information resources and capabilities created through CRM technology may be one of the most valuable resources a company has for uncovering new value-creating opportunities for customers and for developing market understanding and insights ahead of the competition. As a further resource for developing and exploiting market sensing capabilities, CRM systems have enormous potential, which many organizations are beginning to exploit to build competitive advantage.

Ethics and Social Responsibility in Strategic Marketing

We noted in Chapter 1 that interest and concerns about ethics and social responsibility are escalating rapidly. Large numbers of business organizations throughout the world are directing attention and efforts to these important concerns. In part, the issues are driven by the belief that businesses should behave in an ethical way, because it is the right thing to do, and that they should deliver social benefits as well as meeting their business goals. However, it is also the case that perceptions of a seller's ethical standing and social contribution can have a direct impact on its attractiveness to customers and their willingness to buy. Ethics and social responsibility questions are increasingly significant to the creation of effective customer relationships, in part because of the impact on corporate reputation.

Corporate Reputation

The level of scrutiny of the ethical standards and corporate social responsibility initiatives undertaken by companies has never been so searching. The attention of pressure groups and the media given to company behavior is unprecedented, continually escalating and frequently hostile. Damage to corporate reputation of a business—because of ethics violations or failure to provide societal benefits—can substantially reduce its ability to compete and can undermine the value of a company.

For example, Communications Consulting Worldwide estimates the difference corporate reputation makes to the value of a company, predicting that if Wal-Mart had the reputation of Target, its stock would rise 4.9 percent (boosting market value by $9.7 billion); if Coca-Cola had the reputation of Pepsi, its stock would rise 3.3 percent (worth $4 billion); if Colgate had the reputation of Procter & Gamble, its stock would rise 6.2 percent (increasing market value by $2 billion).[33] Reputational risk is already subject to systematic management attention in major companies because of the impact of reputation on market value and the ability to compete.[34] The reputational damage to companies like BP (plant safety issues, environmental damage); Siemens, Volkswagen, and Samsung (bribery and corruption allegations), Mattell (safety issues in childrens' toys); discount fashion retailers (unacceptable employment conditions in overseas factories); and Merck & Co. (the "Dodgeball" sales training package to prepare salespeople to duck and dodge doctors' questions about the pain drug Vioxx's links to heart and stroke risks[35]) is considerable and requires a strategic response. A major concern is that companies may be uncertain how to

---

[33]Pete Engardio and Michael Arndt, "What Price Reputation?"*BusinessWeek,* July 9 and 16, 2007, 70–79.
[34]Robert G. Eccles, Scott C. Newquist, and Roland Scatz. "Reputation and Its Risks," *Harvard Business Review,* February 2007, 104–114.
[35]Christopher Bowe, "Steer Clear of Flippancy – Or Pay the Price," *Financial Times,* September 6, 2005, 14.

repair damaged reputations—it may take a careful analysis of what is causing reputational damage, which constituencies are affected (customers, investors, employees), and what needs to be fixed.[36]

Importantly, the strength or weakness of an organization's corporate reputation significantly impacts customer perceptions of how attractive it is to do business with that company. In addition, reputation influences investors, the capital markets, the ability to recruit talented people, and the influential commentary of investment analysts and the media. In several ways, corporate reputation is about the ability to compete.

A poor corporate reputation—regarding handling of suppliers and customers, honesty and fairness in making deals, behavior toward the environment, working standards for employees in the value chain, and similar judgments—can make a company unattractive to customers. Customers may reject a potential supplier because they do not want to be contaminated by association or to face the criticisms of their own customers and investors. Conversely, a strong corporate reputation can make a company more attractive than competitors to some customers because they benefit by association, i.e., corporate reputation adds to the value of the customer relationship by providing the customer with assurance as to a supplier's good standing and that it is safe to deal with that company without risking their own reputation.

Ethical standards and corporate responsibility initiatives are an important foundation for an attractive corporate reputation, which impacts positively on relationships with consumers and business-to-business customers.

Ethical Imperatives

Ethical behavior is concerned with good conduct. In a business context, ethics refer to the rules or standards guiding the behavior of the members of a profession or organization.[37] It is important to understand ethics and its relevance in an organization. Moreover, management needs to be proactive in building an ethical environment and employee commitment to ethical behavior. Importantly, ethical practices help to create and sustain trust with consumers and value chain members. There have been extensive public concerns about poor ethical practices in business organizations, fueled by highly publicized scandals such as those at Enron, Siemens, and others.

Defining Ethical Standards

Business ethics are concerned with "ethical rules and principles, moral or ethical problems, and special duties and obligations that apply to persons engaged in commerce.[38] Marketing ethics focus on those ethical situations that fall within the scope of marketing operations in an organization. Marketing's involvement outside the organization with customers and value chain members often exposes it to situations where ethical and moral issues are particularly evident.

For example, salespeople have been frequent targets for criticism regarding ethical standards—they are exposed to more ethical pressures than people in other jobs; they work in relatively unsupervised settings; they typically face demanding sales revenue targets; and many are largely "paid by results." A survey of sales managers by *Sales & Marketing Management* revealed that 49 percent of managers said their salespeople had lied on a sales call, 34 percent said their salespeople made unrealistic

[36]George Anders, "Companies Seem Uncertain How to Restore Tarnished Reputations," *Wall Street Journal*, January 9, 2008, 6.
[37]*The American Heritage Dictionary* (Boston: Houghton Mifflin Company), 1985.
[38]Dhruv Grewal and Michael Levy, *Marketing* (New York: McGraw-Hill, 2009), 43.

promises to customers, and 22 percent reported that their salespeople had sold products their customers did not need.[39] It is now widely accepted that that a salesperson's ethical behavior plays a critical role in forming and sustaining long-term customer relationships.

More broadly than salesforce issues, evaluating the ethical questions surrounding a marketing strategy, decision, or practice may require senior executives to ask probing questions about the nature and consequences of decisions being made in the following form:

- Who are all the people affected by this issue—employees, managers, shareholders, competitors, other third parties, and the wider community and environment?

- Does our position on this issue actually or potentially cause harm to any of those affected, beyond the acceptable effects of fair competition?

- Has our behavior been deceptive? Would you regard it that way if you were in the position of any of the other stakeholders?

- Are there disguised conflicts of interest between the parties directly involved and those affected by the issue?

- If everyone behaved in the way we are behaving, what would happen? If harm would result from everyone treating customer, third parties, shareholders, and others as we are doing, should we refrain from continuing this behavior?[40]

There may be advantages in incorporating such approaches in the training and development of executives and addressing them in personal appraisal processes. Importantly, executives may be encouraged to consider ethics as a determinant of business success.[41]

Furthermore, in common with most professional institutes, the American Marketing Association (AMA) has a statement of ethics proposing ethical norms and values for its members. This statement covers a range of ethical values including honesty, responsibility, fairness, respect, transparency, and citizenship. Each value category includes several specific items. For example, the ethical value of *honesty*—to be forthright in dealings with customers and stakeholders, mandates that we will

- Strive to be truthful in all situations and at all times.
- Offer products of value that do what we claim in our communications.
- Stand behind our products if they fail to deliver their claimed benefits.
- Honor our explicit and implicit commitments and promises.[42]

Increasingly, companies are developing their own codes of ethics, often featured on their websites. The codes may range from a paragraph to a detailed code like the AMA statement. General Electric, for example, does not simply publish an ethical code, it also releases its audit of ethical violations and reports integrity concerns annually.[43]

---

[39]Sergio Roman and Jose Luis Munuera, "Determinants and Consequences of Ethical Behaviour: An Empirical Study of Salespeople," *European Journal of Marketing,* 39(5–6), 2005, 473–495.

[40]Adapted from Avinash Persaud and John Plender, *All You Need to Know About Ethics and Finance: Finding a Moral Compass in Business Today* (London: Longtail Publishing, 2006). John Plender and Avinash Persaud, "Good Ethics Means More than Ticking Boxes," *Financial Times,* August 23, 2005, 10.

[41]A. Singhapakdi, "Perceived Importance of Ethics and Ethical Decisions in Marketing," *Journal of Business Research,* 45, 1999, 89–99.

[42]http://www.Marketingpower.com

[43]Alison Maitland, "GE to Release Audit of Ethical Violations," *Financial Times,* May 19, 2005, 29.

Nonetheless, the subjectivity of ethical judgments and the potential changes in views of "right and wrong" create serious dilemmas around "integrity landmines." A recent review of the dilemma faced by companies concludes:

> "The changes in laws, regulations, stakeholder expectations, and media scrutiny that have taken place in the past decade can now make a major lapse in integrity catastrophic. Fines, penalties and settlements are counted in the hundreds of millions (or billions) of dollars. . . . And worse, in some cases (as Enron and Arthur Anderson demonstrated)—a company can actually implode."[44]

Many business and marketing practices regarded as wholly acceptable in the past—for example, "corporate hospitality"—may now be enough to undermine or destroy buyer/seller relationships. The impact is magnified by growing transparency and information availability.

Interestingly, the concept of "moral intensity" describes the extent of the moral imperative perceived in a specific situation, and suggests that people may disagree regarding the existence of an ethical issue in that situation and in making judgments regarding its seriousness.[45] It may not be immediately obvious that a situation has a moral or ethical dimension that executives should consider. For example, in examining strategic account relationships, typically between suppliers and their largest and most important business-to-business customers, analysis suggests several serious ethical concerns regarding the sharing of proprietary information and favoring some customers at the expense of others, which are not conventionally prominent in managerial concerns in this area.[46]

Drivers of Ethical Demands

The "green" and "ethical" consumer has become a vocal force in many markets. For example, a five-country survey conducted by market research group GfK NOP suggests that consumers in five of the world's leading economies believe that business ethics have worsened in the past five years, and they are turning to "ethical consumerism" to make companies more accountable.[47] Respondents believe that brands with "ethical" claims would make business more answerable to the public, and that companies should "promote ethical credentials more strongly."[48]

Commentators on branding suggest that ethical consumption is one of the most significant branding issues in modern markets, and underlies change in the automotive sector, food, retailing, technology, and health and beauty sectors. Its influence is behind the strong sales growth of hybrid cars, "cruelty-free" beauty products, and dramatic growth in sales of organic food. The conclusion appears to be that ethical and environmental questions are being posed by growing numbers of consumers, and they are often skeptical about corporate responses.[49] The impact of "ethical consumerism" is large, and of escalating significance. For example, the Daimler miniature Smart car had a troubled history, but the 2008 launch in the United States has been a big success—the vehicle has exactly the right green credentials to appeal to buyers for a city car in trendy cities like Boston and San Francisco.[50]

---

[44]Bob W. Heineman, Jr., "Avoiding Integrity Land Mines," *Harvard Business Review,* April 2007, 100–101.

[45]A. Singhapakdi, "Perceived Importance of Ethics and Ethical Decisions in Marketing," *Journal of Business Research,* 45, 1999, 89–99.

[46]Nigel F. Piercy and NIkala Lane, "Ethical and Moral Dilemmas Associated with Strategic Relationships Between Business-to-Business Buyers and Sellers," *Journal of Business Ethics,* 72, 2007, 87–102.

[47]Carlos Grande, "Businesses Behaving Badly, Say Customers," *Financial Times,* February 20, 2007, 24.

[48]Carlos Grande, "Ethical Consumption Makes Mark on Branding," *Financial Times,* February 20, 2007, 24.

[49]Andrew Edgecliffe-Johnson, "Scepticism Grows Over Claims on Ethics," *Financial Times,* May 27, 2008, 3.

[50]"Americans Get Smart," *Sunday Times,* December 9, 2007, 3–3.

While not all consumers are driven by ethical concerns, and those who are may be a small part of the market, research suggests that consumers with high ethical standards make up a distinct segment in many markets, with a willingness to pay higher prices for ethical products, and more inclination to "punish" producers of unethical products. Nonetheless, there is some virtue in testing rather than assuming that consumers care enough about moral issues to pay more.[51]

Correspondingly, business-to-business customers are increasingly concerned with ethical standards in supplier companies. Target Corporation prides itself on its high ethical standards and business principles, emphasizing the protection of human rights, and extends these principles and standards to its suppliers. Purchasing officers are required to uphold Target Corporation ethical standards wherever they buy in the world, even when these exceed the requirements of local laws—Target engineers do not just inspect suppliers' factories for product quality, but also for labor rights and employment conditions. Target operates a formal "compliance organization" for its purchasing. Similarly, Home Depot insists that all its wood products are sourced from suppliers who can provide verifiable evidence of their sound forest management practices. Home Depot is one of the largest buyers of wood products in the United States, and the company wants to be seen as taking a strong position on sustainability.[52]

Other pressures to higher ethical standards come from external lobbyists and pressure groups, regulators, employees and executives, and investors, but perhaps the most critical issue remains customer expectations. Interestingly, when asked by researchers what they want from sellers major customers put honesty and integrity at the top the list.[53]

Proactive Responses by Firms

The reality in the modern world is that ethics and social responsibility are important because of their impact on all stakeholders from shareholders and suppliers to employees and customers. Importantly, neglect or poor handling of these issues have a strong possibility of negative backlash. Two trends are particularly indicative of the relevance of ethics and social responsibility to business firms in most industries. A rapidly increasing number of organizations have established ethics executives with responsibility for guiding their firm's ethics and social responsibility initiatives. Moreover, many companies have developed their own codes of ethics and internal procedures to provide a framework for ethics actions. Clearly, there are many different types of unethical practices. Examples of the array of ethical issues include misleading advertising and sales promotion, product deception, misleading discussion with customers and intermediaries, price discrimination, and inappropriate use of entertainment or promotional expenditures.

For example, in the pharmaceuticals business, high sales pressure placed on doctors to prescribe new drugs has resulted in formal training courses in medical schools to teach future doctors how to resist sales pitches.[54] Payments and incentives to clinicians to change their prescribing behavior or purchasing are no longer perceived as acceptable practices. The search in the pharmaceutical industry for new and better ways to get to market, avoids these practices. Companies like Pfizer, Wyeth, Novartis, and GlaxoSmithKlein recognize that the era of "hard sell" is over in their sector and they are working to develop new sales models.

---

[51]Remi Trudel and June Cotte, "Does Being Ethical Pay?" *Wall Street Journal,* May 13, 2008, R2.

[52]Peter Senge, Bryan Smith, Nina Krushwitz, Joe Laur, and Sara Schley, *The Necessary Revolution: How Individuals and Organizations are Working Together to Create a Sustainable World,* London: Nicholas Brealey, 2008.

[53]Christina Galea, "What Customers Really Want," *Sales & Marketing Management,* May 2006, 11–12.

[54]Arlene Weintraub, "Just Say No to Drug Reps," *BusinessWeek,* February 4, 2008, 69.

Organizational Involvement

It is critical that the management of a company must encourage and facilitate effective responses to ethical issues and social responsibilities in order for the whole organization to become actively involved. Serious involvement in ethics and social responsibility by a company includes the following:

- Favorable organization culture
- Assignment of responsibility
- Ethics codes
- Operating processes/guidelines
- Action
- Monitoring and control

We briefly examine each of these areas to describe what is involved in organizational ethics.

Organizational Culture

The culture of a business is an important influence on the extent of involvement of a company in ethics and social responsibility. The firm's culture is influenced to some degree by the society in which it operates. Within this environment, top management and other stakeholders determine the extent of the firm's involvement in ethical and social responsibility activities. Top management must be proactive in creating the firm's ethical environment to provide the leadership needed to be successful in ethics initiatives. Importantly, this commitment to positive ethical behavior must extend to the entire workforce. Problems arise when an employee's personal values conflict with those of the organization. Management should communicate the need and importance of ethics and social responsibility throughout the organization and to other stakeholders. The focus should be on the value and importance of these issues and actions in the current societal and organizational environment.

Assignment of Responsibility

Many companies have designated ethics and social responsibility officers to guide and coordinate activities throughout the organization. Such individuals are concerned with gaining an understanding of the status of ethics awareness and actions. They can provide the direction for proactive efforts to strengthen and build ethics programs throughout the firm. Ethics and social responsibility are company-wide in scope. While marketing is likely to have a major involvement in these activities and concerns, all other business functions encounter ethics situations and are involved in social responsibility initiatives.

Ethics Codes

Many companies have developed ethics statements and codes, which may range from a brief statement to a more extensive set of guidelines. The purpose of written and widely distributed expressions of ethical conduct is to guide the entire workforce regarding ethical behavior. Grewal and Levy indicate that "The process of creating a strong ethical climate within a marketing firm (or in the marketing division of any firm) includes having a set of values that guides decision making and behavior. . . . Everyone within the firm must share the same understanding of these values and how they translate into the business activities of the firm, and they must share a consistent language to discuss them."[55] However, the reality is that there are situations where individuals may not behave ethically. The challenge is to develop guidelines and processes for use in preventing unethical practices and coping with those that occur.

---

[55]Grewal and Levy, 43.

Guidelines and Operating Processes

In addition to a code of ethics, companies may develop additional ethics guidelines and operating processes. The type of business, frequency of unethical situations, and management preferences are likely to influence the nature and extent of the ethics structure that is developed. The objective is to prevent unethical situations from occurring. This can be facilitated by appropriate communications with employees and other stakeholders. In some cases meetings may be needed. An ethics officer is useful in coordinating and managing these activities. A first step in deciding how extensive a firm's efforts should be regarding ethics is to determine the nature and extent of an organization's ethics situations. How frequently have unethical problems developed in the past? How serious where the problems and how were they resolved? The objective is to evaluate an organization's opportunity for improving control over ethics problems.

Action

It is important to have in place a clear understanding of how (and by whom) actions will be taken to resolve unethical situations. This will depend, in part, on how formalized are the organization's ethical guidelines and operating processes. Well managed and socially responsible firms have a history of responding quickly and extensively to ethics situations that are potentially unethical in nature and scope. Their managements recognize the damage unethical practices can have on brands, companies, and stakeholders.

Monitoring and Control

It is important to track how well things are going concerning ethics performance in the organization. Are problems declining (or increasing)? Are changes needed in ethics guidelines and processes? Is training of employees and executives needed? Importantly, high ethical standards perceived may be linked closely to corporate reputation and a company's ability to do business in its target markets. Ethical dilemmas are expected to grow in importance. Increasing complexity of business operations will create new ethics situations. Globalization will impose new ethics situations and additional complexity in adapting to the ethical priorities of different national cultures. Societal differences will compound ethics challenges. Companies will need to continue to strengthen their ethics programs and procedures.

Corporate Social Responsibility Initiatives

In a similar way to ethical questions, corporate social responsibility (CSR) has moved to a high level of relevance and importance in the social and business environment.[56] Social responsibility spans economic, legal, ethical, and philanthropic concerns by an organization and its stakeholders.[57] The objective is to have a favorable impact on society and eliminate or reduce the negative effects which a business may have. Importantly, while at one time CSR was mainly an issue of "corporate philanthropy,"[58] or entirely a question of moral obligation or pure altruism, CSR has been increasingly recognised as a source of competitive advantage, as well as an important part of how competitive relationships operate.

---

[56]Nigel F. Piercy and Nikala Lane, "Corporate Social Responsibility: Impacts on Strategic Marketing and Customer Value," *The Marketing Review,* 9(4) 2009, 335–360.

[57]Archie Carroll, "The Pyramid of Corporate Social Responsibility: Toward the Moral Management of Organizational Stakeholders," *Business Horizons,* 34(4) July/August 1991, 42.

[58]Michael E. Porter and Mark R. Kramer, "The Competitive Advantage of Corporate Philanthropy," *Harvard Business Review,* December 2002, 57–68.

Defining CSR

CSR is generally understood to encompass company activities that integrate social and environmental concerns into business operations, and into the company's interaction with other stakeholders, on a voluntary basis.[59] The 21st century has seen issues of social responsibility and the morality and ethics of company practices become a key element of managing customer relationships and how companies are perceived and understood by their customers. However, research suggests that an integrated approach to CSR in marketing is largely missing in both theory and practice.[60]

Drivers of CSR

Factors underpinning the growing attention by executives to issues of corporate social responsibility are: the new concerns and expectations of consumers, public authorities, and investors in the context of globalization and industrial change; social criteria increasingly influencing the investment decisions of individuals and institutions; increased concern about the damage caused by economic and business activity to the physical environment, and the transparency of business activities brought about by media and new information and communication technologies.[61] Business norms across the world have moved CSR into the mainstream of business practice. Non-governmental organizations like the World Resources Institute (WRI), AccountAbility, Global Reporting Initiative (GRI), International Standards Organization (ISO 14000), and the United Nations, all have major initiatives aimed at improving the social involvement and performance of the world's business community.[62] Indeed, there is an increasingly widespread view that sustainability is now the key driver of innovation for companies.[63]

Importantly, effective CSR can provide significant and measurable benefits for companies. Some commentators suggest that after years of skepticism, big companies are genuinely acting to cut waste, cut carbon emissions, find sources of renewable energy, and develop sustainable business models.[64] An increasingly widespread view is that there is a business case underpinning social initiatives—behind the drive for sustainability lies a growing belief that environmental and social projects not only improve corporate reputations, but also foster innovation, cut costs, and open up new markets.[65] Unilever's Pureit low-cost water purification machine is illustrative—it cleans water to provide drinking water without boiling or the use of mains electricity, and purifies water more cheaply than boiling. Developed by Hindustan Unilever in India, the social and health benefits of lower costs for clean drinking water are evident, but also the potential market for the product in the rural areas of emerging markets is huge.

Company approaches to CSR vary from the defensive to the more strategic. We examine each approach.

---

[59]Piercy and Lane, 2009, op cit.

[60]Isabelle Maignan, O. C. Ferrell, and Linda Ferrell, "A Stakeholder Model for Implementing Social Responsibility in Marketing," *European Journal of Marketing,* 39(9–10, 2005, 956–977).

[61]Commission of the European Communities, *Green Paper: Promoting a European Framework for Corporate Social Responsibility* (COM, July 2001), 6.

[62]Paul C. Godfrey and Nile W. Hatch, "Researching Corporate Responsibility: An Agenda for the 21st Century," *Journal of Business Ethics,* 70, 2007, 87–98.

[63]R. Nidumolo, C. K. Prahalad, and M. R. Rangaswami, "Why Sustainability is Now the Key Driver of Innovation," *Harvard Business Review,* September 2009, 56–64.

[64]Peter Senge, Bryan Smith, Nina Krushwitz, Joe Laur, and Sara Schley, *The Necessary Revolution: How Individuals and Organizations are Working Together to Create a Sustainable World* (London: Nicholas Brealey), 2008.

[65]Michael Skapinker, "Why Companies and Campaigners Collaborate," *Financial Times,* July 8, 2008, 15.

Defensive CSR

If a firm is essentially, defensive in its stance on social responsiveness, then its primary concerns will be the protection of relationships. For example, relationship protection dominates with consumers, business-to-business customers, influential lobby or pressure groups, suppliers, employees and managers, and relative position against competitors. Nonetheless, Porter and Kramer warn that companies seeing CSR only as a way to placate pressure groups often find that this approach turns into a series of short-term public relations actions, with minimal social benefit and no strategic benefit for the business. They suggest the most common corporate responses to CSR have not been strategic and are often little more than cosmetic.[66]

The environmental issues at Coca-Cola are illustrative. Coke has attracted negative publicity: the alleged mistreatment of workers in Columbia; the use of water in drought-stricken parts of India; delaying acceptance of responsibility for contaminated product in Belgium in 1999; violently ejecting shareholder activists from the AGM; and playing a major role in fueling the childhood obesity epidemic sweeping the developed world. Coke has been actively boycotted on university campuses throughout North America and in parts of Europe. The company was in danger of replacing Nike and McDonalds as the chief corporate villain for the antiglobalization movement. The problem recognized by management was negative perceptions of the company progressively undermining the value of the brand. The new CEO of Coke mandated a proactive company approach to social issues, with a goal of making Coke the "recognized global leader in corporate social responsibility." The company has undertaken an audit of labor practices throughout its supply chain, launched several water conservation projects, embraced industry guidelines restricting the sale of sugary drinks in schools, and supported initiatives to encourage physical exercise among children. Nonetheless, critics still claim the company is pursuing these initiatives under pressure, not because they believe they are the right things to do.[67]

The goal in defensive CSR mode is to anticipate and develop appropriate responses to social demands from any source that threatens to undermine the value and credibility of brands, the attractiveness of the competitive position on which the company's strategy depends, and the viability of the marketing strategy itself. Management attention can usefully be given to examining the links between CSR stance and the impacts on consumers, business-to-business customers, investors, lobby groups, suppliers, employees and managers, and competitors.

Strategic CSR

In examining the potential for a more strategic view of CSR, Michael Porter and Mark Kramer[68] have made a compelling case that businesses should not simply be pursuing CSR as an end in itself, but should be embedding it into their strategy to help build competitive advantage. Porter notes that

> all too often, large companies see corporate social responsibility as something entirely separate from their business goals. As high unemployment, rising poverty, and dismay over corporate greed breed contempt for the capitalist market system. . . . Serving the intersecting needs of business and the community is the only path to winning back respect.[69]

---

[66]Michael E. Porter and Mark R. Kramer, "Strategy and Society: The Link Between Competitive Advantage and Corporate Social Responsibility," 78–92.

[67]Andrew Ward, "Coke Joins the Battle for the Brand Corporate Responsibility," *Financial Times,* November 21, 2006, 10.

[68]Porter and Kramer, "Strategy and Society: The Link Between Competitive Advantage and Corporate Social Responsibility," *Harvard Business Review,* December 2006, 78–92.

[69]Michael E. Porter, "How Big Business Can Help Itself by Helping its Neighbors," *Bloomberg BusinessWeek,* May 31–June 6, 2010, 56.

At a strategic level, the logic is the transformation of value chain activities to benefit society, while at the same time reinforcing the company's strategy, and making strategic moves that leverage corporate capabilities competitiveness. Strategic CSR may involve the introduction of radically different new products—the Toyota Prius hybrid car responded to consumer concerns about car emissions pollution, and provided both competitive advantage for Toyota and environmental benefits. However, the broader goal of strategic CSR is to invest in social aspects of the company's context to strengthen company competitiveness. This is achieved, in part, by adding a social dimension to the company's value proposition and ways of doing business.

Indeed, some companies have made high-profile efforts to position as socially responsible, as an explicit part of their strategy. Some go even further in advocating the combination of business and social goals. Rosabeth Moss Kanter uses the term "vanguard companies" to describe those which are ahead of the rest and provide a model for the future, because they aspire to be both big and human, efficient but innovative, global but concerned about local communities, using their power and influence to develop solutions to problems the public cares about. She concludes from her studies of companies like IBM, Procter and Gamble, Publicis, Cemex, and Diageo that humanistic values and attention to societal needs provide the starting point for effective strategy in the global information age. Nonetheless, social purpose creates strategic advantages only if those social commitments have an economic logic that attracts resources to the firm.[70]

Some of the ways in which a company can combine social benefits with business goals are shown in the strategy pursued by Unilever and the chief executive vision on which the strategy is based, described in the STRATEGY APPLICATION.

Creating Shared Value

Interestingly, Porter and Kramer propose an extension to their earlier view of CSR in the form of creating shared value. They argue that societal needs, not just economic needs, define markets, and that viewing markets through the lens of shared value opens up innovation and growth opportunities.[71] Their logic rests on closely linking social goals with business goals. They define shared value as policies and operating practices that enhance a company's competitiveness while simultaneously improving the economic and social conditions in the communities in which the company operates. They argue that creating shared value supersedes CSR. Shared value initiatives are underway at companies like Google, IBM, Intel, Johnson & Johnson, Unilever, and Wal-Mart. Addressing societal concerns can provide major productivity improvements for the firm. For example, by reducing its packaging and cutting 100 million miles from its truck delivery routes, Wal-Mart both lowered carbon emissions and saved $200 million in costs. Shared value opportunities are created from re-conceiving products and markets and redefining productivity in the value chain.

Customer Value and Competitive Positioning

Escalating transparency underlines the importance of CSR to a company's competitive position with customers. For example, the GoodGuide website provides an online database of verified information regarding the health, environmental, and social impacts of 65,000 common products, allowing consumers and rivals to trace the provenance of products.[72]

---

[70]Rosabeth Moss Kanter, *Supercorp: How Vanguard Companies Create Innovation, Profits, Growth and Social Good,* (London: Profile Books, 2009).

[71]Michael E. Porter and Mark R. Kramer, "Creating Shared Value," *Harvard Business Review,* January–February 2011, 62–77.

[72]Paul Tyrell, "Technology Lets Buyers Unravel the Ethics Behind the Brand," *Financial Times,* September 16, 2010, 16.

In 2010, Chairman of Unilever, Paul Polman, outlined his "sustainable living plan" for multinational company Unilever, focused on sustainability and environmental protection, and said to the international investment community:

Unilever has been around for 100-plus years. We want to be around for several hundred more years. So, if you buy into this long-term value-creation model, which is equitable, which is shared, which is sustainable, then come and invest with us. If you don't buy into this, I respect you as a human being, but don't put your money in our company.

Unilever aims to do well by doing good and believes companies can profit by selling low-cost products to the poorest people in the world. Illustrative examples include:

In African countries like Kenya, Tanzania, Senegal, and Benin, Unilever participates in a public-private partnership coordinated by the World Bank to promote handwashing, particularly after going to the toilet and before handling food. Other participants include Unicef, USAid, the London School of Hygiene and Tropical Medicine, and the Bill and Melinda Gates Foundation. Unilever's contribution is marketing expertise to replace unsuccessful methods of public health education with more sophisticated ways of understanding and shaping consumer behavior. Unilever is, however, also clear that by making washing hands with antibacterial soap a habit in these countries, they will increase sales of the company's Lifebuoy soap.

- Unilever has pledged to buy materials like the palm oil used in its soaps and margarine from sustainable sources. In part this responds to a Greenpeace campaign accusing Unilever of destroying Indonesian rainforests for palm oil and parodying the company's advertising, but it also reflects the logic that Unilever's sales growth cannot be maintained unless its suppliers in emerging markets use their land in a way that helps them to carry on producing what the company needs.

- In rural India, about 35,000 women sell low-priced soaps, shampoos, and detergents to fellow villagers in a program operated by Hindustan Unilever. Benefits include turning the poor into microconsumers and small-scale entrepreneurs to combat poverty, but also providing Unilever with access to new consumers of its products in markets otherwise difficult to reach.

Sources: Barney Jopson, "Unilever Look to Clean Up in Africa," *Financial Times*, November 15, 2007, 20. Michael Skapinker, "Long-Term Corporate Plans May be Lost in Translation," *Financial Times*, November 23, 2010, 15. Alison Damast, "BOP Theory Makes the Grade," *BusinessWeek*, August 20, 2007, 16.

A major impact of corporate social responsibility imperatives is in encouraging the development of new business models that address both commercial and social needs at the same time. Adding a social dimension to the value proposition adds a new frontier for thinking about competitive positioning and competitive advantage in business and marketing strategy. The number of industries and companies whose competitive advantage can involve social value propositions is rapidly growing.

In some sectors, the emergence of "eco-entrepreneurs" is transforming traditional business models with new technologies. Fast-moving "eco-upstarts" may be better positioned than established companies to pursue social goals with commercial benefits:

- PlanetTran is a chauffeur service that uses only hybrid cars and aims to save the planet "one car journey at a time." Successful with the eco-conscious business community in Boston and San Francisco, PlanetTran supplies corporate clients with quarterly reports measuring the environmental benefits of using PlanetTran compared to traditional transport arrangements.

- In the consumer transportation sector, the merger of Zipcar and Flexcar in 2007 created the largest U.S. car-sharing service with 180,000 members. Car-sharing allows members to rent vehicles for periods as short as an hour, collecting vehicles from locations like rail stations and shopping mall car parks, and accessing the vehicles with smartcards. Zipcar has already opened in London with the goal of creating the first pan-European car sharing service. Convenient car-sharing services may replace car ownership altogether for many city dwellers. Zipcar estimates that each car it adds to its fleet can keep 20 private cars off the road. Nonetheless, with revenues running at $100 million in 2008, Zipcar is not in profit, though interestingly Hertz and Enterprise are now imitating the Zipcar model in their own operating models.

- The fastest-growing transportation mode in the United States is curbside buses operated by companies like Megabus, operating a model with street-side pick-up, express travel between major cities and cut-rate fares. Estimates suggest curbside carriers already reduce national fuel consumption by 11 million gallons annually, the equivalent of taking 24,000 cars off the road. The new bus riders are young, well-educated, and digitally connected.

Sources: R. Knight, "Green Entrepreneurs with the Drive to Transform Travel," *Financial Times,* September 26, 2008, 16. B. Simon, "Zipcar and Flexcar Gear Up for Merger," *Financial Times,* November 1, 2007, 27. A. Aston, "Growth Galore, But Profits Are Zip," *BusinessWeek,* September 8, 2008, 62. Ben Austen, "The Megabus Effect," *Bloomberg BusinessWeek,* April 11–17, 2011, 62–67.

From a strategic marketing perspective it is important to ask how CSR impacts on the customer value proposition. CSR may do good for society in its own right, but we emphasize value-creation through CSR which resonates with the development of new business models that combine social and business goals. The value proposition describes the unique offer made to the customer, with all its hard and soft dimensions, and is at the center of how a company aims to differentiate itself from competitors in its target market segments. In fact, there are indications that many companies have a poor understanding of their customers' real concerns about social and environmental issues surrounding their businesses. High-performing companies show a deeper understanding of their customers' CSR expectations.[73] Businesses need new sources of operational, supply chain and customer information to gain the new levels of insight required to meet objectives in areas like sustainability.[74]

---

[73]G. Pohle and J. Hittner, *Attaining Sustainable Growth Through Corporate Social Responsibility* (Somers, NY: IBM Institute for Business Value, February 2008).

[74]IBM, *Leading A Sustainable Enterprise* (Somers, NY: IBM Institute for Business Value, 2009).

A key question is how a supplier's CSR initiatives align with customer priorities and thus drive value for the customer. Consider the case of Philips environmentally friendly Alto industrial lighting tubes. While containing less toxicity, the Alto product was more expensive than competing light tubes, and conventional suppliers sold on price and bulb life to purchasing officers. Telling buyers that the tube is more environmentally friendly or that it is more environmentally friendly than competitors' products provides little leverage with purchasing officers accustomed to evaluating alternatives on price and bulb life. However, appealing to, for example, shopping mall developers on the basis of reduced disposal costs (because the green product is less toxic) and environmental image (the cleaner lighting becomes part of their environmental appeal to consumers) is effective. Alto replaced more than 25 percent of the U.S. market for traditional fluorescent lamps.[75]

Examples of how companies and entrepreneurs are developing new business models in the transportation sector, combining social and business goals with customer value are illustrated in the INNOVATION APPLICATION.

Summary

To some, CRM means little more than building relationships with customers to match the product offer better with customer needs. Others see CRM as concerned with developing a unified and cohesive view of the customer, no matter how the customer chooses to communicate with the organization (in person, by mail, Internet, or telephone), and emphasizing enhanced customer service and the use of call centers to provide consistency in how the company interacts with customers. To others, CRM focuses on the creation and use of a customer database to support decision makers.

Understanding customer relationship management begins with recognizing that CRM seeks to increase the value of an organization's customer base by developing and retaining better relationships with customers. CRM may involve the use of databases but includes much more than technology. CRM makes it possible to examine individual customers or narrowly defined groups (microsegments) and calculate what each offers the company in potential profits. The resulting customer lifetime value (CLV) can be used to focus marketing and promotional efforts.

CRM strategy can be viewed from company-wide, customer-facing, and functional perspectives. The company-wide or strategic perspective provides the most complete view of CRM. Designing the CRM strategy follows a sequence of initiatives: gaining organizational commitment to CRM, forming the project team, analyzing business needs, and determining the CRM strategy to be pursued by the organization.

CRM strategy includes the value proposition to be offered, the business case, the customer strategy, the enterprise transformation plan, and responsibilities to other stakeholders. CRM strategy implementation involves integration of sales, marketing, and service functions across all media and value chain members, creation of a data warehouse, decision guidelines for use of CRM analyses, determination of performance benchmarks, and integration of cross-functional operations.

Several hurdles to successful CRM implementation include implementing before creating a customer strategy, launching CRM before making essential organizational changes, asssuming that more CRM technology is necessarily better, and investing time and resources with disinterested customers. CRM is a major undertaking that is complex and demanding.

---

[75]K. W. Chan and R. Mauborgne, "Creating Market Space," *Harvard Business Review,* January–February 1999, 83–93.

CRM is a value-creation process consisting of the value the customer receives and the value the organization receives. The benefits the customer receives are expressed in the value proposition. The value the organization receives is determined by a penetrating analysis of the profitability of the customer base. Customer lifetime value is the basis of the assessment.

CRM is an important aspect of strategic marketing, recognizing that CRM is an enterprise spanning initiative. It is essential that CRM be carefully integrated with marketing strategy. CRM has a vital role to play in market targeting and marketing program positioning strategies.

Finally, we examine several aspects of ethics and social responsibility. Companies are developing and implementing programs and processes to reduce ethical problems and deal with those that occur. Many companies have appointed ethics officers, developed codes of ethics, and operating process and guidelines. Social legitimacy in all its forms is a major impact of the ability of a seller to establish and maintain effective customer relationships.

Questions for Review and Discussion

1. How should CRM be defined to provide a complete strategy perspective?
2. Discuss the value of considering CRM at different organizational levels.
3. What is involved in estimating customer lifetime value (CLV)?
4. Discuss the process of developing a CRM strategy.
5. What are the important issues in CRM implementation?
6. Discuss how CRM creates value for the firm's stakeholders.
7. What is the relationship between CRM and market segmentation?
8. Discuss the role of the cross-functional CRM team.
9. In what ways can perceptions of poor ethical standards inhibit a company's ability to build customer relationships and compete effectively?
10. How can it be right for a company to invest resources in social responsibility projects, when its primary role is to deliver value to its shareholders?

Internet Applications

A. Visit the website of SalesForce.com. Based on the information provided discuss how SalesForce.com can contribute to a company's CRM.
B. Visit one of the websites discussed in Exhibit 4.3. Discuss how the website may be useful to a company in its CRM activities.

Application

A. Critically evaluate the "Net Promoter" concept of customer satisfaction used by the General Electric Co. What role does customer experience information play in GE's CRM?

Chapter 5

Capabilities for Learning About Customers and Markets

Market-oriented companies display superiority in understanding customers, markets and competitors. "Every discussion of market orientation emphasizes the ability of the firm to learn about customers, competitors, and channel members in order to continually sense and act on events and trends in present and prospective markets."[1] Market-driven companies display innovative skills in gathering, interpreting, and using information of all kinds to guide their business and marketing strategies and to achieve competitive advantage.

Strategic agility, demanded by rapidly changing markets, mandates strategic sensitivity—awareness of what is happening and what is going to happen next, as a basis for rapidly developing effective responses to change or new opportunities.[2] Agility means a company can consistently identify and seize opportunities more quickly and effectively than rivals, and emphasizes the ability to make sense of the outside world and spot opportunities as they emerge.[3] Industry-based research by the Business Performance Management Forum suggests that companies fail to respond to fast-changing markets because they are unable to understand and adjust to what their customers want. The failure of executives to "read" their markets means their companies struggle to meet the demands of increasingly competitive international markets and sophisticated customers.[4]

Importantly, learning about markets is concerned with interpreting information as well as collecting data. With resources like online Internet searches, in-company information and intelligence systems, marketing research agency reports and surveys, ethnographical research techniques, and burgeoning technical literature in most fields, executives may be in danger of being overwhelmed by information. Research suggests that for

---

[1]George S. Day, "The Capabilities of Market-Driven Organizations," *Journal of Marketing,* October, 1994, 43.

[2]Yves Doz and Mikko Kosonen, *Fast Strategy: How Strategic Agility Will Help You Stay Ahead of the Game* (Philadelphia PA: Wharton School Publishing), 2007.

[3]Donald Sull, "From Lines to Loops: An Iterative Approach to Strategy," in *Strategy, Innovation and Change: Challenges for Management,* Robert Galavan, John Murray and Costas Markides, eds. (Oxford: Oxford University Press), 2008.

[4]Francesco Guerrera, "US Groups 'Fail To Understand Customer Needs,'" *Financial Times,* June 5, 2006, 27.

strategy, and the organizational changes that follow strategy, the way executives interpret and understand information about their environments may be more important than accuracy. Investments in enhancing and shaping interpretation may create a more durable competitive advantage than investments in obtaining additional information.[5] An imperative in market-led strategy is the quest is for superior interpretation and market understanding.

Procter and Gamble illustrates the competitive strength that comes from superior customer knowledge. Since 2000, P&G has experienced a transformation. The company has pushed up-market in the West and down-market in developing countries, concentrated resources in the top brands, and through merger with Gillette, has become the world's biggest consumer goods company, outperforming rivals Colgate and Unilever. In 2011, air freshener Febreze became the 24th P&G brand to achieve $1 billion in annual sales. P&G has become innovative and outward-looking, with the mantra "The customer is boss" and is committed to delivering more than brands—it must deliver a consumer experience. P&G invests less in formal marketing research and more in talking to people one-to-one in their homes, or in facilities that replicate the home environment—like the Consumer Village, where P&G meets consumers and works to identify desired consumer experiences with products. For example, research teams spent time in homes across the United States, watching people clean baths, resulting in the Mr Clean Magic Reach—an extendible tool with changeable cleaning pads to reach high areas and tight corners in bathrooms. Researchers have spent weeks in the homes of low-income consumers to understand what it is like to live on $50 a month—for example, resulting in Tide Clean White in China for hand-washing of clothes. P&G's virtual reality Cave is a walk-in three-dimensional room where computer-generated imagery allows P&G researchers to test alternative retail concepts and experiences. In addition, P&G has launched new social networking sites to gain insight into consumer habits and preferences in online forums for women. In launching its eStore website selling products direct to consumers, the emphasis is on creating a live, online learning laboratory to listen, learn, and collaborate with the online shopper. Impressive innovation and responsiveness at P&G is built on processes for continuous learning and knowledge generation.[6]

A theme linking the success of companies in many sectors is their capabilities for superior market sensing and their ability to develop competitive advantage from their learning processes. The challenge for executives is increasingly one of knowledge management to build company-wide understanding of the marketplace and enhanced responsiveness, rather than simply collecting information. Market sensing and learning are core competencies underpinning market-driven strategy.

The importance to executives of challenging how well customers and markets are understood and how well a company can identify the threats and opportunities emerging in markets is emphasized in the STRATEGY APPLICATION. Conventional approaches may be inadequate in turbulent environments and achieving a deep understanding of customers and markets and how they are changing can be challenging.

---

[5] Kathleen M. Sutcliffe and Klaus Weber, "The High Cost of Accurate Knowledge," *Harvard Business Review,* May, 2003, 74–82.

[6] This illustration is adapted from: Andrew Davidson, "The Razor-Sharp P&G Boss," *The Sunday Times,* December 3, 2006, 3–6. Alan Mitchell, "P&G Takes Hoppers to Another World in the War of the Brands," *Financial Times,* October 18, 2006, 10. Lisa Cornwell, "P&G Launches Two Social Networking Sites," *Marketing News,* February 1, 2007, 21. Jonathan Birchall, "P&G Goes Online to Compete for Sales," *Financial Times,* May 20, 2010, 20. Ellen Byron, "P&G Makes Febreze a $1 Billion Dollar Brand," *Wall Street Journal,* March 10, 2011, p. 19.

In his now-famous book, Nassim Nicholas Taleb introduced the idea of the *Black Swan*—the impact of highly improbable events. The analogy comes from the 17th century when the black swan issue fascinated philosophers, and when news of the first sighting of a black swan in Australia trickled back to Europe. At that time, philosopher John Stuart Mill observed "No amount of observation of white swans can allow the inference that all swans are white, but the observation of a single black swan can refute that conclusion."

Taleb's logic is that black swan events are highly unpredictable—they are outliers beyond the realm of normal expectations. Yet they have massive impact when they occur, and after the event, we try to make it appear less random and more predictable that it actually was, and thus avoid learning. In these terms, both Google and 9/11 are black swans.

The black swan analogy has attracted much attention and challenges executives to understand a major limitation to what we learn from observations and experience, and the fragility of knowledge.

Black swan logic makes what you do not know more relevant than what you do know, yet many approaches to marketing research measurement and market assessment specifically exclude the possibility of a black swan because it appears improbable. Taleb's rationale is that people misunderstand randomness and risk. At the heart of his logic is the challenge of unlikely but not impossible events for which we fail to plan. If our knowledge is restricted to the irrelevant and inconsequential, then large events will continue to surprise us.

Sources: Nassim Nicholas Taleb, *The Black Swan: The Impact of the Highly Improbable* (New York: Random House), 2007. David Smith, "When Catastrophe Strikes Blame a Black Swan," *Financial Times,* May 6, 2007, 24. Nassim Taleb. "Fear of a Black Swan," *Fortune,* April 14, 2008, 44–45.

In this chapter we examine how continuous learning about markets improves competitive advantage. First, we look at the relationship among market-driven strategy, market sensing, and learning processes. Then, we overview marketing information and knowledge development resources, including marketing research and information systems. Next, we look at marketing intelligence and knowledge management. Finally, several important issues are highlighted concerning the ethical issues that surround the collection and use of information in strategic marketing.

Market-Driven Strategy, Market Sensing, and Learning Processes

The ability to learn from customers underpins market-driven strategy. Market-driven firms are characterized by their ability to sense and respond to events and trends in their markets.[7] Market sensing is a key capability of the market-driven organization, concerned with the ability of organizations to continuously learn about their markets, and acts as an antecedent to market orientation.[8] Companies like P&G illustrate the close relationship between a market-oriented culture and organizational learning. Market orientation is both a culture and a process committed to achieving superior customer value (see Chapter 1). The process consists of information acquisition, broad information dissemination, and shared diagnosis leading to coordinated action.[9]

---

[7]George S. Day, "Managing the Market Learning Process," *Journal of Business and Industrial Marketing,* 17(4), 2002, 240–252.

[8]George S. Day, "The Capabilities of Market-Driven Organizations," *Journal of Marketing,* 56 (October), 1994, 37–52.

[9]Stanley F. Slater and John C. Narver, "Market Orientation, Customer Value, and Superior Performance," *Business Horizons,* March–April, 1994, 22–27.

Market-Sensing Processes

Importantly, market-driven companies deploy multiple approaches to understand the opportunities and threats emerging in their markets, and to predict how customers will react to changes in marketing strategy. They include:

- **Building open-minded inquiry processes**—market-driven organizations show an openness to studying change, avoiding complacency
- **Analyzing competitors' actions**—giving detailed attention to rivals' tactics and strategies to develop understanding of their plans and capabilities
- **Listening to front-line employees**—motivating the involvement of staff who are in contact with customers in building understanding of change and new opportunities and threats
- **Searching for latent customer needs**—finding unserved needs through dialogue, observation, and engagement with customers
- **Scanning the periphery of the market**—actively looking for new opportunities in the market
- **Encouraging experimentation**—building culture and process around continuous curiosity and new ideas.[10]

Many of the world's most successful companies show how the risk in markets can be shaped by paying continuous attention to how customers are changing, and evaluating more deeply how markets are developing. Market-oriented companies have a "knowledge intensity," in which revealing and relevant data are gathered and studied frequently. Knowledge intensity identifies both market risk and new opportunities for growth:

> It's answering the question: what do we know about customers that others don't? And then using that knowledge to make and keep profitable customers for life.[11]

Many of the characteristics of robust market-sensing strategy and market knowledge intensity are illustrated in the market learning strategy at Best Buy. This is described in the INNOVATION APPLICATION. Market-sensing activities and the generation of market knowledge are important learning processes, often associated with the learning organization.

Learning Organizations

Our understanding of learning organizations is not complete. However, it is clear that these organizations share several important characteristics, relevant to superior market sensing capabilities:

> Learning organizations are guided by a shared vision that focuses the energies of organizational members on creating superior value for customers. These organizations continuously acquire, process, and disseminate throughout the organization knowledge about markets, products, technologies, and business processes. They do not hesitate to question long held assumptions and beliefs regarding their business. Their knowledge is based on experience, experimentation, and information from customers, suppliers, competitors, and other sources. Through complex communication, coordination, and conflict resolution processes, these organizations reach a shared interpretation of the information, which enables them to act swiftly and decisively to exploit opportunities and defuse problems. Learning organizations are exceptional in their ability to anticipate and act on opportunities in turbulent and fragmenting markets.[12]

[10]George S. Day, "Managing the Market Learning Process," *Journal of Business and Industrial Marketing,* 17(4), 2002, 240–252.
[11]This illustration is based on Adrian Slywotsky and Karl Weber, *The Upside: From Risk Taking to Risk Shaping* (New York: Crown Business), 2007.
[12]Day, 1994, 71.

Best Buy is the world's largest consumer electronics retailer. To stay up with agile rivals like Wal-Mart, Amazon, and Costco in the United States, Best Buy has shifted its focus from products to consumers, in a business model aimed at building a strong position with the most attractive consumer groups. The Best Buy strategy emphasizes treating each customer as a unique individual, developing solutions to meet their needs, and engaging employees to serve them. The strategic goal is to match rivals on price, while delivering better levels of customer service and more accessible and focused stores.

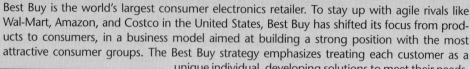

New ideas come from listening to customers and employees more closely—ideas that previously would never have reached corporate headquarters. More than 120,000 employees act as agents of the customer not the product manufacturer. Employees closely engaged with consumers identify new growth opportunities. Those with the highest potential have included small business customers, new services offerings, and international growth—worth $230 billion by revenue in 2007. One key insight for Best Buy underpins the new emphasis on "connectivity"—stores are being remodeled to demonstrate potential connections between devices previously merchandized in separate departments, such as televisions and computers.

Best Buy has actively engaged with social media—the company's chief executive talks to employees and customers personally on Facebook every night and operates Twitter and Linked-In pages, as well as providing a blog called Brian's Whiteboard on the Best Buy corporate website.

Importantly, Best Buy shares its customer knowledge with manufacturers and product developers. The company has assembled a team of engineers, technologists, and product experts from Apple, Xerox, Kodak, and other leading R&D companies, focused on meeting new customer needs. Best Buy executives participate in product development and design, at companies like Hewlett-Packard and Toshiba, to provide insights into translating technology for customer needs and enhancing the customer experience.

A core competency for innovation at Best Buy is gathering and synthesizing customer intelligence. This advances collaboration with suppliers, while building Best Buy's private label business in consumer electronics.

Sources: Devendra Mishra, "How Best Buy Uses Customer Input to Develop Private Label Line," www.dealerscope.com/story, June 14, 2006. Matthew Boyle, "Best Buy's Giant Gamble," *Fortune*, April 3, 2006. Cliff Edwards, "Tech Bows to Best Buy," *Bloomberg BusinessWeek*, December 2, 2009, 50–56. Diane Brady, "Hard Choices," *Bloomberg BusinessWeek*, December 5–12, 2010, 104. Jonathan Birchall, "Well Connected to His Company," *Financial Times*, May 3, 2010, 14.

Continuing research promises to further expand our knowledge about these complex and relevant organizational processes.

Learning and Competitive Advantage

The advantage gained from learning is that the organization is able to quickly and effectively respond to opportunities and threats, and to satisfy customers' needs with new products and improved services. Learning capabilities and skills are central to business agility.[13] Learning drastically reduces the time necessary to accomplish projects such as new product development. For example, Swedish fashion retailer H&M can get new designs into its stores in as little as 3 weeks, compared to the 6 months needed by traditional clothing retailers. H&M's designers carefully watch fashion trends and identifying a new trend leads to immediate action—sketches and patterns that go electronically to fabrics buyers and production units worldwide. Executives in charge can conceive and produce new fashions on their own authority.[14] Superior learning capabilities and speed of learning create a new competitive advantage, which may be extremely difficult for competitors to imitate or equal.

Interestingly, market sensing capabilities and knowledge generation may directly create competitive advantage. United Parcel Service (UPS) has a joint venture with the largest domestic marketing research agency in China. UPS used this relationship to sponsor two major studies of urban, middle-class Chinese consumers, to identify the demand in different market segments for U.S. consumer products. The research reports were made available to small and medium-sized U.S. exporting firms identifying new business opportunities. The goal is to gain recognition of UPS as the knowledge leader on the subject, and the premier carrier flying to more points in China than any other U.S. airline.[15] It is increasingly common with large customers that suppliers are required to identify end-use market opportunities for their buyers, and market learning and knowledge developments are key elements of competing.

Learning About Markets

Learning about markets requires developing processes throughout the organization for obtaining, interpreting, and acting on information from sensing activities. The learning processes of market-oriented companies include a sequence of activities beginning with open-minded inquiry.[16]

- **Objective Inquiry.** One danger to be avoided is not exploring new views about markets and competition, because they are not taken seriously. Search for information is of little value if management already has a fixed view, on which new information will have no influence whatever it indicates. Not all companies see the value in continuous learning about markets. Managers who are not part of market-driven cultures may be unwilling to invest in information to improve their decision-making results. The same companies often encounter problems because of faulty or incomplete market sensing. Developing processes for continuous learning allows firms to capture more information about customers, suppliers, and competitors.[17] This capability provides the potential for growth based on informed decisions and a more complete mapping and analysis of the competitive environment. Firms can respond much more quickly to competitors' actions and take advantage of situations in the marketplace. Open-minded inquiry also helps to anticipate value migration threats, which are frequently initiated by competitors from outside the traditional market or industry.[18] The earlier STRATEGY APPLICATION

---

[13]Yves Doz and Mikko Kosonen, *Fast Strategy: How Strategic Agility Will Help You Stay Ahead of the Game* (Philadelphia PA: Wharton School Publishing), 2007.

[14]Steve Hamm, "Speed Demons," *BusinessWeek,* March 27, 2006, 67–76.

[15]Michael Fielding, "Special Delivery: UPS Conducts Surveys to Help Customers Export to China," *Marketing News,* February 1, 2007, 13.

[16]The following discussion is based on Day, "The Capabilities of Market-Driven Organizations." See also Stanley F. Slater and John C. Narver, *Market-Oriented Isn't Enough: Build a Learning Organization,* Report No. 94–103 (Cambridge, MA: Marketing Science Institute, 1994).

[17]Nigel F. Piercy and Nikala Lane, "Marketing Implementation: Building and Sustaining A Real Market Understanding," *Journal of Marketing Practice: Applied Marketing Science,* 2(3), 1996, 15–28.

[18]Adrian J. Slywotzky, *Value Migration* (Boston: Harvard Business School Press), 1996.

concerning Black Swan theory underlines the importance of objective and open-minded enquiry to effective learning.

- **Information Distribution for Synergy.** The widespread distribution of information in the organization can leverage the value of the information by cutting across business functions to share information on customers, channels of distribution, suppliers, and competitors. Synergistic distribution works to remove functional hurdles and practices. Cross-functional teams are useful to encourage transfer of information across functions. The explosion in information connectivity (access) facilitates widespread information distribution.[19] Unbundling information from its physical carrier, such as salespeople, will provide access as well as speed in organizations. This will help cross-functional teams and alter hierarchical structures and proprietary information systems. Expanded information connectivity promises to encourage cooperation among functions, reduce the power of information possession, and enhance organizational learning.

- **Mutually Informed Interpretations.** The mental model of the market guides managers' interpretation of information. The intent is to reach a shared vision about the market and about the impact that new information has on this vision. Market-oriented culture encourages market sensing, but the process requires more than gathering and studying information. "This interpretation is facilitated by the mental models of managers, which contain decision rules for deciding how to act on the information in light of anticipated outcomes."[20] The mental model reflects executives' vision about the forces influencing the market and likely future directors of change. Learning occurs as members of the organization evaluate the results of their decisions based on their vision at the time the decisions were made. Deciding to take the high risk of cutting-edge ventures requires managers to reach a shared vision about uncertain future market opportunities.

- **Accessible Memory.** This part of the learning process emphasizes the importance of keeping and gaining access to prior learning. The objective is not to lose valuable information that can continue to be used. Doing this involves integrating the information into the organizational memory, and not losing information when people leave the organization. Information storage technology is an important facilitator, but the human factor remains critical.

Barriers to Market Learning Processes

In some situations learning processes may be ineffective. If managers do not understand or accept the value of new information and insight from the marketplace, they are likely to maintain existing perspectives and reject new ones. Rigid organizational structures and inflexible information systems may stand in the way of learning and knowledge sharing in an organization. Political interests may defend the status quo, or the pressure of existing business operations may block the capacity of managers to take on new ideas. For example, Donald Sull describes companies falling prey to "active inertia"—responding to market shifts by accelerating activities that succeeded in the past—with the result that the market changes but the company does not and performance declines.[21] While investment in a market-sensing and -learning process is mandated by both market orientation and the speed of market change, it is important to recognize that making these processes effective may require decisive management action to address organizational barriers.

[19]Philip B. Evans and Thomas S. Wurster, "Strategy and the New Economics of Information," *Harvard Business Review,* September–October, 1997, 70–82. See also, Philip Evans and Thomas S. Wurster, *Blown To Bits: How the New Economics of Information Transforms Strategy* (Boston: Harvard Business School Press), 2000.
[20]Day, "The Capabilities of Market-Driven Organizations," 43.
[21]Donald Sull, *Why Good Companies Go Bad and How Great Managers Remake Them* (Cambridge MA: Harvard Business School Press), 2005.

Understanding and adjusting to cultural differences between markets has always been a challenge in marketing consumer products internationally. Many errors have been made:

- To sell a low-priced version of a best-selling U.S. auto to India, one company removed rear seat electric window controls to cut costs. Sales were poor because the company failed to understand that while the rear seat is low status in the west (it is where the children sit), it is high status in India (because the wealthy have chauffeurs).
- Western breakfast cereals sell poorly in India because local families want hot breakfasts and Western cereals do not survive contact with hot milk.
- P&G struggled with diaper sales in Brazil—in the Unites States parents demand add-ons like scents and biodegradable materials, but in Brazil many babies sleep in the parents' bed, so dryness is the top priority. A cheap, ultra-watertight diaper with no add-ons did well in the Brazilian market.

Tellingly, Intel employs a cultural anthropologist with the job title "director of interaction and experience research," with the goal of helping the chip maker power new devices, make new software, and enter new markets by providing technologists with better understanding of how people all over the world use computers, phones, and other devices.

Her studies include examining how people behave when they watch television, impacting on Intel's Smart-TV products. In studying the cellphone market, she recounts meeting a Muslim boy in Kuala Lumpur using his cellphone to orient him towards Mecca for prayer. She found a ceremonial store in Malaysia selling paper facsimiles of the latest cellphones, to be burned at funerals so dead relatives could talk to each other in the afterlife. She says "Technology is starting to manifest itself in every part of our lives, not just at work and home but in religious practices, our love lives, and how we keep secrets."

Intel is not alone in searching for much deeper understanding of how people use technology, to change how new products are developed. Microsoft, IBM, and Hewlett-Packard have anthropologists and ethnologists working alongside systems engineers and software developers.

Frog Design in San Francisco employs anthropologists to understand why the poorest people in the world buy cellphones and how they use them. Their research was the first to document the use of airtime as a currency, which led Vodafone to launch a money transfer system in Kenya and Afghanistan.

In parallel, in the pharmaceutical business, drug companies are focusing on the consumer experience as well as the medicine, using ethnography and semiotics to understand how patients really use medications. One result is the more discreet insulin "pen" to replace old-fashioned hypodermics, and bright colored plastic skins to wrap around insulin pens to make them less threatening to childhood diabetes sufferers.

Sources: Gillian Tett, "The Brazilian Nappy Challenge," *FT/Magazine,* February 12/13, 2011, 54. Michael V. Copeland, "Intel's Cultural Anthropologist," *Fortune,* September 27, 2010, 16–17. Andrew Jack, "An Experiment in Design," *Financial Times,* August 26, 2010, 10. Jessi Hempel, "Technology's Roving R&D Man," *Fortune,* December 6, 2010, 28.

The development of effective market-driven strategy is closely related to market-sensing capabilities and market-learning processes. Learning is increasingly proving to be a core capability of successful organizations. Nonetheless, it is important to recognize that learning and knowledge creation disrupt existing business models and open the way to new ones. Consider, for example, the impact of anthropological insights in international markets described in the GLOBAL APPLICATION.

Next, we examine the various methods of acquiring and processing information for use in marketing decision making. The objective is to show how the various information capabilities assist decision makers in strategic and operating decisions. A good marketing information management strategy takes into account the interrelationship of these capabilities.

Marketing Information and Knowledge Resources

Some marketing information resource development activity is concerned with creating processes for continuous scanning of markets rapidly note significant trends, events, and changes. Other activities may undertake specific, focused studies to answer management questions—such as the effectiveness of an advertising campaign in a market. Marketing information resources can be generated internally—for example, in analyzing company records, or conducting market research studies—or externally—using marketing research agencies and consultants. Enhancing the marketing information resources available to executives may involve using information sources that are already in existence—for example, a Google search for competitor offerings—or the development of new information resources through observation studies or survey work. There is a wide variety of potential information sources in enhancing market learning processes, and the marketing information system provides a way of integrating these.

Importantly, marketing research and information resources should be seen as a model for innovation and change, rather than simply supporting the incremental administration of brands.[22] Marketing information may challenge the assumptions managers make about customers and provide them with new insights to guide strategy choices. Illustrations of the search for market insights, the surprises uncovered, and their impact on management decisions are given in the STRATEGY APPLICATION.

Scanning Processes

Information resource development may be concerned with building processes for continuous monitoring of customers and markets to quickly identify and explain changes, new trends, and important events to which executives should respond. Effective scanning must balance the need to provide executives with relevant intelligence, while at the same time not attempting to report everything that happens in a market and overloading executives with information. Nonetheless, scanning may require watching for new opportunities outside the existing core markets.[23] The strategic challenge is to watch for the signals of disruptive change in the marketplace, which predict competitive battles to come, or highlight major strategic choices that executives must make about marketing strategy.[24] Scanning activities will vary across companies—from fashion trend spotting at H&M and Zara to daily monitoring of steel prices in different markets at companies like ArcelorMittall.

Recent advances in monitoring and customer feedback center on Internet-based conversations, and particularly those on blogging sites and social networks like Facebook and

---

[22]Peter Lorange, "Memo to Marketing," *Sloan Management Review,* Winter 2005, 16–20.

[23]George S. Day and Paul J. H. Shoemaker, "Scanning the Periphery," *Harvard Business Review,* November 2005, 135–148.

[24]Clayton M. Christensen, Scott D. Anthony, and Erik A. Roth, *Seeing What's Next: Using the Theories of Innovation to Predict Industry Change* (Boston: Harvard Business School Press), 2004.

Successful companies exploit many innovative approaches to generate new market insights, many of which do not rely on sophisticated technology:

- Toyota employees were asked to study autos in junkyards. One common problem was broken side view mirrors. That insight led to the invention of the folding mirror.

- In 2009, Morgan Stanley in London commissioned a paper on media and communications from a 15-year-old intern called Matthew Robson. His views were scrutinized by analysts everywhere from the *Huffington Post* to *The Hindu,* and were blogged on, twittered about, and discussed in boardrooms and investment offices around the world. The 15-year-old's insights were that his peers see online advertising as extremely annoying and pointless, they cannot be bothered to read newspapers, they never buy CDs or use Yellow Pages directories, and generally try to avoid paying for anything except concerts and cinema tickets. Teenagers do not buy smartphones for fear of losing them, and do not use Twitter because it uses up too much credit on the phone. The insights severely challenge assumptions that underpin many new business models. Some point out that executives should have asked their own children.

- The Lcafe in Tokyo is the country's first marketing café, targeting trend-conscious young people with samples of new products to collect feedback. The Lcafe target is Japanese women their 20s and 30s, who have an influential role in shaping new trends. Participants receive tokens to exchange for new product samples and provide their feedback and opinions.

- Pantone Color Institute is a division of Pantone Inc., employing people to travel the world to predict what colors will best sell products. Long before orange became a hot color in the United States, Pantone researchers had noticed its use in unlikely places like fences and front doors in Italy and Germany, in Morocco's natural dyes, and on monks cloaked in saffron robes. At the time in the United States orange was a color for discount stores not one associated with spirituality or trendiness. Since, orange has gone mainstream, covering such products as video cameras, KitchenAid blenders, and Ford's F-150 SVT Raptor. The Pantone goal is to predict the next trendy color that will grab consumer attention.

Sources: Beth Kowitt, "Innovation Education," *Fortune,* April 11, 2011, 16. Andrew Edgecliffe-Johnson, "The Text of a Generation," *Financial Times,* July 18–19, 2009, 11. Miho Inada, "Tokyo's Sample Café Targets Trend Makers," *Wall Street Journal,* August 24, 2009, 24. Alyssa Abkowitz, "The Color Committee Gets to Work," *Fortune,* October 26, 2009, 22–24.

Twitter. Examples of companies exploiting consumer feedback through social media are shown in the STRATEGY APPLICATION.

Organizing scanning effectively as a component of market sensing and learning may involve a number of initiatives or approaches:[25]

- Making **existing functional groups** responsible for scanning—though with the risk they will focus only on the familiar, not the periphery.

- **Create ad hoc issue groups**—identify important questions to address and assign them to task forces.

- **A high-level lookout**—IBM has a facility called the "Crow's Nest," a team scanning specific topics at the periphery of the organization and sharing insights with top management.

---

[25]This illustration is adapted from George S. Day and Paul J. H. Shoemaker, "Scanning the Periphery," *Harvard Business Review,* November 2005, 135–148.

The growth in social media networks like Facebook, Twitter, and others offers an innovative platform for interaction with consumers and the generation of insightful feedback to company offerings.

- Moxie.com is an online fashion boutique uses its "buyerchat" events to make decisions about products to stock. For example, to choose between two versions of a retro-style gingham dress from Los Angeles–based fashion label Knitted Dove, the buyer interrupts the sales meeting to put photographs on the social messaging site Twitter to get instant feedback from consumers. The chief excutive describes that as a radical embracing of the concept of crowdsourcing via social media, but inviting the site's customers to help influence the process of buying the next season's lines. The most committed participants get "junior buyer" and "buyer in training" online badges and gift vouchers.

- Fresh & Easy, the California-based grocery chain owned by Tesco from the U.K., conducts regular evening wine-tasting events, during which participants gather on Twitter at a fixed time, equipped with a preannounced selection of wines, and then share their reactions.

- Online reviews are becoming a valued source of direct feedback for retailers and manufacturers. Samsung Electronics started hosting reviews on its U.S. website in 2008, using technology provided by Bazaar-Voice, which is the dominant supplier of third-party review services in the United States, working with more than 500 brands including Wal-Mart, Home Depot, and Procter & Gamble. Samsung has changed the way it works as a result of very speedy customer review feedback—for example, moving flat-screen TV speakers from the side to the bottom of the product to better fit existing customer cabinets.

- In the hard-pressed fashion business, First Sight is a Pittsburgh firm that invites a retailer's customers to play an online game. They set up a virtual fashion store and stock and price merchandise the retailer is considering stocking. Feedback on their choices goes to the retailer in as little as 2 days. The goal of the online gaming is to alert retailers when to get into a trend and when to get out.

Sources: Jonathan Birchall, "Would You Buy This Dress? Online retailer Puts Its Wares to the Twitter Test," *Financial Times,* December 31, 2010, 11. Jonathan Birchall, "Customer Views You Can Use," *Financial Times,* September 3, 2009, 12. Jessica Shambora, "The Wisdom of Fashionistas," *Fortune,* September 27, 2010, 10.

- **New initiatives**—Shell created its Game Changer Program in 1996, to encourage managers to envision and test new opportunities beyond the core business: In its first 6 years it commercialized 30 technologies and created three new businesses.

- **Investing in start-ups**—modest investments may build a clear view of emerging technologies and markets.

- **Outsource**—use consultants for fresh perspectives on the business to be incorporated in strategic decision making.

One approach to presenting the result of scanning to executives is shown in Exhibit 5.1. The market-sensing grid can be used as a participative, cross-functional structure for capturing insights from scanning (and other marketing information resources as they become available). The process is to identify significant market events impacting on the business (or part of it) over a 3- to 5-year period, and to position events by estimated probability and impact. By including external views, such as suppliers, technology experts, distributors,

EXHIBIT 5.1
A Grid for Market Sensing

Probability of the Event Occurring

	High	Medium	Low
7			
6	Utopia		Field of Dreams
5			
4		Things to Watch	
3			
2	Danger		Future Risks
1			

Effect of the Event on the Company*

* 1 = Disaster, 2 = Very bad, 3 = Bad, 4 = Neutral, 5 = Good, 6 = Very good, 7 = Ideal.

customers, it is possible to build a picture of the marketplace that may challenge existing company beliefs and management assumptions, and identifies the highest priorities for further scanning and other information collection activities.[26]

Specific Marketing Research Studies

Marketing research is "the systematic gathering, recording, processing, and analyzing of marketing data, which—when interpreted—will help the marketing executive to uncover opportunities and to reduce risks in decision making."[27] Strategies for obtaining marketing research information include collecting existing information, using standardized research services, and conducting special research studies.

The starting point in undertaking specific marketing research studies is carefully defining the problem to be studied, indicating specific objectives, and determining what information is needed to help solve the problem. A problem definition framework to guide marketing research studies is shown in Exhibit 5.2.

Internal and External Marketing Information Resources

Marketing information resources exist internal to the company, as well as being collected from external sources.

Internal Information Resources

The internal information system of the firm affects the extent and ease of the collecting existing information. The nature and scope of the information and the information system

---

[26]Nigel F. Piercy and Nikala Lane, "Marketing Implementation: Building and Sustaining a Real Market Understanding," *Journal of Marketing Practice: Applied Marketing Science,* 2(3), 1996, 15–28.
[27]William R. Dillon, Thomas J. Madden, and Neil H. Firtle, *Marketing Research in a Marketing Environment,* 3rd ed. (Homewood, IL: Richard D. Irwin, 1994), 737.

EXHIBIT 5.2
Problem Definition to Guide Marketing Research Studies

Research Project and Scope	Research Objectives	Research Questions	Planned Outcomes
Describe the topic for the study and the background.	Set specific goals for the study - why is it being undertaken?	Identify the specific pieces of information required and the questions that need to be asked to obtain that information	When completed how should the results be presented for management use?

network will vary greatly from firm to firm and among industries. Even simple information systems are able to generate analyses of sales and cost data. Many firms have extensive internal information systems, or at least the capability to implement such systems. Recall the new customer information resources being created by CRM systems (see Chapter 4). There is a powerful case that successful companies fully exploit the customer information they have already collected and stored, which can be shared and reinterpreted for new insights, and which may even identify new product opportunities.[28]

Major organizations maintain internal marketing research units to undertake studies as required, although the trend in recent years has been to outsource at least part of the research process to external providers (marketing research agencies). Nonetheless, evidence suggests as much as 10 percent of many companies' research budgets stays in-house.[29]

External Information Resources

External marketing information resources include open source resources (freely available data on the Internet or in print sources), information services (paid-for, standardized reports and databases), and specific studies undertaken by marketing research agencies and consultants (for example, surveys of consumers). In the use of marketing research agencies for specific studies, it is important for executives to carefully manage relationships with these third-party providers of information resources.

Relationships with External Marketing Research Providers

Marketing information providers are likely to be marketing research firms. In the global marketing research industry in 2009, the top 25 marketing research firms had worldwide revenues of $17.4 billion.[30] These top 25 organizations accounted for approximately 56 percent of world expenditure through commercial firms for research purposes. Exhibit 5.3 shows the top ten U.S. agencies in 2010. Agency research commonly spans market measurement studies, media audience research, and customer satisfaction measurement. Research into the impact of the Internet on markets is growing rapidly.

With the increasing globalization of brands and international competition, growing emphasis is being placed on a global perspective on marketing research. Particular interest is being shown in research in China and India, but also in Latin America and parts of Africa, as well as eastern Europe and Russia. Particular problems in global research

---

[28]Ranjay Gulati, James Oldroyd, and Phanish Puranam, "Staring You in the Face," *Wall Street Journal,* September 22, 2008, R7.
[29]Jack Honomichl, "The 2011 Honomichl Top 50 Report," *Marketing News,* June 30, 2011, 11–19.
[30]Jack Honomichl, *Honomichi Global 25,* Special Section of the *Marketing News,* August 30, 2010, 1–59.

EXHIBIT 5.3 **Top Ten U.S. Marketing Research Firms in 2010**

Source: Extracted from Jack Honomichl, "The 2011 Honomichl Top 50 Report" *Marketing News,* June 30, 2011, p. 17.

U.S. Rank 2010	Organization	Headquarters	Website	U.S. research revenue ($ millions)	Global research revenue ($ millions)
1	The Nielsen Co.	New York	Nielsen.com	2,407	4,958
2	Kantar	London & Fairfield, Conn.	kantar.com	915	3,184
3	IMS Health Inc.	Norwalk, Conn.	imshealth.com	801	2,210
4	SymphonyIRI Group	Chicago, Ill.	symphonyiri.com	457	720
5	Westat Inc.	Rockville, Md.	westat.com	455	455
6	Arbitron Inc.	Columbia, Md.	arbitron.com	390	395
7	Ipsos	New York	ipsos-NA.com	380	1,513
8	GfK USA	New York	Gfkamerica.com	291	1,718
9	Synovate	London, U.K.	synovate.com	236	885
10	The NPD Group Inc.	Port Washington, N.Y.	NPD.com	174	240

relate to cross-cultural differences that impact on information quality and characteristics. For example, an industry rule of thumb is that in the Americas the farther north you go, the more reserved consumers are in what they express. The same consumer perception of the quality of a product might receive high scores in Latin America, average marks in the United States, and less favorable reviews in Canada, because of cultural differences. For companies in international markets, making allowances for such cultural differences in examining global marketing research is an important challenge.[31] Recall the earlier STRATEGY APPLICATION concerned with cultural anthropology in understanding how products are used in different cultures.

Formal research studies follow a step-by-step process beginning with defining the problem to be investigated and the objectives of the research. A project proposal should indicate the objectives, research method, sampling plan, method of analysis and cost. In deciding whether to undertake a special marketing research study and when interpreting the results, several considerations are important:

- **Defining the Problem.** Care must be exercised in formulating the research problem. It is essential to spell out exactly what information is needed to solve the problem. If this cannot be done, exploratory research should be conducted to help define the research problem and determine the objectives of the project. Caution should be exercised to avoid defining a symptom rather than the underlying problem—do falling sales reflect declining market size, new competitive activity, or ineffective promotion? It is useful to prepare a written statement of the research problem, specific objectives, the information that is needed, information sources, and when the information is needed. When companies contract with research firms to do the research, it is important that the supplier be as familiar as possible with the problem to be studied. Management needs to clearly define the intended project and may choose to involve the research supplier in defining the problem. Failure to adequately define and clarify the problem to be studied may undermine relationships between client and research agency.

---

[31]Catherine Arnold, "Global Perspective," *Marketing News,* May 15, 2004, 43.

- **Understanding the Limitations of the Research.** Most studies are unable to do everything that the user wishes to accomplish and also stay within the available budget. Priorities for the information that is needed should be indicated. Also, obtaining certain information may not be feasible. For example, measuring the impact of advertising on profits may not be possible due to the influence of many other factors on profits. Research suppliers should be able to indicate the limitations that may exist for a particular project. Discussions with a potential supplier are advisable before making a final commitment to the project. This will be useful in finalizing information need priorities.

- **Quality of the Research.** There are many challenges to obtaining sound research results. The available evidence indicates that some studies are not well designed and implemented and may contain misleading results. Factors that affect the quality of study results include the experience of the research personnel, skills in carefully managing and controlling the data collection process, the size of the sample, the wording of questions, and how the data are analyzed.

- **Costs.** Customized research studies are frequently expensive. The factors that affect study costs include sample size, the length of the questionnaire, and how the information will be obtained. The complexity of the study objectives and the analysis methods also increase the professional capabilities required in research personnel. Costs must be compared carefully to the likely benefits of the research to executives in making decisions.

- **Evaluating and Selecting Suppliers.** When selecting a marketing research supplier, it is useful to talk with prior clients to determine their satisfaction with the research firm. It is also important to identify consultants who are experienced in conducting the particular type of research needed by the user. Familiarity with the industry may also be important. Spending some time in evaluating a potential research supplier is very worthwhile. Experience and qualifications are important in selecting the supplier. Several useful screening questions are shown in Exhibit 5.4. These could be used to evaluate possible suppliers before asking for a detailed research proposal from the supplier.

- **Research Methods.** It is important to recognize that the research problem to be addressed indicates the appropriateness of different research methods. Large-scale consumer/company surveys may not be the most appropriate approach. Qualitative research methods, rather than surveys and other quantitative methods, may be more appropriate in some circumstances. The use of focus groups is a typical way of collecting rich qualitative data, as compared to the more representative information from a survey or market test.

EXHIBIT 5.4
Screening Potential Marketing Research Suppliers

Research agency screening issues:
- Recommendations from other clients.
- Industry and manager opinions about the agency.
- Agency size and resources.
- Agency experience in this type of marketing research.
- Agency online capabilities.
- Sub-contracting arrangements at the agency.
- Interviewer training and supervision.
- Arrangements for validating data collected, e.g., by interviewers.
- Quality of research instruments for the project, e.g., questionnaires.
- Adequate arrangements for sampling.
- Quality of reports produced for other clients (if not confidential).
- Warranties and guarantees provided.

Existing Marketing Information Sources

In-Company Resources

There is considerable value and potential in using the information in the organization's current system. Management should structure information systems to capture value. Information is a scarce and valuable resource that affects the future success or failure of the firm. Management may not have control over the actions of competitors or consumers, but an effective information system provides a way to anticipate and react.

The product mix and the nature of business operations influence what type of internal marketing information system is appropriate in a particular firm. The system needs to be designed to meet the information needs of the organization. Manufacturers have different information requirements from retailers or wholesalers. The size and complexity of the firm also influence the composition of the information system.

The costs and benefits of the information must be evaluated for both short-term and long-term planning. Incremental efforts and expenditures in the early stages of creating an internal information system may avoid future costly modifications. It is critical to consider a long-term perspective in evaluating information system decisions.

Harrah's Entertainment is an interesting example of a company developing market-led strategy on the basis of existing information. Harrah's is the largest gaming corporation in the world and operates 52 casinos in the United States and overseas and in 2007 had $11 billion in revenue. In a sector known for fickle customers, Harrah's built a strategy based on customer loyalty. Harrah's has used the data in their customer loyalty program—the Total Gold card— to uncover consumer preferences based on tracking the millions of individual transactions conducted. Harrah's found that 26 percent of their customers generated 82 percent of their revenues. These were not the high-rollers targeted by competitors, they were former teachers, doctors, bankers, and machinists—middle-aged and senior adults with discretionary time and income who enjoy income. They typically do not stay in casino hotels, but visit a casino on the way home from work or on a weekend night out. They respond differently to marketing and promotions because they enjoy the anticipation and excitement of gambling itself. The data show that women gamble more than men and older women out-gamble everyone. Harrah's strategy provides visibly higher levels of service to the customers with greatest value to the company. The transactional data can even be used to see which particular customers are playing which slot machines and to identify what it was about the particular machine that appealed to them. Harrah's successful strategy is driven by leveraging an existing information source to build competitive differentiation. Nonetheless, a leveraged buy-out in 2008 immediately prior to a collapse in consumer spending has left Harrah's with a high debt burden at a time of reduced revenues, which will further test the robustness of its strategy.[32]

Open Source Resources

A wide and rich variety of information resources exist in the form of published information that can be accessed freely or at low cost. Government and international agencies provide valuable statistical sources on such areas as population trends, economic development, household purchasing, and international market differences. Universities, private research firms, industry and trade organizations, and consultants often publish useful information.

---

[32]Gary Loveman, "Diamonds in the Data Mine," *Harvard Business Review,* May 2003, 109–113. Karl Taro Greenfeld, "How to Survive in Vegas," *Bloomberg BusinessWeek,* August 9–15, 2010, 70–75.

Internet Resources

Frequently information can be accessed online. For example, the World Bank (www .worldbank.com) and the U.S. Central Intelligence Agency publication *The World Factbook* (www.cia.gov/library) both provide concise and high-quality data on the economic performance, governmental characteristics, communications, and infrastructure for the majority of countries in the world. The Internet also provides more general search facilities, using Google or other search engines, to identify sources of information on topics of interest. Online databases like Wikipedia, the online encyclopedia, can indicate prior research conducted on the topic of interest and further sources of information. While charges may apply to access some proprietary databases, many are available for no cost.

Naturally, some care is needed to evaluate the quality and objectivity of Internet information sources, but they should not be ignored as a marketing information resource.

Research Agency Resources

A wide variety of marketing information is available for purchase in special publications and on a subscription basis from research agencies. A key advantage to the standardized information in these resources is that the costs of collection and analysis are shared by many users. The major limitation is that the information may not correspond well with the user's individual needs. Many services allow online access to data, enabling subscribers to automatically input external information into their own information systems.

Many standardized information services are available to meet a wide range of decision making needs.[33] For example,

> The Nielsen Group (www.nielsen.com) offers *Consumer Watch* services—audience measurement and analytical services related to TV, online and mobile devices, providing audience data to the media and advertising industries; and *Consumer Buy* services—retail scanner and consumer panel-based measurement and a wide range of analytics to allow clients to manage their brands, uncover new sources of demand, launch and grow new products, improve their marketing programs and establish more effective consumer relationships. The consumer panel, for instance, collects data from more than 250,000 household panelists across 27 countries, who use in-home scanners to record purchases from every shopping trip.

Using the large data banks collected and organized by these services, many different analyses can be made, depending on a company's information needs. The cost of the information for use by one company would be prohibitive. By sharing the database, a wide range of company information needs can be met.

Creating New Marketing Information

When existing marketing information resources do not address executives' research needs, then the requirement may be to collect new information. Approaches may include observation and ethnographic studies, quantitative research surveys, or Internet-based data collection. These data collection methods may require marketing research agency resources or be carried out by analysts inside the company.

Observation and Ethnographic Studies

Studies involving observation include, for example, counting customer traffic flows in a retail store, measuring waiting times for service in a shop, or the reaction of exhibition visitors to display stands.

---

[33] A description of the top 25 companies in the global marketing research industry can be found in the *Honomichi Global 25,* Special Section of the *Marketing News,* August 30, 2010, 1–59.

Considerable attention is being given to the use of ethnographic approaches in collecting marketing information. Research suggests that it may be mistaken for executives to assume that consumers think in a well-reasoned or rational way, or that they can readily explain their thinking and behavior.[34] Accordingly, asking customers direct questions may give misleading results, and observational techniques like ethnography may be more insightful.

Ethnography is a social science based on anthropology and its use in marketing studies is based on the idea that richer information and insight can be generated by immersion in the consumer's life. For example, one ethnography project examined the behavior of parents and children shopping together by observing them in stores and recording basic information such as what they said to each other.[35]

Similarly, when WD-40 wanted to reposition a product line as essential bathroom cleaners, the company undertook open-ended research to try to understand how consumers clean and how they shop. In-home ethnographies and focus groups examined consumer cleaning habits and product usage. They found consumers engage in two types of cleaning—weekly deep cleans and quick daily cleaning—and liked the idea of a brand focused on the bathroom. The brand's new positioning—X14 as The Bathroom Expert—and its competitive differentiation, come directly from insights into how people clean.[36]

There are a growing number of cases where traditional research approaches have failed to identify the insights important to new marketing strategy initiatives, but where qualitative, ethnographic research has proved effective:

> Marriott used an ethnographic research agency to rethink the hotel experience for an increasingly important customer segment: the young, technology sophisticated "road warrior." A team including a designer, an anthropologist, a writer and an architect spend six weeks touring hotels in twelve cities. They loitered in hotel lobbies, cafes and bars, and asked guests to graph what they were doing hour by hour. The findings were: hotels are generally good at serving large parties, but not small groups of business travelers; hotel lobbies tend to be dark and poorly designed for doing business; Marriott lacked places where guests could comfortably combine work with pleasure outside their rooms. The result was the reinvention of the lobbies of Marriott and Renaissance Hotels, creating for each a social zone, with small tables, brighter lights and wireless Web access. Another area allows solo travelers to work in larger, quiet, semiprivate spaces.
>
> General Electric used ethnographic research to develop its competitive positioning in the plastic fibers business—providing material for high value products like fire-retardant jackets and bulletproof vests. Researchers interviewed presidents, managers and engineers at textile makers, touring their offices and photographing their plants. One major insight caused GE to rethink their strategy: GE thought that the fibers industry was a commodity business based on obtaining the cheapest materials. What it found instead was an artisan-based industry where customers wanted to collaborate from the earliest stages to develop high-performance materials—these are people with curiosity who like to get their hands dirty. GE now shares prototypes with customers, by-passing executives, and working closely with engineers on technical questions. A considerable advantage has been achieved in access to a new market.[37]
>
> Intel used ethnographic research to examine the use of computers by children in China. The work involved a two-and-a-half year study of Asian families in seven countries,

---

[34]Gerald Zaltman, *IIow Customers Think: Essential Insights Into the Mind of the Market,* (Boston: Harvard Business School Press), 2003.

[35]Rupert Steiner, "Homing in On Consumers," *Sunday Times,* August 25, 2002, S3, 8.

[36]Michael Fielding, "A Clean Slate," *Marketing News,* May 1, 2007, 9.

[37]Spencer E. Ante, "The Science of Desire," *BusinessWeek,* June 5, 2006, 98–106.

examining their lives and values. In the US the conventional parents' belief is that a child should be bought a computer in the early stage of his/her development—exposing the child to computing at the earliest age. In China, parents believe the opposite—they want children to learn Mandarin, and the computer is a distraction from this. This insight led Intel designers to launch a PC aimed at the Chinese home educational market, which has a touch-sensitive screen that allows users to write in Mandarin, tracing the order in which the character is being written (correct stroke order being an important part of the learning process). Chinese parents also had misgivings about allowing children unlimited Internet access. Locks and keys are important symbols of authority in China. Instead of installing a software-based key on the PC, Intel included a physical locking mechanism, visible elsewhere in the room, and reassuring to parents.[38]

The strength of qualitative research, such as ethnography, is in the richness of the data, which can create important insights into the market. The weakness is that the small numbers of subjects studied means that it is difficult to know if the results are representative of the wider market. Qualitative approaches of this kind may be followed by more conventional, quantitative studies to confirm and validate findings.

Research Surveys

Research surveys are initiated in response to problems or special information needs. Examples include market segmentation, new-product concept tests, product use tests, brand-name research, and advertising recall tests. Studies use field surveys involving personal, phone, or mail interviews with respondents who represent target populations.

Internet-Based Research

The impact of Internet resources on the ability to collect new market information is considerable. New and speedy ways of conducting survey studies using electronic questionnaires, e-mail questionnaires, and electronic panels are expanding rapidly. By the mid-2000s expenditure on Internet-based marketing research exceeded $1.2 billion annually, and there are some indications that internet-based research now accounts for more than 50 percent of all marketing research expenditure.[39]

Online market research services, offer less expensive and more rapidly available market research surveys. For example, Insight Express provides clients with a survey template to build an online questionnaire, allowing them to sample from a panel of 100 million with a patented sampling methodology, pay by credit card, and download results within a few days. An online research project may cost a small fraction of a traditional research project. Ice cream company Ben & Jerry's is an Insight Express client that transferred to online research because traditional data collection was too slow. An in-house database of Ben & Jerry's loyal customers is sampled alongside an Insight Express panel to test new flavors and new products. While reservations exist regarding the quality of the data produced by some online services, they provide a relatively inexpensive route to sensing the market quickly.

Useful insights can also be built by examining customer online behavior. Key words entered into search engines provide insight into competitive preferences and purchase intentions, bearing in mind that nearly 80 percent of all online purchases start at a major search engine. User clicks on a company's website can be counted to identify successful promotions and cross-sells between products. The website can be used as a platform for

---

[38]Kim Thomas, "Anthropologists Get to the Bottom of Customers' Needs," *Financial Times,* August 24, 2005, 9.
[39]Allison Enright, "Web Consumer Habits Yield Real-World Results," *Marketing News,* November 1, 2006, 20.

experimentation—comparing the impact of alternate content on site visitors. The importance of online research of this kind is underlined by customer multiple channel behavior—it is estimated that almost 90 percent of online shoppers actually complete their purchase by buying offline at the store.[40]

For example, Anglo-Dutch food and personal products company Unilever spends around $400 million a year on marketing research. It now conducts more than 80 percent of its U.S. research online. The policy is to exploit the speed and low cost of the Web to research consumer behavior. Unilever's estimate is that the Web is 10 to 20 percent cheaper than traditional data collection methods. The company expects increasingly to shift to Internet projects in other countries—the trigger is when a minimum of half the population has Internet access. Unilever data testing suggests Internet responses were more honest than those produced by traditional methods, and the company is moving from brand research into more strategic work in Internet research projects.[41]

Proactive uses of Internet-based data concerning customer behavioral data are illustrated in the INTERNET APPLICATION, although these approaches may rely on marketing research agency support. Patterns of online behavior provide a rich source of market insight and tracking technologies are rapidly developing in sophistication.

Marketing and Management Information Systems

Enhanced technology capabilities have led many companies to invest in formalized information systems to exploit their data resources. Important issues include the establishment of specialized marketing information systems, as well as more general management information systems, and the potentials for marketing decision support systems and expert systems.

Marketing Information Systems

The marketing information system provides a mechanism for integrating marketing information and intelligence resources. A marketing information system "consists of people, equipment, and procedures to gather sort, analyze, evaluate and distribute needed, timely, and accurate information to marketing decision makers"—it is developed from internal company records, marketing intelligence activities, and marketing research.[42]

Importantly, while companies have invested heavily in developing information systems, inward-oriented firms emphasize enhanced operating efficiency and reduced costs through automating information processing. The market-oriented firm, however, looks for ways in which information systems can make them more effective in the marketplace.[43]

Databases are a particularly relevant form of information resource, frequently supported by CRM systems. For example, in its European retail operation, supermarket Tesco uses its loyalty club data to indicate demographic, income, and housing characteristics of consumers in the catchment area of a store to design appropriate product assortments—stores near large universities may concentrate on high-value ready-meal replacements from pizzas to take-away and precooked curries, while stores in family residential areas emphasize extensive food choices, cooking ingredients, and products for babies and children. Recall the growing role of customer relationship management (CRM) technology in building new databases (see Chapter 4)—or data warehouses—from the company's own customer contacts.

[40]Eric J. Hansen, "Apply Online Market Data for Offline Insights," *Marketing News,* April 1, 2007, 30.

[41]Carlos Grande, "Unilever to Cash In on Benefits of Web Research," *Financial Times,* April 17, 2007, 18.

[42]Philip Kotler and Kevin Lane Keller, *A Framework for Marketing Management,* 3rd ed (Upper Saddle River NJ: Pearson/Prentice-Hall, 2007), 41.

[43]Noel Capon and James M. Hulbert, *Marketing Management in the 21st Century* (Upper Saddle River NJ: Prentice-Hall, 2001).

By dissecting online behavioral data about Internet users, new generations of predictive technology are developing, fueled by growing streams of data from mouse clicks to search queries. Analysis looks at patterns of clicks, searches, purchases, and other variables to establish patterns and develop new insights into consumer behavior.

Intense interest in personal data about Internet users is booming, along with the practice of "scraping"—using sophisticated software to harvest online conversations and collect personal details from social networking sites, resume sites, and online forums where people share their lives. Tracking peoples' activities online to gather details of their behavior and personal interests has become big business. There is even software to match peoples' real names to the pseudonyms they use on blogs, social nets, and online forums.

Nielsen Buzzmetrics is a leader in social media monitoring, collecting data from 130 million blogs, 8,000 message boards, Twitter, and social networks. Its services include Threat-Tracker, which alerts a company if its brand is being discussed in a negative way.

A new tool is collecting the equivalent of fingerprints from every computer, cellphone, and TV in the world—every device will have a "reputation" based on its owner's online behavior, shopping habits, and demographics. This will be more difficult for users to block than earlier tools to monitor online behavior, such as browser cookies. Similarly, "deep packet inspection" technology provides a powerful way of reading packets of data traveling across the Internet to track not just Web browsing but all online activity.

The growth of social networks like Facebook and Twitter has led to companies scrambling to decode the new data about peoples' online relationships to develop new insights. They are finding that a person is more likely to buy something if online "friends" have bought it. For example, San Francisco company Rapleaf harvests data from blogs, online forums, and social networks, following the network behavior of 480 million people, and advises companies on promotions. Rapleaf found from "friendship" data that borrowers are a better bet if their friends have higher credit ratings.

Insurance companies are, for example, preparing to use people's Facebook profiles as a way of setting premiums based on lifestyles—online data about food purchases, activities, and social groups provide an indicator of life expectancy.

Sources: Stephen Baker, "What's a Friend Worth?" *BusinessWeek,* June 1, 2009, 32–36. Stephen Baker, "The Web Knows What You Want," *BusinessWeek,* July 27, 2009, 48–49. Julia Angwin and Steve Stecklow, "'Scrapers Dig Deep on web for Data that Companies Covet," *Wall Street Journal,* October 13, 2010, 16–17. Robin Henry, "Insurers Use Facebook to Vet Lifestyles," *Sunday Times,* December 5, 2010, S1, 18. Julia Angwin and Jennifer Valentino-DeFries, "New Online Tracking Frontier," *Wall Street Journal,* December 2, 2010, 14–15. Steve Stecklow and Paul Sonne, "Shunned Profile Method is on the Verge of a Comeback," *Wall Street Journal,* November 25, 2010, 16–17.

These new data sources are the focus of many data-mining exercises and can create new insights into customer behavior.

Companies vary considerably in the degree and way to which they have formalized marketing information systems. It is useful to consider the nature of more general management information systems and moves toward the development of marketing decision-support systems for additional insight. The marketing information system may operate as an independent entity, or as a component of the more general management information system.

Management Information Systems

Management information systems (MISs) provide raw data to decision makers throughout a firm. The system collects data on the transactions and operations of the firm and may include competitor and environmental information. The decision makers (and systems analysts) are responsible for extracting the data relevant for a decision and in the appropriate format to facilitate the process. The system can provide information for decisions at all levels of the organization. Lower- and middle-level managers are likely to use the system most often for operating decisions. The system may generate routine reports for frequent operating decisions, such as weekly sales by product, or may be queried for special analyses on an as-needed basis. Nonroutine decisions may consist of tracking the sales performance of a sales district over several months, determining the number of customer returns for a particular good, or listing all customers or suppliers within a given geographic area. The basic MIS collects data and allows for retrieval and manipulation of format in an organized manner. Typically, the MIS does not interact in the decision-making process. More advanced MIS capabilities provide important decision analysis capabilities.

Marketing Decision-Support Systems

A decision-support system (DSS) assists in the decision making process using the information captured by the MIS. A marketing decision-support system (MDSS) integrates data that are not easily found, assimilated, or formatted or readily manipulated with software and hardware into a decision-making process that provides the marketing decision maker with assistance when needed.[44] The MDSS allows the user flexibility in applications and in format. An MDSS can be used for various levels of decision making ranging from determining reorder points for inventory to launching a new product.

Expert systems are an extension of decision support systems and apply a variety of sophisticated models to make inferences from a knowledge base, which are significant to marketing decisions.[45] These tools have considerable potential for leveraging the value of marketing information.

Marketing Intelligence and Knowledge Management

Extracting the maximum sensing and learning value from marketing information resources is enhanced by efforts to develop formal information systems. However, in the pursuit of this goal, increasing attention is also being given to active marketing intelligence gathering and knowledge management approaches. The potential for a chief knowledge officer to manage learning processes is a relevant development, with the goal of leveraging customer knowledge for competitive advantage.

Marketing Intelligence

Importantly, we have shown that the emphasis on market sensing in market-driven companies does not rely on hard data alone. For example, many companies have invested in in-company intelligence units to coordinate and disseminate "soft" or qualitative data and improve shared corporate knowledge.[46] Intelligence may come from published materials in trade and scientific journals, salesperson visit reports, programs of customer visits by executives, social contacts, feedback from trade exhibitions and personal contacts, or even

[44]Nikolaos F. Matsatsinis and Y. Siskos, *Intelligent Support Systems for Marketing Decisions* (New York, Springer, 2002). Berend Wierenga and Gerrit van Bruggen, *Marketing Management Support Systems: Principles, Tools and Implementation* (New York: Springer, 2000).

[45]Arvind Rangaswamy, Raymond R. Burke, Jerry Wind, and Jehoshua Eliashberg, *Expert Systems for Marketing,* Marketing Science Institute Working Paper 87-107 (Cambridge, MA: Marketing Science Institute, 1987). Luiz Moutinho, Bruce Curry, Fiona Davies and Paulo Rita, *Computer Modelling and Expert Systems in Marketing* (London: Routledge, 1995).

[46]Thomas A. Stewart, "Getting Real About Brainpower," *Fortune,* November 27, 1995.

rumor in the marketplace. Formal marketing intelligence gathering activities may be an important element of the scanning processes we discussed earlier.

Knowledge Management

There is increasing recognition that knowledge about customers should be managed as a strategic asset, because competitive advantage can be created by not merely possessing current market information but by knowing how to use it. Market knowledge is inextricably linked to organizational learning and market orientation in the market-driven company.[47]

Peter Drucker argues, for example, that often 90 percent of the information that companies collect is internal—market research and management reports that only tell executives about their own company—while the real challenge is to build knowledge about new markets they do not yet serve and new technologies they do not yet possess.[48] Knowledge that builds competitive advantage involves major emphasis on rigorous customer perspectives and competitor comparisons.[49]

Role of the Chief Knowledge Officer

To meet this challenge, some companies have established positions with titles such as chief knowledge officer or chief learning officer. While the titles and the job responsibilities vary, all appear linked to improving an organization's knowledge management and learning processes. This may be a staff position with only a few people involved, or instead, responsibility for databases, a technical infrastructure, and related knowledge functions.[50] The position may report to chief executive officer, information officer, or other high level executive.

Other organizations have developed a management role described as a chief learning officer, with a more general role in developing and enhancing company-wide learning processes. For example, Shell Oil has appointed a head of global learning to stimulate individual and organizational skills in learning, focused on business improvement.[51] Interestingly, the Shell initiative underlines the cross-functional nature of organizational learning processes, and the potential role of human resource development functions in working with departments like marketing to enhance learning processes.

While there appear to be differences between the role and functions of knowledge and learning officers, both positions do not occur in the same company.[52] Knowledge management is concerned with knowledge (information) collection and linking information within the organization. While the future of the position is not clear, as it develops there is likely to be a relationship between knowledge management and the discussion in this chapter of continuous learning about markets.

Leveraging Customer Knowledge

One study is illustrative of methods being employed by companies to improve the availability and use of customer knowledge in impacting strategic decisions.[53]

---

[47]Rohit Deshpande, "From Market Research Use to Market Knowledge Management," in Rohit Deshpande, ed., *Using Market Knowledge* (Thousand Oaks, California: Sage, 2001), 1–8.

[48]Peter Drucker, *Peter Drucker on the Profession of Management* (Boston: Harvard Business School Press, 1998).

[49]George S. Day, "Learning About Markets," in Rohit Deshpande, ed., *Using Market Knowledge* (Thousand Oaks, California: Sage, 2001), 9–30.

[50]Thomas A. Stewart, "Is This Job Really Necessary?" *Fortune,* January 12, 1998, 154–155.

[51]See http://sww-learn.sshel.com.

[52]Thomas Stewart, *Fortune,* ibid.

[53]Eric Lesser, David Mundel, and Charles Wiecha, "Managing Customer Knowledge," *Journal of Business Strategy,* November–December, 2000, 35–37.

Creating "Customer Knowledge Development Dialogues"

For example, Chrysler's Jeep division runs customer events called "Jeep Jamborees," attracting enthusiasts for the vehicle. Jeep employees connect with customers through informal conversations and semi-formal round-tables. Engineers and ethnographic researchers focus on the Jeep owner's relationship with the vehicle, driving changes to existing models and plans for new models.

Operating Enterprise-Wide "Customer Knowledge Communities"

IBM, for example, uses collaborative Internet workspace called the CustomerRoom with major accounts, where individuals throughout its divisions and functions can exchange knowledge with each other and with the customer.

Capturing Customer Knowledge at the Point of Customer Contact

Customer Relationship Management systems capture customer behavior and response information which offers rich potential for better insights into issues like customer defection and competitors' strengths, as well as emerging customer needs and perceptions.

Management Commitment to Customer Knowledge

Management responsibility includes investing resources, time, and attention in maintaining customer dialogs and communities as a commitment to enhanced organizational understanding of the customer. For example, approaches by some companies include planned programs of customer visits for cross-functional teams of executives as a systematic way of acquiring customer information, but also building superior understanding and responsiveness to customer perspectives.[54]

Ethical Issues in Collecting and Using Information

Lastly, important privacy and ethical issues concerning the role of information in the organization need to be assessed by managers and professionals. Questions regarding ethical and socially responsible behavior are escalating in importance for individual executives and organizations. These questions may impact particularly on approaches to collecting customer information, and the uses made of that information.

Invasion of Customer Privacy

The dramatic increase in use of databases has generated concerns about the invasion of privacy of individuals. Companies have responded to the issue by asking customers to indicate their preferences concerning mailing lists and other uses of the information. Nonetheless, concerns about this issue will undoubtedly continue as the sophistication of communications technology and software continues to develop.

Consider, for example, the use of patient information in the drug industry. Database marketing by pharmaceutical companies is guided by information obtained from toll-free number calls, subscription to magazines, and pharmacy questionnaires.[55] This information can be used to guide database marketing programs, targeting people with specific health concerns such as depression, arthritis, and other problems. Some patients are objecting

---

[54]Edward F. McQuarrie and Shelby H. McIntyre, "Implementing the Marketing Concept Through a Program of Customer Visits," in Rohit Deshpande, ed., *Using Market Knowledge* (Thousand Oaks, California: Sage, 2001), 163–190.

[55]William M. Bulkeley, "Prescriptions, Toll-Free Numbers Yield a Gold Mine for Marketers," *Wall Street Journal,* April 17, 1998, B1 and B3.

about the use of their prescription data to guide direct mail and other promotional efforts. Yet further objections relate to the possible sharing of medical information databases of this kind with other parties, such as insurance companies who may want to determine premiums on the basis of health data for existing patients and their children.

Indeed, public concern about identity theft abuses surrounding companies holding and selling personal information is leading to greater regulatory control of individual information use.[56] Further privacy dilemmas are raised, for example, by the potential for using radio frequency identification (RFID) tags to monitor consumer products throughout their life—RFID tags in clothes could be used to track the wearer's movements and activities throughout the life of the apparel. While the data possibilities are rich, concerns exist over invasion of privacy and inappropriate use of the data collected.[57] While the Google search engine generates rich and valuable data about individuals' Web behavior of considerable relevance to advertising and marketing decisions, critics are concerned that Google has unwittingly created a form of privatized surveillance well suited to government use in countries like China.[58] While companies have responded to the mood of the public concerning environmentalism and ethical consumerism, individual privacy rights may also be a leading issue.

Information and Ethics

Related to the issue of invasion of privacy is the issue of how companies and research suppliers should respond to ethical issues. For example, should a prospective client share a supplier's detailed project proposal with a competing supplier? A central issue concerns which organization pays for the cost of preparing the proposal. If the proposal is prepared at the expense of the supplier, then the proposal is the property of the supplier.[59] Sharing the proposal with its competition would be an issue of questionable ethics.

Other issues relate to the ways in which information is collected and from whom it is collected. There are major professional restrictions, for example, on collecting marketing information from children. The possible use of Internet chat rooms to create dialogues with child consumers avoids conventional restrictions, but poses a substantial ethical dilemma for executives presented with such data, as well as risks to corporate reputation.

In terms of the dilemmas that may emerge in how information is collected, consider the use of medical brain-scanning technology to capture clues as to consumer product preferences and reactions to marketing messages described in the ETHICS APPLICATION. The use of brain-scanning technology promises very useful marketing information. Brain-scanning studies have examined predicting memory recall based on the amount of memory encoding taking place when a person scans a product or package; comparing brain responses to new products compared to existing versions; providing quantitative evaluation of the memorability and comprehensibility of advertisements placed in different media; and providing flavor and fragrance houses with physiological evidence that their fragrances really do induce the mood swings they claim.[60] Executives face difficult issues in deciding if "neuromarketing" is an acceptable use of medical technology or whether it breaches the individual's right to privacy.

---

[56]Stephanie Kirchgaessner, "Access Denied: The Data Industry May Face New Restrictions After Privacy Breaches," *Financial Times,* May 20, 2005, 14.

[57]Jon Ungoed-Thomas, "Hidden Surveillance Chips Can Keep Tabs on Shoppers," *Sunday Times,* February 5, 2006, 1–7.

[58]John Lanchester, "Big Google Is Watching You," *Sunday Times,* January 29, 2006, 5–3.

[59]Dillon, Madden, and Firtle, *Marketing Research in a Marketing Environment,* 48. Elizabeth MacDonald and Joanne S. Lublin, "In the Debris of a Failed Merger: Trade Secrets," *Wall Street Journal,* March 10, 1998, B1 and B10.

[60]Gemma Calvert, "It's a No-Brainer," *The Marketer,* December 2006, 19–21.

Medical research has created the magnetic resonance imaging (MRI) scanner to detect injury and disease associated with the brain. However, recent uses of scanning technology leads some to suggest they should be redefined as "market research imaging" machines.

- MRI technology and software allows the machine to picture the flow of blood in the brain in response to visual stimuli—almost a picture of thoughts pinpointing what part of the brain recognizes things, enabling researchers to understand better the very essence of the mind and how it thinks, decides, and feels. This is "functional" MRI technology (fMRI).

- A controversial use of fMRI is probing customer preferences—sometimes called "neuromarketing"—researchers at Harvard, Emory, Caltech, and Baylor are studying how consumer preferences for different kinds of products track with activity in different parts of the brain, as well as reactions to marketing messages.

- A company in California offers a service to Hollywood studios to test audiences as they watch movie trailers to see which generate the most "brain buzz."

- Consumer watchdog Gary Ruskin complains "it's wrong to use a medical technology for marketing, not healing."

- Other ethical concerns include the issue of privacy.

- Prominent neurobiologist, Donald Kennedy, former head of the U.S. Food and Drug Administration, urges caution in collecting brain data: "our brains are us, marking out the special character of our personal capacities, emotions and convictions. . . . As to my brainome, I don't want anyone to know it for any purpose whatsoever."

- A further issue is whether brain scan data should be made available to insurers, employers, and even law enforcement agencies.

Sources: Joan O'C Hamilton, "Journey to the Center of the Mind," *BusinessWeek,* April 19, 2004, 66–67. Aili McConnon, "If Only I Had a Brain to Scan," *BusinessWeek,* January 22, 2007, 19.

Information sharing with research suppliers, other external contractors, strategic alliance partners, and acquisition/merger prospects often involves highly confidential information. There are many possible situations that present ethical questions and concerns. Companies normally sign confidentiality agreements. Nonetheless, revealing trade secrets is a risk that relies primarily on the ethical behavior of the participants. Moreover, these situations offer excellent opportunities for learning.

Importantly, the generation, collection, and application of intelligence and information resources in strategic marketing must be conducted within a framework provided by corporate ethical guidelines and social responsibility initiatives, as well as the individual ethical standards of executives and the expectations of stakeholder groups like shareholders and employees. Attention to the appropriateness of behavior in this area is a growing concern.

Summary

Developing and enhancing market learning processes are critical activities in the market-oriented company and underpin the development of effective market-driven strategies. Responding effectively to fast-changing markets and intense competition demands deep customer knowledge and insight. Market knowledge management is a core capability for companies pursuing a market-driven approach to strategy.

Market-sensing processes are the foundation for the learning organization and developing competitive advantage from superior customer understanding. The basis for superior customer knowledge is a range of marketing information and knowledge resources. These resources include active scanning processes, as well as specific marketing research studies. Information and intelligence resources are both internal to the company and external in the marketplace, and both require management attention. Where external information resources are accessed through the use of a marketing research agency, careful attention should be given to managing the relationship with the information provider.

A useful distinction is between existing and new information resources. Existing resources include in-company records, open source resources like online databases, and published research agency studies. Creating new marketing information may involve observation and ethnographic studies, research surveys, and Internet-based research. Marketing and management information systems provide frameworks for integrating information resources and displaying them to decision makers.

Underpinning the effective management of market learning processes are active approaches to marketing intelligence gathering and to knowledge management. The role of the chief knowledge officer or the chief learning officer is becoming increasingly relevant to developments in developing a company's learning capabilities. The goal is leveraging customer knowledge effectively.

There is growing attention to the ethical issues surrounding the collection and use of market and customer information. Individual rights to privacy, information sharing, collecting data from the vulnerable, and invasive data collection approaches are illustrative. Corporate ethical frameworks and the ethical standards of individual executives are important in ensuring responsible behavior in this area.

Questions for Review and Discussion

1. Discuss how an organization's marketing information skills and resources contribute to its distinctive capabilities.

2. How would you explain to a group of top-level executives the relationship between market-orientation and continuous learning about markets?

3. Outline an approach to developing an effective market sensing capability for a regional full-service bank.

4. Compare and contrast the use of standardized information services as an alternative to special research studies for tracking the performance of a new packaged food product.

5. Suppose the management of a retail floor covering (carpet, tile, wood) chain is considering a research study to measure household awareness of the retail chain, reactions to various aspects of wallpaper purchase and use, and identification of competing firms. How could management estimate the benefits of such a study in order to determine if the study should be conducted?

6. Are there similarities between marketing intelligence and the operations of the U.S. Central Intelligence Agency? Do companies ever employ business spies?

7. What obstacles may be faced in enhancing a company's ability to learn more and better about its customers, and how should they be addressed?

8. Why would a company consider observational or ethnographic research in preference to conventional surveys?

9. Data mining from databases is receiving increased attention in many companies. Discuss the underlying logic of data mining.

10. What are the relevant issues that need to be considered when obtaining the services of an outside supplier for a marketing research project?

11. What do you consider to be the proper ethical limits on the collection and use of customer information by companies?

Internet Applications

A. Revisit the list of major marketing research agencies in Exhibit 5.3. Visit several of the websites listed. Examine the major types of information provided both as standardized services and special study capabilities. List these and identify the ways in which such resources can impact on marketing decisions.

B. Select a well-known company or brand and use a search engine to find Web pages that include its name. Review the content of blogs and online reviews, and examine the lessons that the company should learn from this feedback. Discuss the impact of Internet-based information on traditional ideas about confidentiality and privacy.

Applications

A. Revisit the INTERNET APPLICATION "The Growth in Internet Information Resources for Market Sensing." What are the major advantages of the Web in developing marketing information resources, but what are the potential disadvantages? How do these two lists balance against each other?

B. Examine the marketing information example described in the ETHICS APPLICATION "Neuromarketing." Should limits be placed on the ability of commercial organizations to capture and exploit information about individuals for reasons of privacy? Why should such issues concern marketing executives?

Designing Market-Driven Strategies

Chapter 6

Market Targeting and Strategic Positioning

Deciding which buyers in the market to target and how to position a company's products for each market target are core decisions of market-driven strategy, guiding the entire organization in its efforts to deliver superior value to customers. Effective targeting and positioning strategies are critical in gaining and sustaining superior business performance. When these decisions are faulty, they weaken business and marketing performance.

Whole Foods Market Inc. is an interesting example of successful market targeting and positioning in the very competitive retail grocery market in the United States.[1] The first store was opened in Austin, Texas, in 1980. The retailer specializes in natural and organic foods, although the prepared foods and many other products it sells are not organic. The high-end grocer targets middle-class buyers who have strong value preferences for natural foods and are willing to pay premium prices for the products that are not often available from other grocery retailers. Whole Foods offers its foods in stores with appealing earth-toned hues and soft lighting. The corporate culture encourages a strong commitment to environmental issues.

Many well-known food brands are not offered in Whole Foods' over 300 health food–oriented stores in the United States, Canada, and Great Britain in 2011, with 1,000 stores as a growth target. Whole Foods sales and profit performance is impressive in the tight profit margin retail grocery market. The retailer has grown from $1.84 billion in sales in 2000 to an estimated $11.27 billion in 2012. Net profit increased from $29 million in 2000 to $246 million in 2010. However, Whole Foods has some major future challenges including conventional supermarkets aggressively moving into the specialty foods market and questions as to whether buyers will sustain their preferences for natural foods, particularly during economic slowdowns.

In analyzing successful marketing strategies of companies like Whole Foods, one feature stands out. Each has market targeting and positioning strategies that are positive contributors to gaining a strong market and financial position for the firm. Examples of effective targeting and positioning strategies are found in all kinds and sizes of businesses, including companies marketing industrial and consumer goods and services in domestic and international markets.

---

[1]This example is based on *The Value Line Investment Survey, Ratings and Reports,* April 22, 2011, 1959; "Eating Too Fast at Whole Foods," *BusinessWeek,* October 24, 2005, 82, 84.

We first examine market targeting strategy and discuss how targets are selected. A discussion of targeting in different market environments follows. Next, we consider strategic positioning and look at what is involved in determining a positioning strategy for each market target. We conclude with a discussion of evaluating positioning effectiveness.

Market Targeting Strategy

The market targeting decision identifies the people or organizations in a product-market toward which an organization directs its positioning strategy initiatives. Selecting one or more promising market targets is a very demanding management challenge. For example, should the organization attempt to serve all buyers who are willing and able to buy a particular good or service, or instead selectively focus on one or more subgroups (segments)? Whole Foods management adopted a selective market targeting strategy.

Consider, for example, the development of Numis Network's marketing strategy of targeting coin collector's using direct selling customer contact. Numis' market initiatives are described in the STRATEGY APPLICATION. The company was founded in 2009 and is off to a strong market entry. This is an interesting example of the launch of an exciting and successful new market entry.

Targeting and positioning strategies consist of (1) identifying and analyzing the segments in a product-market, (2) deciding which segment(s) to target, and (3) designing and implementing a positioning strategy for each target.

Many companies use some form of market segmentation (see Chapter 3), since buyers have become increasingly differentiated regarding their value requirements. Micro-segmentation (finer segmentation) is becoming popular, aided by effective segmentation and targeting methods based on customer relationship management. The Internet offers an opportunity for direct access to individual customers and online peer-to-peer groups. In the following discussion we assume that the market of interest is segmented on some basis.

Targeting Alternatives

The targeting decision determines which customer group(s) the organization will serve. A specific marketing effort (positioning strategy) is directed toward each target that management decides to serve. For example, Pfizer's targeting strategy for the launch of its new prescription pain relief product Relpax was as follows:

> Pfizer for the first time launched a new product—Relpax—without any TV advertising at all. Relpax is a prescription medicine for migraine headache relief. Pfizer identified **active young mothers as the prime target group** for Relpax and adjusted its media mix accordingly. "They are listening to the radio in the car, [going] on the Internet late at night, or reading a magazine in a quiet moment," says Dorothy L. Weitzer, a Pfizer marketing vice-president. "They are not watching TV."[2]

Market targeting approaches fall into two major categories: (1) segment targeting when segments are clearly defined; and (2) targeting based on product differentiation. As shown by Exhibit 6.1, segment targeting ranges from a single segment to targeting all or most of the segments in the market. American Airlines uses extensive targeting in air travel services, as does General Motors with its different brands and styles of automobiles. An example of selective targeting is Autodesk's targeting of architects with its line of computer-aided design software.

---

[2]Anthony Bianco, "The Vanishing Mass Market," *BusinessWeek,* July 12, 2004, 63.

Numis Network, a direct selling company, was founded in 2009 by three experienced entrepreneurs. The products are gold and silver highly collectible coins. The coins are graded, certified, and government issued. The market target is the coin collector.

Numis was launched around the exclusive Silver Coin of the Month Club. The product inventory includes 200 coins and related items (coin watches, coin necklaces, Forever Crystal gift sets, and ancient coins). Numis is the first direct selling company to offer high-quality, government-minted collectible coins at competitive prices.

Numis uses a traditional network marketing approach. People are recruited by inviting others to observe the operations, join the club, and make money. Personal websites and social networking sites are available to all Numis sales representatives. Training of new representatives is very customized utilizing highly qualified personal-development trainers and an array of training videos. The world-class training program is called Numis University. More than 15,000 people joined the direct seller in the first 18 months of operation. Sales representatives are in all 50 U.S. states and Canada. Plans are to expand in 2012 into Europe and Australia.

The firm's success ingredients are an exciting and unique product coupled with a highly competent management team and financial resources. Numis has a proactive social responsibility program through a variety of local charitable initiatives.

Source: Tori Brown, "Putting the Cool in Coin Collecting," *Direct Selling News,* April 2011, 37–44.

While segment targeting is used more extensively than product differentiation, the latter may be appropriate in certain situations. When segments are difficult to identify, even though diversity in preferences may exist, companies may appeal to buyers through product specialization or product variety. While differences may exist in needs and wants, buyers' preferences are diffused, making it difficult to define segments.[3] Specialization involves offering buyers a product differentiated from competitors' products and designed to appeal to customer needs and wants not satisfied by competitors. Using a product variety strategy, the Vanguard Group offers a wide range of mutual funds to investors, which are not targeted to particular investor segments.

EXHIBIT 6.1
Market Targeting Approaches

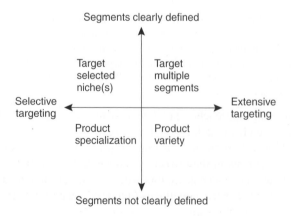

---

[3]Ravi S. Achrol, "Evolution of the Marketing Organization: New Forms for Turbulent Environments," *Journal of Marketing,* October 1991, 82–83.

Factors Influencing Targeting Decisions

Market segment analysis discussed in Chapter 3 helps to evaluate and rank the relative attractiveness of the segments under consideration as market targets. These evaluations include customer information, competitor strengths and positioning, and the financial and market attractiveness of the segments. An important guide in targeting is determining the value requirements of the buyers in each segment. Market segment analysis is essential in evaluating both existing and potential market targets.

Management needs to decide if it will target a single segment, selectively target a few segments, or target all or most of the segments in the product-market. Several factors may influence the choice of the targeting strategy:

- Stage of product-market maturity.
- Extent of diversity in buyer value requirements.
- Industry structure.
- The firm's capabilities and resources.
- Opportunities for gaining competitive advantage.

Since the relevance and importance of these factors is likely to vary according to stage of product-market maturity, we use maturity as the basis for considering different targeting situations. The objective is to look at how each factor affects the market target strategy.

Targeting in Different Market Environments

The product-market environment is influenced by the extent of concentration of competing firms, the stage of maturity, and exposure to international competition. Four life cycle stages illustrate the range of product-market structures:

Emerging. Product-markets that are newly formed are categorized as emerging and are created by factors such as a new technology, the changing needs of buyers, and the identification of unmet needs by suppliers. The Segway battery-powered one-person scooter targets commercial users such as postal carriers.

Growing. These product-markets are experiencing rapid growth. Flat-panel TVs are in an advanced stage of growth, accounting for worldwide sales in 2006 of 44 million units out of a total of 185 million TVs.[4] Competition consists of several firms and one or more may be gaining a leading market position.

Mature. These product-markets are shifting from growth to maturity, as indicated by the product life cycles of the products. Growing rapidly until reaching high levels of household penetration, microwave ovens are now in the maturity stage.

Declining. A declining product-market is actually fading away instead of experiencing a temporary decline or cyclical changes. Fax machines are rapidly declining as Internet technology and e-mail dominate the product-market.

The four product-market stages of evolution are neither exhaustive nor mutually exclusive. Moreover, changing environmental and industry conditions may alter a product-market classification. Also, rapid growth may occur in some countries while growth is mature or declining in other countries or regions. Because of these variations a global perspective concerning product-markets is important.

---

[4]Evan Ramstad, "Flat-Panel TVs, Long Touted, Finally are Becoming the Norm," *Wall Street Journal,* April 15–16, 2006, A1.

The four different market environments discussed above are closely related to the product life cycle (PLC) stages. Looking at competition during the stages of the product life cycle and at different product-market levels (generic, product type, and variant) provides insights into different types and intensities of competition. We know that products, like people, move through life cycles, and products' life cycles are increasingly shorter due to the rapid pace of technological change in the 21st century.

The life cycle of a typical product is shown in Exhibit 6.2. Sales begin at the time of introduction and increase over the pattern shown. Profits initially lag sales, since expenses often exceed sales during the initial stage of the product life cycle as a result of heavy introductory expenses. Total sales and profits decline after the product reaches the maturity stage. Typically, profits fall off before sales.

Emerging, growth, and mature market environments are discussed to illustrate different targeting situations. Also, several targeting and positioning issues in global markets are considered.

Emerging Markets

Knowledge about an emerging market is very limited. The market is new and is relatively small. The number of competitors initially consists of the first market entrant and one or two other firms. Growth patterns are uncertain and the emerging market may eventually disappear. Market definition and analysis are rather general in the early stages of product-market development. Buyers' needs and wants are not highly differentiated because they do not have experience with the product. Determining the future scope and direction of growth of product-market development may be difficult, as will forecasting the size of market growth.

There are two types of emerging markets: (1) a totally new product-market and (2) a new product technology entering an existing product-market. In the first situation, the emerging market is formed by people/organizations whose needs and wants have not been satisfied by available products. A cure for the AIDS virus is an example. In the second situation, the market entry provides an alternative value proposition to buyers in an existing market. The entry of digital photography into the traditional camera and film market is an example of the second entry situation.

Buyer Diversity

The similarity of buyers' preferences in the emerging market often limits segmentation efforts. It may be possible to identify a few broad segments. If segmentation is not feasible, an alternative is to define and describe an average or typical user, directing marketing efforts toward these potential buyers.

EXHIBIT 6.2
Life Cycle of a Typical Product

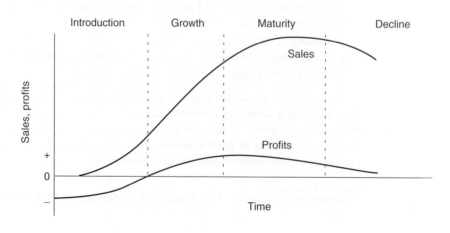

Product-Market Structure

New enterprises are more likely to enter a new product-market than are large, well-established companies. The exception is a major innovation in a large company coupled with strong entry barriers. The pioneers developing a new product-market "are typically small new organizations set up specifically to exploit first-mover advantages in the new resource space."[5] These entrepreneurs often have limited resources and must pursue product-market opportunities that require low levels of investment. Industry development is influenced by various factors, including attractiveness of the market, rate of acceptance of the product by buyers, entry barriers, performance of firms serving the market, and future expectations.

Capabilities and Resources

A firm entering an existing product-market with a new product is more likely to achieve a competitive edge by offering buyers unique benefits rather than lower prices for equivalent benefits, though cost may be the basis of superior value when the new product is a lower-cost alternate technology to an existing product. For example, Voiceover Internet Protocol represented a potential threat to the pricing models of the telecommunications industry.

Entry of disruptive technologies into existing product-markets may present competitive threats to the incumbent firms, because the value proposition of the new technology (e.g., digital photography) may eventually attract buyers away from incumbent firms.[6] We discuss disruptive technology in Chapter 8.

Targeting Strategy

Targeting in an emerging market is likely to focus on a preference or use situation that corresponds to the value proposition offered by the new product. The targeting decision will depend, in part, on whether a totally new product-market or new product technology is involved. Targeting in the former situation is likely to focus on an average or typical user. Targeting for a new technology in an existing market may require trying to link the value offered by the technology to buyers expected to benefit most from the value offered. Market entry experimentation may be needed to refine the targeting strategy.

Growth Markets

Segments are likely to be found in the growth stage of the market. Identifying customer groups with similar value requirements improves targeting, and "experience with the product, process, and materials technologies leads to greater efficiency and increased standardization."[7] During the growth stage the market environment moves from highly uncertain to moderately uncertain. Further change in the market is likely, but there is a level of awareness about the forces that influence the size and composition of the product-market.

Patterns of use can be identified and the characteristics of buyers and their use patterns can be determined. Segmentation by type of industry (use situation) may be feasible in industrial markets. Demographic characteristics such as age, income, and family size may identify broad segments for consumer products such as food and drugs. Analysis of the characteristics and preferences of existing buyers yields useful guidelines for estimating market potential.

---

[5]Mary Lambkin and George S. Day, "Evolutionary Processes in Competitive Markets: Beyond the Product Life Cycle," *Journal of Marketing,* July 1989, 4.

[6]Clayton M. Christensen and Michael E. Raynor, *The Innovator's Solution* (Boston: Harvard Business School Press, 2003), Chapter 1.

[7]Lambkin and Day, "Evolutionary Processes in Competitive Markets," 14.

Product-Market Structure

We often assume that high growth markets are very attractive, and that early entry offers important competitive advantages. Nevertheless, there are some warnings for industry participants:

> First, a visible growth market can attract too many competitors—the market and its distribution channel cannot support them. The intensity of competition is accentuated when growth fails to match expectations or eventually slows. Second, the early entrant is unable to cope when key success factors or technologies change, in part because it lacks the financial skills or organizational skills.[8]

For example, the fiber-optic cable network market in the United States attracted far too many competitors (some 1,500). Most of the networks were not being used in the early 2000s due to significant overbuilding.

Existing companies are likely to enter new product-markets at the growth stage. They have the resources to support market entry, and if there is a good capabilities/customer value requirements match, and the growth market offers high potential, entry is likely. Recall, for example, the various existing firms that entered the digital photography market at the growth stage. Later entrants also have the advantage of evaluating the attractiveness of the product-market during its initial development.

Capabilities and Resources

The firms competing in growth markets are likely to follow one of these strategies: (1) pursuit of a market leadership strategy or (2) follow very selective targeting and positioning strategies. Eastman Kodak is following the leadership strategy in the digital photography market, whereas Pentax is using a more focused strategy.

Targeting Strategy

There are at least three possible targeting strategies in growth markets: (1) extensive market coverage by firms with established businesses in related markets, (2) selective targeting by firms with diversified product portfolios, and (3) very focused targeting strategies by small organizations serving one or a few market segments.[9]

A selective targeting strategy is feasible when buyers' needs are differentiated or when products are differentiated. The segments that are not served by large competitors provide an opportunity for a small firm to gain competitive advantage. The market leader(s) may not find a small segment attractive enough to seek a position in the segment. If the buyers in the market have similar needs, a small organization may gain advantage through specialization, concentrating on a specific product or component.

Mature Markets

Not all firms that enter the emerging and growth stages of the market survive in the maturity stage. The needs and characteristics of buyers also change over time. Market entry at the maturity stage is less likely than in previous life cycle stages, although firms with disruptive technologies are likely to enter at this stage.

Buyer Diversity

Segmentation is often essential at the maturity stage of the life cycle. The product-market is clearly defined, indicating buyers' preferences and the competitive structure. The factors that drive market growth are recognized, and the market is not likely to expand or decline

---

[8]Elaine Romanelli, "New Venture Strategies in the Minicomputer Industry," *California Management Review,* Fall 1987, 161.
[9]Lambkin and Day, "Evolutionary Processes in Competitive Markets," 12.

rapidly. Nonetheless, eventual decline may occur unless actions are taken to extend the product life cycle through product innovations.

Identification and evaluation of market segments are necessary to select targets that offer each firm a competitive advantage. Since the mature market has a history, information should be available concerning how buyers respond to the marketing efforts of the firms competing in the product-market. Knowledge of the competitive and environmental influences on the segments in the market helps to obtain accurate forecasts and guide positioning strategies.

The maturity of the product-market may reduce its attractiveness to the companies serving the market, so a market-driven organization may benefit from (1) scanning the external environment for new opportunities that are consistent with the organization's skills and resources (core competencies), (2) identifying potential disruptive technology threats to the current technologies for meeting customer needs, and (3) identifying opportunities within specific segments for new and improved products. These initiatives become even more urgent when market growth shifts to decline.

Wal-Mart, the world's largest retailer, altered its targeting and positioning strategies in 2006 to target six groups of buyers in the mature U.S. retail market.[10] The six demographic groups consist of affluent buyers, empty-nesters, African-Americans, Hispanics, suburbanites, and rural residents. Management grouped its 3,400 stores into six different models. Products and other positioning efforts were matched to each target group.

Buyers in mature markets are experienced and increasingly demanding. They are familiar with competing brands and display preferences for particular brands. The key marketing issue is developing and sustaining brand preference, since buyers are aware of the product type and its features. Many top brands like Coca-Cola, Gillette, and McDonald's have held their leading positions for more than half a century. This highlights the importance of obtaining and protecting a lead position at an early stage in the development of a market.

Product-Market Structure

Mature product-markets typically experience intense competition for market share, emphasis on cost reduction, continuing needs for new products, international competition, tight profit margins, and increases in the role and importance of value chain strategies. Deciding how to compete successfully in a mature product-market is a demanding challenge.

The typical mature industry structure consists of a few companies that dominate the industry and several other firms that pursue market selectivity strategies. The larger firms may include a market leader and two or three competitors with relatively large market positions compared to the remaining competitors. Acquisition may be the best way of market entry rather than trying to develop products and marketing capabilities. Mature industries are increasingly experiencing pressures for global consolidation. Examples include automobiles, foods, household appliances, prescription drugs, and consumer electronics.

Capabilities and Resources

Depending on the firm's position in the mature market, management's objective may be cost reduction, selective targeting, or product differentiation. Poor performance may lead to restructuring the corporation to try to improve financial performance. If improvement is not feasible, the decision may be to exit from the business.

---

[10]Ann Zimmerman, "To Boost Sales, Wal-Mart Drops One-Size-Fits-All Approach," *Wall Street Journal,* September 7, 2006, A1, A7.

Audi AG implemented a major turnaround strategy in the mid-1990s designed to appeal to more automobile buyers with an exciting image. The midrange Audi A4 introduced in 1995 attracted new buyers and was part of a major new product strategy to increase sales and profits. Leveraging Audi's capabilities and resources, the A4's initial entry was very successful. Supported by a major advertising campaign, the new model attracted younger buyers. Appealing to this target was a major objective of the new marketing strategy. Audi's A6 and A8 models were targeted to additional market segments.

Targeting

Both targeting and positioning strategies may change in moving from the growth to maturity stages of the product-market. Targeting may be altered to reflect changes in priorities among market targets. Positioning within a targeted market may be adjusted to improve customer satisfaction and operating performance.

The retailer Best Buy implemented an interesting microsegmentation targeting strategy, focusing on customer groups patronizing its nearly 1,000 individual stores in combination with national targeting.[11] Individual store employees identified new customer groups (e.g., European shipworkers at Baytown's busy port, retiree clubs, newly returned military). Headquarters provides financial modeling software for store managers to use in evaluating targeting options.

Targeting segments is appropriate for all firms competing in a mature product-market. The strategic issue is deciding which segments to serve. Market maturity may create new opportunities and threats in a company's market target(s). The STRATEGY APPLICATION describes Levi Strauss's challenges in the mature jeans market.

Firms pursuing extensive targeting strategies may decide to exit from certain segments. The targets that are retained in the portfolio can be prioritized to help guide new product planning, value chain strategy, pricing strategy, and promotion strategy and expenditures.

Global Markets

Understanding global markets is important regardless of where an organization decides to compete, since domestic markets often attract international competitors. The increasingly smaller world linked by instant communications, global supply networks, and international finance markets mandates evaluating global opportunities and threats. In selecting strategies for global markets, there are two primary options for consideration: (1) the advantages of global integration and (2) the advantages of local responsiveness.[12]

Global Integration

This strategy considers the extent to which standardized products and other strategy elements can be designed to compete on a global basis. The world is the market arena and buyers are targeted without regard to national boundaries and regional preferences. The objective is to identify market segments that span global markets and to serve these opportunities with global positioning strategies.

Local Responsiveness

While local responsiveness is a relevant issue, the central consideration is how to segment global markets. Increasingly, the basis for global segmentation is not by country.[13]

---

[11]Jena McGregor, "At Best Buy, Marketing Goes Micro," *BusinessWeek,* May 26, 2008, 52, 54.
[12]Philip R. Cateora, Mary C. Gilly, and John L. Graham, *International Marketing,* 15th ed. (New York, NY: McGraw-Hill Irwin, 2011), Chapter 12.
[13]Ibid., 21–23.

Levi Strauss experienced major sales and profit declines after the mid-1990s. Revenues fell from $7 billion in 1996 to $4 billion in fiscal 2003 and were running at $4.4 billion in 2010.

For years the Levi brand targeted the middle price and quality market, avoiding discounters like Wal-Mart, Target, and Kohl's. Management also failed to recognize the significance of the boom in high-fashion denim. In a surprising turnaround initiative Levi has expanded its jeans market coverage to target both price and fashion-conscious buyers.

The new Levi Signature brand was designed for Wal-Mart, Target, and other discounters. The more expensive Premium Red Tab was targeted to up-scale customers of retailers like Nordstrom and Neiman-Marcus.

In 2010 Levi's launched its first global brand outside the United States—Denizen—targeting Asian consumers with a better fitting jean. Denizen follows the model of pricing in the middle of the market—more expensive than cheap casual wear, but cheaper than luxury brands, notwithstanding the warning that Chinese consumers love luxury and bargains but not the area in between. The Denizen brands reaches the United States in 2011 as a low-cost jean sold in Target.

Attempting to appeal to a wide range of market targets with a variety of poorly differentiated Levi jeans brands is risky. A potential consequence is damage to the Levi brand, and the initiative may not have a major impact on Levi's sales and profits.

Levi Strauss's very slow response to changes in its core jeans market is illustrative of the challenges of competing in highly competitive mature markets. Recognizing the seriousness of the problem, management hired a turnaround consulting firm in late 2003.

Sources: Wendy Zellner, "Lessons from a Faded Levi Strauss," *BusinessWeek,* December 15, 2003, 44. Patti Waldmeir, "Levi Woos Asia with Tailored Brand," *Financial Times,* August 19, 2010, 19. Barney Jopson and Patti Waldmeir, "Levi's Chinese Jeans Poised for US Market Launch," *Financial Times,* April 12, 2011, 23.

Instead, other segmentation variables are often more important. Examples include climate, language group, media habits, and income. Nestlé's skills in local responsiveness have been very important in generating strong revenue and profit performance.

Targeting

Strategies for competing in international markets range from targeting a single country, regional (multinational) targeting, or targeting on a global basis. The strategic issue is deciding whether to compete internationally, and if so, how to compete. Also, the choice of a domestic focus requires an understanding of relevant global influences on the domestic strategy.

The GLOBAL APPLICATION describes the remarkable success of the Harry Potter books in competing in global markets in an unconventional way and crossing national boundaries to reach the target market.

The global success of Harry Potter books—stories of a schoolboy wizard—is based on high levels of reader enthusiasm and unconventional marketing approaches.

- Harry Potter's publishers (Scholastic Corp in the United States and Bloomsbury in the U.K. covering the rest of the world) have sold more than 450 million Potter books worldwide. Scholastic had a 12 million print run for the sixth Potter book.

- The seventh Potter book was launched in 2007, with the fifth movie out a few weeks later, and plans for a Harry Potter attraction in Orlando, Florida, expected to cost half a billion dollars. The first six Harry Potter movies generated $5.4 billion in worldwide box office receipts, with the remaining two movies launched in 2011 and 2012.

- Escalating worldwide sales have been driven by Warner's massive marketing spend for the Potter movies, but especially the word-of-mouth reader recommendations to families and children.

- Sales in the United States and the U.K. have seen deep price cutting by retailers like Amazon.com, Wal-Mart, and Tesco—each seeking to get consumers into the store or onto the website to sell other products. Amazon alone preordered a million copies of the final book.

- Sales in China and other non-English-speaking countries have been supported by growing numbers of people learning to read and speak English—and using the Harry Potter books as a way to get children to learn.

- The author—J. K. Rowling—hardly promotes the books, and has withdrawn more from promotional efforts with each new book.

- Strict embargos prevent fans anywhere in the world from gaining access to the book before the official publication date. Scholastic's book launch campaigns to "tease" fans in the United States have involved a complete blackout on advance information, no review copies, and no author interviews allowed, while juicy plot details were "leaked" to the press. Some booksellers were allowed to display the volume before the publication day—but in locked cages.

The Harry Potter books and movies (as well as merchandise) have succeeded with crossing international boundaries in reaching the market target of child readers, and boys in particular.

Sources: Diane Brady, "The Twisted Economics of Harry Potter," *BusinessWeek*, July 2, 2007, 38–39. Ben Fenton, "Potter Sets Another Bloomsbury Record," *Financial Times*, Friday, June 29, 2007, 23. Stephen Brown, "Torment Your Customers (They'll Love It)," *Harvard Business Review*, October 2001, 83–88. Matthew Garrahan, "Spellbound Fans Break Records for Harry Potter," *Financial Times*, November 21, 2010, 19.

Positioning Strategy

Positioning strategy is discussed in the rest of the chapter. First, we provide an overview of strategic positioning and consider selection of the positioning concept. Next, we examine the composition of positioning strategy and how the positioning components are combined into an integrated strategy. Finally, we look at how positioning effectiveness is evaluated.

Positioning may focus on an entire company, a mix of products, a specific line of products, or a particular brand, although positioning is often centered on the brand. Positioning initiatives are closely linked to business strategy because strategic positioning comprises the efforts of the business to deliver superior value to its customers. The major initiatives necessary in strategic positioning are described in Exhibit 6.3. The buyers in the market target are the focus of the positioning strategy designed for the target. The *positioning*

EXHIBIT 6.3
Strategic Positioning
Initiatives

POSITIONING CONCEPT

How management wants
buyers in the market target
to position the product
(brand)

**MARKET
TARGET**

**POSITIONING
EFFECTIVENESS**

How well management's
positioning objectives are
achieved for the market target

**POSITIONING
STRATEGY**

The combination of marketing
actions used to communicate
the positioning concept to
targeted buyers

concept indicates management's desired positioning of the product (brand) in the eyes and minds of the targeted buyers. It is a statement of what the product (brand) means guided by the value requirements of the buyers in the market target.[14] Positioning is intended to deliver the value requirements appropriate for each market target pursued by the organization. For example, Gatorade is targeted to active people experiencing hot and thirsty use situations. The drink is positioned as the best thirst quencher and replenisher, backed by scientific tests, and Gatorade's 80 percent market share attests to effective positioning of the brand. Selecting the desired positioning requires an understanding of buyers' value requirements and their perceptions of competing brands.

The *positioning strategy* is the combination of marketing program (mix) strategies used to portray the positioning desired by management to the targeted buyers. This strategy includes the product (good or service), supporting services, distribution channels, price, and promotion actions taken by the organization. *Positioning effectiveness* considers how well management's positioning objectives are being achieved in the market target. This includes determining the metrics to be used in assessing effectiveness.

As shown in Exhibit 6.4 the positioning objective is to have each targeted customer perceive the brand distinctly from other competing brands and favorably compared to the other brands. Of course, the actual positioning of the brand is determined by the buyer's perceptions of the firm's positioning strategy (and perceptions of competitors' strategies).

EXHIBIT 6.4
How Positioning
Works

Objective	Match the organization's distinctive capabilities with the customer value requirements for the market target. (How do we want to be perceived by targeted buyers?
Desired Result	Gain a relevant, distinct, and enduring position by the targeted buyers that they consider important
Actions by the Organization	Design and implement the positioning strategy (marketing program) for the market target.

[14]C. Whan Park, Bernard J. Jaworski, and Deborah J. Macinnis, "Strategic Brand Concept-Image Management," *Journal of Marketing,* October 1986, 135–145.

It's 1:30 p.m. on a Monday in the bustling H&M store on Manhattan's Fifth Avenue, and Alma Saldana, a 28-year-old makeup artist from Houston, is stuffing three tiny vests into her black H&M shopping bag. That's on top of blouses, jackets, and pants. Saldana is in a buying frenzy. This is her first visit to H&M, the Stockholm-based fashion retailer, and it's everything she had hoped for. "Somebody told me you find great fashion at a very cheap price, and it's true!" she exclaims.

Such enthusiasm has made H&M one of the hottest fashion companies around. Central to its success is its ability to spot shifts in demand and respond with lightning speed. While traditional clothing retailers design their wares at least 6 months ahead of time, H&M can rush items into stores in as little as 3 weeks. Most of the work is done ahead, too. But when it sees consumers scooping up something like vests, it speeds a slew of new variations into stores within the same season, to the delight of shoppers like Saldana. "Speed is important. You need to have a system where you can react in a short lead time with the right products," says Chief Executive Rolf Eriksen.

How does it work? H&M designers had included a couple of cropped vests in their autumn/winter collections. In August, shortly after the vests went on sale, they started "flying out of the stores," says Margareta van den Bosch, H&M's head of design. H&M's designers in Stockholm (it has more than 100) spotted the trend in the company's worldwide sales reports, published internally every Monday. About half of them immediately started sketching new styles. As quickly as designs came off their desks, pattern makers snipped and pinned, pressing employees into service as live models. At the same time, buyers ordered fabrics. The designs were zoomed electronically to workers at H&M's production offices in Europe and Asia, which then selected manufacturers that could handle the jobs quickly. In less than two months most H&M stores had five to ten new vest styles in stock.

One of the secrets to H&M's speed is decisiveness. The people in charge of each collection can dream up and produce new fashions on their own authority. Only huge orders require approval from higher ups. "We have a flat organization. We have a shorter way to a decision," says Sanna Lindberg, president of H&M Hennes & Mauritz USA. That makes H&M fashionable in more ways than one.

H&M's closest competition is Zara (Spain) with 5,000 stores in 77 countries. Zara may even be faster than H&M. However, in countries where H&M has gained market position such as Germany, the Netherlands, and Austria, its market penetration is higher than Zara. H&M was slow in moving into Asia which in 2011 accounts for only 3 percent of revenues.

Sources: Steve Hamm, "SPEEDDEMONS," *BusinessWeek,* March 27, 2006, 70–71. "Global Stretch," *The Economist,* March 12, 2011, 76.

The desired result is to gain a relevant, distinct, and enduring position that is considered important by the buyers that are targeted. Management must design and implement the positioning strategy to achieve this result. A company's positioning strategy (marketing program) works to persuade buyers to favorably position the brand.

Achieving a distinct and valued position with targeted buyers is a pivotal initiative for the Stockholm based fashion retailer, Hennes & Mauritz (H&M), as described in the INNOVATION APPLICATION. The specialty retailer's effectiveness in getting different functions of the business to work together in designing products is impressive. H&M's positioning strategy also benefits from effective market sensing and speed of response. H&M is a formidable competitor for Gap and other specialty retailers.

Selecting the Positioning Concept

The positioning concept indicates how management wants buyers to perceive the company's brand. Selecting the positioning concept is a key marketing and business strategy decision:

> The position can be central to customers' perception and choice decisions. Further, since all elements of the marketing program can potentially affect the position, it is usually necessary to use a positioning strategy as a focus for the development of the marketing program. A clear positioning strategy can insure that the elements of the marketing program are consistent and supportive.[15]

Choosing the positioning concept is an important first step in designing the positioning strategy. The positioning concept of the brand is "the general meaning that is understood by customers in terms of its relevance to their needs and preferences."[16] The positioning strategy is the combination of marketing mix actions that is intended to implement the desired positioning of the brand concept to achieve a specific position with targeted buyers.

Positioning Concepts[17]

The positioning concept should be linked to buyers' value requirements. The focus of the concept may be *functional, symbolic,* or *experiential.* A *functional* concept applies to products that solve consumption-related problems for externally generated consumption needs. Examples of brands using this basis of positioning include Crest toothpaste (cavity prevention), Clorox liquid cleaner (effective cleaning), and a checking account with ABC Bank (convenient services). *Symbolic positioning* relates to the buyer's internally generated need for self-enhancement, role position, group membership, or ego-identification. Examples of symbolic positioning are Rolex watches and Louis Vuitton luxury goods. Finally, the *experiential* concept is used to position products that provide sensory pleasure, variety, and/or cognitive stimulation. BMW's automobile brands are positioned using an experiential concept that emphasizes the driving experience.

Three aspects of positioning concept selection are important.[18] First, the positioning concept applies to a specific brand rather than all of the competing brands in a product classification such as toothpaste. Second, the concept is used to guide positioning (marketing program) decisions over the life of the brand, recognizing that the brand's specific position may change over time. However, consistency over time is important. Third, if two or more positioning concepts, for example, functional and experiential, are used to guide positioning strategy, the multiple concepts are likely to confuse buyers and perhaps weaken the effectiveness of positioning actions. Of course, the specific concept selected may not fall clearly into one of the three classifications.

Positioning Decision

In deciding how to position a brand, it is useful to study the positioning of competing brands using attributes that are important to existing and potential buyers of the competing brands. The objective is to try to determine the preferred (ideal) position of the buyers in each market segment of interest and then compare this preferred position with the actual positions of competing brands. Marketing research (e.g., preference maps) may be

---

[15]David A. Aaker and J. Gary Shansby, "Positioning Your Product," *Business Horizons,* May–June 1982, 56–62.

[16]C. W. Park and Gerald Zaltman, *Marketing Management* (Chicago: The Dryden Press, 1987), 248.

[17]This discussion is based on Park, Jaworski, and Macinnis, "Strategic Brand Concept-Image Management," 136–137; and David A. Aaker, *Building Strong Brands* (New York: The Free Press, 1996), 95–101.

[18]Ibid.

The online retailer Zappos.com was founded in 1999, and throughout its life has extolled its "wow" customer service and distinct corporate culture.

The organization lives and breathes customer service (the basis for the company's positioning) which is driven by its unique corporate culture. The company is managed around passion and excitement and the culture is shaped by ten core values, including "create fun and a little weirdness," as well as "do more with less" and "deliver 'wow' through service."

Company investments in supply chain resources have developed the business model to focus on enhancing the customer experience and continue to deliver the promised "wow" experience.

By 2008, Zappos reached $1 billion in sales, and expanded into clothes and other categories where customer service could be the differentiator. Late 2009 the company was sold to Amazon for $1.2 billion, but continues to operate as an independent entity.

Source: Winter Nie and Beverley Lennox, "Creating a Distinct Corporate Culture, *Financial Times*, February 17, 2011, 14.

necessary in identifying customers' ideal positioning. Management then seeks a distinct position that matches the firm's distinctive capabilities with buyers' preferred position in the target of interest.

The INTERNET APPLICATION describing Zappos.com is an interesting example of an innovative online retailer's positioning strategy.

Determining the existing positioning of a brand by targeted buyers and deciding whether the position satisfies management's objectives are considered later in the chapter. First, we discuss developing the positioning strategy.

Developing the Positioning Strategy

The positioning strategy integrates the marketing program (mix) components into a coordinated set of initiatives designed to achieve the firm's positioning objective(s). Developing the positioning strategy includes determining the activities and results for which each marketing program component (product, distribution, price, promotion) will be responsible, choosing the amount to spend on each program component, and deciding how much to spend on the entire program.

Selecting the positioning strategy may be guided by a combination of management judgment and experience, analysis of prior activities and results, trial (e.g., test marketing), and field research. We consider several issues regarding targeting and supporting activities, followed by deciding how to develop the positioning strategy.

Scope of Positioning Strategy

The positioning strategy is usually centered on a single brand (Colgate's Total toothpaste) or a line of related products (kitchen appliances) for a specific market target. Whether the strategy is brand-specific or greater in scope depends on such factors as the size of the product-market, characteristics of the good or service, the number of products involved, and product interrelationships in the consumer's use situation. For example, the marketing programs of Johnson & Johnson, Procter & Gamble, and Sara Lee focus on positioning each of their various brands, whereas firms such as General Electric Company, Caterpillar, NIKE, and Samsung use the corporate name to position the product-line or product-portfolio.

When serving several market targets, an umbrella strategy covering multiple targets may be used for certain of the marketing program components. For example, advertising may be designed to appeal to more than a single target, or the same product (coach airline seats) may be targeted to different buyers through different distribution channels, pricing, and promotion activities.

Marketing Program Decisions

A look at Nokia Corporation's positioning strategy illustrates how the Finland based global cellular phone producer combines its marketing mix components into a coordinated strategy.[19]

Nokia is the world's largest producer by volume, of cell phones, with 2007 sales of $75 billion, up from nearly $30 billion in 2001. Profits during the same period grew from $2.8 billion to $8.3 billion. Nokia's positioning strategy includes aggressive innovation initiatives, a very effective global value chain network, competitive pricing, and effective promotion strategies matched to its major global markets in Asia, Europe, Middle East, Africa, and the Americas. However, Nokia began to encounter intense competitive pressures and slower growth in 2004.

Product Strategy

In addition to cell phones, Nokia develops and produces infrastructure equipment and systems for wireless and fixed networks. It has an active new product development program designed to excel over competition. Nokia is emphasizing radio technology and mobile-phone software in R&D efforts. Midway in the decade cell phones accounted for 63 percent of Nokia's revenues and nearly 90 percent of profits. In 2007 Nokia launched Ovi—an online music service to compete with Apple's iTunes, allowing music downloads to cell phones.

Value Chain Strategy

Nokia manages the value chain from supplier to end-user, integrating its global supply network with phone company partners. The network is very efficient although complex due to the numerous components that are part of each cell phone. The value chain has over 60 billion components moving through it each year. Nokia has been particularly effective in connecting with end-user consumers in China.

Pricing Strategy

Nokia's pricing strategy was rigid in the early 2000s but became more flexible as intense competition developed. The company's market share dropped from 35 percent, which it held for several years to a low of 29 percent in 2004. It has since regained market share through innovative products and competitive pricing.

Promotion Strategy

Nokia has two important customers—end-users of cell phones and service providers. The company made some mistakes with providers who wanted their phones to be identified as a provider brand. Nokia resisted while smaller competitors responded to gain market share

---

[19]This illustration is based on Christopher Lawton, "Investors Hang Up on Nokia," *Wall Street Journal,* June 1, 2011, B1–B2; Peter Burrows, "Elop's Fable," *Bloomberg BusinessWeek,* June 6–June 12, 2011, 56–61; Tom Simonite, "Smart-Phone Operating Systems Control More Consumer Electronics,"*technologyreview,* May–June 2011, 72–73; Bruce Einhorn and Nandini Lakshman, "Nokia Connects," *BusinessWeek,* March 27, 2006, 44–45, "Will Rewiring Nokia Spark Growth?" *BusinessWeek,* February 14, 2005, 46–47; and "The Giant in the Palm of Your Hand," *Economist,* February 12, 2005, 67–69.

so Nokia eventually adopted a more flexible position with its partners. Nokia had to decentralize its distribution to end-users in China, going from 3 sales offices to 70 to counter the sales efforts of local phone producers. It also introduced China-specific phone models with special software. These initiatives gained Nokia a strong preference over Motorola and Samsung. However, by 2011 Android had cut into Nokia's smartphone position in Asia. Android increased from a 5 percent share in 2009 to 38 percent in 2010.

Competitive Advantage

Nokia's management made some mistakes and responded too slowly with change initiatives after gaining feedback from the marketplace. Offering an innovative array of fashionable and functional cell phones is a continuing challenge. Most impressive are the firm's skills in managing a global value chain network. Nonetheless, Nokia faces tough global competition. Its positioning strategy for each market target will be an important competitive advantage that management must continue to strengthen and adapt in the complex and dynamic market and competitive space.

By 2010 it was apparent that Nokia's cell phone business needed to be recharged. Nokia lost 75 percent of its market value from 2007 to 2011. A new CEO had been recruited from Microsoft. The mobile phone giant would partner with Microsoft to strengthen the smartphone portfolio. Nokia's management recognized the key role of the operating system in mobile technology. While still the world's leading producer of cell phones, Nokia has lost market share since 2007. A key need was to develop very profitable, upscale products to compete with Apple's *iPhone* and smartphones that run Google's Android operating system. The new products were essential to improve Nokia's margins and profits. The Nokia experience illustrates the continuing challenge of competitive positioning in dynamic markets. The new CEO is making several business strategy changes including a new management team and organizational design.

An overview of the various decisions that are made in developing a positioning strategy is shown in Exhibit 6.5. Several of these decision initiatives are described in the Nokia illustration. We examine each positioning component in Chapters 9–13. The present objective is to show how the components fit into the positioning strategy. The positioning concept is the core focus for designing an integrated strategy, which indicates how (and

EXHIBIT 6.5
Positioning Strategy Overview

Product/Brand Strategy

Salesforce/ Internet/Direct Strategy

Value Chain Strategy

MARKETING PROGRAM POSITIONING STRATEGY

Advertising/ Sales Promotion Strategy

Pricing Strategy

The Reebok business was bought by Adidas in 2006 providing an opportunity to expand in the challenging U.S. market.

Management's goal was to position Reebok as a premium American fitness and training brand to build market share in the United States.

But Reebok was overdistributed—management did not want to be in places like Wal-Mart and other discount retailers anymore because it undermined a premium brand positioning.

Moreover, about 30 percent of sales was at price levels for $39 dollars and below. Low prices do not support a premium positioning or make money.

However, addressing these problems led to Reebok losing market share and declining sales, alarming financial analysts and investors. Further difficulties came with the financial crisis impacting consumer spending negatively.

Furthermore, the brand needed investment in new products to support a premium positioning. For example, 2009 saw the launch of the Reebok EasyTone footwear collection that allows consumers to "take the gym with them." The EasyTone technology involves two balance pods under the heel and forefoot of the shoe that create a natural instability with every step, which Reebok claims forces the muscles to adapt and develop tone.

Also in 2009, Reebok launched JUKARI Fit to Fly, an innovative gym workout designed to make fitness for women fun again. JUKARI, the result of a long-term relationship between Reebok and renowned entertainment company, Cirque du Soleil, is an hour-long workout created on a specially designed piece of equipment called the FlySet, which simulates the sensation of flying while exercising. In parallel, Reebok also created two collections of high quality women's fitness apparel and footwear called On the Move and the Reebok-Cirque du Soleil collection. Both lines consist of products that can be worn for a range of fitness disciplines.

Reebok prices will have to increase because of rising raw material costs, but the brand is back in demand. Time will tell if the positioning has been effective.

Source: Diane Brady, "Hard Choices," *Bloomberg BusinessWeek,* April 11–17, 2011, 88.

why) the product mix, line, or brand is to be positioned for each market target. This strategy includes:

- The product (good or service) strategy, including how the product/brand will be positioned against the competition in the market target.
- The value chain (distribution) strategy to be used.
- The pricing strategy, including the role and positioning of price relative to competition.
- The advertising and sales promotion strategy and the objectives which these promotion components are expected to achieve.
- The sales force strategy, direct marketing strategy, and Internet strategy, indicating how they are used in the positioning strategy.

Designing the Positioning Strategy

It is necessary to determine the major strategy guidelines for each marketing program component. What is the role of each positioning component and the objective(s) for each? What are the major strategy initiatives and which organizational unit(s) will be responsible? What are the estimated costs? Typically, the positioning strategy will be a continuation of the existing strategy, although as discussed in the Nokia illustration, changes may be necessary (e.g., shifting to more competitive pricing). The STRATEGY APPLICATION concerning Reebok is an interesting example of positioning strategy.

Cross-Functional Relationships

Responsibilities for the positioning strategy components (product, distribution, price, and promotion) are often assigned to various functional units within a company or business unit. This separation of responsibilities (and budgets) highlights the importance of coordinating the positioning strategy. Responsibility should be assigned for coordinating and managing all aspects of the positioning strategy. Some companies use strategy teams for this purpose. Recall in the INNOVATION APPLICATION the close interfunctional coordination by H&M in identifying new apparel designs and quickly moving them into the retailer's stores. Product and brand managers may be given responsibility for coordinating the positioning strategy across functional units.

Determining Positioning Effectiveness

Estimating how the market target will respond to a proposed marketing program, and, after implementation, determining program effectiveness are essential in selecting and managing positioning strategies. Positioning evaluation should include *customer analysis, competitor analysis,* and *internal analysis.*[20] Importantly, these analyses need to be conducted on a continuing basis to determine how well the positioning strategy is performing. Nokia's declining cell phone market share in the United States and other areas is illustrative. Positioning shows how the company or brand is differentiated from its competitors. The objective is to appeal to the value requirements of the targeted buyers. Buyers position companies and brands in responding to specific attributes or dimensions about products or corporate values. Management's objective is to gain (or sustain) a distinct position that corresponds to customers' value preferences for the brand or company being positioned in the market target of interest.

Several methods and metrics are available for analyzing positioning alternatives and determining positioning effectiveness. These include customer and competitor research, market testing of proposed strategies, and the use of analytical techniques (see Exhibit 6.6).

EXHIBIT 6.6
Determining Positioning Effectiveness

Customer and Competitor Research

Methods for Assessing Positioning Effectiveness

Analytical Positioning Techniques

Test Marketing

---

[20]Aaker, *Building Strong Brands,* Chapter 6.

Customer and Competitor Research

Research studies provide customer and competitor information which may be helpful in designing positioning strategy and evaluating strategy results. Several of the research methods discussed in Part 2 can be used to determine the position of a brand. For example, preference maps can guide analysis in considering alternative marketing program strategies by mapping customer preferences for various competing brands compared to customers' ideal preferences.

Methods are available for considering the effects on sales of different marketing program components. For example, multivariate data analysis, can be conducted to identify important causal factors affecting market response.[21] The advantage of these analyses is examining the effects of several factors at the same time. For example, a medical equipment producer identified seven factors considered to be possible influences on the sales of a new product for use by surgeons in the operating room.

The effect of each factor can be measured using field tests to vary the amount (level) of the factor exposed to targeted buyers. For example, the high level of training consisted of a training initiative, whereas the low level was no training. A fractional factorial experimental design was used to evaluate the effects of the seven factors. Different factor combinations were tested. One factor combination included no training, a monetary incentive, no vacation incentive, no mailing to physicians, mailing to operating room supervisors, letter from the president, and offering the standard product (rather than a customized version). A sample of 64 salespeople was randomly selected, and groups of eight were randomly assigned to each of the eight treatment combinations, which were intended to enable testing the effects of each factor plus the influence of various combinations of factors.

One useful finding from the tests was that several of the factors had no impact on sales. For example, the customized product did not sell as well as the standard product. This information saved the firm an estimated $1 million in expenses by eliminating the need to offer customized product designs. Before conducting the tests, management had planned to customize the product for surgeons' use. The other results of the screening experiment were useful in designing the positioning strategy for the product. Interestingly, the vacation incentive for the salespeople had the largest effect on sales of all of the factors, surpassing even a financial incentive.

Test Marketing

Test marketing generates information about the commercial feasibility of a promising new product or about new positioning strategies for new products. The research method can also be used to test possible changes in the marketing program components (e.g., different amounts of advertising expenditures). Conventional test marketing is conducted in one or more cities where the product is marketed and data are collected to determine probable sales and/or profitability. In addition to the standard test market there are other types of market tests including controlled, electronic, simulated, and virtual tests.[22] The alternative forms of tests provide different options concerning test reality and costs. Electronic technology offers some attractive options to standard tests.

While usually less costly than a national market introduction, conventional test marketing is very expensive. Market tests of packaged consumer products often cost $2 million or more depending on the scope of the tests and locations involved. The competitive risks

[21]See Joseph F. Hair, Jr., William C. Black, Barry J. Babin, Rolph E. Anderson, and Ronald L. Tatham, *Multivariate Data Analysis,* 6th ed. (Upper Saddle River, NJ: Pearson Education Inc., 2006).
[22]Donald R. Cooper and Pamela S. Schindler, *Marketing Research* (Burr Ridge, IL: McGraw-Hill/Irwin, 2006), 321–327.

of revealing one's plans must also be weighed against the value of test market information. The major benefits of testing are risk reduction through better demand forecasts and the opportunity to fine-tune a marketing program strategy. We continue the discussion of test marketing of new products in Chapter 8.

Analytical Positioning Techniques

Obtaining information about customers and prospects, analyzing it, and then developing strategies based on the information coupled with management judgment is the crux of positioning analysis. Some promising results have been achieved by incorporating research data into formal models for decision analysis. These models are developed using historical sales and marketing program data. A wide range of software is available for marketing model applications (e.g., advertising media allocation models).[23]

Determining Positioning Effectiveness

How do we know if we have a good positioning strategy? Information is needed as to whether the strategy yields the results which are expected concerning sales, market share, profit contribution, growth rates, customer satisfaction, and other competitive advantage outcomes. Developing a positioning strategy that cannot be easily copied is an essential consideration. For example, a competitor would need considerable resources—not to mention a long time period—to duplicate the powerful Revenue Management decision support system developed by American Airlines. In contrast, an airline can respond immediately with a price cut to meet the price offered by a competitor.

Companies do not alter their positioning strategies on a frequent basis, although adjustments are made at different stages of product-market maturity and in response to environmental, market, and competitive forces. Recall the changes made by Nokia to gain market share. Even though frequent changes are not made, a successful positioning strategy should be evaluated on a 1- to 3-year basis to identify shifting buyer preferences, changes in competitor's strategies, and positioning weaknesses.

Faulty positioning can subvert a company's marketing strategy. Positioning errors include:

- *Underpositioning*—when customers have only vague ideas about the company and its products and do not perceive anything distinctive about them.
- *Overpositioning*—when customers have too narrow an understanding of the company, product, or brand. For example, Mont Blanc sells pens for several thousand dollars, but it is important to the company that the consumer is aware that Mont Blanc pens are available in much cheaper models.
- *Confused positioning*—when frequent changes and contradictory messages confuse customers regarding the positioning of the brand.
- *Doubtful positioning*—when the claims made for the product or brand are not regarded as credible by the customer.[24]

It is a challenge for a company with a clear positioning and segment choice in place to also target additional acquisitions which may undermine the strength of positioning in the existing business. This issue may be particularly important to maintaining growth in

---

[23]Gary L. Lilien and Arvind Rangaswamy, *Marketing Engineering: Computer Assisted Marketing Analysis and Planning* (Reading, MA: Addison-Wesley, 1998).

[24]Graham J. Hooley, Nigel F. Piercy, and Brigitte Nicoulaud, *Marketing Strategy and Competitive Positioning*, 5th ed. (London Pearson, 2011), 186, Exhibit 8.3.

From acquiring his first steel mill in Indonsia in 1976, Lakshmi Mittal has grown ArcelorMittal to a dominant force in the global steel business. Mittal supplies more than 30 percent of the steel used by U.S. car companies and by 2011 was the world's largest steelmaker. Between 1989 and 2004, Mittal made 17 deals across the globe, buying the unwanted assets of bigger steel groups or down-at-heel state-owned plants. Revenues increased from $59 billion in 2006 to $78 billion in 2010. Acquisitions have spanned Asia, the Caribbean, the former Eastern Europe, the United States (International Steel Group and Ispat Inland), and Europe. Mittal's business turns around failing steel plants through a program of replacing existing management, fixing liquidity by reestablishing credit with suppliers, improving operations, shifting production to higher-value output, forming regional groups to boost purchasing power, and selling off non-core subsidiaries. Importantly, Mittal's long-term strategy is to challenge the existing business model prevalent in the steel industry— conventional industry thinking was dominated by tonnages of steel produced, not profits, and regional supply chains. Mittal's view was that only large steel companies could negotiate advantageously with suppliers of iron ore and coal, and major customers such as automakers. Through a strategy of consolidation, a rigorous program of continued improvement, and the deployment of a superior knowledge-sharing network across the global business, Mittal has reinvented the steel sector and created new ways to achieve superiority in customer value and competitive.

Sources: Thomas Biesheuvel, "ArcelorMittal Advances to Nine-Month High on Outlook," tbiesheuvel@ bloomberg.net. February 8, 2011. *Standard & Poors,* "ArcelorMittal 'A'", March 19, 2011. Stanley Reed, "Mittal & Son," *BusinessWeek,* April 16, 2007, 44–50. Stanley Reed, "The Raja of Steel," *BusinessWeek,* December 20, 2004, 18–22.

mature markets. The STRATEGY APPLICATION describing the business strategy challenges confronting ArcelorMittal is illustrative.

Positioning and Targeting Strategies

Positioning strategies become particularly challenging when management decides to target several segments. The objective is to develop an effective positioning strategy for each targeted segment. The use of a different brand for each targeted segment is one way of focusing a positioning strategy. The Gap employs this strategy with its Gap, Banana Republic, and Old Navy brands.

Summary

Choosing the right market target strategy can affect the performance of the enterprise. The targeting decision is critical to guiding the positioning strategy of a brand or company in the marketplace. Moreover, locating the firm's best match between its distinctive capabilities and a market segment's value requirements may require a detailed analysis of several segments. Targeting decisions establish key guidelines for business and marketing strategies.

The market targeting options include a single segment, selective segments, or extensive segments. Choosing among these options involves consideration of the stage of product-market maturity, buyer diversity, product-market structure, and the organization's distinctive capabilities. When segments cannot be clearly defined, product specialization or product variety strategies may be used.

Market targeting decisions need to take into account the product-market life cycle stage. Risk and uncertainty are high in the emerging market stage because of the lack of experience in the new market. Targeting in the growth stage benefits from prior experience, although competition is likely to be more intense than in the emerging market stage. Targeting approaches may be narrow or broad in scope based on the firm's resources and competitive advantage. Targeting in mature markets often involves multiple targeting (or product variety) strategies by a few major competitors and single/selective (or product specialization) strategies by firms with small market shares. Global targeting ranges from local adaptation to global reach.

The positioning concept describes how management wants buyers to position the brand, and is based on the targeted buyers' value requirements. The concept used to position the brand may be based on the functions provided by the product, the experience it offers, or the symbol it conveys. Importantly, buyers position brands, whereas companies seek to influence how buyers position brands. Success depends on how well the organization's distinctive capabilities match the value requirements of each targeted segment.

Developing the positioning strategy requires integrating the product, value chain, price, and promotion strategies to focus them on the market target. The result is an integrated strategy designed to achieve management's positioning objectives while gaining the largest possible competitive advantage. Shaping this bundle of strategies into an integrated set of initiatives is a major challenge for marketing decision makers. Since the strategies span different functional areas and responsibilities, close cross-functional coordination is essential.

Building on an understanding of the market target and the objectives to be accomplished by the marketing program, the positioning strategy matches the firm's capabilities to buyers' value preferences. These programming decisions include selecting the amount of expenditure, deciding how to allocate these resources to the marketing program components, and making the most effective use of resources within each mix component. The factors that affect marketing program strategy include the market target, competition, resource constraints, management's priorities, and the stage of the product life cycle. The positioning strategy consists of the initiatives that will be pursued to achieve the desired positioning relative to the competition.

Central to the positioning decision is examining the relationship between the marketing effort and market response. Positioning analysis is useful in estimating the market response as well as in evaluating competition and buyer preferences. The analysis methods include customer/competitor research, market testing, and positioning models. Analysis information, combined with management judgment and experience, are the basis for evaluating the positioning strategy.

Questions for Review and Discussion

1. Discuss why it may be necessary for an organization to alter its targeting strategy over time.
2. What factors are important in selecting a market target?
3. Discuss the considerations that should be evaluated in targeting a macro-market segment whose buyers' needs vary versus targeting three microsegments within the macro segment.
4. How might a medium-sized bank determine the major market targets served by the bank?
5. Select a product and discuss how the size and composition of the marketing program might require adjustment as the product moves through its life cycle.
6. Suggest an approach that can be used by a regional family restaurant chain to determine the firm's strengths over its competitors.
7. Describe a positioning concept for three different brands/products that corresponds to functional, experiential, and symbolic positioning.

8. Discuss some of the more important reasons why test market results may *not* be a good gauge of how well a new product will perform when it is launched in the national market.

9. "Evaluating marketing performance by using return-on-investment (ROI) measures is not appropriate because marketing is only one of several influences upon ROI." Develop an argument against this statement.

10. Two factors complicate the problem of making future projections as to the financial performance of marketing programs. First, the flow of revenues and costs is likely to be uneven over the planning horizon. Second, sales may not develop as forecasted. How should we handle these factors in financial projections?

11. Discuss the relationship between the positioning concept and positioning strategy.

12. Select a product type product-market (e.g., ice cream). Discuss the use of functional, symbolic, and experiential positioning concepts in this product category.

13. Discuss the conditions that might enable a new competitor to enter a mature product-market.

14. Competing in the mature market for air travel promises to be a demanding challenge in the 21st century. Discuss the marketing strategy issues facing American Airlines during the next decade.

15. Assume you are assisting Nokia in determining information needs for monitoring its cell phone targeting and positioning strategies. What are your recommendations?

Internet Applications

A. PepsiCo competes in the United States and many other countries. Consider how Pepsi may utilize maps in analyzing and selecting market targets (see tiger.census.gov and www.nationalgeographic.com).

B. Go to www.johnsandjohnson.com and click on "Background" and then on "Principal Global Operations." Identify the positioning strategies of the different companies.

C. Go to www.mcdonalds.com and analyze McDonald's positioning initiatives and discuss important positioning issues for McDonalds.

D. Based on information available at www.cisco.com, describe Cisco Systems' positioning strategy.

Application

A. H&M's initiatives described in the INNOVATION APPLICATION could be accomplished by competitors like Gap. Why have competitors failed to recognize these opportunities?

7

Strategic Relationships

The formation of strategic relationships among suppliers, producers, distribution channel organizations, and customers (intermediate customers and end-users) occurs for several reasons. The goal may be gaining access to markets, enhancing value offerings, reducing the risks caused by rapid technological change, sharing complementary skills, learning and acquiring new knowledge, building sustained close relationships with major customers, or obtaining resources beyond those available to a single company. Strategic relationships of these kinds are escalating in importance because of the complexity and risks in a global economy, the skill and resource limitations of a single organization, and the power of major customers to insist on collaborative relationships with their strategic suppliers. Strategic alliances, joint ventures, and strategic account collaborations are examples of cooperative relationships between independent firms.

An important transformation of business has taken place in industry after industry driven by two factors. First, the age of mass production is over and customers demand unique value, so value is shifting from products to solutions and experiences, and consequently relationships are taking over as the central element of exchange. Second, no single business is likely to be big enough to cope with complex and diverse customer demands. This underlines the importance of alliances and networks to deliver customer value—constellations of suppliers that can be configured in different ways to meet different customer needs. Success will involve managing through new collaborative networks.[1]

Increasingly, business and marketing strategies involve more than a single organization. A key element of IBM's business services strategy has been to multiply collaborative projects across all the major parts of the business: top U.S. science and engineering universities are funded to create a new academic discipline called Services Science; a partnership with Sony and Toshiba produced a new processor that is in Sony's Playstation and Toshiba's TVs, and will be the foundation for IBM's next generation of computers; computer code is given to external developers; IBM programmers are paid to work on the Linux open source operating system and key patents have been given to Linux; "collaboratories" are joint ventures for research with countries, companies, and independent research establishments throughout the world. Other parts of the business have been grown through key acquisitions. Collaborating with customers and even competitors to invent new technologies is part of IBM's strategy of openness. Sharing intellectual property in the form of software, patents, and ideas is aimed to stimulate industry growth and create opportunities for IBM to sell high-value products and services that meet new demands. Through its collaborative

---

[1]C. K. Prahalad and M. S. Krishnan, *The New Age of Innovation: Driving Co-Created Value Through Global Networks* (McGraw-Hill Professional, 2008).

EXHIBIT 7.1
Strategic
Relationships

strategy IBM has been transformed into a borderless organization working globally with partners to enhance the value of offerings to customers on a worldwide basis.[2]

In this chapter we examine the nature and scope of the strategic relationships among various types of partners. We consider the full range of strategic relationships shown in Exhibit 7.1. First, we consider the rationale for interorganizational relationships and discuss the logic underlying collaborative relationships. Next, we look at different kinds of organizational relationships, followed by a discussion of several considerations that are important in developing effective interorganizational relationships. We emphasize the risks and strategic vulnerabilities that new types of business relationship strategy may create. Finally, we examine several important issues concerning global relationships.

The Rationale for Interorganizational Relationships

At one time companies mainly established relationships with other organizations to achieve tactical objectives, such as selling in smaller overseas markets. However, the modern reality is that strategic relationships among organizations relate to the key elements of overall competitive strength—technology, costs, and marketing. Unlike tactical relationships, the effectiveness of these strategic agreements among companies can affect their long-term performance and even survival.

Several factors create a need to establish cooperative strategic relationships with other organizations. These influences include the opportunities to enhance value offerings to customers; the diversity, turbulence, and risk in the global business environment; the escalating complexity of technology; the existence of large resource requirements; the need to gain access to global markets; and the availability of appropriate information technology for coordinating complex intercompany operations. As shown in Exhibit 7.2, the various drivers of relationships fall into four broad categories: (1) opportunities to enhance value by combining the competencies of two or more organizations, (2) environmental complexity, (3) competitive strategy, and (4) skills and resource gaps.

Opportunities to Enhance Value

The opportunity present in many markets today is that organizations can couple their competencies to offer superior customer value. Even when partnering is not required, a

[2]This illustration is based on David Kirkpatrick, "IBM Shares Its Secrets," *Fortune,* September 5, 2005, 60–67. Steve Hamm, "Big Blue Goes for Big Win," *BusinessWeek,* March 10, 2008, 63–65. "Globalization's Offspring," Economist.com, April 4, 2007. Samuel J. Palmisano, "The Globally Integrated Enterprise," *Foreign Affairs,* 85(3), 2006, 127–138. Jessi Hempel, "IBM's Super Second Act," *Fortune,* March 21, 2011, 55–61.

Strategy Application

Microsoft and Nokia Alliance

Google first unleashed Android, a key piece of mobile telephone strategy in the form of a package of open Linux-based software designed to make it easier and cheaper to build the next generation of smartphone and mobile services, and then pioneered the Open Handset Alliance to compete against Nokia and Microsoft systems. The logic is that open handsets, running any applications users want, weakens the conventional mobile telephone business model. Google is trying to make the value chain in wireless mobile like the broadband Internet market, where applications are developed independently of device manufacturers and network operators.

In 2009, Microsoft and Nokia—once fierce rivals in the mobile telecommunications business—announced an alliance to bring advanced business software to smartphone to counter the strength of BlackBerry and the Apple iPhone. The alliance also responds to Google's moves into free online software aimed at Microsoft's business customers, and the threat of the Open Handset Alliance.

The partnership between the world's largest software company and the largest mobile phone maker (at the time) means that the latest online versions of Microsoft's Office suite will be available on a range of Nokia handheld devices.

By teaming up, Microsoft and Nokia aim to compete more effectively with Android and Apple than they could do separately. Faced with declining market share in smartphones, Nokia specifically looks to sharpen its response to the iPhone, and device rivals using Google's Android operating system, while at the same time reducing its software development costs. Nokia looks to regain lost ground, while sharing the execution cost with Microsoft.

Nonetheless, critics fear that Nokia's abandonment of its "burning platform" (its own Symbian operating system) in favor of Microsoft's Windows, will condemn the company to a future as a commoditized hardware producer with low margins.

Sources: Mike Harvey, "Microsoft and Nokia Team Up to Challenge Dominance of Rivals' Smartphone Devices," *Times,* August 13, 2009, 40. Andrew Ward, "Nokia Points to Android as the Biggest Threat," *Financial Times,* April 23–24, 2011, 18. Andrew Ward, "Nokia's Microsoft Tie-Up Still Under Scrutiny," *Financial Times,* April 8, 2011, 23.

relationship strategy may result in a much more attractive value offering. The STRATEGY APPLICATION describes alliance between Microsoft and Nokia. In the fiercely competitive smartphone market, these companies have identified greater opportunities to enhance customer value by collaborating rather than competing. Microsoft wants its online

EXHIBIT 7.2
Drivers of Interorganizational Relationships

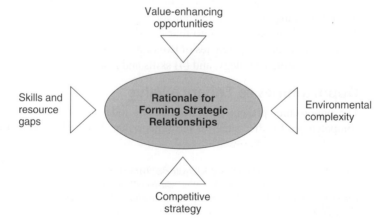

Value-enhancing opportunities

Skills and resource gaps

Rationale for Forming Strategic Relationships

Environmental complexity

Competitive strategy

business software on new generations of smartphones, and Nokia wants access to Microsoft's operating system.

In manufacturing business, modularity in product and process design offers a useful basis for leveraging interorganizational capabilities to create superior customer value. It consists of "building a complex product or process from smaller subsystems that can be designed independently yet function together as a whole."[3] A key feature of modularity is the flexibility gained by designers, producers, and product users. Companies are able to partner with others in design and production of modules or subsystems. The computer industry has led in advancing the use of modularity: chip designers, computer manufacturers, component specialists, and software firms are able to make unique contributions to product design, manufacture, and use by working within the framework of an integrated architecture, which indicates how the modules fit together and the functions each will perform.

Environmental Complexity

The theme of the changing and turbulent global business environment is examined in several chapters, so the present discussion is brief. Environments display escalating turbulence and diversity. Diversity refers to differences between the elements in the environment, including people, organizations, and social forces affecting resources.[4] Interlinked global markets create important challenges for companies. Coping with diversity involves both the internal organization and its relationships with other organizations. Environmental diversity reduces the capacity of an organization to respond quickly to customer needs and new product development.[5] Organizations meet this challenge by (1) altering their internal organization structures (see Chapter 14) and (2) establishing strategic relationships with other organizations.

Procter and Gamble has reconfigured itself from being an inward-facing company to an outward-facing organization that is open to collaboration. More than 50 percent of its innovation output comes from outside the company. When a revolutionary food wrapping technology was developed, P&G chose not to follow the old model of launching its own brand. The CEO took the view that this would not maximize value for the company, and instead entered a joint venture with a key competitor, who already had brand, sales, and distribution strengths in this market.[6]

Environmental diversity makes it difficult to link buyers and the goods and services that meet buyers' needs and wants in the marketplace. Because of this, companies are teaming up to meet the requirements of fragmented markets and complex technologies. These strategies may involve supplier and producer collaboration, strategic alliances between competitors, joint ventures between industry members, and network organizations that coordinate partnerships and alliances with many other organizations.[7]

[3]Carliss Y. Baldwin and Kim B. Clark, "Managing in an Age of Modularity," *Harvard Business Review,* September–October 1997, 84–93 at 84.

[4]Ravi S. Achrol, "Evolution of the Marketing Organization: New Forms for the Turbulent Environments," *Journal of Marketing,* October 1991, 78–79.

[5]Ibid.

[6]Rod Newing, "From Inward to Outward," *Financial Times Report: Understanding the Culture of Collaboration,* June 29, 2007, 14.

[7]Frederick E. Webster, Jr., "The Changing Role of Marketing in the Organization," *Journal of Marketing,* October 1992, 1–17.

Competitive Strategy

In some cases, working with other organizations may be a key element of how an organization competes. There are several examples suggesting this factor is of increasing importance. The "hollow organization" competes primarily through its relationships with other organizations to deliver value to end-users. The "hollow" airline, for example, is one where the airline itself owns little more than its brand, network and Internet site—engineering and maintenance services are outsourced; aircraft are leased by the hour from the manufacturer; airport services are provided by third-party suppliers; food and catering services are bought-in; sales and distribution channels are online; and alliances with other airlines provide access to a network of destinations. The entirely hollow airline does not yet exist, but many companies in this sector already display several of its characteristics. This strategy relies on the ability to manage an array of strategic relationships with outsourcers, suppliers, and alliances.

Skills and Resource Gaps

The skills and resource requirements of technologies in many industries often surpass the capabilities of a single organization. Even those companies that can develop the capabilities may do so faster via partnering. The sharing of complementary technologies and risks are important drivers for strategic partnerships.

The INNOVATION APPLICATION describing the development of software applications around Apple's iPhone and iPad devices is an interesting illustration of the power of collaboration. The "apps," which are worth $2.4 billion a year, drive Apple's device sales, but are provided by independent software developers working at their own risk.

Technology Constraints

Technology constraints impact industry giants as well as smaller firms. Small companies with specialized competitive strengths are able to achieve impressive bargaining power with larger firms because of their high levels of competence in specialized technology areas, and their ability to substantially compress development time. The partnerships between large and small pharmaceutical companies are illustrative. The small firm gains financial support, while the large firm gets access to specialized technology.

Access to technology and other skills, specialization advantages, and the opportunity to enhance product value are important motivations for establishing relationships among organizations. These relationships may be vertical between suppliers and producers or horizontal across industry members.

Financial Constraints

The financial needs for competing in global markets are often greater than the capacity of a single organization. As a result, many companies must seek partners in order to obtain the resources essential for competing in many industries, or to spread the risks of financial loss with another firm.

For example, Astron Clinica is a small British technology company with 28 employees. It developed the Siascope machine—a device that scans the skin for melanomas. Scientists from P&G's beauty products division recognized the potential for the machine to evaluate skin conditions in the choice of beauty care products. The device was developed into the Siascope handheld scanner branded under the Olay name (P&G's first ever cobranding). The companies now have a research collaboration as well as a commercial agreement. Alone Astron Clinica could not have taken the product to market—nor afforded the costly one-page U.S. national newspaper advertisements, provided by P&G, for their machines.[8]

---

[8]Jenny Wiggins, "Why Little and Large Teamed Up on Skincare," *Financial Times,* November 8, 2006, 14.

Apple's innovatory devices, particularly the iPhone smartphone and the iPad tablet computer have been globally successful. Underpinning this success has been the opening of the Apple platform to applications "apps" developers across the world.

Apps have provided Apple with the ability to disrupt the established order in computers, music, cellphones, and video games to date, and possibly publishing next. The apps phenomenon may be the most important thing that Apple has ever created. They have created a new ecosystem around devices that people want and the App Store that makes them easy to find and buy. The App Store offers more than 185,000 apps for sale.

More than 100,000 apps drive sales of the iPhone and iPad with users installing an average of 10 apps a month. The apps drive device sales which in turn drives device sales. Apps extend into business software—Salesforce.com saw 200,000 downloads of its customer relations app to the iPhone in 2010, which is a driver of growing corporate sales of the Apple apps.

In 2010, a video game produced by San Francisco developers called Pocket God became the number one download from the Apple App Store—in a single year 2.1 billion people downloaded the game at a price of 99 cents.

Apple offers software developers direct access to the consumer via the real estate of the iPhone and iPad screen. Developers set the price and Apple takes a 30 percent cut of the income.

Apple was able to demand that network carriers like AT&T give up control over the programs that could operate on their airwaves. The company in effect took the control of handsets won from the carriers and gave it to a teeming mass of independent programmers. The potential audience drew in tens of thousands of registered programmers.

More then 125,000 developers work to make apps for Apple products. Apple pays them nothing. They sign contracts agreeing to Apple's rigorous terms, and hope users will buy their apps or view ads on them.

By 2010, the Apple apps economy was worth £2.4 billion, with $200 million sold per month.

Apple's value chain is underpinned by the company's ability to manage strategic relationships with network carriers, independent developers, and other content providers. But Apple's future depends as much on managing its collaborators as beating its competitors.

Sources: Joseph Menn, "Store Set to be the Apple of Master's Eye," *Financial Times,* October 21, 2009, 18. Dominic Rushe, "Apps Generation Makes a Killing from Apple," *Sunday Times,* January 31, 2010, S3, 9. Peter Burrows, "Apple's Endlessly Expanding Universe," *Bloomberg BusinessWeek,* April 26–May 2, 2010, 92–99.

Market Access

Interorganizational relationships are also important in gaining access to markets. Products have traditionally been distributed through marketing intermediaries such as wholesalers and retailers in order to access end-user markets. These vertical channels of distribution are important in linking supply and demand. Horizontal relationships have often been established between competing firms to access global markets and domestic market segments not served by the cooperating firms. These cooperative marketing agreements expand the traditional channel of distribution coverage and gain the advantage of market knowledge in international markets.

Standard Chartered Bank is an interesting example of a company establishing a strong competitive position in emerging markets through a combination of internal growth, strategic alliances, and acquisitions. Standard Chartered was formed by the 1969 merger of The Standard Bank of British South Africa and the Chartered Bank of India, Australia, and China. It derives 90 percent of its profits from Asia, Africa, and the Middle East. It is expanding aggressively in India and China. The unique network built by the bank combines deep local knowledge with global capability to offer innovative products and services in the consumer and wholesale banking markets. Standard Chartered has outmaneuvered and outperformed larger rivals in building its positioning in emerging markets, and delivered remarkably robust performance during the recession of the late-2000s compared to many banks.[9]

International strategic alliances are used by many companies competing throughout the world. Commercial air travel is one of the more active industries involving overseas partners and competing through strategic alliances. This sector provides an interesting example also of the creation of new corporate brands through strategic alliances, where the alliance becomes the brand.[10] Around 77 percent of the global airline market is taken by the three major alliances: *oneworld* (12 member airlines built around American Airlines and British Airways), with 23 percent of the global market; *Skyteam* (14 members built around Delta and Air France/KLM), taking 25 percent of the market; and *Star Alliance* (built around Lufthansa, United, US Airways, and Continental with 27 member airlines), taking 29 percent of the market.[11] These strategic relationships have become central to competing in this industry. In effect, competition is between alliances rather than between individual organizations.

Nonetheless, gaining international market access through alliance and joint venture is not always straightforward and requires careful evaluation and management. The GLOBAL APPLICATION describes oil giant BP's difficult experiences in its alliances in the Russian market. The legacy of a highly conflictual joint venture, entangled with complex governmental politics and impacted by organized crime, is a major strategic constraint on other developments by the company in this very important market, on which it has a high level of dependence.

Information Technology

Information technology makes establishing interorganizational relationships feasible in terms of time, cost, and effectiveness. Advances in information technology provide an important resource for improving the effectiveness of both internal and interorganizational communications. Information systems enable organizations to effectively communicate even though the collaborating firms are widely dispersed geographically. In particular, the Internet provides a powerful means, for example, to reduce product development times by sharing designs for components and subassemblies with suppliers, customers and collaborators throughout the world. Internet collaboration tools allow unified communications (combining information systems with voice and text messaging), the development operation of global virtual teams, video and Web conferencing, and asynchronous communication (where people interact over a period of time rather than responding instantly to questions of information). These tools facilitate working across traditional corporate boundaries.[12]

---

[9]Peter Thal Larsen, "One-Time 'Banana-Skin' Bank Blossoms," *Financial Times,* May 25, 2007, 19. Patricia Kownsmann and Chester Yung, "Standard Chartered Net Rises," *Wall Street Journal,* March 4, 2010, 25.
[10]Hong-Wei He and John M. T. Balmer, "Alliance Brands: Building Corporate Brands Through Strategic Alliances," *Journal of Brand Management,* 13(4–5), 2006, 242–256.
[11]www.tourismfuturesintl.com, access July 16, 2011.
[12]Rod Newing, "The Great Enabler," *Financial Times Report: Understanding the Culture of Collaboration,* June 29, 2007, 18–19.

BP's global strategy involves a number of strategic relationships, particularly in emerging markets like Russia. These relationships have proved to be problematic and extremely difficult for the company to manage. Alliances in Russia have to be placed in the context also of close involvement by the national government.

BP led a joint venture in Russia—TNK-BP—with 50 percent owned by a quartet of powerful Russian oligarchs trading as AAR. TNK-BP owns more than 200 important oil licenses and six refineries, and accounts for a quarter of BP's total worldwide oil reserves. The CEO of the TNK-BP venture was U.S. executive Bob Dudley. The venture was characterized by conflict, friction, and a struggle for control of the company from the outset, leading to open war between BP and its Russian partners over dividend payments in particular. A strategic triumph for BP was rapidly turning into an expensive trap.

Disputes came to head when in 2008, Dudley had to flee Moscow and run the business from a secret location for several months following harassment from the Russian authorities and a visa dispute, leading to the threat of imprisonment. He appeared to have misinterpreted arcane Kremlin politics and underestimated the influence of his oligarch partners.

In 2010, now-CEO of BP, Dudley announced an ambitious deal with Rosneft (a state-owned Russian oil group) for an Arctic exploration project and share swap. Its TNK-BP partners objected to this deal and won a tribunal injunction to block it, claiming exclusive rights to BP activities in Russia under their shareholder agreement.

BP looked to buy out its TNK-BP partners, though the Russian government did not want TNK-BP to be wholly foreign owned. The support of Russian Prime Minister Putin and Deputy Prime Minister Sechin for the Rosneft deal counted for little in the political infighting leading up to the 2012 presidential elections.

In 2011, BP offered its TNK-BP partners participation in the Arctic alliance with Rosneft if they removed their legal objections, but the partners wanted the Rosneft deal as part of the TNK-BP venture and refused to cooperate. In June 2011, Mr Sechin reported in the *Wall Street Journal* that the Rosneft deal was dead. As the deal with BP collapsed, Rosneft started to look for a new partner for the Arctic project. Investors started to demand a breakup of the BP business.

Sources: Danny Fortson, "Torments of Bob Dudley." *Sunday Times,* April 17, 2011, S3, 5. Guy Chazan and Jacob Gronholt-Pedersen, "BP Presses for Time as Rosneft Eyes New Partner," *Wall Street Journal,* April 14, 2011, 1. Catherine Belton and Sylvia Pfeifer, "Dudley Faces Backlash Over Russian Failure," *Financial Times,* April 14, 2011, 21.

Evaluating the Potential for Collaboration

Collaborative relations may include shared activities such as product and process design, cooperative marketing programs, applications assistance, long-term supply contracts, and just-in-time inventory programs. The amount of collaboration may vary substantially across industries and individual companies. Moreover, in a given competitive situation a firm may pursue different degrees of collaboration across its customer base. For example, some customer relationships are transactional, but the same supplier may seek collaborative relationships with other customers.

Several criteria are relevant when considering possible collaborative relationships with other organizations. We examine each factor, indicating important issues concerning how the factor may impact a strategic relationship.

What Is the Strategy?

Partnering is the result of two organizations working together toward a common objective such as sharing technologies, market access, or compressing new product development time. For example, a supplier may benefit from a customer's leading-edge application of

P&G is creatively using partnerships and collaborative relationships with other organizations to refine and extend its Web business. Strategic relationships underpin a new business model and value chain for P&G.

- In 2008, P&G started swapping employees with Google—teams from the two companies sitting in on each others training and planning meetings.
- P&G, the biggest advertising spender in the world has woken up to the fact that the next generation of laundry, detergent, toilet paper, and skin cream buyers spends more time online that watching television.
- Google wants a bigger slice of P&G's $8.7 billion advertising spend.
- The employee swap has surprised both sides—the Google team was astounded that P&G would promote the Pampers brand without inviting "motherhood" bloggers to the press conference; the P&G executives were amazed that their Google counterparts did not recognize Tide's signature orange-colored packaging as a key part of the brand's image.

Not long after the Google initiative, P&G took a stake in the U.K. online grocery retailer Ocado—its first ever investment in a retail business. P&G's goal was to use Ocado as a testing ground to better understand how consumers use the Internet.

P&G is testing its ability to use the Internet to sell toothpaste, household cleaners, and diapers direct to U.S. households, in a long-term challenge to its retail partners. The company is using a third party to operate the Essentials.com site that is exclusively selling P&G brands. The Essentials site is one of the hot links from the community-focused websites P&G runs for its brands.

In 2010, P&G started selling brands direct to the U.S consumer for the first time from its "eStore" site, bringing the company into direct competition with the e-commerce sites of its retailers customers like Wal-Mart, Target, CVS, and Walgreens. The site also supports online brand building through social networks like Facebook.

Sources: Jonathan Birchall, "P&G Web Moves Challenge Partners," *Financial Times,* October 20, 2008, 6. Ellen Byron, "A New Odd Couple: Google and P&G Swap Workers to Spur Innovation," *Wall Street Journal,* November 29, 2008, 16–17. Elizabeth Rigby, "P&G Takes a Stake in Lossmaking Ocado in Boost to Online Retailer," *Financial Times,* November 27, 2008, 19. Jonathan Birchall, "P&G Goes Online to Compete for Sales," *Financial Times,* May 20, 2010, 20.

the supplier's product. The key issue is that there should be a strong underlying strategic logic for collaboration. The alignment between alliance strategy and business strategy is crucial to success in partnering.[13] Many alliance failures show a management concern for the alliance as an end in itself, rather than as a means toward achieving a broader strategic goal.[14]

The INTERNET APPLICATION describing P&G's move into direct online marketing to consumers is illustrative. A strategy of opening up the direct distribution of consumer products involves collaborative relationships with Google, online retailer Ocado, and third-party website operators, leading to the launch of P&G's own online offering. The exercise has been one of steady learning and progression by P&G.

---

[13]Salvatore Parise and John C. Henderson, "Knowledge Resource Exchange in Strategic Alliances," *IBM Systems Journal,* 40(4), 2001, 908–924.

[14]James D. Bamford, Benjamin Gomes-Casseres, and Michael S. Robinson, *Mastering Alliance Strategy: A Comprehensive Guide to Design, Management and Organization* (Somerset NJ: Jossey-Bass, 2002).

Research by Accenture on alliance issues and trends finds that for nearly half the companies involved in strategic alliances, learning was seen as the critical goal. Achieving learning goals through alliances is highly associated with successful alliances.[15] Consider the strategic rationale for alliance between Boeing and Lockheed Martin to promote the advancement of the future of air transportation in the United States. Rapid expansion of air traffic in the United States identifies an opportunity in developing new generations of air traffic control systems to enable this growth. The collaboration brings together Lockheed Martin's air traffic management experience with Boeing's strengths in aircraft systems, avionics, aviation operations, and airspace simulation and modeling.[16] While the challenges in meeting the goals of the alliance are considerable, there is a clear and compelling strategic logic from the outset.

The Costs of Collaboration

This factor considers the costs as well as the benefits of partnering with customers, suppliers, and competitors. Strategic relationships are demanding in terms of both time and resources. The relationship may require substantial investments by the partners, which may not easily be transferred to other business relationships. Accordingly, the benefits need to be candidly assessed and compared to the costs. This requires careful planning of the relationship to spell out activities, participants, and costs.

Opportunity costs should form part of this calculation—participation in an alliance may restrict a company's freedom to pursue other strategies. Alliance partners may object to strategic moves by other alliance members, even though they are outside the scope of the alliance agreement. For example, alliances have become a central part of competitive strategy in the auto industry, particularly in addressing emerging markets. But 2008 saw Mahindra & Mahindra pulling out of a $1 billion joint venture with Renault and Nissan, because Mahindra was unhappy with Renault's tie-up with Indian motorcycle maker Bajaj, established a few months earlier. While multiple alliances are the norm in Indian business, Mahindra saw a conflict of interest.[17] As networks of alliances and partnerships develop, the potential for partners to perceive conflicts of interest escalates.

Is Relationship Strategy Essential?

Normally, relationships are formed because the partners believe that combining their efforts is essential, and that pursuing the project alone is not feasible. However, experience indicates that strategic relationships are more likely to succeed when dependence is important and equivalent between the collaborating organizations.

Are Good Candidates Available?

Promising partners may be unwilling to collaborate or already involved with other organizations. For example, in global airlines many of the most desirable alliance partners have established relationships, as detailed earlier, and partnering with weaker companies is increasingly undesirable and risky in this sector.

Do Relationships Fit Our Culture?

The corporate cultures of the partners should be adaptable to the partnership. This issue is particularly important for partners from countries with substantial national cultural differences—recall the BP situation in its Russian partnerships described in the earlier

---

[15]Nick Palmer, "Alliances: Learning to Change," www.accenture.com, January 2003.
[16]"Boeing and Lockheed Martin Form Strategic Alliance," *Airline Industry Information,* January 23, 2007, 1.
[17]Amy Yee, "Mahindra Pulls Out of $1bn Joint Venture," *Financial Times,* January 8, 2008, 17.

GLOBAL APPLICATION. The partners' approach to business activities and priorities should be compatible.

For example, the global alliance between British Telecom (BT) and AT&T aimed to combine resources around "Concert"—a product to provide multinational corporations with a single, global telecoms source based on "virtual private networks," with target sales of $10 billion. BT had a history of failed partnerships in its globalization history. AT&T lacked experience in collaborative situations, and its earlier global alliance—Unisource—had broken down over AT&T's reluctance to cooperate with foreign partners or commit to common investment with them. After a relationship of persistent squabbling between BT and AT&T, the Concert alliance collapsed after only 2 years. Costs to BT of unwinding from the alliance were estimated at $2.1 billion, with charges of $5.5 billion to AT&T from Concert's demise.[18]

We will discuss shortly the related question of partnering capabilities. It is becoming clear that the ability to operate effective relationship strategies between organizations relies on skills and capabilities that vary considerably between organizations.

Forms of Organizational Relationships

The types of organizational relationships that may be formed by a firm are shown in Exhibit 7.3. Included are supplier and customer partnerships (vertical relationships), lateral (horizontal relationships), and internal relationships. Relationships are both interorganizational (between organizations) and intraorganizational (internal relationships). Supplier relationships include those companies providing goods and services, some of which may be regarded as strategic suppliers or outsourcers, because they impact on the focal firm's ability to deliver value to its customers. Customer partnerships include both intermediate customers (e.g., distributors) and end-use customers (consumers of the product). Lateral relationships may be with competitors, unrelated companies at the same stage of the value chain, or governmental organizations. Internal partnerships include relationships with strategic business units, functional departments, and employees within the business.

A useful way to examine organizational relationships is to consider whether the tie between firms is *vertical* or *horizontal*. The focal firm may participate in both vertical and horizontal relationships. We first look at vertical relationships among organizations, and then, strategic alliances and joint ventures, followed by internal relationships.

EXHIBIT 7.3
Vertical and Lateral Organizational Relationships

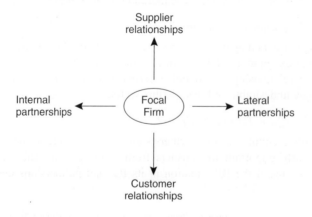

[18]"Concertina'd," *Financial Times,* October 17, 2001, 28.

Supplier Relationships

Moving products through various stages in the value-added process often involves linking suppliers, manufacturers, distributors, and consumer and business end-users of goods and services into vertical channels. Functional specialization and efficiency create the need for different types of organizations. For example, wholesalers stock products in inventory and deploy them when needed to retailers, thus reducing the delays of ordering direct from manufacturers.

Over recent years the use of collaborative relationships with suppliers has expanded in many industries. While problems such as industrial secrets, labor objections, and loss of control have occurred, the benefits of leveraging distinctive capabilities of partners are substantial in developing new products and manufacturing processes. These relationships are extensively used in the automotive and computer industries.

The complexity and importance of effective management of supplier relationships in the value chain is illustrated in the RELATIONSHIP APPLICATION concerning Boeing's "Dreamliner," the 787 model. The 787 is a highly innovative design, which has sold very well to airlines, yet the complexity of the supply chain has repeatedly led to delays in product launch and the fracturing of relationships between Boeing and its airline customers. The first delivery was promised for 2011,3 years behind schedule, though with some questions over whether Boeing can produce the aircraft fast enough to meet the backlog of orders.

Strategic Suppliers

Relationships with suppliers are often managed by a company's procurement function. However, when a supplier has a major impact on the company's value offering and its relationships with its own customers, the supplier may be regarded as strategic. In some situations, managing supplier relationship management systems closely linked to customer relationship management systems may be mandated. In such cases, the involvement of marketing executives in supplier relationships may be vital.[19]

Outsourcing

The outsourcing of activities, such as transportation, repair and maintenance services, information systems, and human resources functions has become widely used. Outsourcing parts of the value chain process to partners is a form of leveraged growth—it allows a company to expand sales without capital investment in all stages of the value chain.[20] The suppliers and buyers of a vast array of raw materials, parts and components, equipment, and services (e.g., consulting, maintenance) are linked together in vertical channels of distribution. In recent years a considerable amount of outsourcing activity has located manufacturing and systems like call centers in emerging markets with very low costs. In many cases outsourcing operations has been followed by outsourcing R&D and design— for example, Taiwanese companies design and manufacture most laptop computers sold worldwide; GlaxoSmithKline and Eli Lilly are teaming up with Asian biotechnology companies to cut the $500 million cost of bringing a new pharmaceutical to market.[21]

---

[19]Nigel F Piercy, "Strategic Relationships Between Boundary-Spanning Functions: Aligning Customer Relationship Management with Supplier Relationship Management," *Industrial Marketing Management,* 18, 2009, 857–864. Frederick E. Webster, Jr., "The Changing Role of Marketing in the Organization," *Journal of Marketing,* October 1992, 1–17.

[20]John Hagel, "Leveraged Growth: Expanding Sales Without Sacrificing Profits," *Harvard Business Review,* October 2002, 69–77.

[21]Pete Encardio and Bruce Einhorn, "Outsourcing Innovation," *BusinessWeek,* March 21, 2005, 46–53.

The Boeing 787—the Dreamliner—was developed as the Boeing challenge to the Airbus A380 superjet. The Dreamliner is a radical design shift, built out of lightweight carbon-reinforced plastics. It promises a 20 percent reduction in fuel, as well as a quieter and more comfortable ride for passengers.

When the first 787 was displayed in Seattle in July 2007, Boeing had logged 642 orders, and was effectively sold out until 2014. However, as the 2008 delivery dates loomed, it became clear there would be substantial delays in delivering the aircraft on time, because of problems in completing the final assembly—it emerged that the first aircraft displayed in July 2007 was actually held together with temporary fasteners. Major design difficulties left U.S. workers struggling to rework parts sent from global suppliers.

If faced with delays in deliveries, airlines have no hesitation in resisting supplier "rationing" and switching purchase to another manufacturer, or demanding large penalty payments. Boeing had expected customers to accept "modest delays" in agreed delivery dates but in January 2008 Qantas became the first airline to announce it was seeking damages from Boeing for late delivery of the 787 and was rapidly followed by others.

A key element of the Dreamliner strategy is the widespread outsourcing of manufacture. Boeing itself is responsible for only about 10 percent of manufacturing (by value)—the tail fin and final assembly. The rest is done by 40 partners, with the wings built in Japan, the carbon composite fuselage in Italy and the United States, and the landing gear in France. Boeing is positioned as the "systems integrator" rather than manufacturer—70 percent of the components in the Dreamliner are sourced from outside the United States. The Dreamliner has 367,000 parts, sourced from a global network of 900 suppliers. The Dreamliner is the first plane in Boeing's history to be designed largely by other companies. Managing a supply chain this complex stretched Boeing's capabilities, and there have been major problems with missing and poorly fitted components and delays.

By March 2008, Boeing was struggling with redesign of the attachment of the wings to the plane, promising further delays. The selling point of novelty and economy achieved through outsourcing has turned out to be the biggest source of problems for Boeing. The Dreamliner project has been delayed through unsolved technical problems and manufacturing holdups in the supply chain. By 2010, Boeing had secured 847 orders for the 787, making it the most successful new commercial aircraft launch in history but was running more then 2 years late in deliveries. The first delivery to Air Nippon in 2011 was 3 years behind schedule.

The aircraft business is demanding and involves high-technology, international competition and is severely affected by economic and currency conditions. Nonetheless, the Dreamliner issues that are most problematic rely on relationship management capabilities more than technology and selling. For future designs, Boeing plans to give suppliers a long-term look at where they will need to invest to meet Boeing's demands for parts, and to monitor suppliers more closely.

Sources: John Gapper, "A Cleverer Way to Build A Boeing," *Financial Times,* July 9, 2007, 11. Keith Epstein and Judith Crown, "Globalization Bites Boeing," *BusinessWeek,* March 24, 2008, 32. Jeremy Lemer, "Dreamliner Test Flights Halted," *Financial Times,* November 11, 2010, 21. Hal Weitzman, "At Full Throttle," *Financial Times,* July 6, 2011, 11. Hal Weitzman, "Boeing's 787 Ready for Take-Off After Three-Year Delay," *Financial Times,* July 19, 2011, 22.

Outsourcing may be a key element of business strategy. For example, in the highly competitive 3D television market, Sony and Samsung are pursuing quite different sourcing approaches. Sony is committed to outsourcing TV production to cut costs and enhance profits, while Samsung uses in-house manufacture of TVs to retain control and achieve internal efficiencies. Both companies believe their approach will deliver competitive edge in different ways.[22]

Nonetheless, there are strategic risks in outsourcing key activities like manufacturing to third parties. While there are attractions in reducing manufacturing costs by outsourcing, and focusing on R&D, product design, and marketing, contract manufacturers may become competitors or share information with rivals. It may be difficult to quickly replace contract manufacturers under these conditions.[23]

Intermediate Customer Relationships

Intermediate customers may include marketing intermediaries (e.g., wholesalers and retailers) and producers assembling products for the end-use market. Vertical relationships also occur between producers and marketing intermediaries). Value chain relationships provide access to consumer and organizational end-users. Interorganizational relationships vary from highly collaborative to transactional ties. We discuss value chain relationships in Chapter 10.

Value chain considerations may motivate new strategic relationships. The Gap has sales problems in its traditional markets in North America and Europe. Gap Inc. has developed franchise arrangements to open stores in Singapore and Malaysia, partnering with local retailer F J Benjamin Holdings. The move is based on the logic that Gap has a strong following among consumers from these markets who shop at Gap when they are abroad, who can now shop in local franchised Gap outlets.[24]

Nonetheless, in a tough postrecession environment, many intermediate customer relationships remain dominated by cost-cutting and consolidating global sourcing of products. In 2010, Wal-Mart started an initiative to reduce its costs by 5 to 15 percent across its entire supply chain (worth \$4–\$12 billion), mainly by increasing the proportion of goods it buys direct from manufacturers rather than through third-party procurement companies or suppliers.[25]

End-User Customer Relationships

The driving force underlying strategic relationships is that a company may enhance its ability to satisfy customers and cope with a rapidly changing business environment through partnering. For example, Boeing involves airlines and even passengers in design choices for its airframes; Marriott partners with corporate customers to add value to corporate travel; and Harley-Davidson has a Harley Owners Group with more than 100,000 members.

Some believe that the future of competition lies in co-creation initiatives with customers—only by letting individual corporate customers and consumers shape products and service can real fit with customer needs be achieved.[26]

[22]Moon Ihlwan, "Sony and Samsung's Strategic Split," *Bloomberg BusinessWeek,* January 18, 2010, 52.
[23]Benito Arruñada and Xosé H. Vásquez, "When Your Contract Manufacturer Becomes Your Competitor," *Harvard Business Review,* September 2006, 135–144.
[24]Kevin Lim, "Gap To Open First Stores in Asia Outside Japan," *Wall Street Journal,* August 2, 2006.
[25]Jonathan Birchall, "Walmart Looks to Cut Billions from Supply Costs," *Financial Times,* January 4, 2010, 19.
[26]C. K. Prahalad and Venkat Ramaswamy, *The Future of Competition: Co-Creating Unique Value With Customers* (Cambridge, MA: Harvard Business School Press, 2004).

Although building collaborative relationships may not always be the best course of action, this avenue for gaining a competitive edge is increasing in popularity. However, an important issue is selecting the customers with which to develop relationships since some may not want to partner and others may not offer enough potential to justify partnering with them. A look at Marriott's partnering strategy is illustrative.

> Building customer relationships is the core sales strategy of Marriott International, Inc.'s Business Travel Sales Organization. The travel manager is the target for the selling activities of the 2,500 person sales organization. The key features of the major account sales strategy are: (1) choose customers wisely (Marriott follows a comprehensive customer evaluation process); (2) build customer research into the value proposition (understanding what drives customer value and satisfaction); (3) lead with learning by following a step-by-step sales process; (4) invest in the customer's goal setting process, rather than Marriott's; and (5) develop a relationship strategy with a sense of purpose, trust, open access, shared leadership, and continuous learning. Marriott's management recognizes that customers who regularly purchase the company's services are valuable assets who demand continuous attention by high-performance teams. Rapidly changing markets and customer diversity add to the importance of developing strong ties with valuable customers to stay in touch with their changing requirements.[27]

Relationship strategies need to recognize differences in the value of customers to the seller as well as the specific requirements of customers.[28] Marriott's emphasis on carefully selecting customers with whom to partner illustrates the importance of prioritizing sales strategies by segmenting accounts for corporate influence and profit. Relationship building is appropriate when large differences exist in the value of customers. Valuable customers may want close collaboration from their suppliers concerning product design, inventory planning, and order processing, and they may proactively pursue collaboration. The objective is to develop buyer and seller relationships so that both partners benefit from the relationship.

Strategic Customers[29]

In the management of relationships with large corporate customers, many organizations have moved to the adoption of strategic/key account management structures and global account management approaches as ways of building teams dedicated to managing the relationship with the most valuable customers.[30] Procter and Gamble's 200-person team to manage its relationship with Wal-Mart, its biggest retailer customer, is illustrative. Strategic, key, and global accounts (customers) are increasingly considered strategic partners.

Dominant Customers

Importantly, some customers may dominate a supplier's customer portfolio. These customers may pose major challenges because of their ability to exert considerable influence and control over suppliers. For example, more than 450 suppliers have established offices in Wal-Mart's home town of Bentonville, Arkansas, in order to be close to their largest customer.[31] Nonetheless, it may be mistaken to regard dominant customers as strategic

[27]David W. Cravens, "The Changing Role of the Salesforce in the Corporation," *Marketing Management,* Fall 1995, 50.
[28]Ibid.
[29]This section is based on: Nigel F Piercy and Nikala Lane, *Strategic Customer Management: Strategizing the Sales Organization* (Oxford: Oxford University Press, 2009).
[30]Noel Capon, *Key Account Management and Planning* (New York: Free Press, 2001).
[31]Jenny Wiggins and Elizabeth Rigby, "New Neighbour Disney Knocks at Tesco's Door," *Financial Times,* December 9–10, 2006, 3.

relationships or partners—they are simply very large accounts with a conventional, though possibly imbalanced, buyer-seller relationship with suppliers. These sales relationships are examined in Chapter 13.

The strategic significance of dominant customers should not be underestimated. The merger of Gillette with Procter and Gamble in 2006 created the world's largest consumer brands group, with a combined portfolio of brands that gives the company a much stronger bargaining position with major retailers like Wal-Mart, Carrefour, and Tesco. However, the merger also represents a significant change to P&G's business model with a new focus on lower-income consumers in markets like India and China. In positioning in these emerging markets, P&G is deliberately not partnering with powerful global retailers. In China, Gillette offers P&G access to a huge distribution system staffed by individual Chinese entrepreneurs—what P&G calls a "down the trade" system ending up with a one-person kiosk in a small village selling shampoo and toothpaste. The result of P&G's strategy should be to achieve growth in Asian markets and reduce dependence on mature markets dominated by powerful dominant retailers.[32]

Strategic Account Management

Strategic customers are those with which the relationship is based on collaboration and joint decision making, where both buyer and seller invest time and resources in the strategic relationship. For a growing number of companies strategic account management (SAM) provides an innovative model for managing relationships with their most important customers. The importance of these developments is underlined when customers actively promote concentration in their supply base and attempt to restrict supplier numbers. For example, in September 2005, Ford Motor announced its intention to reduce its supply base of 2,000 by around half to reduce its $90 billion purchasing budget and to improve quality. By 2009, Ford more than halved its global supply base from 3,300 in 2004 to 1,600, with a goal of quickly getting down to 750 suppliers. Ford targets seven "key suppliers" covering about half its parts purchasing, with enhanced access to Ford's engineering and product planning. Ford will work more closely with selected suppliers, consulting them earlier in the design process and giving them access to key business plans on future vehicles, and committing to giving them business to allow them to plan their own investments.[33] Interestingly, Ford cut the development cost of seats for the Focus sedan by awarding the entire global contract to a single supplier—Johnson Controls.[34]

The rationale for SAM is that a supplier's most important customers require dedicated resources and special value-adding activities (such as, joint product development, business planning, consulting services) in the value offering. SAM is seen a new business model that goes beyond conventional buyer-seller relationships to establish partnership and joint decision making between the customer and supplier. Nonetheless, there are substantial risks in high levels of dependence on strategic customers. Investments should be weighed against the risks of customer disloyalty and strategic change, as well as the perception of strategic customer privileges by the rest of the customer base. The attraction of SAM may rest on a degree of market and relationship stability which may not exist.

---

[32]Jeremy Grant, "Mr Daley's Mission: To Reach 6Bn Shoppers and Make Money," *Financial Times,* July 15, 2005, 32.

[33]James Mackintosh and Bernard Simon, "Ford To Focus On Business From 'Key Suppliers,'" *Financial Times,* September 30, 2005, 32. Bernard Simon and Julie MacIntosh, "Chrysler Turns the Screw on Beleaguered Parts Makers," *Financial Times,* February 2, 2009, 20.

[34]Bernard Simon, "Carmakers Explore Fresh Terrain with Suppliers," *Financial Times,* May 5, 2010, 23.

For example, in 2005 Apple Computer announced an end to its long-term strategic relationship with IBM as supplier of microprocessors for Apple desktop computers, and named Intel as the replacement. Apple believes that Intel can provide components for the products of the future, with higher performance and lower prices. Supplier switch is increasingly viewed as a strategic move by companies like Apple to leverage their competitive position, which takes higher priority than loyalty to existing strategic suppliers. Indeed, a supplier switch of this kind may be an inevitable consequence of strategic change.[35]

Strategic Alliances

A strategic alliance between two organizations is an agreement to cooperate to achieve one or more common strategic objectives. Strategic alliances play a major role in almost every industry, and the typical corporation relies on alliances for 15–20 percent of its total revenues, assets or income.[36] The relationship is horizontal in scope, between companies at the same level in the value chain. While the term alliance is sometimes used to designate customer partnerships, it is used here to identify collaborative relationships between companies that are competitors or in related industries. The alliance relationship is intended to be long term and strategically important to both parties. The following discussion assumes an alliance between two parties, though recognizing that a company may have several alliance partners.

Each organization's contribution to the alliance is intended to complement the partner's contribution. The alliance requires each participant to yield some of its independence. The rationale for the relationship may be to gain access to markets, utilize existing distribution channels, share technology development costs, or obtain specific skills or resources. The alliance is not a merger between two independent organizations, although the termination of an alliance may eventually lead to an acquisition of one partner by the other partner. It is different from a joint venture launched by two firms or a formal contractual relationship between organizations. Moreover, the alliance involves more than purchasing stock in another company. Instead, it is a commitment to actively participate on a common project or program that is strategic in scope.

Alliance Success

The competitive realities of surviving and prospering in the complex and rapidly changing business environment encourage companies to form strategic alliances in many different industries. Some strategic partnerships have endured for substantial periods—an ongoing Fuji-Xerox joint venture was established in 1962, and Samsung and Corning have been working together since 1973.[37]

Nonetheless, the record of success of alliances is not favorable, and success rates of less than 50 percent have often been found by researchers.[38] While the alliance is a promising strategy for enhancing the competitive advantage of the partners, several failures have occurred due to the complexity of managing these relationships.

Alliance Weaknesses

Weaknesses in alliances may come from several causes. For example, collaborations suffer from the potential threat of opportunistic behavior by one of the partnering organizations. For example, recall the BP problems with relationships with its partners in Russia

---

[35]Scott Morrison and Richard Waters, "Time Comes to 'Think Different.'" *Financial Times,* June 7, 2005, 25.
[36]David Ernst and James Bamford, "Your Alliances Are Too Stable," *Harvard Business Review,* June 2005, 133–141.
[37]Loren Gary, "A Growing Reliance on Alliance," *Harvard Management Update,* April 2004, 3–4.
[38]Salvatore Parise and John C. Henderson, "Knowledge Resource Exchange in Strategic Alliances," *IBM Systems Journal,* 40(4), 2001, 908–924.

in the GLOBAL APPLICATION. Weak alignment of objectives, performance metrics, and clashes of corporate cultures can all undermine alliance effectiveness. Poorly structured partnerships may be extremely damaging to all concerned.

Types of Alliances

An alliance typically involves marketing, research and development, operations (manufacturing), and/or financial relationship between the partners. Capabilities may be exchanged or shared. In addition to functions performed by the partners, other aspects of alliances may include market coverage and effectively matching the specific characteristics of the partners. The alliance helps each partner to obtain business and technical skills and experience that are not available internally. One partner contributes unique capabilities to the other organization in return for needed skills and experience. The intent of the alliance is that both parties benefit from sharing complementary functional responsibilities rather than independently performing them.

Requirements for Alliance Success

The success of the alliance may depend heavily on effectively matching the capabilities of the participating organizations and on achieving the full commitment of each partner to the alliance. The benefits and the trade-offs in the alliance must be favorable for each of the partners. The contribution of one partner should fill a gap in the other partner's capabilities.

One important concern in the alliance relationship is that the partner may gain access to confidential technology and other proprietary information. While this issue is important, the essential consideration is assessing the relationship's risks and rewards and the integrity of the alliance partner. A strong bond of trust between the partners exists in most successful relationships. The purpose of the alliance is for each partner to contribute something distinctive rather than to transfer core skills to the other partner. It is important for the managers in each organization to evaluate the advisability and risks concerning the transfer of skills and technologies to the partner.

Alliance Vulnerabilities

Relatedly, it is important to recognize that alliance relationships may be fragile and difficult to sustain effectively, particularly if there is a lack of trust or mutuality of interest between partners. Moreover, careful analysis is required of the impact of a failed alliance on a company's remaining ability to compete and survive. The higher the level of dependence on a partner organization, the greater the strategic vulnerability created if the alliance fails.

Joint Ventures

Joint ventures are agreements between two or more firms to establish a separate entity. These relationships may be used in several ways: to develop a new market opportunity; to access an international market; to share costs and financial risks; to gain a share of local manufacturing profits; or to acquire knowledge or technology for the core business. For example, Coca-Cola has a longstanding joint venture with Nestlé—Beverage Partners Worldwide (formerly Coca-Cola and Nestlé Refreshments), established in 2001—to take its tea and coffee brands into global markets alongside Nestlé products. In 2007, this venture was refocused on the ready-to-drink tea market—Nestlé tea brands are licensed to Coca-Cola outside the United States, but Nestlé and Coca-Cola compete in coffee and nontea beverages worldwide and in the ready-to-drink tea market in the United States. In some cases, joint ventures can grow valuable assets—in 2001 Xerox was able to sell half its stake in Fuji Xerox Co. to Fuji for $1.3 billion, to counter liquidity problems.[39]

While joint ventures are similar to strategic alliances, a venture results in the creation of a new organization. Environmental turbulence and risk set the rationale for the venture more so than a major skill/resource gap, although both pressures may be present. Lack of success in the management of joint ventures often reflects a lack of adequate attention to planning and executing the launch of the venture, leading to strategic conflicts between partners, governance problems, and missed operational synergies. A dedicated team focused on managing alignment of strategic interests of the partners and creating a shared governance system improves the chances of building a high-performing joint venture.[40]

For example, in 2006 consumer electronics giant Best Buy launched a strategic relationship with Carphone Warehouse in Europe, in a joint venture to open more than 200 cellphone retail stores in the United States, mainly within existing Best Buy stores, to boost Best Buy's mobile phone sales using Carphone's technology and expertise. By 2008, Best Buy had made a further $2.2 billion investment in an expanded joint venture with Carphone to establish Best Buy stores in Europe, as part of its globalization strategy.[41]

Internal Partnering

Internal partnerships may occur between business units, functional departments, and individual employees. The intent is to encourage and facilitate cross-functional cooperation rather than specialization. Key internal processes such as new product development benefit from cross-functional cooperation in areas such as research and development, marketing, purchasing, finance, and operations working together to identify, evaluate, develop, and commercialize new product concepts.

The success of internal relationship strategies requires developing strong internal collaboration that cuts across functional boundaries. As noted in earlier chapters, many companies are using teams of people from various functions to manage processes such as new-product development, customer relationships, order processing, and delivery of products. As we discussed in Chapter 1, a market-oriented organization is committed to delivering superior customer value through market sensing, interfunctional cooperation, and shared decision making. The relationship strategy requires attention to the internal structure. The starting point is building a collaborative customer-driven internal culture. Research suggests that organizations that collaborate well internally perform better in meeting customer needs, accommodating special customer requests, and introducing new products. As a result, they are perceived more favorably by customers.[42]

Four steps may be important to evaluating internal partnering: (1) a cost-benefit analysis of the potential gains from improved internal synergies; (2) investigation of why collaboration is not happening—personal relationship difficulties, competing priorities, resource constraints, skills gaps; (3) assessment of what is needed to unblock the problem—restructuring, personnel changes, senior management intervention; and (4) consideration of the possible downside of efforts to enhance internal collaboration before acting—distraction costs, loss of accountability, initiative, and motivation.[43]

---

[39]Matthew Schifrin, "Partner or Perish," *Forbes,* May 21, 2001, 26–28.

[40]James Bamford, David Ernst, and David G. Fubrini, "Launching A World-Class Joint Venture," *Harvard Business Review,* February 2004, 90–100.

[41]Jonathan Birchall, "Piggyback Strategies Bring Home the Bacon," *Financial Times,* November 10–11, 2007, 18. Jonathan Birchall, "Best Buy Plots Its Global Strategy," *Financial Times,* May 12, 2008, 14.

[42]Richard Wilding, "Playing to the Tune of Shared Success," *Financial Times Report: Understanding Collaboration,* November 10, 2006, 2–3.

[43]Andrew Campbell, "Why In-House Collaboration Is So Difficult," *Financial Times,* February 13, 2006, 14.

Managing Interorganizational Relationships

Forming and managing effective collaborative partnerships between independent organizations is complex, so we need to look further into the process of developing effective relationships. Key elements of this process are indicated in Exhibit 7.4. The objective of the relationship is first considered, followed by a discussion of several relationship management guidelines.

Objective of the Relationship

In some situations collaborative action may be an option rather than a requirement. Several possible strategic objectives of relationships are discussed below.

New Technologies and Competencies

This objective is a continuing challenge for many companies because of the increasing complexity of technology and the short time span between identifying and commercializing new technologies. Alliance with others may provide a rapid approach to learning about new technologies and their potentials.

Developing New Markets and Building Market Position

Alliances and other collaborative relationships may be promising alternatives for a single company interested in developing a market or entering a global market. This strategy requires finding potential partners that have strong marketing capabilities, and/or market position. Collaboration may be used to enter a new product market or to geographically expand a position in a market already served.

For example, Coca Cola and PepsiCo are both targeting the high-growth ready-to-drink coffee market. PepsiCo has extended its U.S. partnership with Starbucks to cover international markets starting with China—Starbucks develops the products like Frappuccino and Double-Shot canned and bottled coffees, and PepsiCo provides distribution and marketing capabilities. Coca Cola's response has been to form a partnership with the Illycaffe Group—one of Italy's most famous names in coffee—to challenge the successful PepsiCo/Starbucks combine.[44]

Market Selectivity

Competing in mature markets often involves either market domination or market selectivity strategies. Competition in these markets is characterized by a small core of major firms

EXHIBIT 7.4
Managing Organizational Relationships

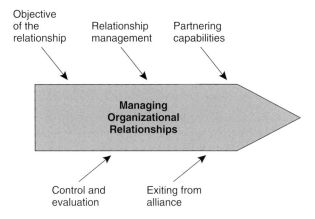

---

[44]Paul Betts, "Coke Aims to Give Pepsi a Roasting in Cold Coffee War," *Financial Times,* October 17, 2007, 26.

and several smaller competitors that concentrate their efforts in market segments. Firms with small market position need to adopt strategies that enable them to compete in market segments where they have unique strengths and/or the segments are not of interest to large competitors. Cooperative relationships may be appropriate for these firms. The possible avenues for relationships include purchasing components to be processed and marketed to one or a few market segments, subcontracting to industry leaders, and providing distribution services to industry leaders.

Restructuring and Cost-Reduction

Competing in international markets often requires companies to restructure and/or reduce product costs. Restructuring may result in forming cooperative relationships with other organizations. Cost-reduction requirements may encourage the firm to locate low-cost sources of supply. Many producers in Europe, Japan, and the United States establish relationships with companies in newly industrialized countries such as Korea and Taiwan. These collaborative relationships enable companies to reduce plant investment and product costs.

Relationship Management

While collaborative relationships are increasingly necessary, the available concepts and methods for managing these partnerships are limited. Contemporary business management skills and experience apply primarily to a single organization rather than offering guidelines for managing interorganizational relationships. However, the experience that companies have gained in managing distribution-channel relationships provides a useful, although incomplete, set of guidelines.

Planning

Comprehensive planning is critical when combining the skills and resources of two independent organizations to achieve one or more strategic objectives. The objectives must be specified, alternative strategies for achieving the objectives evaluated, and decisions made concerning how the relationship will be structured and managed. To determine the feasibility and attractiveness of the proposed relationship, the initiating partner may want to evaluate several potential partners before selecting one.

Trust and Self-Interest

Successful partnerships involve trust and respect between the partners and a willingness to share with each other on various self-interest issues. Confrontational relationships are not likely to be successful. Prior informal experience may be useful in showing whether participants can cooperate on a more formalized strategic project.

Conflicts

Realizing that conflicts will occur is an important aspect of the relationship. The partners must respond when conflicts occur and work proactively to resolve the issues. Mechanisms for conflict resolution include training the personnel who are involved in relationships, establishing a council or interorganizational committee, and appointing a mutually acceptable ombudsman to resolve problems.

For example, Suzuki Motor and Volkswagen formed a partnership in 2009 to cooperate on small autos and new technologies. VW had the chance to build its presence in the small-auto markets in India and Japan and Suzuki looked to gain access to VW's diesel and hybrid electric car technology. However, tensions between the partners led to no cooperative projects emerging. Suzuki managers were angered to be listed as an "associate" in VW's annual report, and did not believe that VW was keeping to the agreement that the companies would be equal and independent partners and accused the German company of trying to take control.[45]

Reputational Risk

Care is required that a partnership should not be with companies where there may be risk of damage by association, for example because of the partner's ethical standards or ineffective social responsibility (see Chapter 4). In some cases there may be substantial damage. Anadarko was the U.S. partner to BP in its Macondo oil well in the Gulf of Mexico, the site of the Deepwater Horizon oil spill disaster. After the disaster, Anadarko was not simply facing sharing clean-up costs with BP, but also a major threat to its growth plans and possibly its existence, because of the relationship with BP.[46]

Leadership Structure

Strategic leadership of the partnership can be achieved by (1) developing an independent leadership structure, or (2) assigning the responsibility to one of the partners. The former may involve recruiting a project director from outside. The latter option is probably the more feasible of the two in many instances.

Flexibility

Recognizing the interdependence of the partners is essential in building successful relationships. Relationships change over time. The partnership must be flexible in order to adjust to changing conditions and partner requirements.

Cultural Differences

Strategic relationships among companies from different nations are influenced by cultural differences. Both partners must accept these realities. If partners fail to respond to the cultural variations, the relationship may be adversely affected. These differences may be related to stage of industrial development, political system, religion, economic issues, and corporate culture.

For example, the joining of U.S. automaker Chrysler with Daimler-Benz in Germany had a compelling strategic logic—combining Daimler's luxury auto skills with Chrysler's volume manufacturing abilities. Nonetheless, the relationship was terminated in 2007 with the sale of Chrysler to the private equity company Cerberus. Chrysler held a large public celebration to mark the end of its relationship with Daimler. The DaimlerChrysler relationship was dogged by poor collaboration and in-fighting between the companies. Difficulties stemmed in part from the national cultural differences and traditions between German and U.S. managers. Collaboration barriers were associated with culture differences in individualism (high for U.S. managers and much lower for Germans) and uncertainty avoidance (high for German executives and much lower for Americans).[47]

---

[45]Michiyo Nakamoto and Chris Bryant, "Suzuki Questions Future of VW Tie-Up," *Financial Times,* July 19, 2011, 22.

[46]Carola Hoyos, "Anadarko Approved Key BP Well Designs," *Financial Times,* June 30, 2010, 17. Edward Klump and Stanley Reed, "How BP's Spill Tarred Anadarko," *Bloomberg BusinessWeek,* July 26–August 1, 2010, 19–20.

[47]Tom Lester, "Masters of Collaboration," *Financial Times Report: Understanding the Culture of Collaboration,* June 29, 2007, 8.

Similarly, alliance between the Swedish pharmaceutical company Pharmacia and U.S. firm Upjohn developed serious problems because of cultural differences between managers. The Swedes practiced a gradualist style of management, favoring consensus, which clashed with the U.S. style, emphasizing decisive action and results. The Americans could not understand why the Swedes went on holiday for the entire month of August, and the Swedes could not understand why the Americans banned alcohol at lunch. Small disagreements escalated in major ones.[48]

Technology Transfer

When the partnership involves both developing technology and transferring the technology into commercial applications, special attention must be given to implementation. Important issues include organizational problems, identifying a commercial sponsor, appointing a team to achieve the transfer, and building transfer mechanisms into the plan. Planners, marketers, and production people are important participants in the transfer process.

Learning from a Partner's Strengths

Finally, the opportunity for an organization to expand its skills and experience should be exploited. Asian companies have been particularly effective in taking advantage of this opportunity.

Partnering Capabilities

In addition to establishing a sound process for designing and managing alliances, it is important to consider what is necessary to build an organizational competence in strategic alliance. The capability to manage effectively through partnerships does not exist in all organizations. Partnering effectively with other organizations is a key core competence, which may need to be developed. Eli Lilly is recognized as a company that generates value from its alliances, and this company addresses the skills gap by running partnership training classes for its managers and for its partners. Other successful alliance strategies are operated by companies like Hewlett-Packard and Oracle by establishing a dedicated strategic alliance function in the company.[49]

Control and Evaluation[50]

Many conventional approaches to control and evaluation are inappropriate and ineffective in managing interorganizational collaborations. Alliance performance evaluation is a critical success factor, which requires the development and implementation of a formal evaluation process that reflects the unique differences between alliances and more traditional organizational forms. A "balanced scorecard" approach allows evaluation criteria to be specified in financial, customer focus, internal business process, and learning and growth dimensions. The goal is to have measurement metrics with both short- and long-term importance, and to incorporate both quantitative measures (e.g., sales, growth, costs) but also important qualitative measures that speak to the strength and sustainability of the alliance (e.g., trust, communications flows, conflicts, culture gaps). Importantly, particularly in the early stages of an alliance relationship, qualitative metrics may be the most significant predictors of success.

---

[48]Morgan Witzel, "The Power of Difference," *Financial Times Report: Understanding Collaboration,* November 10, 2006, 13.

[49]Jeffrey H. Dyer, Prashant Kale, and Harbir Singh, "How To Make Strategic Alliances Work," *Sloan Management Review,* Summer 2001, 37–43.

[50]This discussion is based on Karen Cravens, Nigel Piercy, and David Cravens, "Assessing the Performance of Strategic Alliances," *European Management Journal,* 18(5), 2000, 529–541.

The challenge of developing appropriate ways to assess alliance performance and strength is considerable. It is useful to consider measures and metrics against the following principles:

- Metrics should be comparable across alliances.
- Metrics should be defined and discussed with alliance partners.
- There should be clarity about the implications of alliance performance.
- A process for auditing alliance performance should be implemented.
- Alliance performance should be linked to individual performance review.
- A forum should be created for reviewing and acting on alliance performance data.[51]

Poorly constructed relationships may show up in a variety of alliance difficulties: a lack of learning and innovation; project delays, dissatisfaction with the partner's performance, missed milestones, unresponsiveness to changes in the marketplace and perceptions that the alliance is not adding value. These indications of problems may reflect poor relationship quality.[52]

There is a strong argument that the performance of alliances should be subject to regular review to establish where problems exist, and where restructuring arrangements may be advantageous. Companies may miss opportunities to reduce costs and generate additional income by failing to: (1) *launch a process*—scan major alliances for signs they need restructuring; (2) *diagnose performance*—assess the venture's strategic fit and the attractiveness of continuing the alliance; (3) *generate restructuring options*—decide whether to fix, grow or exit the alliance; or (4) *execute the changes*—assign accountability for making changes.[53]

Exiting from Alliance

Specific collaborations and alliances may come to the end of their useful lives when the relationship fails to deliver value, or the market opportunity declines. One attraction of strategic alliances is that they can be fluid and temporary arrangements to take advantage of opportunities when they occur. Effective management of strategic relationships should pay attention to managing the termination of alliances when necessary. Research suggests that executives often persist with alliances, even though measures indicate the collaboration is no longer attractive.[54] This may reflect the sunk costs in the alliance, the desire to imitate competitors' alliance successes, and the high external visibility of the alliance.

Early preparations for the eventual end of the alliance are recommended. The lack of agreement about how the alliance should be ended when appropriate suggests that when tensions arise between partners, alliance managers are reluctant to alert their superiors and risk being blamed for the failure and instead focus their tensions on alliance counterparts. The outcome is likely to be a dysfunctional strategic alliance marked by deep animosity between alliance managers. Discussions about alliance termination are likely to be emotionally charged and ineffective.[55]

---

[51]Jonathan Hughes, *Implementing Alliance Metrics: Six Basic Principles,* Vantage Partners' White Paper, www.vantagepartners.com/publications, 2002.

[52]Stuart Kliman and Christopher Hiserman, *Creating an Alliance Management Capability* (Boston: Vantage Partners, 2005).

[53]David Ernst and James Bamford, "Your Alliances Are Too Stable," *Harvard Business Review,* June 2005, 133–141.

[54]Andrew Delios, Andrew C. Inkpen, and Jerry Ross, "Escalation in Strategic Alliances," *Management International Review,* 44(4), 2004, 457–479.

[55]Ranjay Gulati, Maxim Sytch, and Parth Mehrotra, "Preparing for the Exit: When Forming a Business Alliance, Don't Ignore One of the Most Crucial Ingredients—How to Break Up," *Wall Street Journal,* March 3, 2007, R-1.

The assignment of responsibility for disengagement from strategic partnerships may usefully be given to senior executives not linked to establishing the original alliance. A successful disengagement plan, agreed between partners at the establishment of the alliance, should consider:

- Identifying and agreeing on the events that will trigger exit from the alliance
- Detailed description of the rights of each partner to alliance assets and products on disengagement
- Design of the disengagement process
- A communication plan for continuous flow of information to alliance partners, customers, suppliers and other involved parties during the alliance dissolution.[56]

Failure risks in alliances and potential losses from failures mandate careful attention to the costs and processes of ending strategic relationships when this becomes a more attractive option than continuing.

Global Relationships Among Organizations

Many organizations compete in global markets. For example, the multinational corporation organization form operates in several countries, using a separate organization in each country. Examples of joint ventures and strategic alliances competing in international markets are discussed throughout the chapter. Collaboration and cooperation between international businesses have become the norm in many industries. The increasing globalization of a company based in emerging markets India and China is especially important. Effective global relationships offer significant advantages in gaining market access and leveraging the capabilities of individual firms. Nonetheless, it is important to recognize that global relationships may operate in significantly different ways to those in the domestic marketplace.

The Global Integrated Enterprise

IBM is a highly internationalized business. It has over 50,000 employees in India—IBM's second biggest operation outside the United States. The company has moved its head of procurement from New York to Shenzen in China.[57]

Samuel Palmisano, IBM's chairman and CEO, has defined a vision for the globally integrated enterprise (GIE), as the 21st century successor to the multinational corporation.[58] Palmisano argues that businesses are changing in fundamental ways—structurally, operationally, and culturally—in response to imperatives for globalization and the impact of new technology. The emerging GIE is a company that shapes its strategy, management, and operations in pursuit of a new goal: the integration of production and value delivery worldwide. Shared business practices and connected business activities make it possible for companies to transfer work from in-house operations to outside specialists. Global integration forces companies to choose where they want work performed geographically, and whether they want it performed in-house or by an external partner. The center of the GIE is global collaboration both with commercial partners and governments. Palmisano's vision at IBM provides substantial support for the emphasis we have placed on the development

[56]Ibid.
[57]"Globalization's Offspring," Economist.com, April 4, 2007.
[58]Samuel J. Palmisamo, "The Globally Integrated Enterprise," *Foreign Affairs,* 85(3), 2006, 127–138.

of strategic relationships to deliver superior value to customers. Importantly, he places this imperative in a global or worldwide context.

Similarly, lowered barriers to international trade and technological developments suggest companies must concentrate their areas of expertise, while collaborating globally with others specializing in different activities. The goal is to find ways of working with suppliers not simply to cut costs but to collaborate on product innovation. Li & Fung is a Hong Kong–based clothing supplier described as a "process orchestrator." The company produces goods for Western companies drawing on a network of 7,500 partners—yarn from Korea, dyed in Thailand, woven in Taiwan, cut in Bangladesh, assembled in Mexico, with a zipper from Japan. Importantly, these companies are partners to Li & Fung rather than simply suppliers. By operating as a network, the partners help each other innovate in both design and manufacture.[59]

Inter-Nation Collaborations

Inter-nation partnerships may create significant market change and shifts in international trading patterns. Consider the relationship between Korea and China. In the 1990s Korea's focus was on the U.S. market and its foreign relations were centered on Washington, D.C. Increasingly in the 21st century, Korea looks at China as the regional leader in diplomacy and statecraft. In 2003, South Korean businesses invested more in China—$4.4 billion—than U.S. companies, which put $4.2 billion into China. Some 25,000 Korean companies manufacture in Korea. Companies like Samsung and LG are using China as a major manufacturing base to produce goods more cheaply and increase global market share for their electronics products and appliances. While some fear the effects of the export of Korean jobs and technology to China, the relationship between the two countries has major global implications for the future.[60]

Interestingly, the Airbus Industrie A380 airliner project—creating the largest passenger airliner ever built—was based on an innovative cross-national alliance, greatly favored by European governments, with jobs spread over Germany, France, Britain, and Spain. The alliance has been plagued by defections—British Aerospace sold its stake in 2006—senior management losses, cross-border wrangles, and weak governance. The project has received large government subsidies, leaving Boeing in the United States feeling substantially disadvantaged. However, it appears that the price of government subsidy has been constant political meddling reducing efficiency and leading to huge production mistakes.[61] Technical problems, which should have been avoided, and production delays to the A380 suggest in this situation the coupling of cross-national difficulties and government interference may offset much of the advantage achieved through public subsidy.

The Strategic Role of Government

While the role of the government in the United States is largely one of facilitating and regulating free enterprise, governments in several other countries play a proactive role with business organizations.

Government Interventions

Government interventions range from indicating preferred strategies to companies through to the full subsidy of commercial enterprises to achieve political ends. For example, in

---

[59]John Hagel III and John Seely-Brown, *The Only Sustainable Edge: Why Business Strategy Depends on Productive Friction and Dynamic Specialization* (Boston: Harvard Business School Press, 2005).

[60]Moon Ihlwan and Dexter Roberts, "Korea's China Play," *BusinessWeek,* March 29, 2004, 48–52.

[61]Carol Matlock, "Snafus: Wayward Airbus," *BusinessWeek,* October 23, 2006, 46–48.

Traditionally De Beers, the world's largest diamond miner, acted to set diamond prices and to control supply—acting as buyer of last resort for other producers. However, the opening of big mines outside its control in the 1990s shifted De Beers's focus away from controlling the supply of rough diamonds to fostering demand for them.

De Beers has 120 years experience of weaving its way through African politics, from founder Cecil Rhodes's imperialist dreams, to the company's dealings with South Africa's apartheid regime, and now to the demands from African governments for a share of the business.

The loosening of De Beer's control on the market was driven by the powerful trend of "beneficiation"—the demand by African states for a greater share of their diamond wealth. The political imperative of "beneficiation" has led to the location of profitable operations like diamond cutting and manufacturing in countries where the stones are mined. Only by cooperating with governments' development aims has De Beers maintained its market position as the biggest producer of rough diamonds.

In Botswana, location of two of De Beer's most valuable mines, diamond sorting has been placed in a desert estate next to Gaborne's airport. The decision to "Africanize" a function previously conducted in London was made by the Botswana government. Beneficiation is also taking place in Namibia, the Democratic Republic of Congo, and Angola. In South Africa, a black empowerment consortium owns 26 percent of the De Beers mining operations. De Beers's managing director says: "Beneficiation is not about altruism but about good business; it creates much closer relationships with our partners."

Close cooperation with partners saw De Beers weather the decline in demand for diamonds in the economic downturn by reducing supply, to take some loss-making years but to get back to profit in 2011.

Sources: William MacNamara, "De Beers Cedes Diamond Grip to African States," *Financial Times,* November 29, 2007, 6. Michael Skapinker, "De Beers Chief Seeks Fresh Settings," *Financial Times,* March 17, 2008, 14. William MacNamara, "De Beers Rediscovers Its Sparkle," *Financial Times,* February 12–13, 2011, 17.

Japan the aerospace industry has been reduced over several years to the role of licensees and parts suppliers. To rebuild the sector for the benefit of Japan economically and politically, the government is supporting a regional jet project with Mitsubishi Heavy Industries—the MRJ will be the first jet-powered commercial passenger aircraft designed and built in Japan. The government's role is to provide a third of the development cost. Analysts suggest it is unlikely that the project will break even.[62]

Nonetheless, in international markets working effectively with local governments may be essential. The STRATEGY APPLICATION describes how diamond producer De Beers has worked with local governments in Africa to reshape the value chain in ways compatible with government ambitions for local prosperity.

However, there are some concerns in the environment experienced globally as countries recover from economic recession that government interventions in business may escalate.[63] Many executives looking to identify growth prospects emphasize the importance of international growth, particularly in the emerging markets. However, drastic reductions

---

[62]Jonathan Soble, "Japanese Aerospace Makes Ready for Take-Off," *Financial Times,* July 5, 2007, 7.

[63]Nigel F. Piercy, David W. Cravens, and Nikala Lane, "Marketing Out of the Recession: Recovery is Coming, But Things Will Never Be the Same Again," *The Marketing Review,* 10(1), 2010, 3–23.

in cross-border lending by banks, as they focus on their domestic markets, means even as risk-taking returns, world finance is likely to be depressed for many years, leading to a "deglobalization" pressure.[64] The Bank for International Settlements reports that the sharp withdrawal of banks from international lending is unprecedented and poses serious risks to global trade and finance.[65]

Further, from the onset of the downturn, there have been concerns that recession would bring with it 1930s-style curbs on trade. Already there has been a marked increase in trade investigations against China and other nations in a trend suggesting a surge in protectionist measures.[66] The Global Trade Alert database is tracking protectionist reforms and underlines an outbreak of discriminatory measures like rises in tariffs that importers must pay or bans on products and preferences for local suppliers. The World Trade Organization also reports a global increase in trade-restricting measures introduced by governments to support and protect key sectors.[67] Interestingly, trade restrictions are favored mainly by the small, emerging markets being targeted by Western companies, rather than large developed countries.

There are distinct signs that because of economic downturn, nationalism has become a stronger force, leading to regulations, trade barriers, and even sovereign-wealth funds, with the effect that national barriers have risen as states increase control over resources and protect their own industries from foreign competition and investment. While trade restrictions by governments to protect their own companies may be seen as temporary, it may be more difficult politically to reverse such policies once they are in place.

The impact of changing government policies on the ability of companies to trade internationally is a growing area of concern in the postrecession environment. Understanding local and national government priorities is critical in emerging markets.

Competing With State-Owned Enterprises

Nations may operate government-owned corporations, though in recent years a trend toward privatization of these corporations occurred in the United Kingdom, Australia, Mexico, and many other countries. Nevertheless, government-supported corporations continue to compete in various global industries, including air transportation, chemicals, computers, and consumer electronics. Not surprisingly, competitors often are critical of government organizations claiming they receive unfair advantage resulting from government financial support.

The impact of state involvement in enterprise may be considerable. In the petrochemicals/energy market, the term "the seven sisters" was once used to describe the Western companies that controlled oil supplies in the Middle East. By the 2000s only four of the original seven sisters remained: ExxonMobile and Chevron in the United States and BP and Royal Dutch Shell in Europe. These companies control around 10 percent of the world's oil and gas and hold 3 percent of reserves. These companies have been sidelined by a new "seven sisters." The new players are largely state-owned and they control almost one-third of the world's oil and gas production, and more than one-third of oil and gas reserves. The new "seven sisters" are Saudi Aramco, Russia's Gazprom, CNPC of China, BIOC of Iran, Venezuala's PDVSA, Brazil's Petrobas, and Petronas of Malaysia. Two-thirds of the world's new refining capacity will be located in Asia and the Middle East, with the biggest

---

[64]John Plender, "Homeward Bound," *Financial Times,* April 30, 2009, 9.

[65]Nina Koeppen, "Banks May Create a Global Threat," *Wall Street Journal,* July 24–26, 2009, 17.

[66]Sarah O'Connor, "Recession Prompts Rise in Protectionist Probes," *Financial Times,* July 23, 2009, 5.

[67]Joshua Chaffin, "WTO Sees Global Increase in Protectionism," *Financial Times,* July 2, 2009, 6.

Corporate social responsibility initiatives have led to several industry-based alliances to tackle environmental and social risks—Hewlett-Packard, Dell, IBM, and others have launched an industry code of conduct for suppliers; big brands like Mattel and Hasbro have said their suppliers must meet the jointly agreed standards of the International Council of Toy Industries.

The idea is to pool experience and to reduce the inefficiencies when all companies in a sector attempt to individually audit suppliers environmental and employment practices.

Nonetheless, the collaborative nature of these arrangements means participants must pay attention to competition legislation. If companies are regarded as too deeply entwined, regulators may find that competition between them has weakened and take action.

Industry alliances for any purpose must avoid certain behaviors:

- **Market manipulation**—Corporate alliances must demonstrate that their joint activities do not lead to price fixing or other forms of market limitation
- **Boycotts**—Codes of conduct must be voluntary and individual companies must address issues of breach of the code by suppliers
- **Benefits**—An alliance should demonstrate the low risk of anticompetitive harm and procompetitive benefits and efficiencies to be gained
- **"Comfort letters"**—Alliances can seek an official letter from bodies like the U.S. Justice Department stating the authority does not intent to challenge the activities of the alliance.

Sources: Sarah Murray, "Alliances Heed Anti-Trust Traps," *Financial Times,* January 5, 2006, 10.
Robert Wright, "Competition Spotlight Could Fall on 'Partners,'" *Financial Times,* April 22–23, 2006, 21.

projects led by state-owned national oil companies. In effect, control of this sector has changed hands.[68]

Collaborating With State-Owned Enterprises

Internationalization imperatives will place many companies in the position where they consider potentials for developing strategic relationships with enterprises actually owned by foreign governments, or that have recently been taken out of state ownership, and which may remain closely linked to local political infrastructure. Considerable care is required in evaluating the potential gains from such relationships, and understanding the different requirements for managing them.

For example, the Chinese government has relaxed regulations to allow foreign market entrants to form joint ventures, and to allow foreigners to acquire state-owned enterprises (SOEs). Research suggests that several factors are important in developing strategic relationships with Chinese enterprises of this kind. First, Chinese SOEs tend to have substantial organizational slack, which may indicate either inefficiencies or potential for improved performance. Second, many Chinese SOEs maintain three sets of books: one set exaggerates performance to impress administrative superiors, one underreports performance for tax purposes, and one set is fairly accurate for use by managers themselves.

---

[68]Carola Hoyas, "The New Seven Sisters: Oil and Gas Giants That Dwarf the West's Top Producers," *Financial Times,* March 12, 2007, 15. Carola Hoyus, "East to Crack West's Grip on Refining," *Financial Times,* November 14, 2008, 26. Brian O'Keefe, "The Next Oil Colossus," *Fortune,* March 21, 2011, 63–70.

Foreign negotiators are likely to be shown the "bragging books." Finally, the belief that ethnic Chinese managers from overseas Chinese economies will be the best choice for managing joint ventures is misplaced—local staff are quite capable of responding well to Western managers, while Chinese managers may struggle with an ambiguous managerial identity.[69]

Government Regulation

There have been notable advances in recent decades in slackening government control of business. Nonetheless, antitrust laws in the United States and Europe prohibit certain kinds of cooperation among direct competitors in an industry. The intense global competition and loss of competitiveness in many industries seem to be changing the traditional view of lone-wolf competition among companies. While antitrust laws continue to be in place, there may be more flexibility by government agencies in interpreting whether collaboration among firms in an industry is an antitrust issue. For example, even the pursuit of corporate social responsibility initiatives on a collaborative basis raises several antitrust issues. This situation is described in the ETHICS APPLICATION.

Summary

The competitive realities of surviving and prospering in the complex and rapidly changing business environment encourage teaming up with other companies, so collaborative strategic relationships among independent companies are escalating in importance. The major drivers of interorganizational relationships are value opportunities, environmental complexity, competitive strategy, and skills and resource gaps. Enhanced value offers to customers may be achieved more effectively through collaboration with other organizations than independently. Complex environments mandate altering internal organizational structures and establishing strategic relationships with other organizations. Alliance and collaboration may be a key part of how an organization differentiates itself and competes. Technology and financial constraints, the need to access markets, and the availability of information technology all contribute to skill and resource gaps, which may be filled through collaboration.

In examining the potential for collaborative relationships several criteria need to be evaluated. Important criteria include determining the underlying strategic logic of the proposed relationship, deciding whether partnering is the best way to achieve the strategic objective in the light of the real costs of collaboration, assessing how essential is the relationship, determining if good candidates are available, and considering whether collaborative relationships are compatible with the corporate culture.

Relationships between organizations range from transactional exchange to collaborative partnerships. These relationships may be vertical in the value-added chain or horizontal within or across industries. Vertical relationships involve collaboration between customers and suppliers and distribution channel linkages among firms. Dominant customers and differences between customers in prospects for the future encourage the development of strategic account management approaches. Horizontal partnerships may include competitors and other industry members. The horizontal or lateral relationships include strategic alliances and joint ventures.

Collaborative relationships are complex, and not surprisingly, generate conflicts. Many horizontal relationships have not been particularly successful, even though the number of these partnerships is escalating throughout the world. Trust and commitment between the

---

[69]Mike W Peng, "Making M&A Fly in China," *Harvard Business Review,* March 2006, 26–27.

partners are critical to building a successful relationship. Planning helps to improve the chances of success. The capability to manage effectively through partnerships requires distinct skills and new approaches not available in all organizations.

Several objectives may be achieved through strategic relationships, including gaining access to new technologies, developing new markets, building market position, implementing market segmentation strategies, and pursuing restructuring and cost-reduction strategies. The requirements for successfully managing interorganizational relationships include planning, balancing trust and self-interest, recognizing conflicts, defining leadership structure, achieving flexibility, adjusting to cultural differences, facilitating technology transfers, and learning from partners' strengths. The development of appropriate control and evaluation approaches, and the design of appropriate exit paths for these new business forms has become a priority.

Global relationships among organizations may include conventional organizational forms, alliances, joint ventures, network corporations, and trading companies. The global integrated enterprise describes a new organizational form, which may replace the conventional multinational company model. A strategy of developing global relationships internationally needs to account for the complexities of inter-nation collaborations and the role of overseas governments in facilitating and encouraging these developments. Important issues also relate to the role of interventionist governments overseas and the challenges of competing with, or collaborating with, state-owned enterprises. Antitrust regulation is also a relevant concern in developing strategic relationships internationally.

Questions for Review and Discussion

1. Discuss the major factors that encourage the formation of strategic partnerships between companies.

2. Compare and contrast vertical and horizontal strategic relationships between independent companies.

3. Discuss the similarities and differences between strategic alliances and joint ventures.

4. A German electronics company and a Japanese electronics company are discussing the formation of a strategic alliance to market the other firm's products in their respective countries. What are the important issues in making this relationship successful for both partners?

5. What are the attractions and possible problems in developing a strategic relationship with a major customer in the form of strategic account management?

6. To what extent is it reasonable for a partner organization to attempt to exert control over your strategic choices in areas not part of the alliance or joint venture?

7. Establishing successful interorganizational relationships is difficult, according to authorities. Will the success record improve in the future as more companies pursue this strategy?

8. Are vertical relationships more likely to be successful than horizontal relationships? Discuss.

9. Suppose you are seeking a Japanese strategic alliance partner to market your French pharmaceutical products in Asia. What characteristics are important in selecting a good partner?

10. Discuss how alliances may enable foreign companies to reduce the negative reaction that is anticipated if they tried to purchase companies in other countries.

11. Discuss how government may participate in helping domestic companies develop their competitive advantages in an industry such as aerospace products.

12. Identify and discuss important issues in deciding whether to create internal cross-functional relationships.

Internet Applications

A. Visit the website www.alliancestrategy.com and review the presentations and material available at the site. Summarize what factors should be considered in making alliances between organizations effective.

B. Go to the investor information and company history information on www.amazon.com. Identify the evolving network of strategic relationships with customers, suppliers, and collaborators both on the Web and with conventional organizations. Which of these relationships are the most important to Amazon?

Applications

A. Review Microsoft and Nokia alliance described in a STRATEGY APPLICATION in this chapter. Identify the strategy underpinning this alliance. Is this an effective counter to the strength of competitors like Google and Apple? What conclusions can be drawn about the strategic vulnerabilities of alliances?

B. Examine the material presented in the GLOBAL APPLICATION concerning BP's Russian alliances. Use an Internet search to update on the status of BP's Russian ventures. What does this case illustrate about the challenges in operating joint ventures and alliances in emerging markets overseas? Are there issues in this case, which may be worth considering by other companies with global ambitions?

Chapter

8

Innovation and New-Product Strategy

Creativity and innovation are essential to all organizations' growth and performance in the global marketplace. Innovation takes many forms including new goods and services, organizational processes, and business models. Importantly, even when the critical role of innovation is recognized by managers, deciding which innovation opportunities to pursue is a demanding challenge. Companies must create a culture of innovation and develop effective processes to identify innovation opportunities and transform ideas into new-product successes.

Consider, for example, the pervasive impact of this innovation. A potentially powerful process capability in new manufacturing technology has emerged which is forecast to have a powerful impact on manufacturing processes.[1] The innovation, called additive manufacturing, enables producing a product by building it up a layer at a time. The exciting aspect of the technology is that costs are reduced by eliminating production lines and waste is substantially reduced. It is not necessary to produce large quantities in order to gain cost advantages. Product parts (e.g., aircraft wings) can be made in configurations that existing production techniques cannot produce. The technology is very limited currently but the potential is exciting. Moreover, the technology is likely to be disruptive wherever it is applied. It promises to significantly impact the economics of manufacturing.

The economic pressures and market turbulence that impacted companies in a wide range of industries during the early years of the 21st century shifted many executives' strategic priorities away from the development of cutting edge new products.[2] The innovation processes of companies like Boeing, Kodak, and Motorola were not meeting the challenges of aggressive development of new products. Instead, short-term, bottom-line performance was the center of attention. These short-term cost initiatives may sometimes be necessary, but it is essential to also pursue long-term innovation strategies. Innovation creates competitive advantage for the organization and value for customers.

Based on a survey of CEOs and government leaders on the topic of innovation, IBM Chairman Samuel J. Polmisano highlights the following innovation initiatives as important success factors:[3]

---

[1]"Print Me a Stradivarius," *The Economist,* February 12, 2011, 11.
[2]Thomas D. Kuczmarski, Erica B. Seamon, Kathryn W. Spilotro, and Zachary T. Johnson, "The Breakthrough Mindset," *Marketing Management,* March–April 2003, 38–43.
[3]"Innovation: The View from the Top," *BusinessWeek,* April 3, 2006, 52 and 54.

- Innovation is a mandatory avenue to successful business performance due to the intense pressures of global competition and commoditization of products and processes.
- Business model innovation plays a critical role in gaining a unique position in markets and competitive space. Product differentiation is only a short-term competitive advantage.
- Collaboration relationships within the organization and among value chain members, competition, government, and other relevant groups are essential in achieving successful innovation results.
- The Chief Executive Officer must personally lead the organization's innovation culture initiatives.

In this chapter we consider the planning of new products beginning with a discussion of innovation as a customer-driven process. Next, we discuss the steps in new-product planning, including generating ideas, screening and evaluating the ideas, business analysis, product development and testing, designing the market entry strategy, market testing, and new-product introduction. The chapter concludes with a discussion of variations in the generic new-product planning process.

Innovation as a Customer-Driven Process

New-product opportunities that offer superior value to customers range from totally new innovations to incremental improvements in existing products. We discuss the different types of innovations, the importance of finding customer value opportunities, and essential drivers of successful innovations.

Types of Innovations

Innovations can be classified according to (1) newness to the market and (2) the extent of customer value created, resulting in the following types of innovations:[4]

- *Transformational Innovation:* Products that are radically new and the value created is substantial. Examples include additive manufacturing, Google, and digital cameras.
- *Substantial Innovation:* Products that are significantly new and create important value for customers. Examples include Kimberly Clark Huggies/Nappies and Diet Coke.
- *Incremental Innovations:* New products that provide improved performance or greater perceived value (or lower cost), such as a new flavor Coca-Cola.

A company's new-product initiatives may include innovation in one or more of the three categories. The reality is that many new products are extensions of existing product lines and incremental improvements of existing products rather than totally new products. These extensions and improvements account for as much as 70 to 80 percent of all innovations. The new-product-planning process that we discuss in this chapter applies to any of the three categories and is used in planning new services as well as tangible goods.

The INNOVATION APPLICATION describes several interesting innovation initiatives pursued by Google, the Internet search leader. Google is an impressive success story driven by innovative people like Marissa Mayer. Not surprisingly, in 2010 Google was No. 2 on *Fortune* magazine's list of The World's Most Admired Companies, and ranked 2nd on Bloomberg *BusinessWeek's* list of the 50 most innovative companies in the world.[5]

---

[4]Suzanne Treville, "Improving the Innovation Process," *OR/MS Today,* December 1994, 29.
[5]Geoff Colvin, "The World's Most Admired Companies," *Fortune,* March 31, 2011, 39–52. Michael Arndt and Bruce Einhorn, "The 50 Most Innovative Companies," *Bloomberg BusinessWeek,* April 25, 2010, 34–40.

Marissa Mayer joined Google in early 1999 as a programmer when the workforce totaled 20. By 2007 Google had 5,700 employees and expected sales of $16 billion. As Director of Consumer Web Products Marissa is a champion of innovation, and she favors new-product launches that are early and often.

HOW GOOGLE INNOVATES

The search leader has earned a reputation as one of the most innovative companies in the world of technology. These are illustrative of the ways Google hatches new ideas:

FREE (THINKING) TIME

Google gives all engineers one day a week to develop their own pet projects, no matter how far these projects are from the company's central mission. If work gets in the way of free days for a few weeks, they accumulate. Google News came out of this process.

THE IDEA LIST

Anyone at Google can post thoughts for new technologies of businesses on an ideas mailing list, available company-wide for input and vetting. But beware: Newbies who suggest familiar or poorly thought-out ideas can face an intellectual pummeling.

OPEN OFFICE HOURS

Think back to your professors' office hours in college. That's pretty much what key managers, including Mayer, do two or three times a week, to discuss new ideas. One success born of this approach was Google's personalized home page.

BIG BRAINSTORMS

As it has grown, Google has cut back on brainstorming sessions. Mayer still holds them eight times a year, but limits hers to 100 engineers. Six concepts are pitched and discussed for ten minutes each. The goal: To build on the initial idea with at least one complementary idea per minute.

ACQUIRE GOOD IDEAS

Although Google strongly prefers to develop technology in-house, it has also been willing to snap up small companies with interesting initiatives. In 2004 it bought Keyhole, including the technology that let Google offer sophisticated maps with satellite imagery.

Source: "Managing Google's Idea Factory," *BusinessWeek,* October 3, 2005, 88–90.

New-product initiatives are guided by customer needs analysis. Even transformational innovations should have some relationship to needs that are not being met by existing products. However, as we discuss shortly, potential customers may not be good sounding boards for radically new innovations. Importantly, these transformational innovations may have a disruptive impact on existing products.

Finding Customer Value Opportunities

Customer value requirements provide important information for determining where opportunities exist to develop new products. Market segment identification and analysis help find segments that offer new-product opportunities to the organization. Extensive study of existing and potential customers and the competition are vital in guiding effective new-product planning.

EXHIBIT 8.1
Finding New-Product Opportunities

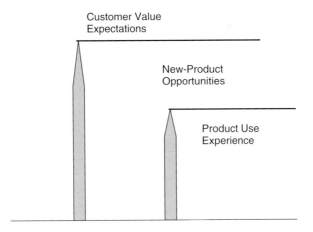

We know that customer value is the combination of benefits provided by a product minus all of the costs incurred by the buyer (see Chapter 1). Customer satisfaction indicates how well the product use experience compares to the value expected by the buyer. The closer the match between expectations and the use experience, the better the resulting value delivery.

Customer Value

The objective of customer value analysis is to identify needs for (1) new products, (2) improvements in existing products, (3) improvements in the processes that produce the products, and (4) improvements in supporting services. The intent is to find gaps (opportunities) between buyers' value expectations and the extent to which they are being met based on product use experience (see Exhibit 8.1). Everyone in the organization needs to be involved in this process. Google's innovation initiatives are illustrative. This market-driven approach to product planning helps to avoid a mismatch between technologies and customer needs.

Finding New-Product Opportunities

A difference between expectations and use experience may indicate a new product. For example, an alert U.S. Surgical Corporation (USS) salesperson saw an opportunity to satisfy a surgical need that was not being met with existing products. USS is a unit of Tyco Healthcare Group L.P. Its products include wound closure products and advanced surgical devices. The close working relationship of USS sales representatives with surgeons in operating rooms, nurses, and administrators gives USS a critical competitive advantage.[6] The salesperson identified the new-product opportunity by observing surgeons' early use of self-developed instruments to perform experiments in laparoscopy. Using this procedure, the surgeon inserts a tiny TV camera into the body with very thin surgical instruments. USS responded quickly to this need by designing and introducing a laparoscopic stapler. The product is used in gall bladder removal and other internal surgical applications.

Matching Capabilities to Value Opportunities

Each value opportunity should be considered in terms of whether the organization has the capabilities to deliver superior customer value. Organizations will normally have the

---

[6]"Getting Hot Ideas from Customers," *Fortune,* May 18, 1992, 86–87.

capabilities needed for product line extensions and incremental improvements. Developing products for a new-product category requires realistic assessment of the organization's capabilities concerning the new category. Partnering with a company that has the needed capabilities is an option concerning the addition of a new-product category.

Transformational Innovations

Customers may not be good guides to totally new-product ideas that may be called radical or breakthrough innovations since they create new families of products and businesses.[7] When such ideas are under consideration, potential customers may not understand how the new product will replace an existing product. The problem is that customers may not anticipate a preference for a revolutionary new product.[8] For example, initial response from potential users of optical fibers, video cassette recorders, Federal Express, and CNN was not encouraging. In these situations, management must form a vision about the innovation and be willing to make the commitment to develop the technology as Corning Inc. did with optical fiber technology. The risk, of course, is that management's vision may be faulty.

Incremental product improvements are guided by analyzing customer value opportunities (see Exhibit 8.1), whereas these approaches to finding new-product opportunities are not very useful in evaluating potential transformational innovations:

> The familiar admonition to be customer-driven is of little value when it is not at all clear who the customer is—when the market has never experienced the features created by the new technology. Likewise, analytic methods for evaluating new-product opportunities (e.g., discounted cash flow and market diffusion analyses) appear to be much more appropriate for incremental than for discontinuous innovation.[9]

Radical innovations have the potential of disrupting existing (sustaining) technologies and creating negative impacts on the leading firms that pursue new-product strategies using existing technologies.[10] Examples of disruptive innovations include Amazon.com., jetBlue (airline), Salesforce.com (customer management software), and steel minimills. Disruptive technologies are often not considered to be threats by firms pursuing sustaining technologies. Clayton Christensen and Michael E. Raynor in *The Innovator's Solution* offer a compelling analysis of these threats and provide important guidelines for managing disruptive innovations.[11] The challenge for companies confronted with potential disruptive opportunities and threats is recognizing that product planning processes differ for sustaining and disruptive innovations. Executives must manage both processes. It may be necessary to position the disruptive technology in a separate organization independent from the core business.

Commoditization and intense global competition are creating pressures for change. The evolution of a creative company toward a new corporate model might logically follow the steps shown in Exhibit 8.2.[12] When products become commodities, profit margins decline and differentiated advantages are difficult to achieve.

Unless proactive initiatives are taken, the existing technology in the core business is likely to dominate innovation activities. A good market/technology match is important in being successful with radical technologies. Priority should be given to market niches that

[7]Gary S. Lynn, Joseph G. Morone, and Albert S. Paulson, "Marketing and Discontinuous Innovation: The Probe and Learn Process," *California Management Review,* Spring 1996, 8–37.
[8]Ibid.
[9]Ibid., 11.
[10]Clayton M. Christensen and Michael E. Raynor, *The Innovator's Solution* (Boston: Harvard Business School Press, 2003).
[11]Ibid.
[12]Bruce Nussbaum, "How to Build Innovative Companies," *BusinessWeek,* August 1, 2005, 62–63.

EXHIBIT 8.2
The Evolution of the Creative Company A new corporate model is taking shape—focusing on creativity and innovation

Source: Bruce Nussbaum, "How to Build Innovative Companies," *BusinessWeek,* August 1, 2005, 62–63.

STEP 1

Technology and information become commoditized and globalized. Suddenly, the advantage of making things "faster, cheaper, better" diminishes, and profit margins decline.

STEP 2

With commoditization, core advantages can be shipped abroad. Outsourcing to India, China, and Eastern Europe sends a growing share of manufacturing and even the Knowledge Economy overseas.

STEP 3

Design Strategy begins to replace Six Sigma as a key organizing principle. Design plays key role in product differentiation, decision-making, and understanding the consumer experience.

STEP 4

Creative innovation becomes the key driver of growth. Companies master new design thinking and metrics and create products that address consumers' unmet, and often unarticulated, desires.

STEP 5

The successful Creative Corporation emerges, with new Innovation DNA. Winners build a fast-moving culture that routinely beats competitors because of a high success rate for innovation.

the traditional technology does not serve well. Christensen and Raynor also propose that products developed from disruptive technologies which are not currently valued by customers may match future value requirements very well. The eventual strong preference for digital photography displayed by buyers is illustrative.

Interestingly, one impact of the changing relationships with emerging markets like India and China and others is that they are perceived increasingly not simply as target markets for new products, but as sources of innovation and new products with a global impact. The geography of innovation is changing from a time when the locus of leading-edge thinking was the United States and Europe to one where the rise of Asia is beginning to dominate innovation.[13] The link between emerging markets and "reverse innovation" (the flow of innovation from emerging markets to the west) is highlighted in the GLOBAL APPLICATION.

Initiatives of Successful Innovators

Certain companies seem to consistently excel over others in developing successful new products. Importantly, successful innovators often pursue similar initiatives.

Creating an innovative culture is essential to generating successful new products. Research findings constantly point to the importance of an innovative organizational climate and culture.[14] This requires top management to position innovation as a distinct organizational priority and communicate the importance of innovation to all employees. Moreover, deciding the right innovation strategy involves defining the product, market, and technology scope of the organization. This requires determining corporate purpose

---

[13]John Kao, *Innovation Nation: How America Is Losing Its Innovation Edge, Why It Matters, and What We Can Do to Get it Back* (New York: Free Press, 2007).

[14]Robert Cooper, "Benchmarking New Product Performance: Results of the Best Practices Study," *European Management Journal,* February 1998, 1–7; "Producer Power," *The Economist,* March 4, 1995, 70; Kuczmarski et al. "The Breakthrough Mindset."

Emerging markets like India and China impact innovation in several ways. Countries like these are providing western companies not only with faster growth prospects, but also originating new products, services, manufacturing methods, and business processes.

Greater spending power in emerging markets makes them an attractive market for new products. Companies like Unilever and Nestlé are fast moving their R&D to emerging markets.

Companies like GE take the view that for years the company sold modified Western products to emerging markets, but now it is pursuing a reverse innovation or "trickle-up innovation" strategy—developing products in countries like China and India and selling them globally.

The result is reverse flows of innovation from emerging markets to the developed world.

- One example is Nestlé's Knorr bouillon jellies. Research highlighted the Chinese like long-boiled, dense soups. Knorr's conventional cubes and granules did not deliver depth of taste or dissolve quickly enough. The solution was creating small pots of jellied bouillon. This led to the subsequent and successful launch of the bouillon jellies in Europe and the rest of the world.

- Pulpy, a fruit-based drink, is Coca-Cola's first international product to be developed in the emerging world and to make a significant impact on group-wide sales. Originated in China by Coke's Minute Maid unit, it was then rolled out over Asia, Latin America, and eastern Europe. It is an unfamiliar Coke brand in London or New York, but all the rage in Shanghai, Jakarta, and Mexico City.

- Siemens in India has developed a low-cost X-ray scanner that is being rolled out to the developed world because of its quality and low cost.

- GE sells Indian-developed electrocardiograms and Chinese-devised ultrasound scanners around the world. The Indian electrocardiogram device sells for $1,000 (a tenth of the price of the original and bulkier U.S.-developed machine). The Chinese scanner sells for $15,000, vastly cheaper than the model GE used to try and sell the Chinese market.

- Nokia uses Indian and Chinese software skills to develop smartphones.

- Vodaphone launched a mobile money transfer system called M-Pesa from its Kenyan affiliate, which has reached the unbanked consumer in Africa and India—it may be offered to the 17 million unbanked individuals in the United States.

Good ideas and new products from emerging markets are being plugged into global systems of manufacture and marketing, impacting on a company's competitiveness in emerging markets but also in the industrialized countries.

Sources: Jeffrey R. Immelt, Vijay Govindarajan, and Chris Trimble, "How GE is Disrupting Itself," *Harvard Business Review,* October 2009, 56–65. Louise Lucas, "New Accent on Consumer Tastes," *Financial Times,* December 14, 2010, 16. Stefan Wagstyl, "Replicators No More," *Financial Times,* January 6, 2011, 11.

and scope which set important guidelines and boundaries for new-product planning. High-quality new-product-planning processes are essential to operationalize the organization's innovation strategy. Importantly, achieving successful new-product outcomes requires allocating adequate resources to new-product initiatives. Finally, the extent to which the organization can leverage its capabilities into promising new-product and market opportunities enhances innovation performance (if the leveraging efforts are successful). Procter and Gamble has been particularly effective in getting its different businesses to collaborate in leveraging their capabilities to develop new products.

EXHIBIT 8.3
Characteristics
of Successful
Innovators

Apple is consistently ranked at or near the top of innovative companies. A key feature is easy to use software that will run on all of its mobile devices.[15] The strategic initiatives shown in Exhibit 8.3 have consistently been good predictors of successful innovative organizations based on research studies, management judgment and experience, and analysis of specific companies' innovation experience.

Innovation Through Collaboration

In complex and fast-moving markets, many organizations are pursuing innovation through collaborative relationships with others (see Chapter 7). For example, Eli Lilly in pharmaceuticals created the Innocentive online forum posting difficult chemical and molecular problems to a global, virtual R&D talent pool, and paying for solutions, rather than relyng on in-house R&D expertise.[16] IBM's performance is underpinned by a strategy of collaborating with customers and rivals to create new technologies, with multiple collaborative projects in all the company's major segments and creating dozens of joint ventures for R&D called "collaboratories."[17] Innovation at P&G was led by a "connect and develop" strategy of working with external partners, replacing its history of relying on in-house R&D.[18] The underlying link is recognition of an "era of open innovation," where searching for ideas and developing strategic relationships outside the organization underpin success.[19]

As companies increasingly collaborate with outsiders to innovate, there are several forms of collaboration to consider:

- The **elite circle**—in which a company chooses participants, defines the problem and chooses the solution.

- The **innovation mall**—where a company posts a problem and anyone can propose a solution.

[15]Brian Bergstein, "Inventing New Technologies and Markets," *technology review,* March–April 2011, 36.
[16]Daniel Burrus and John David Mann, "Rethink the Model for Innovation," *Financial Times,* January 27, 2011, 14.
[17]David Kirkpatrick, "IBM Shares Its Secrets," *Fortune,* September 5, 2005, 60–67.
[18]Richard Evans, "Reach Out in an Era of Open Innovation," *Financial Times,* June 21, 2007, 14
[19]Deborah Ancona and Henrik Bresnan, *X-Teams: How to Build Teams That Lead, Innovate, and Succeed* (Boston: Harvard Business School Press, 2007).

- The **innovation community**—where anybody can propose problems, offer solutions and decide which solutions to use,
- The **consortium**—which operates like a private club with participants jointly selecting problems, deciding how to work on them and choosing solutions.[20]

Different forms of collaboration fit with different situations faced by innovators, and it is likely that needs will change over time.

Recognizing the Realities of Product Cannibalization

Cannibalization occurs when a new product attracts sales from an existing product. Executives may be hesitant to develop improved products because of their successful existing products. Instead, proactive cannibalization is often a viable strategy. Proactive cannibalization consists of the pursuit of a deliberate, ongoing strategy of developing and introducing new products that attract the buyers of a company's existing products. The strategic logic of this concept is offering buyers a better solution to a need currently being satisfied. Executive resistance to cannibalization is driven by the belief that it is unproductive for a company to compete with its own products and services. Nonetheless, the reality is that changes in market requirements and customer value opportunities will result in competitor threats for existing products and technologies.

There are various examples of the negative consequences of avoiding cannibalization initiatives in the communications, financial services, retailing, and other sectors. Illustrative is Sony's continued support of its Trinitron TVs even though it was apparent that consumers favored flat-panel TVs. Proactive cannibalization may be essential to many firms to sustain a competitive advantage and achieve financial performance and growth objectives. In support of the logic of proactive cannibalization, research sponsored by the Marketing Science Institute indicates that managers of successful firms proactively resist the instinct to retain the value of past investments in product development.[21] They pursue proactive cannibalization initiatives.

New-Product Planning

A new product does not have to be a high-technology breakthrough to be successful but it must deliver superior customer value. Post-it Notes became a big winner for 3M Company.[22] The familiar notepaper pads come in various sizes and each page has a thin strip of adhesive which can be attached to reports, telephones, walls, and other places. The idea came from a 3M researcher. He had used slips of paper to mark songs in his hymnbook, but the paper kept falling out. To eliminate the problem, the employee applied an adhesive that had been developed in 3M's research laboratory, which, interestingly, failed to provide the adhesive strength needed in the original application. The adhesive worked fine for marking songs in the book. Initially, office-supply vendors saw no market for the sticky-back notepaper. The 3M Company employed extensive sampling to show the value of the product. Over the signature of the CEO's administrative assistant, samples were sent to executive assistants at all Fortune 500 companies. After using the supply of samples, the executive assistants wanted more. Post-it-Notes quickly became indispensable in both offices and homes.

---

[20]Gary P. Pisana and Robert Verganti, "Which Kind of Collaboration is Right for You?" *Harvard Business Review,* December 2008, 78–86.

[21]Rajesh K. Chandy and Gerald J. Tellis, "Organizing for Radical Product Innovation," MSI Report No. 98–102 (Cambridge, MA: Marketing Science Institute, 1998).

[22]Lawrence Ingrassia, "By Improving Scratch Paper, 3M Gets New-Product Winner," *Wall Street Journal,* March 31, 1983, 27.2.

Creating an innovative culture is an important foundation for successful innovation (see Exhibit 8.3). It is also necessary to set some boundaries concerning the types of new products to be considered for possible development. We examine these issues followed by a discussion of the activities that comprise the new-product-planning process.

Developing a Culture and Strategy for Innovation

Open communications throughout the organization and high levels of employee involvement and interest are characteristic of innovative cultures. Recognizing the importance of developing a culture and innovation strategy, Google has pursued several actions intended to encourage innovation initiatives (see earlier INNOVATION APPLICATION). Evidence of innovative cultures may be found in corporate mission statements, advertising messages, presentations by top executives, and case studies in business publications.

Innovation Culture

Creating (and strengthening) an innovation culture can be encouraged by several interrelated management initiatives:[23]

- Plan and implement a two-day innovation workshop of top executives to develop an innovation plan. This would involve use of cross-functional teams, resource allocations, rewards, and innovation performance metrics.
- Develop an innovation statement highlighting the company's objectives and senior management's roles and responsibilities.
- Conduct innovation training programs for employees and managers to encourage commitment and involvement.
- Communicate the priority of innovation via articles, newsletters, and presentations to employees, shareholders, and customers.
- Schedule innovation speakers on a regular basis to expose employees to innovation authorities.

Strategy for Innovation

The organization's innovation strategy spells out management's choice of the organization's most promising opportunities for new products. This strategy should take into account the organization's distinctive capabilities, relevant technologies, and the market opportunities that provide a good customer value match with the organization's capabilities.

A major benchmarking study of 161 business units across a broad range of industries in the United States, Germany, Denmark, and Canada indicates that a carefully formulated and communicated new-product innovation strategy is a cornerstone of superior new-product performance.[24] A successful new-product strategy includes:

1. Setting specific, written new-product objectives (sales, profit contribution, market, share, etc.).
2. Communicating throughout the organization the role of new products in contributing to the goals of the business.
3. Defining the areas of strategic focus for the corporation in terms of product scope, markets, and technologies.
4. Including longer-term, transformational projects in the portfolio along with incremental projects.

---

[23]Kuczmarski et al. "The Breakthrough Mindset," 43.
[24]Cooper, "Benchmarking New Product Performance."

The aversion to "Big I" growth strategies is rooted in the belief that potential rewards will be accrued too far in the future at too high a risk. This belief imposes costs that need to be understood. Even though the actual rewards may be realized far in the future, the equity markets account for them in their expectations of (suitably discounted) earnings. If the firm is viewed as mired in slow-growth markets, vulnerable to emerging technologies, and lacking a compelling story about its future growth thrust, the stock price will surely suffer.

Balancing Risk and Reward along the Growth Path

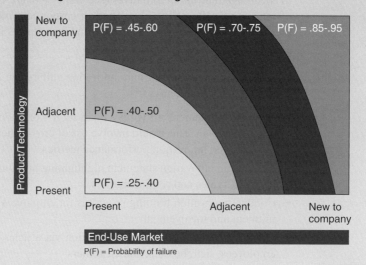

P(F) = Probability of failure

As the risk matrix shows, it is far less risky for a business to launch a new product or technology into a familiar served market than to adapt a current product to a new end-use market. Market risks are much greater than product risks because there are more dimensions of uncertainty, including competitors, channels, and consumers. If the market is entirely unfamiliar, the firm doesn't even know what it doesn't know—and the knowledge is hard to acquire. Market risks also tend to arise much later in the product development process, and are harder to resolve. A further complication is that an existing brand name may have no meaning in a "new to the company" market. Because prospective buyers lack any experience, they view the new entrant as risky and need special inducements to try the new product.

Some firms have been able to overcome the centripetal pull of innovation resources toward cautious, lower-yield "small i" growth initiatives and improve their organic growth rate. This requires visible and vocal top management commitment, supported with resources and incentives. A disciplined organic growth process is also needed to deliberately shift the balance of the portfolio of growth initiatives toward opportunities with higher risk-adjusted returns.

Many steps were taken to encourage fresh thinking at General Electric including diversifying the top ranks with outsiders (in a break from their "promote-from-within" history), keeping executives in their positions longer so they become deeply immersed in their industries, and tying executive compensation to new ideas, improved customer satisfaction, and top-line growth. The leaders of each GE business were required to submit at least three "Imagination Break-Through" proposals per year promising at least $100 million in additional growth.

Source: George S. Day, "Closing the Growth Gap: Balancing 'Big I' and 'Small i' Innovation," Report No. 06–121, *Marketing Science Institute*, 2006, pp. 5–7.

Adopting these strategy guidelines should assist management in selecting the right innovation strategy.

The STRATEGY APPLICATION on balancing innovation initiatives discusses the importance of considering innovation projects that include search into three domains for organic growth: deeper market penetration, expansion into adjacent markets, and exploration beyond adjacencies as shown by the risk matrix. Support for the matrix logic is provided by many sources.

Developing Effective New-Product-Planning Processes

Creating the right culture and selecting the right innovation strategy are essential but not sufficient initiatives in pursuing successful innovation initiatives (see Exhibit 8.3). Innovation is achieved through the processes put in place by the organization. The previously discussed benchmarking study found that having a high-quality new-product development process in place is the most important cornerstone of new-product-planning performance.

Developing successful new products requires systematic planning to coordinate the many decisions, activities, and functions necessary to identify and move a new-product idea to commercial success. A basic (generic) planning process can be used in planning a wide range of new products. There may be necessary modifications in the process in certain situations and these issues are discussed in the last section of the chapter. The major stages in the planning process are shown in Exhibit 8.4. Later in the chapter we examine each stage to see what activities are involved, how the stages depend on each other, and why cross-functional participation and coordination of new-product planning are very important.

Successful new-product planning requires (1) generating a continuing stream of new-product ideas that will satisfy the organization's requirements for new products and (2) putting in place people, processes, and methods conducting activities and evaluating new-product ideas as they move through each of the planning stages.

The following initiatives are important in effectively applying the planning process to develop and introduce new products. First, the process involves different business functions, so it is necessary to develop ways of coordinating and integrating cross-functional activities in the planning process. Second, compressing the time span for product development creates an important competitive advantage. For example, U.S. Surgical's quick response

EXHIBIT 8.4
New-Product-Planning Process

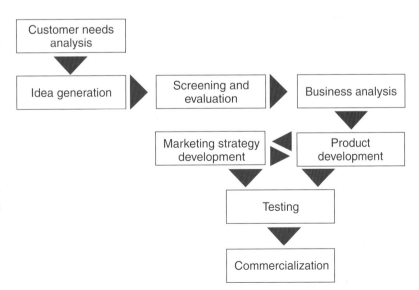

to laparoscopy equipment development enabled the company to establish first position in the market. Third, the product planning activities require resources and must be managed so that the results deliver high levels of customer satisfaction at acceptable costs. Finally, the planning process can be used for new service development as well as physical products.

Responsibility for New-Product Planning

Since new-product development involves different business functions such as marketing, finance, operations, human resources, and research and development (R&D), ways of encouraging cross-functional interaction and coordination are essential. Various organizational designs may be employed to coordinate interfunctional interactions that are necessary in developing successful new products, including:[25]

- Coordination of new-product activities by a high-level business manager.
- Cross-functional coordination by a new-product-planning team.
- Creation of a cross-functional project task force responsible for new-product planning.
- Designation of a new-products manager to coordinate planning among departments.
- Formation of a matrix organizational structure for integrating new-product planning with business functions.
- Creation of a design center which is similar in concept to a new-product team, except the center is a permanent part of the organization.

The design team and design center are more recent new-product coordination mechanisms. Though cross-functional teams are widely cited as promising new-product planning

EXHIBIT 8.5 **Attributes of Different Products and Their Associated Development Efforts***

Source: Karl T. Ulrich and Stephen D. Eppinger, *Product Design and Development,* 3rd ed. (Burr Ridge, IL: Irwin/McGraw-Hill, 2004), 5.

	Stanley Tools Jobmaster Screwdriver	Rollerblade In-Line Skate	Hewlett-Packard DeskJet Printer	Volkswagen New Beetle Automobile	Boeing 777 Airplane
Annual production volume	100,000 units/ year	100,000 units/year	4 million units/year	100,000 units/year	50 units/ year
Sales lifetime	40 years	3 years	2 years	6 years	30 years
Sales price	$3	$200	$300	$17,000	$130 million
Number of unique parts (part numbers)	3 parts	35 parts	200 parts	10,000 parts	130,000
Development time	1 year	2 years	1.5 years	3.5 years	4.5 years
Internal development team (peak size)	3 people	5 people	100 people	800 people	6,800 people
External development team (peak size)	3 people	10 people	75 people	800 people	10,000 people
Development cost	$150,000	$750,000	$50 million	$400 million	$3 billion
Production investment	$150,000	$1 million	$25 million	$500 million	$3 billion

*All figures are approximate, based on publicly available information and company sources.

---

[25]Eric M. Olsen, Orville C. Walker, Jr., and Robert W. Ruekert, "Organizing for Effective New-Product Development: The Moderating Role of Product Innovativeness," *Journal of Marketing,* January 1995, 48–62.

mechanisms, research findings suggest that they may be most appropriate for planning truly new and innovative products.[26] The more traditional bureaucratic structures (e.g., new-products manager) may be better in planning line extensions and product improvements. The danger of the traditional structure is failing to identify new-product opportunities outside the scope of existing new-product planning, and not identifying potential disruptive threats.

The nature and scope of new-product projects may influence how the responsibilities are allocated. Illustrative characteristics of various new-product development efforts are described in Exhibit 8.5.

Idea Generation

Guided by the new-product innovation strategy, finding promising new ideas is the starting point in the new-product development process (see Exhibit 8.4). Idea generation ranges from incremental improvements of existing products to transformational products. As discussed earlier encouraging a commitment to innovation throughout the organization is an important catalyst for new idea generation. Exhibit 8.6 describes how General Electric's innovation champion pursues this objective.

Sources of Ideas

New-product ideas come from many sources. Limiting the search for ideas to those generated by internal research and development activities is far too narrow an approach for most

EXHIBIT 8.6
An Innovation Champion in Action at GE

Source: Bruce Hussbaum, "How to Build Creative Companies," *BusinessWeek,* August 1, 2005, 77.

Beth Comstock calls herself "a little bit of the crazy, wacky one" at corporate headquarters. And it's an apt description when you realize she works at General Electric Co. Comstock, 44, is charged with transforming GE's culture, famously devoted to process, engineering, and financial controls, to one that's more agile and creative. Chairman and CEO Jeffrey R. Immelt tapped the former communications chief to become GE's first-ever chief marketing officer almost three years ago. The job came with a critical twist: the goal of driving innovation through the company's 300,000-plus ranks.

"Creativity is still a word we're wrestling with," Comstock concedes. "It seems a bit undisciplined, a bit chaotic for a place like GE." More comfortable territory is the term "imaginative problem-solving"—encouraging people to think "what if"—yet always with the aim of driving growth. One of Comstock's first moves was to bring in anthropologists to audit GE's culture. They came back with praise for GE's famous work ethic but noted that employees wanted more "wow"—more discoveries from the company founded by Thomas Edison.

Comstock has a role whose importance is spreading throughout Big Business—that of innovation champion. She began by studying the best practices at companies such as Procter & Gamble, FedEx, and 3M. She brought in a raft of creativity consultants, futurists, and design gurus to lead sessions with different operations. Their names were jolting for GE types: Play, a Richmond (VA.) group that helps execs think differently, and Jump, based in San Mateo, CA., which researches how people use things. GE is expanding its army of designers to bring businesses closer to customers. And Comstock is staging "dreaming sessions" where Immelt, senior execs, and customers debate future market trends. Comstock concedes some managers view the workshops as a waste of time. "We have a long way to go," she says. But for GE, there's no turning back.

By Diane Brady in New York

---

[26]Ibid.

Innovation is an increasingly global game. It can involve a worldwide research and development operation like Microsoft's Advanced Technology Center outside Beijing, or IBM's labs in China, Israel, Switzerland, Japan, and India.

Or innovation can be the product of a much more amorphous structure—global innovation networks—bringing together in-house engineers, contract designers and manufacturers, university scientists, and technology suppliers for a particular project.

Because technology crosses borders faster than ever, thanks to the Internet, inexpensive telecom links, and advances in interactive design software, the location of R&D facilities matters far less than who controls these networks and where the benefits accrue. By mobilizing scattered R&D teams, companies can speed development cycles, and more rapidly bring technologies to market.

Procter & Gamble uses online networks to get in touch with thousands of experts worldwide to support its rapid new-product innovation process. It found a professor in Bologna, Italy, who had invented an ink-jet method for printing edible images on cakes. P&G used this method to create Pringles potato chips with jokes and pictures printed on them—boosting the product's growth. The new product came out in one year rather than the usual three or four.

In 2006, IBM organized its online Innovation Jam—trying to get the opinions of 100,000 minds—clients, consultants, and employee family members across the world—to tinker with its technology in the pursuit of new ideas.

Sources: Pete Engardio, "Scouring the Plant for Brainiacs," *BusinessWeek,* October 11, 2004, 62–66. Jessi Hempel, "Big Blue Brainstorm," *BusinessWeek,* August 7, 2006, 79. Steve Hamm, "Speed Demons," *BusinessWeek,* March 27, 2006, 67–76.

firms. Sources of new-product ideas include R&D laboratories, employees, customers, competitors, outside inventors, acquisition, and value chain members. Both solicited and spontaneous ideas may emerge from these sources. Increasingly, companies are developing "open-market innovation" approaches to generating ideas using licensing, joint ventures, and strategic alliances.[27] By opening their boundaries to suppliers, customers, outside researchers, even competitors, businesses are increasing the import and export of new ideas to improve the speed, cost, and quality of innovation. For example, when Pitney-Bowes was challenged with protecting consumers and postal workers from envelopes tainted with anthrax spores by terrorists, they had no in-house response—their expertise is in secure metering systems to protect postal revenues. They collected ideas from fields as diverse as food handling and military security, before working with outside inventors to introduce new products and services to secure mail against bioterrorism—specialized scanners and imaging systems to identify suspicious letters and packages.

Importantly, generating new-product ideas and developing them into new products involves many companies in developing international collaborations and networks. The GLOBAL APPLICATION illustrates this globalization of innovation efforts.

The Search Process

It is essential to establish a proactive idea-generation and evaluation process that meets the needs of the enterprise. Answering these questions is helpful in developing the idea-generation program:

- Should idea search activities be targeted or open-ended? Should the search for new-product ideas be restricted to ideas that correspond to the firm's new-product strategy?

---

[27]Darrell Rigby and Chris Zook, "Open-Market Innovation," *Harvard Business Review,* October 2002, 80–89.

- How extensive and aggressive should new-product idea search activities be?
- What specific sources are best for generating a regular flow of new-product ideas?
- How can new ideas be obtained from customers?
- Where will responsibility for new-product idea search be placed? How will new-product idea generation activities be directed and coordinated?
- What are potential threats from disruptive technologies that may satisfy customers better than our products?

For most companies, the idea search process should be targeted within a range of product and market involvement that is consistent with corporate mission and objectives and business unit strategies. While some far-out new-product idea may occasionally change the future of a company, more often open-ended idea search dissipates resources and misdirects efforts. However, management should be proactive in monitoring potentially disruptive innovations and opportunities beyond the core product and market focus.

Idea Sources

Identifying the best sources of ideas depends on many factors including the size and type of firm, technologies involved, new-product needs, resources, management's preferences, and the organization's capabilities. Management needs to consider these factors and develop a proactive strategy for idea generation that will satisfy the firm's requirements. Creating an innovative culture should encourage generating new-product ideas. The innovation strategy provides idea generation guidelines.

Many new-product ideas originate from the users of products and services. Lead user analyses offer promising potential for the development of new products.[28] The objective is to identify the companies and product users that pioneer new applications and to study their requirements to guide new-product development in product-markets that change rapidly. Lead users identify gaps between their value expectations and available products and then pursue initiatives to meet their needs. Implementing this approach to idea generation requires major internal and external initiatives. The benefits can be significant for an organization's idea generating activities. The intent is to satisfy the lead users' needs, thus accelerating new-product adoption by other companies.

Web-search inquiries represent a relatively new source of information concerning buyers' product preferences. For example, analysis of search terms may indicate product characteristics and features that are of interest to buyers. Search research may be useful in generating ideas and providing new-product design information.

Involving customers in the innovation process goes beyond obtaining direct customer feedback. Some companies have gone to the extent of equipping customers with the tools to develop and design their own products—ranging from minor modifications to major innovations. For example, Bush Boake Allen (BBA) is a global supplier of specialty flavors to food companies like Nestlé.[29] BBA has developed a toolkit which enables customers to create their own flavors, which BBA then manufactures.

---

[28]Stefan H. Thomke, *Managing Product and Service Development* (Burr Ridge, IL: McGraw-Hill/Irwin, 2007), 189–198. Eric von Hippell, *Democratizing Innovation* (Cambridge, MA: The MIT Press, 2005).
[29]Ibid., 359–381.

Methods of Generating Ideas

There are several ways of obtaining ideas for new products. Typically, a company considers multiple options in generating product ideas.

Search

Utilizing several information sources may be helpful in identifying new-product ideas. New-product idea publications are available from companies that wish to sell or license ideas they do not wish to commercialize. New technology information is available from commercial and government computerized search services. News sources may also yield information about the new-product activities of competitors. Many trade publications contain new-product announcements. Companies need to identify the relevant search areas and assign responsibility for idea search to an individual or team.

Marketing Research

Surveys of product users help to identify needs that can be satisfied by new products. The focus group is a useful technique to identify and evaluate new-product concepts, and this research method can be used for both consumer and industrial products. The focus group consists of 8 to 12 people invited to meet with an experienced moderator to discuss a product use situation. Idea generation may occur in the focus group discussion of user requirements for a particular product use situation. Group members are asked to suggest new-product ideas. Later, focus group sessions may be used to evaluate alternative product concepts intended to satisfy the needs identified in the initial session. More than one focus group can be used at each stage in the process. Ethnographic research approaches are also relevant to the search for unsatisfied customer needs (see Chapter 5).

Another research technique that is used to generate new-product ideas is the advisory panel. The panel members are selected to represent the firm's target market. For example, such a panel for a producer of mechanics' hand tools would include mechanics. Companies in various industries, including telecommunications, fast foods, and pharmaceuticals use customer advisory groups.

Internal and External Development

Research and development laboratories continue to generate many new-product ideas. The United States is the leading spender on industrial research and development in the world and, with the exception of countries like Japan and Korea, very few countries allocate a higher percentage of gross domestic product to R&D. Escalating R&D costs are driving innovative companies to explore new ways of matching R&D resources to value opportunities—through "open source innovation," strategic alliances, joint ventures, and the global search for promising innovation prospects.

Pharmaceutical, semiconductor, software, and biotech companies spend significantly more percentage-wise on R&D than other industries.[30] For example, in 2004 Microsoft's R&D was 21 percent of sales compared to 3 percent by General Motors. Microsoft spent $7,779 million on R&D in 2004. Also relevant is the amount of R&D expenditures allocated to longer-term projects.

New-product ideas may originate from development efforts outside the firm. Sources include inventors, government and private laboratories, and small high-technology firms. Strategic alliances between companies may result in identifying new-product ideas, as well as sharing responsibility for other activities in new-product development.

---

[30]"R & D 2005," *technology review,* September 2005, 50–52.

Other Idea-Generation Methods

Incentives may be useful to get new-product ideas from employees, marketing partners, and customers. Management should also guard against employees leaving the company and developing a promising idea elsewhere. For this reason many firms require employees to sign secrecy agreements.

Finally, acquiring another firm offers a way to obtain new-product ideas. This strategy may be more cost-effective than internal development and can substantially reduce the lead-time required for developing new products. Procter and Gamble's purchase of the battery powered Crest SpinBrush from the inventor and Glide dental floss from the Gore Company are examples.

Idea-generation identifies one or more new-product opportunities that are screened and evaluated. Before comprehensive evaluation, the idea must be transformed into a defined concept, which states what the product will do (anticipated attributes) and the benefits that are superior to available products.[31] The product concept expresses the idea in operational terms so that it can be evaluated as a potential candidate for development into a new product.

Interestingly, there is an emerging view that the corporate social responsibility and ethical initiatives (which we discussed in Chapter 4) have a direct link to innovation in products, value chains, and processes, particularly in identifying new ideas and ways of doing business. The relationship between social responsibility initiatives and new-product innovation is illustrated in the ETHICS APPLICATION.

Screening, Evaluating, and Business Analysis

Management needs a screening and evaluation process that will eliminate unpromising ideas as soon as possible while keeping the risks of rejecting good ideas at acceptable levels. Moving too many ideas through too many stages in the new-product planning process is expensive. Costs build up from the idea stage to the commercialization stage, whereas the risks of developing a bad new product decline as information accumulates about product performance and market acceptance. The objective is to eliminate the least promising ideas before too much time and money are invested in them. However, the tighter the screening procedure, the higher the risk of rejecting a good idea. Based on the specific factors involved, it is necessary to establish a level of risk that is acceptable to management.

Evaluation should occur regularly as an idea moves through the new-product planning stages. Since the objective is to eliminate the poor risks as early as possible, evaluation is necessary at each stage in the planning process. We discuss several evaluation techniques. Typically, evaluation begins by screening new-product ideas to identify those that are considered to be most promising. These ideas become concepts and are subjected to more comprehensive evaluation. Finally, business analysis determines whether to move the concept into the new-product development stage (see Exhibit 8.4).

Screening

A new-product idea receives an initial screening to determine its strategic fit in the company or business unit. Two questions need to be answered: (1) is the idea compatible with the organization's mission and objectives and (2) is the product initiative commercially

---

[31]C. Merle Crawford and C. Anthony Di Benedetto, *New Products Management,* 10th ed. (New York: McGraw-Hill/Irwin, 2011), Chapter 4.

Corporate social responsibility initiatives and the growing emphasis on sustainability among public policy makers and interests groups underline new types of innovation opportunities for companies.

Behind the drive for sustainability, there is a growing opinion that environmental and social projects not only improve corporate reputations but also foster innovation, cut costs, and open up new markets.

Climate change and greener consumers mean organizations can turn sustainability into innovation's new frontier.

Sustainability leads to environmentally friendly policies that lower costs and increase revenues and should be the touchstone for innovation

Companies making sustainability a goal may tap new areas of competitive advantage by rethinking business models as well as products, technologies and processes.

The pursuit of sustainability involves five stages:

- **Viewing compliance with environmental regulation as opportunity**—using compliance as the chance to experiment with sustainable technologies, materials and processes.
- **Making value chains sustainable**—developing sustainable sources of raw materials, increasing the use of clean energy, finding innovative uses for returned products.
- **Designing sustainable products and services**—for example, in product development and packaging.
- **Developing new business models**—finding novel ways to capture value and compete differently.
- **Creating next-practice platforms**—question through the sustainability lens the dominant logic of the business.

Sources: Michael Skapinker, "Virtue's reward? Companies Make the Business Case for Ethical Initiatives," *Financial Times,* April 28, 2008, 9. Ram Nidumolu, C. K. Prahalad, and M. R. Rangaswami, "Why Sustainability is Now the Key Driver of Innovation," *Harvard Business Review,* September 2009, 56–64.

---

feasible? The compatibility of the idea considers factors such as internal capabilities (e.g., development, production, and marketing), financial needs, and competitive factors. Commercial feasibility considers market attractiveness, technical feasibility, financial attractiveness, and social and environmental concerns. The number of ideas generated by an organization is likely to influence the approach utilized in screening the ideas. A large number of ideas call for a formal screening process.

Screening eliminates ideas that are not compatible or feasible for the business. Management must establish how narrow or wide the screening boundaries should be. For example, managers from two similar firms may have very different missions and objectives as well as different propensities toward risk, so an idea could be strategically compatible in one firm and not in another. Also, new-product strategies and priorities may be revised when top management changes. For example, when Vice-Chairman Robert A. Lutz joined General Motors in 2001 his primary charge was to build collaborative relationships with design and engineering managers with the objective of developing exciting new styling concepts.[32] Collaboration initiatives were a departure from past practices at GM.

---

[32]"GM's Design Push Picks Up Speed," *BusinessWeek,* July 18, 2005, 40–42.

After identifying relevant screening criteria, scoring and importance-weighting techniques may be used to make a composite evaluation of the factors considered in the screening process. By summing the weighted scores, an evaluation is obtained for each idea being screened. Management can set ranges for passing and rejecting. The effectiveness of these methods is highly dependent on including all of the relevant criteria and gaining agreement on the relative importance of the screening factors from the people involved in the evaluation process.

Concept Evaluation

The boundaries concerning idea screening, concept evaluation, and business analysis are often not clearly drawn. These evaluation stages may be combined, particularly when only a few ideas are involved. After completing initial screening, each idea that survives becomes a new-product concept and receives a more comprehensive evaluation. Several of the same factors used in screening may be evaluated in greater depth, including buyers' reactions to the proposed concept. A team representing different business functions should participate in concept evaluation.

Importance of Concept Evaluation

Extensive research on companies' new-product-planning activities highlights the critical role of extensive market and technical assessments *before* beginning the development of a new-product concept.[33] These "up-front" evaluations should result in a clearly defined new-product concept indicating its market target(s), customer value offering, and positioning strategy. Research concerning product failures strongly suggests that many companies do not devote enough attention to up-front evaluation of product concepts.

The failure of the handheld CueCat scanner offers compelling evidence of the value and importance of concept evaluation. The purpose of CueCat was to read a bar code and when attached to a personal computer, provide a direct access to a Web page for the product. The founder of Digital Convergence Corp. raised $185 million from investors to commercially launch CueCat.[34] Large investors included Belo Corp. ($37.5 million), Radio Shack ($30 million), and Young & Rubicam ($28 million). The business plan was to give away 50 million CueCats ($6.50 cost) and obtain revenues from advertisers and licensing fees. Four million CueCats were distributed but few were used. People did not want to carry the scanner around and could quickly access Web sites by typing the address. CueCat did not fill a consumer need. Importantly, this weakness could have been identified by concept evaluation before large expenditures were made to produce and distribute the product.

Several concept evaluation issues are highlighted in Exhibit 8.7. Evaluation includes more than concept tests. For example, the new-product team may perform competitor analyses, market forecasts, and technical feasibility evaluations. The questions indicated in Exhibit 8.7 are helpful in deciding how to evaluate the new-product concept.

Concept Tests

Concept tests are useful in evaluation and refinement of the characteristics of proposed new products. The purpose of concept testing is to obtain a reaction to the new-product concept from a sample of potential buyers before the product is developed. More than one

---

[33]Cooper, "Benchmarking New Product Performance."

[34]Elliot Spagat, "A Web Gadget Fizzles Despite a Salesman's Dazzle," *Wall Street Journal,* June 27, 2001, B1, B4.

EXHIBIT 8.7
Concept Evaluation Issues

- What is the objective (purpose) of concept evaluation?
- How much time/resources should be allocated to evaluation?
- What are the risks?
- Who will perform the evaluation?
- Who decides the outcomes?
- What evaluation techniques are most useful?

concept test may be used during the evaluation process. The technique supplies important information for reshaping, redefining and coalescing new-product ideas.[35] Concept tests help to evaluate the relative appeal of ideas or alternative product positionings, supply information for developing the product and marketing strategy, and identify potential market segments.

The concept test is a useful way to evaluate a product idea very early in the development process. The costs of these tests are reasonable, given the information that can be obtained. Since the actual product and a commercial setting are not present, the evaluation is somewhat artificial. The concept test is probably most useful in identifying very favorable or unfavorable product concepts. The research method also offers a basis for comparing two or more concepts. An important requirement of concept testing is that the product (good or service) can be described in words and visually, and the participant must have the experience and capability to evaluate the concept. The respondent must be able to visualize the proposed product and its features based on a verbal or written description and/or picture. An example of a Mail Concept Test Format is shown in Exhibit 8.8.

Computer technology offers very promising capabilities for visual testing of new-product concepts. Potential customers can be provided with multimedia virtual buying environment. For example, virtual methodology was used to evaluate the potential of new electric cars: "Respondents viewed multimedia presentations, read on-line articles about the new product, talked with users of the vehicle, visited a showroom, and were able to virtually get into the vehicle and talk with salespeople."[36]

Business Analysis

Business analysis estimates the commercial feasibility of the new-product concept. Obtaining an accurate financial projection depends on the quality of the revenue and cost forecasts. Business analysis is normally accomplished at several stages in the new-product planning process, beginning at the business analysis stage before the product concept moves into the development stage. Financial projections are refined at later stages.

Revenue Forecasts

The newness of the product, the size of the market, and the competing products all influence the accuracy of revenue projections. In the case of an established market, such as breakfast cereals, snack foods, and toothpaste, estimates of total market size are usually available from industry information. Industry associations often publish forecasts and government agencies such as the U.S. Commerce Department forecast sales for various industries. The more difficult task is estimating the market share that is feasible for a new-product entry.[37]

[35]William R. Dillon, Thomas J. Madden, and Neil H. Firtle, *Marketing Research in a Marketing Environment,* 3rd ed. (Burr Ridge, IL: Richard D. Irwin, Inc., 1994).
[36]Glen L. Urban, *Digital Marketing Strategy* (Upper Saddle River, NJ : Pearson Prentice Hall, 2004), 96.
[37]David Welch, "Why Hybrids Are Such a Hard Sell," *BusinessWeek,* March 19, 2007, 45.

EXHIBIT 8.8   **Mail Concept Test Format—Plain Verbal Description of the Product and It's Major Benefits**

Source: C. Merle Crawford and C. Anthony Di Benedetto, *New Products Management,* 10th ed. (New York: McGraw-Hill/Irwin, 2011), 217.

A major soft drink manufacturer would like to get your reaction to an idea for a new diet soft drink. Please read the description below before answering the questions.

> New Diet Soft Drink
> Here is a tasty, sparkling beverage that quenches thirst, refreshers, and makes the mouth tingle with a delightful flavor blend of orange, mint, and lime.
> It helps adults and kids two control weight by reducing the craving for sweets and between meal snacks, and best of all, it contains absolutely no calories.
> Comes in 12 ounce cans or bottles and costs 60 ¢ each.

1. How different, if at all, do you think this diet drink would be from other available products on the market that might be compared with it?

   ❑ Very different

   ❑ Somewhat different

   ❑ Slightly different

   ❑ Not at all different

2. Assuming you tried the product described above and like it, about how often do you think you would buy it?

   Check one

   ❑ More than once a week

   ❑ About once a week

   ❑ About twice a month

   ❑ About once a month

   ❑ Less often

   ❑ Would never buy it

A range of feasible share positions can be forecast at the concept stage and used as a basis for preliminary financial projections. Managers may have success norms based on prior experience.

In certain situations major difficulties may exist in forecasting the demand for new products. Consider, for example, the dilemma that faced telecom companies with third-generation (3G) mobile phone services. European carriers spent some $250 billion buying 3G rights and new networks. Notwithstanding efficient data connections at broadband speeds, cheaper voice calls, Internet access, photo messaging, games, streaming video clips, and videoconferencing on 3G phones, consumers have shown limited interest in buying mobile multimedia. There is a possible risk that levels of business achieved may never pay back the cost of the 3G licenses acquired in 2001 and 2002.[38] After a very slow start-up the forecasts in 2004 became cautiously optimistic, indicating an evolution rather than revolution.

---

[38]Almar Latour, "Disconnected," *Wall Street Journal,* June 5, 2001, A1, A8; "Vision Meet Reality," *The Economist,* September 4, 2004 63–65.

Preliminary Marketing Plan

An initial marketing strategy should be developed as a part of the business analysis. Included are market target(s), positioning strategy, and marketing program plans. While this plan is preliminary, it is an early guide to strategy development and coordination among marketing, design, operations, and other business functions. The choice of the marketing strategy is necessary in developing the revenue forecast.

Cost Estimation

Several different costs occur in the planning and commercialization of new products. One way to categorize the costs is to estimate them for each stage in the new-product planning process (see Exhibit 8.4). The costs increase rapidly as the product concept moves through the development process. Expenditures for each planning stage can be further divided into functional categories (e.g., marketing, research and development, and operations).

Profit Projections

Analyses appropriate for new-product evaluation include break even, cash flow, return on investment, and profit contribution. Management can use break-even analysis as a basis for assessing whether it is feasible to reach and exceed break even. Business analysis estimates should take into consideration the probable flow of revenues and costs over the time span used in the analysis. Typically, new products incur heavy costs before they start to generate revenues.

Product and Process Development

After completing the business analysis, management must decide either to begin product development or abort the project. During the development stage the concept may be transformed into one or more prototypes. The prototype is the actual product, but may be custom produced rather than by an established manufacturing process. Use testing of the product may occur during the development stage.

Our earlier discussion of customer-guided new-product planning emphasizes the importance of transforming customer preferences into internal product design guidelines. Product design decisions need to be guided by customer preferences and analysis of competitor advantages and weaknesses. Product development should involve the entire new-product planning team.

Product Development Process

The development of the new product includes product design, industrial design (ease-of-use and style), process (manufacturing) design, packaging design, and decisions to make or outsource various product components. Development typically consists of various technical activities, but also requires continuing interaction among R&D, marketing, operations, finance, and legal functions. The relative importance of the activities differs according to the product involved. For example, product and process design are extensive for complex products like large commercial aircraft. In contrast line extensions (e.g., new flavors and package sizes) of food products do not require extensive design activities.

Importantly, the effective management of lean product development processes that take products to market more rapidly has become a competitive imperative. In many sectors the time taken to bring a product to market has been halved. At Nissan Motor Co. the development of new cars used to take 21 months, now the process is completed in 10 1/2 months.

In cell phones, Nokia, Motorola, and others used to take 12 to 18 months to develop basic models, now this takes 6 to 9 months. Faster product development processes are mandated in many markets.[39]

When the new product is a service there are similarities in the development process and also some differences relative to physical products. New financial services must be designed and processes developed for making them available to customers. However, the service is not tangible so its design must take this into account. Use testing may be particularly important for services such as software. The reality is that many products today are combinations of goods and services. Starbucks, the world's largest coffee chain, is illustrative. The Starbucks experience is more than drinking a cup of expensive coffee.

Product Specifications

Product specifications describe what the product will do rather than how it should be designed. This information indicates the product planners' expectations regarding the benefits provided by the product based on customer analysis, including essential physical and operating characteristics.[40] These guidelines help the technical team determine the best design strategy for delivering the benefits. The more complete the specifications for the product, the better the designers can incorporate the requirements into the design. The specifications also provide a basis for assessing design feasibility. In some situations benefit/cost assessments may require changing the specifications.

Industrial Design

Many companies are placing increasing emphasis on the ease-of-use and style of products. Design consultants assist companies on various design initiatives. Industrial design has become a major part of the new-product development process for many products. Design was an important contributor to Apple's success in the early 2000s. The design process of the consultant IDEO, the industry leader, is described in the RELATIONSHIP APPLICATION.

Prototype

The technical team uses the product specifications to guide the design of one or more physical products. Similar information is needed to guide software design and design of new services. At this stage the product is called a prototype since it is not ready for commercial production and marketing. Many of the parts may be custom built, and materials, packaging, and other details may differ from the commercial version. Nevertheless, the prototype needs to be capable of delivering the benefits spelled out in the specifications. Scale models are used for some products such as commercial aircraft, which can be tested in wind tunnels to evaluate their performance characteristics. Computer technology is also used in testing and evaluation of new products such as automobiles and aircraft.

Use Tests

When testing of the prototype is feasible, designers can obtain important feedback from users concerning how well the product meets the needs that are spelled out in the product specifications. A standard approach to use testing is to distribute the product to a sample of users, asking them to try the product. Follow-up occurs after the test participant has had sufficient time to evaluate the product. The design of new industrial products may include

[39]Steve Hamm, "Speed Demons," *BusinessWeek,* March 27, 2006, 67–76.
[40]Crawford and Di Benedetto, *New Products Management,* Chapter 12.

A company goes to IDEO with a problem. Management wants a better product, service, or space—no matter. IDEO puts together an eclectic team composed of members from the client company and its own experts who go out to observe and document the consumer experience. Often, IDEO will have top executives play the roles of their own customers.

Execs from food and clothing companies show off their own stuff in different retail stores and on the Web. Health-care managers get care in different hospitals. Wireless providers use their own—and competing—services.

The next stage is brainstorming. IDEO mixes designers, engineers, and social scientists with its clients in a room where they intensely scrutinize a given problem and suggest possible solutions. It is managed chaos: a dozen or so very smart people examining data, throwing out ideas, writing potential solutions on big Post-its that are ripped off and attached to the wall.

IDEO designers then mock up working models of the best concepts that emerge. Rapid prototyping has always been a hallmark of the company. Seeing ideas in working, tangible form is a far more powerful mode of explanation than simply reading about them off a page. IDEO uses inexpensive prototyping tools—Apple-based iMovies to portray consumer experiences and cheap cardboard to mock up examination rooms or fitting rooms. "IDEO's passion is about making stuff work, not about being artists," says design guru Tucker Viemeister, CEO of Dutch-based designer Springtime USA. "Their corporate customers really buy into it."

Source: Bruce Nussbaum, "The Power of Design," *BusinessWeek,* May 17, 2004, 91.

the active involvement of users in testing and evaluating the product at various stages in the development process. The relatively small number of users in industrial markets compared to consumer markets makes use testing very feasible. Use tests are also popular for gaining reactions to new consumer products such as foods, drinks, and health and beauty aids. Clinical trials may also be conducted to support performance claims of products such as foods offering therapeutic benefits.

Unlike a market test, the use test normally does not identify the brand name of the product or the company name. While it is less accurate in gauging market success compared to the market test, the use test yields important information such as preferences, ratings, likes/dislikes, advantages/limitations, unique features, usage and users, and comparisons with competing products.

Process Development

The process for producing the product in commercial quantities must be developed. Manufacturing (producing) the product at the desired quality level and cost is a critical determinant of profitability. The new product may be feasible to produce in the laboratory but not on a full-scale basis because of costs, production rates, and other considerations. Initial production delays can also jeopardize the success of a new product. Airbus experienced delays in producing its new A-380 superjumbo jet and this created concerns for several customers.

The feasibility to *mass customize* and *modularize* may have a major impact on product and process design.[41] Mass customization enables customizing product offerings at relatively low costs. Modularity involves developing and producing a product using interrelated modules, thus facilitating mass customization. The system architecture for the product links the modules together, but each part can be designed and produced independently within the organization or by outsourcing. Modularity was pioneered by the computer industry, but is applicable to many other products.

Marketing Strategy and Market Testing

Developing the marketing strategy for a new product varies depending on whether it is an incremental improvement or new to the market and/or the company. The latter requires complete targeting and positioning strategies (see Chapter 6). The incremental product improvement may only need a revised promotion strategy to convey to target buyers information about the benefits offered by the improved product. It is also important to consider how the new product will relate to the firm's existing products. Regardless of the newness of the product, reviewing the proposed marketing strategy helps to avoid market introduction problems.

Marketing Strategy Decisions

Evaluation efforts (e.g., concept and use tests) conducted during concept evaluation and product development supply information that may be helpful in designing the marketing strategy. Examples of useful planning guidelines include user characteristics, product features, advantages over competing products, types of use situations, feasible price range, and potential buyer profiles. Marketing strategy planning begins at the concept evaluation stage and continues during product development. Activities such as packaging, name selection, environmental considerations, product information, colors, materials, and product safety must also be decided between design, operations, and marketing.

Market Targeting

Selection of the market target(s) for the new product range from offering a new product to an existing target, to identifying an entirely new group of potential users. Examining available marketing research information for the new product may yield useful insights as to targeting opportunities. It may also be necessary to conduct additional research such as market testing before finalizing the market targeting strategy.

An interesting example of product development targeting an existing user group with a new application of established technology is shown in the INNOVATION APPLICATION, describing Nestlé's extension of its highly successful Nespresso coffee making machines into the baby formula preparation market.

Positioning Strategy

The core of this strategy is how management wants the new product to be positioned in the eyes and minds of the targeted buyers. Several positioning decisions are made

---

[41]See, for example, James H. Gilmore and B. Joseph Pine II, "The Four Faces of Mass Customization," *Harvard Business Review,* January–February 1997, 91–101; and Kathleen M. Eisenhardt and Shona L. Brown, "Time Pacing: Competing in Markets That Won't Stand Still," *Harvard Business Review,* March–April 1998, 67.

Nestlé has built its Nespresso home espresso makers into a $3.9 billion business offering high-quality coffee through an innovative value chain.

The Swiss company's new BabyNes machine heats capsules of Nestlé baby formula, eliminating clumps that happen when mixing powdered formula, and dispenses a precise amount into a feeding bottle. It can be operated with one hand, leaving the other free to tend to the hungry child.

The new product is rolling out globally in 2012 after successful launch in Switzerland in 2011.

The machines are premium priced at around $300, and the capsules of Nestlé formula cost triple the price of coffee capsules, placing the BabyNes among the ranks of high-end baby products.

Source: Thomas Mulier, "A Nespresso Machine for the Diaper Set," *Bloomberg BusinessWeek,* July 4–July 10, 2011, 26–27.

during marketing strategy development. Issues such as packaging, name selection, sizes, and other aspects of the product must be decided. The value chain strategy determines the customer access channels to be used. It is also necessary to select a price strategy and to develop the advertising and sales promotion strategy. Testing of ads may occur at this stage. Decisions must be made concerning use of the Internet. Finally, sales management must design a personal selling strategy including deciding about sales force additions and training and allocation of selling effort to the new product.

The market introduction of the new high-definition digital video disk players presented some interesting targeting and positioning challenges. Sony offered its Blu-ray format while Toshiba had the HD-DVD format, selling at $499 compared to Sony players at $1,000.[42] A key positioning challenge was whether one format would eventually become the market standard. Blu-ray had some superior features but the question was whether they would be valued by buyers at double the price of Toshiba's players? The question was resolved in 2008, when Warner Brothers studios made a decision to exclusively release its movies in Sony's Blu-ray format, and Wal-Mart and Best Buy indicated their preference for Blu-ray players. Toshiba opted to stop making HD-DVD players.[43] The situation was similar to the battle between VHS and Beta technologies in the 1980s. VHS became the standard even though the Beta technology was considered superior.

Market Testing

"A test market is a controlled experiment conducted in a carefully chosen marketplace (e.g., website, store, town, or other geographical location) to measure marketplace response and predict sales or profitability of a product."[44] Market testing can be considered after the product is fully developed, assuming the product is suitable for market testing. Market tests gauge buyer response to the new product and evaluate one or more positioning strategies. Test marketing is used for consumer products such as foods, beverages, and health and beauty aids. Market tests can also be conducted for business-to-business goods and

---

[42]Andrew Simons, "HD-DVD Takes an Early Lead in Sales Race Against Blu-ray," *Wall Street Journal,* April 26, 2006, B3B.

[43]Mariko Sanchanta, "Sony Wins Next-Generation DVD Battle," *Financial Times,* February 20, 2008, 28.

[44]Donald R. Cooper and Pamela S. Schindler, *Marketing Research* (Burr Ridge, IL: McGraw-Hill/Irwin, 2006), 321.

services. Several methods of testing are available including simulated test marketing, scanner based tests, and conventional tests.

A description of the different new-product evaluation methods is shown in Exhibit 8.9. The testing tools for each of the stages are indicated. Note how market testing fits into the planning process. The exhibit also provides an overview of the marketing plan development.

Simulated Tests

The distinguishing feature of simulated tests is that they are conducted in a simulated shopping environment and may be used in place of or before a full-scale market test.[45] Typically, a research facility is used to provide a simulated shopping experience in order to obtain feedback from the participants. Not surprisingly, the findings are not as accurate as actual market tests.

Simulated tests offer several advantages including speed, low costs ($50,000 to $150,000 compared to $1 million or more for traditional market tests), and the tests yield relatively accurate forecasts of market response. The tests also eliminate the risk present in conventional testing of competitor exposure.

Scanner-Based Tests

These tests are conducted in an actual market environment. The test product must be made available in each test city. Information Resources Inc.'s BehaviorScan system pioneered the use of cable television and a computerized database to track new products during these tests. The system uses information and responses from recruited panel members in each test city. Each member has an identification card to show to participating store cashiers. Purchases are electronically recorded and transmitted to a central data bank. Cable television enables BehaviorScan to use controlled advertisement testing. Some viewers can be exposed to ads while the ads are being withheld from other viewers.

EXHIBIT 8.9
How Market Testing Relates to the Other Testing Steps

Source: Chart from C. Merle Crawford and C. Anthony Di Benedetto, *New Products Management*, 10th ed. (New York: McGraw-Hill/Irwin, 2011), 455.

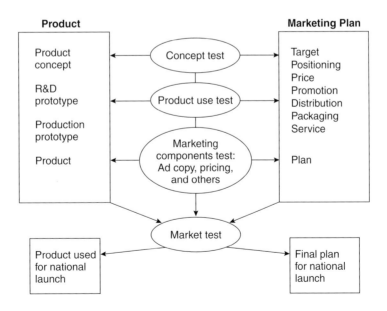

---

[45]Ibid., 325–326.

Traditional Tests

This method of market testing introduces the product under actual market conditions in one or more test cities.[46] It is typically used for frequently purchased consumer products. The time required for the tests ranges from a year to 18 months or more. Test marketing employs a complete marketing program including advertising and personal selling. Product sampling is often an important factor in launching the new product in the test market. The product is marketed on a commercial basis in each city, and test results are then projected to the national or regional target market. Because of its high cost, conventional test marketing represents the final evaluation before full-scale market introduction. Management may decide not to test market in order to avoid competitor awareness and high testing costs, and to speed up the new-product introduction.

Web-Enabled Tests

While these tests offer less control than other tests, they are increasingly used due to speed and relatively low costs. Procter and Gamble initially offered Crest Whitestrips via the product's dedicated website.[47] The research information obtained during an 8-month campaign was valuable in guiding P&G's full-scale market introduction of the successful product. The Internet has become an important basis for market testing.

Testing Industrial Products

Market testing can be used for industrial products. Selection of test sites may need to extend beyond one or two cities to include sufficient market coverage. For example, a region of a country might be used for testing. The test firm has substantial control of an industrial products test through the use of direct mail, the Internet, and personal selling. The relatively small number of customers also aids targeting of marketing effort.

Selecting Test Sites

Test sites for consumer products should exhibit the buyer and environmental characteristics of the intended market target. Since no site is perfect, the objective is to find a reasonable match between the test and market target for the new product. These criteria are often used to evaluate potential test sites for consumer products.

1. Representation as to population size.
2. Typical per capita income.
3. Typical purchasing habits.
4. Stability of year-round sales.
5. Relative isolation from other cities.
6. Not easily disrupted by competitors.
7. Typical of planned distribution outlets.
8. Availability of retailers that will cooperate.
9. Availability of media that will cooperate.
10. Availability of research and audit service companies.[48]

---

[46]Ibid., 323–324.
[47]Ibid., 327.
[48]Dillon, Madden, and Firtle, *Marketing Research,* 582–584.

The highest-ranked metropolitan areas for test markets in the United States are Albany, New York; Rochester, New York; Greensboro, North Carolina; Birmingham, Alabama; and Syracuse, New York.[49]

External Influences

Probably the most troublesome external factor that may affect test market results is competition that does not compete on a normal basis. Competitors may attempt to drive test market results awry by increasing or decreasing their marketing efforts and making other changes in their marketing actions. It is also important to monitor the test market environment to identify other unusual influences such as major shifts in economic conditions.

Commercialization

Introducing new products into the market requires finalizing the marketing plan, coordinating market entry activities across business functions, implementing the marketing strategy, and monitoring and controlling the product launch. Procter & Gamble's entry into Japan's dish soap market in 1995 is an interesting example of an international new-product venture.[50] P&G's Joy brand gained a leading 20 percent share of the $400 million dish-soap market by 1997. The successful strategy included offering new technology, packaging that retailers liked, attractive margins for retailers, and heavy spending on innovative commercials that got consumers' attention. At the time of market entry, Kao and Lion (Japanese companies) together had nearly 40 percent of the market. P&G developed a highly concentrated formula for Joy to eliminate consumers' concerns about Joy's strengths compared to other brands. Encouraged by commercials to try the new product, Japanese homemakers were pleased with Joy's performance.

The Marketing Plan

Market introduction requires a complete marketing strategy that is spelled out in the marketing plan. The plan should be coordinated with the people and business functions responsible for the introduction, including salespeople, sales and marketing managers, and managers from other functional areas such as operations, distribution, R&D, finance, and human resources. Responsibility for the new-product launch is normally assigned to a marketing or product manager. Alternatively, companies may assign responsibility to product planning and market introduction teams.

The timing and geographical scope of the launch are important decisions. The options range from a national market introduction to an area-by-area rollout. In some instances, the scope of the introduction may extend to international markets. The national introduction is a major endeavor, requiring a comprehensive implementation effort. A rollout reduces the scope of the introduction and enables management to adjust marketing strategy based on experience gained in the early stages of the launch. Of course, the rollout approach, like market testing, gives competition more time to react.

Monitoring and Control

Real-time tracking of new-product performance at the market entry stage is extremely important. Standardized information services (e.g., Information Resources Inc.) are available for monitoring sales of products such as foods, health and beauty aids, and prescription

---

[49]Acxiom Corporation, www.acxiom.com/testmarkets, 2005.
[50]Norhiko Shirouzu, "P&G's Joy Makes an Unlikely Splash in Japan," *Wall Street Journal,* December 19, 1997, B1 and B8.

- Ecoimagination was launched in 2005 by Jeffrey Immelt, GE's Chief Executive Officer, to highlight GE's focus on green issues—placing green technology products under a single brand.
- By 2007, GE had doubled its sales of environmentally friendly products to $12 billion over the previous two years—this includes wind-turbines, water-purification systems, and energy-efficient appliances.
- Immelt had $50 billion of projects in the pipeline and was on track to meet its target of $20 billion in "green" sales by 2010.
- In 2006, GE invested $900 million of its $3.7 billion R&D budget on green projects.
- The focus on green products is part of Immelt's priority to reduce GE's exposure to low-growth industries and move to more profitable areas.
- In managing the Ecoimagination initiative, GE is rigorous in selecting projects that are wanted by customers and are financially viable, but that also meet the criterion that they must significantly and measurably improve customers' environmental and operating performance.

Sources: Francesco Guerra, "Turning Green Requires a Lot of Imagination," *Financial Times,* Friday, May 24, 2007, 28. Fiona Harvey, "GE Looks Out for a Cleaner Profit," *Financial Times,* Friday, July 1, 2005, 13.

drugs. Information for these services is collected through store audits, consumer diary panels, and scanner services. Special tracking studies may be necessary for products that are not included in standardized information services. The Internet is rapidly becoming an essential new-product information gathering and monitoring capability. These activities include private online communities and research panels that provide companies with shoppers' feedback.

It is important to include product performance metrics and performance targets in the new-product plan to track how well the product is performing. Often included are profit contribution, sales, market share, and return on investment objectives—including the time horizon for reaching objectives. It is also important to establish benchmarks for objectives that indicate minimum acceptable performance. For example, market share threshold levels are sometimes used to gauge new-product performance. Repeat purchase data are essential for tracking frequently purchased products. Regular measures of customer satisfaction are also relevant in tracking market performance.

Management vision for the strategic direction to be taken by the business is also a significant influence on innovation. The ETHICS APPLICATION describes the pursuit of sustainable product development at General Electric, as part of its Ecoimagination corporate responsibility initiative. Many companies now include sustainability goals in their product development and innovation strategy.

Variations in the Generic New-Product-Planning Process

The new-product-planning process (see Exhibit 8.4) is based on the logic of being market driven and focused on customer needs. While a market-oriented focus is always important, some variations in the generic process may be necessary due to the new-product strategy of a particular company. The major impact of the variants is on the types of ideas that are considered by the firm. Several variations from the generic process are described in Exhibit 8.10.

EXHIBIT 8.10   **Summary of Variants of the Generic Development Process**

Source: Karl T. Ulrich and Stephen D. Eppinger, *Product Design and Development,* 3rd ed. (Burr Ridge, IL: Irwin/McGraw-Hill, 2004), 19.

Process Type	Description	Distinct Features	Examples
Generic (Market-Pull) Products	The team begins with a market opportunity and selects appropriate technologies to meet customer needs.	Process generally includes distinct planning, concept development, system-level design, detail design, testing and refinement, and production ramp-up phases.	Sporting goods, furniture, tools.
Technology-Push Products	The team begins with a new technology, then finds an appropriate market.	Planning phase involves matching technology and market. Concept development assumes a given technology.	Gore-Tex rainwear, Tyvek envelopes.
Platform Products	The team assumes that the new product will be built around an established technological subsystem.	Concept development assumes a proven technology platform.	Consumer electronics, computers, printers.
Process-Intensive Products	Characteristics of the product are highly constrained by the production process.	Either an existing production process must be specified from the start, or both product and process must be developed together from the start.	Snack foods, breakfast cereals, chemicals, semiconductors.
Customized Products	New products are slight variations of existing configurations.	Similarity of projects allows for a streamlined and highly structured development process.	Motors, switches, batteries, containers.
High-Risk Products	Technical or market uncertainties create high risks of failure.	Risks are identified early and tracked throughout the process. Analysis and testing activities take place as early as possible.	Pharmaceuticals, space systems.
Quick-Build Products	Rapid modeling and prototyping enables many design-build-test cycles.	Detail design and testing phases are repeated a number of times until the product is completed or time/budget runs out.	Software, cellular phones.
Complex Systems	System must be decomposed into several subsystems and many components.	Subsystems and components are developed by many teams working in parallel, followed by system integration and validation.	Airplanes, jet engines, automobiles.

The variants set some boundaries on the types of ideas considered by a company. For example, PepsiCo's beverage division has a focus on drinks in its idea seeking activities. Pepsi's introduction of Sierra Mist carbonated beverage is an example of a process-intensive new product. The generic new-product-planning process (see Exhibit 8.4) is relevant to all of the product variants other than limiting to some extent the types of ideas to be considered.

Summary

New-product planning is a vital activity in every company, and it applies to services as well as physical products. Companies that are successful in new-product planning follow a step-by-step process of new-product planning combined with effective organization designs for managing new products. Experience and learning help these firms to improve product planning over time.

Several key initiatives are pursued by companies that are successful innovators. These include (1) creating an innovative culture, (2) selecting the right innovation strategy, (3) developing and implementing effective new-product processes, (4) making resource commitments, and (5) leveraging distinctive capabilities.

Top management often defines the product, market, and technology scope of new-product ideas to be considered by an organization. The steps in new-product planning include customer needs analysis, idea generation and screening, concept evaluation, business analysis, product development and testing, marketing strategy development, market testing, and commercialization (see Exhibit 8.4).

Idea generation starts the process of planning for a new product. There are various internal and external sources of new-product ideas. Ideas are identified by information search, marketing research, research and development, incentives, and acquisition. Screening, evaluation, and business analysis help determine if the new-product concept is sufficiently attractive to justify proceeding with development.

Design of the product and use testing transform the product from a concept into a prototype. Product development creates one or more prototypes. Product testing obtains user's reactions to the new product. Production development determines how to produce the product in commercial quantities at costs that will enable the firm to price the product at a level attractive to buyers. Marketing strategy development begins early in the product planning process. A new marketing strategy is needed for a totally new product. Product line additions, modifications, and other changes require a less extensive strategy development.

Completion of the product design and marketing strategy moves the process to the market testing stage. At this point management may decide to obtain some form of market reaction to the new product before full-scale market entry. Testing options include simulated test marketing, scanner-based test marketing, and conventional test marketing. Industrial products are not market tested as much as consumer products. Instead, use tests of product prototypes are more typical for industrial products. Commercialization completes the planning process, moving the product into the marketplace to pursue sales and profit performance objectives.

The market-driven, customer-focused generic planning process provides the basic guide to developing new products. Nonetheless, some variations may be necessary in applying the process when technology, production processes, and other limiting factors define the scope of ideas considered by a particular firm.

Questions for Review and Discussion

1. Explain the relationship between customer satisfaction and customer value.
2. In many consumer products companies, marketing executives seem to play the lead role in new-product planning, whereas research and development executives occupy this position in firms with very complex products such as electronics. Why do these differences exist? Do you agree that such differences should occur?
3. Discuss the features and limitations of focus group interviews for use in new-product planning.
4. Identify and discuss the important issues in deciding how to organize for new-product planning.

5. Discuss the issues and trade-offs of using tight evaluation versus loose evaluation procedures as a product concept moves through the planning process to the commercialization stage.

6. What factors may affect the length of the new-product planning process?

7. Compare and contrast the use of scanner tests and conventional market tests.

8. Is the use of a single city test market appropriate? Discuss.

9. Examine the new-product-planning process assuming a platform strategy is being used by the organization (see Exhibit 8.10). How does the use of a platform strategy alter the planning process?

10. Discuss the potential role of the Internet in the new-product-planning process. Which stages of the process may benefit most from Internet initiatives?

Internet Applications

A. Visit the website of the Gap (www.gap.com). Discuss how the Web can be used in new-product planning for a bricks-and-mortar retailer such as the Gap.

B. Virgin Group Ltd. is an interesting corporate conglomerate headed by British tycoon, Richard C. N. Branson. Visit Virgin.com and develop a critical analysis of Virgin's new-product strategy of launching a portfolio of online businesses.

C. Dell, Inc. is expanding its product portfolio. Go to www.dell.com and describe the product categories in which Dell competes.

D. Visit the Hennes & Mauritz website and compare H&M's product offerings with those offered by Gap (www.gap.com).

Applications

A. The Google INNOVATION APPLICATION describes how the company manages its idea factory. Are there risks of expanding too far beyond the core search business? How should new-product planners avoid this problem without disregarding all potential opportunities beyond the core business?

B. The RELATIONSHIP APPLICATION describes how the design consultant IDEO assists companies in new-product design. Discuss the advantages and limitations of having this activity performed by a consultant rather than internally.

Part 4

Market-Driven Program Development

Chapter

Strategic Brand Management

Products play an important role in generating sales and profits and creating growth opportunities for all companies. Moreover, management initiatives for new and existing products are closely interrelated. Many companies have several products and/or brands in their portfolios. The objective is to achieve the highest overall performance from the portfolio of products offered by the firm. This requires successful new product introductions, effective targeting and positioning of existing products, selecting metrics and tracking performance of the portfolio, and improving or eliminating poor performing products. Strategic brand management of the portfolio is an ongoing challenge, involving executives from all business functions.

Estimates suggest that brand power can account for as much as 10 percent of the change in a company's stock price. The best global brands typically outperform the stock market by significant margins. For example, McDonalds' beats the S&P 500 by an average of 20 percentage points a year.[1]

PepsiCo has been very successful in its strategic brand management in recent years, with sales increasing from $24 billion in 2001 to $64.4 billion in 2011 in an extremely competitive environment. At the core of Pepsi's brand management initiatives is an impressive array of beverage and snack products. One of Pepsi's strengths is not being dependent on only beverages for profits and growth. It has 16 brands that each accounts for $1 billion in annual sales. Pepsi's competitive advantage is a carefully formulated and executed brand management strategy.[2] Pepsi's acquisition of Quaker Oats and Gatorade (80 percent market share) enhanced its portfolio. Coke had the lead opportunity to acquire Quaker but declined due to lack of the board of directors' support. However, Coke is the world's largest beverage company with over 500 non-alcohol beverage brands. Pepsi's strategic brand management initiatives, guided by excellent market sensing capabilities, established Aquafina in the lead position in the bottled water market. Interestingly, snacks account for nearly half of Pepsi's profits generated by Frito Lay and Quaker Oats. Remaining profit is contributed by Pepsi's very successful overseas operations. One of Pepsi's major brand management challenges is getting its brand managers to collaborate on sales and marketing

[1]"Stick With the big Names," *BusinessWeek,* August 3, 2009, 56.
[2]This illustration is based in part on *The Value Line Investment Survey, Ratings & Reports,* Issue 10, April 29, 2011, 1974. Katrina Brooker, "The Pepsi Machine," *Fortune,* February 6, 2006, 68–72

programs. This initiative was designated the "Power of One," and is considered as a key strategic growth initiative.

Strategic brand management requires several interrelated initiatives designed to build strong brands and a powerful portfolio. First, we examine the challenges of brand management, and discuss the importance and scope of strategic brand analysis. Next, we look at brand identity strategies, and consider what is involved in managing each brand over time and managing the portfolio of brands. The chapter is concluded with a discussion of brand leveraging initiatives.

Strategic Brand Management

It is important to distinguish between the terms *product* and *brand*. In practice they are often used interchangeably, although there are differences in meaning. A *product* is intended to meet the needs of buyers in the product-market. It may consist of objects, services, organizations, places, people, and ideas. This view of the product covers a wide range of situations, including tangible goods and intangible services. Thus, political candidates are products, as are travel services, medical services, refrigerators, gas turbines, and computers.

A *brand* is the product offered by a specific company. The American Marketing Association defines a brand as follows (www.marketingpower.com):

> A name, term, design, symbol, or any other feature that identifies one seller's good or service as distinct from those of other sellers. The legal term for brand is *trademark*. A brand may identify one item, a family of items, or all items of that seller. If used for the firm as a whole, the preferred term is *trade name*.

While the products of some companies are not identified as brands, most have some form of brand designation. Throughout the chapter when discussing a company's product, product line, or product mix (portfolio) we assume that the products have a brand identity.

In the past differences between goods and intangible services have been emphasized by highlighting how services are different (e.g., intangible, consumed when they are produced, and variable consistency). However, a compelling logic has been proposed that the distinction between goods and services should be replaced by a view that services are the dominant perspective in the 21st century, consisting of both tangible and intangible components.[3] The service-centered logic integrates goods with services and these offerings deliver value to customers. Thus, the important issue is understanding the composition of the value offering being made to buyers by a brand.

First, we look at the strategic role of brands. A discussion follows of brand management challenges. Next, we consider where responsibility for brand management is placed in an organization. Finally, the initiatives involved in strategic brand management are examined.

The Strategic Role of Brands

Strategic brand management is a key issue in many organizations and is not the domain only of consumer packaged goods companies. Apple pursues an interesting and very effective brand management strategy with its impressive array of app developers.[4] It works

---

[3]Stephen L. Vargo and Robert F. Lusch, "Evolving to a New Dominant Logic for Marketing," *Journal of Marketing,* January 2004, 1–17.

[4]"How Apple Feeds Its Army of App Makers," *Bloomberg Businessweek,* June 19, 2011, 39–40.

aggressively to motivate its developers to be involved and loyal. Apple's support services include extensive technical specifications, manuals, and programming tools for use by the developer in writing aps. The result is Apple's ecosystem of third-party software developers providing a major advantage against competitor Android.

A strategic brand perspective requires executives to decide what role brands play for the company in creating customer value and shareholder value. This role should be the basis for directing and sustaining brand investments into the most productive areas. It is important to distinguish between the functions of brands for buyers and sellers.[5] For buyers, brands reduce

- Customer search costs, by identifying products quickly and accurately.
- The buyer's perceived risk, by providing an assurance of quality and consistency (which may then be transferred to new products).
- The social and psychological risks associated with owning and using the "wrong" product, by providing psychological rewards for purchasing brands that symbolize status and prestige.

For sellers, brands play a function of facilitation, by making easier some of the tasks the seller has to perform. Brands facilitate

- Repeat purchases that enhance the company's financial performance, because the brand enables the customer to identify and re-identify the product compared to alternatives.
- The introduction of new products, because the customer is familiar with the brand from previous buying experience.
- Promotional effectiveness, by providing a point of focus.
- Premium pricing by creating a basic level of differentiation compared to competitors.
- Market segmentation, by communicating a coherent message to the target audience, telling them for whom the brand is intended and for whom it is not.
- Brand loyalty, of particular importance in product categories where loyal buying is an important feature of buying behavior.

Interestingly, several global corporate social responsibility initiatives have been linked to strong branding strategies (see Chapter 4). The Fairtrade initiative involves licensing the Fairtrade brand to food product brand owners like Cadbury, Starbucks, and Ben & Jerry's as a way of supporting farmers in the developing world by guaranteeing them minimum prices for their crops, and associating the brands with this cause. Frequently, Fairtrade branded products command premium prices from ethically minded consumers. Although Fairtrade accounts for only a tiny percentage of worldwide food and beverage sales, it has shown impressive revenue growth, even during a period of economic downturn. Similarly, Wal-Mart and Unilever look to the Rainforest Alliance to help them certify the coffee and tea that they sell, to reassure consumers about environmental issues.[6] Another interesting example is the Product Red development described in the ETHICS APPLICATION.

---

[5]The discussion in this section is based on Pierre Berthon, James M. Hulbert, and Leyland F. Pitt, *Brands, Brand Managers, and the Management of Brands: Where to Next?* Boston: Marketing Science Institute, Report No. 97–122, 1997.

[6]Michael Skapinker, "No Markets Were Hurt in Making This Coffee," *Financial Times,* November 9, 2010, 15. Michael Skapinker, "Why Companies and Campaigners Collaborate," *Financial Times,* July, 8, 2008, 15.

- In 2006, a start-up run by Irish rock star, Bono, and Californian backer, Bobby Shriver, set itself the ambitious task of creating a brand that would save thousands of Africans from dying from disease.
- Product Red raises money by licensing its logo to brands including Apple, Motorola, Emporio Armani, Dell, Gap, Converse, Nike, American Express, and Hallmark—in return for payments that go to the Geneva-based Global Fund to Fight Aids, Tuberculosis, and Malaria.
- Each partner company creates a product with the Product Red logo. In return for the opportunity to increase its own revenue through the Product Red products that it sells, a percentage of the profit is given to the Global Fund.
- The companies involved say the Red branding helps them reach new consumers and to appeal to a rising interest in ethical consumption among their existing buyers.
- Since its launch, Product Red has generated over $170 million for the Global Fund and over 7.5 million people have been impacted by HIV and AIDS programs supported by Red purchases.

Sources: Alan Beattie, "Challenges Ahead for Bono's Brand," *Financial Times,* December 1–2, 2007, 14. http://www.joinred.com/aboutred, accessed July 25, 2011.

The opportunity for using brand strength to build customer value and competitive advantage has encouraged managers to focus attention on global estimates of the value of brands and the concept of brand equity. The financial value of brands is an important indication of how well a brand is being managed by a company.[7] Interbrand (branding consultant) each year ranks the value of the top 100 global brands based on a company's financial condition. A formula based on net operating profit after tax is used. Also considered are consumer-polling data on brand preferences. The 2010 top ranked brands were Coca-Cola Co., International Business Machines Corp., Microsoft Corp., Google, Inc., and General Electric Co. In 2009 GE was 4th instead of Google, and Nokia was 5th. (Recall our discussion of Nokia's performance problems in Chapter 6). *BusinessWeek* publishes the top 100 brand ranking each year.

Strong brands are major contributors to the distinctive capabilities of companies like BMW, Google, Hewlett-Packard, General Electric, and Toyota. Sustaining and building brand strengths is a continuing challenge for managers. The TECHNOLOGY APPLICATION describes International Business Machine's 100 years of success. IBM's secret has been perceptively packaging technology for use by businesses.

Brand Management Challenges

Several internal and external forces create hurdles for product and brand managers in their efforts to build strong brands:[8]

- **Intense Price and Other Competitive Pressures.** Deciding how to respond to these pressures shifts managers' attention away from brand management responsibilities.
- **Fragmentation of Markets and Media.** Many markets have become highly differentiated in terms of customer needs. Similarly, the media (advertising and sales promotion)

---

[7]Suzanne Vranica, "Brands Recover, with Some Casualties," *Wall Street Journal,* September 16, 2010, B9.
[8]David A. Aaker, *Building Strong Brands* (New York: The Free Press, 1996), 26–35.

International Business Machines is a century-long success story. This performance is particularly impressive in the fast-moving field of technology. The core strategy is to package technology for use by businesses.

The IBM strategy began with punch-card machines. This was followed by magnetic-tape systems, mainframes, PCs, and today services and consulting. Part of the success may be luck, but at the core were impressive top management choices. CEO Lou Gerstner's shift from products to services is a powerful example of recognizing the critical need of changing strategic direction. The important focus has been building IBM around an idea instead of a specific technology.

Under Sam Palmisano, Gerstner's successor, IBM has grown earnings and stock value impressively, and taken IBM into new countries, expanding hot businesses like supercomputing and analytics. IBM sits at no. 12 on *Fortune*'s 2010 list of the *World's Most Admired Companies*. The modern IBM is characterized by bold imagination and sets the agenda for enterprise technology.

Sources: "The Test of Time," *The Economist,* June 11, 2011, 20. Jessi Hempel, "IBMs's Super Second Act," *Fortune,* March 21, 2011, 55–61.

available to access market segments have become very fragmented and specialized. The Internet has compounded market targeting and access complexity.

- **Complex Brand Strategies and Relationships.** Multiple additions to core brands have created complex brand management situations. These complexities may encourage managers to alter strategies rather than building on the existing strategies.
- **Bias Against Innovation.** Brand complacency may result in a failure to innovate. Innovation may be avoided to prevent cannibalism of existing products.
- **Pressure to Invest Elsewhere.** A strong brand may generate complacency and cause management to shift resources to new initiatives.
- **Short-Term Pressures.** Managers encounter many short-term pressures that shift their attention and resources away from important brand-building programs. Top management's need to achieve quarterly financial targets is illustrative.

The key to reducing these negative impacts on brand-building strategies is developing brand strategy guidelines, tracking initiatives on a regular basis, and critically assessing potential challenges that shift management attention away from core strategies.

Importantly, brand strategy cannot neglect the fundamental impact of online media like social networks and blogs. Online experiences can be a vital part of the brand experience for consumers, and online interactions can shape the perception and meaning of a brand to users. Some examples are shown in the INNOVATION APPLICATION.

Brand Management Responsibility

Responsibility for strategic brand management extends to several organizational levels. Three management levels often are found in companies that have strategic business units, different product lines, and specific brands within lines.

Product/Brand Management

Responsibilities for these positions consist of planning, managing, and coordinating the strategy for a specific product or brand. Management activities include market analysis, targeting, positioning strategy, performance analysis and strategy adjustment, identification of new product needs, and management and coordination of product/brand marketing

Innovation Application

Brand Engagement and Social Media

One impact of Internet-based social media is on the way consumers engage with brands and how they become involved.

- Stephanie Meyer's Twilight books about a teenage vampire have been a major publishing success linked to social networking sites and online discussion groups—the first social networking bestseller. The author engages directly with readers online to answer detailed questions about the plots and readers have responded by creating an entire world of Twilight on the Web with blogs, discussions, and news sites. The online impact is a central part of what the brand means to consumers.

- HBO's hit series *True Blood,* concerning vampires living among humans came to market through a viral marketing campaign, including blogs, online videos, online discoveries, and opinions about story lines. The core marketing message is surrounded by new online story content, fictional online worlds, and user-generated campaigns. Co-branding includes a Gillette promotion for a "True Blood special edition" of its Fusion Power razor with the slogan "Dead Sexy"; and the convertible Mini-Cooper inviting readers to "Feel the wind in your fangs," as well as a fake advertisement for vampire dental care. The creation of a community and new experiences are part of the brand.

- To target deodorant at young "degree-using males," Unilever used online poker. Poker is popular with young men and is the ultimate game of risk—showing good fit for a brand targeting "men who take risks." Unilever partnered with ESPN to create the "Degree Men—All in a Moment" feature during the World Series of Poker, and worked with ESPN.com and MSN.com to integrate the brand into their online poker games.

- Provoking online debate makes a brand stand out. The challenge is linking a brand with a sufficiently interesting idea. The Unilever Dove personal care products campaign challenges conventional ideas of beauty. Dove's "Evolution" viral film reached 21 million U.S. consumers and spread globally within hours.

Sources: Simon Clift, "Brand New World," *Wall Street Journal,* March 13, 2008, 12. Heather Green, "Harry Potter With Fangs—And a Social Network," *BusinessWeek,* August 11, 2008, 44–46. Andrew Edgecliffe-Johnson, "Marketers Tap into New Vein for Brands," *Financial Times,* June 11, 2009, 12.

---

activities. Marketing plans for specific brands are often developed at this level. Product or brand managers typically do not have authority over all brand management activities, but they have responsibility for the performance of their brands. These managers are sponsors or advocates of specific products, negotiating and collaborating on behalf of their product/brand strategies with the salesforce, research and development, operations, marketing research, and advertising and sales promotion managers.

Product Group/Marketing Management

A business that has several product categories and/or brands may assign responsibility for coordinating the initiatives of product or brand managers to a product director, group manager, or marketing manager. This person coordinates and monitors the activities and approves the recommendations of a group of product or brand managers. The executive's responsibilities are to manage the brand portfolio. Additionally, the product group manager coordinates product management activities and decisions with the business unit management.

Product Portfolio Management

This responsibility is normally assigned to the chief executive of the strategic business unit (SBU), the corporate level of an organization, or a team of top executives. Illustrative decisions include product acquisitions, research and development priorities, new-product decisions, product drop decisions, and resource allocation. Evaluation of brand/product portfolio performance may also be centered at this level. In a corporation with two or more SBUs, top management may coordinate and establish product management guidelines for the SBU management. We look further into the organization of marketing activities in Chapter 14.

Market-Driven Management

Increasingly, changes are being made by companies to integrate sales, marketing, and other business functions into cross-functional teams.[9] A study by the Boston Consulting Group indicated that 90 percent of the responding companies have restructured their marketing departments. It is apparent that traditional product and brand-based organizations will increasingly evolve into customer and market-based approaches to implement more effectively the mandate for customer focus.

Strategic Brand Management

Strategic brand management decisions are relevant to all businesses, including suppliers, producers, wholesalers, distributors, and retailers. While many of these decisions involve the evaluation, selection, and dropping of products from suppliers, retailers may also develop new goods and services, such as Gap and Target have done. These retailers are involved in designing some of their own products. Moreover, suppliers are faced with important brand management decisions.

The importance of strategic brand management is illustrated by Sony, the troubled Japanese electronics giant. The GLOBAL APPLICATION describes how Sony's management launched its turnaround strategy. The core challenge is customer value-driven innovation.

Strategic brand management consists of several interrelated initiatives as shown in Exhibit 9.1.[10] We briefly describe each activity, examining it in greater depth in the following sections of the chapter.

EXHIBIT 9.1
Strategic Brand Management

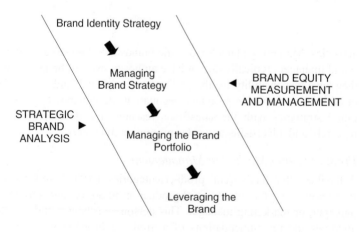

---

[9]Berthon et al. *Brand Managers and the Management of Brands.*
[10]David A. Aaker, *Building Strong Brands* (New York: The Free Press, 1996), 26–35.

Sir Howard Stringer, a Welsh-born American citizen, was appointed CEO of Sony, the troubled Japanese electronics giant, in 2005. Sony's past strategic brand management initiatives had failed to close the digital gap between software/services/content/devices. During the CEO's first year several cost reduction and portfolio initiatives were implemented to launch the turnaround strategy:

The Aibo, a beloved robotic pet, was put to sleep. They shut down the Qualia line of boutique electronics that included a $4,000 digital camera and a $13,000 70-inch television. They eliminated 5,700 jobs and closed nine factories, including one in south Wales. (He took some flak back home for that.) They have sold $705 million worth of assets. You probably didn't know that Sony owned a chain of 1,221 cosmetics salons and the 18 Japanese outlets of the Maxim's de Paris restaurant chain. They're gone. Gone, too, is a group of salary-men in their 60s, 70s, and 80s who, after retiring from senior management positions, were given the title of "advisor," a tradition established by Sony's founders. "That was very symbolic," says Hideki (Dick) Komivama, a Sony executive and key ally of Stringer's. The 45 advisors each had a secretary, a car and driver, and worst of all, the ability to gum up decision making and second-guess people doing real jobs. No more.

Sir Howard's actions clearly improved Sony's performance. However, by 2009 Sony had lost billions in TVs and game consoles. Sales increased from $64 billion in 2005 to $86 billion in 2010. In 2011 near term profits were impacted by production slowdowns caused by Japan's earthquake and tsunami damages. While 2012 sales were projected at $89 billion, Sony by 2011 had experienced three years of losses.

Sources: Marc Gunther, "The Welshman, the Walkman, and the Salary Men," *Fortune,* June 12, 2006, 72. Bert Helm, "100 Best Global Brands," *BusinessWeek,* September 25, 2009, 52. *The Value Line Investment Survey,* Issue 10, April 29, 2011, 1992. Daisuke Wakabayashi and Juro Osawa, "Struggling Sony Cuts CEO's Pay," *Wall Street Journal,* June 29, 2011, B4.

Strategic Brand Analysis

Analysis provides essential information for decision making for each of the brand management activities shown in Exhibit 9.1. Analysis includes market/customer, competitor, and brand information.

Brand Equity Measurement and Management

Each of the strategic brand management initiatives shown in Exhibit 9.1 may have a positive or negative impact on the value of the brands in the portfolio. Brand equity recognizes the importance of brand value and identifies the key dimensions of equity. The objective is to build brand equity over time.

Brand Identity Strategy

The intent of brand identity is to determine "a unique set of brand associations that the brand strategist aspires to create or maintain."[11] The identity may be associated with the product, the organization, a person, or a symbol. Identity implementation determines what part of the identity is to be communicated to the target audience and how this will be achieved. The brand positioning statement describes the identity information to be used to position the brand in the eyes and minds of targeted buyers.

---

[11]Ibid., 68.

Managing Brand Strategy

A brand must be managed from its initial launch throughout the brand's life cycle. While the brand strategy may be altered over time, the intent is to pursue consistent initiatives, build the strength of the brand, and avoid damaging the brand. Target's management has been very successful in managing the retailer's brand, whereas Kmart's faulty brand management eventually contributed to its bankruptcy.

Managing the Brand Portfolio

This initiative consists of coordinating the organization's portfolio or system of brands with the objective of achieving optimal system performance. The focus is on the performance of the portfolio and its brand interrelations rather than an individual brand. Procter and Gamble has been particularly impressive in managing its very successful brand portfolio.

Leveraging the Brand

Leveraging involves extending the core brand identity to a new addition to the product line, or to a new product category. Nike's leveraging the core footwear brand into apparel and sports equipment is illustrative of extending the brand to new product categories.

Strategic Brand Analysis

A company may have a single product, a product line, or a portfolio of product lines. In our discussion of managing existing products, we assume that product/brand strategy decisions are being made for a SBU. The product composition of the SBU consists of one or more product lines and the specific product(s) that make up each line.

Strategic brand analysis includes market and customer, competitor, and brand analysis. Since Chapter 2 considers market and customer and competitor analysis, the present discussion centers on brand analysis. Various aspects of the brand may be examined including performance, portfolio interrelationships, leveraging strengths and weaknesses, and brand values.

Evaluating the performance of the brand portfolio helps guide decisions on new products, modified products, and eliminating products. Consider, for example, Apple's decision to drop the Newton handheld computer.[12] Apple invested an estimated $500 million in the brand extension beginning in 1987. The core concept was a computer that could convert the user's handwriting into electronic format. Introduced in 1993 at around $1,000, the Newton was too expensive for many users and there were problems with the handwriting recognition feature. Competition eventually emerged from the successful Palm Pilot introduced in 1996. Over 1 million units were sold in a 2-year period. The designers created a handheld unit that could do a few things well. Apple's Message Pad was never profitable, although some industry observers suggest that Apple could have been the market leader by continuing product improvement. The Personal Digital Assistant units were a disruptive technology that required time to develop a position in the mainstream market (see Chapter 8).

Tracking Brand Performance

Evaluating the products in the brand portfolio requires tracking the performance of each brand as shown in Exhibit 9.2. Management needs to establish the performance objectives and benchmarks for tracking performance. We discuss brand metrics in Chapter 15. Objectives

---

[12]Jim Carlton, "Apple Drops Newton, An Idea Ahead of Its Time," *Wall Street Journal,* March 2, 1998, B1 and B8.

EXHIBIT 9.2
Tracking Brand Performance

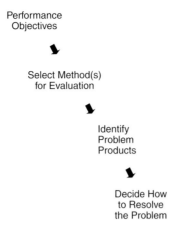

may include both financial and nonfinancial factors. Because of the demand and cost inter-relationships among products, it is necessary to sort out the sales and costs attributable to each product to show how well it is doing. Activity-based cost analysis is useful for this purpose.[13]

The next step in tracking performance is selecting one or more methods to evaluate product performance. Several useful techniques are shown in Exhibit 9.3. The results of the analyses should identify problem products as well as those performing at or above management's expectations. Finally, management must decide how to resolve the problem.

An interesting application of performance analysis for a service is the revenue management system used by American Airlines to evaluate route performance. Each route (e.g., Los Angeles—Dallas/Fort Worth) is a unit in the route system or network. Based on performance, forecasts of demand and competition, and other strategic and tactical considerations,

EXHIBIT 9.3
Methods for Analyzing Product Portfolio Performance

---

[13]Robert Cooper and Robert S. Kaplan, "Measure Costs Right: Make the Right Decisions," *Harvard Business Review,* September–October 1998, 96–103.

the airline makes decisions to expand, reduce, or terminate service throughout the route network. Each analyst is responsible for a group of routes. Based on management guidelines, the analyst determines how many seats on each flight are to be allocated to AA advantage miles and those assigned to various fare classifications. American Airlines pioneered this system and is recognized throughout the industry for its distinctive revenue management capabilities. Assisting analysts are powerful computer models developed using experience data and management science techniques.

We look at product life-cycle analysis, product grid analysis, and positioning analysis to illustrate methods for diagnosing product performance and identifying alternatives for resolving problems. Standardized information services, research studies, and financial analysis are discussed in previous chapters.

Product Life-Cycle Analysis

As discussed in Chapter 6 the major stages of the product life cycle (PLC) are introduction, growth, maturity, and decline. Relevant issues in PLC analysis include

- Determining the length and rate of change of the product life cycle.
- Identifying the current PLC stage and selecting the product strategy that is appropriate for this stage.
- Anticipating threats and finding opportunities for altering and extending the PLC.

Rate of Change

Product life cycles are becoming shorter for many products due to new technology, rapidly changing preferences of buyers, and intense competition. Cycles also vary for different products. A clothing style may last only one season, whereas a new commercial aircraft may be produced for many years after introduction. Determining the rate of change of the PLC is important because of the need to adjust the marketing strategy to correspond to the changing conditions.

Product Life-Cycle Strategies

The PLC stage of the product has important implications regarding all aspects of targeting and positioning (see Chapter 6). Different strategy phases are encountered in moving through the PLC. In the first stage, the objective is to establish the brand in the market through brand development activities such as advertising, coupons, and sampling. In the growth stage, the brand is reinforced through marketing efforts. During the maturity/decline stage, product repositioning efforts may occur by adjusting size, color, and packaging to appeal to different market segments. Analysis of the growth rate, sales trends, time since introduction, intensity of competition, pricing practices, and competitor entry/exit information are useful in PLC stage analysis.

Product Performance Analysis

Performance analysis considers whether each product is measuring up to management's minimum performance criteria, and assesses the strengths and weaknesses of the product relative to other products in the portfolio. The comparative analysis of products can be performed by incorporating market attractiveness and competitive strength assessments using two-way (horizontal and vertical) grids. These analyses highlight differences among products. After identifying the relative market attractiveness and competitive strength of the products in the portfolio, more comprehensive analysis of specific performance factors may also be useful.

Brand Positioning Analysis

Perceptual maps are useful in comparing brands. Preference mapping offers useful guidelines for strategic targeting and product positioning. The analyses can relate buyer preferences to different brands and indicate possible brand repositioning options. New-product opportunities may also be identified in the analysis of preference maps. Positioning studies over time can measure the impact of repositioning strategies.

Toyota faced an interesting brand positioning problem which led to the introduction of the Scion brand in 2002. The problem was that Toyota and Lexus buyers had an average age of 54, and Toyota needed to attract younger auto consumers, many of whom perceived Toyotas as autos for older people. Scion, based in California considered its "funky" cars as the first stepping stone in a young auto buyer's journey. Scion positioned itself as a "guerrilla brand" linked to the lifestyle of younger buyers. Scion established its own record label and designer clothing range. The average age of Scion buyers was thirty-one years, but the challenge for Toyota is how many Scion buyers will migrate in time to Toyota and Lexus.[14]

Brand Equity Measurement and Management

Measuring Brand Equity

Aaker proposes several measures to capture all relevant aspects of brand equity:[15]

- Loyalty (price premium, satisfaction/loyalty).
- Perceived quality and leadership/popularity measures.
- Associations/differentiation (perceived value, brand personality, organizational associations).
- Awareness (brand awareness).
- Market behavior (market share, price and distribution indices).

These components provide the basis for developing operational measures of brand equity.

Several methods for brand valuation have been proposed. Interbrand's approach brand value estimates is discussed earlier in the chapter. Young & Rubicam (Y&R) has developed a brand evaluation tool, the Brand Asset Valuator (BAV).[16] The technique uses the brand's vitality (relevance and differentiation) and brand stature (esteem and familiarity) to gauge the health of the brand. Y&R has conducted studies with 30,000 consumers and 6,000 brands in 19 countries.

Brand Health Reports

It is important to consider absolute brand values and investments, and the change in brand value over time, in the evaluation of brand health. Several major companies have adopted brand health report cards, which provide indicators to monitor the direction of change in brand equity and identify the key issues to be addressed. Brand health reports can be compiled for individual brands or the entire brand portfolio.[17] The brand report card can assess

---

[14]Bernard Simon, "Scion Brand Greases the Wheels for Toyota," *Financial Times,* April 26, 2006, 10.

[15]David A. Aaker, *Managing Brand Equity* (New York: The Free Press, 1991), 15.

[16]Kevin L. Keller, *Strategic Brand Management,* 2nd ed. (Upper Saddle River, NJ: Prentice Hall, 2003), 509–511.

[17]Kevin Lane Keller, "The Brand Report Card," *Harvard Business Review,* January–February 2000, 147–157.

the brand against the characteristics of the strongest brands by scoring against the following key criteria of brand strength:

- The brand excels at delivering the benefits customers truly desire.
- The brand stays relevant.
- The pricing strategy is based on consumers' perceptions of value.
- The brand is properly positioned.
- The brand is consistent.
- The brand portfolio and hierarchy make sense.
- The brand makes use of and coordinates a full repertoire of marketing activities to build brand equity.
- The brand's managers understand what the brand means to consumers.
- The brand is given proper support and that support is sustained over the long run.
- The company monitors sources of brand equity.[18]

Others suggest that brand health assessment measures should include market position (e.g., market share and repeat purchase behavior), perception (e.g., awareness, differentiation), marketing support (e.g., share of advertising spending in the sector compared to market share), and profitability.[19] Brand health reports need to be produced on a regular and systematic basis to alert managers to necessary changes in strategy and new market opportunities.

Brand Identity Strategy

Determining the most promising brand identity strategy for an organization's products is a very important strategic initiative (see Exhibit 9.2). Brand identification should span a long time horizon, providing a foundation for building brand equity:

> Brand identity is a unique set of brand associations that the brand strategist aspires to create or maintain. These associations represent what the brand stands for and imply a promise to customers from the organization members.[20]

We first discuss alternatives for brand identification and consider the role of the value proposition in brand identity. Next, options for focusing brand identity are described. Finally, we look at how brand identity is implemented.

Alternatives for Brand Identification

In addition to identifying the brand based on the product or the organization, David Aaker extends brand identification options to the brand as a person and the brand as a symbol.[21] The brand as a person (brand personality) perspective recognizes that strong brands may have an identity beyond the product or the company, which has positive impacts on the customer relationship and perception of value. The brand as a symbol underlines the role in brand building of visual imagery, metaphors, and brand heritage. For example, consider Nike's "swoosh" visual symbolism, the Energizer bunny metaphor for long battery life, and Starbuck's Seattle coffee house tradition. This involves "getting to the heart of the brand" to understand the promise that the brand makes to the customer and the brand's

---

[18]Ibid., 148–149.

[19]Noel Capon and James M. Hulbert, *Marketing Management in the 21st Century* (Upper Saddle River, NJ: Prentice-Hall, 2001).

[20]Aaker, *Building Strong Brands,* 68.

[21]This discussion is based on Aaker, *Building Strong Brands,* Chapter 3.

value proposition.[22] A clear and effective brand identification strategy is a foundation for building brand strength.

While employing all four brand identity perspectives may not be appropriate for an organization, it is important to consider identity options beyond only a product focus. Moreover, it is essential to recognize that brand identity articulates how management would like the brand to be perceived.

The value proposition conveys the benefit(s) offered by the brand. These benefits may be functional, emotional, or self-expressive.[23] Recall our discussion of these alternative positioning concepts in Chapter 6. The intent is to consider the benefits that distinguish the brand from its competition. The value proposition expresses the underlying logic of the relationship between the brand and the customer.

Brand Focus

One of several options as to where to focus the brand identity may be appropriate for a company. We look at the features of each. The major alternatives include product-line, corporate, and combination bonding.

Product-Line Branding

This strategy places a brand name on one or more lines of related products representing different product categories (e.g., Crest toothpaste, brushes, and floss). This option provides focus and offers cost advantages by promoting the entire line rather than each product. One feature of product-line branding is that additional items (line extensions) can be introduced utilizing the established brand name.

Corporate Branding

This strategy builds brand identity using the corporate name to identify the entire product offering. Examples include IBM in computers, BMW in automobiles, and Victoria's Secret in intimate apparel. Corporate branding has the advantage of using one advertising and sales promotion program to support all of the firm's products. It also facilitates the introduction and promotion of new products. The shortcomings of corporate branding include a lack of focus on specific products and possible adverse effects on the product portfolio if the company encounters negative publicity for one of its products.

Interestingly, in the postrecession environment of the 2010s, groups like Procter & Gamble, Unilever, and Nestlé are making new efforts to emphasize their corporate brands. Corporate branding allows groups to deliver broader messages and cross-product information to customers. In 2011, P&G launched campaigns in the United States, U.K., China, France, and Brazil, which, for the first time in P&G history, emphasized to consumers the link between P&G and the brands in its portfolio. Unilever and Nestlé have adopted such approaches for several years. The logic is to transfer qualities of trust and reliability across the entire brand portfolio. For P&G, corporate branding is linked to the company's Olympics Games sponsorship. Further, as companies like Nestlé put increasing effort into corporate social responsibility initiatives and sustainability, they want consumers to know about these efforts. Nonetheless, the risks remain in corporate branding if things go wrong.[24]

---

[22]Don E. Schultz, "Getting to the Heart of the Brand," *Marketing Management,* September–October 2000, 8–9.
[23]Aaker, *Building Strong Brands,* 102.
[24]Louise Lucas, "People Meet the Parents," *Financial Times,* April 21, 2011, 16.

Combination Branding

A company may use a combination of product-line and corporate branding. Sears, for example, employs both product-line and corporate branding (e.g., the Kenmore appliance and Craftsman tool lines). Combination branding benefits from the buyer's association of the corporate name with the product or line brand name.

Private Branding

Retailers with established brand names, such as Costco, Krogers, Target, and Wal-Mart Stores, Inc., contract with producers to manufacture and place the retailer's brand name on products sold by the retailer. Called private branding, the major advantage to the producer is eliminating the costs of marketing to end-users, although a private-label arrangement may make the manufacturer dependent on the firm using the private brand. Nevertheless, the arrangement can yield benefits to both the producer and the value chain member. The retailer uses its private brand to build store loyalty, since the private brand is associated with the retailer's stores.

Indeed, the power of retailers to challenge traditional leading brands is growing. AC Nielson research confirms that two-thirds of customers around the world believe that supermarkets' own brands are a good alternative to other brands.[25] Kumar and Steenkamp identify private labels as: (1) *"value"* or generic at a basic level; (2) *copycat brands,* which imitate the qualities of premium brands at a lower price; (3) *premium store brands,* which sell at the same or higher price as manufacturers' premium bands; or (4) *value innovators,* like IKEA, offering their unique value for money proposition.[26] Retailer market sensing in positioning different types of private labels and opening up new markets underlines an important challenge to traditional brand owners.

Identity Implementation

Identity implementation involves deciding the components of the brand identity and value proposition to be included in the brand position statement. These questions should be answered in formulating the identity implementation strategy:[27]

1. Select a brand position that will be favorably recognized by customers and will differentiate the brand from its competitors.
2. Determine the primary and secondary target audiences.
3. Select the primary communication objectives.
4. Determine the points of advantage.

Determination of the brand position is the core of the implementation strategy. This decision involves selecting the part of the core identity to be communicated to the target audiences, including points of leverage and key benefits.[28]

Managing Brand Strategy

Proactive efforts should be devoted to managing each brand over time. Analyzing performance shows how well the existing brand strategy is performing, helps management to identify new product needs, and points to where the existing strategy should be altered.

---

[25]Stefan Stern, "Quality Becomes Commodity in Brand Battle," *Financial Times,* Wednesday, March 14, 2007, 12.
[26]Nirmalya Kumar, Jan-Benedict, and E. M. Steenkamp, *Private Label Strategy* (Cambridge, MA: Harvard Business School Press, 2007).
[27]Aaker, *Building Strong Brands,* 183.
[28]Ibid., Chapter 6.

The P&G purchase of Gillette shows that innovation is key to branding and marketing is more diffuse and personal. Five new lessons for branding:

- **Innovate, Innovate, Innovate**—Why tinker with Tide? To build a widening family of detergents and cleaners including everything from Tide Coldwater for cold water washing to Tide Kick, a combination measuring cup and stain penetrator.

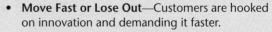
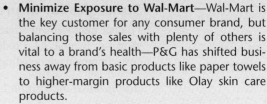

- **Move Fast or Lose Out**—Customers are hooked on innovation and demanding it faster.

- **Minimize Exposure to Wal-Mart**—Wal-Mart is the key customer for any consumer brand, but balancing those sales with plenty of others is vital to a brand's health—P&G has shifted business away from basic products like paper towels to higher-margin products like Olay skin care products.

- **The New Media Message**—P&G has mastered "surround-sound marketing"—using everything from in-store demos to pitches on Wal-Mart TV, to online innovations, to target specific customers and to fit the medium to the message.

- **Think Broadly**—P&G is a solver of problems in the home, and doesn't define itself by products. While toothpaste rival Colgate-Palmolive was focusing on the toothpaste tube, P&G grabbed greater "share of mouth" with innovations such as the inexpensive spin toothbrush and premium-priced Whitestrips teeth-whitening kits.

Dropping unprofitable brands may also be important. In 2009 P&G's CEO was stepping up the search for divestiture candidates. Possible brands were Braun small appliances, Iams pet food, and others.

Sources: Nanette Byrnes, Robert Berner, Wendy Zellner, and William C. Symonds, "Branding: Five New Lessons," *BusinessWeek,* February 14, 2005, 26–28. Jeffrey McCracken and Ellen Bryon, "P&G Considers Booting Some Brands," *Wall Street Journal,* October 29, 2009, B1 and B9.

The challenging and dynamic process of successfully managing brand strategy is illustrated by Procter and Gamble and the lessons apparent in P&G strategy after the Gillette merger. These lessons are described in the INNOVATION APPLICATION.

Brands that have been successful over a long time period offer useful insights about brand strategy management. Established brands like Budweiser, Hershey, IBM, and Intel continue to build strong market positions. The performance records of powerful brands are the result of (1) marketing skills, (2) product quality, and (3) strong brand preference developed through years of successful advertising.[29] The brand equity that has been built for a company's brands is a valuable asset. A common characteristic of many enduring brands is that the targeting and positioning strategy initially selected has generally been followed during the life of each brand. Consistency in the marketing strategy over time is very important.[30]

---

[29]Ronald Alsop, "Enduring Brands Hold Their Allure by Sticking Close to Their Roots," *Wall Street Journal,* Centennial Edition.
[30]Ibid.

Burberry PLC is an interesting example of the challenges of managing a brand over time. The Burberry plaid is one of the most recognized logos throughout the world.[31] The tan plaid fabric design performed a key role in transforming Burberry from a raincoat producer to a luxury fashion brand offering everything from dresses to dog collars. A new CEO joined the company in 2006, and quickly decided plaid overexposure was a major brand symbol problem. Part of a series of initiatives, Burberry is strategically diversifying into new icons. For example, an equestrian knight and the signature of founder Thomas Burberry are being added to handbags, shoes, and scarves. Importantly, the intent is to surpass rather than replace Burberry's trademark tartan. Burberry was performing well by 2011, driven by booming sales in Asia and South America.

Strategies for Improving Product Performance

Product improvement strategies include decisions for each product in the product line as shown in Exhibit 9.4. Product-line actions may consist of adding a new product, reducing costs, improving the existing product, altering the marketing strategy, or dropping the product.

Additions to the Product Line

Management may decide to add a new product to the line to improve performance. As discussed in Chapter 8, the new product concept should be carefully evaluated before it is developed and introduced in the market.

Cost Reduction

We know that lower costs give a company a major advantage over the competition. A product's cost may be reduced by changes in its design, manufacturing improvements, reduction of the cost of supplies, and improvements in marketing productivity. Costco, the warehouse retailer, is continually working to lower the costs of its products through inventory management, operating improvements, and other initiatives. Interestingly, Costco's average store sales are about double that of Wal-Mart's competing Sam's Club.

Product Improvement

Products are often improved by changing their features, quality, and styling. Automobile features and styles are modified on an annual basis. Many companies allocate substantial resources to the regular improvement of their products. Compared to a decade ago, today's products, such as disposable diapers, cameras, computers, and consumer electronics show vast improvements in performance and features. For example, the Skoda automobile brand was associated with low mechanical standards and reliability, until acquired by Volkswagen whose engineering and production expertise has transformed the Skoda product into one of the leading European brands.

EXHIBIT 9.4
Strategies for Improving Product Performance

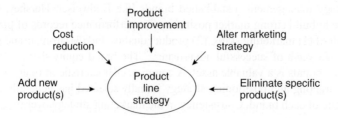

---

[31]Cecilie Rohwedder, "Burberry's New CEO Seeks Alternate Brand Symbols as Famed Tartan Grows Trite," *Wall Street Journal,* July 7, 2006, B1, B3. "A Checkered Story," *The Economist,* January 22, 2011, 68–69.

One way to differentiate a brand against competition is with unique *features.* Another option is to let the buyer customize the features desired in a product. Optional features offer the buyer more flexibility in selecting a brand. The capability to produce products with varied features that appeal to market diversity is an important competitive advantage.

Style may offer an important competitive edge for certain product categories. The impact of intangibles like style should not be underestimated. Trackers of trends have been surprised by the influence of Japanese design and culture in the 2000s. Japanese designs are impacting fields as diverse as toys (e.g., small dolls); cars (e.g., Toyota's gas-electric Prius); and fashion (e.g., Louis Vuitton's Murakami bags). Japanese-style comics called *manga,* as thick as paperback books, selling for $10 in Target and Borders, are at the center of pop culture, along with *anime,* the distinctive Japanese-style cartoons.[32]

Marketing Strategy Alteration

Changes in market targeting and positioning may be necessary as a product moves through its life cycle. However, the changes should be consistent with the core strategy. Problems or opportunities may point to adjusting the marketing strategy during a PLC stage. Tylenol's marketing strategy over its life cycle has been altered while maintaining a consistent positioning on its strong association with doctors and hospitals.

Product Elimination

Dropping a problem product may be necessary when cost reduction, product improvement, or marketing strategy initiatives are not feasible for improving poor performance of the product. In deciding to drop a product, management may consider a variety of performance criteria in addition to the product's sales and profit contribution. Elimination may occur at any PLC stage, although it is more likely to occur in either the introduction or decline stages. Risks are involved in eliminating products that have loyal buyers, so the exit strategy should be carefully planned and implemented.

Environmental Effects of Products

Environmental issues concerning product labeling, packaging, use, and disposal need to be considered. Protection of the environment involves a complex set of trade-offs among social, economic, political, and technology factors (see coverage in Chapter 4).

Managing the Brand Portfolio

Portfolio management is concerned with enhancing the performance of all the brands and product lines offered by a company. Initiatives include changing brand and product-line priorities, adding new product lines or brands, and deleting product lines or brands. Companies that have several different brands and product categories should manage them as a portfolio rather than pursuing independent brand strategies:

> The brand portfolio strategy specifies the structure of the brand portfolio and the scope, roles, and interrelationships of the portfolio brands. The goals are to create synergy, leverage, clarity within the portfolio and relevant, differentiated, and energized brands.[33]

The importance of a brand portfolio perspective is illustrated by DaimlerBenz's response to a new product test failure. In the late 1990s management targeted the small car market with the

---

[32]Christopher Palmeri and Nanette Byrnes, "Is Japanese Style Taking Over the World?" *BusinessWeek,* July 26, 2004, 96–98.
[33]David A. Aaker, *Brand Portfolio Strategy* (New York: The Free Press, 2004), 13.

new A-Class Baby Benz, alongside the prestigious Mercedez-Benz C- and E-Class lines.[34] In 1997, wholly unexpectedly, in a test drive a Swedish journalist rolled the A-Class Benz when simulating a swerve around an imaginary elk (the "Elk Test"). The company quickly responded with expensive changes to the vehicle including new tires and electronic stabilizing as standard. Nonetheless, after 3,000 canceled orders the car was taken off the market for three months to undertake chassis modifications. Rumors spread that the company had stretched itself too far too quickly to get into the mass car market. Nonetheless, the company survived the crisis and its responsive and careful approach protected the brand portfolio from long-term damage.

Determining Roles of Brands

A brand portfolio perspective encourages the use of brands to support the entire portfolio as well as the support of each brand:

> A key to managing brands in an environment of complexity is to consider them as not only individual performers, but members of a system of brands that must work to support one another. A brand system can serve as a launching platform for new products or brands and as a foundation for all brands in the system.[35]

The major objectives of brand portfolio management are shown in Exhibit 9.5. Importantly, the focus is the entire portfolio rather than specific brands.

Strategies for Brand Strength

A cohesive and clearly defined brand portfolio is essential to achieving strong portfolio performance. The importance of a strategic brand management perspective is described:

> Brand portfolio strategy becomes especially critical as brand contexts are complicated by multiple segments, multiple products, varied competitor types, complex distribution channels, multiple brand extensions, and the wider use of endorsed brands and subbrands.[36]

Nestlé, the world's largest food company, has over 8,000 brands.[37] Starting in 2001 management pursued initiatives to streamline operations to reduce cost, strengthen key

EXHIBIT 9.5
Brand Portfolio Management Objectives

Source: David A. Aaker, *Building Strong Brands,* New York: The Free Press, 1996, 241–242.

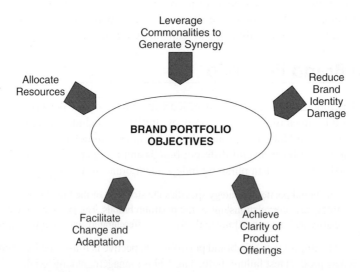

[34]David Woodruff, "A-Class Damage Control at DaimlerBenz," *BusinessWeek,* November 24, 1997, 62. Rufus Olins and Matthew Lynn, "A-Class Disaster," *Sunday Times,* November 16, 1997, 54.

[35]Aaker, *Building Strong Brands,* 241.

[36]Aaker, *Brand Portfolio Strategy,* 13.

[37]"Nestle Is Starting to Slim Down at Last," *BusinessWeek,* October 27, 2003, 56–57.

product groups via acquisitions, outsource activities such as tomato canning and pasta production, and develop new products. By 2003, $1.5 billion in cost reductions had been achieved. Some critics observed that significantly expanded marketing expenditures may offset the cost reductions.

Strategies for building brand strength and sustaining that strength for the brand portfolio require attention to the implementation of brand identification, revitalizing brands in the later stages of their life cycles, and recognizing the strategic vulnerabilities of core brands to competitive attack or changing market conditions.

Adding a New Line

The motivation for adding a new product line may be to

- Increase the growth rate of the business.
- Offer a more complete range of products to wholesalers and retailers.
- Gain marketing strength and economies in distribution, advertising, and personal selling.
- Leverage an existing brand position.
- Avoid dependence on one product line or category.

The product portfolio may be expanded through internal development or by purchase of an entire company or a line of products. Purchase may be a favorable option compared to the costs of internal development. Acquisition is also a faster means of expanding the product mix. Strategic alliances may also be used to expand product lines.

Brand Building Strategies

The essence of strategies for brand strength is that management should actively "build, maintain, and manage the four assets that underlie brand equity—awareness, perceived quality, brand loyalty, and brand association."[38] Critical to this process is developing the brand identification strategy and implementing that identity throughout the company and the marketplace.

Attention is frequently needed in coordinating the brand identity across the organization, the various media it uses, and the different markets and segments it serves.[39] For example, IBM's corporate brand identifies a great number of products and company divisions in diverse end-user markets. The challenge is to implement the brand identification consistently across these different situations. The risk of failing to do so is customer confusion and reduced brand equity.

Fighter Brands

In the harsh market conditions faced by some branded goods in postrecession conditions, one option is the launch of a "fighter brand," aimed to combat low-price competitors while protecting the company's premium priced offerings. For example, Busch beer helped Anheuser-Busch retain value-conscious customers who would otherwise have defected to Budweiser's cheaper competitors. While value-oriented customers and new low-price competitors may encourage brand owners to consider fighter brand possibilities, evidence suggests this is a high-risk strategy and many approaches of this kind fail. Among the risks to evaluate are that the fighter brand may cannibalize the company's premium offering, may fail to impact on the competition, may lose money, may be unattractive to customers, and may consume excessive amounts of management time for little pay-back.[40]

---

[38]Aaker, *Building Strong Brands,* 35.
[39]Ibid., 340.
[40]Mark Ritson, "Should You Launch a Fighter Brand," *Harvard Business Review,* October 2009, 86–94.

Brand Revitalization

Mature brands that are important in the company's overall strategy may require rejuvenation. For example, Procter & Gamble's Oil of Olay has over half-a-century-long brand history and retains a strong position in the skin care market by adding products that link to the brand heritage.[41] Similarly, when P&G acquired the mature Old Spice men's fragrance brand, it was underperforming in its target market of older consumers. P&G successfully repositioned the brand to attract younger consumers and rebuilt market share.[42]

Removing Orphan Brands

On occasion, consumer goods companies face the issue of a long tail of brands, possibly as a result of mergers and acquisitions, which do not fit well with the brand portfolio. The strategic decision to remove "orphan brands" aims to build more sales under the strongest brands remaining in the portfolio. For example, P&G took the view that Pringles potato snacks did not fit well with their personal care and cleaning products and sold the brand to Diamond Foods in 2011, to fit with Diamond's nut and popcorn products. This sale marked P&G's final withdrawal from the conventional food business, following its spin-off of Folgers coffee in 2008. P&G aims to invest in brands with innovation potential, leverage as leaders with major retailers, and attractive margins.[43]

Strategic Brand Vulnerabilities

A strategic perspective on brands also requires that decision makers be aware of the vulnerability of brands. When Skoda cars were first launched in the United Kingdom, with a heritage of low-quality vehicles assembled in part by convict labor in a then-Communist country, consumer tests revealed that perceived value was actually lower when the brand was known, than when the brand identification was removed from the cars.

In the early 1990s, *Encyclopedia Britannica* rebuffed an approach from Microsoft to produce a digital version of their encyclopedia. In less than 2 years Microsoft's Encarta dominated the market. When *Encyclopedia Britannica* approached Microsoft to re-open negotiations, Microsoft's management indicated that research findings showed that Britannica had negative brand equity and would have to pay Microsoft to have its name on a joint product.[44]

Proactive market sensing efforts by a company are essential in identifying and responding to strategic brand vulnerabilities. For example, in the mid-1990s Limited Brands, the specialty apparel retailer, determined that the apparel market was becoming very competitive and unprofitable. Management perceptively recognized that Limited's brand emphasis should shift from apparel to accessories as described in the STRATEGY APPLICATION. Interestingly, in early 2007 there was speculation that the retailer was considering the sale of its apparel brands, and by 2010 this had been accomplished.

An important issue in managing brand portfolios is deciding how many brands should comprise the system. Four questions are relevant in deciding whether to introduce a new brand name:

1. Is the brand sufficiently different to merit a new name?
2. Will a new name really add value?

---

[41]Dana James, "Rejuvenating Mature Brands Can Be a Stimulating Exercise," *Marketing News,* August 16, 1999, 16–17.

[42]James Heckman, "Don't Let the Fat Lady Sing: Smart Strategies Revive Dead Brands," *Marketing News,* January 4, 1999, 1.

[43]Barnet Jopson and Louis Lucas, "Finding a Home for Orphan Brands," *Financial Times,* April 11, 2011, 22.

[44]L. Downes and C. Mui, *Unleashing the Killer App: Digital Strategies for Market Dominance* (Boston: Harvard Business School Press, 1998).

- In 1995 apparel represented 70 percent of Limited's sales. By 2005, 70 percent of sales were from skin-care products, cosmetics, and lingerie.
- Clothes are increasingly out of fashion—after declines for 3 years, U.S. apparel sales increased only 4 percent in 2004 to $172.8 billion.
- Apparel dollar sales declines are due to discount pricing and households spending more on electronics, home improvement, and spa services.
- Limited was trying to make itself over as a high-end Procter & Gamble.
- Victoria's Secret is adding hair and cosmetics lines to its beauty business (has three of the top ten selling fragrances in the United States).
- One new product was "Tutti Dolci" (all sweets), food-inspired scents—lotion and lip gloss in fragrances like lemon meringue, angel-food cake, and chocolate fondue.
- Victoria's Secret has also accelerated new product development.
- From 2003 through 2005 Intimate Brands (lingerie and beauty products) accounted for all the corporation's operating income.
- Limited was also partnering with other companies to sell its brands and develop new products.
- Limited has three business groups:
  - Beauty and Personal Care
  - Lingerie
  - Apparel
- Apparel is a continuing challenge with 2004 operating margins at 1.4 percent compared to over 19 percent for Bath & Body Works and Victoria's Secret.
- Limited had about 3,700 stores in 2005 and sales were nearly $9.7 billion with net profits at $600 million.

Sources: Limited Brands 2005 Annual Report; Value Line Investment Survey, 2011; and Amy Merrick, "For Limited Brands Clothes Become the Accessories," *Wall Street Journal*, March 8, 2005, A1 and A14.

3. Will the existing brand be placed at risk if it is used on a new product?
4. Will the business support a new brand name?[45]

Brand Leveraging Strategy

Established brand names may be useful to introduce other products by linking the new product to an existing brand name. The primary advantage is immediate name recognition for the new product. Methods of capitalizing on an existing brand name include line extension, stretching the brand vertically, brand extension, co-branding, and licensing.

Line Extension

This leveraging strategy consists of offering additional items in the same product class or category as the core brand. Extensions may include new flavors, forms, colors, and package

---

[45] Aaker, *Building Strong Brands*, 264–266.

sizes. Coca-Cola Blak (Coffee Coke) is an example. The primary danger is overextending the line and weakening the brand equity. Many new products are line extensions.

Line extensions are attractive options for many companies. They help expand the market opportunity for the product line by offering more variety. The extensions are useful in countering competitors' efforts. Some extensions may encourage cannibalization as illustrated by Gillette's introduction of its Fusion razor in 2006. It will attract sales from the Mach3 razor although Fusion's higher price may discourage purchases. Soundly conceived and well-executed extensions strengthen the brand's position in the marketplace. However, relying on line extensions as the primary basis for innovation may be risky.

Stretching the Brand Vertically[46]

This form of line extension may include moving up or down in price/quality from the core brand. It may involve subbrands that vary in price and features. The same name may be used (e.g., BMW 300, 500, 700), or the brand name linked less directly (Courtyard by Marriott). The advantages of this strategy include expanded market opportunities, shared costs, and leveraging distinctive capabilities. The primary limitations are damage to the core brand when moving lower (e.g., lower-price/quality versions of a premium brand) or difficulty in moving the brand to a higher-price/quality level.

Moving the brand down is more likely to affect buyers' perceptions than other brand management options. It is an attractive option because of the size of the lower-price/quality market, and this initiative is relatively easy to pursue since it benefits from the image of the higher-level brand. Gap tried it with its discount Gap but quickly recognized the risks exceeded the benefits and instead launched Old Navy. Several risks of moving down are shown in Exhibit 9.6.

Moving the brand up is also risky. Pursuing a questionable vertical move upward in price and quality, Volkswagen introduced its luxury $75,000 sedan in the United States in late 2003, investing $1 billion to develop the Phaeton. VW has a strong brand image but not the right logo for a luxury automobile. Moreover, Phaeton was competing with VW's Audi A8 luxury sedan. In late 2005 management announced plans to withdraw the Phaeton from the U.S. market, and its future in Europe was questionable.

Brand Extension

This form of leveraging benefits from buyers' familiarity with an existing brand name in a product class to launch a new product line in another product class.[47] The new line may or may not be closely related to the brand from which it is being extended. Examples of

**EXHIBIT 9.6
Moving Down Is
Easy but Risky**

Source: David A. Aaker,
Building Strong Brands (New
York: The Free Press, 1996),
279–281.

- Affects perceptions of the brand—perhaps even more significantly than other brand management options.
  We are influenced more by unfavorable information than by favorable information.
- The brand's ability to deliver self-expressive benefits may be reduced.
- Potential cannibalization problem.
- Potential failure risk.
- Problem when the line extension is perceived to be inconsistent with the quality expected from the brand.

[46] Aaker, *Brand Portfolio Strategy,* Chapter 7.
[47] Ibid.

related extensions include Ivory shampoo and conditioner, Nike apparel, and Swiss Army watches. Critics of brand extensions indicate that these initiatives often do not succeed and may damage the core brand. There are several potential risks associated with brand extensions: (1) diluting existing brand associations; (2) creating undesirable attribute associations; (3) failure of the new brand to deliver on its promise; (4) an unexpected incident (e.g., product recall); and (5) cannibalization of the brand franchise.[48] Among the more successful brand extensions of the 1990s were the various lines of Healthy Choice foods.

Regardless of the possible dangers of brand extension, it continues to be very popular. Two considerations are important. There should be a logical tie between the core brand and the extension. It may be a different product type, while having some relationship to the core brand. The extension also needs to be carefully evaluated as to any negative impact on the brand equity of the core brand.

An interesting example of how the Virgin Group in the United Kingdom is extending the brand into new industries is described in the RELATIONSHIP APPLICATION. Sir Richard Branson, CEO of Virgin Group, launched Virgin USA, a discount airline, in 2007.

Co-Branding

This strategy consists of two well-known brands working together in promoting their products. The brand names are used in various promotional efforts. Airline co-branding alliances with credit card companies are illustrative. The advantage is leveraging the customer bases of the two brands. Joint products may be involved or instead a composite product may be co-branded.

Co-branding may involve business-to-business partners although, more commonly co-branding is used to link consumer brands. Disney, for example, is co-branding breakfast cereals, toaster pastries, and waffles with Kellogg, as well as Disney Xtreme! Coolers with Minute Maid.[49]

"Co-branding occurs when brands from different organizations (or distinctly different businesses within the same organization) combine to create an offering in which brands from each play a driver role."[50] Promotional budgets can be shared and new product introductions facilitated. The important challenge is selecting the right brand combination and coordinating the implementation between two independent companies. An effective co-branding arrangement is a strong competitive strategy.

Licensing

Another popular method of using the core brand name is licensing. The sale of a firm's brand name to another company for use on a noncompeting product is a major business activity. The firm granting the license obtains additional revenue with only limited costs. It also gains free publicity for the core brand name. The main limitation to licensing is that the licensee may create an unfavorable image for the brand. Licensing may be used for corporate, product line, or specific brands.

Global Branding

Companies operating in international markets face various strategic branding challenges. For example, European multinational Unilever reduced its brand portfolio from 1,600 to 400, to focus on its strong global brands like Lipton, while acquiring more global brands for its portfolio: SlimFast, Ben & Jerry's Homemade, and Bestfoods (Knorr, Hellmans).

---

[48]Ibid., 210–213.

[49]Stephanie Thompson, "The Mouse in the Food Aisle," *Advertising Age,* September 10, 2001, 73.

[50]Aaker, *Brand Portfolio Strategy,* 20.

An Experienced Virgin

Virgin Group is one of the greatest examples of extending a brand into new industries without diverging from its core values—irreverent, unconventional, creative, entertaining, active. "Each time Virgin entered a new business," explains John Mathers, director, Sampson Tyrrell Enterprise, "all the commercial pundits suggested it was stretching the brand too far. They reasoned that few people would want to buy financial services, for example, from a youth brand with a rock and roll image." But ever since its inception in the early 1970s, Virgin has been racking up an impressive number of notches on its corporate bedpost.

Virgin's businesses now include book publishing, radio and television broadcasting, hotel management, entertainment retail, trading and investments, and an airline—"a highly successful migration of core values that are very much the product of an ideology," says Interbrand's Tom Blackett.

Andrew Welch of Landor cites an example of how the Virgin megastore in Paris has been able to transcend its boundaries of being purely a retailer: "It has become a temple for young consumers and youth culture. Paris youth place their trust in Virgin for guidance on what is contemporary culture. As such, Virgin is considered the consummate specialist in all things for youth fashion and fashionability."

"Virgin has succeeded in many markets in creating a new reality that its competitors have been compelled to follow because it touches the consumer in a fundamental way," summarizes Blackett, "which may actually be the key to shaking up mature environments in the future."

Source: Excerpt from Stephen J. Garone, *Managing Reputation with Image and Brands* (New York: The Conference Board, 1998), 11. Reprinted with permission from The Conference Board.

The company's global brand strategy is intended to position it favorably with international retailers.[51]

Interestingly, the strength of branding of products from China and other emerging markets has dramatically increased. The GLOBAL APPLICATION underlines this escalation.

Increasingly cosmopolitan consumers in many countries with similar tastes drawn from exposure to similar media and the economies of scale of global brand identification and communications, encourage the development of global brands. However, global brand identity may also create barriers to building strong identification with local markets, so both a global and local perspective may be important.

Aaker and Joachimsthaler argue that global brand strategy is often misguided, and the priority should not be building global brands (although they may result). Instead, the priority should be working for global brand leadership—strong brands in all markets supported by effective, strategic global brand management.[52] Nonetheless, this may involve different approaches to those successful in the domestic market.

Multinational operations increasingly face the challenge of managing brand portfolios containing global, regional and national brands. For example, Nestlé manages a four-level brand portfolio: 10 worldwide corporate brands (e.g., Nestlé, Carnation, Buitoni); 45 worldwide strategic brands (e.g., KitKat, Polo, Coffee-Mate), which are the responsibility of general management at the strategic business unit level; 140 regional strategic brands

---

[51]Richard Tomkins, "Manufacturers Strike Back," *Financial Times,* June 16, 2000, 14.
[52]David A. Aaker and Erich Joachimsthaler, *Brand Leadership* (New York: The Free Press, 2000).

As global wealth shifts, major brands are more likely to grow out of Asia, the Middle East, or South America than the United States or Europe.

Research by consultants Wolff Olins identifies five food and drink brands from emerging markets likely to soon become global brands:

- **Juan Valdez Café**—a Colombian coffee chain
- **Almarai**—a Saudi dairy and fruit-juice company
- **Patchi**—a Lebanese boutique chocolate chain
- **ChangYu**—China's largest wine producucer
- **United Spirits**—India's largest liquor group

In more and more product categories strong Chinese brands are emerging to compete both domestically and internationally: **Haier** (appliances); **Lenovo** (computers), **TCL** (TVs, mobile phones); **Wahaha** (beverages); **Gome** (electronics); **Geely** (cars); **Bird** (mobile phones; **Tsingtao** (beers); **Li-Ning** (clothing, shoes); **Yonghe King** (fast food).

Interestingly, when the Hollywood blockbuster sequel *Transformers 3: Dark Side of the Moon* opened in 2011, household brand names loomed large in a product placement push. But they were Chinese brands. The movie's protagonist Sam, wears a T-shirt from Meters/bonwe, a midlevel clothing retailer in China. The film's main robot, Brains, transforms from a Lenovo Edge computer (sold by China's largest PC maker). At one point, a scientist tells Sam to finish his Shuhua Low Lactose milk (a product of Yili, one of China's largest dairy companies). The Chinese companies are looking for both greater international awareness and domestic market credibility by placement in a Hollywood movie.

Many Western companies are looking to collaborate with or in some cases acquire strong brands from the emerging markets.

Sources: Dexter Roberts, "China's Power Brands," *BusinessWeek,* November 8, 2004, 44–49. Jenny Wiggins, "World's Next Top Brands Set to Rise in the East," *Financial Times,* July 20, 2009, 19. Kathrin Hille, "Chinese Brands Star in Hollywood Movie," *Financial Times,* July 20, 2011, 17.

(e.g., Stouffers, Contadina, Findus), which are the responsibility of strategic business units and regional management; and 7,500 local brands (e.g., Texicana, Brigadeiro, Rocky), which are the responsibility of managers in local markets.[53] While some observers believe Nestlé's brand strategy may be overly complex, the performance of the world's largest food company has been favorable.

Internet Brands

Some controversy surrounds the issue of branding on the Internet, relating mainly to the sustainability of brands that exist only on the Internet, but extending to how the Web can impact the brand equity of conventional brands. It is all but impossible for the decision maker to ignore the linkage between the brand and the Internet. Interestingly, successful online brands may be those adopting brand strategies that rely on traditional, offline forms of communications. For example, the career website Monster.com makes successful use of sponsoring the halftime report at the Super Bowl backed by advertising spots in the pregame and during the game. Monster's target is men and women aged 18 to 49, and the Super Bowl event gives excellent coverage, which coincides with the time of the year when many people are thinking of changing their jobs.[54]

---

[53]"A Dedicated Enemy of Fashion," *The Economist,* August 31, 2002, 47–48; A. J. Parsons, "Nestle: The Visions of Local Managers," *The McKinsey Quarterly,* No. 2 1996, 5–29.
[54]Michael Krauss, "Monster.com Exec Shares Vision for Brand," *Marketing News,* May 1, 2004, 6.

The Web provides those hostile to a company or a brand an international distribution system, no barriers to entry, and little censorship or accountability. Unofficial websites and blogs are set up to scrutinize individual companies, creating online communities where customers and employees can share information and vent opinions. The dilemma for companies is if, and how, to respond.

- Companies like Lenovo, Southwest Airlines, and Dell have specialists dedicated to engaging or co-opting online critics.
- Dell has made blogger outreach such a discipline, the company's team sat down in Austin, Texas, for drinks with the blogger who ignited the Dell Hell customer-service crusade with his rants about the company.
- Companies like BuzzLogic use algorithms to analyze which bloggers and social media are driving the conversation around issues that matter to brand owners.
- Home Depot found itself being accused of being a "consistent abuser" of peoples' time by an MSN columnist, which sparked 10,000 angry e-mails and 4,000 Web posts. A heartfelt and repentant online apology letter was sent to all Home Depot customers.

Sources: Michell Conlin, "Web Attack," *BusinessWeek,* April 16, 2007, 54–56. Allison Enright, "Knock, Knock: Who's There?" *Marketing News,* June 1, 2007, 11–12.

The Internet can play a pivotal role in enhancing brand relationships and corporate reputation, by offering customers a new degree of interactivity with the brand, and speed and adaptability in the relationship-building process.[55] Nonetheless, interactivity also brings threats to the brand to which brand managers may need to respond. The INTERNET APPLICATION describes some of the attributes of blogs in relation to brands.

While much remains to be learned about the requirements for effective brand building on the Internet, these initiatives should be included in strategic brand management responsibilities.

Brand Theft

Counterfeit brands represent a huge global business that negatively impacts authentic brands. The fakes negatively impact brand equity and attract sales from the real brands. A wide range of fake brands are sold including software, apparel, electronics, watches, and many other products. Much of the counterfeit merchandise is produced in China, although other Asian countries are also involved in the value chain. International trade in counterfeit and pirated goods was estimated at over $600 billion in 2007.[56]

Counterfeiting is as profitable as selling drugs and much less likely to result in major jail terms if participants are arrested. Software is a very attractive product since it is easy to copy for fake sales. Law enforcement officials are far more interested in drug trafficking than fake goods. The high margins and lower law enforcement concerns have attracted organized crime to distribution of counterfeit brands.

---

[55]Larry Chiagouris and Brant Wansley, "Branding on the Internet," *Marketing Management,* Summer 2000, 34–38.
[56]"Knock-offs Catch On," *The Economist,* March 6, 2010, 81.

Passing off counterfeits as genuine is easier on the Internet because customers cannot physically inspect the goods, and they are often sold under the image of the genuine product. Internet counterfeiters are hard to trace.

- The Internet is estimated to account for 14 percent ($90 billion) of the annual $624 billion global counterfeit trade.
- There is a booming trade in online sales of counterfeit medicines and pharmaceuticals, particularly "lifestyle" drugs like Viagra to treat impotence.
- World Wrestling Entertainments (WWE) is one of many brand owners struggling to stem the tide of counterfeit goods sold over the Internet.
- Every morning WWE goes online to find about 3,500 auctions selling fake WWE T-shirts, DVDs, and other accessories.
- Estimates suggest 90 percent of Louis Vuitton and Christian Dior items listed on eBay are fakes. The brand owners are suing eBay.
- The "brand new" Vuitton holdall bag listed at $188 on eBay is certainly cheap compared to the genuine article which retails at $885 in select stores like Neiman Marcus.
- A French court in 2005 ordered Google Inc. to pay nearly $400,000 in damages to Vuitton/Dior owner LVMH because the search engine had displayed advertising from merchants selling fake Vuitton goods.

Sources: Maija Palmer, "Cyberspace Fakes Make Brands Truly Worried," *Financial Times,* April 11, 2007, 10. Eric Schine, "Faking Out the Fakers," *BusinessWeek,* June 4, 2007, 76–80. Carol Matlack, "Fed Up With Fakes," *BusinessWeek,* October 9, 2006, 56–57.

Brand counterfeiting has been fueled by the ease with which counterfeit products can be sold on the Internet. In 2010 software companies were using lower prices in China to lure users away from illegal copies.[57] The ETHICS APPLICATION describes some aspects of the online counterfeit brand threat.

Summary

Strategic brand management provides guidelines in selecting strategies for each of the components of the positioning strategy, forming the leading edge of efforts to influence buyers' positioning of the company's brands. Brand strategy needs to be matched to the right value chain, pricing, and promotion strategies. Product decisions shape both corporate and marketing strategies, and are made within the guidelines of the corporate mission and objectives. The major product decisions for a strategic business unit include selecting the mix of products to be offered, deciding how to position a SBU's product offering, developing, and implementing strategies for the products in the portfolio, selecting the branding strategy for each product, and managing the brand portfolio.

Most successful corporations assign an individual or organizational unit responsibility for strategic brand management. Product managers for planning and coordinating product activities are used by many companies, although new customer- and market-based structures are increasing in popularity.

Brand equity is a valuable asset that requires continuous attention to build and protect the brand's value. The equity of a brand includes both its assets and liabilities, including brand loyalty, name awareness, perceived quality, brand associations, and proprietary

---

[57]Owen Fletcher, "Fighting China's Pirates," *Wall Street Journal,* October 26, 2010, B6.

brand assets. Increasingly, companies are measuring brand equity to help guide product portfolio strategies, and adopting regular brand health checks. Mature brands may require specific revitalization approaches. Managers must be aware also of existing and emerging strategic brand vulnerabilities.

Analysis of a company's brand strategy helps to establish priorities and guidelines for managing the product portfolio. The analysis methods include portfolio screening, analysis of the product life cycle, product performance analysis, positioning analysis, and financial analysis. It is necessary to decide for each product if (1) a new product should be developed to replace or complement the product; (2) the product should be improved (and, if so, how); or (3) the product should be eliminated. Strategy alternatives for the existing products include cost reduction, product alteration, marketing strategy changes, and product elimination. Product mix modification may also occur.

Strategic brand management is guided by brand equity value and brand strategy analysis. The strategy consists of (1) brand identity strategy, (2) managing each brand over time, (3) managing the brand portfolio, and (4) leveraging the brand. These interrelated initiatives need to be managed as a process.

Brand identity may focus on the product, the organization, a person, or a symbol. The brand identification used by a firm involves deciding among corporate branding, product-line branding, specific product branding, and combination branding. Brand identification in the marketplace offers a firm an opportunity to gain a strategic advantage through brand equity building and brand leveraging opportunities.

Each brand needs to be managed over time but coordinated and integrated with the brands in the portfolio. Management is concerned with the combination and effectiveness of brands in the portfolio. Each brand should contribute to the portfolio as well as benefiting from it. The objective should be to coordinate strategies across the portfolio rather than managing each brand on an independent basis.

Opportunities for leveraging brands include line extensions in the existing product class, extending the line vertically up or down, extending the brand to different product classes, co-branding with other brands, and licensing the brand name. Line extensions are widely used alongside the other forms of leveraging. For companies with international operations, additional concerns relate to global branding issues. Increasingly, attention is also required concerning the role of the Internet in implementing brand identification. Brand theft is an escalating major challenge on a global basis.

Questions for Review and Discussion

1. Eli Lilly & Company manufactures a broad line of pharmaceuticals with strong brand positions in the marketplace. Lilly is also a manufacturer of generic drug products. Is this combination branding strategy a logical one? If so, why?

2. Discuss the advantages and limitations of following a branding strategy of using brand names for specific products.

3. What is the role of strategic brand analysis in building strong brands?

4. To what extent are the SBU strategy and the product strategy interrelated?

5. Suppose that a top administrator of a university wants to establish a product-management function covering both new and existing services. Develop a plan for establishing a product-planning program.

6. Many products like Jell-O reach maturity. Discuss several ways to give mature products new vigor. How can management determine whether it is worthwhile to attempt to salvage products that are performing poorly?

7. How does improving product quality lower the cost of producing a product?

8. Why do some products experience long successful lives while others have very short life cycles?

9. How can a company combine the strengths of global brands with the need to adapt to local market requirements in a multinational operation?

10. Discuss the underlying logic of managing brand portfolios.

11. What are the strengths and limitations in moving the Marriott brand vertically upward and downward in terms of price and quality?

Internet Applications

A. Examine the Fortune Brands website (www.fortunebrands.com). Analyze and evaluate the strategic initiatives used by Fortune Brands in their strategic brand management.

B. Visit the website of lastminute.com (www.lastminute.com). Map the business model used by this Web brand. Review the strengths and weaknesses of the model, and consider how the brand has been established and how it may be extended.

C. Go to www.e4m.biz, operated by the U.K.'s Marketing Council. Register at the site and choose the Business-to-Consumer area, and the Brand Consistency option under Strategy Area. Review several of the short cases describing how major companies are striving for consistency in their brand identification while using multiple channels including the Internet. What conclusions can you draw regarding the requirements for brand consistency across multiple channels?

D. Visit the Yahoo Inc. website. Describe Yahoo's brand portfolio.

Applications

A. Review the IBM Centenary APPLICATION. What are the important issues confronting IBM's management in managing the company's brand portfolio? How can a brand portfolio perspective assist in meeting these challenges?

B. The RELATIONSHIP APPLICATION describing the brand extension initiatives of Virgin Group indicates entry into many new markets, several of which are unrelated. Have the different markets created any problems for the extension initiatives?

Chapter 10

Value-Chain Strategy

The group of vertically aligned organizations that add value to a good or service in moving from basic supplies to finished products for consumer and organizational end-users is the value chain. Strategic choices in value-chain options are an important part of market-led strategy. We use the term value chain in preference to others, which describe distribution activities from other perspectives (such as that of manufacturing or operations functions), to underline the central purpose of superior customer value. Terms such as physical distribution management, logistics, distribution, and supply chain management are all used to identify certain aspects of the value chain and its management as well as new organizational units found in many companies. The term value chain focuses attention on the whole system of processes, activities, organizations, and structures that combine to create value for customers as products move from their point of origin to the end-user.

The value chain (or network) is the configuration of distribution channels linking value-chain members with end-users. We examine the decisions faced by a company in developing a channel of distribution strategy. Channels of distribution are a central issue in managing the value chain. An effective and efficient distribution channel provides the member organizations with an important strategic edge over competing channels. Distribution strategy concerns how a firm reaches its market targets. We also emphasize the need for marketing decision makers to incorporate into their thinking the impact of innovations in supply chain strategy and digital channels. An important goal is maintaining the ability of the market-driven company to realign its value chain, when this is necessary to meet the changing needs of its customers and markets.

Importantly, a strategic logic is emerging based on factors other than the traditional economic advantages of traditional channel intermediaries. These include the critical importance of brands, competitive advantage gained from enhanced market sensing capabilities and closeness to the customer, the impact of escalating consumer power, the priorities for effective supply chain configuration, and strategic "fit." These factors contribute to a new strategic logic for value-chain reinvention that is influencing a growing number of companies. The design of value chains is linked directly to positioning and market segmentation strategies. As precise positioning against competitors becomes a high priority and as new segmentation models develop, long multilevel value chains are too slow and unresponsive to change to allow effective implementation of manufacturer positioning and segmentation initiatives. For many producers, a value-chain priority is to facilitate the development of new growth platforms for the future, rather than achieving only efficiencies in distribution.[1]

The strategic importance of value-chain decisions and realignment is illustrated by developments at Dell Inc. in the computer business. Throughout the 1990s and early 2000s, Dell was renowned for the power of the "Dell direct business model." Leveraging outstanding supply chain efficiency, Dell delivered superior value to (mainly corporate) customers through a flow model, in which customer orders generated the production and assembly of products. The direct business model allowed customers more choices in specifying products to their precise needs, and reduced stocks held in the value chain to an absolute minimum—Dell ran its global operation on 5 or 6 days' stock. The direct business model was a formidable value-chain innovation, promoting outstanding supplier connectedness, superior learning, and responsiveness to customer needs.

Nonetheless, Dell now faces slowing sales growth, loss of market share to Hewlett-Packard, and new competitive imperatives. In key target markets like China, the direct model is not favored by customers who prefer personal service. Low levels of service associated with the direct model have attracted criticism, particularly in the consumer market. Faced with these challenges, Dell is broadening its business model to target computer re-sellers—specialty vendors who design and install computer systems for corporate customers. In addition, Dell is developing a global retail strategy that includes selling computers in Best Buy, Carrefour, and Wal-Mart stores and wireless companies like AT&T. Experimental Dell own-branded stores are expanding, along with the kiosks located inside shopping malls and traveling shows. The company aims to develop from a computer distributor to a broader supplier of technology to businesses. Redesigning its value-chain strategy is critical to Dell achieving its strategic goals, particularly in overseas markets and the technology services business, to rebuild the company's competitive position.[2]

We look at the role of distribution channels in marketing strategy and discuss several channel strategy issues. Next, we examine the process of selecting the type of channel, determining the intensity of distribution, and choosing the channel configuration of organizations. A discussion of managing the distribution channel follows. We then look at distributing through international channels.

Strategic Role of Value Chain

A good distribution network creates a strong competitive advantage for an organization. Value-chain design may be a critical part of how companies compete in the harsh environment characterizing many markets coming out of recession. Importantly, companies can drive competitive differentiation and advantage through the design of value chains which outmaneuver their competitors. The STRATEGY APPLICATION describes the successful expansion of Forever 21 in the fast fashion business, positioned against strong competitors like H&M, Zara, and Gap with an innovative and distinctive value chain.

In Chapter 7 we discussed partnering between international airlines to gain market access. However, the airlines example also underlines the impact of the Internet on distribution

---

[1]Nigel F. Piercy, David W. Cravens, and Nikala Lane, "Peek-a-Boo: Finding and Connecting with your Customers," *Marketing Management,* Summer 2010, 18–24.

[2]Kevin Allison, "Dell To Target Indirect Sales," *Financial Times,* May 17, 2007, 27. Kevin Allison and Chris Nuttall, "Dell to Sell Its Computers at Wal-Mart," *Financial Times,* May 25, 2007, 24. Cliff Edwards, "Dell's Do-Over," *BusinessWeek,* October 26, 2009, 37–40. Ben Worthen, "Deals Offer Dell Many Paths to Grow," *Wall Street Journal,* September 8, 2010, 21.

Forever 21 is a Los Angeles-based fashion retailer with revenues of more than $3 billion a year from its 500 stores, with ambitions to have 1,000 stores globally. From its 450 U.S. store base, the "cheap chic teen retailer" is trading in South Korea, Japan, the Middle East, and Canada, with pushes next into Europe and China. The business is privately owned by the Korean-American Change family, and debt-free with profits invested into global expansion. The business has quadrupled in size in the last decade.

The company has been quick to take advantage of the misfortunes of other retailers, moving into premises vacated by Saks, Sears, Mervyns, Dillard's, Circuit City, Virgin Megastore, and HMV. Locations include Manhattan's Fifth Avenue, London's Oxford Street, and Times Square.

In the "fast fashion" business, taking on H&M and Zara, Forever 21 stands for constantly changing styles and very low prices. The company famously shuns sales, working to the philosophy "the first price should be the right price." Fast stock turnaround gives higher volumes compensating for lower margins.

The fast-changing collections aim to instill a "once it's gone, it's gone" mentality in young consumers. A typical Forever 21 stores can turn over 20 percent of its merchandise in a week—twice as much as many retailers. The company's constantly brings in new styles—between 10 and 100 products a day—so the promise of something new lures shoppers in, on average twice a week.

While discounters offer low-price value, Zara offers high fashion and H&M offers range, Forever 21 aims to combine all those strengths under one brand.

The company grew out of the Korean-American ecosystem in Los Angeles including garment manufacturing, wholesaling, and retailing. Now, Forever 21 manufactures only 20 to 30 percent of its products in Los Angeles (those needing a fast turnaround) and manufactures in China, Pakistan, Vietnam, and other countries.

For many Forever 21 consumers, being able to find cheap copies of celebrity outfits and runaway fashions is a major attraction. Forever 21 attracts some controversy because it has frequently been accused of not just following trends but selling copies of clothes created by trendy designers. The tight-knit community of clothing manufacturers and vendors that dominates the garment industry in Los Angeles has been accused of underpaying workers. The company has never been found guilty of copyright infringement.

Risks to the business include its investment in large stores with operational complexity, and trying to be all things to all people.

Sources: Susan Berfeld, "Steal This Look!" *Bloomberg BusinessWeek,* January 24–30, 2011, 90–96. Kate Walsh, "Praise the Lord and Pass the Miniskirt," *Sunday Times,* July 24, 2011, S3, 8. Claer Barrett and Barney Jopson, "Forever 21 Changes the Game for UK Fast Fashion," *Financial Times,* July 28, 2011.

---

channels. For a growing number of airlines, an e-mailed reservation number has replaced the multipart ticket that the traveler had to collect from a travel agent or receive through the mail. Significantly, European no-frills airlines like easyJet and Ryanair are working to achieve 100 percent direct Internet booking and ticketing, replacing the traditional functions of the travel agent. Channels are a major element of how airlines compete. We consider the impact of digital channels as part of the choices executives face in developing distribution strategy.

We describe the distribution functions in the channel and then look at the distribution of services. We also examine several factors affecting the choice of whether to use distribution intermediaries or go direct to end users.

Distribution Functions

The *channel of distribution* is a network of value-chain organizations performing functions that connect goods and services with end-users. The distribution channel consists of *interdependent* and *interrelated* institutions and agencies, functioning as a system or network,

EXHIBIT 10.1
Value Chain
Structures

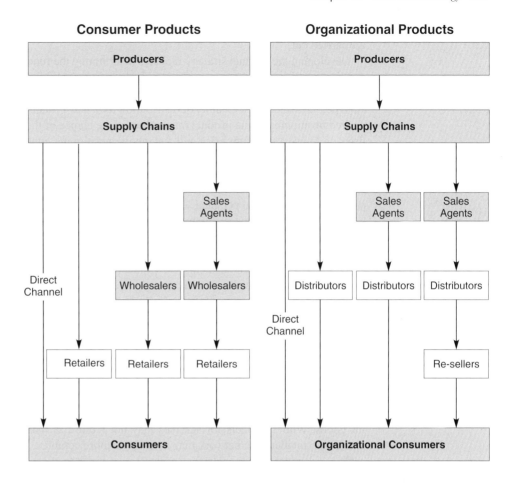

cooperating in their efforts to produce and distribute a product to end-users. Examples of channels of distribution for consumer and industrial products are shown in Exhibit 10.1. Direct and indirect channels may both have digital, or Internet-based elements. Commonly, a company may use several channel links to reach different types of customers. In addition to the intermediaries that are shown, many facilitating organizations perform services such as financial institutions, transportation firms, advertising agencies, and insurance firms.

Several value-added activities are necessary in moving products from producers to end-users. *Buying and selling* activities by marketing intermediaries reduce the number of transactions for producers and end-users. *Assembly* of products into inventory helps to meet buyers' time-of-purchase and variety preferences. *Transportation* eliminates the locational gap between buyers and sellers, thus accomplishing the physical distribution function. *Financing* facilitates the exchange function. *Processing and storage* of goods involves breaking large quantities into individual orders, maintaining inventory, and assembling orders for shipment. *Advertising and sales promotion* communicate product availability, location, and features. *Pricing* sets the basis of exchange between buyer and seller. *Reduction of risk* is accomplished through mechanisms such as insurance, return policies, and futures trading. *Personal selling* provides sales, information, and supporting services. *Communications* between buyers and sellers include personal selling contacts, written orders and confirmations, and other information flows. Finally, *servicing and repairs* are essential for many types of products. Increasingly, the Internet provides an enabling and information-sharing technology, changing the way in which these value-adding functions are carried out.

Developing the channel strategy includes determining the functions that are needed and that organizations will be responsible for each function. Middlemen offer important cost and time advantages in the distribution of a wide range of products.

When first selecting a channel of distribution for a new product, the pricing strategy and desired positioning of the product may influence the choice of the channel. For example, a decision to use a premium price and a symbolic positioning concept calls for retail stores that buyers will associate with this image.

Once the channel-of-distribution design is complete and responsibilities for performing the various marketing functions are assigned, these decisions establish guidelines for pricing, advertising, and personal selling strategies. For example, the manufacturers' prices must take into account the requirements and functions of middlemen as well as pricing practices in the channel. Likewise, promotional efforts must be matched to the various channel participants' requirements and capabilities. Consumer-products manufacturers often direct advertising to consumers to help *pull* products through distribution channels. Alternatively, promotion may be concentrated on middlemen to help *push* the product through the channel. Intermediaries may also need help in planning their marketing efforts and other supporting activities.

Channels for Services

Services such as air travel, banking, entertainment, health care, and insurance also involve distribution channels. The service provider renders the service to the end-users rather than it being produced like a good and moved through marketing intermediaries to the end-user. Because of this, the distribution networks for services differ somewhat from those used for goods. While channels for services may not require as many levels (e.g., producer, distributor, retailer), the network may actually be more complex.

The objectives of channels for services are similar to those for goods, although the functions performed in channels differ somewhat from those for goods. Services are normally rendered when needed rather than placed into inventory. Similarly, services may not be transported although the service provider may go to the user's location to render the service. Processing and storage are normally not involved with services. Servicing and repair functions may not apply to many services. The other functions previously discussed apply to both goods and services (e.g., buying and selling, financing, advertising and sales promotion, pricing, reduction of risk [e.g., lost baggage insurance], and communications).

Nonetheless, value chain innovation opportunities exist in services sectors. The INNOVATION APPLICATION describes the development of mobile virtual network operators in the cell phone business.

Direct Distribution by Manufacturers

We consider channel of distribution strategy from a manufacturer's point of view, although many of the strategic issues apply to firms at any level in the value chain—supplier, wholesale, or retail. Manufacturers are unique because they may have the option of going directly to end-users through a company salesforce or serving end-users through marketing intermediaries. Manufacturers have three distribution alternatives: (1) direct distribution, (2) use of intermediaries, or (3) situations in which both (1) and (2) are feasible. The Internet direct channel makes alternative (1) open to many more companies. The factors that influence the distribution decision include buyer considerations, product characteristics, and financial and control factors.

- Companies like Ikea, Virgin, and Tesco have joined the ranks of mobile virtual network operators (MVNOs), who purchase cell phone capacity at wholesale from the network operators and sell them as branded products at low cost to retail customers.
- The virtual operator is able to offer comprehensive coverage without having to invest in infrastructure.
- The low-cost cell phone deal provides the retailer MVNO the opportunity to send marketing messages offering promotions and discounts to customers and sign them up for loyalty programs.
- While Disney has withdrawn from the MVNO market in the United States, Virgin Mobile US is an MVNO—a joint venture between Virgin Group and Sprint Nextel. Virgin Mobile targets the youth market with a distinctive prepaid service that includes youth-oriented content.
- In the U.K., Tesco Mobile is run on the O2 network and runs a no-frills, pay-as-you-go service. The company focuses on value for money deals aimed at less affluent consumers, but in practice offers tariffs comparable with other operators, particularly rival virtual operator Virgin Mobile, based on the T-Mobile network. By 2011, Tesco Mobile had 2.6 million customers.

Sources: Paul Taylor, "Mobile Phone Resellers Forced to Take Stock," *Financial Times,* October 3, 2007, 25. Rob Minto, "'Virtual' Operators Use Low-Price Plans as Marketing Tool," *Financial Times,* August 29, 2008, 4.

Buyer Considerations

Manufacturers look at the amount and frequency of purchases by buyers, as well as the margins over manufacturing costs that are available to pay for direct selling costs. Customers' needs for product information and applications assistance may determine whether a company salesforce or independent marketing intermediaries can best satisfy buyers' needs.

Competitive Considerations

Distribution channels are an important aspect of how a company differentiates itself and its products from others, and this may impel decision makers toward increased emphasis on direct channels. The Internet can change the economics of distribution in favor of direct marketing.

For example, recent years have shown substantial growth in custom online ordering, a form of mass customization. On its website www.mymms.com, Masterfoods USA (the division of Mars that makes M&M's), offers consumers a palette of 25 colors to coat M&M's—for example, in their school colors—and to add printed messages and pictures. The cost is nearly three times that of regular M&M's, but it provides a growing niche business.

Product Characteristics

Companies consider product characteristics in deciding whether to use a direct or distribution-channel strategy. Complex goods and services often require close contact between customers and the producer, who may have to provide application assistance, service, and other supporting activities. For example, chemical-processing equipment, mainframe computer systems, pollution-control equipment, and engineering-design services are often marketed directly to end-users via company salesforces. Another factor is the range of products offered by the manufacturer. A complete line may make distribution by the manufacturer economically feasible, whereas the cost of direct sales for a single product may be prohibitive. High-volume purchases may make direct distribution feasible for a single product. Companies whose product designs change because of rapidly changing technology often adopt direct sales approaches. Also qualified marketing intermediaries may not be available, given the complexity of the product and the requirements of the customer. Direct contact with the end-user provides feedback to the manufacturer about new product needs, problem areas, and other concerns. Many supporting services may be Web-based.

Financial and Control Considerations

It is necessary to decide if resources are available for direct distribution, and, if they are, whether selling direct to end-users is the best use of the resources. Both the costs and benefits need to be evaluated. Direct distribution gives the manufacturer control over distribution, since independent organizations cannot be managed in the same manner as company employees. This may be an important factor to the manufacturer.

For example, several high-technology manufacturers have opened retail outlets. By 2011, Apple Computer had opened more than 300 stores—spanning the United States, Europe, and Japan. The goal is to educate consumers about the company's computers, music players and other product innovations. It is a response to the threat of commoditization in electronics—the consumer with little brand loyalty who buys the cheapest possible product. Similar motives underpin the opening of retail outlets by Sony Electronics and Microsoft—the aim is to reinforce the brands with affluent consumers and gain better insight into fast-changing trends in consumer electronics. These moves underline the importance of market access and market learning in sustaining competitive differentiation.[3]

Other reasons for manufacturers entering the retail marketplace focus on the need to manage the brand experience more closely than could be achieved through independent retailers. The INNOVATION APPLICATION examines novel ventures by Nestlé, Dyson, and Heineken in building their own retail operations.

Exhibit 10.2 highlights several factors favoring distribution by the manufacturer. A firm's financial resources and capabilities are also important considerations. The producers of business and industrial products are more likely than producers of consumer products to utilize company distribution to end-users. This is achieved by a direct to the end-user network of company sales offices and a field salesforce or by a vertically integrated distribution system (distribution centers and retail outlets) owned by the manufacturer. Companies with superior Internet capabilities may also favor the direct channel more than others.

Channel Strategy

The decisions that are necessary in developing a channel of distribution strategy include (1) determining the type of channel arrangement, (2) deciding the intensity of distribution, and (3) selecting the channel configuration (see Exhibit 10.3).

Management may seek to achieve several objectives through channel of distribution strategy. While the primary objective is gaining access to end-user buyers, other related objectives may also be important. These include providing promotional and personal selling support, offering customer service, obtaining market information, and gaining favorable revenue/cost performance. Recall the moves into retail by Apple, Sony, and others to build brand values with consumers.

---

[3]Cliff Edwards, "Boutiques for the Flagging Brand," *BusinessWeek,* May 24, 2004, 68.

Several brand owners are extending their channel strategy from reliance on conventional retailers to establish positions at the retail level of the value chain:

- Nespresso, a subsidiary of Nestlé, has established "coffee boutiques." Located at prestigious addresses like New York's Madison Avenue and London's Beauchamp Place, the boutiques are lined with dark wood paneling, discreetly lit, with plush interiors. Nespresso previously sold coffee capsules for espresso machines by mail-order (and online) to members of the "Nespresso Club," and then started selling branded coffee machines.

- Nespresso plans further retail expansion—taking the brand into hotels, restaurants, offices, and first-class airline lounges. The goal is to enable an increasing number of people to experience the brand firsthand. The brand experience is aimed to lead to purchase of the coffee machines and accessories. Nespresso's objective is establish a lifestyle brand and this is reflected in its channel strategy.

- By 2011, Nespresso had a network of more than 250 retail outlets with sales hitting $3.6 billion. The brand has created a luxury product niche in a mass market with a distinctive distribution strategy.

- Innovative appliance manufacturer Dyson uses temporary "pop-up" retail outlets to let consumers get their hands on new appliances, quiz company engineers, and see how things work.

- In a similar move, Heineken, the premium beer company, has opened a restaurant on the Champs Elysée in Paris, to link beer with food. It plans Heineken bars at international airports, to follow the model it has established at Hong Kong airport—the first branded beer bar developed for an airport.

The strategic logic for such moves is that branded consumer goods companies are often at the mercy of third-party retailers when it comes to the marketing and placement of their products. The goal is to move beyond selling a "product in a box" to offering a superior "service experience."

Sources: Jenny Wiggins and Haig Simonian, "How To Serve A Bespoke Cup of Coffee," *Financial Times,* April 3, 2007, 10. Neil Craven, "Dyson Fills the Vacuum as Pop-ups Get Posher," *Mail on Sunday,* December 27, 2009, 71. Paul Betts, "Nespresso What Else—Probably Not that Cup of Tea," *Financial Times,* May 21, 2010, 21. Haig Simonian, "Perks Up in US Amid Robust Sales," *Financial Times,* March 19–20, 2011, 19.

EXHIBIT 10.2
Factors Favoring Direct Distribution by the Manufacturer

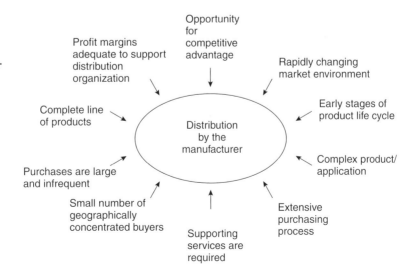

EXHIBIT 10.3
Channel Strategy
Selection

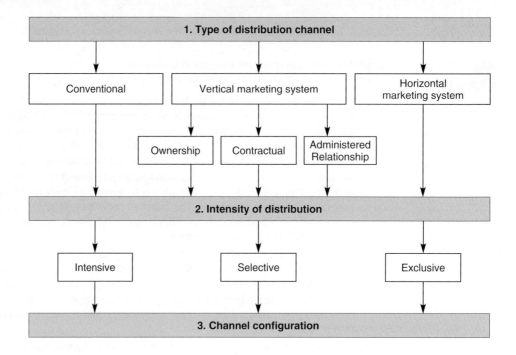

Types of Channels

The major types of channels are conventional channels and vertical marketing systems, although horizontal marketing systems are important in some situations, along with emerging digital channels.

Conventional Channel

The conventional channel of distribution is a group of vertically linked independent organizations, each trying to look out for itself and with limited concern for the total performance of the channel. Relationships between the conventional channel participants are rather informal and the members are not closely coordinated. The focus is on buyer-seller transactions rather than close collaboration throughout the distribution channel.

Some of the problems faced in the fast-moving fashion industry by a company using a conventional channel strategy, faced with new competitors adopting direct channel strategy, are illustrated by the experiences of Benetton in its struggle to compete with H&M and Zara. This illustration is summarized in the STRATEGY APPLICATION.

Vertical Marketing Systems

The second type of distribution channel is the vertical marketing system (VMS). Marketing executives in an increasing number of firms realize the advantages to be gained by managing the channel as a coordinated system of participating organizations. We consider later the influence of supply chain management approaches and the Internet on the operations of channels. These vertical marketing systems dominate U.S. retailing and are significant factors in the business and industrial products and services sectors.

A primary feature of a VMS is the management (or coordination) of the distribution channel by one organization. Programming and coordination of channel activities and functions are directed by the firm that is the channel manager. Operating rules and guidelines indicate the functions and responsibilities of each participant. Management

- Italian fashion company Benetton became one the world's best-known brands in the 1980s, based on distinctive casual wear and provocative advertising.
- The company saw itself as manufacturer, not a retailer, with a traditional business model based on the wholesale distribution of clothes to franchisees.
- The channel strategy was based on regional agents—regarded as strategic partners—that managed the franchisees selling Benetton products, while Benetton avoided the risks of running or owning retail outlets. The model worked well in Italy but not in other markets like the United States.
- In the 1990s, Benetton was left behind by new competitors like Zara from Spain and H&M from Sweden, getting new fashion design into their own stores in a matter of weeks and at bargain prices.
- With Benetton falling out of fashion, store owners who sold the brand began to cut back on orders rather than risk steep markdowns. Benetton closed stores in the United States, where it struggled to compete on price.
- In the 2000s, under a new CEO, Benetton has worked to improve its relationships with store owners by selling them products at cheaper wholesale prices so they could make higher profits, which hurt Benetton's own profits—they considered it worthwhile to get longer-term loyalty.
- Investments have been made in supply chain efficiency—some production outsourced to China, inventory broken into smaller shipments to be sent to stores in line with changes in consumer demand.
- New designs to make Benetton "hip" again are fueled by a network of trend-spotters across Europe and Asia, and the high-end cat walks of Paris, Milan, and London.
- Nonetheless, by 2011, Benetton stock continued to perform weakly, greatly below the 2000 value. The company was looking to emerging markets for renewed performance by offering classic, timeless style rather than fashion.
- Faster fashion is helping Benetton get back on track, though the brand that once set trends must now follow them.

Sources: Gail Edmonson, Jack Ewing, and Christina Passariello, "Has Benetton Stopped Unraveling?" *BusinessWeek,* June 23, 2003, 22–23. Stacy Meichtry, "Benetton Picks Up the Fashion Pace," *Wall Street Journal,* April 10, 2007, B-1. Margareta Pagnano, "Benetton Looks to Nguyen to Put Colour Back into the Brand," *Independent on Sunday,* June 12, 2011, 86.

assistance and services are supplied to the participating organizations by the firm that is the channel leader.

Three types of vertical marketing systems may be used: *ownership, contractual,* and *administered*. During recent years, a fourth form of VMS has developed in which the channel organizations form collaborative relationships rather than control by one organization. We consider this as a *relationship* VMS.

Ownership VMS

Ownership of distribution channels from source of supply to end-user involves a substantial capital investment by the channel coordinator. This kind of VMS is also less adaptable to change compared to the other VMS forms. Nonetheless, market turbulence and shortages of materials and components encourages some companies to pursue strategies of vertical control or integration to gain control over raw materials, manufacturing and distribution. For example, in the high-end tourism business, Tui, a German-based company, has a vertically integrated value chain incorporating its own retail/online operations to sell customized tours, with ownership of the aircraft and real estate that deliver the product to consumers. Tui directly owns travel agencies, hotels, airlines, cruise ships and retail stores, and the company's strategy is to leverage this owned value chain for competitive advantage.[4]

However, a less risky and capital-intensive alternative may be developing collaborative relationships with channel members (e.g., supplier/manufacture alliances). Such arrangements tend to reduce the coordinator's control over the channel but overcome the disadvantages of control through ownership. Nonetheless, in highly competitive markets, the need for control of distribution may make channel ownership more attractive. Globally, many auto manufacturers are establishing their own retail outlets and establishing Internet sales, and buying out independent franchisees and distributors, to regain channel control by building an ownership VMS, replacing conventional channels.

Contractual VMS

The contractual form of the VMS may include various formal arrangements between channel participants including franchising and voluntary chains of independent retailers. Franchising is popular in fast foods, lodging, and many other retail lines. Traditional automobile dealerships are another example of a contractual VMS. Wholesaler-sponsored retail chains are used by food and drug wholesalers to establish networks of independent retailers. Contractual programs may be initiated by manufacturers, wholesalers, and retailers.

Administered VMS

The administered VMS exists because one of the channel members has the capacity to influence channel members. This influence may be the result of financial strengths, brand image, specialized skills (e.g., marketing, product innovation), and assistance and support to channel members. For example, De Beers has managed the worldwide distribution of rough diamonds through its marketing cartel for over a century, acting as "buyer of last resort" to achieve market stability and steady price appreciation for diamonds. No longer a cartel, De Beers controls about 50 percent of global diamond production. In 2007, De Beers cut the number of clients (distributors, cutters and traders) to which it sells diamonds by around 20 percent, to concentrate the product on the distributors De Beers judged best able to stimulate demand for diamond jewelry.[5]

Relationship VMS

This type of channel shares certain characteristics of the administered VMS, but differs in that a single firm does not exert substantial control over other channel members. Instead, the relationship involves close collaboration and sharing of information. The relationship VMS may be more logical in channels with only two or three levels.

The economic performance of vertical marketing systems is likely to be higher than that in conventional channels, if the channel network is properly designed and managed. However, the participating firms in the channel must make certain concessions and be willing to work toward overall channel performance. There are rules to be followed, control is exercised in various ways, and generally there is less flexibility for the channel members. Also, some of the requirements of the total VMS may not be in the best interests of a particular participant. Nonetheless, competing in a conventional distribution channel

---

[4]Roger Blitz and Gerrit Wiessman, "Thomas Cook Chief Intends to Travel Lighter," *Financial Times,* June 19, 2007, 21.

[5]James Lamont, "De Beers to Reduce Its Client List," *Financial Times,* June 9, 2007, 23. William MacNamara, "De Beers Rediscovers Its Sparkle," *Financial Times,* February 12–11, 2011, 17.

against a VMS is a major competitive challenge, so a channel member may find membership in a VMS to be beneficial.

Horizontal Marketing Systems

The horizontal marketing system exists when two or more unrelated companies put together resources or programs to exploit a marketing opportunity.[6] For example, Kroger Co., the largest U.S. grocery retailer, has introduced an extended range of financial services—home loans, pet insurance, identity theft products—in partnership with U.S. Bank. The horizontal marketing system is a relevant issue in reviewing channel strategy, but is close in its characteristics to the partnering, joint venture and strategic alliance arrangements considered as strategic relationships in Chapter 7, and is not discussed further in this chapter.

Digital Channels

A further relevant development is the digital—or Internet-based—distribution channel. While online selling has become commonplace, there are several emerging issues meriting attention.

First, product digitization is important in many more markets. Where a traditional product can be converted to digital format, then it can be constructed and delivered to the user directly through the Internet, and conventional distribution may be avoided. Examples include music and software downloads, where the need for a conventional CD to be physically handled by distributors or retailers is reduced or removed. Similar developments include business and consumer information services, insurance and other financial services, e-books, education and training, computer games, television services, and movie rental and purchase. Interestingly, after some years of hesitation, video content creators like Hollywood studios are moving into digital distribution channels, creating services allowing consumers to watch films when and where they want. These moves are stimulated by the goal of new revenue streams and concern that traditional distribution models are declining.[7] Similarly, Sony is cutting U.S. jobs and reviewing its business model to react to the shift of the computer games industry from sales of packaged software in retail stores to networking and online distribution.[8]

Second, while product digitization goes hand in hand with the digitization of channel functions, it is not a prerequisite. Consider the airline ticket example. While the airline still provides a seat on the aircraft, many of the traditional distribution functions carried out by travel agents or airline retail outlets are replaced by an online reservation number and an online, preprinted boarding card, and online choice of seats, food, and entertainments. Opportunities exist more broadly to digitize certain channel functions for both products and services. The idea of "lean consumption" underlines the emergence of these opportunities to minimize customer time and effort and to deliver exactly what they want, when and where they want it.[9]

The digitization of products and channel functions is not necessarily associated with the process of disintermediation—replacing distributors with direct manufacturer-owned channels. Rather, companies like iTunes and online insurance brokers are creating new types of online distributor—a process of reintermediation. Indeed, digitization

---

[6]Philip Kotler and Kevin Lane Keller, *A Framework for Marketing Management,* 5th ed. (Upper Saddle River NJ: Pearson/Prentice Hall, 2011).
[7]Paul Taylor, "Coming Soon: Films on File," *Financial Times,* May 31, 2006, 12.
[8]Mariko Sanchanta, "Sony to Cut US Jobs to Prop Up PS3," *Financial Times,* June 8, 2007, 28.
[9]James P. Womack and Daniel T. Jones, "Lean Consumption," *Harvard Business Review,* March 2005, 59–68.

of distribution functions can work closely with conventional channel arrangements—instore online ordering of out-of-stock products, or collecting online purchases from retail outlets are illustrative developments.

Distribution Intensity

The second step in channel strategy is selecting distribution intensity (see Exhibit 10.3). Distribution intensity is best examined in reference to how many retail stores (or industrial product dealers) carry a particular brand in a geographical area. If a company decides to distribute its products in many of the retail outlets in a trading area that might normally carry such a product, it is using an intensive distribution approach. Typical examples would be consumer food or beverage products. A trading area may be a portion of a city, the entire metropolitan area, or a larger geographical area. If one retailer or dealer in the trading area distributes the product, then management is following an *exclusive* distribution strategy. Examples include Lexus automobiles and Caterpillar industrial equipment. *Selective* distribution falls between the two extremes. Rolex watches and Louis Vuitton fashion goods are distributed on a selective basis.

Choosing the right distribution intensity depends on management's targeting and positioning strategies and product and market characteristics. The major issues in deciding distribution intensity are

- Identifying what is feasible, taking into account the size and characteristics of the market target, the product, and the requirements likely to be imposed by prospective intermediaries (e.g., they may want exclusive sales territories).
- Selecting the alternatives that are compatible with the proposed market target and marketing program positioning strategy.
- Choosing the alternative that (1) offers the best strategic fit, (2) meets management's financial performance expectations, and (3) is attractive enough to intermediaries so that they will be motivated to perform their assigned functions.

The characteristics of the product and the market target to be served often suggest a particular distribution intensity. For example, an expensive product, such as a Toyota Lexus luxury automobile, does not require intensive distribution to make contact with potential buyers. Moreover, several dealers in a trading area could not generate enough sales and profits to be successful due to the luxury car's limited sales potential.

The distribution intensity should correspond to the marketing strategy selected. For example, Estée Lauder distributes cosmetics through selected department stores that carry quality products. Management decided not to meet Revlon head-on in the marketplace, and instead concentrates its efforts on a small number of retail outlets. In doing this, Estée Lauder avoids huge national advertising expenditures and uses promotional tactics to help attract its customers to retail outlets. Buyers are frequently offered free items when purchasing other specified items.

Strategic requirements, management's preferences, and other constraints help determine the distribution intensity that offers the best strategic fit and performance potential. The requirements of intermediaries need to be considered, along with management's desire to coordinate and motivate them. For example, exclusive distribution is a powerful incentive to intermediaries and also simplifies management activities for the channel leader. But if the company granted exclusive distribution rights is unable (or unwilling) to fully serve the needs of target customers, the manufacturer will not take advantage of the sales and profit opportunities that could be obtained by using more intermediaries.

Channel Configuration

The third step in selecting the distribution strategy is deciding: (1) how many levels of organizations to include in the vertical channel and (2) the specific kinds of intermediaries to be selected at each level (see Exhibit 10.3). The type (conventional or VMS) of channel and the distribution intensity selected help in deciding how many channel levels to use and what types of intermediaries to select. Different channel levels are shown in Exhibit 10.1. As an example, an industrial products producer might choose between distributors and sales agents (independent organizations that receive commissions on sales) to contact industrial buyers, or some combination of these intermediaries. Several factors may influence the choice of one of the channel configurations shown in Exhibit 10.1.

End-User Considerations

It is important to know *where* the targeted end-users might expect to purchase the products of interest. The intermediaries that are selected should provide an avenue to the market segment(s) targeted by the producer. Analysis of buyer characteristics and preferences provides important information for selecting firms patronized by end-users. This, in turn, guides decisions concerning additional channel levels, such as the middlemen selling to the retailers that contact the market target customers.

Product Characteristics

The complexity of the product, special application requirements, and servicing needs are useful in guiding the choice of intermediaries. Looking at how competing products are distributed may suggest possible types of intermediaries, although adopting competitors' strategies may not be the most promising channel configuration. The breadth and depth of the products to be distributed are also important considerations since intermediaries may want full lines of products.

Manufacturer's Capabilities and Resources

Large producers with extensive capabilities and resources have a lot of flexibility in choosing intermediaries. These producers also have a great deal of bargaining power with the middlemen, and, the producer may be able (and willing) to perform certain of the distribution functions. Such options are more limited for small producers with limited capabilities and resource constraints.

Required Functions

The functions that need to be performed in moving products from producer to end-user include various channel activities such as storage, servicing, and transportation. Studying these functions is useful in choosing the types of intermediaries that are appropriate for a particular product or service. For example, if the producer needs only the direct-selling function, then independent manufacturers' agents may be the right middlemen to use. Alternatively, if inventory stocking and after-sales service are needed, then a full-service wholesaler may be essential.

Availability and Skills of Intermediaries

Evaluation of the experience, capabilities, and motivation of the intermediaries that are under consideration for channel membership is also important. Firms within the same industry often vary in skills and experience. Also, qualified channel members may not be available. For example, some types of middlemen will not distribute competing products. The more complex the channel network, the more challenging it is to complete various distribution functions. Nevertheless, using specialists at two (or more) levels (e.g., brokers, wholesalers, dealers) may offer substantial economies of scale through the specialization of functions. The channel configuration that is selected typically takes into account several important trade-offs.

Channel Maps

It is often useful to produce a map of existing or planned channel strategy, to allow comparison with competitors and to identify new opportunities. For example, Exhibit 10.4 shows an illustrative channels map for one region's annual use of central heating units. There are two customer groups: construction companies using heating units in new buildings and domestic customers upgrading their residences. The customers are reached through independent distributors, small hardware retailers, large retail hardware chains, construction sub-contractors, and direct sales by the manufacturers. A well-constructed channel map indicates clearly the end-user customers and shows the relative roles of distributors, construction subcontractors, retailers, and other marketing intermediaries in reaching end-users. Channel map analysis should emphasize end-users.

The figures shown in the channel map are for all suppliers to the market in the region. They can be compared to existing and planned sales of an individual company through each channel link to identify areas of weakness and strength against competitors—for example, by calculating market share for each channel link—and to aid establishing channel priorities. Profitability data will highlight differences between channels, from an industry and an individual company perspective. Trend and forecasts can be incorporated to highlight shifts in channel importance and necessary changes in channel strategy. Anticipated changes in product use by different customers will also impact channel configuration choices.

Selecting the Channel Strategy

The major channel-strategy decisions we have examined are summarized in Exhibit 10.3. Management (1) chooses the type(s) of channel to be used, (2) determines the desired intensity of distribution, and (3) selects the channel configuration. One of the first issues

EXHIBIT 10.4
Illustrative Channel Map for All Producers of Heating Units

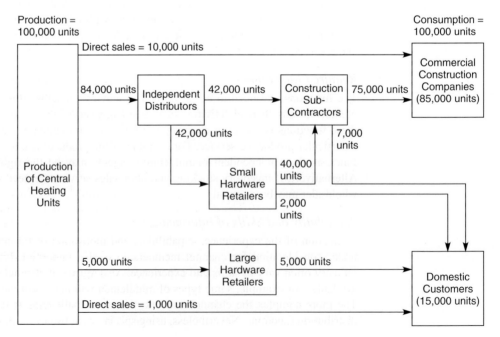

to be resolved is deciding whether to manage the channel, partner with other members, or instead to be a participant. This choice often rests on the bargaining power a company can exert in negotiating with other organizations in the channel system and the value (and costs) of performing the channel management role. The options include deciding to manage or coordinate operations in the channel of distribution, becoming a member of a vertically coordinated channel, or becoming a member of a conventional channel system. The following factors need to be assessed in the choice of the channel strategy.

Market Access

Market target decisions need to be closely coordinated with channel strategy, since the channel connects products and end-users. The market target decision is not finalized until the channel strategy is selected. Information about the customers in the market target can help eliminate unsuitable channel-strategy alternatives. Multiple market targets may require more than a single channel of distribution. One advantage of middlemen is that they frequently have an established customer base. When this customer base matches the producer's choice of market target(s), market access is achieved very rapidly.

Value-Added Competencies

The channel selected should offer the most favorable combination of value-added competencies. Making this assessment requires looking at the competencies of each participant and the trade-offs concerning financial and flexibility and control considerations.

Financial Considerations

Two financial issues affect the channel strategy. First, are the resources available for launching the proposed strategy? For example, a small producer may not have the money to build a distribution network. Second, the revenue-cost impact of alternative channel strategies needs to be evaluated. These analyses include cash flow, income, return on investment, and operating capital requirements (see Appendix to Chapter 2).

Flexibility and Control Considerations

Management should decide how much flexibility it wants in the channel network and how much control it would like to have over other channel participants. An example of flexibility is how easily channel members can be added (or eliminated). A conventional channel offers little opportunity for control by a member firm, yet there is a lot of flexibility in entering and exiting from the channel. The VMS offers more control than the conventional channel. Legal and regulatory constraints also affect channel strategies in such areas as pricing, exclusive dealing, and allocation of market coverage.

Channel Strategy Evaluation

Suppose a producer of industrial controls for fluid processing (e.g., valves, regulators) is considering two channel strategy alternatives: (1) using independent manufacturer's representatives (agents) versus (2) recruiting a company salesforce to sell its products to industrial customers. The representatives receive a commission of 8 percent on their dollar sales volume and have to be trained. Salespeople will cost an estimated $150,000 in annual salary and expenses. Salespeople must be recruited, trained, and supervised.

An illustrative channel strategy evaluation is shown in Exhibit 10.5. The company salesforce alternative is more expensive (using a 2-year time frame) than the use of independent sales agents. Assuming both options generate contributions to profit, the trade-off of higher expenses needs to be evaluated against flexibility and control considerations, and the higher quality of selling efforts with the direct salesforce option. One possibility that is

EXHIBIT 10.5
Illustrative Channel
Strategy Evaluation

Evaluation Criteria	Strategy 1:* Manufacturer's Representatives	Strategy 2:* Company Sales Force
Market Access	Rapid market coverage	One- to three-year development time
Value-added Competencies	Medium	High
Sales Forecast (2 years)	$20 million	$30 million
Forecast Accuracy	High	Medium/Low
Estimated Costs	$2 million**	$3.6 million#
Selling Expenses (Costs/Sales)	10%	12%
Flexibility	Good	Limited
Control	Limited	Good

*Two-year time span.
#Includes $150,000 each for ten salespeople (including salary and costs) plus management time.
**Includes 8 percent commission plus management time in recruiting and training representatives.

often used by manufacturers seeking access to a new market is to initially utilize manufacturer's representatives with a longer-term strategy of converting to a company salesforce. This offers an opportunity to gain market knowledge while keeping selling expenses in line with actual sales.

Changing Channel Strategy

The issue of flexibility in channel strategy has been a considerably higher priority for many companies in recent years. The Dell example discussed at the beginning of this chapter is illustrative of the need to change channel strategy in response to new marketing strategy requirements, competitive pressures, and customer change.

Channel Strategy Modification

Channel strategy should be reviewed regularly, since modifications may be required when marketing strategy has changed market targets and priorities; distribution is not working as planned; new channel possibilities have developed; customer buying patterns have changed; market structure or segmentation changes; new competitors have entered; or the product moves into a later product life cycle stage. It is unlikely that any channel will remain effective through the product life cycle—early buyers may be prepared to pay for high added-value channels, but later buyers are likely to favor low-cost channels. The optimal channel strategy will almost certainly change over time. Modifications may encompass adding or dropping channel members, adding or dropping specific channels, or adopting new channels and sales approaches.[10]

Avon Cosmetics is the world's leading direct selling company, operating in 143 countries with global sales revenue of $10 billion. Channel strategy is dominated by 6.5 million part-time, mainly female, salespeople selling cosmetics from a catalog direct to consumers in their homes. Nonetheless, faced with intense competition and the impact of greater female participation in the workforce in developed countries (meaning they are not home for the direct sell), Avon has made significant changes to its channel strategy. While the direct selling operation remains dominant—particularly in emerging markets like Latin America and China—Avon products can be purchased online from eRepresentatives, and depending

---

[10]Philip Kotler and Kevin Lane Keller, *A Framework for Marketing Management*, 5th ed. (Upper Saddle River, NJ: Pearson/Prentice Hall, 2011).

on geographic location they can be bought in kiosks in shopping malls, beauty centers and beauty boutiques, and in outlets and department stores.[11]

Channel Migration

Channel migration refers to the strategic shift from one channel to another (for example, the move in low-cost airlines like Ryanair away from selling tickets through travel agents to selling only in the Internet—98 percent of Ryanair tickets are now sold online[12]). Companies face a challenge in responding to opportunities for channel migration when a new channel possibility opens up.[13] New possibilities range from Internet channels, to direct selling opportunities, to working with new types of marketing intermediary. Essential questions to consider are (1) whether the new channel complements or replaces existing distribution channels and (2) if the new channel enhances or undermines the company's existing capabilities and value chain. The answers to these questions should indicate the necessary channel migration strategy.

For example, the emergence of an Internet channel may have one of several effects: it may be complementary to existing channels and fit with existing capabilities (Dell's transition from conventional direct selling to the Internet is illustrative); it may be complementary to new channels, but require new capabilities (such as the transition from branch-based retail banking to online banking); it may replace existing channels but still enhance existing capabilities (as the case with online travel booking/agencies); or it may replace existing channels and require new capabilities (the situation faced by traditional music production companies and retailers).[14]

Channel migration indicates the need to add or drop channels, reinforce or develop new channel capabilities, and the resistance or conflict to be faced with existing channel members.

Importantly, channel migration decisions are not restricted to the online and off-line channel balance. In the mid-2000s, Liz Claiborne, the clothing and accessories company operated a portfolio of 44 brands and the business was divided between direct retail and wholesale channels. The wholesale business was hit by shifts in the U.S. department store landscape, including the merger of Federated and Macy's stores, and increased private label competition from stores like Target, JC Penney, and Kohl's. In 2007, the company decided to dispose of its 16 wholesale brands, sold through department stores and other outlets, and to focus on developing its own retail businesses through its four leading brands—Mexx, Juicy Culture, Lucky Brand denim, and Kate Spade. The goal is to operate as a specialty retailer with no wholesale channel, though the risks in this migration strategy are high.[15]

Channel Innovation

Economic downturn and emerging recovery are leading to strategic realignments in value chains in pursuit of sustainable competitive advantage. One aspect of strategic renewal occurring in these harsh market conditions is direct value chain amendments for products traditionally dominated by conventional channels of distribution involving retailers,

---

[11]Dominic Rushe, "Avon Calling," *Sunday Times,* January 15, 2006, S3, 5. Nanette Byrnes, "Avon: More Than Cosmetic Changes," *BusinessWeek,* March 12, 2007, 62–63. Andrew Davidson, "The Avon Lady with a Calling," *Sunday Times,* October 17, 2010, S3, 9.

[12]Kerry Capell, "Wal-Mart with Wings," *BusinessWeek,* November 27, 2006, 44–46.

[13]Nirmalya Kumar, *Marketing as Strategy: Understanding the CEO's Agenda for Driving Growth and Innovation* (Boston: Harvard Business School Press, 2004).

[14]Ibid., 89.

[15]Jonathan Birchall, "Liz Claiborne to Cut Brands and Focus on Retail Business", *Financial Times,* July 12, 2007, p. 26. Suzanne Kapnor, "Liz Claiborne's Extreme Makeover", *Fortune,* December 8, 2008, pp. 69–72.

wholesalers and other types of distributive intermediary. The reinvented distribution channel is likely to be an important part of postrecession marketing strategy for many companies. There are some indications, for example, that vertical integration strategies may be back in fashion as companies look to seek greater control over raw materials, manufacturing, and distribution.

The array of possibilities for reinvention in value chain strategies includes the development of digital options in distribution and the construction of multiple routes to end-users operating in parallel (multichannels). The possibilities extend to more extreme options of channel invasion, where one channel participant moves to play an additional role in the channel system, and to a full-scale channel reinvention involving a new business model. Clearly, these decisions are often driven by gaining the ability to control the value chain or the intent to achieve this control. There are interesting signs that leading companies are actively exploring opportunities created by channel digitization, multichanneling, enhanced value-chain control, superior market sensing capabilities, and new business models based on innovative distribution platforms.[16] Examples of value-chain innovation moves are shown in Exhibit 10.6.

Channel Audit

Channel modification and migration decisions require careful analysis. The channels map discussed earlier (see Exhibit 10.4) provides a starting point for evaluation. The map provides a tool for monitoring the amount of business going through different channels to different customer types, and to include new channel possibilities in the model. Developing trends and new channels provide a trigger for considering channel strategy change. Nonetheless, channel strategy change needs to make sense in the context of overall marketing strategy, and implementation must be achievable even if there are conflicts with existing channels.

For example, direct Internet sales compete with distributors and salespeople in the value chain. One of Dell Inc.'s key advantages in growing the computer business with its direct business model was that it was very difficult for existing market leaders like IBM and H-P to operate a direct business model—they were tied to traditional distribution channels and were reluctant to compete with their own distributors. There was a considerable delay before competitors migrated their own channels to incorporate Internet sales and distribution.

EXHIBIT 10.6
Value-Chain Reinvention

Source: Adapted from Nigel F. Piercy, David W. Cravens, and Nikala Lane, "Peek-a-Boo: Finding and Connecting with Your Customers," *Marketing Management,* Summer 2010, 18–24.

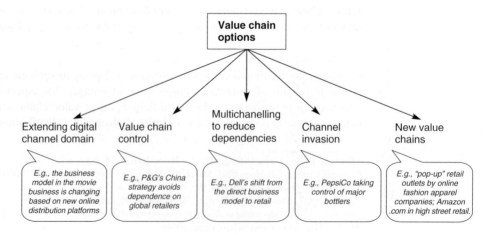

[16]Piercy, Cravens, and Lane, ibid.

Managing the Channel

After deciding on the channel design, the channel participants are identified, evaluated, and recruited. Finding competent and motivated intermediaries is critical to successfully implementing the channel strategy. Channel management activities include choosing how to assist and support intermediaries, developing operating policies, providing incentives, selecting promotional programs, and evaluating channel results. To gain a better insight into channel management, we discuss channel leadership, management structure and systems, physical distribution and supply chain management, channel relationships, conflict resolution, channel performance, and legal and ethical considerations.

Channel Leadership

Some form of interorganization management is needed to ensure that the channel has satisfactory performance as a competitive entity.[17] One firm may gain power over other channel organizations because of its specific characteristics (e.g., size), experience, and environmental factors, and its ability to capitalize on such factors. Gaining this advantage is more feasible in a VMS than in a conventional channel. Performing the leadership role may also lead to conflicts arising from differences in the objectives and priorities of channel members. Conflicts with retailers created by the channel strategy changes are illustrative. The organization with the most power may make decisions that are not considered favorable by other channel members.

Management Structure and Systems

Channel coordination and management are often the responsibility of the sales organization (see Chapter 13). For example, a manufacturer's salespeople develop buyer-seller relationships with wholesalers and/or retailers. The management structure and systems may vary from informal arrangements to highly structured operating systems. Conventional channel management is more informal, whereas the management of VMS is more structured and programmed. The VMS management systems may include operating policies and procedures, information system linkages, various supporting services to channel participants, and setting performance targets.

Physical Distribution Management

Physical distribution (logistics) management has received considerable attention from distribution, marketing, manufacturing, and transportation professionals. The objective is improving the distribution of supplies, goods in process, and finished products. Physical distribution is a key channel function and thus an important part of channel strategy and management. Management needs to first select the appropriate channel strategy. Once the strategy is selected, physical distribution management alternatives can be examined for the value-chain network. Many organizations now address physical distribution issues as part of a supply chain strategy.

Supply Chain Strategy[18]

The impact of supply chain strategies has extended beyond issues of transportation, storage and stock-holding issues to influence relationships between channel members

---

[17]For a complete discussion of channel management see Anne Coughlin, Erin Anderson, Louis W. Stern, and Adel I. El-Ansary, *Marketing Channels,* 7th ed. (Englewood Cliffs, NJ: Prentice Hall, Inc., 2006).

[18]This section of the chapter benefited from the advice and insightful contributions of Niall C. Piercy, School of Management, University of Bath, U.K.

and customer value. For example, the Efficient Consumer Response (ECR) program is a cooperative partnership between retailers and manufacturers to reduce supply chain costs—lower stock levels; fewer damaged goods; simpler transaction management. ECR approaches have achieved impressive cost savings, particularly for retailers. Collaboration and information sharing has become central to supply chain design. Integrating processes across organizational boundaries is essential to building the seamless supply chain.[19]

A major development in supply chain management came from Japanese management approaches, and the example of Toyota in the *lean supply chain*.[20] The basis of the lean supply chain is defining value from the perspective of the end-customer, to identify the value stream of activities in the supply chain that are needed to place the correctly specified product with the customer. All non-value-creating activities are "muda" or waste and should be eliminated. Attention is given to continuous flow of products in the supply chain, instead of traditional "batch and queue" approaches, to eliminate time wasting, storage and scrap. Products are not produced upstream in the supply chain until ordered by the downstream customer, that is, pulled through the supply chain, removing the need for large inventories and customer waiting time. The goal is to remove demand instability through collaboration between suppliers and distributors, and ultimately to allow customers to order direct from the production system.[21] The ECR initiative is an example of a lean supply chain model.

Nonetheless, in response to the impact of turbulent volatile markets, some emphasis has been placed on creating *agile supply chains,* which are not lengthy and slow-moving "pipelines," but agile and responsive to market change.[22] Supply chain agility means using market knowledge and a virtual corporation to respond to marketplace volatility, as opposed to the lean approach that seeks to remove waste and manage volatility out of the supply chain by leveling demand.[23] The agile supply chain reserves capacity to cope with unpredictable demand.[24] While lean supply chains require long-term partnership with suppliers, the agile model mandates fluid and market-based relationships to enhance responsiveness to the market and capacity for rapid change.[25] Agile supply chain models emphasize customer satisfaction rather than meeting a more limited set of value criteria based on reduced costs.

Harsh trading conditions are influencing major companies to rethink the relationship between supply chains and other aspects of strategy, driven in part by the potential for greater efficiencies and in part by awareness of the risks and vulnerabilities in supply chains; for example, the global impact of the tsunami and earthquakes in Japan disrupting supplies in sectors like automotive and electronics.[26]

Supply chain strategies impact on several critical issues for marketing strategy and the value chain: product availability in the market; speed to market with innovations; the range of product choices offered to customers; and product deletion decisions, prices, and

---

[19]Martin Christopher, *Marketing Logistics,* 2nd ed. (Oxford: Butterworth-Heinemann, 2003).

[20]James P. Womack and Daniel T. Jones, *Lean Thinking: Banish Waste and Create Wealth in Your Corporation* (New York: Simon and Schuster, 1996).

[21]Daniel T. Jones, "The Route to the Future," *Manufacturing Engineer,* February 2001, 33–37.

[22]Martin Christopher, "The Agile Supply Chain," *Industrial Marketing Management,* 29(1), 2000, 37–44.

[23]J. B. Naylor, M. M. Naim, and D. Berry, "Leagility: Interfacing the Lean and Agile Manufacturing Paradigm in the Total Supply Chain," *International Journal of Production Economics,* 62, 1999, 107–118.

[24]Martin Christopher and Denis R. Towill, "Supply Chain Migration from Lean to Functional to Agile and Customized," *Supply Chain Management,* 5(4), 2000, 206–221.

[25]B. Evans and M. Powell, "Synergistic Thinking: A Pragmatic View of 'Lean' and 'Agile,'" *Logistics and Transport Focus,* 2(10), December 2000, 26–32. Mark Whitehead, "Flexible: Friend or Foe," *Supply Management,* January 6, 2000, 24–27.

[26]Peter Marsh, "Tsunami Highlights Danger to Supplies," *Financial Times,* April 13, 2011, 23.

competitive positioning. In the market-driven company, a strategic value chain perspective requires collaboration and integration between marketing and supply chain management.[27]

E-Procurement

The development of Internet-based supply chain management highlights the growing role of e-procurement—where customers search and buy online, accessing a far greater choice of suppliers. The major impact is with business-to-business customers, including retailers and purchasers of industrial products. Industry portals and complex e-procurement systems offer very specific supplier search facilities. E-procurement is associated with supplier base reduction and the use of devices like online auctions and exchanges. The impact of e-procurement is being felt both in direct and indirect channels, and is an increasingly significant factor in managing channels.

Channel Relationships

Chapter 7 considered various forms of strategic relationships between organizations, examining the degree of collaboration between companies, the extent of commitment of the participating organizations, and the power and dependence ties between the organizations. We now look at how these issues relate to channel relationships.

Degree of Collaboration

Channel relationships are often transactional in conventional channels but may become more collaborative in VMSs. The extent of collaboration is influenced by the complexity of the product, the potential benefits of collaboration, and the willingness of channel members to work together as partners. Supply chain models encourage collaboration and information-sharing between suppliers and producers.

Commitment and Trust Among Channel Members

The commitment and trust of channel organizations is likely to be higher in VMSs compared to conventional channels. For example, a contractual arrangement (e.g., franchise agreement) is a commitment to work together. Yet, the strength of the commitment may vary depending on the contract terms. For example, contracts between manufacturers and their independent representatives or agents typically allow either party to terminate the relationship with a 30-day notification.

Highly collaborative relationships among channel members call for a considerable degree of commitment and trust between the partners. The cooperating organizations provide access to confidential product plans, market data, and other trade secrets. Trust normally develops as the partners learn to work with each other and find the relationship to be favorable to each partner's objectives.

Power and Dependence

In VMSs, power is concentrated with one organization and the other channel members are dependent on the channel manager. This concentration of power does not exist with the relationship VMS. Power in conventional channels is less concentrated than in VMSs, and channel members are less dependent on each other. Conventional channel relationships may, nevertheless, result in some channel members possessing more bargaining power than others.

In many sectors, suppliers face unprecedented pressure from powerful channel members. New merchandizing strategies with this effect include house branding and category

---

[27]Nigel F. Piercy, "Marketing Implementation: The Implications of Marketing Paradigm Weakness for the Strategy Execution Process," *Journal of the Academy of Marketing Science,* 26(3), 1998, 222–236.

killers.[28] House branding includes retailers who have established the retail store network as the brand, such as Gap, Banana Republic, and Victoria's Secret. These retailers rely on contract manufacturers to produce their brands. Category killers are companies like Toys'R'Us, Home Depot, Staples, and Linens 'n Things that attempt to dominate one segment of the market, often with very low prices. Suppliers may have substantially less control over these channels than in the past. Responses may include suppliers reclaiming important value-added services from distributors to build stronger relationships with end-users; eliminating layers in the conventional channel; or creating new channels.

Channel Globalization

Significantly for consumer goods suppliers, many major retail chains have expanded internationally. The globalization of distribution channels is underlined by the launch of Internet-based online exchanges. With the ability to source and merchandize globally, efficient supply chains, and powerful information technology, major retailers have more bargaining power than many of their suppliers. Domestic suppliers face global competition.

Agentrics (a merger of the Global Exchange Network GlobalNetXchange and Worldwide Retail Exchange), brings together more than 50 of the world's largest retailers and over 80,000 suppliers, with a goal of streamlining and automating sourcing globally, and supporting collaboration between retailers and suppliers. It is estimated that Internet-based procurement systems may cut 30 percent off costs.[29] In an increasing number of business-to-business situations, suppliers unable or unwilling to make the transition to Web-based commerce are locked out of doing business with major customers.[30]

Suppliers face competition at a global level in what would once have been seen as domestic business. Buyers able to access online exchanges or participate in online reverse auctions have in effect globalized the distribution channel.

Multichanneling

An important trend in distribution is the use of multiple channels to gain greater access to end-user customers. Increasingly suppliers face the challenge of managing relationships between the multiple channels used in the same market. The problem is to define innovative channel combinations that best meet customer needs. However, in many situations the way channels are used is defined by customer choice. Customers may "channel surf"—Forrester Research estimates that as many as half of all customers shop for information in one channel, then defect from that channel to make the purchase in another medium. Where customers have become more adversarial, buy more strategically, and have the information and technology to make more informed decisions, it may be risky to assume that discrete channels serving static market segments is a sustainable option. Channel decisions must be informed by understanding the various paths buyers follow as they move through the purchase process.[31]

Home furnishings and cookware retailers Williams Sonoma, for instance, has a cross-channel selling strategy with sales split 60/40 between retail outlets and online/catalog sales direct to the consumer. The company continues to find ways of improving each channel so it drives results in the others—catalogs do not simply sell products, by acting as

[28]Robert Meehan, "Create, Revise Channels for Customers," *Marketing News,* October 23, 2000, 48.
[29]Jonahan Fenby, "B2B, Or Not to Be?" *Sunday Business,* March 26, 2000, 79.
[30]Weld Royal, "Death of a Salesman," www.industryweek.com, May 17, 1999, 59–60.
[31]Paul F. Nunes and Frank V. Cespedes, "The Customer Has Escaped," *Harvard Business Review,* November 2003, 96–105.

- Channel hopping is where customers flit between Internet and phone shopping, home deliveries or call and collect, or use the conventional store.
- Research suggests that people use technology at home to find the right products at attractive prices in the most time-efficient way, and then decide how to purchase.
- A Yankee Group study commissioned by Siemens suggests 70 percent of consumers want to be able to use social media like Facebook and Twitter to interact with retailers.
- In retail banking, it is not unusual for a customer to choose different channels for different product needs, ending up with face-to-face contact for some purchases, branch-based services for others, online access for others, and the use of third-party intermediaries for yet other needs.
- Apple's retail outlets emphasize a "high touch" customer service. Nonetheless, at busy times, there are not enough experts at the in-store Genius Bar to deal with customer service issues—so customers are offered an in-store, live, interactive Internet link to an expert sales agent located in another store or call centre.
- At Mothercare, a British mother-and-baby retailer, customers use an in-store computer to order on the Internet items not in stock at the store, not available in smaller stores, or that they simply do not want to carry home (but do want to see in the store before purchasing).
- The multiple channels used by consumers place priority on cross-functional planning by companies to ensure that are customer touchpoints are coordinated.

Sources: Jonathan Birchall, "Are You Being e-Served?" *Financial Times,* January 3, 2007, 8. Lucy Killgren and Tom Braithwaite, "Mothercare's Growth Continues," *Financial Times,* April 5, 2007, 21. Jonathan Birchall, "The New Profit Pick-Me-Up," *Financial Times,* June 21, 2006, 15. *Social Media Means Serious Business* (Yankee Group Research, Inc., 2010).

in-home advertising they bring the company to the attention of new customers who are encouraged to use the stores. The goal is a personalized and cohesive customer experience across multiple channels and multiple brands.[32] Relatedly, the INTERNET APPLICATION describes the "channel hopping" behavior of consumers, to which some retailers are successfully responding and building new value offers for consumers.

Care is required in managing channels which may in part compete with each other—the website, the salesperson, and the distributor may all share the same target customer. Attention is required to ensure that incentives and rewards are aligned with the channel strategy. For example, should salespeople be incentivized to put business onto the direct Internet channel; should prices be varied across channels to reflect costs or customer expectations; should customer choice of channel option be actively managed?

Conflict Resolution

Conflicts may occur between channel members, and in multichanneling between channels, because of differences in objectives, priorities, and corporate cultures. Looking at a proposed channel relationship by each participating organization may identify areas (e.g., incompatible objectives) that are likely to lead to major conflicts. In such situations, management may decide to seek another channel partner. Effective communications before and after establishing channel relationships can also help to eliminate or reduce conflicts.

Several methods are used to resolve actual and potential conflicts. One useful approach is to involve channel members in the decisions that will affect the organizations. Another

---

[32] Ibid.

helpful method of resolving or reducing conflict is developing effective communications channels between channel members. Pursuing objectives that are important to all channel members also helps to reduce conflict. Finally, it may be necessary to establish methods for mediation and arbitration.

Channel Performance

The performance of the channel is important from two points of view. First, each member is interested in how well the channel is meeting the member's objectives. Second, the organization that is managing or coordinating the channel is concerned with its performance and the overall performance of the channel. Tracking performance for the individual channel members includes various financial and market measures such as profit contribution, revenues, costs, market share, customer satisfaction, and rate of growth. Several criteria for evaluating the overall performance of the channel are shown in the METRICS APPLICATION.

Companies gain a strategic advantage by improving distribution productivity. Reducing distribution costs and the time in moving products to end-users are high-priority action areas in many companies. Recall the development of Forever 21 described in the earlier STRATEGY APPLICATION.

Monitoring the changes that are taking place in distribution and incorporating distribution strategy considerations into the strategic planning process are essential strategic marketing activities. Market turbulence, global competition, and information technology create a rapidly changing distribution environment. Furthermore, multichanneling creates new challenges in measuring channel effectiveness.[33]

Legal and Ethical Considerations

Various legal and ethical considerations may impact channel relationships. Legal concerns by the federal government include arrangements between channel members that substantially lessen competition, restrictive contracts concerning products and/or geographical coverage, promotional allowances and incentives, and pricing practices.[34] State and local laws and regulations may also impact channel members, both domestically and overseas.

The importance of ethical standards and the emergence of corporate social responsibility initiatives was underlined in Chapter 4. Escalating demands for accountability from external stakeholders, the goals of managers themselves, and the aspirations of entrants to management professions, all support close attention to standards of behavior and the impact of societal demands on business practices. Many organizations have formal statements of ethical positioning and many have appointed executives with responsibility for monitoring compliance and reporting performance against these standards to shareholders.[35]

Channel decisions that impact other channel members may create ethical situations. Complexity increases in international channels crossing different cultures. The ETHICS APPLICATION describes the migration of ethical and moral imperatives through the value chains in several sectors.

---

[33]Matt Hobbs and Hugh Wilson, "The Multi-Channel Challenge," *Marketing Business,* February 2004, 12–15.

[34]An expanded discussion of these issues is available in Anne Coughlin, Erin Anderson, Louis W. Stern, and Adel I. El-Ansary, *Marketing Channels,* 7th ed. (Englewood Cliffs, NJ: Prentice Hall, Inc., 2006), Chapter 12.

[35]Alison Maitland, "GE to Release Audit of Ethical Violations," *Financial Times,* May 19, 2005, 29. Joseph Weber, "The New Ethics Enforcers," *BusinessWeek,* February 13, 2006, 76–77.

Performance Objective	Possible Measure(s)	Applicable Product and Channel Level
Product Availability		
• Coverage of relevant retailers	• Percent of effective distribution	• Consumer products (particularly convenience goods) at retail level
• In-store positioning	• Percent of shelf-facings or display space gained by product, weighted by importance of store	• Consumer products at retail level
• Coverage of geographic markets	• Frequency of sales calls by customer type; average delivery time	• Industrial products; consumer goods at wholesale level
Promotional Effort		
• Effective point-of-purchase (POP) promotion	• Percent of stores using special displays and POP materials, weighted by importance of store	• Consumer products at retail level
• Effective personal selling support	• Percent of salespeople's time devoted to product; number of salespeople receiving training on product's characteristics and applications	• Industrial products; consumer durables at all channel levels; consumer convenience goods at wholesale level
Customer Service		
• Installation, training, repair	• Number of service technicians receiving technical training; monitoring of customer complaints	• Industrial products, particularly those involving high technology; consumer durables at retail level
Market Information		
• Monitoring sales trends, inventory levels, competitors' actions	• Quality and timeliness of information obtained	• All levels of distribution
Cost-Effectiveness		
• Cost of channel functions relative to sales volume	• Middlemen margins and marketing costs as percent of sales	• All levels of distribution

Source: Harper W. Boyd, Jr., Orville C. Walker, Jr., and Jean-Claude Larréché, *Marketing Management,* 3rd ed. (New York: Irwin/McGraw-Hill, 1998), 317. Copyright © The McGraw-Hill Companies, Used with permission.

Ethical and social responsibility imperatives are migrating through many value chains, when a pressure to comply affects value chain partners.

- The world's largest retailers—Wal-Mart, Best Buy, Tesco, Carrefour, and Metro—with more than $500 billion in aggregate annual sales, are working together to develop a code of standards called the Global Social Compliance Program—a business-driven program for the continuous improvement of working and environmental conditions in global supply chains. The new code covers both food and nonfood production and focuses on the employment and working conditions of suppliers, and labor abuse.

- Growing "green consumer" pressure on supermarkets to reduce environmental impact is reflected in mandates to suppliers to reduce packaging and the choice of local and regional suppliers to reduce the "carbon footprint" of transporting food over long distances.

- Some of the world's largest clothing and footwear manufacturers are collaborating to create a scheme where apparel sold globally is labeled to show how the items production and usage impact the environment. Participants in the ecological labeling initiative include Wal-Mart, JC Penney, Levi Strauss, Nike, Marks & Spencer, Adidas, H&M, and Li & Fung.

- Microsoft drops suppliers who do not meet the software company's standards on employee diversity. Suppliers have been told that the supplier base has to represent all the peoples of the world: male, female, different ethnicities, different cultures, different backgrounds. Vendors who fail to heed the request are being reduced or terminated.

- Companies like Azco, one of the world's biggest chemicals businesses, and TNT and DSM in the Netherlands, have started to roll out executive bonus schemes linked directly to meeting sustainability targets.

- The incoming CEO of Coke mandated a proactive company approach to social issues, with a goal of making Coke the "recognized global leader in corporate social responsibility." The company has undertaken an audit of labor practices throughout its supply chain, launched several water conservation projects, embraced industry guidelines restricting the sale of sugary drinks in schools, and supported initiatives to encourage physical exercise among children.

Sources: Andrew Ward, "Coke Joins the Battle for the Brand Corporate Responsibility," *Financial Times,* November 21, 2006, 10. Jonathan Birchall and Elizabeth Rigby, "Big Retailers Join Forces in an Effort to Fight Labour Abuses," *Financial Times,* January 11, 2007, 1. Andrew Taylor, "Microsoft Drops Suppliers Over Diversity Policy," *Financial Times,* March 24–25, 2007, 5. M. Goodman, "Azko's Fresh Basis for Bonus," *Sunday Times,* June 27, 2010, S3, 9. Peter Marsh, "Big Names in Clothing Eco-Label Plan," *Financial Times,* March 1, 2011, 26.

International Channels

Distribution channels available in international markets are not totally different from the channels in a country like the United States. Uniqueness is less a function of structural alternatives and more related to the vast range of operational and market variables that influence channel strategy.[36] Several channel of distribution alternatives are shown in Exhibit 10.7. The arrows show the many possible channel networks linking producers, middlemen, and end-users.

---

[36]Philip R. Cateora and John Graham, *International Marketing,* 13th ed. (Burr Ridge, IL: McGraw-Hill/Irwin, 2006).

EXHIBIT 10.7
International Channel of Distribution Alternatives

Source: Phillip R. Cateora, and John L. Graham, International Marketing, 12th ed. (Burr Ridge, IL: McGraw-Hill/Irwin, 2005), 414, Copyright © The McGraw-Hill Companies. Used with permission.

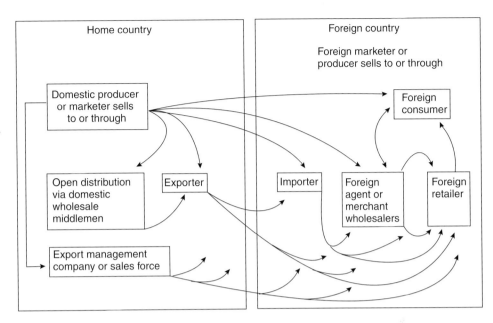

Examining International Distribution Patterns

While the basic channel structure (e.g., agents, wholesalers, retailers) is often similar across countries, there are many important differences in distribution patterns among countries. Examining actual distribution patterns indicates the complexity of the international distribution task.[37] Generalization about distribution practices throughout the world is obviously not possible. Nonetheless, in some cases, competitive advantage may be created by value chain innovation in international markets—consider, for example, Nestlé's microselling and other initiatives in the Brazil marketplace, described in the GLOBAL APPLICATION.

Studying the distribution patterns in the nation(s) of interest is important in obtaining guidelines for distribution strategy. Various global trends such as enhanced global communications, globally available news, entertainment and advertising media, the Internet, regional cooperative arrangements (e.g., European Union), and transportation networks (e.g., intermodal services) impact distribution systems in various ways reflecting globalization. Global market turbulence and corporate restructuring create additional influences on distribution strategies and practices. Channel maps for overseas markets can be insightful (see Exhibit 10.4).

Global Market Structure Differences

Importantly, market structures may be significantly different in global markets. For example, in the food market, notwithstanding the strong position of Wal-Mart and up-market innovators like Whole Foods Market and Trader Joe's, many U.S. retail chains are relatively weak and fragmented and lack the scale to bargain with food companies or to produce their own labels. Many have in effect rented out their shelves to food companies such as Heinz and Kraft.[38] This market structure gives food product manufacturers considerable scope to manage channels and channel members, for example, in a VMS arrangement. By contrast, in Europe, each country market is relatively small, and retail concentration is extremely high. In the United Kingdom, for example, one retailer (Tesco) controls more than 30 percent of

---

[37]Cateora and Graham, ibid.

[38]John Gapper, "America's Time-Warp Supermarkets," *Financial Times,* June 11, 2007, 11.

Sales of Nestlé "bottom of the pyramid" products in Brazil are growing at around 27 percent a year—twice the national average and four times the global rate. Nestlé's "bottom of the pyramid products are 140 of the company's 1,500 products aimed at low-income consumers. The company has succeeded in tapping into a new source of sales growth.

In Brazil, Nestlé is actively promoting its products in unusual ways:

- The company has established a network of microdistributors and resellers—microdistributors recruit dozens of commission-based freelance, door-to-door resellers incentivized with cell phones, bicycles, and free river cruises for the best performers.

- The result is recruitment of 8,000 frontline female resellers in an innovative program called "Nestlé ate voce" (Nestlé comes to you).

- Resellers push blue and white carts through the streets to bring cookies, cakes, and dairy products to the doors of Brazilian consumers. Resellers access the fast-growing Brazilian working-class population—with carefully targeted products and incentives of free gifts and 15 days credit. Training focuses on how the products can improve the quality of peoples' lives.

- The company has launched "Nestlé comes to you onboard"—a floating supermarket that travels to isolated communities along the Amazon river, stocking only Nestlé products.

- Nestlé vending racks are suspended next to the drivers at the front of buses in Rio de Janeiro.

- An itinerant cinema offers free cookies to customers who bring proof of previous purchase of Nestlé products.

- Health and nutrition events are held for school children, with the Nestlé logo prominently displayed.

Nestlé has countered criticisms that it is promoting a trend to more unhealthy unprocessed foods in Brazil by offering healthier products than its rivals and the establishment of its "wellness strategic unit" staffed by trained nutritionists.

Source: Andrew Jack, "Brazil's Unwanted Growth," *FT.Com/Magazine,* April 9–10, 2011, 28–33. http://www.Nestlé-nordic.com/corporate/nordic/ourResponsibility/projects/brazil.htm, accessed July 30 2011.

---

the national grocery market, and the top five firms (Tesco, Asda, Sainsbury and Morrisons) control 75 percent of the market.[39] Similar concentration is seen in other European countries with the impact of French retailers like Carrefour. The ability for manufacturers to control channel members is quite different when powerful retailing companies control such high shares of the market, and different channel strategy choices are necessary.

Distribution in Emerging Markets

Furthermore, some of the most attractive prospects are in emerging markets, where local market conditions may be substantially different to those in developed countries. The importance of channel strategy in adapting to these local conditions may be a critical factor

---

[39]Elizabeth Rigby, "Food Retailing Recovery on Special Offer," *Financial Times,* November 16, 2006, 21.

Global Application

Competing in India

India, with a huge population and a rapidly globalizing economy, is a key target market for many companies. Firms like Wal-Mart, Vodaphone, and Citigroup are placing multi-million-dollar bets on the country—lured by the 300 million strong middle class. Western fast-food companies like McDonald's and Subway are growing business in India at almost 30 percent a year. India has a young and increasingly wealthy population.

The realities of developing effective channel strategy in India identify challenges:

- The infrastructure has received little investment—many roads are crumbling, airports are jammed, power blackouts are common, water supplies are limited. Improvements are slowed by the sheer scale, by corruption in many public bodies, and by cost.

- Seventy percent of India's population lives in the rural countryside. The population is poor, and the infrastructure at its worst in these areas. Successes have been products adapted to these conditions—4 cent sachets of soap, salt, and tea from Hindustan Lever; $20 wind-up radios from Philips; the $900 Hero-Honda Splendour motor cycle—sold in small shops, bus-stop stalls, and roadside cafes.

- Outside the educated middle class, Internet usage is remarkably low among the Indian population, holding back the expected boom in Internet shopping.

- Foreign retailers like Tesco and Wal-Mart are not permitted by Indian law to wholly own businesses in India and must proceed through joint-ventures with Indian companies.

- Foreign companies have many horror stories:

  - Nokia saw thousands of cell phones ruined when a shipment from its factory in Chennai was soaked by rain because there was no room to warehouse the crates at the airport.

  - Suzuki says trucking its cars 900 miles from the Gurgaon factory to the port in Mumbai can take up to 10 days—because of delays on three state borders on the way, and big rigs are banned from congested cities during the day—and once at the port, the autos can wait weeks for the next outbound ship, because there is not enough dock space for cargo carriers to load and unload.

  - When GE sent executives to survey a potential site for a factory to manufacture locomotives in partnership with India Railways, they returned discouraged—it took 5 hours to drive the 50 miles from the airport to the site, and when they got there they found nothing—no roads, no power, no schools, no water, no hospitals, no housing.

Source: Steve Hamm, "The Trouble with India," *BusinessWeek*, March 19, 2007, 49–58. Manjeet Kripalani, "Rural India, Have a Coke," *BusinessWeek*, May 27, 2002, 30–31. Amy Kazmin, "Western Fast-Food Chains Aim to Cater for India's Youth," *Financial Times*, March 17, 2011, 24.

for success. The GLOBAL APPLICATION illustrates some of the problems faced by companies entering the India market, relating to the lack of infrastructure and other barriers.

Nonetheless, major differences exist between infrastructure in different emerging markets—India and China, for example, are quite different and it is important to ask the right questions regarding distribution potentials.[40]

Tapping into the huge demand potential in emerging markets may require originality and innovation in value chain design. For example, Nuru, a London-based company, is making high-efficiency LED lighting affordable in rural Rwanda, replacing traditional high-pollution kerosene lighting, by recruiting an army of local entrepreneurs. The local

---

[40]Jagdish N. Sheth, *Chindia Rising: How China and India Will Benefit Your Business* (Atlanta, GA: Incore Publishing, 2008).

313

entrepreneur not only sells the lights (for around $6) but also runs a business pedaling a small generator that charges the lights (earning around $4 a day—more than triple the average daily income in rural Rwanda). As a result, users get safe, clean lighting at one-tenth the cost of kerosene.[41]

Factors Affecting Global Channel Selection

The channel strategy analysis and selection process presented in the chapter can be used for developing or evaluating international channel strategy, recognizing that many situational factors affect channel decisions in specific countries. The factors affecting the choice of international channels include cost, capital requirements, control, coverage, strategic product-market fit, and the likelihood that the middlemen will remain in business over a reasonable time horizon.[42] The political and economic stability of the country is, of course, very important. Stability needs to be evaluated early in the decision to enter the country. Increasingly, global security considerations have become important factors in choosing the route to market.[43]

Global Issues Regarding Multichannel Strategies

The impact of the Internet and efficient global communications systems highlight the need to consider the relationship between domestic channels and global channels. The international company is automatically multichanneling. Problems may occur when there are differences between domestic and global channels in prices and product availability. If the product is cheaper in the domestic market than overseas, then overseas customers may seek to access the lower priced product through online sales. Correspondingly, if the product is cheaper through global channels, then domestic buyers may attempt to access the product online from the global channel, or even import the product back into the domestic market if price differences are large enough. It may be very difficult to prevent customers from pursuing these practices. Similar issues arise if product availability varies between domestic and global channels. It is increasingly challenging to differentiate the value offerings between domestic and global channels, and there may be considerable risks to customer relationships in maintaining this channel strategy.

Summary

The value chain consists of the organizations, systems, and processes that add to customer value in moving products to end-users. A strategic value-chain perspective aims to align a company's value chain with changing customer and competitive requirements. The core of the value chain is the channel of distribution. A strong channel network is an important way to gain competitive advantage. The choice between company distribution to end-users and the use of intermediaries is guided by end-user needs and characteristics, product characteristics, and financial and control considerations.

Manufacturers select the type of channel to be used, determine distribution intensity, design the channel configuration, and manage various aspects of channel operations. These channels are either conventional or vertical marketing systems (VMSs). The VMS, the dominant channel for consumer products, is increasing in importance for business and industrial products. In a VMS, one firm owns all organizations in the channel, a contractual arrangement exists between organizations, one channel member is in charge of channel

---

[41]Brian Dumaine, "Lighting Up Africa," *Fortune,* July 5, 2010, 14.
[42]Cateora and Graham, ibid.
[43]Stephen Fidler, "Appetite for Risk Drives Industry," *Financial Times* Special Report: *Corporate Security,* June 27, 2007, 1.

administration, or members develop collaborative relationships. Digital channels are of growing importance in many sectors. Channel decisions also include deciding on intensity of distribution and the channel configuration.

The choice of a channel strategy begins when management decides whether to manage the channel or to assume a participant role. Strategic analysis identifies and evaluates the channel alternatives. Several factors are evaluated, including access to the market target, channel functions to be performed, financial considerations, and legal and control constraints. The channel strategy adopted establishes guidelines for price and promotion strategies. Channel modification or migration strategies mandate regular review of channel strategy.

International channels of distribution may be similar in structure to those found in the United States and other developed countries. Nevertheless, important variations exist in the channels of different countries because of the stage of economic development, government influence, and industry practices. The Internet has a dramatic impact on the globalization of channels of distribution.

Questions for Review and Discussion

1. In the late 1990s several airlines started selling tickets using the Internet. Discuss the implications of this method of distribution for travel agencies.

2. Distribution analysts indicate that costs for supermarkets equal about 98 percent of sales. What influence does this high break-even level have on supermarkets' diversification into delis, cheese shops, seafood shops, and flowers?

3. Why do some large, financially strong manufacturers choose not to own their dealers but instead establish contractual relationships with them?

4. What are the advantages and limitations of the use of multiple channels of distribution by a manufacturer?

5. Discuss some likely trends in the distribution of automobiles in the 21st century, including the shift away from exclusive distribution arrangements.

6. In the late 1990s Radio Shack initiated co-branding strategies with Compaq Computer and SPRINT. Discuss the logic of this strategy, pointing out its strengths and shortcomings.

7. Identify and discuss some of the factors that should increase the trend toward collaborative relationships in vertical marketing systems.

8. Why might a manufacturer choose to enter a conventional channel of distribution?

9. Discuss what is meant by channel migration and the issues that a manufacturer faces in dealing with migration issues.

10. Suppose the management of a raw material supplier is interested in performing a financial analysis of a distribution channel comprised of manufacturers, distributors, and retailers. Outline an approach for doing the analysis.

11. Discuss some of the important strategic issues facing a drug manufacturer in deciding whether to distribute veterinary prescriptions and over-the-counter products through veterinarians or distributors.

12. Consider the differences in retail concentration between the United States and Europe. How do those differences impact on manufacturers' channel strategies?

Internet Applications

A. Examine the Web sites of Aveda (www.aveda.com) and The Body Shop (www.bodyshop.com). Compare and contrast the distribution networks of these two retailers.

B. Go to the site of the Agentrix (www.agentrix.com) and review the public pages describing the history, membership, and operation of this international online exchange for retailers (combining the earlier online exchanges the Global Exchange Network and the Worldwide Retail

Exchange). Identify and list the ways in which the exchange alters distribution strategy for suppliers, and the impact on consumers.

Applications

A. Review the STRATEGY APPLICATION describing retail ventures being started by manufacturers. Consider what motivates such ventures. Are there other examples that you can identify? Develop a list of the market and customer factors that may cause manufacturers to add direct channels.

B. One of the GLOBAL APPLICATIONS describes certain local market conditions in India, particularly rural India. What adaptations should international marketers review when planning channel strategy in emerging markets and how can they find out what is required?

Chapter

11

Pricing Strategy

Determining appropriate pricing strategies for products is challenging and dynamic in many firms because of deregulation in some markets, more informed buyers, intense global competition, slow growth in some markets following economic downturn and recession, and the opportunity for firms to strengthen market position.

Price directly impacts financial performance and is an important influence on buyers' positioning of brands. For example, a major challenge in rebuilding market position at the Starbucks coffee chain was countering a high-price image at a time of economic downturn and facing strong new competition from lower-priced McDonald's—in fact, Starbucks' actual prices were lower than consumers' perceptions of its prices.[1]

In some cases, price may become a proxy measure for product quality, when buyers have difficulty in evaluating the quality of complex products. A similar effect occurs with luxury products when high price may be linked to exclusivity and other brand-specific values. Pricing outcomes may not always follow simple economic logic—price increases may be associated with higher demand if customers interpret this as a signal of more price rises on the way, and falling prices may be linked to reduced demand if customers read this as an indicator that prices will soon fall further. Many conventional assumptions about pricing should be questioned in increasingly complex postrecession markets.[2]

For some companies, low price is an important and highly visible way of attracting customers. Ryanair is the leading European no-frills airline, which has taken the low-cost flying model to an extreme. Ryanair has pursued an aggressive growth strategy based on very low prices. Fares are often no more than $20 one-way for European flights and a significant proportion of tickets are given away free (in some cases, the price is actually negative, because the airline pays airport duties and charges for the passenger). Importantly, approximately one-fifth of Ryanair's revenue comes from ancillary services (such as hotel bookings, car rentals, travel insurance, in-flight gambling, in-flight product sales, checked-in baggage charges, Internet-booking charges). The company has an extremely vigorous cost-cutting approach that includes employees (who pay for their own uniforms), operating costs (pursuing large discounts on everything from aircraft to airport charges), and customers (proposals include charges for using the bathroom on the aircraft, in addition to already high charges for checking-in baggage and other utilities, and possibly even "standing" cabins with vertical seats). The harsh economic conditions of the late-2000s

---

[1] Janet Adamy, "Starbucks Counter Pricey Image," *Wall Street Journal,* February 10, 2009, 28.
[2] Nigel F. Piercy, David W. Cravens, and Nikala Lane, "Thinking Strategically About Pricing Decisions," *Journal of Business Strategy,* 31(5), 2010, 38–48. Nigel F. Piercy, David W. Cravens, and Nikala Lane, "Marketing Out of the Recession: Recovery Is Coming, But Things Will Never Be the Same Again," *Marketing Review,* 10(1), 2010, 3–23.

saw Ryanair cutting costs further, focusing on the most profitable routes in Europe, and aggressively pricing yet lower to gain market share at the expense of weakened rivals, several of which have since ceased trading. Over the past decade, while the global airline industry collectively lost nearly $50 billion, Ryanair was in profit for 9 out of 10 years, and lays claim to being the most profitable airline in the world. Over 15 years, from a small base flying out of Ireland, Ryanair has become the largest short-haul airline in Europe (by passenger miles flown). Ryanair's low-price model has significantly expanded travel on most of its routes, as well as taking business away from higher priced airlines in Europe and other low-cost operators.[3]

Importantly, not all value-based strategies require low prices. But pricing decisions have important consequences for most companies. Once implemented, it may be difficult to alter price strategy—particularly if the change calls for a significant increase in prices. Nonetheless, price has many possible uses as a critical strategic instrument in business strategy.

First, we examine the strategic role of price in marketing strategy and discuss several pricing situations. Next, we describe and illustrate the steps to developing or modifying pricing strategy. We then examine situation analysis for pricing decisions, using several application situations to highlight the nature and scope of pricing analysis and consider deciding which pricing strategy to adopt. Finally, we discuss pricing policies and look at several special pricing issues, including pricing considerations in global markets.

Strategic Role of Price

In some companies, price plays a dominant role in marketing strategy, while, in other situations, price may perform a more passive role. Nevertheless, the strategic role of price is too often not recognized: "Part of the reason that pricing is misused and poorly understood is the common practice of making it the last marketing decision. We think that we must design products, communication plans, and a method of distribution before we have something to price. We then use pricing tactically to capture whatever value we can."[4] Taking a wholly tactical view of price neglects the important strategic role pricing can play in marketing strategy. Strategic choices about market targets, positioning strategies, and products and distribution strategies set guidelines for both price and promotion strategies. Product quality and features, type of distribution channel, end-users served, and the functions performed by value chain members all help establish a feasible price range. When an organization forms a new distribution network, selection of the channel and intermediaries may be driven by price strategy.

Importantly, the global economic downturn and recession of the late-2000s and early 2010s encouraged many companies to direct renewed attention to the use of price to maintain sales volume, or at least to protect market share, as buyers reduce purchase levels and competitors reduce their prices. During the downturn, most developed countries experienced an unprecedented decline in prices—although there were different price falls in different sectors and for different companies. The economic downturn underlined the competitive importance of pricing decisions for many companies where price has traditionally been seen as a largely tactical tool. Among the reasons for this change in perspective is the unprecedented level of investor, public, media, and regulatory scrutiny of prices.

---

[3]This illustration is based on: Felix Gillette, "The Duke of Discomfort," *Bloomberg BusinessWeek,* September 6–12, 2010, 58–61. Pilita Clark, "Ryanair's Talk of a Spree on Aircraft Casts Cloud Over Dividend Hopes," *Financial Times,* September 8, 2010, 1. Quentin Fottrell, "Ryanair Banks on Rivals' Pains," *Wall Street Journal,* February 2, 2010, 28.

[4]Thomas Nagle, "Making Pricing a Key Driver of Your Marketing Strategy," *Marketing News,* November 9, 1998, 4.

Kodak's Printer and Cartridge Pricing   Kodak has challenged industry convention with low prices for the ink cartridges for its newest printers. The conventional approach by printer manufacturers is a "razor and blades" price strategy (cheap printers but expensive cartridges). Kodak charges slightly more for the printer and substantially less for replacement ink cartridges. While the traditional approach means high-volume users effectively subsidize low-volume users, Kodak is targeting high-volume printer users with a better deal based on a different pricing architecture. The pricing strategy is linked to a social networking campaign "Pricey Ink Stinks."

Payment-by-Results for Medicines   British drug company Janssen-Cilag, a subsidiary of Johnson & Johnson, has led the way toward payment by results for medical treatment. The company offers to cover the cost of a $50,000 cancer drug if the patient fails to show adequate progress. The hospital only pays for the drug if the patient responds well. This price strategy allows the company to maintain the nominal price for the product (a global price benchmark in the sector) and receive payment only when the patient benefits. Sharing the risk makes the drug more affordable for the hospital. This value offer has generated a raft of new pricing models from competitors aimed at value-based pricing in healthcare.

À la Carte Pricing by Airlines   Faced with more thrift-oriented passengers and the commoditization of their product, U.S. airlines are moving toward pricing "extras" separately from the price of the ticket—charging for checking baggage and selling pillows and bottled water. The attraction is a better deal for passengers who do not use these services, and additional revenue from those who do.

Infosys's New Outsourcing Price Model   Infosys Technologies' pricing strategy moves away from the traditional outsourcing industry model of charging clients based on the number of staff needed for the job—the "body shop" approach. The company is looking for new ways of driving sales growth in a "software-assisted-services" approach. Rather than just developing software and selling it to the client, Infosys retains ownership of the software and charges the client on a pay-per-use basis. This saves the customer the cost of maintaining and hosting the software, while Infosys gets a longer-term revenue stream from the product.

Demand-Based Pricing for Restaurants   Private supper clubs in London and premier restaurant Alinea in Chicago are among those adopting a new pricing model for meals—diners buy tickets for meals in advance rather than paying after eating, and pay lower prices for less popular dining slots. Groupon participates in this model by negotiating discounts with restaurants and taking payments upfront from diners. This pricing model protects venues from last-minute cancellations and allows better food planning and less wastage.

Sources: Paul Taylor, "The Wicked Price of Print," *Financial Times,* June 1, 2007, 18. Nicholas Timmins, "Drugmaker's Proposal to NHS: We'll Pay if Cancer Treatment Fails," *Financial Times,* June 4, 2007, 1. Scott McCartney, "U.S. Airlines Are Moving to a la Carte Model," *Wall Street Journal,* September 16, 2008, 6. Joe Leahy, "Infosys Develops New Pricing Models," *Financial Times,* January 12–13, 2008, 20. Rose Jacobs, "Restaurant Goers Sign Up to Pre-Paid Dining Experience," *Financial Times,* October 23–24, 2010, 14.

Companies in many situations are aiming to use price in new and more creative ways to establish advantage and to deliver superior value to customers. The INNOVATION APPLICATION provides some examples of the creative use of pricing strategy to impact on positioning in the market and to deliver superior value. It is likely that responding effectively to the new competitive imperatives of the postrecession era will require many more companies to develop new business models in which price plays a different type of role. Far from operating as a tactical tool, price is becoming a key part of reinvention in redesigning the process of how products are taken to market. The core issue is finding new and better ways to create superior customer value. As a result, the role of price is increasingly central to positioning.[5]

Price in the Positioning Strategy

Price is an important part of positioning strategy, and pricing decisions need to be coordinated with decisions for all of the positioning components. Importantly, this pricing perspective mandates understanding how pricing is viewed and understood by customers. Interestingly, A.T. Kearney research suggests that because of the complexity of negotiated prices for business-to-business products—volume discounts, payment terms, local deals, freight and handling, service calls, and so on—the actual price paid by customers may be half the product's list price, and importantly executives in the seller organization may not know what that price is—which underlines the importance of close management involvement in pricing.[6]

Importantly, while price may be a decisive positioning issue because it impacts buyer choices in some situations, it is relatively rarely the only factor that impacts customer value. Consider, for example, the dilemma at P&G in the harsh trading conditions of the late-2000s. A goal is to maintain the premium prices of major brands, but at the same time the company must compete effectively with the retail price discounters and generic retailer brands, who are taking market share with low prices. This case is described in the STRATEGY APPLICATION.

Product Strategy

Pricing decisions require analysis of the product mix, branding strategy, and product quality and features to determine the effects of these factors on price strategy. When a single product is involved, the pricing decision is simplified. Yet, in many instances, a line or mix of products must be priced. The prices for products in a line do not necessarily correspond to the cost of each item. For example, prices in supermarkets are based on a total mix or assortment strategy rather than individual item pricing. Understanding the composition of the mix and the interrelationships among products is important in determining pricing strategy, particularly when the brand identity is built around a line or mix of products rather than on a brand-by-brand basis. Consider a situation involving a product and consumable supplies for the product. One popular strategy is to price the base product at competitive levels and set higher margins for replacement supplies. Examples include parts for automobiles and razor blades.

Product quality and features affect price strategy. A high-quality product may benefit from a high price to help establish it as a prestige position in the marketplace and satisfy management's profit performance requirements. Alternatively, a manufacturer supplying private-branded products to a retailer like Wal-Mart or Target must price competitively in order to obtain sales.

Innovation in value for customers influences feasible prices. The product strategy challenge is innovation at the right price. For example, Henkel's Purex detergent brand is succeeding in getting customers to spend more on their laundry, even in times of austerity, by adding antistatic fabric sheets to the Purex offering. Similarly, Colgate-Palmolive has launched packs of disposable mini-toothbrushes and a mouth freshener called Wisp, to

---

[5]Piercy, Cravens and Lane, ibid.
[6]Tom Lester, "Find the Right Pricing Strategy," *Financial Times,* December 5, 2005, 16.

During the economic downturn, major consumer goods companies like Procter & Gamble moved toward value rather than price-based competition. In fact, P&G has increased prices during the downturn to protect profit margins from the effect of declining sales in developed markets.

P&G is pursuing "performance-based value messaging," which communicates to frugally minded customers that it is worth paying more for products like Tide detergent and Bounty towels because they save money by doing a better job. It may also be that consumers will pay more for products that have ethical and environmental values.

The challenge is differentiating products to prove to customers that they are "better" than alternatives, rather than simply cutting prices. P&G's head of consumer and market research believes that changes in consumer attitudes as a result of economic recession will be a long-term development signaling higher consumer engagement as they ask more questions about the value of the products they are offered.

One P&G innovation is Olay Pro-X—a range of clinical anti-ageing products that sell for around twice the price of its regular Olay creams. Pro-X is aimed at more prosperous consumers, accustomed to paying much more for similar products in department stores rather than in drug stores. P&G sees Pro-X as one of its "big ideas" that represent superior value to the specific target consumer. Pro-X has taken around 5 percent of the U.S. anti-ageing clinical market.

Nonetheless, though traditionally able to charge a premium, P&G has also introduced cheaper products to compete directly with retailer own-label brands and discounters. P&G is launching products like Tide Basic to compete with retailer own-labels. By late-2009, P&G's CEO implemented a price-cutting strategy in reaction to market share losses across its portfolio in the United States—less expensive versions of household products had dented market share, with Tide costing as much as twice the cost of private label versions. A growing challenge is pursuing radically different value propositions with different customer target groups.

By 2011, as raw material price increases pushed P&G prices higher, the strength of the brand led to the acceptance of these price increases by consumers, notwithstanding unprecedented levels of price promotions and discounts by competitors in some sectors.

Sources: Jonathan Birchall and Jenny Wiggins, "Retail Suppliers Chase the Value in a Shift to Thrift," *Financial Times,* May 7, 2009, 15. Ellen Byron, "P&G Plans Price Cuts, Expansion," *Wall Street Journal,* September 11–13, 2009, 7. Ellen Byron, "Tide Turns Toward 'Basic' as P&G Battles Downturn," *Wall Street Journal,* August 7–9, 2009, 12–13. Barney Jopson, "Consumers Take P&G Price Rises in Stride," *Financial Times,* August 6–7, 2011, 12.

address the unmet need for "on-the-go tooth cleaning." At launch, Wisp took 7 percent of the U.S. toothbrush market.[7] Value innovation judgments are central to price choices.

Distribution Strategy

Type of channel, distribution intensity, and channel configuration also influence pricing decisions. The functions performed and the motivation of intermediaries need to be considered in setting prices. Value-added resellers require price margins to pay for their activities and provide incentives to obtain their cooperation. Pricing is equally important when distribution is performed by the producer. Pricing in coordinated and managed channels reflects total channel considerations more so than in conventional channels. Intensive distribution

---

[7]Jonathan Birchall, "Out to Launch in a Downturn," *Financial Times,* June 4, 2009, 16.

is likely to call for more competitive pricing than selective or exclusive distribution. In multichannel situations, pricing may pose a particular challenge. For example, if the website offers a lower price than conventional channels, how will members of those channels react? Pricing decisions must take into account these issues.

Responsibility for Pricing Decisions

Responsibility for pricing decisions varies across organizations. Marketing executives determine pricing strategy in many companies. Pricing decisions may be made by the chief executive officer in some firms, such as aircraft producers and construction firms. Manufacturing and engineering executives may be assigned pricing responsibility in companies that produce custom-designed industrial equipment. The vital importance of pricing decisions argues strongly for cross-functional participation. Pricing impacts all business functions. Operations, engineering, finance, and marketing executives should participate in strategic pricing decisions, regardless of where responsibility is assigned. Coordination of strategic and tactical pricing decisions with other aspects of marketing strategy is also critical because of the marketing program interrelationships involved.

Because responsibility for pricing has often split between the corporate center and operating units, and also between marketing, sales, finance, and manufacturing functions, there have been recommendations for the establishment of a central pricing function to provide expertise and a bridge between marketing, finance, and sales.[8] Achieving a strategic perspective on price mandates clear senior management involvement in pricing. This responsibility should encompass explicit decisions on price levels and changes and close monitoring of unit revenues obtained in different segments and with different customers. From a strategic perspective, price effectiveness cannot be delegated to lower levels in the organization. Nonetheless, involvement in the pricing process by lower levels is essential.[9]

Pricing Situations

Pricing strategy requires continuous monitoring because of changing external conditions, the actions of competitors, and the opportunities to gain a competitive edge through pricing actions. Various situations require pricing actions such as

- Deciding how to price a new product, or line of products.
- Evaluating the need to adjust price as the product moves through the product life cycle.
- Changing a positioning strategy that calls for modifying the current pricing strategy.
- Deciding how to respond to the pressures of competitive threats.

Decisions about pricing for existing products may include increasing, decreasing, or holding prices at current levels. Understanding the competitive situation and possible actions by competitors is important in deciding if and when to alter prices. Demand and cost information are strong influences on new-product pricing. Deciding how to price a new product also should include considering competing substitutes, since few new products occupy a unique position in the market.

Roles of Pricing

Prices perform various roles in the marketing program—as a signal to the buyer, an instrument of competition, a means to improve financial performance, and a substitute for other marketing program functions (e.g., promotional pricing).

[8]Kent B. Monroe, *Pricing: Making Profitable Decisions,* 3rd ed. (Burr Ridge IL: Irwin/McGraw-Hill, 2003).
[9]Piercy, Cravens, and Lane, ibid.

Signal to the Buyer

Price offers a fast and direct way of communicating with the buyer. The price is visible to the buyer and provides a basis of comparison between brands. Price may be used to position the brand as a high-quality product or instead to pursue head-on competition with another brand.

Instrument of Competition

Price offers a way to quickly attack competitors or, alternatively, to position a firm away from direct competition. For example, off-price retailers use a low-price strategy against department stores and other retailers. Price strategy is always related to competition whether firms use a higher, lower, or equal price.

This pricing role is particularly important in hard economic conditions of slowdown and recession. In the late-2000s, companies like Hewlett-Packard, Southwest Airlines, and FedEx all pursued tactics of aggressive pricing (as well as hiring extra salespeople, publicizing competitors' cutbacks to customers as indicating reduced service levels, and entering new markets), to take business away from competitors. The logic is that while such aggressive pricing strategies depress short-term profits, they gain market share, which can be held for the longer-term—market share is most up for grabs in a downturn, when competitors are too hard-pressed to defend their position vigorously. We saw at the start of the chapter, Ryanair price cuts in economic downturn were aimed at capturing market share.[10]

Improving Financial Performance

Since prices and costs determine financial performance, pricing strategies need to be assessed as to their estimated impact on the firm's financial performance, both in the short and long run. Importantly, both revenues and costs need to be taken into account in selecting pricing strategies.

Marketing Program Considerations

Prices may substitute for selling effort, advertising, and sales promotion. Alternatively, price may be used to reinforce these promotion activities in the marketing program. The role of pricing often depends on how other components in the marketing program are used. For example, prices can be used as an incentive to channel members, as the focus of promotional strategy, and as a signal of value. In deciding the role of pricing in marketing strategy, management evaluates the importance of prices to competitive positioning, probable buyers' reactions, financial requirements, and interrelationships with other components in the marketing program.

Pricing Strategy

The major steps in selecting a pricing strategy for a new product or altering an existing strategy are shown in Exhibit 11.1. Strategy formulation begins by determining pricing objectives, which guide strategy development. Next, it is necessary to analyze the pricing situation, taking into account demand, cost, competition, and pricing objectives. These analyses indicate how much flexibility there is in pricing a new product or changing the pricing strategy for an existing product. Finally, specific prices and operating policies are determined to implement the strategy. Each step in the pricing strategy that is shown in Exhibit 11.1 is discussed in more detail in the rest of the chapter.

The dilemma faced in pricing strategy for a new product is illustrated by Apple's difficulties in pricing the now-iconic iPhone at launch. The goal of getting to new

---

[10]Ibid.

EXHIBIT 11.1
**Steps in Selecting
a Pricing Strategy**

Set Pricing
Objectives

Analyze the
Pricing
Situation

Select
Pricing
Strategy

Determine
Specific Prices
and Policies

platform into as many hands as possible as quickly as possible, led Apple to quickly revise downward the price of the iPhone, two months after launch, and to make further moves down in price with the 3G iPhone in 2008. Even with an extremely enthusiastic fan-base of Apple customers and an innovative product, the company appeared to misread the price the market would bear. This example is discussed in the INNOVATION APPLICATION.

Pricing Objectives

Pricing strategies are expected to achieve specific objectives. More than one pricing objective is usually involved, and sometimes the objectives may conflict with each other. If so, adjustments may be needed on one of the conflicting objectives. For example, if one objective is to increase market share by 30 percent and the second objective is to obtain a high profit margin, management should decide if both objectives are feasible. If not, one must be adjusted. Objectives set essential guidelines for pricing strategy.

Pricing objectives vary according to the situational factors present (e.g., intensity of competition, economic conditions, etc.) and management's preferences. A high price may be set to recover investment in a new product. This practice is typical in the pricing of new prescription drugs. A low price may be used to gain market position, discourage new competition, or attract new buyers. Several examples of pricing objectives follow.

Gain Market Position

Low prices may be used to gain sales and market share. Limitations include encouraging price wars and reduction (or elimination) of profit contributions. Recall the earlier discussion of Ryanair's pricing strategy.

Achieve Financial Performance

Prices are selected to contribute to financial objectives such as profit contribution and cash flow. Prices that are too high may not be acceptable to buyers—recall the Apple iPhone dilemma described earlier in the INNOVATION APPLICATION.

Product Positioning

Prices may be used to enhance product image, promote the use of the product, create awareness, and other positioning objectives. The visibility of price (high or low) may contribute to the effectiveness of other positioning components such as advertising.

The 2007 U.S. launch of Apple's iPhone was very impressive—despite consumer gripes about the then-$600 price, and other issues.

In the first 36 hours of availability, iPhones were selling at a rate of 125 a minute, which was a record for any Apple product debut.

A few weeks later, Apple surprised many by slashing the iPhone's price by $200 and eliminating another version of the phone with smaller storage capacity.

The uproar over the price cut promoted Apple to offer a $100 Apple store credit to those who bought the phone at the original price.

The pricing model for this innovative product was a big challenge for Apple. Why in such high demand, would Apple cut the price by 33 percent after only two months on the market? Steve Jobs claimed he just wanted to get as many iPhones out there as quickly as possible.

But the abrupt markdown provoked lawsuits and rubbed up some of Apple's early adopter fans the wrong way. Early purchasers besieged Apple with complaints they had been taken advantage of and overcharged, bringing an apology from CEO Steve Jobs.

The iPhone launch in Europe and Japan—at higher prices than in the United States—saw slow take-up by consumers, because of the high price.

The 2008 launch of a new iPhone saw significantly lower prices in the United States, and Apple bowing to pressure from phone operators to allow them to subsidize the latest iPhone—AT&T was looking at a $200 subsidy on the handset, allowing it to sell to the consumer for $200 or less.

Apple's efforts to boost sales of the iPhone handset meant offering an aggressively priced new model with faster Internet speeds, and dropping its insistence on revenue-sharing with wireless carriers.

Sources: Ben Charny, "iPhone Debut in Europe Calls for a New Approach," *Wall Street Journal,* November 14, 2007, 31. Brent Schlender, "The iPhone on Training Wheels," *Fortune,* November 26, 2007, 26. Andrew Parker, Paul Taylor and Richard Waters, "Apple Relents on Subsidy for iPhone," *Financial Times,* June 7–8, 2008, 1. Nick Wingfield, "Will Masses Embrace New iPhone?" *Wall Street Journal,* June 11, 2008, 4.

Stimulate Demand

Price is used to encourage buyers to try a new product or to purchase existing brands during periods when sales slow down (e.g., recession). A potential problem is that buyers may balk at purchasing when prices return to normal levels. It has been estimated that even for non-premium products, once discounting has been implemented, it takes 3 to 5 years to get consumers to pay full prices again.[11] Discount coupons for new products may help stimulate demand without actually lowering listed prices.

Influence Competition

The objective of pricing actions may be to influence existing or potential competitors. Management may want to discourage market entry or price cutting by current competitors. Alternatively, a price leader may want to encourage industry members to raise prices. One problem is that competitors may not respond as predicted.

Intel employed an interesting strategy for competing with inexpensive semiconductors that offered rapid graphics processing and posed a threat to Intel's flagship Pentium chip.[12] Rather than lowering the Pentium price to appeal to the price-sensitive market segment, Intel developed the Cirrus chip based on the Pentium platform, which eliminated additional

[11]John Gapper, "When Not Cutting Prices Is a Luxury," *Financial Times,* May 28, 2009, 13.
[12]This illustration is based on George E. Cressman, Jr., and Thomas T. Nagle, "How to Manage an Aggressive Competitor," *Business Horizons,* March–April 2002, 26.

design and tooling costs. Some of the Pentium capabilities were not activated in the new chip, which was priced to compete with competitors' products. Intel stimulated demand without lowering the price of its premium chip.

Analyzing the Pricing Situation

Thorough and systematic pricing analysis is essential in evaluating new product concepts, developing test marketing strategy, and designing a new product introduction strategy. Pricing analysis is also important for existing products because of changes in the market and competitive environment, unsatisfactory market performance, and modifications in marketing strategy over the product's life cycle. Intel's analysis of pricing in the price-sensitive chip market segment is illustrative. The factors influencing the pricing situation include (1) customer price sensitivity, (2) product costs, (3) current and potential competitive actions, and (4) pricing objectives (see Exhibit 11.2). We examine each factor and illustrate what is involved in the analyses.

Customer Price Sensitivity

One of the challenges in pricing analysis is estimating how buyers will respond to different prices. The pricing of Procter & Gamble Company's analgesic brand, Aleve, illustrates this situation. The product was introduced in a highly competitive $2.38 billion market.[13] Aleve was the over-the-counter version of Naprosyn (developed by Syntex Corporation). P&G estimated first-year sales of $200 million. A $100 million marketing effort spearheaded Aleve's market entry. The pricing was the same as Advil though Aleve lasts 8 to 12 hours compared to Advil's 8 hours. Aggressive promotional pricing (coupons) was anticipated from the leading competitors, Tylenol ($700 million sales) and Advil ($330 million). Some industry authorities expected Aleve to pose a greater threat to the weaker brands (Bayer, Bufferin, and Nuprin) rather than the two leading competitors.

Analysis of buyers' price sensitivity should answer the following questions:

1. How big is the product-market in terms of buying potential?
2. What market segments and market targeting strategy is to be used?
3. What is the sensitivity of demand in each segment to changes in price?

EXHIBIT 11.2
Factors Impacting the Pricing Situation

[13]Laura Bird, "P&G's New Analgesic Promises Pain for Over-the-Counter Rivals," *Wall Street Journal,* June 16, 1994, B9.

4. What is the importance of nonprice factors, such as features and performance?
5. What is estimated sales at different price levels?

Let's examine these questions for Aleve. The analgesic market was growing at about a 3 percent annual rate. Aleve offers extended relief benefits to arthritis sufferers and people with sore muscles. P&G apparently wanted to stress the brand's performance (value proposition) rather than encourage price competition. Management's $200 million sales estimate would position Aleve in third place behind Tylenol and Advil.

The core issue in pricing is finding out what value requirements (benefits-costs) the buyer places on the product or brand.[14] Pricing decision makers need this information in order to determine the pricing strategy. Basing price only on cost may lead to pricing too high or too low compared to the value perceived by the buyer. Buyers see different values depending on their use situation so market segment analysis is essential. For example, people who want an analgesic that lasts longer are likely to perceive a high value provided by Aleve.

Price Elasticity

Price elasticity is the percentage change in the quantity sold of a brand when the price changes, divided by the percentage change in price. Elasticity is measured for changes in price from some specific price level so elasticity is not necessarily constant over the range of prices under consideration. Surprisingly, research indicates that in some situations people will buy more of certain products at *higher* prices, thus displaying a price-quantity relationship that slopes upward to the right, rather than the typical downward sloping volume and price relationship. In these instances, buyers seem to be using price as a measure of quality because they are unable to evaluate the product.

Estimating the exact shape of the demand curve (price-quantity relationship) is probably impossible in most instances. Even so, there are ways to estimate the sensitivity of customers to alternative prices. Test marketing can be used for this purpose. Study of historical price and quantity data may be helpful. End-user research studies, such as consumer evaluations of price, are also used. These approaches, coupled with management judgment, help indicate the responsiveness of sales to different prices in the range of prices that is under consideration.

An interesting discussion of the challenges in obtaining information from potential buyers about their willingness to purchase a product at different prices is provided in Exhibit 11.3. The differences in people's responses based on how price questions are presented highlight the importance of experience and research skills in customer pricing research.

Nonprice Factors

Factors other than price may be important in analyzing buying situations. For example, buyers may be willing to pay a premium price to gain other advantages or, instead, be willing to forgo certain advantages for lower prices. Factors other than price that may be important are quality, uniqueness, availability, convenience, service, and warranty.

The value offered to the buyer by a brand is relevant information in setting price and determining pricing strategy.[15] Customer value mapping (CVM) estimates value as the

---

[14]Robert J. Dolan, "How Do You Know When the Price Is Right," *Harvard Business Review,* September–October, 1995, 174–183.
[15]This discussion is based on Gerald E. Smith and Thomas T. Nagle, "A Question of Value," *Marketing Management,* July–August 2005, 39–43.

EXHIBIT 11.3
**Effects of Price
Presentation**

Source: Kent B. Monroe,
Pricing. 3rd ed. (Burr Ridge,
IL: McGraw-Hill/ Irwin, 2003),
223. Copyright © The McGraw-
Hill Companies. Used with
permission.

One problem in conducting price research is how to get information from respondents about their willingness to purchase a product at different prices. Ideally, we would like to know how the individual would respond to different prices. However, once they realize that we are trying to estimate their demand curve individuals may provide answers that reflect their understanding of the traditional demand curve—that they buy more at lower prices and less or none at higher prices. The problem is that price is presented as a cost or sacrifice to potential buyers, not as an attribute. To present price as an attribute means that other product or service information must be presented to the respondents.

One research study looked at a range of prices, but the researchers varied whether only one price was presented to respondents or whether multiple prices were presented. In the multiple price situation, prices were presented sequentially, either high to low or low to high. As the graph indicates, substantial differences occurred in the estimates. Presenting multiple prices produced downward sloping demand curves, but a single price presentation revealed increasing estimated usage between $3 and $9, declining thereafter.

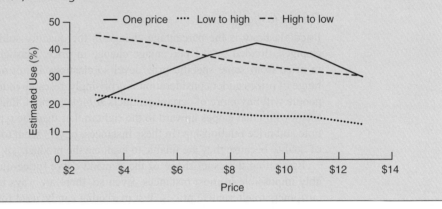

perceived quality buyers obtain per unit of price. In contrast, value using economic value modeling (EVM) consists of the economic savings and gains provided customers due to purchase of the firm's brand instead of competitors' brands. Thus, using EVM price is determined by the value provided and is the recommended basis of assessing value. An illustrative comparison of the two value approaches is shown in Exhibit 11.4. In this illustration using the preferred EVM method, your product offers more value than competitors' products.

The underlying logic of EVM as the better basis for viewing value offered to the customer is that "dollar worth of benefits minus price" is a more realistic view of value than using the price/benefit ratio.[16] CVM does not take into account the differentiated benefits that are offered. Of course, the customer must recognize and have a preference for the differentiated benefits. Economic value is an important frame of reference in communicating with customers and designing a positioning strategy.

In some instances the buying situation may reduce the importance of price in the buyer's choice process. The price of the product may be a minor factor when the cost is small compared to the importance of the use situation. Examples include infrequently purchased electric parts for home entertainment equipment, batteries for appliances, and health and

---

[16]Ibid.

EXHIBIT 11.4
Comparison of Approaches to Value Determination

Source: Gerald E. Smith and Thomas T. Nagle, "A Question of Value," *Marketing Management,* July/August 2005, 40.

Suppose your firm's differentiated product provides $15,000 in value for customers and costs $6,000, whereas competitors' commodity products offer $10,000 in value and cost $3,000.

EVM Value	CVM Price/Benefit Ratio
Your Product:	Your Product:
$15,000 – $6,000 = $9,000	$\dfrac{\$6,000}{\$15,000} = 0.40$
Competitors' Products:	Competitors' Products:
$10,000 – $3,000 = $7,000	$\dfrac{\$3,000}{\$10,000} = 0.30$
Your product offers higher value than competitors' products	Competitors' products offer the most favorable price/benefit

beauty aids during a vacation. The need for important but relatively inexpensive parts for industrial equipment is another situation that reduces the role of price in the buyer's purchase decision. Quick Metal, an adhesive produced by Loctite Corporation, is used by maintenance personnel to repair production equipment such as a broken gear tooth. At less than $40 a tube, the price is not a major concern since one tube will keep an expensive production line operating until a new part is installed.

Other examples of nonprice factors that affect the buying situation include (1) purchases of products that are essential to physical health, such as pain relief; (2) choices among brands of complex products that are difficult to evaluate, such as home electronics (a high price may be used as a gauge of quality); and (3) image-enhancement situations, such as serving prestige brands of drinks to socially important guests.

Forecasts

Forecasts of sales are needed for the price alternatives that management is considering. In planning the introduction of Aleve, P&G's management could look at alternative sales forecasts based on different prices and other marketing program variations. These forecasts, when combined with cost estimates, indicate the financial impact of different price strategies. The objective is to estimate sales in units for each product (or brand) at the prices under consideration.

Controlled tests can be used to forecast the effects of price changes. For example, a fast-food chain can evaluate the effects of different prices on demand using tests in a sample of stores. Methods for analyzing the effects of positioning strategy components and positioning results are discussed in Chapter 6.

Cost Analysis

Cost information is essential in making pricing decisions. A guide to cost analysis is shown in Exhibit 11.5.

Composition of Product Cost

First, it is necessary to determine the fixed and variable costs involved in producing and distributing the product. Also, it is important to estimate the amount of the product cost accounted for by purchases from suppliers. For example, a large portion of the cost of a personal computer are the components purchased from suppliers. It is

EXHIBIT 11.5
Cost Analysis for
Pricing Decisions

- Determine the components of the cost of the product.
- Estimate how cost varies with the volume of sales.
- Analyze the cost competitive advantage of the product.
- Decide how experience in producing the product affects costs.
- Estimate how much control management has over costs.

useful to separate the costs into labor, materials, and capital categories when studying cost structure.

Activity-based costing (ABC) is a technique that provides information for pricing strategy. Many firms have adopted ABC as a costing mechanism to more appropriately assign indirect costs to goods and services. The key component of ABC is to assign costs based on the activities that are performed to create the good or provide the service being examined. With ABC, decision makers obtain a much more accurate representation of product costs. This information is useful in pricing decisions and comparisons across product lines and customer groups. Since ABC estimates the cost of the product in terms of a collection of activities, it is much easier to evaluate pricing for particular attributes or service levels. Similarly, it is possible to make comparisons to competitors by evaluating the costs of activities necessary to offer product enhancements.

Firms that successfully implement ABC do so initially as an accounting technique, yet the ultimate objective is to facilitate activity-based management (ABM). In this manner, the cost data become an integral part of the product strategy in terms of considering the entire value chain, encompassing suppliers, customers, and competitors. For example, products that may require packaging or delivery modifications incur additional costs. With ABM, decision makers have a better understanding of these additional costs, can price accordingly, and can consider these costs in conjunction with the offerings of competitors.

Volume Effect on Cost

The next part of cost analysis examines how costs vary at different levels of production or quantities purchased. Can economies of scale be gained over the volume range that is under consideration, given the target market and positioning strategy? At what volume levels are significant cost reductions possible? Are there points when costs of increasing capacity for additional volume production go up in steps? Volume effect analysis determines the extent to which the volume produced or distributed should be taken into account in estimating costs.

Competitive Advantage

Comparing key competitors' costs is often valuable. Are their costs higher, lower, or about the same? Although such information may be difficult to obtain, experienced managers can often make accurate estimates. In some industries such as commercial airlines cost information is available. It is useful to place key competitors into relative product cost categories (e.g., higher, lower, same). Analysts may be able to estimate competitive cost information from knowledge of types of costs, wage rates, material costs, production facilities, and related information.

Interestingly, when the Apple iPhone was launched in June 2007, early customers included companies like iSuppli in California, whose goal was to smash the product into pieces to identify which companies had won contracts to supply internal components. This intelligence is of enormous value to other handset manufacturers, but also to stock market investors. The data identify little-known suppliers who may benefit from the iPhone's runaway success, and also allow predictions of how Apple's cost of manufacturing for the device may fluctuate.[17]

Experience Effect

It is important to consider the effect of experience on costs. Experience or learning-curve analysis (using historical data) indicates whether costs and prices for various products decline by a given amount each time the number of units produced doubles. However, price declines may be uneven because of competitive influences. When unit costs (vertical axis) are plotted against total accumulated volume (horizontal axis), costs decline with volume if an experience effect is present.[18] This occurs when experience over time increases the efficiency of production operations.

Control Over Costs

Finally, it is useful to consider how much influence an organization may have over its product costs in the future. To what extent can research and development, bargaining power with suppliers, process innovation, and other improvements help to reduce costs over the planning horizon? These considerations are interrelated with experience-curve analysis, yet may operate over a shorter time range. The bargaining power of an organization in its channels of distribution, for example, can have a major effect on costs, and the effects can be immediate.

Competitor Analysis

Each competitor's pricing strategy needs to be evaluated to determine (1) which firms represent the most direct competition (actual and potential) for buyers in the market targets that are under consideration; (2) how competing firms are positioned on a relative price basis and the extent to which price is used as an active part of their marketing strategies; (3) how successful each firm's price strategy has been; and (4) the key competitors' probable responses to alternative price strategies.

The discussion in Chapter 2 considers guidelines for competitor identification. It is important to determine both potential and current competitors. The success of a competitor's price strategy is usually gauged by financial performance. One problem with using this metric to gauge pricing success is accounting for influences other than price on profits.

The most difficult of the four questions about competition is predicting what rivals will do in response to alternative price actions. No changes are likely unless one firm's price is viewed as threatening (low) or greedy (high). Competitive pressures, actual and potential, often narrow the range of feasible prices and rule out the use of extremely high or low prices relative to competition. In new-product markets, competitive factors may be insignificant, although very high prices may attract potential competitors.

The retail consumer electronics market offers an interesting look at the effects of intense competition. Wal-Mart Inc. launched a competitive battle against Best Buy Co. and Circuit City Stores Inc. in 2005 using much lower prices for TV and computer service contract warranties.[19] The initiative is part of Wal-Mart's strategy to upscale its merchandise, including the interiors of many of its electronics departments and addition of high-end products. The extended warranty on electronics products is a retailer's most profitable line

---

[17]Chris Hughes, "Banks Delve Deep to Locate Esoteric Data," *Financial Times,* September 14, 2007, 23.
[18]A guide to determining experience curves is provided in Kent B. Monroe, *Pricing: Making Profitable Decisions,* 3rd ed. (McGraw-Hill/Irwin, Burr Ridge, IL, 2003), Chapter 13.
[19]Robert Berner, "Watch Out, Best Buy and Circuit City," *BusinessWeek,* November 21, 2005, 46 and 48.

In late 2005 Wal-Mart Inc. launched extended warranties on TVs and computers selling above $300: Wal-Mart warranty prices are creating challenges for Best Buy and Circuit City profit margins. Here are service contract price comparisons on a per-year basis (for the same or similar items).

PRODUCT		Wal-Mart	Best Buy	Circuit City
		SERVICE CONTRACT PRICE		
RCA 52-inch HDTV projection TV	About $1000	$29.44	$62.49	$100.00
Toshiba notebook computer	$996 to $1,250	$34.44	$83.33	$92.50
Hewlett-Packard desktop computer package	$629 to $748, including rebates	$29.44	$69.99	$82.49

(Data: Wal-Mart, Best Buy, and Circuit City websites)

The pricing options for Best Buy and Circuit City are to: (1) not change their prices and face possible sales losses; or (2) reduce warranty prices and negatively impact profits.

Source: Robert Berner, "Watch Out, Best Buy and Circuit City," *BusinessWeek,* November 21, 2005, 46 and 48.

of business. As shown in the STRATEGY APPLICATION Wal-Mart's warranty prices are on the average 50 percent lower than Best Buy and Circuit City.

Game theory is a promising method for analyzing competitors' pricing strategy options. The technique became very popular in the 1990s. An interesting application of game theory is discussed in the STRATEGY APPLICATION. Game theory was used to design the auction process for the simultaneous sale of several third-generation (3G) wireless phone licenses in Britain.[20] The process was very successful for the government. After 150 rounds of bidding, final bidders for five licenses paid a total of $34 billion, more than seven times the amount initially anticipated by the government.

Pricing Objectives

Management's objectives may affect the extent of pricing flexibility and should be included as the last part of analyzing the pricing situation. For example, an objective of gaining market position where low prices are used to increase sales and market share would narrow the range of pricing options even if the demand-cost gap is wide. Similar assessments are needed depending on the pricing objectives set by management. Importantly, if one or more of the pricing objectives cannot be achieved based on the assessments of customer price sensitivity, costs, and competitors' likely responses (see Exhibit 11.2), the feasibility of the objective(s) may need to be evaluated.

---

[20]Almar Latour, "Disconnected," *Wall Street Journal,* June 5, 2001, A1 and A8.

A popular exercise in seminars and executive briefings we hold is to ask executives to participate in a prisoner's dilemma pricing game. Each team must decide whether to price its products high or low compared to those of another team in 10 rounds of competition. The objective is to earn the most money; results are determined by the decision that two competitors make in comparison with each other.

The game fairly accurately simulates a typical profit/loss scenario for price competition in mature markets. The objective is to impart several lessons in pricing competition, the first being that pricing is more like playing poker than solitaire. Success depends not just on a combination of luck and how the hand is played but also on how well competitors play their hands. In real markets, outcomes depend not only on how customers respond but, perhaps more important, on how competitors respond to changes in price.

If a competitor matches a price decrease, neither the initiator nor the follower will achieve a significant increase in sales and both are likely to have a significant decrease in profits. In developing pricing strategy, managers need to anticipate the moves of their competitors and attempt to influence those moves by selectively communicating information to influence competitive behavior.

The second lesson is that managers must adopt a very long time horizon when considering changes in price. Once started, price wars are difficult to stop. A simple decision to drop price often becomes the first shot in a war that no competitor wins. Before initiating a price decrease, managers must consider how it will affect the competitive stability of markets.

The third lesson from the prisoner's dilemma is that careful use of a value-based marketing approach can reverse a trend toward price-based marketing. This is accomplished through signaling, a nonprice competitive tactic that involves selectively disclosing information to competitors to influence their behavior. The steel and airline industries provide prominent examples of the signaling strategy's use. They often rely on announcements that conveniently appear on the front pages of the *Wall Street Journal* to signal competitors of pending price moves and provide them with opportunities to follow. The strategy takes time to implement, but it provides a far better long-term competitive position for marketers who employ it.

Source: Excerpt from Reed Holden and Thomas T. Nagle, "Kamikaze Pricing," *Marketing Management,* Summer 1998, 34. Reprinted with permission of the American Marketing Association.

Selecting the Pricing Strategy

Analysis of the pricing situation provides essential information for selecting the pricing strategy. Using this information management needs to (1) determine extent of pricing flexibility and (2) decide how to position price relative to costs and how visible to make the price of the product. The pricing strategy needs to be coordinated with the development of the entire marketing program since in most, if not all, instances there are other important marketing program component influences on buyers' purchasing behavior.

How Much Flexibility Exists?

Demand and cost factors determine the extent of pricing flexibility. Within these upper and lower boundaries, competition and pricing objectives also influence the choice of a specific pricing strategy. Exhibit 11.6 illustrates how these factors influence flexibility. The price gap between demand and cost may be narrow or wide. A narrow gap simplifies the decision; a wide gap provides a greater range of feasible pricing options. Choice of the pricing strategy is influenced by competitors' strategies, present and future, and by management's pricing objectives. Management must determine where to position price within the flexibility band shown in Exhibit 11.6. In competitive markets the feasibility range may be very narrow.

EXHIBIT 11.6
**Determinants
of Pricing
Flexibility**

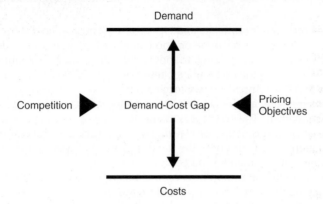

Recall, for example, P&Gs pricing of Aleve, which was priced the same as a key competitor's brand. New markets or emerging market segments in established markets may allow management more flexibility in strategy selection.

A pricing strategy situation is described in the RELATIONSHIP APPLICATION. Several important pricing issues are highlighted. Before reading the next paragraph identify the issues that you believe need to be considered in deciding what action to take concerning the pricing of Novaton. Also decide whether you agree or disagree with the decision made by Novet's pricing team.

The Novaton illustration highlights several issues to consider in analyzing the pricing situation (see Exhibit 11.2). A key question is why Novaton is not selling well in the market.[21] The problem may be price but it could also be very low customer awareness (25 percent). Surprisingly, the team's pricing analyses did not consider customers' perceptions of Novaton. Depending on how customers position the brand, a price cut may not be effective. The information about Holycon's plans may be correct but the team is basing a very important pricing decision on extremely limited intelligence. Similarly, the competitor's manufacturing capacity information came from only one person. Finally, the competitor's costs were estimated by assuming Holycon had similar operations to Novaton's. This premise may be faulty.

Thus, there are several serious questions about Fritz's pricing strategy.[22] It was later determined after Holycon entered the market that the underlying problem causing the low sales was low awareness. Interestingly, customers actually considered Novaton to be better than Holycon. Novet's market sensing information was faulty. Holycon's costs were 60 percent less than Novet's costs for Novaton. Holycon came into the market at prices 40 percent below Novaton's original price. After 2 years of tough price competition Novet dropped out of the market. This might have been avoided if the pricing team had recognized that a better pricing strategy would have been to position Novaton as offering superior value worth its original price and aggressively communicate the value proposition to build awareness with potential buyers.

Price Positioning and Visibility

A key decision is how far above cost to price a new product within the flexibility band (see Exhibit 11.6). A relatively low market entry price may be used with the objective of building volume and market position, or instead, a high price may be selected to generate large margins. The former is a "penetration" strategy whereas the latter is a "skimming" strategy. Analysis of the results of low price strategies in highly competitive markets indicates

---

[21]The following issues are based on George E. Cressman, "Snatching Defeat from the Jaws of Victory," *Marketing Management,* Summer 1997, 10–11.

[22]Ibid.

Relationship Application

Can You Identify the Pricing Issues in This Decision Situation?

The meeting was held on a snowy day in January. Novet's corporate offices, located in a large midwestern city, were quiet as people arrived late because of the new snowstorm. Mary Fritz, a marketing manager, started the discussion: "Let me review our progress on Novaton. We introduced it 18 months ago to a marketplace containing no competitive products, and we knew this product would be really valuable to our customers. We set our initial price at $250 per unit, expecting to sell 5,000 units in our first year, an additional 20,000 units this year, and 40,000 units next year. We just knew that as customers started to use the product, they would tell others. And word of mouth would be our best advertisement.

"We know this new product is really great," Fritz said, "and the customers who bought it like it a lot. But we've only sold 492 units so far. Now we're hearing Holycon Inc. is about to introduce a competing unit called the H-200. Some of our distributors have seen the H-200 and say it's just as good. Holycon has told the distributors they will price at 15 percent below us. In other markets where we've faced Holycon, we've had to be really aggressive in cutting prices in order to keep share. This time, we would like to get ahead of them, and use a preemptive strategy."

Fritz's group manager, Nina Pacofsky, responded: "OK, what do you suggest? And don't forget, we've committed to some very hefty profit goals this year. I'm not ready to tell Division we're not going to make it—especially this early in the year."

"Well, here's what we propose," said Fritz. "Since Holycon has always cut prices in the past, we're going to cut prices first this time and make it hard for them to compete. We propose to cut prices by 30 percent. In order to keep our profitability level, we're going to cut back on advertising. And, we figure that the lower price will not only discourage Holycon, but be so attractive when combined with our features that volume will go way up. We'll actually exceed our projected profit level for the year."

John Fine, the product manager, asked what the awareness level was for Novaton. Fritz didn't know, but Sally Olson found a note in a market research report indicating that awareness was about 25 percent.

Pacofsky hesitated. "Does anyone know if Holycon has actually built manufacturing facilities for their product?"

James Busky, the manufacturing manager, responded: "I heard from an extruder salesman that he had sold two extruders to Holycon. The salesman told me what the extruders were and said they were for a secret project. But, based on the type of extruders, they could only be used to compete with us. And, given the size of the extruders, Holycon's capacity will probably be about 40,000 units per year, almost 60 percent of our capacity."

Pacofsky wanted to know what Holycon's costs were likely to be and also wondered whether Holycon would be able to make any money if Novaton's prices were 30 percent lower.

"Based on our costs, and the fact that Holycon invested two years after us, we believe Holycon will have a margin of 3 percent on sales," said Tom Jeffries, the group competitive intelligence and market research specialist. "Because we were first to market, and customers know us better, we think Holycon will not get enough share to justify its entry. We think they'll drop out of the market if we cut our prices."

"OK," Pacofsky said. "Go ahead with the price cut. We know Holycon always cuts prices, and it's clear we're not getting customers to buy because our prices are too high. Keep me up-to-date on sales. And we've got to keep our profits up."

The meeting adjourned. Mary Fritz headed off to draft new price lists and announcements to the sales force. Heading to her office, she dropped into the advertising manager's office, and asked him to stop all advertising on Novaton.

Source: George E. Cressman Jr., "Snatching Defeat from the Jaws of Victory," *Marketing Management,* Summer 1997, 10. Reprinted with permission of the American Marketing Association.

that while the strategies are sometimes necessary, they should be used with considerable caution.[23] Recall our earlier discussion of the consequences of game theory.

Lack of knowledge about the probable market response of buyers to the new product complicates the pricing decision. Several factors may affect the choice of a pricing approach for a new product, including the cost and life span of the product, the estimated responsiveness of buyers to alternative prices, and assessment of competitive reaction. The dangers of faulty assessment of these factors are illustrated by the RELATIONSHIP APPLICATION about the Novaton product.

A decision should also be made about how visible price will be in the promotion of the new product. The use of a low entry price requires active promotion of the price to gain market position. When firms use a high price relative to cost, price often assumes a passive role in the marketing mix, and performance in combination with other attributes of the product are stressed in the marketing program.

Illustrative Pricing Strategies

The pricing strategy selected depends on how management decides to position the product relative to competition, and whether price will perform an active or passive role in the marketing program. The use of price as an active (or passive) factor refers to whether price is highlighted in advertising, personal selling, and other promotional efforts. Many firms choose neutral pricing strategies (at or near the prices of key competitors), emphasizing non-pricing factors in their marketing strategies.[24] The neutral pricing strategy seeks to remove price as the basis of choosing among competing brands. We examine the four illustrative strategies shown in Exhibit 11.7, describing their characteristics and features.

High-Active Strategy

Emphasizing a high price in promotional activities is intended to convey to the buyer that the expensive brand offers superior value. While used on a very limited basis, this pricing strategy has been employed to symbolically position products such as high-end alcoholic beverages. Making price visible and active can appeal to the buyer's perceptions of quality, image, and dependability of products and services. A firm using a high-price strategy is also less subject to retaliation by competitors, particularly if its brand is differentiated from other brands. Louis Vuitton handbags and accessories are an example of successful high-active pricing strategy.

EXHIBIT 11.7
Role of Price

	Active	Passive
High	High-Active e.g. value superiority	High-Passive e.g. emphasize nonprice competitive factors
Low	Low-Active e.g. discounters	Low-Passive e.g. avoid price comparisons

Role of Price / Price Level

[23]Reed K. Holden and Thomas T. Nagle, "Kamikaze Pricing," *Marketing Management,* Summer 1998, 31–39.
[24]Ibid.

High-Passive Strategy

High prices may be essential to gain the margins necessary to serve small target markets, produce high-quality products, or pay for the development of new products. Relatively high-priced brands are often marketed by featuring nonprice factors rather than using high-active strategies. Product features and performance can be stressed when the people in the target market are concerned with product quality and performance. Expensive Swiss watches are marketed using the high-passive pricing strategy. Illustrative of the importance to these companies of vigorously defending their price positioning, manufacturers of the world's most expensive watches pay high prices to buy back their own watches at auctions to maintain high prices, allowing the launch of high-price new lines without damaging competition from the used watch market.[25]

Low-Active Strategy

Several retailers use this pricing strategy, including Home Depot (home improvement), Dollar General Stores (apparel), Office Depot (office supplies), and Southwest Airlines (air travel). The low-active strategy is also popular with discount stock brokers. When price is an important factor for a large segment of buyers, a low-active price strategy is very effective, as indicated by the rapid growth of discount retailers. It is a more attractive option when competition for the market target is not heavy or when a company has cost advantages and a strong position in the product-market. Southwest Airlines has performed very well using the low-active pricing strategy for its city-to-city route network. Once positioned here, it may be difficult to move. When ConAgra Foods passed on rising costs and drove the retail price of Banquet dinners from $1 to $1.25, consumers stopped buying the product and the company had to cut costs to get back to a $1 dinner, because this appears to be its value positioning in the consumer's mind.[26]

Low-Passive Strategy

This strategy may be used by small producers whose brands are not familiar to buyers and have lower-cost features than other suppliers. By not emphasizing a low price, the firm runs less danger that potential buyers will assume the brand is inferior to other brands. Some firms participating in conventional distribution channels may not spend much on marketing their products and, thus, can offer low prices because of lower costs. An illustration is retailer "secret sales," when customers receive special price offers by e-mail or similar means, thus allowing price cuts without alerting the market to this happening.

The Exhibit 11.7 framework emphasizes the importance of active search and analysis for strategic positioning alternatives which may have been overlooked.

Legal and Ethical Considerations

A wide variety of laws and regulations affect pricing actions. Legal constraints are important influences on the pricing of goods and services in many different national and cooperative regional trade environments. Pricing practices in the United States that have received the most attention from government include:

Price Fixing

A conspiracy among firms to set prices for a product is termed price fixing. Pricing fixing is illegal under the Sherman Act. When two or more competitors collude to explicitly or implicitly set prices, this practice is called *horizontal price fixing*. On the other hand, *vertical price fixing* involves controlling agreements between independent buyers and sellers (a manufacturer and a retailer) whereby sellers are required to not sell products below a

---

[25]B. Bourne, "Auction Dodge Pushes Up Luxury Watch Prices," *Sunday Times,* October 28, 2007, S1, 3.
[26]J. Weber, "Over a Buck for Dinner? Outrageous," *BusinessWeek,* March 9, 2009, 57.

minimum retail price. This practice, called *resale price maintenance,* was declared illegal in 1975 under provisions of the Consumer Goods Pricing Act.

Price Discrimination

The Clayton Act as amended by the Robinson-Patman Act prohibits price discrimination—the practice of charging different prices to different buyers for goods of like grade and quality. However, not all price differences are illegal; only those that substantially lessen competition or create a monopoly are deemed unlawful.

Deceptive Pricing

Price deals that mislead consumers fall into the category of deceptive pricing. Deceptive pricing is outlawed by the Federal Trade Commission. *Bait and switch* is an example of deceptive pricing. This occurs when a firm offers a very low price on a product (the bait) to attract customers to a store. Once in the store, the customer is persuaded to purchase a higher-priced item (the switch) using a variety of tricks, including (1) degrading the promoted item and (2) not having the promised item in stock or refusing to take orders for it.

Predatory Pricing

Predatory pricing is charging a very low price for a product with the intent of driving competitors out of business. Once competitors have been driven out, the firm raises its prices. Proving the presence of this practice has been difficult and expensive because it must be shown that the predator explicitly attempted to destroy a competitor and the predatory price was below the defendant's average cost.[27]

Ethical issues in pricing are more subjective and difficult to evaluate than legal factors. Companies may include ethical guidelines in their pricing policies. Deciding what is or is not ethical is often difficult. Possible ethical issues should be evaluated when developing a pricing strategy.

In some cases, ethical and legal issues may overlap. Consider, for example, Amazon's struggle to avoid adding sales tax to its prices in the United States, described in the ETHICS APPLICATION. The commercial issue is maintaining competitively low prices, the legal issue is unclear, but the moral question is whether the company should be pursuing such active policies designed to avoid sales taxes (and risking damage to its reputation in the process).

Ethics concerning the pricing of prescription drugs are a continuing challenge for the industry. The drug producers are under continuing pressure from consumers, elected officials, and special interest groups concerning high drug prices. Drug pricing raises possible ethical issues, although the companies indicate their high prices are necessary due to large research and development expenses. Price controls have been proposed by consumer groups. The pharmaceutical industry has been criticized for high spending on promotion, public relations, advertising, and drug samples and payments to doctors, and for maintaining high prices in emerging markets where many of the world's poorest consumers live.[28]

Determining Specific Prices and Policies

The last step in pricing strategy (see Exhibit 11.1) is selecting specific prices and formulating policies to help manage the pricing strategy. Pricing methods are first examined, followed by a discussion of pricing policy.

---

[27]Robert A. Kerin, Stephen W. Hartley, and William Rudelius, *Marketing: The Core* (Burr Ridge, IL: McGraw-Hill/Irwin, 2004), 272.
[28]Andrew Jack, "A Sugared Pill," *Financial Times,* March 9, 2011, 11.

Amazon.com, the world's largest online retailer, hasn't charged sales tax in most states in the United States since its inception in 1994.

The company has taken extreme steps to ensure it stays that way: staff traveling around the United States are required to consult a company map that shades each state red, yellow, or green based on their sales tax policies. Amazon staff need permission from a manager to enter "red" states, where a worker's actions might trigger laws that force Amazon to collect taxes in those states. Activities like soliciting new customers and promoting products are banned while in those states. Amazon has ended relationships with affiliates, where that relationship could have obliged the company to charge sales taxes in those states.

Credit Suisse estimates that if Amazon were forced to collect sales taxes in all U.S. states, it would lose as much as $650 million in sales a year.

As an online retailer, Amazon says it is obliged to charge taxes only on purchases from residents of states where Amazon has physical retail operations (warehouses do not count). The business model is designed not to have to collect state sales taxes.

Several chain retailers, including bookstore Borders Group Inc. have also tried to avoid charging sales tax online, arguing online sales were separate from regular retail, but have been blocked. Borders is looking at bankruptcy and liquidation. Several online retailers, smaller than Amazon, charge sales taxes in states where they have warehouses.

Legal experts say that Amazon's approach is aggressive but within the law.

Source: Adapted from: Stu Woo, "Amazon Battles States in U.S. Over Uncollected Sales Tax," *Wall Street Journal,* August 4, 2011, 14–15.

Determining Specific Prices

It is necessary to either assign a specific price to each product item or to provide a method for computing price for a particular buyer-seller transaction. Many methods and techniques are available for calculating price.

Price determination is normally based on *cost, demand, competition,* or a *combination* of these factors. Cost-oriented methods use the cost of producing and marketing the product as the basis for determining price. Demand-oriented pricing methods consider estimated market response to alternative prices. The most profitable combination of price and market response level is selected. Competition-oriented methods use competitors' prices as a reference point in setting prices. The price selected may be above, below, or equal to competitors' prices. Typically, one method (cost, demand, or competition) provides the primary basis for pricing, although the other factors are also considered.

Cost-Oriented Approaches

Break-even pricing is a cost-oriented approach that may be used to determine prices. The initial computation is as follows:

$$\text{Break-even (units)} = \text{Total fixed costs divided by Unit price} - \text{Unit variable cost}$$

When using this method, we select a price and calculate the number of units that must be sold at that price to cover all fixed and variable costs. Management must assess the feasibility of exceeding the break-even level of sales to generate a profit. One or more possible prices may be evaluated. Break-even analysis is not a complete basis for determining price, since both demand and competition are important considerations in the pricing decision. With break-even price as a frame of reference, demand and competition can be evaluated. The price selected is at some level higher than the break-even price.

Another popular cost-oriented pricing method is cost-plus pricing. This technique uses cost as the basis of calculating the selling price. A percentage amount of the cost is added to cost to determine price. A similar method, popular in retailing, markup pricing, calculates markups as a percentage of the selling price. When using markup pricing, this formula determines the selling price.

$$Price = Average\ unit\ cost\ divided\ by\ (1 - Markup\ percent)*$$

*Percent expressed in decimal form.

Competition-Oriented Approaches

Pricing decisions are always affected by competitors' prices and their potential actions. Pricing methods that use competitors' prices in calculating actual prices include setting prices equal to or at some specified increment above or below the competition's prices. In industries such as air travel, one of the firms may be viewed by others as the price leader. When the leader changes its prices, other firms follow with similar prices. American Airlines has attempted to perform such a leadership role in the United States, although its pricing changes are not always adopted by competing airlines. Another form of competition-oriented pricing is competitive bidding where firms submit sealed bids to the purchaser. This method is used in the purchase of various industrial products and supplies.

Reverse auction pricing is an interesting competitive form of Internet pricing. Buyers benefit through savings and suppliers expand their market coverage. This method of determining price involves sellers bidding for organizational buyers' purchases.

Many times, supplier performance is rated, and these ratings are presented by the site as a benefit to current and prospective buyers. Freemarkets.com conducts online auctions of industrial parts, raw materials, commodities, and services. Suppliers bid lower prices in real time until the auction is closed to fill the purchase orders of large buying organizations.[29]

The sharing of information benefits both buyers and sellers, although the buyer controls the process. The underlying logic is that prices continue to fall due to declining bids until a stable market price is reached.

While considering competitive price levels is a necessary part of setting prices effectively, it is important to avoid any form of collusion or cooperation with competitors in setting prices. In most parts of the world such practices are illegal and offenders face severe punishments if these practices are detected by regulatory authorities.

Demand-Oriented Approaches

The buyer is the frame of reference for these methods. One popular method is estimating the value of the product to the buyer. The objective is to determine how much the buyer is willing to pay for the product based on its contribution to the buyer's needs or wants. Recall our earlier discussion of estimating value provided to the customer (EVM). This approach is used for both consumer and business products. Information on demand and price relationships is needed in guiding demand-oriented pricing decisions. Internet auction pricing is a demand-oriented method of pricing.

Many pricing methods are in use, so it is important to select specific prices within the guidelines provided by price strategy and to incorporate demand, cost, and competition considerations. Other sources provide extensive coverage of pricing decisions.[30]

---

[29]Jeffrey F. Rayport and Bernard J. Jaworski, *e-Commerce* (New York: McGraw-Hill/Irwin, 2001), 157.

[30]See, for example, Monroe, *Pricing;* and Thomas T. Nagle and Reed K. Holden, *The Strategy and Tactics of Pricing,* 3rd ed. (Englewood Cliffs, NJ: Prentice Hall, 2002).

Establishing Pricing Policy and Structure

Determining price flexibility, positioning price against competition, and deciding how active price will be in the marketing program do not provide the operating guidelines necessary for implementing the pricing strategy. Policy guidelines must be determined for use in guiding pricing decisions and pricing structure.

Pricing Policy

A pricing policy may include consideration of discounts, allowances, returns, and other operating guidelines. The policy serves as the basis for implementing and managing the pricing strategy. The policy may be in written form, although many companies operate without formal pricing policies.

Pricing Structure

When more than one product item is involved, management must determine product mix and line-pricing interrelationships in order to establish price structure. Pricing structure concerns how individual items in the line are priced in relation to one another: The items may be aimed at the same market target or different end-user groups. For example, department stores often offer lower priced store brands and premium national brands. In the case of a single product category, price differences among the product items typically reflect more than variations in costs. For example, commercial airlines must work with an array of fares in the pricing structure.

Once product relationships are established, some basis for determining the price structure must be selected. Many firms base price structure on market and competitive factors as well as differences in the costs of producing each item. Some use multiple criteria for determining price structure and have sophisticated computer models to examine alternate pricing schemes. American Airlines' revenue management system is illustrative. Other companies use rules of thumb developed from experience.

Most product line pricing approaches include both cost considerations and demand and competitive concerns. For example, industrial-equipment manufacturers sometimes price new products at or close to cost and depend on sales of high-margin items such as supplies, parts, and replacement items to generate profits. The important consideration is to price the entire mix and line of products to achieve pricing objectives.

Pricing Management

Pricing strategy is an ongoing process rather than a once-a-year budgeting activity. Several principles of pricing management are outlined in Exhibit 11.8. Importantly, pricing strategy is an interrelated process requiring central management direction and control.

Special pricing situations may occur in particular industries, markets, and competitive environments. Some examples follow.

Price Segmentation

Price may be used to appeal to different market segments. For example, airline prices vary depending on the conditions of purchase. Different versions of the same basic product may be offered at different prices to reflect differences in materials and product features. Recall our earlier discussion of Intel's PC chip strategy. Industrial-products firms may use quantity discounts to respond to differences in the quantities purchased by customers. Price elasticity differences make it feasible to appeal to different segments.

Value-Chain Pricing

The pricing strategies of sellers in the value chain should include consideration of the pricing needs (e.g., flexibility and incentives) of producers and facilitating firms (e.g., wholesalers).

EXHIBIT 11.8
Managing Pricing Strategy

Source: Adapted from Kent B. Monroe, *Pricing*, 3rd ed. (Burr Ridge, IL: McGraw-Hill/Irwin, 2003) 624–626.

1. The more that competitors and customers know about your pricing, the better off you are. In an information age, it is necessary to be transparent about prices and the value of a firm's offerings.
2. In highly competitive markets, the focus should be on those market segments that provide opportunities to gain competitive advantage. Such a focus leads to a value-oriented pricing approach.
3. Pricing decisions should be made within the context of an overall marketing strategy that is embedded within a business or corporate strategy.
4. Successful pricing decisions are profit oriented, not sales volume or market share oriented.
5. Prices should be set according to customers' perceptions of value.
6. Pricing for new products should start as soon as product development begins.
7. The relevant costs for pricing are the incremental avoidable costs.
8. A price may be profitable when it provides for incremental revenues in excess of incremental costs.
9. A central organizing unit should administer the pricing function. Generally, it is better to avoid letting salespeople set price, especially without access to profitability information and specific training in pricing and revenue management.
10. Pricing management should be viewed as a process and price setting as a daily management activity, not a once-a-year activity.

These decisions require analysis of cost and pricing at all value-chain levels. If producer prices to intermediaries are too high, inadequate margins may discourage intermediaries from actively promoting the producer's brand. Margins vary based on the nature and importance of the added value that intermediaries in the channel are expected to provide. For example, margins between costs and selling prices must be large enough to compensate a wholesaler for carrying a complete stock of replacement parts. When a firm uses more than one distribution channel, the question of price differences between channels also has to be considered.

Price Flexibility

Will prices be firm, or will they be negotiated between buyer and seller? Perhaps most important, firms should make price flexibility a policy decision rather than a tactical response. Some companies' price lists are very rigid, while others have list prices that give no indication of actual selling prices. It is also important to recognize the legal and ethical issues in pricing products when using flexible pricing policies.

When considering reducing prices it is important to estimate how operating profits will be impacted. Estimates of how operating profits will be reduced for a 1 percent price cut provided by McKinsey & Co. consultants are 24 percent for food stores and drugstores, 13 percent for airlines, and 11 percent for computers and office equipment.[31] Smaller operating profit decreases are estimated for tobacco (5 percent) and diversified financials (2.4 percent).

Product Life Cycle Pricing

Some companies have policies to guide pricing decisions over the life cycle of the product. Depending on its stage in the product life cycle, the price of a particular product or an entire line may be based on market share, profitability, cash flow, or other objectives. In many product-markets, price declines (in constant dollars) as the product moves through its life cycle. Because of life-cycle considerations, different objectives and policies may apply to particular products within a mix or line. Price becomes a more active element

---

[31] Janice Revall, "The Price Is Not Always Right," *Fortune*, May 14, 2001, 240.

of strategy as products move through the life cycle and competitive pressures build, costs decline, and volume increases. Life-cycle pricing strategy should be consistent with the overall marketing program positioning strategy used.

Global Issues in Pricing

Developing a global perspective concerning the pricing strategies for many products is increasingly important. Global perspectives on price include both the challenges of pricing in overseas markets and those related to meeting international competition in the domestic marketplace. This priority is underlined by the impact of global customers demanding coherent pricing policies across their international purchasing (see Chapter 7 for a discussion of global customer relationships). The existence of powerful value chain members able to exert considerable influence over other members of the value chain also characterizes some global markets (recall the Chapter 7 discussion of concentration in the European grocery retail business compared to that in the United States).

Pricing Regulation and Restriction in Global Markets

Importantly, while companies in the United States have considerable freedom in making pricing choices and setting their own prices, this freedom of maneuver is often not found in global markets. For example, when conditions pushed food price high in Asia, the Chinese government intervened, mandating producers of "general necessities" should register with local price bureaux if they wanted to increase prices, moving toward centralized government price control. Similarly, Russia imposed food price controls in its territories at this time. The Chinese government continues to control prices for key economic inputs, including power, oil, gas, and water. The wholesale price of grain is also regulated in China.[32]

Though less extreme than these emerging market illustrations, the convention of being able to freely set prices is relatively recent even in much of Europe. The GLOBAL APPLICATION describes the restrictions on retail pricing and competition for Christmas in several European countries. This environment is considerably different from that in the United States and requires careful consideration by companies operating globally.

The Impact of Emerging Markets

In a growing number of sectors, it is important to understand the impact on developed country markets like the United States, Europe, and Japan, of products produced in BRICPlus countries. (BRICPlus includes leading emerging markets Brazil, Russia, India, and China, but also rapidly growing countries with similar emerging market characteristics, such as Mexico, Indonesia, and South Africa.) Recall the discussion in Chapter 8 of "trickle-up" innovation, where products developed and produced in emerging markets enter the global market, typically at very low prices. BRICPlus countries can effectively compete with very low wages coupled with high-technology capabilities, and produce a growing range of consumer and business products. In countries like China, competitive edge is further strengthened by an enormous domestic market.[33]

Nonetheless, it should be recognized that in some cases very low product prices from emerging markets may be associated with undesirable employment conditions for local workers, unattractive levels of environmental pollution by production units, and compromised

---

[32]Raphael Minder and Joe Leahy, "Asia Battles with Surging Food Costs," *Financial Times,* January 10, 2008, 9. Richard McGregor and Javiar Blas, "Beijing Pledges Action to Rein in Soaring Staples," *Financial Times,* January 10, 2008, 9.
[33]Pete Engardio and Dexter Roberts, "The China Price," *BusinessWeek,* December 6, 2004, 104–105.

- In contrast to the United States, where pre-Christmas price cuts are a key part of retailers' strategies and shoppers' plans, holiday sales are a revolution in European retailing.
- For decades, European retailers could cut prices only during certain periods set by the government. Winter sales were in the new year, not at Christmas.
  - German law changed in 2004 to allow stores to hold sales when they pleased, but most retailers kept prices high in the holiday season.
  - German law still mandates by its "Price Labelling Decree" that anything in a shop window must carry a price tag so consumers instantly know an item's affordability.
  - In France, the government still regulates the setting of retail prices and sets minimum prices that retailers must pay suppliers.
  - In Germany, it took years of debate to eliminate laws that prohibited haggling and put limits on bonus schemes like store-loyalty cards—designed to protect small shopkeepers from large stores.
- Some retailers in Europe like Galeries Lafayette in Paris and Harrods in London still stick to a full-priced Christmas, on the grounds it makes little sense to discount when people are desperate to buy.
- In many European countries, the hours stores are open is also regulated by local and central government—even in Britain, one of the most deregulated European states, stores can only open 6 hours on Sundays.
- The European retail situation is changing as a result of European Union efforts to harmonize states' laws, the impact of global competition, and the rise of Internet retailing.

Source: Cecilie Rohwedder, "European Shoppers Enjoy Novelty: Christmas Sales," *Wall Street Journal,* December 24–26, 2007, 1–2.

standards in product safety and quality.[34] Consumer criticisms of the social responsibility stance of fashion retailers sourcing products in very low cost markets is illustrative. Major product recalls, like those implemented by Mattel in the toys industry in 2007 because of lead paint contaminating Barbie doll accessories, and the recall of household textiles contaminated with cancer-causing chemicals are illustrative of the problems that may be faced in sourcing products from emerging markets. However, the demand from consumers for very low price products remains strong, and showed clear signs of increasing during the economic downturn of the late-2000s.

Relationships between companies in the West and emerging markets are frequently framed by ethical considerations. Recall the earlier discussion of the pricing of prescription pharmaceuticals and the criticism of companies that maintain globally uniform prices, so poor customers pay as much as rich customers across the world. Furthermore, consider the

---

[34]Tom Braithwaite, "Delays in Toyshops as Chinese Retest Stocks," *Financial Times,* Thursday August 30, 2007, 4. Peter Smith, "Scare Spurs Australian Crackdown on Clothing and Textiles," *Financial Times,* Friday August 24, 2007, 7. Claire Newell and Robert Winnett, "Revealed: Topshop Clothes Made with 'Slave Labour,' " *Sunday Times,* August 12, 2007, S1, 3.

- The global tobacco industry supports about 100,000 jobs worldwide and duties on tobacco products provide huge tax revenues for governments throughout the developed world.
- Tobacco companies describe their product as "a legal and widely enjoyed consumer product," while also recognizing that cigarette smoking poses a severe health risk for both users and "passive smokers."
- Cigarette smoking is declining in many developed countries, but remains at high levels in the developing world.
- The industry is implementing several important initiatives in the developing world: campaigns against child labor in tobacco cultivation; is involved in programs to alleviate indigenous diseases in developing countries; encourages environmental protection.
- The dilemma is whether tobacco companies should be actively supporting cigarette smoking in developing countries, and the role of low-priced brands in developing these markets, compared to the effects of tobacco cultivation industry of declining demand.
- Industry response to this dilemma has been to actively promote the switch by developing country tobacco users to more expensive global brands to replace cheaper local brands.
- The only point of agreement between the World Health Organization and the tobacco industry is consensus that there will be more people smoking in the world in 2050 than there are now (driven mainly by population growth in the developing countries).
- These dilemmas are shared with companies who transport and retail tobacco products.

Sources: Pan Kwan Yuk, "Cooper to Focus on Sales Growth As She Takes Imperial's Helm," *Financial Times,* November 11, 2009, 20. Hannah Kuchler, "BAT Benefits from Increased Cigarette Prices," *Financial Times,* February 26, 2010, 22. Rose Jacobs, "Emerging Markets Light up BAT Sales," *Financial Times,* July 29, 2010, 18.

dilemma, for example, facing executives in the tobacco industry and those associated with it, regarding the low pricing of cigarettes in the developing world described in the ETHICS APPLICATION. Emerging markets are attractive prospects for tobacco companies, but pricing at levels that maintain or increase smoking in those countries is morally questionable.

Global Competition from Emerging Market Multinationals

It is also important to recognize that in some sectors global companies from emerging markets may be better prepared to cater for the growing value-for-money segment in post-recession markets in developed countries like the United States, than are Western multinationals. Strong Asian companies like Haier, Cery, and Tata have skills in providing high-value products at very low prices to choosy middle-class Asian customers, and they are quickly bringing their price-oriented propositions to global markets.[35]

For example, Tata produces the lowest-price automobile in the world in India. The development of the Nano is described in the GLOBAL APPLICATION. Produced for the domestic India market, there is no sign yet that the Nano will be marketed overseas but the potential clearly exists. That potential is for a very low price automobile disrupting the auto market in Africa and Latin America, and even parts of Europe and the United States, because it is unlikely that major auto companies in the West can produce a comparable vehicle at this price level. This will be very challenging competition, and competing with the Nano on price will be very difficult.

---

[35]Peter J. Williamson and Ming Zeng, "Value-for-Money Strategies for Recessionary Times," *Harvard Business Review,* March 2009, 66–77.

The Indian auto market is small—one-sixth the size of China's—but growing fast.

Tata Motors is part of the powerful Indian conglomerate Tata Group—98 operating companies and joint ventures that fit seven business sectors.

In 2009, Tata Motors in Mumbai unveiled the Nano—which aspires to be the peoples' car for the developing world. The Nano is the lowest-priced auto in the world.

Priced at one Lakh ($2,900) the Nano is designed to lure India's growing middle class away from their bicycles and motor scooters and into safe, family-sized, weatherproof vehicles.

The Nano had a rocky start—production had to move location within India, sales peaked at 9,000 a month but then fell away requiring additional sales efforts, and there were technical modifications needed. Even by 2011, Nano sales were disappointing, and the company was still looking at how to expand into rural India.

The Nano contains many cost-saving tricks—three lugs instead of four holding the wheels on; multitasking components (e.g., the brace holding the front seats in place also serves as side-impact protection); no radio; no airbags; only one windshield wiper; and the tiny engine is located under the back seat and accessible only by unscrewing six wing nuts.

Labor is Tata's big operational lever—on the final trim line, where Nano seats, instrument panels, and doors are installed, men do the work instead of machines and there is only one robot. Low labor costs gives the Nano a major competitive advantage.

Tata already has thoughts about the Nano in the U.S. market—a more potent version selling for $7,000–$8,000 with a bigger engine, wider stance, and better crash protection.

At the 2011 Geneva Car Show, Tata unveiled an experimental, very small, Indian-built vehicle, roughly the same size as the Nano. Tata has yet to decide whether to launch the concept car in Europe.

Sources: John Reed, "Tata Woos Europe with Micro Concept," *Financial Times,* February 28, 2011, 24. Alex Taylor, "Tata Takes on the World," *Fortune,* May 2, 2011, 61–65. James Fontanella-Khan and James Lamont, "Tata Loses Tread on Domestic Sales," *Financial Times,* August 12, 2011, 16.

Summary

The challenging role of pricing strategies is underlined by pressures from global competition, as well as difficulties in altering prices once they are established and regulatory restrictions on executives' pricing actions. However, price plays a very important role in business strategy. The strategic role of price is underlined by its impact on positioning strategy—particularly relating to product strategy choices and distribution channels. An important question relates to the location of responsibility for pricing decisions, and the need to coordinate tactical and strategic pricing decisions with other aspects of marketing strategy. Pricing requires continuous review because of changing external conditions, competitive moves, and the emergence of opportunities to gain competitive advantage through pricing actions.

Importantly, price plays a number of roles in the market-driven program, acting as a signal to the buyer, providing a competitive mechanism, offering a means to impact financial performance, and acting as a substitute for other marketing program functions. Major steps in constructing a pricing strategy are determining pricing objectives, analyzing the pricing situation, selecting the pricing strategy, and determining specific prices and policies.

Pricing objectives vary according to company priorities and other situational factors, such as intensity of competition and economic conditions, and may address different goals. Analysis of the pricing situation examines the level of customer price sensitivity, product costs, existing and anticipated competitive actions, and pricing objectives. The selection of a pricing strategy must be based on the degree of pricing flexibility that exists for the company with the product and the market being targeted, and the positioning impact of price on the product. Several opportunities exist for combining the role of price visibility in strategy with price level. An extremely important context for selecting pricing strategy is the legal and ethical issues surrounding price. Regulation in most countries prohibits competitors from setting price levels, price discrimination between different buyers, deceptive pricing, and predatory pricing to drive competitors from business. In addition to legal considerations, ethical and moral questions also confront executives in choosing prices.

The determination of specific prices may be based on costs, competition, and/or demand influences. Implementing and managing the pricing strategy also includes establishing pricing policy and structure. Finally, management of pricing strategy is an interrelated process that must be managed on a continuing basis. Several special pricing considerations include price segmentation, distribution channel pricing, price flexibility, and product life-cycle pricing. Pricing for global markets introduces a further set of issues for executives to examine.

Questions for Review and Discussion

1. Discuss the role of price in the marketing strategy for Rolex watches. Contrast Timex's price strategy with Rolex's strategy.
2. The Toyota Camry and the Lexus ES 330 are very similar but the ES 330 is priced substantially higher than the Camry. Discuss the features and limitations of this pricing strategy.
3. Indicate how a fast-food chain can estimate the price elasticity of a proposed new product such as a new chicken sandwich.
4. Real estate brokers typically charge a fixed percentage of a home's sales price. Advertising agencies follow a similar price strategy. Discuss why this may be sound price strategy. What are the arguments against it from the buyer's point of view?
5. Cite examples of businesses to which the experience-curve effect may not be applicable. What influence may this have on price determination?
6. In some industries prices are set low, subsidies are provided, and other price-reducing mechanisms are used to establish a long-term relationship with the buyer. Utilities, for example, sometimes use incentives to encourage contractors to install electric- or gas-powered appliances. Manufacturers may price equipment low, then depend on service and parts for profit contribution. What are the advantages and limitations of this pricing strategy?
7. Discuss why it is important to consider pricing from a strategic rather than a tactical perspective.
8. Discuss some of the ways that estimates of the costs of competitors' products can be determined.
9. Discuss how a pricing strategy should be developed by a software firm to price its business-analysis software line.
10. Suppose a firm is considering changing from a low-active price strategy to a high-active strategy. Discuss the implications of this proposed change.
11. Describe and evaluate the price strategy used for the Lexus 430 European-style luxury sedan.

Internet Applications

A. Explore the website of British Airways (www.ba.com). Consider how the website can facilitate price discrimination.
B. Visit the website of Amazon.com. Evaluate Amazon's pricing strategy. How do its prices compare to those of "brick and mortar" retailers? Critically evaluate the company's product offering and identify potential market segments.
C. Visit the Oracle.com website. Discuss how Oracle considers price in the information provided for its business process software suite.

D. Study the information available from Starbucks' website (www.starbucks.com). Discuss how the website enhances the firm's ability to obtain premium prices.

Applications

A. From the RELATIONSHIP APPLICATION, develop a list of the pricing issues faced by the executives at Novet. What are the arguments that can be made for avoiding the price cutting option?

B. Consider the INNOVATION APPLICATION describing new approaches to the way in which price is presented to customers as part of the value proposition. What other ways can you identify for reinventing the price component of a company's value offering? Are there ways of extending the approaches described in the APPLICATION into other sectors?

Chapter

12

Promotion, Advertising, and Sales Promotion Strategies

The purpose of promotion strategy is to manage the organization's communications initiatives, coordinating and integrating advertising, personal selling, sales promotion, interactive/Internet marketing, direct marketing, and public relations to communicate with buyers and others who influence purchasing decisions. The promotion strategies of many companies are encountering rapid changes and challenges due to the availability of alternative communications channels, rapidly changing markets and competitive space, customer relationship management initiatives, and global expansion of markets. Billions are spent every week around the world on the various promotion activities. Effective management of these expensive resources is essential to gain the optimum return from the promotion expenditures. Integrating the promotion components into a consistent overall strategy requires close coordination across the responsible units in the organization.

Google provides an interesting perspective on how promotion strategy is changing.[1] It is the world's largest search engine. The search engine has transformed itself into a media octopus, generating revenues primarily by delivering targeted advertising. Google has a 31 percent share of online advertising revenue. Revenues have increased from $10.6 billion in 2006 to an estimated $40 billion in 2012. Initially Google linked keywords to advertisers' text ads, and then expanded into print advertising, purchasing print ad space in magazines and selling the space to its ad customers. The company moved into radio ad buying and is testing TV ads. Google's Click-to-Call enables people with Internet phone service to connect to an advertiser's call center. Google's YouTube service is doing well. Driving these initiatives are its more than 25,000 employees. Google's popularity with advertisers is based on cost and accountability of expenditures.

---

[1]This illustration is based on *The Value Line Investment Survey, Ratings, & Reports,* Issue 13, May 20, 2011, 2627; Robert D. Hof, "Is Google Too Powerful?" *BusinessWeek,* April 19, 2007, 47–55; David Kiley, "Google: Searching for an Edge in Ads," *BusinessWeek,* January 20, 2006, 80–92.

The communications activities that make up promotion strategy inform people about products and persuade the company's buyers, value-chain organizations, and the public at large to purchase brands. The objective is to combine the promotion components into an integrated strategy for communicating with buyers and others who influence purchasing decisions. Since each component has certain strengths and shortcomings, an integrated strategy incorporates the advantages of each component into a cost-effective promotion mix.[2]

First, we review promotion strategy and examine the decisions that are involved in designing the strategy. The intent is to develop an integrated view of communications strategy to which each of the promotion components contributes. Next, we discuss each component beginning with the major decisions that comprise advertising strategy and the factors affecting advertising decisions. The final section considers the design and implementation of sales promotion strategies. Personal selling, direct marketing, and Internet strategies are discussed in Chapter 13.

Promotion Strategy

Promotion strategy consists of planning, implementing, and controlling an organization's communications to its customers and other target audiences. The purpose of promotion in the marketing program is to achieve management's desired communications objectives with each audience. An important marketing responsibility is planning and coordinating the integrated promotion strategy and selecting the specific strategies for each of the promotion components. Word-of-mouth communications among buyers and the communications activities of other organizations may also influence the firm's target audience(s).

The Composition of Promotion Strategy

Advertising

Global advertising expenditure for 2011 is estimated at $484 billion, with the greatest growth being shown in the Asia Pacific region, Central and Eastern Europe, and Latin America, and declines in North America and Western Europe over earlier years.[3] Estimates for Internet advertising reached $72 billion for 2011, with online expenditure almost doubling in the period 2007–11.[4] The five years up to 2011 also saw declining expenditure on newspaper, magazine, and radio advertising, but some growth in television spending. Interestingly, mobile advertising expenditure (placing advertising on cell phones and smart phone devices) was $3.3 billion in 2011, but is expected to grow to $21 billion by 2015, with spending dominated by the Asia Pacific region and Japan.[5] In 2011 the United States

---

[2]George E. Belch and Michael A. Belch, *Advertising and Promotion: An Integrated Marketing Communications Perspective,* 9th ed. (Burr Ridge, IL: Irwin/McGraw-Hill, 2011).

[3]ZenithOptimedia Advertising Expenditure Forecasts, www.phorm.com/assets/reports/AdvertisingExpenditure, accessed August 22, 2011.

[4]ZenithOptimedia, ibid.

[5]MobiThinking, "Global Mobile Statistics 2011," www.mobithinking.com/mobile-marketing-tools/latest-mobile-stats, accessed August 22, 2011.

accounted for around 33 percent of global expenditure on advertising, with Western Europe and Asia Pacific each accounting for 24 percent of world-wide spending.[6] Advertisers are shifting expenditure away from traditional media like print and primetime television.

Among the advantages of using advertising to communicate with buyers are the low cost per exposure, the variety of media (newspapers, magazines, television, radio, Internet, direct mail, and outdoor advertising), control of exposure, consistent message content, and the opportunity for creative message design. In addition, the appeal and message can be adjusted when communications objectives change. Internet advertising enables advertisers to target their communications to specific buyers with more focus than other media options. Advertising also has some disadvantages. It cannot interact with the buyer and may not be able to hold viewers' attention. Moreover, the message is fixed for the duration of an exposure.

Personal Selling

Personal selling consists of verbal communication between a salesperson (or selling team) and one or more prospective purchasers with the objective of making or influencing a sale. Annual expenditures on personal selling are much larger than on advertising. U.S. firms spend nearly three times as much on their sales organizations compared to advertising.[7] Importantly, both promotion components share some common features, including creating awareness of the brand, transmitting information, and persuading people to buy. Business-to-business salespeople's compensation and supervision are likely to cost $125,000 or more per person each year. The cost of a sales call may be $400 or more for industrial goods and services, and, typically, multiple calls are necessary to sell the product.[8] Personal selling has several unique strengths: salespeople can interact with buyers to answer questions and overcome objections, they can target buyers, and they have access to market and competitor knowledge and provide feedback.

Sales Promotion

Sales promotion consists of various promotional activities including trade shows, contests, samples, point-of-purchase displays, product placement in films and other media, trade incentives, and coupons. Sales promotion expenditures are much greater than spending on advertising, and as large as sales force expenditures. This array of special communications techniques and incentives offers several advantages: sales promotion can be used to target buyers, respond to special occasions, and create an incentive for purchase. Sales promotion activities may be targeted to consumers, value-chain members, or employees (e.g., salespeople). An active sales promotion initiative is the placement of branded products in films, magazines, videogames and music, and TV.[9] A CBS TV executive estimates that three-fourths of all scripted prime-time network programs will include paid product placement. Expenditures for product placement were less than $5 billion in 2006 but were growing. The expanded use of product placement is because of its appeal to advertisers and television firms' interest in supplementing revenues lost to internet advertising. Pricing and other operating guidelines are fragmented.

Direct Marketing

Direct marketing includes the various communications channels that enable companies to make direct contact with individual buyers. Examples are catalogs, direct mail, telemarketing,

[6]ZenithOptimedia, ibid.

[7]A. A. Zoltners, P. Sinha, and S. E. Lorimer, *Building a Winning Sales Force: Powerful Strategies for Driving High Performance* (New York: AMA COM, 2009).

[8]Mark W. Johnston and Greg W. Marshall, *Sales Force Management,* 9th ed. (Burr Ridge, IL: McGraw-Hill/Irwin, 2009), 47.

[9]"Lights, Camera, Brands," *The Economist,* October 29, 2005, 61–62.

SEARCH WORKS

Google and Yahoo! have demonstrated the power of the Web by using customers' search queries to connect them with advertisers.

CUSTOMERS ARE ONLINE

More than half of American households have always-on Net connections. And the Web reaches millions at the office. The Big Three portals—Yahoo, AOL, and MSN—reach a combined 50 million a day—twice the TV audience of a World Series game.

VIDEO ROCKS

The adoption of broadband, which can handle videos, lets advertisers put TV-like ads online. Longer spots by BMW and Adidas have reached cult status. As demand for video soars, portals sell choice slots in advance, much like TV's up-front sales.

FEEDBACK IS INSTANT

Marketers and online publishers have tools to track an ad's performance in real time, allowing them to make quick adjustments if customers aren't clicking. This turns the Net into a vast marketing lab. And as video grows, it becomes a test bed for TV ads.

CUSTOMERS LEAVE TRAILS

It was an empty promise during the dot-com days, but now advertisers have the technology to follow customers, click by click, and to hit them with relevant ads. The upshot? No wasted money peddling dog food to cat owners.

Source: Stephen Baker, "The On-line Ad Surge," *BusinessWeek,* November 22, 2004, 79.

television selling, radio/magazine/newspaper selling, and electronic shopping. The distinguishing feature of direct marketing is the opportunity for the marketer to gain direct access to the buyer. Direct marketing expenditures account for an increasingly large portion of promotion expenditures.

Interactive/Internet Marketing

Included in this promotion component are the Internet, mobile telephones and devices, CD-ROM, kiosks, and interactive television. Interactive media enable buyers and sellers to communicate with each other. The Internet performs an important and rapidly escalating role in promotion strategy. In addition to providing a direct sales channel, the Internet may be used to identify sales leads, conduct Web-based surveys, provide product information, and display advertisements. The Internet is the platform for a complete business strategy in the case of Internet business models. Marketing strategies are increasingly linked to Internet initiatives.

Interestingly, while Internet ad spending is much less than TV spending, U.S. households spend about the same amount of time viewing each medium.[10] This points to the strong interest of advertisers concerning Internet advertising. Moreover, Internet advertising is booming. The INTERNET APPLICATION highlights several reasons for advertisers' strong interest in the Internet.

---

[10]"Target Practice," *The Economist,* April 2, 2005, 13.

Public Relations

Public relations for a company and its products consist of communications placed in the commercial media at no charge to the company receiving the publicity. For example, a news release on a new product may be published in a trade magazine. The media coverage is an article or news item. The objective of the public relations department is to encourage relevant media to include company-released information in media communications. Public relations activities can make an important contribution to promotion strategy when the activity is planned and implemented to achieve specific promotion objectives. (Public relations activities are also used for publicity purposes such as communicating with financial analysts.) Publicity in the media can be negative as well as positive and cannot be controlled by the organization to the same extent as other promotion components. Since a company does not purchase the media coverage, public relations is a cost-effective method of communication. The media are usually willing to cover topics of public interest. Many companies retain public relations consultants who proactively pursue opportunities to feature their companies and brands. For many companies the active management of "corporate reputation" is a public relations priority because reputation impacts on many of the stakeholders in the company.

Designing Promotion Strategy

Market target and positioning strategies guide promotion decisions as shown in Exhibit 12.1. Several activities are involved in designing an organization's promotion strategy including (1) setting communication objectives; (2) deciding the role each of the components makes in the promotion program; (3) estimating the promotion budget; (4) selecting the strategy for each promotion component; (5) integrating and implementing the promotion component strategies; and (6) evaluating the effectiveness of the integrated promotion strategies. Specific strategies must be determined for advertising, personal selling, sales promotion, direct marketing, Internet, and public relations, and these promotion components need to be carefully integrated and coordinated to achieve communication objectives.

EXHIBIT 12.1
Designing Promotion Strategy

MARKET TARGETING AND POSITIONING STRATEGIES
▽
COMMUNICATION OBJECTIVES
▽
ROLE OF PROMOTION COMPONENTS
▽

Advertising | Sales Promotion | Public Relations | Personal Selling | Direct Marketing | Interactive/Internet Marketing

PROMOTION BUDGET
▽
PROMOTION COMPONENT STRATEGIES ◁ Coordination with Product, Value Chain, and Pricing Strategies
▽
INTEGRATE AND IMPLEMENT STRATEGIES FOR THE COMPONENTS
▽
EVALUATE EFFECTIVENESS OF PROMOTION STRATEGY

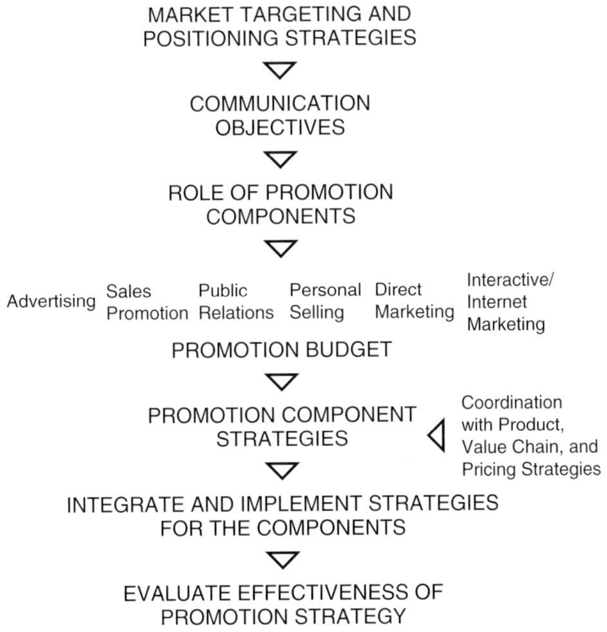

Market targets and product, distribution, and price decisions provide a frame of reference for (1) deciding the role of promotion strategy in the total marketing program and (2) identifying the specific communications tasks of the promotion activities. One important question is deciding the role that the promotion strategy will play in marketing strategy. Advertising and personal selling are often a major part of a firm's marketing strategy. In consumer package goods firms, sales promotion and advertising comprise a large portion of the promotion program. In industrial firms, personal selling often dominates the promotion strategy, with advertising and sales promotion playing a supporting role. The use of sales promotion and public relations varies considerably among companies. The role of direct marketing also differs across companies and industries.

Interestingly, Singapore Airlines performs an important promotion role in marketing the city-nation. The airline is consistently one of the more profitable global airlines, although much smaller than the major carriers.[11] The airline's favorable brand position helps to position the country with executives, government officials, and tourists who experience Singapore Airline's renowned services. The tiny city-state with a small population has a strong brand image, enhanced by the airline's favorable reputation with customers and competitors throughout the world. The airline's advertising in business and travel magazines is designed to favorably position its distinctive bundle of values. Global air travel was expected to double in 2010 compared to 1990, and much of the growth is in Asia.

Communication Objectives

Communication objectives help determine how the promotion strategy components are used in the marketing program. Several illustrative communication objectives follow.

Need Recognition

A communication objective, which is important for new-product introductions, is to trigger a need. Need recognition may also be important for existing products and services, particularly when the buyer can postpone purchasing or choose not to purchase (such as life insurance). For example, P&G emphasized the need to control dandruff in its advertising of Head & Shoulders shampoo in China. The ads focused attention on how dandruff is very visible on people with black hair.

Finding Buyers

Promotion activities can be used to identify buyers. The message seeks to get the prospective buyer to respond. The Internet plays a pivotal role in obtaining instant feedback. Salespeople may be given responsibility for identifying and screening prospects. The use of toll-free numbers is often helpful in identifying customers as well as issues and problems of interest to the callers.

Brand Building

Promotion can aid a buyer's search for information. One of the objectives of new product promotional activities is to help buyers learn about the product. Prescription drug companies advertise to the public to make people aware of diseases and the brand names of products used for treatment. In the past, they targeted only doctors through ads in medical journals and contacts by salespeople. Advertising is often a more cost-effective way to disseminate information than personal selling, particularly when the information can be exposed to targeted buyers by electronic or printed media.

---

[11]"SIA Presses for Higher Yields with New Aircraft, IFE Systems," *Aviation Week & Space Technology,* June 4, 2001, 69–70.

Procter & Gamble aims to inspire meaningful relationships with even the most mundane products:

TIDE Ads convey that women can focus on other things in their lives because Tide is taking care of the laundry.

ALWAYS P&G is using design and wit to elevate the image of the sanitary napkin. One ad bends an Always into a chaise lounge. The copy: "If you're going to sit all day, it better be comfortable."

PAMPERS No longer is pitched as just the most absorbent diaper; Pampers now is sold as helping the development of your baby.

Source: Robert Berner, "Detergent Can Be So Much More," *BusinessWeek,* May 1, 2006, 68.

Evaluation of Alternatives

Promotion helps buyers evaluate alternative brands, and such evaluations may be a primary objective of promotion activities. Both comparative advertising and personal selling are effective in demonstrating a brand's strengths over competing brands. An illustration of this form of advertising is to analyze competing brands of a product, showing a favorable comparison for the brand of the firm placing the ad. For example, Procter & Gamble Co. is pursuing company-wide initiatives to reestablish relationship bonds between customers and its core brands.[12] The intent is to position brands like Tide as offering more value than a commodity detergent. P&G in its promotion activities is seeking to differentiate Tide to avoid comparisons by buyers with competitors based on price and habit. P&G managers and strategists from its advertising agency, Saatchi and Saatchi, went out into the field to talk with and observe women buyers to guide the development of a relationship positioning message for Tide. P&G's brand building initiatives are described in the RELATIONSHIP APPLICATION.

Decision to Purchase

Influencing the buyer's decision to purchase a brand is an important promotion objective. Several of the promotion components may be used to encourage the buyer to purchase a brand. Personal selling is often effective in obtaining a purchase commitment from the buyers of consumer durable goods and industrial products. Direct selling organizations such as Avon (cosmetics) and Cutco (knives) use highly programmed selling approaches to encourage buyers to purchase their products. Communication objectives in these firms include making a target number of contacts each day. Point-of-purchase sales promotions, such as displays in retail stores, are intended to influence the purchase decision, as are discount coupons. One of the advantages of personal selling over advertising is its flexibility in responding to the buyer's objections and questions at the time the decision to purchase is being made.

Customer Retention

Communicating with buyers after they purchase a product is an important objective of promotion for many brands. Follow-up by salespeople, advertisements stressing a firm's

---

[12]Robert Berner, "Detergent Can Be So Much More," *BusinessWeek,* May 1, 2006, 68.

service capabilities, and toll-free numbers placed on packages to encourage users to seek information or report problems are illustrations of post-purchase communications. Hotels leave questionnaires in rooms for occupants to use in evaluating hotel services.

As illustrated, various communication objectives may be assigned to promotion strategy. The uses of promotion vary according to the type of purchase, the stage of the buyer's decision process, the maturity of the product-market, and the role of promotion in the marketing program. Objectives need to be developed for the entire promotion program and for each promotion component. Certain objectives, such as sales and market share targets, are shared with other marketing program components. In the following sections and Chapter 13 we discuss and provide examples of objectives for each promotion component.

Deciding the Role of the Promotion Components

Early in the process of developing the promotion strategy, it is useful to set guidelines as to the expected contribution for each of the promotion components. These guidelines help determine the strategy for each promotion component. It is necessary to decide which communication objective(s) will be the responsibility of each component. For example, advertising may be responsible for creating awareness of a new product. Sales promotion (e.g., coupons and samples) may encourage trial of the new product. Personal selling may be assigned responsibility for getting wholesalers and/or retailers to stock the new product. It is also important to decide how large the contribution of each promotion component will be, which will help to determine the promotion budget.

Determining the Promotion Budget

Isolating the specific effects of promotion may be difficult due to pursuit of multiple promotion objectives, lags in the impact of promotion on sales, effects of other marketing program components (e.g., retailers' cooperation), and the influences of uncontrollable factors (e.g., competition, economic conditions). Realistically, budgeting in practice is likely to emphasize improving promotion effectiveness rather than seeking the optimal size of the budget. Because of this, more practical budgeting techniques are normally used, such as, (1) objective and task, (2) percent of sales, (3) competitive parity, or (4) all you can afford. These same approaches are used to determine advertising and sales promotion budgets. The personal-selling budget is largely determined by the number of people in the salesforce and their qualifications. Direct marketing budgets are guided by the unit costs of customer contact such as cost per catalog mailed.

In many companies, the promotion budget may include only planned expenditures for advertising and sales promotion. Typically a separate budget is developed for the sales organization, which may include sales promotion activities such as incentives for salespeople and value-chain members. Public relations budgets also are likely to be separate from promotion budgeting. Even so, it is important to consider the size and allocation of total promotion expenses when formulating the promotion strategy. Unless this is done, the integration of the components is likely to be fragmented. Internet budgets may be separate or included with the promotion component that utilizes Internet capabilities.

An example of a promotion budget (excluding salesforce and public relations) for a pharmaceutical product is shown in Exhibit 12.2. Note the relative size of advertising and sample expenditures. The sampling of drugs to doctors by salespeople is a substantial amount of the promotion budget. Sampling is an important promotion component in this industry.

EXHIBIT 12.2
Illustrative
Promotion Budget
for a Pharmaceutical
Product

Promotional Activity	2012 Budget
Promotional material	$ 405,000
Samples	810,000
Direct Mail	559,000
Journal advertising	683,000
Total Budget	**$2,457,000**

Objective and Task

This logical and cost-effective method is probably the most widely used budgeting approach. Management sets the communication objectives, determines the tasks (activities) necessary to achieve the objectives, and adds up costs. This method also guides determining the role of the promotion components by selecting which component(s) is appropriate for attaining each objective. Marketing management must carefully evaluate how the promotion objectives are to be achieved and choose the most cost-effective promotion components. The effectiveness of the objective and task method depends on the judgment and experience of the marketing team. The budget shown in Exhibit 12.2 was determined using the objective and task method. The pharmaceutical firm executives involved in the budgeting process include product managers, the division manager, sales management, and the chief marketing executive.

Percent of Sales

Using this method, the budget is calculated as a percent of sales and is, therefore, quite arbitrary. The percentage figure is often based on past expenditure patterns. The method fails to recognize that promotion efforts and results are related. For example, repeating a 10-percent-of-sales budget from the previous year may be too much or not enough promotion expenditures to achieve sales and other promotion objectives. Budgeting by percent of sales can result in too much spending on promotion when sales are high and not enough when sales are low. In a cyclical industry where sales follow up-and-down trends, a strategy of increasing promotion expenditures during low-sales periods may be more appropriate.

Competitive Parity

Promotion expenditures for this budgeting method are guided by how much competitors spend. Yet competitors may be spending too much (or not enough) on promotion. Another key shortcoming of the competitive parity method is that differences in marketing strategy between competing firms may require different promotion strategies. A comparison of promotional strategies of these firms is not very meaningful, since their market targets, promotion objectives, and use of promotion components are different. Interestingly, Louis Vuitton, the largest and most profitable luxury brand in the world, spends only 5 percent of its revenues on advertising which is only half of the industry average.[13]

All You Can Afford

Since budget limits are a reality in most companies, this method is likely to influence all budget decisions. Top management may specify how much can be spent on promotion. For example, the guideline may be to increase the budget to 110 percent of last year's actual promotion expenditures. The objective and task method can be combined with the

---

[13]"The Vuitton Machine," *BusinessWeek,* March 22, 2004, 98–100, 102.

"all-you-can-afford" method by setting task priorities and allocating the budget to the higher priority tasks.

Determining the promotion budget is typically an interactive process among budgeting team members. Trade-offs must be evaluated concerning the expenditure needs of promotion components, priorities among the components, and total budget limits. These discussions by the budgeting team and top management play an important role in promotion strategy integration.

Promotion Component Strategies

The strategies for the promotion components need to be consistent with market targeting strategy and contribute to the desired positioning of the brand. Determining the strategy for each promotion component includes setting objectives and budget, selecting the strategy, and determining the promotion activities (and timing) to be pursued. For example, advertising activities include choosing the creative strategy, formulating the message(s), and selecting the media to carry the ads.

In this chapter we consider advertising and sales promotion strategy determination. Public relations strategy involves similar initiatives to advertising strategy determination and is not discussed. Chapter 13 examines salesforce, Internet, and direct marketing strategies.

Integrating and Implementing the Promotion Strategy

Several factors may affect the composition of the promotion program as shown by Exhibit 12.3. Advertising, public relations, personal selling, direct marketing, Internet, and sales promotion strategies have the potential to be fragmented when responsibility is assigned across several departments. There are differences in priorities, and determining the productivity of each promotion component is difficult. For example, coordination between personal selling and advertising is complicated since each of these promotion components has specific objectives, a separate budget and management, and different measures of effectiveness. Coordinating the activities of the two functions is an important responsibility of higher-level management. The separation of selling and advertising strategies also prevails in a variety of consumer and industrial products firms. An important marketing management issue is how to integrate the promotion strategy components.

EXHIBIT 12.3
Illustrative Factors That Influence the Design of Promotion Strategy

Developing and implementing integrated communications strategies are essential for manufacturers as well as retailers, and for both consumer and business products. Effective management of these strategies has a positive impact on revenues and the productivity of promotion strategy:

> The Integrated Marketing Communications approach to marketing communications planning and strategy is being adopted by both large and small companies and has become popular among firms marketing consumer products and services as well as business-to-business marketers. There are a number of reasons why marketers are adopting the IMC approach. A fundamental reason is that they understand the value of strategically integrating the various communications functions rather than having them operate autonomously. By coordinating their marketing communications efforts, companies can avoid duplication, take advantage of synergy among promotional tools, and develop more efficient and effective marketing communications programs.[14]

Effectiveness of Promotion Strategy

Tracking the performance of promotion strategy involves (1) evaluating the effectiveness of each promotion component and (2) assessing the overall effectiveness of the integrated promotion strategy. In this and the next chapter we discuss measurement of effectiveness of the individual promotion components. Cross-functional teams can be used to assess overall promotion strategy effectiveness. Comparisons of actual results to objectives can be employed in the evaluation of each promotion component and the effectiveness of the integrated promotion strategy.

Advertising Strategy

Management's perception of how advertising can contribute to the communication objectives has an important influence in deciding advertising's role. Estimating the impact on buyers helps to decide advertising's role and scope in the marketing program and to choose specific objectives for advertising.

The nature and scope of advertising is changing as suggested by our lead-in example concerning Google. The CEO of Ogilvy & Mather, one of the world's largest advertising agencies comments on the past and the present:

> Advertising was a straightforward business: agencies had to devise a good idea for an ad and then choose the right publication or broadcast slot in order to catch consumers' attention. Today, advertising is far more complex, thanks to technological advances, social shifts and the far greater sophistication of both the advertisers and audiences. Modern consumers demand to be wooed, not berated.[15]

Identifying and describing the target audiences is the first step in developing advertising strategy. Next, it is important to set specific objectives and estimate the advertising budget. There may be an adjustment (up or down) of this initial budget as the specific advertising activities and media choices are determined. The selection of the creative strategy follows. Specific messages need to be designed for each ad. Ads may be pretested. Choices of the advertising media and programming schedules implement the creative strategy. The final step is implementing the advertising strategy and evaluating its effectiveness. Each

---

[14]George E. Belch and Michael A. Belch, *Advertising and Promotion,* 8th ed. (New York: McGraw-Hill/Irwin, 2009), 12–13.
[15]"Queen of Madison Avenue," *The Economist,* February 24, 2007, 80.

of these activities is examined, highlighting important features and strategy issues. In the discussion we assume that the target audience(s) has been selected.

Setting Advertising Objectives and Budgeting

Advertising Objectives

Our earlier discussion of promotion strategy objectives identified various objectives that may be relevant for advertising. These include need recognition, identifying buyers, brand building, evaluation of alternatives, decision to purchase, and customer retention. More than one objective may be applicable for a particular advertising strategy.

Exhibit 12.4 shows alternative levels for setting advertising objectives. In moving from the most general level (exposure) to the most specific level (profit contribution) the objectives are increasingly more closely linked to buyers' purchase decisions. For example, knowing that advertising causes a measurable increase in sales is much more useful to management than knowing that a specific number of people are exposed to an advertising message. The key issue is whether objectives such as exposure and awareness are related to purchase behavior. For example, how much will exposure to the advertising increase the chances that people will purchase a product? Objectives such as exposure and awareness often can be measured, whereas determining the sales and profit impact of advertising may be more difficult due to the impact of other factors on sales and profits. Because of the ease of measurement, exposure and awareness objectives are used more often than attitude change, sales, and profit objectives.

Several questions that are useful in determining advertising objectives are presented in Exhibit 12.5. The questions consider different uses of advertising ranging from generating immediate sales to brand building. Specific objectives are shown for each of the nine questions.

Budget Determination

The budgeting methods for promotion discussed earlier in the chapter are also used in advertising budgeting. The objective and task method has a stronger supporting logic than the other methods. Consider, for example, the Italian government's advertising program intended to favorably position Italian fashion designers and craftsmen as the worlds finest.[16] The objectives were to increase Italy's share of U.S. imports and enhance the prestige of

EXHIBIT 12.4
Alternative Levels for Setting Advertising Objectives

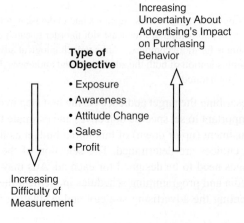

Type of Objective

Increasing Uncertainty About Advertising's Impact on Purchasing Behavior

- Exposure
- Awareness
- Attitude Change
- Sales
- Profit

Increasing Difficulty of Measurement

---

[16]Wendy Bounds and Deborah Ball, "Italy Knits Support for Fashion Industry," *Wall Street Journal,* December 15, 1997, B8.

EXHIBIT 12.5   Determining Advertising Objectives

Source: William Arens, *Contemporary Advertising*, 7th ed. (Burr Ridge, IL: Irwin/McGraw-Hill, 1999), R18. Copyright © The McGraw-Hill Companies. Used with permission.

1. Does the advertising aim at *immediate sales?* If so, objectives might be:

   - Perform the complete selling function.
   - Close sales to prospects already partly sold.
   - Announce a special reason for buying now (price, premium, and so forth).
   - Remind people to buy.
   - Tie in with special buying event.
   - Stimulate impulse sales.

2. Does the advertising aim at *near-term sales?* If so, objectives might be:

   - Create awareness.
   - Enhance brand image.
   - Implant information or attitude.
   - Combat or offset competitive claims.
   - Correct false impressions, misinformation.
   - Build familiarity and easy recognition.

3. Does the advertising aim at building a *long-range consumer franchise?* If so, objectives might be:

   - Build confidence in company and brand.
   - Build customer demand.
   - Select preferred distributors and dealers.
   - Secure universal distribution.
   - Establish a "reputation platform" for launching new brands or product lines.

4. Does the advertising aim at helping increase sales? If so, objectives would be:

   - Hold present customers.
   - Convert other users to advertiser's brand.
   - Cause people to specify advertiser's brand.
   - Convert nonusers to users.
   - Make steady customers out of occasional ones.
   - Advertise new uses.
   - Persuade customers to buy larger sizes or multiple units.
   - Remind users to buy.
   - Encourage greater frequency or quantity of use.

5. Does the advertising aim at some specific step that leads to a sale? If so, objectives might be:

   - Persuade prospect to write for descriptive literature, return a coupon, enter a contest.
   - Persuade prospect to visit a showroom, ask for a demonstration.
   - Induce prospect to sample the product (trial offer).

6. How important are supplementary benefits of advertising? Objectives would be:

   - Help salespeople open new accounts.
   - Help salespeople get larger orders from wholesalers and retailers.
   - Help salespeople get preferred display space.
   - Give salespeople an entrée.
   - Build morale of sales force.
   - Impress the trade.

7. Should the advertising impart information needed to consummate sales and build customer satisfaction? If so, objectives may be to use:

   - "Where to buy it" advertising.
   - "How to use it" advertising.
   - New models, features, package.
   - New prices.
   - Special terms, trade-in offers, and so forth.
   - New policies (such as guarantees).

8. Should advertising build confidence and goodwill for the corporation? Targets may include:

   - Customers and potential customers.
   - The trade (distributors, dealers, retail people).
   - Employees and potential employees.
   - The financial community.
   - The public at large.

9. What kind of images does the company wish to build?

   - Product quality, dependability.
   - Service.
   - Family resemblance of diversified products.
   - Corporate citizenship.
   - Growth, progressiveness, technical leadership.

its brands. The Italian Trade Commission budgeted $25 million on advertising and other promotion activities in the 5-year period through 1997 to achieve these objectives. The aggressive campaign generated positive results with an increase in Italy's U.S. imported apparel share from 4.5 to 5.9 percent. Much larger increases in apparel share were obtained by the more expensive imports like Versace and Giorgio Armani.

Budget determination, creative strategy, and media/programming strategy are closely interrelated, so these decisions need to be closely coordinated. A preliminary budget may be set, subject to review after the creative and media/programming strategies are determined. Using objective and task budgeting, creative plans and media alternatives should be examined in the budgeting process.

Creative Strategy

The range of advertising objectives shown in Exhibit 12.5 indicates the possible focus of the creative strategy. For example, if the objective is to enhance the image of a brand, then the message conveyed by the ad would seek to strengthen the brand image. This theme is illustrated by one of BMW's magazine ads introducing the new X5 4.8 which stated: "No matter how we disguise it, its heritage keeps showing through."

The creative strategy is guided by the market target and the desired positioning for the product or brand. Recall, in Chapter 6, we discuss positioning according to the *functions* performed by the brand, the *symbol* to be conveyed by the brand, or the *experience* provided by the brand. The creative theme seeks to effectively communicate the intended positioning to buyers and others influencing the purchase of the brand.

There are several successful advertising campaign themes that have been used for many years. Examples include Nike's "Just Do It" and Wheaties' "Breakfast of Champions."[17] Interestingly, some of the highest-rated and lowest-rated ads have been created by the same advertising agency (we discuss the agency's role later in the chapter).

Creative advertising designs enhance the effectiveness of advertising by providing a unifying concept that binds together the various parts of an advertising campaign. Advertising agencies are experts in designing creative strategies. The agency professionals may design unique themes to position a product or firm in some particular way or use comparisons with competition to enhance the firms' brands. Choosing the right creative theme for the marketing situation can make a major contribution to the success of an advertising program. While tests are used to evaluate creative approaches, the task is more of an art than a science. Perhaps the best guide to its creativity is an agency's track record and the success of its tests of creative approaches.

Several challenges are impacting the creative process and changing the design of creative strategies:

> The new generation of advertising creatives will face a world of ever-growing complexity. They must handle many challenges of integrated marketing communications (IMC) as they help their clients build relationships with highly fragmented target markets. They will need to understand the wide range of new technologies affecting advertising (computer hardware and software, electronic networking, high-definition television, and more). And they have to learn how to advertise in emerging international markets.[18]

The earlier illustration describing P&G's initiatives to develop creative strategies for the firm's core brands highlights the importance of this part of advertising strategy.[19] In their field

---

[17]Belch and Belch, *Advertising and Promotion,* 8th ed. (New York: McGraw-Hill/Irwin, 2009), 268.
[18]William F. Arens, *Advertising,* 9th ed. (Burr Ridge, IL: McGraw-Hill/Irwin, 2004), 384.
[19]Berner, "Detergent Can Be So Much More," 66, 68.

studies of buyers, executives followed buyers as they shopped and sat in on sessions to listen to them talk about their lives. This information was very useful in designing creative ads.

Media/Scheduling Decisions

A company's advertising agency or media placement organization normally guides media selection and scheduling decisions. These professionals have the experience and technical ability to match media and scheduling to the target audience(s) specified by the firm. The media, timing, and programming decisions are influenced largely by two factors: (1) access to the target audience(s) and (2) the costs of reaching the target group(s).

The audience coverage of different media varies considerably so the access provided to the target audience is also important. The various media provide extensive profile information on their viewers. *Standard Rates and Data Services* publishes advertising costs for various media. The costs are determined by circulation levels and the type of publication. In deciding which medium to use, it is important to evaluate the cost per exposure and the match of the characteristics of the subscribers to market targets. The medium should provide coverage of the buyers in the market target for the product or brand being advertised. High media costs help explain why companies may transfer resources to online advertising, such as banners and click-throughs, where production and media costs are much lower.

Media models are available to analyze allocations and decide which media mix best achieves one or more objectives. These models typically use an exposure measure (see Exhibit 12.4) as the basis for media allocation. For example, cost per thousand exposures can be used to compare alternative media. The models also consider audience characteristics (e.g., age group composition) and other factors. The models are useful in selecting media when many advertising programs and a wide range of media are used.

The fragmentation of many consumer markets is driving significant amounts of advertising spending from traditional mass media to more focused narrowcast media. The INNOVATION APPLICATION describes some of these changes.

New types of Internet-based media are becoming very significant to media scheduling choices. Social networking websites like MySpace, Facebook, and YouTube are becoming important media for reaching audiences not easily accessed through conventional print and TV approaches. Publisher Random House, for example, created a Web page on MySpace for Hannibal, to promote the publication of Thomas Harris's novel *Hannibal Rising* about Hannibal Lector. The aim was to reach young readers who are resistant to traditional advertising media and even official websites. Social networking sites provide options for branded viral marketing campaigns to be pasted on personal pages and passed around within the social networking community. Viral marketing—distributing promotional video clips across the Internet—is increasingly used by advertisers, for example, Unilever's Axe deodorant, Volkswagen, Diageo's Smirnoff Raw Tea, and Virgin Money. Viral marketing is also known as "word-of-mouse" or "buzz" marketing and involves releasing a compelling, but branded, video-clip or computer game, hoping that Internet users will distribute it widely to friends and contacts.[20]

Role of the Advertising Agency

Advertising agencies perform various functions for clients including developing creative designs and selecting media. In addition to creative skills and media selection, full-service agencies offer a range of services including marketing research, sales promotion, marketing

[20]Allison Enright, "Viral Campaign Hooks Potential Users," *Marketing News,* May 15, 2007, 9–10; Matthew Garahan, "A Hunt for Revenue in the Ecosystem," *Financial Times,* Monday, April 30, 2007, 24; Danuta Kean, "Vampires and Cannibals Find Prey Online," *Financial Times,* Tuesday, November 7, 2006, 12.

- The decline in prime-time television audience ratings and newspaper circulation since the 1970s has been accompanied by the development of a proliferation of digital and wireless communication channels: hundreds of narrowcast cable TV and radio channels; thousands of specialized magazines; millions of computer terminals, video game consoles, personal digital assistants, and cell phone screens.
- In the 1960s an advertiser could reach 80 percent of U.S. women with a spot aired simultaneously on CBS, NBC, and ABC, while now an ad would have to run on 100 TV channels to get near this feat.
- Mass media's share of advertising is declining as marketers boost spending on more targetable, narrowcast media.
- The fastest form of online advertising is "paid search"—the search engine used displays paid advertisements or "sponsored links" with the search results. Internet users can be targeted by region and city.
- Online media are interactive, so advertisers can gather invaluable personal information from consumers and get a more precise measurement of advertising impact.
- A study by Sanford C. Bernstein & Co. predicted by 2010 marketers would spend more for advertising on cable and the Internet, than on network TV or on magazines.

Source: Anthony Bianco, "The Vanishing Mass Market," *BusinessWeek,* July 12, 2004, 58–62.

planning. The traditional basis of compensation is a 15 percent fee on media expenditures. For example, $1 million of advertising provides a commission of $150,000. The agency pays the $850,000 for the media space and bills the client $1,000,000.

Agency Relationship

The relationship between a corporate client and an agency is a cooperative effort. The client briefs the agency on the marketing strategy and the role of advertising in the marketing program. In some instances agency executives may be involved in the design of marketing strategy. The better the agency understands the company's targeting and positioning strategies, the more effective the agency can be in providing advertising services. The agency may assign one or more professionals full-time to a client with a large advertising budget.

Choosing an advertising agency is an important decision. It is also necessary to evaluate the relationship over time, since a company's advertising requirements change. Good agency relationships are usually the result of collaboration with an agency that has the capabilities and commitment needed by the client. The American Association of Advertising Agencies examined in a major study how agencies and clients determine value of the relationship and the agency activities that deliver the best value to the client's business.[21] The top seven activities identified in the study are shown in Exhibit 12.6.

The increasing demands for integrated marketing communications strategies, and the development of complex multimedia campaigns, may require reevaluation of the traditional client/agency relationship. Traditional agencies may not be strong in areas like online advertising. The consumer goods company Unilever, for example, has established internal teams to cope with rapid changes in advertising media—in the form of communications planning and digital advertising operations units. As the use of TV advertising

---

[21]Belch and Belch, *Advertising and Promotion,* 94.

EXHIBIT 12.6
How Advertising Agencies Add Value to the Relationship

Source: Report on the Agency-Advertiser Value Survey, American Association of Advertisers and Association of National Advertising, August 2007.

1. Developing and producing creative ideas that are fresh and appropriate.
2. Ensuring that agency disciplines and functions are integrated and that agency teams and divisions collaborate well on behalf of the client.
3. Working in a collaborative way with the client by creating an environment of low egos and high mutual respect.
4. Developing ideas and programs that can be integrated into multiple communication channels.
5. Assigning its best people to the client's business and making its top executives available when needed.
6. Evaluating brand drivers like awareness, consideration, and purchase intent.
7. Providing guidance and solutions in new media and technologies.

declines—down from 85 percent of the global advertising spent in 2000 to 65 percent in 2006—Unilever is developing "holistic" campaigns that make use of a wider range of marketing tools.[22]

Agency Compensation

Most agencies operate on some type of commission arrangement, though the arrangement may involve a commission for media placement and a separate arrangement for other services. For example, media placement would receive a 5 percent commission, whereas other services associated with the advertising would yield an additional 10 percent. These changes in the original 15 percent commission are because advertising specialists are available (e.g., media buying) and offer reduced fees for specific services. Projects such as research studies are priced on an individual basis.

Clients may work out flexible payment arrangements with their agency. The agency may keep a record of its costs and the client will pay for the services it requires. The resulting compensation may be greater or less than the traditional 15 percent commission. In some situations agencies may share cost savings with the client.

Industry Composition

Large, full-service agencies like Dentsu in Tokyo and Young and Rubicam in New York account for the dominant portion of billings. Nonetheless, several local and regional agencies have created pressures for change throughout the industry. Concerns of clients about arbitrary commission rates and lack of flexibility in client services have led to placing business with small specialty agencies that provide media buying, creative design, and other services. There are many local and regional agencies that serve small and medium-size clients.

Ad agencies are experiencing major changes driven by clients' shifting media priorities and the emergence of new competitors like Google. Ad-skipping technology provided by TiVo and other firms helps TV viewers skip commercials. Internet advertising is experiencing huge growth trends. Some critics indicate that clients and their agencies have lost contact with consumers. Turbulence and change are likely to continue to impact traditional agencies in the future.

Implementing the Advertising Strategy and Measuring Its Effectiveness

Before an advertising strategy is implemented, it is advisable to establish the criteria that will be used for measuring advertising effectiveness. Advertising expenditures are wasted if firms spend too much or allocate expenditures improperly. Measuring effectiveness

---

[22]Gary Silverman, "Unilever in Advertising Shake-Up," *Financial Times,* Tuesday, March 14, 2006, 23.

provides necessary feedback for future advertising decisions. Importantly, the quality of advertising can be as critical to getting results as the amount of advertising.

Tracking Advertising Performance

As previously discussed, advertising's impact on sales may be difficult to measure because other factors also influence sales and profits. Most efforts to measure effectiveness consider objectives such as attitude change, awareness, or exposure (see Exhibit 12.4), although Internet advertising is changing performance measurement opportunities. Comparing objectives and results helps managers decide when to alter or stop advertising campaigns. Services such as Nielsen's TV ratings are available for the major media. These ratings have a critical impact on the allocation of advertising dollars, although recent research findings question the accuracy of the ratings. Various measurement concerns are causing several changes in the rating process.

Methods of Measuring Effectiveness

Major emphasis by several companies is being placed on developing better methods of measuring the effectiveness of advertising. Companies are seeking ways for choosing between alternative methods of promotion such as displays in supermarkets versus radio advertising. Classification of testing methods of effectiveness measurement are shown in the METRICS APPLICATION.

Several methods are used to evaluate advertising results. Analysis of historical data identifies relationships between advertising expenditures and sales using statistical techniques such as regression analysis. Recall tests measure consumers' awareness of specific ads and campaigns by asking questions to determine if a sample of people remembers an ad. Longitudinal studies track advertising expenditures and sales results before, during, and after an advertising campaign. Controlled tests are a form of longitudinal study in which extraneous effects are measured and/or controlled during the test. Test marketing can be used to evaluate advertising effectiveness. Effort/results models use empirical data to build a mathematical relationship between sales and advertising effort.

Interestingly, one of the leading full-service global advertising companies, WPP Group, is applying statistical analysis (econometric models) to measure the effectiveness of advertising expenditures.[23] The search for more effective measurement techniques is driven by concerns about the effectiveness of TV advertising, pressures on costs, and changing media technologies.

Sales Promotion Strategy

Sales promotion expenditures are increasing more rapidly than advertising in many companies. Both advertising and sales promotion initiatives are receiving major attention by companies in their attempts to boost productivity and reduce costs. Sales promotion activities provide extra value or incentives to consumers and value-chain participants.[24] The intent is to encourage sales. Sales promotion is some form of inducement (e.g., coupon, contest, rebate, etc.). Importantly, sales promotion activities can be targeted to various points of influence in the value chain.

To pursue its goal of doubling its market share to 10 percent of light trucks in the U.S. Toyota favored sales promotion strategy over conventional advertising. The head of marketing at Toyota claimed "We can have the most beautiful advertising but that's not going

---

[23]Aaron O. Patrick, "Econometrics Buzzes Ad World as a Way of Measuring Results," *Wall Street Journal,* August 16, 2005, B8.
[24]Belch and Belch, *Advertising and Promotion,* Chapter 16.

Pretests

Laboratory Methods

Consumer juries	Theater tests	Readability tests
Portfolio tests	Rough tests	Comprehension and reaction tests
Physiological measures	Concept tests	

Field Methods

Dummy advertising vehicles   On-air tests

Postests

Field Methods

Recall tests	Single-source tests	Recognitions tests
Association measures	Inquiry tests	Tracking studies

Source: George E. Belch and Michael A. Belch, *Advertising and Promotion,* 8th ed. (New York: McGraw-Hill/Irwin, 2009), 621.

to change people's minds. The only way you can do that is in person."[25] Rides in the Tundra were offered at fishing shows and tournaments, and at dirt-bike races. Test-drives can also be arranged at a big chain of building materials stores. The market targets for the Tundra are people with outdoor interests and owners of building and construction businesses. Specially trained "truck champions" are available at dealerships. Additionally, negative perceptions of the truck as an import are being countered with sponsorship of Brooks and Dunn, a top country music act, and sponsorship of the Texas Football Classic, a high school tournament.

We look at the nature and scope of sales promotion, the types of sales promotion activities, their advantages and limitations, and the decisions involved in determining sales promotion strategy.

Nature and Scope of Sales Promotion

Purchase rebates are one of the most active forms of sales promotion. Rebates are popular with companies, although consumers dislike the hassles of submitting rebate forms, providing proof of purchase, and delays in obtaining the rebates. The STRATEGY APPLICATION examines the realities of mail-in rebates.

The responsibility for sales promotion activities often spans several marketing functions, such as advertising, merchandising, product planning, and sales. For example, a sales contest for salespeople is typically designed and administered by sales managers, and the costs of the contest are included in the sales department budget. Similarly, planning and coordinating a new product sampling or coupon refund program may be assigned to a product manager. Point-of-purchase promotion displays in retail stores may be the responsibility of the field sales organization.

Total expenditures for sales promotion by business and industry in the United States are likely more than double advertising expenditures. The complete scope of sales promotion is often difficult to identify because the activities are included in various departments and

---

[25]Bernard Simon, "Consumers Get to Meet the New Toyota Pickup," *Financial Times,* September 15, 2006, 12.

- Consumers hate the hassles, companies love unredeemed rebates, and regulators are investigating the consumer complaints.
- As much as 40 percent of rebates never get redeemed.
- Some 400 million rebates are offered each year with a total value of $6 billion.
- Unclaimed rebates translate into more than $2 billion of *extra* revenue for retailers and their suppliers each year.
- Complex filing rules and long delays discourage consumers.
- Companies emphasize the filing processes that are intended to discourage fraud.
- The largest rebate processor monitors 10,000 addresses suspected of submitting bogus rebates.
- Rebates offer companies an opportunity to promote small discounts without marking the products down.
- Rebates have become very popular with computer and consumer-electronics companies.
- The value of rebates has also increased.
- Regulators are intensifying their scrutiny of the companies offering rebates.
- The developing backlash against rebates is pushing some companies to halt rebate strategies.
- Others are encouraging online filing.
- Fulfillment houses are revising their processing systems, using computer technology to validate claims.
- Consumers would like mail-in rebates to go away but want the best price they can get.

Source: Brian Grow, "The Great Rebate Runaround," *BusinessWeek,* December 5, 2005, 34, 36, and 37.

budgets. Unlike advertising, sales promotion expenditures are not published in business publications or on the Internet.

A relevant issue is deciding how to manage the various sales promotion activities. While these programs are used to support advertising, pricing, channel of distribution, and personal selling strategies, the size and scope of sales promotion suggest that the responsibility for managing sales promotion should be assigned to one or a team of executives. Otherwise, sales promotion activities become fragmented, and may not be properly integrated with other promotion components. The chief marketing executive should assign responsibility for coordination and evaluation of sales promotion activities.

Sales Promotion Activities

Many activities may be part of the total promotion program, including trade shows, specialty advertising (e.g., imprinted calendars), contests, point-of-purchase displays, coupons, recognition programs (e.g., awards to top suppliers), and free samples. Companies may direct their sales promotion activities to consumer buyers, industrial buyers, value-chain members, and salespeople, as shown in Exhibit 12.7. Sales promotion programs fall into three major categories: incentives, promotional pricing, and informational activities.

Promotion to Consumer Targets

Sales promotion is used in the marketing of many consumer goods and services, and includes a wide variety of activities, as illustrated in Exhibit 12.7. A key management

EXHIBIT 12.7
Sales Promotion
Activities Targeted
to Various Groups

Sales Promotion Activity	Targeted to:			
	Consumer Buyers	Industrial Buyers	Channel Members	Salespeople
Incentives				
Contests	X	X	X	X
Trips	X	X	X	X
Bonuses			X	X
Prizes	X	X	X	X
Advertising support			X	
Free items	X	X		
Recognition			X	X
Promotional Pricing				
Coupons	X			
Allowances		X	X	
Rebates	X	X	X	
Cash	X			
Informational Activities				
Displays	X			
Demonstrations	X	X	X	
Selling aids			X	X
Specialty advertising (e.g., pens)	X	X	X	
Trade shows	X	X	X	

concern is evaluating the effectiveness of promotions such as coupons, rebates, contests, and other awards. The large expenditures necessary to support these programs require that the results and costs be objectively assessed.

The sponsoring of sports events and individuals is a major initiative by various companies and brands. Sales promotion results from the association of the brand with the event or person. An example is PepsiCo's sponsorship of the Pepsi 400 NASCAR race. Similarly, sports celebrities may be sponsored. The strategy issue is determining the benefits versus costs of these sales promotion activities.

Product-placement activities are expanding in popularity with product sponsors. Viewing a product on a TV show provides interesting use exposure if the placement is in a realistic setting. Companies may be interested in positioning the product in a typical use setting rather than the immediate generation of sales. General Motors obtained an impressive product placement opportunity in the movie *Transformers.*[26] Interestingly, the stars of the movie are GM cars that are transformed into robots fighting evil. Leveraging the sales promotion opportunity, movie fans are able to create their own transformers at Chevyautobot.com.

Promotion to Industrial Targets

Many of the sales promotion methods that are used for consumer products also apply to industrial products, although the role and scope of the methods may vary. For example, trade shows perform a key role in small- and medium-sized companies' marketing strategies. The advantage of the trade show is the heavy concentration of potential buyers at one

[26]Dorothy Pomerantz, "Best Ad Ever," *Forbes,* June 18, 2007, 44.

location during a very short time period. The cost per contact is much less than a salesperson calling on prospects at their offices. While people attending trade shows also spend their time viewing competitors' products, an effective display and buyer/seller interactions offer a unique opportunity to hold the prospects' attention.

The Internet has many of the features of trade shows while eliminating certain of their limitations. For example, the Web enables the French woolens manufacturer, Carreman, to provide its customers fabric samples in one day.[27] The company posted its top fabrics on the Etexx website for online sample ordering. Management is optimistic that its customers will respond favorably to the initiative. Etexx, a start up based in Nice, France, created an e-marketplace for buyers and sellers of fabrics.

Sales promotion programs that target industrial buyers may consume a greater portion of the marketing budget than advertising. Many of these activities support personal selling strategies. They include catalogs, brochures, product information reports, samples, trade shows, application guides, and promotional items such as calendars, pens, and calculators.

Promotion to Value-Chain Members

Sales promotion is an important part of manufacturers' marketing efforts to wholesalers and retailers for such products as foods, beverages, and appliances. Catalogs and other product information are essential promotional components for many lines. The Internet offers an alternative way to make catalog information available. Promotional pricing is often used to push new products through channels of distribution. Various incentives are popular in marketing to value chain members. Specialty advertising items such as calendars and memo pads are used in maintaining buyer awareness of brands and company names.

Promotion to the Salesforce

Incentives and informational activities are the primary forms of promotion used to assist and motivate company salespeople. Sales contests and prizes are popular. Companies also make wide use of recognition programs like the "salesperson of the year." Promotional information is vital to salespeople. Presentation kits help salespeople describe new products and the features of existing products to customers.

A high-tech promotion tool with exciting potential is the automated sales presentation created with integrated use of sound, graphics, and video briefcase computers. These multimedia or interactive techniques give salespeople powerful presentation capabilities, allowing them access to a complete product information system available on the notebook computer.

Advantages and Limitations of Sales Promotion

Because of its wide array of incentive, pricing, and communication capabilities, sales promotion has the flexibility to contribute to various marketing objectives. A marketing manager can target buyers, value-chain members, and salespeople, and the sales response of the sales promotion activities can be measured to determine their effectiveness. For example, a company can track its coupon redemption or rebate success. Many of the incentive and price promotion techniques trigger the purchase of other products.

Sales promotion is not without its disadvantages. In most instances, rather than substituting for advertising and personal selling, sales promotion supports other promotional efforts. Control is essential to prevent some people from taking advantage of free offers, coupons, and other incentives. Value-added resellers may build inventories on products that receive manufacturers' trade discounts. Incentives and price-promotional activities need to

---

[27]"Streamlining," *BusinessWeek,* E.Biz, September 18, 2000, EB70.

be monitored. An effective advertisement can be run thousands of times, but promotional campaigns are usually not reusable. Thus, the costs of development must be considered in evaluating benefits and costs.

Sales Promotion Strategy

The steps in developing the sales promotion strategy are similar to the design of advertising strategy. First, it is necessary to define the communications task(s) that the sales promotion program is expected to accomplish. Next, specific promotion objectives are set for awareness levels and purchase intentions. It is important to evaluate the relative cost-effectiveness of feasible sales promotion methods and to select those that offer the best results/cost combination. Both the content of the sales promotion and its timing should be coordinated with other promotion activities. Finally, the program is implemented and is evaluated on a continuing basis. Evaluation examines the extent to which objectives are achieved. For example, trade show results can be evaluated to determine how many show contacts are converted to purchases.

Summary

Promotion strategy is a vital part of the marketing positioning strategy. The components—advertising, sales promotion, public relations, personal selling, direct marketing, and interactive/Internet marketing—offer an impressive array of capabilities for communicating with market targets and other relevant audiences. However, promotion activities are expensive. Management must decide the size of the promotion budget and allocate it to the promotion components. Each promotion activity offers certain unique advantages and also shares several characteristics with the other components.

Promotion strategy is guided by the market targeting and positioning strategies. Communication objectives must be determined and the role of each promotion component selected by marketing management. Budgeting indicates the amount and allocation of resources to the promotion strategy components. The major budgeting methods are objective and task, percent of sales, competitive parity, and all you can afford. Objective and task is the recommended method. Several product and market factors affect whether the promotion strategy will emphasize advertising, sales promotion, personal selling, or seek a balance between the forms of promotion. The effective integration of the communications program is a major challenge for many firms. Finally, the effectiveness of the promotion strategy is evaluated.

The steps in developing advertising strategy include identifying the target audience, deciding the role of advertising in the promotional mix, indicating advertising objectives and budget size, selecting the creative strategy, determining the media and programming schedule, and implementing the program and measuring its effectiveness. Advertising objectives may range from audience exposure to profit contribution. Advertising agencies offer specialized services for developing creative strategies, designing messages, and selecting media and programming strategies. Measuring advertising effectiveness is essential in managing this expensive resource.

Our discussion of sales promotion highlights several methods that are available for use as incentives, advertising support, and informational activities. Typically, firms use sales promotion activities in conjunction with advertising and personal selling rather than as a primary component of promotion strategy. Sales promotion programs may target consumer buyers, industrial buyers, value chain organizations, and salespeople. Sales-promotion strategy should determine the methods that provide the best results/cost combinations for achieving the communications objectives.

Questions for Review and Discussion

1. Compare and contrast the role of promotion in an international public accounting firm with promotion by American Airlines.

2. Identify and discuss the factors that are important in determining the promotion program for the following products:

   a. Video tape recorder/player.

   b. Personal computer.

   c. Boeing 7E7 Dreamliner commercial aircraft.

   d. Residential homes.

3. What are the important considerations in determining a promotion budget?

4. Under what conditions is a firm's promotion strategy more likely to be advertising/sales promotion–driven rather than personal selling–driven?

5. Discuss the advantages and limitations of using awareness as an advertising objective. When may this objective be appropriate?

6. Identify and discuss the important differences between advertising and sales promotion strategies in promotion strategy.

7. Coordination of advertising and personal selling strategies is a major challenge in large companies. Outline a plan for integrating these strategies.

8. Discuss the role of sales promotion methods in the promotion strategy of a major airline.

9. How and to what extent is the Internet likely to be useful in companies' promotion strategies?

Internet Applications

A. Discuss how Godiva Chocolatier's website (www.godiva.com) corresponds to the brand image portrayed by its retail stores. What are the promotion objectives that Godiva's management seems to be pursuing on the website?

B. Go to the websites of NBC and the BBC (www.nbc.com and www.bbc.co.uk). Contrast the ways NBC and the BBC promote their daily TV programs online. Which similarities and differences do you detect? Suggest ways of improvement considering the respective cultural frame of reference and target market for NBC and BBC.

C. Discuss how Apple's (www.apple.com) marketing strategy for iPod Mini is enhanced by a Web-based approach.

Applications

A. Consider the online promotion activities described in the INTERNET APPLICATION. Discuss how these initiatives offer compelling advantages over traditional promotion strategies.

B. Review the RELATIONSHIP APPLICATION concerning Procter & Gamble's advertising efforts designed to avoid its core brands such as Tide detergent becoming commodity products. Consider whether it is possible for consumers to genuinely engage with products of this kind.

Chapter

13

Sales, Digital, and Direct Marketing Strategies

Sales organizations in many companies around the world have experienced significant changes in how the selling function is being performed over the last decade. Many transactional selling activities are handled by the Internet, while salespeople are more focused on collaborative and consulting relationships with customers. Contrary to some forecasts the role of selling has not deteriorated. More than a few companies and business units have shifted resources from marketing to sales because management considers the sales organization vital in attaining marketing and business strategy objectives.[1] Personal selling, the Internet, and direct marketing initiatives are being impacted by many changes in the 21st century. The Internet has become an important and expanding avenue of direct contact between customers and companies selling goods and services, particularly through social media like Facebook and Twitter. Management may use a combination of salespeople, direct marketing, and the Internet to perform selling and sales support functions. Coordinating an organization's activities across multiple customer contact initiatives is essential to avoid conflicts and enhance overall results.

Hewlett-Packard Co.'s (H-P) salesforce organizational changes are illustrative of the market-driven initiatives underway in many companies.[2] In 2006 H-P's then-new CEO had received feedback from 400 customers and internal executives, which caused a major overhaul of H-P's salesforce strategy and structure. Before the changes H-P had eleven layers of managers between the CEO and customers; sales team efforts were fragmented and duplicative. Seventy percent of H-P's revenues are from companies, yet salespeople were not actively seeking their business. New initiatives included product specialization by salespeople, salesperson customer responsibility assignment and reduction of the number of accounts, and standardization of account management software. H-P's salesforce now spends more time in front of customers, responds faster to their needs, and is winning more

[1]Frederick E. Webster, Alan J. Malter, and Shankar Ganesan, "The Decline and Dispersal of Marketing Competence," *MIT Sloan Management Review,* 46(4), 2005, 35–43.
[2]Pui-Wing Tam, "Hurd's Big Challenge at H-P: Overhauling Corporate Sales," *Wall Street Journal,* April 3, 2006, A1, A13. Cliff Edwards, "How HP Got the Wow! Back," *BusinessWeek,* December 22, 2008, 60–61.

corporate sales deals. H-P's performance has improved and greater gains are expected from the sales strategy and structure changes.

In this chapter we first discuss developing and implementing salesforce strategy. Next, we consider the issues and initiatives concerning Internet strategy. Finally, we describe and illustrate the various methods used in direct marketing to customers.

Salesforce Strategy

The strategic role of sales and selling resources is evolving rapidly in many companies. We consider this strategic sales perspective. The management of sales efforts linked to strategic marketing goals is examined as salesforce strategy.

Strategic Sales Perspective

Sales organizations in many firms are undertaking a major transformation, as companies search for new organizational approaches that meet escalating customer and competitive pressures. The emergence of the strategic sales organization can be explained by several factors: changing customer relationship requirements; the changing sales task, which emphasises customer relationship strength as well as sales transactions; and the importance of strategic sales capabilities to cope with technology complexity, growing customer sophistication, commoditization pressures, and the need for radically different selling approaches. The underlying need is to manage customers strategically includes the need to understand the opportunities and risks in the customer portfolio, and the need to implement appropriate strategies with strategic customers (see Chapter 7). The result is the emergence of new sales organization models reflecting both reshaping and restructuring of existing functions to better meet market requirements, but also the development of new types of customer business development and process-based organizational forms (see Chapter 14). New types of more strategic sales organizations provides a means to achieve better alignment of sales and customer processes with business and marketing strategy.[3]

Escalating customer demands for enhanced service, new types of relationships with vendors, and greater added-value by business-to-business suppliers of all kinds are indicated in the H. R. Chally consultancy's *World Class Sales Excellence Research Report,*[4] which investigates the views of corporate purchasers and their expectations for the relationship with the salesperson from a supplier. These findings are summarized in Exhibit 13.1. The Chally characterizes how the best salesforces are distinguished in the eyes of their customers. The research points to a customer environment that has radically different requirements from those of the transactional selling approaches of the past, and that poses substantially different management challenges in managing customer relationships. Sales and service organizations that meet these customer demands and expectations and develop sustainable and attractive customer relationships are likely to be considerably different to those of the past, and to operate differently.

For example, Procter & Gamble has been transformed from a slow-moving, inward-looking company into a nimble, innovative, and aggressive competitor. Part of that

---

[3]Nigel F Piercy and Nikala Lane, "The Evolution of the Strategic Sales Organization," in David W. Cravens, Kenneth Le-Meunier-Fitzhugh, and Nigel F Piercy, *The Oxford Handbook of Strategic Sales and Sales Management* (Oxford: Oxford University Press, 2011), 19–50. Nigel F. Piercy and Nikala Lane, *Strategic Customer Management: Strategizing the Sales Organization* (Oxford: Oxford University Press, 2009).
[4]H. R. Chally, *The Chally World Class Sales Excellence Research Report* (Dayton, OH: The H. R. Chally Group, 2006).

EXHIBIT 13.1
Customer Demands for New Sales Relationships

Source: Adapted from H. R. Chally, *World Class Sales Excellence Research Report* (Dayton, OH: The H. R. Chally Group, 2006).

The Chally Report investigates the views of major corporate purchasers and their expectations for the relationship with the vendor salesperson from a supplier, and their requirements the salesperson should

Be personally accountable for our desired results—the sales contact with the supplier is expected to be committed to the customer and accountable for achievement.

Understand our business—to be able to add value, the supplier must understand the customer's competencies, strategies, challenges, and organizational culture.

Be on our side—the salesperson must be the customer's advocate in his or her own organization, and operate through the policies and politics to focus on the customer's needs.

Design the right applications—the salesperson is expected to think beyond technical features and functions to the implementation of the product or service in the customer's environment, thinking beyond the transaction to the customer's end state.

Be easily accessible—customers expect salespeople to be constantly connected and within reach.

Solve our problems—customers no longer buy products or services, they buy solutions to their business problems, and expect salespeople to diagnose, prescribe, and resolve their issues, not just sell them products.

Be creative in responding to our needs—buyers expect salespeople to be innovators, who bring them new ideas to solve problems, so creativity is a major source of added value.

transformation has been the creation of customer business development (CBD) organizations at the front of the business. The goal of CBD is to transform the old, narrow idea of buyer-seller relationships with customers into a multifunctional, collaborative approach designed to achieve mutual volume, profit, and market share objectives. CBD teams work with customers to develop the customer's plans and strategies to the advantage of both customer and P&G. CBD team members work collaboratively with experts from finance, management systems, customer service, and brand management to develop and implement business strategies that deliver sustainable competitive advantage for P&G brands.[5]

Similarly, when Sam Palmisano took over as CEO at IBM, one of his early moves was to implement a thorough overhaul of the 38,000-person salesforce. In the 1990s salespeople representing the various IBM business units essentially worked on their own, looking for opportunities to sell individual products or services. Palmisano "reintegrated" IBM in front of customers by bringing together specialists from computers, software, consulting, and research into teams that meet with customers to help solve their business problems and develop new business strategies. Collaborating with customers, suppliers, and even rivals is part of his plan to invent new technologies to create new markets.[6]

The role of the sales organization in many companies is shifting from order-taking and managing transactions to business development and effective customer relationship management. Sales organizations are playing an active role in creating and shaping marketing

---

[5]This example is based on Piercy and Lane, *Strategic Customer Management: Strategizing the Sales Organization*, 20–21.
[6]This illustration is based on Steve Hamm, "Beyond Blue," *BusinessWeek,* April 18, 2005, 36–42. Steve Hamm, "Big Blue Goes for the Big Win," *BusinessWeek,* March 10, 2008, 63–65.

Ethics Application

Challenges in Selling and Sales Management

strategy, rather than implementation. There is an emerging opportunity and challenge for executives:

> Today's competitive environment demands a radically different approach. Specifically, the ability of firms to exploit the true potential of the sales organization requires that company executives adopt a new mindset about the role of the selling function within the firm, how the sales force is managed, and what salespeople are expected to produce. The sales function must serve as a dynamic source of value creation and innovation within the firm.[7]

Furthermore, when examining salesforce strategy and its impact on strategic marketing it is increasingly important to recognize that salespeople's interactions with many customers and the geographical dispersion of salespeople are likely to create more ethical issues than are experienced in other types of jobs (see Chapter 4). The level of scrutiny of the ethical and social responsibility standards of companies has never been so searching. Sales managers may encounter a wide range of ethical situations as discussed in the ETHICS APPLICATION. Issues of integrity and social responsibility in seller behavior are a high priority for many business leaders. Indeed, research suggests that when major customers are asked what they want from sellers, honesty and integrity are ranked highest.[8]

Salesforce Strategy

As well as concerns for strategic sales organization transformation, salesforce strategy requires clear decisions about how to use personal selling to contact sales prospects, generate sales, and develop the types of customer relationships that management considers necessary to accomplish the organization's salesforce objectives. Personal selling activities vary considerably across companies based on how personal selling contributes to marketing positioning strategy and promotion strategy. For example, a pharmaceutical salesperson maintains regular contact with doctors and other professionals, but actual purchases are made at retail outlets where the prescriptions are filled. Nonetheless, salespeople play a vital role in the

---

[7]The Sales Educators, *Strategic Sales Leadership: Breakthrough Thinking for Breakthrough Results* (Mason, OH: Thomson, 2006), 1.

[8]Christina Galea, "What Customers Really Want," *Sales & Marketing Management,* May 2006, 11–12.

EXHIBIT 13.2
Salesforce Strategy

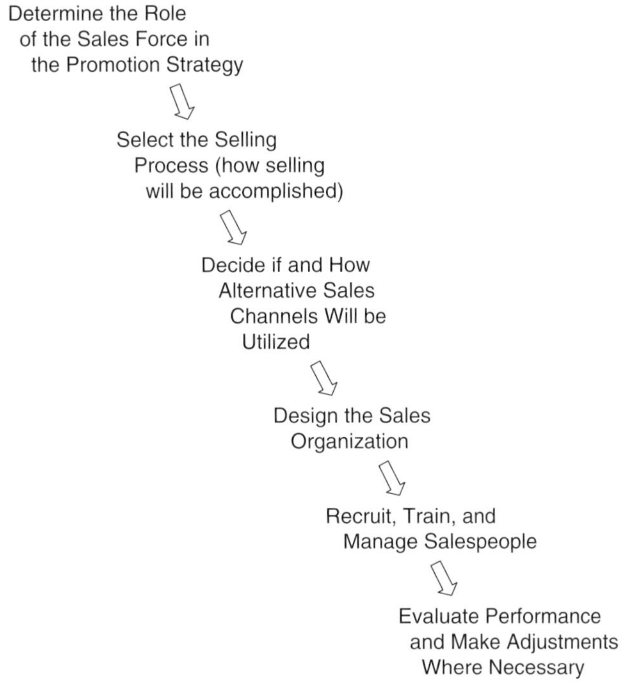

Determine the Role
of the Sales Force in
the Promotion Strategy

Select the Selling
Process (how selling
will be accomplished)

Decide if and How
Alternative Sales
Channels Will be
Utilized

Design the Sales
Organization

Recruit, Train, and
Manage Salespeople

Evaluate Performance
and Make Adjustments
Where Necessary

pharmaceutical company's marketing strategy. The drug salesperson provides information on new products, distributes samples, and works toward building long-term relationships.

Salesforce strategy includes six major initiatives, as shown in Exhibit 13.2. First, the role of the salesforce in the promotion strategy is determined. This requires deciding how personal selling is expected to contribute to the marketing program. Second, the selling process must be determined, indicating how selling will be accomplished with targeted customers. Third, in selecting sales channels, management decides how the sales organization, major account management, telemarketing, and the Internet will contribute to the selling process. Fourth, the design of the sales organization must be determined and assessed over time to determine its effectiveness. Recall H-P's redesign initiatives discussed in the lead-in illustration. Fifth, salespeople are recruited, trained, and managed. Finally, the results of the selling strategy are evaluated and adjustments are made to narrow the gap between actual and desired results.

The Role of Selling in Promotion Strategy

Salespeople's responsibilities may range from taking orders from customers to extensive collaboration as consultants to customers. While management has some flexibility in choosing the role and objectives of the salesforce in the marketing program, several factors often guide the role of selling in a firm's integrated marketing communications strategy, as shown in Exhibit 13.3. Recall our discussion of integrated marketing communications (IMC) in Chapter 12. Considerable direction as to how personal selling will be used is provided by the target market, product characteristics, distribution policies, and pricing policies. The selling effort needs to be positioned into the integrated communications program. It is also useful to indicate how the other promotion-mix components, such as advertising, support and relate to the salesforce. Sales management needs to be aware of the plans and activities of other promotion components.

The objectives assigned to salespeople frequently involve management's expected sales results. Sales quotas are used to state these expectations. Companies may give incentives to

EXHIBIT 13.3
**Factors Influencing
the Role of Personal
Selling in a Firm's
IMC Strategy**

Source: Mark W. Johnston and
Greg W. Marshall, *Sales Force
Management,* 9th ed. Burr
Ridge, IL: McGraw-Hill/Irwin,
2009, 94.

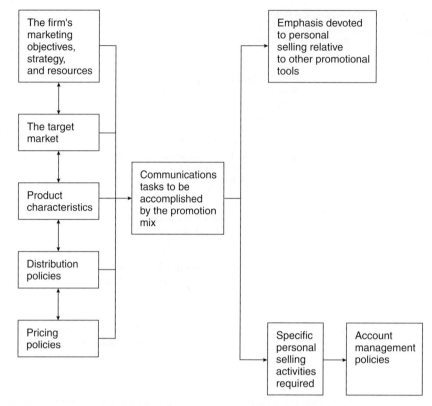

salespeople who achieve their quotas. Team selling incentives may also be used. Objectives other than sales are important in many organizations. These include increasing the number of new accounts, providing services to customers and channel organizations, retaining customers, selecting and evaluating value chain intermediaries, and obtaining market information. The objectives selected need to be consistent with marketing strategy and promotion objectives and measurable so that salesperson performance can be evaluated.

Selling roles range from transactional selling to consulting-type relationships. The Internet is replacing salespeople in transactional selling, whereas it may be used to provide support for relationship-type selling roles. Transactional selling is not restricted to small, low-volume buyers. The important issue is how much direct contact with the salesperson is needed by the buyer. For example, physicians may need detailed assistance on new drugs from salespeople, whereas transactional selling via the Internet is preferred for older and less complex products prescribed by doctors. Importantly, companies may need to utilize different types of selling for the same customer.

Types of Sales Jobs

The salespeople who sell to ultimate consumers (door-to-door sales, insurance sales, real estate brokers, retail store sales, etc.) comprise a major portion of the number of salespeople, but a much greater volume of sales is accounted for by business-to-business salespeople.[9] B2B sales may be to resellers (e.g., retail chains), business users, and institutions.

---

[9]The following discussion is based on Mark W. Johnston and Greg W. Marshall, *Sales Force Management,* 9th ed. (Burr Ridge, IL: McGraw-Hill/Irwin, 2009), 49–50.

Consumer and organizational sales are similar in several respects, but B2B sales may involve more complex products, more extensive purchasing processes, different selling skills, and more collaborative management processes (e.g., training, coaching, directing, and evaluating).

Illustrative sales positions for salespeople include new business selling, trade selling, missionary selling, and consultative/technical selling.[10]

New Business Selling

This selling job involves obtaining sales from new buyers. The buyers may be one-time purchasers or repeat buyers. For example, recruiting a new online business customer by an Office Depot salesperson is an illustration of a one-time selling situation. Alternatively, the selling strategy may be concerned with obtaining new buyers on a continuing basis. Commercial insurance and real estate sales firms frequently use this strategy.

Trade Selling

This form of selling provides assistance and support to value chain members rather than obtaining sales. A producer marketing through wholesalers, retailers, or other intermediaries may provide merchandising, logistical, promotional, and product information assistance. For example, PepsiCo's field sales organization assists retailers in merchandising and support activities and builds relationships with fast food and other retailers selling drinks on premises.

Missionary Selling

A strategy similar to trade selling is missionary selling. In these selling situations, a producer's salespeople work with the customers of a channel member to encourage them to purchase the producer's product from the channel member. For example, commercial airline sales representatives contact travel agencies, providing them with schedule information on new routes and encouraging agencies to book flights on their airline.

Consultative/Technical Selling

Firms that use this strategy sell to an existing customer base and provide technical and application assistance. These positions may involve the sales of complex equipment or services such as management consulting. Importantly, consultative selling requires giving sales professionals authority in negotiating sales as illustrated by sales of Boeing's large commercial aircraft.[11] These sales relationships involve high-level consultative selling strategies as described in the RELATIONSHIP APPLICATION.

An organization may use more than one of the selling strategies. For example, a transportation services company might use a new business strategy for expanding its customer base and a missionary selling strategy for servicing existing customers. The skills needed by the salesperson vary according to the selling strategy used.

Important changes are underway in many sales organizations. These initiatives require redesigning the traditional sales organization, leveraging information technology to lower costs and provide quick response, designing the sales strategy to meet different customer needs, building long-term relationships with customers and business partners, and responding proactively to global competitive opportunities and challenges. The salesforce continues to be essential in many organizations, although salespeople are being asked to assume new responsibilities and the methods for keeping score are changing.

---

[10]Ibid.

[11]Stanley Holmes, "Boeing's Jet Propellant," *BusinessWeek,* December 26, 2005, 40.

During the 2000s Boeing experienced an intense competitive battle against Airbus for control of the commercial jetliner market. Airbus was winning the battle until 2005 when Boeing's Asia-Pacific jet sales were $26 billion compared to Airbus' $9 billion.

Under a new CEO management gave salespeople much more control over selling strategy compared to previous tight and rigid control by top management. Boeing lost many sales to Airbus because of top management's unwillingness to give competent sales professionals flexibility in negotiating sales. Larry Dickenson, Boeing's top salesman who covers the Asia-Pacific market, builds on over eighteen years of relationships with airlines like Cathay Pacific, Quantas Airways Ltd., and Singapore Airlines Ltd., to negotiate winning contracts.

Importantly, Dickenson carefully plans and executes each sales campaign, overseeing every detail in the process that may span several years. The strategy is a combination of attractive pricing, financing, and leasing arrangements in combination with training and service packages.

Source: Stanley Holmes, "Boeing's Jet Propellant," *BusinessWeek,* December 26, 2005, 40.

Defining the Selling Process

Several selling and sales support activities are involved in moving from identifying a buyer's needs to completing the sale and managing the postsale relationships between buyer and seller. This selling process includes (1) prospecting for customers, (2) opening the relationship, (3) qualifying the prospect, (4) presenting the sales message, (5) closing the sale, and (6) servicing the account.[12] The process may be very simple, consisting of a routine set of actions designed to close the sale, such as supermarket purchases. Alternatively, the process may extend over a long time period, with many contacts and interactions between the buyers, other people influencing the purchase, the salesperson assigned to the account, and technical specialists in the seller's organization. The selling process for Boeing aircraft is illustrative (RELATIONSHIP APPLICATION).

Sales management guides the selling process by indicating the customers and prospects the firm is targeting and providing guidelines for developing customer relationships and obtaining sales results. This process is management's strategy for achieving the salesforce objectives in the selling environment of interest. Salespeople implement the process following the guidelines set by management, such as the product strategy (relative emphasis on different products), customer targeting and priorities, and the desired selling activities and outcomes.

The selling process is normally managed by the salesperson who has responsibility for a customer account, although an increasing number of companies are assigning this responsibility to customer relationship management teams. Account management includes planning and execution of the selling activities between the salesperson and the customer or prospect. Some organizations analyze this process and set guidelines for use by salespeople to plan their selling activities. Selling process analysis may result in programmed selling steps or alternatively, may lead to highly customized selling approaches where the salesperson develops specific strategies for each account. A company may also use team selling (e.g., product specialists and salesperson), major account management, telemarketing, and Internet support systems.

---

[12]Johnston and Marshall, *Sales Force Management,* 2009, 51–55.

Indications of a possible need for a change in the sales process include faulty forecasting, sales declines, lost customers, new customers from acquisitions, drops in profit margins, and price wars. The changes made by FedEx Corp. are illustrative.[13] Management combined its air and ground freight salesforces in 2000. Rather than deploying separate salesforces, customers are contacted by salespeople representing both air and ground services. The changes provide more uniform coverage and eliminate costly duplicated customer contacts. Notwithstanding the impact of global economic downturn, FedEx has experienced strong sales and profit growth, moving to an estimated $39 billion in sales for 2011 and more than $1.5 billion in net profit. These changes are illustrative of customer management initiatives being implemented by several companies. Recall also our earlier discussion of sales organization changes at P&G and IBM.

The selling process provides guidelines for salesforce recruiting, training, allocation of effort, organizational design, and the use of selling support activities such as telemarketing and the Internet. Understanding the selling process is essential in coordinating all elements of the marketing program.

Sales Channels

An important part of deciding the personal selling strategy is selecting the alternative channels to end-user customers. Management must decide (1) which channel(s) to use in contacting value chain members and end-users and (2) how telemarketing, Internet, and direct marketing will be used to support the field salesforce. For example, management may decide to contact major accounts using national or global account managers, manage regular accounts using the field salesforce, and service small accounts via telemarketing or the Internet. The reality is that direct contact by face-to-face salespeople is very expensive and the need for this resource should be evaluated in terms of benefits and costs.

The choice of a particular sales channel is influenced by the buying power of customers, the selling channel threshold levels, and the complexity of buyer-seller relationships. The buying power of a supplier's total customer base may range from several major accounts to a large number of very low-volume purchasers. Customers and prospects can be classified into: (1) major accounts, (2) other customers requiring face-to-face contact, and (3) accounts whose purchases (or potential) do not justify regular contact by field salespeople. Many companies are serving these accounts using the Internet.

The number of customers in each buying power category influences the selection of selling channels. The need for a multiple selling channel strategy should be determined. For example, the amount of telemarketing effort that is needed determines whether a telemarketing or electronic support unit should be considered. Similarly, enough major accounts should exist in order to develop and implement a major account program. If the customer base does not display substantial differences in purchasing power and servicing requirements, then the use of a single salesforce channel may be appropriate.

There is a trend toward greater use of customer management strategies by many companies. For example, Newell Rubbermaid Inc., producer of a range of consumer household products, undertook a major salesforce initiative underway to introduce new products and build stronger relationships with retailers.[14] The salespeople work with stores in spotlighting Newell Rubbermaid products and conducting product comparisons in the stores for end-users. Hundreds of college graduates have been recruited to strengthen relationships with retailers.

---

[13]Rick Brooks, "FedEx Fiscal Fourth-Quarter Profit Rose by 11%, Surpassing Expectations," *Wall Street Journal,* June 29, 2000, B2. Value Line Investment Survey, Ratings and Reports, December 2, 2011, 309.

[14]Erik Ahlberg, "Newell Rubbermaid Rebirth Is a Work in Progress," *Wall Street Journal,* November 27, 2002, B3A.

Another significant trend is the use of external third-party salesforces to outsource selling, most frequently applied to transactional selling.[15] Sales outsourcing providers include manufacturers' representatives, contract sales organizations, sales agents, and sales outsourcing consultants. Sales outsourcing can be applied to part of the sales process (e.g., generating leads), particular customer segments (e.g., geographical areas difficult to reach with conventional sales efforts), or sales of particular products lines (e.g., parts and maintenance for equipment). Sales outsourcing is particularly important for companies in the electronics, communications, and technology sectors as a way of rapidly gaining market coverage.[16] For example, in the United States, Procter & Gamble has a 200-person team wholly dedicated to Wal-Mart (the single customer that constitutes 20 percent of P&G's business), but nonetheless, outsources routine sales visits to retail stores to a third-party sales organization.[17] Sales and marketing firm Acosta employs 13,000 people to sell client products across 130,000 North American retail stores—clients include P&G, Nestlé, Kellogg, and Starbucks.[18]

Designing the Sales Organization

Designing the sales organization includes selecting an organizational structure and deciding the number and deployment of salespeople to geographical areas and/or customers and prospects.

Organizational Design

The organizational design adopted should support the firm's salesforce strategy. As companies adjust their selling strategies, organizational structure may also require changes. FedEx's shift to a single salesforce for its air and ground services is illustrative. There is a significant trend toward a greater focus on customers' (market-driven) designs rather than products or geography as the basis for the design of the sales organization.

The characteristics and requirements of the customer base, the product(s), and the geographic location of buyers are the more important influences on the design of the sales organization. The answers to several questions are helpful in narrowing the choice of an organizational design.

1. What is the selling job? What activities are to be performed by salespeople?
2. Is specialization of selling effort necessary according to type of customer, different products, or salesperson activities (e.g., sales and service)?
3. Are channel of distribution relationships important in the organizational design?
4. How many and what kinds of sales management levels are needed to provide the proper amount of supervision, assistance, and control?
5. Will sales teams be used, and if so, what will be their composition?
6. How and to what extent will sales channels other than the field salesforce be used to contact and serve customers?

The salesforce organizational design needs to be compatible with the selling strategy and other marketing program strategies. Several illustrative types of organization designs

---

[15]Erin Anderson and Bob Trinkle, *Outsourcing the Sales Function: The Real Cost of Field Sales* (Mason, OH: Thomson/South-Western, 2005).

[16]Accenture, *A Structured Approach to Reaching New Customers and Growing Revenues,* www.accenture.com/us-en/Pages/insight-indirect-sales-channels-revenues.aspx, accessed August 18, 2011.

[17]Anderson and Trinkle, 2005.

[18]Matthew Boyle, "Who's Really Stocking Your Grocer's Shelf?" *Bloomberg BusinessWeek,* March 28–April 3, 2011, 34–35.

EXHIBIT 13.4
Sales Organization Designs

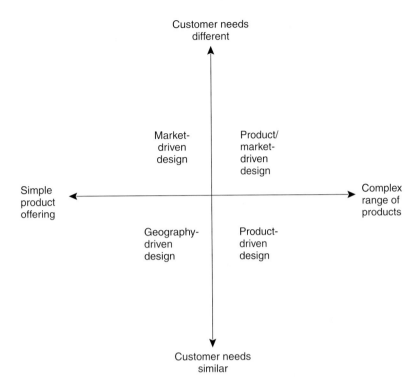

are shown in Exhibit 13.4. These designs should take into account the scope of the product portfolio and differences in customer needs. Whenever the customer base is widely dispersed, geography is likely to be relevant in the organizational design. The market-driven design is heavily influenced by the customer base, although geographical location may also influence the design. The product/market design takes both factors into account in determining how the organization is structured. Similar customer needs and a complex range of products point to the product-driven design. If the product or the customer base does not dominate design considerations, a geographical organization is used. The assigned geographical area and (or) accounts that are the responsibility of each salesperson comprise the sales territory or work unit.

Sales Force Deployment

Sales management must decide how many salespeople are needed and how to deploy them to customers and prospects. Several factors outside the salesperson's control often affect his or her sales results, such as market potential, number and location of customers, intensity of competition, and market (brand) position of the company. Salesforce deployment analysis should consider both salesperson factors and the relevant uncontrollable factors.

There is a compelling amount of evidence indicating that sales unit design has a strong impact on sales unit performance. The better the sales unit is designed, the higher the performance of the unit assigned to a manager and the assigned salespeople (typically ten or less). Studies conducted involving over 1,000 field sales managers in eight countries around the world support the strong role of sales unit design.[19]

---

[19]David W. Cravens, Nigel F. Piercy, and George S. Low, "Globalization of the Sales Organization: Management Control and Its Consequences," *Organizational Dynamics* (3), 2006, 1–14.

Salesforce.com is an interesting example of a dot-com start-up that has developed a successful business model supplying customer management software over the Net for use by salespeople.

A key feature of the software is that it is sold as a service to customers at a monthly charge for each individual user. Salesforce.com has over 72,000 customers in more than 70 countries.

Salesforce.com illustrates how Internet information technology can enhance the capabilities and efforts of salespeople. By replacing large up-front software purchases with monthly service charges Salesforce.com offers customers a compelling value opportunity.

Salesforce.com's core business is software that helps salespeople keep track of how much they have sold to specific customers, when they need to call again, and if they have met their quota. Since this feature can be duplicated by software competitors such as Microsoft and SAP, Salesforce.com faced difficulty sustaining its competitive edge.

In 2005 the company launched AppExchange— an online marketplace enabling software firms and customers to trade and sell applications they develop. There will be no charge for the eBay-like service but Salesforce.com expects it to expand demand for the firm's software. This was followed in 2008 by Force.com—a web-based platform allowing other companies to build their own online services using Salesforce.com technology.

Effectively, Salesforce.com has become an enterprise cloud computing company, with three main businesses: the Sales Cloud and the Service Cloud applications for sales and customer service (also known as customer relationship management); Force.com, a cloud-based platform for building and running business applications; and Chatter, an enterprise collaboration application.

Sources: www.salesforce.com, accessed August 18, 2011. "An eBay for Business Software," *BusinessWeek,* September 19, 2005, 78–79. Vaujini Vara, "An Early Adopter's New Idea: Salesforce.com Sees Future Built on 'Platforms,'" *Wall Street Journal,* January 22, 2008, B3, Value Line Investment Survey, Ratings & Reports, July 22, 2011, 1808.

Salesforce.com is an interesting example of a software service designed to help salespeople manage their customer relationships and their productivity. The software can easily be implemented in large and small organizations as described in the INTERNET APPLICATION.

Several methods are available for analyzing salesforce size and the deployment of selling effort including: (1) revenue/cost analysis, (2) single-factor models, (3) sales and effort response models, and (4) portfolio deployment models. Normally, sales and/or costs are the basis for determining salesforce size and allocation.

Revenue/cost analysis techniques require information on each salesperson's sales and/or costs. One approach compares each salesperson to an average break-even sales level, thus helping management to spot unprofitable territories. Another approach analyzes the profit performance of accounts or trading areas, to estimate the profit impact of adding more salespeople, or to determine how many people a new sales organization needs. These techniques are very useful in locating high- and low-performance territories.

Single-factor models assume that size of the salesforce and/or effort deployment are determined by one factor, such as market potential or workload (e.g., number of calls required), whose values can be used to determine required selling effort. Suppose there are two territories, X and Y. Territory X has double the market potential (opportunity for business) of territory Y. If selling effort is deployed according to market potential, X should get double the selling effort of Y.

EXHIBIT 13.5

Sales Force
Deployment Analysis
Illustration for
Jones's and Smith's
Territories

Trading Area[†]	Present Effort (percent)	Recommended Effort (percent)	Estimated Sales* Present Effort	Estimated Sales* Recommended Effort
Jones:				
1	10%	4%	$ 19	$ 13
2	60	20	153	120
3	15	7	57	50
4	5	2	10	7
5	10	3	21	16
Total	100%	36%	$ 260	$ 206
Smith:				
1	18%	81%	$ 370	$ 520
2	7	21	100	130
3	5	11	55	65
4	35	35	225	225
5	5	11	60	70
6	30	77	400	500
Total	100%	236%	$ 1,210	$ 1,510

*In $000.
[†]Each territory is made up of several trading areas.

Consideration of multiple influences (e.g., market potential, intensity of competition, and workload) on market response can improve salesperson deployment decisions. Several promising *sales and effort response models* are available to assist management on sales-force size and deployment decisions.[20] Exhibit 13.5 shows the information provided by one of these models. The analysis indicates that Jones' territory requires only about 36 percent of a person whereas Smith's territory can support about 2.36 people. The inadequate sales coverage in Smith's territory is risky in terms of dissatisfaction and loss of customers, whereas expensive salesperson effort is being wasted in Jones's territory. Also, too much contact may irritate customers. The allocations are determined by incrementally increasing selling effort in high-response areas and reducing effort where sales response is low. Note that Exhibit 13.5 includes only two territories of a large sales organization. Sales response is determined from a computer analysis of the selling effort-to-sales response relationship.

We know that salespeople differ in ability, motivation, and performance. Managers are involved in selecting, training, monitoring, directing, evaluating, and rewarding sales-people. A brief look at each activity illustrates the responsibilities and functions of a sales manager.

Finding and Selecting Salespeople

In a major study, the chief sales executives in over 100 firms selling business-to-business products indicated on a 1 to 10 scale how important 29 salesperson characteristics are to the success of their salespeople.[21] The executives indicated that the three most significant success characteristics are (1) being customer-driven and highly committed to the job;

---

[20]Johnston and Marshall, *Sales Force Management,* Chapter 5, 2009.
[21]David W. Cravens, Thomas M. Ingram, Raymond W. LaForge, and Clifford E. Young, "Hallmarks of Effective Sales Organizations," *Marketing Management,* Winter 1992, 56–67.

EXHIBIT 13.6

Characteristics Related to Sales Performance in Different Types of Sales Jobs

Source: Mark W. Johnston and Greg W. Marshall, *Sales Force Management,* 9th ed. Burr Ridge, IL: McGraw-Hill/Irwin, 2009, 276.

Type of Sales Job	Characteristics That Are Relatively Important	Characteristics That Are Relatively Less Important
Trade selling	Age, maturity, empathy, knowledge of customer needs and business methods	Aggressiveness, technical ability, product knowledge, persuasiveness
Missionary selling	Youth, high energy and stamina, verbal skill, persuasiveness	Empathy, knowledge of customers, maturity, previous sales experience
Technical selling	Education, product and customer knowledge—usually gained through training, intelligence	Empathy, persuasiveness, aggressiveness, age
New business selling	Experience, age and maturity, aggressiveness, persuasiveness, persistence	Customer knowledge, product knowledge, education, empathy

(2) accepting direction and cooperating as a team player; and (3) and being motivated by one's peers, financial incentives, and oneself.

Exhibit 13.6 describes several salesperson characteristics that are often important for different types of selling situations. The characteristics vary based on the type of selling strategy being employed, so we must first define the job that is to be performed. Managers use application forms, personal interviews, rating forms, reference checks, physical examinations, and various kinds of tests to assist them in making hiring decisions. The personal interview is widely acknowledged as the most important part of the selection process for salespeople.

Training

Some firms use formal programs to train their salespeople, while others use informal on-the-job training. Factors that affect the type and duration of training include type of sales job, product complexity, prior experience of new salespeople, and management's commitment to training. Training topics may include selling concepts and techniques, product knowledge, territory management, and company policies and operating procedures.

In training salespeople, companies may seek to (1) increase productivity, (2) improve morale, (3) lower turnover, (4) improve customer relations, and (5) enable better management of time and territory.[22] These objectives are concerned with increasing the results from the salesperson's effort and/or reducing selling costs. Sales training should be evaluated concerning its benefits and costs. Evaluations may include before-and-after training results, participant critiques, and comparison of salespeople receiving training to those that have not been trained. Product knowledge training is probably more frequently used than any other type of training.

Supervising and Motivating Salespeople

The manager who supervises salespeople has a key role in implementing a firm's selling strategy. She or he faces several important management issues. Coordinating the activities of a field salesforce is difficult due to lack of regular contact, although Internet access

---

[22]Johnston and Marshall, *Sales Force Management,* Chapter 10, 2009.

overcomes to some extent the lack of face-to-face contact. Compensation incentives are often used to encourage salespeople to obtain sales. However, salespeople need to be self-motivated. As discussed earlier, sales executives want salespeople who are customer-driven; committed to the company and to team relationships; and motivated by peers, incentives, and themselves.

The most widely used basis of compensation is a combination of salary and incentive pay. In situations where sales management wants to exercise control over salesperson activities, 75 percent salary and 25 percent incentive pay is a typical arrangement. The compensation plan should be fair to all participants and create an appropriate incentive. Salespeople also respond favorably to recognition programs and special promotions such as vacation travel awards.

Managers assist and encourage salespeople, and incentives highlight the importance of results, but the salesperson is the driving force in selling situations. Sales management must match promising selling opportunities with competent and self-motivated professional salespeople while providing the proper company environment, leadership, and collaborative support. Although most sales management professionals consider financial compensation the most important motivating force, research findings indicate that personal characteristics, environmental conditions, and company policies and procedures are also important motivating factors.[23]

A major study involving a large (1,000 +) sample of business-to-business salespeople found that salespeople who experienced higher levels of management monitoring and directing by managers displayed higher performance, job satisfaction, and organizational commitment.[24] Importantly, the management control efforts are collaborative and appear to be favorably received by many salespeople. These findings suggest that higher levels of management control are associated with favorable salesperson attitudes and behavior.

Salesforce Evaluation and Control

Sales management is continually working to improve the productivity of selling efforts. During the last decade personal selling costs increased much faster than advertising costs, so achieving high salesforce performance is important. The evaluation of salesforce performance considers sales results, costs, salesperson activities, and customer satisfaction. Several issues are important in evaluation, including where to focus the analysis, measures of performance, performance standards, and taking into account factors that the sales organization and individual salespeople cannot control.

Over a considerable period of time many pharmaceutical companies expanded their salesforces, reaching over 100,000 salespeople worldwide in 2004.[25] However, several of these companies have re-evaluated the productivity and strategy of their salesforces. The pharmaceutical industry has searched for new and better ways to get to market. Companies like Pfizer, Novartis, and GlaxoSmithKlein have recognized the need for radically new sales models.[26] The STRATEGY APPLICATION describes how Wyeth (now part of Pfizer) changed its selling strategy and reduced the size of its salesforce.

[23]Ibid., Chapter 7.
[24]David W. Cravens, Greg W. Marshall, Felicia G. Lassk, and George S. Low, "The Control Factor," *Marketing Management,* 13(1), January–February 2004, 39–44.
[25]Scott Hensley, "Wyeth to Revamp, Cut Its Sales Force," *Wall Street Journal,* June 20, 2005, A3, A6.
[26]Arlene Weintraub, "Just Say No to Drug Reps," *BusinessWeek,* February 4, 2008, 69.

- Wyeth's changes in the sales organization are driven by concerns of physicians about duplicated sales coverage and the need to improve salesforce productivity.
- The prior approach of multiple salespeople calling on doctors to market the same drugs is being changed.
- Out of Wyeth's salesforce of 5,000, about half call on primary-care doctors. As many as 750 may be cut or reassigned.
- The selling strategy is to reduce the frequency of sales calls, while making each more worthwhile.
- Initiatives include assigning each salesperson responsibility for more drugs, reducing sales calls on the doctors who write the fewest prescriptions, and utilizing a part-time salesforce for coverage of selected accounts, and use of Internet-based seminars.
- Other pharmaceutical companies are expected to follow Wyeth's salesforce strategy initiatives.

Source: Scott Hensley, "Wyeth to Revamp, Cut Its Sales Force," *Wall Street Journal,* June 20, 2005, A3, A6.

Where to Focus the Analysis

Evaluation extends beyond the salesperson to include other organizational units, such as districts and branches. Selling teams are used in some types of selling. Companies that use teams focus evaluations on team results. Product performance evaluation by geographical area and across organization units is relevant in the firms that produce more than one product. Individual account sales and cost analyses are useful for customers such as national accounts and accounts assigned to salespeople.

Performance Measures

Management needs yardsticks for measuring salesperson performance. For example, the salesforce of a regional food processor that distributes through grocery wholesalers and large retail chains devotes most of its selling effort to calling on retailers. Since the firm does not have information on sales of its products by each individual retail outlet, evaluations are based on the activities of salespeople rather than sales outcomes. This type of control system focuses on "behavior" rather than "outcomes."

Sales managers may use both activity (behavior) and outcome measures of salesperson performance. Research indicates that multiple item measures of several activities and outcomes are useful in performance evaluation.[27] Illustrative areas include sales planning, expense control, sales presentation, technical knowledge, information feedback, and sales results. Achievement of the sales quota (actual sales/quota sales) is a widely used outcome measure of sales performance. Other outcome measures include new business generated, market share gains, new product sales, and profit contributions.

Performance evaluation is influenced by the sales management control system used by the organization. Emphasis may be placed on salesperson activities, on outcomes, or a combination of activities and outcomes. The objective is to use the type of control that is most effective for the selling situation. Direct selling organizations like Avon and Mary Kay focus more on outcome control. Companies like American Airlines and Pfizer include

---

[27]Cravens et al., "The Control Factor."

both activity and outcome control. An important aspect of management control is the compensation plan. When salespeople are compensated primarily by commission earnings on sales results, pay becomes the primary management control mechanism.

Setting Performance Standards

Although internal comparisons of performance are frequently used, they are not very helpful if the performance of the entire salesforce is unacceptable. A major problem in setting sales performance standards is determining how to adjust them for factors that are not under the salesperson's control (i.e., market potential, intensity of competition, differences in customer needs, and quality of supervision). A competent salesperson may not appear to be performing well if assigned to a poor sales territory (e.g., salesperson Jones Exhibit 13.5), when the low performance may not be due to the salesperson. Such differences need to be included in the evaluation process since territories often are not equal in terms of opportunity and other uncontrollable factors.

We know that evaluating performance is one of sales management's more difficult tasks. Typically, performance tracking involves assessing a combination of outcome and behavioral factors. In compensation plans other than straight commission, performance evaluation may affect the salesperson's pay, so obtaining a fair evaluation is important.

By evaluating the organization's personal selling strategy, management may identify various problems requiring corrective action as illustrated by the Wyeth example (STRATEGY APPLICATION). Problems may be linked to individual salespeople or to decisions that impact the entire organization. A well-designed information system helps in the diagnosis of performance and guides corrective actions when necessary.

Digital Strategy

We now consider digital or Internet-based marketing strategy, examining the alternatives, integration of Internet-based initiatives with marketing and promotion strategies, options for measuring effectiveness, and the expanding role of digital models in business and marketing strategies. Also, recall our discussion of the topic in earlier chapters.

The Internet is a worldwide means of exchanging information and communicating through a series of interconnected computers.[28] It offers a fast and versatile communications capability. Internet-based initiatives span a wide range of global industries and companies, and there have been successes but also many failures, stimulated by over-optimistic expectations and faulty implementation. Initiatives have been pursued by both traditional enterprises and new business designs. Business-to-business use of the Internet is far more extensive than consumer adoption of the Internet, although consumer use of the Internet for information on products and actual purchase is expanding rapidly. The impacts of the Internet on business organizations in the future are expected to continue to be both transformational as well as incremental in scope.

The impact of digital change is expected to be much greater for companies and organizations that are very dependent on the flow of information, for example, information services. The impact of the Internet promises to be revolutionary for certain industries and incremental for others.[29] We have experienced the impact of the Internet on sales of books,

---

[28]George E. Belch and Michael A. Belch, *Advertising and Promotion,* 8th ed. (New York: McGraw-Hill Irwin, 2009), 483–484.
[29]Michael J. Mandel and Robert D. Hof, "Rethinking the Internet," *BusinessWeek,* March 26, 2001, 117–122.

EXHIBIT 13.7
E-Tailing Finally Hits Its Stride

Source: "E-Tailing Finally Hits Its Stride," *BusinessWeek,* December 20, 2004, 36–37.

The E-Tail Effect

How e-commerce is shaking up the retail landscape:

The Big Guns Arrive

After early struggles, online sales at brick-and-mortar giants such as Wal-Mart, Sears, and Gap are soaring. These chains are also using the Web to test new products and move into new markets.

Niches Go National

More and more niche players are succeeding by offering variety rivals can't match. Luggage seller eBags, for example, is able to stock 12,000 styles, compared with 250 in a typical store.

Search Lends a Hand

Using Google and similar websites, consumers can search far and wide for specialized products – say, stainless-steel farm sinks. That's creating markets for lesser known brands and new merchants.

More Pricing Pressures

Shoppers are increasingly using price-comparison sites such as Shopping.com and Shopzilla. The result: Ever more cutthroat competition for brick-and-mortar and online stores alike.

music, and air travel. Internet evolutions forecast for the future include jewelry, payments, telecom, hotels, real estate, and software.[30] Several effects on retailing of e-commerce are discussed in Exhibit 13.7.

Certainly, the Internet has encouraged the development of "consumer-generated content" for some advertising. For example, The Hub is a Wal-Mart site, jointly sponsored by Sony, aiming to reach out to fashion-conscious young consumers. High school students are invited to create their own Web pages and videos, the winners to be used in Wal-Mart's cable TV and cinema advertising. Targeting young males as consumers of Doritos, Frito-Lay invited consumers online to create Doritos ads, with the winners broadcast on CBS during the NFL Superbowl in 2006. The advertising spot they filled is estimated to cost more than $2 million. The goal is to tap into the creativity and engagement of consumers, though the approach carries some risks.[31]

Nonetheless, the early 2000s saw the collapse of many Internet-based businesses, and there are concerns that there may be another Internet "bubble" likely to burst in the early 2010s.[32] The earlier Internet shakeout may have been inevitable because of the race to develop Internet capabilities and business designs. Acknowledging the setbacks, it is apparent that Internet initiatives will continue to expand:

> Although the specific details are unpredictable and unimportant, digital technology will inevitably accelerate, intensify, and reduce the cost of marketing activities. What is important is that marketing managers will help guide the company's customers toward better utilization of the company's products and services.[33]

---

[30]Timothy J. Mullaney, "E-Biz Strikes Again," *BusinessWeek,* May 10, 2004, 80–90.

[31]Jon Fine, "What Makes 'Citizen Ads' Work?" *BusinessWeek,* February 19, 2007, 24; Aline van Duyn and Jonathan Birchall, "Wal-Mart's Amateur Advertisers," *Financial Times,* Friday, July 21, 2006, 8.

[32]Bijan Khezri and Howard Jones, "Internet Wars: Version 2," *Wall Street Journal,* August 5–7, 2011, 17.

[33]Glen L. Urban, *Digital Marketing Strategy* (Upper Saddle River, NJ: Pearson Prentice Hall), 2004, 180.

Strategy Development

The first step in Internet strategy development is to determine the role of the digital strategies in the organization's overall business and marketing strategies. This role may involve a separate business model, a value-chain channel, a marketing communications tool, or an advertising medium:

> Marketers lured by the Internet's promise of immediacy, interactivity, availability, customization, and global reach need to evaluate when it really pays to reach customers through the Internet and how the Internet best fits into overall marketing strategy. To do so, they need to pay even closer attention to customers and rethink how to evaluate market opportunities, set marketing strategy, and deploy marketing programs.[34]

Importantly, while company goals are not normally directly shaped by Internet-based potentials, it is clear that there have been major changes in the "communications landscape." For example in the fragmentation of the audiences for many traditional media (television, newspapers) and the rapid expansion of expenditure in online applications (Internet, mobile telephones, and pad computers), and the transformational impact of social media like Facebook and Twitter on communications with customers (business-to-customer) and between customers (peer-to-peer).[35] The changed environment has important implications for implementing innovative and effective communications as part of marketing strategy.[36]

A New Communications Landscape

Digitization has impacted throughout the value chain for many companies and in particular has brought radical changes to the way in which information is disseminated and interpreted in society.[37] The rapid growth in social media offers both challenges and opportunities in marketing communications strategy.

Advertising Agency Role

Some companies have faced difficulties regarding the Internet and social media capabilities of conventional advertising agencies.[38] Major advertising agencies have made extensive efforts to incorporate digital capabilities effectively into traditional activities, in some cases by acquiring digital specialist agencies.[39] Nonetheless, some major advertisers, such as Unilever, have brought digital advertising expertise in-house to avoid dependence on conventional advertising agencies.[40] P&G, Dell, and Johnson & Johnson have all tried to create new types of advertising groups that blend different functions to support their move from traditional to digital media.[41] The availability of digital advertising expertise that integrates with conventional advertising capabilities remains a serious concern.

The Impact of Social Media

While the center of the social media evolution is social platforms like Facebook and Bebo, they are linked to a complex of blogging and news sites (e.g., Digg.com), networking sites (e.g., Twitter, LinkedIn for professionals), content sites like Flickr and YouTube, and social

---

[34]Bernard Jaworski and Katherine Jocz, "Rediscovering the Customer," *Marketing Management,* September–October 2002, 24.

[35]Anthony Bianco, "The Vanishing Mass Market," *BusinessWeek,* July 12, 2004, 58–62.

[36]Maurice Saatchi, "The Strange Death of Modern Advertising," *Financial Times,* June 22, 2006, 17.

[37]Michael E. Porter, "Strategy and the Internet," *Harvard Business Review,* March 2001, 62–78.

[38]Suzanne Vranica, "Big Marketers Go On Hunt for New Agencies," *Wall Street Journal,* October 26, 2009, 6.

[39]Felix Gillett, "Don Draper's Revenge," *Bloomberg BusinessWeek,* November 29–December 5, 2010, 75–80.

[40]Gary Silverman, "Unilever in Advertising Shake-Up," *Financial Times,* March 14, 2006, 23.

[41]Suzanne Vrenica, "Transformed by the Internet," *Wall Street Journal,* January 2, 2008, 28.

- Facebook reached the half a billion member level in 2010.
- The average Facebook user creates 90 pieces of content each month.
- Flickr is growing at 25 percent a year and at the end of 2010 was hosting more than 5 billion images.
- Twitter claims 175 million registered users, and 95 million Tweets are written every day.
- LinkedIn has over 100 million professionals using its platform worldwide.
- More than 1 million companies have LinkedIn Company pages.

Source: www.pamorama.net/2011/01/30/65-terrific-social-media-infographics/, accessed August 19, 2011.

gaming sites like Zynga. The common characteristic between these media is the connectedness and dynamic conversations between users.

The considerable reach of social media websites like Facebook, LinkedIn, and Twitter offers the potential to engage in direct consumer contact at relatively low cost compared to traditional media.[42] The scale of social media activity is illustrated by the social media statistics in the INNOVATION APPLICATION.

Importantly, there is a compelling logic suggesting that social media can play a bigger role than providing a new communications channel. Social media may augment the product offering to create a new category or position in the market. In social media–based positioning attempts, the goal is to create a community providing not only functional benefits, but also emotional, social and self-expressive benefits. The new category that may be created by these efforts relies on a social media element that makes competitors brands irrelevant from a customer perspective. The social media efforts at Dell to augment the technology product offering are described in the INTERNET APPLICATION. Innovative social media efforts by others like Pampers, Harley-Davidson, and Southwest Airlines are also impressive.[43]

New Business Models

The Internet offers potential not simply for new ways of communicating as part of marketing strategy, but new types of communication based on peer-to-peer relationships and communications. For example, social shopping where networks of individuals share product preferences and purchasing behavior is becoming important. The potential for developing new types of business model may be substantial in some industries.

For example, Groupon is a strong competitor in the "daily deals" or online coupon business, offering customers discounts by purchasing vouchers from the Groupon site, and offering suppliers access to the combined purchases of a group of consumers. Nonetheless, the innovative Groupon business model faces formidable potential competition in this business. The development of Groupon is described in the INNOVATION APPLICATION.

---

[42]Andreas M. Kaplan and Michael Haenlein, "Users of the World Unite! The Challenges and Opportunities of Social Media," *Business Horizons,* 53, 2010, 59–68.

[43]David Aaker, *Brand Relevance: Making Competitors Irrelevant* (San Francisco: Jossey-Bass, 2011). David Aaker, "Beyond Communication to Changing the Marketplace," *Marketing News,* July 30, 2011, 14.

Dell has eight different types of social media efforts from online communities to support forums and Facebook and Twitter accounts. Consumers can interact with Dell however they find most comfortable, rewarding, and useful.

Dell has become a social media brand through

- The IdeaStorm online community in which consumers can post innovation ideas for Dell to consider, and evaluate existing ideas.
- Dell maintains blogs, including Direct2Dell, in which participants communicate directly with the company, as well as blogs like Enterprise IT Perspectives, Health Care and Education that are focused on particular topics.
- Dell sponsors several online communities, focused on such topics as digital entertainment, gaming, and small and medium business, as well as the Dell Management Console community, which allows a peek at the future of Dell technology.
- Dell has three owners' clubs—Streak, Alienware, and XPS—in which users can share their experiences with Dell's offerings.
- There are several support forums allowing users to ask questions about nearly a dozen offering areas, such as mobile devices, servers, and laptops.
- With multiple Twitter handles, Dell has more than 1.5 million followers and Twitter deals have generated more than $1 million in revenue.
- An active Dell Facebook page has more than 600,000 fans.
- Dell's YouTube channel has more than 6,000 subsribers.

Dell's social media efforts are more than tactics to communicate and provide product support. The strategic opportunity is to change the category or brand. Dell is moving from offering computer hardware and software to offering hardware and software surrounded by a responsive computer-based support system, connected to a social network, providing social, emotional, and self-expressive benefits as well as functional benefits.

Competing brands that lack such a linked social network may no longer be relevant to customers.

Sources: David Aaker, *Brand Relevance: Making Competitors Irrelevant* (San Francisco: Jossey-Bass, 2011). David Aaker, "Beyond Communication to Changing the Marketplace," *Marketing News,* July 30, 2011, p. 14. www.dell.com.

Deciding Internet Objectives

The capabilities of the Internet fall into two broad categories: a communications medium and a direct response medium enabling users to purchase and sell products. The communications features of the Internet include the following.[44]

Creating Awareness and Interest

Advertising on the Internet offers important advantages to many companies. The opportunity for global exposure provides a compelling brand-building capability.

Disseminating Information

Providing product, application, and company information via the Internet is essential in the competitive marketplace. This capability offers an opportunity for direct one-on-one contact.

---

[44]The following is based on Belch and Belch, *Advertising and Promotion,* 486–488.

Groupon is one of the most popular coupon sites on the Internet offering cut-price deals on everything from holidays to chicken sandwiches. The staples are spa treatments and restaurant deals. Groupon's turnover was between $3 billion and $4 billion in 2011, up from $750 million in 2010.

In a typical Groupon deal, consumers buy a voucher for a meal or salon service for a 50 percent discount. When the Chicago-based group discount website launched the daily deal craze in 2008, it typically shared sales revenues with merchants 50:50.

As more and more players have entered the online coupon market—LivingSocial, Foursquare, Loopy, as well as Google, Facebook, and AT&T—margins have fallen to around the 20 percent level. In its IPO prospectus, Groupon admits to accepting lower gross margins in the race to acquire new subscribers.

Shrinking revenue shares for daily deals sites are commonest among local businesses that are strong brands in their communities. Groupon was initially pitched as a mechanism to help businesses grow and acquire new customers, but daily deal companies are increasingly haggling with merchants who already have established brand reputations and strong customer bases to differentiate their daily deal offers.

In 2010, Groupon turned down a $6 billion offer from Google, and is rumored to be valuing the business at $25 billion in a planned initial public offering. There are concerns this valuation may be too high.

Predictions are that larger companies like Facebook and Google, and LivingSocial backed by Amazon.com investment, with the resources to innovate in daily deals will become the dominant players, even though Groupon was the first to build a deals platform. Groupon has not evolved enough in its mobile and social offerings to remain competitive.

Fears are that Groupon will become the MySpace of daily deals.

Sources: Brad Stone and Douglas MacMillan, "Are Four Words Worth $25 billion?" *Bloomberg BusinessWeek,* March 21–27, 2011, 70–75. Richard Waters, "LivingSocial Raises $400m for Expansion," *Financial Times,* April 6, 2011, 22. April Dembosky, "Daily Deal Groups Start to Feel the Heat," *Financial Times,* August 13–14, 2011, 11.

Obtaining Research Information

The Internet offers a very cost-effective means of obtaining information, such as user profiles. However, concerns have been voiced about invasion of consumer privacy.

Brand Building

Access to users provides an opportunity to build a brand that is unique compared to other media. This highlights the importance of developing effective designs for websites.

Improving Customer Service

The Internet provides an important avenue of after-the-sale customer contact.

We now consider what is involved in developing digital capability. This initiative may be pursued by an existing company such as Avon Products Corp. or a new Web-based business model.

Digital Strategy

Designing and launching new digital business that enables buyers to purchase products is a major initiative. Recall, faulty evaluation of market opportunities and inadequate planning have resulted in many Web-based business failures. Several interrelated decisions must be made:

1. Which customer groups should I serve?
2. How do I provide a compelling set of benefits to my targeted customer? How do I differentiate my "value proposition" versus online and offline competitors?

3. How do I communicate with customers?

4. What is the content, "look-and-feel," level of community, and degree of personalization of the website?

5. How should I structure my organization? What business services and applications software choices do I need to consider?

6. Who are my potential partners? Whose capabilities complement ours?

7. How will this business provide value to shareholders?

8. What metrics should I use to judge the progress of the business? How do I value the business?[45]

The intent of the present discussion is to describe what is involved in a digital initiative; an extensive coverage of the topic is provided by several other sources.[46]

Value Opportunities and Risks

The earlier discussion highlights several unique features of the Internet as a communications medium. Properly designed and managed, Web-based initiatives provide important opportunities for offering superior customer value. These include[47]

1. Very focused targeting is possible via the Web.

2. Messages can be designed to address the needs and preferences of the target audience.

3. The Web offers a compelling opportunity for interaction and feedback.

4. A core value offering of the Internet is access to a wide range of information.

5. The sales potential offered by the Internet is substantial.

6. The Internet provides an exciting opportunity for communications innovation.

7. The exposure opportunities of the Internet are significant, enabling many small companies and professionals to attain cost-effective access to customers and prospects.

8. The speed of response via the Internet is impressive.

The extensive value opportunities offered by the Web explain the many initiatives pursued by companies. Nonetheless, there are some risks associated with the use of the Internet as a communications medium.[48] These include difficulties in effectiveness measurement, changes in audience characteristics, access and response delays, multiple-ad exposure, potential for deception, and costs that may be higher than traditional media. There are also concerns that Internet users may become weary of more online advertising and change their behavior to avoid it, for example, move from one social network to another.

Measuring Internet Effectiveness

Measurement of effectiveness problems associated with the Internet are particularly challenging. This is not surprising given the explosive growth of Web-based initiatives and the limited experience with the medium. Nonetheless, there are many sources of measurement data. Evaluating the quality and relevance of alternative measurement sources requires careful assessment by the organization pursuing Internet strategies.

---

[45]Jeffrey F. Rayport and Bernard J. Jaworski, *e-Commerce* (New York: McGraw-Hill/Irwin, 2001), 12.
[46]See, for example, Glen L. Urban, *Digital Marketing Strategy* (Upper Saddle River, NJ: Pearson Prentice Hall), 2004.
[47]Belch and Belch, *Advertising and Promotion,* 500–501.
[48]Ibid., 501–503.

Measures of effectiveness of the Internet include Internet-specific measures (e.g., clicks), cross-media studies, and traditional measures (recall and retention, surveys, sales, and tracking).[49] Thus, the Internet has specific criteria to gauge effectiveness and traditional measures can be utilized.

Direct Marketing Strategies

The purpose of direct marketing is to make direct contact with end-user customers through alternative media (e.g., computer, telephone, mobile devices like smartphone and pads, mail, and kiosks). Many direct marketing methods are available, each offering certain advantages and limitations. The rapid growth of direct marketing indicates the importance placed by many companies on these direct avenues to customers. The growth in multichaneling strategies (see Chapter 10) often involves combining direct marketing approaches with other methods of reaching buyers. For example, Williams-Sonoma, the kitchenware retailer, generates over 40 percent of its annual revenues from catalog and Internet sales. The company first builds a catalog customer base in a metro-area. Williams-Sonoma may open a retail store when sufficient catalog shoppers are identified, targeting catalog buyers with store promotion mailings.

First, we look at several considerations in the use of direct marketing. Next, the major direct marketing methods are discussed. Finally, we consider at how direct marketing strategies are developed and implemented.

Reasons for Using Direct Marketing

The popularity of direct marketing methods is driven by a combination of factors such as socioeconomic trends, low costs, databases, and buyers' demands for value. We examine how these influences affect companies' use of mail, phone, media, and computers to contact individual buyers.

Socioeconomic Trends

Several trends make the availability of direct marketing purchases attractive to many buyers. Having two working spouses imposes major time constraints on households, so purchase via direct channels is a useful way of saving time as well as making contact at the convenience of the customer. Many single-person households also favor direct marketing purchases. Buyers can shop at home, save time, and avoid shopping congestion. Rapid response to order processing and shipping enables buyers to obtain their purchases in a few days. Liberal exchange policies reduce the risks of direct purchases.

Low Access Costs

While the cost per contact varies according to the method of direct contact, costs are often much lower than face-to-face sales contact. The availability of databases that can target specific customer groups enables companies to selectively target buyers. Companies like American Express can market products to their credit card users. Similarly, airline frequent flyer mailing lists provide cost-effective access to buyers. The availability of credit cards simplifies the payment process.

---

[49]Ibid., 498–499.

Database Management

The availability of computerized databases is an important determinant of successful direct marketing (see Chapter 4). The information in the systems includes internal data on customers and purchased data on customers and prospects. The customer and prospect information contained in databases can be used to generate mailing lists and prospect lists and to identify market segments. These segments offer a direct communications channel with customers and prospects.

Value

The shopping information provided via direct marketing, convenience, reduced shopping time, rapid response, and competitive prices gives buyers an attractive bundle of value in many buying situations. Effective database management enables direct marketing to identify buyers who purchase on a continuing basis.

The differentiated needs and wants of buyers can be addressed through direct marketing, thus enhancing the value offered by the direct marketer. Offerings may be mass-customized when the direct marketer has the capability to modularize the product offering. For example, kiosks can be linked to information networks that transmit customized orders to customers.

Direct Marketing Methods

The major direct marketing methods are shown in Exhibit 13.8. We briefly examine each method to highlight its features and limitations.

Catalogs and Direct Mail

Contact by mail with potential buyers may generate orders by phone or mail, or instead encourage buyers to visit retail outlets to view goods and make purchases. Examples of companies using catalogs and other printed matter to encourage direct response include L.L. Bean (outdoor apparel and equipment) and the American Marketing Association (marketing seminars and conferences).

Notwithstanding the importance of Internet initiatives, the rate at which catalogs are sent out by companies continues to rise. Companies are using catalogs alongside websites to provide tangibility to consumers—L.L. Bean's 2006 catalog included a fabric swatch to demonstrate the softness of its fleece fabric. Catalogs may be about brand building and attracting customers, while the website is the ideal place to place orders.[50]

EXHIBIT 13.8
Direct Marketing Methods

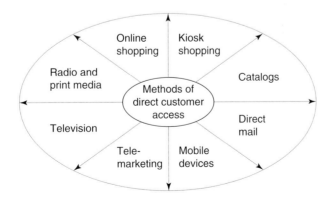

[50]Louise Lee, "Catalogs, Catalogs Everywhere," *BusinessWeek,* December 4, 2006, 32–34.

Victoria's Secret is a very successful U.S. retailer of women's wear, intimate apparel, and beauty products. The company is part of Limited Brands with sales of more than $5 billion a year.

The company is famed for its annual fashion show but also its catalog, both of which feature top fashion models. Victoria's Secret sells direct from the catalog, online, and through a global chain of retail stores.

Victoria's Secret dispatches around 400 million catalogs a year.

Catalogs are so important to Victoria's Secret, the company even lists the cost of mailing, paper, and printing as a "risk factor" in its financial statements, because an increase in costs could damage earnings.

The company sales revenue is around $4 billion from the retail stores, and $1.5 billion in direct sales from the catalog and Web page (although the impact of the catalog and website on building retail store traffic is not known).

In recent years the Victoria's Secret catalog operation has been criticized by forest conservation groups, and the company has made considerable efforts to use recycled materials in catalogs.

Sources: Louise Lee, Catalogs, Catalogs, Everywhere," *BusinessWeek,* December 4, 2006, 32–34. www.limitedbrands.com, accessed August 19, 2011.

The continuing impact of high-profile catalog strategies is illustrated by intimate apparel retailer, Victoria's Secret. This is described in the STRATEGY APPLICATION.

Mobile Devices

The rapid diffusion of smartphones (e.g., Blackberry, iPhone) and pad devices (e.g., iPad) provides a growing method of gaining direct access to targeted individuals. It is estimated that there are 5.3 billion mobile users in the world (around 77 percent of the world population), with growth led by India and China. Access to mobile users emphasizes texting and instant messaging as well as e-mail. In the United States, Google is the main recipient of mobile advertising revenues, estimated at $1 billion in 2011.[51] Mobile technology is quickly developing payment and banking systems, as well as several ticketing and couponing approaches. The INNOVATION APPLICATION describes the growing use of "placecasting" and other ways of making direct contact with consumers through their mobile phones. It is likely that expanding ownership of mobile devices will encourage further developments. Leading retailers including Wal-Mart, Sears, and Gap have launched mobile versions of their websites, together with shopping and browsing applications for iPhones and Blackberrys. Other retailers, such as JC Penney and Sephora, participate in Facebook's initiative to allow users to populate their Facebook pages with product, information, images, and reviews, and access their mobile devices, even when in the store.[52]

Telemarketing

This form of direct marketing consists of the use of telephone call contact between the buyer and seller to perform all or some of the selling function. Telemarketing offers two key advantages—low contact cost and quick access by both buyer and seller. It may be

---

[51]MobiThinking, "Global Mobile Statistics 2011," www.mobithinking.com/mobile-marketing-tools/latest-mobile-stats, accessed August 22, 2011.

[52]Jonathan Birchall, "Codes Open New Front in Retail Wars," *Financial Times,* May 18, 2010, 23.

Starbucks and L'Oréal are among leading brands developing placecasting to places messages direct with European consumers.

Placecasting involves consumers receiving offers and discounts over their mobile phones by text message.

Placecasting uses a "geofencing" system that directs text messages to consumers' mobile phones when they are in the proximity of stores.

The system uses technology developed by Placecast, a private U.S. company, which has used brand-specific geofencing systems in the United States for North Face, the outdoor clothing brand, and American Eagle, the youth clothing brand.

Several major retailers, including Best Buy, Macy's, and Target, are trialing Shopkick, a system that uses a nonaudible audio signal to send promotions to selected participating customers' mobile phones when they enter the store.

Supermarket Kroger and discounter Target, have begun issuing "digital coupons" on the Internet that can be downloaded to mobile phones and scanned against purchases at the store checkout.

Quick Response codes can be scanned by a smartphone camera to link the device to a retailer's mobile website. Youth-oriented cosmetics retailer, Sephora, uses this to link customers' phones to its Tarina Tarantino website and also has a mobile phone link for customer-generated product reviews, which can be uploaded to Facebook.

Sources: Jonathan Birchall, "Codes Open New Frontiers in Retail Wars," *Financial Times,* May 18, 2010, 23. Jonathan Birchall, "Placecast Signals Change for Shop Offers," *Financial Times,* October 15, 2010, 23.

used as the primary method of customer contact or as a way to support the field salesforce. Telemarketing has escalated in importance and is a vital part of the selling activities of many companies. Telemarketing, like the Internet, is a potential avenue of conflict with an organization's face-to-face salesforce, and may be an annoyance for consumers. Legal restrictions exist in the United States, and several countries have arrangements for consumers to "opt out" of commercial telephone messages.

Direct Response Media

Many companies use television, radio, magazines, and newspapers to obtain sales from direct buyers. Direct response from the advertising is obtained by mail, telephone, and fax or online. People see the ads, decide to buy, and order the item from the organization promoting the product.

Magazines, newspapers, and radio offer a wide range of direct marketing advertisements. The intent of the direct response communications is to persuade the person reading or hearing the ad to order the product. The advantage of using these media is the very low cost of exposure. While the percent of response is also low, the returns can be substantial for products that buyers are willing to purchase through these media.

Online Shopping

Two major methods of direct marketing are (1) computer ordering by companies from their suppliers and (2) consumer and business shopping via the Internet, as discussed earlier in the chapter. Online purchasing by business buyers is appropriate when the customer's requirements involve routine repurchase of standard items, and direct access to the buyer is not necessary. Electronic capabilities may be used to support a field salesforce rather than as the sole method of customer contact. Computer ordering helps the seller establish a close link to customers and reduces order cycles (time from order placement to receipt) and inventory stocks. Computer ordering enables the buyer to reduce inventory levels, cut costs, and monitor customer preferences. For example, Wal-Mart's computerized scanning equipment in its stores informs the retailer about what (and where) customers are buying and meeting their needs, via the computerized ordering system. While some customers may resist becoming dependent on suppliers through electronic linkages, there is a strong trend toward closer ties between suppliers and organizational buyers.

As discussed earlier in the chapter virtual shopping on the Internet has developed rapidly during the last few years. Many companies are taking advantage of the potential opportunities of direct marketing to computer users. The business-to-business sector accounts for the largest portion of total Internet sales. There are three types of networks: (1) the *Internet* itself is a global interlink of computer networks that have a common software standard; (2) an *Intranet* is a company internal capability using Internet software standards; and (3) an *Extranet* consists of providing external partners access to the Intranet. For example, a retail chain may serve customers via the Internet, coordinate store operations via the Intranet, and utilize the Extranet to interact with freelance product designers and other external partners.

Kiosk Shopping

Similar in concept to vending machines, kiosks offer buyers the opportunity to purchase from a facility (stand) located in a retail complex or other public area (e.g., airport). Kiosks frequently have Internet linkages. Airline tickets and flight insurance are examples of products sold using kiosks. In some instances, the order may be placed at the kiosk but delivered to the customer's address. The advantage to the seller is exposure to many people, and the buyer benefits from the shopping convenience. Kiosks are best suited for selling products that buyers can easily evaluate due to prior experience.

Advantages of Direct Marketing

It is apparent that direct marketing offers several advantages for sellers.[53] This marketing approach enables selective reach and segmentation opportunities. Considerable flexibility in accessing potential buyers is provided via direct marketing. Timing contact can be managed and personalized. Importantly, the effectiveness of direct marketing can be measured from direct response.

Direct marketing also has certain limitations.[54] It may have negative image factors (e.g., junk mail, "spam" e-mails). Accuracy of targeting is only as good as the lists used to access potential buyers. There may also be limited content support in direct-response advertising. Also, postal rates and access charges tend to increase over time.

---

[53]Belch and Belch, *Advertising and Promotion,* 475–476.
[54]Ibid.

Direct Marketing Strategy

As highlighted in our discussion, direct marketing promotion has the primary objective of obtaining a purchase response from individual buyers. While the methods differ in nature and scope, all require the development of a strategy. Market target(s) must be identified, objectives set, positioning strategy developed, communication strategy formulated, programs implemented and managed, and results evaluated against performance expectations.

The direct marketing strategy should be guided by the organization's marketing strategy. Direct marketing provides the way of reaching the customer on a one-to-one basis. Product strategy must be determined, prices set, and distribution arranged. Direct marketing may be the primary avenue to the customer as in the case of L.L. Bean, Inc., in its targeting of outdoor apparel buyers using catalog marketing. Other companies may use direct marketing as one of several ways of communicating with their market targets. Dell Inc. employs direct sales contact with business customers, telephone sales, and Internet sales. The Internet may also be used by Dell's customers to obtain information before placing an order by phone.

Summary

Management analyzes the firm's marketing strategy, the target market, product characteristics, distribution strategy, and pricing strategy to identify the role of personal selling in the promotion mix. New business, trade selling, missionary selling, and consultative/technical selling strategies illustrate the possible roles that may be assigned to selling in various firms. The selling process indicates the selling activities necessary to move the buyer from need awareness to a purchase decision. Various sales channels are used in conjunction with the field salesforce to accomplish the selling process activities.

Salesforce organizational design decisions include the type of organizational structure to be used, the size of the salesforce, and the allocation of selling effort. Deployment involves decisions regarding salesforce size and effort allocation. Managing the salesforce includes recruiting, training, supervising, and motivating salespeople. Evaluation and control determine the extent to which objectives are achieved and determine where adjustments are needed in selling strategy and tactics.

The Internet provides a unique and compelling means of electronic contact between buyers and sellers. The core capability of the Internet is communicating with buyers and prospects via an interactive process. The Internet is a relatively new medium and companies are learning how to obtain its advantages and avoid its risks. The key organizational decision is determining what role the Internet will play in the business and marketing strategies. The options range from a separate business model to a promotional medium.

The Internet offers several communications features including disseminating information, creating awareness, obtaining research information, brand building, encouraging trials, improving customer service, and expanding distribution. Developing an Internet business model is a major initiative involving the design of a new business. Faulty evaluation of market opportunities and inadequate planning have resulted in many Web-based failures.

The Internet's unique features offer important opportunities for providing superior customer value. It also has some potential risks in its use as a communications medium. A major challenge is measuring the effectiveness of Internet initiatives.

The purpose of direct marketing is to obtain a sales response from buyers by making direct contact using mail, telephone, advertising media, or computer. The rapidly expanding adoption of direct marketing methods that occurred in the last decade is the consequence of several influences including socioeconomic trends, low costs of exposure, computer technology, and buyers' demands for value. Direct marketing is used by many companies to contact organizational and consumer buyers.

Direct marketing offers several advantages including selective reach, segmentation opportunities, flexibility, timing control, and effectiveness measurement. However, certain direct methods may convey a negative image.

Companies have many options available for direct marketing to buyers. The methods include catalogs, direct mail, telemarketing, television, radio, magazines/newspapers, electronic shopping, and kiosk shopping. Developing a strategy for using each method includes selecting the market target(s), setting objectives, selecting positioning strategy, developing the communications strategy, implementing and managing the strategy, and evaluating results.

Questions for Review and Discussion

1. What information does management require to analyze the selling situation?
2. Suppose an analysis of salesforce size and selling effort deployment indicates that a company has a salesforce of the right size but that the allocation of selling effort requires substantial adjustment in several territories. How should such deployment changes be implemented?
3. What questions would you want answered if you were trying to evaluate the effectiveness of a business unit's salesforce strategy?
4. Discuss some of the advantages and limitations of recruiting salespeople by hiring the employees of companies with excellent training programs.
5. Is incentive compensation more important for salespeople than for product managers? Why?
6. Select a company and discuss how sales management should define the selling process.
7. What are the unique capabilities offered by the Internet to business users of the communications medium?
8. Discuss whether the Internet may replace conventional catalogs and direct mail methods of promotion.
9. Direct marketing is similar in many ways to advertising. Why is it important to view direct marketing as a specific group of promotion methods?
10. Discuss the reasons why many companies are interested in the marketing potential of the Internet.
11. Select one of the direct marketing methods and discuss the decisions that are necessary in developing a strategy for using the method.
12. Suppose you have been asked to evaluate whether a regional camera and consumer electronics retailer should obtain Internet space. What criteria should be used in the evaluation?

Internet Applications

A. Examine the website of Salesforce.com. Discuss how the Internet service provider can assist sales managers in their sales force management activities.
B. Visit Nokia's U.S. website (www.nokiausa.com). Evaluate Nokia's sales approach online. How does Nokia enhance its direct marketing strategy through Web-based offerings? How could the company increase traffic to its online sales platform without creating channel conflict?
C. Review the website of Merrill Lynch (www.ml.com). How does Merrill Lynch leverage its global position to adjust to local markets through the Internet? Why is the Internet particularly relevant for firms in the financial services industry?

Applications

A. Review the STRATEGY APPLICATION concerning Wyeth's salesforce initiatives. Discuss how these changes should be integrated with the drug company's promotion and marketing strategies.
B. The ETHICS APPLICATION highlights several aspects of ethics that are relevant to salespeople. Discuss why salespeople are more likely to be confronted with ethical situations than manufacturing employees.

Implementing and Managing Market-Driven Strategies

Chapter 14

Designing Market-Driven Organizations

Aligning the strategy and capabilities of the organization with the market, in order to provide superior customer value, is a priority in many companies.[1] Often substantial and innovative organizational change is essential to achieve this objective. The market-driven organization must reflect customer value requirements in its design, roles, and activities.

Recent decades have seen a period of unprecedented organizational change, and this activity promises to continue. Companies have realigned their organizations to establish closer contact with customers, improve customer service, bring the Internet into operations and marketing, reduce unnecessary layers of management, decrease the time span between decisions and results, and improve organizational effectiveness in other ways. Organizational changes include the use of information technology to reduce organizational layers and response time, use of multifunctional teams to design and produce new products, development of new roles and structures, and creation of flexible networks of organizations to compete in turbulent business environments. Emphasis has changed from formal structure and systems to the processes needed to enhance creativity and innovation in companies.

Closely associated with Procter & Gamble's market-driven business and marketing strategy initiatives are critically important organizational changes.[2] At the end of the 1990s, P&G faced intense competition throughout the world and loss of position in several key product markets. To turn the business around, P&G completed a massive global restructuring plan aimed to improve the company's innovation and competitiveness. The reorganization cost an estimated $2 billion.

Previously organized into four business units covering the regions of the world, in 1998 seven new executives reporting to the CEO were given profit responsibility for global product units such as baby care, beauty, and fabric and home care (Global Business Units). Several of the Global Business Units are headquartered overseas. The Global Business Units have the authority to develop new products and marketing programs. The new design

---

[1]George S. Day, *Aligning the Organization with the Market,* Marketing Science Institute Report 05-003 (Cambridge, MA: Marketing Science Institute, 2005).

[2]This illustration is based in part on the following sources: Patricia Van Arnum, "Procter & Gamble Moves Forward With Reorganization," *Chemical Market Reporter,* February 1, 1999, 12. John Bissell, "What Can We Learn From P&G's Troubles," *Brandweek,* July 10, 2000, 20–22. Christine Bittar, "Cosmetic Changes," *Brandweek,* June 18, 2001, 2. Jack Neff, "P&G Outpacing Unilever in Five Year Battle," *Advertising Age,* November 3, 2003, 1–2. Jack Neff, "Well-Balanced Plan Allows P&G to Soar," *Advertising Age,* December 12, 2005, 2–4.

concept also includes eight Market Development Units intended to tackle local market issues (e.g., supermarket retailing in South America), as well as Global Business Services and corporate functions. The regional units can leverage P&G's scale through a single sales-force, multibrand marketing efforts, and consolidated media and communications planning and buying. Key objectives are to increase the speed of decision making and move new products into commercialization faster, as well as managing the business on a global basis.

"Change agents" work across the Global Business Units to lead cultural and business change by helping teams to work together more effectively through using real-time col-laboration tools. Virtual innovation teams are linked by intranets, which can be accessed by senior executives to keep up with developments. The program involves considerable down-sizing in personnel and substantial change. The sales organization is designed to focus salesperson attention more directly on individual brands. The organization design supports strategies articulated clearly so all business disciples—from product supply to purchasing—can work together. P&G is working to develop more career marketing experts.

With its new organization design in place, P&G shows solid sales growth across all its major businesses and geographies. P&G is targeting profitable market segments through-out the world, where previously competitors were virtually unchallenged. The considerable savings from restructuring have been plowed back into market development. The company is focused on big brands in big categories (laundry, hair care, diapers, and feminine pro-tection); big developed markets; emerging, developing markets; and partnerships with big retailers. P&G's changes in organizational design underline the nature of the fundamen-tal changes facing many companies in realigning their structures and processes with the requirements of turbulent and intensely competitive environments.

First, we examine several important trends in organization strategy, and then consider major issues impacting on organizing for market-driven strategy. We discuss changing roles for the marketing function/department in companies, and alternative organization designs. Finally, we look at several organizing issues related to global marketing and global customers.

Trends in Organization Strategy

Organizational requirements to create and implement effective market-driven strategy should be considered as part of the broader shifts in the way in which organizations are being shaped and managed. Organization design is increasingly recognized as an impera-tive for senior management, and a key element of corporate strategy. There is major concern that traditional approaches to organizational structure make critical aspects of organizational working more complex and less efficient. If organizing models lag behind the demands of new strategies, there are limits on how well a company can perform in implementing strategy.[3]

While flatter organizations (fewer management levels) are expected, together with more disaggregated organizations (more functions outsourced to partners), and traditional hier-archies are likely to be broken down, the debate about the characteristics of the new organi-zation and the shape it will take continues.[4] Several relevant themes are considered before examining the organizational imperatives for market-driven strategy.

Importantly, the shaping and processes of new organizations will reflect changing views about work and how goals are best accomplished. The INNOVATION APPLICATION

[3]Lowell L. Bryan and Claudia I. Joyce, *Mobilizing Minds: Creating Wealth from Talent in the 21st-Century Orga-nization* (New York: McGraw-Hill, 2007).
[4]Peter Doyle and Phil Stern, *Marketing Management and Strategy,* 4th ed. (Harlow: Pearson Education, 2006).

The Conference Board reports that companies are now being forced to constantly reorganize to stay competitive.

The ways in which companies reorganize reflect major changes driven by globalization and technology. New challenges include:

- Off-shoring means that work can be broken into smaller tasks and redistributed around the world but that brings the challenge of welding vast, globally dispersed workforces into superfast, efficient organizations.

- For international businesses, the task is learning how to build productive international teams.

- The rapid growth of broader, richer channels of communication—including virtual worlds—is transforming what it means to be "at work."

- But talented people are still in high demand and they are motivated by self-fulfilment not fear, so the era of standardized benefits and work practices is vanishing.

- Companies like IBM, Nokia, and Dow Chemicals have faced up to how to get an organization full of people from different cultures and backgrounds to collaborate efficiently and effectively.

- Indian companies like Infosys Technologies and Satyam Computer Services provide models of how to recruit, train, and retain workers in a hypercompetitive environment.

- But the goal is to strip complexity out of organizations, not to make them more complex and unwieldy.

Sources: Robert Kramer, *Designing Organizations That Execute New Strategies and Create Capabilities for Change* (New York, The Conference Board, 2007). Peter Coy, "The Future of Work," *BusinessWeek,* August 20 & 27, 2007, 41–95. Ron Ashkenas, "Simplicity-Minded Management," *Harvard Business Review,* December 2007, 101–109. Jenny Mero, "The Evolution of Work," *Fortune,* September 29, 2008, 103–105.

reviews some topical ideas about the future of work. This is the evolving and relevant context for considering organizational change.

The New Organization[5]

Traditional Structures

Conventional approaches to organizing consist of business units, operating similarly but separately, controlled by a central authority (head office) that determines strategy and watches over implementation. This is a system of "command and control," made visible in organization charts that lay down organizational hierarchy. Even when companies decentralize decision making and accountability, they often recentralize when they run into hard times like economic downturns.

The main failing of the traditional approach is that it creates barriers to the spread of knowledge and to the achievement of economies of scale. Ideas and commands flow vertically between the center and the business unit, creating "silos" with little communication across the business units (or silos). Globalization frequently leads to attempts to add a "matrix overlay." For example, Philips established both national geographic organizations and product divisions, held together with coordinating committees designed to resolve

---

[5]This section is adapted from *The New Organization: A Survey of the Company,* Special Report: *The Economist,* January 21, 2006.

conflicts between the two lines of command. The matrix overlay has proved problematic, and Philips is pulling back to a more conventional structure.[6] Effective organization design requires more than ad hoc structural changes.

In traditional organizational structures, units were either within the organization and closely connected to other units, or they were outside the organization and not connected at all. Transactions with external suppliers were at arm's length. The line between what was inside and outside the organization has become blurred with the rapid growth in joint ventures, alliances, and other strategic relationships (see Chapter 7). Partnering underlines the need for new organizational approaches.

The move by companies away from traditional organizational structures may involve substantial change and realignment. Consider, for example, the organizational strategy seen at oil major Shell, described in the STRATEGY APPLICATION.

Organizational Design Shifts

Many organizations have implemented major changes in the way they manage and organize, and many others are examining their needs for rethinking their policies.

Changes in the ways in which companies are organized are driven by communications technology, the globalization of production and sales, and the transfer of responsibility to outsiders for core business functions, through outsourcing, joint ventures, and alliances. Change is also mandated by the way in which individuals work to carry out their job responsibilities, and the emergence of the "networked worker"—working electronically from a knowledge base and constantly communicating.

Innovation

Key in shaping the new organizational form is the imperative for enhanced rates and effectiveness in innovation to achieve organic growth. Increasingly, innovation is achieved by companies looking outside their boundaries for knowledge and expertise, rather than relying on internal R&D or marketing initiatives. We noted earlier companies like IBM and P&G have opened their organizations up to partner with innovation drivers from outside their companies. The management of cross-boundary relationships frequently requires new approaches to organizing.

The Knowledge-Based Worker

Innovation and growth depend increasingly on knowledge workers or professionals. Knowledge workers have "thinking-intensive" jobs.[7] They represent a growing proportion of the employees of large companies—possibly as much as 25 percent of employees in financial services, media, and pharmaceuticals.[8] Knowledge workers may operate more effectively as "internal partners" rather than conventional employees (see Chapter 7). Knowledge workers have been identified as the source of future wealth for companies, but a resource that requires different organizational approaches to achieve effectiveness. The management of knowledge workers may put less emphasis on formal structure and reporting lines, and more emphasis on (1) leadership, concerned with the individual, the team, and goals; (2) talent management, to provide career development paths in flattened organizations, and to retain talent in the organization; and (3) a culture of innovation and creativity. "Talent marketplaces" inside the organization allow capable employees to plot their own career paths internally.[9]

---

[6]Nelson D. Schwartz, "Lighting Up Philips," *Fortune,* January 2, 2007, 31–35.
[7]Bryan and Joyce, 2007.
[8]Ibid.
[9]Ibid.

Royal Dutch Shell, the Anglo-Dutch oil major, had ambitious production targets, yet has a stock value indicating underperformance compared to the global oil sector.

Uncertainties in 2010 saw Shell cutting jobs and refining capacity, faced with weak gas prices and depressed margins on refined oil products. This followed drastic actions by the incoming CEO in 2009 to cut 5,000 jobs, including 150 senior managers, and to put in place a new organizational structure.

Shell has often been criticized for its cumbersome structure compared to its rivals—particularly ExxonMobil—and the company's new CEO, Peter Voser, initiated an organizational change initiative "Transition 2009" soon after taking the post.

"Transition 2009" was designed to simplify Shell's structure, reduce bureaucracy, and improve efficiency. The CEO was convinced that Shell was too "consensus-oriented" and its costs simply too high, and that tough new conditions required greater centralization like that at ExxonMobil and Total.

Restructuring involved the merger of the three upstream businesses into two new geographically focused divisions: Upstream International and Upstream Americas. The downstream division (which primarily refines and markets oil products) was expanded to include trading, biofuels, and solar energy. A new division, called projects and technology, manages the design of all major projects, upstream and downstream.

The restructuring aimed to cut layers of management, speed up decision making, and ensure projects come on-stream faster with better execution. This is a key objective in a company heavily criticized for delays and cost overruns at some of its most important oil and gas ventures.

The CEO's explanatory statement to *The Times* of London in July 2009 was: "We simply have too many people doing business with each other and not with the outside world. We are stripping away layers and overlaps that are of no value and putting more emphasis on frontline activities. . . . This really means fewer people thinking about strategy and more people implementing."

Sources: Robin Pagnamenta and David Robertson, "Middle Managers Next in Line as Shell Gets Set to Axe Thousands of White Collar Jobs," *The Times,* July 31, 2009, 45. Benoit Falcon and Maarten Van Tartwijk, "Shell Tells Staff to Expect Substantial Job Cuts," *Wall Street Journal,* September 7, 2009, 4. Kate Mackensie, "Shell's Rivals Prove a Hard Act to Follow," *Financial Times,* October 30, 2009, 21. Christopher Thompson and Sylvia Pfeifer, "Shell Sets Ambitious Targets for Expansion," *Financial Times,* March 16, 2011, 19.

Managing Culture

The active management of the culture of an organization may be a key element of achieving and sustaining competitive advantage. Toyota provides an interesting example. The company aims to have employees who are self-motivating and to a high degree self-directing, and the "Toyota Way" embodies the values and culture that guide decision making. Toyota's progress has been characterized by initiatives that focus on avoiding complacency and emphasizing change. The priority for avoiding complacency is underlined by recent Toyota product recalls. The Toyota Way and a recent culture initiative are described in the STRATEGY APPLICATION.

Collaborative Working

Many companies emphasize the importance of organizing around teams. Executives are increasingly expected to work as team members, but also to be skilled at constructing effective teams. Recall the imperatives identified in the INNOVATION APPLICATION

Toyota's distinct business beliefs and methods have origins in the five principles laid down in 1935 by the founder, Sakichi Toyoda, though not formally documented until 2001, when the company recognized that the growing number of Toyota employees outside Japan needed to be trained in its use.

PILLAR I

Challenge—We form long-term vision, meeting challenges with courage and creativity to realize our dreams.

Kaizen: "Continuous improvement"—We improve our business operations continuously, always driving for innovation and evolution.

Genchi Genbutsu: "Go and see for yourself"—We go to the source to find the facts to make correct decisions, build consensus, and achieve our goals.

PILLAR II

Respect—We respect others, make every effort to understand each other, take responsibility, and do our best to build mutual trust.

Teamwork—We stimulate personal and professional growth, share the opportunities for development, and maximize individual and team performance.

Everything Matters Exponentially

In 2007, Toyota launched a far-reaching initiative called EM^2 "Everything Matters Exponentially" in the United States. EM^2 is a total re-examination of product planning, customer service, sales and marketing, and involves retraining all U.S. factory workers. The key is a relentless reinforcement of a culture that avoids the "big company disease" of complacency, and lets bad habits set in.

Sources: Thomas A. Stewart and Anand P. Raman, "Lessons from Toyota's Long Drive," *Harvard Business Review*, July–August 2007, 74–83. David Welch, "Staying Paranoid at Toyota," *BusinessWeek*, July 2, 2007, 80–82.

earlier. IBM has, for example, made transformational changes to get rid of the command and control structure of the past, and to build a culture of connection and collaboration—within the company as well as outside.

Informal Networks

Culture change and effective teamwork requires insight into the informal networks that employees create outside their company's formal structure. Mapping networks shows most people combine with clusters of eight to ten people with whom they communicate most, and with whom they feel "safe." Some influential individuals move across network clusters—they are "knowledge mules" who carry ideas from one corporate silo to another and thereby generate new ideas. Knowledge "mules," or brokers, are critical to innovation. Higher levels of interaction between employees are associated with the ability to solve complex organizational problems.

Organizational Diversity and External Relationships

New organizations are likely to contain contradictions—some parts centralized, others not; close and loose relationships between business units will coexist in the same company. Organization structures in the future may consist of some strategically aligned businesses linked closely where there are opportunities to create value from leveraging shared capabilities, but other business units with loose relationships because greater value lies in a differentiated focus.

EXHIBIT 14.1
Alternative Organizational Structures

Source: George S. Day, "Aligning the Organization to the Market," in *Reflections on the Future of Marketing,* Donald R. Lehmann and Katherine E. Jocz, eds. (Cambridge, MA: Marketing Science Institute, 1997), 69–73.

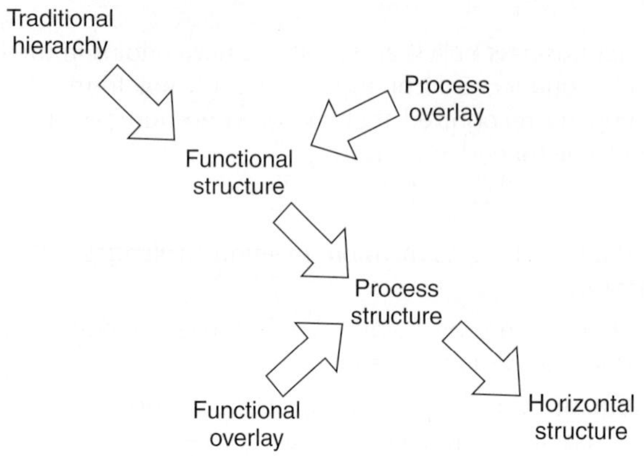

Traditional hierarchy

Functional structure

Process overlay

Process structure

Functional overlay

Horizontal structure

Outsourcing core business functions to partner organizations poses another collaborative working challenge. Dependence among businesses creates new sources of uncertainty and risk. Companies may develop extended organizational forms to cope. One type of structure may manage outsourced operations, and another structure may work better for internal activities. We examined several relevant partnering issues in Chapter 7.

Managing Organizational Process

A key characteristic of new organizations is an emphasis on managing organizational process, rather than a primary emphasis on structure. Exhibit 14.1 shows possible new structures as companies move away from traditional hierarchical structures. The prevailing organizational forms appeared to be the hybrid overlay structures.[10]

As shown in Exhibit 14.1 the structures of large established companies are moving toward horizontal business processes while retaining integrating functions (marketing, human resources) and specialist functions (research and development, marketing).[11] Processes are major clusters of strategically important activities such as new product development, order generation and fulfillment, and value/supply-chain management. As companies adopt process-based approaches, various organizational changes occur, including fewer levels and fewer managers, greater emphasis on building distinctive capabilities using multifunctional teams, customer-value-driven processes and capabilities, and continuously changing organizations that reflect market and competitive environment changes.[12]

This hybrid organizational form may take the form shown in Exhibit 14.2, which is based on observations of several major companies moving their organizations in this direction. The names given to major processes vary but are concerned with defining, creating, and delivering value. Processes are led by senior executives. Support for processes comes from resource groups, which may be conventional functional departments or business units, or external collaborators. Coordination mechanisms link process management with resource group management, such as business plans and planning groups or cross-functional teams.

---

[10]George S. Day, "Aligning the Organization to the Market," in *Reflections on the Futures of Marketing,* Donald R. Lehman and Katherine E. Jocz, eds. (Cambridge MA: Marketing Science Institute, 1997), 69–72.
[11]Ibid., 70–71.
[12]Ibid.

EXHIBIT 14.2
An Illustration of a Process-Based Organization Structure

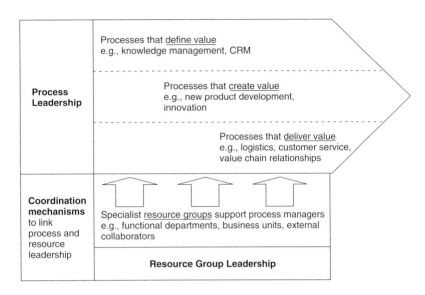

Consumer packaged goods companies such as Kraft Foods have pioneered the move toward hybrid structures, and away from traditional product and brand management approaches in order to place greater emphasis on customer management:

> Teams are organized around three core processes: (1) the consumer management team, replacing the brand management function, is responsible for customer segments; (2) customer process teams, replacing the sales function, serve the retail accounts; and (3) the supply management team, absorbing the logistics function, ensures on-time delivery to retailers. There is also a strategic integration team, to develop effective overall strategies and coordinate the teams. Although this team relies on deep understanding of the market, it might not be in the marketing function. While functions remain, their roles are to coordinate activities across teams to ensure that shared learning takes place, to acquire and nurture specialized skills, to deploy specialists to the cross-functional process teams, and to achieve scale economies.[13]

Organizational Agility and Flexibility

The pressure on companies to rapidly realign strategies and structures with market change may be considerable. Examine, for example, the imperatives for strategic and organizational change that are faced by the Hollywood movie producers as the consumer market shifts from buying movies to leasing them, which is described in the STRATEGY APPLICATION. Interesting questions surround the new business models and corresponding organizational forms that will provide the Hollywood studios with effective responses to this market change.

Considerable emphasis is placed on flexibility and agility in the new organization. Markets and competitive scenarios that change rapidly place a priority on speed and responsiveness. Traditional organizational forms may be too slow in response to exploit new opportunities as they occur and respond effectively to competitive threats. Speed may require finding new ways to identify opportunities, launching initiatives with agile teams, breaking the unwritten rules of the organization, outsourcing tasks to specialists, and using the same business model again to exploit further opportunities.[14]

[13]Ibid., 72.
[14]Steve Hamm, "Speed Demons," *BusinessWeek,* March 27, 2006, 68–76.

Hollywood generated a $11.7 billion trade surplus for the United States in 2008, larger than industries such as telecommunications, consulting, legal, and professional services.

Even 5 years ago, Hollywood studios were rich in cash and booming DVD sales meant that even movies that flopped at the box office would make their money when released on DVD.

Times have changed. DVDs used to generate more than $20 billion a year, but since 2006 sales have fallen by more than $6 billion. Attempts to reverse the decline—including the new higher-quality Blu-ray disc format—have largely failed. A failure to replace DVD revenues with digital sales means that fewer movies will be made.

The big question is whether consumers are willing to spend money to own movie and TV content any more or will choose to rent online instead. It may be the consumer wants access to movies and TV content without the burden of ownership.

Hollywood's latest venture, backed by all the big studios except Disney, is a cloud-based "rights locker" and authentication system called UltraViolet. Major retailers like Best Buy, and technology groups such as H-P, Intel, and Cisco are on board, as are phone makers Nokia and Motorola. Meanwhile Apple and Disney are working on their own cloud-based rights locker.

UltraViolet allows consumers to buy movies online and stream them to any device of their choosing (smartphone, tablet, PC, Internet-enabled TV). UltraViolet may be Hollywood's last chance to preserve its retail business model. Hollywood wants to continue selling movies because the profit margin on a DVD sale is more than 65 percent—almost double the margin on a rental. Selling an electronic format is even more profitable because there are no manufacturing costs and minimal distribution costs.

However, in a digital world it may be that consumers want to rent not buy movies. Importantly, purchasing a movie may cost $15 when it can be rented for $3–$4—and most people watch a movie only once. Netflix, for example, already offers a DVD and online movie streaming for a fixed monthly price, giving access to an unlimited mix of older movies and newer titles. Globally, more than 30 online retailers have stopped selling movies online.

Like the music business, the Internet has empowered consumers and taken power away from the Hollywood studios, who now face the challenge of aligning themselves with what consumers want.

Sources: Ronald Grover, "Hollywood Ponders a Post-DVD Future," *BusinessWeek,* March 2, 2009, 56. Matthew Garrahan, "And the Loser Is . . .," *Financial Times,* February 20, 2009, 9. Matthew Garrahan, "A Cloud Up in the Air," *Financial Times,* August 1, 2011, 7.

The advantage of doing things faster than the competition is clearly established in various kinds of business. For example, fashion leader Zara's skill in moving women's apparel from design to the store in weeks instead of months enables the retailer to market new designs ahead of its competitors.

Organizations that set themselves up to do things faster have a competitive advantage. Business agility provides a competitive strength based on flexible technology and structures, and new working practices that allow organizations to remove bottlenecks and points of rigidity. Recall the earlier discussion of agile supply chains (see Chapter 10). Increasingly, organizations are being designed for agility and responsiveness.[15] In the past, organizations were designed with stability in mind. The priority now is to build organizations that

---

[15]"Business Agility," *The Sunday Times,* Special Report, February 26, 2006. "Understanding Business Agility," Financial Times Special Report, May 8, 2003.

Generational groups include the **Traditionalists** (born between 1928 and 1945); the **Baby-boomers** (born post-War to the 1960s); **Generation X** (born between 1965 and 1979); **Generation Y** or the **"Millennials"** (born 1980 to 1995); and the Internet generation (still in their teens).

The millennials are moving into positions of power.

The millennial generation lives, buys, plays, and socializes online. Social networking websites are a way of life. Currently out of their teen years, this generation will be the staff of our major organizations within a few years.

The children of the baby-boomers are already marching into the workplace.

They are ambitious, demanding, and question everything. They are different. They have tattoos and piercings. When it comes to loyalty, the company is the last on the list. They always seem to be at the gym. The idea of a "work ethic" doesn't work. Home is the only safe place to be (so many continue living with their parents). If they don't like the job—they quit (because the worst that can happen is moving back home).

Work/life balance is very important. They want interesting work from the first day, and for people to notice and react to their performance.

The relentless questioning of the millennials (generation why?) is a managerial challenge to the more conformist generation X-ers (too young to have been part of the hippy protest era and too old to be idealists).

The millennials are expected to be the most high-maintenance workforce in the history of the world, but also the most high-performing.

Sources: Jessi Hempel, "The MySpace Generation," *BusinessWeek,* December 12–19, 2005, 63–70. Nadira A. Hira, "You Raised Them, Now Manage Them," *Fortune,* May 28, 2007, 26–33. Tamara Erickson, *What's Next, Gen X?* (Cambridge, MA: Harvard Business School Press, 2009).

are capable of changing. One of the strengths of self-managing teams and small, close-to-the-customer business units, is greater organizational responsiveness and speed in adapting to changed circumstances.[16]

Employee Motivation

The effective design of new organizations is, in part, related to the motivation and aspirations of the people who work at all levels in the company. Booz, Allen & Hamilton research underlines that for talented people in Western companies today, financial incentives matter far less than nonfinancial factors—esteem, a challenging and varied job, the chance to work on teams, the opportunity to interact with interesting people. It is dangerous to assume that people are motivated only by money and to design organizations and processes on that basis. For example, IBM has shifted the emphasis in annual bonus schemes from the performance of the employee's individual unit and toward that of the company as a whole.

The life aspirations of individuals entering professional and management roles are also significant. Designing organizations in which the most-talented individuals cannot work productively is a danger with conventional approaches. For example, the RELATIONSHIP APPLICATION describes some of the issues faced in working with and managing employees from the "Millennial Generation."

---

[16]Edward Lawler and Christopher Worley, *Built to Change: How to Achieve Sustained Organizational Effectiveness* (San Francisco: Jossey-Bass, 2006).

Organizing for Market-Driven Strategy

Trends in organizational strategy provide the context for examining the organizational conditions favorable to market-driven strategy. We consider the link between strategic marketing and organization structure, moves to enhance the alignment of organizations with their markets, the role of marketing as an organizational process owner as well as a functional specialization, and particularly the cross-functional role of marketing in achieving internal partnerships and integration of company resources around customer value.

Strategic Marketing and Organization Structure

As strategies change and evolve in a company, it is increasingly important to examine organizational issues in the implementation of marketing strategy. Across many business sectors, several factors lead companies to rethink how they organize for effective marketing—to counter performance shortfalls by better integration; to globalize products and brands effectively; to bring sales and marketing closer together; to focus on brands and products.

Importantly, organizational change may be more easily achieved also when there are major strategic shifts to respond to weakening business performance. The radical reshaping of the Cadbury Schweppes' confectionery and beverages business is illustrative. Reducing organization costs is a major part of recovering competitiveness. The Cadbury organization strategy is described in the METRICS APPLICATION.

Organizational change is a continuing process in many companies. We have described the trend away from vertical structures toward flat horizontal structures with greater emphasis on managing processes (for example, new product development) and less emphasis on functional specialization. These observations are highly relevant to implementing market-driven strategy effectively.

Aligning the Organization With the Market[17]

Organizations are evolving toward closer alignment with their markets as a result of new marketing strategies and increasingly assertive customers demanding more accountability and responsiveness. Market change is reinforcing the customer dimension of organization, and companies are structuring operations around customer groups. Research suggests three stages of evolution: (1) improving alignment through informal lateral integration, (2) using integrating mechanisms such as key account or segment managers, and (3) full customer alignment with customer-based units at the front of the organization or matrix structures around segments. Many organizations will stop short of the third phase.

In stage 1, the functional or product organization is retained, but sales or product management takes informal steps to cross silos and solve customer problems. Stage 2 gains partial alignment with customers through integrating functions like global account coordinators and market segment specialists breaking away from a focus on products. The third stage involves comprehensive approaches to get full structural alignment with the market, using customer-based front-end units or matrix structures with segment champions. The customer-based front-end unit structure is illustrated in Exhibit 14.3.

Market alignment by matrix structures is illustrated by Sony in the U.S. consumer electronics market. With five products divisions operating largely independently, Sony overlaid a market segment structure onto the existing product structure. The head of each product

---

[17]This section is based on George S. Day, *Aligning the Organization with the Market,* Marketing Science Institute Report 05-003 (Cambridge MA: Marketing Science Insititute, 2005).

- Cadbury was the world's largest confectionery business. Under competitive pressure and the attentions of activist shareholder Nelson Peltz, Cadbury aimed to radically reshape its business.
- The restructuring cost was around $900 million.
- The U.S. beverages business—Dr Pepper, 7-Up, and Snapple—was hived off.

- The goal was to find savings of around $500 million a year from the remaining confectionery business, including closing some global manufacturing operations.
- Cadbury had relatively low profit margins compared to competitors—Cadbury's average was 10 percent, compared to 18 percent at Wrigley and Hershey. The low margins were linked to Cadbury's complex operating structure, with many brands and manufacturing sites.
- The biggest focus of reorganization was on overheads—sales, general, and administrative costs. Some administrative functions were outsourced.
- Under investor pressure, an entire management level under the CEO was removed.
- The organizational structure was too complex with too many overlaps. Organizational costs accounted for 20 percent of turnover, as compared to 12 percent for Cadbury's rivals.

In 2010 the Cadbury confectionery business was acquired by Kraft Foods in a hostile takeover bid. A large number of former-Cadbury executives left the company at this point. While Cadbury sales remain weak, Kraft's management team is actively pursuing organizational savings through consolidation and integration of the Cadbury business within the Kraft group. Actions include factory closure and separating the faster growing snacks business (Oreo, Cadbury, Trident gum) from the slower growing North American grocery business (Kraft macaroni and cheese, Philadelphia cheese products).

Sources: Ben Laurence, "Cadbury Sheds 5,000 Jobs in Drastic Revamp," *Sunday Times,* June 17, 2007, S3, 1. Jenny Wiggins, "Cadbury Sweet Talk on Confectionery Revival Fails to Move Sceptics," *Financial Times,* June 20, 2007, 22. Louise Lucas and Elizabeth Rigby, "Kraft's Rosenfeld Snubs UK Inquiry," *Financial Times,* March 11, 2011, 17. Helen Thomas and Alan Rappaport, "Kraft to Spin Off Grocery Arm," *Financial Times,* August 5, 2011, 13.

EXHIBIT 14.3
Customer-Based Front-End Organization

Source: Adapted from George S. Day, *Aligning the Organization with the Market,* Marketing Science Institute Report 05–003 (Cambridge MA: Marketing Science Institute, 2005).

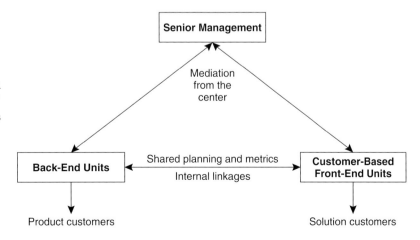

business unit was given added responsibility for one of the market segments—the head of digital imaging products became the champion for the "double income, no kids" segment and the head of personal mobile products was champion for the generation Y consumer segment. The dual focus for these executives was supported through the reward system.

Structural alignment around markets is likely to be disruptive and add organizational costs, and executives should consider the imperatives to

- Have a strategic rationale for realignment, such as providing better solutions to customers or gaining deeper knowledge of their needs.
- Keep everyone focused on the customer experience, with clear accountabilities for the quality of relationships with major customers, integration, and tracking lost customers.
- Adjust the pace of alignment to allow for anticipated obstacles and ways to overcome them.
- Keep realigning in response to market change and advances in technology.

Marketing Functions Versus Marketing Processes

While the existence of conventional marketing functions or departments remains important to achieve efficiency in carrying out operational marketing tasks, there is increasing evidence that when considering marketing strategy, marketing should be seen as a set of processes that work across the organization and its partners to shape and implement strategy.[18] Indeed, some of the most admired firms in the world underline the strategic importance of marketing processes. At GE, marketing was a "lost function" under Jack Welch, while CEO Jeff Immelt has revitalized the marketing organization as a driver of growth rather than a support function.[19] At Microsoft, Steve Balmer emphasizes the marketing organization's lead role in making Microsoft "value propositions shine through for customers." At Intel the transition is from an engineering mind-set of relentlessly increasing microprocessor speed to a marketing-led approach of designing microprocessors for specific customer end-use applications like mobility and entertainment.[20] A process perspective underlines the cross-functional role of marketing.

Marketing as Cross-Functional Process

In providing leadership in market-driven strategy, marketing is increasingly seen as a cross-functional activity working across traditional organizational boundaries to develop and implement strategy. Challenges of internal partnership between functional specialists and achieving integration of organizational capabilities around customer value creation are highly relevant.

Marketing executives are challenged to span the "silos" represented by traditional functions, product organizations, and geographic divisions to create cooperation, synergy, and appropriate resource allocation across business units. At companies like IBM, McDonalds', and Sony, "silo spanning" efforts are linked to rejuvenation of their organizations. This may represent one of the most important challenges for chief marketing officers.[21]

---

[18]Nirmalya Kumar, *Marketing as Strategy: Understanding the CEO's Agenda for Driving Growth and Innovation* (Boston MA: Harvard Business School Press, 2004).

[19]Beth Comstock, Ranjay Gulati, and Stepehn Liguori, "Unleashing the Power of Marketing," *Harvard Business Review,* October 2010, 89–98.

[20]Mohan Sawney, "Five Steps That Take Marketing to the Next Level," A Microsoft and Kellogg School of Management Collaboration, www.microsoft.com/business/executive circle, 2006.

[21]David Aaker, *Spanning Silos: The New CMO Imperative* (Cambridge MA: Harvard Business School Press, 2008).

Integration Challenges

There have been several problems related to integration between marketing and other activities in companies. Effectiveness depends on developing strong linkages between marketing and other functional units. This may involve a variety of approaches.

Many traditional approaches to organization have hindered the ability of companies to coordinate and integrate activities around customer needs. In some organizations, there are major barriers to effective communication between marketing and other units, leading to misunderstanding and conflict, such as poor use of market information by R&D departments for reasons of rivalry and political behavior.[22] Additionally, the integration problem may be exacerbated by "ownership" of key activities by other functions: (1) customer relationship management systems span departments and systems to integrate customer knowledge; (2) critical new product "pipelines" may place priority on leveraging R&D capabilities faster than the competitor; (3) the implementation of digital commerce may leave traditional marketing behind; and (4) many of the people and processes that impact on customer value are outside the control of the marketing area.[23]

Linking Marketing to Other Functional Units

Increasingly, marketing and sales professionals must display superior skills in coordinating and integrating their activities with other functional areas of the business. Priorities will depend on the situation faced and the strategy in question, but illustrative examples of critical cross-functional relationships include:

- *Marketing and Finance/Accounting*—Viewing customers as assets that impact on shareholder value provides a shared basis for avoiding traditional conflicts dialogue on marketing resource allocation, and lining internal system up with customer value imperatives.
- *Marketing and Operations*—The challenge is matching internal capabilities in operations and supply chain management, for example, in speed, flexibility, quality management, operational systems—with market opportunities.
- *Marketing and Sales*—In many situations the salesforce represents the ability of the company to implement marketing strategy, which is constrained by lack of "buy-in," and traditional sales management practices that do not support strategic change.
- *Marketing and R&D*—The challenge is building structures to link innovation and research capabilities with market opportunities.
- *Marketing and Customer Service*—Customer service operations may represent the most important point of contact between a customer and the company and impact directly on customer perceptions of value, mandating alignment with strategic initiatives.
- *Marketing and Human Resource Management*—The key issue may be building competitive advantage through the quality of the people in the company, with major implications for aligning processes of recruitment, selection, training, development, evaluation, and reward with business strategy requirements.[24]

Effective cross-functional working is the key to many of the examples we have discussed. Many successful companies display characteristics of cross-functional effectiveness; Costco,

---

[22]Elliot Maltz, William E. Souder, and Ajith Kumar, "Influencing R&D/Marketing Integration and the Use of Market Information by R&D Managers," *Journal of Business Research,* 51(2), 2001, 69–82.

[23]Nigel F. Piercy, *Market-Led Strategic Change: Transforming the Process of Going To Market,* 4th ed. (Oxford: Butterworth-Heinemann, 2009), 435–436.

[24]James Mac Hulbert, Noel Capon, and Nigel F. Piercy, *Total Integrated Marketing: Breaking the Bounds of the Function,* (New York: The Free Press, 2003).

Zara, and Toyota are illustrative. This capability may be a key attribute of the market-led company of the future. The move toward process-based organizations further underlines this requirement.

Approaches to Achieving Effective Integration

Organizational mechanisms for enhancing the quality of marketing's links with other functional units include effective cross-functional teams, shared goals, superior internal communications, high levels of top management support, and attention to resolving internal disputes and conflicts.[25] Several approaches to building effective integration may be considered as part of organization design. Formal mechanisms for integration include:

- Relocation and design of facilities to encourage communication and exchange of information.
- Personnel movement using joint training and job rotation to facilitate managers' understanding of other functions.
- Reward systems that prioritize higher levels goals (e.g., company profits from a cross-functional project) not just functional objectives.
- Formal procedures, for example requiring coordinated input from marketing, finance, operations, and IT to complete project documentation.
- Social orientation facilitating nonwork interaction between personnel from different functions.
- Project budgeting to centralize control over financial resources so they are channeled, for example, to a project or process team not to a functional department.[26]

Evidence relating to the effectiveness of these approaches is mixed. Nonetheless, the initiatives emphasize the need to examine more than simple structural choices in designing the effective market-driven organization. Interestingly, several routes to enhanced integration—for example, increased personal communication, spatial proximity, and social interaction—will become progressively more difficult in the intranet-based, hollow organization. In such cases, integration issues may become a high priority for management attention. Building the "customer-engaged" organization may be one of the most formidable challenges facing marketing executives.[27]

These challenges may also be integrated with other corporate initiatives, such as corporate social responsibility (see Chapter 4). The "greening" of strategy at German engineering giant Siemens, as part of its intense rivalry with GE, is illustrative. Siemens faced damage from ethics violations and recessionary markets, but has restructured as an environmentally-focused infrastructure provider. This innovatory organizational shift is described in the ETHICS APPLICATION.

Marketing Departments

Marketing capabilities and competencies in an organization are important resources that create value in a company. One topical issue is whether those resources should be grouped into a formal marketing function and where this should be located in the

[25]Hulbert, Capon, and Piercy, 2003.

[26]Elliot Maltz and Ajay Kohli, "Reducing Marketing's Conflict With Other Functions: The Differential Effects of Integrating Mechanisms," *Journal of the Academy of Marketing Science,* Fall 2000, 479–492.

[27]William Band and John Guasperi, "Creating the Customer-Engaged Organization," *Marketing Management,* July–August 2003, 35–39.

Siemens is Europe's largest engineering group. The mid-2000s were when regulators found Siemens had for years paid bribes to win government infrastructure contracts in countries like Iraq and Russia. Having paid fines of $2.5 billion and facing the risk of governments barring it from receiving future contracts, Siemens recruited as CEO Peter Löscher, then a GE executive.

Soon after arriving at the company as CEO, Löscher seized on the large bribery scandal to radically change the company's culture—replacing the entire top management team, bringing in outside managers, creating structures that improved accountability, selling off noncore areas, and cutting personnel and purchasing costs.

While jettisoning the telecommunications and information technology businesses from the Siemens portfolio, Löscher has increased the part of Siemens that sells sustainability-focused consumers everything from lightbulbs to high-speed trains to factory control systems. About a quarter of its 400,000 employees are what Siemens calls "green collar workers," who produce or market its portfolio of resource-efficient products.

The company's new focus on low-cost products for emerging markets (more than 30 percent of Siemens' sales) emphasizes the company's shift from its traditional focus on engineering process toward marketing products.

Löscher has used the recession years to reshape the business, from a strategic perspective, to refocus on core markets and reposition the firm as a "green infrastructure" company ready for economic recovery, emphasizing the company's roots as a leading innovator and underlining the vast growth potential in supplying infrastructure such as trams, smart power grids, and water treatment facilities.

In 2011 in a major organizational shift, the company created an Infrastructure and Cities sector, from several existing units (high-speed and urban trains, building technologies, and energy distribution) to focus on a new customer segment and accelerate growth in this area by creating a fourth business arm.

A key part of Siemens' strategy, like that of rival GE, is a big bet that increasing green consciousness will fuel future sales in the engineering business.

Sources: Maria Bartiromo, "Siemens CEO Löscher Looks to the Future," *BusinessWeek,* October 19, 2009, 17–18. Richard Weiss and Benedikt Kammel, "How Siemens Got Its Geist Back," *Bloomberg BusinessWeek,* January 31–February 6, 2011, 18–20. Daniel Schäfer, "Siemens Targets Growth with Latest Reshuffle," *Financial Times,* March 30, 2011, 19.

organization. The existence of a marketing department does not necessarily indicate that a company displays high levels of market orientation. Nor does the absence of a formal marketing department indicate that a company is not market oriented. Conventionally, we expect that a market-driven company will have some formal marketing organization, but there are some indications that forward-thinking companies are revisiting this issue. P&G, for example, has moved from conventional marketing departments to its customer business development structure to focus marketing and selling resources on major retailer customers.

Important organization design choices relate to the centralization or decentralization of marketing tasks and activities, the integration or diffusion of marketing responsibilities, organizing contingencies, and the role to be played by marketing in the organization.[28]

---

[28]This section is adapted from Ajay K. Kohli and Rohit Deshpandé, *Marketing Organizations: Changing Structures and Roles,* Marketing Science Institute Special Report No. 05-200 (Cambridge MA: Marketing Science Institute, 2005).

Centralization Versus Decentralization

Companies with two or more business units may have corporate marketing organizations as well as business unit marketing organizations. Corporate involvement may range from a coordinating role to one in which the corporate staff has considerable influence on business unit marketing operations. Also, the chief marketing executive and staff may participate in varying degrees in strategic planning for the enterprise and the business unit.

While many of the goals of organizational realignment for new market realities are compatible with higher degrees of decentralization, there may also be attractions in more centralized structures. Consider the different organizational strategies pursued at BP and ExxonMobil, described in the STRATEGY APPLICATION. There are strengths and weaknesses in both approaches, which require careful evaluation.

The corporate role of marketing is influenced by top management's approach to organizing the corporation, as well as the nature and complexity of business operations. Marketing strategy decisions are typically centered at the business-unit and product-market levels. Even so, it is very important for the top management team to include strategic marketing professionals. The market-driven nature of business strategy requires the active participation of marketing professionals.

A major organizational design issue is whether marketing tasks and activities should be centralized (at the corporate level) or decentralized (at the business unit level) in a multi-business organization.

Research suggests that when marketing tasks across business units are highly related, the marketing function tends to be centralized at the corporate level.[29] Nonetheless, there are also signs that organizations are increasingly structuring marketing activities around customer-centric arrangement, such as key account teams and segment managers in a less centralized format.[30] Influenced by the general trend in organizations toward decentralized management approaches, many corporations are moving marketing functions away from the corporate level to the business unit level. Decentralization is a better way to cope with growing product and market complexity, and to enhance speed of response to market changes.[31] The available evidence suggests that there is no one best way to structure marketing activities, and that managers should consider strategic requirements as well as the capabilities and cultural requirements for the two approaches.[32]

Integration or Diffusion

A further major issue concerns whether marketing tasks and activities should be diffused (performed by people in different departments/functions) or focused (performed by individuals belonging to the marketing department/function). Research suggests that in practice there are signs that in many organizations marketing activities are moving from the marketing function to cross-functional teams and other functions (such as R&D or sales).[33] The integration of marketing functions associated with adopting the marketing concept, may be followed by the *dis*integration of marketing functions to achieve greater cross-functional effectiveness in delivering superior value to customers. The diffusion of marketing

---

[29]John P. Workman, Christian Homburg, and Kjell Gruner, "Marketing Organization: An Integrative Framework of Dimensions and Determinants," *Journal of Marketing,* 62(July), 1998, 21–41.

[30]Christian Homburg, John P. Workman, and Ove Jensen, "Fundamental Changes in Marketing Organization: The Movement Toward a Customer-Focused Organizational Culture," *Journal of the Academy of Marketing Science,* 28 (Fall), 2000, 459–478.

[31]Peter Doyle and Phil Stern, *Marketing Management and Strategy,* 4th ed. (London: Pearson Education, 2006).

[32]Kohli and Deshpandé, 2005.

[33]Homburg, Workman, and Jensen, 2000.

ExxonMobil's organizational strategy emphasizes **centralization:**

- Exxon is organized on functional lines, for example, worldwide exploration operation is a single division.
- This structure helps spread best practice and new technology rapidly around the company.
- Senior management is close to operations and can review performance throughout the business and quickly contact responsible executives.
- Throughout the business there are consistent strategies and approaches, consistent expectations for high standards in safety and operational performance.
- Exxon is recognized as the global leader in safety and engineering excellence.

Exxon's rival, **BP**, has a far more **decentralized** approach:

- Decentralization encourages entrepreneurialism and initiative, facilitates integration of acquisitions into the business, and helps drive down costs to deliver outstanding financial performance.
- But decentralization has inhibited BP's ability to get projects executed and completed on time/budget.
- Decentralized management approaches have limited BP's ability to share best practice around the Group.
- Senior management has struggled to know exactly what is happening on the ground and lack of detailed knowledge is linked to major safety defaults.
- Business unit leaders are incentivized to behave independently and conceal problems and top management lacks information to monitor their actions closely.

Source: Ed Crooks, "BP Faces Sea Change on Way to Recovery," *Financial Times,* July 24, 2007, 21.

activities across multiple functions is more common in market-oriented businesses serving business customers, and operating in uncertain markets with uncertain technologies.[34]

There are attractions in achieving a "customer mind-set" among all employees in a firm, not just marketing employees, suggesting that marketing tasks and activities should be the responsibility of multiple functions, not just the marketing department.[35]

Contingencies for Organizing

The formalization of marketing as an organizational function and the centralization/decentralization and diffusion/focused possibilities underline the need to consider organizational and market contingencies to guide decisions. For example, a classic view of four organizing concepts is shown in Exhibit 14.4. Note the usage context and performance characteristics of each structure. Since strategy implementation may involve a usage context that combines two of the structures, trade-offs are involved. The adopted organization structure may facilitate the implementation of certain activities and tasks. For example, the bureaucratic form should facilitate the implementation of repetitive activities such as telephone processing of air

---

[34]Workman, Homburg, and Gruner, 1998.
[35]Karen N. Kennedy, Felicia G. Laask, and Jerry R. Goolsby, "Customer Mind-Set of Employees Throughout the Organization," *Journal of the Academy of Marketing Science,* 30(Spring), 2002, 159–171.

EXHIBIT 14.4 **Four Archetypical Marketing Organizational Forms**

Source: Robert W. Ruekert, Orville C. Walker, Jr., and Kenneth J. Roering, "The Organization of Marketing Activities: A Contingency Theory of Structure and Performance," *Journal of Marketing,* Winter 1985, 20. Reprinted with permission of the American Marketing Assocation.

	Market Versus Hierarchical Organization	
	Internal Organization of Activity	**External Organization of Activity**
	Bureaucratic Form	Transactional Form
Centralized Formalized Nonspecialized	*Appropriate usage context* • Conditions of market failure • Low environmental uncertainty • Tasks that are repetitive, easily assessed, requiring specialized assets *Performance characteristics* • Highly effective and efficient • Less adaptive *Examples in marketing* • Functional organization • Company or division sales force • Corporate research staffs	*Appropriate usage context* • Under competitive market conditions • Low environmental uncertainty • Tasks that are repetitive, easily assessed, with no specialized investment *Performance characteristics* • Most efficient form • Highly effective for appropriate tasks • Less adaptive *Examples in marketing* • Contract purchase of advertising space • Contract purchase of transportation of product • Contract purchase of research field work
	Organic Form	Relational Form
Structural Characteristics **Decentralized Nonformalized Specialized**	*Appropriate usage context* • Conditions of market failure • High environmental uncertainty • Tasks that are infrequent, difficult to assess, requiring highly specialized investment *Performance characteristics* • Highly adaptive • Less efficient *Examples in marketing* • Product management organization • Specialized sales force organization • Research staffs organized by product groups	*Appropriate usage context* • Under competitive market conditions • High environmental uncertainty • Tasks that are nonroutine, difficult to assess, requiring little specialized investment *Performance characteristics* • Highly adaptive • Highly effective for nonroutine, specialized tasks • Less efficient *Examples in marketing* • Long-term retainer contract with advertising agency • Ongoing relationship with consulting firm

travel reservations and ticketing. Once management analyzes the task(s) to be performed and the environment in which they will be done, it must determine its priorities. For example, is the objective performance and short-run efficiency or adaptability and longer-term effectiveness?

Activities in different categories should be structured differently whenever feasible. Some firms appear to be moving in this direction, as shown by reports of cuts in corporate staff departments, the shifting of more planning and decision-making authority to individual business unit and product-market managers, and the increased use of ad hoc task forces to deal with specific markets or problems—all of which indicate a shift toward more decentralized and flexible structures.[36]

---

[36]Quote from Robert W. Ruekert, Orville C. Walker, Jr., and Kenneth J. Roering, "The Organization of Marketing Activities: A Contingency Theory of Structure and Performance," *Journal of Marketing,* Winter 1985, 23–24.

Corporate culture may also have an important influence on implementation. For example, implementing new strategies may be more difficult in highly structured, bureaucratic organizations. General Motors' difficulty in responding to the global competitive pressures during the last decade is illustrative. Management should consider its own management style, accepted practices, specific performance of executives, and other unique characteristics in deciding how to design the organization.

Evaluating Organization Designs

The design of the marketing organization is influenced by several contingencies: market and environmental factors, the characteristics and capabilities of the organization, and the marketing strategy followed by the firm. In evaluating the adequacy of an organizations design, the following factors provide guidelines:

- The organization should correspond to the strategic marketing plan. For example, if the plan is structured around markets or products, then the marketing organizational structure should reflect this same emphasis.

- Coordination of activities is essential to successful implementation of plans, both within the marketing function and with other company and business unit functions. The more highly specialized that marketing functions become, the more likely coordination and communications will be hampered.

- Specialization of marketing activities leads to greater efficiency in performing the functions. As an illustration, a central advertising department may be more cost-efficient than establishing an advertising unit for each product category. Specialization can also provide technical depth. For example, product or application specialization in a field sales force will enable salespeople to provide consultative-type assistance to customers.

- The organization should be structured so that responsibility for results will correspond to a manager's influence on results. While this objective is often difficult to fully achieve, it is an important consideration in designing the marketing organization.

- Finally, one of the real dangers in a highly structured and complex organization is the loss of flexibility. The organization should be adaptable to changing conditions. Consider the rationale for the venture marketing organization described later in the chapter.

Since some of these characteristics conflict with others, organizational design requires looking at priorities and balancing conflicting consequences.

Structuring Marketing Resources

Whether marketing activities are centralized or decentralized, and whether they involve a fully integrated marketing department or a marketing unit with more limited responsibilities, structuring the array of marketing resources in a formal organization design involves important management choices. We consider several structuring issues, before discussing traditional organization designs available, and several of the newer marketing roles being identified in some companies.

Structuring Issues

Functional specialization is often the first consideration in selecting an organizational design for marketing resources. Specialist functions are attractive because they develop expertise, resources, and skills in a particular activity. Emphasis on functions may be less appropriate when trying to direct activities toward market targets, products, and customers. Market targets and product scope also influence organizational design. When two or more targets and/or a mix of products are involved, companies often depart from functional organizational designs that place advertising, selling, research, and other supporting services into functional units. Similarly, distribution channels and sales force considerations may influence the organizational structure adopted by a firm. For example, the marketing of home entertainment products targeted to business buyers of employee incentives and promotional gifts might be placed in a unit separate from a unit marketing the same products to consumer end-users. Geographical factors have a heavy influence on organization design because of the need to make the field supervisory structure correspond to how the sales force is assigned to customers.

The major forms of marketing organizational designs are *functional, product, market,* and *matrix* designs.

Functional Organizational Design

This design assigns departments, groups, or individuals, responsibility for specific activities, such as advertising and sales promotion, pricing, sales, marketing research, and marketing planning and services. Depending on the size and scope of its operations, the marketing organization may include some or all of these activities. The functional approach is often used when a single product or a closely related line is marketed to one market target.

Product-Focused Design

The product mix may require special consideration in the organizational design. New products often do not receive the attention they need unless specific responsibility is assigned to the planning and coordination of the new-product activities. This problem may also occur with existing products when a business unit has several products and there are technical and/or application differences. We examine several approaches to organizing using a product focus.

Product/Brand Management

The product or brand manager, sometimes assisted by one or a few additional people, is responsible for planning and coordinating various business functions for the assigned products. Typically, the product manager does not have authority over all product-planning activities but may coordinate various product-related activities. The manager usually has background and experience in research and development, engineering, or marketing and is normally assigned to one of these departments. Product managers' titles and responsibilities vary widely across companies.

Product management structures continue to be used in many organizations even though there is a trend toward process designs.[37] The product management system assigns clear responsibility for product performance, and the system encourages coordination across business functions. Nonetheless, the product focus may take emphasis away from the market. Also, there may be a short-term focus on financial performance. An example of a product-focused structure is shown in Exhibit 14.5.

Category Management

Associated with the new approaches to efficient supply chain management (see Chapter 10), a development in product-focused organization is the adoption of category management structures. Categories are groups of products defined by consumer purchase behavior patterns. For example, Nestlé and Interbrew are working with retailers to develop categories structures within which their brands can be developed, and restructuring their organizations around the categories.[38]

---

[37]Donald R. Lehmann and Russell S. Winer, *Product Management,* 4th ed. (Chicago: McGraw-Hill/Irwin, 2004).
[38]"FMCG Firms Need to Focus on Category before Brand," *Marketing,* September 27, 2001, 5.

EXHIBIT 14.5
Product-Focused
Structure

Source: Donald R. Lehmann
and Russell S. Winer, *Product
Management,* 2nd ed. (Chicago:
Richard D. Irwin, 1997), 4.
Copyright © The McGraw-
Hill Companies. Used with
permission.

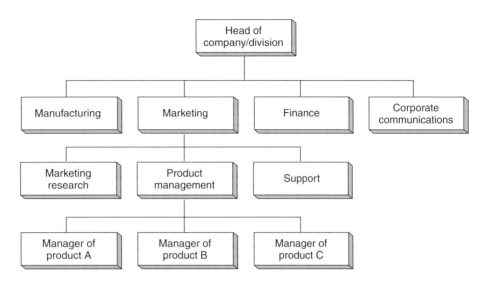

Venture Teams

The venture team requires the creation of an organizational unit to perform some or all of the new-product-planning functions. This unit may be a separate division or company created specifically for new-product or new business ideas and initiatives. Venture teams offer several advantages, including flexibility and quick response. They provide functional involvement and full-time commitment, and they can be disbanded when appropriate. Team members may be motivated to participate on a project that offers possible job advancement opportunities.

New-Product Teams

The new-product team is similar to a venture team in that it is comprised of functional specialists working on a specific new-product development project. The product team has a high degree of autonomy with the authority to select leaders, establish operating procedures, and resolve conflicts. The team is formed for a specific project although it may be assigned subsequent projects. Successful innovation at 3M is based on cross-functional new-product teams.[39]

Factors that often influence the choice of a product organization design are the kinds and scope of products offered, the amount of new-product development, the extent of coordination necessary among functional areas, and the management and technical problems previously encountered with new products and existing products. For example, a firm with an existing functional organizational structure may create a temporary team to manage and coordinate the development of a major new product. Before or soon after commercial introduction, the firm will shift responsibility for the product to the functional organization. The team's purpose is to allocate initial direction and effort to the new product so that it is properly launched.

Market-Focused Design

This approach is used when a business unit serves more than one market target (e.g., multiple market segments) and customer considerations are an important factor in the design of the marketing organization. For example, the customer base often affects the structuring of the field sales organization. A key advantage of this design is its customer focus.[40] Greater use of

---

[39]Peter Doyle and Phil Stern, *Marketing Management and Strategy,* 4th ed. (London: Pearson Education, 2004).
[40]Lehmann and Winer, *Product Management.*

organization designs that focus on customer groups is predicted.[41] A potential conflict may exist if a company also has in place a product management system. Some firms appoint market managers and have a field salesforce that is specialized by type of customer. The market manager operates much like a product manager, with responsibility for market planning, research, advertising, and salesforce coordination. Market-oriented field organizations may be deployed according to industry, customer size, type of product application, or in other ways to achieve specialization by to end-user groups. Conditions that suggest a market-oriented design are (1) multiple market targets being served within a strategic business unit, (2) substantial differences in the customer requirements in a given target market, and/or (3) each customer or prospect purchasing the product in large volume or dollar amounts.

Matrix Design

This design utilizes a cross-classification approach to emphasize two different factors, such as products and marketing functions (see Exhibit 14.6). Field sales coverage is determined by geography, whereas product emphasis is obtained using product managers. In addition to working with salespeople, product managers coordinate other marketing functions such as advertising and marketing research. Of course, other matrix schemes are possible. For example, within the sales regions shown in Exhibit 14.6, salespeople may be organized by product type or customer group. Also, marketing functions

EXHIBIT 14.6
A Matrix Marketing Organization Based on a Combination of Functions and Products

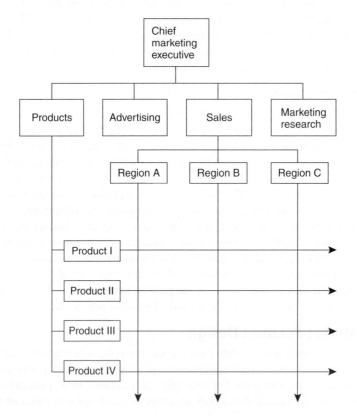

---

[41]Christian Homburg, John P. Workman, and Ove Jensen, "Fundamental Changes in Marketing Organization: The Movement Toward a Customer-Focused Organizational Structure," *Journal of the Academy of Marketing Science,* 28(4), 2000, 459–478.

may be broken down by product category, such as appointing an advertising supervisor for Product II.

Combination approaches are effective in that they respond to important influences on the organization and offer more flexibility than the other traditional approaches. A major difficulty with these designs is establishing lines of responsibility and authority. Product and market managers frequently complain that they lack control over all marketing functions even though they are held accountable for results. Nevertheless, matrix approaches are popular, so their operational advantages must exceed their limitations.

New Marketing Roles

As we discussed early in the chapter, the use of self-managing employee teams, emphasis on business processes rather than activities, and the application of information technology are creating major changes in organization design. There are several new roles and organizing approaches relevant to structuring marketing resources.

New Marketing Specializations

The identification of *new specialist roles* in marketing processes raises the question of appropriate location in the organization structure (within the marketing function or more broadly in the business unit). Examples include the chief knowledge or information officer in marketing, and the possible role of the chief relationship officer. Some companies have, for example, appointed a chief customer officer, whose job focuses only on customer interactions and the customer experience. One possible structure for the marketing organization of the future reflecting these concerns is illustrated in Exhibit 14.7. Large investment in CRM and its utilization in building relationship marketing strategy (see Chapter 4) may lead to the division of marketing into activities associated with customer acquisition processes and those focused on customer retention, since these are often very distinct and different processes.[42] The introduction of such roles requires attention to organizational positioning, and the potential for new coordination and communication requirements.

A number of major organizations have also developed *strategic account management* structures (see Chapter 13). Customer-based organization designs of this kind are becoming more widely used.[43] In the most advanced form, strategic account management involves a new collaborative relationship with major accounts, focused on the customer's strategy and

EXHIBIT 14.7
Illustration of a New Organization Structure for Marketing

Source: Adapted from Russell S. Winer, "A Framework for Customer Relationship Management," *California Management Review,* 43(4), 2001, 89–105.

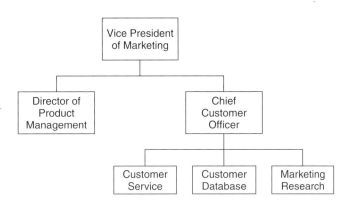

[42]Russell S. Winer, "A Framework for Customer Relationship Management," *California Management Review,* 43(4), 2001, 89–105.
[43]Nigel F. Piercy and Nikala Lane, *Strategizing the Sales Organization* (Oxford: Oxford University Press, 2009).

sources of competitive advantage. The strategic account manager in these cases has a strategic responsibility for managing all contact between the seller and customer organization and planning jointly with the customer. Strategic key account management positions are senior positions that may not fit easily into the conventional sales organization, and which carry major marketing and cross-functional responsibilities.[44]

In many companies an additional issue is where and how to position *Internet-based channels* in the marketing organization and the business unit. Early approaches isolated Internet channels from the rest of the business, while the real challenge for most companies is how to integrate the Internet into the core business.[45] Major "bricks and clicks" companies like Staples are rethinking the policy of separating their dot.com operations from the rest of the business, and bringing them back into the main operation.[46] The Web operations of successful retailers like Walgreens in the United States and Tesco in the U.K. are closely integrated with their retail stores. Several important organizational issues are involved in achieving that integration.

Venture Marketing Organizations

An interesting approach adopted by some companies extends the idea of venture teams, as a way of responding to high priority opportunities faster than conventional organizational approaches allow. The venture marketing organization (VMO) adopts the principles of venture capitalism: they aggressively seek new opportunities, allocate resources to the best, but cut their losses as they go. The VMO has a number of defining characteristics:

- Fluidity—to keep pace with the market, the VMO continually reconfigures, with little formal structure or fixed membership in opportunity teams
- People are allocated roles not jobs—the issue is managing talent within the organization and applying it to promising opportunities
- Fast decision making is made from the top
- Opportunity identification is everyone's job

Resources are focused on the highest payback opportunities and losers are quickly pruned.[47]

The impressive impact of a VMO-style approach to new market opportunities at Starbucks is described in the INNOVATION APPLICATION.

Partnering with Other Organizations

Selecting or modifying marketing organization design should take into consideration the trade-offs between performing marketing functions within the organization and having external organizations perform the functions. For example, many organizations are outsourcing all or some of their sales functions to third parties. In 1999, Intel broke with its tradition of employee salespeople, and committed a segment of its market to outsourced sales organizations. By 2003, Intel was using 25 outsourcers to generate $800 million in sales on four continents.[48]

The discussion of relationship strategies in Chapter 7 examines the use of partnering to perform various business functions. Contractual arrangements are often made for

---

[44]Noel Capon, *Key Account Management and Planning* (New York: The Free Press, 2001). Christian Homburg, John P. Workman, and Ove Jensen, "A Configurational Perspective on Key Account Management," *Journal of Marketing,* April 2002, 38–60.

[45]Michael Porter, "Strategy and the Internet." *Harvard Business Review,* March 2001, 63–78.

[46]Andrew Edgecliffe-Johnson, "Staples Brings Dotcom Back Into Fold," *Financial Times,* April 4, 2001.

[47]Nora A. Aufreiter, Teri L. Lawver, and Candance D. Lun, "A New Way to Market," *The McKinsey Quarterly,* Issue 2, 2000, 52–61.

[48]Erin Anderson and Bob Trinkle, *Outsourcing the Sales Function: The Real Cost of Field Sales* (Mason OH: Thomson/South-Western, 2005), 55.

Innovation Application

Venture Marketing Organization at Starbucks

The venture marketing organization (VMO) is a fluid approach to identifying new opportunities and concentrating resources on the best. Starbucks has a VMO-style approach to innovation.

- Starbucks approaches new opportunities by assembling teams whose leaders often come from the functional areas most critical to success. The originator of the idea may take the lead role only if qualified.
- If teams need skills that are not available internally they look outside. To lead the "Store of the Future" project, Starbucks hired a top executive with retail experience away from Universal Studios; and to develop its lunch service concept, it chose a manager from Marriott.
- After the new product is launched, some team members may stay to manage the venture, while others are redeployed to new-opportunity teams or return to line management. Success on a team is vital for promotion or a bigger role on another project.
- Teamwork extends to partner organizations. When pursuing a new ice cream project, Starbucks quickly realized they lacked the in-house packaging and channel management skills to move quickly. Teaming up with Dreyer's Grand Ice Cream got the product to market in half the normal time, and within four months it was the top-selling brand of coffee ice cream.
- Starbucks emphasizes the importance of identifying new opportunities throughout its organization. Anyone in the company with a new idea for an opportunity uses a one-page form to pass it to a senior executive team. If the company pursues the idea, the originator, regardless of tenure or title, is usually invited onto the launch team as a full-time member.
- In its first year, Starbucks' Frappuccino, a cold coffee drink, contributed 11 percent of company sales. The idea originated with a frontline manager in May 1994, gaining high-priority status from a five-person senior executive team in June. The new team developed marketing, packaging, and channel approaches in July. A joint venture arrangement with PepsiCo was in place by August. The first wave of rollout was in October 1994, with national launch in May 1995.
- A high-level steering committee meets every two weeks to rate new opportunities against two simple criteria: impact on company revenue growth and effects on the complexity of the retail store. The committee uses a one-page template to assess each idea, relying on a full-time process manager to ensure the information is presented consistently.

Sources: Nora A. Aufreiter, Teri L. Lawver, and Candance D. Lun, "A New Way to Market," *The McKinsey Quarterly,* Issue 2, 2000, 52–61. Nora Aufreiter and Teri Lawver, "Winning the Race for New Market Opportunities," *Ivey Business Journal,* September–October 2000, 14–16.

advertising and sales promotion services, marketing research, and telemarketing. Services are also available to perform marketing functions in international markets. Outsourcing various business functions is an active initiative in many companies due to cost-reduction pressures, availability of competent services, increased flexibility, and shared risk. There are various marketing functions that may be provided by independent suppliers. Examples include telemarketing, database marketing, field sales, logistics, website design and management, and information services.

Internal units provide more control of activities, easier access to other departments, and greater familiarity with company operations. The commitment of the people to the organization is often higher since they are part of the corporate culture. The limitations of internal units include difficulty in quickly expanding or contracting size, lack of experience in other business environments, and limited skills in specialized areas such as advertising, marketing research, Web design, and database management.

External organizations offer specialized skills, experience, and flexibility in adapting to changing conditions. These firms may have lower costs than an organization that performs the function(s) internally. Obtaining services outside the firm also has limitations, including loss of control, longer execution time, greater coordination requirements, and lack of familiarity with the organization's products and markets. Identifying core competencies, coordinating relationships, defining operating responsibilities, establishing good communications, and monitoring and evaluating performance are essential to gaining effective use of external organizations.

Networked Organizations

The marketing coalition company has been proposed as another new organization form for marketing.[49] The marketing coalition company is an horizontally aligned organization acting as the control center for organizing a network of specialist firms. The core of this organization is a functionally specialized marketing capability that coordinates a network of independent functional units. They perform such functions as product technology, engineering, and manufacturing. No pure forms of the marketing coalition company are known to exist, although several Japanese companies have certain characteristics of the coalition company.

The marketing coalition design is an example of a network organization. Networks are groups of independent organizations that are linked together to achieve a common objective.[50] They are composed of a network coordinator and several network members who typically are specialists. Network organizations occur in new ventures and reformed traditional organizations. The underlying rationale for network formation is leveraging the skills and resources of the participating organizations. Many of the aspects of strategic alliances discussed in Chapter 7 are highly relevant to considering networked organizations.

Organizing for Global Marketing and Global Customers

Implementing the global strategies of companies creates several important organizational issues. A key issue is the degree to which products and marketing strategies and programs are standardized across domestic and international markets, as compared to being adapted to local market requirements. Of critical importance is the development of global customers— for example, in retailing and in the IT and automotive sectors.

Consider the challenges faced at P&G in organizing for its rapid international expansion in both developed and emerging markets, described in the GLOBAL APPLICATION.

Many strategic alliances involve global relationships (see Chapter 7). Expanded use of various types of alliances is expected to continue, particularly as a way of competing

---

[49]Ravi S. Achrol, "Evolution of the Marketing Organization: New Forms for Turbulent Environments," *Journal of Marketing,* October 1991, 77–93.

[50]David W. Cravens, Nigel F. Piercy, and Shannon H. Shipp, "New Organization Forms for Competing in Highly Dynamic Environments, the Network Paradigm," *British Journal of Management,* 7, 1996, 203–218.

More than $40 billion of P&G's annual sales are outside the United States. The priority for success and growth in emerging market sales influences P&G's organizational structure. P&G gets a third of its business from developing regions and targets 50 percent by 2020. Importantly, P&G aims to make money not just from the newly rich in the emerging markets, but also from the very poor, with innovative value offerings and distribution approaches.

In its international business, P&G is shifting to a "hub and spoke" approach to managing businesses in regions such as south-east Asia and the Balkans in place of the single-country model of the past.

Efforts are focused on the 40+ brands with global sales of more than $500 million, such as Tide detergent and Swiffer cleaning products, that account for more than 90 percent of profits.

The remaining brands are divided into three categories; **"future stars"**—with the potential for growth; **"local jewels"**—strong in particular countries or regions, and **"underperformers"**—to be discontinued or divested. Only top-performing brands and countries, such as Russia and China, can increase overhead expenditure.

Sources: Jonathan Birchall, "P&G Staff Cuts and Revamp to Lift Productivity," *Financial Times,* February 25, 2008, 25. Jennifer Reingold, "Can P&G Make Money in Places Where People Earn $2 a day?" *Fortune,* January 17, 2011, 58–63.

internationally. The effectiveness of the alliance depends on how well operating relationships are established and managed on an on-going basis, and how well the partners can work together. These principles are highly relevant to the organizational change involved in globalizing.

It is clear that international experience and proven capabilities will increasingly be required for executive advancement in the 21st century.[51] The global marketing strategy context underlines the importance for the market-driven company of nurturing and retaining superior management talent. International experience promises to become increasingly important to marketing executives' career development.

Organizing for global marketing strategies is examined followed by a discussion of the importance of appropriate organizational designs for managing relationships with global customers. Much of the earlier material in the chapter applies to international operations. This discussion highlights several additional considerations.

Organizing for Global Marketing Strategies

The important distinction in marketing throughout the world is that buyers differ in their needs, preferences, and priorities. Since such differences exist *within* a national market, the variations between countries are likely to be greater. Brands like Budweiser beer and Levi's jeans have significantly different market positions in international markets compared to those they occupy in the United States. Global market targeting and positioning strategies create several marketing organizational issues.

Business Functions

Global decisions concerning production, finance, and research and development are often more feasible than making the marketing decisions that span these markets. Marketing

---

[51]Morgan W. McCall and George P. Hollenbeck, *Developing Global Executives: The Lessons of International Experience* (Boston, MA: Harvard Business School Press, 2001).

strategies often require sensitivity to cultural and linguistic differences. Foreign currencies, government regulations, and different product standards further complicate buyer-seller relationships. The important issue is recognizing when standardized marketing strategies can be used and when they must be modified.

Organizational Issues

The marketing organization selected for competing in national markets is influenced by the market *scope* (e.g., single-country, multinational, or global strategy), and by the market *entry strategy* (export, licensing, joint venture, strategic alliance, or complete ownership). The adoption of a global strategy using joint ventures, alliances, or complete ownership presents the most complex organizational challenge.

The marketing organization design in international operations may take one of three possible forms: (1) a global product division; (2) geographical divisions, each with product and functional responsibilities; or (3) a matrix design incorporating (1) or (2) in combination with centralized functional support or instead a combination of area operations and global product management.[52] The global form corresponds to rapid growth situations for firms that have a broad product portfolio. The geographic form is used to obtain a close relationship with national and local governments. The matrix form is utilized by companies reorganizing for global competition. An example of a combination organization design is shown in Exhibit 14.8.

Coordination and Communication

Organizing marketing activities to serve international markets creates important coordination and communication requirements. Language and distance barriers complicate organizational relationships. For many companies, growing emphasis on effective global teamwork is replacing traditional concepts of domestic versus international divisions. Many of the constraints to organizing globally have lessened, even for companies with a

EXHIBIT 14.8
Global Marketing Organization Plan Combining Product, Geographic, and Functional Features

Source: Philip R. Cateora and John L. Graham, *International Marketing,* 12th ed. (Burr Ridge, IL: McGraw-Hill/Irwin, 2005), 336. Copyright © The McGraw-Hill Companies. Used with permission.

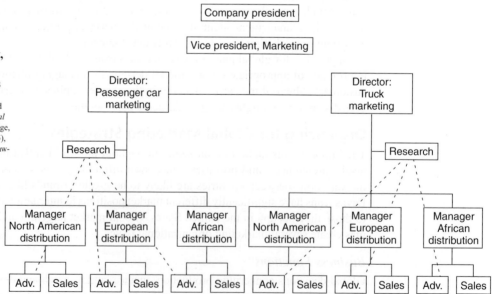

---

[52]This discussion is based on Philip R. Cateora and John Graham, *International Marketing,* 12th ed. (Burr Ridge, IL: McGraw-Hill/Irwin, 2005), 335–338.

limited international involvement. Enabling technology provided by the Internet and collaboration software facilitates the operation and management of global teams.

For example, to reflect the growing internationalization of its business, in 2007 PepsiCo restructured its business to break down the divisions between its North American and Latin American businesses. The new PepsiCo Americas Beverages and Americas Food divisions aim to link developed and developing markets to share brands and best practices. PepsiCo becomes one of the first major U.S. consumer products companies to link up its operations in the United States/Canada with those in Latin America, although it is expected this type of realignment will become more common.[53]

Organizing for Global Customers

A major challenge for many companies is the growing importance of global customers, who expect to buy on a global basis and to receive favorable treatment across all their worldwide locations. This challenge is illustrated by the growth of global retailing businesses and the development of global account management organizations.

The Growth of Global Retailers

In the consumer goods sector, the growth of global retailers has been substantial. In consumer packaged goods, Ahold (Netherlands), Carrefour (France), and METRO (Germany) each operate in more than 25 countries. Aldi (Germany), Auchan (France), Rewe (Switzerland), Tesco (United Kingdom), and Wal-Mart each operate in 10 or more countries. Similar globalization trends are apparent in industries as diverse as apparel, chemicals, entertainment, financial services, and personal computers. Powerful global customers expect coverage, speed, consistent and high-quality service, and extraordinary attention from their suppliers that reflect their buying power. These expectations require suppliers to provide a single point of contact, uniform terms of trade, and worldwide standardization of products and services.[54]

Global customers demand more uniform and transparent global prices from suppliers. In 2000, British supermarket Tesco acquired a small supermarket chain in Poland called Hit. Hit was obtaining better prices from its suppliers than was Tesco. The lack of a logical worldwide pricing structure allows global customers like Tesco to demand retrospective discounts when they discover anomalies.[55]

Global Account Management Structures

We considered earlier the challenges of managing strategic customer relationships (see Chapter 7) and channel strategy (see Chapter 10). However, the growth in importance of global customers has led many suppliers to develop specialized organizational units and processes to manage their relationship. Global account management is "an organizational form and process in multinational companies by which the worldwide activities serving one or more multinational customers are coordinated centrally by one person or team within the supplier company"[56]

In some companies, global account managers have been developed in parallel to strategic account management functions (see Chapter 7). Procter & Gamble, for example, has established global customer development teams to present a single face to the global customer.

---

[53]Jonathan Birchall, "PepsiCo Links Up Operations in Americas," *Financial Times,* November 6, 2007, 27.

[54]Nirmalya Kumar, *Marketing as Strategy: Understanding the CEO's Agenda for Driving Growth and Innovation* (Boston MA: Harvard Business School Press, 2004).

[55]Ibid., 119.

[56]George S. Yip and Audrey J. M. Bink, *Managing Global Customers: An Integrated Approach* (Oxford: Oxford University Press, 2007), 9.

Global account management (GAM) puts a single executive or team in charge of a single customer and all its global needs. This executive must be able to call on all the company's resources and be able to market all its products to the customer.

GAM involves a relationship with the customer that doesn't just find solutions for operational needs, but builds strategies for the future and develops new business.

Main tasks in initiating GAM are selecting the accounts, developing corporate structure that make GAM a distinct company operation, and recruiting account managers.

Microsoft began introducing GAM in 2000, and focuses on multi-million-dollar, global corporate customers that depend heavily on information technology.

To be a Microsoft global account, candidates must have enough revenue potential to justify Microsoft's allocating significant resources. Account size is only one criterion, the candidate must:

- be willing to collaborate;
- be ready to share information for developing new products and processes;
- be willing to establish multilevel relationships with Microsoft;
- be a leader in their industry (to leverage Microsoft's reputation);
- possess superior skills and knowledge and be early adopters of new technology;
- and already have global organizational coordination.

Microsoft encourages its senior managers to develop relationships with senior decision makers in the global account and to be active in ensuring that GAM initiatives get all the resources they require from within Microsoft.

At Microsoft, account managers, called global business managers, are encouraged to be innovative and have their own budgets. They work across business units, functions, and organizations, and get support in marshalling resources from a headquarters team of ten, and support from a broader group of 150 people worldwide, who contribute in various ways to account planning and operational management.

Source: Adapted from Christoph Senn and Axel Thoma, "Worldy Wise: Attracting and Managing Customers Isn't the Same When Business Goes Global," *Wall Street Journal,* March 3, 2007, R.5.

P&G's global customer teams operate in parallel with the company's business units and country organizations, in a form of matrix. The customer teams have specialists in IT, retail merchandizing, finance, sales, supply chain, marketing, and marketing research. The teams manage relationships with global retailers and develop joint plans with them, as well as working with business units and country managers to deliver against strategic goals for the customer in each product category and geographic location.

Global account management teams are multi-functional and can only operate effectively by addressing cross-functional coordination and communication around the strategy development for the global customers. Global account managers frequently report to very senior levels of the organization. Effective organizational responses to the global customer and becoming extremely important in a wide range of companies. The approach to managing global accounts at Microsoft is described in the GLOBAL APPLICATION.

Increasing globalization of organizations driven by the factors we have described means that for an increasing number of marketing executive's global experience will be an important step in career development. Skills in managing internationally and developing effective global customer relationships will be at a premium.

Summary

Market-driven organizations reflect customer value requirements in their design, roles, and activities. This is a foundation for implementing and managing market-driven strategy. For many companies organizational change is a constant process aimed at achieving this alignment.

The market-driven organization is related in part to major trends in organization design on a broader front. Traditional structures—dominated by vertical "silos"—are increasingly inadequate to meet the requirements of new strategies in complex and turbulent environments. New organizing imperatives are driven by communications technology, the globalization of production and sales, and the transfer of responsibility to outside organizations for core business functions. Organizational designs emphasize innovation, the productivity of the knowledge worker, the management of culture in line with strategy, collaborative working inside and outside the company, informal networks, and organizational mechanisms to manage external relationships with partner organizations. The design and management of organizational processes has become a key issue in design. Organizations are being designed to achieve agility and flexibility, and to accommodate new challenges in employee engagement and motivation.

These trends in organizational design are relevant to organizing for market-driven strategy and achieving effective strategy implementation. In particular, the impact of the customer on design choices mandates consideration to the alignment of the organization with the market, and developing structures to achieve this goal. Considerable emphasis is placed on managing marketing processes that cut across traditional organizational boundaries and underline high priorities for cross-functional partnering and effective integration around the drivers of customer value.

Several important questions center on the organization of marketing resources. Design choices are faced in the centralization or decentralization of the marketing organization, and the integration of diffusion of responsibility for marketing tasks. No one way of structuring matches all situations, and important contingent factors surround this design choice. Within marketing resource groups, the major structural choices are between functional, product, market or matrix designs. Consideration must also be given to the identification of new marketing roles and specializations as the role of marketing evolves in a company. One major issue is partnership, both internally, for example in venture marketing organizations, but also externally in working with marketing partners. In some cases, the networked organization will be an important development.

Global marketing strategy and the global customer identify several additional organizational imperatives. Global marketing frequently relies on strategic alliances. Global programs imply organizational choices regarding the international location of business functions and designing appropriate organizational forms to meet the additional challenges of international coordination and communication. The growing globalization of customers in many sectors leads to the organizational response of developing global account management structures and processes. New buyer expectations for a single point of contact with a supplier, together with uniform terms of trade and worldwide standardization of products and services frequently indicate the need for an organizational design at a global level to manage these customer relationships.

Questions for Review and Discussion

1. The chief executive of a manufacturer of direct-order personal computers is interested in establishing a marketing organization in the firm. A small salesforce handles sales to mid-sized businesses and advertising is planned and executed by an advertising agency. Other than the CEO, no one inside the firm is responsible for the marketing function. What factors should the CEO consider in designing a marketing organization?

2. Of the various approaches to marketing organization design, which one(s) offers the most flexibility in coping with rapidly changing market and competitive situations? Discuss.

3. Discuss the conditions where a matrix-type marketing organization would be appropriate, indicating important considerations and potential problems in using this organizational form.

4. Assume that you have been asked by the president of a major transportation services firm to recommend a marketing organizational design. What important factors should you consider in selecting the design?

5. Discuss some of the important issues related to integrating marketing into an organization such as a regional women's clothing chain compared to accomplishing the same task in Limited Brands.

6. What are possible internal and external factors that may require changing the marketing organization design?

7. Is a trend toward more organic organizational forms likely in the future?

8. Summarize and chart the current and future impact of the Internet on marketing processes and organization.

9. Discuss the important organizational design issues in establishing an effective strategic alliance between organizations.

10. What are the major approaches to organizing the marketing function for international operations? Discuss the factors that may affect the choice of a particular organization design.

11. As companies begin to replace functions with processes, what are the possible effects on organizational designs?

12. What characteristics would you seek in a candidate for a global account management position?

Internet Applications

A. Visit the website of the Strategic Account Management Association (www.strategicaccounts .org) and review some of the research library resources available at the site. What is the basis for suggesting that the strategic/key account manager is anything more than a senior salesperson working on major accounts—why is it any different? Where can a strategic account manager be positioned in the marketing and sales organization?

B. Go to the website of Coca-Cola Inc (www.cocacola.com). Use the corporate information pages (Our Company, Our Brands, and Around the World) to identify the growth in brands marketed by the company and its geographic emphasis. Identify the challenges for this company in organizing marketing for a growing brand portfolio in a diverse global marketplace.

C. Consultants Booz Allen and the Association of National Advertisers have an online tool for assessing the "DNA" of marketing organizations—www.marketingprofiler.com. Visit this site and consider if the questions asked in the diagnostic provide a good basis for evaluating a marketing organization. Use the profiling diagnostic to evaluate a marketing organization that you know.

Applications

A. Read the INNOVATION APPLICATION "Venture Marketing Organization at Starbucks." What lessons can be learned about the organizational requirements for rapid and effective innovation?

B. Consider the STRATEGY APPLICATION "The Toyota Way." Can other companies learn from the Toyota approach to managing its organization, or is the success of the approach unique to Toyota?

Chapter 15

Strategic Marketing Implementation and Control

How well marketing strategy is implemented and managed on a continuing basis is the ultimate test of the robustness of market targeting and positioning decisions. Putting strategy into action and making adjustments to eliminate performance gaps are essential stages in strategic marketing. Strategy and implementation are interdependent activities concerned with matching capabilities with opportunities and this interdependence is critical:

> Drawing a line between strategy and execution almost guarantees failure. . . . It's a commonly held idea that strategy is distinct from execution, but this is a flawed assumption. The idea that a strategy can be brilliant and its execution poor is simply wrong.[1]

The importance of effective processes for both strategy and implementation is illustrated by the strategic turnaround at car-maker Fiat in Italy. Turin saw the launch of the Fiat 500 in Europe in mid-2007—a modern mini-car designed to resemble the tiny 1957 Cinquecento that put many Italians on the road for the first time.[2] Yet when Sergio Marchionne was appointed Fiat CEO in 2004, Fiat was deeply in debt and making substantial financial losses. The reputation of Fiat vehicles was for terrible quality and reliability, considerable market share had been lost, and the Fiat Group had diversified into everything from banking and insurance to energy. In the early 2000s, Fiat actively considered leaving the auto industry altogether.

Marchionne's strategy started with a radical restructuring and dismantling of Fiat's management and bureaucracy. Young managers were taken from lower levels of the organization to take charge of new units for each of Fiat's car brands. He negotiated his way out of an alliance with General Motors, and advertisements proclaimed to customers and employees "Fiat is all-Italian again." R&D and operations were overhauled and updated— the Fiat Bravo progressed from design to production in a record 18 months, about half the usual time.

[1]Roger L. Martin, "The Execution Trap," *Harvard Business Review,* July–August 2010, 64–71, quotation from 66.
[2]This illustration is based on Ray Hutton, "Fiat Back from the Brink," *Sunday Times,* July 1, 2007, —S3, 11. John Reed, "Fiat Paints a Picture with Rebirth of a Street Icon," *Financial Times,* July 4, 2007, 21.

Marchionne has launched a range of strategic relationships in cooperative ventures and technology licence deals. Strategically, Fiat is widely seen as a brand that has regained its sense of direction. The brand credibility does not rely on expensive cars. Fiat is succeeding with small cars, on which other manufacturers find it hard to make money, because it is very efficient at making them. Fiat is trying to position itself as a leader in cleaner cars. Management has succeeded in implementing radical change in a short time period. Fiat is back in profit, regaining market share, and reducing its mountain of debt.

In 2009 Marchionne took on the challenge of applying his strategic change capabilities at Chrysler, where he has rapidly adopted unconventional methods like fostering internal competition by making each Chrysler brand a separate company.[3] Marchionne took day-to-day management control of Chrysler when it emerged from bankruptcy after U.S. government financial support, with Fiat taking a 20 percent ownership stake, and he is working on a vigorous revival plan for Michigan's smallest carmaker.[4]

We begin by examining the strategic role of the chief marketing officer in managing the implementation of targeting and positioning choices and then review issues relating to the development of strategic marketing plans and management of the planning process. Next, we discuss strategy implementation and building implementation effectiveness, including consideration of internal marketing approaches. Then we overview strategic evaluation and control in marketing. This is followed by an evaluation of the measurement of marketing performance, including the development of marketing metrics and the management dashboard. Finally, we consider several global marketing aspects of planning, implementation and control.

The Strategic Role of the Chief Marketing Officer

In the turbulent global marketplace now faced by many companies, and with the continued impact of economic downturn and recession on different markets, a high priority is effective and insightful leadership by the chief marketing officer (CMO). Mandates for "higher-ambition leaders" include powerful strategic vision drawing on a broad view of a company's heritage, and cultural, organizational and social assets; building widespread commitment and capabilities to achieve that vision by an organization with shared purpose, emotional connection, trust and respect; and the strength to commit to the strategic vision over the longer term.[5] Importantly, the CMO role extends beyond compelling strategic vision to effective strategy implementation and managing organizational change.

Strategic CMO Capabilities

Research by McKinsey underlines the challenges for CMOs in adapting to a rapidly changing marketing environment resulting from unprecedented proliferation in new media, market segments, and distribution channels—consequently priorities include enhancing the capabilities and flexibility of organizations, emphasizing portfolios rather than single brands, and promoting consistency across the marketing organization.[6]

---

[3]David Welch, David Kiley, and Carol Matlack, "Tough Love at Chrysler," *BusinessWeek,* August 24 & 31, 2009, 26–28.

[4]Bernard Simon and John Reed, "Italy's Villain of the Piece is Toast of Motown," *Financial Times,* January 16, 2011, 14.

[5]Nathanial Foote, Russell Eisenstat, and Tobias Fredberg, "The Higher Ambition Leader," *Harvard Business Review,* September 2011, 95–102.

[6]David Court, "Confronting Proliferation: A Conversation with Four Senior Marketers," *McKinsey Quarterly,* No. 3, 2007 18–27.

The average tenure for CMOs in major organizations is less than 2 years. Rapid technological change and senior management concerns for profitability place priority on CMO abilities: to *mobilize marketing* across the organization (for example, in 2009, Best Buy's CMO created the Twelpforce to allow any employees to handle customer service or product queries via Twitter); to act as a *futurist* (for example, Walgreen's first-ever CMO in 2008 has repositioned the company as a premium health care brand, rather than a convenience store with a pharmacy in the back, achieving 14 percent sales growth in spite of the sluggish economy); and to track the *financial returns* on marketing expenditures.[7]

Core CMO Tasks

A recent study suggests that there are seven key tasks expected of the CMO, although our understanding of some of these roles remains only partial:

- Establishing the role of marketing in the firm
- Owning the voice of the market
- Responsibility for marketing strategy
- Coordinating marketing with other areas of the firm
- Running the marketing organization
- Identifying and leading the marketing transformation effort
- Establishing a marketing scorecard and performance metrics[8]

While the earlier chapters have been concerned with the first five of these tasks facing the CMO, the emphasis in this chapter is on the tasks of leading transformation and establishing appropriate performance metrics.

Planning, Implementation, and Accountability

We have discussed creating effective marketing strategies and examined some of the organizational issues central to strategic marketing (see Chapter 14). The developing and strategic role of the CMO is underlined by this coverage. We now examine the strategic marketing planning process as a mechanism for implementing strategy and marketing metrics for performance measurement and meeting new pressures for greater marketing accountability in the firm.

The Strategic Marketing Planning Process

The strategic marketing plan indicates marketing objectives and the strategy and tactics for accomplishing the objectives, and guides implementation and control. The Appendix to Chapter 1 presents a step-by-step planning process. Our perspective at this stage is more on implementation and control than analysis.

Marketing Plans Guide Implementation

The relationships between marketing strategy and the annual marketing plan are shown in Exhibit 15.1. The planning cycle is continuous. Plans are developed, implemented, evaluated, and revised to keep the marketing strategy on target. Since a strategy typically extends beyond 1 year, the annual plan is used to guide short-term marketing activities. An annual planning period is necessary, since several of the activities shown require action within 12 months or less, and budgets also require annual planning.

---

[7]Jessica Shambora, "Wanted: Fearless Marketing Execs," *Fortune,* August 15, 2011, p. 10.
[8]Bernard J. Jaworski, "On Managerial Relevance," *Journal of Marketing,* 75, July 2011, 211–224.

EXHIBIT 15.1
Strategy and
Planning
Relationships

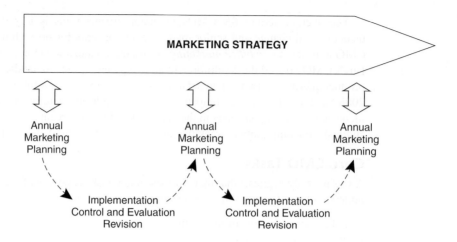

A look at the marketing planning process used by a large pharmaceutical company illustrates how planning is done, as summarized in the STRATEGY APPLICATION.

Contents of the Marketing Plan

An outline for developing the marketing plan is presented in the Appendix to Chapter 1 (see Exhibit 1A.1). Many plans follow this general format. Planning activities include making a situation assessment, identifying market targets, setting objectives, developing targeting and positioning strategies, deciding action programs for the marketing-mix components, and preparing supporting financial statements (budgets and profit-and-loss projections).

The typical planning process involves considerable coordination and interaction among functional areas. Team planning approaches like the pharmaceutical company's planning workshop are illustrative. Successful implementation of the marketing plan requires a broad consensus among various functional areas.[9] For example, a consensus is essential between product managers and sales management. Collaboration between product managers and sales managers is essential to provide sales coverage for the product portfolio. Multiple products require negotiation in reaching agreement on the amount of sales force time devoted to various products. Recall the Chapter 14 discussion of the importance of efforts to secure the integration of marketing with other functions and units in the organization, and approaches to achieving this.

Managing the Planning Process

A useful perspective is to consider that planning is an organizational process in which interactions and discussions between executives shape outcomes. Examining planning as an organizational process can provide several insights into improving planning effectiveness. Planning involves more than analytical techniques and computation. Insight into problems faced in making marketing planning effective may be addressed by considering the behavior of executives in conducting planning and the organizational context in which planning is done, as well as by formal training in planning techniques and procedures.[10] An effective planning process is closely linked to successful implementation. Exhibit 15.2

---

[9]James Mac Hulbert, Noel Capon, and Nigel F. Piercy, *Total Integrated Marketing: Breaking the Bounds of the Function* (New York: The Free Press, 2003).
[10]Nigel F. Piercy and Neil A. Morgan, "The Marketing Planning Process: Behavioral Problems Compared to Analytical Techniques in Explaining Marketing Planning Credibility," *Journal of Business Research,* 29, 1994, 167–178.

- Product managers are responsible for coordinating the preparation of marketing plans.
- A planning workshop is conducted midyear for the kick-off of the next year's plans.
- The workshop is attended by top management and by product, research, sales, and finance managers. The firm's advertising agency manager also participates in the workshop.
- The current year's plans are reviewed and each product manager presents the proposed marketing plan for next year.
- The workshop members critique each plan and suggest changes.
- Since the requested budgets may exceed available funds, priorities are placed on major budget components. Each product manager must provide strong support for requested funds.
- The same group meets again in 90 days and the revised plans are reviewed. At this meeting, the plans are finalized and approved for implementation.
- Each product manager is responsible for coordinating and implementing the plan.
- Progress is reviewed throughout the plan year and when necessary the plan is revised.

EXHIBIT 15.2

Dimensions of Marketing Planning Process

Source: Adapted from Nigel F. Piercy, *Market-Led Strategic Change: Transforming the Process of Going to Market,* 4th ed. (Oxford: Elsevier, 2009), 461.

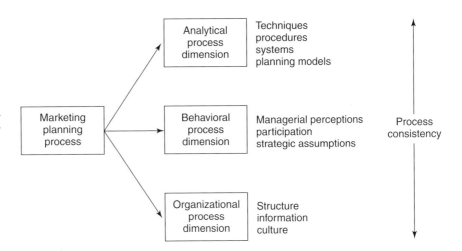

shows three dimensions of planning process—analytical, behavioral, and organizational dimensions—that should be managed consistently.

The analytical dimension of planning process consists of the tools for systematic planning—analytical techniques, formal procedures and systems—that are needed to develop robust and tested plans and strategies. The behavioral dimension of planning is concerned with how managers perceive planning activities and the strategic assumptions they make, as well as the degree and extent of participation in planning. Correspondingly, the organizational dimension of planning is concerned with the organizational structure in which planning is carried out, along with the associated information resources and corporate culture. One challenge to management is to manage all these aspects of the planning process in a consistent way—the conduct of planning should fit with

3M is a global enterprise manufacturing more than 60,000 products from a base of 112 technology platforms, and 28 autonomous business units, of which Abrasive Systems Division (ASD) is one. ASD is 3M's original business and operates in a mature market, supplying abrasives mainly to manufacturing companies.

- At 3M (UK), the early 1990s saw ASD market share falling, accompanied by declining staff morale (compared to other company units and benchmark companies outside 3M).

- The appointment of Stuart Lane as ASD business unit manager in 1992 had three key goals: to restore sales growth to a minimum of 5 percent per year, to return gross margin to the levels of the 1980s, and to bring the employee satisfaction level to at least the company average.

- Lane's first observations were that people felt they were not treated with respect or thanked for jobs well done; they lacked freedom to use initiative and make decisions; there was little information sharing and too much bureaucracy.

- Lane's first decision was to double ASD's sales growth target from the 25 percent required by senior management (for 1992–1996) to 50 percent.

- In collaboration with 3M's Corporate Marketing business planners he designed what he describes as "a semi-formal, structured, iterative process" of planning for ASD.

- The new planning process started with a two-day planning workshop in spring 1992, followed by five workshops over the following three months. Lane considers the workshops as critical to developing a robust plan for ASD, but also the team-building, ownership, enthusiasm, and commitment to make the plan happen, and confidence among the team members that they were going to achieve the ambitious, "stretch" goals for ASD. Lane was prepared to sacrifice some sophistication in planning in favor of simplicity and involvement to win people's support.

- The planning was linked directly to an implementation process with three key elements:

  1. A written plan, presented to management, but also reduced to an index card containing the essence of the plan in simple and memorable terms.

  2. The launch of the new plan to the ASD organization at the annual sales conference, and distribution of the index cards to be kept at the front of people's diaries.

  3. The introduction of Segment Action Teams (with a member of the management team as leader, but including people from sales, marketing, customer service and technical services from different levels in the organization), to take responsibility for segment-specific tactics and programmes. The Segment Action Teams have evolved into a key and permanent part of the ASD structure.

The results achieved by 1996 were a 53 percent growth in sales, a 100 percent growth in gross margin contribution, a 30 percent increase in market share, and employee satisfaction 12 percent above the company average. This was achieved, recall, in a mature market showing little growth.

Source: Adapted from Stuart Lane and Debbie Clewes, "The Implementation of Marketing Planning: A Case Study in Gaining Commitment at 3M (UK) Abrasives," *Journal of Strategic Marketing* 8(3), 2000, 225–240. Reprinted with permission of Taylor & Francis Ltd., www.tandf.co.uk/journals.

other organizational characteristics, executives should be trained and supported in developing plans.

The INNOVATION APPLICATION describes how a manager addressed planning process issues at an SBU of the 3M Corporation in the United Kingdom. It illustrates the advantages of linking the planning process to implementation issues.

Implementing the Strategic Marketing Plan

The effectiveness of strategy implementation determines the outcome of marketing planning. The management of the planning process may enhance implementation effectiveness by building commitment and "ownership" of the plan and its execution. For example, actively managing the participation of different functions and executives from different specializations may improve the fit between the plan and the company's real capabilities and resources, and avoid implementation barriers. Planning and execution are interdependent parts of strategic change.[11]

Marketing managers increasingly function as boundary-spanners both internally between functional areas and externally with suppliers, organizational partners, and customers (see Chapter 14). Additional efforts to make the strategy implementation process more effective are a high priority in many companies. Estimates suggest as many as 70 percent of new strategic initiatives in companies fail at the implementation stage.[12] Many companies now recognize that implementation capabilities are an important corporate resource that requires detailed management attention.[13]

Implementation Process

Research underlines the influence of two sets of factors on marketing strategy implementation: *structural* issues, including the company's marketing functions, control systems, and policy guidelines, and *behavioral* issues, concerning marketing managers' skills in bargaining and negotiation, resource allocation, and developing informal organizational arrangements.[14] We consider several organizational and interpersonal aspects of effective implementation process.

The link between planning and implementation in a product manager's marketing planning is illustrated in the STRATEGY APPLICATION. A good implementation process spells out the activities to be implemented, who is responsible for implementation, the time and location of implementation, and how implementation will be achieved (see Exhibit 15.3).

The marketing plan can be used to identify the organizational units and managers that are responsible for implementing the various activities in the plan. Deadlines indicate the time available for implementation. In the STRATEGY APPLICATION case, the sales manager is responsible for implementation through the sales force.

Building Implementation Effectiveness

Managers are important facilitators in the implementation process, and some are better implementers than others. Planners and implementers often have different strengths

[11]Lawrence G Hrebiniak, "Obstacles to Effective Strategy Implementation," *Organizational Dynamics,* 35(1), 2006, 12–31.

[12]David Miller, "Successful Change Leaders: What Makes Them?" *Journal of Change Management,* 2(4), 2002, 359–368.

[13]Nigel F. Piercy, "Marketing Implementation: The Implications of Marketing Paradigm Weakness for the Strategy Execution Process," *Journal of the Academy of Marketing Science,* 26(3), 1998, 222–236. Nigel F. Piercy and Frank V. Cespedes, "Implementing Marketing Strategy," *Journal of Marketing Management,* 12, 1996, 135–160.

[14]Charles H. Noble and Michael P. Mokwa, "Implementing Marketing Strategies: Developing and Testing a Managerial Theory," *Journal of Marketing,* October 1999, 57–73.

EXHIBIT 15.3
The Implementation Process

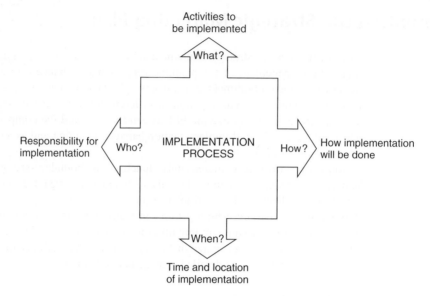

Activities to be implemented

What?

Responsibility for implementation

Who?

IMPLEMENTATION PROCESS

How?

How implementation will be done

When?

Time and location of implementation

and weaknesses. An effective planner may not be good at implementing plans. Desirable implementation skills include:

- The ability to understand how others feel, and good bargaining skills.
- The strength to be tough and fair in putting people and resources where they will be most effective.
- Effectiveness in focusing on the critical aspects of performance in managing marketing activities.
- The ability to create a necessary informal organization or network to match each problem with which they are confronted.[15]

Research underlines the importance of engendering a sense of role significance among those responsible for implementation.[16] In addition to skillful implementers, several factors facilitate the implementation process. These include *organizational design, incentives,* and *effective communications.* The features of each factor are highlighted.

Organizational Design

Certain types of organizational designs aid implementation. For example, product managers and multifunctional coordination teams are useful implementation methods. Management may create implementation teams consisting of representatives from the business functions and/or marketing activities involved. The flat, flexible organization designs discussed in Chapter 14 offer several advantages in implementation, since they encourage interfunctional cooperation and communication. These designs are responsive to changing conditions.

As organizations shift from functional to process structures, the resulting changes promise to strengthen as well as complicate implementation strategies.[17] The use of cross-functional teams will aid implementation activities. The challenges of process definition,

---

[15]Thomas V. Bonoma, "Making Your Marketing Strategy Work," *Harvard Business Review,* March–April 1984, 75.
[16]Noble and Mokwa, 71.
[17]David W. Cravens, "Implementation Strategies in the Market-Driven Strategy Era," *Journal of the Academy of Marketing Science,* Summer 1998, 237–238.

Consider the following statement from a product manager's marketing plan:

Sales representatives should target all accounts currently using a competitive product. A plan should be developed to convert 5 percent of these accounts to the company brand during the year. Account listings will be prepared and distributed by product management.

- In this instance, the salesforce is charged with implementation
- An objective (5 percent conversion) is specified but very little information is provided as to *how* the accounts will be converted
- A strategy is needed to penetrate the competitors' customer base
- The salesforce plan must translate the proposed actions and objective (5 percent conversion) into assigned salesperson responsibility (quotas), a timetable, and selling strategy guidelines.
- Training may be necessary to show the product advantages—and the competitors' product limitations—that will be useful in convincing the buyer to purchase the firm's brand.

design, and management call for new skills and a multifunctional perspective, which will make implementation activities more complex and require careful attention by management.

Incentives

Various rewards may help achieve successful implementation. For example, special incentives such as contests, recognition, and extra compensation are used to encourage salespeople to push a new product. Since implementation often involves teams of people, creation of team incentives may be necessary. Performance standards must be fair, and incentives should encourage something more than normal performance. Focusing incentives on the achievement of overall plan goals rather than individual efforts is particularly relevant.[18]

Communications

Rapid and accurate movement of information through the organization is essential in implementation. Both vertical and horizontal communications are needed in linking together the people and activities involved in implementation. Meetings, status reports, and informal discussions help to transmit information throughout the organization. Computerized information and decision-support systems like corporate intranets help to improve communications' speed and effectiveness.

Problems often occur during implementation and may affect how fast and how well plans are put into action. Examples include competitors' actions, internal resistance between departments, loss of key personnel, supply chain delays affecting product availability (e.g., supply, production, and distribution problems), and changes in the business environment. Corrective actions may require appointing a person or team for trouble shooting the problem, increasing or shifting resources, or changing the original plan.

Importantly, implementation and change operate in a wider company context. Consider, for example, the implementation issues faced in the execution of Google's acquisition of

---

[18]Hay Group, *Work on Your Winning Strategy: Its Time for Variable Pay to Deliver the Best Returns,* www .haygroup,com, accessed August 25, 2011.

In mid-2011, Google Inc. agreed to acquire Motorola Mobility Holdings for $12.5 billion, allowing Google, as creator of the fast-growing Android operating system, to build its own smartphones and tablet computers.

The strategic move underlines the strength of vertical integration between software producers and hardware manufacturers (e.g., to compete with Apple's integrated model and the Nokia/Microsoft alliance). Motorola also brings Google 17,000 Motorola patents, important to defending its technology.

But the execution risks are substantial. Software company Google will now face issues such as running manufacturing plants, managing inventory, and relationships with carriers and retailers.

In addition, the Motorola acquisition makes potential rivals out of some existing Google partners that already license its Android operating system, although Google says it plans to run Motorola as a separate business on an equal footing with other partners.

When Google attempted to manufacture laptops running its Chrome operating system, to rival Microsoft's Windows, it faced considerable challenges in executing the plan, and eventually chose to work with brand-name hardware manufacturers like Acer Inc. and Samsung.

Larry Page of Google described the Motorola initiative: "Together, we will create amazing user experiences that supercharge the entire Android ecosystem for the benefit of consumers, partners and developers. I look forward to welcoming Motorolans to our family of Googlers."

However, Google and Motorola are separated by half a continent, a different cultural legacy (Google is a software company and Motorola an 80-year-old hardware operation), and very different corporate cultures.

Sources: Amir Efrati and Matt Jarzemsky, "Google Deal Upends Mobile Sector," *Wall Street Journal*, August 16, 2011, 1. Shatdni Raice, "Google-Motorola Tie-Up to Test Corporate Style," *Wall Street Journal*, August 18, 2011, 22. Lucy Kellaway, "Chief Googler's 'Amazing' Clichés Are Dull and Void," *Financial Times*, August 22, 2011, 10.

Motorola, described in the STRATEGY APPLICATION. Google faces some interesting challenges in managing relationships with its acquisition across a cultural divide, working effectively in the hardware manufacturing business, and maintaining productive relationships with its existing Android partners.

Internal Marketing

One approach to enhancing strategy implementation effectiveness is the adoption of internal marketing methods. Internal marketing involves developing programs to win line management support for new strategies; changing the attitudes and behavior of employees working at key points of contact with customers; and gaining the commitment of those whose problem-solving skills are important to superior execution of the strategy. Research suggests many organizations fail to deliver their planned brand experience because of insufficient internal marketing.[19] Exhibit 15.4 shows internal marketing and external marketing programs as parallel outputs from the planning process. While external marketing positions the strategy in the customer marketplace, internal marketing is aimed at the internal customer within the company. Internal marketing goals may include promoting the external marketing

---

[19]"Survey Reveals 'Inadequate' State of Internal Marketing," *Marketing Week*, July 3, 2003, 8.

EXHIBIT 15.4   Internal Marketing

Source: Reprinted from *Market-Led Strategic Change: A Guide to Transforming the Process of Going to Market,* Nigel F. Piercy, Copyright 2009, with permission from Elsevier.

strategy and how employees contribute, developing better understanding between customers and employees (regardless of whether they have direct contact), and providing superior internal customer service to support external strategy.[20]

An internal marketing approach involves examining each element of the external marketing program to identify what changes will be needed in the company's internal marketplace and how these changes can be achieved. If used as part of the planning process, analysis of the internal marketplace can isolate organizational change requirements (e.g., new skills, processes, organizational structures), implementation barriers (e.g., lack of support and commitment in key areas of the company), and new opportunities (by uncovering organizational capabilities otherwise overlooked).[21] Internal marketing is a promising way of identifying and resolving some of the implementation issues associated with the move from functional to process-based organizational designs. The importance of gaining the buy-in of all employees and managers to strategy is illustrated in the RELATIONSHIP APPLICATION, which describes the impressive performance culture at steelmaker Nucor.

We examined market orientation as a key aspect of the market-driven company in Chapter 1. Interestingly, recent suggestions are that in addition to external market orientation of the conventional type, executives' attention should also be devoted to internal market orientation—aligning managerial behaviors with the employee behaviors and outcomes important to strategy implementation. The intention is to better align external market objectives with internal capabilities.[22]

One developing aspect of internal marketing is the opportunity to actively market plans and strategies not only inside the company, but also with partner organizations and their employees. Effective implementation may rest also on company-wide and network-wide efforts to put marketing plans and strategies into effect.

---

[20]Dana James, "Don't Forget Staff in Marketing Plan," *Marketing News,* March 13, 2000, 10–11.

[21]Nigel F. Piercy, *Market-Led Strategic Change: Transforming the Process of Going to Market,* 4th ed. (Oxford: Elsevier, 2009), 495–510.

[22]Ian N. Lings and Gordon E. Greenley, "Measuring Internal Market Orientation," *Journal of Services Research,* 7(3), 2005, 290–305. Spiros P. Gounaris, "Internal-Market Orientation and Its Measurement," *Journal of Business Research,* 59(4), 2006, 432–448.

Nucor is the largest producer of steel in the United States and the world's foremost steel recycler. Performance in sales growth, productivity, and profitability is outstanding.

In a Rust Belt industry, Nucor has nurtured a dynamic and engaged workforce. Nucor's flattened hierarchy and emphasis on pushing power to the front-line lead its employees to adopt the mind-set of owner-operators.

Nucor Corporation's mission statement is: "Nucor Corporation is made up of 11,900 teammates whose goal is to 'Take Care of Our Customers.' We are accomplishing this by being the safest, highest quality, lowest cost, most productive and most profitable steel and steel products company in the world. We are committed to doing this while being cultural and environmental stewards in our communities where we live and work. We are succeeding by working together."

Nucor bases the majority of most workers' income on their performance. Nucor's management style is based on the belief that employees will make extraordinary efforts if rewarded richly, treated with respect, and given real power.

Nucor is an example of outstanding strategy execution. Managers have abandoned the command-and-control model that has dominated American business for the better part of a century, trust their people, and do a better job of sharing corporate wealth.

Nucor places a premium on teamwork and idea-sharing between frontline workers and management, to create a highly profitable partnership.

Key elements of the Nucor approach are

- Pay for performance—even with the risks of lower income in bad times.
- Listen to the front line—the best ideas come from the factory floor.
- Push authority down in the organization.
- Protect your culture—cultural compatibility is a big focus in acquisitions.
- Try unproven technologies—it is important to take risks.

Sources: Nanette Byrnes, "The Art of Motivation," *BusinessWeek,* May 1, 2006, 57–62. www.nucor.com, accessed August 25, 2011.

A Comprehensive Approach to Improving Implementation

One comprehensive way to deal with difficulty in the implementation of the marketing plan is to employ the balanced scorecard method.[23] This process is a formalized management control system that implements a given business unit strategy by means of activities across four areas: financial, customer, internal business process, and learning and growth (or innovation).

The balanced scorecard was created in reaction to the difficulties that many managers experienced when trying to implement a particular strategy. A strategy is often not defined in a manner that describes how it might be achieved. Merely communicating the strategy to employees does not provide any instruction as to what actions they must take to help achieve the strategy. More importantly, managers might even take action to the detriment of other areas in an organization when attempting to implement the strategy. The balanced scorecard provides a framework to minimize such an occurrence by encouraging implementation of a common strategy, which is communicated and coordinated across all major areas of the organization. The "balanced" component of the balanced scorecard reflects the

---

[23]Robert S. Kaplan and David P. Norton, *The Strategy-Focused Organization: How Balanced Scorecard Companies Thrive in the New Business Environment* (Boston: Harvard Business School Press, 2001).

need to consider how all areas of the organization function together to achieve a common goal of strategy implementation.

The major benefit of the balanced scorecard is that an often aggregate, broadly defined strategy is translated to very specific actions. Through execution and monitoring of these actions, management can assess the success of the strategy and also modify and adjust the strategy if necessary. Another major benefit of the balanced scorecard methodology is that it is feasible for any business unit level strategy and provides a means to link performance evaluation to strategy implementation.

Our marketing plan outline (see Exhibit 1A.1) can be adapted to the balanced scorecard format. A marketing plan is designed to achieve specific objectives through a set of strategies. Often a difficult area is determining which activities will lead to achieving market segment objectives, and ensuring that activities in one area do not interfere with activities in another area. The balanced scorecard approach allows consideration of specific activities that will accomplish the objective, but also formally includes an assessment of the strategy component across all aspects of the business unit at the same time. This assessment helps to include performance measures and targets that are more long-term oriented and are not solely financially based. In this way, a consideration of activities to execute a marketing strategy would also involve how these activities affect four major areas of the company: (1) the financial perspective, (2) the customer, (3) internal business processes, and (4) learning and growth. This integrated assessment considers how the strategy would affect all major areas of the company and what performance indicators should be monitored in each of the four major areas. In this manner, it is much easier to integrate the marketing plan with the overall business strategy.

Internal Strategy-Organization Fit

It is important that the organization's competitive and marketing strategy is compatible with the internal structure of the business and its policies, procedures, and resources (see Chapter 14).

Organizational Stretch

The absence of good fit between marketing strategy and organizational characteristics is likely to be a significant barrier to effective strategy implementation. "Organizational stretch" to execute strategy should be considered; that is, the degree to which structures, capabilities, systems, processes, and resource allocation may require adjustment to deliver the strategy. Marketing strategy must also be considered in the context provided by corporate strategy and business strategies being pursued by other business units, since lack of compatibility may be problematic.[24]

The importance of internal fit is shown by Hennes and Mauritz (H&M), the largest apparel retailer in Europe and a highly successful global fashion business. H&M sells "cheap chic"—very new, very extreme, very cheap fashion clothes to younger buyers. As well as outsourcing manufacturing to a huge network of garment shops in low-wage locations, H&M is run on principles of frugality internally. Overheads are minimized

---

[24]Nigel F. Piercy, *Market-Led Strategic Change: Transforming the Process of Going to Market,* 4th ed. (Oxford: Elsevier, 2009), 486–488.

everywhere—executives rarely fly business class; taking cabs is frowned upon; all employee cell phones were taken away in the 1990s and even now only a few key employees have them. The fit between H&M's strategy and positioning, and its internal culture and management approach, may help explain its success.[25]

The Role of External Organizations

The implementation of marketing strategy is affected by external organizations such as strategic alliance partners, marketing consultants, advertising and public relations firms, channel members, and other organizations participating in the marketing effort (see Chapter 7). These outside organizations may present a major coordination challenge when they actively participate in marketing activities. Their efforts should be identified in the marketing plan and their roles and responsibilities clearly established and communicated. There is a potential danger in not informing outside groups of planned actions, deadlines, and other implementation requirements. For example, the organization's advertising agency account executive and other agency staff members need to be familiar with all aspects of promotion strategy as well as the major aspects of marketing strategy (e.g., market targets, positioning strategies, and marketing-mix component strategies). Withholding information from participating firms hampers their efforts in strategy planning and implementation.

The development of collaborative relationships between suppliers and producers improves implementation. Supply chain management strategies encourage reducing the number of suppliers and building strong relationships (see Chapter 10). We noted earlier that internal marketing is playing a growing role in sustaining alliance and network-based organizations based on partnering. Companies that are effective in working with other organizations are likely to also do a good job with implementation inside the organization, since they have skills in developing effective working relationships. Total quality programs also encourage internal teamwork among functions.

Strategic Marketing Evaluation and Control

Marketing strategy must respond effectively to changing conditions. Evaluation and control keep the strategy on target and show when adjustments are needed. Managers need to continually monitor performance and, when necessary, revise their strategies due to changing conditions. Strategic marketing planning requires information from ongoing monitoring and evaluation of performance.

Discussion of strategic evaluation has been delayed until this stage in order to first clarify the strategic areas that require evaluation and to identify the kinds of information needed for assessing marketing performance. The earlier chapters establish an essential foundation for building a strategic evaluation program. We now examine the impact of customer relationship management systems, an overview of evaluation activities, and the role of the strategic marketing audit.

Customer Relationship Management

Recall that the widespread adoption of customer relationship management (CRM) systems to integrate all customer data from different sources, in combination with electronic point-of-sale customer data capture, offers several new and powerful resources for strategic evaluation and control (see Chapter 4). Penetrating analysis of databases may reveal

---

[25]Kerry Capell and Gerry Khermouch, "Hip H&M," *BusinessWeek,* November 11, 2002, 39–42.

important purchasing patterns and the effect of marketing actions. The ability to identify profitability at the level of the individual customer by combining CRM and purchase data with other databases is becoming an especially important capability of strategic appraisal for marketing management. CRM systems have the potential to greatly expand the measures of performance used, and to take a more fine-grained look at marketing effectiveness related to customer acquisition and defection rates, customer tenure, customer value and worth, proportion of inactive customers, and cross-selling.[26]

Overview of Control and Evaluation Activities

Control and evaluation consumes a high proportion of marketing executives' time and energy. Evaluation may seek to (1) find new opportunities or avoid threats, (2) keep performance in line with management's expectations, and/or (3) solve specific problems that exist.

An example of a threat identified via product-market analysis for Royal Doulton, a premier brand of formal chinaware famed for its expensive dinner plates, is the move by consumers toward informal dining. This change in preferences is a major threat for Royal Doulton. An example of information to keep performance in line with management expectations is closely tracking innovation in Web applications and earnings from acquisitions at Cisco Systems Inc. Finally, evaluating the effectiveness of alternative TV commercials is an example of solving specific problems.

The major steps in establishing a strategic control and evaluation program are described in Exhibit 15.5. Strategic and annual marketing plans set the direction and guidelines for the evaluation and control process. A strategic marketing audit may be conducted when setting up an evaluation program, and periodically thereafter. Next, performance standards and metrics need to be determined, followed by obtaining and analyzing information for the purpose of performance-gap identification. Actions are initiated to pursue opportunities or avoid threats, keep performance on track, or solve a particular decision-making problem.

The Strategic Marketing Audit

A marketing audit is useful when initiating a strategic evaluation program. Since evaluation compares results with expectations, it is necessary to lay some groundwork before setting up a tracking program. The audit can be used to initiate a formal strategic marketing planning program, and it may be repeated on a periodic basis. Normally, the situation analysis is part of the annual development of marketing plans. Audits may be conducted every 3 to 5 years, or more frequently in special situations (e.g., acquisition/merger).

A guide to conducting the strategic marketing audit is shown in Exhibit 15.6. This format can be adapted to meet the needs of a particular firm. For example, if a company does

EXHIBIT 15.5 **Strategic Marketing Evaluation and Control**

Conduct strategic marketing audit → Select performance criteria and choose relevant marketing metrics → Obtain and analyze information → Assess performance and take necessary action

---

[26]Lawrence A. Crosby and Sheree L. Johnson, "High Performance Marketing in the CRM Era," *Marketing Management,* September–October 2001, 10–11.

EXHIBIT 15.6 **Guide to Conducting the Strategic Marketing Audit**

I. CORPORATE MISSION AND OBJECTIVES

   A. Does the mission statement offer a clear guide to the product-markets of interest to the firm?

   B. Have objectives been established for the corporation?

   C. Is information available for the review of corporate progress toward objectives, and are the reviews conducted on a regular (e.g., quarterly, monthly) basis?

   D. Has corporate strategy been successful in meeting objectives?

   E. Are opportunities or problems pending that may require altering marketing strategy?

   F. What are the responsibilities of the chief marketing executive in corporate strategic planning?

II. BUSINESS COMPOSITION AND STRATEGIES

   A. What is the composition of the business (business segments, strategic planning units, and specific product-markets)?

   B. Have business strength and product-market attractiveness analyses been conducted for each planning unit? What are the results of the analyses?

   C. What is the corporate strategy for each planning unit (e.g., develop, stabilize, turn around, or harvest)?

   D. What objectives are assigned to each planning unit?

   E. Does each unit have a strategic plan?

   F. For each unit what objectives and responsibilities have been assigned to marketing?

III. MARKETING STRATEGY (FOR EACH PLANNING UNIT)

   A. Strategic planning and marketing:

      1. Is marketing's role and responsibility in corporate strategic planning clearly specified?

      2. Are responsibility and authority for marketing strategy assigned to one executive?

      3. How well is the firm's marketing strategy working?

      4. Are changes likely to occur in the corporate/marketing environment that may affect the firm's marketing strategy?

      5. Are there major contingencies that should be included in the strategic marketing plan?

   B. Marketing planning and organizational structure:

      1. Are annual and longer-range strategic marketing plans developed, and are they being used?

      2. Are the responsibilities of the various units in the marketing organization clearly specified?

      3. What are the strengths and limitations of the key members of the marketing organization? What is being done to develop people? What gaps in experience and capabilities exist on the marketing staff?

      4. Is the organizational structure for marketing effective for implementing marketing plans?

   C. Market target strategy:

      1. Has each market target been clearly defined and its importance to the firm established?

      2. Have demand, industry, and competition in each market target been analyzed and key trends, opportunities, and threats identified?

      3. Has the proper market target strategy been adopted?

      4. Should repositioning or exit from any product-market be considered?

   D. Objectives:

      1. Are objectives established for each market target, and are these consistent with planning-unit objectives and the available resources? Are the objectives realistic?

      2. Are sales, cost, and other performance information available for monitoring the progress of planned performance against actual results?

EXHIBIT 15.6—(*continued*)

   3. Are regular appraisals made of marketing performance?
   4. Where do gaps exist between planned and actual results? What are the probable causes of the performance gaps?

   E. Marketing program positioning strategy:
   1. Does the firm have an integrated positioning strategy made up of product, channel, price, advertising, and sales force strategies? Is the role selected for each mix element consistent with the overall program objectives, and does it properly complement other mix elements?
   2. Are adequate resources available to carry out the marketing program? Are resources committed to market targets according to the importance of each?
   3. Are allocations to the various marketing mix components too low, too high, or about right in terms of what each is expected to accomplish?
   4. Is the effectiveness of the marketing program appraised on a regular basis?

IV. MARKETING PROGRAM ACTIVITIES

   A. Product strategy:
   1. Is the product mix geared to the needs and preferences that the firm wants to meet in each product-market?
   2. What branding strategy is being used?
   3. Are products properly positioned against competing brands?
   4. Does the firm have a sound approach to product planning and management, and is marketing involved in product decisions?
   5. Are additions to, modifications of, or deletions from the product mix needed to make the firm more competitive in the marketplace?
   6. Is the performance of each product evaluated on a regular basis?

   B. Channel of distribution strategy:
   1. Has the firm selected the type (conventional or vertically coordinated) and intensity of distribution appropriate for each of its product-markets?
   2. How well does each channel access its market target? Is an effective channel configuration being used?
   3. Are channel organizations carrying out their assigned functions properly?
   4. How is the channel of distribution being managed? What improvements are needed?
   5. Are desired customer service levels being reached, and are the costs of doing this acceptable?

   C. Pricing strategy:
   1. How responsive is each market target to price variations?
   2. What role and objectives does price have in the marketing mix?
   3. Should price play an active or passive role in program positioning strategy?
   4. How do the firm's pricing strategy and tactics compare to those of the competition?
   5. Is a logical approach used to establish prices?
   6. Are there indications that changes may be needed in pricing strategy or tactics?

   D. Advertising and sales promotion strategies:
   1. Have a role and objectives been established for advertising and sales promotion in the marketing mix?
   2. Is the creative strategy consistent with the positioning strategy that is being used?
   3. Is the budget adequate to carry out the objectives assigned to advertising and sales promotion?

(*continued*)

EXHIBIT 15.6—(*continued*)

> 4. Do the media and programming strategies represent the most cost-effective means of communicating with market targets?
> 5. Do advertising copy and content effectively communicate the intended messages?
> 6. How well does the advertising program measure up in meeting its objectives?
>
> E. Sales force strategy:
>
> 1. Are the role and objectives of personal selling in the marketing program positioning strategy clearly specified and understood by the sales organization?
> 2. Do the qualifications of salespeople correspond to their assigned roles?
> 3. Is the sales force of the proper size to carry out its function, and is it efficiently deployed?
> 4. Are sales force results in line with management's expectations?
> 5. Is each salesperson assigned performance targets, and are incentives offered to reward performance?
> 6. Are compensation levels and ranges competitive?
>
> V. IMPLEMENTATION AND MANAGEMENT
>
> A. Have the causes of all performance gaps been identified?
> B. Is implementation of planned actions taking place as intended? Is implementation being hampered by marketing or other functional areas of the firm (e.g., operations, finance)
> C. Has the strategic audit revealed areas requiring additional study before action is taken?

not use indirect channels of distribution, this section of the audit guide will require adjustment. Likewise, if the salesforce is the major part of a marketing program, then this section may be expanded to include other aspects of salesforce strategy. As the role of the Internet in strategy evolves, social media impact on performance, and new value chains and market segments become important, the structure of the audit should also change. The items included in the audit correspond to the strategic marketing plan because the main purpose of the audit is to appraise the effectiveness of strategy being followed. The audit guide includes several questions about marketing performance. The answers to these questions are incorporated into the design of the strategic tracking program.

There are other reasons besides starting an evaluation program for conducting a strategic marketing audit. Corporate restructuring may bring about a complete review of strategic marketing operations. Major shifts in business activities such as entry into new product and market areas or acquisitions may require strategic marketing audits. The growing impact of Internet-based business models may also encourage management to undertake an audit.

The results of the strategic marketing audit provide the basis for selecting performance criteria and choosing relevant marketing metrics to assess actual performance against plans and strategic intent.

Marketing Performance Measurement

As marketing plans are developed, performance criteria need to be selected to monitor performance. Specifying the information needed for marketing decision making is important and requires management's concentrated attention. In the past, marketing executives could develop and manage successful marketing strategies by relying on intuition, judgment, and experience. Successful executives in the 21st century need to combine judgment and experience with information and decision support systems (see Chapter 5).

The purpose of objectives is to state the results that management is seeking and also provide a basis for evaluating the strategy's success. Objectives set standards of performance. Progress toward the objectives in the strategic and short-term plans is monitored on a continuing basis. In addition to information on objectives, management requires other kinds of feedback for use in performance evaluation. Some of this information is incorporated into regular tracking activities (e.g., the effectiveness of advertising expenditures). Other information is obtained as the need arises, such as a special study of consumer preferences for different brands.

Examples of performance criteria are discussed in several earlier chapters. Criteria should be selected for the total plan and its important components. Illustrative criteria for total performance include sales, market share, profit, expense, and customer satisfaction targets. Brand-positioning map analyses may also be useful in tracking how a brand is positioned relative to key competitors. These assessments can be used to gauge overall performance and for specific market targets. Performance criteria are also needed for the marketing mix components. For example, new-customer and lost-customer tracking is often included in sales force performance monitoring. Pricing performance monitoring may include comparisons of actual to list prices, extent of discounting, and profit contribution. Since many possible performance criteria can be selected, management must identify the key measures that will show how the firm's marketing strategy is performing in its competitive environment and point to where changes are needed. Recall that the growing impact of CRM systems offers management access to a larger number of performance measures, particularly those relating to customer retention and defection (see Chapter 4).[27]

The importance of monitoring performance against objectives and demonstrating the added-value achieved through marketing efforts has led many organizations to make substantial investments in systems of marketing metrics to evaluate marketing's contribution. Marketing metrics use both internal and external information sources to provide a structure for monitoring the effectiveness of marketing activities and strategies.

The Importance of Marketing Metrics

In the majority of organizations, marketing executives are under growing pressure to demonstrate their contribution to firm performance. This pressure reflects a mandate for greater accountability in the use of company resources, but also impacts the professional standing of the marketing organization within the firm. The goal is to make better causal links between marketing activities and financial returns to the business.[28] Research suggests that the ability to measure marketing performance, through appropriate systems and metrics, is significantly and positively related to company performance, profitability, stock returns, and to marketing's stature within the organization.[29]

The Use of Marketing Metrics

The quantitative measurement of marketing performance is not a simple task. Most useful marketing metrics require some data from sources external to the firm. Some potentially useful measures like customer lifetime value require complex modeling and statistical

---

[27]Larry Yu, "Successful Customer-Relationship Management," *Sloan Management Review,* Summer 2001, 18–29.
[28]Wayne R. McCullough, "Marketing Metrics," *Marketing Management,* Spring 2000, 64.
[29]Don O'Sullivan and Andrew V. Abela, "Marketing Performance Measurement Ability and Firm Performance," *Journal of Marketing,* April 2007, 79–93.

analysis, which may be hard to sell to top management and other parts of the organization. Linking marketing metrics to firm performance and value has proved problematic in the past.[30]

Research from a five-country study (United States, U.K., Germany, Japan, France) of large companies finds that the majority of companies report one or more marketing metrics to their boards of directors. Most frequently the reported measures are market share, and product/service quality. Least used were more complex metrics like customer or segment lifetime value. Respondents in the study concurred that metrics reporting would increase in the future.[31]

Nonetheless, identifying valid and reliable metrics that indicate performance on key dimensions of strategy is often not straightforward. Consider, for example, the problems faced by Wal-Mart is developing a "sustainability index" to rank the environmental impact of consumer products, described in the ETHICS APPLICATION.

Critical questions to consider in developing a metrics-based reporting system related to marketing performance are

- Does what we report to management actively probe end-user behavior (customer retention, acquisition, usage) and why consumers behave that way (awareness, satisfaction, perceived quality)?
- Are the results of end-user research routinely reported and in a format integrated with financial metrics?
- In these reports, are results compared with levels previously forecast in business plans?
- Are the results compared with the levels achieved by competitors on the same indicators?
- Is short-term performance adjusted according to the change in brand equity?[32]

Types of Marketing Metrics[33]

There are several ways of grouping marketing metrics. Some measures are associated with assessing competitive position and effectiveness with the customer, while others address product profitability, product and portfolio performance, customer profitability, sales and channel effectiveness, pricing, promotion, advertising and Web activities, and financial performance. Also, some emphasis has been placed on metrics which address brand equity as a summary measure of marketing performance. Metrics have also been developed to monitor internal market characteristics like innovation health, employee-based equity, and internal process performance. The Appendix to this chapter provides more detail of these different types of marketing metrics.

Selecting Relevant Metrics

The choice of the most relevant metrics is critical. Guidelines suggest that choices should be made in the light of the need to (1) measure performance relative to strategy, (2) track performance relative to competitors, (3) track performance relative to customers, (4) track

[30]Donald R. Lehmann, "Linking Marketing Decisions to Financial Performance and Firm Value," in *Executive Overview* (Cambridge MA: Marketing Science Institute, March 2002).

[31]Patrick Barwise and John U. Farley, *Which Marketing Metrics Are Used and Where?,* Report 03-002, (Cambridge MA: Marketing Science Institute, 2003).

[32]Tim Ambler, "Marketing Metrics," *Business Strategy Review,* 11(2), 2000, 59–66.

[33]This section is based on Paul W. Ferris, Neil T. Bendle, Philip E. Pfeifer, and David J. Reibstein, *Marketing Metrics: 50+ Metrics Every Executive Should Master* (Upper Saddle River NJ: Wharton School Publishing/Pearson Education, 2006). This book provides a definitive guide to the identification and computation of relevant metrics.

In 2009, Wal-Mart's CEO announced an initiative to create a "sustainability index" to measure the environmental and social impact of every product sold in its stores. Wal-Mart has spent $5 million creating the Sustainability Consortium with Arizona State University and the University of Arkansas.

Progress in creating a rigorous sustainability metric has been hampered by underlying dilemmas: all products, no matter how "green" have some environmental impact; products have to be evaluated all the way from raw materials to final consumption; trade-offs exist between different forms of sustainability—is soil erosion more or less important than carbon emissions? Examples of the problems in creating a metric include:

	+	−
Aquafina 1-liter bottle (PepsiCo)	Aquafina's bottles are 100% recyclable	How green can this be when 80% of water bottles are not recycled?
Compact Fluorescent lightbulbs (GE)	A CFL bulb uses 75% less energy than a traditional incandescent bulb	Is the energy saved worth the risk of mercury exposure from a broken CFL?
Barbie Doll (Mattel)	Barbie has accessories made from excess fabric and trimmings from other Barbie products	How green is Barbie, if you don't know the origins of the skirt?
Crest Cavity Protection Toothpaste (P&G)	Crest's lightweight tube saves energy in shipping	Is that saving offset by the cardboard box needed to protect the tube?

Wal-Mart is aiming for a simpler approach of providing more sustainability information to consumers.

Source: Adapted from Paul Keegan, "The Trouble with Green Product Ratings," *Fortune,* August 15, 2011, 32–36.

performance over time, (5) model performance (to test the impact of different elements of strategy being changed).[34]

A single performance metric is unlikely to meet all these needs. The goal is to implement better ways of measuring marketing performance. Clarifying objectives and the business model (which shows the links between inputs such as financial expenditure and competitive activities and outputs in expected results) is prerequisite. Measures of these key steps, or the objectives themselves, become the metrics that should be used to monitor performance and form part of future plans. Research suggests that for a large firm, 8 to 10 is usually about the right number of metrics, while a smaller firm will need fewer.[35]

Importantly, metrics should be chosen to reflect strategic priorities and the issues most closely linking marketing investments with profits. For example, for monitoring external

---

[34]Bruce H. Clark, "A Summary of Thinking on Measuring the Value of Marketing," *Journal of Targeting, Measurement and Analysis for Marketing,* 9(4), 2001, 357–369.

[35]Tim Ambler and John Roberts, *Beware the Silver Metric: Marketing Performance Measurement Has to be Multidimensional,* Marketing Science Institute Report 06-003 (Cambridge MA: Marketing Science Institute, 2006).

market performance, footwear retailer Payless ShoeSource uses two types of marketing metrics: spending efficiency and effectiveness (e.g., ROI by advertising medium, advertising to sales spending ratios); and, business building (e.g., customer traffic, ratio of loyal to new customers). On the other hand, at food company Cadbury, in the Managing for Value program, key measures include performance against strategic milestones, market share, advertising spending, brand and advertising awareness, average purchases, and percent of total volume from new products.[36] Many major organizations are developing new sets of metrics to give top management better insight into performance against competitors and the value achieved from marketing investments.

In some cases, choice of metrics may be tied closely to specific marketing activities. For example, Shell's large expenditure on sponsoring Ferrari in Formula One motor racing underlines the need for financial justification for this expenditure. Before signing a new 5-year sponsorship contract, Shell management evaluated costs and benefits in five ways:

- Comparing attitudes toward the Shell brand of those who were aware of the Ferrari link, and those who were not
- Examining change in purchasing behavior associated with shifts in attitudes toward the brand
- Commissioning an independent evaluation of brand value, including branding, sales, price premium, and advertising effects
- Making country-by-country comparisons—different Shell companies had merchandized the sponsorship locally to varying extents, so if the sponsorship was profitable, those who promoted it more should have obtained more benefit
- Surveying manager opinion and their ratings of the impact of the sponsorship on return on investment

After top management review, Shell approved continued sponsorship as an important part of the company's marketing strategy.[37]

In other situations, the selection of metrics may reflect the need to provide management with a continuous monitoring process for evaluating the effectiveness of marketing strategy.

Designing a Marketing Management Dashboard

As formal marketing performance measurement becomes more central to planning and control activities, because it documents and drives the effectiveness of marketing actions, a "dashboard" for senior managers is often becoming integral. The dashboard takes its name from a comparison with the instrument panel of an automobile, which also presents key data in an easily understandable way.[38]

The dashboard may be a conventional report or a software product. The dashboard requires that senior management agree to a restricted set of key marketing metrics to communicate and evaluate the company's marketing performance. The dashboard facilitates control of short-term activities and longer-term planning. Objectives and processes should be aligned with the marketing dashboard.[39]

---

[36]Tim Ambler, 2000, ibid.

[37]"Marketers Still Lost in the Metrics," *Marketing,* August 10, 2000, 15–17.

[38]Ferris et al., 331.

[39]Bruce H. Clark, Andrew V. Abela, and Tim Ambler, "Behind the Wheel," *Marketing Management,* May–June 2006, 19–23.

The attraction of the dashboard concept is to provide decision makers with a reduced set of vital measures in a form that is easy to interpret and apply. Advanced software packages can display critical information in easy-to-read graphics, assembled in real time from corporate information systems.[40]

For strategic decision makers, the marketing dashboard should contain metrics related to the main business drivers, the factors that directly and predictably affect performance, and should reflect the pipeline of growth ideas—how knowledge of customers is translated into a strategy for sustaining growth—and review the marketing talent pool. The main business drivers might include share of customer wallet, or retention, compared to competitors. The pipeline of growth section could indicate new products in the pipeline and expected revenues and profits from them. The marketing talent pool addresses the marketing skills the company needs and its inventory of talent.[41]

At an operational level, managers might choose dashboard metrics more closely related to strategy implementation. For example, Exhibit 15.7 shows marketing dashboard for the senior managers at a manufacturer of branded luggage distributed through retail stores, over a 4-year period, showing five critical measures. The brand shows strong sales growth and has maintained its margins at attractive levels, even though selling less expensive items. However, returns for the retailer have fallen dramatically, while inventory levels at the retail level have escalated. Sales per store has fallen substantially. The price premium for the brand has fallen and a growing proportion of sales are on promotional deals. The metrics underline concerns about the company's ability to maintain its distribution without reversing these trends, knowing that weaker distribution will hit future sales and margins.

Nonetheless, there remains a concern that the use of marketing dashboards should be monitored carefully. There is a danger that the dashboard contains metrics relevant to assessing past performance rather than those which give insight into present performance and future developments. The uses of marketing dashboards at several major companies are illustrated in the METRICS APPLICATION.

Interpreting Performance Measurement Results

When actual results achieved are compared with planned results, if performance gaps are too large, corrective actions may be required. The process of interpretation and decision on appropriate actions is critical.

Opportunities and Performance Gaps

Strategic evaluation activities seek to (1) identify opportunities or performance gaps and (2) initiate actions to take advantage of the opportunities or to correct existing and pending problems. The real test of marketing evaluation and control approaches is whether they help management to identify performance problems early enough that remedial action is possible. In monitoring, there are two critical factors to take into account.

Problem/Opportunity Definition

Strategic analysis should lead to a clear explanation of an opportunity or problem since this will be needed to guide whatever strategic action may be taken. Often it is easy to confuse problem symptoms with problem causes.

---

[40]Spencer E. Ante, "Giving the Boss the Big Picture," *BusinessWeek,* February 13, 2006, 48–51.

[41]Gail J. McGovern, David Court, John A, Quelch, and Blair Crawford, "Bringing Customers into the Boardroom," *Harvard Business Review,* November 2004, 70–80.

EXHIBIT 15.7

Illustrative Marketing Dashboard for a Branded Luggage Product

Source: Paul W. Ferris, Neil T. Bendle, Philip E. Pfeifer and David J. Reibstein, *Marketing Metrics: 50+ Metrics Every Executive Should Master,* (Upper Saddle River NJ: Wharton School Publishing/Pearson Education, 2006), 332.

Revenue and Margins

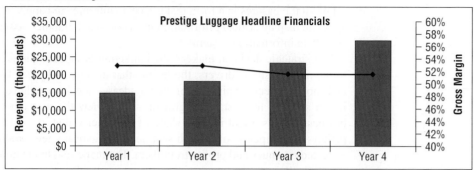

The financial metrics look healthy, revenue showing good growth while margins are almost unchanged.

Manufacturer Prices to Store Prices

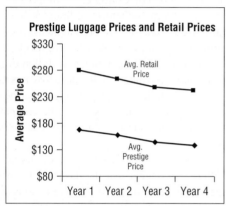

Prestige Luggage is selling less expensive items.

Store Inventory and GMROII

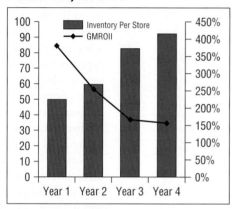

Prestige Luggage is making diminishing returns for retailer.

Distribution

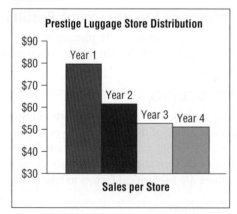

We are moving into smaller stores.

Pricing and Promotions

Prestige Luggage is becoming reliant on promotion.

Interpreting Information

Management must also separate normal variations in performance from significant gaps in performance, since the latter are the ones that require strategic action. For example, how much of a drop in market share is necessary to signal a performance problem? Limits need to be set on the acceptable range of strategic performance.

"Dashboards are one of management's key techniques to make sure an organization is performing according to its objectives"—Kan Rau, Bay Area Consulting Group.

Steve Balmer, MICROSOFT

- Ballmer requires his top officers to bring their dashboards with them into one-to-one meetings. Ballmer zeroes in on such metrics as sales, customer satisfaction, and status of key products under development.
- More than half of Microsoft employees use dashboards.

Ivan Seidenberg, VERIZON

- Seidenberg and others can choose from 300 metrics to put on their dashboards, from broadband sales to wireless defections. Managers pick the metrics they want to track, and the dashboard flips the pages twenty-four hours a day.

Jeff Immelt, GENERAL ELECTRIC

- Many GE executives use dashboards to run their day-to-day operations, monitoring profits per product line and fill rates for orders. Immelt occasionally looks at a dashboard, but he relies on his managers to run the businesses, so he can focus on the bigger picture.

Larry Ellison, ORACLE

- A fan of dashboards, Ellison uses them to track sales activity at the end of a quarter, the ratio of sales divided by customer service requests, and the number of hours that technicians spend on the phone solving customer problems.
- Although all 20,000 of Oracle's salespeople use dashboards, some 20 percent of them refuse to enter their sales leads into the system. Salespeople don't want to be held accountable for a lead that is not converted into a sale. This makes it harder to get a true picture of the demand for Oracle's products, and Ellison has even considered refusing to pay commission on a sale if the lead is not entered into a dashboard.

Source: Spencer E Ante, "Giving the Boss the Big Picture," *BusinessWeek*, February 13, 2006, 48–51.

No matter how extensive the information resources may be, they cannot interpret the strategic importance of the information. This is the responsibility of management.[42]

The Exhibit 15.7 illustration of a marketing dashboard provides an example of strategic problem identification. An illustration of opportunity monitoring is provided by the emergence of concerns about environmental and "green" issues in many countries. Environmental concerns are ongoing areas of strategic evaluation. Companies must identify important areas of concern and implement strategies that take into account consumer, public policy, and organizational priorities. Major changes in perceptions of environmental responsibility may also create important opportunities. The change in direction at Interfaces Inc. described in the ETHICS APPLICATION is an interesting example of a CEO effectively combining his environmental and ethical judgment with responsiveness to customer concerns, and measuring the results achieved.

---

[42]An interesting evaluation of providing decision makers with support in the interpretation of evidence is found in D. V. L. Smith and J. H. Fletcher, *The Art and Science of Interpreting Market Research Evidence* (Chichester: Wiley, 2004).

- Ray C. Anderson is founder and now chairman of Atlanta-based Interface Inc., the world's largest manufacturer of commercial carpet tiles.
- In the mid-1990s, Interface was peppered by questions from interior designers about the dangers in the materials and processes it was using.
- Anderson convened a task force to answer his customers' questions. The members of the task force asked him for his environmental vision. Anderson comments, "But I had no vision, absolutely none . . ."
- He found his environmental vision in a book describing the need for sustainability to protect the earth's limited resources.
- Anderson pledged that by 2020 Interface would be a completely sustainable company, producing no dangerous waste, no harmful emissions, and using no oil.
- By 2004, Interface's eco-scorecard looked like this:

INTERFACE'S ECO-SCORECARD

A decade ago, Interface founder, Ray Anderson, pledged that his $924 million company would stop using the earth's natural resources, eliminate waste, and emit no harmful emissions by 2020. Reductions made so far:

Waste	Down 80%
Water intake	Down 78%
Emission of greenhouse gases	Down 46%
Energy consumption	Down 31%
Use of petroleum-based materials	Down 28%
Total Savings	$231 million

Source: Michelle Conlin, "From Plunderer to Protector," *BusinessWeek,* July 19, 2004, 62–62.

Determining Normal and Abnormal Variability

However, it is important to recognize that operating results and metrics such as sales, market share, profits, order-processing time, and customer satisfaction, are likely to display normal up- and down-fluctuations. The issue is determining whether these variations represent random variation or instead are due to special causes. For example, if a salesperson's sales over time remain within a normal band of variation, then the results are acceptable under the present operating conditions. Random high and low variations do not indicate unusually high or low performance. If this range of performance is *not* acceptable to management, then the system must be changed. This may require salesperson training, redesign of the territory, improvement in sales support, or other changes in the salesperson's operating system.

Statistical process-control concepts and methods are useful in determining when operating results are fluctuating normally or instead are out of control. Quality-control charts can be used to analyze and improve results in marketing performance measures such as the number of orders processed, customer complaints, and territory sales.[43] Control-chart

---

[43] Mac Hulbert, Capon, and Piercy, 2003.

analysis indicates when the process is experiencing normal variation and when the process is out of control.

The basic approach to control-chart analysis is to establish average and upper and lower control limits for the measure being evaluated. Examples of measures include order-processing time, district sales, customer complaints, and market share. Control boundaries are set using historical data. Future measures are plotted on the chart to determine whether the results are under control or instead fall outside the acceptable performance band determined by the upper and lower control limits. The objective is to continually improve the process that determines the results.

Deciding What Actions to Take

Many corrective actions are possible, depending on the situation. Management's actions may include exiting from a product-market, new-product planning, changing the target-market strategy, adjusting marketing strategy, or improving efficiency.

Avon Products Inc., the leading direct selling cosmetics organization faced falling sales across the world in 2005.[44] After several years of solid growth, sales had stalled in the United States, but also at the same time in developing markets like Central Europe and Russia, which had been very successful for Avon. Big problems for Avon around the world had remained unrecognized. CEO, Andrea Jung, faced the challenge of turning this business around. Among the changes implemented, she reorganized Avon's management structure, taking away much autonomy from country managers, in favor of globalized manufacturing and marketing. Previously, Avon country managers ran their own plant, developed their own new products, and created their own advertising, often relying as much on instinct as numbers. Jung trimmed out seven layers of management, and importantly launched return-on-investment analysis to study performance market by market in a more rigorous way. New recruits came from larger, more analytical consumer products companies such as Gillette, Procter & Gamble, PepsiCo, and Kraft. New approaches to data at Avon surfaced surprises: the number of products for sale in Mexico had ballooned to 13,000; decreasing average pay for new representatives had stalled the U.S. business. Key elements of Jung's recovery strategy were a more data-centric approach to making strategic decisions, increased advertising and new product development expenditure, and opening the China market.

Progress continues in rebuilding Avon's competitive position. The company's experience underlines the importance of basing strategic realignment on rigorous analysis of evidence regarding marketing performance and the underlying drivers of performance.

Managing in a changing environment is at the center of strategic marketing. Anticipating and responding effectively to change is the essence of evaluation and control. Executives develop innovative marketing strategies and monitor their effectiveness, altering the strategies as a result of changing conditions.

Global Issues for Planning, Implementation, and Control

The coverage of strategic marketing planning, implementation, and control processes in this chapter is relevant to global marketing strategy. Nonetheless, there are several additional issues which arise regarding the international situation.

[44]This illustration is based on Nanette Byrnes, "Avon: More Than Cosmetic Changes," *BusinessWeek,* March 12, 2007, 62–63. Dominic Rushe, "Avon Calling," *Sunday Times,* January 15, 2006, S3, 5.

Global Marketing Planning

While the underlying process of planning is the same, international plans frequently necessarily make simplifying assumptions to cope with the additional complexity of planning for the global situation. For example, global plans often use regional identities as the planning unit. Many companies refer to "EMEA," as a global market for which plans are formed. EMEA stands for Europe, Middle East, and Africa. This region contains country-markets that are substantially different in economic development, infrastructure, and culture. While regional plans may be a necessity, it is important to look in more detail at the countries and cultures within these regions to identify opportunities and trends. The same applied to designations like "PRA" (Pacific Rim and Asia," or "ROW" (Rest of World—all areas outside the domestic market).

Planning globally must also accommodate more substantial variation in marketing strategies and programmes than is the case domestically. Situations will differ regarding the balance between standardizing strategy internationally and adapting to local market conditions, but it is important that the chosen level of adaptation and variability should not be obscured by the way in which plans are constructed. Strategy variation between markets may be extreme. Consider, for example, the major shift in Microsoft's business model for the China market, which is a radical departure from to how the company operates elsewhere, described in the GLOBAL APPLICATION.

It is also often the case that information regarding global markets is not available in the same quantity or at the same quality that would be expected in the domestic market. Many of the most promising market prospects are in emerging markers, where high-quality market information may be least available.

Implementation Globally

The implementation of global strategies must often address issues related to market differences in national culture, economic development, and political characteristics. The GLOBAL APPLICATION case is illustrative. Particular issues concern the relationships between managers in the domestic market and executives located in overseas markets. Recall, for example, the Avon Products Inc. recovery strategy described earlier, and the company's moves to reduce local management autonomy to develop a more globally unified brand.

Performance Measurement and Control Globally

Performance measurement and control follows the same general principles but in the global market situation must additionally consider market differences—in local marketing arrangements, in product or market life cycle stage, in the availability of information, and in the strength of the relationships between local and central management. A particular risk is that measurement approaches and metrics chosen for the domestic market may not be the most relevant for international markets. If the product is in an earlier life cycle stage in international markets than at home, then the most relevant metrics may be different. Culture-based differences in attitudes toward control activities may also be a consideration.

For example, assessing global sales operations effectiveness is more complex because individual salespeoples' ability to adjust to local conditions and culture may differ significantly and impact performance. In some countries, teamwork is favored over individual accomplishment, rendering individual salesperson evaluation metrics of questionable value. In the global marketplace, cultural skills appear more relevant to evaluating sales operations than technical and managerial capabilities.[45]

---

[45]Earl D. Honeycutt, John B. Ford, and Antonis C. Simintiras, *Sales Management: A Global Perspective* (London: Routledge, 2003).

To develop its position in China, Microsoft has developed a new business model, which is radically different from how it operates elsewhere.

The problem faced in China was not brand acceptance—everyone was using Windows, but mainly counterfeit copies bought for a few dollars. China's weak intellectual property–enforcement laws meant Microsoft's usual pricing strategies were doomed to fail. Another problem for Microsoft was when Beijing's city government started installing free open-source Linux operating systems on workers' PCs.

- Microsoft entered China in 1992, but its business there was a disaster for more than a decade.

- Almost none of the policies that had made Microsoft market leader in the United States and Europe made sense in China. In China, Microsoft has had to become "un-Microsoft."

- Prices for Microsoft products are rock-bottom in China. Instead of charging hundreds of dollars for its Windows operating system and Office applications, it sells a $3 package of Windows and Office to students. In China's back alleys, Linux often costs more than Windows, because it requires more disks.

- Microsoft's China strategy abandons the centerpiece of its public policy approach elsewhere—the protection of its intellectual property at all costs. Tolerating piracy has become part of Microsoft's long-term strategy.

- In China, Microsoft is partnering closely with the government, instead of fighting it, as it does in the United States and Europe—which has opened the company to criticism from human rights groups.

Nonetheless, China remains problematic for Microsoft and performance in other Asian markets like India has been far better. The protection of intellectual property rights in China is high on Microsoft's agenda again, and Microsoft has been pursuing illegal copiers of its software in the Chinese courts.

Sources: David Kirkpatrick, "How Microsoft Conquered China," *Fortune,* July 23, 2007, 76–82. Bruce Einhorn and Mark Lee, "Ballmer: China Can't Get a Lot Worse," *Bloomberg BusinessWeek,* May 31–June 6, 2010, 35. Kathrin Hille, "Microsoft to Collect Damages for Piracy in China," *Financial Times,* April 23, 2010, 22.

The interpretation of performance, for example, against the metrics used in the domestic marketplace is extremely important. For example, consider the situation where an international market has adverse metrics on expenses, profitability, and sales—expenses metrics indicate that expenditure in this market is very high compared to other markets, and sales and profits are relatively low. These indicators could indicate (1) an international market where performance is weak, and withdrawing from the market should be considered, or (2) a market that has excellent prospects where the company is investing to build a strong competitive position. The GLOBAL APPLICATION illustrates a case where conventional performance metrics would make the China market position appear untenable, yet for the company this is a critically important long-term market prospect. Interpreting performance measures and making appropriate control decisions can only be done in the context of the strategy being pursued in a specific global market.

Increasingly, marketing strategy planning, implementation, and control will involve a global dimension for more companies. While the general approaches we have discussed are relevant, there may be additional issues to consider in the global marketing context.

Summary

Marketing strategy implementation and control are vital links in a series of strategic marketing activities. These tasks emphasize the continuing process of planning, implementing, evaluating, and adjusting marketing strategies. Market-driven strategy and implementation are interdependent activities concerned with matching a company's capabilities with market opportunities. Strategic evaluation of marketing performance is the first step in strategic marketing planning and the last step after launching a strategy. Marketing strategy planning, implementation, and control issues build on the concepts, processes, and methods developed in Chapters 1 through 14. The leadership role of marketing executives in organizational change to deliver superior customer value is escalating in importance.

The strategic marketing planning process was examined earlier in the book (see Appendix to Chapter 1). The strategic marketing plan guides strategy implementation. Plans are developed, implemented, evaluated, and revised to keep the marketing strategy on target. Planning activities involve making a situation assessment, identifying market targets, setting objectives, developing targeting and positioning strategies, deciding action programs for marketing mix components, and preparing financial statements. The planning process typically involves considerable coordination and interaction between functional areas. Since planning is an organizational process as well as analytical techniques, consideration should be given to the roles and behaviors of executives in planning, and to the organizational context in which planning is carried out. The goal is consistency between these dimensions of planning to enhance effectiveness.

The effectiveness of strategy implementation determines the outcome of marketing planning. Many strategy initiatives in organizations fail because of inadequate attention to the structural and behavioral issues surrounding implementation process. An effective implementation process spells out the activities to be implemented, who is responsible for implementation, the time and location of implementation, and how implementation will be achieved. Enhanced implementation effectiveness is related to managerial skills in execution, but also organizational design choices, providing relevant incentives, and effective communications. Internal marketing programs provide a structure for addressing implementation processes. The balanced scorecard approach provides a comprehensive approach to improving implementation. The fit achieved between strategy implementation requirements and organization characteristics and external partnerships may be decisive.

Strategic marketing evaluation and control is concerned with finding new opportunities or avoiding threats, keeping performance in line with management's expectations, or solving specific problems that have been identified. Planning sets the direction and provide guidelines for evaluation and control. A strategic marketing audit may be relevant to establishing appropriate evaluation and control approaches. Performance standards and metrics need to be determined, followed by acquiring necessary information for analysis of performance gaps, leading to the choice of appropriate actions.

Measuring marketing performance compares objectives to achievement using marketing metrics of several kinds. The ability to measure marketing performance is positively related to company performance. Metrics have been developed around customer and competitor issues, profitability, products and portfolios, customer profitability, sales and channels, pricing, promotion, advertising, media and Web performance, and financial results. Particular emphasis has been placed on developing a set of metrics that assesses brand equity. Marketing metrics can also be used to evaluate internal processes like innovation and internal communications. Selecting the most relevant metrics for a particular situation has been linked to the development of management dashboards focused on the main business drivers. Interpreting performance measurement results requires careful attention to identifying performance problems that are not normal variability and require remedial action. Corrective actions may then follow.

In global marketing, the general principles for planning, implementation, and control are the same. Nonetheless, there are several additional issues in considering international markets related to market diversity and differences in national cultures and stage of economic development.

Questions for Review and Discussion

1. Discuss the similarities and differences between strategic marketing *planning* and *evaluation.*
2. What is involved in managing marketing planning as a process? What issues should be addressed in managing planning process in a company manufacturing high-technology components for the automotive sector?
3. Selecting the proper performance criteria for use in tracking results is a key part of a strategic evaluation program. Suggest performance criteria for use by a fast-food retail chain to monitor strategic marketing performance.
4. What justification is there for conducting a marketing audit in a business unit whose performance has been very good? Discuss.
5. Examination of the various areas of a strategic marketing audit shown in Exhibit 15.6 would be quite expensive and time-consuming. Are there any ways to limit the scope of the audit?
6. Why would senior managers concerned with strategic marketing review marketing metrics concerned with internal processes?
7. One of the more difficult management control issues is determining whether a process is experiencing normal variation or is actually out of control. Discuss how management can resolve this issue.
8. What role can internal marketing play in enhancing the effectiveness of both planning and implementation?
9. How can the "balanced scorecard" methods assist managers in their implementation efforts?
10. Discuss how management control differs for a strategic alliance compared to internal operations.
11. What are the important factors that managers should take into account to improve the implementation of strategies?
12. How would the marketing dashboard differ between a business-to-business company marketing computer software and a producer of packaged consumer products?

Internet Applications

A. Visit the website for 1-800-FLOWERS (www.1800flowers.com). How does this company employ its website to adapt to a constantly changing environment?
B. Enter the phrase "marketing implementation" into your search engine and review the first 20 sites indicated. View several of those representing consultants and agencies offering products and services to support marketing implementation. Which sound likely to be effective? What role, if any, can external agencies play in developing effective marketing strategy implementation initiatives?
C. Identify suppliers of marketing dashboard software on the Web. Does this type of decision support system replace management judgment on the most appropriate performance criteria for their businesses?

Applications

A. Review the ETHICS APPLICATION describing the environmental strategy implemented at Interfaces Inc. List the attractions from a marketing perspective of adopting an environmentally responsible position. Discuss whether companies can undertake environmental initiatives unless there is a commercial advantage.
B. Read the RELATIONSHIP APPLICATION describing Nucor Steel. Do "happy employees" always mean "happy customers"? Identify and list situations where you do not believe that this is true.
C. Examine the company examples in the METRICS APPLICATION concerning uses of marketing dashboards. What are the possible limitations to the dashboard concept?

Appendix **15A**

Marketing Metrics

Marketing Metrics Focusing on Marketing Operations[1]

Competitive and Customer Metrics

Measures of competitiveness include market share (in revenue and volume, and relative to competitors), though this can be decomposed, for example, into market share with heavy users or share of customer product requirements (share of wallet). It is also possible to develop development indices for brands and categories (sales within a specified segment compared to the rest of the market), and measures of penetration (e.g., purchasers of a brand as a percentage of the total population). Consumer metrics include measures of awareness, knowledge beliefs, purchase intentions, loyalty, willingness to recommend, satisfaction, and willingness to search. By assessing the share of customer "hearts and minds," the dynamics behind market share can be explained and more valid predictions made for the future.

Profitability Metrics

Measures relating to profitability include the margin on a unit of product and on products sold through different channels. Average price per unit sold and variable and fixed costs can be included. Analyzing marketing expenditure components can be linked to contribution margins and break-even sales level calculations. Target volumes and revenues (to break-even) can be evaluated. The Appendix to Chapter 2 provides guidance on financial analysis for marketing planning and control.

Product and Portfolio Metrics

Product- and portfolio-related questions include what volumes can be expected from a new product; how sales of existing products will be affected by the launch of a new offering; whether brand equity is increasing or decreasing; what customers really want and what

are they prepared to sacrifice to get it. Metrics relevant to addressing these questions include measures of the trial of a product and repeat purchases, penetration (percentage of the population buying), and volume projections. Measures to assess the health of the brand also include growth rates, cannibalization rates (percentage of new product sales taken from the existing product line), and brand equity evaluation. Utilities-related metrics consider the relative value customers place on different attributes of the product offering—in total and by segment.

Customer Profitability Metrics

Other metrics examine the performance of individual customer relationships. These range from number counts of customers, recency of purchase, and retention rates to measures of customer profit. More complex metrics evaluate customer lifetime value (the present value of future cash flows attributed to the customer relationship), prospect lifetime value (lifetime value of an acquired customer less the cost of prospecting), as well as average acquisition and retention costs.

Sales and Channel Metrics

These measures assess the adequacy and effectiveness of the systems that provide customers with reasons and opportunities to buy the product. The most common salesforce metrics focus on whether salesforce effort level and coverage are adequate and the sales pipeline (number of customers at different stages of the sales cycle). Distribution metrics are concerned with measures of product distribution and availability (e.g., the percentage of potential outlets that stock the product). Logistics metrics track the operational effectiveness of the systems that service retailers and distributors—inventory turnover, out-of-stocks, service levels.

Pricing Metrics

Several metrics are relevant to evaluating pricing alternatives. There are several methods for calculating price premiums (prices relative to alternatives). Demand functions can be addressed through reservation prices metrics (e.g., the maximum an individual is prepared to pay for the product) and percent good value measures (e.g., the proportion of customers who consider the product to be good value). Price elasticity is the market response to changes in price, which may also allow for competitive reactions to price changes.

[1]This section is based on Paul W. Ferris, Neil T. Bendle, Philip E. Pfeifer, and David J. Reibstein, *Marketing Metrics: 50+ Metrics Every Executive Should Master* (Upper Saddle River, NJ: Wharton School Publishing/Pearson Education, 2006). This book provides a definitive guide to the identification and computation of relevant metrics.

Promotion Metrics

Metrics evaluating the effectiveness of sales promotion distinguish between baseline and incremental sales to isolate the lift achieved through the promotional activity. Metrics include the redemption rate on coupons and rebates, the costs of coupons and rebates, and the percentage of sales made using coupons and rebate. The pass-through of rebates to the consumer by retailers and distributors can also be calculated, as well as the impact on average price paid.

Advertising, Media, and Web Metrics

Media metrics reveal how many people may be exposed to an advertising campaign, how often those people have an opportunity to see the ads, and the cost of each potential impression made, for example, cost per thousand impressions (CPM). Measures also consider frequency response function (how often an individual has to see the ad before there is a response), effective reach of the advertising, and the share of voice (compared to competitors). A variety of metrics have also been developed to track online advertising performance, such as "cost per click" (advertising costs divided by the number of clicks generated), cost per order, as well as website characteristics like number of visits and abandonment rate (rate of purchases started but not completed).

Financial Metrics

As discussed in the Chapter 2 Appendix, several measures can be used to assess the financial implications of marketing effort. These include net profit (sales revenue less total costs), return on sales (net profit as a percentage of sales revenue), return on investment (net profits over the investment needed to generate the profits), economic profit (net profit after tax less the costs of capital), payback (time taken to return the initial investment), net present value (the value of future cash flows after accounting for the time value of money), internal rate of return (the discount rate at which the net present value of an investment is zero), and return on marketing investment (incremental revenue attributable to marketing over the marketing spending). It should be noted that return on marketing investment remains an ambiguous concept and as a metric is addressed in several different ways.

Brand Equity Metrics

Particular attention has focused on groups of metrics, indicating brand equity as an overall indicator of marketing performance. For many companies,

brand equity is one of the largest and most valuable assets—for some leading organizations, brand value is more than 50 percent of total market capitalization. Brand value is often as important for business-to-business companies as for consumer businesses—25 percent of the market capitalization of Microsoft is accounted for by the brand; the IBM brand accounts for 47 percent of IBM's market value.[2] The importance of brand as an intangible corporate asset underlines the importance of marketing metrics related to brand value.

Important questions regarding brand equity are whether potential customers are aware of the brand, what proportion of the population has bought the brand, how customers rate the brand's quality, how satisfied customers are with the brand experience, whether customers are loyal to the brand, and how easy it is to locate and buy the brand. General brand equity metrics and measures to address these questions include:[3]

Consumer metric	Measured by
• Familiarity	• Familiarity relative to other brands in the set being considered
• Penetration	• Number of customers or number of active customers as a percentage of the intended market
• What they think about the brand	• Brand preference as a percentage of preference of other brands within the set being considered, or those with intention to buy, or those with brand knowledge
• What they feel	• Customer satisfaction compared to the average for other brands
• Loyalty	• Either behavioral (repeat buying, retention) or intermediate (commitment, engagement)
• Availability	• Distribution, for example, weighted percentage of retail outlets carrying the brand

[2]Jane Simms, "Intangible Revolution," *The Marketer,* April 2007, 20–23.
[3]Tim Ambler, *Marketing and the Bottom Line,* 2nd ed. (Harlow: Pearson, 2003).

Innovation Metrics

Other metrics are concerned with internal measurements inside the organization. One consideration is the potential for developing and reporting metrics that relate to both the quality and quantity of innovation in the organization—"innovation health"—since effective innovation in product and process is critical to marketing performance in many organizations. Metrics proposed in this area include:[4]

• Strategy	• Awareness of goals • Commitment to goals • Active innovation support • Perceived resource adequacy
• Culture	• Appetite for learning • Freedom to fail
• Outcomes	• Number of initiatives in process • Number of innovations launched • % revenue due to launches in the last 3 years

Internal Market Metrics

There is increasing recognition of "internal branding" in organizations and consequently internal brand equity. These concerns reflect the link between company

[4]Ibid.

performance and employee attitudes. There are metrics available to assess employee-based equity:[5]

- Awareness of corporate goals
- Perceived caliber of employer
- Relative employee satisfaction
- Commitment to corporate goals
- Employee retention
- Perceived resource adequacy
- Appetite for learning
- Freedom to fail
- Customer-brand empathy

Internal Process Metrics

When particular internal processes have been identified as critical to marketing performance, metrics can be developed to evaluate and monitor process performance and links to marketing goals. For example, internal communications have been linked to cross-functional working effectiveness, such as between marketing and sales. Metrics can be developed to monitor the quantity of cross-functional communications and their perceived quality as a monitoring approach for this important organizational characteristic.[6]

[5]Ibid.
[6]Elliot Maltz and Ajay K. Kohli, "Reducing Marketing's Conflict With Other Functions: The Differential Effects of Integrating Mechanisms," *Journal of the Academy of Marketing Science*, Fall 2000, 479–492.

Cases for Part 6

Case 6-1

Facebook

Three years ago 1-800-Flowers, long a pioneer in Internet marketing, became the first national florist to create a fan page on Facebook. It used the free page to build relationships with customers and sell selected products, but it spent very little money advertising on the site. In January, however, the company began buying a different kind of Facebook advertisement. "Sponsored stories," as they're called, let marketers pay to turn actions people take on Facebook into promotional content. When members click a thumbs-up button to signal that they "like" a product or brand, for example, a simple ad appears on their friends' pages: "Julia Smith likes 1-800-Flowers.com." Those friends can click a Like button on that ad, which then shows up on *their* friends' pages, and so on.

Thanks in part to those ads, the company now has more than 125,000 Facebook fans, more than twice as many as it had at the start of the year. Now, says 1-800-Flowers president Chris McCann, "We look at Facebook as core to our marketing program."

So do dozens of other major brands, including Ford, Procter & Gamble, Starbucks, and Coca-Cola. Suddenly, large companies are running multimillion-dollar ad campaigns on Facebook. Startups, such as the social-game maker Zynga and the daily-deal service Groupon, are mounting similar though smaller campaigns, and so are hundreds of thousands of local businesses, such as fitness salons and photographers. Facebook ads hauled in nearly $2 billion in revenues last year, according to the business information service eMarketer, and a leaked document belonging to investor Goldman Sachs revealed that the privately held company made a profit of about $500 million in the same period. This year, revenues are on track to reach $4 billion—making the $75 billion valuation investors are placing on Facebook seem slightly less crazy.

It's a stunning performance for a company many observers thought would never make much money, let alone become a major force in advertising. *(We were wrong, too. See "Social Networking Is Not a Business," technology review, July/August 2008.)* But cofounder and CEO Mark Zuckerberg and his ad executives are just getting started. Chief operating officer Sheryl Sandberg and David Fischer, vice president of advertising and global operations, intend to create something quite different from the two dominant types of advertising online: the search (or keyword) ads on Google and the display (or banner and video) ads everywhere else on the Internet.

Most of the ads on Facebook today—little rectangles running down the right side of the page, each holding a tiny image and up to 160 characters of text—barely hint at the huge bet Sandberg and Fischer are making. Facebook aims to be not just a place to advertise but an entirely new way to advertise—one that uses the power of social networks to create and amplify brand messages. In essence, the company is pushing a highly charged version of word of mouth, long seen as the most valuable of all marketing because people view friends' recommendations as more credible than marketers'.

Conventional word of mouth reaches only a limited number of people. Facebook, where each of an estimated 600 million active users is connected to an average of 130 friends, changes all that by lending personal recommendations enormous reach. After all, anything a user does on the site can be broadcast automatically to all that person's friends. "This is in many ways the Holy Grail of marketing: making your customers your marketers," says Sandberg, who joined Facebook in early 2008 after building up Google's ad sales operation from four people to 4,000. "For the first time, you can do word-of-mouth marketing at massive scale."

To put it another way, when we use Facebook we no longer just view the ad; we become the ad. It's a notion that disturbs some people, especially as Facebook continues to challenge social norms about privacy and use of personal data. Indeed, one reason advertisers love Facebook is that ads can be precisely targeted to specific audiences on the basis of their stated interests, location, "likes," and much more. "A lot of data is being harvested and monetized by Facebook and its advertisers, but users have no idea," says Jeff Chester, executive director of a nonprofit digital-marketing watchdog called the Center for Digital Democracy.

Zuckerberg believes that these new, more personal forms of marketing are the only way advertisers can adapt to the increasingly social nature of the Internet. On average, users spend more than six and a half hours a month on Facebook, significantly more time than they spend on other major sites—mostly because they are so engrossed in communicating with their friends. There's an implicit contract in social media that people not be interrupted by commercial pitches, just as it would be inappropriate to start hawking Tupperware without warning at a dinner party, suggests Ted McConnell, a former longtime P&G marketing executive who's now executive vice president of digital for the Advertising Research Foundation. This means the attention-grabbing kind of image-based advertising that still dominates television, magazines, and even major websites could be an artifact of one-way broadcast media—which is to say, all media that preceded the Internet.

On the Internet, not only can consumers talk back to advertisers, but they can talk to each other about products, services, and brands. Ford sought to harness that kind of activity last year when it unveiled its 2011 Explorer sport utility vehicle not at an auto show but on Facebook. "We wanted to avoid the traffic jam of the auto shows," says Scott Monty Ford's head of social media. The company put up a teaser page on Facebook, with videos, photos, a sweepstakes to win a car, and, on the day of the "reveal," live chats with CEO Alan Mulally and other executives. And it ran ads on Facebook encouraging people to "like" the Explorer. The result, according to the auto-website network Jumpstart Automotive Group: the share of SUV shoppers, on Jumpstart sites who researched Fords jumped 52 percent, more than triple the increases other automakers saw after spending $2.5 million apiece on 30-second televised Super Bowl ads.

Shiny New Object

What sets Facebook apart from online rivals, especially Google, is that its advertising is aimed not at influencing immediate purchases but at branding, something online ads have never done very well. "We're not really demand fulfillment, when you've already figured out what you're going to buy—that's search," explains Sandberg, bounding up to a whiteboard to circle the bottom of a classic "marketing funnel," representing the stage at which a purchase is completed. Circling the top half of the funnel, where consumers become aware of brands and consider buying their products,

she adds: "We're demand generation, before you know you want something."

If she and Fischer can deliver on their plans, Facebook could capture significant chunks of the $500 billion advertising market from television, now the dominant medium for brand marketing. Dwayne Chambers, chief marketing officer at Krispy Kreme, for instance, recently told *Advertising Age* that Facebook, where the doughnut company has more than three million fans, now looks like a more attractive place to advertise than TV.

It surely won't move all its ads there right away, though. A lot of Facebook's current advertising is anything but revolutionary. For one thing, even Facebook concedes that most of the ads aren't yet very social. They may promote a brand or provide a link to a brand site, as other display ads do, but many still don't carry friends' recommendations or even a Like button. What's more, many of the ads aren't even used for branding; they merely try to get people to play a game or fill out an e-mail registration. Facebook's ability to target audiences according to their interests and site activities makes these ads attractive enough to direct marketers, but it's hardly unique: advertising networks run by Google, Yahoo, and others distribute similar ads to targeted audiences on thousands of websites.

Another challenge is that very few people click on Facebook ads. The analytics firm Webtrends recently estimated that these ads on average draw clicks only once every 2,000 times they're viewed—about half the industry average for display advertising. Though ads with a friend's name attract more clicks, the performance is still nowhere near that of Google ads, which on average get a click for every 50 times they're viewed. That's mostly due to the nature of search ads, which are served up to people who have often signaled their readiness to purchase with the very words they type into the search box. But the inescapable result is that Google still grossed more in a month in 2010 than Facebook did all year, even though people spent more time on Facebook.

Right now, many advertisers are embracing Facebook anyway—the returns are good enough, and they don't want to be left behind. "Social media is the shiny new object," says Jascha Kaykas-Wolff, VP of marketing for Involver, which supplies technology to help brands manage their social-media presence. But other advertisers remain wary, and for good reason. Advertising on social-networking pages means relinquishing a lot of control. An ad might be displayed alongside pictures of a college kid getting wasted, or a "sponsored story" on Facebook might turn out to republish negative feedback from a customer. "Buy an ad—you don't get to write it," Sandberg says, laughing at how such a pitch must sound to advertisers. Some marketers also want to be more creative with their ads than what's permitted on Facebook, whose plain ad designs are intended to avoid annoying users. "I would like [ads] to be more eloquent and elegant," says Seth Greenberg, Intuit's vice president of global media and digital marketing.

If Facebook's leaders hope to reinvent marketing in the age of social media, then, it's clear they must still persuade marketers—as well as the people those marketers want to reach—that social marketing has real value. But its early efforts to develop this new form of marketing suggest how difficult this will be.

Privacy Debacle

On November 6, 2007, Mark Zuckerberg mounted a stage at a New York event space called Loft Eleven and declared, "The next hundred years will be different for advertising, and it starts today." Engineers had been working day and night on a "completely new way of advertising online," called Facebook Ads. Companies including Coca-Cola, Blockbuster, and CBS had already signed on. Advertisers would be able to set up free brand pages enabling people to become their "fans." "Social ads" would combine actions posted by Facebook members, such as a purchase or a restaurant review, with the advertiser's message. And a system called Beacon would post on the news feeds of a logged-in Facebook user's friends whenever that user took an action on some 40 other websites, such as buying a movie ticket on Fandango or listing an item for sale on eBay.

People could opt out of Beacon on these individual partner sites, but that wasn't enough to prevent a wave of outrage from privacy advocates and users. Some were furious, for example, to find their gift purchases broadcast to recipients. Coke, among other advertisers, quickly bowed out of Beacon. Within a month of the announcement, Zuckerberg apologized and changed the system to give users more control over how their actions were tracked. But the fallout was a big blow to Facebook's strategy of using participants' activities to target ads. Although Facebook's revenues would hit $300 million by the end of 2008, according to published accounts, they were dwarfed by those of its rival MySpace, whose

banner ads and flashy homepage takeovers were widely estimated to have grossed $600 million.

Nonetheless, Facebook kept focusing on ads that tapped its social graph, the term Zuckerberg used to describe the way relationships on the site could be mapped. It even gave users a chance to click thumbs-up or thumbs-down buttons on ads. In August 2008 the company launched "engagement ads," which prompted users to comment, sign up as a Facebook fan of the advertiser, or take part in a poll; those actions would show up in friends' news feeds. Those ads were slow to catch on, but in 2009 Facebook added other features for marketers. Among them was a new design for brand pages that made them look more like user profile pages—implicitly turning brands into peers.

These efforts increased Facebook's appeal to marketers without antagonizing users. After attending a January 2010 meeting between venture capitalists and P&G executives, David Hornik, a partner with August Capital, wrote that P&G had come to view Facebook as a "must-have for digital advertising and brand building" for which it was "willing to pay dearly." The following month, in a powerful sign that Facebook was putting all its chips on social ads, the company not only ended its three-year-old banner-ad deal with Microsoft but announced that it would stop running generic banner ads, saying that "ad formats that feature social actions perform better and provide a better user experience."

Now that advertisers were warming to Facebook, the company needed to build up its sales operation, and fast. So in March 2010, just as it overtook Google as the Web's most visited site (according to the market watcher Hitwise), the company hired Fischer for its top sales job—luring him away from Google, where he had been Sandberg's deputy and then her successor. One key task: attracting sales talent to Facebook's famously geeky culture. Fischer has since expanded international offices and brought the company's sales force to more than 500 people.

Meanwhile, that April Facebook made its most ambitious attempt yet to spread its vision: Zuckerberg announced Open Graph, a set of technologies that he called "the most transformative thing we've ever done for the Web." Open Graph would integrate other participating sites with Facebook in an entirely new way. In particular, the company revealed that it was making the Like button available to any other site that wanted to add it; a page a user "liked" on any of those sites would generate a link to be shared with friends in that person's Facebook feed. Logged-in Facebook members arriving on a site like CNN would be able to see which stories friends had enjoyed. The personalized music service Pandora would be able to take the songs and bands a user had "liked" into account when making recommendations. Meanwhile, the things users did on those sites would be fed back into Facebook. The universal Like button has since become the centerpiece of Facebook's plans to make marketing more of a conversation between brands and consumers *(see TRIO: Social Indexing, p. 42).*

By summer, Facebook's user base had reached 500 million and its number of advertisers, the company said,

SOCIAL GRAPHS

Facebook's audience is growing faster than those of other popular websites, but its revenues are not yet comparable to its rivals'.

People have increasingly flocked to Facebook, partly at the expense of MySpace, which is part of News Corp.'s Fox Interactive group.

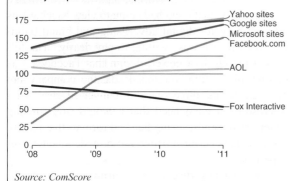

Monthly unique U.S. visitors (millions)

Source: ComScore

As more people have joined the site, it's become more useful. Now it accounts for about one-eighth of the time that people spend online.

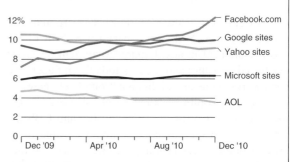

Share of online time spent at top five U.S. Web properties

Source: ComScore

These trends have made Facebook more appealing to advertisers...

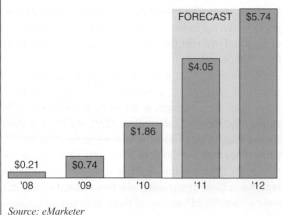

Facebook ad revenues, 2009–2012 ($ billions)

Source: eMarketer

...but Facebook hasn't capitalized on that as it might.

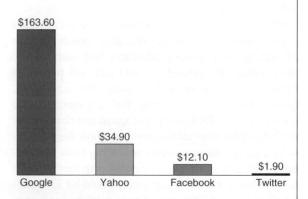

Annual revenue per monthly unique U.S. visitors

Sources: Company filings; eMarketer; ComScore

had tripled in 18 months. Many of those advertisers were small, but that is not necessarily a bad thing; Google's ad network was built on small and medium-size businesses that like its cost-effectiveness. On Facebook, those businesses can now afford to place branding ads more efficiently. Says Fischer: "We're bringing brand marketing to a much broader set of marketers than was ever possible before—expanding that top of the funnel."

To underline what Facebook could do for traditional brand marketers, in September Sandberg addressed an audience of marketers and agencies at a New York conference hosted by an online-ad trade group called the Interactive Advertising Bureau. "The social graph," she said in an expansion of Zuckerberg's definition, "is not just connections between people but between people and the things they love." Give people a chance to help shape your brands' products and image, she said, and they'll view ads as useful, engaging content, not commercial interruptions.

She came armed with figures from Nielsen, which had worked with Facebook over the past year to compare the impact of Facebook social ads and standard ads in the same campaign. In one study of 14 campaigns, Nielsen found that people who viewed ads displaying a friend's endorsement were 68 percent more likely to remember the ad than were people who saw a plain display ad. What's more, they were more than four times as likely to say they intended to purchase the advertised product.

Moneyball Marketing

Despite Facebook's momentum, doubts remain about whether it can persuade more big brands to open their wallets—a question that's especially important given investors' expectations. Maurice Lévy, CEO of the French advertising firm Publicis, told the *New York Times* this spring that he didn't know if any business model that emerged from social media could be "as successful as people are expecting, or as successful as Google with

search." Moreover, the recession has forced brands to find cheaper ways to reach consumers—and social media is one of them. Sandberg cites company after company that has built brand value using Facebook pages and Like buttons. But, of course, those services are free.

Consider what Intuit did last year to promote its signature program, TurboTax. The company inserted a Like button in the application that users could click when they finished their taxes; about 100,000 people clicked either that button or the Like button on the company's Facebook page. People who saw that a friend "liked" TurboTax were four times as likely to click on a link to the product as those who saw a standard display ad. Some 30 percent of those who clicked the link bought the program, and 79 percent of them were new customers. All great for Intuit—but the company didn't pay Facebook for any of this.

"It's really the *Moneyball* era of marketing," says Cory Treffiletti, president of the San Francisco marketing agency Catalyst S+F, referring to Michael Lewis's 2003 book about how the Oakland Athletics used player data to assemble a successful baseball team on the cheap.

One potential moneymaker for Facebook would be an ad network, which would syndicate its ads to other websites in return for a cut of the revenues they generate. Google's AdSense network, for example, grossed $9 billion last year. But the company says it has no plans for an ad network. So Facebook's biggest challenge remains coming up with new kinds of advertising that will appeal to both marketers and users.

Sandberg and Fischer admit they've not yet fully cracked that nut. If Facebook's strategy of making us all willing marketers is to do the trick, the company will have to find a way to marry the science of the social graph to the art of the advertising it's trying to replace.

Source: Robert D. Hof, "You Are the Ad," technology review, May/June 2011, 64–69.

Case 6-2
Wentworth Industrial Cleaning Supplies

Wentworth Industrial Cleaning Supplies (WICS), located in Lincoln, Nebraska, is experiencing a slowdown in growth; sales of all WICS products have leveled off far below the volume expected by management. Although total sales volume has increased for the industry, WICS's share of this growth has not kept pace. J. Randall Griffith, vice president of marketing, has been directed to determine what factors are stunting growth and to institute a program that will facilitate further expansion.

WICS is a division of Wentworth International, competing in the janitorial maintenance chemical

EXHIBIT 1
Institutional
Maintenance
Chemical Market

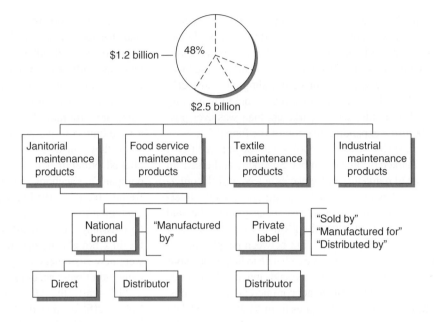

market. According to trade association estimates, the total market is roughly $2.5 billion in 2007. Exhibit 1 shows the nature of this market. Four segments comprise the institutional maintenance chemical market, which consists of approximately 2,000 manufacturers providing both national and private labels.

Total industry sales volume in dollars of janitorial supplies is approximately $1.3 billion. Exhibit 2 shows the breakdown by product type for the janitorial market. WICS addresses 75 percent of the market's product needs with a line of high-quality products. The composition of WICS's product line is as follows:

Special purpose cleaners	46%
Air fresheners	9
General purpose cleaners	16
Disinfectants	15
Other	14

The janitorial maintenance chemical market is highly fragmented; no one firm, including WICS, has more than 10 percent market share. Agate and Marshfield Chemical sell directly to the end-user, while Lynx, Lexington Labs, and WICS utilize a distributor network. Most of WICS's competitors utilize only one channel of distribution; only Organic

Labs and Swanson sell both ways. Most private-label products move through distributors. Sanitary supply distributors (SSDs) deliver 65 percent of end-user dollars, while direct-to-end-user dollar sales are 35 percent (Exhibit 3).* The following shows the sales breakdown by target market by type of distribution:

Distributor Sales

Retail	20%
Industrial	18
Healthcare	18
Schools	11
Building supply contractors	10
Restaurants	3
Hotels	3
Other	17

Direct Sales

Retail	47%
Building supply contractors	35
Health care	15
Hotels	2
Restaurants	1

Trade association data plus information from other sources estimate the number of SSDs to be between 5,000 and 6,000. The following shows the sales

This case was written by Neil M. Ford, University of Wisconsin-Madison. Joan Russler and Jeffrey Forbes, MBAs-Marketing, University of Wisconsin-Madison, assisted in the preparation of this case. Copyright © 2001 Neil M. Ford. Updated 2007.

*Includes paper supply distributors that carry janitorial supplies.

EXHIBIT 2
WICS "Served"
Portion of
the Janitorial
Maintenance
Chemical Market

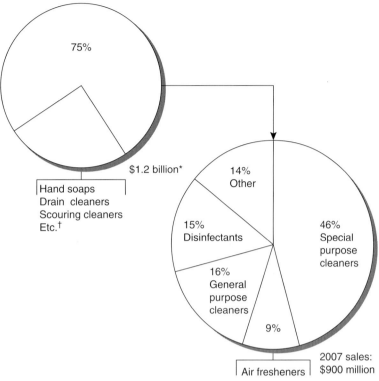

*End-user dollars.
†Includes some general purpose cleaners and air fresheners that WICS does not
 manufacture.

EXHIBIT 3
Janitorial
Maintenance
Chemical Market
(End-User Dollars)

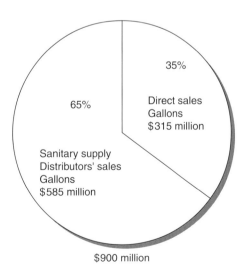

volume breakdown for the SSDs based on an average of 5,500:

Size in Sales Volume

Less than $100,000	1,210
$100,000–499,999	2,475
$500,000–1,000,000	1,375
More than $1,000,000	400
Total	5,500

According to a recent analysis of end-users, WICS provides cleaning supplies for approximately 20,000 customers. WICS's sales force is expected to call on these accounts as well as prospects for new business. These 20,000 end-users receive product from the SSDs who supply cleaning supplies manufactured by WICS and others as well. About one-third of the average SSD's total sales is accounted for by WICS's products. An exception is the paper supply distributor, where WICS's products account for an average of 10 percent of sales.

The typical SSD carries other related items. In fact, according to a survey conducted by an independent firm, SSDs almost always carry a private-label line of cleaning supplies plus one to two additional branded products besides the WICS line. This survey revealed that 60 percent of the SSDs carry a private-label line along with WICS and a private label. The private label may be a regional label or the SSD's own label.

WICS places almost total reliance on selling through the SSDs, although a small amount of sales (less than 10 percent) are made direct. WICS sells its janitorial maintenance products through roughly 400 distributors, who in turn "see" 65 percent of the end-user dollar market. Thus, 65 percent of sales in the total janitorial maintenance market are made through SSDs (35 percent are direct sales); and the 400 SSDs used by WICS provided 65 percent coverage. The market seen by each distributor, referred to as his or her *window* on the market, is a function of the following:

Product lines carried (paper versus chemical).

Customer base (type and size).

Nature of business (specialization by market versus specialization by sales function).

The combination of these factors produces end-user market coverage of 42 percent (65 percent distributor sales × 65 percent coverage). WICS has very limited direct sales.

To reach its market, WICS uses a sales force of 135 area managers, 21 territory managers, and 4 regional managers (Exhibit 4). Regional managers are located in San Francisco, Denver, Chicago, and Boston. Although WICS is viewed as a giant in the industry, it does not produce a complete line of janitorial chemicals. Janitorial chemicals are rated on the basis of their performance. WICS produces products that have average to premium performance ratings; WICS has no products in the economy class. Moreover, due to various factors, WICS's coverage in the average and premium classes is not complete. The emphasis on premium and average products results in providing only 75 percent of the market's product needs.

EXHIBIT 4   **WICS's Access to the Market**

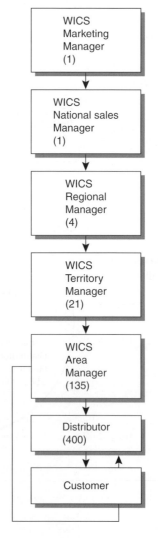

EXHIBIT 5
End-User Product Coverage

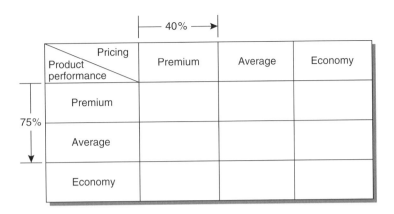

To provide high distributor margins and extensive sales support, WICS charges premium prices. Recent estimates reveal that only 40 percent of the served market is willing to pay these premium prices. The impact of WICS's limited product line coupled with its premium prices is evident in Exhibit 5.

An overall description of WICS's marketing program shows that it has focused on market development. Distributors receive high margins (30 to 40 percent) and sales costs are high (10 to 15 percent) due to emphasis on selling technical benefits, demonstrations, and cold calls. Area managers call on prospective end-users to develop the market for the SSD. By comparison, WICS's competitors offer SSDs low margins (15 to 20 percent) and incur low sales costs (5 to 8 percent).

Griffith recently received a memo from Steve Shenken, WICS's national sales manager, reporting on a study of the effectiveness of SSDs. Territory managers evaluated each SSD in their respective regions on a basis of reach (advertising and promotional programs) and frequency of sales calls. The composite report indicated distributors as a whole were doing an excellent job servicing present accounts. In other words, 400 SSDs provide WICS with a sizable share of the market.

Area managers (AMs) represent WICS in distributor relations. The AMs' "prime focus is to sell and service existing key end-user accounts and selected new target accounts in their assigned territories." According to a recent study, maintenance of current accounts comprises approximately 80 percent of the AMs' time (Exhibit 6). In addition to handling old accounts, the AM makes cold calls on prospective distributors as directed by the territory managers. However, the number of cold calls made monthly has decreased

substantially in the past year since the major SSDs now carry WICS products. A study of AM and SSD attitudes, conducted by MGH Associates, management consultants, is presented in Appendixes A and B. Some of the sales management staff question the use of AM time; however, there has been no indication that formal changes will be made in the future regarding sales force organization and directives. The AM job description has seen few revisions, if any, during the firm's past 10 years of rapid growth (Exhibit 7).

Area managers are compensated with a straight salary, enhanced periodically by various incentive programs and performance bonuses. Incentive

EXHIBIT 6
Allocation of Area Manager Duties*

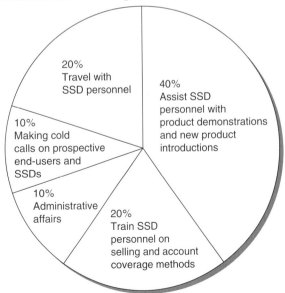

*Based on an analysis of call reports.

EXHIBIT 7 **Wentworth Industrial Cleaning Supplies Position Description**

Date: January 1, 2007
Approved by: (1) _____
            (2) _____
            (3) _____

Position: Area Manager, Maint. Prods.
Incumbent: 135 Positions Nationally
Division: Janitorial Maintenance
                   Products Division
                   Reports to: Territory Manager
                               Janitorial Maintenance
                               Products Division

Position Purpose:

To sell and service user accounts and authorized distributors in an assigned territory to assure that territory sales objectives are attained or exceeded.

Dimensions:

Annual sales:	$300 M (average)
Number of distributors:	4 (average)
Number of distributor salesmen:	12 (average)
Annual expense budget:	$4.2 M (average)
Company assets controlled or affected:	$8 M (average)

Nature and Scope

This position reports to a territory manager, janitorial maintenance products. Each district is subdivided into sales territories that are either assigned to an individual member of the district or to a team effort, based on market and/or manpower requirements.

The janitorial maintenance products division is responsible for developing and marketing a broad line of chemical products for building maintenance purposes.

The incumbent's prime focus is to sell and service existing key-user accounts and selected new target accounts in his assigned territory. He multiplies his personal sales results by spending a major portion of his time working with distributor sales personnel, selling WICS maintenance products and systems to key accounts such as commercial, industrial, institutional, governmental accounts, and contract cleaners. When working alone, he sells key-user accounts through an authorized distributor as specified by the user customer.

The incumbent plans, schedules, and manages his selling time for maximum sales productivity. He interviews decision makers and/or people who influence the buying decision. He identifies and evaluates customer needs through careful observation, listening and questioning techniques to assure proper recommendations. He plans sales strategy to include long-term/quick-sell objectives and develops personalized user presentations to meet individual sales situations, utilizing product literature, manuals, spot demonstrations, and sales aids to reinforce presentations. This position sells systems of maintenance to major volume user accounts through the use of surveys and proposals, test programs, and other advanced sales techniques. He develops effective closing techniques for maximum sales effectiveness. This position trains custodial personnel in product usage techniques through the use of product demonstrations and/or audiovisual training to assure customer satisfaction. He follows up promptly on customer leads and inquiries. He services customer and distributor complaints or problems and provides technical support as required. On a predetermined frequency basis, he surveys and sells assigned local accounts currently being sold on national contract. He represents the division in local custodial clinics and trade shows as required. He maintains an adequate current supply of literature, forms, and samples and maintains assigned equipment and, sales tools in a businesslike condition.

The incumbent is responsible for training, developing, and motivating distributor sales personnel. This is accomplished by frequent on-the-job training in areas of product knowledge, selling skills, and demonstration techniques. He sells distributor management and assists distributors to maintain an adequate and balanced inventory of the full product line. He introduces marketing plans and sells new products and sales promotions to distributor management. He participates in distributor sales meetings to launch new products or sales promotions, or for training and motivational purposes. He keeps abreast of pertinent competitive activities, product performance, new maintenance techniques, and other problems and opportunities in the territory. Periodically, he communicates Wentworth growth objectives versus distributor progress to distributor management (i.e., sales coverage, volume and product sales, etc.). He assists the distributor to maintain a current and adequate supply of product literature, price lists, and sales aids.

(continued)

EXHIBIT 7   Wentworth Industrial Cleaning Supplies Position Description (*concluded*)

The incumbent prepares daily sales reports, weekly reports, travel schedules, weekly expense reports, and the like, and maintains territory and customer records. He maintains close communication with his immediate supervisor concerning products, sales, distributor and shipping problems.

He controls travel and business expenses with economy and sound judgment. He handles and maintains assigned company equipment and territory records in a businesslike manner.

Major challenges to this position include maintaining established major users, selling prospective new target accounts and strengthening distribution and sales coverage to attain or exceed sales objectives.

The incumbent operates within divisional policies, procedures, and objectives. He consults with his immediate supervisor for recommendations and/or approval concerning distributor additions or terminations, exceptions to approved selling procedures, and selling the headquarters level of national or regional accounts.

Internally, he consults with the editing office concerning distributor shipments, credit, and so forth. Externally, he works closely with distributor personnel to increase sales and sales coverage and with user accounts to sell new or additional products.

The effectiveness of this position is measured by the ability of the incumbent to attain or exceed territory sales objectives.

This position requires an incumbent with an in-depth and professional knowledge of user account selling techniques, product line, and janitorial maintenance products distributors, and a minimum of supervision.

Principal Accountabilities

1. Sell and service key-user accounts to assure attainment of territory sales objectives.
2. Sell, train, develop, and motivate assigned distributors to assure attainment of product sales, distribution, and sales coverage objectives.
3. Plan, schedule, and manage personal selling efforts to assure maximum sales productivity.
4. Plan and develop professional sales techniques to assure maximum effectiveness.
5. Train custodial personnel in the use of Wentworth products and systems to assure customer satisfaction.
6. Maintain a close awareness of territory and market activities to keep the immediate supervisor abreast of problems and opportunities.
7. Perform administrative responsibilities to conduct an efficient territory operation.
8. Control travel and selling expenses to contribute toward profitable territory operation.

programs generally require that AMs attain a certain sales level by a specified date. For example, the Christmas Program necessitated that AMs achieve fourth-quarter quotas by November 15; on completion of this objective, the AM received a gift of his or her choice, such as a color television. To date, management considers the Zone Glory Cup the most effective incentive program. The Glory Cup is an annual competition among areas within territories, which entails meeting or exceeding sales objectives by a specified date. An all-expense-paid vacation at a plush resort for area, territory, and regional managers and their legal spouses is the prize for the winning team. However, management at WICS believes that prestige is the prime motivator in this competition and the underlying reason for the program's success.

In a recent meeting, Terry Luther, executive vice president of the WICS division of Wentworth International, expressed his concern to Griffith about WICS's mediocre performance. Luther indicated corporate cash flow expectations from WICS were not being met

and that a plan was needed from Griffith concerning how WICS could improve its overall operating performance. Griffith was quite aware that Wentworth International would make personnel changes to meet corporate objectives and that selling off divisions not able to meet corporate expectations was not unlikely. Griffith informed Luther that an action plan would be developed and be on his desk within 30 days.

Griffith's first step was to approve an earlier request made by Mike Toner, sales and distributor relations manager, for a study of sales force and distributor attitudes and opinions (Appendixes A and B). Next, the memo in Exhibit 8 was sent, discussing Griffith's assignment from Luther.

Staff reaction to Griffith's memo (Exhibit 8) was one of frustration and anger. Several managers thought they had already complied with Griffith's request. One person commented, "I've told Randy numerous times what we need to do to turn the division around, and all he does is nod his head. Why go through this 'wheel-spinning' exercise again?" Another said, "The

EXHIBIT 8   Griffith's Memo

Intra-Office Memorandum

To: Steve Shenken, National Sales Manager
    Caitlin Smith, Manager—Sales Analysis
    Ryan Michaels, Manager—Sales Training
    Calla Hart, Manager—Special Sales Program
    Charlotte Webber, Senior Product Manager
    Mike Toner, Sales and Distributor Relations Manager

From: Randall Griffith, Vice President—Marketing

Subject: WICS Performance Review

    As you all know, our performance has not met corporate expectations. To rectify this situation, before we all lose our jobs, we need to meet to discuss ways for improving our market performance.

    At our next meeting, I want each of you to develop proposals for your areas of responsibility. These proposals need not be detailed at this time. For the moment, I am seeking ideas, not final solutions.

only time old J. R. listens to us is when the top brass leans on him for results." Despite staff reaction, the meeting would be held, and everybody would have suggestions for consideration.

To provide adequate time, Griffith scheduled an all-day meeting to be held at Wentworth's nearby lodge, located on Lake Woebegone. Griffith started the meeting by reviewing past performance. Next, he asked each manager to outline his or her proposal. First to speak was Steve Shenken, who indicated that Mike Toner would present a proposal combining both of their ideas. Shenken also said he would listen to all sales force proposals and try to combine the best parts into an overall plan.

Mike Toner's Proposal

Toner's proposal was rather basic. If improving market share was WICS's objective, then more SSDs are needed in all territories. According to Toner,

Each area manager serves, on the average, four SSDs. Since we can only get so much business out of an SSD, then to increase sales we need more SSDs. I suggest that each area manager add two more distributors. Of course, this move will require that we either add more area managers or that we hire and train a special group to call on new end-users and new distributors. It's difficult to attract new SSDs unless we show them a group of prospective end-users who are ready to buy WICS's products. Now, I have not made any estimates of how many more people are needed, but we do know that present AMs do not have enough time to adequately seek new business.

After Toner presented this proposal, Griffith asked if the existing AMs could not be motivated to apply more effort toward securing new business. Calla Hart thought the AMs could do more and that her proposal, if adopted, would alleviate the need for expansion of the AMs and SSDs.

Calla Hart's Proposal

As expected, Hart's proposal revolved around her extensive experience with WICS's incentive programs. This satisfactory experience led Calla to suggest the following:

If I thought that the AMs and the SSDs were working at full capacity, I would not propose more incentive programs. But they are not! We can motivate the AMs to secure more new business, and we can get more new business from our distributors. We all know that the SSDs are content to sit back and wait for the AMs to hand them new business. Well, let's make it worthwhile to the SSDs by including them in our incentive programs. For the AMs I suggest that we provide quarterly incentives much like our Christmas Program. AMs who achieve their quotas by the 15th of the second month of the quarter would receive a gift.

In addition, we need to develop a program for recognizing new end-user sales. Paying bonuses for obtaining new end-user accounts would be one approach. For example, let's reward the AM from each territory who secures the highest percentage increase in new end-user accounts. At the same time, we need to reward the distributor from each territory who achieves the highest percentage increase in new end-user sales dollars. And let's recognize these top producers each quarter and at year end as well. Our incentive programs work. We know that, so let's expand their application to new sales.

Finally, on a different note, I support establishing quotas for our distributors. We have quotas for our sales force, and we enforce them. AMs who do not make quotas do not stay around very long. Why not the same procedures for some of our SSDs? We all know that there are some distributors who need to be replaced. Likewise, I have not made any cost estimates but feel that we are just searching for new ideas.

Griffith thanked Hart for her comments. He wondered whether applying more pressure to the distributors was the most suitable approach. He agreed with Hart that WICS's incentive programs seemed to be very popular but questioned if other techniques might not work. Griffith then asked Ryan Michaels for his comments.

Ryan Michael's Proposal

During his short time with WICS, Michaels has gained respect as being very thorough and analytical. He is not willing to accept as evidence such comments as "We know it works" as a reason for doing something. Determining the value of sales training, Michaels's area of assignment, has caused him considerable concern. He knows it is useful, but how useful is the question he is trying to answer. According to Michaels, WICS needs to examine the basic selling duties of the area managers:

Before we recruit more AMs and SSDs, or try to motivate them to obtain more new business with incentive programs, we need to examine their job activities. I favor doing a job analysis of the area manager. Some evidence that I have seen indicates that job descriptions are outmoded. AMs do not perform the activities detailed in the job descriptions. For example, most AMs spend very little time calling on prospective end-users. Accompanying distributor sales reps on daily calls does not lead to new end-user business. Possibly the AMs could better spend their time doing new account development work. But before we make any decisions concerning time allocation, we need to conduct a job analysis. And, while we are collecting data, let's ask the AMs what rewards are important to them. How do they value promotions, pay increases, recognition, and so forth? Maybe the AMs do not want more contests.

Griffith agreed that the job descriptions were out of date. He also contended this is typical and nothing to

be concerned about in the short run. The idea of finding out what rewards AMs value intrigued Griffith. Next, Griffith asked Charlotte Webber for her reactions to WICS's market share problem.

Charlotte Webber's Proposal

Webber's proposal was more strategic in nature than the previous suggestions. Her experience as a product manager led her to consider product-oriented solutions and to suggest the following:

I think we can increase market share and sales volume through the expansion of current lines and the addition of a full line of economy-based products. We can expand our present premium and average lines to cover 100 percent of the product class by adding air fresheners and general purpose cleaners. In addition we must introduce the economy-based products to counter competition.

The proposed plan would not be costly because we could use our existing distributor network. If additional SSDs are necessary, we can select those in the $500,000 to $1,000,000 sales volume range. I feel that through these extensions and an increased number of SSDs we can address 75 percent of the SSD end-user dollars.

Griffith agreed that line extensions were a viable means of achieving some corporate goals. He expressed concern over entry into the low-quality segment of the market due to WICS's present customer perceptions of the company as a high-quality producer. Griffith turned to Caitlin Smith for additional suggestions on how to increase market share.

Caitlin Smith's Proposal

Smith's proposal came as no surprise to those attending the meeting. Her position in sales analysis made her critically aware of WICS's high cost of sales. It was only recently, however, that she developed a plan incorporating market share and cost of sales. Her views were accurate, but often given little weight due to her inexperience. According to Smith,

Our costs of sales are currently running at 10 to 15 percent, while our competitors' costs average 5 to 8 percent. As many of you know I am in favor of changing the job description of the area manager and the sales presentation. These changes are necessary due to our products' stage in the life cycle and customer service level preferences. Recently I have become convinced that there is another means of reducing sales costs. By reducing prices we could increase sales volume and reduce the cost of sales. This strategy would also increase penetration and market share.

Griffith conceded that price reductions were a possibility but expressed concern over the possibility of weakening consumer perceptions of WICS as a high-quality manufacturer. He also questioned Smith's assumption that the industrial cleaning supplies industry was presently in the mature stage of the product life cycle.

Following these comments, Griffith thanked the participants for their input and adjourned the meeting. On retiring to his room, he reflected on the suggestions presented during the meeting and his own beliefs. He knew he must begin to formulate an action plan immediately since the 30-day deadline was drawing near.

Appendix A

Conclusions of Study of Area Manager Attitudes

MGH Associates, management consultants, was retained by WICS to investigate attitudes and opinions of field personnel and sanitary supply distributors. Initially, MGH conducted lengthy interviews with selected individuals, followed by the administration of a comprehensive questionnaire. The results below identify role expectations and attitudes toward their reasonableness.

Territory Manager's Role Expectations

MGH Associates's interviews included territory managers because the territory manager is really the only management level contact the distributor has.

The territory manager interprets his or her role to be that of an overseer, to assure that WICS objectives are achieved and that quotas are met.

The territory manager interprets his or her role to include,

- Training the area managers to sell WICS products.
- Training and motivating the distributor sales force.
- Coordinating area manager activities with headquarters in Lincoln.
- Hiring and firing area managers.
- Striving for new product commitments from the distributors.

- Acting as referee for competition between distributors.
- "Building the book" for the adding or deleting of distributors.
- Submitting the study to the regional manager, who writes a proposal based on the territory manager's study. It is submitted to corporate management, where the final decision is made.

Area Manager's Role Expectations

The following is the area manager's view of the role he or she believes WICS management expects to be performed:

- Multiply sales effort through distributor's sales force (listed first because it was consistently mentioned first).
- Teach and motivate the distributor's sales force to sell WICS products.
- Introduce new products to the market through:
  - Direct calls on end-users.
  - Distributors.
- Keep margins high to keep distributors happy. If they are happy, they will push WICS.
- Follow through on direct sales responsibilities.
- Collect information for management.
- Fulfill responsibilities relating to incentives:
  - New gallon sales.
  - Repeat gallon sales.
  - Demonstrations.
  - 30, 35, 40? calls/week.
  - Major account calls.
  - Cold calls—"to develop business the distributor is reluctant to go after."

Area Manager's Role Problems

The area manager's perception of what management expects does not imply that the area manager feels that management's approach is working. In general, the sales force appears frustrated by a sales role they see as ineffective:

- A sales role that stresses:
  - New gallon sales.
  - Cold calls on end-users.

- Product demonstrations.
- New product introduction.
- "Checking the boxes" rather than being "creatively productive":
  - 15 demos.
  - 10 cold calls.
  - 5 distributor training sessions.
- Incentives stress selling techniques that may not be the most productive ways to sell.
  - Emphasis is on new gallon sales over repeat gallon sales. Incentives weight new gallons over repeat gallons (two to one).
  - Emphasis to "demonstrate as often as possible" for the points. Demonstrate to show you are a "regular guy" who gets his or her hands dirty, not necessarily to show product benefits.
- Bonus incentives appear to be a "carrot" only for those who don't regularly make bonus, that is, "hit 106 for maximum bonus and minimum quota increase."
- The sales role gives the area manager little ability to impact his or her own success to:
  - Change distribution.
  - Move distributor outside his or her window.
- The area manager describes his or her role as:
  - A "lackey."
  - A "chauffeur."
  - A "caretaker of old business."

Area Manager's Role: Making Cold Calls

One of the causes of area manager frustration is the general ineffectiveness of their cold calls sales role:

- The area manager makes cold calls on end-users not presently sold by the WICS distributor, with the difficult objective of moving these accounts to the WICS distributor.
- If the area manager succeeds in moving this account over to WICS products, chances are small that the distributor will keep the business:
  - Without a major portion of the account's total purchases, the distributor cannot afford to continue to call on the account.
  - Distributor sales rep is on commission.

- After five calls, will stop calling if purchases have not begun to increase.
- The distributor that lost the account will try extremely hard to get back the business. This may mean giving the product away to keep control of the account—maintain majority of the account's purchases. Past experience indicates it is very difficult to move distributors outside their window.

Appendix B

Conclusions of Study of WICS Sanitary Supply Distributor Attitudes

WICS Distributor's Role Expectations

The following is the WICS distributor's role as outlined by WICS management and sales force:

- Act as an extension of the WICS sales force.
- Push and promote WICS product line in a specified area:
  - Sell WICS over other brands.
  - Always sell the premium benefits of WICS products to the end-user, instead of distributor's private label.
  - Be aware that the WICS line could be lost if private label sales grow too large.
- Actively market new WICS products.

Distributor's Role Problems

Distributors have been angered by WICS's attempt to run their businesses ("WICS is trying to tell me what to do").

- WICS makes demands—"uses pressure tactics":
  - Distributors say they are told "our way or no way."
  - Distributors feel they are forced to carry products they don't want:
    - High minimum buy-ins.
    - "Won't see area manager if we don't carry the new product."
  - Distributors say WICS management doesn't "realize we make our living selling all our products—not just WICS."

- Communication is poor with WICS management.
  - One way—"Our opinions never reach Lincoln."
- "WICS uses the distributor as a testing ground for new products":
  - Distributor is not told what to expect.
  - After 14-week blitz, "You never hear about the product again."
  - The distributor sales force is not trained to sell to, and cannot afford to call on, certain segments of the market.
- Growth takes the distributor into new geographical market areas, and WICS may elect not to go/grow with the distributor:
  - New branch in different city.
- Growth may take distributor sales personnel out of area manager's district:
  - Receives no support from WICS.
- Worst case—distributor sales rep's territory is completely outside district:
  - No WICS representative at any accounts.
- Prefer to sell other than WICS.
- WICS does not realize that a distributor's total business extends beyond "its own backyard" in many markets.

Distributor's Role Selling Costs

Distributors have shown concern over the high cost of selling WICS products. Sales costs are approximately 45 percent of the total operating costs.

- "WICS products are basically no better than anyone else's."
- Yet WICS asks distributors to switch competitor's accounts over to WICS products:
  - Price advantage is very rare.
  - A problem must exist.
  - A demonstration is required.
- All these make the "problem-solving" sale time-consuming and costly.
- Result: When a WICS product is sold, it is easy for competitive WICS distributors to cut price to try to get the business:
  - They have very low sales costs.
- Required action: Original distributor must cut margin to keep the business:
  - This frustrates distributor salespeople.
  - Causes them to sell private label.

Case 6-3

General Electric Appliances*

Larry Barr had recently been promoted to the position of district sales manager (B.C.) for G.E Appliances, a division of Canadian Appliance Manufacturing Co. Ltd. (CAMCO). One of his more important duties in that position was the allocation of his district's sales quota among his five salesmen. Barr received his quota for 2002 in October 2001. His immediate task was to determine an equitable allocation of that quota. This was important because the company's incentive pay plan was based on the salesmen's attainment of quota. A portion of Barr's remuneration was also based on the degree to which his sales force met their quotas.

Barr graduated from the University of British Columbia in 1993 with the degree of bachelor of

commerce. He was immediately hired as a product manager for a mining equipment manufacturing firm because of his summer job experience with that firm. In 1996, he joined Canadian General Electric (C.G.E) in Montreal as a product manager for refrigerators. There he was responsible for creating and merchandising a product line, as well as developing product and marketing plans. In January 1999, he was transferred to Coburg, Ontario, as a sales manager for industrial plastics. In September 2000, he became administrative manager (Western Region) and when the position of district sales manager became available, Barr was promoted to it. There his duties included development of sales strategies, supervision of salesmen, and budgeting.

Background

Canadian Appliance Manufacturing Co. Ltd (CAMCO) was created in 1998 under the joint ownership of Canadian General Electric Ltd. and General Steel

*Copyright © 2002 Richard W. Pollay, John D. Claxtoan, and Rick Jenkner. Adapted with permission.

Wares Ltd. (G.S.W.). CAMCO then purchased the production facilities of Westinghouse Canada Ltd. Under the purchase agreement, the Westinghouse brand name was transferred to White Consolidated Industries Ltd., where it became White-Westinghouse. Appliances manufactured by CAMCO in the former Westinghouse plant were branded Hotpoint (See Exhibit 1).

The G.E, G.S.W., and Hotpoint major appliance plants became divisions of CAMCO. These divisions operated independently and had their own separate management staff, although they were all ultimately accountable to CAMCO management. The divisions competed for sales, although not directly, because they each produced product lines for different price segments.

Competition

Competition in the appliance industry was vigorous. CAMCO was the largest firm in the industry, with approximately 45 percent market share, split between G.E, G.S.W. (Moffatt & McClary brands), and Hotpoint. The following three firms each had 10 to 15 percent market share: Inglis (washers and dryers only), W.C.I. (makers of White-Westinghouse, Kelvinator, and Gibson), and Admiral. These firms also produced appliances under department store brand names such as Viking, Baycrest, and Kenmore, which accounted for an additional 15 percent of the market. The remainder of the market was divided among brands such as Maytag, Roper Dishwasher, Gurney, Tappan, and Danby.

EXHIBIT 1 Organization Chart

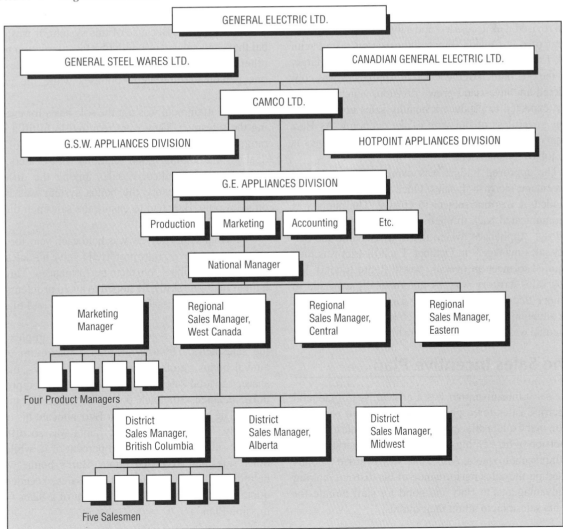

G.E marketed a full major appliance product line, including refrigerators, ranges, washers, dryers, dishwashers, and television sets. G.E appliances generally had many features and were priced at the upper end of the price range. Their major competition came from Maytag and Westinghouse.

The Budgeting Process

G.E Appliances was one of the most advanced firms in the consumer goods industry in terms of sales budgeting. Budgeting received careful analysis at all levels of management.

The budgetary process began in June of each year. The management of G.E. Appliances division assessed the economic outlook, growth trends in the industry, competitive activity, population growth, and so forth to determine a reasonable sales target for the next year. The president of CAMCO received this estimate, checked and revised it as necessary, and submitted it to the president of G.E. Canada. Final authorization rested with G.E. Ltd., which had a definite minimum growth target for the G.E. branch of CAMCO. G.E. Appliances was considered an "invest and grow" division, which meant it was expected to produce a healthy sales growth each year, regardless of the state of the economy. As Barr observed, "This is difficult, but meeting challenges is the job of management."

The approved budget was expressed as a desired percentage increase in sales. Once the figure had been decided, it was not subject to change. The quota was communicated back through G.E. Canada Ltd., CAMCO, and G.E. Appliances, where it was available to the district sales managers in October. Each district was then required to meet an overall growth figure (quota), but each sales territory was not automatically expected to achieve that same growth. Barr was required to assess the situation in each territory, determine where growth potential was highest, and allocate his quota accordingly.

The Sales Incentive Plan

The sales incentive plan was a critical part of General Electric's sales force plan and an important consideration in the quota allocation of Barr. Each salesman had a portion of his earnings dependent on his performance with respect to quota. Also, Barr was awarded a bonus based on the sales performance of his district, making it advantageous to Barr and good for staff morale for all his salesmen to attain their quotas.

The sales force incentive plan was relatively simple. A bonus system is fairly typical for salesmen in any field. With G.E., each salesman agreed to a basic salary figure called "planned earnings." The planned salary varied according to experience, education, past performance, and competitive salaries. A salesman was paid 75 percent of his planned earnings on a guaranteed regular basis. The remaining 25 percent of salary was at risk, dependent on the person's sales record. There was also the possibility of earning substantially more money by selling more than quota (see Exhibit 2).

The bonus was awarded such that total salary (base plus bonus) equaled planned earnings when the quota was just met. The greatest increase in bonus came between 101 and 110 percent of quota. The bonus was paid quarterly on the cumulative total quota. A holdback system ensured that a salesman was never required to pay back previously earned bonus because of a poor quarter. Because of this system, it was critical that each salesman's quota be fair in relation to the other salesmen. Nothing was worse for morale than one person earning large bonuses while the others struggled.

Quota attainment was not the sole basis for evaluating the salesmen. They were required to fulfill a wide range of duties including service, franchising of new dealers, maintaining good relations with dealers, and maintaining a balance of sales among the different product lines. Because the bonus system was based on sales only, Barr had to ensure the salesmen did not neglect their other duties.

A formal salary review was held each year for each salesman. However, Barr preferred to give his salesmen continuous feedback on their performances. Through human relations skills, he hoped to avoid problems that could lead to dismissal of a salesman and loss of sales for the company.

Barr's incentive bonus plan was more complex than the salesmen's. He was awarded a maximum of 75 annual bonus points broken down as follows: market share, 15; total sales performance, 30; sales representative balance, 30. Each point had a specific money value. The system ensured that Barr allocate his quota carefully. For instance, if one quota was so difficult that the salesmen sold only 80 percent of it, while the other salesmen exceeded quota, Barr's bonus would be reduced, even if the overall area sales exceeded the quota. (See Appendix, "Development of a Sales Commission Plan.")

EXHIBIT 2
Sales Incentive
Earnings Schedule:
Major Appliances
and Home
Entertainment
Products

Sales Quota Realization (percent)	Percent of Base Salary Total	Sales Quota Realization (percent)	Incentive Percent of Base Salary Total
70 %	0 %	105%	35.00%
71	0.75	106	37.00
72	1.50	107	39.00
73	2.25	108	41.00
74	3.00	109	43.00
75	3.75	110	45.00
76	4.50	111	46.00
77	5.25	112	47.00
78	6.00	113	48.00
79	6.75	114	49.00
80	7.50	115	50.00
81	8.25	116	51.00
82	9.00	117	52.00
83	9.75	118	53.00
84	10.50	119	54.00
85	11.25	120	55.00
86	12.00	121	56.00
87	12.75	122	57.00
88	13.50	123	58.00
89	14.25	124	59.00
90	15.00	125	60.00
91	16.00	126	61.00
92	17.00	127	62.00
93	18.00	128	63.00
94	19.00	129	64.00
95	20.00	130	65.00
96	21.00	131	66.00
97	22.00	132	67.00
98	23.00	133	68.00
99	24.00	134	69.00
100	25.00	135	70.00
101	27.00	136	71.00
102	29.00	137	72.00
103	31.00	138	73.00
104	33.00	139	74.00
		140	75.00

Quota Allocation

The total 2002 sales budget for G.E. Appliances division was about $100 million, a 14 percent sales increase over 1999. Barr's share of the $33 million Western Region quota was $13.3 million, also a 14 percent increase over 1999. Barr had two weeks to allocate the quota among his five territories. He needed to consider factors such as historical allocation, economic outlook, dealer changes, personnel changes, untapped potential, new franchises or store openings, and buying group activity (volume purchases by associations of independent dealers).

Sales Force

There were five sales territories within B.C. (Exhibit 3). Territories were determined on the basis of number of customers, sales volume of customers, geographic size, and experience of the salesman. Territories were altered periodically to deal with changed circumstances.

One territory was comprised entirely of contract customers. Contract sales were sales in bulk lots to builders and developers who used the appliances in housing units. Because the appliances were not resold at retail, G.E took a lower profit margin on such sales.

EXHIBIT 3
G.E. Appliances—
Sales Territories

Territory Designation	Description
9961 Greater Vancouver (Garth Rizzuto)	Hudson's Bay, Firestone, Kmart, McDonald Supply, plus seven independent dealers
9962 Interior (Dan Seguin)	All customers from Quesnel to Nelson, including contract sales (50 customers)
9963 Coastal (Ken Block)	Eatons, Woodwards, plus Vancouver Island north of Duncan and upper Fraser Valley (east of Clearbrook) (20 customers)
9964 Independent and Northern (Fred Speck)	All independents in lower mainland and South Vancouver Island, plus northern B. C. and Yukon (30 customers)
9967 Contract (Jim Wiste)	Contract sales Vancouver, Victoria, All contract sales outside 9962 (50–60 customers)

G.E. Appliances recruited M.B.A. graduates for their sales force. They sought bright, educated people who were willing to relocate anywhere in Canada. The company intended that these people would ultimately be promoted to managerial positions. The company also hired experienced career salesmen to get a blend of experience in the sales force. However, the typical salesman was under 30, aggressive, and upwardly mobile. G.E.'s sales training program covered only product knowledge. It was not felt necessary to train recruits in sales techniques.

Allocation Procedure

At the time Barr assumed the job of district sales manager, he had a meeting with the former sales manager, Ken Philips. Philips described to Barr the method he had used in the past to allocate the quota. As Barr understood it, the procedure was as follows.

The quota was received in October in the form of a desired percentage sales increase. The first step was to project current sales to the end of the year. This gave a base to which the increase was added for an estimation of the next year's quota.

From this quota, the value of contract sales was allocated. Contract sales were allocated first because the market was considered the easiest to forecast. The amount of contract sales in the sales mix was constrained by the lower profit margin on such sales.

The next step was to make a preliminary allocation by simply adding the budgeted percentage increase to the year-end estimates for each territory. Although this allocation seemed fair on the surface, it did not take into account the differing situations in the territories, or the difficulty of attaining such an increase.

The next step was examination of the sales data compiled by G.E Weekly sales reports from all regions were fed into a central computer, which compiled them and printed out sales totals by product line for each customer, as well as other information. This information enabled the sales manager to check the reasonableness of his initial allocation through a careful analysis of the growth potential for each customer.

The analysis began with the largest accounts, such as Firestone, Hudson's Bay, and Eatons, which each bought over $1 million in appliances annually. Accounts that size were expected to achieve at least the budgeted growth. The main reason for this was that a shortfall of a few percentage points on such a large account would be difficult to make up elsewhere.

Next, the growth potential for medium-sized accounts was estimated. These accounts included McDonald Supply, Kmart, Federated Cooperative, and buying groups such as Volume Independent Purchasers (V.I.P.). Management expected the majority of sales growth to come from such accounts, which had annual sales of between $150,000 and $1 million.

At that point, about 70 percent of the accounts had been analyzed. The small accounts were estimated last. These had generally lower growth potential but were an important part of the company's distribution system.

Once all the accounts had been analyzed, the growth estimates were summed and the total compared to the budget. Usually, the growth estimates were well below the budget.

The next step was to gather more information. The salesmen were usually consulted to ensure that no potential trouble areas or good opportunities had been overlooked. The manager continued to revise and adjust the figures until the total estimated matched the budget. These projections were then summed by territory and compared to the preliminary territorial allocation.

Frequently, there were substantial differences between the two allocations. Historical allocations were then examined and the manager used his judgment in adjusting the figures until he was satisfied that the allocation was both equitable and attainable. Some factors that were considered at this stage included experience of the salesmen, competitive activities, potential store closures or openings, potential labor disputes in areas, and so forth.

The completed allocation was passed on to the regional sales manager for his approval. The process had usually taken one week or longer by this stage. Once the allocations had been approved, the district sales manager then divided them into sales quotas by product line. Often, the resulting average price did not match the expected mix between higher- and lower-priced units. Therefore, some additional adjusting of figures was necessary. The house account (used for sales to employees of the company) was used as the adjustment factor.

Once this breakdown had been completed, the numbers were printed on a budget sheet and given to the regional sales manager. He forwarded all the sheets

for his region to the central computer, which printed out sales numbers for each product line by salesman, by month. These figures were used as the salesmen's quotas for the next year.

Current Situation

Barr recognized that he faced a difficult task. He thought he was too new to the job and the area to confidently undertake an account-by-account growth analysis. However, due to his previous experience with sales budgets, he did have some sound general ideas. He also had the records of past allocation and quota attainment (Exhibit 4), as well as the assistance of the regional sales manager, Anthony Foyt.

Barr's first step was to project the current sales figures to end-of-year totals. This task was facilitated because the former manager, Philips, had been making successive projections monthly since June. Barr then made a preliminary quota allocation by adding the budgeted sales increase of 14 percent to each territory's total (Exhibit 5).

Barr then began to assess circumstances that could cause him to alter that allocation. One major problem was the resignation, effective at the end of the year, of one of the company's top salesmen, Ken Block. His territory had traditionally been one of the most difficult,

EXHIBIT 4 Sales Results

Territory	1999 Budget (× 1,000)	Percent of Total Budget	1999 Actual (× 1,000)	1999 Variance from Quota (V%)
9967 (Contract)	$2,440	26.5%	$2,267	(7)%
9961 (Greater Vancouver)	1,790	19.4	1,824	2
9962 (Interior)	1,624	17.7	1,433	(11)
9963 (Coastal)	2,111	23.0	2,364	12
9964 (Ind. dealers)	1,131	12.3	1,176	4
House	84	1.1	235	–
Total	$9,180	100.0%	$9,299	1%

Territory	2000 Budget (× 1,000)	Percent of Total Budget	2000 Actual (× 1,000)	2000 Variance from Quota (V%)
9967 (Contract)	$2,587	26.2%	$ 2,845	10%
9961 (Greater Vancouver)	2,005	20.3	2,165	8%
9962 (Interior)	1,465	14.8	1,450	(1)
9963 (Coastal)	2,405	24.4	2,358	(2)
9964 (Ind. dealers)	1,334	13.5	1,494	12
House	.52	0.8	86	—
Total	$9,848	100.0%	$10,398	5%

EXHIBIT 5 Sales Projections and Quotas, 2001–2002

Projected Sales Results 2001

Territory	Oct. 2001 Year to Date	2001 Projected Total	2001 Budget	Percent of Total Budget	Projected Variance from Quota (V%)
9967	$2,447	$ 3,002	$ 2,859	25.0%	5%
9961	2,057	2,545	2,401	21.0	6
9962	1,318	1,623	1,727	15.1	(6)
9963	2,124	2,625	2,734	23.9	(4)
9964	1,394	1,720	1,578	13.8	
House	132	162	139	1.2	—
Total	**$9,474**	**$11,677**	**$11,438**	**100.0%**	**2%**

Preliminary Allocation 2002

Territory	2001 Projection	2002 Budget*	Percent of Total Budget
9967	$ 3,002	$ 3,422	25.7%
9961	2,545	2,901	21.8
9962	1,623	1,854	13.9
9963	2,625	2,992	22.5
9964	1,720	1,961	14.7
House	162	185	1.3
Total	**$11,677**	**$13,315**	**100.0%***

*2002 budget = 2001 territory projections + 14% = $13,315.

and Barr believed it would be unwise to replace Block with a novice salesman.

Barr considered shifting one of the more experienced salesmen into that area. However, that would have disrupted service in an additional territory, which was undesirable because it took several months for a salesman to build up a good rapport with customers. Barr's decision would affect his quota allocation because a salesman new to a territory could not be expected to immediately sell as well as the incumbent, and a novice salesman would require an even longer period of adaptation.

Barr was also concerned about territory 9,961. The territory comprised two large national accounts and several major independent dealers. The buying decisions for the national accounts were made at their head offices, where G.E.'s regional salesmen had no control over the decisions. Recently, Barr had heard rumors that one of the national accounts was reviewing its purchase of G.E. Appliances. If it were to delist even some product lines, it would be a major blow to the salesman, Rizzuto, whose potential sales would be greatly reduced. Barr was unsure how to deal with that situation.

Another concern for Barr was the wide variance in buying of some accounts. Woodwards, Eatons, and McDonald Supply had large fluctuations from year to year. Also, Eatons, Hudson's Bay, and Woodwards had plans to open new stores in the Vancouver area sometime during the year. The sales increase to be generated by these events was hard to estimate.

The general economic outlook was poor. The Canadian dollar had fallen to 92 cents U.S. and unemployment was at about 8 percent. The government's anti-inflation program, which was scheduled to end in November 2002, had managed to keep inflation to the 8 percent level, but economists expected higher inflation and increased labor unrest during the postcontrol period.

The economic outlook was not the same in all areas. For instance, the Okanagan (9,962) was a very depressed area. Tourism was down and fruit farmers were doing poorly despite good weather and record prices. Vancouver Island was still recovering from a 200 percent increase in ferry fares, while the lower mainland appeared to be in a relatively better position.

In the contract segment, construction had shown an increase over 2000. However, labor unrest was common. There had been a crippling eight-week strike in 2000, and there was a strong possibility of another strike in 2002.

With all of this in mind, Barr was very concerned that he allocate the quota properly because of the bonus system implications. How should he proceed? To help him in his decision, he reviewed a note on development of a sales commission plan that he had obtained while attending a seminar on sales management the previous year (see Appendix below).

Appendix: Development of a Sales Commission Plan

A series of steps are required to establish the foundation on which a sales commission plan can be built. These steps are as follows:

A. Determine Specific Sales Objectives of Positions to Be Included in Plan

For a sales commission plan to succeed, it must be designed to encourage the attainment of the business objectives of the component division. Before deciding on the specific measures of performance to be used in the plan, the component should review and define its major objectives. Typical objectives might be:

- Increase sales volume.
- Do an effective balanced selling job in a variety of product lines.
- Improve market share.
- Reduce selling expense to sales ratios.
- Develop new accounts or territories.
- Introduce new products.

Although it is probably neither desirable nor necessary to include all such objectives as specific measures of performance in the plan, they should be kept in mind, at least to the extent that the performance measures chosen for the plan are compatible with and do not work against the overall accomplishment of the component's business objectives.

Also, the relative current importance or ranking of these objectives will provide guidance in selecting the number and type of performance measures to be included in the plan.

B. Determine Quantitative Performance Measures to Be Used

Although it may be possible to include a number of measures in a particular plan, there is a drawback to using so many as to overly complicate it and fragment the impact of any one measure on the participants. A plan that is difficult to understand will lose a great deal of its motivation force, as well as be costly to administer properly.

For those who currently have a variable sales compensation plan(s) for their salespeople, a good starting point would be to consider the measures used in those plans. Although the measurements used for sales managers need not be identical, they should at least be compatible with those used to determine their salespeople's commissions.

However, keep in mind that a performance measure that may not be appropriate for individual salespeople may be a good one to apply to their manager. Measurements involving attainment of a share of a defined market, balanced selling for a variety of products, and control of district or region expenses might fall into this category.

Listed in Exhibit 6 are a variety of measurements that might be used to emphasize specific sales objectives.

For most components, all or most of these objectives will be desirable to some extent. The point is to select those of greatest importance where it will be possible to establish measures of standard or normal performance for individuals, or at least small groups of individuals working as a team.

If more than one performance measurement is to be used, the relative weighting of each measurement must be determined. If a measure is to be effective, it must carry enough weight to have at least some noticeable effect on the commission earnings of an individual.

As a general guide, it would be unusual for a plan to include more than two or three quantitative measures with a minimum weighting of 15 to 20 percent of planned commissions for any one measurement.

C. Establish Commission Payment Schedule for Each Performance Measure

1. Determine appropriate range of performance for each measurement. The performance range for a measurement defines the percent of standard performance (%R) at which commission earnings start to the point where they reach maximum.

EXHIBIT 6
Tailoring
Commission Plan
Measurements to
Fit Component
Objectives

Objectives	Possible Plan Measurements
1. Increase sale/orders volume	Net sales billed or orders received against quota.
2. Increase sales of particular lines	Sales against product line quotas with weighted sales credits on individual lines.
3. Increase market share	Percent realization (%R) of shares bogey.
4. Do balanced selling job	%R of product line quotas with commissions increasing in proportion to number of lines up to quota.
5. Increase profitability	Margin realized from sales.
	Vary sales credits to emphasize profitable product lines.
	Vary sales credit in relation to amount of price discount.
6. Increase dealer sales	Pay distributor, sales people, or sales manager in relation to realization of sales quotas of assigned dealers.
7. Increase sales calls	%R of targeted calls per district or region.
8. Introduce new product	Additional sales credits on new line for limited period.
9. Control expense	%R of expense to sales or margin ratio. Adjust sales credit in proportion to variance from expense budget.
10. Sales teamwork	Share of incentive based upon group results.

The minimum point of the performance range for a given measurement should be set so that a majority of the participants can earn at least some incentive pay and the maximum set at a point that is possible of attainment by some participants. These points will vary with the type of measure used and the degree of predictability of individual budgets or other forms of measurement. In a period where overall performance is close to standard, 90 to 95 percent of the participants should fall within the performance range.

For the commission plan to be effective, most of the participants should be operating within the performance range most of the time. If a participant is either far below the minimum of this range or has reached the maximum, further improvement will not affect his or her commission earnings, and the plan will be largely inoperative as far as he or she is concerned.

Actual past experience of %R attained by participants is obviously the best indicator of what this range should be for each measure used. Lacking this, it is better to err on the side of having a wider range than one that proves to be too narrow. If some form of group

measure is used, the variation from standard performance is likely to be less for the group in total than for individuals within it. For example, the performance range for total district performance would probably be narrower than the range established for individual salespeople within a district.

2. Determine appropriate reward to risk ratio for commission earnings. This refers to the relationship of commission earned at standard performance to maximum commission earnings available under the plan. A plan that pays 10 percent of base salary for normal or standard performance and pays 30 percent as a maximum commission would have a 2 to 1 ratio. In other words, the participant can earn twice as much (20 percent) for above-standard performance as he or she stands to lose for below-standard performance (10 percent).

Reward under a sales commission plan should be related to the effort involved to produce a given result. To adequately encourage above-standard results, the reward to risk ratio should generally be at least 2 to 1. The proper control of incentive plan payments lies in the proper setting of performance standards, not in the setting of a low maximum payment for outstanding results that provides a minimum variation in individual earnings. Generally, a higher percentage of base salary should be paid for each 1%R above 100 percent than has been paid for each 1%R up to 100%R to reflect the relative difficulty involved in producing above-standard results.

Once the performance range and reward to risk ratios have been determined, the schedule of payments for each performance measure can then be calculated. This will show the percentage of the participant's base salary earned for various performance results (%R) from the point at which commissions start to maximum [sic] performance. For example, for measurement paying 20 percent of salary for standard performance:

Percent Base Salary Earned		Percent of Sales Quota
1% of base salary for each + 1%R	0% 20%	80% or below 100% (standard performance)
1.33% of base salary for each + 1%R	60%	130% or above

D. Prepare Draft of Sales Commission Plan

After completing the above steps, a draft of a sales commission plan should be prepared using the outline below as a guide.

Keys to effective commission plans

1. Get the understanding and acceptance of the commission plan by the managers who will be involved in carrying it out. They must be convinced of its effectiveness to properly explain and "sell" the plan to the salespeople.

2. In turn, be sure the plan is presented clearly to the salespeople so that they have a good understanding of how the plan will work. We find that good acceptance of a sales commission plan on the part of salespeople correlates closely with how well they understood the plan and its effect on their commission. Salespeople must be convinced that the measurements used are factors they can control by their selling efforts.

3. Be sure the measurements used in the commission plan encourage the salespeople to achieve the marketing goals of your operation. For example, if sales volume is the only performance measure, salespeople will concentrate on producing as much dollar volume as possible by spending most of their time on products with high volume potential. It will be difficult to get them to spend much time on introducing new products with relatively low volume, handling customer complaints, and so on. Even though a good portion of their compensation may still be in salary, you can be sure they will wind up doing the things they feel will maximize their commission earnings.

4. One good solution to maintaining good sales direction is to put at least a portion of the commission earnings in an "incentive pool" to be distributed by the sales manager according to his or her judgment. This "pool" can vary in size according to some qualitative measure of the sales group's performance, but the manager can set individual measurements for each salesperson and reward each person according to how well he or she fulfills the goals.

5. If at all possible, you should test the plan for a period of time, perhaps in one or two sales areas or districts. To make it a real test, you should actually pay commission earnings to the participants, but the potential risk and rewards can be limited. No matter how well a plan has been conceived, not all the potential pitfalls will be apparent until you've actually operated the plan for a period of time. The test period is a relatively painless way to get some experience.

6. Finally, after the plan is in operation, take time to analyze the results. Is the plan accomplishing what you want it to do, both in terms of business results produced and in realistically compensating salespeople for their efforts?

Case 6-4

China and India: Opportunities and Challenges

It may not top the must-see list of many tourists. But to appreciate Shanghai's ambitious view of its future, there is no better place than the Urban Planning Exhibition Hall, a glass-and-metal structure across from People's Square. The highlight is a scale model bigger than a basketball court of the entire metropolis—every skyscraper, house, lane, factory, dock, and patch of green space—in the year 2020.

There are white plastic showpiece towers designed by architects such as I.M. Pei and Sir Norman Foster. There are immense new industrial parks for autos and petrochemicals, along with new subway lines, airport runways, ribbons of expressway, and an elaborate riverfront development, site of the 2010 World Expo. Nine futuristic planned communities for 800,000 residents each, with generous parks, retail districts, man-made lakes, and nearby college campuses, rise in the suburbs. The message is clear. Shanghai already is looking well past its industrial age to its expected emergence as a global mecca of knowledge workers. "In an information economy, it is very important to have urban space with a better natural and social environment," explains Architectural Society of Shanghai President Zheng Shiling, a key city adviser.

It is easy to dismiss such dreams as bubble-economy hubris—until you take into account the audacious goals Shanghai already has achieved. Since 1990, when the city still seemed caught in a socialist time warp, Shanghai has erected enough high-rises to fill Manhattan. The once-rundown Pudong district boasts a space-age skyline, some of the world's biggest industrial zones, dozens of research centers, and a bullet train. This is the story of China, where an extraordinary ability to mobilize workers and capital has tripled per capita income in a generation, and has eased 300 million out of poverty. Leaders now are frenetically laying the groundwork for decades of new growth.

Invaluable Role

Now hop a plane to India. It is hard to tell this is the world's other emerging superpower. Jolting sights of extreme poverty abound even in the business capitals.

A lack of subways and a dearth of expressways result in nightmarish traffic.

But visit the office towers and research and development centers sprouting everywhere, and you see the miracle. Here, Indians are playing invaluable roles in the global innovation chain. Motorola, Hewlett-Packard, Cisco Systems, and other tech giants now rely on their Indian teams to devise software platforms and dazzling multimedia features for next-generation devices. Google principal scientist Krishna Bharat is setting up a Bangalore lab complete with colorful furniture, exercise balls, and a Yamaha organ—like Google's Mountain View (Calif.) headquarters—to work on core search-engine technology. Indian engineering houses use 3-D computer simulations to tweak designs of everything from car engines and forklifts to aircraft wings for such clients as General Motors Corp. and Boeing Co. Financial and market-research experts at outfits like B2K, OfficeTiger, and Iris crunch the latest disclosures of blue-chip companies for Wall Street. By 2010 such outsourcing work is expected to quadruple, to $56 billion a year.

Even more exhilarating is the pace of innovation, as tech hubs like Bangalore spawn companies producing their own chip designs, software, and pharmaceuticals. "I find Bangalore to be one of the most exciting places in the world," says Dan Scheinman, Cisco Systems Inc.'s senior vice-president for corporate development. "It is Silicon Valley in 1999." Beyond Bangalore, Indian companies are showing a flair for producing high-quality goods and services at ridiculously low prices (page 64), from $50 air flights and crystal-clear 2¢-a-minute cell-phone service to $2,200 cars and cardiac operations by top surgeons at a fraction of U.S. costs. Some analysts see the beginnings of hyper-competitive multinationals. "Once they learn to sell at Indian prices with world quality, they can compete anywhere," predicts University of Michigan management guru C.K. Prahalad. Adds A. T. Kearney high-tech consultant John Ciacchella: "I don't think U.S. companies realize India is building next-generation service companies."

Simultaneous Takeoffs

China and India. Rarely has the economic ascent of two still relatively poor nations been watched with such a mixture of awe, opportunism, and trepidation. The postwar era witnessed economic miracles in Japan and South Korea. But neither was populous enough to power worldwide growth or change the game in a complete spectrum of industries. China and India, by contrast, possess the weight and dynamism to transform the 21st-century global economy. The closest parallel to their emergence is the saga of 19th-century America, a huge continental economy with a young, driven workforce that grabbed the lead in agriculture, apparel, and the high technologies of the era, such as steam engines, the telegraph, and electric lights.

But in a way, even America's rise falls short in comparison to what's happening now. Never has the world seen the simultaneous, sustained takeoffs of two nations that together account for one-third of the planet's

population. For the past two decades, China has been growing at an astounding 9.5% a year, and India by 6%. Given their young populations, high savings, and the sheer amount of catching up they still have to do, most economists figure China and India possess the fundamentals to keep growing in the 7%-to-8% range for decades (Exhibit 1).

Barring cataclysm, within three decades India should have vaulted over Germany as the world's third-biggest economy. By mid-century, China should have overtaken the U.S. as No.1. By then, China and India could account for half of global output. Indeed, the troika of China, India, and the U.S.—the only industrialized nation with significant population

EXHIBIT 1

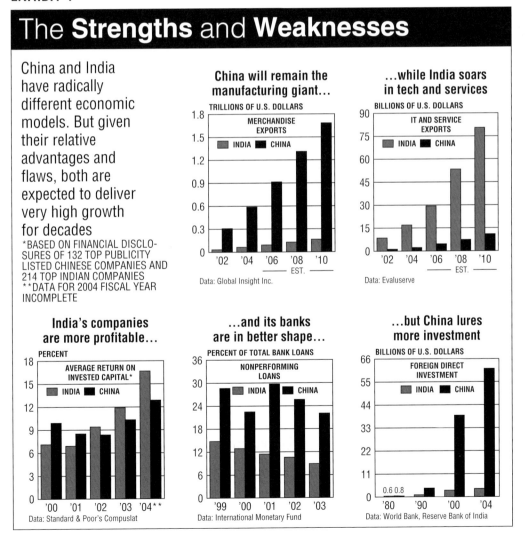

The **Strengths** and **Weaknesses**

China and India have radically different economic models. But given their relative advantages and flaws, both are expected to deliver very high growth for decades

*BASED ON FINANCIAL DISCLOSURES OF 132 TOP PUBLICLY LISTED CHINESE COMPANIES AND 214 TOP INDIAN COMPANIES
**DATA FOR 2004 FISCAL YEAR INCOMPLETE

China will remain the manufacturing giant...
TRILLIONS OF U.S. DOLLARS
MERCHANDISE EXPORTS
INDIA ■ CHINA
Data: Global Insight Inc.

...while India soars in tech and services
BILLIONS OF U.S. DOLLARS
IT AND SERVICE EXPORTS
INDIA ■ CHINA
Data: Evalueserve

India's companies are more profitable...
PERCENT
AVERAGE RETURN ON INVESTED CAPITAL*
INDIA ■ CHINA
Data: Standard & Poor's Compustat

...and its banks are in better shape...
PERCENT OF TOTAL BANK LOANS
NONPERFORMING LOANS
INDIA ■ CHINA
Data: International Monetary Fund

...but China lures more investment
BILLIONS OF U.S. DOLLARS
FOREIGN DIRECT INVESTMENT
INDIA ■ CHINA
Data: World Bank, Reserve Bank of India

EXHIBIT 2

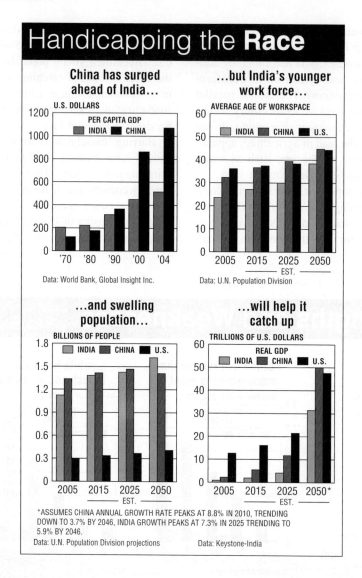

Handicapping the **Race**

China has surged ahead of India...

U.S. DOLLARS

PER CAPITA GDP
INDIA ■ CHINA

Data: World Bank, Global Insight Inc.

...but India's younger work force...

AVERAGE AGE OF WORKSPACE
INDIA ■ CHINA ■ U.S.

EST.

Data: U.N. Population Division

...and swelling population...

BILLIONS OF PEOPLE
INDIA ■ CHINA ■ U.S.

EST.

*ASSUMES CHINA ANNUAL GROWTH RATE PEAKS AT 8.8% IN 2010, TRENDING DOWN TO 3.7% BY 2046, INDIA GROWTH PEAKS AT 7.3% IN 2025 TRENDING TO 5.9% BY 2046.

Data: U.N. Population Division projections

...will help it catch up

TRILLIONS OF U.S. DOLLARS
REAL GDP
INDIA ■ CHINA ■ U.S.

EST.

Data: Keystone-India

growth—by most projections will dwarf every other economy (Exhibit 2).

What makes the two giants especially powerful is that they complement each other's strengths. An accelerating trend is that technical and managerial skills in both China and India are becoming more important than cheap assembly labor. China will stay dominant in mass manufacturing, and is one of the few nations building multibillion-dollar electronics and heavy industrial plants. India is a rising power in software, design, services, and precision industry. This raises a provocative question: What if the two nations merge into one giant "Chindia?" Rival political and economic ambitions make that unlikely. But if their industries

truly collaborate, "they would take over the world tech industry," predicts Forrester Research Inc. analyst Navi Radjou.

In a practical sense, the yin and yang of these immense workforces already are converging. True, annual trade between the two economies is just $14 billion. But thanks to the Internet and plunging telecom costs, multinationals are having their goods built in China with software and circuitry designed in India. As interactive design technology makes it easier to perfect virtual 3-D prototypes of everything from telecom routers to turbine generators on PCs, the distance between India's low-cost laboratories and China's low-cost factories shrinks by the month. Managers in the vanguard of globalization's new wave say the impact will be nothing less than explosive. "In a few years you'll see most companies unleashing this massive productivity surge," predicts Infosys Technologies CEO Nandan M. Nilekani.

To globalization's skeptics, however, what's good for Corporate America translates into layoffs and lower pay for workers. Little wonder the West is suffering from future shock. Each new Chinese corporate take-over bid or revelation of a major Indian outsourcing deal elicits howls of protest by U.S. politicians. Washington think tanks are publishing thick white papers charting China's rapid progress in microelectronics, nanotech, and aerospace—and painting dark scenarios about what it means for America's global leadership.

Such alarmism is understandable. But the U.S. and other established powers will have to learn to make room for China and India. For in almost every dimension—as consumer markets, investors, producers, and users of energy and commodities—they will be 21st-century heavyweights (Exhibit 3). The growing economic might will carry into geopolitics as well. China and India are more assertively pressing their interests in the Middle East and Africa, and China's military will likely challenge U.S. dominance in the Pacific.

One implication is that the balance of power in many technologies will likely move from West to East (Exhibit 4). An obvious reason is that China and India graduate a combined half a million engineers and scientists a year, vs. 60,000 in the U.S. In life sciences,

projects the McKinsey Global Institute, the total number of young researchers in both nations will rise by 35%, to 1.6 million by 2008. The U.S. supply will drop by 11%, to 760,000. As most Western scientists will tell you, China and India already are making important contributions in medicine and materials that will help everyone. Because these nations can throw more brains at technical problems at a fraction of the cost, their contributions to innovation will grow (Exhibit 5).

Consumers Rising

American business isn't just shifting research work because Indian and Chinese brains are young, cheap, and plentiful. In many cases, these engineers combine skills—mastery of the latest software tools, a knack for complex mathematical algorithms, and fluency in new multimedia technologies—that often surpass those of their American counterparts. As Cisco's Scheinman puts it: "We came to India for the costs, we stayed for the quality, and we're now investing for the innovation."

A rising consumer class also will drive innovation (Exhibit 6). This year, China's passenger car market is expected to reach 3 million, No. 3 in the world. China already has the world's biggest base of cell phone subscribers—350 million—and that is expected to near 600 million by 2009. In two years, China should overtake the U.S. in homes connected to broadband. Less noticed is that India's consumer market is on the same explosive trajectory as China five years ago. Since 2000,

EXHIBIT 3

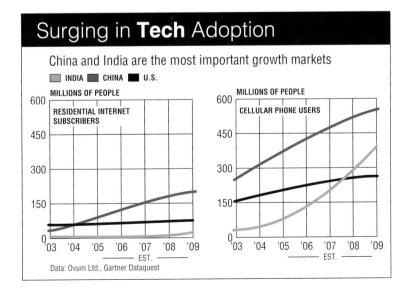

Surging in **Tech** Adoption

China and India are the most important growth markets

INDIA CHINA U.S.

MILLIONS OF PEOPLE — RESIDENTIAL INTERNET SUBSCRIBERS

MILLIONS OF PEOPLE — CELLULAR PHONE USERS

Data: Ovum Ltd., Gartner Dataquest

EXHIBIT 4

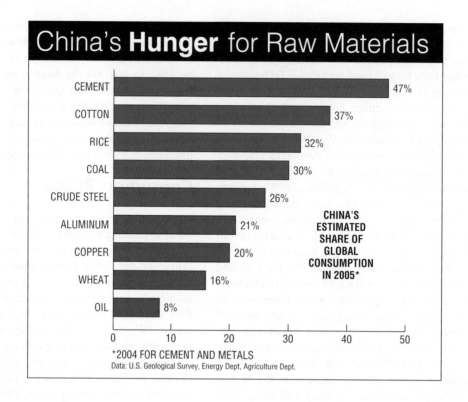

China's **Hunger** for Raw Materials

CEMENT — 47%
COTTON — 37%
RICE — 32%
COAL — 30%
CRUDE STEEL — 26%
ALUMINUM — 21%
COPPER — 20%
WHEAT — 16%
OIL — 8%

CHINA'S ESTIMATED SHARE OF GLOBAL CONSUMPTION IN 2005*

0   10   20   30   40   50

*2004 FOR CEMENT AND METALS
Data: U.S. Geological Survey, Energy Dept, Agriculture Dept.

EXHIBIT 5

Booming **Growth** in Young Professionals

China and India are racing ahead of the U.S. in numbers of young professionals*

INDIA   CHINA   U.S.

FINANCE AND ACCOUNTING — MILLIONS — 3.0, 2.4, 1.8, 1.2, 0.6, 0 — '03 '04 '05 '06 '07 '08 — EST.

ENGINEERING — MILLIONS — 2.5, 2.0, 1.5, 1.0, 0.5, 0 — '03 '04 '05 '06 '07 '08 — EST.

LIFE SCIENCES — THOUSANDS — 900, 800, 700, 600, 500, 0 — '03 '04 '05 '06 '07 '08 — EST.

*CUMULATIVE TOTAL NUMBER OF UNIVERSITY GRADUATES WITH SEVEN OR FEWER YEARS OF EXPERIENCE
Data: McKinsey Global Institute

the number of cellular subscribers has rocketed from 5.6 million to 55 million.

What's more, Chinese and Indian consumers and companies now demand the latest technologies and features. Studies show the attitudes and aspirations of today's young Chinese and Indians resemble those of Americans a few decades ago. Surveys of thousands of young adults in both nations by marketing firm Grey Global Group found they are overwhelmingly optimistic about the future, believe success is in their hands,

EXHIBIT 6

Source: *BusinessWeek*

A Profile of **Youth** in India and China

CHINA	INDIA
66% OF YOUNG CHINESE ADULTS REGARD THEMSELVES AS INDIVIDUALISTS	**62%** OF YOUNG SINGLE WOMEN SAY IT IS O.K. TO HAVE FAULTS THAT OTHERS CAN SEE
23% OF YOUNG CHINESE ADULTS SAY IT IS NOT IMPORTANT TO HAVE A CHILD	**76%** OF YOUNG SINGLE WOMEN SAY THEY SHOULD DECIDE WHEN TO HAVE A CHILD
64% OF YOUNG ADULTS SAY MARRIED MEN SHOULD DO HOUSEWORK	**51%** OF YOUNG URBAN WOMEN SAY A BIG HOUSE AND CAR ARE KEY TO HAPPINESS

Data: Grey Global Group

and view products as status symbols. In China, it's fashionable for the upwardly mobile to switch high-end cell phones every three months, says Josh Li, managing director of Grey's Beijing office, because an old model suggests "you are not getting ahead and updated." That means these nations will be huge proving grounds for next-generation multimedia gizmos, networking equipment, and wireless Web services, and will play a greater role in setting global standards. In consumer electronics, "we will see China in a few years going from being a follower to a leader in defining consumer-electronics trends," predicts Philips Semiconductors Executive Vice-President Leon Husson.

For all the huge advantages they now enjoy, India and China cannot assume their role as new superpowers is assured. Today, China and India account for a mere 6% of global gross domestic product—half that of Japan. They must keep growing rapidly just to provide jobs for tens of millions entering the workforce annually, and to keep many millions more from crashing back into poverty. Both nations must confront ecological degradation that's as obvious as the smog shrouding Shanghai and Bombay, and face real risks of social strife, war, and financial crisis. Increasingly, such problems will be the world's problems. Also, with wages rising fast, especially in many skilled areas, the cheap labor edge won't last forever. Both nations will go through many boom and harrowing bust cycles. And neither country is yet producing companies like Samsung, Nokia, or Toyota that put it all together, developing, making, and marketing world-beating products.

Both countries, however, have survived earlier crises and possess immense untapped potential. In China, serious development only now is reaching the 800 million people in rural areas, where per capita annual income is just $354. In areas outside major cities, wages are as little as 45¢ an hour. "This is why China can have another 20 years of high-speed growth," contends Beijing University economist Hai Wen.

Very impressive. But India's long-term potential may be even higher. Due to its one-child policy, China's working-age population will peak at 1 billion in 2015 and then shrink steadily. China then will have to provide for a graying population that has limited retirement benefits. India has nearly 500 million people under age 19 and higher fertility rates. By mid-century, India is expected to have 1.6 billion people—and 220 million more workers than China. That could be a source for instability, but a great advantage for growth if the government can provide education and opportunity for India's masses. New Delhi just now is pushing to open its power, telecom, commercial real estate and retail sectors to foreigners. These industries could lure big capital inflows. "The pace of institutional changes and industries being liberalized is phenomenal," says Chief Economist William T. Wilson of consultancy Keystone Business Intelligence India. "I believe India has a better model than China, and over time will surpass it in growth."

For its part, China has yet to prove it can go beyond forced-march industrialization. China directs massive investment into public works and factories, a wildly successful formula for rapid growth and job creation. But considering its massive manufacturing output, China is surprisingly weak in innovation. A full 57% of exports are from foreign-invested factories, and China underachieves in software, even with 35 software colleges and plans to graduate 200,000 software engineers a year. It's not for lack of genius. Microsoft Corp.'s 180-engineer R&D lab in Beijing, for example, is one of the world's most productive sources of innovation in computer graphics and language simulation.

While China's big state-run R&D institutes are close to the cutting edge at the theoretical level, they have yet to yield many commercial breakthroughs. "China has a lot of capability," says Microsoft Chief Technology Officer Craig Mundie. "But when you look under the covers, there is not a lot of collaboration with industry." The lack of intellectual property protection, and Beijing's heavy role in building up its own tech companies, make many other multinationals leery of doing serious R&D in China.

China also is hugely wasteful. Its 9.5% growth rate in 2004 is less impressive when you consider that $850 billion—half of GDP—was plowed into already-glutted sectors like crude steel, vehicles, and office buildings. Its factories burn fuel five times less efficiently than in the West, and more than 20% of bank loans are bad. Two-thirds of China's 13,000 listed companies don't earn back their true cost of capital, estimates Beijing National Accounting Institute President Chen Xiaoyue. "We build the roads and industrial parks, but we sacrifice a lot," Chen says.

India, by contrast, has had to develop with scarcity. It gets scant foreign investment, and has no room to waste fuel and materials like China. India also has Western legal institutions, a modern stock market, and private banks and corporations. As a result, it is far more capital-efficient. A *BusinessWeek* analysis of Standard & Poor's Compustat data on 346 top listed companies in both nations shows Indian corporations have achieved higher returns on equity and invested capital in the past five years in industries from autos to food products. The average Indian company posted a 16.7% return on capital in 2004, vs. 12.8% in China.

Small-Batch Expertise

The burning question is whether India can replicate China's mass manufacturing achievement. India's info-tech services industry, successful as it is, employs fewer than 1 million people. But 200 million Indians subsist on $1 a day or less. Export manufacturing is one of India's best hopes of generating millions of new jobs.

India has sophisticated manufacturing knowhow. Tata Steel is among the world's most-efficient producers. The country boasts several top precision auto parts companies, such as Bharat Forge Ltd. The world's biggest supplier of chassis parts to major auto makers, it employs 1,200 engineers at its heavily automated

Pune plant. India's forte is small-batch production of high-value goods requiring lots of engineering, such as power generators for Cummins Inc. and core components for General Electric Co. CAT scanners.

What holds India back are bureaucratic red tape, rigid labor laws, and its inability to build infrastructure fast enough. There are hopeful signs. Nokia Corp. is building a major campus to make cell phones in Madras, and South Korea's Pohang Iron & Steel Co. plans a $12 billion complex by 2016 in Orissa state. But it will take India many years to build the highways, power plants, and airports needed to rival China in mass manufacturing. With Beijing now pushing software and pledging intellectual property rights protection, some Indians fret design work will shift to China to be closer to factories. "The question is whether China can move from manufacturing to services faster than we can solve our infrastructure bottlenecks," says President Aravind Melligeri of Bangalore-based QuEST, whose 700 engineers design gas turbines, aircraft engines, and medical gear for GE and other clients.

However the race plays out, Corporate America has little choice but to be engaged—heavily. Motorola illustrates the value of leveraging both nations to lower costs and speed up development. Most of its hardware is assembled and partly designed in China. Its R&D center in Bangalore devises about 40% of the software in its new phones. The Bangalore team developed the multimedia software and user interfaces in the hot Razr cell phone. Now, they are working on phones that display and send live video, stream movies from the Web, or route incoming calls to voicemail when you are shifting gears in a car. "This is a very, very critical, state-of-the-art resource for Motorola," says Motorola South Asia President Amit Sharma.

Companies like Motorola realize they must succeed in China and India at many levels simultaneously to stay competitive. That requires strategies for winning consumers, recruiting and managing R&D and professional talent, and skillfully sourcing from factories. "Over the next few years, you will see a dramatic gap opening between companies," predicts Jim Hemerling, who runs Boston Consulting Group's Shanghai practice. "It will be between those who get it and are fully mobilized in China and India, and those that are still pondering."

In the coming decades, China and India will disrupt workforces, industries, companies, and markets in ways that we can barely begin to imagine (Exhibit 7). The upheaval will test America's commitment to the global

EXHIBIT 7

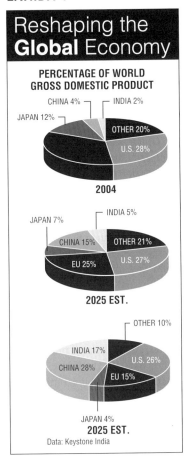

Reshaping the **Global** Economy

PERCENTAGE OF WORLD GROSS DOMESTIC PRODUCT

CHINA 4% — ⌐ INDIA 2%
JAPAN 12%
OTHER 20%
U.S. 28%
2004

JAPAN 7% ⌐ INDIA 5%
CHINA 15%   OTHER 21%
EU 25%   U.S. 27%
2025 EST.

⌐ OTHER 10%
INDIA 17%
CHINA 28%   U.S. 26%
EU 15%
JAPAN 4%
2025 EST.
Data: Keystone India

trade system, and shake its confidence. In the 19th century, Europe went through a similar trauma when it realized a new giant—the U.S.—had arrived. "It is up to America to manage its own expectation of China and India as either a threat or opportunity," says corporate strategist Kenichi Ohmae. "America should be as open-minded as Europe was 100 years ago." How these Asian giants integrate with the rest of the world will largely shape the 21st-century global economy.

Growth Obstacles

Plenty of forces can still throw the Chinese and Indian economies far off course. The economic fundamentals of both nations, with their enormous populations of young workers and consumers, point to strong growth for decades under almost every forecast. But it is instructive to remember that financial crashes, coups, political strife, and plain bad management have derailed many

other miracle economies from Southeast Asia to Latin America. And the same huge populations that can translate into economic power for China and India also could prove to be a double-edged sword if social, political, and environmental challenges are not deftly managed. Indeed, growth doesn't have to slow all that much to pose serious social problems. Both China and India need annual growth of at least 8% just to provide jobs for the tens of millions joining the workforce each year. Fear of worker unrest is a big reason Beijing has kept stoking its boom with massive lending and growth in the money supply, despite economists' warnings that it is setting the stage for a nasty bust. If India grows only 6.5% a year, which seems a respectable rate, its jobless rate would still jump, resulting in another 70 million unemployed by 2012, forecasts India's Planning Commission.

Slower growth also could keep China and India from fulfilling the widespread predictions that they will become superpowers. For example, in forecasting that India will rank just behind the U.S. as the world's No. 3 economy by mid-century, with a gross domestic product of $30 trillion, Goldman, Sachs & Co. assumes 8.5% average annual growth. But what if India grows at less than 6%, its average for the past 20 years? By 2050, it would have only a $7.3 trillion economy—smaller than Taiwan's even then and just 2.6% of global GDP, notes Stephen Howes, the World Bank's former chief India economist. Worse, India's masses would remain extremely poor. "If you don't grow fast enough, will you have social forces that bring everything to a stalemate?" asks Infosys Technologies Ltd. CEO Nandan M. Nilekani. "That's the worry."

To achieve the high growth predictions, China and India will have to overcome formidable challenges. Some of the biggest:

Environment

Both countries have paid a steep ecological price for rapid industrial and population growth, with millions of deaths attributed to air and water pollution each year. Air quality in big cities like New Delhi, Chongqing, and Bombay is among the world's worst. And forests are vanishing at alarming rates.

Enforcement of environmental laws in both nations is poor. Many power plants and factories depend on coal and don't invest in clean technologies. China is one of the world's most wasteful users of oil. If it does not act quickly, the long-term costs of health problems linked to the environment and the required cleanup will skyrocket. A growing scarcity of water in both nations could slow industry within two decades.

Political Backlash

China's Communist Party harshly represses dissent. But virtually each week brings new reports of big protests in cities and villages over corruption, pollution, or worker abuse. They underscore China's lack of democratic institutions and the widening gap between rich and poor. Serious challenges to Communist rule can still erupt, especially if the economy stalls. Judging from history, the process could be tumultuous.

India has a democracy, but it also has extremely unbalanced growth and rampant corruption. The surprise electoral defeat of the ruling Bharatiya Janata Party by a more populist coalition led by Sonia Gandhi's Congress Party in 2004 served as a warning of mass discontent. The new government also is reform minded, but the pace of economic liberalization has slowed. Further electoral setbacks for reformers are possible if the poor don't see the benefits of growth. Tensions between Hindus and Muslims have eased after bloody riots in 2003 and 2004. But communal violence remains a threat.

Financial Crisis

Debt and currency crises have derailed many high-flying emerging markets. India needed an International Monetary Fund bailout in 1991. China withstood the 1997 Asian financial crisis mainly because they lack convertible currencies. Also, Beijing controls the banks. Bailouts and the banks' near-monopoly over China's vast domestic savings have kept them solvent despite mountains of bad loans to state firms.

In 2006, however, Beijing will start letting foreign banks compete for deposits and domestic loans. That could put more financial pressure on state banks. China also is starting to loosen its currency controls a bit. China has plenty of foreign reserves now. But if Beijing can't whip its banks into shape, there's a danger that financial market liberalization will go wrong, leading to a crash. India's financial system is in stronger shape, but its public finances remain a mess, with budget deficits at the federal and state level reaching 10% of GDP.

Health

Perhaps China's biggest worry over the long term is inadequate medical care for its rapidly aging population (Exhibit 8). In 20 years, China will have an estimated 300 million people age 60 or older. Yet only one in six Chinese workers now has a pension plan, and just 5% have guaranteed medical benefits. What's more, many retirees will not be able to rely on children for support. Beijing promises to build a broader safety net, but adequate health care and pensions could consume a huge portion of GDP and deplete China's economic strength in the future.

Both nations also could face full-blown crises with AIDS, tuberculosis, avian flu, and other infectious diseases, and their health systems have been slow to mobilize. At least 5 million Indian adults are infected with HIV, one of the world's highest rates outside sub-Saharan Africa. India's National Intelligence Council predicts the number could pass 20 million in 2010. The U.N. estimates the number of Chinese with HIV could hit 10 million in five years. Some 200,000 Chinese also die annually of TB. And a serious flu epidemic could kill millions. "Many investors don't appreciate the economic damage a serious outbreak would cause in our crowded cities," says Subroto Bagchi, chief operating officer of Bangalore infotech services firm MindTree Consulting Ltd.

War

India and neighboring Pakistan have fought three times since their independence in 1947—and have had many

EXHIBIT 8

Source: *BusinessWeek*

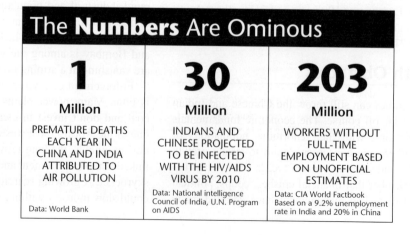

The **Numbers** Are Ominous

1 Million	**30** Million	**203** Million
PREMATURE DEATHS EACH YEAR IN CHINA AND INDIA ATTRIBUTED TO AIR POLLUTION	INDIANS AND CHINESE PROJECTED TO BE INFECTED WITH THE HIV/AIDS VIRUS BY 2010	WORKERS WITHOUT FULL-TIME EMPLOYMENT BASED ON UNOFFICIAL ESTIMATES
Data: World Bank	Data: National intelligence Council of India, U.N. Program on AIDS	Data: CIA World Factbook Based on a 9.2% unemployment rate in India and 20% in China

border skirmishes over Kashmir. Now, both nations possess nuclear weapons, so a war could be catastrophic. New Delhi and Islamabad have recently eased tensions and begun peace talks. But the rise to power of a radical Islamic regime in Pakistan, or election of a stridently Hindu nationalist government in India, could easily reignite tensions. China's biggest flash point remains Taiwan. Beijing has cooled its fiery rhetoric lately, but still vows to invade should the island declare independence. Any war in the Taiwan Strait would likely involve the U.S. and possibly Japan—China's

two biggest trade partners—and paralyze shipping in and out of China's southern ports. It also would likely result in long-term Sino-U.S. tensions that would spill into trade.

It's too much to expect for any developing nation to avoid military, financial, environmental, and health crises for decades. But the test for a great power is how well it manages a great crisis.

Source: Pete Engardio, "Crouching Tigers, Hidden Dragons," *BusinessWeek*, August 22/29, 2005, 52–61.

Case 6-5

Toyota

Yoi Kangae, Yoi Shina! that's Toyota-speak for "Good thinking means good products." The slogan is emblazoned on a giant banner hanging across the company's Takaoka assembly plant, an hour outside the city of Nagoya. Plenty of good thinking has gone into the high-tech ballet that's performed here 17 hours a day. Six separate car models—from the Corolla compact

to the new youth-oriented Scion xB—glide along on a single production line in any of a half-dozen colors. Overhead, car doors flow by on a conveyor belt that descends to floor level and drops off the right door in the correct color for each vehicle. This efficiency means Takaoka workers can build a car in just 20 hours.

The combination of speed and flexibility is world class (Exhibit 1). More important, a similar dance is happening at 30 Toyota plants worldwide, with some able to make as many as eight different models on the same line. That is leading to a monster increase

EXHIBIT 1 Global Push

Data: Toyota Motor, 2002 sales figures

Toyota's on the offensive around the globe. Here's a look at its worldwide operations:

North America

SALES: 1.94 million
Toyota's products keep gaining on the Big Three's models, while Lexus is a luxury leader. Toyota employs 35,000 people and runs 10 factories in the region, and has 11.2% of the U.S. market.

Europe

SALES: 756,000
Has a 4.4% market share, led by the **Yaris** compact and a new **Avensis** with a cleaner diesel engine. Plans to boost production in Britain and France. Lexus though, is struggling.

Southwest Asia

SALES: 268,000
Builds cars in Bangladesh, India, Pakistan, and Turkey. The durable **Qualis** SUV is a big hit in India, and Toyota plans to start building transmissions there in mid-2004.

Southeast Asia

SALES: 455,000
Assembles cars in seven countries and is expanding its factories in Thailand and Indonesia. Plans to export trucks, engines, and components from the region to 80 countries.

South America

SALES: 97,000
Builds cars in Argentina, Brazil, Colombia, and Venezuela. Regionwide revenues fell 10% last year because of economic troubles in Argentina, but sales in Brazil grew after the launch of a new **Corolla**.

Africa

SALES: 140,000
Has manufacturing plants in Kenya and South Africa. Last year, it saw sales across the continent jump 10.5%, thanks to a new **Corolla** sedan and **Prado** SUV.

China

SALES: 58,000
Playing catch-up with rivals Volkswagen and GM. In April, it agreed with FAW to make the **Land Cruiser, Corolla**, and **Crown**. Share today is about 1.5%, but Toyota wants 10% by 2010.

Japan

SALES: 1.68 million
Has maintained 40%-plus market share for five years running. New models this year include the **Sienta** compact minivan, the sportier **Wish** minivan, and a revamped **Harrier** SUV.

EXHIBIT 2   Way Ahead of the Pack

Data: Bloomberg Financial Markets, Harbour & Associates, J.D. Power & Associates, Toyo Keizai, Dresden Kleinwort, Burnham Securities. Research assistance by Susan Zegel.

	Market Cap*	Operating Profit*	Hours per Vehicle**	Defects***
Toyota	$110	$12.7	21.83	196
Nissan	54	7.5	16.83	258
Honda	40	6.1	22.27	215
DaimlerChrysler	38	5.7	28.04[†]	311
GM	24	3.8	24.44	264
Ford	22	3.6	26.14	287

*Billions
**Average assembly time (North America)
***Problems per 100 vehicles on year 2000 models
[†]Chryster only

in productivity and market responsiveness—all part of the company's obsession with what President Fujio Cho calls "the criticality of speed."

Remember when Japan was going to take over the world? Corporate America was apoplectic at the idea that every Japanese company might be as obsessive, productive, and well-managed as Toyota Motor Corp. We know what happened next: One of the longest crashes in business history revealed most of Japan Inc. to be debt-addicted, inefficient, and clueless. Today, 13 years after the Nikkei peaked, Japan is still struggling to avoid permanent decline. World domination? Hardly.

Except in one corner. In autos, the Japanese rule (Exhibit 2). And in Japan, one company—Toyota—combines the size, financial clout, and manufacturing excellence needed to dominate the global car industry in a way no company ever has. Sure, Toyota, with $146 billion in sales, may not be tops in every category. GM is bigger—for now. Nissan Motor Co. makes slightly more profit per vehicle in North America, and its U.S. plants are more efficient. Both Nissan and Honda have flexible assembly lines, too. But no car company is as strong as Toyota in so many areas.

Of course, the carmaker has always moved steadily forward: Its executives created the doctrine of *kaizen,* or continuous improvement (Exhibit 3). "They find a hole, and they plug it," says auto-industry consultant Maryann Keller. "They methodically study problems, and they solve them." But in the past few years, Toyota has accelerated these gains, raising the bar for the entire industry. Consider:

- Toyota is closing in on Chrysler to become the third-biggest carmaker in the U.S. Its U.S. share, rising steadily, is now above 11%.

- At its current rate of expansion, Toyota could pass Ford Motor Co. in mid-decade as the world's No. 2 auto maker. The No. 1 spot—still occupied by General Motors Corp., with 15% of the global market—would be the next target. President Cho's goal is 15% of global sales by 2010, up from 10% today. "They dominate wherever they go," says Nobuhiko Kawamoto, former president of Honda Motor Co. "They try to take over everything."

- Toyota has broken the Japanese curse of running companies simply for sales gains, not profit. Its operating margin of 8%-plus (vs. 2% in 1993) now dwarfs those of Detroit's Big Three. Even with the impact of the strong yen, estimated 2003 profits of $7.2 billion will be double 1999's level. On Nov. 5, the company reported profits of $4.8 billion on sales of $75 billion for the six months ended Sept. 30. Results like that have given Toyota a market capitalization of $110 billion—more than that of GM, Ford, and DaimlerChrysler combined (Exhibit 4).

- The company has not only rounded out its product line in the U.S., with sport-utility vehicles, trucks, and a hit minivan, but it also has seized the psychological advantage in the market with the Prius, an eco-friendly gasoline-electric car. "This is going to be a real paradigm shift for the industry," says board member and top engineer Hiroyuki Watanabe. In October, when the second-generation Prius reached U.S. showrooms, dealers got 10,000 orders before the car was even available.

- Toyota has launched a joint program with its suppliers to radically cut the number of steps needed to make cars and car parts. In the past year alone, the

EXHIBIT 3   Kaizen in Action

Data: Toyota Motor

Data: *BusinessWeek*, Edmunds.com Inc.

Toyota stresses constant improvement, or *kaizen,* in everything it does. Here's how the company revamped the 2004 Sienna minivan after the previous generation got disappointing reviews.

- The 3.3-liter, 230 hp engine is bigger and more powerful than before, but it gets slightly better gas mileage.
- Now has five-speed transmission instead of four.
- The 2004 is nimbler with a turning diameter of 36.8 feet—3.2 feet shorter than the previous model.
- At $23,495, it's $920 cheaper than the 2003.
- Third-row seats fold flat into the floor. On the older model they had to be removed to maximize cargo space.
- The new model is longer and wider than the 2003, with more headroom, leg room, and 12% more cargo space.

Camry

Bland? Sure, as bland as the bread and butter it is to Toyota. This reliable family sedan has been America's top-selling car in five of the past six years. $19,560–$25,920

Yaris

The snub-nosed compact is Toyota's top-seller in Europe. Its Euro-styling has made it a hit in Japan too, where it's known as the Vitz. $11,787–$14,317

Prius

A funky-looking and earth-friendly gas-electric hybrid that gets 55 mpg—but offers the power and roominess of a midsize sedan. $20,510

Tundra

This full-size pickup has built a loyal following as it has grown in bulk and power. A Double Cab model due in November will up the ante. $16,495–$31,705*

Scion xB

An attempt to be hip and edgy included underground marketing for this new car aimed at young people. Sales have been double Toyota's forecasts. $14,165–$14,965

Lexus RX330

The first Lexus built in North America, this luxury SUV boasts a smooth, car-like ride and nimble handling. It has been Lexus' U.S. sales leader. $35,700–$37,500

*Doesn't include Double cab model, which isn't yet priced.

EXHIBIT 4   Toyota's Money Machine

Data: Toyota Motor Corp., Lehman Brothers Inc.

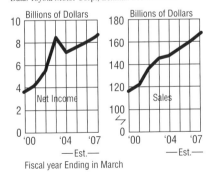

Fiscal year Ending in March

company chopped $2.6 billion out of its $113 billion in manufacturing costs without any plant closures or layoffs. Toyota expects to cut an additional $2 billion out of its cost base this year.

- Toyota is putting the finishing touches on a plan to create an integrated, flexible, global manufacturing system. In this new network, plants from Indonesia to Argentina will be designed both to customize cars for local markets and to shift production to quickly satisfy any surges in demand from markets worldwide. By tapping, say, its South African plant to meet a need in Europe, Toyota can save itself the $1 billion normally needed to build a new factory.

If Cho gets this transformation right, he'll end up with an automotive machine that makes the Americans and Germans quake. Cost-cutting and process redesign will chop out billions in expenses. That will keep margins strong and free up cash to develop new models and technologies such as the Prius, to invest in global manufacturing, and to invade markets such as Europe and China. New models and new plants will build share, which will build more clout. And if there's a hiccup—well, there's a cash-and-securities hoard of $30 billion. "This is a company that does not fear failure," says Cho.

Roadblocks?

Can anything stop Toyota? There are some potential roadblocks. Toyota doesn't always get it right: Its early attempts at the youth market, minivans, and big pickup trucks all disappointed. It remains dependent on the U.S. business for some 70% of earnings. Its Lexus luxury sedans are losing ground to BMW, though Lexus' strong SUV sales are keeping the division in the game. The average Toyota owner is about 46, a number the company must lower or risk going the way of Buick. And most of Toyota's big sellers aren't exactly head-turners.

Meanwhile, Toyota's rivals are hardly sitting still. GM is finishing up a $4.3 billion revamp of Cadillac, and a revival is in the works: Overall GM quality is on an upswing too. "Toyota is a good competitor, but they're not unbeatable," says GM Chairman G. Richard Wagoner Jr. Over at Nissan, CEO Carlos Ghosn doubts Toyota's big bet on hybrids will pay off. "There will be no revolution," he predicts. And Detroit's Big Three are praying that a strong yen will batter Toyota. If the yen sticks at 110 to the dollar over the next 12 months, Toyota could see its pretax profits shrink by $900 million.

A strengthening yen might have hammered Toyota in the 1980s, and it will certainly have an impact next year. But today, three decades after starting its global push, Toyota can't be accused of needing a cheap yen to subsidize exports. Since starting U.S. production in 1986, Toyota has invested nearly $14 billion there. What's more, many of its costs are now set in dollars: Last year, Toyota's purchases of parts and materials from 500 North American suppliers came to $19 billion—more than the annual sales of Cisco Systems Inc. or Oracle Corp. The U.S. investment is an enormous natural hedge against the yen. "About 60% of what we sold here, we built here," Toyota Chairman Hiroshi Okuda said in a Sept. 10 speech in Washington.

Better for Toyota, those cars are also among the industry's biggest money-makers. Take SUVs: Ten years ago, Toyota had a puny 4% share. Today, it owns nearly 12% of that high-margin segment with eight models ranging from the $19,000 RAV4 to the $65,000 Lexus LX 470—and makes as much as $10,000 on each high-end model it sells. The company is steadily robbing Ford, Chrysler, and GM of their primacy in the cutthroat U.S. SUV market and has largely sat out the latest round of rebates:

Toyota's average incentive per car this fall is just $647, compared with $3,812 at GM and $3,665 at Ford, according to market watcher Edmunds.com. This is one war of attrition where Detroit is clearly outgunned.

Toyota's charge into SUVs indicates a new willingness to play tough in the U.S., which it considers vital to its drive for a global 15% share. "The next era is full-size trucks and luxury, environmental, and youth cars," predicts James E. Press, chief operating officer at Toyota Motor Sales USA Inc. Toyota is already intent on boosting its 4.5% market share in pickups, the last profit refuge of the Big Three. Toyota is building an $800 million plant in San Antonio, Tex., that will allow it to more than double its Tundra output, to some 250,000 trucks a year by 2006, with rigs powerful and roomy enough to go head to head with Detroit's biggest models.

Toyota plans to extend its early lead in eco-cars by pushing the Prius and adding a hybrid Lexus RX 330 SUV next summer. The Lexus will get as much as 35 miles per gallon, compared with roughly 21 mpg for a conventional RX 330. And Toyota is vigorously attacking the youth market with the $14,500 Scion xB compact, which surprised Toyota-bashers with its angular, minimalist design. Since the Scion's U.S. launch in California in June, Toyota has sold nearly 7,700 of them, 30% better than forecast. Toyota Vice-President James Farley says three out of four buyers of the brand had no intention of buying a Toyota when they started looking. "That's exactly why we started the Scion," he says.

The Scion is evidence that Toyota's growing cash cushion gives it the means to revamp its lack-luster designs. When Cho traveled through Germany in 1994, he recalls being asked: Why are Toyota cars so poorly styled? Part of the problem, says Cho, is that too many Toyotas were designed with Japanese consumers in mind and then exported. Some worked; some flopped.

These days, design teams on the West Coast of the U.S., in southern France, and back home compete for projects. That has paid off with models such as the Yaris, Toyota's best-seller in Europe, where the company now has a 4.4% share, compared with less than 3% a decade ago. The Yaris was designed by a Greek, Sotiris Kovos, then imported successfully to Japan because of its "European" look. "Toyota has finally recognized that buyers want to feel like they have some level of style," says Wesley Brown, a consultant with auto researcher Iceology. The redesigned Solara sports coupe is getting high grades, too: A V-shape line flowing up from the grille gives it a more muscular silhouette, and its interior is 20% roomier than before.

Toyota Man

Leading Toyota to this new level of global vigor is Cho. He's Toyota Man personified: Self-effacing, ever smiling, but an executive whose radar seems to pick up every problem and opportunity. "Cho understands as much as anyone I've ever seen what's actually happening on the factory floor," says manufacturing consultant Ronald E. Harbour, whose firm's annual report on productivity is the industry bible.

That feel for the factory didn't come naturally. The 66-year-old company lifer studied law, not business, at the prestigious University of Tokyo and could have easily ended up as a faceless bureaucrat at the Ministry of Finance. But Cho learned the car business—and clearly learned it well—at the knee of Taichi Ohno, the creator of the legendary Toyota Production System, a series of in-house precepts on efficient manufacturing that changed the industry. Ohno, a brilliant but notoriously hot-headed engineer, lectured Cho about the need to be flexible and to look forward.

That advice is something Cho found invaluable when he was tapped to oversee the 1988 launch of Toyota's key U.S. plant in Georgetown, Ky., now the company's biggest U.S. factory and the maker of the Camry sedan. The good-natured and unpretentious Cho regularly worked the plant floor, making sure to shake hands with each line worker at Christmas to show his appreciation. He spoke at Rotary Club meetings and stopped to make small talk with the folks in Georgetown.

Given Toyota's booming U.S. sales in the late 1990s, few inside the company were surprised when Cho won the top job. Yet equally few had any clue that the new president was about to unleash so many powerful changes. Like his predecessor Okuda, Cho had long been frustrated by Toyota's glacial decision-making process and cultural insularity. Those had led to missed opportunities, such as when product planners at headquarters in Japan resisted calls from their U.S. colleagues to build an eight-cylinder pickup truck. Cho is rectifying that deficiency with a vengeance with the San Antonio plant.

Then three years ago, as Ghosn—"le cost killer"—was slashing billions at rival Nissan and cutting its supplier ranks in half, Cho had a revelation: If Nissan could do it, Toyota could do it better. The resulting program, called Construction of Cost Competitiveness for the 21st Century, or CCC21, taps into the company's strengths across the board to build cars more efficiently. It's also turning many operations inside out.

No Detail Too Small

Toyota has always valued frugality. It still turns down the heat at company-owned employee dormitories during working hours and labels its photocopy machines with the cost per copy to discourage overuse. But cost-cutting was often a piecemeal affair. With CCC21, Cho set a bold target of slashing prices on all key components for new models by 30%, which meant working with suppliers and Toyota's own staff to ferret out excess. "Previously, we tried to find waste here and there," says Cho. "But now there is a new dimension of proposals coming in."

In implementing CCC21, no detail is too small. For instance, Toyota designers took a close look at the grip handles mounted above the door inside most cars. By working with suppliers, they managed to cut the number of parts in these handles to five from 34, which helped cut procurement costs by 40%. As a plus, the change slashed the time needed for installation by 75%—to three seconds. "The pressure is on to cut costs at every stage," says Takashi Araki, a project manager at parts maker Aisin Seiki Co.

Just as Cho believes he can get far more out of suppliers, he thinks Toyota can make its workers vastly more productive. This is classic *kaizen*, but these days it has gone into overdrive (Exhibit 5). In the middle of the Kentucky plant, for instance, a *Kaizen* team of particularly productive employees works in a barracks-like structure. The group's sole job is coming up with ways to save time and money. Georgetown employees, for instance, recommended removing the radiator support base—the lower jaw of the car—until the last stage of assembly. That way, workers can step into the engine compartment to install parts instead of having to lean over the front end and risk straining their backs. "We used to have to duck into the car to install something," explains Darryl Ashley, 41, a soft-spoken Kentucky native who joined Toyota nine years ago.

In Cambridge, Ont., Cho is going even further: He's determined to show the world that Toyota can meet its own highest standards of excellence anywhere in its system. It was once company doctrine that Lexus could only be made in Japan. No longer. Production of the RX 330 suv started in Cambridge on Sept. 26. If the Canadian hands can deliver the same quality as their Japanese counterparts, Toyota will be able to chop shipping costs by shifting Lexus production to the market where the bulk of those cars are sold (Exhibit 6).

EXHIBIT 5
Deciphering
Toyota-Speak

A handy glossary for understanding the company's vernacular.

Kaizen

Continuous improvement. Employees are given cash rewards for ferreting out glitches in production and devising solutions.

PDCA

Plan, do, check, action. Steps in the development cycle aimed at quick decision-making in a task such as designing a car.

Obeya

Literally, "big room." Regular face-to-face brainstorming sessions among engineers, designers, marketers, and suppliers.

Pokayoke

Mistake-proofing. Use of sensors to detect missing parts or improper assembly. Robots alert workers to errors by flashing lights.

CCC21

Construction of Cost Competitiveness for the 21st century. A three-year push to slash costs of 170 components that account for 90% of parts expenses.

GBL

Global Body Line. A manufacturing process that holds auto frames together for welding with one brace instead of the 50 braces previously required.

EXHIBIT 6   Lexus: Still Looking for Traction in Europe

When Dirk Lindermann was looking for a new luxury sedan last summer, he considered Mercedes and BMW before settling on a $40,000, black Audi A4. Lexus, though, didn't even enter into the game. "Lexus has no personality," says the 40-year-old Berlin advertising executive.

That's a problem for Toyota Motor Corp. The company's smooth-driving Lexus sedans sprinted from zero to luxury-market leader in the U.S. during the 1990s, overtaking German rivals Mercedes and BMW—as well as Cadillac and Lincoln—by offering better quality and service at a lower price. But Lexus is going nowhere fast in Europe: After 12 years in showrooms, last year it registered sales of just 21,156 cars—down 11% from 2001—compared with more than 234,000 in the U.S.

Toyota itself is fast shedding any *arriviste* stigma in the Old World. Since it began producing cars on the Continent in the '90s, European sales are up nearly 60%, to 734,000. Now it wants to crack the high-end with a renewed push for Lexus. The goal is to triple sales of the six Lexus models Toyota offers there by 2010, to at least 65,000 cars. "The potential in Europe for Lexus is every bit as great as in the U.S.," says Stuart McCullough, director of Lexus Europe.

To make Lexus a success, though, Toyota needs to establish it as a separate brand. Until now, the car has been sold in Europe mainly through Toyota's 250 dealerships, along with the far less lustrous Yaris, Corolla, and Avensis models. So Toyota is trying to set up dealerships that offer luxury-car buyers the kind of white-glove service they demand. "Lexus has to establish its own heritage, not just chase BMW and Mercedes," says Tadashi Arashima, president and chief executive of Toyota Motor Marketing Europe.

Will image-conscious Europeans warm up to Lexus if the cars are sold in tony showrooms? In Spain, where exclusive Lexus dealerships have been operating since 2000, sales are up 9% so far this year, though the brand sold just 969 vehicles in the country. "We've been able to show that these cars can compete with the big German brands in quality and also offer a lot more in terms of price," says Jorge Merino, head of sales at Axel, a three-year-old Lexus dealership in Madrid.

One big selling point is Lexus' six-year warranty. And the carmaker includes three years of free checkups, maintenance, and roadside assistance. That compares with a standard guarantee of two years at most luxury brands. "I like BMW and Mercedes, but I have a feeling I may get more for my money with Lexus," says Ignacio Redondo, a legal consultant in Madrid who drives a Saab 900 but is mulling a new Lexus for the first time.

Harder, though, will be conforming to the European concept of luxury. Americans love comfort, size and dependability, while Europeans think luxury means attention to detail and brand heritage. "The biggest selling point for Lexus is that it doesn't break down," says Philipp Rosengarten, analyst at Global Insight Inc.'s automotive group. That's not enough to succeed in Europe. Instead, Lexus needs to create a desire to own the car—and even with plush dealerships and extended warranties, it has kilometers to go before reaching that goal.

By Gail Edmondson in Frankfurt, and Karen Nickel Anhalt in Berlin with Paulo Prada in Madrid

The Japanese bosses put the Canadians through their paces. The 700 workers on the RX 330 line trained for 12 weeks, including stints in Japan for 200 of them. There, the Canadians managed to beat Japanese teams in quality assessment on a mock Lexus line. Cambridge has taken Toyota's focus on *poka-yoke,* or foolproofing measures, to another level. The plant has introduced "Circle L" stations where workers must double- and triple-check parts that customers have complained about—anything from glove boxes to suspension systems. "We know that if we can get this right, we may get to build other Lexus models," says Jason Birt, a 28-year-old Lexus line worker.

The Cambridge workers are aided by a radical piece of manufacturing technology being rolled out to Toyota plants worldwide. The system, called the Global Body Line, holds vehicle frames in place while they're being welded, using just one master brace instead of the dozens of separate braces required in a standard factory. No big deal? Perhaps, but the system is half as expensive to install. Analysts say it lets Toyota save 75% of the cost of refitting a production line to build a different car, and it's key to Toyota's ability to make multiple models on a single line. Better yet, the brace increases the rigidity of the car early in production, which boosts the accuracy of welds and makes for a more stable vehicle. "The end results are improved quality, shortened weld-

ing lines, reduced capital investment, and less time to launch new vehicles," says Atsushi Niimi, president of Toyota Motor Manufacturing North America.

Cho and his managers are not just reengineering how Toyota makes its cars—they want to revolutionize how it creates products. With the rise of e-mail and teleconferencing, teams of designers, engineers, product planners, workers, and suppliers rarely all convened in the same place. Under Cho, they're again required to work face to face, in a process Toyota calls obeya—literally, "big room." This cuts the time it takes to get a car from the drawing board to the showroom. It took only 19 months to develop the 2003 Solara. That's better than 22 months for the latest Sienna minivan, and 26 months for the latest Camry—well below the industry average of about three years.

If all this sounds like Toyota is riding a powerful growth wave, well, it is. While Cho is as mild-mannered and modest as they come, the revolution he has kicked off is anything but. Toyota is in the midst of a transformative makeover—and if Cho succeeds, the entire global auto industry is in for one, too.

With Kathleen Kerwin in Detroit, Christopher Palmeri in Los Angeles, and Paul Magnusson in Washington

Source: Brian Bremner and Chester Dawson, "Can Anything Stop Toyota?" *BusinessWeek,* November 17, 2003, 114–122.

Case 6-6

Samsung Electronics Co.

The office park in northern New Jersey hardly looks like a place that plays a role in cutting-edge design. Hard by a highway interchange, the two-story building is about as distinctive as white rice. But climb the stairs to the second floor, and you'll see designers from Samsung Electronics Co. studying in pains-taking detail the American consumer psyche. There, engineer Lee Byung Moo watches from behind a two-way mirror as three women and two men stuff a stainless steel refrigerator with the contents of a half-dozen bags of groceries. After the five have finished and given their opinions on several potential configurations of drawers and compartments, Lee and two others rush into the room to take photographs and note exactly where the "shoppers" have put the ice cream, chicken, beer, milk,

and other food. "We want to know the tastes of American customers because we need to develop products that fit their lifestyle," says Lee.

Half a world away, Choi Won Min sits in a windowless room on the ground floor of a Seoul skyscraper—an equally unlikely spot to find the leading edge of design. He spends his days (and often his nights) in front of two piano keyboards, a phalanx of mixing consoles, and dozens of synthesizers. With his headphones on, he hits a note, listens intently, then tweaks a few settings and hits another key. His primary mission in the two-year-old lab: coming up with a suite of bells, boings, beeps, and buzzes for digital gadgets that will immediately say "Samsung" to users worldwide. In the past, "simple sounds seemed to be sufficient, but now we realize how important sounds are in user interfaces," Choi says.

Lee and Choi are foot soldiers in Samsung's continuing assault on the world of cool. In recent years, the South Korean company has begun gearing all it does, from financing to decision-making to training and labs, to make Samsung a finely tuned receptor of all the things that make its products must-haves in an increasingly competitive marketplace. Hundreds of millions of dollars have been spent spiffing up the look, feel, and function of everything from refrigerators and washing machines to cell phones and MP3 players. And the focus has been on research of the sort Lee and Choi are doing: finding out what's likely to sell before consumers even know they want it. The effort has paid off. Samsung has grown from a me-too producer of electronics and appliances into one of the world's leading brands—in large part because of its focus on design. "We want to be the Mercedes of home electronics," says Yun Jong Yong, Samsung's chief executive.

The way Samsung's moving, you'd think it wants to be the Ferrari. This year, Samsung won five citation in the Industrial Design Excellence Awards (IDEA)—making it the first Asian company to win more prizes than any European or American rival. (The competition is sponsored by *BusinessWeek,* which publishes the results, but the laureates are selected by the Industrial Designers Society.) And since 2000, Samsung has earned a total of 100 citations at top design contests in the U.S., Europe, and Asia. Brokerage Hyundai Securities expects Samsung to earn $10.3 billion on sales of $52.8 billion this year, up from profits of $5.2 billion and $39.8 billion in revenues last year. (Although much of that increase comes from the semiconductor division, the company's snazzy consumer products also helped.) "Samsung is the poster child for using design to increase brand value and market share," says Patrick Whitney, director of the Institute of Design at the Illinois Institute of Technology.

The change started in 1993, when Chairman Lee Kun Hee visited retailers in Los Angeles and saw that Samsung products were lost in the crowd, while those from Sony Corp. and and a few others stood out. So he ordered his managers to concentrate less on cost saving and more on coming up with unique products. The bottom line: Great design could catapult Samsung to the top ranks of global brands.

Decade of Determination

The boss spoke. Samsung listened. And the company's design push was under way. To attract better, younger designers, Samsung in 1994 moved its design center to Seoul from sleepy Suwon, a small city an hour south of the capital. That same year, Samsung hired U.S. design firm IDEO to help develop a computer monitor—the first

of many such collaborations with IDEO and other leading consultancies. Then in 1995, the company set up the Innovative Design Lab of Samsung, an in-house school where promising designers could study under experts from the Art Center College of Design in Pasadena, Calif, one of the top U.S. design schools. Samsung designers were dispatched to Egypt and India, Paris and Frankfurt, New York and Washington to tour museums, visit icons of modern architecture, and explore ruins.

Just as important, Samsung's designers have broken through the barriers of Korea's traditional Confucian hierarchies. Although Korea has loosened up as democracy has taken hold in the last 15 years, respect for elders and a reluctance to speak out of turn are still the norm, and Samsung as a whole still holds lots of meetings where Confucian order prevails. But the design center is different. Located several minutes' walk from company headquarters, it's a place with no dress code, where some younger staffers dye their hair green or pink, and where everyone is encouraged to speak up and challenge their superiors. Designers work in three- to five-person teams, with members from various specialty areas and levels of seniority—all working as equals.

The wrenching departure from tradition has paid off. Virtually all of the 19 IDEA awards Samsung has won since 2000 are the fruit of such teams. Helped by its innovative designs and egalitarian approach, Samsung has emerged as the best-selling brand in high-end TVs in the U.S., and the world's largest LCD computer monitor producer, with 17% of the global market. And Samsung has sold more than 10 million SGHE700s—the first clamshell phone with a hidden antenna—racking up some $1.2 billion in profits since its debut 14 months ago. "Good design is the most important way to differentiate ourselves from our competitors," says CEO Yun.

Many of the new design ideas are coming from outside. Last year, Samsung started sending designers abroad to spend a few months at fashion houses, cosmetics specialists, or design consultancies to stay current with what's happening in other industries. Lee Yun Jung, a senior designer who works on colors and finishes, spent last autumn in residence at a furniture designer in Italy. While she gathered plenty of ideas for product surfaces, the real eye-opener was the relaxed culture of the place. "A 23-year-old novice could interrupt the 60-year-old master," she marvels. Since returning, Lee has tried to be more open to ideas percolating up from the bottom of her department.

Today, Samsung knows it can't afford to let up. It's the first Asian company outside of Japan to use design to vault to the first tier of global companies. But in the Digital Age it's not too hard for strivers such as Lenovo of China and BenQ to make products that approach the quality of long-standing industry giants such as Sony, Panasonic, or Philips Electronics. Samsung, of course, was an upstart itself not long ago. It was the transition from analog to digital that gave the Korean company the opening it needed. "In the analog age, Samsung devoted most of its energy trying to catch up with Japanese leaders, but the arrival of digital put everybody on the same starting line," says Chin Dae Je, Korea's Information & Communication Minister and president of Samsung Electronics before joining the Cabinet last year.

These rivals—whether newcomer or veteran—aren't standing still. The newbies often hire U.S., Japanese, or Italian design consultancies to help them shape products that won't get lost in the crush of goods at Best Buy or Circuit City Stores. And those Asian upstarts are all looking to Samsung as a role model for their own transformation into global brands. The likes of Sony and Matsushita, meanwhile, are also placing a renewed emphasis on creating stand-out products. "Sony has been losing some of its edge in design," says Makoto Kogure, head of the Japanese giant's TV division. "Now we're drastically changing and [creating a] Sony identity."

Front-Loaded Design

So Samsung must continue to reinvent itself. In the past four years, the company has doubled its design staff, to 470, adding 120 of those just in the past 12 months (Exhibit 1). And since 2000, its design budget has been increasing 20% to 30% annually. To keep an eye on trends in its most important markets, Samsung now has

EXHIBIT 1

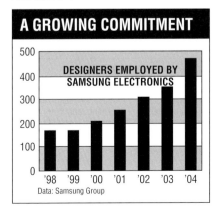

design centers in London, Los Angeles, San Francisco, and Tokyo, and this year it opened one in Shanghai. More important, Samsung is changing the processes and procedures in its design department and giving designers more power to influence not just how products look but also what gets built (Exhibit 2). "Just as a lizard cuts off its own tail to move on, we will have to break with the past to move forward," says Chung Kook Hyun, the senior vice-president who runs design operations.

Samsung's designers these days no longer have to find a way to put their boxes around the devices that engineers cook up. Instead, they often give concepts to engineers, who must then build the machine inside the box dreamed up by the designers. James Choe, for instance, recently studied research showing that consumers prefer printers in which the paper lies flat rather than feeding in vertically. Engineers working on the same project, however, preferred a vertical model because it would cut the production cost of a $110 printer by about 10%. Before Choe started at Samsung three years ago, the engineers might have won. But when the desktop laser printer rolled out last year, Choe's design had prevailed. "The engineers didn't like it, but in the end management listened to us," he says.

Sometimes the designers come up with entirely new product categories. Kang Yun Je thought Samsung could do better than its rivals with a sleek, silver, rear-projection TV sporting a curved back and superthin edges, so that when viewed from an angle it looks as thin as an LCD TV. "When we first came up with the design, we had no guarantee it could be made," says Kang, a shaggy 36-year-old who sports a goatee and wears his shirt untucked. "So I went to the head of engineering, and he said that if I could give him some time and resources, he'd try to do it."

Where to get the resources? To make sure designers get heard, Samsung has created the post of chief design officer—something few other companies have bothered to do. And to make sure top execs stay attuned to the importance of the issue, CEO Yun holds quarterly design meetings where the chiefs of all the business units review new products and evaluate their designs. So Kang was able to simply call Choi Gee Sung, head of Samsung's TV, computer, and audio businesses and chief design officer since January, to secure backing for the TV project. A few years ago, Kang says, a designer at his level would have had to go through the marketing department and midlevel execs before reaching top management. Choi liked what he saw and gave Kang the go-ahead on the TV. Smart move: The TV,

EXHIBIT 2

Redesigning Samsung

Here's how Samsung is continuing to reinvent itself to keep its product designs at the leading edge

PIPELINE TO THE TOP	DESIGN-LED INNOVATION	QUESTION AUTHORITY
Designers can now go straight to top managers with ideas for new products. An award-winning rear-projection TV was developed by a designer who pitched it to the TV unit chief.	Designers no longer have to build boxes around engineers' devices. Instead, engineers now often find a way to stuff the right parts inside the designer's boxes.	Samsung is shedding its traditional Confucian hierarchy, encouraging younger designers to challenge their superiors when they think something needs to be changed.
BACK TO SCHOOL	**GLOBAL REACH**	**BEYOND HARDWARE**
Designers are sent to work at furniture, fashion, and industrial design houses to keep on top of the latest trends.	Since 2000, Samsung has opened or expanded design centers in San Francisco, London, Tokyo, Los Angeles, and this year in Shanghai.	Samsung studies everything about how consumers actually use products—from owners' manuals to packaging to the beeps, buzzes, and bells that digital devices make.

code-named L7, won a silver prize in the IDEA competition this year and is expected to be a big seller.

Samsung's design focus goes well beyond just the look and feel of its products. The company is working to improve the way people use and control gadgets, and two years ago it opened what it calls a "usability laboratory" in downtown Seoul (Exhibit 3). There, across the hall from where Choi Won Min taps away at his synthesizers in search of the perfect sound, engineers and consumers alike test everything from getting products out of the box to the icons and menus on screens. "In the past, physical design was the focal point," says Chief Design Officer Choi (no relation to the sound designer). "In the future, the user interface will be emphasized more."

The usability lab was built to provide a lifelike forum for tests. It looks like a typical living room,

EXHIBIT 3

From Laggard to Leader

How Samsung ratcheted up its design emphasis

1969 Samsung Electronics established as maker of TVs with technology borrowed from Sanyo.	**1977** Samsung introduces its first color TV.	**1980s** Focuses on undercutting Japanese rivals with me-too products. Design is an afterthought.
1988 Launches first mobile phone.	**1993** Chairman Lee Kun Hee tells execs to reinvent Samsung through design.	**1994** Hires U.S. design consultancy IDEO to help develop computer monitors.
1995 Sets up in-house design school, the Innovative Design Lab of Samsung.	**1996** Lee declares "Year of Design Revolution," stressing that designers should lead in product planning.	**1998** Asian financial crisis dents Samsung's ambitions; design staff cut by 28%.	**2000** Samsung once again focuses on design, and CEO Yun Jong Yong calls for design-led management.
2001 Yun initiates quarterly design meetings for top execs; opens design labs in Los Angeles and London.	**2002** Samsung's "usability laboratory" inaugurated in downtown Seoul.	**2004** Samsung wins a total of 33 awards at top design contests in the U.S., Europe, and Asia.	

with a kitchen in the corner for testing cooking appliances. Entering the room, designers and engineers kick off their shoes just as they do in a Korean home. On a recent fall day, one engineer padded around in her slippers making rice in a Samsung steamer, another checked out a washing machine, and a third played with the controls on a computer monitor. Behind a two-way mirror, an engineer controlled four high-definition cameras that can zoom in on any corner of the room to record the sessions and save them for later study.

It's that commitment to research that has given Samsung its edge. Many designers sit in on focus groups and watch closely as potential customers provide feedback on their new models. And each foreign lab has a researcher on site—unusual in the industry. Hwang Chang Hwan, Samsung's principal mobile-phone designer, faced complaints about the SPH-S2300, a three-megapixel camera phone. Techies and camera aficionados liked the optical zoom lens—a first in a camera phone—but other consumers didn't like the thickness of the lens. Most of all, young users hated the clumsy keypad, which was laid out in two rows of six keys along the bottom of the screen in order to keep the phone short enough to fit in a pocket. So when it came time to upgrade the phone, Samsung's designers listened. The new, five-megapixel successor sports a smaller lens that allows for a slimmer body, and it slides open, exposing a larger screen but leaving room for the traditional layout of three keys by four.

Can Samsung stay on top of its design game? Some skeptics say the company still doesn't have the breadth and depth in design of Sony, or the ingrained design culture of Apple Computer Corp. "Samsung has improved, but I don't see an identity in their design that really speaks to consumers," says Jim Wicks, Motorola Inc.'s vice-president in charge of designing cell phones. Still, few would deny that Samsung has managed to inject the importance of design into its corporate DNA. In this era of cutthroat competition, that may be just what it takes to create a lasting advantage.

Source: David Rocks and Moon Ihlwan, "Samsung Design," *BusinessWeek,* December 6, 2004, 88–96.

Case 6-6 Epilogue

The Next Big Bet

SEOUL

The world's biggest information-technology firm is diving into green technology and the health business. It should take care; its rivals should take notice.

In 2000 Samsung started making batteries for digital gadgets. Ten years later it sold more of them than any other company in the world. In 2001 it threw resources into flat-panel televisions. Within four years it was the market leader. In 2002 the firm bet heavily on "flash" memory. The technology it delivered made the iPhone and iPad a reality, and made Samsung Apple's biggest supplier—and now its biggest hardware competitor.

The handsome payoffs from these ballsy bets made the South Korean company a colossus; last year its sales passed $135 billion. Now it is embarking on a similarly audacious plan to move away from electronics into technologies where it barely has a presence today. It intends to spend $20 billion over ten years on solar panels, light-emitting diodes (LEDS) used for lighting, electric-vehicle batteries, medical devices and biotech drugs. These businesses shift Samsung away from easily substitutable gadgets towards more essential industrial goods (see table), or from "infotainment" to "lifecare," as the company puts it. Just as electronics defined swathes of the 20th century, the company believes green technology and health care will be central to the 21st.

With these plans Samsung sees itself bringing technologies that are vital for society into much broader use. The company has always had an eye for more than just the bottom line, seeking both to epitomise and to further the progress of its home country. Now it talks idealistically of improving the world by driving down the costs of zero-carbon power and providing poor countries and rural areas with medical equipment and drugs that they cannot afford today.

But the plans are also an ambitious industrial power play, one that challenges some of the world's biggest companies. Success would raise Samsung to new heights. Failure could lead to the firm losing what it already has, no longer able to flourish just as a maker of commodity gadgets and components.

The 83 firms that are tied together in Samsung's remarkably complex structure provide 13% of South Korea's gross exports. Samsung Electronics, the biggest of them, started making transistor radios in 1969, and has since evolved into the world's leading manufacturer of televisions and much else. It is on track to unseat Nokia as the biggest maker of mobile phones by volume next year. Interbrand, a consultancy which seeks to calculate brand value, puts it in the world's top 20, ahead of Sony and Nike. It has come second only to IBM in the number of patents earned in America for five years running.

Yet Samsung wants to diversify away from consumer electronics, a market that suffers from falling prices, thin margins, fast product cycles and fickle customers. Chinese rivals may do to Samsung what Samsung did to Western and Japanese firms in the past. "The majority of our products today will be gone in ten years," Samsung's patriarch and chairman, Lee Kun-hee, told executives in deliberately alarmist tones last January.

To survive, he said, the company must not only go into the new businesses it has identified, but open itself up to work with partners and even make acquisitions. Samsung has long been a closed world from that point of view, a disposition reinforced after the disastrous acquisition of a PC maker in the 1990s. But now the company knows it needs new skills, sales channels and customers.

Doing It the Samsung Way

By 2020 Samsung's Mr Lee wants the five new business areas to provide $50 billion of revenue, and Samsung Electronics to be a $400 billion company (for all his provocations to his staff, there are still going to be a lot of flat screens and memory sold). It is a brash goal, admits Inkuk Hahn of Samsung's strategy team. But ten years ago people were incredulous when Mr Lee insisted that Samsung, which then had sales of $23 billion, could be the number-one technology company, with sales of $100 billion. It claimed that crown just eight years later. "This is why you have to believe us," Mr Hahn insists.

The new businesses look remarkably disparate, but they share a need for big capital investments and the capacity to scale manufacture up very quickly, talents the company has exploited methodically in the past.

Samsung's successes come from spotting areas that are small but growing fast. Ideally the area should also be capital-intensive, making it harder for rivals to keep up. Samsung tiptoes into the technology to get familiar with it, then waits for its moment. It was when liquid-crystal displays grew to 40 inches in 2001 that Samsung took the dive and turned them into televisions. In flash memory, Samsung piled in when new technology made it possible to put a whole gigabyte on a chip.

When it pounces, the company floods the sector with cash. Moving into very high volume production as fast as possible not only gives it a price advantage over established firms, but also makes it a key customer for equipment makers. Those relationships help it stay on the leading edge from then on.

The strategy is shrewd. By buying technology rather than building it, Samsung assumes execution risk not innovation risk. It wins as a "fast follower,"

slipstreaming in the wake of pioneers at a much larger scale of production. The heavy investment has in the past played to its ability to tap cheap financing from a banking sector that is friendly to big companies, thanks to implicit government guarantees much complained about by rivals elsewhere.

From Crisis to Crisis

Competitors also balk at the way that Samsung scales up quickly to supply parts to other firms as well as to price its own gadgets keenly. Supplying the rest of industry drives down Samsung's costs yet further, with its rivals in effect financing its success. This strategy can create problems. Samsung is Apple's most important supplier in the smartphone and tablet-computer markets. Samsung components, which include all the product's application processors, account for 16% of the value of an iPhone. It is also Apple's greatest competitor in those markets. Apple is now suing the socks off the company for copying the look and feel of its products. At the same time it is urgently seeking new ways to diversify its supply chain.

Many companies saw the potential of technologies such as liquid-crystal panels, flash memory and rechargeable batteries. But few could or would invest billions in a single shot. That Samsung could is in large part due to a cult of personality around Mr Lee, who likes to keep things shaken up. "Change everything but your wife and children," he exhorted managers in 1993. Three years later he lit a bonfire of 150,000 gadgets because some were defective. Other bosses often need to face a crisis—a "burning platform," in the memorable phrase of Stephen Elop, Nokia's boss—before they make changes. Samsung does so when things are going well. The company has pushed out older managers and restructured its divisions over the past two years despite posting record profits even in the global financial crisis.

Management by perpetual crisis is perhaps a reflection of the company's national roots. In 1960, when the Samsung companies were taking off, South Korea, battered by recent war, had a GDP the same size as Sudan's; its last dictatorship fell only two years before the Berlin Wall. Today, though it enjoys one of the world's highest living standards, South Korea is still an emerging market in some ways, with endemic corruption and some economic structures that border on the feudal.

Samsung, like its host country, has a foot in both the industrialised and developing worlds, which it has used to its advantage. While it has always produced things for major IT firms and Western consumers, it has aimed products at poor countries, too. This not only gave Samsung scale, but also market shares in the world's fastest-growing economies. Whereas Western firms reeled in the recent recession, Samsung flourished, buoyed by sales in markets that never stopped growing.

From Laptop to Rooftop

Some of the five new businesses Samsung has set its sights on are not that far from what the company does already. Its experience in semiconductors and flat-screen televisions fits easily with solar cells and LED lighting: the technology, materials and production processes are similar. Likewise, its expertise in batteries for gadgets smooths the way for making car-sized ones. The firm wants to apply the magic of ever cheaper chips to medical devices as it did mobile phones. Even drugs aren't so far afield when one sees them in business-process terms: high-volume manufacturing with low defect rates. In all these fields Samsung believes it can sit—rather as Korea does geographically—in between China, with its cheap products, and Japan, with its costly, high-quality ones.

In solar energy Samsung plans to make panels for both domestic and industrial use. Producing panels for "utility-scale" projects may allow it to lower prices for the residential market. Changsik Choi, who heads the business, also speaks optimistically of a "brand halo effect": consumers whose living rooms are stuffed with Samsung products may choose the company for their rooftops too.

Samsung's dominance of the television market has already made it the world's second-largest maker of LED components (Japan's Nichia is the first). Since they consume a fraction of the power of conventional light bulbs, last longer and avoid some of the drawbacks of compact fluorescents, the first-generation alternative, LEDs are expected eventually to become the norm for all sorts of lighting; the market is growing by 65% a year. Samsung already sells LED lighting in South Korea and plans soon to expand abroad. In this market it will hew to its strategy of supplying parts to others, thereby lowering costs for its own products.

In electric-vehicle batteries Samsung has joined forces with Bosch, the world's biggest supplier of car parts and a fount of expertise on power- and engine-management. Samsung sees their partnership, SB LiMotive, as crucial since the car business relies on close ties between carmakers and their suppliers. Some carmakers, like Nissan and Toyota, will continue developing their own batteries, but Samsung thinks that many carmakers will not want to be in the battery business, just as they are not in the petrol business, and that they will be a rich source of demand. Chrysler and BMW are among SB LiMotive's first customers.

For medical devices Samsung aims to use information technology to lower costs, add features and make devices accessible to more people, particularly the poor. For example, it is developing x-ray machines that expose patients to less radiation and do away

Fresh fields

Samsung's new business areas			Targets for 2020		
Sector	Investment, $bn	Ownership	Sales, $bn	Jobs	Status
Solar panels	5.1	100% Samsung SDI	8.5	10,000	Production began in January
LED lighting	7.3	50% Samsung Electronics, 50% Samsung Electro-Mechanics	15.2	17,000	Already selling in South Korea
E-vehicle batteries	4.6	50% Samsung SDI, 50% Bosch	8.7	7,600	Initial operations began in November 2010
Biotech drugs	1.8	40% Samsung Electronics, 40% Samsung Everland, 10% Samsung C&T, 10% Quintiles	1.5	1,000	Factory to begin in 2013; developing biosimilars now for patents expiring in 2016
Medical devices	1.0	100% Samsung Electronics	8.5	10,300	Blood-testing unit available, X-ray machine ready in 1-2 years, acquired ultrasound maker

Sources: Samsung; *The Economist*

with physical film. Last year Samsung began selling a machine for testing patients' blood chemistry that is smaller, cheaper, uses less power and offers more functions than rivals' devices. In April it bought Medison, a South Korean maker of ultrasound equipment, as a way to get further into the market: it is looking at buying body-scanner firms too.

In biotech drugs the company plans to begin as a contract manufacturer of biosimilars (generic versions of biotech drugs) and has partnered with Quintiles, a drug outsourcer. The strategy lets Samsung gain experience while assuming little commercial risk. It is building a factory outside Seoul and has already begun developing biosimilars for medicines with patents that expire in 2016.

Incumbents and Incomers

The markets are certainly promising, but they entail huge risks. Nor is the size of Samsung's commitment quite on a par with the overwhelming force it has deployed in the past. The solar and LED businesses already struggle with oversupply, meaning Samsung may get walloped by the same dramatic price erosion as it has seen in liquid-crystal flat panels. Electric-vehicle batteries may be in similar straits if demand for the cars they might power remains sluggish. They are also in the crosshairs of Chinese companies, as are medical devices and drugs. In a bid to escape the vagaries of consumer electronics, Samsung may be ploughing headlong into the areas most ripe for invasion by a new breed of emerging-market titans.

Acquisitions, a way of life in the drug business, are also a challenge: knowing what to buy and when is a skill that Samsung has never developed. The same applies to dealing with government regulators: Samsung's towering importance at home may give it a false confidence in its ability to handle governments elsewhere.

Its position as a domestic titan could be a hindrance in other ways. Working with partners entails sharing information and a view of joint success that is at odds with its insular corporate culture. The international talent the company will need to attract is also less likely to be moved by the admonishments and appeals to national grandeur that Mr Lee has used to build Samsung's success. They might, indeed, find such things wearisome.

Samsung's rivals are ready for a fight. Philips and GE have been preparing to compete with firms in emerging markets for years, devising cheap products and building on existing relationships with clients.

Toshiba plans to spend an extra $9 billion in the energy and environment sectors over the next three years on top of its normal capital expenditure, research and acquisitions. Fumio Ohtsubo, Panasonic's boss, praises his Samsung rivals for their low prices but believes his company develops superior technology. "If we can get the same conditions in terms of free-trade agreements, low corporate taxes and other incentives, then we should be able to compete," he says.

In medical devices Samsung will be up against firms like Philips, Siemens, Toshiba, Hitachi and GE (for which Samsung made medical equipment between 1984 and 2004). GE's Indian office famously reduced the cost of an electrocardiogram machine from $2,000 to $400. And the fact that hospitals prefer to buy different equipment from a single vendor so that, in principle, everything works together puts a maker of this-and-that at a disadvantage, even if it is cheap.

Perhaps the biggest challenge, though, will be one of succession. The 69-year-old chairman's son, Jay Y. Lee, 43, was named president last December. Educated in Japan (like his father and grandfather, the firm's founder) and at Harvard Business School, he has been groomed from the start. His first test will be reforming the jumble of opaque, interlocking relationships and conflicts of interest that passes for Samsung's corporate governance.

The "Samsung group," as it is often known, has no legal identity. The 83 firms sit under an umbrella company called Everland, in which the Lee family has a controlling 46% stake. The family also has minority positions in other Samsung firms, which often hold shares in other members of the group, and indeed in Everland. For example, the family and related interests own 21% of Samsung's life-insurance firm, which owns 26% of its credit-card business, which in turn owns 26% of Everland. Get it? Nobody other than the Lees really does.

The company must change if only to avoid South Korea's devastating 50% inheritance tax after the elder Lee's passing (his father died at the age of 77). That would further whittle the family's stakes, notes Shaun Cochran of CLSA, a broker. He expects a holding company to be formed, so investors have clearer exposure to the different parts of Samsung's businesses. The younger Lee will also need to root out corruption, which his father often complained about without rising above it; the elder Lee's 2008 conviction for tax evasion was pardoned in 2009 on the ground of his importance to the country.

When the Dealing's Done

Chairman Lee's fear is that successful companies get flabby when they hit middle age. He saw that in Sony, founded in 1946, which has been struggling since the 1990s. Samsung Electronics turned 40 in 2009, which prompted Mr Lee to lay the groundwork for the five new growth areas. Diversification is essential. In the mid-1990s almost all of its profits came from DRAM memory chips: when the market soured in 1996, its profits shrivelled by 95%.

Samsung may be swapping "infotainment" for "lifecare"—but it is still in the hardware business, and that may leave it more vulnerable than it thinks. Many of today's computer and electronics giants are getting out of the manufacturing businesses altogether, IBM has shifted to services, trailed by Japan's Fujitsu, while Philips and Siemens both sold their IT businesses to focus on other areas. But getting out of things is not something Samsung is good at. Despite a commitment to perpetual crisis, a mixture of implicitly subsidised capital, weak shareholder pressure and family control has allowed it to stick too long with dodgy decisions—such as its move into cars, brought short only by the Asian financial crisis, and its only-now-ended commitment to hard-drive manufacture.

Even with a $20 billion bankroll, bets can be spread too thin. Perhaps the biggest risk for Samsung is not that none of its wagers will win, but that it won't be able to stop betting on the ones that don't. Knowing the right time to bet is a great gift. So is knowing the right time to walk away.

Source: "The next big bet," *The Economist,* October 1, 2011, 75–77.

Case 6-7

Keurig Inc.

A Wednesday afternoon in February 2003 found Keurig Inc.'s president and CEO Nick Lazaris heading south on Interstate 89 back toward his Wakefield, Massachusetts, office and mulling over the day's events in preparation for a briefing with his senior management team (see Exhibit 1 on page 520). He realized that the next two weeks would be critical to the success of the company's newest product initiative in the single-cup coffee market. Lazaris had just wrapped up a presentation to the Green Mountain Coffee Roasters Inc. (GMCR) management team, one of the company's strategic partners and an investor in its business. While reviewing the company's progress toward the launch of its innovative coffee-brewing system into the at-home consumer market, GMCR had asked Keurig to reconsider its decision to use a different version of the coffee portion pack, known as a K-Cup, in the consumer market. In making its request, GMCR had offered a number of compelling reasons for using the existing commercial portion pack in both channels.

As he drove, Lazaris passed a new Starbucks and reflected on how gourmet coffeehouses had helped pave the way for Keurig's single-serve brewing system. The proliferation of soft drinks since the 1960s had caused coffee to lose its place as a central component of social gatherings, spurring a precipitous drop in coffee consumption to an all-time low of 6.1 pounds per capita in the mid-1990s from a peak of 16.5 pounds per capita in the mid-1940s.[1] The entrance of gourmet coffeehouses had reinvigorated the market, developing a distinct subculture of coffee drinkers and educating younger consumers about great traditional coffees as well as espresso and milk-based specialty beverages. As a result, by 2003 an estimated twenty million Americans were drinking gourmet coffee on a daily basis.

Keurig's launch of a single-cup brewing system in the office coffee service market in the late 1990s had benefited from coffee drinkers' increasing sophistication. Office employees could appreciate the greater variety, freshness, and convenience derived from the ability to brew a single cup of coffee on demand. Office managers recognized the advantages garnered from less coffee waste, increased employee productivity, and decreased hassle associated with tending the coffee machine.

February 2003 found Keurig poised to launch its new model B100 system in the at-home segment with hopes of repeating its success in a much larger but more competitive market. With rumors of other single-cup competitors ready to enter the market, Lazaris knew Keurig needed to move quickly in order to obtain its desired positioning in the emerging single-cup consumer market. Revisiting the decision to proceed with a two-K-Cup strategy had the potential to derail the company's launch efforts and demanded rapid attention by Lazaris and the senior management team. Reevaluation of the K-Cup

[1] United States Department of Agriculture.

EXHIBIT 1 **Keurig Senior Management Team**

Source: Keurig, Inc.

NICK LAZARIS: PRESIDENT, CHIEF EXECUTIVE OFFICER, AND DIRECTOR

Lazaris joined Keurig in 1997. His more than twenty years of business experience includes president/CEO- and VP-level experience in marketing, sales, finance, and business development in the home furnishings and office products industries. Prior to Keurig he was president/CEO of MW Carr, a photo frame manufacturer/marketer, and VP and divisional GM for Tech Specialists, a contract professional staffing firm. Earlier in his career, Lazaris served as chief of staff for West Virginia Governor Jay Rockefeller. In 2001 and 2003 he was a regional finalist for Ernst & Young's Entrepreneur of the Year. He received his BS from MIT and his MBA from Harvard Business School, and is a licensed CPA.

DICK SWEENEY: CO-FOUNDER AND VICE-PRESIDENT, ENGINEERING AND OPERATIONS

Sweeney co-founded Keurig in 1993 and joined the company full time as VP of engineering in 1996. He brought to Keurig more than 25 years of experience in manufacturing, product development, and consulting for industrial and consumer appliances, including espresso machines. Prior to Keurig he was VP of manufacturing for Canrad-Hanovia, a manufacturer of scientific and UV lighting. Before that he was VP of operations for V-M Industries, a consumer appliances manufacturer and importer. Sweeney received his BS from New Jersey Institute of Technology and his MBA from Fairleigh Dickinson University.

CHRIS STEVENS: VICE-PRESIDENT OF SALES

Stevens joined Keurig in 1996. He brought to Keurig more than 20 years of experience in consumer goods sales and marketing, as well as general management. After beginning his sales career with seven years at Procter & Gamble, he became president of the August A. Busch Co., a subsidiary of Anheuser-Busch. After also serving as a divisional manager with A-B, he was executive VP and general manager for United Liquors before becoming executive director of the Sports Museum of New England. Stevens received his BS from Notre Dame and completed the Executive Education program at Columbia Business School.

DAVE MANLY: VICE-PRESIDENT OF MARKETING

Manly joined Keurig in 2002. He brought to Keurig more than 20 years of experience in consumer goods sales and marketing. His experience included VP and GM positions building well-known consumer brands in the food products and consumer goods industries via innovative marketing approaches. Manly has held marketing positions at Nexus EnergyGuide, EnergyUSA, LoJack Corporation, Boston Whaler Boat Company, and Procter & Gamble (food products division). Manly received his BS from DePauw University and his MBA from Purdue University.

JOHN WHORISKEY: VICE-PRESIDENT, GENERAL MANAGER—AT-HOME DIVISION

Whoriskey joined Keurig in 2002. He brought to Keurig more than twenty years of experience that included president- and VP-level experience in marketing and sales in the home furnishings, gift, and consumer products industries. Prior to Keurig he was president of Fetco Home Décor and president of Optelec Inc. Prior to that, he worked in VP-level positions for Honeywell Consumer Products, Tucker Housewares, The First Years, and Polaroid. Whoriskey received his BS and an MBA from Boston College.

---

decision would also force them to rethink other elements of their product plans, including pricing and marketing. With less than six months until the September launch, time was of the essence.

The Company and Its Products

Keurig Inc. had been founded to develop an innovative technique that would allow coffee lovers to brew one perfect cup of coffee at a time. Beginning with the company's inception in 1992, the word "Keurig," from the Dutch word for excellence, had been the guiding principle behind the development of its products and services. The company leveraged investments from venture capital funds to transform its concept for a single-cup brewing system into a commercially viable business with the development and patenting of a single-portion pack and a revolutionary new coffee brewer. The first brewer targeting the office coffee service market, the B2000, was launched in 1998.

EXHIBIT 2
B2003 Commercial Brewer and Keurig K-Cups

Source: Keurig, Inc.

A licensing agreement allowed GMCR to pack its specialty coffees in Keurig's patented container, the K-Cup (see Exhibit 2). Eight varieties of coffee were originally available for sale to offices. Keurig continued to expand its relationships with roasters such as GMCR, using a selective but nonexclusive strategy. This ongoing effort had expanded the number of roaster partnerships to five, resulting in the largest variety of coffees available with a single-cup system in the market in 2003.

In February 2002 the ownership structure of Keurig changed through agreements with two of its roaster partners. Keurig sold stock to Van Houtte Inc. to raise nearly $10 million to support the launch of the at-home business. This investment provided Van Houtte with nearly a 28 percent ownership stake in Keurig. At the same time, GMCR acquired and executed options to purchase a large number of Keurig shares from existing shareholders, enabling Keurig to consolidate to a smaller number of significant shareholders. GMCR obtained a 42 percent stake in Keurig. With these moves, Van Houtte and GMCR joined Memorial Drive Trust (MDT) as the three largest shareholders of Keurig. MDT, an investment advisory firm that managed a U.S. based profit-sharing plan, had served as the lead venture investor in Keurig since 1995 and led Keurig's board of directors. As provided for in separate shareholder agreements with MDT, neither GMCR nor Van Houtte was allowed to have a seat on the board of directors. Lazaris reinforced the company's position

with respect to these roaster shareholders in a letter to its authorized distributors and other roaster partners:

> We do not plan to allow any roaster or other commercial business partner to sit on our board of directors. Our core strategy remains unchanged: we are committed to a multiroaster strategy that relies on strong relationships with selected gourmet coffee roasters who take a great deal of pride in the coffee consumption experience that supports the meaning of their brand to consumers.[2]

Single-Cup Brewing Technology

Keurig's single-portion system hinged on three key elements: a coffee brewer that perfectly controlled the amount, temperature, and pressure of water to provide a consistently superior-tasting cup of coffee; a unique portion-pack system containing ground coffee beans as well as filter paper; and a varied coffee selection to replicate the choices available in a gourmet coffeehouse.

The Keurig commercial-market brewer included an "always-on" feature, enabling it to brew a cup of coffee in less than one minute at any time of day. Plumbed to a water line, the automatically refillable water reservoir maintained up to twelve cups of water at brewing temperature. After the customer inserted a K-Cup in a drawer, positioned the 8-ounce cup to receive the brewed coffee, and pressed the "brew" button, the brewer would pierce the K-Cup, inject pressurized hot water, and brew

[2]Internal memo dated February 5, 2002.

the coffee. The K-Cup, evolved from an initial mock-up design based on a modified yogurt cup, contained a built-in cone-shaped filter and the exact amount and grind of coffee to fresh-brew a single 8-ounce cup. K-Cups were impermeable to air, moisture, and light to ensure the contents stayed fresh for at least six months.

A key differentiator for Keurig's brewing system was the broad coffee selection available through licensing arrangements with a variety of gourmet coffee roasters. Coffee roasters controlled the quality of their coffee and the number of varieties available through K-Cup production lines. A production line might be owned by the coffee roaster or leased from Keurig. K-Cups were produced by five roasters with six brands and more than 75 coffee varieties.[3] Roaster partners included Green Mountain Coffee Roasters, Diedrich Coffee, Van Houtte, Timothy's World Coffee, and Ueshima Coffee Company. For each K-Cup sold, the roaster paid Keurig a royalty of approximately $.04.

The Art of Cupping

"Cupping" was a method of tasting the finished (or brewed) coffee product used by roasters and many large retailers to evaluate the flavor profile of a coffee. Similar to wine tasting, cupping involved swishing coffee around in the mouth to evaluate elements of the flavor profile. Expert "cuppers" could taste as many as 10 to 20 varieties a day and perform an analysis that included taste, brightness (degree of acidity), fragrance and aroma, body, and finish. The process began with the roasting and grinding of a small batch of beans. Once the ground beans were placed in a cup, hot water was poured over them and the analysis process began. The cupping process could be supplemented by state-of-the-art machinery to ensure product consistency.

In the world of gourmet coffees, roasters offered a variety of coffees tailored to the different tastes of gourmet coffee drinkers. For each variety of coffee offered, cuppers had established an expected flavor profile. The process by which that profile was achieved was closely controlled by the cupper during the cupping process. However, those same controls could not always be achieved in the traditional home brewing process. The desired flavor profile could be affected by a number of factors beyond the control of the roaster or cupper: the amount of coffee or water used by the consumer, variations in the temperature throughout brewing, or the amount of time the coffee sat in the coffee pot prior to being consumed. Through close control of critical elements in the coffee brewing process, the Keurig system enabled that flavor profile to be re-created on a consistent basis and ensured that the coffee drinker had the same taste experience time after time.

Away-From-Home Market

Keurig's market included two broad target customers: office users and households.[4] Keurig chose to focus first on the away-from-home commercial segment of office users in the hopes that a successful rollout would provide a springboard for launch into the at-home segment. The groundwork for launching into the away-from-home office coffee service (OCS) market was laid by Starbucks and other specialty coffee purveyors. They had successfully educated consumers about good-quality coffee and made it acceptable to pay $1.50 or more for a cup of coffee and even more for coffee-based specialty beverages. This behavior opened the door for Keurig and others to offer a single-cup system into offices, capitalizing on people's desire to have the same great taste in the office as they got at a coffeehouse.

In 2002 the OCS market reached $3.46 billion in total revenues.[5] At the same time, acceptance of the single-cup brewing technology was evident in surveys of OCS distributors. In 2000 only 14.8 percent of distributors had offered a single-cup system, but that figure had increased to 44.8 percent in 2001.[6] By 2003 total single-cup brewer placements had reached 143,200 (see Exhibit 3).

Since the launch of its first commercial brewer in 1998, Keurig had quickly moved to a leading position in the sales of single-cup brewing systems. After five years in the market at the end of 2002, Keurig had shipped more than 33,000 brewers in North America, equal to 1 percent of all OCS brewers. In comparison to the competition, Lazaris was quick to point out the speed with which Keurig had penetrated the market:

> It took Filterfresh twenty years to ship 45,000 units in North America. And in its first five years, Flavia shipped only 8,000 units in North America. In addition, our expansion into Asia at the end of 2001 provided us an added opportunity for growth. In partnership with the top Asian roaster, UCC, our initial sales in Japan and Korea had been more than 2,700 brewers.

---

[3]Currently there were three leased-production lines and an additional eight roaster-owned lines. Three additional lines were planned.

[4]From early trial activities, Keurig had determined its single-serve brewing system was not well aligned with the needs of food service establishments serving a large volume of coffee.

[5]International Coffee Organization, London, UK.

[6]*Automatic Merchandiser* 2002 Coffee Service Market Report.

EXHIBIT 3   U.S. Single-Cup Brewer Placements by OCS Distributors

Source: *Automatic Merchandiser,* February 2002, July 2004.

Manufacturer	Product(s)	1999/2000	2000/2001	2001/2002	2002/2003
Cafection	Avalon	7,500	11,000	13,000	16,000
Crane	Cafe System	22,500	23,000	11,000	12,000
Filterfresh	Filterfresh/Keurig	23,000	24,000	26,500[a]	30,000[b]
Flavia	Flavia	8,000	19,000	32,000	40,000
Keurig	Keurig	13,000	23,000	30,000	33,000
Newco	Gevalia	0	1,000	1,200	1,300
Progema	Venus	0	0	1,000	2,400
Unibrew	Unibrew	3,200[c]	3,200	3,200	3,200
Zanussi	Brio/Colibri	5,000	6,400	8,000	10,000
Other		1,100	1,600	516	4,600
Total		83,300	112,200	126,416	143,200

[a]Includes 1,484 Keurig units.
[b]Includes 2,300 Keurig units.
[c]Available to Filterfresh franchisees only.
Note: Table has been modified to exclude espresso machine sales.

A second measure of Keurig's achievements in the OCS market was shipment of its patented K-Cups. In 2002 Keurig's roaster partners shipped more than 125 million K-Cups, bringing total K-Cup shipments since launch to more than 340 million. Also in the works was the launch of an offering of teas in T-Cups, with the first being the "Celestial Seasonings" teas.

Away-from-Home Channel of Distribution

The office coffee market was served by a network of approximately 1,700 distributors that were responsible for placement and maintenance of office brewers and ongoing coffee supply. Keurig worked with a total of 180 Keurig authorized distributors (KADS) for sales throughout North America. A small number of KADS handled customers throughout the United States or North America, while the majority covered smaller regions.

The purchasing decision was handled by office managers. "Office managers are all about eliminating headaches. The variety of coffees, convenience of brewing, and negligible clean-up of the Keurig system mean fewer employee complaints and greater productivity," explained Chris Stevens, away-from-home vice-president of sales, who was responsible for managing Keurig's day-to-day relationship with its network of KADS. Customer relationships were managed by the KADS and feedback on problems or desired new features was funneled through the KADS to share with Keurig.

The KADS purchased commercial brewers from Keurig at a wholesale price that ranged from $500 to $1,000. The brewer was placed in offices free of charge or with a low monthly rental in exchange for ongoing coffee sales. Typically there was no formal contract between the KAD and the office manager, although the KAD established expected volumes based on the number of employees in the office. If volumes fell below expected levels, the KAD could remove the brewer from the office or raise the price of the K-Cups. The KAD was also responsible for ongoing repairs of the brewer.

The KAD provided a variety of coffees to offices, based on their individual consumption profiles. KADS entered into direct relationships with one or more licensed roasters for the purchase of K-Cups. Typically, KADS paid roasters $0.25 per K-Cup and sold K-Cups to office managers for $0.40–$0.50. Roasters then paid Keurig a royalty of $0.04 per K-Cup sold.

Away-from-Home Single-Cup Competition

There were two primary competitors in the away-from-home market.

Filterfresh

Hopper-based single-cup technology was pioneered by Westwood, Massachusetts-based Filterfresh Coffee Service Inc. in the late 1980s. Filterfresh was a U.S. subsidiary of Canadian-based Van Houtte (a Keurig shareholder), a leading gourmet coffee roaster, marketer, and distributor in North America. The Filterfresh commercial single-cup system was based on the "French press" method of brewing. Ground coffee beans were loaded into a storage hopper in the machine. Once a button was pressed for a cup of coffee, an amount of ground beans would be measured from the hopper and mixed with hot water. The mixture would then be strained to remove the grounds and a single cup of coffee resulted. No brewed coffee was left to sit and become waste as was common in a traditional glass pot system, and a person enjoyed a freshly brewed cup of coffee each time. Regular tending of the coffee system was required to remove used coffee grounds and reload ground beans into the storage hopper. Filterfresh established its relationship with Keurig in October 2001 to market Keurig's commercial brewer and offer a system that could provide a greater variety of single-cup coffees and teas.

Flavia

Flavia was owned by Mars Inc. It introduced its first single-cup brewer to offices in Britain in 1985 and expanded to Europe and Japan before introducing its "Brew-by-Pack" system in the United States and Canada in 1996. Similar to the Keurig brewer, the S350 commercial brewer utilized a single-serving pack. Each Filterpack contained its own filter and the appropriate measure of ingredients, which were foil-sealed, protecting them against air and moisture. A selection of twenty-four coffee varieties was available with the system.

At-Home Market

Building on its success in the OCS market, Keurig viewed the at-home consumer market as a logical extension to its business strategy. John Whoriskey joined Keurig as general manager and vice-president of the at-home division in 2002. He brought with him more than 20 years of experience in consumer goods sales and marketing. "I fell in love with Keurig and

its brewing system," he commented. "I don't consider myself a gourmet coffee drinker, but I do like a good cup of coffee. I would drive a mile out of my way to work to pick up a good cup of coffee. With a Keurig brewer, we can offer convenience benefit with taste assurance, in the comfort of your own home."

The at-home market represented an enormous opportunity for Keurig. Leading market research firms estimated the total size of the retail coffee market at approximately $18.5 billion in 2000. At-home retail consumption was a $6.9 billion market, with at-home gourmet coffee accounting for $3.1 billion (see Exhibit 4). Away-from-home gourmet coffee represented a $3.9 billion market and was typically sold by the cup at cafes such as Starbucks or in other food service venues such as restaurants. At the same time, estimates showed 157 million Americans drank coffee, with 60 percent predominantly drinking previously ground coffee and another 10 percent using freshly ground whole bean coffee.[7] Profiles of coffee drinkers varied by product type, with consumers of whole-bean coffee exhibiting an upscale profile (see Exhibit 5). In addition, about eighteen million coffee makers were purchased annually in the United States, representing about $450 million in retail sales. Coffee makers represented one of the largest-volume small appliances sold for home use.[8]

Previously the purview of upscale outlets—coffee/tea stores, gourmet/specialty stores, kitchenware stores, and coffeehouses—gourmet coffees had increasingly been sold in mass-retail outlets. At the same time, the growing popularity of whole-bean coffee had been driving the launch of a variety of roasts, blends, and flavors. Starbucks, for example, showed growth of whole-bean sales in excess of 100 percent in 2000.[9]

[7] Simmons Market Research Bureau (2000).

[8] Keurig company information.

[9] *The U.S. Market for Freshly Brewed Coffee Beverages,* Packaged Facts, March 2004.

EXHIBIT 4
U.S. Retail At-Home Coffee Market

Source: *Packaged Facts Market Profile: The U.S. Coffee and Tea Market,* September 2001.

Year	Mass Market Coffee Sales ($ in Millions)	Pound Volume (in Millions)	Gourmet Coffee Sales ($ in Millions)	Pound Volume (in Millions)
2000	3,815	840	3,100	320
1999	3,800	850	3,000	310
1998	3,975	830	2,800	290
1997	4,205	845	2,500	270
1996	3,905	850	2,200	255

EXHIBIT 5
Demographic
Characteristics by
Product Form

Source: *Packaged Facts Market Profile: The U.S. Coffee and Tea Market,* September, 2001.

Factor	Ground	Instant	Whole Bean
Age	55–64	NS	45–54
Race	NS	Black; Hispanic	Asian; Other
Marital status	NS	Widowed	Married
Household income (in thousands)	NS	$10–$15	$75+
Education	NS	Not high school graduate	College graduate
Employment status	Retired	Homemaker	Full-time
Occupation	NS	NS	Professional/managerial
Household size	NS	NS	NS
Region	Midwest	NS	West

Notes: U.S. adults. NS is no statistically significant differences.

Coffee advertising centered on two major themes: good taste and positive stimulation. Taglines such as Maxwell House's "Good to the last drop" reflected the emphasis on the taste experience. Positive stimulation focused on the benefits caused by drinking a particular cup of coffee. As an example, the well-known tagline "The best part of waking up is Folgers in your cup" suggested that the stress and challenges in your life could be overcome by taking that first sip.

At-Home Single-Cup Market Research

Keurig commissioned a variety of market research studies on the at-home product concept from 1999 to 2001 prior to moving ahead with any significant development efforts. "We wanted to get an understanding of the acceptability of the single-cup approach, gain some insight into pricing of the K-Cup and the brewer, and profile our prime consumer prospects," explained Lazaris. This research was executed in a variety of formats, including intercept surveys, Internet-based surveys, surveys of current OCS users, and surveys and focus groups of home use testers.

Intercept interviews were conducted in three cities in the summer of 2000. Lazaris explained the study's focus: "We were interested in speaking with regular gourmet coffee drinkers so respondents were selected based on

coffee brewing habits and coffee consumption." To qualify for the intercept survey, consumers had to drink gourmet coffee, which included coffee from freshly ground whole beans, from gourmet coffee roasters, and from premium coffee cafes such as Starbucks, Dunkin' Donuts, Seattle's Best, or Caribou Coffee. All participants had to drink at least one cup of coffee per day.

While nearly 94 percent of respondents indicated that they were satisfied with the coffee they drank at home, 88 percent expressed an interest in the product concept. Interest focused primarily on convenience, particularly quick brewing, ease of use, and minimal clean-up, sources of the most dissatisfaction with current home brewing systems. Based on explanation of the product alone, more than three-quarters of respondents said they would be likely to purchase a system like the one proposed. The product demonstration had a huge impact on this figure. More than 90 percent of respondents indicated that the demonstration increased their likelihood of buying the product. Key factors rated highest in the demonstration included the time it took to prepare coffee and the time it took to clean up.

Keurig had gained some initial insight into brewer pricing from previous market research (see Exhibit 6). It now wanted to explore product pricing with consumers

EXHIBIT 6
Initial Market
Research

Source: Company-sponsored market research.

Brewer Pricing	Awares % (N = 170)	Nonawares % (N = 601)
$199	6	1
$449	9	7
$ 99	31	18

Note: Results from early street intercept testing were segmented between "Keurig-awares," people familiar with the Keurig system, and "Keurig-nonawares."

EXHIBIT 7   Intercept Testing Market Research

Source: Company-sponsored market research.

Table 7A: Willingness to Pay for Coffee

Survey respondents were asked how much they would be willing to pay for a cup of coffee like the one they tasted. Interviewers guided the respondents and started the price point inquiry at $0.55. The percentages of respondents represent the cumulative percentages of people willing to pay each price.

Initial Pricing	Percentage of Respondents (Cumulative)
$0.55	43.8
0.50	53.5
0.45	60.0
0.40	69.5
0.35	79.3
0.30	87.3
0.25	97.8

Table 7B: K-Cup Pricing Based on Coffee Consumption

Survey respondents were asked how much they would be willing to pay for a K-cup. The percentages of respondents represent the cumulative percentages of people willing to pay each price. Responses include only customers who were very or somewhat likely to purchase system.

K-Cup Pricing	1 Cup/Day[a] (N = 78) %	2+ Cup/Day[a] (N = 446) %
$0.55+	5.1	14.6
0.50–0.54	16.7	30.7
0.45–0.49	20.5	33.6
0.40–0.44	22.0	41.5
0.35–0.39	28.2	48.2
0.30–0.34	41.0	58.5
0.25–0.29	60.3	75.6

Table 7C: Brewer and K-Cup Pricing Based on Coffee Consumption

This table reflects the percentages of respondents willing to pay certain prices for the brewer. Information is segmented based on their previously stated K-cup pricing and coffee consumption. Responses include only customers who were very or somewhat likely to purchase system.

K-Cup Pricing	1 Cup/Day[a] (N = 78)%			2+ Cups/Day[a] (N = 446)%		
	< $100	$100–$129	$130+	< $100	$100–$129	$130+
< $0.30	34.1	9.4	5.9	22.2	8.9	6.3
0.30–0.39	7.1	8.2	2.4	6.2	5.3	5.2
0.40–0.49	2.4	2.4	4.7	5.7	2.5	1.9
0.50+	10.6	5.9	1.2	9.9	9.5	10.1
Don't Know	5.9			6.3		

[a]Coffee consumption per weekday.

who considered the system (brewer and K-Cups) and also experienced a product demonstration. Among intercept respondents, the self-reported daily consumption rate of coffee was an average of two to three cups. When asked about their willingness to pay for a cup of coffee like the one they tasted, 44 percent indicated they would pay $0.55 (see Exhibit 7 on page 526). Later in the survey, respondents were asked about their willingness to pay for both K-Cups and the brewer. More than 30 percent of respondents who were interested in the system were willing to pay $0.50 or more for a K-Cup. Before obtaining input on brewer pricing, respondents were told that high-quality coffee makers sold in the range of $69 to $149. Approximately one-fourth of the respondents were willing to pay more than $130 for the brewer. Consumers who drank more coffee were more willing to pay for both the K-Cup and the brewer.

An Internet-based survey used as its basis a Keurig system summary (see Exhibit 8) that was shown to people who drank coffee on a daily basis. It found that the concept had strong appeal, with 67 percent of respondents expressing interest. The main differentiating factor revolved around the speed of brewing a cup of coffee. Of second highest importance was the convenience of no preparation or clean-up. As part of the study, a price point of $149.99 was tested. The 9 percent of respondents who indicated that they "definitely would buy" or "probably would buy" the coffee system at this price were classified as "core customers." These respondents tended to be younger and most were male. Follow-up survey questions revealed that the average price core customers were willing to pay for the coffee system was $125.

For the home use test, a commercial model brewer was placed in the homes of gourmet coffee drinkers. The testers were then required to purchase K-Cups at a retail price of $0.50 via fax, e-mail, or phone for their own individual coffee consumption. Subsequent interviews and focus groups found that users consistently referenced great-tasting coffee with a system that was fast and convenient. Additional attributes of the product highlighted included taste consistency, coffee variety, and cleanliness of preparation. Of particular note was the fact that coffee consumption at home increased with the presence of the Keurig brewer. On average, 2.25 cups of coffee were consumed per day at home. Not only were participants drinking more coffee in the morning, but they were purchasing less coffee outside the home. An acceptable price range for the brewer was determined to be in the $129–$199 range, with a price exceeding $200 triggering a reaction that the item would become a luxury purchase for which more consideration would be required. K-Cup pricing, however, did not appear to be an issue.

EXHIBIT 8   **Internet Survey Concept Description**

Source: Keurig, Inc.

Introducing a Revolutionary New Home Coffee-Making System Coffee House Taste by the Cup™
Fresh
Fast
Convenient
Delicious
• *The System*—A revolutionary coffee-making system that uses individual portion packs of freshly roasted and ground coffee with a unique coffeemaker designed to brew GREAT cups of coffee, one cup at a time. Each user picks the brand and variety of coffee they want and makes a fresh, piping hot cup in just 30 seconds.
• *Delicious and Fresh*—Individual portion packs come in over 36 varieties of branded coffees from Green Mountain Coffee Roasters, Diedrich Coffee, and Gloria Jean's Coffees. The coffee is roasted, ground, and packed at the roasters' facilities into an individual portion pack where freshness is sealed in. The pack provides an oxygen, light, and moisture barrier to ensure fresh-ground quality that is guaranteed for six months. Whether you prefer light roasts, dark roasts, blends, decafs, or flavored coffees, this system serves you the coffee you prefer, brewed to perfection every time.
• *Convenient*—The entire brewing process takes place in the portion pack. There is no waste, no pot or filters to clean, and no hassle. Just discard the used portion pack after brewing.
• *Fast*—Just press a button and in 30 seconds you'll have a fresh cup of hot coffee. The machine is always plugged in and powered on with hot water ready to brew your cup of coffee.

At-Home Single-Cup Competition

A key element of Keurig's strategy in the at-home market was being one of the first entrants in the product category. In establishing itself as a pioneer in the upscale single-cup brewing category, Keurig envisioned that subsequent press coverage would naturally include a reference to the Keurig system as a single-cup pioneer and enhance its visibility in the upscale market.

In the traditional consumer coffee market, Procter & Gamble (P&G) and Kraft were the market share leaders with distribution largely through grocery stores (see Exhibit 9). In advertising expenditures, the two companies represented 84 percent of total expenditures of $163 million.[10] In the coffee maker appliance market, appliance brands targeted either upscale or mass market retailers. In the upscale segment, Cuisinart, Krups, Braun, DeLonghi, and Bunn had strong distribution. In the mass channel, through which about 70 percent of all coffee makers were sold, Mr. Coffee, Black & Decker, Sunbeam, and Hamilton Beach had strong positions.

Market indicators had led Keurig to believe that a number of these large established consumer products companies were preparing to enter the emerging single-cup market. In addition to the growth of the single-cup system in the away-from-home market, recent trends in Europe were showing the adaptation of traditional espresso pod systems for American-style coffee brewing.

[10] *Packaged Facts Market Profile: The U.S. Coffee and Tea Market,* September 2001.

EXHIBIT 9   Coffee Market Share

Source: *Packaged Facts Market Profile: The U.S. Coffee and Tea Market,* September 2001.

Company	Market Share (%)
Procter & Gamble[a]	36.9
Philip Morris/Kraft	31.8
Nestlé[b]	5.0
Starbucks	3.7
Chock Full o'Nuts[c]	3.1
Tetley[d]	2.1
Community Coffee	1.8
Private Label	7.5
Other	8.1
Total	100.0

[a]Includes sales of Folgers and Millstone ground regular.
[b]Nestlé sold its ground brands to Sara Lee in late 2000.
[c]Chock Full o'Nuts sold to Sara Lee in 2000.
[d]Tetley sold off its coffee brands in 2000.

In each case, including Keurig, the systems were proprietary, with individual brewers working only with compatible coffee pod systems.

Salton, with 2002 sales of $922 million, was a leading domestic designer, marketer, and distributor of a broad range of branded, small appliances. Under its licensed brand name, Melitta, it had formally announced plans for a May 2003 launch of a new brewing system: One:One. The One:One brewer would brew coffee utilizing Javapods, small round packets of filter paper in which the grounds were sealed. Salton's expected retail brewer pricing was $49 with pod pricing of about $0.25 per pod.

Sara Lee, a U.S.-based consumer packaged products company with sales of $17.6 billion in 2002, had been active primarily in the European coffee market, but, through a series of acquisitions completed in 2000, had become a stronger force in the U.S. market. Its two best-known brands were Chock Full o'Nuts and Hills Brothers. Sara Lee had stated that the Senseo-Crema pod system might be in the U.S. market in the second half of 2003. Previously introduced in Europe, the Senseo Coffee Pod System used coffee pods of a different size than the Salton Javapods. The Sara Lee pods were bulk-packed in a bag made with a very thin layer of aluminum to preserve freshness. Sara Lee had placed almost two million Senseo pod systems in Europe since the product's introduction. The company's experience in the consumer market gave it the potential to be a formidable competitor. Senseo's European pricing suggested a U.S. retail price of about $70 and a pod price of about $0.20 (with two pods required to deliver an 8-ounce serving).

There were also rumors that P&G had partnered with an appliance marketer to launch its own proprietary pod system. It was expected that P&G would focus on mass channel distribution of both its pod brewers and pods, given P&G's strength in the grocery channel. P&G's pricing and distribution were expected to be similar to Salton's and Sara Lee's.

Nespresso, developed by Nestlé, was a European capsule-based single-cup espresso brewing system. It offered similar benefits to the Keurig system including taste, variety, and convenience. Since its introduction in 1987, more than 500,000 units had been sold, largely in Europe, using direct fulfillment via phone, fax, and Internet. Keurig wondered whether Nestlé would decide to enter the American-style single-cup coffee market, based on its experience with single-cup espresso.

Is the Cup Half-Full or Half-Empty?

Keurig did not have the resources to launch its B100 brewing system through the retail channel. However, it felt it could develop a direct marketing approach using an e-commerce-enabled Web site to sell both the brewer and K-Cups in conjunction with leveraging the distribution capabilities of roasters and KADs. In pursuing this strategy, Keurig had encountered a number of channel issues that could jeopardize its established business in the away-from-home OCS market. Chris Stevens explained the challenge of balancing the needs of the OCS channel with the development of the new at-home business:

> Feedback from our KADs indicated that they would interpret our entry into the at-home market with a direct sales approach as a first step towards a direct approach in the OCS market in the long term. Concern about this would diminish the KADs' marketing efforts in both the OCS and at-home markets, resulting in erosion of our installed base and revenue stream from our core OCS segment and a less effective launch in the at-home market. At the same time, we were worried about loss of pricing control with KADs underpricing Keurig and the roasters because they had no brewer investment to recover. In addition, there was concern that the office managers would not support our at-home marketing efforts for fear of theft of K-Cups for use in the home brewer.

Given these issues, Keurig's goal had been to introduce a controlled distribution of brewers and portion packs that would maximize the launch of the at-home business while protecting the away-from-home OCS channel. Key in this strategy had been the introduction of a second portion pack as the basis for production differentiation—a new Keurig-Cup for the at-home market—and that decision had driven its development efforts to date. The K-Cup would work only in the commercial brewer, while the Keurig-Cup worked only in the at-home brewer (see Exhibit 10). Further distinction was made with the color of the two portion packs: the K-Cups were white while the Keurig-Cups were tan. These two portion packs would be manufactured on the same packaging lines. Design of the necessary tooling to thermoform the new cup bases had been completed at a cost of about $400,000. In addition, new parts for the packaging lines at licensed roasters had been manufactured by Keurig at a cost of just under $60,000 per packaging line to enable the lines to manufacture both the Keurig-Cups and the K-Cups. While the new B100 brewer was targeted for both lower-volume OCS customers and for at-home use, different cup holder inserts and different color drawers would differentiate the brewer products in the two markets.

Building off this product differentiation, Keurig's controlled distribution strategy allowed roasters to sell Keurig-Cups in direct and indirect markets and KADs to sell them in direct markets, assuming certain volume commitments were met on sales of the associated

EXHIBIT 10
K-Cup (left) and Proposed Home Keurig-Cup (right)

Source: Keurig, Inc.

Note: Cups are shown upside down to illustrate difference in design.

brewer. KAD brewer volume commitments ensured that parties selling Keurig-Cups would be equally vested in brewer sales and focused on marketing an entire system. Roasters would manufacture Keurig-Cups for Keurig to resell directly to at-home users over the Internet. In addition to providing necessary assurances to KADS about Keurig's future plans, the two-portion-pack strategy eliminated office manager concerns over the potential theft of portion packs for use in home brewers, increasing the likelihood of their participation in in-office promotions of the Keurig system.

Unfortunately, the plan had reached a roadblock at that afternoon's meeting with GMCR. Lazaris later summed up GMCR's concerns to the senior management team in an e-mail, "We reviewed the controlled distribution structure with GMCR's management team. GMCR responded that it was complicated and resulted in doubling the number of portion pack products they would have to manufacture and warehouse. There could also be the potential for customer dissatisfaction resulting from using a portion pack in the wrong brewer. GMCR preferred the one-cup model based on long-term simplicity and the desire to move quickly because of the competitive systems coming to market. Clearly, GMCR has the same interests we do—it has the largest share of the OCS K-Cup business and can't afford to alienate the channel. It has an ownership interest in Keurig and wants to see long-term value creation. But going back to the board to discuss a major change at this point will not be easy."

At-Home Product Pricing

Another issue being wrestled with by the senior management team in early 2003 was determination of the pricing strategy for the Keurig-Cup and B100 brewer for the at-home market. A decision on the one-cup vs. two-cup approach challenged by GMCR would have a direct impact on Keurig's portion pack pricing strategy. One benefit of the controlled distribution strategy utilizing two distinct portion packs was increased control of the pricing, specifically for the Keurig-Cup. "We were interested in using a direct sales model for the at-home market," explained John Whoriskey. "With the Keurig-Cup, we could set pricing for the consumer market without having to worry about erosion of our established revenue base in the OCS market." Without the product distinction, office managers would have the opportunity to purchase portion packs from their current KAD or directly from the Keurig Web site, potentially drawing away sales from the KADs and

jeopardizing their relationships with their accounts. Regardless of the one-cup vs. two-cup approach, Keurig needed to set a price for its direct sales of coffee.

Equally challenging was the pricing of the B100 brewer. Early market research suggested that consumers paid greater attention to the pricing of the brewer and it would have a direct impact on their decision to invest in the Keurig system. In price testing, upscale consumers appeared to react favorably to pricing in the $149 to $170 range, providing Keurig with the target price for its product development and business plan forecasts. With an estimated launch of September 2003, Keurig had forecasted at-home brewer shipments of about 20,000 through year-end. Just under two-thirds of those sales were expected to be through direct Keurig sales activities, with the remainder being driven by roasters and KADs either selling B100s to at-home consumers or driving leads to Keurig by referring potential customers to the Keurig Web site. Additionally, Keurig expected KADS to buy about 3,000 B100 brewers for placement in small offices in the OCS channel. Keurig-Cup and K-Cup sales were expected to follow the same at-home/away-from-home distribution split as the brewers.

Yet another issue was the manufacturing costs of the new brewer. Development efforts on the at-home brewer were put on hold in 2002 to speed development of a smaller commercial brewer called the B1000 that was launched in December 2002. Under the leadership of Engineering Development Vice-President Dick Sweeney, development of the new B100 at-home brewer was restarted after the B1000 brewer was launched. While the B100 could also be used in offices, it was targeted at the at-home consumer market. The B1000 brewer had costs greater than $300 and some significant design issues. Sweeney explained, "Product development always has the dark cloud of unexpected consequences. What distinguishes a company is how it resolves issues and moves on. In this case, our experiences with the B1000 brewer provided valuable insight into the development of the B100 at-home brewer." Even so, the latest reports from the manufacturing partner had projected costs at $220. Additional engineering efforts were focused on reducing those costs to $200.

As a result, Keurig's senior management team and board of directors were struggling with the pricing of the B100. The three key price points being reviewed were $199, $249, and $299. The company could simply not afford to sell at the desired $149 price point and it was too late to redesign the brewer for lower costs. At $299, there would be a small profit margin to apply toward marketing and infrastructure costs. At $199, there would be a large immediate loss on brewer sales, but marketing research had shown the $199 price to be more attractive than $200 or more. While Keurig's business model allowed the recovery of losses on the brewer through the royalties on K-Cups, the degree of losses impacted cash. Lazaris wondered, "If we price high, we can always lower the price, but we may not have the time to correct the pricing, given competitive pressures."

Marketing Plan for At-Home Launch

Unlike the OCS market, the at-home market did not include a single source for both brewer and coffee sales. Traditionally, consumers made separate purchases. Brewer distribution was through small appliance retailers like department stores, mass merchants, and kitchen specialty stores, while coffee distribution was through grocery stores, gourmet food retailers, and coffee shops. Each product was promoted independently and essentially all brewers worked with all coffees. The Keurig brewer and its patented single-portion pack presented unique distribution challenges. To accomplish a Keurig system sale would require either direct distribution or a great deal of investment to develop traditional channels and to place enough brewers to pull portion packs through retail shelves. To complicate matters, market research had made it clear that the Keurig system was a "demonstration-driven product." The question was how best to demonstrate the system to the target market of gourmet coffee drinkers.

"Based on the market research and the unique challenges of the Keurig system, leveraging our current OCS penetration was a primary focus of our at-home launch strategy. We planned to target Keurig office users, people already familiar with the benefits of the Keurig system, and convert them to at-home buyers in order to build critical mass to support channel expansion," explained VP of away-from-home marketing Dave Manly. With more than 30,000 commercial brewers in place, Keurig had about one million people to focus on in its direct marketing efforts.

Critical to the success of direct marketing efforts to "Keurig-aware" coffee drinkers was the support and involvement of the Keurig authorized distributors. The KADs maintained relationships with office managers where commercial brewers were placed and had knowledge of each office's size. Keurig would not be able to market to coffee drinkers in the offices without the KADs' assistance. As a result, Keurig had designed

EXHIBIT 11
Point-of-Sale Display

Source: Keurig, Inc.

a KAD referral program that gave them attractive incentives to support the marketing of the new brewer.

The KAD referral program was to be driven by point-of-sale (POS) advertising that had been developed for display on or near the office brewer (see Exhibit 11). In exchange for placement of the POS materials, the KAD would be compensated $15 for each home brewer sale attributed to that KAD's OCS accounts and would be paid a two-cent-per-K-Cup (or Keurig-Cup) annuity on subsequent coffee sales that Keurig made to that customer for three years. Chris Stevens outlined the company's expectations: "We anticipated that about 60 percent of our KADs would participate in our joint marketing program with sales of two brewers for each office where advertising was placed. We estimated that the remaining 40 percent would already be planning their own marketing program and would want to maintain more control of their customers."

A second avenue for marketing to "Keurig-awares" would be via an Internet direct marketing campaign. Since the launch of the commercial brewer in the OCS market, Keurig had received unsolicited e-mails from more than 12,000 users of its office system who wanted to know when a similar system would be available for home use. Keurig planned to market to these people directly and expected 20 percent of them to purchase a home brewer in the first three months of the launch. Finally, a public relations campaign coupled with additional marketing activities by roasters such as placement in their retail stores, catalogs, and Web sites would provide additional avenues for sales to gourmet coffee drinkers.

Lazaris's Dilemmas

As Lazaris reflected on Keurig's strategy for the launch of its at-home brewer in preparation for the senior management meeting, he wondered:

1. How should we respond to GMCR's request to switch to the single K-Cup approach? What do we really need to know to make this decision? How will our other roasters and the KADS respond? Can our team really implement a new game plan at this late date and still launch in six months? Can we afford the write-off on the new Keurig-Cup and packaging line tooling?

2. What is the right price for the brewer? Is there a way to afford a $149 price point on the brewer that we have not thought of?

3. How should we price the at-home portion pack? If we have one cup in all markets, what pricing is optimal? If we have both the K-Cup and the Keurig-Cup, what pricing makes sense and optimizes our market opportunity?

4. Have we taken the necessary steps for our marketing plan to succeed? Is there another avenue that we are overlooking?

Source: Elizabeth L. Anderson, Keurig at Home: Managing a New Product Launch, Kellogg School of Management, January 27, 2006. One-time permission to reproduce granted by Kellogg School of Management.

Case 6-8

Tesco

Tesco is the UK's dominant retailer, taking around 30% of the national grocery market, and the company has overtaken Argos/Homebase to become the UK's biggest retailer of non-food items. It is the world's third largest retailer after Wal-Mart and Carrefour. Its annual group sales are pushing £53 billion, with profits of £2.75 billion in 2008. Tesco.com is one of the world's most successful Internet retailing models with 850,000 customers and sales growing at around 30% a year. The company's growth and business performance up to the mid-2000s has been outstanding.

After a decade of extraordinary growth, Tesco is nearly twice the size of its nearest competitors, Asda and Sainsbury, and takes £1 in every £8 spent in Britain's shops. However, for much of that time Tesco has faced only weak competition—Morrisons was embroiled in the problematic acquisition of Safeway, Sainsbury had a legacy of major operational problems and even Asda wobbled after it was bought by Wal-Mart. For this decade, Tesco appeared unbeatable and unstoppable. However, by mid-2008 there were growing signs that Tesco's performance could be faltering. A slowdown in

This case was written by Nigel F. Piercy, Warwick Business School, The University of Warwick.

sales growth over Christmas 2007 saw £1 billion wiped off Tesco's market value. Underlying sales growth in the UK was running at 3–4% compared to the 5–6% of earlier years, as rivals like Morrisons and Sainsbury have bounced back. Profit forecasts in the City have been trimmed, and Tesco had lost market share for three quarters in a row. Tesco shares fell 15% in the first quarter of 2008. Full year results were stronger, but investors were also unhappy to see a steady stream of senior executives leaving Tesco to join its rivals.

Tescopoly in the UK

Tesco has become a profoundly unpopular company. In 2008, when Tesco collected awards at the Retail Week "industry Oscars"—leader of the year for CEO Sir Terry Leahy and "consumers' favourite retailer'—on the walk to the stage the Tesco executives were booed by their peers not cheered. Anti-Tesco protests are widespread among local communities resisting the arrival of new superstores in their towns and fighting the growing dominance of Tesco Express local stores in suburban areas. Some 2000 small independent food shops close every year because of supermarket competition. Competition Commission recommendations appear aimed directly at curbing Tesco's growth. Tesco's reputation is one of aggressive treatment of competitors, brutal almost feudal treatment of suppliers, and transgressions like collusion to fix prices in the dairy business. In

2008, when the *Guardian* newspaper published articles alleging that Tesco was avoiding paying UK taxes, the company moved rapidly to silence its critics through the courts, leading the *Guardian* to observe: "It is hard to think of another large public company that would resort to such bullying tactics." Tesco's 2008 AGM saw angry critics flying in from India, China and the USA to attack Tesco strategy, as well as a TV chef demanding better conditions for Tesco's battery-farmed chickens, amid much television and press publicity.

Internationalizing Tesco

In the 1990s Leahy started serious efforts to develop the Tesco business abroad. It has grown to a portfolio of around 12 different markets, employing 450,000 people, with the international business generating £7.6 billion in sales and £370 million profit. Tesco is increasingly looking to its international businesses to drive growth. About 80% of group capital is being spent on overseas expansion. While internationalization has been part of Tesco's strategy for some time, the way conditions are developing for the company in the UK now makes success in the international operations a much higher imperative. In 2008 the UK still accounted for 76% of Tesco sales and 78% of profits.

International growth at Tesco has a mixed history. A purchase of the French supermarket chain Catteau in 1993 was a disaster, and the company pulled out of its Taiwan operation because of poor results in the face of competition from Carrefour. However, the company has growing businesses in Eastern Europe—the Czech Republic, Poland, Slovakia and Hungary. In 2007 Tesco began rolling out Tesco-Express type stores in Japan, suggesting after four years of trying they had finally found an effective format. The company is looking for aggressive expansion in the world's second-biggest economy. It has around 150 stores in Japan—of which about 50 are its own-branded Tesco Express outlets. Tesco entered Japan in 2004, through acquisition of the Tsurakame chain of discount supermarkets. The venture was dogged by early setbacks, and returns were the lowest of all Tesco's international markets. Japan is not an easy market—Carrefour withdrew in 2005 and Wal-Mart is struggling.

Tesco operates around 50 hypermarkets in China, on the east coast between Beijing and Shenzhen. In 2008 Tesco took its Express convenience chain into China as well—the first Tesco Legou Express opening in February. China became the eighth overseas market to get the Tesco Express format, joining Thailand, Japan, South Korea, Ireland, Turkey, the Czech Republic and Hungary. The multi-format approach increasingly characterizes Tesco's international strategy. In 2008 the company acquired the South Korean discount chain Homeover for just under £1 billion, adding 36 stores to its existing Korean business.

The importance of international success underlines the significance of Tesco's entry into the USA with its Fresh & Easy retail concept. Leahy's international strategy has been based on only entering emerging markets with fragmented local competition, a large population and potential for rapid economic growth to boost consumer spending. Entry to the USA is a major departure from this successful strategy.

Tesco's American Adventure

The USA has been the graveyard for many British retailers' international strategies. It is a fiercely competitive marketplace and entries by firms like Marks & Spencer and Sainsbury have been disasters. Nonetheless, Tesco has committed £1.25 billion over five years to its new Fresh & Easy convenience store format in the USA. Leahy stands to make an £11.5 million bonus if the venture pays off. The goal is to have 200 stores open by the end of the 2008/9 financial year, though it could be a chain of 1,000 stores by 2012 if the retail format is favoured by US consumers. A rapid roll-out is important to making the low-margin business model work. Initial store openings were in California in 2007, with plans for more in Arizona and Nevada, and possibly Mexico. This rate of expansion is unprecedented for Tesco—its next biggest overseas market is Thailand, where it took 9 years to open 220 stores. Tesco has almost no brand recognition in the USA—when the F&E team first went to the USA they could not even lease cars easily—people would say "are Tesco good for the money?"

The Fresh & Easy Concept

Tesco's US market entry is based on a small-store format—loosely based on the Tesco Express, but emphasizing low price for high quality and healthy food—operating as Fresh & Easy (F&E) not as Tesco branded stores.

Developing Market Understanding . . .

The Tesco commitment to its US strategy is underlined by the intense efforts to build an understanding of the US market. Researchers probed the refrigerator contents of and lifestyles of US families, checking the time they got up, what they ate for breakfast and when they shopped. The retailer even prepared meals for them. For two weeks 50 senior Tesco directors and managers lived the "American dream"—shopping and eating with US families on the West Coast, even sharing their leisure activities. Amid intense secrecy a prototype store was built in Los Angeles—the cover story was that they were making a movie, and executives used plastic bags of cash rather than corporate credit cards to buy things for the mock store, rather than risk tipping off rivals what they were doing. People were flown in from San Francisco, Las Vegas and Phoenix to test new ideas and products—more than 200 focus groups toured the store. Interestingly, part of the F&E strategy is to open its small stores in poor inner-city areas largely unpopulated by rival retailers—the US "grocery gap," where areas like South Central Los Angeles lack supermarkets and the city's poorest residents pay the highest prices for food at small local stores with limited access to fresh food.

Fresh & Easy's Market Positioning...

The F&E positioning is between the discount, cut-price supermarkets and the trendy, upscale "organic" food stores. The major competitors in the health-conscious market are Trader Joe's and Ralphs, featuring attractive stores with unpackaged fresh produce and expansive salad bars. The business model positions F&E as a hard discounter, with costs kept low by keeping product ranges and store formats identical across the chain. The goal is to undercut competitors like Trader Joe's by 10–25%. F&E CEO Tim Mason notes "The brand is designed to be as fresh as Whole Foods, with value like a Wal-Mart, the convenience of a Walgreens and product range of a Trader Joe's." Nonetheless, initial reactions were mixed—some consumers complained that the "Fresh & Easy" name sounded more like a chain of chicken ranches, or a tampon.

The Fresh & Easy Value Proposition...

The proposition is low-cost fresh food. Much of the fresh produce and premium ready meals are locally-sourced—F&E sells large sushi packs for under £2 and Australian wine for £1. Prices are low because stores are located in low-rent areas. Some locations are planned for "food deserts"—areas like Compton in Los Angeles, which other retailers have avoided. The F&E stores are small by comparison with normal supermarkets—at 10,000 square feet they are less than a third the size of the average supermarket. Many of the ideas like the

free-sample and recipe kitchen and signs about being a good neighbour are very similar to Trader Joe's and Whole Foods, but the prices are substantially lower. For the USA, F&E is a radical innovation in the form of a neighbourhood convenience store with a distinctive offering. While related to the Tesco Express format, the goal was not to transfer the Tesco format from Britain to America, but to design an American store for American consumers.

As in all its operations, Tesco adapts to local market conditions. In the US chain there are no British products and no Tesco logos. The US operation in California is painfully "hip." The head office has life-sized surf boards pinned to the walls, middle-aged executives are squeezed into tight jeans, and CEO Tim Mason from the UK, normally "suited and booted," has taken to wearing friendship bracelets. The stores are predominantly painted green and include parking spaces reserved for hybrid cars and bicycle racks.

For the first time in its history, Tesco has become directly involved in food production. It operates a food preparation facility—dubbed the Fresh & Easy Kitchen—at its central distribution centre near Los Angeles. The company decided to set up its own kitchen because of concerns about using third-party suppliers who did not meet their standards. Forty percent of the ingredients for the kitchen, as well as prepacked fresh products for the stores, are provided by Wild Rocket Foods and 2 Sisters Food Group. These two UK suppliers have each invested $100 million in setting up food processing plants adjacent to the Tesco distribution "campus." None of Tesco's US competitors operates similar kitchen facilities.

The Underlying Relationship Network...

The F&E operation rests on a complex set of strategic relationships and networks, some of which provide the strengths of the F&E business model, and some of which underline weaknesses in Tesco's US operation.

The **consumer relationship** is potentially problematic. F&E is mainly own-brand, which is a risk with brand-obsessed US consumers. The stores are utilitarian and basic in a country where this is far from the usual food retail expectation. There are few staff on hand to assist, which is unusual for US stores and their service culture. The F&E stores use self-service checkouts to reduce costs, which is difficult for the elderly and non-English speaking consumers-Americans are used to being served. Neither are there any of the money-off coupons and vouchers to which US consumers are accustomed. There may be good reasons why other retailers in the USA have decided not to try to change middle America's shopping and eating habits.

The **competitor relationships** are critical to F&E's survival. Initially, it seemed that the push-back from US competitors was muted, and Tesco believed that the local retailers assumed that F&E was so radical it would not be a threat to them. In fact, the F&E venture is being closely tracked by US competitors. Some analysts suggested that lining your tanks up on Wal-Mart's front lawn and expecting them to be ignored was a little optimistic. Wal-Mart is planning small-format grocery stores in the Phoenix area and Safeway is launching small stores in northern California. Indeed, Wal-Mart has hired a former Tesco executive to head its defence. The signs are that Wal-Mart's first-ever small stores under the banner "Marketside" will adopt a green logo with a stylized tomato, egg and grape design, suggesting a greater emphasis on healthy eating and fresh produce—and indicating an all-out war with Tesco's F&E operation. The first Wal-Mart Marketside locations are close to F&E sites. The Wal-Mart Marketside stores will be built around a "premium offering" rather than low cost—with less focus on price than F&E and more emphasis on "meal solutions," with food prepared in-store. The Safeway "Market by Vons" small-store format has been launched in California—described as "very pretty" but "very expensive" by Tesco's Tim Mason. The competitive responses by both Wal-Mart and Safeway are avoiding the F&E low price position.

Part of the F&E strategy relies on a new approach to **supplier relationships.** One critical part of the strategy developed by Tesco was to bring UK-based suppliers with them to the USA. This has the strength of securing expertise in the type of product preparation required for Fresh & Easy. However, it also has the attraction of avoiding dependence on local suppliers in the USA, who would likely be in the pocket of Wal-Mart or other US supermarkets—being a new, small customer for suppliers dealing with US retail giants would be a very weak and vulnerable position likely to lead to product shortages, short deliveries and poor service from suppliers. Tesco avoided this problem by bringing with them suppliers already trained to toe the Tesco line—unlikely to cause problems and risk their standing with Tesco in the UK. Relatedly, back-office functions have been outsourced to Bangalore in India to keep administration costs low.

There have been some problems regarding existing **partnership relationships.** One cost of Tesco's entry into the USA was the demise of collaborative relationships that had been established over time with US companies. A joint venture with Safeway in home shopping—Grocery Works—was ended by Safeway because of the F&E venture. Tesco owns 84% of Dunnhumby, the loyalty card research firm, and their largest client in the US—Krogers—was evaluating the viability of the relationship in the light of Tesco's entry into US food retailing.

Perhaps the most problematic part of the F&E relationship network relates to **relationships with employees and trades unions.** The main grocery workers' union—the United Food and Commercial Workers Union—represents almost 90,000 people in southern California. It is part of the Alliance for Healthy and Responsible Grocery Stores—a coalition of community groups, faith-based organizations and unions. The alliance was formed after a long strike by California grocery workers in 2003, and has since succeeded in blocking Wal-Mart superstore developments.

This alliance is a vocal critic of Tesco, accusing the company of arrogance, being out of touch with local communities, and failing to appreciate the close ties between consumers and grocery workers. The deal-breaker is Tesco's employment of non-unionized staff. Notwithstanding requests from the unions for meetings, backed by letters from Hillary Clinton and Barack Obama, Tesco has refused to meet union representatives. Obama urged Tesco to work with local communities to develop community-benefits agreements—written pledges of the rewards a store opening would bring to local areas. As he moved ever closer to the US Presidency, Obama renewed his pleas direct to Leahy on union membership, though with no discernible effect on the company's position. The union is also looking to British Labour MPs to support its campaign.

The union stepped up its campaign, dubbing the Tesco chain "Fresh & Queasy" and questioning the freshness of its products (using television programme evidence about shortcomings in hygiene and waste control in Tesco's UK food stores). The union's website accuses Fresh & Queasy of being the "Wal-Mart of the UK" with a "bad record" on selling organic foods. The union was behind the establishment of a new group called Health First, which was the group that brought a successful court case against Tesco on the basis that its main warehouse did not meet environmental planning law—similar tactics have been used to stop the expansion of Wal-Mart in California.

The Early F&E Results

Tesco declined to honour an earlier undertaking to break out the US results in its 2008 annual report, fuelling growing rumours that the early performance of F&E was falling short of expectations. Tesco strongly rebutted such claims. In March 2008, after a frenetic opening programme of 61 stores in five months, Tesco announced a three month "pause" in store openings on the west coast (although store openings resumed in July in Los Angeles). F&E losses up to February 2009 were predicted at £100 million compared to £62 million the previous year. Jeff Adams (former Tesco chief in Thailand) was parachuted into the US business as Chief Operating Officer—with plans he should be used in Chicago and the Midwest, once the California, Nevada and Arizona operation reaches critical mass. In April 2008 Tesco announced plans to cash in on part of its property portfolio by selling off some UK stores, to help fund its international expansion.

Suppliers were reporting disappointing sales at F&E, and that F&E stores were struggling to attract customers. While Tesco had targeted weekly sales at $12–$22 a square foot, one analyst reported sales densities in F&E were as low as $5 a square foot. One unsourced report suggested F&E was missing internal targets by as much as 70%. Analysts began to predict that F&E losses would escalate in 2009—possibly to more than double previous estimates. Consumer blogs described the F&E stores as "boring, sterile and depressing," and branded goods suppliers (frustrated by the fact that more than half F&E's 3,500 products are own-label) have not been slow to spread rumours that the chain is on its knees. Others suggest that the F&E retail concept is flawed and cannot succeed.

Tim Mason used the break in store openings to "tweak" the F&E model: **prices**—consumers did not get the low price image, so "extra-low price" promotions have been introduced—what Mason calls "turning up the volume on price;" **promotion**—introducing discount couponing around stores offering $5 off a $20 shop; **products**—new fresh food lines added; **shopping trolleys**—bigger trolleys outside the stores because small trolleys suggest small shopping trips; and **store design**—more colours to make the stores "warmer" and less sterile. He is also fighting very high wastage rates with fresh products.

Nonetheless, in April 2008 the company announced plans for a second distribution centre and kitchen in northern California. Leahy was positively gushing in presenting his 2008 report, claiming F&E was ahead of budget and that the F&E stores already had a "special place" with US consumers.

These judgements are grossly unfair, based on the first few months' trading of a new business. It will not be clear for a considerable period of time whether F&E will succeed. However, the issue becomes whether pressures will lead to premature exit from the business and the potentially disproportionate effect of the F&E venture's performance on Tesco's UK and other overseas businesses.

Dilemmas for Tesco's Fresh & Queasy

The F&E positioning is between the discount supermarkets (e.g., Wal-Mart) and upmarket, stylish "gourmet" retailers like Trader Joe's (and to a lesser extent the much larger Whole Foods Market and Bristol Farms). F&E offers more fresh and organic foods than the discounters, but is cheaper than the gourmet outlets. The classic dilemma is whether they have found a profitable and defensible new market space, or whether they have in effect created a "stuck in the middle" operation that is neither one thing nor the other, which will lose out on price to the discounters and on product quality to the gourmet stores. If F&E has uncovered a new market space, then the question remains whether it can be defended or whether it will simply be invaded by new formats developed by established US competitors or by new entrants. There appears little in the F&E format that could not be copied and bettered by competitors. These issues have not been resolved and will determine whether F&E survives competitive attacks. It is noteworthy that the new formats developed by Wal-Mart and Safeway to compete with F&E have avoided low price positioning.

Certainly, the factors that drove Tesco's initial success in the UK (radical price discounting) and then allowed the company to sustain and consolidate its position (market power used against suppliers, blocking competitors access to new sites, and political clout) simply do not exist in the USA. To local suppliers, Tesco is a small, new entrant with little buying power and they are unlikely to tolerate the aggressive attitudes to which Tesco exposes suppliers at home. Tesco has no record of working with trades unions and local communities, which is a requirement in the California marketplace. Tesco's clout in the UK is backed by muscle weight which it simply does not have in the USA. It remains to be seen if the company can adjust to these realities and develop new ways of working.

In the short-term, Tesco faces the problem of whether the retail format it has piloted in the south-west USA, in the form of Fresh & Easy will be capable of successful expansion elsewhere in America. Will a format that matches the characteristics of California and Arizona consumers really travel to Oklahoma, Wisconsin and New York? Unlike the UK, there are relatively few genuinely national food retailers in the USA, reflecting this market diversity in America. Moreover, while the early operation in the south-west has several important protections built into the business model—most importantly the import of European suppliers to make the supply chain secure—there is a major question mark over the extent to which these protections can be maintained in a larger expansion in the USA. If Fresh & Easy has to change supply chain strategy to expand, dealing mainly with local suppliers, then the viability of the operation becomes more questionable.

However, perhaps the largest dilemma for Tesco to confront with Fresh & Easy in the USA is not simply "will it work?" but "how much will it hurt us if it fails?" The immediate costs of failure in the USA would not be devastating—stores could be disposed of, and so on. The real damage would be the impact of failure on the rest of the business. It would raise the question that if Tesco can be beaten in one market, then perhaps it can be beaten in another—perhaps even in the UK. At a time when the Tesco UK juggernaut is beginning to slow, and Leahy is coming towards the end of his tenure as CEO with no obvious successor apparent, this is potentially a major new vulnerability for the business. The F&E operation is minute in terms of the total Tesco business, but with its very high profile underlining its strategic importance, failure would have a disproportionate effect on Tesco's strength. Certainly, if Tesco cannot succeed in the USA, then its aspirations towards being a genuine global competitor to Wal-Mart are at an end.

In particular (much to Leahy's disgust) Tesco went through the late-1990s and started the 2000s with its shares considerably undervalued by the stock market. This largely reflected the market's nervousness about Tesco's aggressive expansion strategy. A public failure in the USA would provoke an unprecedented crisis for the business, and would very likely depress its share value yet again. In these circumstances, Tesco would become an attractive target for a strategic investor.

The opportunities for an aggressive investor to release value for shareholders would be very attractive, for example: spinning off as separate businesses the different retail formats, the international operation and the Internet operation; selling assets like the land and property bank (estimated value of £14 billion alone); selling key operating retail sites to competitors. Such moves would transform the Tesco business, release huge value for shareholders, and probably meet with the wholehearted approval of the British regulators and critics of Tesco's market dominance. However, the legacy business would be nothing like the current Tesco operation, and Leahy's strategy would be in tatters. The incoming CEO would find that the Tesco business model was broken.

This scenario would be attractive to many suppliers who have had their profit margins crushed by Tesco's aggressive and oppressive use of its market power. Some might even play a role in orchestrating and supporting the investor-led restructuring of Tesco, as a way of reducing their dependence on the company. If Sainsbury were finally to be purchased by private equity interests and to undergo a similar type of restructuring, the UK retail grocery market would be a very different prospect for suppliers.

The F&E platform is intended to form a launch pad for a broader push against Wal-Mart, both in the USA and in other global markets where the two retailers compete against each other. If F&E fails, then Tesco is left without this component of its global competition strategy. This is an urgent issue. Tesco has placed India top of its target list after the USA. Its talks with local partner Bharti collapsed, and Bharti went on to partner with Wal-Mart, leaving Tesco to identify another possible partnership and play "catch-up" to Wal-Mart again.

Sources: Jenny Davey and William Kay, "Tesco Fails to Find America Easy," *Sunday Times,* April 6 2008, p. 3–8. Elizabeth Rigby, "Tesco's Trolley May Have Started to Wobble," *Financial Times,* April 5/6 2008, p. 19. Jonathan Birchall and Tom Braithwaite, "Tesco Denies Claims of US Troubles," *Financial Times,* February 27 2008, p. 22. Elizabeth Rigby and Jonathan Birchall, "Tesco US Subsidiary Moves Into Food Production," *Financial Times,* December 2 2007, p. 22. Jenny Davey, "Tesco Drives Into America," *Sunday Times,* June 10 2007, p. 3–1. Kerry Capell, "Tesco: California Dreaming?," *BusinessWeek,* February 27 2006, p. 38. Aaron O. Patrick, "Tesco Alleges Libel by Guardian in Tax Stories," *Wall Street Journal,* April 7 2008, p. 4. Elizabeth Rigby, "Leahy Hits Back Over Fresh & Easy," *Financial Times,* April 16 2008, p. 21. Elizabeth Rigby, "US Tesco Chief Dons Lucky Shirt to Fend Off Criticism," *Financial Times,* June 16 2008, p. 17.

Case 6-9
Wal-Mart[1]

Richard Ivey School of Business
The University of Western Ontario

Introduction

With US$312.4 billion in 2006 sales from operations spanning 15 countries, Wal-Mart Stores, Inc. (Wal-Mart) was the world's largest retailer. Wal-Mart's supply chain, a key enabler of its growth from its beginnings in rural Arkansas, was long considered by many to be a major source of competitive advantage for the company. In fact, when Wal-Mart was voted "Retailer of the Decade" in 1989, its distribution costs were estimated at 1.7 percent of its cost of sales, comparing favorably with competitors such as Kmart (3.5 percent of total sales) and Sears (five percent of total sales).[2]

But by 2006, competitors were catching up. Many of Wal-Mart's management techniques, which it borrowed and refined after having seen them in action at innovative retailers, were now being copied by others. By 2006, most retailers were using bar codes, shared sales data with suppliers, had in-house trucking fleets to enable self distribution, and possessed computerized point-of-sale systems that collected item-level data in-real-time.

Although Wal-Mart continually searched for cost saving initiatives, in the most recent quarters the company had been unable to meet its self-imposed target of holding inventory growth to half the level of sales growth. Wal-Mart's new executive vice-president of logistics, Johnnie C. Dobbs, wondered what he could do to ensure that Wal-Mart's supply chain remained a key competitive advantage for his firm.

Retail Industry

U.S. retail sales, excluding motor vehicles and parts dealers, reached US$2.8 trillion in 2005. Major categories in the U.S. retail industry included the following:[3]

Category	2005 (US$ billions)
General merchandise stores	525.7
Food and beverage	519.3
Food services and drinking places	396.6
Gasoline	388.3
Building materials and gardening equipment and supplies	327.0
Furniture, home furnishings, electronics and appliances	211.7
Health and personal care	208.4
Clothing and clothing accessories	201.7
Sporting goods, hobby, book, music	81.9

In the United States, retailers competed at local, regional and national levels, with some of the major chains such as Wal-Mart and Costco counting operations in foreign

[3]www.census.gov, accessed 23 August 2006.

---

[1]This case has been written on the basis of published sources only. Consequently, the interpretation and perspectives presented in this case are not necessarily those of Wal-Mart or any of its employees.
[2]*Discount Store News, "Low distribution costs buttress chain's profits,"* 18 December 1989.

countries as well. In addition to the traditional one-store owner-operated retailer, the industry included formats such as discount stores, department stores (selling a large percentage of soft goods, i.e., clothing), variety and convenience stores, specialty stores, supermarkets, supercentres (combination discount and supermarket stores), Internet-retailers and catalogue retailers. Major retailers competed for employees and store locations, as well as for customers. The 10 biggest global retailers were as follows:

Retailer	2006 Sales (US$ billions)	Head quarters
Wal-Mart Stores, Inc.	312.4	U.S.
Carrefour SA	88.2	France
The Home Depot, Inc.	81.5	U.S.
Metro AG	66.0	Germany
Tesco	63.7	U.K.
The Kroger Co.	60.6	U.S.
Costco	53.0	U.S.
Target Corp.	52.6	U.S.
Royal Ahold	52.2	Netherlands
Aldi Group	37.0 (est.)	Germany

Source: Company reports, www.hoovers.com

The top 200 retailers accounted for approximately 30 percent of worldwide retail sales.[4] For 2005, retail sales were estimated to be US$3.7 trillion[5] in the United States and CDN$572 billion in Canada.[6]

Background of Wal-Mart Stores, Inc.[7]

Based in Bentonville, Arkansas and founded by the legendary Sam Walton, Wal-Mart was the world's largest retailer with more than 6,500 stores worldwide, including stores in all 50 states as well as international stores in Argentina, Brazil, Canada, Costa Rica, El Salvador,

[4]http://www.uneptie.org/pc/sustain/reports/Retail/Nov4Mtg 2002/Retail_Stats.pdf, accessed 10 May 2006.
[5]http://www.census.gov/mrts/www/data/pdf/annpub06.pdf, accessed 10 May 2006.
[6]http://www.cardonline.ca/tools/cma_retail.cfm, accessed 10 May 2006.
[7]The information contained in the background and history section is similar to that found in "Wal-Mart Stores, Inc.," 9B06M068.

Guatemala, Honduras, Mexico, Nicaragua, Puerto Rico and the United Kingdom, as well as joint venture agreements in China and a stake in a leading Japanese retail chain. The company had 1.3 million employees (known as "associates") in the United States and a total of 1.8 million worldwide. It was estimated that Wal-Mart served more than 138 million customers each week. Exhibit 1 presents a summary of Wal-Mart historical financial statements.

Wal-Mart's strategy was to provide a broad assortment of quality merchandise and services at "everyday low prices" (EDLP) and was best known for its discount stores, which offered merchandise such as apparel, small appliances, housewares, electronics and hardware, but also ran combined discount and grocery stores (Wal-Mart Super Centers), membership-only warehouse stores Sam's Club), and smaller grocery stores (Neighborhood Markets). In the general merchandise area, Wal-Mart's competitors included Sears and Target, with specialty retailers including Gap and Limited. Department store competitors included Dillard, Federated and J.C. Penney. Grocery store competitors included Kroger, Albertsons and Safeway. The major membership-only warehouse competitor was Costco Wholesale.

The Development of Wal-Mart's Supply Chain

Before he started Wal-Mart Stores in 1962, Sam Walton owned a successful chain of stores under the Ben Franklin Stores banner, a franchisor of variety stores in the United Although he was under contract to purchase most of his merchandise requirements from Ben Franklin Stores, Walton was able to selectively purchase merchandise in bulk from new suppliers and then transport these goods to his stores directly. When Walton realized that a new trend, discount retailing—based on driving high volumes of product through low-cost retail outlets—was sweeping the nation, he decided to open up large, warehouse-style stores in order to compete. To stock his new warehouse-style stores, initially named "Wal-Mart Discount City," Walton needed to step up his merchandise procurement efforts. As none of the suppliers were willing to send their trucks to his stores, which were located in rural Arkansas, self-distribution was necessary.

As Wal-Mart grew in the 1960s to 1980s, it benefited from improved road infrastructure and the inability of its competitors to react to changes in legislation, such as the removal of "resale price maintenance," which had prevented retailers from discounting merchandise.

EXHIBIT 1 Wal-Mart Key Financial Figures (2000–2006)

Source: Wal-Mart annual reports

Fiscal Year Ended January 31	2000	2001	2002	2003	2004	2005	2006
Operating Results							
Net sales	156,249	180,787	204,011	229,616	256,329	285,222	312,427
Cost of sales	121,825	140,720	159,097	78,299	198,747	219,793	240,391
Operating, selling, general and administrative expenses	26,025	30,822	35,147	39,983	44,909	51,248	56,733
Interest expense, net	840	1,196	1,183	927	832	986	1,172
Effective tax rate	36.8%	36.5%	36.2%	35.2%	36.1%	34.7%	33.4%
Income from continuing operations	5,394	6,087	6,448	7,818	8,861	10,267	11,231
Net income	5,324	6,235	6,592	7,955	9,054	10,267	11,231
Financial Position							
Current assets of continuing operations	23,478	25,344	26,615	29,543	34,421	38,854	43,824
Inventories	19,296	20,987	22,053	24,401	26,612	29,762	32,191
Property, equipment and capital lease assets, net	35,533	40,461	45,248	51,374	59,023	68,118	79,290
Total assets of continuing operations	68,983	76,231	81,549	92,900	105,405	120,154	138,187
Current liabilities of continuing operations	25,525	28,366	26,795	32,225	37,840	43,182	48,826
Long-term debt	13,653	12,489	15,676	16,597	17,102	20,087	26,429
Long-term obligations under capital leases	3,000	3,152	3,044	3,000	2,997	3,171	3,742
Shareholders' equity	25,878	31,407	35,192	39,461	43,623	49,396	53,171

Purchasing

As his purchasing efforts increased in scale, Walton and his senior management team would make trips to buying offices in New York City, cutting out the middleman (wholesalers and distributors). Wal-Mart's U.S. buyers, located in Bentonville, worked with suppliers to ensure that the correct mix of staples and new items were ordered. Over time, many of Wal-Mart's largest suppliers had offices in Bentonville, staffed by analysts and managers supporting Wal-Mart's business.

In addition, Wal-Mart started sourcing products globally, opening the first of these offices in China in the mid-1980s. Wal-Mart's international purchasing offices worked directly with local factories to source Wal-Mart's private label merchandise. Private label sales at Wal-Mart, first developed in the 1980s, were believed to account for 20 percent of 2005 sales. Private label products appealed to customers since they were often priced at a significant discount to brand name merchandise; for Wal-Mart, the private label items generated higher margins than did the suppliers' branded products.

Every quarter, buyers met in Bentonville to review new merchandise, exchange buying notes and tips and review a fully-merchandised prototype store, located within a warehouse. In order to gather field intelligence, buyers toured stores two or three days a week, working on the sales floors to help associates stock and sell merchandise.

Wal-Mart wielded enormous power over its suppliers. For example, observers noted that increased bargaining clout was a contributing factor in Procter & Gamble's (P&G) acquisition of chief rival Gillette.[8] Prior to the acquisition, sales to Wal-Mart accounted for 17 percent of P&G's revenues and 13 percent of Gillette's revenues.[9] On the other hand, these two suppliers combined accounted for about eight percent of Wal-Mart's sales.[10]

---

[8] http://www.newyorker.com/talk/content/?050214ta_talk_surowiecki, accessed 7 Feb 2005.
[9] Larry Dignan, "Procter & Gamble, Gillette Merger Could Challenge Wal-Mart RFID Adoption," Extremetech.com, accessed 31 January 2005.
[10] Mark Roberti, "P&G-Gillette Merger Could Benefit RFID," *RFID Journal,* 4 February 2005.

Some viewed Wal-Mart's close co-operation with suppliers in a negative light:

> Wal-Mart dictates that its suppliers…accept payment entirely on Wal-Mart's terms…share information all the way back to the purchasing of raw materials. Wal-Mart controls with whom its suppliers speak, how and where they can sell their goods and even encourages them to support Wal-Mart in its political fights. Wal-Mart all but dictates to suppliers where to manufacture their product, as well as how to design those products and what materials and ingredients to use in those products.[11]

When negotiating with its suppliers, Wal-Mart insisted on a single invoice price and did not pay for co-operative advertising, discounting or distribution.

Globally, Wal-Mart was thought to have around 90,000 suppliers, of whom 200—such as Nestle, P&G, Unilever and Kraft—were key global suppliers. With Wal-Mart's expectations on sales data analysis, category management responsibilities and external research specific to their Wal-Mart business, it was not uncommon for a supplier to have several dozen employees working full-time to support the Wal-Mart business.

Distribution

Wal-Mart's store openings were driven directly by its distribution strategy. Because its first distribution centre in the early 1970 was a significant investment for the firm, Walton insisted on saturating the area within a day's driving distance of the distribution centres in order to gain economies of scale. Over the years, competitors copied this "hub-and-spoke" design of high volume distribution centres serving a cluster of stores. This distribution-led store expansion strategy persisted for the next two decades as Wal-Mart added thousands of U.S. stores, expanding across the nation from its headquarters in Arkansas.

Stores were located in low-rent, suburban areas, close to major highways. In contrast, key competitor Kmart's stores were thinly spread throughout the United States and were located in prime, urban areas. By the time the rest of the retail industry started to take notice of Wal-Mart in the 1980s, it had built up the most efficient logistics network of any retailer.

Wal-Mart's 75,000-person logistics division and its information systems division included the largest private truck fleet employee base of any firm—7,800 drivers, who delivered the majority of merchandise sold at stores. Wal-Mart's 114 U.S. distribution centres, located throughout the United States, were a mix of general merchandise, food and soft goods (clothing) distribution centres, processing over five billion cases a year through its entire network.

Product was picked up at the suppliers' warehouse by Wal-Mart's in-house trucking division and was then shipped to Wal-Mart's distribution centres. Shipments were generally cross-docked, or directly transferred, from inbound to outbound trailers without extra storage. To ensure that cases moved efficiently through the distribution centres, Wal-Mart worked with suppliers to standardize case sizes and labeling. The average distance from distribution centre to stores was approximately 130 miles. Each of these distribution centres was profiled in a store-friendly way, with similar products stacked together Merchandise purchased directly from factories in offshore locations such as China or India was processed at coastal distribution centres before shipment to U.S. stores.

On the way back from stores, Wal-Mart's trucks generated "back-haul" revenue by transporting unsold merchandise on trucks that would be otherwise empty. Wal-Mart's backhaul revenues—its private fleet operated as a for-hire carrier when it was not busy transporting merchandise from distribution centres to stores—were more than US$1 billion per year.[12]

Because its trucking employees were non-unionized and in-house, Wal-Mart was able to implement and improve upon standard delivery procedures, co-ordinating and deploying the entire fleet as necessary. Uniform operating standards ensured that miscommunication between traffic co-ordinators, truckers and store level employees was minimized.

Retail Strategy

Wal-Mart's first stores were filled with merchandise that had been bought by Walton in bulk, as he was convinced that a new trend—discounting merchandise off the suggested retail price—was here to stay. In the 1960s, Wal-Mart grew rapidly as customers were attracted by its assortment of low-priced products. Over time, the company copied the merchandise assortment strategies of other retailers, mostly through observation as a result of store visits.

Unlike its competitors in the 1970s and 1980s, Wal-Mart implemented an "everyday low prices" (EDLP)

[11]Barry C. Lynn, "Breaking the chain," *Harper's Magazine,* July 2006, page 34.

[12]http://www.dcvelocity.com/articles/july2004/inbound.cfm, accessed 19 Aug 2006.

policy, which meant that products were displayed at a steady price and not discounted on a regular basis. In a "high-low" discounting environment, discounts would be rotated from product to product, necessitating huge inventory stockpiles in anticipation of a discount. In an EDLP environment, demand was smoothed out to reduce the "bullwhip effect." Because of its EDLP policy, Wal-Mart did not need to advertise as frequently as did its competitors and was able to channel the savings back into price reductions. To generate additional volume, Wal-Mart buyers worked with suppliers on price rollback campaigns. Price rollbacks, each lasting about 90 days, were funded by suppliers, with the goal of increasing product sales between 200 and 500 percent. A researcher remarked: "Consumers certainly love Wal-Mart's low prices, which are an average of eight percent to 27 percent lower than the competition."[13]

The company also ensured that its store-level operations were at least as efficient as its logistics operations. The stores were simply furnished and constructed using standard materials. Efforts were made to continually reduce operating costs. For example, light and temperature settings for all U.S. stores were controlled centrally from Bentonville.

As Wal-Mart distribution centres had close to real-time information on each store's in-stock levels, the merchandise could be pushed to stores automatically. In addition, store-level information systems allowed manufacturers to be notified as soon as an item was purchased. In anticipation of changes in demand for some items, associates had the authority to manually input orders or override impending deliveries. In contrast, most of Wal-Mart's retail competitors did not confer merchandising responsibility to entry-level employees as merchandising templates were sent to stores through head office and were expected to be followed precisely. To ensure that employees were kept up-to-date, management shared detailed information about day/week/month store sales with all employees during daily 10-minute-long "standing" meetings.

The display of merchandise was suggested by a storewide template, with a unique template for each store, indicating the layout of Wal-Mart's various departments. This template was created by Wal-Mart's merchandising department, after analysing historical store-sales and community traits. Associates were free to alter the merchandising template to fit their local store requirements. Shelf space in Wal-Mart's different departments—from shoes to household appliances to automotive supplies—was divided up, each spot allocated to specific SKUs.

Each Wal-Mart store aimed to be the "store of the community," tailoring its product mix to appeal to the distinct tastes of that community. Thus, two Wal-Mart Stores a short distance apart could potentially stock different merchandise. In contrast, most other retailers made purchasing decisions at the district or regional level.

In order to harness the knowledge of its suppliers, key category suppliers, called "category captains," were introduced in the late 1980s, and they provided input on shelf space allocation. As an observer noted:

> One obvious result [of using category captains] is that a producer like Colgate-Palmolive will end up working intensively with firms it formerly competed with, such as Crest manufacturer P&G, to find the mix of products that will allow Wal-Mart to earn the most it can from its shelf space. If Wal-Mart discovers that a supplier promotes its own products at the expense of Wal-Mart's revenue, the retailer may name a new captain in its stead.[14]

Information Systems

Walton had always been interested in gathering and analysing information about his company operations. As early as 1966, when Walton had 20 stores, he attended an IBM school in upstate New York with the intent of hiring the smartest person in the class to come to Bentonville to computerize his operations.[15]

Even with a growing network of stores in the 1960s and 1970s, Walton was able to personally visit and keep track of operations in each one, due to his use of a personal airplane, which he used to observe new construction development (to determine where to place stores) and to monitor customer traffic (by observing how full the parking lot was).

In the mid-1980s, Wal-Mart invested in a central database, store-level point-of-sale systems, and a satellite network. Combined with one of the retail industry's first chain-wide implementation of UPC bar codes, store-level information could now be collected instantaneously and analysed. By combining sales data with

---

[13]William Beaver, "Battling Wal-Mart: How Communities Can Respond," *Business and Society Review,* New York: Summer 2005. Vol. 110, Issue 2; pg. 159.

[14]Barry C. Lynn, "Breaking the chain," Harper's Magazine, July 2006, page 33.
[15]http://www.time.com/time/time100/builder/profile/walton2.html, accessed 23 August 2006.

EXHIBIT 2 **Wal-Mart's Retail Link Database**

Source: Casewriter

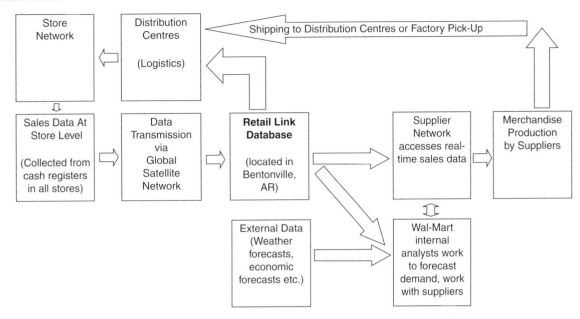

external information such as weather forecasts, Wal-Mart was able to provide additional support to buyers, improving the accuracy of its purchasing forecasts.

In the early 1990s, Wal-Mart developed Retail Link. At an estimated 570 terabytes—which Wal-Mart claimed was larger than all the fixed pages on the Internet—Retail Link was the largest civilian database in the world. For a description of how Retail Link fits in with Wal-Mart's supply chain, see Exhibit 2. Retail Link contained data on every sale made at the company during a two-decade period. Wal-Mart gave its suppliers access to real-time sales data on the products they supplied, down to individual stock-keeping items at the store level.

In exchange for providing suppliers access to these data, Wal-Mart expected them to proactively monitor and replenish product on a continual basis. In 1990, Wal-Mart became one of the early adopters of collaborative planning, forecasting and replenishment (CPRE), an integrated approach to planning and forecasting by sharing critical supply chain information, such data on promotions, inventory levels and daily sales.[16] Wal-Mart's vendor-managed inventory (VMI)

program, (also known as continuous replenishment) required suppliers to manage inventory levels at the company's distribution centres, based on agreed-upon service levels. The VMI program started with P&G diapers in the late 1980s and, by 2006, had expanded to include many suppliers and SEUs.[17] In some situations, particularly grocery products, suppliers owned the inventory in Wal-Mart stores up to the point that the sale was scanned at checkout.

To support this inventory management effort, supplier analysts worked closely with Wal-Mart's supply chain personnel to co-ordinate the flow of products from suppliers' factories and resolved any supply chain issues, from routine issues such as, ensuring that products were ready for pickup by Wal-Mart's trucks, and arranging for the return of defective products, to last-minute issues such as managing sudden spikes in demand for popular items. When Wal-Mart buyers met, on a frequent basis, with a supplier's sales teams, two important topics of review were the supplier's out-of-stock rate and inventory levels at Wal-Mart, indication of how well replenishment was being handled.

[16]Johnson, A.H., "35 Years of IT Leadership: A New Supply Chain Forged," *Computerworld,* September 30, 2002, pp. 38–39.

[17]Andel, T., "Partnerships With Pull," Transportation and Distribution, July 1995, pp. 65–74.

Suppliers were provided with targets for out-of-stock rates and inventory levels.

In addition to managing short-term inventory and discussing product trends, Wal-Mart worked with suppliers on medium-to long-term supply chain strategy including factory location, co-operation with downstream raw materials and suppliers and production volume forecasting.

Wal-Mart's satellite network, in addition to receiving and transmitting point-of-sale data, also provided senior management with the ability to broadcast video messages to the stores. Although the bulk of senior management lived and worked in Bentonville, Arkansas, frequent video broadcasts to each store in their network kept store employees informed of the latest developments in the firm.

In an effort to emulate Wal-Mart's ability to share information with suppliers, Wal-Mart's competitors relied on a system similar to Retail Link. Agentrics LLC, a software service provider, developed, in conjunction with several of global retailers, a software platform called "Retail Interface," which collected store level sales data which could then be shared with suppliers. Agentrics' customer base included many of the world's top retailers—including Carrefour, Tesco, Metro, Costco, Kroger and Walgreen's–who were also investors in Agentrics.

Human Resources

By visiting each store and by encouraging associates to contribute ideas, Walton was able to uncover and disperse best practices across the company in the 1960s and 1970s. To ensure that best practices were implemented as soon as possible, Walton held regular "Saturday morning meetings," which convened his top management team in Bentonville. At 7 a.m. each Saturday, the week's business results were discussed, and merchandising and purchasing changes were implemented. Store layout resets were managed on the weekend, and the rejigged stores were ready by Monday morning. Walton and his management team often toured competitors' stores, looking for new ideas to "borrow."

Wal-Mart believed that centralization had numerous benefits, including lower costs and improved communications between different divisions. All of Wal-Mart's divisions, from U.S. stores, International, Sam's Club, to its logistics and information systems division were located in Bentonville, a town of 28,000 people in Northwest Arkansas. Regional managers and in-country presidents were the few executives who were stationed outside of Bentonville.

Another key to Wal-Mart's ability to enjoy low operating costs was the fact that it was non-union. Without cumbersome labor agreements, management could take advantage of technology to drive labor costs down and make operational changes quickly and efficiently. Being non-union, however, had its drawbacks. As its store network encroached on the territory of unionized–grocers, unions, such as the United Food and Commercial Workers' Union, started to become more aggressive in their anti-Wal-Mart publicity campaigns, funding so-called, grassroots groups whose goals were to undermine Wal-Mart's expansion. Wal-Mart's size also made it a target for politicians every stumble was magnified and played up in the press.

Wal-Mart in 2006

Wal-Mart operated approximately 3,900 stores in the United States and 2,600 stores in 13 other countries. As store level, the company stocked more than 100,000 SKUs. Two of Wal-Mart's key supply chain improvement initiatives include "Remix" and RFID (radio frequency identification tags).

Remix

Remix, which was started in the fall of 2005 and targeted for completion in 2007, aimed to reduce the percentage of out-of-stock merchandise at stores by redesigning its network of distribution centres. As Wal-Mart stores increased their line-up of grocery items (it was the United States' largest grocer in 2005), it became apparent that, as employees sorted through truckloads of arriving merchandise to find fast-selling items, delays in restocking shelves occurred.[18]

Moving from its original model of having distribution centres serve a cluster of stores, Wal-Mart envisioned that fast-moving merchandise such as paper towels, toilet paper, toothpaste and seasonal items would be shipped from dedicated "high velocity" food distribution centres. Food distribution centres—designed to handle high-turn food items—differed from general merchandise distribution centres in the following ways: they were smaller, they had temperature controls and they had less automation. In contrast, general merchandise distribution centres required automation and conveyor belts to move full pallets of goods.

[18]Kris Hudson, "Wal-Mart's Need for Speed," *The Wall Street Journal,* 26 September 2005.

Wal-Mart did not elaborate on how much savings this move was expected to generate, but it was believed to be an incremental improvement to the current system. Wal-Mart's current chief information officer (CIO), Rollin Ford, stated:

> We could have done nothing and been fine from a logistics standpoint ... but as you continue to increase your sales per square foot, you've got to do things differently to make those stores more productive.[19]

RFID

Mandating RFID tags on merchandise shipped by Wal-Mart's top 100 suppliers was an attempt to increase the ability to track inventory, with the goal of increasing in-stock rates at store level. Privately, suppliers and observers chafed at the mandate, as it would cost them millions of dollars to implement. Publicly, Wal-Mart trumpeted RFID as a way to increase in-stock rates and reduce tracking costs. Simon Langford, Wal-Mart's manager of RFID strategy, was enthusiastic about RFID:

> It gives us visibility as to where the product is. Smart applications will be able to direct our associates to where the product is, so we can replenish shelves sooner. We're still working through most of the issues. There's technology available now that's deployable in some areas. But the readers, for example, are an issue[20] and we're asking our (RFID technology) suppliers to accelerate their development.[21]

RFID tags would allow Wal-Mart to increase stock visibility as stock moved in trucks, through the distribution centres and on to the stores. Wal-Mart would be able to track promotion effectiveness within the stores while cutting out-of-stock sales losses and overstock expenses. The company placed RFID tag readers in several parts of the store: at the dock where merchandise came in, throughout the backroom, at the door from the stockroom to the sales floor, and in the box-crushing area where empty cases eventually wound up. With those readers in place, store managers would know what stock was in the backroom and what was on the sales floor.

According to researchers, about 25 percent of out-of-stock inventory in the United States was not really out-of-stock: the items could be misplaced on the floor or mis-shelved in the backroom. U.S.-wide, about eight percent of merchandiser was out of stock at any given time, leading to lost sales for retailers. In a study performed by the University of Arkansas, Wal-Mart stores with RFID showed a net improvement of 16 percent fewer out-of-stocks on the RFID-tagged products that were tested. However, RFID tags cost approximately 17 cents each.[22]

Keeping Inventory Growth Slower Than Sales Growth

In 2006, Wal-Mart continued to seek improvements to its supply chain. Although the company publicly declined to outline its targets for inventory reduction, its suppliers stated that Wal-Mart's top executives spoke in January 2006 about eliminating as much as $6 billion in excess inventory.[23]

In the past few years, however, Wal-Mart's internal goal had called for cutting its inventory growth rate to half of its sales growth rate. In its 2006 fiscal year ended January 31, the company posted a sales increase of 9.5 percent from the previous year while its inventory grew 8.2 percent. During the previous year, its sales increased by 11.3 percent, while its inventory grew 11.8 percent. The figures suggested Wal-Mart was falling short of its self-imposed target, and in April 2006, Wal-Mart's chief financial officer, Tom Schoewe, stated:

> If you look back at the last six or eight quarters, we have not met that objective. I think the chances of meeting that objective are greater this year than they have ever been before.[24]

Wal-Mart's performance in international markets was also mixed. In Mexico and Canada, it was the largest retailer and enjoyed strong profits. In March 2006, it purchased a majority share in Central American Holding Company (CARHO), giving it control over 37S supermarkets and stores in Central America.

However, Wal-Mart had been faring less well in other markets. For example, in the United Kingdom,

---

[19]http://cincom.typepad.com/simplicity/2005/09/index.html, accessed 23 Aug 2006.
[20]Wal-Mart needs readers in different sizes and shapes for different locations, and they have to be designed so that antennas cannot be knocked off when a forklift backs up or lifts a pallet load. http://www.networkworld.com/news/2003/0616walmart.html?page=3.
[21]Ibid.

[22]http://knowledge.wpcarey.asu.edu/index.cfm?fa=viewfeature &id=1205, 8 June 2006.
[23]Kris Hudson, "Wal-Mart Aims To Sharply Cut Its Inventory Costs," *The Wall Street Journal,* 20 April 2006.
[24]Kris Hudson, "Wal-Mart Aims To Sharply Cut Its Inventory Costs", *The Wall Street Journal,* 20 April 2006.

EXHIBIT 3   **Competitors' Financial Information**

Source: Annual Reports

(2005 Figures Except for Federated Department Stores [2004]) in Millions of Dollars

Company	Segment	Sales	COGS	SC & A	Net Income	Inventories	Assets
Albertsons Inc.	Grocery	40,358	29,038	10,082	446	3,036	17,871
Costco Wholesale Corp.	Wholesale	52,935	46,347	5,044	1,063	4,015	16,514
Federated Department Stores	Department	22,390	13,272	6,980	1,406	5,459	33,168
Gap Inc.	Clothing	16,023	10,154	4,124	1,113	1,696	8,821
Kroger Co.	Grocery	60,553	45,565	11,027	958	4,886	20,482
Sears Holdings Corp.	General merchandise	49,124	35,505	10,759	858	9,068	30,573
Safeway Inc.	Grocery	38,416	27,303	11,113	561	2,766	15,757
Target Corp.	General merchandise and grocery	52,620	34,927	11,185	2,408	5,838	34,995
Wal-Mart Stores	General merchandise and grocery	312,427	240,391	56,733	11,231	32,191	138,187

Wal-Mart's ASDA unit accounted for half of Wal-Mart's international sales. ASDA, the United Kingdom's second-largest supermarket chain, to continued to lag behind Tesco PLC as the latter added to its market-leading share in the country, while Sainsbury held third spot. In May 2006, a retail analyst commented that Tesco was ahead of ASDA in the lucrative and fast-growing non-food markets such as personal care, house wares, music and video.[25] U.K. based union publication commented:

> Right now, ASDA seems to be fighting a losing battle for second place in British retailing. Trailing marker leader Tesco by far, ASDA Wal-Mart has seen Salisbury's closing up through its much faster growth rate. The nervousness in Wal-Mart's Bentonville headquarters has been shown by CEO Lee Scott's repeated calls for a British government intervention against Tesco's strong market presence. What Mr. Scott prefers not to talk about is his own company's dominant position in global retailing.[26]

In May 2006, Wal-Mart pulled out of South Korea, selling its 16 stores to the country's biggest discount chain. Wal-Mart Vice-chairman Mike Duke claimed

EXHIBIT 4   **Comparable Same Store Sales for Retail Competitors**

Comparable Store Sales	Most recent fiscal year
Albertsons Inc.	0.3%
Costco Wholesale Corp.	7.0%
Federated Dept. Stores*	2.6%
Gap Inc.	−5.0%
Kroger Co.	5.9%
Sears Holdings Corp.	−5.3%
Safeway Inc.	5.9%
Target Corp.	5.6%
Wal-Mart Stores (U.S. Stores)^	3.0%
Wal-Mart-Sam's Club (U.S. Stores)^	5.0%

*Last available prior to merger.
^Wal-Mart's U.S. stores accounted for 67.2 percent of total firm sales. SAM'S Club and International accounted for 12.7 percent and 20.1 percent respectively.
Source: Annual Reports.

that the firm was focusing on where it could achieve most growth. He stated:

> It became increasingly clear that in South Korea's current environment, it would be difficult for us to reach the scale we desired.[27]

[25]http://www.forbes.com/home/feeds/afx/2006/05/23/afx2768414.html, accessed 23 August 2006.
[26]http://www.union-network. org/unisite/sectors/commerce/Multinationals/Wal-Mart_Asda_warehouse_workers_vote_on_strike.htm, accessed 23 August 2006.

[27]http://news.bbc.co.uk/2/hi/business/5005542.stm, accessed 23 August 2006.

In August 2006, Wal-Mart exited the German market with losses of about $1 billion after eight years of failing to turn around its two acquisitions, purchased in 1997 and 1998. Wal-Mart's performance in its core domestic market was also suffering. In mid-August 2006, Wal-Mart posted its first profit decline in a decade.[28]

[28]http://www.startribune.com/535/story/615563.html, accessed 23 August 2006.

Case 6-10
British Airports Authority

BAA (the British Airports Authority) owns Heathrow, Gatwick and four other UK airports, including Glasgow and Edinburgh. The UK airports group was privatized in 1987, but became a subsidiary of an international consortium led by Spain's Grupo Ferrovial in 2006. The consortium includes CDP, the Canadian pensions institution, and the private equity arm of the Government of Singapore Investment Corporation. BAA styles itself "the world's leading airport company."

BAA has become one of the most vilified brands and companies in the UK. The organization is closely linked to the deplorable standards of service for passengers at British airports, excessive charges for airlines using their airports, failing miserably in managing airport security emergency measures, and an obsession with manipulating passengers "trapped" in their airports to spend money at BAA's retail operations and concessions.

The company has experienced difficulties in retaining managers, reflecting growing tensions between BAA and its Spanish owners, and vocal critics range from the airlines to the government (the latter concerned not simply about anti-competitive practices at BAA, but also the negative impact of British airport standards on the success of the 2012 Olympics on which many British politicians' futures rest). The attention of regulators both at the Civil Aviation Authority and the Competition Commission was focused on the company from 2007 onwards.

Certainly, Heathrow is world-renowned for having the longest queues, the worst baggage restrictions, the surliest staff, the most unpleasant security shambles, the dirtiest public areas, the fewest lounges, the highest

This case was written by Nigel F. Piercy, Warwick Business School, the University of Warwick.

Competitors such as Target Stores and Costco seemed to be catching up, growing comparable store sales faster than Wal-Mart. For competitors' financials, see Exhibit 3; for comparable same store sales, see Exhibit 4.

prices for food and drink and the most misdirected luggage of any airport in the developed world. Nonetheless, Heathrow is the busiest airport in the world and the second most profitable airport. In fact, many of the worst aspects of BAA's performance actually reflect the issue of airport capacity—Heathrow, for example, in 2007 handled 67 million passengers in facilities designed for 40–45 million. In particular, lack of runway capacity will inevitably continue to constrain further growth and cause delays. Heathrow has only two runways, compared to four in Paris and six in Amsterdam.

Hopes that the opening of the new Terminal 5 in 2008 would recover some of BAA's reputation were misplaced, since the March opening was surrounded by chaos and judged to be a fiasco—thousands of lost bags, hundreds of flights cancelled and more delayed, passengers forced to fly without their bags, escalators and lifts paralysed. BA was looking at a bill of at least £50 million for cancelled flights, but a more serious dent in its long-term reputation and that of its Heathrow hub. One commentator noted at the time: "The basic problem is that you are dealing with two horribly inefficient organizations in the form of BA and BAA. When you put them together, you get something like this." BA was looking at delaying its full transfer to Terminal 5 until October 2008 and for financial compensation from BAA. Both BA and BAA stood accused in Parliament of undermining "UK plc" as a result of the T5 catastrophe.

The Role of Ferrovial

Spanish-based infrastructure group Ferrovial bought BAA in 2006 for £10.3 billion, and took the company off the stock market. Only some £500,000 was Ferrovial's own funds, the remainder of the purchase was funded by debt. BAA chief executive, Mike Casper, who had led the fight to maintain the independence of BAA, was replaced by Stephen Nelson—previously retail director at BAA, and earlier marketing director at supermarket company Sainsbury. In the first 18 months of Ferrovial ownership the company was surrounded by a storm of criticism from the media and from the airlines, which pay substantial fees for using BAA's airports.

The Security Problem...

Ferrovial's ownership of BAA had barely started when the government instigated an airport security clampdown triggered by an alleged terrorist plot to blow up transatlantic flights, which resulted in the worst kind of abject chaos at London's airports. As flights were cancelled and security procedures intensified, the inadequacy of BAA's infrastructure was exposed. The company faced a storm of criticism from passengers, media commentators and airline bosses. Ryanair, in particular, accused BAA of ignoring the needs of its customers, refusing to devote enough staff to security screening, and inflating its charges—Ryanair took particular exception to the hand-written photocopied note given by the BAA duty manager to passengers who had missed their flights stating "BAA is not responsible for compensating passengers for missing flights. Please refer to your airline." British Airways, Virgin, BMI and American Airlines produced a litany of similar complaints.

There is a strong case that the British government has shown a complete lack of planning regarding security—instead creating a kind of "security theatre" by playing catch-up to a succession of perceived threats. Government concerns are dominated by appeasing media critics and creating an illusion of security, regardless of the effect of their policies in imposing chaos on airport management. At times security queues at Heathrow have exceeded a quarter of a mile. Nonetheless, in February 2008 Greenpeace campaigners appeared to have little problem evading BAA's "high security" systems and procedures, to get air-side, climb on the tail of a BA aircraft and festoon it with banners protesting about the climate effects of the proposed third Heathrow runway.

Tensions between the new owners and BAA management have led to a series of high-profile departures by senior and middle-management BAA executives. Initial tensions centred on the interference by the Spanish owners in local publicity and PR activities. However, Ferrovial's poor handling of the security crisis triggered a second wave of high-profile management departures.

Financing Issues...

Ferrovial faces substantial problems in refinancing the package used to buy BAA. The consortium took out big loans to buy BAA, planning to quickly refinance the deal. It could have cut the cost of borrowing by issuing bonds backed by future Heathrow and Gatwick revenues. However, uncertainties over the CAA's position on BAA prices and profits, and the wider international credit squeeze prevented this happening. In the first nine months of the 2007/8 financial year, BAA generated cash of £800 million, but paid out £890 million on its capital spending plans, and faced an interest bill of £329 million.

BAA is saddled with £6 billion in debt, which Ferrovial continues to struggle to restructure. Meantime, BAA's credit rating has been downgraded, and Ferrovial's net income plunged 48.5% in 2007. There are some fears that the real problem is that having borrowed so heavily to make the purchase, Ferrovial is starving BAA of cash. There were suspicions that BAA was in breach of the covenants on some of its loans at the end of 2007. By the middle of 2008, it was clear that BAA could run out of operating cash by the end of 2009 without additional financing. Early in 2008, BAA was looking for a £1 billion loan secured against its regional airports.

Ferrovial has had to conduct a fire sale of businesses to reduce its debt burden. The BAA World Duty Free chain was sold to Italy's Autogrill for £547 million in March 2008, but other sales include: Bristol Airport stake—gone for £105 million; Sydney airport stake—gone for £408 million; Budapest Airport—gone for £1.3 billion; six Australian airports—one for £343 million; BAA property arm—going for an estimated £600 million; and jointly owned airport office space and other development sites—gone for £265 million.

BAA, as well as refinancing the loans taken out to buy the company, also has to find a new capital expenditure financing package to pay for its ambitious spending plans. Along with the completion of Terminal 5 at Heathrow, costing more than £4 billion, BAA plans to demolish and rebuild the airport's Terminal 2, and also to refurbish and expand Gatwick. In the longer-term, the company wants to build a controversial third runway and sixth terminal at Heathrow, likely to cost around £9 billion if it is approved by the government.

The problem is that as Ferrovial sells assets it is diluting both its value and its cash flow. BAA's operational cash flow, some £1 billion in 2007, remains insufficient to meet debt service requirements as well as its tax and capital expenditure bill. Additional borrowing will be necessary to deliver the capital expenditure investment programme BAA has promised the regulator. Mid-2008 Ferrovial secured fresh financing of £7.65 billion for BAA, in the form of a loan from nine banks over a five to six year period.

Opposition to Expansion...

In fact, BAA faces opposition to its expansion plans both from environmental campaigners and from the local communities around airports, who will be exposed to yet more noise. BAA has worked jointly with the Department for Transport in its environmental modelling to test the effects of Heathrow expansion (indeed BAA has paid for some of the work) and producing the DoT report, to which BAA is now asked to "respond." BAA suggests that there is no local noise problem, while critics suggest that the figures have been "managed" somewhat strangely to permit this conclusion to be drawn.

Documents leaked to the *The Sunday Times* in March 2008 revealed that BAA had colluded with government officials to "fix" evidence in favour of a new third runway at Heathrow. This could account for the surprising consultation document conclusion that it would be possible to bolt a new airport the size of Gatwick onto Heathrow without any adverse environmental impact. The leaked documents show even the government's own watchdog—the Environment Agency—criticizes the flawed and incomplete evidence in the Department for Transport (DfT) report. The picture emerging is one where BAA colluded with the DfT: BAA providing instructions to DfT officials on how to "strip out" data that indicated environmental targets would be breached by the airport; BAA repeatedly selected alternative data showing negligible impact on noise and pollution; the DfT gave BAA unprecedented access to confidential reports and allowed the company to help rewrite the consultation document; and the final document significantly reduced forecasts of anticipated carbon emissions caused by the proposed new runway by not including incoming international flights.

BAA has also used an extensive network of lobbying and PR groups, headed by senior Labour figures, with access to the government, to promote its plans for the third Heathrow runway. Critics of the company see this as a cynical attempt by BAA to sustain its profits and its grip on the market, irrespective of the impact on the environment and residents. Concerns also surround the degree of collusion between a government department and a private company to deceive the public and policy-makers. Ruth Kelly, Transport Secretary, was in daily contact with

BAA management but refused to meet protestors against the Heathrow expansion. In a move that underlines the company's alignment with the Labour government, BAA's chief executives launched a public attack on the opposition Conservative party for daring to express concerns about the plans for a third Heathrow runway.

One emerging fact from documents reluctantly released by the government under the Freedom of Information Act was that runway expansion would create an "island of noise" over the Queen's residence at Windsor Castle. BAA appears willing to risk even snarling Corgi-power. In addition, although the relevant maps were omitted from the consultation documents, it also transpired that the Heathrow expansion planned to make part of the M25 motorway the crash zone for the third Heathrow runway.

More seriously for BAA, the fiasco of the Terminal 5 opening in March 2008 raised major questions about BAA's competence to manage expansion and the undesirability of allowing them to expand with a third Heathrow runway.

Abuse of Power...

BAA is also accused of abusing its monopoly in its airports by the way it treats potential competitors. BAA has moved into the lucrative area of off-airport car parking. Critics suggest it is abusing its legal powers by overcharging for access to airport forecourts and threatening to seize rival car parking operators' land under compulsory purchase orders. For example, in 2008 one independent car parking operator at BAA's Glasgow airport was looking at charges levied by BAA rising from £5,000 a year to £150,000 a year, simply for using the roads that give access to the airport forecourt. BAA denies accusations of bullying behaviour on the grounds they are simply looking out for their own interests.

Employee Reactions...

In 2008 BAA found itself in conflict with employees over its attempts to close their final salary pension scheme, among other changes in their employment conditions. About 5,000 workers, including fire-fighters, security, maintenance, administrative and clerical staff were threatening to close Britain's biggest airports in 2008. While the first strikes threatened in 2008 were cancelled at the last minute, the threat of industrial action by employees to cripple airports continues. The inability of BAA management to deal effectively with the problem of outdated working practices lies at the heart of the company's failure to root out inefficiencies in the operation. For example, union opposition to flexible working deals makes it difficult for BAA to roster staff to deal with fluctuating passenger demand. Unions are in a strong position at airports – even a short stoppage is seriously damaging. For example, a single day's stoppage at Heathrow costs British Airways alone £20 million, plus the knock-on effects on ticket sales and general confidence. The unions claim that BAA is only interested in cost-cutting, not improving conditions for employees or passengers.

The Heathrow Hassle—Making a Bad Joke of Customer Service with a Snarl

The most violent criticisms of BAA relate to the "Heathrow hassle"—the sheer, nightmare-like, unpleasantness of travelling through the airport. It does not help that, among its other ploys for both annoying and extracting revenue from airline passengers, BAA is renowned for managing security systems in ways that allegedly provide for commercial advantage. For example, there is an interesting synergy between BAA-employed "security" staff confiscating cosmetics and personal care products from passengers (using complex "regulations" about permitted package sizes, and the "essential" enclosure of the packages of hand cream in small plastic envelopes, which apparently prevents them from becoming a threat to aircraft security), which allows passengers to go through security, forfeit their possessions and then replace their cosmetics at high prices at the BAA-owned retail concessions air-side.

Interestingly, BAA maintains that it has solved the queuing problems at Heathrow and Gatwick—notwithstanding the views of the airlines and their passengers. In particular, BAA claims that security queue measurements show waiting times of less than 10 minutes (the threshold at which they become liable for financial penalties). Unfortunately, investigations by Booz Allen Hamilton for the CAA suggest that BAA achieved this remarkably improved performance by simply not measuring the queues from the back, but from near the front. BAA's passenger survey—its Quality Service Monitor—apparently shows very high customer satisfaction levels throughout the past five years, regardless of security alerts and other problems. Airline chiefs at Virgin and BMI suggest that BAA is systematically manipulating and distorting the data to achieve these effects, and that BAA figures are wildly at odds with those collected by independent surveys.

A 2008 ploy of subjecting passengers in the new Terminal 5, as well as in Terminal 1, to the intrusive and humiliating process of being fingerprinted and photographed in the terminal, is illustrative of BAA's passenger policies. The fingerprinting and photographing of passengers is claimed to be for "security." In fact, it is a way of mixing domestic and international passengers to maximize the traffic in the duty free and other retail outlets in the terminal. As pointed out by the Information Commissioner, fingerprinting passengers in this way is almost certainly illegal under the Data Protection Act. The Home Office denies that fingerprinting is required for security purposes. BAA appears happy to invade personal privacy to achieve greater retail sales. BAA says that those who refuse fingerprinting will not be allowed to fly. Abusing security concerns for commercial gain underpins the BAA approach. BAA backed off from fingerprinting in the new Terminal 5, 24 hours before it opened. The company says it has "postponed" fingerprinting, and apparently intends to go ahead with this process at all its airports, whether it is illegal or not.

The BAA Viewpoint

Critics take the view that Ferrovial has squeezed the maximum profit out of the British airports it controls, for the minimum investment. The BAA perspective is that the fees charged to airlines are just about the lowest in Europe, and that the operational airport problems reflect capacity and infrastructure problems that they inherited, and that Ferrovial cannot be held responsible for these problems. They argue that the current problems reflect many years of lack of investment, which preceded Ferrovial's purchase of BAA.

Whose Fault?...

The BAA view is that flight delays and poor passenger experience at Heathrow and Gatwick reflect the same failings identified in 2002, which simply have continued to get worse in the following five years. Indeed, Ferrovial makes the point that if the airports had not been such a mess, then they would not have been an attractive purchase. They claim that their much criticized retail operations at the airports actually heavily subsidize airport services. BAA blames the airlines (which are actually their main customers) for many of the problems, and the Home Office for the delays and mismanagement of airport security and immigration control—indeed, they appear to blame everybody but themselves. BAA CEO Stephen Nelson was adamant in 2007 that BAA had no responsibility for 94% of the delays at Heathrow. He argued that the major hold-ups occur at check-in (responsibility of the airlines) and immigration (responsibility of the Home Office).

Price Increases...

In 2007/8 BAA made it clear that they wanted a substantial hike in the prices charged to airlines, as a prerequisite for investment in improved services (and BAA profitability). This move predictably attracted much hostile criticism from the airlines. Nonetheless, BAA maintained the position that there would be no further investment, and the Heathrow improvements would be postponed, without higher prices. The Competition Commission backed a CAA decision not to allow BAA the price increases it wanted. BAA management dropped heavy hints that without the price increases there would be no additional investment in improving Heathrow facilities in the lead-up to the 2012 Olympics (a matter of considerable sensitivity to the Labour government).

In the event, BAA was allowed a 23.5% rise in Heathrow prices for the 12 months from April 2008, likely to produce an additional cost of £20 a ticket in landing fees. Charges will continue to increase in each of the following four years by 7.5% above the rate of retail inflation. Gatwick charges will rise by 8.2% in 2008 and 2% above inflation for the following four years. This ruling allows charges at Heathrow to rise by 86% over five years at Heathrow, and 49% at Gatwick. In effect, although BAA's rate of return is pushed down, large price increases were permitted. The regulators pushed down the cost of capital from 7.75% to 6.2% (i.e., how much the regulator thinks BAA has to pay for the capital it needs to run and invest in the business). BAA complains that this does not take into account the risks involved in running airports—accusing the CAA of creating "regulatory shock," a sudden and unjustified drop in the cost of capital that will disrupt the company. The CAA shows no sign of relenting on this issue—it told Ferrovial during the bid process that they should not assume the cost of capital would remain the same.

Furthermore, BAA claims the price increases are inadequate, while the airlines claim that the regulators continue to reward BAA for its inefficiencies. BAA claimed its ability to refinance its £10 billion debt pile was placed in jeopardy because of the price control proposals for Heathrow and Gatwick.

The Competition Commission did, however, criticize BAA, demanding greater transparency over its World Duty Free retail operation, and warning that failure to fix the Heathrow delays would result in large financial penalties. Even under existing arrangements, BAA was fined a further £146,000 by the CAA in 2007 for the delays and poor customer service at Heathrow, bringing its total in regulatory penalties to £4 million since July 2003. Nonetheless, the financial penalties are relatively trivial compared to the price increases allowed. The potential for being fined £7 million in 2009 is small in comparison with the £925 million it will earn in charges in 2008–9.

As far back as 2002, the Competition Commission expressed concern that BAA's World Duty Free shops concession was operated by a subsidiary of BAA in the absence of competitive tendering, and a lack of competition between outlets selling duty-free products. BAA operates a "single till" system where its highly profitable commercial activities, mainly rental income from its retail and other concessions, subsidize the airport charges levied on airlines.

BAA's Bargaining Power...

The unexpectedly generous price increases allowed to BAA reflect a number of unusual factors. Ferrovial's rocky financial position may have helped. Reeling from the disastrous collapse of Northern Rock in 2007, the Labour government had no desire to see BAA collapse to become its "Southern Rock." Interestingly, it was only after the CAA approval of its price increases that BAA revealed that it would not be able to complete the Heathrow East upgrade in time for the London Olympics.

The Reactions...

CAA's unexpectedly generous ruling on prices was followed by several reactions. With uncharacteristic unanimity, leaders of four of Britain's leading airlines—easyJet, bmi, Virgin Atlantic and Ryanair—shared the same stage with the same message: calling for the break-up of the "highly indebted" and "financially unstable" BAA operation. They met with Transport Secretary Ruth Kelly to urge her to reform airport regulation and order the break-up of BAA. Along with BA, these airlines want BAA's monopoly removed to allow separate airport owners to compete for business from the airlines. easyjet retained law firm Lane & Partners as adviser and notified BAA of its intention to seek a judicial review of the price increases. They were also threatening to refuse to pay the higher charges.

Soon after, MPs on the Commons' Transport Select Committee called for BAA's break-up on the grounds that its monopoly was "bad for passengers and bad for aviation." On the same day that Terminal 5 was opened by the Queen, MPs were accused of effectively hanging a "For Sale" sign on Gatwick airport. The MPs were confident that an airport sell-off would happen—whether voluntarily or by force. City commentators suggest that what Ferrovial has done is to overpay for a business, gear it as highly as possible, then wait for the regulator to bail them out—which CAA has effectively done by allowing airport charges at Heathrow and Gatwick to reach around £6.8 billion over the next five years. In April 2008, as the initial report by the Competition Commission made the prospect of a break-up of Ferrovial's British airport monopoly more likely, Commission investigators censured BAA for trying to improperly influence consultants advising the Commission.

But, Do Popularity Points Bring Prizes?...

BAA appears to have sacrificed customer satisfaction in order to cut costs and avoid investment. However, under existing arrangements, BAA has neither the incentives nor the desire to provide anything more than the most basic level of service for passengers, as opposed to shoppers, in the airport. The issue is whether the company faces a backlash resulting from their unquenchable thirst for cash from "imprisoned" shoppers in the airport. Critics contrast the image of broken travelators, inadequate seating, filthy toilets and constant queues with BAA's enthusiasm for maximizing the profit it makes from its shopping concessions.

The new Terminal 5, for example, is a major attempt to increase passenger expenditure on the ground, through a retail-and-restaurant offering. The new Terminal boasts a Gordon Ramsay restaurant and personal shoppers at its Harrod's outlet. The terminal will have more advertising than almost any other airport in the world—BAA research suggests that anxious travellers are particularly susceptible to advertising messages, so they will be exposed to 50–120 ads in the time from when they arrive to when they can finally escape onto their flights. The T5 billboards are offered to advertisers for £1.5 million a year.

BAA maintains that T5 will solve many of the problems at Heathrow. Nonetheless, more than half the passengers using T5 will have to suffer the extreme inconvenience of being bussed to their planes—the highest proportion at any major European terminal. The new terminal offers no additional Heathrow capacity (as it opens, other areas will be closed for overdue refurbishment—the £3.4 billion Heathrow East project to revamp terminals 1 and 2), but it does have 112 shops, and about the same retail square footage as out-of-town shopping sites like Bluewater and Lakeside.

The retail revenue stream is vitally important to BAA—it is worth more than £600 million a year. BAA takes a double-digit cut of the sales of leased retail areas—sometimes as high as 40% of retail spend. In return, retailers enjoy a low competition environment, in which stores do not compete with each other in significant product categories. Critics suggest T5 is more a bazaar of upmarket retail outlets than a serious attempt to improve passenger service standards. BAA has a vested interest in maximizing the amount of passenger shopping time in its terminals, and employs various ploys to achieve this goal.

BAA is very unpopular. But the company is under little or no incentive to improve passenger satisfaction levels. More satisfied passengers will not spend more, increase revenue streams by recommending use of the airport to others, or provide any other tangible benefit to BAA. Dissatisfied passengers may complain and be more difficult to deal with, but they cannot easily impact on BAA's revenues and profits. Those who complain too much or too loudly can anyway be removed from the airport and prevented from travelling by BAA staff, calling on their "security" rationale for passenger bullying and assault, backed-up by aggressive armed airport police (apparently the latter are people who like guns but are not qualified to be employed as police officers outside the airports).

Indeed, many of the factors about which passengers complain most—flight delays, extra-long check-in times, confiscation of property in the name of security—have a positive commercial benefit for BAA, by increasing the time people have to shop in the airport and their need to replace personal products. It is unlikely that any more than a marginal effect could be felt by passengers choosing not to fly at all because the airport experience is so horrible. Some international passengers may be able to arrange travel so as to avoid BAA airports, and Heathrow in particular, but the numbers are not likely to be high enough to worry BAA. Passengers have become resigned to the fact that the unhelpful airport staff, surly "security" people, loutish "police officers" and ineffective cleaners, really do not care what passengers think, because they do not *have* to care.

The only real sign of competition is that a new, faster train service would become increasingly attractive for short-haul travellers with journeys within the UK or to near Europe. British Airways has already voiced its concerns that growing numbers of business travel passengers may avoid Heathrow by avoiding air travel. However, the reality of this competitive threat depends on the growth and improvement of the key rail services, which does not seem imminent.

BAA's main paying customers are, of course, the airlines. The airlines do care very much that passengers are subjected to unpleasant experiences at the hands of BAA; they do care about flight delays and cancellations; they do care about lost baggage. The airlines are in a situation where substandard BAA behaviours, over which the airlines have little or no control, impact on passenger satisfaction with the airlines, and consequent airline choices and volume of business. British Airways, for example, is particularly concerned that business travellers paying premium business-class and first-class fares will go out of their way to avoid Heathrow (and consequently choose alternative airlines), for example, choosing to make Amsterdam the hub instead of Heathrow, and favouring KLM/Air France over BA as a consequence. Nonetheless, the airlines have relatively little choice other than to accept BAA's behaviour—there is no alternative to using the facilities provided by BAA. They can complain, and frequently do, but other than that they have little leverage to impact on BAA.

The only parties with any real power to hurt BAA are the Civil Aviation Authority and the Competition Commission—who effectively set the prices BAA can charge the airlines and the rules of the game, such as whether BAA should be forced to divest some of the airports it controls to encourage greater competition. The critical issue for BAA is whether passenger service levels and the vocal complaints of airlines will actually make any difference to the airport and competition authorities. Could a position be reached where, for example, the CAA was prepared to levy massive fines on BAA, whenever it inconvenienced passengers, as some critics have urged?

Theoretically, the government and the airport authorities have three options for improving the British airport situation. *First,* they could break BAA's monopoly of the London airports—for example, forcing the company to sell its Gatwick interests. BAA says this would make no difference because the basic problem of capacity and airport infrastructure would not change. *Second,* they could overhaul the regulatory regime, to promote better service and provide incentives for BAA performance improvement as an airport operator. However, the relevant authority—the Civil Aviation Authority—is feeble, and unlikely to have the nerve to undertake this approach to any real extent that exceeds the current token fines. *Third,* the government could force a more rational allocation and pricing of flight slots at Heathrow, to reflect their scarcity. On the grey market, Heathrow take-off

slots have often changed hands for more than £5 million a pair in the past, depending on the arrival and departure times, but the looming "open skies" free-for-all finds airlines willing to pay more than £20 million a pair for scarce and desirable take-off and landing slots. In 2008, as a result of the "open-skies" treaty to liberalize transatlantic aviation, Continental paid a record $209 million for four pairs of take-off and landing slots at Heathrow. This could provide the resources needed to finance airport service improvements. However, it looks as though Whitehall has no appetite for a fight of this kind. In particular, while one way to improve London's airports would be to price the growth out of flying, to bring demand back in line with capacity, it is unlikely that any government would have the political will to do this.

The Dilemmas for BAA

BAA remains in the strange position of having inherited the infrastructure of a publicly owned airports authority—particularly responsibility for matters of airport security in which there is, and should be, no commercial advantage—and the type of monopoly position (control of all of London's major airports) appropriate to a public authority, but arguably less appropriate to a commercial company seeking to make a return on its investment for shareholders. The airports authority also finds itself being held in part responsible for the image of the country presented to foreign visitors (particularly by a government keen to justify its support for the 2012 Olympics), and the government desire for greater airport capacity.

Ferrovial's ownership started with a poorly managed crisis, which has shaped relationships since. The investors clearly expected this to be a sleepy infrastructure investment, but in fact it has proved to be a political minefield. This was never going to be a comfortable position to occupy—which the CAA was at pains to point out to Ferrovial when the purchase was negotiated. Ferrovial's most serious omission was to think that the regulators would not seize on the highly leveraged BAA deal and clamp down on BAA's returns, after years of relative *laissez-faire.*

Certainly, BAA is in a position where it is vulnerable to attack from those representing passengers and from vocal airlines protesting about increases in airport fees impacting on fares, and the poor service they receive. Nonetheless, to remedy the infrastructure that drives the poor performance of the airports, BAA needs access to increased capital and robust revenue streams. Stakeholders fighting to limit BAA's revenue and capital sources are the same ones who are the most critical of BAA's performance, and who most want to see increased investment for performance improvement. The biggest threat to BAA is action by the government and regulatory bodies, stimulated and supported by stakeholder attacks on BAA, before the company has the opportunity to address the factors underlying its problems. BAA price increases to airlines have been restricted by the CAA and it remains subject to the threat of the break-up of the company as a result of Competition Commission investigation. There is a possible scenario in which Ferrovial "walks away" from the airports operation.

Part of the BAA problem is that while the airlines and passenger groups have vociferously called for the break-up of the BAA London airports monopoly, such a move has previously been rejected by government ministers, who look to BAA to provide more airport capacity. Environmental protestors opposing the expansion of air travel have called the House of Commons building the "headquarters of BAA," underlining what they believe to be an over-close and corrupt relationship between ministers and the airports authority.

An additional complication is that research by the UK air regulatory authorities—the CAA and National Air Traffic Services—suggests that there is a further constraint to airport growth, which needs to be addressed. Their models suggest that with new runways at Heathrow and Stansted, there will simply not be enough room in the skies over London for all the extra flights which are planned—the third Heathrow runway would add 230,000 flights a year. Their submission to the Competition Commission notes that air traffic expansion in the southeast "would not [leave] sufficient airspace capacity to accommodate the scale of predicted traffic growth on the basis of current and predicted technology." They offer the prospect of London's air traffic noise spreading to homes in the south Midlands and East Anglia to deal with the overspill. This threatens BAA's plans for achieving higher performance through capacity expansion.

Early in 2008 rumours spread that the government was alarmed by the scale of the opposition to expansion at Heathrow and Stansted, and was secretly quite happy with BAA threats to delay further investment if facing tough new financial targets set by the CAA. Faced with an imminent general election and a weak position in the polls, Labour ministers were concerned about the political consequences of proceeding. The political prospect was raised (not for the first time) of building an additional London airport, possibly in the Thames estuary, away

from residential areas and allowing 24 hour flight take-offs and landings. A new airport would bring to an end expansion plans at BAA-owned Heathrow, Gatwick and Stansted. The only obstacles to this happening are political will, rather than financial or technological challenges. While the government and BAA have long enjoyed a cosy relationship—BAA's communications strategy director is Tom Kelly who was formerly official spokesman for Tony Blair, and several key Labour officials have worked for BAA or pro-aviation lobby groups—if expansion at Heathrow becomes a big vote loser, this relationship may become less friendly.

BAA executives appear to have been shocked by the hostility the company faces from the public and from business, particularly over Heathrow. Even the staid *Financial Times* is prepared to regard Heathrow as Britain's most hated facility and BAA the country's most hated company. Heathrow's failings have topped the agenda several times in talks between big business and Prime Minister Gordon Brown. In September 2007 Ferrovial earmarked £17 million for "fix the basics" at Heathrow—mainly for painting and cleaning—in an attempt to head-off further criticisms. A BAA management shake-up in 2007 included the appointment of Sir Nigel Rudd, lately chair of Alliance Boots and one of the leading figures in British business, as chairman. In late-2007 BAA launched a "charm offensive" with CEO Stephen Nelson touring the boardrooms of leading companies to explain BAA's poor performance. By 2008 it appeared increasingly as though time was running out for BAA.

A torrid week for BAA at the end of February 2008 saw: figures released by the Association of European Airlines showing that passengers at Heathrow and Gatwick suffered the worst flight delays among all leading European airlines in 2007; a *Sunday Times* article and a Channel 4 TV documentary, authored by investigative journalist Andrew Gilligan, accusing BAA of rigging satisfaction and service quality statistics, bullying competitors and failing to provide adequate airport security; and front-page stories showing Greenpeace protestors climbing over an airplane on the runway at Heathrow, having evaded security procedures. At this point, BAA's chief executive, Stephen Nelson, stepped down as a result of a management shake-up instigated by chairman Sir Nigel Rudd as his first big decision at the company. He may have had his hurt feelings assuaged by the £2.6 million he was paid in his last year with BAA.

Mr Nelson was replaced by Colin Matthews, bringing experience in both the utility and airline sectors. Rudd's goal was to exchange Mr Nelson, with his background in retail and consumer industries, for Mr Matthews, former head of water company Severn Trent, and with experience at British Airways. Mr Matthews brings a track record of working within a regulated utility and of dealing with irate stakeholders, and has overseen business break-ups at Severn Trent and Hays, the business services group. He moved into the CEO position on April Fool's Day 2008. Any hope he would have a good start following a successful opening of Terminal 5 was misplaced—it was a disaster. Mr Matthews first public statement was an apology for the T5 mess. And he still faces the major challenges of pricing issues at Heathrow and Gatwick, responses to BAA's application for an extra runway and capacity expansion at Stansted, and the Competition Commission's conclusions regarding BAA ownership of London's main airports. Rudd is looking to Matthews to fix the Heathrow problems, but there are bigger concerns that the sheer scale of the problems faced by BAA may make its current business model unworkable and unsustainable. Certainly, in mid-2008, former BA CEO Robert Ayling concluded that BAA had a flawed business model that has contributed to the bankruptcy and near collapse of many airlines, and has turned Heathrow into a "national disgrace." He firmly opposes further expansion at Heathrow.

Sources: Dominic O'Connell, "BAA May Run Out of Cash, Warns Bank," *Sunday Times,* January 27 2008, p. 3–3. Philip Stevens, "British Airways Catches the Heathrow Disease," *Financial Times,* December 18 2007, p. 13. Dominic O'Connell, "Aviation Chiefs Trim BAA's Wings," *Sunday Times,* October 7 2007, p. 3–7. Martin Wolf, "Break-Up of BAA Is Not the Answer," *Financial Times,* August 24 2007, p. 11. Andrew Gilligan, "BAA "Rigged Figures" to Hide Airport Delays," *Sunday Times,* February 24 2008, p. 1–10. Kevin Done, "Latest Chief Poised to Steer Course Through Minefield," *Financial Times,* February 28 2008, p. 3. Dominic O'Connell, "Squeeze on BAA Could be Terminal," *Sunday Times,* March 2 2008, p. 3–7. Jon Ungoed-Thomas and Marie Woolf, "Revealed: The Plot to Expand Heathrow." *Sunday Times,* March 9 2009, p. 1–1. Jon Ungoed-Thomas and Marie Woolf, "The Great Heathrow Evidence Fit-Up," *Sunday Times,* March 9 2008, p. 1–7. Dominic O'Connell, "Airlines Unite to Push for BAA Break-Up," *Sunday Times,* March 16 2008, p. 3–2. Jon Ungoed-Thomas, "Labour's Flying Club Lobbies for BAA," *Sunday Times,* March 16 2008, p. 1–10. "Who Wants a Third Runway After This?," *Sunday Times,* March 30 2008, pp. 1-12–1-13. James Stack, "Fingerprint Plan for Terminal 5 Passengers Could Breach Data Laws," *Daily Mail,* March 24 2008, p. 11. Kevin Done, "BAA Chief to Attack Tories on Heathrow," *Financial Times,* June 25 2008, p. 4. Bob Ayling, "Third Runway Is a Flight of Fancy," Sunday *Times, May* 4 2008, p. 1–21. Dominic O'Connell, "BAA Censured for "Interfering" In Break-up Probe," *Sunday Times* April 27 2008, p. 3–1.

Case 6-11

California Credit Life Insurance Group

Diane Flanagan, vice president of human resources at California Credit Life Insurance Group (CCLI), had just returned to her office after a lengthy conversation with Kevin Stark, vice president of sales. Flanagan and Stark had spent many hours reviewing the results of several reports that described the problems and opportunities experienced by women in sales.

The reports came from a variety of sources and were based on one-on-one discussions between women and men in sales and another person such as a reporter or a human resource manager. In some cases, the information resulted from focus group interviews. Flanagan

and Stark hoped to gain a comprehensive understanding of the environment faced by women in sales.

Toward the end of their meeting, Flanagan received a rather urgent telephone call from Shelley Ryan, a lawyer from CCLI's legal staff. Ryan was calling to inform Flanagan that Suzette Renoldi, a sales rep in the southeastern region, had just filed a sexual discrimination suit against James Bradford, CCLI area sales manager from the southeastern region. Ryan called to Flanagan's attention that this was not the first complaint of sexual discrimination involving Bradford. Flanagan was aware of this and, in addition, knew of another situation that could have led to sexual harassment charges being brought against Bradford. The person involved, Ilse Rieboldt, declined to pursue the matter for a variety of reasons. Diane Flanagan had been unable to assure Ilse Rieboldt that bringing charges would be very reasonable, based on the description of the events. After an excellent start with CCLI, Riebolt quit in 1997 and took a position with a competitor.

This case was written by Professor Neil M. Ford, University of Wisconsin-Madison.

California Credit Life prided itself on being an equal opportunity employer and wanted to avoid any adverse publicity. Flanagan was very concerned about the veracity and implications of the suit. On the other hand, she was not interested in any attempts to cover up the situation if the charges were true.

According to company policy and advice provided by Shelley Ryan, the first action to be taken should be a thorough investigation of the charges and of all available data. Ryan urged Flanagan to gather the necessary information as quickly and as quietly as possible.

Initially, Flanagan determined she would need a vast amount of information. CCLI's computerized customer relationship management system (CRM) would be a source of much of the needed data. The CRM system contained such files as sales performance, quotas, expenses, salaries, and commissions for all of CCLI's sales reps across the country. A separate data management system in the human resources department contained the data from studies conducted on such subjects as job satisfaction, role conflict, role ambiguity, and other subjects.

The Company

California Credit Life Insurance Group was incorporated in Los Angeles in 1961. CCLI's initial product line included all types of life insurance. Since its inception, CCLI has expanded its product line to include all types of insurance such as health, automobile, professional liability, pension and retirement programs, commercial packages, and related financial services.

In 1997, CCLI decided to open an office in the southeastern area of the United States as soon as all staffing and physical details could be resolved. The southeastern region became a reality in 2001, with James Bradford selected to be area sales manager. Bradford had been a sales rep in the Dallas region and had been selected for the new position based on his excellent sales performance and his strong interpersonal skills. Shortly after Bradford accepted the position, it became apparent to Diane Flanagan that he did not wholeheartedly support CCLI's position concerning equal opportunity. In fact, it became necessary to instruct Bradford that one-third of his sales force would be female, a figure in line with CCLI's experience in its other regional offices.

California Credit Life Insurance has 15 regional offices and 230 sales representatives. Area sales managers typically supervise 15 people, a large number but manageable given the nature of the selling job. The sales reps work independently and do not need day-to-day supervision or contact with their area sales manager. CCLI requires two performance evaluations each year. Area sales managers have hiring authority and can set base salaries with approval from CCLI. Promotional opportunities are limited, and turnover among the area sales managers has been very low.

Area sales managers can recognize excellent performance by increasing the base salary and modifying a

EXHIBIT 1   Total Sales and Sales to Quota, 2001–2007*

	2001 Total Sales	Percent to Quota	2002 Total Sales	Percent to Quota	2003 Total Sales	Percent to Quota
Suzette Renoldi	$228,800	101.4	$247,104	102.1	$261,930	101.4
Stuart Pletz	215,600	97.3	219,912	99.4	230,908	99.9
Alvin Polard	100,000	96.7	101,000	97.2	103,020	100.0
Ted Hervington	350,000	100.3	346,500	95.4	343,035	99.6
Tim Hart	264,900	99.8	270,198	100.4	275,602	100.9
Brett Moore	234,000	98.9	231,660	96.7	231,660	99.0
Shari Swaggert	375,000	105.3	397,500	103.5	413,400	102.6
Mark Hoffton	189,000	101.2	192,780	100.6	198,563	101.1
Bob Pizzano	250,100	100.1	257,603	101.0	265,331	101.8
Felicia Abler	289,650	100.8	309,926	104.5	325,422	103.2
Kathy Levenhagen	190,000	103.8	209,000	106.2	223,630	103.5
Jeff Birdest	195,640	95.4	205,422	100.4	211,585	102.9
Larry Green	320,000	99.6	326,400	99.7	336,192	102.4
Chris Brackett	296,430	101.3	311,252	102.4	326,815	103.6
Ilse Rieboldt	287,500	102.4	296,125	105.3	T	
Mike Peck					100,412	102.3
Jeff Martin						
Cliff Arlen						
Kim Babler						

*Terminations are noted by T.

(continued)

sales rep's territory to cover better accounts. Sales reps receive a 3 percent commission on sales in addition to their base salaries. Yearly bonuses are distributed by the area sales manager based on a sales rep's performance. Records indicated Bradford's bonus allocation did not reflect sales volume and seemed to be determined by taking the total bonus award and dividing it by 15. This process added an average of $1,750 to each sales rep's income.

The Suzette Renoldi Matter

Renoldi joined CCLI in 2001 after graduating with a business degree from the University of South Carolina. Her initial performance was strong, and she made quota each year except for the last two years. Quotas are set by the area sales manager based on guidelines handed down from Kevin Stark, vice president of sales, and negotiations between the area sales manager and each sales representative.

Diane Flanagan contacted Shelley Ryan to determine what was behind Renoldi's legal action against CCLI and Bradford. Ryan informed her that she had not seen the actual complaint but knew that Renoldi had asked for territory changes so that her sales opportunities would be greater, a request that Bradford denied. Bradford allegedly told Renoldi that her unwillingness to entertain clients, especially males, was the reason her sales had fallen off and not because of a lack of

sales potential. Renoldi refuted this accusation and claimed Bradford's territory assignment was discriminatory from the start. Flanagan knew she would need to see the complete complaint and personally discuss the situation with both Renoldi and Bradford. Meanwhile, Flanagan started compiling as much information as possible from company sources.

The first documents received by Flanagan revealed sales volumes for each sales representative (Exhibit 1), expense account data (Exhibit 2), number of performance evaluations (Exhibit 3), and base salaries (Exhibit 4). Her office conducts various personnel studies, and she had available the summary results of a recent job satisfaction survey for the entire company. She requested a breakout based on region and sex, knowing that the small number of women in the southeastern region posed a statistical problem. Exhibit 5 presents job satisfaction scores for the sales representatives by sex for the southeastern region and the entire company. Flanagan was somewhat pleased with the results for the entire company but disappointed with the southeastern region's showing. At this juncture, Flanagan decided to summarize some of the studies she and Stark had been reviewing.

The first study, conducted by HBRS (a research company), was based on a series of focus group interviews with women sales reps from a variety of selling positions. HBRS also conducted focus group sessions with men. No attempt was made to conduct sessions with both men and women because it was believed this

EXHIBIT 1 Total Sales and Sales to Quota, 2001–2007* (*concluded*)

2004 Total Sales	Percent to Quota	2005 Total Sales	Percent to Quota	2006 Total Sales	Percent to Quota	2007 Total Sales	Percent to Quota
$267,169	102.3	$264,340	101.1	$282,844	99.6	$288,500	98.5
242,453	101.1	245,442	101.6	262,623	98.4	288,885	100.2
106,111	100.3	107,500	100.6	115,025	100.3	124,227	100.6
T							
281,114	100.8	282,445	101.2	302,216	102.0	326,395	102.7
232,818	98.1	T					
417,534	102.1	410,890	99.8	T			
204,520	100.8	204,800	100.7	219,136	100.1	230,093	100.4
273,291	101.2	275,364	101.6	294,639	102.1	318,210	102.0
326,724	103.4	322,745	101.9	345,337	102.9	348,790	98.7
230,339	103.9	225,990	102.1	241,809	100.1	265,990	99.0
217,932	101.6	218,500	101.7	233,795	101.4	252,110	101.7
347,959	102.3	348,660	102.0	373,066	103.1	414,103	102.5
339,887	103.0	342,110	103.4	366,057	104.1	406,323	103.8
253,117	101.6	241,553	99.1	281,313	101.8	305,014	102.4
213,419	99.1	235,017	100.2	279,106	101.2	312,844	102.8
		185,442	97.1	214,877	99.3	264,651	98.1
				204,913	98.4	278,228	100.2

would limit discussion. Flanagan read the following verbatim comments:

Karen R. (computer sales): *I really enjoy the challenge of selling high-priced, high-tech computers. It feels great to help somebody solve a problem. But I still get questions from my friends when I tell them about my travel demands.*

Margaret M. (medical equipment sales): *I don't mind the travel, but at times it is all lumped together. Making child care arrangements can be a hassle.*

Sherry W. (office equipment sales): *This travel thing is bad news at my house. My husband becomes aloof the minute I mention that I have to be gone overnight. He's still aloof after I return. I know he wants me to quit and get a job with no travel.*

Martha W. (cosmetics sales): *I don't have a husband to contend with, but with my travel schedule I don't have much of a social life either. My biggest problem was deciding what to pack and lost luggage. I'm supposed to carry a sample case that weighs 35 pounds plus a garment bag and my briefcase.*

Deirdre B. (insurance sales): *I rarely travel outside of the city. My major headache is the guy who thinks that I should be home sewing and cooking or, if I have to work, in the typing pool.*

Karen R. (computer sales): *I've made quota every year for the last five years only to confront men who say I'm lucky. One guy told me that I make more sales because customers want to see what a female sales rep looks like; then when I'm making my presentation, I rely on my feminine wiles to make the sale.*

Cherie I. (aluminum sales): *I've had the credibility problem too. One purchasing agent informed me that my predecessor stood 6 feet, 2 inches, weighed 195 pounds, and had a beard. I was really flustered with that comment and even more so when he asked me if I was busy in the evening. No doubt he wanted to explain the intricacies of aluminum to me.*

Laura W. (advertising sales): *Being hassled comes with the territory. And I don't have to leave the office either. But I've adapted. I either play naive or ignore the comments. I told one fellow laughingly that he could do better than me. But I do get tired of the hassle.*

Candace S. (commercial lending): *The surprises never end. My first attempt at customer entertaining was a shocker. The customer said he would join me for dinner if he could bring his wife along. I was dumbfounded. Do I take both and report the expenses? I did, but business talk was very limited. I got the account, but it was weird.*

EXHIBIT 2 **Expense Account Data, 2001–2007***

	2001	2002	2003	2004	2005	2006	2007
Suzette Renoldi	$1,800	$1,875	$1,820	$1,830	$1,790	$1,933	$1,905
Stuart Pletz	1,100	1,367	1,450	1,690	1,855	2,078	2,210
Alvin Polard	1,250	1,462	1,667	1,723	1,775	1,988	1,995
Ted Hervington	1,790	1,890	1,993	T			
Tim Hart	2,000	2,134	2,177	2,189	2,950	3,304	3,380
Brett Moore	2,500	2,578	2,673	2,774	T		
Shari Swaggert	1,540	1,603	1,615	1,672	1,715	T	
Mark Hoffton	1,778	1,800	1,829	1,950	2,059	2,306	2,384
Bob Pizzano	1,892	1,966	1,998	2,150	2,331	2,611	2,673
Felicia Abler	1,224	1,250	1,282	1,354	1,332	1,439	1,461
Kathy Levenhagen	1,452	1,466	1,562	1,432	1,455	1,571	1,543
Jeff Birdest	1,970	1,980	2,155	2,245	2,778	3,111	3,260
Larry Green	2,145	2,256	2,347	2,355	2,679	3,000	3,114
Chris Brackett	2,234	2,457	2,679	2,789	2,887	3,233	3,211
Ilse Rieboldt	1,234	1,423	T				
Mike Peck			1,131	2,046	2,811	2,270	2,413
Jeff Martin				1,548	2,060	2,316	2,385
Cliff Arlen					1,440	2,119	2,376
Kim Babler						1,804	2,223

*Terminations are noted by T.

EXHIBIT 3 Performance Evaluations, 2001–2007*

	2001		2002		2003		2004		2005		2006		2007	
	1st	2nd	1st	2nd	1st	2nd	1st	2nd	1st	2nd	1st	2nd	1st	2nd
Suzette Renoldi	Y	N	Y	Y	Y	Y	Y	Y	N	Y	Y	N	Y	Y
Stuart Pletz	Y	Y	Y	Y	Y	Y	Y	Y	Y	Y	Y	Y	Y	Y
Alvin Polard	Y	Y	Y	Y	Y	N	Y	Y	Y	Y	Y	Y	Y	Y
Ted Hervington	Y	Y	N	Y	Y	Y	T							
Ted Hart	Y	Y	Y	Y	Y	Y	Y	Y	Y	Y	Y	Y	Y	Y
Brett Moore	Y	Y	Y	Y	Y	Y	Y	Y	T					
Shari Swaggert	Y	Y	Y	Y	Y	Y	Y	Y	N	Y	T			
Mark Hoffton	Y	Y	Y	Y	Y	Y	Y	Y	Y	Y	Y	N	Y	Y
Bob Pizzano	Y	Y	N	Y	Y	Y	Y	Y	Y	Y	Y	Y	Y	Y
Felicia Abler	Y	Y	Y	Y	Y	Y	Y	Y	N	Y	N	Y	N	Y
Kathy Levenhagen	Y	N	Y	Y	N	Y	Y	Y	Y	Y	Y	Y	N	Y
Jeff Birdest	Y	N	Y	Y	Y	Y	Y	Y	Y	Y	Y	Y	Y	Y
Larry Green	Y	Y	Y	Y	Y	Y	Y	Y	Y	Y	Y	Y	Y	Y
Chris Brackett	Y	Y	Y	N	Y	Y	Y	Y	Y	N	Y	Y	N	Y
Ilse Rieboldt	Y	Y	N	Y	T									
Mike Peck						Y	Y	Y	Y	Y	Y	Y	Y	Y
Jeff Martin							Y	Y	Y	Y	Y	Y	Y	Y
Cliff Arlen									Y	Y	Y	Y	Y	Y
Kim Babler										Y	N	Y	N	Y

*Terminations are noted by T.

559

EXHIBIT 4   Base Salaries for All Sales Reps in the SE Region, 2001–2007*

	2001	2002	2003	2004	2005	2006	2007
Suzette Renoldi	$25,000	$27,600	$29,200	$29,200	$29,250	$29,300	$30,750
Stuart Pletz	25,000	27,300	28,900	29,150	29,860	30,580	32,750
Alvin Polard	25,000	28,930	29,600	29,990	30,650	31,320	33,850
Ted Hervington	25,000	26,000	26,700	T			
Tim Hart	25,000	25,780	26,750	26,890	26,900	27,000	29,700
Brett Moore	25,000	25,900	26,200	26,750	T		
Shari Swaggert	25,000	29,000	29,500	29,750	29,800	T	
Mark Hoffton	25,000	26,200	27,150	27,450	27,900	28,500	30,500
Bob Pizzano	25,000	27,100	28,450	28,600	28,770	28,900	31,300
Felicia Abler	25,000	28,750	29,200	29,450	29,500	29,750	31,500
Kathy Levenhagen	25,000	28,450	28,750	28,950	29,340	29,750	31,500
Jeff Birdest	25,000	25,700	26,500	27,800	29,100	31,000	33,750
Larry Green	25,000	25,900	28,000	28,750	30,100	31,500	34,000
Chris Brackett	25,000	27,000	27,800	28,900	29,900	31,000	33,750
Ilse Rieboldt	25,000	26,200	T				
Mike Peck			26,000	27,500	28,300	28,750	30,000
Jeff Martin				26,500	27,500	28,250	29,500
Cliff Arlen					27,000	27,500	28,250
Kim Babler						27,250	28,000

*Terminations are noted by T.

EXHIBIT 5
Job Satisfaction Summary, 2007*

*All scores are standardized at a mean of 50. The higher the score, the more sales representatives are satisfied.

	Southeastern Region			Total Company		
	Male	Female	Total	Male	Female	Total
1. Job	54.06	45.13	52.16	53.84	50.19	53.61
2. Fellow workers	58.35	49.63	55.82	57.98	51.11	57.39
3. Supervisor	59.91	41.24	57.33	54.13	48.54	51.43
4. Company policy and management support	61.58	52.28	60.17	58.91	53.28	56.46
5. Pay	49.31	52.39	50.07	49.88	51.65	49.92
6. Promotion and advancement	59.41	48.37	57.30	58.28	49.87	57.06
7. Customer	53.70	48.44	51.19	54.07	48.56	52.09
Total	59.47	48.14	59.12	58.19	50.23	57.48

Laura W. (advertising sales): *Entertaining has been a problem with me too, especially when it comes to paying the check. Some men must feel threatened by this.*

Brenda S. (building supply sales): *Remember when we were girls? The boys wouldn't let us join their stupid clubs. Not much has changed, has it? Now it's the country club where decisions are made. And, damn it, don't tell me that I have to take up golf. I may get good and win. I remember my boss's reaction when I clobbered him in tennis.*

Roseann S. (textbook sales): *Speaking of bosses, my manager's evaluation of my performance is an embarrassment. He is absolutely unable to criticize my performance. Most reviews have been late too.*

Karla H. (software programs): *This is my second sales job. My first put me into a "pioneer" situation, industrial equipment. To succeed with that company you had to be a "superwoman" and become "one of the guys." I was told that I could not succeed without experience. What a catch-22! I can't get experience without succeeding.*

Peggy T. (chemical sales): *You know, I've experienced a lot. This is my tenth year with_____. And I've been hassled, rejected, had to cancel a sales call due to a sick child, but I wouldn't trade it for anything. Your sales manager is really key. Mine treats me the same as he treats everybody else, but he does recognize that there are gender differences.*

The male commentators had this to say:

Bill M. (computer sales): *Well, I can tell you this much. When the first women showed up, I was really surprised. Not that women cannot sell computers, after all many of my customers are women and most of them are really sharp, but we weren't informed that a woman had been hired.*

Joe M. (machine tool sales): *Yeah, I was surprised too. But this "little thing" wanted to set the pace. You know, be the first woman ever to sell heavy-duty machinery costing $250,000 and up. She just didn't look the part, flowery dresses, heels, perfume. One of her customers called my boss and asked him to send a man the next time.*

Frank C. (office furniture sales): *We have several women in my district. Like everybody else, some are super, some are average. I think that it has been a good move. We are now selling accounts that we were unable to sell before. And our national sales manager had us attend several company training sessions on how to integrate women into the sales force.*

John R. (tractor sales): *I know this is going to sound strange, but I don't like it. A woman's place is in the home, not out selling and taking up space that some man could occupy. They have no business selling tractors!*

Mike R. (pharmaceutical sales): *Talk about problems. We now have several women in our sales force. You should have seen the other reps when the first one was introduced at a sales meeting. You would have thought that she was the first gal these guys had ever seen. But I just about lost it when she comes up to me one day and asks if I would help her carry some boxes to her car. "Carry them yourself" is what I should have said.*

Paul T. (building materials sales): *The thing that bugs me is the equal rights stuff, or should I say unequal rights. I'd like to see what happens if I call the boss or a customer and tell them I can't keep an appointment because my babysitter is sick.*

Not only that, Susan just got back from maternity leave—something I'll never get—and I had to cover her accounts while she was gone.

Mack H. (stockbroker): *I don't want to play "Can You Top This," but we have a similar situation. Karen comes back off of maternity leave (this was her second child) and then decides that full-time is too much for her. She asks (and gets it too) to work only from Tuesday to Thursday. And she still gets full benefits but at a reduced salary.*

Calvin H. (chemical sales): *We have a few women in the sales force, and the problems have been minimal. Management handled it well. They even had discussions with the sales force about how to call on customers who are women. Our purchasing agents, production engineers—they're all men—have had sessions on how to deal with women sales reps.*

Brad M. (food product sales): *Well, with women in my group we've had the usual mess. Office romance, you know. He was married—was, that is—and now he's divorced, and she is working for another company. I think she was fired, but nobody will admit it.*

Bob R. (aluminum sales): *Yeah, I can identify with that. It almost caused a divorce in my house. I was expected to travel with Beth and show her the ropes. Well, my wife wanted to know what "ropes" I was going to show her. All I had to do was mention that I was going to travel with Beth, and things went to hell. It's OK now, but it was shaky for a while.*

Todd B. (commercial lending sales): *I've made joint calls with Katherine, and I've learned a lot. I thought I knew all the answers, but watching Kate interact with customers has been a real treat. She's good and really has a knack for finding out customer needs. My own sales have increased as a result, I'm sure.*

Flanagan finished her review of the HBRS report and thought that most of the comments reinforced what she suspected were the major problems confronting women in sales. Other reports she reviewed supported the findings of the HBRS report. She wondered if she could get the remaining women in the southeastern region to discuss their feelings, attitudes, and problems with her or with a neutral third party. She knew the legal proceedings might prevent her from contacting the women. Shelley Ryan and CCLI's legal staff suggested she could bring in several women from different regions for a focus group or one-on-one sessions. Ryan told her to bring in some men too since their perceptions will be valuable. Flanagan decided to adopt this strategy. After all, regardless of the outcome of the Renoldi case, CCLI should learn as much as possible about the subject to avoid future incidents.

Flanagan decided to retain a research firm to conduct the focus group interviews with samples of women and men sales reps. Six groups of 10 sales reps each participated in the project. The sessions lasted approximately two hours. Dana Moore and Bill Carson moderated the focus groups and reported to Flanagan that they felt very positive about the process and the results. The report was accompanied with videotapes so Flanagan could see and hear the proceedings. To remain objective, Flanagan did not review the tapes and asked Moore and Carson to prepare their verbatim comments without identifying the respondent.

Flanagan reviewed the report, hoping to find some insight as to how CCLI might avoid future problems such as the one existing in the southeastern region. Many of the comments coincided with those from the HBRS report, although a few provided additional insight concerning the problem in the southeastern region. Flanagan read with great interest the following verbatim comments from the women:

Sales rep #1: *Basically, I like my job a lot. But it has taken me much time to get to that point. And it's been my doing, all the way, especially with the limited support that I get from my manager.*

Sales rep #2: *Speaking of support, some of the guys I work with view me as a threat to their precious power structure. One guy told me that I should be home making soup and not taking up space that a man could fill.*

Sales rep #3: *I can relate to that. My manager at my last sales job was the only woman district sales manager in the company. She was told that she should not take credit for work done by the men who worked for her.*

Sales rep #4: *It's not just how I relate to my manager but the whole support issue. I don't feel like I'm part of the company. Why just the other day, a customer asked about a new policy that he knew about but nobody told me about. I asked one of the men in our office, and he knew.*

Sales rep #5: *I had a similar situation just the other day, and I don't like having to say, "I don't*

know the answer, but I'll find out for you." But I knew that the customer expected an answer then, not later.

Sales rep #6: *I'd like to think that if I needed an answer my manager would be the logical source. But in my office I ask one of the other women.*

Sales rep #7: *I really question the ability of the higher-ups to tell me what's going on. It would be great to have a mentor or someone that I could rely on for the straight scoop.*

Sales rep #8: *Hey, I don't want to seem odd, but my manager is really supportive. I told him about my problem taking a customer to dinner and getting into the hassle about who pays the bill. The customer just would not let a woman buy him dinner. My manager said I should join the Capital Club and take customers there where the bill doesn't come to the table. It works like a charm.*

Sales rep #9: *I've had a similar experience. A customer, a good one, sent me a bottle of Passion perfume and a cashmere sweater. I was dumbfounded and asked my manager what to do, since I didn't recall hearing anything about receiving gifts during our training program. He gave me several suggestions, and I decided which one to try. It worked, and I still have the account.*

Sales rep #10: *My manager is pretty supportive. But he can't eliminate the hassling that goes on with some customers. Do the purchasing agents and others with CCLI treat women sales reps the same?*

Sales rep #11: *I'd really like a chance to move into sales management. That's why I got into sales to begin with. Now, all I have to do is figure out what it takes to get promoted. It's a big mystery at CCLI. And if something doesn't happen soon, I'll go elsewhere.*

Sales rep #12: *This whole performance evaluation process is a joke. My manager is usually late, and on top of it the review is so general and vague that I have no idea what I'm supposed to do to better myself. And our annual bonuses show no relation to contribution. We all get the same bonus.*

The comments from the men did not add anything to her understanding of CCLI's problems. They were very similar to those provided by HBRS, plus they duplicated many of the comments made by the women concerning performance evaluations and promotion policies.

The report suggested to Diane Flanagan that CCLI has much work ahead if it is going to avoid problems similar to those in the southeastern region. Although names were not given in the report, Flanagan thought she could associate many of the comments with James Bradford, CCLI's problem sales manager. She did not learn anything from the focus groups that would help with the legal proceedings in the Suzette Renoldi matter. But, for certain, she wanted to change things to avoid future problems.

Case 6-12

Home Depot Inc.

Don D. Ray is one tough hombre. The 39-year-old Kentucky native spent three years with the 82nd Airborne Div., one of the U.S. Army's elite units, serving at the head of a maintenance crew during the first Gulf War and an additional seven years on active duty. Then, after the September 11 terrorist attacks, Ray suited up for service again, this time as the commander of a special forces A-team that followed the U.S.-led invasion into Afghanistan. His 12-man squad of snipers, demolition experts, and communications specialists hunted renegade al-Qaeda and Taliban. Combing mountain villages, he grew a thick beard, wore traditional Afghan garb, and rode on horseback to blend in with local Muslims. Ray and his men never killed anyone, he says, but they arrested dozens of suspected militants.

Nowadays, Ray commands a different kind of operation. He has replaced crack-of-dawn physical training and green Army fatigues with sunrise store openings and an orange Home Depot apron. A store manager in Clarksville, Tenn., Ray runs a 110,000-square-foot box with 35,000 products and a 100-member staff, 30 of them former military. Many days start at 4 a.m. That's when he wakes, eats breakfast, catches some CNBC news, then heads to the store, where the doors open at 6. Although Ray's bookish round glasses and pressed khakis make him look more like a teacher than a one-time terrorist hunter, he exudes a steely confidence. Former soldiers on his staff call him "sir." "In the military, we win battles and conquer the enemy," says Ray. At Home Depot, "we do that with customers."

Military analogies are commonplace at Home Depot Inc. these days. Five years after his December, 2000, arrival, Chief Executive Robert L. Nardelli is putting his stamp on what was long a decentralized, entrepreneurial business under founders Bernie Marcus and Arthur Blank. And if his company starts to look and feel like an army, that's the point. Nardelli loves to hire soldiers. In fact, he seems to love almost everything about the armed services. The military, to a large extent, has become the management model for his entire enterprise. Of the 1,142 people hired into Home Depot's store leadership program, a two-year training regimen for future store managers launched in 2002, almost half—528—are junior military officers. More than 100 of them now run Home Depots. Recruits such as Ray "understand the mission," says Nardelli. "It's one thing to have faced a tough customer. It's another to face the enemy shooting at you. So they probably will be pretty calm under fire."

Built like a bowling ball, Nardelli is a detail-obsessed, diamond-cut-precise manager who, in 2000, lost his shot at the top job at General Electric Co. to Jeffrey R. Immelt. He is fond of pointing out that if Home Depot were a country, it would be the fifth-largest contributor of troops in Iraq. Overall, some 13% of Home Depot's 345,000 employees have military experience, vs. 4% at Wal-Mart Stores Inc. And that doesn't even count James E. Izen, 38, a lieutenant colonel in the U.S. Marine Corps stationed outside Nardelli's door, is part of a Marine Corps Corporate Fellows program that Home Depot joined in 2002.

Importing ideas, people, and platitudes from the military is a key part of Nardelli's sweeping move to reshape Home Depot, the world's third-largest retailer, into a more centralized organization. That may be an untrendy idea in management circles, but Nardelli couldn't care less (Exhibit 1). It's a critical element of his strategy to rein in an unwieldy 2,048-store chain and prepare for its next leg of growth. "The kind of discipline and maturity that you get out of the military is something that can be very, very useful in an organization where basically you have 2,100 colonels running things," explains Craig R. Johnson, president of Customer Growth Partners Inc., a retail consulting firm.

Rivals such as Wal-Mart are plunging deeper into home improvement products, while archenemy No.1, Lowe's Cos., is luring Home Depot customers to its 1,237 bright, airy stores. Even as other companies seek to stoke creativity and break down hierarchies, Nardelli is trying to build a disciplined corps, one predisposed

EXHIBIT 1

Full Metal Apron

Nardelli is building an army at Home Depot. Here are the new marching orders for America's biggest home improvement store:

Issue Clear Commands

On Monday afternoons, Home Depot's in-house television station broadcasts *The Same Page*, a 25-minute live show emphasizing the week's top priorities.

Expel Underachievers

There's little room for error at the Home Depot. Weak managers are routinely booted. Of the top 170 executives, 98% of Nardelli's team are new to their positions since 2001.

Hire Warriors

Home Depot is on a military hiring spree. The number of former troops hired by Nardelli, who loves their discipline, has risen steadily from 10,000 in 2003 to 17,000 in 2005.

Quantify It

Home Depot now measures everything from gross margin per labor-hour for store workers to the number of "greets" at its front doors. Nardelli's predecessors, **Marcus** and **Blank**, relied more on instinct.

Centralize Control

Before Nardelli arrived, managers ran stores as individual fiefdoms. Now he is centralizing the operation, spending $1.1 billion on technology that helps to give Atlanta greater control over most tasks.

Borrow Military Ideas

What other company looks to Marine Corps literature for management wisdom? That's what Home Depot Marine Fellow **James Izen** did in helping to craft motivational messages for more than 300,000 store workers.

to following orders, operating in high-pressure environments, and executing with high standards. Home Depot is one company that actually lives by the aggressive ideals laid out in *Hardball: Are You Playing to Play or Playing to Win?* the much discussed 2004 book co-authored by Boston Consulting Group management expert George Stalk (Exhibit 2).

The cultural overhaul is taking Home Depot in a markedly different direction from Lowe's, where managers describe the atmosphere as demanding—but low-profile, collaborative, and collegial. Lowe's does not have formal military-hiring programs, says a company spokeswoman, nor does it track the number of military veterans in its ranks. Observes Goldman, Sachs & Co. analyst Matthew Fassler: "Bob believes in a command-and-control organization."

In Nardelli's eyes, it's a necessary step in Home Depot's corporate evolution. Even though founders Marcus and Blank were hardly a pair of teddy bears, they allowed store managers immense autonomy. "Whether it was an aisle, department, or store, you were truly in charge of it," says former store operations manager and Navy mechanic Bryce G. Church, who now oversees 30 Ace Hardware stores. And the two relied more on instincts than analytics to build the youngest company

ever to hit $40 billion in revenue, just 20 years after its 1979 founding. In the waning years of their leadership in the late 1990s, however, sales stagnated. The company "grew so fast the wheels were starting to come off," says Edward E. Lawler III, a professor of business at the University of Southern California. These days every major decision and goal at Home Depot flows down from Nardelli's office. "There's no question; Bob's the general," says Joe DeAngelo, 44, executive vice-president of Home Depot Supply and a GE veteran.

Although he has yet to win all the hearts and minds of his employees, and probably never will, Nardelli's feisty spirit is rekindling stellar financial performance (Exhibit 3). Riding a housing and home-improvement boom, Home Depot sales have soared, from $46 billion in 2000, the year Nardelli took over, to $81.5 billion in 2005, an average annual growth rate of 12%, according to results announced on Feb. 21. By squeezing more out of each orange box through centralized purchasing and a $1.1 billion investment in technology, such as self-checkout aisles and in-store Web kiosks, profits have more than doubled in Nardelli's tenure, to $5.8 billion. Home Depot's gross margins inched up from 30% in 2000 to 33.5% last year. But fast-growing Lowe's is still Wall Street's darling, in large part because analysts are

EXHIBIT 2

Take No Prisoners

Home Depot's cultural makeover echoes some of the guiding principles of *Hardball: Are You Playing to Play or Playing to Win?* co-authored by **George Stalk.**

Raise the costs of your competitors

Maneuver them into pursuing customers they believe are more profitable but aren't. Your competitors' costs increase, and profits decrease.

Devastate your rivals' profit sanctuaries

Influence the behavior of competitors by knowing where their most lucrative business niches are: then, when needed, use that knowledge to constrict their cash flow.

Take it and make it your own

Recognize the value of an existing idea, practice, or business model from another industry and deploy the insight to create an unassailable advantage.

Break the compromises your industry accepts

Customers rarely see past standard operating procedures. Instead, they accept them as "the way the industry works." Breaking those compromises can release huge cometitive advantages.

Unleash massive, overwhelming force

Establish a resource advantage over competitors, then engage them in wars of attrition. Warning: Can be costly to carry out.

EXHIBIT 3   **Work in Progress**

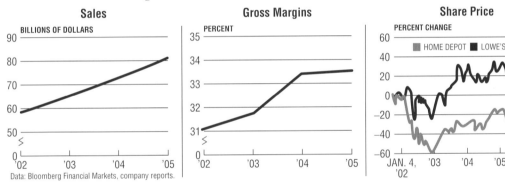

Data: Bloomberg Financial Markets, company reports.

only now getting comfortable with Nardelli's strategy. Based in Mooresville, N.C., Lowe's has seen sales grow an average of 19% a year since 2000, and it has narrowed the gap in gross margins vs. Home Depot. Since the day before Nardelli's arrival on Dec. 14, 2000, Lowe's split-adjusted share price has soared 210%. Home Depot's is down 7%.

One way Nardelli plans to kick-start the stock: move beyond the core U.S. big-box business and conquer new markets, from contractor supply to convenience stores to expansion into China. On Jan. 19, Home Depot announced plans to scale back the growth of new stores from more than 180 per year to about 100. The slowdown will let him plow extra resources into beefing up Home Depot Supply (HDS), a wholesale unit hawking pipes, custom kitchens, and building materials to contractors and repairmen. It's a fragmented market worth

$410 billion per year, according to Home Depot, where Wal-Mart and Lowe's are AWOL and the only competitors are regional companies. Already, Nardelli has spent $4.1 billion buying 35 companies to bulk up HDS, and it plans to plunk down a further $3.5 billion to buy Orlando-based Hughes Supply Inc. By 2010, HDS sales are expected to reach $23 billion, accounting for 18% of Home Depot's total, up from 5% in 2005.

The scope of the task is staggering. Nardelli, in essence, is building a whole new company—in a market twice the size of do-it-yourself retail—to service a prickly customer: professional contractors who want low prices, great quality, and instant service. Success in this field will require pinpoint execution, and Nardelli knows it. But his ambitions make some analysts nervous. "He's moving out of retail into services," says Deborah Weinswig, an analyst at Citigroup. "If it was just retail, a lot of us would be more comfortable."

"Culture of Fear"

The high stakes of Home Depot's services gambit is one of the main reasons Nardelli has pushed his cultural makeover so hard in the five years since he has been at the helm. But not all have embraced him, or his plans. *BusinessWeek* spoke with 11 former executives, a majority of whom requested anonymity lest the company sue them for violating nondisclosure agreements. Some describe a demoralized staff and say a "culture of fear" is causing customer service to wane. Nardelli's own big-time pay package, $28.5 million for the year ended Jan. 30, 2005, rubs many workers the wrong way. His guaranteed bonus, the only locked-in payout at the company, rose to $5.8 million in 2004, from $4.5 million in 2003, at a time when Home Depot's stock price finished below its yearned price in 2000, when Nardelli took over.

Before he arrived, managers ran Home Depot's stores on "tribal knowledge," based on years of experience about what sold and what didn't. Now they click nervously through Black-Berrys at the end of each week, hoping they "made plan," a combination of sales and profit targets. The once-heavy ranks of full-time Home Depot store staff have been replaced with part-timers to drive down labor costs. Underperforming executives are routinely culled from the ranks. Since 2001, 98% of Home Depot's 170 top executives are new to their positions and, at headquarters in Atlanta, 56% of job changes involved bringing new managers in from outside the company. Says one former executive: "Every single week you shuddered when you looked at e-mail because another officer was gone."

As a manager, Nardelli is relentless, demanding, and determined to prove wrong every critic of Home Depot. He treats Saturdays and Sundays as ordinary working days and often expects those around him to do the same. "He's the hardest-working guy you'll ever see," says his former boss, Jack Welch. "If I was working late at GE and wanted to feel good at 9 p.m., I would pick up the phone and call Bob. He would always be there." Privately, Nardelli admits that the move to Home Depot has sometimes been a tough slog. When he first took over—having no retail experience and replacing the beloved Bernie and Arthur—he often felt as though he were fighting a lonely, up-hill battle to convert Home Depot's legions of workers to his new vision for the company.

Nardelli's history of surrounding himself with military recruits goes back to his GE days. At GE Transportation

in the 1980s, he pioneered a program of hiring junior military officers, in part because few people were willing to move to "Dreary Erie, Pa.," where the unit is headquartered. Former grunts, used to sitting in mud holes, found the locale less of a problem. William J. Conaty, senior vice-president for corporate human resources at GE, says: "Places like Erie or Fort Wayne, Ind., didn't look desolate to these guys." Welch soon expanded the program throughout GE.

Welch characterizes Nardelli as "an unusual patriot… a true flag-waving American." Nardelli's father, Raymond, served in Europe during World War II with the Pennsylvania Keystone unit of the National Guard. As a freshman at Rockford Auburn High School in Rockford, Ill., Nardelli joined the Reserve Officers' Training Corps (ROTC) and eventually became company commander and a member of the rifle team. He also played football. "You could either take gym class or ROTC," recalls Nardelli. "I took ROTC and enjoyed the hell out of it." When it came time for college, he applied to the U.S. Military Academy at West Point, N.Y. But the Army academy accepts applicants in part by congressional district, and the young Nardelli missed the cut by one person: He was the first alternate from his region of Illinois. Instead he attended Western Illinois University in Macomb. After graduating in 1971, his draft number was called, but, he says, he did not pass his physical. Later he went on to the University of Louisville for an MBA.

As an adult, Nardelli's passion for the military persists. At Home Depot headquarters, 1,800 "blue star banners" hang in the main hallway in honor of employees serving in Afghanistan, Iraq, and elsewhere. He is frequently shadowed by Marine Fellow Izen. During one recent project to help Home Depot hone its motivational message to 317,000 store troops, Izen consulted the *Marine Corps Doctrinal Publication 1* on "War-Fighting." MCDP *1,* as it's called in the Marines, includes a chapter on "developing subordinate leaders," which Izen found a handy guide for Home Depot workers, too. "It's about how to out-think your enemy," says Izen.

The military, says Nardelli, trains its recruits to be leaders and think on their feet, skills he wants in Home Depot stores. "Having personally been on the flight deck of an aircraft carrier where 18-year-olds are responsible for millions of dollars worth of aircraft," says Nardelli, "I just think these are folks who understand the importance of training, understand the importance of 'you're only as good as the people around you.' In their case, their life depends on it many times. In our case, our business depends on it many times."

Indeed, the Home Depot of Bob Nardelli is being run with military-style precision (Exhibit 4). These days everyone at Home Depot is ranked on the basis of four performance metrics: financial, operational, customer, and people skills. The company has placed human resources managers in every store, and all job applicants who make it through a first-round interview must then pass a role-playing exercise. Dennis M. Donovan, Home Depot's executive vice-president for human resources and a GE alumnus, measures the effectiveness of Home Depot workers by using an equation: $VA = Q \times A \times E$. Its meaning? According to Home Depot, the value-added (VA) of an employee equals the quality (Q) of what you do, multiplied by its acceptance (A) in the company, times how well you execute (E) the task. The goal is to replace the old, sometimes random management style with new rigor. "Bob's creating a second culture [at Home Depot]," says DeAngelo.

While Nardelli is careful to say that the military is just one pipeline of talent into Home Depot—the company also recruits senior citizens through the AARP and Latinos through four Hispanic advocacy groups—he is clearly imbuing the company with "Semper Fi" spirit. If Nardelli is the four-star general, then Carl C. Liebert III is his chief of staff. A graduate of the U.S. Naval Academy at Annapolis, Md., where he played college basketball with NBA star David Robinson, Liebert, 40, stands 6 ft., 7 in. and is every bit as intense as his boss. After running Six Sigma programs at GE's Consumer Products unit, followed by a stint at Circuit City Stores Inc., he took over Home Depot's stores in the U.S. and Mexico in 2004. Now, with Lowe's and Wal-Mart picking off Home Depot's customers, Liebert is moving quickly to whip the troops into shape. "What worked 20 years ago may not work today," says Liebert. "It's as simple as warfare. We don't fight wars the way we used to."

Simple Slogans

To win the customer service war, Liebert has adjusted his tactics. At the annual store managers' meeting in Los Angeles on Mar. 8, Home Depot plans to roll out a 25-page booklet dubbed *How to Be Orange Every Day*. All store employees will be expected to keep it in their apron pocket. It contains aphorisms such as "customers cannot buy what we do not have," "we create an atmosphere of high-energy fun," and "every person, penny and product counts." Liebert hopes such simple slogans will help shore up Home Depot's once-vaunted customer service. To Liebert's mind, they recall the four basic responses to an officer's question in the Navy: "Yes, sir"; "No, sir"; "Aye, aye, sir"; and "I'll find out, sir." He calls it an effort to "align" all Home Depot workers on the same page when it comes to serving customers. "I think about that line from *A Few Good Men* when Jack Nicholson says: 'Are we clear?' and Tom Cruise says: 'Crystal,'" chuckles Liebert. "I love that."

But drilling workers in how to treat customers may not be enough. The University of Michigan's annual American Customer Satisfaction Index, released on Feb. 21, shows Home Depot slipped to dead last among major U.S. retailers. With a score of 67, down from 73 in 2004, Home Depot scored 11 points behind Lowe's and three points lower than much-maligned Kmart. "This is not competitive and too low to be sustainable. It's very serious," says Claes Fornell, professor of business at the University of Michigan and author of the 12-year-old customer satisfaction survey, which uses a 250-person sample and an econometric model to rate companies on quality and service. Fornell believes that the drop in satisfaction is one reason why Home Depot's stock price has declined at the same time

EXHIBIT 4

Buzz Words

Nardelli's cultural transformation has prompted some new lingo among Home Depot workers, some of it unflattering:

The "Aprons"	"Bob's Army"	"Bobaganda"
Like "troops," a term used by some senior executives to refer to Home Depot store workers (who wear aprons)	Slang for the "store leadership program," wherein almost 50% of the 1,142 trainees hired are ex-military personnel	The always-on Home Depot television channel, a.k.a. HD-TV, shown in rooms where employees take their breaks

"Home Despot"	"Home GEpot"	"Orange Belt"
For the most disenchanted workers, the moniker bestowed on the mighty home-improvement chain	A snarky reference to the swelling ranks of General Electric alumni Nardelli has wooed	The entry level for employees studying Six Sigma, the quality management system Nardelli imported from GE

Lowe's has soared. A former executive who spoke on condition of anonymity says that Nardelli's effort to measure good customer service, instead of inspiring it, is to blame: "My perception is that the mechanics are there. The soul isn't."

Nardelli angrily disputes the survey. "It's a sham," he says, jabbing his finger in the air for emphasis. Nardelli notes that, in 2003, Fornell shorted Home Depot stock in his personal portfolio, before his survey results came out. Fornell says the trades were part of his research into a correlation between companies' customer-satisfaction scores and stock price performance. The University of Michigan banned the practice the next year. Home Depot executives add that internal polling shows customer satisfaction is improving, but they won't release complete results. They point to Harris Interactive's 2005 Reputation Quotient, an annual 600-person survey that combines a range of reputation-related categories, from customer service to social responsibility. The survey ranked Home Depot No. 12 among major companies and reported that customers appreciated Home Depot's "quality service." Still, Home Depot appears to know it has serious customer-service problems. Store chief Liebert's back-to-basics plan includes a push to improve even the "genuineness" of the greeting that customers receive at the door.

Some of the same former managers who blame Nardelli's hardball approach for corroding the service ethic at Home Depot describe a culture so paralyzed with fear that they didn't worry about whether they would be terminated, but when. One night last year, an unnamed executive in the lighting department at Home Depot headquarters left fliers on desks and in elevators containing a litany of complaints about Home Depot, including Nardelli's giant pay package and the high level of executive turnover. The rebel, say other former executives, was tracked down by security cameras and immediately fired. Citing concerns about the employee's privacy, Home Depot declined to comment on the incident. In break rooms, the company pipes in HD-TV, short for Home Depot television. But employees have mocked it as "Bobaganda," referring to Nardelli, for its constant drone of tips, warnings, and executive messages. Every Monday night, for example, store chief Liebert and Tom Taylor, executive vice-president for marketing and merchandising, host a 25-minute live broadcast for senior store staff on the week's most important priorities called *The Same Page*. "These are [their] marching orders for the week," says Liebert.

Command of Details

Still, it's hard even for Nardelli critics, including ones he has fired, not to admire his unstinting determination to follow his makeover plan in the face of scores of naysayers. They describe being "in awe" of his command of minute details. But some of them question whether the manufacturing business model that worked for him at GE Transportation and GE Power Systems—squeezing efficiencies out of the core business while buying up new business—can work in a retail environment where taking care of customers is paramount. "Bob has brought a lot of operational efficiencies that Home Depot needed," says Steve Mahurin, chief merchandising officer at True Value Co. and a former senior vice-president for merchandising at Home Depot. "But he failed to keep the orange-blooded, entrepreneurial spirit alive. Home Depot is now a factory."

Can his plan work? "Ab-so-lute-ly," says Nardelli. "This is the third time this business model has been successful." He rejects the idea that he has created a culture of fear. "The only reason you should be fearful is if you personally don't want to make the commitment," says Nardelli. "Or there's a bolt of reality that you're in a position, based on the growth of the company, that you can't deliver on those commitments." He says Home Depot is dealing with the challenges of being a more centralized company just fine. And he makes no apologies for laying off the ranks of underperforming store workers and executives to achieve aggressive financial objectives. "We couldn't have done this by saying, 'Run slower, jump lower, and just kind of get by,' " insists Nardelli, hardening his gaze. "So I will never apologize for setting the bar high."

John N. Pistone, 35, is on the elite team. A graduate of West Point and former company commander in the Army's First Cavalry Div., he served in Kuwait in 2000 and was an ROTC instructor at Boston College. Now a district manager running eight Home Depot stores on the east side of Atlanta, with 1,200 staffers, he's on the fast track, in part because of his cool demeanor and always-on smile that endears him to employees. "A private in the Army is a lot like an $8-an-hour cashier," he says. But there's another reason Pistone is on the rise: As he clicks through his BlackBerry on a Monday morning, he remarks, with a sigh of relief, that his eight stores "made plan" the previous week. "This is a quarterly business that we worry about hourly," he says. As Bob Nardelli builds his new army at Home Depot, that's a sentiment he loves to hear.

A Lab in a Secure, Undisclosed Spot

In a bland office park not far from Home Depot Inc.'s Atlanta headquarters lies a squat, unmarked building. It could easily be mistaken for the uninspiring home of an insurance firm. That's fine by the steady stream of spit-and-polish Home Depot executives who file through the entrance, many of whom don orange aprons once safely inside. What they don't want you to know is that behind this unassuming facade is Home Depot's secret weapon: an 88,000-square-foot Innovation Center, where the chain tests everything from riding lawn mowers to displays for patio furniture sets before they hit stores.

Since it opened quietly in September, 2004, the Innovation Center has become a key command center in Chief Executive Robert L. Nardelli's push to overhaul the giant retailer. "This is our working laboratory," says Thomas V. Taylor Jr., Home Depot's executive vice-president for marketing and merchandising. Bringing new and better products to its 2,048 stores is critical for Home Depot, in its battle to out-innovate archrival Lowe's Cos., which has its own product testing center on its Mooresville (N.C.) campus, and voracious juggernaut Wal-Mart Stores Inc.

So sensitive is this Home Depot-owned site that reporters are requested not to disclose its address. Hard-nosed Nardelli boasts about how outsiders must pass through a metal detector that scans for camera phones. Once you get past a burly guard stationed at the front door, the Innovation Center emerges as a kind of ersatz, unfinished Home Depot store. Amid soft lighting and wide aisles, 16-ft. racks display vacuum cleaners, power tools, and oven hoods in an effort to learn how they'll look in the real stores. Super-secret projects, in which Home Depot is testing radically new product categories with scant relation to hammers and nails, are watched separately by security personnel and covered with huge tarpaulins.

When Nardelli arrived in 2000, Home Depot had precious little elbow room to experiment. It was risky for executives to tinker with new tools or test-run different types of displays in existing stores, lest they tip their hand to spies from competitors, who are constantly walking the aisles. As a result, they would do demos in the bottom level of a parking garage at Home Depot's headquarters—but the cramped, nine-ft. ceilings made it hard to duplicate the cavernous space of the actual stores.

Now, Taylor and his team have a full-blown Home Depot mock-up to explore new product segments, frequently at blitzkrieg speed. Company officials say they can go from an Innovation Center product test to an in-store pilot project in as little as 30 days. One of the projects soon to make its way out of the Innovation Center: In late March, Home Depot will roll out a special section in 10 stores in Jacksonville, Fla., targeting car buffs with a diverse selection of new products such as Rain-X wiper blades in seven sizes, Master Lock EZ mount towing kits, and Castrol motor oil.

The Innovation Center is also a venue for experimentation. In his relentless drive for "laser execution" at Home Depot, Nardelli has pushed executives to come up with new ways to beat competitors on price, displays, and product assortment. That's why a wall in one aisle at the center is covered, floor to ceiling, with boring white lightbulbs. Each horizontal row of bulbs is set off with tape and labeled with names and price tags: Home Depot, Target, Wal-Mart, Sam's Club, Menard's, and Costco. It's Taylor's marketwide view of what Home Depot is up against—and how, down to the tiniest detail, he can innovate for an advantage.

Source: Didne Brady, Michael Arndt, and Brian Grow, "Renovating Home Depot," *BusinessWeek,* March 6, 2006, 50–58.

Case 6-13
International Business Machines

Through much of the 20th century, under the leadership of founder Thomas J. Watson and his son, Thomas Jnr., International Business Machines (IBM) ruled computing and defined the US multinational. From the days of tabulating machines all the way to the Space Age (when IBM mainframes helped chart the path for man to the moon), IBM was a paragon of power, prestige and far-sightedness.

Bold gambles characterize IBM's history. During the Great Depression, Watson increased manufacturing

This case was written by Nigel F. Piercy, Warwick Business School, The University of Warwick.

capacity for tabulating machines, pushing IBM to the edge of insolvency, but with a big pay-off when the US Social Security Act of 1935 required the government to keep records—only IBM could meet the demand for data-processing machines. In the early 1960s, IBM had reached a plateau, and Watson gambled everything on the first mainframe—the System/360. Costing more than $5 billion to develop, it was the biggest ever privately financed commercial project of its time. It offered the revolutionary new concept of compatibility, allowing customers to use the same printers and other peripherals with any 360 machine.

Around this time, IBM acquired the nickname "Big Blue" because of the colour of its muscular blue mainframe computers (mirrored in the blue suits adopted by IBM executives).

The next big leap of faith was in 1981, when CEO John M. Opel unveiled the IBM Personal Computer. The PC became an overnight sensation, even though IBM was not able to sustain its early success. Indeed, by the 1990s, IBM had become a slow-moving maker of computer hardware, with a services business that was an afterthought to mainframes and PCs. At this stage, the world of information technology appeared to have left IBM behind.

Bringing Big Blue Back from the Brink

Lou Gerstner's turnaround of the giant computer company has become management history. When he arrived at IBM on April Fool's Day 1993, he found a company with 266 book-keeping systems, 128 chief information officers and 339 different surveys for measuring customer satisfaction. IBM lost 200,000 jobs and £10 billion between 1986, when it was at the height of its success, and 1994 when Gerstner's leadership started to have an effect.

When Gerstner arrived at IBM, the company's market share was plummeting, cash was draining fast from the business, the organization was acutely unable, to innovate—a contemporary IBM quip was that "new products don't get launched at IBM, they manage to escape." Senior executives, including Gerstner's predecessor John Akers, had given up on the idea that the group could be saved and were preparing to break it up into a series of "Baby Blues." Gerstner, late of Harvard Business School, McKinseys and American Express, did not break the business up, but turned it around to once again deliver good returns to shareholders.

Source: Getty Images

His central strategy flew in the face of conventional wisdom: IBM would use its size to become an "integrator"—assembling systems from the mass of components provided by its own product divisions and by its competitors. At the time industry thinking was that the future belonged to specialist technology companies that could bring new products to market extremely quickly, and change strategy in an instant. Vertically integrated giants like IBM, making everything from microprocessors through to operating systems and finished computers and software, were thought to have no place in the new fragmented world of technology. IBM's very poor performance from the late-1980s onwards seemed to justify this view.

In fact, Gerstner's services-led strategy aimed to turn IBM into the integrator of choice for large corporations. In the six years up to 2001, Gerstner increased IBM's revenue by 19%, net income by 83% and earnings per share by 250%, adding 100,000 new employees to the payroll. Admittedly, a revenue growth of 4% a year is not spectacular, given this period was one of very high information technology spending growth throughout the world. Nearly all the growth (and all the new jobs) came from IBM Global Services, the consulting and outsourcing unit. Sales of hardware stagnated and software did not do much better. It is also the case that the mid-1990s were a period of drastic and painful middle management blood-letting at IBM.

There are also concerns that Gerstner's focus on making IBM a services business, blinded him to important competitive shifts, in which IBM lost out. For example, Cisco walked away with the multi-billion dollar market for networking equipment, even though much of the technology was developed in IBM laboratories. Similarly, IBM failed to counter Sun Microsystems' spectacular late-1990s push into the Unix server market, and the company was slow to challenge Oracle in relational databases (another invention of IBM laboratories). It may also have been short-sighted to allow new upstarts, like BEA in middleware and EMC in storage, the freedom to become market leaders in these fields.

Moving on from the Trauma of Turnaround

In 2002 Samuel J. Palmisano succeeded Lou Gerstner in the top job at IBM. Following Gerstner's dramatic strategic shift at the company, commentators saw Palmisano as no more than a caretaker of Gerstner's strategy. In fact, Palmisano provided far more in changing IBM structure, management and strategic direction.

Early signs that Palmisano planned to manage the company differently to Gerstner came at the first IBM board meeting of 2003, when he asked the board to cut his 2003 bonus and set it aside as a pool of money to be shared by about 20 top executives, based on their performance as a team. Palmisano also put an end to the 92 year old IBM Executive Management Committee—the 12-person inner sanctum that had presided over IBM's strategy and initiatives. Instead, Palmisano favoured working with three new teams of people, covering operations, strategy and technology, drawn from throughout the company, to bring the best ideas to the table, and to move more quickly than the old IBM bureaucracy permitted. Palmisano is building a flatter organization with fewer bureaucratic levels, and allocating $100 million to teach 30,000 managers to lead, not control their staff.

His goal was to build a new strategy to put IBM back at the forefront of technology. Called "e-business on demand" the initiative aimed to allow IBM to supply computing power as if it were water or electricity. The strategy was to be a unifying force for IBM, bring closer together the almost autonomous "fiefdoms" in software, chips and computers. Palmisano planned to have IBM get back to the position where it set the industry agenda, using its R&D to leap ahead with grid computing and self-healing software. In its first year, "e-business on demand" took a third of IBM's $5 billion R&D budget.

The "e-business on demand" strategy had the potential to cut technology user costs by 50%, though achieving this was dependent on a decade of rolling out new technologies and new ways of doing business: companies would have to simplify into a unified network, based on a small number of server, using open standards so all machines can speak to each other; to achieve efficiency in server and software usage, virtualization (a process in which many machines appear to be one) gets more work out of equipment by farming work out across them; all networks and data centres would have to be linked to create a giant computing grid allowing access to more information and computing power; if a company ran out of capacity, it would buy computing power from a supplier, as needed, instead of building a new data centre; and new Web-based services will speed up tasks yet more.

Nonetheless, while this was a brave initiative, few technology companies have succeeded in falling as far as IBM did, and then getting back to the top. Certainly, many of the heavyweights in technology—from Hewlett-Packard to Microsoft—are pushing research into next-generation computing systems that will rival IBM's. IBM's general manager for "e-business on demand" notes: "in 1996, we had the benefit of being considered irrelevant. [Microsoft's William H.] Gates and [Steven A.] Balmer felt pity on us. Now they are all watching us. If we don't move fast, they will pass us."

The new initiative provided Palmisano with the tool to remake IBM. Gerstner's reforms started the process, by shifting IBM towards software and services, but Palmisano's "e-business on demand" went much further. He was counting on the initiative to create the best IBM sales growth since the 1990s. New offerings already include servers running the free Linux operating system and grid software that pools the power of scores of networked computers into a virtual supercomputer.

Managing the Next Transformation

Far from simply under-studying Lou Gerstner, Palmisano has the goal of freeing IBM from the confines of the $1.2 trillion computer industry, which is growing at just 6 percent a year. Much of the traditional world of computing has become a commodity business. Instead of just selling and servicing technology, IBM is using its resources to help companies rethink and remake how they run their businesses. Palmisano is looking for an annual revenue stream of $50 billion in business consulting and outsourcing services. By packaging low-cost technology augmented with sophisticated software, IBM sells customers business transformation services. IBM aims to ride on top of the commodity wave, rather than drowning in it.

By 2005, the change at IBM was remarkable. The number of employees focused on business services rather than pure technology had gone from 3,500 in 2002 to more than 50,000, out of a total of 330,000 IBM people. After selling the loss-making PC division to China's Lenovo Group, Palmisano has been buying business services companies, including Daksh, a 6,000-employee Indian customer-relations company. The risks are considerable. Mistakes in implementation will give slower growth and lower profits, undermining IBM's research-driven business model and its position in the corporate technology world. Falling short in delivery could put IBM back to where it was in the 1990s.

The initial challenge was to make the grand vision—now known as business process transformation services—into a "must have" for corporates, without offering overly favourable terms—technology companies have a long history of underestimating the actual costs of running customers' computing operations. IBM faces strong competition in a new area. One potent rival is Accenture—the services company that has interests in business process outsourcing. While Accenture cannot rival IBM's technology skills, it is stronger in business expertise. Challenging both IBM and Accenture are aggressive Indian outsourcers like Wipro and Tata Consultancy Services.

Palmisano's vision also involves reinventing the services industry by injecting disciplines of product development and delivery, more usually found in product markets, and doing this on a global scale. Turning services—by definition delivered by people—into repeatable processes is a massive organizational and cultural shift for the business. The move blurs the line between the services and software business models—for example, merging services into software to allow services developed for one project to be applied to others subsequently.

By 2005, in spite of early IBM successes in the outsourcing area, the success of Palmisano's services strategy was far from assured. Sales growth was slow. The era of multibillion dollar outsourcing contracts had come to an end. Critics saw underlying weaknesses exposed in IBM's services strategy: that it did not deliver on the original promise of services; that its method of delivering services did not bring consistent benefits for customers around the world, many of whom actually face very similar problems; and, the lack of a standardized approach had led IBM to miss out on some of the hottest markets, such as security. With services performance continuing to disappoint, in 2006 IBM began shifting executives from its traditional computing business into senior positions in the services arm in an effort to inject new momentum into the flagging division. Meantime, IBM's traditional information technology businesses remained under substantial pressure from low-cost competitors.

Learning to Compete in New Ways

In 2004 almost half IBM's $96 billion revenues came from tech services like outsourcing (after the sale of the PC business to Lenovo). However, increasingly major customers, like Louis Vuitton and Target in retail, were turning to Indian companies like Wipro in Bangalore for tech services solutions. In fact, the services business is less profitable than other IBM activities: operating margins in services in 2004 were 25%, compared to 31%

for hardware and 87% for software. However, only services offer the growth on the massive scale that IBM wants.

The Commoditization Threat...

A major challenge posed by low-cost generic competition like Wipro is commoditization. IBM experienced the effects of commoditization in hardware (the much copied IBM PC, for example), but now is looking at commoditization in services as well. New Indian competitors, for example, operate low-cost, low-wages business models. IBM, on the other hand, had 260,000 employees in the USA and other developed countries (the other 60,000 were in lower-cost regions), and 164,000 pensioned retirees. Palmisano's strategic response has two main components.

Strategic Geographies...

First, to deal with the India-threat, he aimed to challenge newcomers like Wipro by taking the low-cost model right back at them. Following disappointing sales in services in 2004, the company eliminated 14,500 jobs, mainly in Europe, hiring 14,000 people in India in 2005, adding to IBM's increasing staff rosters in emerging markets—"strategic low-cost geographies" in IBM terminology. Of the services group programmers writing customer code, about half (26,000 or so) were already located in India, Brazil or China. By now India accounted for the largest number of IBMers outside the USA. With India-based employment exceeding 50,000, more than a quarter of all services personnel and one-sixth of all IBM employment would be in India—making it larger in India than Wipro, Infosys or Tata Consultancy Services. The head of the IBM services operation positions growth in the developing world as part of implementing a "global delivery model" for services, together with a much tighter "services supply chain." Palmisano is committed to growing IBM revenues 5% a year and earnings per share least 10%—for a company IBM's size, this means adding the equivalent of a Wipro every five months. In 2006 Palmisano unveiled an additional $6 billion investment in India.

By late 2007 IBM was recognized as the leader of the Indian tech services industry, with 10% of the industry workforce, and Bangalore and New Delhi were home to IBM's largest research and development laboratories outside the USA. The IBM Indian workforce of 53,000 constituted 15% of the worldwide total IBM employment. Expansion has been rapid—in the first half of 2007 alone IBM signed up $1.4 billion of long-term contracts in India. In addition, integrating

India into global operations has allowed IBM to eliminate 20,000 jobs in high-cost markets such as the USA, Europe and Japan.

Strategic Collaboration Initiatives...

Second, Palmisano is gambling on a strategy of giving away intellectual property in software, patents and ideas. His thinking is that spreading these riches around means the entire industry will grow faster, opening new opportunities for IBM to sell high-value products and services that meet this new demand. By adopting a strategy of "openness," IBM aims to tap into a major new "spur to innovation itself." The company spends $5.7 billion a year on R&D, but by sharing discoveries wants to make the industry grow faster.

A big part of this sharing plan is collaborating with customers and even rivals to invent new technologies. In hardware, IBM has co-developed with Sony and Toshiba a break-through chip called the Cell, which could eventually transform all IBM computers. In software, embracing Linux and other open-source software has given IBM new platforms on which it is building most of its new high-growth applications.

Giveaways to open-source software groups, customer groups, universities and other IT companies have been extensive and diverse:

- IBM contributed management software to the Apache Geronimo project—a collaboration of programmers aiming to create an open-source version of the software most businesses use to run their most demanding applications.
- The company has organized a "patent commons"—giving away over 500 software patents in 2005, with value at least $10 million, to be used free by anyone working on an open-source project.
- A retail industry group has been given rights to patents for Internet access in stores, to make it easier to collate information about customers as they are served.
- Top university engineering and business schools are receiving money and expertise to create a new academic discipline called Services Sciences, Management and Engineering. By 2005 this programme had cost IBM $10 million.
- IBM research labs has 600 programmers spending all their time improving Linux – but they cost less than the $500 million a year it would take IBM to develop and maintain its own operating system. Funds saved are channelled into proprietary software that works on Linux.

Estimates suggest the IBM giveaways to be worth at least $150 million a year. The secret is that IBM seldom gives away a technology unless it has intellectual property and expertise that will enable it to make money if the technology is widely adopted. The support for open-source software is a challenge to Microsoft's proprietary applications software. For example, in China IBM is working to convince policy-makers and business leaders that using open-source software makes more sense than buying Microsoft's.

Nonetheless, IBM is in a highly competitive marketplace with a growing list of rivals. Dell has started to look at the tech services marketplace, where low-end work like computer maintenance could provide major growth. Although it is only one-third of IBM's size, Accenture is seen by many customers as a better problem solver than IBM.

The New IBM Organization

The strategic evolution of the IBM business model has been reflected in the way the business is managed and what the organization has become. For example, IBM has changed from a company once dominated by lifetime employees selling computer products to a "conglomeration of transient suppliers."

IBM has worked to get rid of the command and control structure of the past, and to build a culture of connection and collaboration—within the company as well as outside. For example, resolving a technical problem in the wake of Hurricane Katrina meant using the company's Blue Pages Plus expertise locator on the corporate intranet, locating the right people, establishing a web page that can be edited by anyone with access to act as a virtual meeting room, and a team of IBM staff in the USA, Germany and the UK designing a solution to the problem.

Global Integration...

IBM is also revamping its "people supply chain." In the 20th century IBM was the pioneer of the multinational business model—creating "mini-IBMs" in each country with their own administration, manufacturing and services operations. But this approach is too top-heavy at a time when lean Indian tech companies and Chinese manufacturers produce high-quality goods and services at a fraction of the costs of multinationals.

IBM now pioneers what it calls "globally integrated operations," with the goal of lowering its costs but also providing superior service. This model groups people around the world into competency centres (collections of people with specific skills), with the aim of having low costs in some places but in others having highly skilled employees close to customers. Rather than each country's business unit having its own workforce entirely, many people are drawn from competency centres. The thinking is that in areas like tech services low-cost labour is essential (to equal Indian and Chinese competitors' costs), but not sufficient (to supply high levels of specialized skills). IBM's radical make-over in its 200,000 person services workforce includes: not being a multinational but a globally integrated enterprise—IBM no longer runs a mini-IBM in each country and region, and has reduced administrative employee numbers and reassigned technical special-ists; moving beyond outsourcing—performing work for clients where it can be done most competitively; assembling A-Teams—when IBM wins a new client, it picks a team to suit that client's needs, selecting people from around the world with the right skills and costs; and avoiding commodity businesses—IBM can-not operate as inexpensively as Indian challengers, so focuses on taking human labour out of tech services.

The Software Bounce

Notwithstanding Palmisano's emphasis on making IBM the leading tech services business in the world, by late 2006 it was apparent that software had become IBM's fastest-growing business. The $16.8 billion soft-ware division—second only to Microsoft in the world software business—was emerging as the most reli-able growth engine. While the overall company grew by 1% in 2006, software grew by 5%. In part fuelled by a rapid sequence of software acquisitions—more than 30 software companies purchased in four years—the plan is to use the acquisitions to tap new soft-ware lines, while milking mature products for profits. Margins are significantly higher for software compared to services. Interestingly, new software products also benefit services—sales often include huge service con-tracts, and customers who buy new software typically spend five times as much on services to install and maintain it.

Software now looks to be the driving force behind improving IBM's performance. Two factors explain this. At the start of the 2000s, the software division performance was held back by the slow decline of the operating systems business. However, by the mid-2000s the focus was on middleware—software that acts as a layer between operating systems and applications, making it possible to run complex IT systems. Middle-ware is more than half IBM software sales. Second, a rapid escalation in acquisitions of software companies has extended software opportunities for IBM.

IBM's software strategy now shows a dramatic con-trast to the business models of rivals like Microsoft, Oracle and SAP. While these companies have been rushing to create vertically integrated "stacks" of soft-ware, extending all the way up to applications used by individual workers, IBM has concentrated on creating a "horizontal" layer of middleware that lies at the centre of IT systems, where most workers never encounter it. The IBM strategy rests on a single belief—that legacy corporate IT systems, measured in trillions of dollars of value, require extensive work as companies try to integrate them better, build on them and adapt them to new business purposes.

IBM has built five middleware brands—Lotus, Tivoli, Websphere, Rational and the DB2 database business—each of which as a standalone business would rank among the world's 25 biggest software businesses. IBM's middleware strategy aims to posi-tion the company to take advantage of the major shift taking place in the global software market—the growth of "service-oriented architecture," or broader and more flexible software platforms on which companies can build more adaptable technology, capable of changing with their business needs.

This market shift vindicates IBM's decision in the late-1990s to move away from the applications busi-ness, instead partnering with other software compa-nies, while it builds broader platforms. However, other broad trends in the software market are more challeng-ing for IBM. Open-source software has been cham-pioned by IBM in its support for the Linux operating system, to challenge Microsoft. However, low-margin open-source software is moving into other parts of middleware. IBM itself offers open-source versions of some of its middleware for the low end of the tech-nology market, like application server software. If more advanced parts of middleware are commoditized, IBM's position could be threatened, unless it can con-tinue to move up into higher value areas of software.

A second challenge for IBM comes from the emerg-ing trend towards "software as a service"—the busi-ness of providing applications online as a service to companies, pioneered by Salesforce.com and taken up by Google. Customers buying these services will no longer need to buy IBM hardware systems and IT integration. This could pressure IBM to step up as a full service provider, which would mean reversing the decision to keep IBM out of the applications business, which has underpinned its profitable partnerships with other software producers.

Late-2007 IBM unveiled its biggest ever acquisition, with the $5 billion cash purchase of software company Cognos—Canada's largest software company with 4,000 employees. The deal represents IBM's response to the rapid consolidation of the business intelligence software market, which was triggered by Oracle's purchase of Hyperion and SAP's agreement to buy Business Objects. The move accelerated IBM's acquisition-based drive to boost the size of its software business, which by this stage accounted for 20% of IBM revenues and 40% of gross profits. Business intelligence software draws data from a range of corporate systems to give managers a view across their operations. It is seen as a strategically important part of the software market. Owning Cognos should help IBM sell more of its other middleware, including its websphere and DB2 database products.

In 2008, in an attempt to restore its position in the $20 billion a year data storage market, IBM bought Moshe Yanai's XIV Corporation for $300 million. Mr Yanai was responsible for one of IBM's most stunning defeats in the 1990s, when he designed computer storage discs for EMC, that displaced IBM's in data centres around the world—IBM's market share went from 80% to 35% in a five-year period and has not recovered. Although XIV has only 50 engineers and a handful of customers, it has the technology that could disrupt the storage industry again. XIV's Nextra technology is more efficient and economical than the current generation of storage, and opens up new opportunities in data storage, such as storing and analysing feeds from security cameras. IBM hopes to be the first with a new storage platform that will fuel growth for companies with very large content archives, such as Google and MySpace.

Evolving Strategy at IBM

By early 2008 Palmisano's review of progress at IBM suggested that the repositioning was going broadly to plan. In Palmisano's first six years at the company, revenue has grown only slowly—in 2008 it was up just 15% from when he took over, although earnings have grown 35%. After a period of decline, IBM stock was back above the $103 level of the date when Palmisano took over.

Palmisano's major emphasis was now on emerging markets. In 2008, IBM was in the process of reorganizing to tailor its structures to the needs of developing countries, where its sales account for 21% of total revenues, but are growing at a 20% annual rate. IBM is creating new markets groups for the Americas, based in Brazil; for the Middle East, Africa and Eastern Europe; and for Asia—breaking them away from the mature US, European and Japanese markets. The separation is aimed to protect the investments from being traded off against issues in the mature markets. The company is looking at 50 target countries which are currently small markets, but which will be big in the future. Mid-2008, the growing emerging markets emphasis provided IBM with some protection against the declining economic situation in the USA, since corporate spending appeared more robust outside America.

The Dilemmas for IBM

IBM exemplifies many of the strategic renewal challenges faced by companies in rapidly changing markets and the types of organizational transformation needed to implement new strategies. However, moving towards the end of the first decade of the 21st century, there are major concerns about the continuing transformation of IBM. Worrying questions are being asked about whether the transition to becoming a tech services company has stalled in the face of low-cost competition, aggressive competition and market change.

While the vision of a new type of globally integrated enterprise focused on new types of service product is compelling, questions surround the ability of the company to implement that vision effectively, globally and rapidly enough to meet competitive threats.

Moving towards a collaborative business model, sharing R&D with customers, developers and competitors, raises the spectre of another Xerox, where new ideas are exploited more effectively by others than by the originators. The commitment to open-source software development and attempts to make open-source the industry standard, may backfire and undermine the strength of the IBM software division, which is currently the main source of revenue growth for the company. Growth driven by acquisition, rather than organically by in-house or collaborative R&D, may undermine the coherence of the business and its knowledge generation for superior IBM service offerings.

Sources: Simon London, "How Big Blue Came Back from the Brink," *Financial Times.* November 12 2002, p. 12. Steve Hamm. "Beyond Blue." *Business Week.* April 18 2005, pp. 36–42. David Kirkpatrick, "IBM Shares Its Secrets," *Fortune,* September 5 2005, pp. 60–67. Richard Waters, "IBM Repackages its Brainpower," *Financial Times,* July 11 2006, p. 12. Richard Waters, "Big Blue Looks to Be More in the Pink after Changing Tack," *Financial Times,* February 28 2008, p. 30.

Richard Waters, "IBM Agrees $5bn Cash Deal for Cognos," *Financial Times,* November 13 2007, p. 33. William M. Bulkeley, "To Play Storage Game, IBM Calls in Old Foe," *Wall Street Journal,* January 11–13 2008, p. 26. William M. Bulkeley, "IBM's Palmisano Eyes Developing Markets," *Wall Street Journal,* February 14 2008, p. 5. William M. Bulkeley. "IBM Earnings Jump on Strong Overseas Sales," *Wall Street Journal,* April 17, 2008, p.5.

Case 6-14

Rover Automobile

Rover dates back a century to when Lord Austin founded the Austin Motor Company, which merged with Morris and Rover in 1952 to create the British Motor Corporation. A string of owners have adopted a variety of business models to try to run Rover-Britain's last volume car-maker, but have never secured its long-term viability. Rover has always been a focus for governments-usually those frightened of the electoral consequences of Rover's demise-the media, the trades unions and the public. The most recent changes in ownership have been from BMW to the Phoenix Group and thence to Shanghai Automotive (SAIC). However, the fate of Rover was probably sealed more than forty years ago in the "British Leyland blunder." Rover's local MP describes the MG Rover saga as "an industrial *Eastenders*—part business story and part soap opera." Nonetheless, Rover and MG are "heritage" brands in the automotive marketplace, with many devoted fans in Europe and the USA.

The Sad History of Rover

The recent history of Rover contains a series of botched rescue attempts, frequent ownership changes and ever-declining performance by the company.

The British Leyland Blunder...

A Labour government in 1968—that of Harold Wilson-engineered the merger of Leyland, Rover's parent company, with the British Motor Corporation, to create a giant national champion in the motor industry—British Leyland. The UK plan backfired. British Leyland never succeeded in welding its mass of component operations into a coherent whole. Importantly, British

This case was written by Nigel F. Piency & Warwick Business School, The University of Warwick.

Leyland took Rover, an upscale brand, into the mass market, but without achieving genuine mass scale. The merged giant was forced into a rights issue in 1972, and was among the first big British companies to collapse after the oil price shock of 1974.

Nationalization...

Nationalization was not successful either. A second Wilson government took British Leyland into state hands in 1975 rather than risk major job losses through private sector restructuring. British Leyland was being torn to pieces by industrial relations disputes at this time-including the infamous "BO strike" triggered by the smell of a worker. The pound appreciated, crippling Rover export sales. Over eight years, the government put £900 million into Rover, to sustain its existence.

Privatization...

When Margaret Thatcher came to power, Sir Michael Edwardes, Rover's executive chairman, took on the unions-firing the plant convenor, known as "Red Robbo." Under the leadership of Thatcher's appointment of Sir Graham Day, the company was renamed as the Rover Group. A partnership with Honda gave Rover a technology lifeline, but at a cost-Rover gave up the right to compete with Honda in markets like the USA, and became dependent on Honda-based cars. Thatcher was determined on political principle to privatize the car business, and leapt at the chance to sell Rover to British Aerospace in 1988. However, privatization did not work either. BAe was a diversified conglomerate and offered Rover no synergies or benefits other than private ownership.

The BMW Years...

BAe sold Rover to BMW in 1994. This was a moment of real hope for Rover-BMW needed to increase its scale without diluting the prestige of its brand, and saw Rover as the answer to this need. But BMW moved slowly in establishing control over Rover, and strong Sterling at the end of the 1990s was a major obstacle.

Some Rover models were selling in Europe, but at a loss. BMW poured £3.4 billion into Rover after buying it in 1994. In 1999, with losses mounting, the Quandt family that controls BMW lost patience, and the BMW CEO who had purchased Rover left BMW. The British government tried desperately to keep BMW at Rover's Longbridge plant with offers of state aid, but BMW was set on a new course-they wanted the Mini brand, but not Rover. In the last year of its ownership, BMW lost £800 million on the Rover operation.

The Phoenix Arises...

By 2000 BMW had given up any hope of turning around the loss-making Rover business, and announced the sale of Rover to Alchemy, a private equity firm led by Jon Moulton—who planned to whittle Rover down to a niche producer of the MG sports car. However, the Alchemy solution was anathema to the Labour government, local councillors and the still vociferous and influential trades unions. Under government pressure, BMW sold instead to Phoenix-a four-man team of local businessmen led by John Towers, a former Rover chief executive. Phoenix claimed that Rover could be saved as a volume car producer, and won control of a rebranded MG Rover for £10—as well as receiving a dowry from BMW to fund job losses.

The Phoenix deal with BMW was complex. Rover was sold for a token price, but also with an interest-free loan of £427 million from BMW, to be repaid by 2049, though earlier if MG Rover made a profit. The plan was that these reserves would allow Phoenix to replace the ageing Rover 25 and Rover 45 models. The Rover 25 and Rover 45 accounted for around two-thirds of MG Rover sales at this time, but were long in the tooth and needed replacing by 2004 or 2005. There was also potential to develop a new model in the Rover 75 line—the Tourer Concept Vehicle—shown at motor shows in 2002.

Phoenix, MG Rover's parent company, lost £187 million pre-tax in 2001. But in the same year, respected trade journal *Autocar* awarded MG Rover its "Achievement of the Year" award to mark the company's turnaround. While sales were continuing to fall-by about 12% in the first year of Phoenix ownership—MG Rover was the unlikely star of the British Motor Show in Birmingham. The MG SV—a 200 mph super-car to take on the likes of Maserati and Porsche—won the plaudits of the motoring press and the public alike. Meanwhile, production workers at Longbridge continued to wonder about the wisdom of spending millions of pounds on Qvale, the Italian sports car company that provided the basic design for the SV.

It was clear to the Phoenix consortium from the outset that Rover could only survive in a world of global car giants if it secured a sustainable partnership with another mass car producer, and this was the major priority.

Phoenix kept Rover going for five years. But they did this by burning through the BMW endowment and cash from asset sales. Losses were cut, but Rover operations continued to bleed cash. By this stage, Rover was producing 150,000 cars a year in an industry where mass market producers need to make 3 million cars a year to be internationally competitive. Phoenix failed to use the BMW cash to produce new models, which might have made Rover an attractive purchase for one of the global car-makers; they were simply rebadging existing models.

Rover survived by cutting costs and selling assets. In addition to the £427 million loan from BMW and stock worth £350 million (in the form of 40,000 unsold cars when it bought Rover), the company sold land, a parts business, engine technology and model rights to Chinese manufacturers. More than £1 billion passed through the company. Certainly, operating losses exceeded £500 million during Phoenix's ownership of Rover. Meanwhile, the Phoenix directors caused outrage by awarding themselves lavish pay and perks, including a £10 million loan note, a £16.5 million pension pot, and control of a lucrative car loans business. Valuable assets were taken out of Rover and put into Phoenix. Phoenix directors paid themselves salaries at a level of twice that paid to the board members of BMW. BMW was furious and branded Phoenix as the "unacceptable face of capitalism" as a result of their treatment of Rover assets. A House of Commons committee later accused the Phoenix directors of "financial sleight of hand."

Rover Runs Out of Road

By 2004 time was running out for Phoenix; the company needed a partner and turned to the emerging markets. A venture with India's Tata did not work out. Talks had focused on making a small Tata car in Britain and selling it as the Rover 15, although an alliance with Tata would not have provided a replacement for the Rover 25. A relationship with China Brilliance wasted more time and money. Yang Rong, a Chinese entrepreneur, first showed interest in buying Powertrain, the engine company that was by now a subsidiary of Phoenix. Then the plan was for MG Rover technology and Yang's investment to provide entry to the Chinese market. The deal failed when Yang was ousted as chairman and CEO of China Brilliance, one of the country's largest vehicle manufacturers.

The Chinese Rescue—Back from, the Brink?...

Rover looked to Shanghai Automotive in China to rescue the situation. The motivation for the purchase of Rover by the Chinese is clear. SAIC was already China's largest car-maker, producing more than 600,000 cars a year, but had nothing to call its own. SAIC started out as a components manufacturer in 1958, made tractors in the 1960s and entered joint ventures to produce cars in the 1980s. SAIC was making cars only in joint ventures with Volkswagen and General Motors-copies of VW and GM designs made to their manufacturing blueprints. SAIC's only brand was Wuling-a line of commercial vehicles. The last SAIC branded car-the Shanghai-had not been produced since 1991. Control of Rover promised SAIC control over its own brand and designs, and freedom from the dictates of Western suppliers-in 2005 90% of the passenger vehicles on the roads of China were foreign makes and the market was growing at around 35% a year. The Rover purchase was also seen as a bridgehead for international expansion.

Rover announced that Shanghai Automotive, which already made cars under licence, would be investing in Rover in return for brands and technology, and that Rover would be rescued from its difficulties by the Chinese. Certainly, SAIC gave MG Rover £67 million in return for access to vehicle technology. This was expected to be part of a much larger deal with SAIC paying MG Rover £200 million in total for rights to use the Rover brand name, Rover's K-series engine technology, and the rights to make Rover models in China. The partners were to commit to designing and building four new models. The plan was to move production of the Rover 25 to China and import it back into the UK, which would have cost 2,000 jobs in the UK. The British government was prepared to offer MG Rover a holiday from VAT and corporation tax payments, and the Chinese regional assistance grants to facilitate the deal. Rover also took advantage of the imminence of a general election to ask the government for further £100 million to keep the deal alive.

In fact, SAIC was baffled by the Rover announcement, since they had only been interested in a joint venture with Rover, and no actual deal had been done. In particular, SAIC was adamant that none of its cash would go to the four owners of Phoenix at any stage, because of the political ramifications. There was also alarm in Shanghai at the prospect of a £400 million black-hole in Rover's pension fund, and the degree of asset-stripping that the Phoenix directors had carried out. SAIC had envisaged two joint ventures, both majority owned by them, but not being exposed to the risk that if MG Rover went bust they would be exposed to liability for pensions, redundancy payments and possible litigation by suppliers. The Blair government agreed the pre-election loan, but with SAIC unwilling to proceed, Rover moved into the hands of the receivers.

The Rover Collapse...

By April 2005 the MG Rover car plant at Longbridge was silent, Rover's 6,100 workers had been told to stay at home, some 70 key suppliers were refusing to send components because they did not believe that they would ever be paid, and the company was moving into administration. Some 19,000 jobs among suppliers in the Midlands were at risk, in addition to the Rover jobs.

As the Rover board met to appoint PriceWaterhouse Coopers as administrators, Patricia Hewitt (then Trade and Industry Secretary) quickly broom-sticked to Birmingham, joined later by Prime Minister Tony Blair and Chancellor Gordon Brown, amid intense media and political interest. The Labour government was looking at the prospect of going into an imminent general election with 12,000 job losses in the West Midlands. When SAIC could not be contacted to step into the breach, under political pressure the Department of Trade and Industry provided a £6.5 million loan to pay staff for another week and give time to clarify the SAIC situation. On April 15 2005, in a letter to Patricia Hewitt, the Chinese made it clear that they were not interested in taking on MG Rover as a going concern.

Rover sales in the last year of its operations had fallen from 356,000 to 106,680, with just 6,500 vehicles sold in the last month. In its last year MG Rover's level of productivity had fallen to just 16.3 cars per year for each employee—compared, for example, to 320 cars per employee at the Nissan plant in Sunderland. The only lifeline was £1 million a day from the government to keep things going-probably designed to delay Rover's final collapse until after the general election in May 2005. The receivers announced in May 2005 that MG Rover had run up liabilities of £1.8 billion, and there was only an estimated £80 million in assets available to the unsecured creditors claiming £1.37 billion. It also became apparent that the Phoenix directors had kept Rover in business by raiding the accounts of Powertrain-the successful engine-making division-which collapsed with debts of £127.6 million, £102 million of which was owed by Rover. While there was no evidence of malpractice, it appeared that MG Rover had been trading while insolvent.

Chinese Whispers and Other Party Games

Having caused the Labour government a pre-election crisis by pulling out of the rescue deal for MG Rover, in late-April 2005 SAIC revealed that it believed it had taken possession of the iconic Rover name as the result of its earlier agreement with the company. This caused some dismay to the government officials still trying to keep MG Rover alive—it robbed them of one of the group's most valuable assets.

An MG Rover spokesman insisted that the brand was still part of the group, while BMW maintained it still had control of the marque, having allowed MG Rover to use it free of charge. SAIC held the position that it had acquired the Rover brand as part of its £67 million deal with the company—building the case that it had the right to the Rover 75 and to produce and sell Rover cars in China. SAIC's claims that it had exclusive rights to the brand and to produce Rover cars and engines-a claim rejected by the bankruptcy administrators-was a substantial barrier to selling all or part of Rover to interested bidders.

The Nanjing Rescue...

In July 2005 Nanjing Automobile, China's oldest vehicle manufacturer, bought MG Rover for £53 million, beating a field of more than a hundred interested buyers, in a bitterly contested and high profile auction. This set the stage for an apparent battle between Nanjing and SAIC, the latter having also bid at a lower price. Nanjing and SAIC were jointly responsible for the collapse of Rover, which was triggered when both withdrew from joint ventures with Rover because of the company's financial weakness. Nanjing planned to ship much of Rover's plant and equipment to China, and to start production again in the West Midlands of the MG TF sports car and the MG ZT saloon. Nonetheless, SAIC still maintained that it owned the designs for Rover's small and large cars and engines.

Nanjing is one of China's most internationally ambitious car-makers, but is widely seen as a weaker performer than rivals like SAIC. Nanjing faced some major challenges in getting Rover production started again:

- **Engineering**—finishing development work on engines to meet new emission standards and testing production lines to ensure they still worked.

- **Purchasing**—finding suppliers for components in Europe, where many had lost money in unpaid bills when Rover collapsed, and could be reluctant to risk the same happening again, or look to Asia for lower cost components.

- **Distribution**—many Rover dealers were owed large sums when Rover collapsed and had moved on to other things, so a network of dealers might have to be established from scratch.

- **Staffing**—recruiting managers and employees familiar with Rover operations could be difficult if they have moved on to other employment, while the alternative of recruiting new staff meant additional training costs.

- **Intellectual property**—design rights for engines, Rover 25 small cars and the large Rover 75 saloon apparently were sold to SAIC for £67 million. Honda (a former Rover partner) had removed or destroyed blueprints for structural parts of the Rover 45 mid-sized car, based in part on the old Honda Civic. The sports car designs were transferred to SAIC in 2005 by mistake. SAIC promised robust action to defend its rights, extending to the MG range, though Nanjing and the Rover administrators believed the MG range was excluded from the deal.

The Rebirth of Rover?

In March 2007 Nanjing, which had shipped several of MG Rover's old assembly lines to China, began production there of a car derived from the MG TF and a saloon for the Chinese market. Nanjing's MG 7 (its version of the Rover 75) was a slow seller in China compared to the near-identical SAIC equivalent. The company had struggled to restart production of the MG TF sportscar in Nanjing and in the UK.

After several postponements, in May 2007 Nanjing Automotive relaunched sportscar production, after a two-year hiatus since Rover's collapse, in a ceremony in MG Rover's old plant in Longbridge. Margaret Hodge, Industry Secretary, was quick to try to take credit by calling the plant reopening "good news for UK manufacturing" and claiming that Nanjing's investment at Longbridge was "re-establishing MG as a global brand" which underlined "the continuing strength of our automotive industry." In fact, Nanjing was using only a fraction of the sprawling Longbridge plant capacity, and employing 130 staff, and a year later full-scale production had still not started.

The chairman of Nanjing's UK operation, Wang Hongbiiao, said he planned to produce 25,000 cars a year at Longbridge by 2008, and twice that number within two years. The company planned to build a network of around 50 MG dealers in the UK, and to begin selling cars on the European continent by 2008. Nanjing had also held discussions about possible assembly of MG cars in Ardmore, Oklahoma. Nonetheless, the CEO of Fiat—Nanjing's foreign joint venture partner—had expressed concerns that the Chinese company was being "distracted" by the MG project, with the result Fiat was considering scrapping its Nanjing partnership in favour of working with another Chinese car-maker.

The SAIC Factor...

Nanjing's regional rival SAIC had also been active in the period since MG Rover's collapse. SAIC had bought Ssangyong, the South Korean producer, in 2005. SAIC also owned the rights to former Rover models, which it produced in China under the "Roewe" brand. One outcome of the muddled sale of MG Rover had been that both SAIC and Nanjing produced versions of the old Rover 75 and the MG ZT sports car. SAIC had the intellectual property rights following a deal done before MG Rover collapsed. Nanjing bought the tooling and equipment to make the cars, as well as rights to the MG name from MG Rover's administrators. SAIC also inherited the planned successor to the mid-sized Rover 45, but was prevented from using the Rover brand by Ford's acquisition of the Rover name (now believed to be part of the Land Rover and Jaguar sales package negotiated with Tata). At a late stage before the 2006 launch of the vehicle, SAIC was forced to rename its version of the Rover 75, the Roewe 750. Around 15,000 Roewe 750s were sold in China in 2007.

Things Come Together...

At the end of 2007 the two halves of MG Rover were reunited with the merger of SAIC and Nanjing Automotive, in what was effectively the take-over of Nanjing by SAIC. SAIC paid $286 million for the core operations of Nanjing, including the MG brand. The Chinese government approved the deal as a way of achieving consolidation in its motor industry and creating a globally competitive car-maker. The combined company has a production capacity of around 1.6 million cars, and has been nicknamed by the motor industry "Chinese Leyland." The deal aimed to lead to a wider range of models carrying the revived MG brand, some to be sold in the UK. Given the unsuitability of the Roewe name for export use, and the problems with using the Rover brand, it is planned new cars will be badged MG.

The merger also brought to an end Nanjing's disappointing car-making joint venture with Fiat, with the Italian group selling its 50% stake but planning to continue cooperation in commercial vehicles and components.

SAIC planned the production of the MG TF roadster in Nanjing in mid-2008, with manufacture at Longbridge to start shortly after that. The long-awaited re-launch was subject to delay as SAIC struggled with quality issues and rebuilding the Rover tooling shipped to China. Serious concerns surrounded the quality of the vehicle. Nonetheless, the relaunch of the MG two-seater, which has a passionate UK and US following, marks the European debut for a Chinese-made car. About 70% of the vehicle, including engines, will be made in China and 30% in Europe.

Dilemmas for the New Chinese Rover Business

Access to the China car market for the MG brand looks promising. The China auto market is second only to the US in terms of vehicles sold, and car sales grew 35% in 2007. Nonetheless, China has dozens of domestic carmakers-many backed by local governments-engaged in fierce competition with the multinational giants which have increasingly targeted the Chinese market. In 2007 both Chinese and foreign companies have cut prices to attract customers, seeking to increase scale and market share. There remain major questions about whether the SAIC/Nanjing merger will create a car business that can take a strong position in this fierce competition.

Internationally, the potential for Chinese producers in the global automotive market is also unproven. Most of the major international players-such as Ford, GM and Chrysler-are going through the painful process of downsizing because production capacity is out of line with international demand for vehicles.

In retrospect, looking at the history of the business, it seems that none of Rover's owners to date-corporatist British Leyland, the government, conglomerate British Aerospace, car genius BMW, or private buyer Phoenix-ever managed to resolve the company's fundamental dilemma. That dilemma is that the brand is too small to succeed in the mass market, and yet too common to retain its prestige position, leading to failure to establish a strong position in international markets. Rover clung to the middle of the market and failed, notwithstanding government interventions which simply postponed the inevitable (usually for matters of political convenience). The question is whether the new ownership can address this fundamental dilemma, and how it can address worries about quality associated with Chinese products.

Sources: Dominic O'Connell, "Why the Chinese Want to Buy Rover," *Sunday Times,* March 13 2005, p. 3–1. Krishna Guha, Jonathan Guthrie, John Griffiths and Jean Eaglesham, "The Wrong and Winding Road: Decades of Blunders That Took Rover to Ignominy," *Financial Times,* April 13 2005, p. 17. Alex Brummer, Dominic O'Connell and Andrew Porter, "The Getaway," *Sunday Times,* April 10 2005, p. 3–5. John Reed, "Nanjing Automobile Begins UK Production of MG Cars," *Financial Times,* May 30 2007, p. 20. Ray Hutton, "China Tie-Up Paves Way for MG Rover Revival," *Sunday Times,* December 23 2007, p. 3–3. Patricia Ho, "SAIC Motor's Parent Sets Accord with Rival Yuejin," *Wall Street Journal,* December 27 2007, p. 2. John Reed, "MG's Two-Seat Roadster Poised to Return," *Financial Times,* February 5 2008, p. 23.

Case 6-15

ESPN

On Sept. 19, millions of fans tuned in to a rare Monday night pro football doubleheader. Interlaced with plays were cutaways to a telethon to help victims of Hurricane Katrina. Viewers of ESPN and ABC saw some of the biggest legends in sports fielding calls from a studio in Manhattan's Times Square: Frank Gifford, Bart Starr, Gale Sayers, John Elway, Eric Dickerson, Donovan McNabb, George Bodenheimer...huh? George Boden-who?

What most folks watching didn't realize was that the stiff-looking guy with the phone in his ear is perhaps the single most influential person in all things sports. As president of the ESPN Networks and ABC Sports, George W. Bodenheimer runs one of the most successful and envied franchises in entertainment, the jewel of Walt Disney Co., and among the most powerful brands of the last quarter-century. While his round-the-clock networks are all about being brash and in-your-face, Bodenheimer is the rare media mogul who is adamant about staying behind the scenes. ESPN's top public-relations executive had to practically drag Bodenheimer out of a production booth and push him in front of the cameras to make an appearance at the Katrina telethon, which he helped pull together with the National Football League in a matter of days. "It's just not about me," he could be heard mumbling as the PR chief made sure his tie was straight.

That modesty has worked well for the 47-year-old Bodenheimer, and ESPN has flourished in his seven years at the helm. Sure, the ESPN he inherited had already extended itself from TV to print, the Internet, and other platforms. And its smart-aleck, testosterone-laden culture was already a trademark. But Bodenheimer's vision of his company, where he started in the mailroom, is as a ubiquitous sports network—and more. To really understand ESPN, you need to see it as a cluster of feisty, creative enterprises under one killer brand (Exhibit 1). Its units, spread out mostly over offices in Connecticut, New York, and Los Angeles, act like startups, full of passionate staffers who are given the freedom to drive forward but always with a mission to keep the customers (rabid and tech-savvy fans like themselves) happy. Bodenheimer "realizes ESPN has to be fast-paced," says Simon Williams, CEO of consultant Sterling Branding. "In his realm, if you stand still you're dead."

So, through 50 different businesses, Bodenheimer has pushed ESPN into broadband, on-demand video, wireless, high-definition, even books. His company has the X Games. It has burgers and fries at ESPN Zone restaurants. Video games are coming soon. All the while, the daily news and highlights show, *SportsCenter,* is as much must-see TV for millions of Americans as the nightly news shows were a generation ago. Put it all together, and Bodenheimer's competitors can't help but express awe. So ESPN has become a model for a wide range of companies, media and others, struggling to make their brands work in new markets. "They have always had a halo to do things like a *SportsCenter* really well," says Jeff Price, chief marketing officer at *Sports Illustrated.* "Nobody has created those touchpoints with consumers like they have." Adds Adam Silver, the top TV executive at the National Basketball Assn.: "George lets others shine, but don't be fooled by the aw-shucks manner. He's an extremely effective

EXHIBIT 1
ESPN The Empire

ESPN The Empire

First, a TV channel, and now.....

MORE CHANNELS Nine TV outlets, including ESPN2, ESPN HD, ESPN Deportes, and ESPN Classic.

ORIGINAL PROGRAMMING ESPN develops its own shows and movies, including ESPN2's *ESPN Hollywood, Cold Pizza,* and the new *Bound For Glory* high school football reality series featuring Dick Butkus.

RADIO The largest U.S. sports-radio network, with more than 700 affiliate stations, features hit shows *Mike & Mike in The Morning* and *The Dan Patrick Show.*

ONLINE ESPN.com gets more than 16 million unique users a month. Includes ESPN Motion, an online video service, and ESPN360, offered via broadband; Verizon is one carrier.

PUBLISHING The biweekly *ESPN The Magazine* won a National Magazine Award for general excellence in 2003. It launched a China edition in the fall of 2004.

WIRELESS Mobile ESPN is an ESPN-branded phone and customized service that rolls out in February.

GAMING Video game leader Electronic Arts has a 15-year deal to be the sole licensee of the ESPN brand in sports games, which will include console, handled, PC, and wireless games.

X GAMES Annual extreme sports competition features motocross, bike stunts, and skateboarding.

ESPY AWARDS Athletes and celebs recognize top achievements in sports and to support The V Foundation for Cancer Research founded by ESPN and late college coach Jim Valvano.

ESPN ZONES Eight sports-themed restaurants operate nationally, with a new one set to open in ESPN's planned $100 million studio facility near the Staples Center in Los Angeles.

INTERNATIONAL The world's largest distributor of sports, ESPN makes its programming available in 11 languages in more than 180 countries.

---

manager who has put his company at the cutting edge of the digital revolution." (Exhibit 2).

Remember to Have Fun

Never one to gloat about the successes, the understated Bodenheimer confesses that the track he has been pounding is getting a whole lot steeper lately. At his back is a slew of rivals gaining momentum. First among them is Comcast Corp., the No. 1 U.S. cable operator. Looking to build a cable sports network to rival ESPN's, Comcast is also ESPN's biggest distributor, so its plans could aggravate what's already a delicate relationship. Right about now, Bodenheimer is placing a hefty bet on an ESPN-branded cell phone and has said that making the new business a winner will be one of his biggest challenges of the year. The cell phone is a move into an alluring market—delivering sports data and images to insatiable fans at all hours. But the pay-off is uncertain at best, and the venture, announced on Sept. 27, could ultimately dent earnings and tarnish the brand. Bodenheimer's angst was turned up a notch or two higher when a key executive, Mark Shapiro,

resigned in August. As head of programming and production, Shapiro was seen as a driven ideas guy who kept new shows flowing and viewers tuning in. He was also an effective bad cop to Bodenheimer's good cop at the negotiating table.

Shapiro is often compared with Bodenheimer's high-energy predecessor, Steve Bornstein, ESPN's president during much of the 1990s. The 26-year-old network's initial blast of growth came under Bornstein, whose swagger infused the place with the cocky culture so strong today (Exhibit 3). Bodenheimer's core strength, say longtime staffers, has been to preserve and encourage that vibe without making it all about George. His message to the staff is something like: ESPN isn't mine, it's yours, so run with it. And remember to have fun.

Bodenheimer is in Brooks Brothers most days, but his operation is anything but buttoned-down. It's more about hoodies and DC skateboarding shoes, which is to say it's all about being young. When *ESPN The Magazine* launched in 1998, designer F. Darrin Perry gave its pages a bold look with bright colors and unconventional type. That high-octane feel extends even to the

EXHIBIT 2

Branding, By George

George Bodenheimer, oversees one of the great brands not only in sports but in all of Corporate America. Here are his tips for nurturing a top brand:

1 DEFINE YOUR MISSION "Serve the fans. That's why we are launching our new cell phone and service, to be able to reach fans wherever they are."

2 KNOW WHAT YOUR BRAND IS "We view ourselves as the world's biggest sports fan. Be fun. That's why we try to keep our programming lively without taking ourselves too seriously."

3 CULTIVATE RELATIONSHIPS WITH YOUR CUSTOMERS "Talk to fans, not at them. We try to do that with our award-winning ad campaigns."

4 DEVELOP AN INCLUSIVE CULTURE "I came up from the mailroom, so I had managers who were listening to me. You need to let everyone contribute."

5 CONTINUALLY ENHANCE YOUR PRODUCT "We have launched three new channels in the past two years, a broadband service, and a cell-phone service. And we are always tweaking our franchise show, *SportsCenter*. We've added more music and highlights recently."

magazine's offices in midtown Manhattan, which are designed to look like a gym, complete with an old school scoreboard. On any given day at the main ESPN campus in Bristol, Conn., now encompassing 100 acres dotted with dozens of satellite dishes, you might find former All-Star second baseman and *Baseball Tonight* host Harold Reynolds waiting in line for brick-oven pizza in the fancy staff cafe, or *SportsCenter* anchor Stuart Scott looking for someone to spot him on the bench press in the state-of-the-art gym. A new $160 million digital center and studio, crammed with robotic cameras and lighting rigs, is ringed with flat screen TVs beaming sports in crisp hi-def. A central control room houses producers at computers editing a constant stream of digital-video game feeds.

The whole scene is NASA meets the bleacher creatures. "People have a passion for sports," says Rich Weinstein, the ESPN account director at ad agency Wieden + Kennedy, which has captured the spirit of ESPN through its award-winning spots for the network. "If your job is your passion, it brings a new perspective to the creative process. George was here when this was a startup, and he has preserved that feeling." True to form, at a strategy session this summer for the new phone, the boss rolled up his sleeves, snapped open a Diet Coke, and burrowed down into every marketing idea the team pitched. Un-mogul-like, he never checked his BlackBerry or cut off discussion. Then he took the group out to a swanky trattoria.

Bodenheimer, who squeezes in a golf game when he can, loves to break the ice by talking about—what else?—sports. He tries to stay engaged with workers across the company without micro-managing. "The great thing about George is that he can stand back and let his managers create," says Gary Hoenig, editor-in-chief of ESPN *The Magazine*. Going up against venerable *Sports Illustrated,* ESPN's seven-year-old biweekly has made great strides. Since 1999, circulation has grown by about 1 million, to 1.8 million, while *SI* has held steady at 3.3 million, according to the Audit Bureau of Circulations (Exhibit 4). Hoenig also credits Bodenheimer with granting him the freedom to develop lucrative specialty newsstand magazines like one on fantasy football.

Tanya Van Court, whom Bodenheimer hired from Cablevision in April, 2004, to oversee a revamp of broadband service, insists, too, that the boss never meddles. During the eight months that the new product ESPN360 was in development, "he would send handwritten notes with suggestions every week and a half or so," she says. "He would offer up [notes like], 'make it the ultimate on demand product for the sports fan and one that is as flexible as possible.' " When ESPN360 launched last January with programming tailored for broadband—including short clips recapping Sunday games—it just may have hit on a new model (Exhibit 5). ESPN insiders liken it to cable TV in its infancy in the 1970s. So far, ESPN360 is available to nearly 5 million users through 14 different broadband providers.

Irresistible Economics

Can Bodenheimer the delegator and his decentralized, free-thinking culture keep up the winning streak? "The next two years will be a real big test for George," says

EXHIBIT 3 **Mr. Touchdown for NFL TV Deals**

If you want to beat the other team, what better way than to put someone in charge who knows their plays? No surprise, then, that when National Football League Commissioner Paul Tagliabue was looking for an executive to renegotiate the league's TV contracts and expand its media presence, he drafted former ESPN President Steve Bornstein.

A 22-year veteran of ESPN and ABC, Bornstein knew every network exec's head fakes and stutter steps. The payoff has been tremendous for the NFL at the bargaining table as well as with the launch of its own cable channel, the NFL Network. Since his arrival at the league in late 2002, Bornstein, 53, has negotiated $24 billion worth of new rights contracts—resulting in a 53% hike over earlier deals. "He's a great auctioneer," says Stephen B. Burke, president of cable operator Comcast. "The NFL has tremendous value. He gives it more."

The Bornstein process isn't always pretty. To be sure, the tough-talking New Jersey native who learned to use sharp elbows to get his shot as a sports cameraman while at the University of Wisconsin, plays hard. He dangles games before competitors and applies pressure like a blitzing strong safety.

Both CBS and Fox agreed to hefty increases last year after Bornstein began talking to NBC, which had dropped broadcasting football but got back in this spring. And heading into talks with his old employer, he knew how much ESPN needed football. If it lost the NFL, the network would have had to pay a 35¢ monthly fee per subscriber back to cable operators, or about $370 million annually. The result: ESPN offered $8.8 billion for a new Monday night package.

What's more, Bornstein is building up the potential competition against his successor, ESPN President George Bodenheimer. He oversees the NFL Network, a cable channel the league launched two years ago. It is seen in 35 million homes, which is still less than half of all cable and satellite households. "He brought a perspective we didn't have," says NFL Executive Vice-President Roger Goodell. The NFL's channel doesn't air regular season games yet, but its shows, like *NFL Total Access,* have that ESPN feel.

What's more, the NFL Network is a strategic asset. The NFL can simply threaten to put its own games on its own channel if it is not getting high enough offers from others. It's also a great way to boost distribution. Satellite operator Direc TV Group, for instance, agreed to distribute the channel to help it negotiate its new $700 million-a-year deal for the Sunday Ticket telecasts.

Bornstein, who lives in the former Fred Astaire mansion in Beverly Hills, shuttles between the NFL's West Coast offices and its Park Avenue digs in New York. "He's still got the entrepreneurial spirit that ESPN had in the '80s and '90s," says NASCAR Vice-President Dick Glover, who worked with Bornstein in the 1990s. Bornstein earned a reputation as a no-nonsense taskmaster who would shoot down underlings by pointing to a "bull-****" meter on a blackboard.

His ability to make ESPN into a money spinner earned Bornstein a ticket upward at parent Walt Disney Co., but his thankless task was to turn around ABC and jump-start Disney's woeful Go.net. "I told him not to take the Internet job, but he really didn't have a choice," says former Cap Cities Chairman Thomas S. Murphy, a Disney board member. "Michael [Eisner] wanted him to do it." But after CEO Eisner picked Robert A. Iger as Disney president, Bornstein resigned.

Within months he had joined the NFL. "It was fun getting back to my roots, starting a cable channel," says Bornstein. Spoken like a guy who's back in the lineup.

—By Ronald Grover in Los Angeles

Sean McManus, head of competing CBS Sports and a friend of Bodenheimer's. All around it, companies are imitating ESPN's cool and edgy packaging of sports. And if live sports is the last great mass market to lure advertisers, then how long can ESPN expect to dominate? Throw in a sports-crazed, often-elusive audience of young men bordering on the fanatic, and the economics are irresistible. That's why so many players are pushing into Bodenheimer's domain, from teams and leagues launching their own channels to cable and satellite operators creating new offerings. "ESPN listens to its audience very closely," says Sterling's Williams. "If it keeps doing that, [that] should be the glue that holds it together."

Even so, the ESPN chief these days finds himself playing more defense than offense to keep games out of competitors' hands. One sign of the times: big hikes in the prices ESPN is paying to lock up new pro football and Major League Baseball rights contracts. The

EXHIBIT 4
Youth Rules

Youth Rules

ESPN wins out vs. *Sports Illustrated* when it comes to drawing younger audiences.
MEDIAN AGE OF VIEWER/READER

31 *ESPN THE MAGAZINE*	**40** *SPORTS ILLUSTRATED*
32 *ESPN.COM*	**38** *SI.COM*
35 *SPORTSCENTER**	*NO SI TV OUTLET*

*11 p.m. show   Data: ESPN Sports Illustrated

EXHIBIT 5   ESPN.Com: Guys and Dollars

The ESPN cable channel, seen in 90 million households, is a must-stop for any channel surfer. But espn.com is the real boys' club. Young men don't show up *en masse* to anything very often, but where they do, advertisers will spend. That's what makes espn.com, with its devoted audience of guys 18 to 34, a coveted spot.

But luring Web users with hot commentators (*Sports Guy* columnist Bill Simmons), cool streaming video (ESPN Motion), the latest scores, and top-notch fantasy-league services, ESPN can use in-house promos to send them back out to its other platforms. "We look at our Web site as being like a bazaar with something always going on," says John Kosner, a senior vice-president.

The 10-year-old site is the biggest Internet draw for sports. In August, espn.com had 16.6 million unique visitors, says ComScore Media Metrix. That's far more than its closest rivals, Fox Sports on MSN (with 12.6 million uniques), nfl.com (12.6 million), and Yahoo! Sports (12.3 million). Sl.com, the Web site of ESPN's magazine rival *Sports Illustrated,* trails at 5 million. The median age of an espn.com user is 32 vs. 38 for Net users in general.

ESPN doesn't disclose revenues, but Kosner says the Web site makes most of its money from ads. "It offers the big three," says Tim Hanlon, a senior vice-president at media-buyer Starcom MediaVest. "Young guys. Sports. And a powerhouse media brand. That's just a home run for advertisers." Subscription revenues at espn.com are growing, too, through its $6.95-a-month Insider and with fantasy services. Broadband's rise will accelerate offerings. And espn360, a customizable high-speed service, showcases super-sharp video and behind-the-scenes coverage. As for rivals, such as a revamped CBS SportsLine. ESPN's Kosner says: Bring it on. "I'd rather be where we are sitting." No kidding.

—*By Tom Lowry in New York*

$2.4 billion, eight-year MLB deal announced on Sept. 14 represents a 50% annual increase in fees. And in April, ESPN ponied up $8.8 billion for a new eight-year *Monday Night Football* deal with the NFL for only one night of football. ABC will no longer broadcast games, including the lucrative Super Bowl; NBC grabbed ESPN's old Sunday night spot. The bottom line: ESPN will pay nearly twice as much a year than it did last time around, though other goodies were included, such as wireless rights that will allow ESPN for the first time to deliver Monday night highlights to cell phones. "You have to ask yourself how much growth will be left if they keep spending like this," says Richard Greenfield, an analyst at Fulcrum Global Partners LLC. Counters Bodenheimer: "Look, we are a sports-media company, and we program sports. It's like saying a seafood restaurant is being defensive when it reorders lobsters."

Bodenheimer, of course, lives in a world that's not totally of his own making. His ESPN is part of a tempest-rocked ship known as Disney. For years, ESPN has been able to do its own thing for one reason: It was the outfit former CEO Michael D. Eisner could count on for the numbers. Now, with Eisner gone, Bodenheimer will work closely with an old friend, new CEO Robert A. Iger, a onetime exec at ABC Sports. The bond between Bodenheimer and Iger is strong, one pro league executive suggests, because they see themselves in each other—"two executives who have always been underestimated." Says Iger: "People sometimes mistake being polite for being easy. That's not the case with George. He's a man of great integrity, but he can be tough." Some speculate that Iger might bring Bodenheimer to Burbank, but for now he needs his friend to stay put, keeping ESPN the financial bulwark it is to counterbalance the fickle businesses of theme parks and hit-driven TV and movies.

Indeed, ESPN revenues alone this year could be about $5 billion, with operating earnings of nearly $2 billion, according to projections from various analysts. The revenues—about 60% from distribution fees and 40% from advertising—would represent about 15% of Disney's total. Analysts estimate that revenues could grow to nearly $6.8 billion in 2008. More important, ESPN is so central to cable menus that it gives Disney bargaining power with distributors to pick up other Disney channels, be they SOAPnet or the ABC Family Channel. Emblematic of ESPN's clout, its longtime head of affiliate sales, Sean R.H. Bratches, was promoted a year ago to oversee distribution for all of Disney's cable channels and broadband services. Using ESPN's leverage was a favorite tactic of Eisner's. So precious was ESPN to the Mouse House that the former CEO told investors several years ago: "We bought the ABC media network and ESPN for $19 billion in 1995. ESPN is worth substantially more than we paid for the entire acquisition."

Muscles Flexed

It's all the more remarkable, then, that ESPN was created with such modest intentions. It was founded in 1979 by former Hartford Whalers play-by-play man Bill Rasmussen on a patch of mud in the blue-collar central Connecticut town of Bristol by putting $9,000 on several credit cards. Rasmussen started the Entertainment and Sports Programming Network (ESPN) as a way to beam University of Connecticut Huskies games to a larger audience using satellite dishes. But it soon became clear to Rasmussen and his son, Scott, that they were on to something with national potential. Getty Oil would kick in $100 million a year after Rasmussen put on the first shows. Five years later, ABC bought out Getty's position (then owned by Texaco Inc.) and in 1988, Hearst Corp. bought a 20% position that was held at the time by RJR Nabisco. Hearst still has a 20% stake, but Disney is the active manager. "Nobody could have anticipated how much of a financial juggernaut ESPN would become," says Fulcrum analyst Greenfield.

Over the years, ESPN began to flex its muscles like the jocks it had helped turn into celebrities. It charged its cable and satellite distributors nearly twice as much for its service than any other channel fetches. (Today, ESPN gets an estimated $2.80 per subscriber per month, vs. about 40¢ for CNN, according to Morgan Stanley.) Double-digit hikes each year created a lot of ill will, culminating in a showdown two years ago that erupted in the halls of Congress. The battle pitted Bodenheimer against James O. Robbins, the outspoken CEO of cable operator Cox Communications Inc., who, acting on behalf of his industry, complained to lawmakers about the steep fees.

The brawl put Bodenheimer in an unwelcome spotlight, where he defended ESPN's pricing by blaming the high cost of rights deals with the leagues. Eventually Cox won lower annual fee increases, down from about 20% to about 7%. But ESPN claimed victory, too: New agreements included the operators' carriage of the latest ESPN channels, such as its Spanish-language outlet ESPN Deportes. "We achieved everything we wanted in that negotiation," says Ed Durso, ESPN's top executive for government and public affairs. "George rose to the occasion."

Bodenheimer knows the next battle is the big one. News Corp. founder Rupert Murdoch, with 15 regional sports channels, is only making noises about a national sports channel. Comcast is making plans. It has held several meetings in recent weeks to talk strategy and has even contacted ESPN executives about jumping ship, say sources close to both companies. Comcast already owns the Philadelphia 76ers, the Philadelphia Flyers, and a bunch of regional sports networks in cities from Philadelphia to Chicago to San Francisco. And it's no secret that

Comcast CEO Brian L. Roberts and President Stephen B. Burke, a former Disney executive, want a piece of the ESPN business model. When the Philadelphia-based cable operator made its unsolicited $54 billion bid for Disney in February, 2004, it was driven in part by a desire to capture ESPN.

Having its own hot sports channel would give Comcast ESPN-like leverage, amplifying its powerful 22 million subscriber base—even if its expertise is largely that of a distributor, not a programmer. For now, it's sticking to plans to convert its relatively unknown Outdoor Life Network, available in 64 million homes, into an ESPN for the new millennium. OLN got some buzz by airing Lance Armstrong's cycling feats every summer from the Tour de France. The rest of the channel's programming, from bull-riding to fishing shows, has niche appeal at best.

But Comcast is moving fast. It signed a $300 million, five-year deal in August to broadcast National Hockey League games on OLN starting this fall, with an option to bail out after two years. (ESPN ditched the sport after its contract expired this year following the acrimonious lockout.) Now, Comcast needs to cinch some of the remaining 60 games available from MLB and win a package of Thursday and Saturday games from the NFL, which draws the largest TV audiences in sports. "Without the NFL, I don't see anybody being a threat to ESPN," says John Mansell, a senior analyst at Kagan Research LLC.

Games in Your Pocket

Even as he fends off rivals, Bodenheimer is about to lead his troops into ESPN's trickiest brand extension so far. The idea is that ESPN could be missing the chance to stay in touch with fans who get off the sofa or walk away from their computer screens. Says Bodenheimer: "We want fans to know you don't have to let the rest of your life get in the way of being a sports fan. You can take it with you." In the past year he has met frequently with the Mobile ESPN development team to sign off on everything from the phone's black-and-red design on a Sanyo handset to the special displays constructed for big retailers. ESPN is leasing network time from Sprint Nextel Corp. and will outsource billing, messaging, and customer service (its price is yet to be announced). The opportunity to partner with ESPN was a no-brainer for Sprint Nextel CEO Gary Forsee. "As proud as we are of our brand, we'd be hard pressed to say Sprint can successfully go after the segments that ESPN [does]," he says. "But ESPN is the world leader, right?"

Still, the risk for ESPN is that if the phone bugs out, users won't be cursing some wireless outfit—they'll be blaming ESPN. "Content providers need to focus on what they do best," says one TV executive. "Hardware plays are fraught with problems." And the venture will require patience. "Sometimes it is up to two years with this kind of business before you reach enough scale with subscribers to be able to turn a profit," says Marina Amoroso, a wireless analyst with researcher Yankee Group. Bodenheimer says he's aware of the perils, "but it is a riskier move not to do this."

The last thing Bodenheimer needs now is to worry about top talent. Yet shortly before programming whiz Shapiro quit, Chief Marketing Executive Lee Ann Daly resigned as well. Losing Shapiro, who quit to join Washington Redskins owner Dan Snyder in remaking Six Flags Inc., is the most problematic. Shapiro's handiwork is all over the network. ESPN Original Entertainment, the cable network's venture into movies, episodic dramas, and talk shows, was his creation. He gave juice to *Sports Century*, the Emmy Award-winning series of profiles of top athletes (and a horse, Secretariat).

In June, Disney heaped new responsibility on Shapiro, promoting him to executive vice-president, overseeing programming at both ESPN and ABC Sports. To all the world it looked as if his next step would be into headquarters. Then, in early August, Shapiro met with Bodenheimer to tell him he was thinking about leaving. He'd had a feeler to head news operations at NBC. A few weeks later he accepted the offer from Snyder. "I knew at some point I was going to go entrepreneurial. It was just a question of when," says Shapiro.

Questions remain about why Bodenheimer and Iger waited so long to lock Shapiro into a new contract. But it is known that top executives at ESPN had been fielding complaints from the brass at pro sports leagues for some time that they could no longer work with Shapiro. Several league officials said they had never dealt with a negotiator as aggressive or as eager to pass himself off as the smartest guy at the table. "ESPN had just had tough relations with their customers, the cable guys," says one TV executive. "They could ill-afford to have bad relations with their suppliers, too. They need the leagues." Shapiro shakes off such criticism. "Of course I'm going to be tough in negotiations. That's my job . . . not to say to [the leagues]: 'Here's a check, fill out how much you want.'" Still, by the end of Shapiro's tenure at ESPN, officials in at least two leagues refused to deal with him unless Bodenheimer was in on the talks.

"Minute-to-Minute Battle"

Shapiro may have also ticked off Disney top brass when he turned down an offer last year to become president of ABC Entertainment, the No. 2 job under then-ABC executive Susan Lyne, who would have become chairman, say sources within the company. The plan was to eventually move out Lyne and put Shapiro in charge, those sources say. Shapiro told Iger he was excited about running prime time—but ultimately turned him down flat. Bodenheimer denies that there was any ill will toward Shapiro at Disney.

Bodenheimer says he is confident that the culture he has fostered, one of tapping ESPN's inner strengths, will ultimately make Shapiro's departure less of a blow. "Mark was obviously a significant contributor," says Bodenheimer. "He's a great talent, but we have a tremendous reservoir of talent here." In fact, Bodenheimer used Shapiro's departure to realign top management in early October into new segments: content, technology,

sales and affiliates, and international. John Skipper, the much-admired senior executive who oversaw advertising and new media, will now run content, assuming much of Shapiro's programming mantle.

How Bodenheimer leads will go a long way in determining whether ESPN remains preeminent, especially as competitors zoom in on niches like volleyball, tennis, you name it. "ESPN will always be a general store of sports," says Brian Bedol, co-founder of college sports channel CSTV, "but it may have to learn to coexist with the leagues and new media companies [that] want to reach fans with very special interests. Technology today is allowing for a direct relationship with those fans."

Nobody wants to understand fans more than Bodenheimer, who will often leave the luxury boxes at games and walk through arenas studying the crowds—unrecognized, of course. "It's a minute-to-minute battle to retain viewers in today's media world," says Bodenheimer. "That's why I want to know what fans are saying—about sports, about ESPN." It's also why the most powerful man in sports needs to stay at the top of his game.

Source: Tom Lowry, "In the Zone," *BusinessWeek,* October 17, 2005, 66–78

Case 6-16

Cowgirl Chocolates

Marilyn looked at the advertisement—a beautiful woman wearing a cowboy hat in a watering trough full of hot and spicy Cowgirl Chocolate truffles (see Exhibit 1). The ad would appear next month in the March/April edition of *Chile Pepper* magazine, the leading magazine for people who liked fiery foods. The ad, the first ever for the business, cost $3,000 to run and Marilyn wondered if it would be her big mistake for 2001. Marilyn allowed herself one $3,000–$6,000 mistake a year in trying to get her now four-year-old business to profitability. Two years ago, it was the pursuit of an opportunity to get her product into Great Britain on the recommendation of the owner of a British

John J. Lawrence, University of Idaho; Linda J. Morris University of Idaho; Joseph J. Geiger University of Idaho.

Reprinted by permission from the *Case Research Journal,* Copyright 2002 by John L. Lawrence, Linda J. Morris, Joseph J. Geiger, and the North American Case Research Association. All rights reserved. John J. Lawrence, et al., "Cowgirl Chocolates" *Case Research Journal,* Volume 22, issue 1, 2002.

biscuit company who loved her chocolates. Despite significant effort and expense, she could not convince anyone in Great Britain to carry her chocolates. Last year it was her attempt to use a distributor for the first time. It was a small, regional distributor, and she had provided them with $5,000 worth of product and had never gotten paid. She eventually got half her product back, but by the time she did it had limited remaining shelf life and she already had enough new stock on hand to cover demand. She ended up giving most of what she got back away.

Marilyn knew it took time to make money at something. She was now an internationally celebrated ceramicist, but it had taken 20 years for her ceramic art to turn a profit. She also knew, however, that she could not wait 20 years for her foray into chocolates to make money, especially not at the rate that she was currently losing money. Last year, despite not paying herself a salary and occasionally bartering her art for services, the small business's revenues of $30,000 did not come close to covering her $50,000+ in expenses. While her art for a long time did not make money, it did not lose that kind of money either. Her savings account was slowly being depleted as she loaned the company money. She knew that the product was excellent—it had won numerous awards from the two

EXHIBIT 1   Cowgirl Chocolate Ad to Appear in *Chile Pepper* Magazine

main fiery food competitions in the U.S.—and her packaging was also excellent and had won awards itself. She just was not sure how to turn her award winning products into a profitable business.

Company History

Cowgirl Chocolates was started in Moscow, Idaho, in 1997 by Marilyn Lysohir and her husband, Ross Coates. Marilyn and Ross were both artists. Marilyn was an internationally known ceramicist and lecturer; Ross was also a sculptor and a professor of fine arts at a nearby university. They had started publishing a once a year arts magazine in 1995 called *High Ground. High Ground* was really a multimedia product—each edition contained more than simply printed words and pictures. For example, past editions had included such things as vials of Mount St. Helen's ash, cassette tapes, seeds, fabric art, and chocolate bunnies in addition to articles and stories. One edition was even packaged in a motion picture canister. With a total production of about 600 copies, however, *High Ground* simply would not pay for itself. But the magazine was a labor of love for Marilyn and Ross, and so they sought creative ways to fund the endeavor. One of the ways they tried was selling hot and spicy chocolate truffles.

The fact that Marilyn and Ross turned to chocolate was no random event. Marilyn's first job, at age 16, was at Daffin's Candies in Sharon, Pennsylvania. The business's owner, Pete Daffin, had been an early mentor of Marilyn's and had encouraged her creativity. He even let her carve a set of animals, including an 8-foot tall chocolate bunny, for display. Her sculptures proved irresistible to visiting youngsters, who would take small bites out of the sculptures. It was at this point that Marilyn realized the power of chocolate.

In addition to loving chocolate, Marilyn loved things hot and spicy. She also was aware that cayenne and other chilies had wonderful health properties for the heart. But it was her brother who originally gave her the idea of combining hot and spicy with chocolate. Marilyn considered her brother's idea for a while, and could see it had possibilities, so she started experimenting in her kitchen. She recruited neighbors, friends and acquaintances to try out her creations. While a few people who tried those early chocolates were not so sure that combining hot and spicy with chocolate made sense, many thought the chocolates were great. Encouraged, and still searching for funding

for *High Ground,* Marilyn found a local candy company to produce the chocolates in quantity, and she and her husband established Cowgirl Chocolates.

The name itself came from one friend's reaction the first time she tasted the chocolates—the friend exclaimed "these are cowboy chocolates!" Marilyn agreed that there was a certain ruggedness to the concept of hot and spicy chocolates that matched the cowboy image, but thought that *Cowgirl* Chocolates was a more appropriate name for her company. Marilyn found the picture of May Lillie that would become the Cowgirl Chocolate logo in a book about cowgirls. May Lillie was a turn of the century, pistol-packing cowgirl, and Marilyn loved the picture of May looking down the barrel of a pistol because May looked so tough. And it certainly was not hard to envision May adopting the Cowgirl Chocolate motto—Sissies Stay Away. That motto had come to Marilyn when a group of friends told her that they really did not like her hot and spicy chocolates. Marilyn was a little disappointed and hurt, and thought to herself 'well, sissies stay away, if you don't like them, don't eat them.'

The Product

Cowgirl chocolate sold its hot and spicy creations in three basic forms: individually wrapped truffles, chocolate bars, and a hot caramel dessert sauce. The individually wrapped truffles were available in a variety of packaging options, with most of the packaging designed to set Cowgirl Chocolates apart. The truffles could be purchased in gift boxes, in drawstring muslin bags, and in a collectible tin. According to Marilyn, this packaging made them "more than a candy—they become an idea, an experience, a gift." The truffles were also available in a plain plastic bag over Cowgirl Chocolate's website for customers who just wanted the chocolate and did not care about the fancy packaging. The chocolate bars and truffles were offered in several flavors. The chocolate bars were available in either orange espresso or lime tequila crunch. The truffles were available in plain chocolate, mint, orange, lime tequila and espresso. The plain chocolate, mint, and orange truffles were packaged in gold wrappers, while the lime tequila truffles were packaged in green wrappers. The espresso truffles were the hottest, about twice as hot as the other varieties, and were wrapped in a special red foil to give customers some clue that these were extra hot. Cowgirl Chocolates' full line of product offerings are described in Exhibit 2 and are shown in Exhibit 3.

EXHIBIT 2   Cowgirl Chocolate Product Offerings with Price and Cost Figures

Item	Approximate Percentage of Total Revenues	Suggested Retail Price[1]	Wholesale Price[1]	Total Item Cost (a + b)	Cost of Chocolate or Sauce (a)	Cost of Product Packaging[2] (b)
Spicy Chocolate Truffle Bars (available in 2 flavors: orange-espresso or lime tequila crunch)	50%	$2.99	$1.50	$1.16	$1.04	$0.12
1/4 pound Muslin Bag (13 truffles in a drawstring muslin bag—available in 3 flavors: assorted hot, lime-tequila, and mild-mannered)	16%	$6.95	$3.50	$2.35	$1.69	$0.66
1/2 pound Tin (assorted hot & spicy truffles in a collectable tin)	12%	$14.95	$7.50	$4.78[3]	$3.25	$1.53
Hot Caramel Dessert Sauce (9.5 oz. Jar)	10%	$5.95	$3.50	$2.50	$2.00	$0.50
Sampler Bag (4 assorted hot truffles in a small drawstring muslin bag)	7%	$2.95	$1.50	$0.97	$0.52	$0.45
1/4 pound Gift Box (assorted hot truffles or mild-mannered truffles in a fancy gift box with gift card)	1%	$8.95	$4.50	$2.95	$1.69	$1.26
1 pound Gift Box (assorted hot truffles or mild-mannered truffles in a fancy gift box with gift card)	1%	$24.95	$12.95	$9.05	$6.37	$2.68
Gift Bucket (tin bucket containing 1/4 pound gift box, 2 truffle bars and 1 jar of caramel sauce)	1%	$39.95	$20.95	$11.02	$5.77	$5.25
Gift Basket (made of wire and branches and containing 1/2 pound tin, 2 truffle bars, 1 jar of caramel sauce and a T-shirt)	1%	$59.95	$30.95	$23.06	$15.29[3]	$7.77
Nothing Fancy (one pound assorted hot truffles or mild-mannered truffles in a plastic bag)	1%	$19.50	N.A.	$7.42	$6.37	$1.05

[1] Approximately 1/3 of sales were retail over the Cowgirl Chocolate website, the remaining 2/3 of sales were to wholesale accounts (i.e., to other retailers).
[2] Packaging cost includes costs of container (bags, tins, or boxes), labels, and individual truffle wrapping. Packaging cost assumes Marilyn packs the items and does not include the packing & labeling fee charged by Seattle Chocolates if they do the packing ($1.00 per 1/2 pound tin or 1 pound box; $0.75 per 1/4 pound box; $0.25 per 1/4 pound bag; $0.20 per sampler bag).
[3] This cost includes the cost of the T-shirt.

EXHIBIT 3
Picture of Cowgirl
Chocolate Products
& Packaging

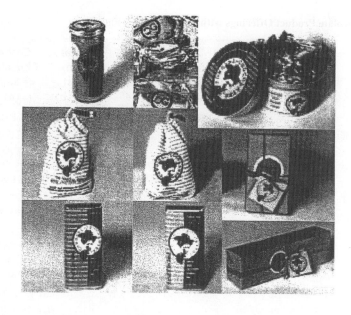

Marilyn was also in the process of introducing "mild-mannered" truffles. Mild-mannered truffles were simply the same fine German chocolate that Marilyn started with to produce all of her chocolates, but without the spice. Marilyn had chosen silver as the wrapper color for the mild-mannered truffles. While she took kidding from friends about how this did not fit with the company's motto—Sissies Stay Away—which was integrated into the company's logo and printed on the back of company t-shirts and hats, she had decided that even the sissies deserved excellent chocolate. Further, she thought that having the mild-mannered chocolate might allow her to get her product placed in retail locations that had previously rejected her chocolates as being too spicy. Marilyn was the first to admit that her chocolates packed a pretty good kick that not everybody found to their liking. She had developed the hot and spicy chocolates based primarily on her own tastes and the input of friends and acquaintances. She had observed many peoples' reactions upon trying her hot and spicy chocolates at trade shows and at new retail locations, and while many people liked her chocolates, the majority found at least some of the varieties to be too hot. In general, men tended to like the hotter truffles much more than women did. Marilyn knew her observations were consistent with what information was available on the fiery foods industry—only approximately 15% of American consumers were currently eating hot and spicy foods

and men were much more inclined to eat hot and spicy foods than were women. In addition to introducing "mild-mannered" chocolates, Marilyn was also thinking about introducing a chocolate with a calcium supplement aimed at woman concerned about their calcium intake.

All of Cowgirl Chocolate's chocolate products were sourced from Seattle Chocolates, a Seattle-based company that specialized in producing European-style chocolate confections wrapped in an elegant package fit for gift giving. Seattle Chocolates obtained all of its raw chocolate from world-renowned chocolate producer Schokinag of Germany. Seattle Chocolates sold its own retail brand plus provided private label chocolate products for a variety of companies including upscale retailers like Nieman Marcus and Nordstroms. Seattle Chocolates was, at least relative to Cowgirl Chocolates, a large company with annual sales in excess of $5,000,000. Seattle Chocolates took Cowgirl Chocolates on as a private label customer because they liked and were intrigued by the company's product and owners, and they had made some efforts to help Cowgirl Chocolates along the way. Seattle Chocolates provided Cowgirl Chocolates with a small amount of its table space at several important trade shows and produced in half batches for them. A half batch still consisted of 150 pounds of a given variety of chocolate, which was enough to last Cowgirl Chocolates for six months at 2,000 sales rates. Marilyn hoped that she could one day convince Seattle Chocolates to manage the wholesale side of Cowgirl Chocolates, but Seattle Chocolates simply was not interested in taking this on at the present time, at least in part because they were not really sure where the market was for the product. Marilyn also knew she would need to grow sales significantly before Seattle Chocolates would seriously consider such an arrangement, although she was not sure exactly how much she would have to grow sales before such an arrangement would become attractive to Seattle Chocolates.

The chocolate bars themselves cost Cowgirl Chocolates $1.04 per bar while the individual chocolate truffles cost $0.13 per piece. Seattle Chocolates also performed the wrapping and packing of the product. The chocolate bar wrappers cost $0.06 per bar. The wrapper design of the bars had recently been changed to incorporate dietary and nutritional information. While such information was not required, Marilyn felt it helped convey a better image of her chocolates. The change had cost $35 to prepare the new printing plates. Including the materials, wrapping the individual truffles cost $0.02 per piece.

The distinctive muslin bags, collector tins and gift boxes also added to the final product cost. The muslin bags cost $0.35 each for the quarter-pound size and $0.32 each for the sampler size. The tamperproof seals for the bags cost an additional $0.05/bag. The minimum size bag order was 500 bags. As with the chocolate bar wrappers, Cowgirl Chocolate had to buy the printing plates to print the bags. The plates to print the bags, however, cost $250 per plate. Each color of each design required a separate plate. Each of her three quarter-pound bag styles (assorted, lime-tequila, and mild-mannered) had a three-color design. One plate that was used to produce the background design was common to all three styles of bags, but each bag required two additional unique plates. There was also a separate plate for printing the sampler bags. Marilyn was planning to discontinue the separate lime-tequila bag, and just include lime-tequila truffles in the assorted bag as a way to cut packaging costs. The lime-tequila bags had been introduced a year ago, and while they sold reasonably well, they also appeared to mostly cannibalize sales of the assorted bags.

The collectible tins cost $0.80 each, and the labels for these tins cost $0.19 per tin. The tape used to seal the tins cost $0.04 per tin. The minimum order for the tins was for 800 units. The company that produced the tins had recently modified the tin design slightly to reduce the chance that someone might cut themselves

on the edge of the can. Unfortunately, this change had resulted in a very small change to the height of the can, which left Cowgirl Chocolate with labels too big for the can. Each label currently had to be trimmed slightly to fit on the can. The alternative to this was to switch to a smaller label. This would require purchasing a new printing plate at a cost of about $35 and might require the purchase of a new printing die (the die holds the label while it is printed), which would cost $360. Marilyn also had hopes of one day being able to get her designs printed directly on the tins. It would make for even nicer tins and save the step of having to adhere the labels to the tins. The minimum order for such tins, however, was 15,000 units.

The gift boxes, including all of the associated wrapping, ribbon, and labels, cost about $1.70 per box. The gift boxes did not sell nearly as well as the tins or bags and were available primarily through Cowgirl Chocolates website. Marilyn was still using and had a reasonable inventory of boxes from a box order she had placed three years ago.

Marilyn currently had more packaging in inventory than she normally would because she had ordered $5,000 worth in anticipation of the possibility of having her product placed in military PX stores at the end of 2000. Seattle Chocolates had been negotiating to get their product into these stores, and there had been some interest on the part of the PX stores in also having Cowgirl Chocolate products. Given the six- to eight-week lead-time on packaging, Marilyn had wanted to be positioned to quickly take advantage of this opportunity if it materialized. While Marilyn was still hopeful this deal might come about, she was less optimistic than she had been at the time she placed the packaging order.

Marilyn was concerned that the actual packing step was not always performed with the care it should be. In particular, she was concerned that not enough or too many truffles ended up in the bags and tins, and that the seals on these containers, which made the packages more tamper resistant, were not always applied correctly. Each quarter-pound bag and gift box was supposed to contain 13 individual truffles, each half-pound tin was supposed to contain 25 individual truffles, and each one-pound gift box was supposed to contain 49 individual truffles. The tins, in particular, had to be packed pretty tightly to get 25 truffles into them. Marilyn had done some of the packing herself at times, and wondered if she would not be better off hiring local college or high school students to do the packing for her to insure that the job was done to her satisfaction. It could also save her some money, as Seattle Chocolates charged her extra for packing the tins and bags. The tins, in particular, were expensive because of the time it took to apply the labels to the top and side of the tin and because of the extra care it took to get all 25 truffles into the tin. Seattle Chocolates charged $1.00 per tin for this step.

Marilyn made the caramel sauce herself with the help of the staff in a commercial kitchen in Sandpoint, Idaho, about a 2½-hour drive north of Moscow. She could make 21 cases of 12 jars each in one day, but including the drive it took all day to do. As with the chocolate, she used only the best ingredients, including fresh cream from a local Moscow dairy. Marilyn figured her costs for the caramel sauce at about $2.50 per jar, which included the cost of the ingredients, the jars, the labeling and the cost of using the Sandpoint kitchen. That figure did not include any allowance for the time it took her to make the sauce or put the labels on the jars. She was considering dropping the caramel sauce from her product line because it was a lot of work to produce and she was not sure she really made any money on it after her own time was factored in. She had sold 70 cases of the sauce in 2000, however, so she knew there was some demand for the product. She was considering the possibility of only offering it at Christmas time as a special seasonal product. She was also looking into the possibility of having a sauce company in Montana make it for her. The company produced caramel, chocolate, and chocolate-caramel sauces that had won awards from the fancy food industry trade association. Marilyn thought the sauces were quite good, although she did not like their caramel sauce as much as her own. The company would sell her 11 oz. jars of any of the sauces, spiced up to Marilyn's standards, for $2.75 per jar. Marilyn would have to provide the labels, for which she would need to have new label designs made to match the jar style the company was set up for, and she would also have to pay a shipping cost of $70–$90 per delivery. The company requested a minimum order size of 72 cases, although the company's owner had hinted that they might be willing to produce in half batches initially.

All of Cowgirl Chocolate's products had won awards, either in the annual Fiery Food Challenges sponsored by *Chile Pepper* magazine or the Scovie Award Competitions sponsored by *Fiery Foods* magazine (the Scovie awards are named after the Scovie measure of heat). All in all, Cowgirl Chocolates had won eleven awards in these two annual competitions. Further, the truffles had won first place in the latest Fiery Food Challenge and the caramel sauce won first place in the latest Scovie competition. The packaging, as distinctive as the chocolate itself, had also won several awards, including the 2000 Award for Excellence for Package Design from American Corporate Identity.

Distribution and Pricing

Marilyn's attempts to get her chocolates into the retail market had met with varying degrees of success. She clearly had been very successful in placing her product in her hometown of Moscow, Idaho. The Moscow Food Co-op was her single best wholesale customer, accounting for 10%–15% of her annual sales. The Co-op sold a wide variety of natural and/or organic products and produce. Many of its products, like Cowgirl Chocolates, were made or grown locally. The Co-op did a nice job of placing her product in a visible shelf location and generally priced her product less than any other retail outlet. The Co-op sold primarily the chocolate bars, which it priced at $2.35, and the quarter-pound muslin bags of truffles, which it priced at $5.50. This compared to the suggested retail prices of $2.99 for the bars and $6.99 for the bags. The product was also available at three other locations in downtown Moscow: Wild Women Traders, a store that described itself as a 'lifestyle outfitter' and that sold high-end women's clothing and antiques; Northwest Showcase, a store that sold locally produced arts and crafts; and Bookpeople, an independent bookstore that catered to customers who liked to spend time browsing an eclectic offering of books and drinking espresso before making a book purchase.

Marilyn was unsure how many of these local sales were to repeat purchasers who really liked the product and how many were to individuals who wanted to buy a locally made product to give as a gift. She was also unsure how much the Co-op's lower prices boosted the sales of her product at that location. At the Co-op, her product was displayed with other premium chocolates from several competitors, including Seattle Chocolates' own branded chocolate bars, which were priced at $2.99. Marilyn knew the Seattle Chocolate bars were clearly comparable in chocolate quality (although without the spice and cowgirl image). Some of the other competitors' comparably sized bars were priced lower, at $1.99, and some smaller bars were priced at $1.49. While these products were clearly higher in quality than the inexpensive chocolate bars sold in vending machines and at the average supermarket checkout aisle, they were made with a less expensive chocolate than she used and were simply not as good as her chocolates. Marilyn wondered how the price and size of the chocolate bar affected the consumer's purchase decision, and how consumers evaluated the quality of each of the competing chocolate bars when making their purchase.

Outside of Moscow, Marilyn had a harder time getting her product placed onto store shelves and getting her product to move through these locations. One other Co-op, the Boise Food Co-op, carried her products, and they sold pretty well there. Boise was the capital of Idaho and the state's largest city. The Boise Museum of Fine Arts gift shop also carried her product in Boise, although the product did not turn over at this location nearly as well as it did at the Boise Co-op. Other fine art museums, gift shops in places like Missoula, Montana, Portland, Oregon, and Columbus, Ohio, carried Cowgirl Chocolates and Marilyn liked having her product in these outlets. She felt that her reputation as an artist helped her get her product placed in such locations, and the product generally sold well in these locations. She thought her biggest distribution coup was getting her product sold in the world-renowned Whitney Museum in New York City. She felt that the fact that it was sold there added to the product's panache. Unfortunately, the product did not sell there particularly well and it was dropped by the museum. The museum buyer had told Marilyn that she simply thought it was too hot for their customers. Another location in New York City, the Kitchen Market, did much better. The Kitchen Market was an upscale restaurant and gourmet food take-out business. The Kitchen Market was probably her steadiest wholesale customer other than the Moscow Co-op. The product also sold pretty well at the few similar gourmet markets where she had gotten her product placed, like Rainbow Groceries in Seattle and the Culinary Institute of America in San Francisco.

Marilyn had also gotten her product placed in a handful of specialty food stores that focused on hot and spicy foods. Surprisingly, she found, the product had never sold well in these locations. Despite the fact that the product had won the major fiery food awards, customers in these shops did not seem to be willing to pay the premium price for her product. She had concluded that if her product was located with similarly priced goods, like at the Kitchen Market in New York City, it would sell, but that if it stood out in price then it did not sell as well. Marilyn was not sure, however, just how similarly her product needed to be priced compared to other products the store sold. It seemed clear to her that her $14.95 half-pound tins were standing out in price too much in the hot and spicy specialty stores that thrived on selling jars of hot sauce that typically retailed for $2.99 to $5.99. Marilyn wondered how her product might do at department stores that often sold half pound boxes of "premium" chocolates for as little as $9.95. She knew her half pound tins contained better chocolate, offered more unique packaging and logo design, and did not give that "empty-feeling" that the competitor's oversized boxes did, but wondered if her product would stand out too much in price in such retail locations.

Several online retailers also carried Cowgirl Chocolates, including companies like Salmon River Specialty Foods and Sam McGee's Hot Sauces, although sales from such sites were not very significant. Marilyn had also had her product available through Amazon.com for a short time, but few customers purchased her product from this site during the time it was listed. Marilyn concluded that customers searching the site for music or books simply were not finding her product, and those who did simply were not shopping for chocolates.

Marilyn also sold her products retail through her own website. The website accounted for about one-third of her sales. She liked Web-based sales, despite the extra work of having to process all the small orders, because she was able to capture both the wholesale and retail profits associated with the sale. She also liked the direct contact with the retail customers, and frequently tossed a few extra truffles into a customer's order and enclosed a note that said "a little extra bonus from the head cowgirl." Marilyn allowed customers to return the chocolate for a full refund if they found it not to their liking. Most of her sales growth from 1999 to 2000 had come from her website.

The website itself was created and maintained for her by a small local Internet service provider. It was a fairly simple site. It had pages that described the company and its products and allowed customers to place orders. It did not have any of the sophisticated features that would allow her to use it to capture information to track customers. Although she did not know for sure, she suspected that many of her Internet sales were from repeat customers who were familiar with her product. She included her website address on all of her packaging and had listed her site on several other sites, like saucemall.com and worldmall.com that would link shoppers at these sites to her site. Listing on some of these sites, like saucemall.com, was free. Listing on some other sites cost a small monthly fee—for the worldmall.com listing, for example, she paid $25/month. Some sites simply provided links to her site on their own. For example, one customer had told her she had found the Cowgirl Chocolate site off of an upscale shopping site called Style365.com. She was not sure how much traffic these various sites were generating on her site, and was unsure how best to attract new customers to her website aside from these efforts.

Marilyn had attempted to get her product into a number of bigger name, upscale retailers, like Dean & Delucca and Coldwater Creek. Dean and Delucca was known for its high-end specialty foods, and the buyers for the company had seemed interested in carrying Cowgirl Chocolates, but the owner had nixed the idea because he found the chocolates too spicy. One of the buyers had also told Marilyn that the owner was more of a chocolate purist or traditionalist who did not really like the idea of adding cayenne pepper to chocolate. Marilyn had also tried hard to get her product sold through Coldwater Creek, one of the largest catalog and online retailers in the country that sold high-end women's apparel and gifts for the home. Coldwater Creek was headquartered just a couple of hours north of Moscow in Sandpoint, Idaho. Like Dean & Delucca, Coldwater Creek had decided that the chocolate was too spicy. Coldwater Creek had also expressed some reservations about carrying food products other than at its retail outlet in Sandpoint. Marilyn hoped that the introduction of mild-mannered Cowgirl Chocolates would help get her product into sites like these two.

Promotion

Marilyn was unsure how best to promote her product to potential customers given her limited resources. The ad that would appear in *Chile Pepper* magazine

was her first attempt at really advertising her product. The ad itself was designed to grab readers' attention and pique their curiosity about Cowgirl Chocolates. Most of the ads in the magazine were fairly standard in format. They provided a lot of information and images of the product packed into a fairly small space. Her ad was different—it had very little product information and utilized the single image of the woman in the watering trough. It was to appear in a special section of the magazine that focused on celebrity musicians like Willie Nelson and The Dixie Chicks.

Other than the upcoming ad, Marilyn's promotional efforts were focused on trade shows and creating publicity opportunities. She attended a handful of trade shows each year. Some of these were focused on the hot and spicy food market, and it was at these events that she had won all of her awards. Other trade shows were more in the gourmet food market, and she typically shared table space at these events with Seattle Chocolates. She always gave away a lot of product samples at these trade shows, and had clearly won over some fans to her chocolate. But while these shows occasionally had led to placement of her product in retail locations, at least on a trial basis, they had as yet failed to land her what she would consider to be a really high volume wholesale account.

Marilyn also sought ways to generate publicity for her company and products. Several local newspapers had carried stories on her company in the last couple of years, and each time something like that would happen, she would see a brief jump in sales on her website. The *New York Times* had also carried a short article about her and her company. The day after that article ran, she generated sales of $1,000 through her website. More publicity like the *New York Times* article would clearly help. The recently released movie *Chocolat* about a woman who brings spicy chocolate with somewhat magical powers to a small French town was also generating some interest in her product. A number of customers had inquired if she used the same pepper in her chocolates as was used in the movie. Marilyn wondered how she might best capitalize on the interest the movie was creating in spicy chocolates. She thought that perhaps she could convince specialty magazines like *Art & Antiques* or regional magazines like *Sunset Magazine* or even national magazines like *Good Housekeeping* to run stories on her, her art and her chocolates. But she only had so much time to divide between her various efforts. She had looked into hiring a public relations firm, but had discovered that this would cost something on the order of $2,000/month. She did not expect that any publicity a public relations firm could create would generate sufficient sales to offset this cost, particularly given the limited number of locations where people could buy her chocolates. Marilyn was considering trying to write a cookbook as a way to generate greater publicity for Cowgirl Chocolates. She always talked a little about Cowgirl Chocolates when she gave seminars and presentations about her art, and thought that promoting a cookbook would create similar opportunities. The cookbook would also feature several recipes using Cowgirl Chocolate products.

In addition to being unsure how best to promote her product to potential customers, Marilyn also wondered what she should do to better tap into the seasonal opportunities that presented themselves to sellers of chocolate. Demand for her product was somewhat seasonal, with peak retail demand being at Christmas and Valentine's Day. But she was clearly not seeing the Christmas and Valentine sales of other chocolate companies. Seattle Chocolates, for example, had around three-quarters of its annual sales in the fourth quarter, whereas Cowgirl Chocolate sales in the second half of 2000 were actually less than in the first half. Likewise, while Cowgirl Chocolates experienced a small increase in demand around Valentine's Day, it was nowhere near the increase in demand that other chocolate companies experienced. Marilyn did sell some gift buckets and baskets through her website, and these were more popular at Christmas and Valentine's Day. The Moscow Co-op had also sold some of these gift baskets and buckets during the 2000 Christmas season. Marilyn knew that the gift basket industry in the U.S. was pretty large, and that the industry even had its own trade publication called the *Gift Basket Review.* But she was not sure if gift baskets were the best way to generate sales at these two big holidays and thought that she could probably be doing more. One other approach to spur these seasonal sales that she was planning to try was to buy lists of e-mail addresses, that would allow her to send out several e-mails promoting her products right before Valentine's Day and Christmas. She had talked to the owners of a jewelry store about sharing the expense of this endeavor and they had tentative plans to purchase 10,000 e-mail addresses for $300.

What Next?

Marilyn looked again at the advertisement that would be appearing soon in *Chile Pepper* Magazine. The same friend who had helped her with her award winning package design had helped produce the ad. It would clearly grab people's attention, but would it bring customers to her products in the numbers she needed?

Next to the ad sat the folder with what financial information she had. Despite having little training in small business accounting and financial management, Marilyn knew it was important to keep good records. She had kept track of revenues and expenses for the year, and she had summarized these in a table (see Exhibit 4). Marilyn had shared this revenue and cost information with a friend with some experience in small business financial management, and the result was an estimated income statement for the year 2000 based upon the unaudited information in Exhibit 4. The estimated income statement, shown in Exhibit 5, revealed that Cowgirl had lost approximately $6,175 on operations before taxes. Combining the information in Exhibits 4 and 5, it appeared that the inventory had built up to approximately $16,848 by December 31, 2000. Marilyn had initially guessed she had $10,000 worth of product and packaging inventory, about twice her normal level of inventory, between what was stored in her garage turned art studio turned chocolate warehouse and what was stored for her at Seattle Chocolates. But the financial analysis indicated that she either had more inventory than she thought or that she had given away more product than she originally thought. Either way, this represented a significant additional drain on her resources—in effect cash expended to cover both the operational loss and the inventory buildup was approximately $23,000 in total (see note 5 of Exhibit 4 for a more detailed explanation). When Marilyn looked at the Exhibits, she could see better why she had to loan the firm money. She also recognized that the bottom line was that the numbers did not look good, and she wondered if the ad would help turn things around for 2001.

If the ad did not have its desired affect, she wondered what she should do next. She clearly had limited resources to work with. She had already pretty much decided that if this ad did not work, she would not run another one in the near future. She was also pretty wary of working with distributors. In addition to her own bad experience, she knew of others in the industry that had bad experiences with distributors, and she did not think

EXHIBIT 4
Summary of
2000 Financial
Information
(unaudited)

Revenues:	
Product Sales	$ 26,000
Revenue from Shipping	4,046 (see Note 1)
Total Revenues	**$ 30,046**
Expenses: (related to cost of sales)	
Chocolate (raw material)	$ 16,508
Caramel (raw material)	2,647
Packaging (bags, boxes, tins)	9,120
Printing (labels, cards, etc)	3,148
Subtotal	$ 31,423 (see Note 2)
Other Expenses	
Shipping and Postage	$ 4,046
Brokers	540
Travel (airfare, lodging, meals, gas)	5,786
Trade shows (promotions, etc.)	6,423
Website	1,390
Phone	981
Office Supplies	759
Photography	356
Insurance, Lawyers, Memberships	437
Charitable Contributions	200
Miscellaneous Other Expenses	1,071
State Taxes	35
Subtotal	$ 22,024
Total Expenses	**$ 53,447**
Cash needed to sustain operations	**$ 23,023** (see Note 3)
Estimated year-end inventory (12/31/00):	
Product Inventory	$ 9,848
Extra Packaging and Labels	7,000
Total Inventory	**$ 16,848**

Notes

(1) The $4,046 Revenue from Shipping represents income received from customers who are charged shipping and postage up front as part of the order. Cowgirl then pays the shipping and postage when the order is delivered. The offsetting operating expense is noted in "Other Expenses."

(2) Of this amount, $14,575 is attributed to product actually sold and shipped. The remaining $16,848 represents leftover inventory and related supplies (i.e., $16848 + $14575 = $31,423).

(3) Marilyn made a personal loan to the firm in the year 2000 for approximately $23,000 to sustain the business's operations.

she could afford to take another gamble on a distributor. She wondered if she should focus more attention on her online retail sales or on expanding her wholesale business to include more retailers. If she focused more on her own online sales, what exactly should she do? If she focused on expanding her wholesale business, where should she put her emphasis? Should she continue to pursue retailers that specialized in hot and spicy foods, try to get her product placed in more Co-ops, expand her efforts to get the product positioned as a gift in museum gift shops and similar outlets, or

focus her efforts on large, high-end retailers like Coldwater Creek and Dean & Delucca now that she had a nonspicy chocolate in her product mix? Or should she try to do something else entirely new? And what more should she do to create publicity for her product? Was the cookbook idea worth pursuing? As she thought about it, she began to wonder if things were beginning to spin out of control. Here she was, contemplating writing a cookbook to generate publicity for her chocolate company that she started to raise money to publish her arts magazine. Where would this end?

EXHIBIT 5   **Cowgirl Chocolates Income Statement (accountant's unaudited estimate for Year 2000)**

			% of Sales
Revenues:			
Product Sales	$26,000		
Miscellaneous Income	$ 4,046		
Total Net Sales		$30,046	100%
Cost of Sales (shipped portion of chocolate, caramel, packaging, and printing)		$14,197	47%
Gross Margin		$15,849	53%
Operating Expenses:			
Advertising & Promotions:			
Trade Shows	6,423		
Website	1,390		
Charitable Contributions	200		
Subtotal		8,013	27%
Travel		5,786	19%
Miscellaneous		1,071	4%
Payroll Expense/Benefits @ 20%	(no personnel charges)	—	0%
Depreciation on Plant and Equipment	(no current ownership of PPE)	—	0%
Continuing Inventory (finished and unfinished)	(not included in income statement)	—	
Shipping & Postage		4,046	13%
Insurance, Lawyers, Professional			
Memberships		437	1.5%
Brokers		540	1.8%
Office Expenses (phone, supplies, photography, taxes)		2,131	7%
Total Operating Expenses		22,024	
Grand Total: All expenses		$36,221	
Profit before Interest & Taxes		($6,175) [see note]	
Interest Expense (short term)		—	
Interest Expense (long term)		—	
Taxes Incurred (Credit @ 18%, approximate tax rate)		($1,124)	
Net Profit After Taxes		($5,051.15)	
Net Profit After Taxes/Sales			–17%

Note: The ($6,175) loss plus the $16,848 in inventory build-up approximates the cash needed ($23,023—see Exhibit 4) to cover the total expenses for year 2000.

Case 6-17

Procter & Gamble Co.

It's Mother's Day, and Alan G. "A.G." Lafley, chief executive of Procter & Gamble Co., is meeting with the person he shares time with every Sunday evening—Richard L. Antoine, the company's head of human resources. Lafley doesn't invite the chief financial officer of the $43 billion business, nor does he ask the executive in charge of marketing at the world's largest consumer-products company. He doesn't invite friends over to watch *The Sopranos,* either. No, on most Sunday nights it's just Lafley, Antoine, and stacks of reports on the performance of the company's 200 most senior executives. This is the boss's signature gesture. It shows his determination to nurture talent and serves notice that little escapes his attention. If you worked for P&G, you would have to be both impressed and slightly intimidated by that kind of diligence.

On this May evening, the two executives sit at the dining-room table in Antoine's Cincinnati home hashing over the work of a manager who distinguished himself on one major assignment but hasn't quite lived up to that since. "We need to get him in a position where we can stretch him," Lafley says. Then he rises from his chair and stands next to Antoine to peer more closely at a spreadsheet detailing P&G's seven management layers. Lafley points to one group while tapping an empty water bottle against his leg. "It's not being felt strongly enough in the middle of the company," he says in his slightly high-pitched voice. "They don't feel the hot breath of the consumer."

If they don't feel it yet, they will. Lafley, who took over when Durk I. Jager was pressured to resign in June, 2000, is in the midst of engineering a remarkable turn-around. The first thing Lafley told his managers when he took the job was just what they wanted to hear: Focus on what you do well—selling the company's major brands such as Tide, Pampers, and Crest—instead of trying to develop the next big thing.

Now, those old reliable products have gained so much market share that they are again the envy of the industry. So is the company's stock price, which has climbed 58%, to $92 a share, since Lafley started, while the Standard & Poor's 500-stock index has declined 32%. Banc of America analyst William H. Steele forecasts that P&G's profits for its current fiscal year, which ended June 30, will rise by 13%, to $5.57 billion, on an 8% increase in sales, to $43.23 billion. That exceeds most rivals'. Volume growth has averaged 7% over the past six quarters, excluding acquisitions, well above Lafley's goal and the industry average.

The conventional thinking is that the soft-spoken Lafley was exactly the antidote P&G needed after Jager. After all, Jager had charged into office determined to rip apart P&G's insular culture and remake it from the bottom up. Instead of pushing P&G to excel, however, the torrent of proclamations and initiatives during Jager's 17-month reign nearly brought the venerable company to a grinding halt.

Enter Lafley. A 23-year P&G veteran, he wasn't supposed to bring fundamental change; he was asked simply to restore the company's equilibrium. In fact, he came in warning that Jager had tried to implement too many changes too quickly (which Jager readily admits now). Since then, the mild-mannered 56-year-old chief executive has worked to revive both urgency and hope: urgency because, in the previous 15 years, P&G had developed exactly one successful new brand, the Swiffer dust mop; and hope because, after Jager, employees needed reassurance that the old ways still had value. Clearly, Lafley has undone the damage at P&G.

What's less obvious is that, in his quiet way, Lafley has proved to be even more of a revolutionary than the flamboyant Jager. Lafley is leading the most sweeping transformation of the company since it was founded by William Procter and James Gamble in 1837 as a maker of soap and candles (Exhibit 1). Long before he became CEO, Lafley had been pondering how to make P&G relevant in the 21st century, when speed and agility would matter more than heft. As president of North American operations, he even spoke with Jager about the need to remake the company.

So how has Lafley succeeded where Jager so spectacularly failed? In a word, style. Where Jager was gruff, Lafley is soothing. Where Jager bullied, Lafley persuades. He listens more than he talks. He is living proof that the messenger is just as important as the message. As he says, "I'm not a screamer, not a yeller. But don't get confused by my style. I am very decisive." Or as Robert A. McDonald, president of P&G's global fabric and home-care division, says, "people want to follow him. I frankly love him like my brother."

Indeed, Lafley's charm offensive has so disarmed most P&Gers that he has been able to change the company profoundly (Exhibit 2). He is responsible for

EXHIBIT 1
Lafley's Vision

Outsourcing If it's not a core function the new P&G won't do it. Info tech and bar-soap manufacturing have already been contracted out. Other jobs will follow.

Acquisitions Not everything has to be invented in company labs. Lafley wants half of all new-product ideas to come from the outside.

Building Staff Managers are under much closer scrutiny, as Lafley scans the ranks for the best and the brightest and singles them out for development.

Brand Expansion The Crest line now includes an electric toothbrush and tooth-whitening products along with toothpaste. Lafley is making similar moves elsewhere.

Pricing P&G isn't just the premium-priced brand. It will go to the lower end if that's where opportunity lies.

EXHIBIT 2 **P&G Turning the Tide**

Data: Banc America securities.

Fabric and Home Care	Beauty Care	Baby and Family Care	Health Care	Snacks and Beverages
Lafley has aggressively cut costs in the company's largest division. But Tide in particular faces intense competition from lower-priced rivals. To compensate, Lafley is introducing high-margin products, such as the Swiffer Duster.	Lafley has quickly expanded this business by acquiring Clairol and Wella. But the company has less expertise here and still has to prove it can grow internally.	P&G now vies with Kimberly-Clark to dominate the disposable-diaper market. But competition has pushed prices down, which is why this division has the slowest profit-margin growth.	With its SpinBrush and tooth-whitening products, P&G has regained the lead in oral care from Colgate. The division will get a lift from distributing heartburn drug Prilosec over the counter. But the pharmaceutical business depends on one big seller, Actonel for osteoporosis.	Because the division generates the company's lowest profit margins many expect Lafley to continue to extricate P&G from these businesses. He has already sold Crisco and Jiff to J.M. Smuckers.
Sales* 29%	Sales 28%	Sales 23%	Sales 13%	Sales 7%
Operating Profit Margin 25%	Operating Profit Margin 23%	Operating Profit Margin 17%	Operating Profit Margin 18%	Operating Profit Margin 15%
Outlook Very Good	Outlook Good	Outlook Good	Outlook Mixed	Outlook Weak

*Share of total sales. Estimates for fiscal year ending June 30, 2003

P&G's largest acquisitions ever, buying Clairol in 2001 for $5 billion and agreeing to purchase Germany's Wella in March for a price that now reaches $7 billion. He has replaced more than half of the company's top 30 officers, more than any P&G boss in memory, and cut 9,600 jobs. And he has moved more women into senior positions. Lafley skipped over 78 general managers with more seniority to name 42-year-old Deborah A. Henretta to head P&G's then-troubled North American baby-care division. "The speed at which A.G. has gotten results is five years ahead of the time I expected," says Scott Cook, founder of software maker Intuit Inc., who joined P&G's board shortly after Lafley's appointment.

Still, the Lafley revolution is far from over. Precisely because of his achievements, Lafley is now under enormous pressure to return P&G to what it considers its rightful place in Corporate America: a company that is admired, imitated, and uncommonly profitable. Nowhere are those expectations more apparent than on the second floor of headquarters, where three former chief executives still keep offices. John Pepper, a popular former boss who returned briefly as chairman when Jager left but gave up the post to Lafley last year, leans forward in his chair as he says: "It's now clear to me that A.G. is going to be one of the great CEOs in this company's history."

But here's the rub: What Lafley envisions may be far more radical than what Pepper has in mind. Consider a confidential memo that circulated among P&G's top brass in late 2001 and angered Pepper for its audacity. It argued that P&G could be cut to 25,000 employees, a quarter of its current size. Acknowledging the memo, Lafley admits: "It terrified our organization."

Lafley didn't write the infamous memo, but he may as well have. It reflects the central tenet of his vision—that P&G should do only what it does best, nothing more. Lafley wants a more outwardly focused, flexible company. That has implications for every facet of the business, from manufacturing to innovation. For example, in April he turned over all bar-soap manufacturing, including Ivory, P&G's oldest surviving brand, to a Canadian contractor. In May, he outsourced P&G's information-technology operation to Hewlett-Packard Co.

No bastion has been more challenged than P&G's research and development operations. Lafley has confronted head-on the stubbornly held notion that everything must be invented within P&G, asserting that half of its new products should come from the outside. (P&G now gets about 20% of its ideas externally—up from about 10% when he took over.) "He's absolutely breaking many well-set molds at P&G," says eBay Inc.'s CEO, Margaret C. "Meg" Whitman, whom Lafley appointed to the board.

Lafley's quest to remake P&G could still come to grief. As any scientist will attest, buying innovation is tricky. Picking the winners from other labs is notoriously difficult and often expensive. And P&G will remain uncomfortably reliant on Wal-Mart Stores Inc., which accounts for nearly a fifth of its sales. Lafley is looking to pharmaceuticals and beauty care for growth, where the margins are high but where P&G has considerably less experience than rivals.

The biggest risk, though, is that Lafley will lose the P&Gers themselves. Theirs is a culture famously resistant to new ideas. To call the company insular may not do it justice. Employees aren't kidding when they say they're a family. They often start out there and grow up together at P&G, which only promotes from within. Cincinnati itself is a small town: Employees live near one another, they go to the same health clubs and restaurants. They are today's company men and women—and proud of it.

Lafley is well aware of his predicament. On a June evening, as he sits on the patio behind his home, he muses about just that. The house, which resembles a Tuscan villa and overlooks the Ohio River and downtown Cincinnati, is infused with P&G history. Lafley bought it from former CEO John G. Smale three years before he was named chief executive. A black-and-gold stray cat the family feeds sits a few feet away and watches Lafley as he sips a Beck's beer. The clouds threaten rain. "I am worried that I will ask the organization to change ahead of its understanding, capability, and commitment," Lafley admits.

For most of its 166 years, P&G was one of America's preeminent companies. Its brands are icons: It launched Tide in 1946 and Pampers, the first disposable diaper, in 1961. Its marketing was innovative: In the 1880s, P&G was one of the first companies to advertise nationally. Fifty years later, P&G invented the soap opera by sponsoring the *Ma Perkins* radio show and, later, *Guiding Light*.

Its management techniques, meanwhile, became the gold standard: In the 1930s, P&G developed the idea of brand management—setting up marketing teams for each brand and urging them to compete against each other. P&G has long been the business world's finest training ground. General Electric Co.'s Jeffrey R. Immelt and 3M's W. James McNerney Jr. both started out on Ivory. Meg Whitman and Steven M. Case were in toilet goods, while Steven A. Ballmer was an assistant product manager for Duncan Hines cake mix, among other goods. They, of course, went on to lead eBay, AOL Time Warner and Microsoft (Exhibit 3).

But by the 1990s, P&G was in danger of becoming another Eastman Kodak Co. or Xerox Corp., a once great company that had lost its way. Sales on most of its 18 top brands were slowing; the company was being outhustled by more focused rivals such as Kimberly-Clark Corp. and Colgate-Palmolive Co. The only way P&G kept profits growing was by cutting costs, hardly a strategy for the long term. At the same time, the dynamics of the industry were changing as power shifted from manufacturers to massive retailers. Through all of this, much of senior management was in denial. "Nobody wanted to talk about it," Lafley says. "Without a doubt, Durk and I and a few others were in the camp of 'We need a much bigger change.'"

When Jager took over in January, 1999, he was hell-bent on providing just that—with disastrous results. He introduced expensive new products that never caught on while letting existing brands drift. He wanted to buy two huge pharmaceutical companies, a plan that threatened P&G's identity but never was carried out. And he put in place a companywide reorganization that left many employees perplexed and preoccupied. Soaring

EXHIBIT 3   **P&G's Family Tree**

The CEOs who preceded Lafley launched ambitious projects but also oversaw a gradual erosion of P&G's core brands.

1981–90	1990–95	1995–99	1999–2000
John Smale moves P&G into the health-care and beauty business, which becomes central to the company. His decision to expand its food and beverage division doesn't amount to nearly as much.	Edwin Artzt helps bring P&&G to the world, and cosmetics to P&G, through the purchase of Max Factor and Cover Girl. But sales of major brands slow—as international expansion and new-product launches take precedence.	John Pepper pushes into developing markets such as China and Russia and starts to revamp the company's international structure. But sales remain weak, and much of P&G's profit gains come from cost-cutting.	Durk Jagar tries to jump-start innovation by launching expensive new products, which flop, and by trying to shake up P&G's stodgy culture, which quickly demoralizes many employees.

commodity prices, unfavorable currency trends, and a techcrazed stock market didn't help either. At a company prized for consistent earnings, Jager missed forecasts twice in six months. In his first and last full fiscal year, earnings per share rose by just 3.5% instead of an estimated 13%. And during that time, the share price slid 52%, cutting P&G's total market capitalization by $85 billion. Employees and retirees hold about 20% of the stock. The family began to turn against its leader.

But Jager's greatest failing was his scorn for the family. Jager, a Dutchman who had joined P&G overseas and worked his way to corporate headquarters, pitted himself against the P&G culture, contending that it was burdensome and insufferable, says Susan E. Arnold, president of P&G's beauty and feminine care division. Some go-ahead employees even wore buttons that read "Old World/New World" to express disdain for P&G's past. "I never wore one," Arnold sneers. "'The old Procter is bad, and the new world is good.' That didn't work."

On June 6, 2000, his 30th wedding anniversary, Lafley was in San Francisco when he received a call from Pepper, then a board member: Would he become CEO? Back in Cincinnati, a boardroom coup unprecedented in P&G's history had taken place.

As Lafley steps into the small study in his house three years later, a Japanese drawing on the wall reminds him of what it was like to become CEO. The room, with its painting of a samurai warrior and red elephant-motif wallpaper, alludes to his stint running P&G's Asian operations. Bookshelves hold leather-bound volumes of Joseph Conrad and Mark Twain. A simple wooden desk faces the window. Lafley focuses on the drawing, which depicts a man caught in a spider's

web; it was given to him by the elder of his two sons, Patrick. "In the first few days, you are just trying to figure out what kind of web it is," he says.

In a sense, Lafley had been preparing for this job his entire adult life. He never hid the fact that he wanted to run P&G one day. Or if not the company, then a company. That itself is unusual since, like almost all P&Gers, Lafley has never worked anywhere else. After graduating from Hamilton College in 1969, Lafley decided to pursue a doctorate in medieval and Renaissance history at the University of Virginia. But he dropped out in his first year to join the Navy (and avoid being drafted into the Army). He served in Japan, where he got his first experience as a merchandiser, supplying Navy retail stores. When his tour of duty ended in 1975, he enrolled in the MBA program at Harvard Business School. And from there, he went directly to Cincinnati.

When he was hired as a brand assistant for Joy dish detergent in 1977 at age 29, he was older than most of his colleagues and he worried that his late start might hinder his rise at P&G. Twice within a year in the early 1980s, Lafley quit. "Each time, I talked him back in only after drinking vast amounts of Drambuie," says Thomas A. Moore, his boss at the time, who now runs biotech company Biopure Corp. On the second occasion, then-CEO John Smale met with Lafley, who had accepted a job as a consultant in Connecticut. Without making any promises, Smale says he told Lafley that "we thought there was no limit on where he was going to go."

Sure enough, Lafley climbed quickly to head P&G's soap and detergent business, where he introduced Liquid Tide in 1984. A decade later, he was promoted to head the Asian division. Lafley returned from

Kobe, Japan, to Cincinnati in 1998 to run the company's entire North American operations. To ease the transition home, he and his younger son, Alex, who was then 12, studied guitar together. Two years later, Lafley was named CEO.

Along the way, he developed a reputation as a boss who stepped back to give his staff plenty of responsibility and helped shape decisions by asking a series of keen questions—a process he calls "peeling the onion." And he retained a certain humility. He still collects baseball cards, comic books, and rock 'n' roll 45s. Whereas some executives might have a garage full of antique cars or Harley-Davidsons; Lafley keeps two Vespa motor scooters. "People wanted him to succeed," says Virginia Lee, a former P&Ger who worked for Lafley at headquarters and overseas.

As CEO, Lafley hasn't made grand pronouncements on the future of P&G. Instead, he has spent an inordinate amount of time patiently communicating how he wants P&G to change. In a company famed for requiring employees to describe every new course of action in a one-page memo, Lafley's preferred approach is the slogan. For example, he felt that P&G was letting technology rather than consumer needs dictate new products. Ergo: "The consumer is boss." P&G wasn't working closely enough with retailers, the place where consumers first see the product on the shelf: "The first moment of truth." P&G wasn't concerned enough with the consumer's experience at home: "The second moment of truth."

Lafley uses these phrases constantly, and they are echoed throughout the organization. At the end of a three-day leadership seminar, 30 young marketing managers from around the world present what they have learned to Lafley. First on the list: "We are the voice of the consumer within P&G, and they are the heart of all we do." Lafley, dressed in a suit, sits on a stool in front of the group and beams. "I love the first one," he laughs as the room erupts in applause.

When he talks about his choice of words later, Lafley is a tad self-conscious. "It's *Sesame Street* language—I admit that," he says. "A lot of what we have done is make things simple because the difficulty is making sure everybody knows what the goal is and how to get there."

Lafley has also mastered the art of the symbolic gesture. The 11th floor at corporate headquarters had been the redoubt of senior executives since the 1950s. Lafley did away with it, moving all five division presidents to the same floors as their staff. Then he turned some of

the space into a leadership training center. On the rest of the floor, he knocked down the walls so that the remaining executives, including himself, share open offices. Lafley sits next to the two people he talks to the most, which, in true P&G style, was officially established by a flow study: HR head Antoine and Vice-Chairman Bruce Byrnes. As if the Sunday night meetings with Antoine weren't proof enough of Lafley's determination to make sure the best people rise to the top. And Byrnes, whom Lafley refers to as "Yoda"—the sage-like *Star Wars* character—gets a lot of face time because of his marketing expertise. As Lafley says, "the assets at P&G are what? Our people and our brands."

Just as emblematic of the Lafley era is the floor's new conference room, where he and P&G's 12 other top executives meet every Monday at 8 a.m. to review results, plan strategy, and set the drumbeat for the week. The table used to be rectangular; now it's round. The execs used to sit where they were told; now they sit where they like. At one of those meetings, an outsider might have trouble distinguishing the CEO: He occasionally joins in the discussion, but most of the time the executives talk as much to each other as to Lafley. "I am more like a coach," Lafley says afterward. "I am always looking for different combinations that will get better results." Jeff Immelt, who asked Lafley to join GE's board in 2002, describes him as "an excellent listener. He's a sponge."

And now, Lafley is carefully using this information to reshape the company's approach to just about everything it does. When Lafley describes the P&G of the future, he says: "We're in the business of creating and building brands." Notice, as P&Gers certainly have, that he makes no mention of manufacturing. While Lafley shies away from saying just how much of the company's factory and back-office operations he may hand over to someone else, he does admit that facing up to the realities of the marketplace "won't always be fun." Of P&G's 102,000 employees, nearly one-half work in its plants. So far, "Lafley has deftly handled the outsourcing deals, which has lessened fear within P&G," says Roger Martin, a close adviser of Lafley's who is dean of the University of Toronto's Joseph L. Rotman School of Management. All 2,000 of the information-technology workers were moved over to HP. At the bar-soap operations, based entirely in Cincinnati, 200 of the 250 employees went to work for the Canadian contractor.

Lafley's approach to selling P&G products is unprecedented at the company, too: He argues that P&G doesn't have to produce just premium-priced goods. So now there's a cheaper formulation for Crest in China. The Clairol deal gave P&G bargain shampoos such as Daily Defense. And with Lafley's encouragement, managers have looked at their most expensive products to make sure they aren't too costly. In many cases, they've actually lowered the prices.

And Lafley is pushing P&G to approach its brands more creatively. Crest, for example, isn't just about toothpaste anymore: There's also an electric toothbrush, SpinBrush, which P&G acquired in January, 2001 (see Appendix). P&G is also willing to license its own technologies to get them to the marketplace faster. It joined with Clorox Co., maker of Glad Bags, last October to share a food-wrap technology it had developed. It was unprecedented for P&G to work with a competitor, says licensing head Jeffrey Weedman. The overall effect is undeniable. "Lafley has made P&G far more flexible," says Banc of America's Steele.

But Lafley still faces daunting challenges. Keeping up the earnings growth, for example, will get tougher as competitors fight back and as P&G winds down a large restructuring program—started under Jager but accelerated under Lafley. Furthermore, some of the gains in profit have resulted from cuts in capital and R&D spending, which Lafley has pared back to the levels of the company's rivals. And already, P&G has missed a big opportunity: It passed up the chance to buy watersoluble strips that contain mouthwash. Now, Listerine is making a bundle on the product.

Nor are all investors comfortable with growth through acquisitions. The deals make it harder for investors to decipher earnings growth from existing operations. Then there's the risk of fumbling the integration, notes Arthur B. Cecil, an analyst at T. Rowe Price Group Inc., which holds 1.74 million P&G shares. "I would prefer they not make acquisitions," he says. Already, Clairol hair color, the most important product in P&G's recent purchase, has lost five points of market share to L'Oréal in the U.S., according to ACNeilsen Corp.

Making deals, however, could be the only way to balance P&G's growing reliance on Wal-Mart. Former and current P&G employees say the discounter could account for one-third of P&G's global sales by the end of the decade. Meanwhile, the pressure from consumers and competitors to keep prices low will only increase. "P&G has improved its ability to take on those challenges, but those challenges are still there," says Lehman analyst Ann Gillin.

Still, Lafley may be uniquely suited to creating a new and improved P&G. Even Jager agrees that Lafley was just what the company needed. "He has calmed down the confusion that happened while I was there," says the former CEO. Jager left a letter on Lafley's desk the day he resigned telling his successor not to feel responsible for his fall. "You earned it," he recalls writing. "Don't start out with guilt."

Lafley says he learned from Jager's biggest mistake. "I avoided saying P&G people were bad," he says. "I enrolled them in change." Lafley, a company man through and through, just can't resist trying out a new slogan.

Source: Robert Berner, "P&G", *BusinessWeek*, July 7, 2003, 52–63.

Appendix to Case 6-17

Darin S. Yates had watched many consumer focus groups at Procter & Gamble Co., but he had never witnessed a response like this. Out of a panel of 24 consumers evaluating a new electric toothbrush, 23 raved about the product, begging to take it home. "We were just blown away," the 36-year-old brand manager recalls.

But Yates, team leader on the new toothbrush, never imagined how successful the Crest SpinBrush would be. While most electric brushes cost more than $50, SpinBrush works on batteries and sells for just $5. Since that focus group in October 2000, it has become the nation's best-selling toothbrush, manual or electric. In P&G's last fiscal year, it posted more than $200 million in global sales, helping Crest become the consumer-product maker's 12th billion-dollar brand. It has also helped Crest reclaim the title as No. 1 oral-care brand in the U.S., a position it lost to Colgate-Palmolive's Colgate brand in 1998. "It's hard for P&G's business models to conceive of a business growing as quickly as SpinBrush," Yates says.

One reason is that P&G didn't conceive SpinBrush to begin with. Four Cleveland-area entrepreneurs developed the gizmo in 1998 with the idea of selling it to P&G. They parlayed a $1.5 million investment into a $475 million payout. Three of them even went on the P&G payroll for a year and a half to shepherd the product— something unheard of at the insular company. Says John Osher, the lead entrepreneur behind SpinBrush: "My job was to not allow P&G to screw it up."

SpinBrush marks a dramatic departure for the 165-year-old company. For once, P&G didn't insist on controlling every step, from product development to pricing. Instead, it harnessed its greatest strength—the ability to market and distribute products—to the innovation and risk-taking ability of a tiny startup that wasn't constrained by the culture inside P&G's Cincinnati headquarters. The strategy is not without risks or cultural challenges. P&G had to bend on how it packaged, manufactured, shipped, and worked its mighty marketing machine. And the story isn't over: The SpinBrush founders question if the product will reach its potential once it is fully enveloped in P&G's big-company culture. "I'm not sure you can teach an elephant to dance," Osher says.

Even so, the acquisition of SpinBrush says a lot about the leadership of Alan G. Lafley, who became chief executive in June 2000, when predecessor Durk I. Jager was ousted. Jager, a combative change agent, had pushed P&G to ramp up development of new products. He shook P&G's identity with proposals to buy two large pharmaceutical companies. In the end he overreached, missing earnings forecasts.

Lafley has been more deft. He has refocused the company on the big brands that drive earnings, including Pampers, Tide, and Crest. Like Jager, he has made acquisitions. But the $4.9 billion purchase of Clairol, P&G's largest ever, and SpinBrush have been closer to P&G's core strengths in hair and oral care than Jager's forays with Iams pet food and PUR water-filter systems.

Those moves have helped Lafley find a balance between sales and profit growth—something that eluded his predecessor. P&G has exceeded Wall Street's earnings estimates in the last three reported quarters, while at the same time increasing share in its markets through higher promotional and ad spending. For the fiscal year ended June 30, analysts expect P&G's operating earnings to climb 9% to $5 billion, reversing a prior-year decline. Such gains will get harder, though, as savings from a $6 billion restructuring started under Jager start to wind down.

Still, Lafley is proving to be a radical strategic thinker by P&G standards. When Kimberly-Clark Corp. launched a moist toilet paper last year, he went against P&G's make-it-here mentality by acquiring a manufacturer of a similar product. That let him parry Kimberly more quickly and tied up less money in the capital-intensive business. Recent negotiations to outsource P&G's 6,000-employee, back-office operations would also have been unlikely at the old P&G. The move reflects Lafley's efforts to focus the company on its core strengths and suggests further payroll cuts ahead.

The SpinBrush saga also shows a new recognition that not all great ideas originate at P&G (Exhibit 4). Lafley has made clear that as many as a third of P&G's new product ideas may come from outside, and he has stepped up efforts to identify and acquire other small companies. But perhaps the biggest change for P&G was in SpinBrush's pricing. P&G usually prices its goods at a premium, based on the cost of technology. But competitors now follow new products more quickly, eroding P&G's pricing power. With SpinBrush, P&G reversed its usual thinking. It started with an aggressive price, then found a way to make a profit. If P&G had conceived SpinBrush, admits Yates, "my gut tells me we would not have priced it where we did."

That's just the opportunity John Osher and his three colleagues saw when they had the SpinBrush brainstorm back in 1998. Osher, 55, had spent most of his career inventing things and selling them to big companies. His latest creation had been the Spin Pop, a lollipop attached to a battery-powered plastic handle, in which the candy spun at the press of a button. He had teamed up on the Spin Pop with John R. Nottingham and John W. Spirk, the principals of a Cleveland industrial design firm, and their in-house patent lawyer, Lawrence A. Blaustein. The Spin Pop had recently sold to Hasbro for millions and the men were looking for another way to utilize the technology.

EXHIBIT 4   Different Strokes for P&G

The marketing giant broke a lot of its own rules when it launched the SpinBrush. Here's what it did:

Looked Outside

SpinBrush wasn't invented at P&G. Instead, the company bought it from a group of entrepreneurs.

Empowered the Inventors

To make sure the new toothbrush didn't get smothered by the P&G bureaucracy, the inventors were hired for the first year to help with everything from packaging to logistics.

Got Aggressive on Price

Instead of starting at the high end and cutting prices as competitors moved in, P&G started low and made it harder for newcomers to steal market share.

They can't remember who came up with the concept, but they know it came from their group walks through the aisles of their local Wal-Mart, where they went for inspiration. They saw that electric toothbrushes, from Sonicare to Interplak, cost more than $50 and for that reason held a fraction of the overall toothbrush market. They reasoned: Why not create a $5 electric brush using the Spin Pop technology? At just $1 more than the most expensive manual brushes, they figured many consumers would trade up. They spent 18 months designing and sourcing a high-quality brush that wouldn't cost more than $5, batteries included. "If it had cost $7.99, we wouldn't have gone forward," Osher says.

They also formulated an exit strategy: Sell it to P&G. In 1998, they saw that Colgate toothpaste was dethroning Crest, the market champ since the early 1960s. Colgate edged out Crest by launching Total and pitching it around the new theme of whitening. P&G, meanwhile, clung to its cavity-fighting message. Colgate gained 5.6 percentage points of market share in 1998, giving the company 29.6% of the market, vs. P&G's 25.6%. "We knew that P&G would be very hungry," says Nottingham.

But first they had to prove the product could sell. They couldn't afford to advertise and sell SpinBrush at that low price. So they resorted to the marketing ploy they used with Spin Pop: packaging that said, "Try Me" and that allowed the consumer to turn the brush on in the store. They also hired a former Clorox salesman, Joseph A. O'Connor, who had years of experience selling to Wal-Mart and other big chains.

When they tested SpinBrush in Meijer Inc., a Midwest discount chain, in October 1999, it outsold the leading manual brush nearly 3 to 1, convincing Meijer to carry it. Using that sales data, they cracked drugstore chain Walgreen Co. and caught the interest of Wal-Mart in early 2000. To help close that deal, O'Connor persuaded a health and beauty aid manager at a Phoenix Wal-Mart to buy 240 SpinBrushes. "They sold out over the weekend," he recalls.

In 2000, the entrepreneurs sold 10 million SpinBrush units, more than triple the existing 3 million U.S. electric toothbrush market. With that record, it wasn't hard for Osher to get an appointment at P&G in July. The company had another reason to take notice: Colgate's recently launched ActiBrush electric toothbrush, at $19.95, was off to a fast start, too.

Yates, a financial manager on the Crest brand, headed a team to evaluate SpinBrush. P&G code-named the project Julius, after basketball great Julius Erving. With approval to negotiate a purchase and focus group

reactions off the charts, Yates moved fast. A deal to buy the startup closed in January, 2001, six months after the first meeting with Osher.

The deal's structure was unprecedented for P&G. Instead of paying a lump sum, P&G would pay $165 million up-front with an "earn-out" payment in three years based on a formula pegged to financial results. The up-front payment alone—nearly four times SpinBrush's prior year sales of $43 million—was rich by P&G's standards. The company paid three times sales for Clairol. But P&G was banking on faster sales growth from SpinBrush.

The deal had another unique feature: Osher, Blaustein, and O'Connor agreed to join the company for the three-year earn-out period with a mandate of keeping the business entrepreneurial. They would become part of a 27-person team headed by Yates that would have authority to bend any P&G rules that interfered with the business. The entrepreneurs would guide the team and had carte blanche to go higher within P&G to resolve conflicts.

And there were conflicts aplenty. Some P&Gers questioned the "Try Me" feature, fearing the batteries would wear out. Others wanted to stop store deliveries for three months so P&G could build inventories. Still others worried about having more automated factories in China. In the end, though, "they would listen to us and fight their own bureaucracy," says Osher.

Yates broke the biggest rule of all for a company whose heritage is in marketing—he didn't advertise SpinBrush for the first seven months. The traditional P&G model for a launch calls for heavy TV advertising from the outset and a high enough price to help carry that cost. But Yates didn't want the ad expense, which could force him to raise prices, until sales could support it. "I didn't want to mess up the economic structure of the business," he says.

P&G now sells SpinBrush in about 35 countries, marking its quickest global rollout ever. And it's added a multitude of models, including ones with replaceable heads. Colgate earlier this year launched Motion, a SpinBrush look-alike, at the same price. In a recent earnings conference call, Colgate CEO Reuben Mark admitted that the company had cut the price of ActiBrush from $19 to $12 because of the competition.

P&G and the SpinBrush founders agreed to an early payout in March, 21 months ahead of schedule. Osher's employment contract ended that month, and O'Connor's and Blaustein's ended in June. P&G pushed for the deal because SpinBrush's sales so far exceeded plans that the company faced the prospect of a much bigger payout if it waited, Osher says. The founders settled on a final payment of $310 million. The total price of $475 million was about 2.3 times last fiscal year's sales, a price some analysts consider a steal.

But Osher and his partners had their own reason for getting out early—they wanted to hedge their bets. They're uncertain whether SpinBrush will live up to its potential as it is further folded into P&G. Osher had an exit interview with Lafley in May in which the CEO vowed to keep SpinBrush on course. Osher has no doubt about Lafley's sincerity. It's just that he is still not sure an elephant can learn to dance.

By Robert Berner in Chicago

Source: "Why P&G's Smile Is So Bright," *BusinessWeek,* August 12, 2002, 58–60.

Case 6-18
Amazom.com Inc.

It was one of the web's typical flash frenzies, a gaggle of geeks seeking the new, new thing. At 2 a.m. on Aug. 24, a new venture called Elastic Compute Cloud quietly launched in test mode. Its service: cheap, raw computing power that could be tapped on demand over the Internet just like electricity. In less than five hours, hundreds of programmers, hoping to use the service to power their MySpace and Google wannabes, snapped up all the test slots. One desperate latecomer instant-messaged a $10,000 offer for a slot to a lucky winner, who declined to give it up. "It's really cool," enthuses entrepreneur Luke Matkins, who will run his soon-to-launch music site on the service. The creator of this *très* cool service: Amazon.com Inc.

Yes, Amazon founder and Chief Executive Jeffrey P. Bezos, the onetime Internet poster boy who quickly became a post-dot-com piñata, is back with yet another new idea. Many people continue to wonder if the world's largest online store will ever fulfill its original promise to revolutionize retailing. But now Bezos is plotting another new direction for his 12-year-old company, which he will lay out on Nov. 8 at San Francisco's Web 2.0 Conference, the annual gathering of the digerati crème. Judging from an advance look he gave *BusinessWeek* on one recent gray day at Amazon's Seattle headquarters, it's so far from Amazon's retail core that you may well wonder if he has finally slipped off the deep end.

Bezos wants Amazon to run your business, at least the messy technical and logistical parts of it, using those same technologies and operations that power his $10 billion online store. In the process, Bezos aims to transform Amazon into a kind of 21st century digital utility (Exhibit 1). It's as if Wal-Mart Stores Inc. had decided to turn itself inside out, offering its industry-leading supply chain and logistics systems to any and all outsiders, even rival retailers. Except Amazon is starting to rent out just about everything it uses to

EXHIBIT 1   Out of the Jungle

OUT OF THE JUNGLE

Amazon has quietly launched a flurry of new businesses, many in the past years, that are seemingly unrelated to its core retail store. Here's a sampling:

COMPUTING	CROWDSOURCING	MEDIA
Amazon's Simple Storage Service and its Elastic Compute Cloud offer startups such as photo-sharing site SmugMug a way to store data and run their programs on Amazon's computers over the Internet.	Amazon Mechanical Turk is a marketplace for piecework. CastingWords pays "Turkers" to transcribe snippets of podcasts that it then assembles for clients. Amazon takes a 10% commission.	Launched in September, Amazon Unbox is software that lets customers download and play movies and TV shows. Amazon.com is also hosting a show with Bill Maher and buying a movie option on a book.
SEARCH	**DISTRIBUTION**	**WEB MEASUREMENT**
After watching Google quickly become a dominant force on the Web, Amazon launched its own search site, A9.com, in 2003. But it never caught on, and Amazon recently cut many of its novel features.	For years, Amazon has run e-commerce operations for the likes of Target and Borders. In September it launched a test of Fulfillment By Amazon. Smaller merchants plug their products into Amazon's distribution system.	Alexa Internet Services provides free Web traffic rankings and other paid services, such as detailed reports on specific sites for 15¢ per 1,000 requests. It is becoming a popular alternative to other measurement services.

run its own business, from rack space in its 10 million square feet of warehouses worldwide to spare computing capacity on its thousands of servers, data storage on its disk drives, and even some of the millions of lines of software code it has written to coordinate all that.

Another big idea from Jeff Bezos? Go ahead and groan. It's fine with him. Even after all these years spent battling back claims that his company would be "Amazon.toast," he's still bounding up and down stairs two at a time to exhort his band of nerds on to the Next Big Thing. And now, more than ever, he's determined to keep going for the big score, even if people think he's crazy. In fact, Bezos, 42, sounds downright eager to confound a new generation of skeptics. "We're very comfortable being misunderstood," he says, letting loose one of his famously thunderous laughs. "We've had lots of practice."

But if techies are wowed by Bezos' grand plan, it's not likely to win many converts on Wall Street. To many observers, it conjures up the ghost of Amazon past. During the dot-com boom, Bezos spent hundreds of millions of dollars to build distribution centers and computer systems in the promise that they eventually would pay off with outsize returns. That helped set the stage for the world's biggest Web retail operation, with expected sales of $10.5 billion this year.

What it didn't translate into was the consistent profit growth many investors had expected by now. Lately profits have fallen, dragged down by spending on new technology projects and on free-shipping offers that Amazon considers marketing in place of TV ads. Analysts expect full-year net income this year to come in at about $180 million, or half of last year's total. Most worrisome to investors is Amazon's three-year-plus binge on new technologies. So far this year its spending on technology and content, including hiring hundreds of engineers and programmers to produce all these new services and buy more servers to run them, is up 52%, to $485 million. As a result, operating margins, at 4.1% for the past four quarters, now come in at less than Wal-Mart's 5.9%. Even Barnes & Noble Inc., that doughty bricks-and-mortar book chain that many expected to get remaindered by the Web, has higher margins, at 5.4%. "I have yet to see how these investments are producing any profit," gripes Piper Jaffray & Co. analyst Safa Rashtchy. "They're probably more of a distraction than anything else."

All that has investors restless and many analysts throwing up their hands wondering if Bezos is merely flailing around for an alternative to his retail operation.

Eleven of 27 analysts who follow the company have underperform or sell ratings on the stock—a stunning vote of no confidence. That number of sell recommendations is matched among large companies only by Qwest Communications International Inc., according to investment consultant StarMine Corp. It's more than even the eight sell opinions on struggling Ford Motor Co.

Neither analysts nor investors think Amazon's business is in danger of collapse. It's just that they're slowly losing confidence in Bezos' promises. The company's 2007 price-to-earnings ratio of 54 is much higher than its peers', even than high-flying Google Inc. at 35. But Amazon's stock is down 20% since the start of the year. A 12% one-day jump on Oct. 24 reflected slightly better-than-expected third-quarter results, but also investor relief that Bezos plans to slow the growth of new tech spending (Exhibit 2).

What's more, at the same time Bezos is thinking big thoughts, Amazon's retail business faces new threats. Its 25% sales growth tracks a little above the pace of overall e-commerce expansion and nearly double its own pace way back in 2001. But other sites are fast becoming preferred first stops on the Web. Google, for one, has replaced retail sites such as Amazon as the place where many people start their shopping. And more personalized and social upstarts such as News Corp.'s MySpace and YouTube, which Google is buying, have become the prime places for many people to gather online—and eventually shop. It's a trend Amazon could have trouble catching up to. Says consultant Andreas Weigend, Amazon's chief scientist until 2004: "The world has shifted from e-business to me-business."

With all those problems, some might view Bezos' latest tech toys as an attempt to take their eye off the ball. But spend some time with Bezos, and it becomes clear there may well be a method to his madness. Amazon has spent 12 years and $2 billion perfecting many of the pieces behind its online store. By most accounts, those operations are now among the biggest and most reliable in the world. "All the kinds of things you need to build great Web-scale applications are already in the guts of Amazon," says Bezos. "The only difference is, we're now exposing the guts, making [them] available to others."

And, he hopes, making money. With its Simple Storage Service, or S3, Amazon charges 15¢ per gigabyte per month for businesses to store data and programs on Amazon's vast array of disk drives. It's also charging other merchants about 45¢ a square foot

EXHIBIT 2
Where's the Payoff?

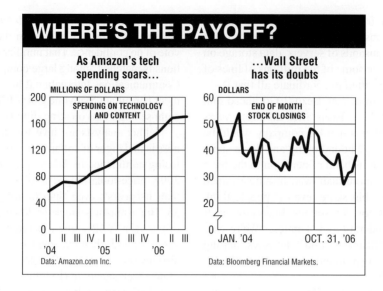

WHERE'S THE PAYOFF?

As Amazon's tech spending soars...

MILLIONS OF DOLLARS

SPENDING ON TECHNOLOGY AND CONTENT

Data: Amazon.com Inc.

...Wall Street has its doubts

DOLLARS

END OF MONTH STOCK CLOSINGS

JAN. '04   OCT. 31, '06

Data: Bloomberg Financial Markets.

per month for real space in its warehouses. Through its Elastic Compute Cloud service, or EC2, it's renting out computing power, starting at 10¢ an hour for the equivalent of a basic server computer. And it has set up a semi-automated global marketplace for online piecework, such as transcribing snippets of podcasts, called Amazon Mechanical Turk. Amazon takes a 10% commission on those jobs.

Bezos is initially aiming these services at startups and other small companies with a little tech savvy. But it's clear that businesses of all kinds are the ultimate target market. Already, Amazon has attracted some high-powered customers. Microsoft Corp. is using the storage service to help speed software downloads, for instance, and the service is helping Linden Lab handle the crush of software downloads for its fast-growing Second Life online virtual world. Highly anticipated search upstart Powerset Inc. plans to use the Amazon computing service, even though it's still in test mode, to supplement its own computers when it launches in mid-November. And the search engine marketing firm Efficient Frontier uses Mechanical Turk to determine the most effective keywords that drive traffic to Web sites.

By all accounts, Amazon's new businesses bring in a minuscule amount of revenue. Although its direct cost of providing them appears relatively low because the hardware and software are in place, Stifel Nicolaus & Co. analyst Scott W. Devitt notes: "There's not going to be any economic return from any of these projects for the foreseeable future." Bezos himself admits as much. But with several years of heavy spending

already, he's making this a priority for the long haul. "We think it's going to be a very meaningful business for us one day," he says. "What we've historically seen is that the seeds we plant can take anywhere from three, five, seven years."

A Dark Horse in a High-Stakes Race

Sooner than that, those initiatives may provide a boost for Amazon's retail side. For one, they potentially make a profit center out of idle computing capacity needed for that retail operation. Like most computer networks, Amazon's uses as little as 10% of its capacity at any one time just to leave room for occasional spikes. It's the same story in the company's distribution centers. Keeping them humming at higher capacity means they operate more efficiently, besides giving customers a much broader selection of products. And the more stuff Amazon ships, both its own inventory or others', the better deals it can cut with shippers.

But there's much more at stake for Bezos than making a few extra bucks selling services that his online store is already providing for itself. This is nothing less than a bid to lead the next wave of the Internet. A dozen years in the making, the economy that has grown up with the Internet by most accounts remains in its infancy. And leadership of that burgeoning economy remains up for grabs.

Google and Microsoft, in particular, are each angling to be the Net's kingpins: Just as Microsoft ruled the PC world (and its profits) with Windows software, so Google and Microsoft want to build what techies call the "platform" for the Web—the powerful layer of basic services on top of which everyone else builds their Web sites. "Amazon's a pretty serious dark horse" in that race, says Internet visionary Tim O'Reilly, CEO of tech publisher O'Reilly Media Inc. "Jeff really understands that if he doesn't become a platform player, he's at the mercy of those who do."

Bezos believes he has identified a unique Amazonian edge: Like no other Internet or computer company today, the e-retailer is in a position to apply the efficiencies of the Net to tangible and corporeal assets like products and people. Bezos envisions embedding the tasks of product distribution and knowledge work right into the flow of more automated business processes such as order taking and payment processing. For instance, a new service called Fulfillment by Amazon lets small and midsize businesses send their inventory to Amazon warehouses. Then when a customer places an order, Amazon gets an automated signal to ship it out—no muss, no fuss, no servers or software or garages full of stuff. "Amazon's in the business of managing complexity," says Amazon director John Doerr of the venture firm Kleiner Perkins Caufield & Byers. "There's no other e-commerce player that does that."

Mundane as these business-focused services may sound, the implications for the economy at large are startling. Google, MySpace, and YouTube cracked open for the masses the means to produce media and the advertising that sustains it, creating tens of billions of dollars in market value and billions more in new revenues. Now, by sharing Amazon's infrastructure on the cheap, Bezos is taking that same idea into the realm of physical goods and human talent, potentially empowering a whole new swath of businesses beyond the Internet itself.

The upshot: While Wall Street yawns, Bezos' pioneering dot-com is actually starting to look almost hip again, at least to the all-important Web 2.0 geek gods who set the Net agenda today. More importantly, some venture capitalists have noticed, and they're encouraging their startups to consider using Amazon services to save money and get to market faster. "Amazon is becoming a very interesting company," says Crosslink Capital general partner Peter Rip. "They're taking their store in the sky and unbundling it."

In any case, this looks like Bezos' biggest bet since he and his wife, MacKenzie, drove west in 1994 to seek fame and fortune on the Net. Since then he has survived the dot-com boom and bust with his ambitions intact. Now with three sons, and a daughter recently adopted from China, Bezos still has managed to find time to start a rocket company, Blue Origin. The venture is building a test facility in West Texas not far from his grandfather's ranch, where he once spent summers branding cattle. A longtime space nut, he made a valedictorian speech in 1982 at Miami Palmetto Senior High School about the need to colonize space.

Amazon, however, commands his full attention, especially now that the groundwork is laid for the company's latest transformation. He began not long after the dot-com bust in 2001 with—big surprise—a huge project to modernize Amazon's massive collection of data centers and the software running on them. The result was that Amazon made it much faster and easier to add new Web site features. Small, fast-moving groups of five to eight Amazon employees now could go hog wild with new ideas, such as customer discussion boards on each product page and software to play music and videos on the site. Since then these "two-pizza teams," which Bezos calls them because each team can be fed with two large pies, have become Amazon's prime innovation engines. "There's a huge value in this small, nimble team approach," says tech consultant and author John Hagel III. "But you can't do that without this kind of computer architecture."

Next came an epiphany: If the new computer setup allowed folks inside to be more creative and independent, why not open it up to outsiders, too? So in 2002, Amazon began offering outside software and Web site developers access to selected Amazon data such as pricing trends, gradually adding more and more until this year. Now it's basically getting free help from more than 200,000 outside Web developers, up 60% from a year ago. They're building new services on top of Amazon technology, further feeding back into Amazon's core retail business. One service, Scanbuy, lets people check Amazon prices on their cell phones to see if they're better than prices in a retail store.

Starting a few months ago, Amazon upped the ante. It began offering not just data but computing power, storage, and more, all intended to turn even more of its internal operations into salable services. One of the most interesting is Amazon Mechanical Turk. A couple of years ago, Amazon needed to make sure photos it took of thousands of businesses for the online Yellow Pages on its A9 search site actually matched the right business. Computers are bad at recognizing and sorting images, but people can do so very quickly. So Amazon set up a Web site where it could farm out the sorting to people for a penny or two per photo, clearly more for fun than for big pay. Last November, it launched the site, naming it after an 18th century chess-playing machine that actually had a real chess master hidden inside it.

New Spark Plugs for Startups

Since its debut, the service has attracted thousands of "Turkers" working for dozens of companies. They're doing jobs that Mechanical Turk Director Peter Cohen says "couldn't be done at all before," because there was no economical way to gather people for these tiny, often ephemeral tasks. Efficient Frontier has used the service to analyze tens of thousands of search keywords to see which best attract potential shoppers to particular Web sites. "There have not been any other services like Mechanical Turk that can do this so efficiently," says software engineer Zachary Mason.

Forget for a moment whether this will eventually turn us all into low-paid piece workers. The important thing is that the service is nurturing startups. Casting-Words co-founder Nathan McFarland uses Turkers—who he says are largely the "bored and nothing-on-TV" set who treat the tasks like crossword puzzles—not only to transcribe 10-minute podcast segments but also to assemble them into full transcriptions and to check the quality. Eighteen-year-old Eric Cranston, a onetime Turker living with his parents in Visalia, Calif., plans to use the service for a company he's starting that will retouch photos for Web sites. Essentially, Bezos sees the thousands of people from all over the world working inside Mechanical Turk's online marketplace as a big "human computer."

Amazon's other new services are getting even more serious attention. Last March, Amazon introduced its Simple Storage Service, which offers cheap space on its disk drives for any programmer or business to use to store data. Right away, Amazon approached an online photo-sharing startup called SmugMug Inc. Ironic choice: President and co-founder Chris MacAskill had fiercely battled Amazon in an earlier startup, an online bookstore called Fatbrain, later bought by Barnesand Noble.com. But his son Don, SmugMug's co-founder and CEO, says that when he heard how easily and cheaply SmugMug could back up its photos on S3, "my eyes got all big." Now, by zapping customers' photos to Amazon to store on its servers, he's avoiding the need to buy more storage devices of his own—and saving $500,000 a year. "Everything we can get Amazon to do, we will get Amazon to do," says Chris MacAskill.

"You're going to see all kinds of startups get a much better and faster start" by using Amazon's services.

They already are. Consider Powerset, the secretive search startup backed by A-list angel investors, including PayPal Inc. co-founder Peter Thiel and veteran tech analyst Esther Dyson. Co-founder and CEO Barney Pell harbors ambitions of out-Googling Google with technology that he says would let people use more natural language than terse keywords to do their searches. By analyzing the underlying meaning of search queries and documents on the Web, Powerset aims to produce much more relevant results than the current search king's.

Problem is, Powerset's technology eats computing power like a child munches Halloween candy. The little 22-person company would have to spend more than $1 million on computer hardware, two-thirds of that just to handle occasional spikes in visitor traffic, plus a bunch of people to staff a massive data center and write software to run it. That's when Pell heard about Elastic Compute Cloud. He was sold. Based on tests so far, using the Amazon site for part of the company's computing power could cut its first-year capital costs alone by more than half.

Not least, Amazon is now opening its vast network of more than 20 distribution centers worldwide to all comers. For years it has handled distribution and even Web site operations for the likes of Target Stores Corp. and Borders Group. Recently it has started providing customized handling, packing, and customer service people for upscale retailers and manufacturers such as fashion boutique Bebe. And with Fulfillment By Amazon, it's opening all that up to small and midsize businesses.

With all these initiatives, Amazon empowers new startups, which are hungry to knock off Internet leaders that happen to be…Amazon competitors. Has Bezos thought about how he may be creating an army of allies to fight his rivals? His answer: "Absolutely!"

It's hard to dismiss another possibility, though: Amazon is biting off more than it can chew. Some of the new tech projects have come out with a thud. Compared with Google's, Amazon's A9.com search site never got traction, and its features were recently downsized. The new Amazon Unbox Video downloading service struck many early reviewers as clunky and slow.

Mostly, it's unclear whether Bezos can escape his and Amazon's linoleum-floor image. Amazon's mission to be the place where "customers can find and discover anything they might want to buy online" doesn't especially mesh with the goal to be the prime source of services needed to run an Internet Age business. By contrast, nearly all of Google's services are clearly aimed

EXHIBIT 3   **Playbook: Best-Practice Ideas**

SURFING THE AMAZON

Jeff Bezos keeps innovation flowing by following these rules:

MEASURE EVERYTHING.	KEEP PRODUCT DEVELOPMENT TEAMS SMALL.	DON'T BE AFRAID OF WEIRD IDEAS.	OPEN UP TO OUTSIDERS.	WATCH CUSTOMERS NOT COMPETITORS.
Decisions are easy when you measure things. Amazon wasn't sure if its TV ads paid off, so it ran a 16-month test in two cities. Result: Bezos nixed the ads and spent the money instead on free-shipping offers.	That forces you to break up projects into doable, measurable chunks. Now most of Amazon's new features and services come from employee teams that can fed on two large pizzas.	It breaks you out of either-or thinking. Publishers said Bezos was nuts to let customers post negative product reviews. Now the reviews, which presaged the social Web craze, are one of the most popular features.	They often will do your innovation for you. Starting in 2002, Amazon began letting outside programmers use its pricing and product data. They've created new services that feed back into Amazon's business.	Customer needs change more slowly, requiring less effort than chasing competitors. By constantly lowering prices, Amazon loses near-term revenue but believes customers will spend more later.

at building the dominant digital utility. Likewise, IBM is much better known as a provider not only of technology services but also of expertise in automating a wider range of business processes, from inventory management to sales tracking. Can Bezos manage a company that simultaneously sells the most routine stuff to consumers and the most demanding business services to entrepreneurs and corporations?

So it is that Jeff Bezos faces a managerial moment of truth. Having saved Amazon from oblivion years ago, he still must prove his latest big bet can help transform the company into something truly enduring. Not only does he make no apologies for such wagers, he revels in them. Every year in his annual letter to shareholders he resurrects his 1997 letter, which reads in part: "We will make bold rather than timid investment decisions where we see a sufficient probability of gaining market leadership advantages" (Exhibit 3).

Today, it's just the same. "We are willing to go down a bunch of dark passageways," he says, "and occasionally we find something that really works." As always, investing in Bezos and his company will require faith that there's light at the end of his newest tunnel—not just a money pit.

Source: Robert D. Hof, "Jeff Bezos' Risky Bet," *BusinessWeek*, November 13, 2006, 52–58.

Case 6-19

Nanophase Technologies Corporation

The 2001 business year was finished and **Nanophase Technologies Corporation,** the industry leader in commercializing nanotechnology, had just reported financial results to shareholders. It was a discouraging year for the Romeoville, Illinois company, with revenues declining to $4.04 million from $4.27 million in 2000. The year was disappointing in other respects as well. **Nanophase** reported a loss of $5.74 million for 2001, even though management had been optimistic about achieving operating profitability. Reflecting on the Statement of Operations shown in Appendix Table 1 and the Balance Sheet in Appendix Table 2, the company's President and CEO, stated:

"2001 was disappointing in terms of revenue growth due to the economic recession, especially in the manufacturing sector that represents our primary customer and business development market, and the events in September, which lingered through the end of the year," stated Joseph Cross, President and CEO. "However we believe that the company had several outstanding accomplishments that provide a solid basis for future revenue growth." (Nanophase Technologies Corporation, Press Release, February 20, 2002)

Nanophase Technologies Corporation was prepared by Dr. Lawrence M. Lamont, Professor Emeritus of Management, Washington and Lee University. Case material is prepared as a basis for class discussion and not designed to present illustrations of either effective or ineffective handling of administrative problems. Used by permission of the author.

The author gratefully acknowledges Nanophase Technologies Corporation for reviewing the accuracy of the case study and granting permission to reproduce certain materials used in the preparation. Copyright 2002.

Later, Cross expanded on the operating results and future prospects when Nanophase hosted a quarterly conference call for investors which was broadcast over the Internet and posted on the company Web site (www.nanophase.com). In the transcript of his prepared remarks, Cross said:

> "Entering 2002, we believe that the company is stronger and better positioned than at any time in its history. We have established the vital delivery capabilities to succeed with our enlarged platform of nanoengineering technologies and delivery capability investments, our market attack is broader and at the same time better focused, the infrastructure - people and equipment are ready to deliver, our processes have been proven demonstrably scalable and robust, and we have strengthened the company's supply chain." (Nanophase Technologies Corporation, Fourth Quarter Conference Call, February 21, 2002)

While Cross was encouraged about the future, there were reasons to be cautious. After all, the company had been in business since 1989 and had not yet earned a profit. Questions arose about 2002, because the U.S. economy was only beginning to emerge from a significant manufacturing recession. Nanophase management remembered that in 2001, after its largest customer had expanded and extended its supply agreement, a weak economy had caused the customer to delay receipt of shipments of zinc oxide powder during the year to adjust inventory. Given the short notice provided by the customer, Cross had indicated that the company would not be able to find additional business to fill the revenue shortfall. Later in 2001, a UK company, Celox, Ltd., failed to fulfill a purchase contract for a catalytic fuel additive which resulted in a substantial loss of revenues and a nonrecurring inventory adjustment. In late November, Nanophase announced a temporary hourly manufacturing furlough until January 7, 2002 to enable the company to reduce existing inventory and lower its cost of operations during the holiday period (Nanophase Technologies Corporation, Press Releases: October 25 and November 14, 2001 and February 20, 2002).

Transition times from start-up to commercialization exceeding ten years were not unusual for companies developing emerging technologies. Typically new high technology firms struggled with product development, experienced set-backs in bringing products to market and were slow to earn profits. Nanophase experienced some of these problems, but the company had managed to achieve a solid record of revenue growth since introducing it's first commercial products in 1997. Exhibit 1 summarizes the revenues, profit (loss) and cost of revenues for the 1993–2001 time period.

Nanophase records revenue when products are shipped, when milestones are met regarding development arrangements or when the company licenses its technology and transfers proprietary information. Cost of revenue generally includes costs associated with commercial production, customer development arrangements, the transfer of technology and licensing fees. It does not include all of the costs incurred by the company. Gross margin, a useful indicator of a businesses move toward profitability, can be calculated as revenue minus cost of revenue divided by revenue.

EXHIBIT 1   Revenue, Costs and Profit (Loss), 1993–2001

Source: SEC form 10-K, 1997 and 2002.

Year	Revenues	Net Profit (Loss)	Cost of Revenues
2001	$4,039,469	$(5,740,243)	$4,890,697
2000	4,273,353	(4,518,327)	4,754,485
1999	1,424,847	(5,117,067)	2,610,667
1998	1,303,789	(5,633,880)	3,221,996
1997	3,723,492	(3,072,470)	3,935,766
1996	595,806	(5,557,688)	4,019,484
1995	121,586	(1,959,874)	532,124
1994	95,159	(1,287,772)	167,746
1993	25,625	(729,669)	61,978

What Is Nanotechnology?

Nanotechnology is the science and technology of materials at the nanometer scale—the world of atoms and molecules. It is a multi-disciplinary science drawing on chemistry, biology, engineering materials, mathematics and physics. Scientists use nanotechnology to create materials, devices and systems that have unusual properties and functions because of the small scale of their structures. Nanophase uses the technology in its patented manufacturing processes to produce nanocrystalline materials, like microfine zinc oxide powder, sold as a component material to producers of industrial and consumer products, such as cosmetics. See Appendix Table 3 for additional description.

Over the next 20–30 years, it is expected that nanotechnology will find applications in chemicals and engineering materials, optical networking, memory chips for electronic devices, thin film molecular structures and biotechnology. Experts predict that the technology could spawn a new industrial revolution. According to Mihail Roco, senior advisor for nanotechnology at the National Science Foundation's Directorate for Engineering: "This is a technology that promises to change the way we live, the way we combat disease, the way we manufacture products, and even the way we explore the universe. Simply put, nanoscale manufacturing allows us to work with the fundamental building blocks of matter, at the atomic and molecular levels. This enables the creation of systems that are so small that we could only dream about their application years ago." "Because of nanotechnology, we'll see more changes in the next 30 years than we saw in all of the last century." (Roco, 2001)

Because nanotechnology promises to impact so many different industries, the National Nanotechnology Initiative has received the financial support of the United States government. The annual letter sent by the Office of Science and Technology Policy and the Office of Management and Budget to all agencies put nanotechnology at the top of R&D priorities for fiscal year 2001. The expenditures have reflected the priority, and in fiscal 2001 actual federal expenditures for nanotechnology were $463.85 million. In 2002, Congress enacted a fiscal year nanotechnology appropriation of $604.4 million. The 2003 budget request was set at $710.2 million, another substantial increase reflecting the continuing interest and commitment to the commercial potential of the technology. (www.nano.gov)

History of Nanophase Technologies Corporation

Nanophase Technologies Corporation traces its beginnings to the mid-1980's and the research of Richard Siegel, who developed the "physical-vapor synthesis" (PVS) method for producing nanocrystalline materials at the Argonne National Laboratory, southwest of Chicago. Siegel, an internationally known scientist, co-founded the company in 1989 after receiving funding from the Argonne National Laboratory-University of Chicago Development Corporation. The mission of Nanophase was to produce nanostructured materials by developing and applying the PVS process. For several years, the company was located in Burr Ridge, Illinois. In 2000, Nanophase expanded its manufacturing capabilities and moved its headquarters to a facility in Romeoville, Illinois. The original Burr Ridge manufacturing facility was also retained and is currently the main source of PVS production. The Romeoville addition enables the company to increase its manufacturing operations and expand its customer application technology to meet future demand. (Stebbins, 2000; www.nanotechinvesting.com; Nanophase Technologies Corporation, 2000 Annual Report)

Developing the Technology

From its beginning as a 1989 start-up, Nanophase emphasized the development of technology, the pursuit of patents and the design of manufacturing processes to transition the company from R&D to a commercial enterprise. Through 1995, the majority of the company's revenues resulted from government research contracts. From this research, the company developed an operating capacity to produce significant quantities of nanocrystalline materials for commercial use. At the same time, Nanophase was involved with potential customers to facilitate the development of products that would utilize the capabilities of the PVS process. During 1996, Nanophase began emerging from product development and in 1997, the first complete year of commercial operations, the company significantly increased its revenues from sales to businesses.

Protecting Intellectual Property

Nanophase was also successful in protecting its technology, equipment and processes with patents. Early in 2002, the company had 38 U.S. and foreign patents, patent applications, or licenses covering core technologies and manufacturing processes. (Nanophase

Technologies Corporation, Fourth Quarter Conference Call, February 21, 2002) Intellectual property such as patents and trade secrets are valuable because they protect many of the scientific and technological aspects of the company's business and result in a competitive advantage.

Reducing Manufacturing Costs

Nanophase placed importance on research and technology development to reduce manufacturing costs. Although the company de-emphasized the pursuit of revenue from government research contracts in 1995, research was funded by the company to improve manufacturing processes for commercial production. For example, in 2001, Nanophase made expenditures to improve PVS manufacturing technology in product quality and output quantity. Nanophase was successful in reducing variable manufacturing cost by 40 to 65% (including a 25% reduction in manufacturing staff) and increased reactor output by 100 to 200% depending on the material. The company was also successful in commercializing a new, lower-cost manufacturing process, trademarked NanoArc Synthesis (TM). The new process promises to further cut some production costs by an estimated 50 to 90%, increase production output rates by estimated factors of 2 to 10 times, and permit the use of less expensive raw materials. The process also will allow Nanophase to increase the variety of nanocrystalline products available for sale and address the needs of potential customers who need nanoparticles in liquid solutions and dispersions. (Nanophase Technologies Corporation, Press Release, February 20, 2002; Fourth Quarter Conference Call, February 21, 2002)

Financing Operations

To date, Nanophase has financed operations from a private offering of approximately $19,558,069 of equity securities and an initial public offering in 1997 of 4,000,000 common shares at $8.00 a share to raise $28,837,936 for continued development of the company. (SEC form 10-K405, 1997) In 2000, Nanophase entered into an agreement with BASF (its largest customer) to borrow $1.3 million to finance the purchase and installation of new equipment to meet the customer's requirements during 2001–2002. (Nanophase Technologies Corporation, Press Release, December 8, 2000)

Nanophase will need additional financing to complete another year of operations. At the end of 2001, the balance sheet indicated that about $7.4 million was available from cash and investments. Nanophase has reported cumulative losses of $34,754,188 from inception through December 31, 2001. (Nanophase Technologies Corporation, 2001 Annual Report)

Transition and Changes in Management

To speed the transition to a commercial venture, executives with experience in developing hightechnology businesses were hired. According to critics, Nanophase had too many development projects under way and did not have enough products and customers to generate a dependable revenue stream. As a result, the company lost its focus and progress fell behind expectations.

Joseph E. Cross came to Nanophase in November 1998 as a Director and President and Chief Operating Officer. In December 1998, Cross was promoted to CEO and he continues to serve in that capacity. Cross brings a background of directing high-technology start-ups and managing rapid growth and turnaround operations. His biography is in Appendix Table 4.

According to Cross, Nanophase was focused more on pure research than on finding practical applications for nanoengineered materials and making money. Cross stated: "We had a bunch of scientists but didn't have any engineers or a sales distribution or manufacturing system." (Stebbins, 2001) Since his appointment, Cross and his management team have been concentrating on six major areas:

1. Emphasizing new business development to expand revenues.
2. Achieving a positive gross margin on products.
3. Increasing the technology and intellectual property base by developing new manufacturing processes and establishing patents and trademarks.
4. Reducing manufacturing costs by using less expensive raw materials, increasing output rates and yields and reducing supply chain costs.
5. Increasing manufacturing skills and the capability to produce products to address current and new market opportunities.
6. And, strategically positioning the company for economic recovery.

Following his appointment to CEO, Cross moved quickly to expand and strengthen the management team in the areas of marketing, manufacturing, technology and engineering. Exhibit 2 shows the executive officers of

EXHIBIT 2   **Profile of Executive Officers**

Company Officer	Title	Joined	Previous Experience
Joseph Cross	Pres. and CEO	1998	Senior Management
Daniel Billicki	VP Sales and Mkt.	1999	Senior Management
Dr. Richard Brotzman	VP R&D	1994	Research Director
Dr. Donald Freed	VP Bus. Development	1995	Senior Marketing
Jess Jankowski	VP and Controller	1995	Controller
Dr. Gina Kritchevsky	Chief Technology Officer	1999	Business Development
Robert Haines	VP Operations	2000	Manufacturing

the company, including their title, year of appointment and previous business experience. At the end of 2001, Nanophase had approximately 51 full-time employees.

Nanophase also attracted an impressive outside Board of Directors to provide management and technical advice to the Company. In addition to Cross, the Board included Donald Perkins, retired Chairman of the Board of Jewel Companies, a Chicago retail supermarket and drug chain; James A. Henderson, former Chairman and CEO of Cummins Engine Company; Richard Siegel, co-founder and internationally known scientist; Jerry Pearlman, retired Chairman of Zenith Electronics Corporation and James McClung, a Senior Vice President and a corporate officer for FMC Corporation. Donald Perkins currently serves as Chairman of the Nanophase Board of Directors. (www.nanophase.com)

The Science of Nanotechnology at Nanophase

Nanotechnology is used to produce nanocrystalline particles in powder form using metallic materials such as aluminum, cerium, copper, iron and zinc. The extremely small size of the particles, combined with the properties of surface atoms gives nanoparticles unusual chemical, mechanical, electrical and optical properties that often exceed those of the original raw materials.

Different technologies are used to achieve these results, but two of the most important are Physical Vapor Synthesis (PVS) and Discrete Particle Encapsulation (DPE). Exhibit 3 illustrates the PVS process patented and used by Nanophase.

The PVS process uses a solid metallic wire or rod which is heated in a reactor to high temperatures (about 3,000 F) using jets of thermal energy. The metal atoms boil off, creating a vapor. A reactive gas is introduced to cool the vapor, which condenses into liquid molecular clusters. As the cooling process continues, the molecular clusters are frozen into solid nanoparticles. The metal atoms in the molecular clusters mix with reactive gas (e.g., oxygen atoms), forming metal oxides such as zinc and aluminum oxide. The nanocrystalline particles are near-atomic size. For example, about nine hundred million zinc oxide crystals could be spread across the head of a pin in a single layer. (Nanophase Technologies Corporation, 2000 Annual Report)

Because of the PVS process, Nanophase is able to produce nanoparticles with properties that are highly desirable to customers. These product features include

EXHIBIT 3   **Nanophase Patented PVS Process**

Source: www.nanophase.com

Thermal Energy Is Applied → Reactive Gas Is Added → Vapor and Gas Are Cooled

Solid Metal ⟹ Vapor Is Formed ⟹ Molecular Clusters Are Formed ⟹ Nanoparticles Are Formed

spherical, nonporous particles of uniform size and large surface area, particles virtually free of chemical residues and particles that flow freely without clustering together. The company is also able to use the PVS process and NanoArc Synthesis (TM) to custom-size the particles for a customer's application.

In some applications, the nanoparticles created by the PVS process require additional surface engineering to meet customer requirements. Nanophase has developed a variety of surface treatment technologies to stabilize, alter or enhance the performance of nano-crystalline particles. At the core of these surface treatment technologies is the patented Discrete Particle Encapsulation (DPE) process. DPE uses selected chemicals to form a thin durable coating around nanoparticles produced by the PVS process to provide a specific characteristic such as preventing the particles from sticking together or enabling them to be dispersed in a fluid or polymer to meet specific customer needs. (SEC form 10-K405, 1997)

Product Markets and Customer Applications

Substantial commercial interest has developed in nanotechnology because of its broad application. Although most companies refuse to disclose their work with the technology, it is likely that materials science, biotechnology and electronics will see much of the initial market development. Nanotechnology has already attracted the interest of large companies like IBM (using the technology to develop magnetic sensors for hard disk heads); Hewlett-Packard (using the technology to develop more powerful semiconductors); 3M (producing nanostructured thin film technologies); Mobil Oil (synthesizing nanostructured catalysts for chemical plants) and Merck (producing nanoparticle medicines). In other applications, Toyota has fabricated nanoparticle reinforced polymeric materials for cars in Japan and Samsung Electronics is working on a flat panel display with carbon nanotubes in Korea. (Roco, 2001)

Nanophase is not active in all of the areas. Instead, the company focuses selectively on products and market opportunities in materials science that can be developed within 12–18 months. Longer range product applications in the 18–36 month time frame were also of interest, but they were pursued mainly to give the company a pipeline of new, future opportunities. Nanophase evaluated markets by using criteria such as revenue potential, time-to-market and whether or not a product developed for one application could be successfully modified for sale in other markets.

Dr. Donald Freed, Vice President of business development, explained the company's strategy for commercializing nanotechnology: "Opportunities for nano-materials will mature at different rates, and there are substantial opportunities in the near term—those with a not too demanding level of technical complexity. There are truly different problems in nanotechnology, such as those falling into the realm of human genetics or biotechnology. So we are successfully pursuing a staged approach to developing products for our customers." Freed further explained that this staged approach to developing customer applications enables the company to build product-related revenues while also expanding its foundations for developing more complicated applications. Nanophase was established in six product markets and was developing one potential market that met its time-to-market criteria of 12 to 18 months. (Nanophase Technologies Corporation, Press Release, October 31, 2000; Nanophase Technologies Corporation, 2000 Annual Report; Analyst Presentation, 2000)

Healthcare and Personal Products

The largest product market for Nanophase was zinc-oxide powder used as an inorganic ingredient in sunscreens, cosmetics and other health care products produced by the BASF cosmetic chemicals group. In early 2001, BASF signed an exclusive long-term purchase contract in which Nanophase agreed to supply a product that met technical and FDA regulatory requirements for active cosmetic ingredients. When added to a sunscreen the specially designed particles are small enough to allow harmless light to pass through the sunscreen while the ultraviolet light bounces off the particles and never makes it to the skin. Zinc-oxide formulations also eliminate the white-nose appearance on the user's skin without a loss of effectiveness. BASF Corporation is a diversified $30 billion global corporation and the third largest producer of chemicals and related products in the United States, Mexico and Canada. Sales to this company accounted for 75.5 percent of Nanophase revenues in 2001. (SEC form 10-Q, May 15, 2002)

In another healthcare application, Schering-Plough Corporation uses Nanophase zinc oxide as an ingredient in Dr. Scholl's foot spray to act as a fungicide and prevent the nozzle from clogging. (Stebbins, 2000) The unique properties of nanoparticles has also enabled their use in antifungal ointments and as odor and wetness absorbents. Both customers continue to explore opportunities for Nanophase products in other areas. The company estimated the market potential for its products in the healthcare and cosmetics market at approximately $45 million. (Nanophase Technologies Corporation, Press Release, October 31, 2000; Nanophase Technologies Corporation, 2000 Annual Report; SEC form 10-K, 2000; Stebbins, 2000)

Environmental and Chemical Catalysts

Nanophase was beginning to sell cerium dioxide to a manufacturing company that supplied one of the three largest automobile companies in the U.S. with catalytic converters for installation on a new car model. The product replaced expensive palladium, which was used in the converters to reduce exhaust emissions. Because a pound of nano-size particles has a surface area of 5.5 acres, less active material was needed to produce comparable emission results saving the customer money and space. Catalysts promised to be a rapidly growing market for Nanophase. Opportunities in industry for new types of nanoparticles to catalyze chemical and petroleum processes and for other environmental applications offered the potential to generate $30–$60 million in revenues. (Nanophase Technologies Corporation, Press Release, October 31, 2000; Nanophase Technologies Corporation, 2000 Annual Report)

Ceramics and Thermal Spray Applications

Nanoparticles were sold for the fabrication of structural ceramic parts and components used in corrosive and thermal environments. The properties of the company's materials enabled the rapid fabrication of ceramic parts with improved hardness, strength and inertness. Fabrication costs were lower because nanoparticles reduced the need for high temperatures and pressures and costly machining during the manufacturing process. Nanophase worked with parts fabricators to design and develop ceramic parts and components using its technologies and materials. (SEC form 10-K405, 1997)

Nanophase products were also used in thermal spray materials to repair worn or eroded metal parts on naval vessels and replace conventional ceramic coatings where properties such as abrasion and corrosion resistance and tensile strength were needed for longer service life. For example, the U.S. Navy uses thermal sprays incorporating aluminum and titanium oxides to recondition worn steering mechanisms in ships and submarines. With less wear and barnacle growth on the bow planes used to steer, the Navy expects to save $100 million a year when the program is fully implemented. Nanophase sells its products to U.S. Navy approved contractors who formulate the spray with nanoparticles and then apply it to critical parts. In addition to the Navy, Nanophase has several development programs with industrial companies involving similar applications. According to Dr. Donald Freed, Vice President of Business Development, "Our materials are being evaluated in such diverse applications as improving wear resistance in the plastics molding industry and in protective coatings for industrial equipment, gas turbine and aircraft engines." The company estimates the potential market for these and similar applications to be in the range of $25 million. (Nanophase Technologies Corporation, Press Release, October 31, 2000)

Transparent Functional Coatings

Nanophase has translated the technology used to make transparent sunscreens into ingredients for coatings designed to improve the scratch resistance of high gloss floor coatings, vinyl flooring and counter tops. Apparently, nanoparticles fit so tightly together that they make vinyl flooring up to five times more scratch resistant than existing products. Additionally, Nanophase is pursuing a number of opportunities for abrasion resistant coatings. Eventually the products may end up in automobile and appliance finishes, eyeglass lense coatings, fabrics and medical products. According to management, the opportunity in transparent functional coatings is estimated at $50–$60 million. (Nanophase Technologies Corporation, Press Release, October 31, 2000; Nanophase Technologies Corporation, 2000 Annual Report)

Conductive and Anti-static Coatings

Nanophase produces indium/tin oxide and antimony/tin oxide formulations for use as conductive and anti-static coatings for electronic products. The nanoparticle coatings are stored and used at room temperatures, which is an economic advantage to manufacturers. Indium/tin oxide is used primarily as a conductive coating to shield computer monitors and television screens from electromagnetic radiation. The world market for indium/tin oxide conductive coatings is estimated at $10–$20 million.

Antimony/tin oxide materials are used for transparent anti-static coatings in electronic component packaging. Nanophase replaced coatings based on carbon black and/or evaporated metals. The key advantage of nanoparticles in this market is that the transparent coatings maintained anti-static protection while enabling end-users to see the contents inside a package. (Nanophase Technologies Corporation, 2000 Annual Report)

Ultrafine Polishing

The newest application for Nanophase was the use of nanoparticles to create ultra smooth, high quality polished surfaces on optical components. The company provided NanoTek (R) metal oxides engineered specifically for polishing semiconductors, memory disks, glass photo masks and optical lenses. The application was made possible because of the 2001 technology advances in the core PVS process, commercialization of the new NanoArc Synthesis (TM) process, and the improved technology for preparation of stable dispersions of nanocrystalline metal oxides. Nanophase received orders of $100,000 and $200,000 for the materials in early 2002 and expected the application to quickly grow to annual revenues of approximately $500,000. (Nanophase Technologies Corporation, Press Release, February 21, 2002)

Nanofibers—A Developing Market

In a developing market called Nanofibers, engineered nanoparticles that could be incorporated directly into fibers for better wear properties and ultraviolet resistance were being developed. It was expected that the customer solution would result in a more stain and wear-resistant fiber with a high level of permanence. The products were being co-developed with leading companies producing nylon, polyester and polypropylene fibers for industrial carpets and textiles. Nanophase estimated that the applications could be commercialized in about 18 months with a potential market opportunity of several million dollars. (Nanophase Technologies Corporation, Fourth Quarter Conference Call, February 21, 2002)

Business Model and Marketing Strategy

Business Model

For most of its revenues, the Nanophase business model used direct marketing to customers. Teams worked collaboratively with prospective customers to identify an unsatisfied need and apply the company's proprietary technology and products to solve a problem. In most cases, the nanocrystalline materials were custom engineered to the customer's application. International and some domestic sales were made through trained agents and distributors that served selected markets. Nanophase was also engaged in on-going research, technology licensing and strategic alliances to expand revenues. The markets served were those where the technology and nanocrystalline materials promised to add the most value by improving the functional performance of a customer's product or the economic efficiency of a process.

Marketing Strategy

The marketing strategy used a business development team to work on nanotechnology applications with new customers. Business development activities included evaluation and qualification of potential markets, identification of the lead customers in each market and the development of a strategy to successfully penetrate the market. Nanophase then formed a technical/marketing team to provide an engineered solution to meet the customer's needs. Since one-third of the company staff had a masters or doctorate in materials-related fields, including chemistry, engineering, physics, ceramics and metallurgy, Nanophase had the expertise to understand the customer's problem, determine the functions needed and apply nanocrystalline technology. The team formed a partnership with the customer to create a solution that delivered exceptional value. After a satisfactory solution was achieved, application engineering and customer management staff were moved to a sales team organized along market lines. The sales team was expected to increase revenue by selling product and process solutions and broadening the customer base in the target market. Customers and applications were carefully selected so the science and materials would represent a technology breakthrough thus enabling the customer to add substantial value to its business, while at the same time making Nanophase a profitable long-term supplier. (Nanophase Technologies Corporation, 2001 Annual Report)

Although Nanophase focused its strategy in the markets previously mentioned, applications existed in related markets where the performance of products could be improved using similar technologies without extensive re-engineering. Based on market research, these included applications in fibers, footwear and apparel, plastics and polymers, paper, pigments and other specialty markets. The company strategy in these instances was to pursue only those applications which fit its primary business strategy and were strongly supported by a significant prospective customer.

Nanophase permitted prospective customers to experiment with small research samples of nanoparticles. About eight different products, branded Nano-Tek (R), were available for sale in quantities ranging from 25 grams to 1 kilogram. The samples included Aluminum Oxide, Antimony/Tin Oxide, Cerium Oxide, Copper Oxide, Indium/Tin Oxide, Iron Oxide, Yttrium Oxide and Zinc Oxide. They were sold by customer inquiry and on the Nanophase web site in different particle sizes and physical properties. Prices for research materials ranged from $0.80 to $10.00 per gram depending on the product and the quantity desired. (www.nanophase.com)

Customer inquiries were initiated by a variety of methods including the Nanophase web page, trade journal advertising, telephone inquiries, attendance and participation at trade shows, presentations and published papers, sponsorship of symposia and technical conferences and customer referrals. Management and staff followed-up on inquiries from prospective customers to determine their needs and qualify the customer and application as appropriate for a nanotechnology solution. Cross described the process as developing a collaborative relationship with the customer. "Our particular sort of chemistry enables people to do things they can't do any other way. To make that happen, you have to have a close relationship with a customer. You have to make it work in their process or their product. So it is indeed providing a solution; not just the powder that we make, which is nanocrystalline in nature. Its formulating the powder to work in a given application." (CNBC Dow Jones Business Video, 1999)

Using management and staff to build collaborative relationships with customers was time consuming and expensive. Exhibit 4 provides the annual selling, general and administrative expenses for the years 1993–2001. While not all of the expenses can be attributed to personal selling, the expenditures are indicative of the substantial growth of the expense category as Nanophase built the business development and marketing capability to commercialize its business. Management expected that these expenses would decrease or stabilize as the markets for the company's products developed.

EXHIBIT 4 **Selling, General and Administrative Expense, 1993–2001**

Source: www.nanophase.com; Nanophase 2001 Annual Report; SEC form 10-K405, 1997.

Year	Expenditures
2001	$3,798,543
2000	3,388,758
1999	3,641,736
1998	3,594,946
1997	2,074,728
1996	1,661,504
1995	1,150,853
1994	799,558
1993	556,616

In a few instances, Nanophase leveraged its resources through partnerships with organizations and individuals focused on market-specific or geographic-specific areas. For example, licensees and agents were used to increase manufacturing, engineering and sales representation. The agents were specialized by geographic region and the types of products they were permitted to sell. Ian Roberts, Director of U.S. and International Sales stated: "The use of experienced sales agents in selected markets is a fast and cost effective way to multiply the Nanophase sales strategy. The agents bring years of industry experience and contacts to the task of introducing nanoparticles to potential customers. We intend to form close partnerships with selected agents for specific products to speed product introduction and horizontal applications." (Nanophase Technologies Corporation, Press Release, November 27, 2000)

In November 2000, Nanophase appointed Wise Technical Marketing, specialists in the coatings industry, to represent the line of NanoEngineered Products (TM) in the Midwest and the Gillen Company LLC to promote the NanoTek (R) metal oxides in Pennsylvania and surrounding areas. Nanophase also announced the appointment of Macro Materials Inc., specialists in thermal spray materials and technology, as its global, nonexclusive agent for marketing and sales of the company's line of NanoClad (TM) metal oxides for thermal spray ceramic coatings.

Nanophase retained international representation in Asia through associations with C.I. Kasei Ltd. and Kemco International of Japan. C.I. Kasei was the second largest customer, accounting for 9.4 percent of

Nanophase revenues in 2001. Kasei was licensed to manufacture and distribute the Company's NanoTek (R) nanocrystalline products, while Kemco represented conductive coatings. Nanophase was also working with customers in Europe and intended to expand its European presence as part of its future marketing strategy. (Nanophase Technologies Corporation, Press Release, November 27, 2000; Nanophase Technologies Corporation, 2000 Annual Report; SEC form 10-Q, May 15, 2002)

Competition

Competition in nanomaterials is not well-defined because the technology is new and several potential competitors are start-up businesses. However, the situation is temporary and eventually Nanophase could face competition from large chemical companies, new start-ups and other industry participants. Five types of industry participation seem to exist.

First, there were several large chemical companies located in the United States, Europe and Asia already involved in manufacturing and marketing of silica, carbon black and iron oxide nanoparticles sold as commodities to large volume users. The companies have a global presence and include prestigious names such as Bayer AG, Cabot Corporation, Dupont, DeGusa Corporation, Showa Denka and Sumitoma Corporation. All of these companies are larger and more diversified than Nanophase and pose a significant threat because they have substantially greater financial and technical resources, larger research and development staffs and greater manufacturing and marketing capabilities.

Second, there are OEMs making nanoparticles for use in their proprietary processes and products. For example,

Eastman Kodak makes nanoparticles for use in photographic film. Similarly, the technology attracted the interest of other large OEM's like IBM, Intel, Lucent Technologies, Hitachi, Mitsubishi, Samsung, NEC, Thermo Electron, Micron Technology, Dow Chemical, Philips Electronics and Hewlett-Packard. They are pursuing applications that involve optical switching, biotechnology, petroleum and chemical processing, computing and microelectronics. These companies are potential competitors in the sense that they could sell nanoparticles not needed in their own operations to outside customers, putting them into competition with Nanophase.

Third, is the group of start-up companies shown in Exhibit 5 that will compete directly with Nanophase. These competitors, funded by venture capital or other private sources, are located in the United States, Canada, Europe and the Middle East. Most were founded in the 1990's after nanotechnology began to gain attention. For example, Oxonica Ltd., Nanopowder Enterprises Inc. and TAL Materials are spin-off firms out of university and government research laboratories. They were founded by scientists and engineers attempting to commercialize a nanotechnology developed while they were employed in a research organization. Richard Laine, a scientist at the University of Michigan, was a driving force behind the founding of TAL Materials. TAL was incorporated to commercialize the nanotechnologies developed in the Science and Engineering Department at the University. (Spurgeon, 2001) Most of the firms listed in Exhibit 5 have not yet reached commercial production. Nanophase is presently the only firm capable of producing substantial quantities of nanoparticles to rigid quality

EXHIBIT 5 **Summary of Potential Nanophase Competitors**

Source: Company Internet Web sites.

Company	Location	Year Founded	Public/Private
Lightyear Technologies Inc.	Vancouver	1996	Private
Argonide Corporation	Florida	1994	Private
TAL Materials Inc.	Michigan	1996	Private
Altair Nanotechnologies Inc.	Wyoming	1999	Private
Nanomat	Ireland	1995	Private
Oxonica Ltd.	England	1999	Private
Nanopowders Industries	Israel	1997	Private
Nanopowder Enterprises, Inc.	New Jersey	1997	Private
Nanosource Technologies, Inc.	Oklahoma	Unknown	Private

standards. The company is acknowledged by industry peers as the world leader in the commercialization of nanomaterials.

Fourth, there are firms that hold process patents or supply commercial equipment to nanotechnology firms, but also have the capability to produce nanomaterials in small quantities using an alternative manufacturing process. These companies, while not competitors at present, could enter the nanocrystalline materials market and compete with Nanophase in the future. Plasma Quench Technologies is an example. This company, which holds a process patent, recently spun out two small development companies, NanoBlok and Idaho Titanium Technologies, to produce titanium powders using the company's patented plasma quench manufacturing process.

Finally, Altair Nanotechnologies is an emerging competitor that has a natural resource position in titanium mineral deposits. Altair is developing the technology to produce nanoparticles such as titanium dioxide in commercial quantities. The company is completing a manufacturing plant and offering its products for sale on an Internet Web site. (www.altairtechnologies.com)

Recent Developments

As the U.S. economy dramatically slowed during 2001, companies around the world delayed the receipt of shipments and rescheduled purchase orders for future delivery. Nanophase was impacted by the slowdown, but the company continued to aggressively pursue applications of nanoparticles with selected customers in each of its product markets. Fortunately, the interest level in nanotechnology remained and some customers continued to move forward on the business development projects already initiated. Despite some setbacks, the results of Nanophase's R&D and intensified business development activities slowly began to show results.

April 24, 2002

On April 24, Joseph Cross, President and Chief Executive Officer, offered some observations about the position of the company:

> Cross said that the company entered 2002 with a wider array of improved technology applications tools than it entered 2001 with, and has significantly increased momentum in business development in several markets. "The improvement in our core PVS Technology, commercialization of our new NanoArc Synthesis (TM) process technology, and multiple

application developments during the last half of 2001 and this far into 2002, provide an integrated platform of nanotechnologies that should allow the company to engineer solutions across more markets," explained Cross. (Nanophase Technologies Corporation, Press Release, April 24, 2002)

May 29, 2002

Nanophase completed a private placement of 1.37 million newly issued shares of common stock for a gross equity investment of $6.85 million. Nanophase plans to use the net proceeds to fund the continued development and capacity expansion of its NanoArc Synthesis (TM) process technology, expand marketing and business development activities, increase process capability and capacity in the PVS process and for general corporate purposes. (Nanophase Technologies Corporation, Press Release, May 29, 2002)

June 26, 2002

Nanophase announced a strategic alliance with Rodel, Inc., a part of the Rohm and Haas Electronic Materials Group. Rodel is a global leader in polishing technology for semiconductors, silicon wafers and electronic storage materials. The company will combine its patented technology with Nanophase's new nanoparticle technology to develop and market new polishing products for the semiconductor industry. The alliance is a five-year partnership and supply agreement with appreciable revenues targeted for 2003 and a planned ramp in volume through 2005 and beyond. Nanophase believes that the revenue opportunities approach the size of the Company's personal care and sunscreen markets. Rodel, headquartered in Phoenix, Arizona, has operations throughout the United States, Asia and Europe. (Nanophase Technologies Corporation, Press Releases, June 26 and June 28, 2002)

July 24, 2002

Nanophase announced financial results for the first two quarters of 2002. Revenues were $3.07 million compared with first half 2001 revenues of $2.12 million for a revenue growth of 45% year-over-year. Gross margin for the first half of 2002 averaged a positive 12% of revenues versus the annual 2001 average of a negative 21%. The company reported a net loss for the first half of 2002 of $2.72 million, or $0.20 per share, compared with a net loss for the first half of 2001 of $2.38 million, or $0.18 per share. Appendix Table 5 shows the comparative results for the first two quarters of operations.

Commenting on the balance of 2002, President Cross noted:

> While we are somewhat concerned with general market conditions and the normal market slowness that we expect during the summer, we remain cautiously positive about 2002. Based on information from current and prospective customers, we currently believe additional orders will be received during July through September toward our annual revenue target. Although orders are always subject to cancellation or change, and these estimates are based on various product mix, pricing, and other normal assumptions, we are maintaining our 2002 revenue target of $7.00 million or an anticipated revenue growth of approximately 75% compared to 2001. (Nanophase Technologies Corporation, Press Release, July 24, 2002)

Synopsis

The 2001 business year had proven to be difficult for Nanophase. The economic recession in the manufacturing sector of the economy had impacted the company's primary customer base; the manufacturing firms using nanomaterials in their processes and products. While interest continued to remain strong in the potential of nanotechnology, it was still difficult to stimulate interest among prospective customers who were also facing economic challenges and declining business activity. Finally, as the third quarter of 2002 rolled in, a slowly improving economic environment was on the horizon. Maybe 2002 and the years that followed would be the breakout years management was planning for.

APPENDIX TABLE 1 **Statements of Operations (Years ended December 31)**

Source: Nanophase Technologies Corporation, 2001 Annual Report.

	2000	2001
Revenue		
Product revenue	$ 3,824,159	$ 3,650,914
Other revenue	449,194	388,555
Total revenue	4,273,353	4,039,469
Operating Expense		
Cost of revenue	4,754,485	4,890,697
R&D expense	1,837,036	1,601,671
Selling, general and administrative expense	3,388,758	3,798,543
Total operating expense	9,980,279	10,290,911
Loss from operations	(5,706,926)	(6,251,442)
Interest income	1,188,599	511,199
Loss before provision for income taxes	(4,518,327)	(5,740,243)
Provision for income taxes	—	—
Net loss	$(4,518,327)	$(5,740,243)
Net loss per share	$ (0.34)	$ (0.42)
Common shares outstanding	13,390,741	13,667,062

APPENDIX TABLE 2   Balance Sheets (Years ended December 31)

Source: Nanophase Technologies Corporation, 2001 Annual Report.

	2000	2001
Assets		
Current Assets:		
Cash and cash equivalents	$ 473,036	$ 582,579
Investments	16,831,721	6,842,956
Accounts receivable	1,238,334	1,112,952
Other receivables, net	144,818	67,449
Inventories, net	892,674	956,268
Prepaid expenses and other current assets	770,200	381,696
Total current assets	20,350,783	9,943,900
Equipment and leasehold improvements, net	3,266,245	8,914,745
Other assets, net	213,135	325,743
Total Assets	$23,830,163	$19,184,388
Liabilities and Stockholders Equity		
Current Liabilities		
Current portion of long-term debts	$ 285,316	$ 714,135
Current portion of capital lease obligations		48,352
Accounts Payable	824,338	1,233,466
Accrued Expenses	884,780	732,427
Total Current Liabilities	1,994,434	2,728,380
Long-term debt	827,984	758,490
Long-term portion of capital lease obligations		53,900
Stockholders' equity		
Preferred stock, $.01 par value; 24,088 authorized and none issued	—	—
Common stock, $.01 par value; 25,000,000 shares authorized and 13,593,914 shares issued and outstanding at December 31, 2000; 12,764,058 shares issued and outstanding at December 31, 1999	135,939	137,059
Additional paid-in capital	49,885,751	50,260,747
Accumulated deficit	(29,013,945)	(34,754,188)
Total stockholders' equity	21,007,745	15,643,618
Total liabilities and stockholders' equity	$23,830,163	$19,184,388

APPENDIX TABLE 3   Nanocrystalline Materials (Nanoparticles)

Source: SEC from 10-K. 2001.

Nanocrystalline materials generally are made of particles that are less than 100 nanometers (billionths of a meter) in diameter. They contain only 1,000s or 10,000s of atoms, rather than the millions or billions of atoms found in larger size particles. The properties of nanocrystalline materials depend upon the composition, size, shape, structure, and surface of the individual particles. Nanophase's methods for engineering and manufacturing nanocrystalline materials results in particles with a controlled size and shape, and surface characteristics that behave differently from conventionally produced larger-sized materials.

APPENDIX TABLE 4   Biographical Profile of Joseph E. Cross, Chief Executive Officer

Source: The Wall Street Transcript, January 22, 2001.

Joseph E. Cross is CEO of Nanophase Technologies Corporation. Mr. Cross has been a Director since November 1998 when he joined Nanophase as President and Chief Operating Officer. He was promoted to Chief Executive Officer in December 1998. From 1993–1998, Mr. Cross served as President and CEO of APTECH, Inc, an original equipment manufacturer of metering and control devices for the utility industry and as President of Aegis Technologies, an interactive telecommunications company. He holds a BS in Chemistry and attended the MBA program at Southwest Missouri University. He brings a background of successfully directing several high-technology start-ups, rapid growth and turnaround operations.

APPENDIX TABLE 5   Statements of Operations (Six months ended June 30)

Source: Nanophase Technologies Corporation, Press Release, July 24, 2002.

	June 30, 2001	June 30, 2002
Revenue		
Product revenue	$ 1,937,489	$ 2,829,773
Other revenue	183,815	239,755
Total revenue	2,121,304	3,069,528
Operating Expense		
Cost of revenue	1,857,122	2,696,720
R&D expense	800,189	1,003,726
Selling, general and administrative, expense	2,226,949	2,091,319
Total operating expense	4,884,260	5,791,765
Loss from operations	(2,762,956)	(2,722,237)
Interest Income	416,616	61,177
Interest Expense	(17,664)	(56,282)
Other, net	(12,000)	(50)
Loss before provision for income taxes	(2,376,004)	(2,717,392)
Provision for income taxes	(30,000)	(30,000)
Net loss	(2,406,004)	(2,747,392)
Net loss per share	$ (0.18)	$ (0.20)
Common shares outstanding	13,628,562	13,980,694

References

Nanophase Technologies Corporation—Press Releases

Nanophase Announces Second Quarter and First Half 2002 Results, July 24, 2002. PRNewswire.

Nanophase Technologies Provides Additional Information at Annual Shareholder Meeting, June 28, 2002. PRNewswire.

Rodel Partners with Nanophase Technologies to Develop and Market Nanoparticles in CMP Slurries for Semiconductor Applications, June 26, 2002. PRNewswire.

Nanophase Technologies Completes Private Equity Financing, May 29, 2002. PRNewswire.

Nanophase Technologies Announces First Quarter 2002 Results, April 24, 2002. PRNewswire.

Nanophase Receives Order for Ultrafine Optical Polishing Application, February 21, 2002. PRNewswire.

Nanophase Technologies Announces Fourth Quarter and 2001 Results, February 20, 2002. PRNewswire.

Nanophase Announces Temporary Hourly Manufacturing Furlough, November 14, 2001. PRNewswire.

Nanophase Technologies Announces Third Quarter 2001 Results, October 25, 2001. PRNewswire.

Nanophase Technologies Announces Capital Investment, December 8, 2000. PRNewswire.

Nanophase Technologies Increases Sales Representation, November 27, 2000. PRNewswire.

Experts From Nanophase Elaborate on New Technology Opportunities, October 31, 2000. PRNewswire.

Online Magazine and Newspaper Articles

Spurgeon, Brad, "Nanotechnology Firms Start Small in Building Big Future," January 29, 2001. *International Herald Tribune.* www.iht.com.

CEO Interview with Joseph E. Cross, January 22, 2001. Reprinted from The Wall Street Transcript. Roco, Mihail C. "A Frontier for Engineering," January, 2001. www.memagazine.org. Stebbins, John, "Nanophase Expects to Turn Tiniest Particles into Bigger Profits," November 5, 2000. www.bloomberg.com

Transcripts of On-line Conference Calls, Analyst Presentations and Personal Interviews

An Interview with Joseph Cross, President and CEO of Nanophase Technologies Corporation, January 2002. www.nanophase.com.

Fourth Quarter Conference Call, February 21, 2002. www.nanophase.com Analyst Presentation, 2000. www.nanophase.com.

CNBC/Dow Jones Business Video, February 9, 1999.

SEC Documents

SEC form 10-K, 2002.
SEC form 10-Q, May 15, 2002.
SEC form 10-K, 2001.
SEC form 10-K, 2000.
SEC form 10-K405, 1997.

Annual Reports

Nanophase Technologies Corporation, 2001 Annual Report.
Nanophase Technologies Corporation, 2000 Annual Report.

Web Sites

www.altairtechnologies.com
www.argonide.com
www.ltyr.com
www.nano.gov
www.nanomat.com
www.nanophase.com
www.nanopowders.com
www.nanopowderenterprises.com
www.nanosourcetech.com
www.nanotechinvesting.com
www.oxonica.com
www.plasmachem.de
www.talmaterials.com

Case 6-20
Hong Kong Disneyland

IVEY

Richard Ivey School of Business
The University of Western Ontario

September 12, 2006, marked the one-year anniversary of the opening of Hong Kong Disneyland (HKD). Amid the hoopla and celebrations, media experts were reflecting on the high points and low points of HKD's first year of operations, including several controversies) that had generate some negative publicity.

At a press conference and interview to discuss the first year of operation, Bill Ernest, HKD's executive vice-president, acknowledged that the park had learnt a lot from its experiences and that the problems had made it stronger. Ernest also announced that HKD attendance for the year had been "well over" five million visitors. Still, this figure was short of the 5.6 million visitors that had earlier been projected by park officials. Ernest stated that the park was on sound financial footing but would not release the details.[1] He also announced the appointment of two non-executive directors Payson Cha Mou-sing, managing director of HKR International, and Philip Chen Nan-lok of Cathay Pacific would be joining the board of directors in a move calculated to counter charges of a lack transparency. The criticisms were, in part, coming from members of the Hong Kong Legislative Council as HKD was 57 percent owned by the Hong Kong Government which had invested HK$23 billion.[2]

Michael N. Young and Donald Liu wrote this case solely to provide material for class discussion. The authors do not intend to illustrate either effective or ineffective handling of a managerial situation. The authors may have disguised certain names and other identifying information to protect confidentiality.

Ivey Management Services prohibits any form of reproduction, storage or transmittal without its written permission. Reproduction of this material is not covered under authorization by any reproduction rights organization. To order copies or request permission to reproduce materials, contact Ivey Publishing, Ivey Management Services, c/o Richard Ivey school of Business, The University of Western Ontario, London, Ontario, Canada, N6A 3K7; phone (519) 661–3208; fax (519) 661–3882; e-mail cases@ivey.uwo.ca.

Copyright © 2007, Ivey Management Services Version: (A) 2007–08–27

[1] Linda Choy and Dennis Eng, "5 Million Visit Disney Park, Short of Target" *South China Morning Post,* electronic edition, September 5, 2006, available at http://scmp.com, accessed December 3, 2006.
[2] In 2006, the Hong Kong dollar was pegged to the U.S. dollar at approximately US$1 = HK$7.80.

Since plans for the-high-profile HKD project were first announced, there had been criticisms of a lack of transparency from Hong Kong government officials, the Consumer Council and members of the public. The dissatisfaction was reflected in a survey conducted by Hong Kong Polytechnic University in March 2006.[3] Although 56 percent of the 524 respondents believed the government's HK$13.6 billion (about US$1.74 billion) investment to be of a "fair" value, 70 percent of respondents had a negative impression of the public investment in HKD. This response was a considerably more pessimistic result than previous surveys. It was in the interests of HKD to turn this situation around.

HKD was the third park that Disney had opened outside of the United States, following the Tokyo Disney Resort and Disneyland Resort Paris. The Tokyo Disney Resort was the most successful of all of the Disney parks worldwide, and indeed one of the most successful theme parks in the world; the Disneyland Paris Resort was much less successful.[4] Pundits had begun to wonder whether the outcome of HKD would more closely resemble that of its successful Far Eastern Japanese cousin or whether it would more closely resemble that of the French park. That outcome depended in part on how well Disney would be able to translate its strategic assets, such as its products, practices and ideologies, to the Chinese context.

[3]May Chan, "Disneyland's Image Has Soured Since Its Opening," *South China Morning Post,* p. CITY3.
[4]Mary Yoko Brannen, "When Mickey Loses Face: Recontextualization, Semantic Fit, and the Semiotics of Foreignness," *Academy of Management Review.* October 2004, pp. 593–616.

Company Background

The Walt Disney Company (Disney) was founded in 1923, and was committed to delivering quality entertainment experiences for people of all ages. As a global entertainment empire, the company leveraged its amazing heritage of creativity, fantasy and imagination established by its founder, Walt Disney. By 2006, Disney's business portfolio consisted of four major segments: Studio Entertainment, Parks and Resorts, Consumer Products and Media Networks. Exhibit 1 summarizes the details of the company's holdings and their respective financial performance in 2005.

Other Disney Parks and Resorts

Disney opened the first Disneyland, Disneyland Resort, at Anaheim, California, in July 1955. The company's second theme park, Walt Disney World Resort, was opened at Lake Buena Vista, Florida, in 1971. After the establishment of these two large theme parks in the United States, Disney sought to expand internationally. Disney's international expansion strategy was straightforward consisting of "bringing the original Disneyland model to a new territory, and then if feasible, adding a specialty theme park."[5] Tokyo Disney Resort was Disney's first attempt at executing this strategy.

Tokyo Disney Resort

Disney opened its first non-US. park in Tokyo, Japan, in 1983. The scope and thematic foundation of the Tokyo park was modeled after the Disney parks in

[5]Sara Bakhshian, "The Offspring", *Amusement Business.* May 2005, pp. 20–21.

EXHIBIT 1 **Current Holdings of the Walt Disney Company**

Source: Annual Report 2005, The Walt Disney Company.

Business Segments	Performance (2005)
Studio Entertainment	This segment had the greatest decrease of 69%, which the company attributed to the overall decline in unit sales in worldwide home entertainment and at Miramax
Consumer Products	This division reported decrease in operating income of 3% due to lower revenue generated from the sales of Disney goods and merchandise
Media Networks	The higher rates paid by cable operators for ESPN and the Disney Channels and higher advertising revenue at ESPN and ABC were the primary factors driving the 27% growth in revenue at the media network unit.
Parks & Resorts	The Parks and Resorts division also enjoyed a 5% increase in revenue, largely due to the higher occupancy at the resorts, theme park attendance, and guest expenditure.

California and Florida. The US$1.4 billion cost to develop Tokyo Disney Resort was financed solely by Oriental Land Co., a land-reclamation company formed under a joint-venture agreement between Mitsui Real Estate Development Co. and Keisei Electric Railway Co.[6] Disney did not assume any ownership of Tokyo Disney Resort to minimize risks. The contract signed in 1979 spelled out Oriental Land as the owner and licensee, whereas Disney was designated as the designer and licensor. Although Disney received a US$100 million royalty every year, this amount was less than would have been the case if Disney were the sole owner or even a co-owner of Tokyo Disney Resort. By 2006, the 23-year-old Tokyo Disney Resort, along with the addition of Tokyo Disney Sea, at an additional cost of US$3 billion in 2000[7] was a huge success, with a combined annual attendance of more than 25 million visitors and an operating income of ¥28,957 million (about US$245.47 million) generated in 2005 alone.[8]

Tokyo Disney Resort was well received by the Japanese, owing in part to the Japanese interest in Western cultures and the Asian love of fantasy and costume. The secret underlying this success was to provide the visitors with "a slice of unadulterated Disney-style Americana," proclaimed Toshio Kagami, president of Oriental Land Co. Tokyo Disney Resort had attracted wide support from the local Japanese, who accounted for more than 95 percent of the annual attendance. Moreover, around 15 percent of the total visitors had visited the park 30 times or more, making Tokyo Disney Resort one of the world's most popular theme parks in terms of annual attendance.[9] The Tokyo Disney Resort also had the highest sales of souvenirs of all the Disney land resorts, in part, because it was the only Disney property to give special admission just for the purpose of purchasing souvenirs.

Disneyland Resort Paris

France was the largest consumer of Disney products outside the United States, particularly in the area of publications, such as comic books.[10] However, this status did not provide much help to Disneyland Resort Paris (formerly named Euro Disney), Disney's second attempt at international expansion. Disneyland Resort Paris came into operation in 1992, after two-and-a-half years of negotiations with the French Government. Disney was determined to avoid the mistake of forgoing majority ownership and profits as had been the case with Tokyo Disney Resort. Thus, Disney became one of the partners in this project. Under the initial financial arrangement, Disney had a 49 percent stake in the project. The French Government provided cash and loans of US$770 million interest rates below the market rates, and financed the majority of the US$400 million infrastructure.

However, cost overruns pushed overall construction costs to US$5 billion—five times the previous estimate of US$1 billion. This increase was due to alterations in design and construction plans. This higher cost, coupled with the theme park's mediocre performance during its initial years of operation and other factors, caused the park severe difficulties between 1992 and 1994. The park did not report a profit until 1995, which was largely due to a reaction of interest costs from US$265 million to US$93 million and the rigorous financial re-engineering efforts in late 1994.[11]

Despite poor results between 1995 and 2001, Disney added a new park, Walt Disney Studios, which brought Hollywood-themed attractions to the French park. At its opening in 2004, the second park attracted only 2.2 million visitors, 5.8 million short of its original projections. At the end of the fiscal year on September 30, 2004, Disneyland Resort Paris announced a loss of €145.2 million (about US$190 million).[12]

Part of the problem with the Paris Resort was the resistance by the French to what they considered America cultural imperialism. French cultural critics claimed that Disney would be a "cultural Chernobyl," and some stated publicly a desire for the park's failure. For example, critic Stephen Bayley wrote:

> The Old World is presented with all the confident big ticket flimflam of painstaking fakery that this bizarre campaign of reverse-engineered cultural imperialism represents. I like to think that by the turn of the

[6]Eva Liu and Elyssa Wong, "Information Note: Tokyo Disneyland: Some Basic Facts," *Research and Library Services Division of the Legislative Council Secretariat*, Hong Kong, 1999, retrieved March 10, 2006 from www.legco.gov.hk/yr99-0/english/sec/library/990in02.pdf.
[7]Ibid.
[8]Oriental Land Co., *2005 Annual Report*, retrieved March 10, 2006 from http://olc.netir-wsp.com/medias/1656486483_OLCAR2005final.pdf.
[9]James Zoltak, "Lots of Walks in the Parks the Past Year," *Amusement Business*. December 2004, pp. 6–7.

[10]Mary Yoko Brannen, "When Mickey Loses Face: Recontextualization, Semantic Fit, and the Semiotics of Foreignness," *Academy of Management Review*. October 2004, pp. 593–616.
[11]James B. Stewart, *Disney War*. Simon & Schuster, New York, 2005.
[12]Jo Wrighton and Bruce Orwall, "Mutual Attractions: Despite Losses and Bailouts, France Stays Devoted to Disney," *Wall Street Journal*. January 26, 2005, p. A1.

century Euro Disney will have become a deserted city, similar to Angkor Wat [in Cambodia].[13]

Disney had to assure the French government that French would be the primary language spoken within the park. Even the French president, Francois Mitterand, joined in the fray, declining to attend the opening-day ceremony, dismissing the expensive new investment with Gallic indifference as "pas ma tasse de the" ("just not my cup of tea").[14]

Robert Fitzpatrick, the first chairman of the Disneyland Resort Paris, was a French-speaking American who knew Europe quite well, in part because of his French wife. Fitzpatrick did not, however, realize that Disney could not approach France in the same way as it had approached Florida when setting up its second theme park. For example, the recruitment process and training programs for its staff were initially not well-adapted to the French business culture. The 13-page manual specifying the dress code within the theme park was apparently unacceptable to the French; the court had even ruled that imposing such a dress code was against the labour laws.

The miscalculations of cultural differences were found in other operational aspects as well. For instance, Disney's policy of banning the serving of alcoholic beverages in its parks, including in California, Florida and Tokyo, was unsurprisingly extended to France. This restriction outraged the French for whom enjoying wine during lunch and dinner was part of their daily custom. In May 1993, Disney yielded to the external pressure, and altered its policy to permit the serving of wines and beers in the theme park. With the renaming and the retooling of the entire theme park complex to better appeal to European taste, Disneyland Resort Paris finally began to profit in 1995.

Why Such Different Outcomes for Tokyo and Paris?

Why was Disney so successful in Tokyo but largely a failure in Paris? Professor Mary Yoko Brannen maintains that it may in part have been due to the way that Disney's strategic assets—such as products, practices and ideology—were translated to and interpreted in the Japanese and French contexts.[15] According to Brannen, the "Americana" represented by Disney was an asset in Japan, where a trip to Disney was seen as an exotic,

foreign-like experience. However, this association with the pure form of all things American was a liability in France, where it was seen as a form of reverse cultural imperialism. The result was a "lost-in-translation" effect for many of Disney's most valued icons and established business practices. For example, Mickey Mouse was seen as a squeaky-clean all-American boy in the United States, and he was viewed as conservative and reliable enough to sell money market accounts in Japan. However, in France, he was seen as a street-smart detective because of the popularity of a comic book series *Le Journal Mickey*.

Likewise, Disney's service training, human resource management (HRM) practices and training required to achieve the "happiest place on earth" were quite easy to implement in Japan, where such practices represented the cultural norm. In France, however, the same training practices were perceived as invasive and totalitarian. Exhibit 2 summarizes how other strategic assets of Disney were recontextualized to the Japanese and French environments. In 2006, it remained to be seen how Disney's strategic assets would translate to, and be interpreted in, the Chinese culture of Hong Kong, the topic to which we turn next.

Mickey Mouse Goes to China

We know we have an addressable market just crying out for Disney products.

—Andy Bird, Walt Disney International president, discussing China's potential[16]

The Chinese "have heard so much about the parks around the world, and they want to experience the same thing," said Don Robinson, the former managing director of HKD. Chinese consumers wanted to connect with the global popular culture and distance themselves from their previous collective poverty and communist dictate. Kevin Wong, a tourism economist at the Hong Kong Polytechnic University, remarked that the Chinese "want to come to Disney because it is American. The foreignness is part of the appeal." The Chinese needed Disney, and Disney needed China. For example, Ted Parrish, co-manager of the Henssler Equity Fund, an investment fund house, said, "If Disney wants to maintain earnings growth in the high teens going forward, China will be a big source of that."[17]

[13]James B. Stewart, *Disney War.* Simon & Schuster, New York, 2006, p. 128.

[14]Ibid.

[15]Mary Yoko Brannen, "When Mickey Loses Face: Recontextualization, Semantic Fit and the Semiotics of Foreignness," *Academy of Management Review.* October 2004, pp. 593–616.

[16]Jeffrey Ressner and Michael Schuman, "Disney's Great Leap into China." *Time.* July 11, 2005, pp. 52–54.

[17]Paul R. La Monica, "For Disney, It's a Small World after All," *CNNmoney.com,* September 12, 2005, retrieved March 10, 2006 from http://money.cnn.com/2005/09/12/news/fortune 500/hongkongdisney/.

EXHIBIT 2 **How Disney's Assets and Practices Recontextualize to Japan and France**

Source: Mary Yoko Brannen, "When Mickey Loses Face: Recontextualization, Semantic Fit and the Semiotics of Foreignness." *Academy of Management Review.* October 2004, p. 593.

Products	United States	Japan	France
Mickey Mouse	Squeaky-clean, all-American boy representing wholesome American values	Safe and reliable (used to sell money market accounts.)	Cunning, street-smart detective epitomized in *Le Journal Mickey*—squeaky clean version is boring
Cowboy	Rugged, self-reliant individualist	Quintessential team player	Carefree, somewhat dim-witted anti-establishment individual
Souvenirs	Fun, part of the experience	Legitimism mementos that fit into the formalized system of gift giving, known as sembetsu	Tacky, waste of money
Practices			
Service	Hypernormal	Cultural norm	Abnormal
Orientation	Hypernormal	Cultural norm	Invasive/illegal
Personnel Management Training	Hypernormal	Cultural norm	Totalitarian
Ideologies			
Disneyland	Modernist theme -fun, clean, wholesome entertainment	Translated modernist theme -fun, clean, safe foreign vacation	Postmodernist theme -resistance to Disney's meta narrative
Foreignness	• Fantasized European roots • Marginalized native and minority others	• Keeping the U.S. exotic • Marginalizing the Asian other	• Politicized repatriation • Schizophrenic relationship with the U.S.

Because the Chinese economy was booming, Disney thought it would be a good time to set up a new theme park there. China's infrastructure was still substandard by work-standards. In addition, the Chinese currency, the renminbi, was not fully convertible. These and, other factors increased the attractiveness of Hong Kong—a Special Administrative Region of China since the handover of sovereignty from the United Kingdom in 1997. Hong Kong had world-class infrastructure and a reputation as an international financial center. Most importantly, Hong Kong had always been a gateway to China. These factors gave Hong Kong an edge as a location for Disney's third international theme park.

The Hong Kong Tourism Industry

Hong Kong, with its unusual blend of East and West, of Chinese roots and British colonial heritage, of ultramodern sophistication and ancient traditions, is one of the most diverse and exciting cities in the world. It is an international city brimming with energy and dynamism yet also a place where peace and tranquility are easily found.[18]

Tourism was one of the major pillars of the Hong Kong economy. In 2005, the total number of visitors was more than 23 million, a new record and approximately a 7.1 percent increase over 2004 (see Exhibit 3). Visitors came from all over the world including Taiwan, America, Africa, the Middle East and Macao (see Exhibit 4). Mainland China was the biggest source of visitors, accounting for 53.7 percent of the total in 2005.[19] The dominance of this group

[18]Hong Kong Tourism Board, www.discoverhongkong.com, accessed August 17, 2007.
[19]Hong Kong Census & Statistics Department, "Hong Kong Monthly Digest of Statistics," Hong Kong Census & Statistics Department, Hong Kong, March 2006.

EXHIBIT 3
**Annual Visitor
Arrivals in
Hong Kong**

Source: Hong Kong
Tourism Board (2006).

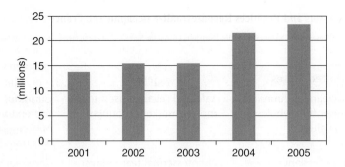

EXHIBIT 4
**Visitor Arrivals by
Country/Territory
of Residence**

Source: Hong Kong
Monthly Digest of Statistics
(March 2006).

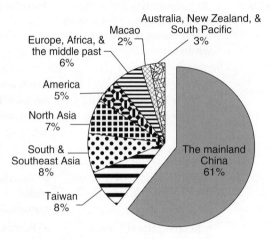

was, in part, supported by the Individual Travel
Scheme[20] introduced in 2003.

Local Attractions

Popular tourist attractions in Hong Kong included,
but were not limited to, Victoria Peak, Repulse Bay,
open-air markets and Ocean Park. Hong Kong's colonial heritage provided several attractions, such as
Cenotaph, Statue Square and the Government House.
Traditional Chinese festivals, such as Tin Hau Festival, Cheung Chau Bun Festival and Temple Fair,
added local flavor. Visitors often took part in the celebration of these annual festive events during their

---

[20]The Individual Travel Scheme was a policy that permitted
urban residents from selected cities in Mainland China to apply
for visas from the Public Security Department to visit Hong
Kong. In 2006, the Scheme covered 38 mainland cities. Until
the implementation of this policy, mainlanders could only visit
Hong Kong through business or travel groups.

stay. The Hong Kong Tourism Board had designated
2006 as "Discover Hong Kong Year" to attract more
travelers and encourage them to extend their stay.
Furthermore, the Asia World-Expo opened in early
2006, and it was expected to attract more business
travelers. Other initiatives included a sky rail to
the world's largest sitting Buddha statue and Hong
Kong Wetland Park. In addition, the Dr. Sun Yat-sen
Museum was being renovated and was scheduled to
reopen in early 2007.

Ocean Park

Ocean Park was another prime attraction in Hong Kong
and was well-recognized worldwide. Prior to Disney's
entry, Ocean Park occupied a quasi-monopoly position
as the only local theme park. Founded in 1977, Ocean
Park was located near Hong Kong's Central district, the
heart of the bustling city. Ocean Park had an annual
attendance of more than four million visitors and had
been ranked recently as one of the top 10 amusement

parks in the world by *Forbes* magazine.[21] Ocean Park sought to blend entertainment with educational elements, thus offering the dual experience for guests termed as "edutainment."

For the 2004/05 fiscal year, Ocean Park's gross revenue was HK$684 million (U$87.8 million), which represented a 12 percent increase over the previous year. The surplus of HK$119.5 million (US$15.3 million) was the best performance ever achieved at the Park.[22] In 2006, Ocean Park received necessary financing for a HK$5.55 billion (about US$0.71 billion) makeover, including a government-guaranteed portion of HK$1.39 billion (about US$0.18 billion).[23] Ocean Park's redevelopment was expected to bring HK$23 billion (about US$2.95 Billion) to HK$28 billion (about US$3.59 billion) over the first 20 years of operation, with visitors projected to increase to more than five million annually by 2011.

Hong Kong's Very Own Disneyland

Hong Kong Disneyland will be the flagship for the Disney brand in this huge and growing country and play a pivotal role helping to bring entertainment to this… part of the world.… It is our first destination opening in a market where [there] isn't a very deep knowledge of Disney culture and stories.

> —Jay Rasulo, chairman of Walt Disney Parks and Resorts[24]

Disney initiated a conversation with the Hong Kong Special Administrative Region (SAR) government in August 1998 about the possibility of setting up a Disney theme park. To avoid a situation like the one encountered by Disneyland Resort Paris, Disney initially planned to simply run the park on a management fee and licensing contract basis. After extended talks and negotiations, however, Disney agreed to take an ownership stake as well.

HKD was expected to bring a number of economic benefits to Hong Kong. First, approximately 18,400 jobs would be created directly or indirectly at HKD's opening, and this number was expected to increase to 35,800 in 20 years. Plus, 3.4 million visitors, mainly from Hong Kong and Mainland China, would be attracted to the park, and attendance was projected to increase to 7.3 million after 15 years. The additional spending by tourists would amount to HK$8.3 billion (about US$1.1 million) in Year 1, rising to HK$16.8 billion (about US$2.2 billion) annually by Year 20 and beyond. There would be "soft" benefits as well, such as with the acquisition of first-class technological innovations and facilities and gaining hands-on experience with quality service training. Over a period of 40 years, it was forecast that HKD would generate an economic benefit equivalent to HK$148 billion (about US$19 billion). This forecast sounded promising during the 1998/99 period when negotiations were taking place, when Hong Kong was still feeling the effects of the 1997 Asian financial crisis.

The Concluded Deal

> This is a happy marriage between a world-class tourism attraction and a world-class tourist destination. We hope that Hong Kong Disneyland will not just bring us more tourists, but also wholesome quality entertainment for local families as well.[25]

After a year of negotiations, the final contract was signed in December of 1999. The theme park and hotels would cost US$1.8 billion to construct over six years. In addition, US$1.7 billion would be spent for land reclamation as no other suitable location was available in the densely populated territory. The park would be situated on Penny's Bay of Lantau Island, the largest of Hong Kong's outlying islands. The Hong Kong Government and Disney would invest US$416 million, and US$ 314 million, respectively. In return, Disney held a 43 percent stake in HKD, and the government held the (remaining 57 percent, which could later be increased to 73 percent by converting subordinate shares further US$1.1 billion was put up in the form of government and commercial loans.

[21]Norma Connolly, "Top 10 Accolade a Boost to Ocean Park." *South China Morning Post,* electronic edition, June 3, 2006, http://www.scmp.com, accessed December 3, 2006.

[22]The Walt Disney Company, *Annual Report. 2005,* retrieved March 10, 2006 from http://corporate. disney. go. com/investors/annual_reports/2005/index.html.

[23]Charis Yau, "Ocean Park Eyes $4.1B Loan to Finance Makeover," *South China Morning Post.* April 13, 2006, p. BIZ1, retrieved May 3, 2006 from WiseNews Database.

[24]Greg Hernandez, "Mickey Gains Recognition in Hong Kong." *Knight Ridder/Tribune Business News,* September 8, 2005, p. 1, retrieved March 10, 2006 from Lexis-Nexis Academic Universe Database.

[25]Stephen Ip, Hong Kong secretary for Economic Services, press release from Hong Kong government, "Hong Kong Disneyland Final Agreement Signed," www.info.gov.hk/gia/general/99912/10/1210286.htm, accessed August 17, 2007.

Hong Kong International Theme Park Limited (HKITP), the joint venture formed between Disney and the Hong Kong Government in December 1999, oversaw the construction and running of HKD. While the government developed the infrastructure, Disney provided master planning, real estate development, attraction and show design, engineering support, production support, project management and other development services. Disney also set up a wholly owned subsidiary, Hong Kong Disneyland Management Limited to manage HKD on behalf of HKITP.

A Rocky Start

There was a palpable excitement when the new Disneyland theme opened, but the skeptics and critics were not so easily impressed. Press reports described the first few months as a "rocky start." Some locals called the park's management policies "absurd."[26]

Four weeks prior to the official opening, HKD invited 30,000 selected individuals per day to visit the park to test the rides and other attractions. During the trial period, a thick haze hovered over the whole park, a result of the air pollutants passing down from Mainland China. This problem was well-recognized by Hong Kong authorities and was particularly acute during low wind periods, which trapped all of Hong Kong in smog.[27] Smog virtually engulfed Sleeping Beauty's Castle.

The first problem noticed was that the capacity limit of 30,000 visitors may have been too high. For example, on September 4, 2005, approximately 29,000 local visitors went to the park. The average queuing time was 45 minutes at the restaurants and more than two hours for the rides. The park faced pressure to lower the daily capacity limit. Instead, the park proposed other measures, such as extending the opening time by an hour and encouraging visits during weekdays by offering discounts, as opposed to reducing the actual limit.[28]

The park faced another problem when inspectors from the Hygiene Department were asked to remove their badges and caps prior to carrying out an official investigation of a food-poisoning case. Park officials later apologized and pledged to operate in compliance with all local regulations and customs. But problems continued. The police could not get into the park—even when deemed when necessary—unless prearranged with the park's security unit.[29]

Operations

Product Offerings

HKD, like its counterparts in the United States Japan and France, symbolized happiness, fantasy and dreams, and sought to offer an unparalleled experience to its visitors. The admission price was initially set at HK$295 (US$38) during the weekdays and HK$350 (US$45) on weekends and peak days, the lowest pricing among the five Disney theme parks. A day pass for a child was HK$250 (US$32), while it was HK$200 (US$27) for seniors aged 65 and above. Tickets were sold primarily via the company's website (http://www.hongkongdisneyland.com), which allowed three-month advance bookings. Tickets were sold through travel agencies. These two measures aimed to control the daily number of visitors and avoiding long queues at the entrance. Only a small portion of ticket were available for walk-in customers.

HKD, like other Disney theme parks, was divided into four parts, including Main Street, U.S.A.; Fantasyland; Adventureland and Tomorrowland. Disney's classic attractions, such as Space Mountain, Mad Hatter Tea Cups and Dumbo, were included in the park. In Main Street, U.S.A., guests could ride a steam train to tour the park. A large part of Fantasyland was the Sleeping Beauty Castle, which included Dumbo and Winnie the Pooh. Guests could find Mickey, Minnie and other popular Disney characters available for photos in the Fantasy Garden, which was unique to HKD. Adventureland was home to Tarzan's tree house, the jungle river cruise and the Festival of the Lion King show. Tomorrowland featured science fiction and space adventures.

To cater to the time-pressed Hong Kong residents, HKD offered a Fastpass ticketing system, which provided a one-hour window to bypass queues for favored rides. Guests preferring an extended stay could check

---

[26]"Mousekeepina." *South China Morning Post.* December 28, 2005, features section, page 12.

[27]Bruce Einhorn, "Disney's Not-so-magic New Kingdom." *Business Week Online.* September 13, 2005, retrieved March 10, 2006 from http://www.businessweek.com/bwdaily/dnflash/sep2005/nf2005/nf20050913_9145_db046.htm?chan=search.

[28]"HK Disneyland Considers Longer Opening Hours to Beat Long Lines." *The Associated Press,* retrieved March 10, 2006, from http://english.sina.eom/taiwan_hk/p/1/2005/0906/44951.html.

[29]Jonathan Hill and Richard Welford, "A Case Study of Disney in Hong Kong." *Corporate Social Responsibility Asia Weekly,* November 16, 2005, retrieved March 10, 2006 from http://www.csr-asia.com/index.php?p=5318.

in to one of the two hotels, HKD Hotel and Disney's Hollywood Hotel, which offered on-site lodging services.

Marketing

HKD collaborated with the Hong Kong Government to jointly promote the theme park. It was estimated that one-third of the visitors would come from Hong Kong, one-third would come from Mainland China and the remaining third would come from Southeast Asian countries.[30] The free-to-air TV program, *The Magical World of Disneyland,* was broadcast in Hong Kong, and could be received in various regions across Southern China. In each episode, famous pop stars from the region (for example, Jacky Cheung, who was also the official ambassador of HKD) would introduce some behind-the-scene stories about HKD, such as interviews with rides designers. Disney believed that the widespread popularity of Jacky Cheung would connect well with the audience in Asia. HKD also launched a special TV channel on local cable TV. This channel included background stories on founder Walt Disney, information about The Walt Disney Company and its evolution, interesting facts about the company's state-of-the-art animated films, and regular updates on the construction progress of the park.

The theme park also introduced a line of Disney-themed apparel at Giordano, a Hong Kong-based clothing retailer with more than 1,500 outlets in Asia, Australia and the Middle Easf.[31] Giordano featured low-price fashionable clothes similar to The Gap in the United States. The Disney line featured adult and children's T-shirts and sweatshirts with popular Disney cartoon characters, such as Mickey Mouse and Nemo. The T-shirts were about HK$80 (US$10) at Giordano much less expensive than comparable items at HKD for HK$380 (US$49).

HKD outsourced part of its marketing effort *Colour Life,* a Guangzhou-based magazine. In September 2005, 100,000 extra copies were printed, featuring the grand opening HKD that month. It was hoped the extra

publicity would increase awareness of the theme park among the-residents of Guangzhou, the major metropolitan area of southern China, just north of Hong Kong. The company also donated 200 HKD umbrellas to key newsstands in Guangzhou to provide even more publicity. In addition, HKD partnered with the Communist Youth, League of China to run special events for children, such as Mickey Mouse drawing contests.

Human Resource Management

The Magical experience of a HKD visit depended upon the quality of service. HKD treated human resource management (HRM) as one of the cornerstones of its competitive advantage. To fill the remaining positions at the park, in April 2005, HKD launched one of the city's largest recruitment events ever. The park screened job candidates according to qualities such as service orientation, language capabilities, passion for excellence and friendliness. Employees were referred to as cast members because "they are always on stage when interacting with guests, and therefore represent a very important element of the show," said Greg Warm, vice-president for HRM at HKD.[32]

In January 2005, HKD sent the first cohort of 500 cultural representatives to Walt Disney World in Orlando for a six-month training program. The cast members would learn about the magical Disney culture and would have a platform to share their Chinese cultural experience with other cast members at Walt Disney World. During their stay at Orlando, the Hong Kong crew was trained according to standards set by The Walt Disney Company worldwide. They also had the opportunity to work in other divisions, including merchandising, food and beverage operations, park operations, custodial services and hotel operations. In addition to training, HKD provided handbooks to each cast member, which literally detailed the regulations from head to toe. For example, male cast members could not have goatees or beards, and female cast members were not allowed to have fingernails longer than six centimeters.

Local Cultural Responsiveness

Given the cultural *faux pas* that occurred with Disneyland Resort Pairs Disney paid special attention to cultural issues pertaining to HKD. Because the prime

[30]Suchat Sritama, "HK Disneyland to Boost Thai Visitor Numbers." *The Nation.* September 13, 2005, retrieved March 10, 2006 from http://www.nationmultimedia.eom/2005/09/13/business/index.php?news=business_18587589.html.

[31]"Hong Kong Disneyland Rolls out Fashions: Hong Kong Disneyland Takes Publicity Blitz to Masses with Fashion Line," *The Associated Press,* retrieved March 10, 2006 from http://abcnews.go.com/Business/wireStory?id=963083&CMP=OTC-RSSFeeds0312, archived at http://news.ewoss.com/articles/D8BFNL1O0.aspx.

[32]Based on: Steven Knipp, "The Magic Kingdom Comes to the Middle Kingdom: What It Took for Hong Kong Disneyland to Finally Open in 2005," *Fun World.* February 2005, retrieved March 10, 2006 from http://www.funworldmagazine.com/2005/february05/features/magic_kingdom/magickingdom.html.

target customer segment was the growing group of affluent Mainland Chinese tourists, *feng shui*[33] masters were consulted for advice on the park layout and design. New constructions often began with a traditional good-luck ceremony featuring a carved suckling pig.[34] One of the main ballrooms was constructed to be 888 square meters since eight was an auspicious number in Chinese culture, signifying good fortune. The hotels deliberately skipped the fourth floor because the Chinese associated four with bad luck. Other finer details were details were incorporates throughout the park to better fit the local culture. For example, theme park sold mooncakes during the Chinese Mid-Autumn Festival. Phyllis Wong, the merchandising director, stated that green hats were not sold at the park because they were a symbol of a wife's infidelity in Chinese culture.[35]

Cast members at HKD were expected to converse proficiently in English, Cantonese and Mandarin, and signs in the park were written in both Chinese and English. Another local adaptation was the squat toilets, which were popular throughout China. "These toilets benefit those Mainland Chinese who prefer squatting and those who don't want to see muddy footprints on toilet seats," commented a Hong Kong visitor.[36]

Restaurants offered a wide variety of food, ranging from American-style burgers and French fries to Chinese dim sum and sweet and sour pork. Although some animal activists groups initially protested, shark fin soup was on the menu as "it is what the locals see as appropriate," said Esther Wong, a spokeswoman of HKD.[37]

[33]Feng shui is the Chinese art and practice of positioning objects in accordance to the patterns of yin and yang, and in flow with chi, the energy source that resides in all matter.
[34]Jeffrey Ressner and Michael Schuman, "Disney's Great Leap into China." *Time.* July 11, 2005, pp. 52–54.
[35]"Disney Uses Feng Shui to Build Mickey's New Kingdom in Hong Kong." *The Associated Press,* retrieved March 10, 2006 from http://english.sina. com/taiwan_hk/1/2005/0907/45097 .html.
[36]"Disneyland with Chinese Characteristics." *Letters from China: China and Independent Travel.* July 22, 2005, retrieved March 10, 2006 from http://voyage.typepad.com/china/2005/ 07/disneyland_with.html.
[37]"HK Disneyland Draws Fire over Soup," *Chinadaily.com.cn.* May 24, 2005, retrieved March 10, 2006 from http://www .chinadaily.com.cn/english/doc/2005-05/24/content_445139 .htm.

Negative Publicity

The Lunar New Year Holiday Fiasco

The park faced several public relations problems during its first year of operations, none bigger than that which occurred during the popular Chinese Lunar New Year holiday period. HKD had introduced a new, discounted, one-day ticket that could be used at any time during a given six-month period. These tickets could not be used on "special days" when the park anticipated an influx of visitors. The first period of special days was the Lunar New Year holidays.[38] In Hong Kong, the 2006 Lunar New Year period started on January 28 (Saturday) and ended on January 31 (Tuesday). However, HKD failed to take into account that the following two days (i.e. February 1 and 2) were still public holidays in Mainland China. Mainland tour agencies had purchased large batches of the discounted tickets and escorted large groups of Mainland tourists to HKD during those two days.

This influx created a major problem for HKD as thousands of mainland tourists clinching their tickets swarmed the front gates of the park. The park could not accommodate the additional guests, and the steel gates were locked shut. Many of these Mainland Chinese tourists had saved all year for this trip and had accompanied their extended families to Hong Kong to experience the Disney magic. Needless to say, they were understandably upset. The crowd turned into an angry mob and brandishing their tickets, started shouting profanities and hurling objects at the police and security guards. Some tourists even tried to climb over the gates, which were topped with sharp spikes. The front page of the local paper the next morning showed a Mainland tourist throwing a young child over the closed gates to his parents who had managed to get inside the park. As one disgruntled customer commented from that fateful day, "I won't come again, even if I am paid to."[39]

To China observers, the behavior was not entirely surprising, given that inland Chinese consumers can be very vocal when they are dissatisfied with a product or service. For example, in 2001, the dissatisfied owner of a

[38]The Lunar New Year Holiday, or Chinese New Year, was one of the most important traditional Chinese festivals. A series of celebrations usually took place during the period, starting from the first day of the first month on the Chinese calendar.
[39]Helen Wu, "Queues Take the Magic out of a Crowded Kingdom." *South China Morning Post.* February 4 2006, p. CITY1.

Mercedes Benz SLK230 had his car towed to the center of town by a pair of oxen, where workers with sledge-hammers demolished the car in front of media crews, creating a publicity nightmare for DaimlerChrysler.[40]

There was plenty of finger-pointing for the fiasco Fengtan Peiling, the commissioner of the Hong Kong Consumer Council, claimed that Disney had failed to learn about the cultural traditions and consumption habits of Chinese people. Wang Shuxin, from the Shenzhen Tourism Tour Group Centre, blamed HKD of falsely accusing the travel agents for the predicament. His center, which oversaw Mainland tourists traveling to Hong Kong had more than claims for compensation through travel agencies. Some agencies wanted to sue HKD for a possible breach of contractual terms.[41] Soon afterwards, the Hong Kong government released a statement requesting the park to improve its ticketing and guest-entry procedures. Bill Ernest, HKD's executive vice-president, later apologized, stating "every market has unique dynamics that must be taken into consideration and must be learned over time," and that Disney was still learning.[42]

Customer Complaints

Customers also complained that the park was too small and that it had too few Hong Kong-themed attractions. HKD had only 22 attractions, 18 fewer than the other Disney theme parks. Other guests claimed that they were mistreated during their stay at the park. Some guests even planned to take legal action against HKD. For example, a park visitor from Singapore alleged negligence and discrimination of Disney's staff because they refused to call an ambulance for her mother who later died of heart failure at an HKD hotel. A spokesperson for HKD denied the allegations, saying that the staff handled the case in the "most appropriate" manner.[43] In another case, a guest and his daughter were in a bakery shop on Main Street, U.S.A. when they were hit by falling debris. The guest stated "the park does not

seem to regard customers' safety as its priority" and threatened to take legal action against HKD, adding that they tried to placate him with a Winnie the Pooh for his daughter.[44]

Working Conditions

The character performers at HKD complained that they were overworked and underpaid. The spokesperson of the staff union stated that workdays of more than 12 hours and inadequate rest breaks had overwhelmed many workers, causing work-related injuries, such as joint and muscles strain. In response, Lauren Jordan, the theme park's vice-president of entertainment, claimed that "there are a few cast members who have found this work to be less rewarding than others and perhaps more physically challenging than they anticipated."

In addition the character performers, who performed in the daily parade and met visitors, were petitioning for the same salaries as stage performers. The entry salaries for parade performers averaged about HK$9,000 per month (US$1,153) per month compared to about HK$11,000 (US$1,409) for stage performers.[45] In response to the staff's concerns, management announced extended breaks of 40 minutes for every 20-minute session with guests during the hot and humid summer season. Cooling vests, designed for the character performers, were also being tested.

Complaints were not limited to the line staff; there was turnover among the executive staff. As one disgruntled executive complained.

> The American make all the key decision and often the wrong ones. Finance is also king here, and when things go wrong they look for local scapegoats. The mood and morale is very low here. I know a lot of us are actively looking for jobs [and many of us] are totally disillusioned.[46]

HKD'S Response

To combat problems highlighted through the media, such as low park attendance, limited attractions, long queues, disgruntled employees and guests' accounts of rude treatment, HKD implemented several recovery strategies.

[40]"Luxury Car Under Hammer," *Herald Sun.* December 28, 2001, retrieved May 3, 2006 from Lexi-Nexis Academic Universe Database.
[41]Meng Chu, "Disneyland Suffers Crowd Problems in Hong Kong." *Voice.* February 10, 2006, retrieved March 10, 2006 from http://bJtoday.ynet.com/article.jsp?oid=7653476.
[42]"HK Disneyland Underestimates Lunar New Year Holiday Potential." *Asia Pulse.* February 6, 2006, retrieved March 10, 2006 from Lexis-Nexis Academic Universe Database.
[43]Patsy Moy and Ravina Shamdasani, "Call for Inquest into Disney Visitor's Death." *South China Morning Post.* February 20, 2006, p. CITY1.

[44]May Chan, "Disney's Pooh Unable to Mollify Irate Father," *South China Morning Post.* December 8, 2005, p. CITY4.
[45]Dennis Eng, "Mickey and Friends Call for a Better Work Environment." *South China Morning Post.* April 10, 2006, p. CITY3.
[46]Dennis Eng, "Two More Executives Quit Disney Park," *South China Morning Post,* p. CITY1.

New Promotion

To boost attendance, HKD adjusted its pricing strategy. In November 2005, the park offered ticket discounts in which the price for local residents was reduced by HK$50 (US$6.41). Moreover, HKD promoted a ticket express package: guests could purchase a one-day rail pass for an extra HK$6.4 over the admission price. This pass gave unlimited rides to and from the park plus a souvenir showcase of the popular Disney characters. Many believed that these new policies were intended to boost attendance but park spokespersons dismissed such a claim.

In mid-2006, 50,000 taxi drivers were invited to HKD free of charge. Every taxi driver who took up the offer was given free admission to the park between May 15 and June 11, 2006. In addition, a 50 percent discount was provided to up to three family members or friends who accompanied each driver. The aim of this promotion was to give taxi drivers a personal experience of the park that they could share with others. The Urban Taxi Drivers Association Joint Committee welcomed this scheme but it was not clear whether it was successful.

HKD also introduced a "one-day trip guide" in Chinese during November of 2005.[47] This initiative was intended to explain HKD to local travel guides. Furthermore, special VIP treatment was extended to local celebrities in the form of a Dining with Disney program. Local TV commercials also featured testimonials of previous guests and enticing scenes from inside HKD.

External Liaison with Mainland Travel Agents

Since Mainland visitors were a primary target of HKD, more proactive and collaborative moves were made with Chinese travel agencies, some of which were reluctant to sell HKD tickets in view of their slim profitability and extensive hassles: when there are problems, [travel agencies] have to eat the cost and other troubles." To overcome this resistance HKD offered Chinese travel agents a 50 percent discount on visits to the park and hotels Incentives of approximately US$2.50 per adult ticket were also given to tour operators who incorporated an HKD visit into their package tours HKD also changed the sales packages to open-ended tickets, from just fixed-date tickets, which offered greater flexibility for visitors and minimized the number of returned tickets.[48]

Setting the Course for Eventual Success

The performance of HKD during its first year of operation had not turned out as good as had been hoped with some potentially devastating mistakes. Tour operations further complained that HKD was not big enough to keep the guests occupied for a whole day. Worse still, HKD had faced much negative publicity: from overcrowding, to customer lawsuits, to chaotic incidents during the Chinese Lunar New Year that were front page news in Hong Kong. Further, a survey of current visitors to HKD revealed that 30 percent of guest opted not to revisit the park, which did not bode well for HKD's future.[49]

Disney had experience in operating parks internationally in both good and bad conditions. Inevitably comparisons had begun being made between HKD and Disneyland Resort Paris in France, which attracted a mere 1.5 million visitors by the end of its second month of operation and nowhere could it match Disney management's original projection of 15 million in the first year. However, some academics believed that it might take another five years to determine whether HKD could be judged as an economic success or failure.

Although maintaining an optimistic public face, the management team at HKD was facing pressures to turn things around. How could HKD steer through the cultural minefield to ensure Hong Kong Disneyland's success? How well had Disney achieved its goal of translating its strategic assets to the Chinese cultural context? What could HKD do to ensure a successful outcome along the lines of Tokyo Disney and avoid the type of embarrassment experienced with Disneyland Paris? What could the company do to rescue the park from the onslaught of continuing negative publicity? The park's management certainly had its challenges cut out for it.

[49]"Feature: Concerns Growing over HK Disneyland's Future." *Knight Ridder/Tribune Business News.* October 20, 2005, p. 1. retrieved March 10, 2006 from Lexis-Nexis Academic Universe Database.

[47]Geoffrey A. Fowler and Merissa Marr, "Hong Kong Disneyland Gets Lost in Translation," *The Wall Street Journal Asia.* February 9, 2006, p. 26.
[48]Ibid.

Source: The initial research and a first draft of this case were completed by Edwina H. S. Chan, Lutricia S.M.Kwok, John C. M. Lee, Jacky W. Y. Shing and Sally P. M. Tsui as an assignment under the direction of Professor Michael Young.

Name Index

Note: Page numbers followed by *n* indicate material in source notes, footnotes, and endnotes.

A

Aaker, David A., 175*n*15, 175*n*17, 180*n*20, 257*n*8, 260*n*10, 261*n*11, 265*n*15, 266*n*20, 266*n*21, 267*n*23, 268*n*27, 268*n*28, 271*n*33, 272*n*35, 272*n*36, 273*n*38, 273*n*39, 275*n*45, 276*n*46, 276*n*47, 277*n*48, 277*n*50, 278*n*52, 392*n*43, 393, 416*n*21
Abdell, Derek F., 43*n*11
Abela, Andrew V., 455*n*28, 458*n*39
Abkowitz, Alyssa, 141
Achrol, Ravi S., 164*n*3, 189*n*4, 430*n*49
Adams, Jeff, 536
Adamy, Janet, 317*n*1
Ahlberg, Erik, 381*n*14
Allison, Kevin, 285*n*2
Alpert, Mark I., 39*n*9
Alsop, Ronald, 269*n*29, 269*n*30
Ambler, Tim, 456*n*32, 457*n*35, 458*n*36, 458*n*39, 469*n*3, 470*n*5
Amoroso, Marina, 587
Ancona, Deborah, 225*n*19
Andel, T., 543*n*17
Anders, George, 119*n*36
Anderson, Chris, 108
Anderson, Elizabeth L., 532
Anderson, Erin, 303*n*17, 308*n*34, 382*n*15, 382*n*17, 428*n*48
Anderson, Ray, 462
Anderson, Rolph E., 181*n*21
Angwin, Julia, 23*n*47, 86*n*30, 152
Anhalt, Karen Nickel, 293
Ante, Spencer E., 149*n*37, 459*n*40, 461
Antoine, Richard L., 600
Aquilano, Nicholas J., 72*n*6
Araki, Takashi, 509
Arashima, Tadashi, 510
Arens, William F., 362*n*18
Arlidge, John, 76, 77
Arndt, Michael, 118*n*33, 219*n*5, 569
Arnold, Catherine, 145*n*31
Arnold, Susan E., 603
Arrunada, Benito, 199*n*23
Artzt, Edwin, 603
Ashkenas, Ron, 406
Ashley, Darryl, 509
Assael, Henry, 80*n*19
Aston, A., 129
Aufreiter, Nora A., 428*n*47, 429

Austen, Ben, 129
Ayling, Bob, 555
Ayling, Robert, 555

B

Babin, Barry J., 181*n*21
Bagchi, Subroto, 504
Baghai, Mehrdad, 71*n*1
Baker, Stephen, 152, 352
Bakhshian, Sarah, 628*n*5
Baldauf, Artur, 36*n*3
Baldwin, Carliss Y., 189*n*3
Ball, Deborah, 360*n*16
Ballmer, Steven A., 602
Balmer, John M.T., 192*n*10
Balmer, Steve, 461, 571
Bamford, James D., 194*n*14, 202*n*36, 204*n*40, 209*n*53
Band, William, 418*n*27
Barr, Larry, 486–491
Barrett, Claer, 286
Bartiromo, Maria, 419
Barwise, Patrick, 456*n*31
Baxter, Sarah, 96*n*44
Bayley, Stephen, 629
Beattie, Alan, 257
Beaver, William, 542*n*13
Bedol, Brian, 588
Belch, George E., 350*n*2, 359*n*14, 362*n*17, 364*n*21, 366*n*24, 367, 389*n*28, 393*n*44, 395*n*47, 395*n*48, 396*n*49, 400*n*53, 400*n*54
Belch, Michael A., 350*n*2, 359*n*14, 362*n*17, 364*n*21, 366*n*24, 367, 389*n*28, 393*n*44, 395*n*47, 395*n*48, 396*n*49, 400*n*53, 400*n*54
Belton, Catherine, 193
Bendle, Neil T., 456*n*33, 460, 468*n*1
Berden, W.O., 6*n*13
Berelson, Bernard, 83*n*25
Berfeld, Susan, 286
Bergstein, Brian, 225*n*15
Berkowitz, Eric N., 84*n*27, 85
Berner, Robert, 269, 331*n*19, 332, 355, 355*n*12, 362*n*19, 605
Berry, D., 304*n*23
Berry, Leonard L., 79*n*15
Berthon, Pierre, 256*n*5, 260*n*9
Betts, Paul, 205*n*44, 291
Bezos, Jeffrey P., 608–613
Bhalla, Gaukav, 4*n*5
Bharat, Krishna, 496
Bhargava, Mukesh, 104*n*1

Bianco, Anthony, 72*n*4, 83, 86*n*29, 163*n*2, 364, 391*n*35
Biesheuvel, Thomas, 183
Bink, Audrey, J.M., 433*n*56
Birchall, Jonathan, 3, 107, 133*n*6, 136, 142, 194, 199*n*25, 204*n*41, 204*n*42, 301*n*15, 307, 310, 321, 321*n*7, 390*n*31, 398*n*52, 399, 431, 433*n*53, 537
Bird, Andy, 630
Bird, Laura, 326*n*13
Birt, Jason, 293
Bissell, John, 404*n*2
Bittar, Christine, 404*n*2
Black, William C., 181*n*21
Blackett, Tom, 278
Blair, Tony, 578
Blank, Arthur, 563–564
Blas, Javier, 343*n*32
Block, Ken, 491–493
Bodenheimer, George W., 581–584, 586–588
Bono, 257
Bonoma, Thomas V., 444*n*15
Bornstein, Steve, 582, 584
Bostillo, Miguel, 90
Bounds, Wendy, 360*n*16
Bourne, B., 337*n*25
Bowe, Christopher, 118*n*35
Boyd, Harper W. Jr., 309
Boyle, Matthew, 72*n*2, 90, 136, 382*n*18
Bradford, James, 555–557
Bradshaw, Tim, 18
Brady, Diane, 35*n*2, 90*n*35, 136, 172, 179
Brady, Didne, 569
Braithwaite, Tom, 307, 344*n*34, 537
Brannen, Mary Yoko, 628, 629*n*10, 630*n*15, 631
Branson, Richard, 277
Bremner, Brian, 511
Bresnan, Henrik, 225*n*19
Brooker, Katrina, 254*n*2
Brooks, Rick, 381*n*13
Broughton, Philip Delves, 108*n*13
Brown, Gordon, 554, 578
Brown, Shona L., 243*n*41
Brown, Stephen, 172
Brown, Tori, 164
Brown, Wesley, 508
Brummer, Alex, 581
Bryan, Lowell L., 405*n*3, 407*n*7, 407*n*8, 407*n*9
Bryant, Chris, 207*n*45
Bryon, Ellen, 269
Buckley, Neil, 87*n*32
Bulkeley, William M., 34*n*1, 155*n*55, 576
Burke, Raymond R., 153*n*45
Burke, Stephen B., 584, 587
Burkitt, Laurie, 22

Burrows, Peter, 177*n*19, 191
Burrus, Daniel, 225*n*16
Bush, Jason, 22, 55*n*16, 87*n*32
Busky, James, 335
Byrnes, Bruce, 604
Byrnes, Nanette, 81, 269, 271*n*32,
    301*n*11, 448, 463*n*44
Byron, Ellen, 133*n*6, 194, 321

C

Calvert, Gemma, 156*n*60
Cameron, Doug, 7
Campbell, Andrew, 204*n*43
Campbell, Kerry, 450*n*25
Capell, Kerry, 3, 301*n*12, 537
Capon, Noel, 100*n*51, 151*n*43, 200*n*30,
    266*n*19, 417*n*24, 418*n*25, 428*n*44,
    440*n*9, 462*n*43
Carlton, Jim, 262*n*12
Carroll, Archie, 124*n*57
Carter, Adrienne, 85*n*28
Carter, Meg, 82*n*22
Case, Steven M., 602
Casper, Mike, 547
Cateora, Philip R., 170*n*12, 170*n*13, 310*n*36,
    311, 311*n*37, 314*n*42, 432*n*52
Cecil, Arthur B., 605
Cespedes, Frank V., 306*n*31, 307*n*32, 443*n*13
Cha, Ariana Eunjung, 72*n*2
Cha Mou-Sing, Payson, 627
Chaffin, Joshua, 213*n*67
Chally, H.R., 374*n*4, 375
Chambers, Swayne, 472
Chan, Edwina H.S., 638
Chan, K.W., 130*n*75
Chan, May, 628, 637*n*44
Chandy, Rajesh K., 226*n*21
Charny, Ben, 325
Chase, Richad B., 72*n*6, 117
Chazan, Guy, 193
Chen Nan-lok, Philip, 627
Chen Xiaoyue, 502
Chester, Jeff, 471
Cheung, Jacky, 635
Chiagouris, Larry, 280*n*55
Chin Dae Je, 512
Cho, Fujio, 506–509, 511
Choe, James, 513
Choi, Changsik, 517
Choi Gee Sung, 513
Choi Won Min, 511, 514
Choy, Linda, 627*n*1
Christensen, Clayton M., 37*n*4, 74*n*10,
    140*n*24, 167*n*6, 222*n*10, 222*n*11
Christopher, Martin, 304*n*19, 304*n*22,
    304*n*24
Chung Kook Hyun, 513
Church, Bryce G., 564

Ciacchella, John, 496
Cjeng, Roger, 37
Clark, Bruce H., 457*n*34, 458*n*39
Clark, Don, 37
Clark, Kim B., 189*n*3
Clark, Pilita, 318*n*3
Claxtoan, John D., 486
Clewes, Debbie, 442
Clift, Simon, 259
Clinton, Hillary, 535
Coates, Ross, 590
Cohen, Peter, 612
Collis, David J., 12*n*29, 13*n*32, 14*n*34
Colton, D.A., 6*n*13
Colvin, G., 114*n*26
Colvin, Geoff, 219*n*5
Comstock, Beth, 231, 416*n*19
Conaty, William J., 566
Conlin, Michelle, 280, 462
Connolly, Norma, 633*n*21
Cook, Scott, 74*n*10
Cooper, Donald R., 181*n*22, 244*n*44,
    245*n*45, 246*n*46, 246*n*47
Cooper, Robert, 223*n*14, 227*n*24, 237*n*33,
    263*n*13
Copeland, Michael V., 139
Cornwell, Lisa, 133*n*6
Cotte, June, 122*n*51
Coughlin, Anne, 303*n*17, 308*n*34
Court, David, 438*n*6, 459*n*41
Cranston, Eric, 612
Craven, Neil, 291
Cravens, David W., 4*n*6, 10*n*25, 36*n*3,
    106*n*10, 200*n*27, 200*n*28, 208*n*50,
    212*n*63, 285*n*1, 302*n*16, 317*n*2,
    320*n*5, 322*n*9, 323*n*10, 374*n*3,
    383*n*19, 385*n*21, 387*n*24, 388*n*27,
    430*n*50, 444*n*16
Cravens, Karen S., 68*n*22, 208*n*50
Crawford, Blair, 459*n*41
Crawford, C. Merle, 235*n*31, 239, 241*n*40
Cressman, George E. Jr., 325*n*12, 334*n*21,
    334*n*22, 335
Crooks, Ed, 421
Crosby, Lawrence A., 451*n*26
Cross, Joseph, 613–614, 616–617, 621, 623,
    625, 626
Crown, Judith, 198
Curry, Bruce, 153*n*45

D

Daly, Lee Ann, 587
Damast, Alison, 128
Davey, Jenny, 3, 537
Davidson, Andrew, 133*n*6, 301*n*11
Davies, Fiona, 153*n*45
Dawson, Chester, 511
Day, George S., 5*n*8, 5*n*10, 7*n*16, 9*n*20,

    41*n*10, 53*n*14, 105*n*5, 132*n*1, 134*n*7,
    134*n*8, 135*n*10, 135*n*12, 137*n*16,
    138*n*20, 140*n*23, 141*n*25, 154*n*49,
    167*n*5, 167*n*7, 168*n*9, 228, 404*n*1,
    410*n*10, 410*n*11, 410*n*12, 411*n*13,
    414*n*17
Day, Graham, 576
DeAngelo, Joe, 564
Delios, Andrew, 209*n*54
Dell, Michael, 26
Demborsky, April, 394
Deshpandé, Rohit, 6*n*12, 154*n*47, 154*n*49,
    155*n*54, 419*n*28
Devitt, Scott W., 610
Di Benedetto, C. Anthony, 235*n*31, 239,
    241*n*40
Dickenson, Larry, 380
Dickson, Peter R., 75*n*11, 88*n*34
Dignan, Larry, 540*n*9
Dillon, William R., 143*n*27, 156*n*59,
    238*n*35, 246*n*48
Dobbs, Johnnie C., 538
Doerr, John, 611
Dolan, Robert J., 327*n*14
Done, Kevin, 555
Donovan, Dennis M., 566
Downes, L., 274*n*44
Doyle, Peter, 2*n*4, 405*n*4, 420*n*31, 425*n*39
Doz, Yves, 132*n*2, 137*n*13
Drucker, Peter F., 13*n*31, 15*n*37, 154*n*48
Du Toit, Gerard, 87*n*33
Dudley, Bob, 193
Duke, Mike, 546
Dumaine, Brian, 314*n*41
Dvorak, Phred, 18
Dyer, Jeffrey H., 208*n*49
Dyson, Esther, 612

E

Eaglesham, Jean, 581
Eccles, Robert G., 118*n*34
Edgecliffe-Johnson, Andre, 86, 121*n*49, 141,
    259, 428*n*46
Edmondson, Gail, 77, 510
Edmonson, Gail, 293
Edwardes, Michael, 576
Edwards, Cliff, 18, 136, 285*n*2, 290*n*3,
    373*n*2
Efrati, Amir, 446
Einhorn, Bruce, 177*n*19, 197*n*21, 219*n*5,
    465, 634*n*27
Eisenhardt, Kathleen M., 243*n*41
Eisenstat, Russell, 438*n*5
Eisner, Michael, 584, 586
El-Ansary, Adel I., 303*n*17, 308*n*34
Eldam, Michael, 77
Eliashberg, Jehoshua, 153*n*45
Ellison, Larry, 461

Elop, Stephen, 516
Encardio, Pete, 112, 197*n*21
Eng, Dennis, 627*n*1, 637*n*45, 637*n*46
Engardio, Pete, 22*n*44, 118*n*33, 232, 343*n*33
Enright, Allison, 150*n*39, 363*n*20
Eppinger, Stephen D., 230, 249
Epstein, Keith, 198
Erickson, Tamara, 413
Eriksen, Rolf, 174
Ernst, Bill, 627, 637
Ernst, David, 202*n*36, 204*n*40, 209*n*53
Evans, B., 304*n*25
Evans, Philip B., 138*n*19
Evans, Richard, 225*n*18

F

Falcon, Benoit, 408
Farley, James, 508
Farley, John U., 456*n*31
Farley, John V., 6*n*12
Fenby, Jonathan, 306*n*29
Fengtan Peiling, 637
Fenton, Ben, 172
Ferrell, Linda, 125*n*60
Ferrell, O.C., 125*n*60
Ferris, Paul W., 456*n*33, 458*n*38,
    460, 468*n*1
Fidler, Stephen, 314*n*43
Fielding, Michael, 137*n*15, 149*n*36
Fine, John, 335
Fine, Jon, 390*n*31
Firtle, Neil H., 143*n*27, 156*n*59, 238*n*35,
    246*n*48
Fitzpatrick, Robert, 630
Flanagan, Diane, 555–557, 563
Flandez, Raymund, 117
Fletcher, Clementine, 3
Fletcher, J.H., 461*n*42
Fletcher, Owen, 281*n*57
Fletcher, Richard, 3
Fontanella-Khan, James, 346
Foote, Nathanial, 438*n*5
Ford, John B., 464*n*45
Ford, Neil M., 476, 555
Ford, Rollin, 545
Fornell, Claes, 567
Forsee, Gary, 587
Fortson, Danny, 193
Foster, George, 68*n*20
Fottrell, Quentin, 318*n*3
Fowler, Geoffrey A., 638*n*47
Fredberg, Tobias, 438*n*5
Freed, Donald, 618–619
Freeman, Hadley, 73*n*7
Fritz, Mary, 334, 335
Frow, Pennie, 104*n*3, 112*n*23, 113*n*24,
    113*n*25, 114*n*28, 115
Fubrini, David G., 204*n*40

G

Galante, Joseph, 55
Galea, Christina, 122*n*53, 376*n*8
Gandhi, Sonia, 504
Ganesan, Shankar, 373*n*1
Gapper, John, 198, 311*n*38, 325*n*11
Garahan, Matthew, 23*n*46, 363*n*20
Garone, Stephen J., 278
Garrahan, Matthew, 172, 412
Gary, Loren, 202*n*367
Gates, William H., 571
Geiger, Joseph J., 588
Gerstner, Lou, 258, 570
Ghosn, Carlos, 294*n*4, 508, 509
Gillett, Felix, 318*n*3, 391*n*39
Gilligan, Andrew, 554, 555
Gillin, Ann, 605
Gilly, Mary C., 170*n*12, 170*n*13
Gilmore, James H., 243*n*41
Ginter, James L., 75*n*11, 88*n*34
Glover, Dick, 584
Godfrey, Paul C., 125*n*62
Gomes-Casseres, Benjamin, 194*n*14
Goodell, Roger, 584
Goodman, M., 310
Goodman, Matthew, 76
Goolsby, Jerry R., 421*n*35
Govindarajan, Vijay, 224
Graham, John L., 170*n*12, 170*n*13,
    310*n*36, 311, 311*n*37, 314*n*42,
    432*n*52
Grande, Carlos, 25*n*54, 121*n*47, 121*n*48,
    151*n*41
Grant, Jeremy, 201*n*32
Grant, Peter, 54*n*15
Greeley, Brendan, 84*n*26
Green, Heather, 18, 259
Greenfield, Karl Taro, 147*n*32
Greenfield, Richard, 586
Greenley, Gordon, 10*n*25, 447*n*22
Grewal, Dhruv, 119*n*38, 123*n*55
Griffith, J. Randall, 475, 479,
    481–484
Griffiths, John, 581
Grobart, Sam, 37
Gronholt-Pedersen, Jacob, 193
Grover, Ronald, 412, 584
Grow, Brian, 368, 569
Gruner, Kjell, 420*n*29, 421*n*34
Guasperi, John, 418*n*27
Guerra, Francesco, 248
Guerrera, Francesco, 132*n*4
Guha, Krishna, 581
Guilding, Chirs, 68*n*22
Gulati, Ranjay, 144*n*28, 209*n*55, 210*n*56,
    416*n*19
Gunther, Marc, 261
Gupta, Mahendra, 68*n*20
Guthrie, Jonathan, 3, 581

H

Haenlein, Michael, 392*n*42
Hagel, John, 197*n*20
Hagel, John III, 211*n*59
Hahn, Inkuk, 516
Hai Wen, 501
Hair, Joseph F. Jr., 181*n*21
Hall, Taddy, 74*n*10
Hamel, Gary, 11*n*27, 58*n*18
Hamilton, Joan O'C., 157
Hamm, Steve, 137*n*14, 174, 187*n*2, 232,
    241*n*39, 313, 375*n*6, 411*n*14, 576
Hanlon, Tim, 585, 586
Hansen, Eric J., 151*n*40
Harbour, Ronald E., 508
Harlow, John, 3
Hart, Calla, 481–483
Hartley, Steven W., 84*n*27, 85, 338*n*27
Harvey, Fiona, 248
Harvey, Mike, 188
Hatch, Nile W., 125*n*62
Heckman, James, 274*n*42
Heineman, Bob W. Jr., 121*n*44
Helm, Bert, 261
Hemerling, Jim, 502
Hempel, Jessi, 139, 232, 258, 413
Henderson, James A., 617
Henderson, John C., 194*n*13, 202*n*368
Henretta, Deborah A., 601
Henry, Robin, 152
Hensley, Scott, 387*n*25, 388
Hernandez, Greg, 633*n*24
Hewitt, Patricia, 578
Hill, Jonathan, 634*n*29
Hille, Kathrin, 279, 465
Hindo, Brian, 25*n*58
Hira, Nadira A., 413
Hiserman, Christopher, 209*n*52
Hittner, J., 129*n*73
Ho, Patricia, 581
Hobbs, Matt, 308*n*33
Hodge, Margaret, 579
Hoenig, Gary, 583
Hof, Robert D., 13*n*30, 349*n*1
Hoff, Robert D., 23*n*48, 389*n*29, 475, 613
Holahan, Catherine, 55
Holden, Reed, 333, 336*n*23, 336*n*24, 340*n*30
Hollenbeck, George P., 431*n*51
Holmes, Stanley, 379*n*11, 380
Holt, Douglas B., 93*n*38
Holycon, 335
Homburg, Christian, 420*n*29, 420*n*30,
    420*n*32, 421*n*34, 426*n*41, 428*n*44
Honeycutt, Earl D., 464*n*45
Hong-Wei He, 192*n*10
Honomichl, Jack, 144*n*29, 144*n*30, 145
Hooley, Graham J., 182*n*24
Hornick, David, 472
Howes, Stephen, 503

Hoyos, Carola, 207n46, 214n68
Hrebiniak, Lawrence G., 443n11
Hudson, Kris, 544n18, 544, 545n23, 545n24
Hughes, Chris, 331n17
Hughes, Jonathan, 209n51
Hulbert, James M., 100n51, 151n43, 256n5, 266n19, 418n25
Hunt, Ben, 18
Hunt, Shelby D., 15n36
Hunter, Gary K., 106n10
Hussbaum, Bruce, 231
Husson, Leon, 501
Hutton, Ray, 437n2, 581
Hwang, Chang Hwan, 514
Hymowitz, Carol, 93n39

I

Iger, Robert A., 584, 586, 588
Ihlwan, Moon, 199n22, 211n60, 515
Immelt, Jeffrey R., 224, 231, 248, 461, 602, 604
Inada, Miho, 141
Ingram, Thomas M., 385n21
Ingrassia, Lawrence, 226n22
Inkpen, Andrew C., 209n54
Ip, Stephen, 633n25
Izen, James E., 563–564

J

Jack, Andrew, 139, 312, 338n28
Jackson, Tony, 108
Jacobs, Robert F., 72n6
Jacobs, Rose, 319, 345
Jager, Durk, 600, 602–603, 606
James, Dana, 274n41, 447n20
Jaworski, Bernard J., 173n14, 175n17, 340n29, 391n34, 395n45, 439n8
Jearzemsky, Matt, 446
Jenkner, Rick, 486
Jensen, Ove, 420n30, 420n32, 426n41, 428n44
Joachimsthaler, Erich, 278n52
Jobs, Steve, 24
Jocz, Katherine E., 8n18, 391n34, 410n10, 410n11, 410n12, 411n13
Johnson, A.H., 543n16
Johnson, Craig R., 563
Johnson, P. Fraser, 538
Johnson, Sheree L., 451n26
Johnson, Zachary T., 218n2, 380n12, 387n23
Johnston, Mark W., 57, 351n8, 376, 378n9, 379n10, 385n20, 386n22
Jones, Daniel T., 295n9, 304n20, 304n21
Jones, Howard, 390n32

Jopson, Barney, 128, 171, 274n43, 286, 321
Joyce, Claudia I., 405n3, 407n7, 407n8, 407n9

K

Kagami, Toshio, 629
Kahn, Barbara E., 96n46, 97n47, 97n48
Kale, Prashant, 208n49
Kale, Sudhir, 104n4, 107n12
Kammel, Benedikt, 419
Kane, Yukari Iwatani, 24
Kang Yun Je, 513
Kanter, Rosabeth Moss, 127n70
Kao, John, 223n13
Kaplan, Andreas M., 392n42
Kaplan, Robert S., 263n13, 448n23
Kapnor, Suzanne, 301n15
Kara, Ali, 96n45
Kartajaya, Hermawan, 2n3
Kawamoto, Nobuhiko, 506
Kay, William, 537
Kaykas-Wolff, Jascha, 472
Kaynack, Erdener, 96n45
Kazmin, Amy, 313
Kean, Danuta, 363n20
Keegan, Paul, 457
Kellaway, Lucy, 446
Keller, Kevin Lane, 151n42, 265n16, 265n17, 266n18, 295n6, 300n10
Keller, Maryann, 506
Kelly, Ruth, 551
Kelly, Tom, 554
Kennedy, Donald, 157
Kennedy, Karen N., 421n35
Kerin, Roger A., 84n27, 85, 338n27
Kerwin, Kathleen, 511
Khermouch, Gerry, 450n25
Khezri, Bijan, 390n32
Kiley, David, 349n1, 438n3
Killgren, Lucy, 307
Kim, W.C., 38n6
Kirchgaessner, Stephanie, 22, 156n56
Kirkpatrick, David, 187n2, 225n17, 465, 576
Kliman, Stuart, 209n52
Klump, Edward, 207n46
Knight, R., 129
Knight, Rebecca, 24n52
Knipp, Steven, 635n32
Knox, Simon D., 106n9, 111n21
Koeppen, Nina, 213n65
Kogure, Makoto, 513
Kohli, Ajay, 418n26, 419n28, 470n6
Komivama, Hideki, 261
Kosner, John, 585
Kosonen, Mikko, 132n2, 137n13
Kotler, Philip, 2n3, 151n42, 295n6, 300n10
Kovos, Sotiris, 508
Kowitt, Beth, 141

Kownsmann, Patricia, 192n9
Kramer, Mark R., 24n50, 25n56, 124n58, 126n66, 126n68, 127n71
Kramer, Robert, 406
Kranhold, Kathryn, 114, 116n31
Krauss, Michael, 2n3, 279n54
Kripalani, Manjeet, 313
Krishnan, M.S., 186n1
Krushwitz, Nina, 122n52, 125n64
Kuchler, Hannah, 345
Kuczmarski, Thomas D., 218n2, 223n14, 227n23
Kumar, Ajith, 417n22
Kumar, Nirmalya, 268n26, 301n13, 301n14, 416n18, 433n54, 433n55
Kumar, V., 108n14, 109n15, 109n18, 110n19, 111
Kwok, Lutricia S.M., 638

L

La Monica, Paul R., 630n17
Laask, Felicia G., 421n35
Lafley, Alan G., 600–606, 608
LaForge, Raymond W., 385n21
Laine, Richard, 622
Lakshman, Nandini, 177n19
Lambkin, Mary, 167n5, 167n7, 168n9
Lamont, James, 294n5, 346
Lamont, Lawrence M., 613
Lanchester, John, 156n58
Lane, Nikala, 4n6, 121n46, 124n56, 125n59, 137n17, 143n26, 200n29, 212n63, 285n1, 302n16, 317n2, 320n5, 322n9, 323n10, 374n3, 375n5, 427n43
Lane, Stuart, 442
Langford, Simon, 545
Larréché, Jean-Claude, 309
Larsen, Peter Thal, 192n9
Lassk, Felicia G., 387n24
Latour, Almar, 54n15, 239n38, 332n20
Laughlin, Jay L., 80n20
Laur, Joe, 122n52, 125n64
Laurence, Ben, 415
Lawler, Edward, 413n16
Lawler, Edward E.III, 564
Lawrence, John L., 588
Lawton, Christopher, 177n19
Lawver, Teri L., 428n47, 429
Lazaris, Nick, 519–525, 531–532
Le Meunier-Fitzhugh, Kenneth, 374n3
Leahy, Joe, 22, 319, 343n32
Leahy, Terry, 532–533, 535–537
Lee, Jay Y., 518
Lee, John C.M., 638
Lee, Louise, 100, 397n50, 398
Lee, Mark, 465
Lee Byung Moo, 511

Lee Kun Hee, 512, 516–519
Lee Yun Jung, 512
Lehman, Donald, 410n10
Lehmann, Donald R., 8n18, 49, 410n11, 410n12, 411n13, 424n37, 425n40, 456n30
LeMenunier-Fitzhugh, Kenneth, 106n10
Lennox, Beverley, 176
Lerner, Jeremy, 198
Lesser, Eric, 154n53
Lester, Tom, 320n6
Levine, Daniel S., 81n21
Lévy, Maurice, 475
Levy, Michael, 119n38, 123n55
Lewis, Michael, 475
Li, Josh, 501
Liebert, Carl C. III, 567
Liguori, Stephen, 416n19
Lilien, Gary L., 182n23
Lillie, May, 590
Lim, Kevin, 199n24
Lindermann, Dirk, 510
Lings, Ian N., 447n22
Liu, Donald, 627
Liu, Eva, 629n6
London, Simon, 14n33, 576
Lorange, Peter, 140n22
Lorimr, S.E., 351n7
Löscher, Peter, 419
Loveman, Gary, 147n32
Low, George S., 383n19, 387n24
Lowry, Tom, 586, 588
Lublin, Joanne S., 156n59
Lucas, Louis, 274n43
Lucas, Louise, 224, 267n24, 415
Lun, Candance D., 428n47, 429
Lusch, Robert F., 2n1, 11n28, 15n38, 255n3
Luther, Terry, 481
Lutz, Ashley, 77n14
Lutz, Robert A., 236
Lynn, Barry C., 541n11, 542n14
Lynn, Gary S., 222n7, 222n8, 222n9
Lynn, Matthew, 272n34
Lysohir, Marilyn, 588–598

M

Mac Hulbert, James, 417n24, 440n9, 462n43
MacAskill, Chris, 612
MacAskill, Don, 612
MacDonald, Elizabeth, 156n59
Macinnis, Deborah J., 173n14, 175n17
MacIntosh, Julie, 201n33
Mackensie, Kate, 408
Mackintosh, James, 201n33
MacMillan, Douglas, 394
MacMillian, Douglas, 55
MacNamara, William, 212, 294n5

Madden, Thomas J., 143n27, 156n59, 238n35, 246n48
Magnusson, Paul, 511
Mahurin, Steve, 568
Maignan, Isabelle, 125n60
Maitland, Alison, 24n51, 120n43, 308n35
Maklan, Stan, 106n9, 111n21
Malter, Alan J., 373n1
Maltz, Elliot, 417n22, 418n26, 470n6
Mandel, Michael J., 389n29
Manly, Dave, 520, 531
Mann, John David, 225n16
Mansell, John, 587
Marchionne, Sergio, 437–438
Marcus, Bernie, 563–564
Markey, Rob, 87n33
Marr, Merissa, 100, 638n47
Marsh, Peter, 304n26, 310
Marshall, Greg W., 57, 351n8, 376, 378n9, 379n10, 380n12, 385n20, 386n22, 387n23, 387n24
Martin, Roger L., 23n49, 437n1
Maslow, A.H., 82n23
Mason, Tim, 534–535, 536
Mason, Zachary, 612
Mathers, John, 278
Matkins, Luke, 608
Matlack, Carol, 281, 438n3
Matlock, Carol, 211n61
Matsatsinis, Nikolaos, 153n44
Matthews, Colin, 554–555
Mattioli, Dana, 34n1
Mauborgne, R., 38n6, 130n75
May, Ed, 100
Mayer, Marissa, 219–220
Mazur, Laura, 9n22
McCall, Morgan W., 431n51
McCann, Chris, 471
McCartney, Scott, 319
McClung, James, 617
McConnan, Aili, 157
McConnell, Ted, 472
McCracken, Jeffrey, 269
McCullough, Stuart, 510
McCullough, Wayne R., 455n28
McDonald, Robert A., 600
McFarland, Nathan, 612
McGovern, Gail J., 459n41
McGregor, Jena, 72n3, 79n16, 170n11
McGregor, Richard, 22, 343n32
McIntyre, Shelby H., 155n54
McManus, Sean, 584
McNerney, W. James Jr., 602
McQuarrie, Edward F., 155n54
Meehan, Robert, 306n28
Meer, David, 73n8, 74n9
Mehrotra, Parth, 209n55, 210n56
Melligeri, Aravind, 502
Meng Chu, 637n41
Menn, Joseph, 24, 191

Merino, Jorge, 510
Mero, Jenny, 406
Merrick, Amy, 275
Meyer, Stephanie, 259
Michaels, Ryan, 483
Mill, John Stuart, 134
Miller, David, 443n12
Miller, Kerry, 112
Minder, Raphael, 343n32
Ming Zeng, 345n35
Minto, Rob, 289
Mishra, Devendra, 136
Mitchell, Adrian, 40
Mitchell, Alan, 133n6
Mitterand, Francois, 630
Mokwa, Michael P., 443n14
Mongtomery, Cynthia A., 12n29
Monroe, Kent B., 322n8, 328, 331n18, 340n30
Montgomery, Cynthia A., 13n32, 14n34
Moore, Thomas A., 603
Moorman, Christine, 4n5, 9n19
Morgan, Neil A., 100n50, 440n10
Morgan, Robert M., 15n36
Moriarity, Rowland T., 93n40
Morone, Joseph G., 222n7, 222n8, 222n9
Morris, Linda J., 588
Morrison, Scott, 202n35
Moulton, Jon, 577
Moutinho, Luiz, 153n45
Moy, Patsy, 637n43
Mui, C., 274n44
Mulier, Thomas, 244
Mullaney, Timothy J., 390n30
Mundel, David, 154n53
Mundie, Craig, 502
Munuera, Jose Luis, 120n39
Murphy, Thomas S., 584
Murray, Sarah, 214

N

Nagle, Thomas, 318n4, 325n12, 327n15, 328n16, 329, 333, 336n23, 336n24, 340n30
Naim, M.M., 304n23
Nairn, Agnes, 100
Nairn, Geoff, 106n8, 114n29
Nakamoto, Michiyo, 207n45
Nardelli, Robert L., 563–569
Narver, John C., 4n7, 5n9, 134n9, 137n16
Naylor, J.B., 304n23
Neff, Jack, 404n2
Nelson, Stephen, 550, 554
Newell, Claire, 344n34
Newing, Rod, 189n5, 192n12
Newquist, Scott C., 118n34
Nicoulaud, Brigitte, 182n24
Nidumolo, R., 125n63

Nidumolu, Ram, 236
Nie, Winter, 176
Niimi, Atsushi, 293
Nilekani, Nandan M., 499, 503
Noble, Charles H., 443*n*14
Norton, David P., 448*n*23
Nottingham, John R., 606
Nunes, Paul F., 306*n*31, 307*n*32
Nussbaum, Bruce, 222*n*12, 223, 242
Nuttall, Chris, 24, 285*n*2

O

Obama, Barack, 535
O'Connel, Dominic, 555, 581
O'Connor, Joseph A., 607
O'Connor, Sarah, 213*n*66
Ohmae, Kenichi, 503
Ohno, Taichi, 508
Ohtsubo, Fumio, 518
O'Keefe, Brian, 214*n*68
Okuda, Hiroshi, 508
Oldroyd, James, 144*n*28
Olins, Rufus, 272*n*34
Olsen, Eric M., 230*n*25, 231*n*26
Olson, Sally, 335
Opel, John M., 570
O'Reilly, Tim, 611
Orwall, Bruce, 629*n*12
Osawa, Juro, 261
Osher, John, 605–608
O'Sullivan, Don, 455*n*29
Ott, John, 87*n*33
Overell, Stephen, 53
Own, Glen, 100

P

Pacofsky, Nina, 335
Page, Larry, 446
Pagnamenta, Robin, 408
Palmer, Jaija, 281
Palmer, Nick, 195*n*15
Palmeri, Christopher, 271*n*32, 511
Palmisamo, Samuel J., 187*n*2, 210–211,
    210*n*58, 258, 375, 570–575
Pan Kwan Yuk, 345
Parise, Salvatore, 194*n*13, 202*n*368
Park, C. W., 175*n*16, 175*n*17
Park, C. Whan, 173*n*14
Parker, Andrew, 325
Parrish, Ted, 630
Patrick, Aaron O., 366*n*23, 537
Paulson, Albert S., 222*n*7, 222*n*8, 222*n*9
Payne, Adrian, 104*n*3, 111*n*21, 112*n*23,
    113*n*24, 113*n*25, 114*n*28, 115
Pearlman, Jerry, 617
Pell, Barney, 612

Peng, Mike W., 215*n*69
Penn, Mark J., 96*n*43
Peppard, Joe, 111*n*21
Pepper, John, 602–603
Peppers, Don, 72*n*5, 106*n*6
Perkins, Donald, 617
Perry, F. Darrin, 582
Persaud, Avinash, 120*n*40, 120*n*41
Pfeifer, Philip E., 456*n*33, 460, 468*n*1
Pfeifer, Sylvia, 193, 408
Phiips, Ken, 490
Piercy, Niall C., 303*n*18
Piercy, Nigel F., 4*n*6, 10*n*26, 36*n*3, 100*n*50,
    106*n*10, 121*n*46, 124*n*56, 125*n*59,
    137*n*17, 143*n*26, 182*n*24, 197*n*19,
    200*n*29, 208*n*50, 212*n*63, 285*n*1,
    302*n*16, 305*n*27, 317*n*2, 320*n*5,
    322*n*9, 323*n*10, 374*n*3, 375*n*5,
    383*n*19, 417*n*23, 417*n*24, 418*n*25,
    427*n*43, 430*n*50, 440*n*9, 440*n*10,
    441, 443*n*13, 447*n*21, 449*n*24,
    462*n*43, 547, 569, 576
Pine, B. Joseph II, 243*n*41
Pisana, Gary P., 226*n*20
Pistone, John N., 568
Pitt, Leyland F., 256*n*5
Plender, John, 120*n*40, 120*n*41, 213*n*64
Pohle, G., 129*n*73
Pollay, Richard W., 486
Polman, Paul, 128
Polmisano, Samuel J., 218–219
Pomerantz, Dorothy, 369*n*26
Porter, Andrew, 581
Porter, Michael, 7*n*15
Porter, Michael E., 23*n*45, 24*n*50, 25*n*56,
    51*n*13, 124*n*58, 126*n*66, 126*n*68,
    126*n*69, 127*n*71, 391*n*37, 428*n*45
Powell, M., 304*n*25
Prada, Paulo, 293
Prahalad, C.K., 38*n*18, 58*n*17, 125*n*63,
    186*n*1, 199*n*26, 496
Press, James E., 508
Pressman, Aaron, 75*n*13
Pritchard, Stephen, 18
Pui-Wing Tam, 38*n*7, 373*n*2
Puranam, Phanish, 144*n*28

Q

Quelch, John A., 93*n*38, 459*n*41

R

Raice, Shatdni, 446
Raman, Anand P., 409
Ramaswami, Sridhar N., 104*n*1
Ramaswamy, Venkat, 199*n*26
Ramstad, Evan, 165*n*4

Ranga, V. Kasturi, 93*n*40
Rangaswami, M.R., 125*n*63, 236
Rangaswamy, Arvind, 153*n*45, 182*n*23
Rappaport, Alan, 415
Rashtchy, Safa, 609
Rasmussen, Bill, 586
Rasulo, Jay, 633
Ray, Don D., 563
Raynor, Michael E., 37*n*4, 38*n*5, 167*n*6,
    222*n*10, 222*n*11
Rayport, Jeffrey F., 340*n*29, 395*n*45
Redondo, Ignacio, 510
Reed, John, 77, 346, 437*n*2, 438*n*4, 581
Reed, Stanley, 39*n*8, 183, 207*n*46
Reibstein, David J., 456*n*33, 468*n*1
Reichheld, Frederick F., 106*n*7, 109*n*16
Reinartz, Werner J., 108*n*14, 109*n*15,
    110*n*19, 111, 112*n*22
Reingold, Jennifer, 431
Renoldi, Suzette, 555, 557, 563
Ressner, Jeffrey, 630*n*16, 636*n*34
Revall, Janice, 342*n*31
Reynolds, Harold, 583
Rigby, Darrell K., 106*n*7, 110*n*20, 112*n*22,
    232*n*27
Rigby, Elizabeth, 194, 200*n*31, 310, 312*n*39,
    415, 537
Rip, Peter, 611
Rita, Paulo, 153*n*45
Ritson, Mark, 273*n*40
Rizzuto, Garth, 490, 492
Robbins, James O., 586
Roberti, Mark, 540*n*10
Roberts, Brian L., 587
Roberts, Dan, 22
Roberts, Dexter, 211*n*60, 279, 343*n*33
Roberts, Ian, 621
Roberts, John, 457*n*35
Robertson, David, 408
Robinson, Don, 630
Robinson, Michael S., 194*n*14
Robson, Matthew, 141
Rockefeller, Jay, 520
Rocks, David, 22*n*43, 515
Roco, Mihail, 615, 626
Roering, Kenneth J., 422*n*36
Rogers, Martha, 72*n*5, 106*n*6
Rohwedder, Cecilie, 270*n*31, 344
Roman, Sergio, 120*n*39
Romanelli, Elaine, 168*n*8
Rosengarten, Philipp, 510
Ross, Jerry, 209*n*54
Roth, M.S., 6*n*13
Rowling, J.K., 86, 172
Royal, Weld, 306*n*30, 307*n*32
Rubens, Paul, 115, 117
Rudd, Nigel, 554
Rudelius, William, 84*n*27, 85, 338*n*27
Ruekert, Robert W., 230*n*25, 231*n*26, 422*n*36
Rush, Dominic, 191

Rushe, Dominic, 100, 108, 301*n*11, 463*n*44
Ruskin, Gary, 157
Rusli, Evelyn M., 37
Rust, Roland T., 4*n*5, 9*n*19
Ryals, Lynette, 106*n*9, 111*n*21, 114*n*27
Ryan, Shelley, 555–557

S

Saatchi, Maurice, 391*n*36
Sanchanta, Mariko, 244*n*43, 295*n*8
Sandberg, Sheryl, 471–475
Sawney, Mohan, 416*n*20
Scatz, Roland, 118*n*34
Schäfer, Daniel, 419
Scheinman, Dan, 496, 499
Schifrin, Matthew, 204*n*39
Schindler, Pamela S., 181*n*22, 244*n*44, 245*n*45
Schine, Eric, 281
Schink, 246*n*46, 246*n*47
Schlender, Brent, 325
Schley, Sara, 122*n*52, 125*n*64
Schoewe, 545
Schroder, Ian, 76
Schultz, Don E., 267*n*22
Schuman, Michael, 630*n*16, 636*n*34
Schwartz, Nelson D., 407*n*6
Scott, Stuart, 583
Seamon, Erica B., 218*n*2
Seely-Brown, John, 211*n*59
Seidenberg, Ivan, 461
Selden, Larry, 114*n*26
Senge, Peter, 122*n*52, 125*n*64
Senn, Christoph, 434
Setiawan, Iwan, 2*n*3
Shah, Neel, 95*n*42
Shambora, Jessica, 142, 439*n*7
Shamdasani, Ravina, 637*n*43
Shansby, J. Gary, 175*n*15
Shapiro, Mark, 582, 588
Sharma, Amit, 502
Shchafter, Phil, 106*n*7
Shenken, Steve, 481
Shet, Jagdish N., 313*n*40
Shing, Jacky W.Y., 638
Shipp, Shannon H., 430*n*50
Shirouzu, Norihiko, 247*n*50
Shocker, Allan D., 39*n*9
Shoemaker, Paul J.H., 140*n*23, 141*n*25
Shriver, Bobby, 257
Siegel, Richard, 615, 617
Silverman, Gary, 365*n*22, 391*n*40
Simintiras, Antonis C., 464*n*45
Simmonds, K., 68*n*21
Simmons, Bill, 585
Simms, Jane, 469*n*2
Simon, B., 129
Simon, Bernard, 18, 75*n*12, 201*n*33, 201*n*34, 265*n*14, 367*n*25, 438*n*4

Simonian, Haig, 291
Simonite, 177*n*19
Simons, Andrew, 244*n*42
Singh, Harbir, 208*n*49
Singhapakdi, A., 120*n*41, 121*n*45
Sinha, P., 351*n*7
Siskos, Y., 153*n*44
Skapinker, Michael, 128, 212, 236, 256*n*6
Skipper, John, 588
Slater, Stanley, F., 4*n*7, 5*n*9, 134*n*9, 137*n*16
Slywotzky, Adrian J., 14*n*35, 135*n*11, 137*n*18
Smale, John G., 602, 603
Smit, Sven, 71*n*1
Smith, Bryan, 122*n*52, 125*n*64
Smith, Caitlin, 483–484
Smith, David, 134
Smith, D.V.L., 461*n*42
Smith, Ethan, 24
Smith, Gerald E., 327*n*15, 328*n*16, 329
Smith, Peter, 344*n*34
Snyder, Dan, 587
Soble, Jonathan, 212*n*62
Somme, Paul, 86
Sonne, Paul, 3, 152
Souder, William E., 417*n*22
Spagat, Elliot, 237*n*34
Spilotro, Kathryn W., 218*n*2
Spirk, John W., 606
Spurgeon, Brad, 626
Sritama, Suchat, 635*n*30
Srivastava, Rajendra K., 39*n*9, 104*n*1
Stack, James, 555
Stark, Kevin, 557
Stebbins, John, 626
Stecklow, 152
Steel, Emily, 23*n*47, 86*n*30
Steele, William H., 600
Steenkamp, E.M., 268*n*26
Steiner, Gary A., 83*n*25
Steiner, Rupert, 149*n*35
Stern, Louis W., 303*n*17, 308*n*34
Stern, Phil, 405*n*4, 420*n*31, 425*n*39
Stern, Stefan, 268*n*25
Stevens, Chris, 523, 529, 531
Stevens, Philip, 555
Stewart, James B., 629*n*11, 630*n*13, 630*n*14
Stewart, Thomas A., 153*n*46, 154*n*50, 154*n*52, 409
Stone, Brad, 394
Strickland, A.J. III, 63
Stringer, Howard, 261
Sull, Donald, 132*n*3, 138*n*21
Sullivan, Allanna, 91*n*36, 92
Sutcliffe, Kathleen M., 133*n*5
Swartz, Gordon S., 93*n*40
Sweeney, Dick, 520, 530
Symonds, William C., 269
Sytch, Maxim, 209*n*55, 210*n*56

T

Tagliabue, Paul, 584
Taleb, Nassim Nichola, 134
Tatham, Ronald L., 181*n*21
Taylor, Alex, 346
Taylor, Andrew, 25*n*53, 310
Taylor, Charles R., 80*n*20
Taylor, Earl L., 93*n*38
Taylor, Paul, 9*n*21, 18, 289, 295*n*7, 319, 325
Taylor, Thomas V. Jr., 569
Tellis, Gerald J., 226*n*21
Tett, Gillian, 139
Thatcher, Margaret, 576
Thiel, Peter, 612
Thomas, Helen, 415
Thomas, Kim, 150*n*38
Thomke, Stefan H., 233*n*28, 233*n*29
Thompkins, Richard, 278*n*51
Thompson, Arthur A. Jr., 63
Thompson, Christopher, 408
Thompson, Stephanie, 277*n*49
Timmins, Nicholas, 319
Tomkins, Richard, 116*n*32
Toner, Mike, 481, 482
Towers, John, 577
Towill, Denis R., 304*n*24
Toyoda, Sakichi, 409
Trachtenberg, Jeffrey A., 86
Treffiletti, Cory, 475
Treville, Suzanne, 219*n*4
Trimble, Chris, 224
Trinkle, Bob, 382*n*15, 382*n*17, 428*n*48
Trudel, Remi, 122*n*51
Tsui, Sally P.M., 638
Tucker, Sundeep, 22
Tyrell, Paul, 127*n*72

U

Ulrich, Karl T., 249
Ungoed-Thomas, Jon, 156*n*57, 555
Urban, Glen L., 238*n*36, 390*n*33, 395*n*46

V

Valentino-DeFreis, Jennifer, 152
Välikangas, Liisa, 11*n*27
Van Arnum, Patricia, 404*n*2
Van Bruggen, Gerrit, 153*n*44
Van Court, Tanya, 583
Van den Bosch, Margareta, 174
Van Duyn, Aline, 390*n*31
Van Horne, James C., 62*n*19
Van Tartwijk, Maarten, 408
Vara, Vaujini, 384
Vargo, Stephen L., 255*n*3
Vascellaro, Jessica E., 18

Vásquez, Xose, 199*n*23
Vence, Deborah, L., 76
Verganti, Robert, 226*n*20
Viemeister, Tucker, 242
Vigerie, Patrick, 71*n*1
Von Hippell, Eric, 233*n*28, 233*n*29
Voser, Peter, 408
Vranica, Suzanne, 257*n*7, 391*n*38
Vrenica, Suzanne, 391*n*41

W

Wagoner, G. Richard Jr., 508
Wagstyl, Stefan, 224
Wakabayashi, Daisuke, 261
Walker, Orville C. Jr., 230*n*25, 231*n*26, 309, 422*n*36
Walsh, Kate, 286
Walton, Sam, 539–540, 542, 544
Wang Hongbiiao, 580
Wang Shuxin, 637
Wansley, Brant, 280*n*55
Ward, Andrew, 126*n*67, 188, 310
Warm, Greg, 635
Warrell, Helen, 86
Watanabe, Hiroyuki, 506
Waters, Richard, 24, 202*n*35, 325, 394, 576
Watson, Thomas J., 569
Watson, Thomas J. Jr., 569
Webber, Charlotte, 483
Weber, J., 337*n*26
Weber, Joseph, 53, 308*n*35
Weber, Karl, 135*n*11
Weber, Klaus, 133*n*5
Webster, Frederick E., 2*n*1, 8*n*18, 11*n*28, 15*n*38, 197*n*19, 373*n*1
Webster, Frederick E. Jr., 189*n*6
Weigend, Andreas, 609

Weinberg, Stuart, 18
Weinstein, Richard, 583
Weinswig, Deborah, 566
Weintraub, Arlene, 122*n*54, 387*n*26
Weiss, Richard, 419
Weitzman, Hal, 198
Welch, Andrew, 278
Welch, David, 238*n*37, 409, 438*n*3
Welch, Jack, 566
Welford, Richard, 634*n*29
Wensley, Robin, 9*n*20, 53*n*14
Whitehead, Mark, 304*n*25
Whitman, Margaret C., 602
Whitney, Patrick, 512
Whoriskey, John, 520, 523, 530
Wierenga, Berend, 153*n*44
Wiessman, Gerrit, 294*n*4
Wiggins, Jenny, 100, 190*n*8, 200*n*31, 279, 291, 321, 415
Williams, Simon, 581
Williamson, Hugh, 80*n*18
Williamson, Peter J., 345*n*35
Willman, John, 25*n*59
Wilson, Hugh, 308*n*33
Wilson, William T., 501
Wind, Jerry, 153*n*45
Winding, Richard, 204*n*43
Winer, Russell S., 49, 107*n*11, 109*n*17, 115*n*30, 424*n*37, 425*n*40, 427*n*42
Wingfield, Nick, 325
Winnett, Robert, 344*n*34
Witzel, Morgan, 208*n*48
Wolf, Martin, 555
Womack, James P., 295*n*9, 304*n*20
Wong, Elyssa, 629*n*6
Wong, Kevin, 630
Wong, Phyllis, 636
Woo, Stu, 339
Woodruff, David, 272*n*34

Woodruff, Robert B., 98*n*49
Woolf, Marie, 555
Workman, John P., 420*n*29, 420*n*30, 420*n*32, 421*n*34, 426*n*41, 428*n*44
Worley, Christopher, 413*n*16
Worthen, Ben, 285*n*2
Wright, Robert, 214
Wrighton, Jo, 629*n*12
Wu, Helen, 636*n*39
Wurster, Thomas S., 138*n*19

Y

Yanai, Moshe, 575
Yang Rong, 577
Yankelovich, Daniel, 73*n*8, 74*n*9
Yates, Darin S., 605, 607
Yee, Amy, 195*n*17
Yip, George S., 433*n*56
Young, Clifford E., 385*n*21
Young, D., 101*n*52
Young, Michael N., 627, 638
Yu, Larry, 455*n*27
Yun Jong Yong, 512
Yung, Chester, 192*n*9

Z

Zalesne, E. Kinney, 96*n*43
Zaltman, Gerald, 149*n*34, 175*n*16
Zellner, Wendy, 7, 171, 269
Zheng Shiling, 496
Zimmerman, Ann, 169*n*10
Zoltak, James, 629*n*9
Zoltners, A.A., 351*n*7
Zook, Chris, 232*n*27
Zuckerberg, Mark, 471–475

Subject Index

A

Abrasive Systems Division (ASD), 442
Accessible memory, 138
Activity-based costing (ABC), 330
Adidas AG, 22, 310
Advertisements, 83
Advertising strategy
    See also Promotion strategy
    creative themes for, 362–363
    Internet-based, 363, 364
    measuring effectiveness of, 365–366, 367
    media/scheduling decisions, 363, 364
    objectives, budgeting for, 360–362
    overview of, 359–360
    role of agencies in, 363, 364–365
    statistics on, 350–351
Agentrics, 306
Agile supply chains, 304
Airbus, 211
Aleve, 326–327
Alexa Internet Services, 608
Alinea Restaurant, 319
Alliances, in organizational relationships,
    202–203
Almarai, 279
Amazon, 24, 37, 338, 339, 608–613
American Airlines, 163, 182, 340, 341
American Marketing Association
    (AMA), 120, 255
Anadarko, 207
Analytical positioning, 182
Android, 188
Anheuser-Busch, 273
Apple, 188, 191, 225, 255–256, 262, 290,
    307, 323–324, 325, 330–331
Apps, 191
Aquafina, 254
ArcelorMittal, 38–39, 183
Astra/Merck, 81
Astron Clinica, 190
AT&T, 196
A.T. Kearney, 320
Audi AG, 170
Autodesk, 163
Avon Cosmetics, 300–301, 355
Avon Products Inc., 463
Azco, 310

B

BabyNes, 244
Bait and switch, 338
Bajaj, 195
Banana Republic, 306

Bazaar-Voice, 142
Belo Corp., 237
Ben & Jerry's, 150, 256, 277
Benetton, 293
Bestfoods, 277
Beverage Partners Worldwide, 203
"Big I, small i" innovation, 228
Bill Me Later, 55
BIOC, 213
Bird, 279
BlackBerry, 18
Black swans, 134
BMW, 175, 257, 267, 576–577
BMW Mini, 77
Boeing, 80, 195, 197–198, 211, 230, 380
Borders Group Inc., 339
Boston Consulting Group, 260
Botswana, 212
BP, 193, 202, 207, 213, 421
Brand Asset Valuator (BAV), 265
Brand building, 354
Brand management. *See* Strategic brand
    management
Brand positioning analysis, 265
Brands
    challenges in managing, 257–258
    co-branding, licensing, 277
    defined, 255
    line extension for, 275–276
    management responsibility, 258–260
    managing, 260–262
    measuring equity of, 265–266
    portfolio management of, 271–275
    strategic role of, 255–257
    theft of, 280–281
    tracking performance of, 262–264
BRICPlus countries, 343
British Aerospace, 211
British Airports Authority (BAA), 546–555
British Telecom (BT), 196
Burberry PLC, 270
Bush Boake Allen (BBA), 233
Business(es)
    composition of, 13–14
    market-driven strategies for, 10–16
Buyer diversity, 168–169
Buyers. *See* Customers
BuzzLogic, 280

C

Cadbury, 256, 415, 458
California Credit Life Insurance Group
    (CCLI), 555–563

Call centers, 112
Canadian Appliance Manufacturing Co. Ltd.
    (CAMCO), 486–488
Cannabalization, 226
Capabilities
    classifying, 8–9
    of organization, 6–8
Carphone Warehouse, 204
Carrefour, 310
Caterpillar Inc., 25, 296
Central American Holding Company
    (CARHO), 545
Centrica, 22
ChangYu, 279
Channels for services, 288, 289
Channel strategy
    changing, 300–302
    configuration of, 297–298
    conflict resolution for, 307–308
    conventional, 292, 293
    digital distribution, 295–296
    globalization, 306
    horizontal marketing systems, 295
    international distribution patterns for,
        310–314
    leadership, management in, 303–305
    legal, ethical considerations
        of, 308, 310
    maps for, 298
    multichanneling, 306–307
    overview of, 290–291
    performance of, 308, 309
    relationships in, 305–306
    selecting, 298–300
    vertical marketing system
        (VMS), 292–295
Chevron, 213
Chief marketing officer (CMO), 438–439
Children, targeting, 100
China
    business opportunities, challenges
        in, 496–505
    counterfeiting in, 280–281
    distribution system in, 201
    emerging brands of, 279
    ethnographic study in, 149–150
    in global market, 21, 22
    income variations in, 45, 46
    and Korea, 211
    Microsoft in, 464, 465
    state-owned enterprises in, 214–215
    UPS in, 137
Christian Dior, 281
Chrysler, 207
Chrysler Jeep, 155
Circuit City Stores Inc., 331–332

Cisco Systems Inc., 37
Citigroup, 313
Clayton Act, 338
Cloud computing, 24
Cluster analysis, 94
CNPC, 213
Co-branding, 277
Coca-Cola, 51, 169, 203, 205, 219, 224,
    254, 257, 276, 310
Colgate-Palmolive, 320–321
Commoditization, 38
Communication, in marketing plan, 445
Competition-oriented pricing, 340
Competitive box, 36
Competitor intelligence, 6
Competitors, analysis of, 99
Competitors, key, 52–54
Complex systems products, 249
ConAgra, 337
Concept testing, 237–238, 239
Confused positioning, 182
Consumer. *See* Customers
Consumer Goods Pricing Act, 338
Corning, 202
Corporate branding, 267
Corporate social responsibility (CSR), 25, 26
Corporations
    and ethical behavior, 23–26
    market-driven strategies for, 10–16
Costco, 268, 270
Cost-oriented pricing, 339–340
Cowgirl Chocolates, 588–599
Crest SpinBrush, 605–608
Cross-classification analyses, 90–91
Cross-functional relationships, 180
Cross-functions, 6
CueCat, 237
Culture
    differences in, 207
    of innovation, 227
    as learning process, 139
    within organizations, 408
Customer business development (CBD), 375
Customer lifetime value (CLV), 9, 107–108
Customer Relationship Management (CRM)
    See also Ethics
    and CLV, 107–108
    and corporate reputation, 118–128
    customer value, competitive positioning,
        127–130
    and database marketing, 106–107
    defensive, 126
    defining, 125
    developing strategy for, 108–112
    development of, 109–110
    drivers of, 125
    implementation of, 110–112
    levels of, 108–109
    and marketing strategy, 17
    and market segmentation, 94

overview of, 104–105
and purchase behavior, 83–85
shared value in, 127
and social responsibility, 118–130
strategic, 126–127
and strategic marketing, 115–118, 450–451
value chain strategy for, 114–115
and value creation process, 112–115
websites for, 113
Customers
    analysis of, 98
    de-selecting, 115, 117
    driven by, 8–10
    and ethics, privacy issues, 155–157
    focus on, 5
    forming groups of, 93–95
    group identification of, 89–93
    identifying, describing, 45–46
    illustrations of, 91–93
    linking sensibilities of, 10
    needs, preferences of, 81–85
    in organizational relationships, 199–202
    perceiving value, 8–9
    price sensitivity of, 326–329
    profiles for, 48
    purchase stages of, 47
    research on, 181–182
    retention of, 355–356
    social media feedback from, 142
    value for, 113
Customer value mapping (CVM), 327–329
Customized products, 249
Cutco, 355

D

The Dad, 81
Daimler, 121
Daimler-Benz, 207, 271–272
Dashboard, marketing management, 458–461
Database marketing, 106–107, 151–152,
    155–156
Data mining, 91
Dba.dk, 55
DeBeers, 212, 294
Deceptive pricing, 338
Decision support system (DSS), 153
Dell Inc., 26, 214, 280, 285, 302, 393
Demand-oriented pricing, 340
Denizen, 171
Dentsu, 365
Diamond Foods, 274
Digital Convergence Corp., 237
Digital distribution channels, 295–296
Digital marketing strategy
    decisions for, 394–395
    development of, 390–393
    expanding initiatives in, 389–390
    Internet objectives for, 393–394

measuring effectiveness of, 395–396
opportunities, risks in, 395
Direct distribution, 288–289
Direct marketing, 351–352
Direct marketing strategies
    advantages of, 400
    catalogs, direct mail, 397–398
    development of, 401
    direct response media, 399–400
    kiosk shopping, 400
    mobile devices as, 398, 399
    online shopping, 400
    placecasting, 399
    purpose of, 396
    reasons for using, 396–397
    telemarketing, 398–399
Disney, 100, 277, 627–638
Distribution functions, 286–288
Dominant customers, 200–201
Doubtful positioning, 182
Dreamliner, 197
Drybar, 95
DSM, 310
Dyson, 291

E

EasyJet, 286
EBay, 55
Ecoimagination, 248
Economic value modeling (EVM),
    328–329, 340
Efficient Consumer Response (ECR), 304
Eli Lilly, 208
EMEA (Europe, Middle East, Africa)
    market, 464
End-user customers, 199–200
Energizer, 266
E-procurement, 305
ESPN, 581–588
Essentials.com, 194
Estée Lauder, 296
E-tailing, 390
Ethics
    See also Customer Relationship
        Management (CRM)
    behavior, standards, 119–121
    and brand counterfeiting, 281
    of channel strategy, 308, 310
    codes, guidelines for, 123–124
    and corporate responsiveness, 23–26
    and CRM, 114, 118–130
    of de-selecting customers, 117
    drivers for, 121–122
    eco-scorecards, 462
    environmental alliances, 214
    and environmentalism, 257
    and information gathering, 155–157
    initiatives for, 124–125

intelligence gathering, 53
monitoring, control of, 124
and new-product development, 248
as organizational priority, 419
proactive responses to, 122–123
in sales strategy, 376
sustainability metrics, 457
targeting children, 100
and the tobacco industry, 345
Ethnographic study, observation, 148–150
Exrax, 22
ExxonMobil, 91, 213, 421

F

Facebook, 23, 152, 471–475
Fairtrade, 256
FedEx, 323, 381
Ferrovial, 547–554
Fiat, 437–438
Filterfresh, 522, 523–524
Financial analysis
break-even, 65, 66
contribution, 65
key financial ratios for, 62
for marketing planning, control, 62–70
model of, 65
planning process for, 67
supplemental, 67–70
units of, 62, 63–64
First Sight, 142
Flavia, 522, 524
Flexcar, 129
Flip, 37, 51
Ford, 201, 472
Forecasts, of sales, 329
Forever 21, 286
Fresh & Easy, 38, 142, 533–537
Frito Lay, 254, 390
Frog design, 139
Fuji, 202, 204
Fulfillment By Amazon, 608
Functional MRI (fMRI) technology, 157

G

Game theory, 332, 333
Gap, 183, 199, 260, 276, 306
Gatorade, 173
Gazprom, 22, 213
GE, 224
Geely, 279
General Electric Appliances, 486–495
General Electric Co., 114, 120, 149, 228,
231, 248, 257, 313, 461
General Motors, 51, 163, 236, 423
Generic (market-pull) products, 249
Geofencing technology, 399

Gillette, 169, 201, 259, 269
Global account management (GAM), 434
Global Fund, 257
Global marketing
branding in retail, 277–278
and brand management, 261, 279
channel strategy, 306, 311–314
and cultural anthropology, 139
escalating, 20–21
expansion, emergence of, 22, 224
global account management (GAM), 434
and innovation, 232
international call centers, 112
and interorganizational relationships, 193
market-driven strategy for, 431
and market targeting, 170–172
pricing issues in, 343–346
strategic marketing in, 464
strategy adaptation in China, 465
Global Social Compliance program, 310
Global Trade Alert, 212
Gome, 279
GoodGuide, 127
Google, 24, 156, 188, 194, 219–220, 227,
257, 281, 349, 398, 446, 472–473
GoreTex, 13
Governments, and business relationships,
211–215
Groupon, 392, 394
GSI Commerce, 55

H

H&M, 137, 174, 286, 293, 310, 449–450
Haier, 279
Harley-Davidson, 199
Harrah's Entertainment, 147
Harry Potter books, 86, 172
Healthy Choice, 277
Heineken, 291
Heinz, 311
Henkel, 320
Hero-Honda Splendour, 313
Hewlett-Packard, 14, 208, 214, 230, 257,
323, 373–374
High-risk products, 249
Hindustan Lever, 313
Home Depot, 280, 306, 337, 563–569
Home Depot Supply, 565
Hong Kong Disneyland (HKD), 627–638
H.R. Chally, 374–375
Hyatt Hotels and Resorts, 76

I

IBM, 141, 155, 186–187, 210, 214, 232,
257, 258, 267, 375, 569–576
iCloud, 24

Identity implementation, 268
IDEO, 242
Ikea, 289
Illycaffe Group, 205
Incentives, 445
Income variations, 45
India
auto market in, 345–346
business opportunities, challenges in,
496–505
channel strategy in, 313
CRM efforts in, 128
in global market, 22
Information distribution, 138
Information gathering, and ethics, 155–157
Information technology, in
interorganizaitonal relationships, 192
Infosys Technologies, 319
Innovation
in advertising, 364
analysis, of concept, 238–240
and brand engagement, 259
in branding, 269
branding in retail, 291
cannabalization, 226
in channel strategy, 301–302
and commericalization, 247–248
and competition, 18
in CRM, 129
culture, strategy for, 227–229
as customer-driven process, 219–226
and customer needs, 40
and customer value, 220–221
and database marketing, 107
disruptive, 37
evaluation, of concept, 237–238
generating ideas, 231–235, 236
marketing strategy, testing, 243–247
and market segmentation, 76
and market-sensing processes, 136
new-product opportunities, 221–223
new-product planning, 226–231
overview of, 218–219
placecasting, 399
in pricing strategy, 319
product development process, 240–243
screening, of concept, 235–237
social media as, 392, 394
in strategic positioning, 174
successful initiatives in, 223–225
through collaboration, 225–226
types of, 219–220
variations in new-product planning,
248–249
in work organizations, 406
Insight Express, 150
Intel, 139, 149–150, 325–326
Intelligence gathering, 53
Interbrand, 257
InterContinental Hotels, 76

Interface Inc., 462
Intermediate customers, 199
Internal marketing, 446–448
Internal partnerships, 204
International Business Machines (IBM), 569–576
International call centers, 112
Internet
  See also Digital marketing strategy
  advertising, marketing on, 352
  attacks on brands, 280
  branding, 279
  channel hopping on, 307
  channel migration to, 301
  cloud computing marketing impact, 24
  competition on, 55
  conducting marketing research on, 150–151, 152
  counterfeiting on, 281
  dynamics of, 22–23
  e-procurement in, 305
  resources on, 148
  return exchange for, 115
  social media efforts on, 392–396
  used by salespeople, 384
  and Web market segments, 86
Interorganizational relationships
  collaboration potential, 193–196
  control, evaluation of, 208–209
  enhancing value in, 187–189
  environmental complexity of, 189
  exiting from, 209–210
  management of, 206–208
  managing, 205
  objectives of, 205–206
  partnering capabilities of, 208
  and skill, resource gaps, 190–193
  strategy for, 190
Interpretations, mutually informed, 138
iPhone, 323–324, 325, 330–331
Ipsco Inc., 22
iTunes Match, 24

J

Janssen-Cilag, 319
Japan, 212
JC Penney, 310
Johnson Controls, 201
Joint ventures, 203–204
Juan Valdez Café, 279
JUKARI, 179

K

Kellogg, 277
Keurig Inc., 519–532
Kimberly Clark, 219

Kiosk shopping, 400
Kmart, 15, 262
Knitted Dove, 142
Knowledge-based worker, 407
Knowledge management, 154–155
Knowledge resources
  creating new marketing information, 148–151
  marketing information resources, 143–146
  marketing information sources, 146–148
  and marketing information systems, 151–153
  overview of, 140
  research studies, 143
  scanning processes for, 140–143
Kodak, 9, 34–35, 168, 319
Korea, 211
Kraft, 311
Krogers, 268
Kurant/Pro, 55

L

LCafe, 141
Lean supply chain, 304
Learning organizations, 135, 136
Lenovo, 22, 38, 279, 280
Levi Strauss & Co, 73, 171, 310
Lexus, 296
LG, 211
Li & Fung, 211, 310
Licensing, 277
Limited Brands, 274–275
Linens 'n Things, 306
Li-Ning, 279
Lipton, 277
Liz Claiborne, 301
L.L. Bean, 397
Lockheed Martin, 195
Loctite Corporation, 329
"The Long Tail," 108
L'Oréal, 399
Louis Vuitton, 281, 296
Lowe's, 563–569

M

Magnetic resonance imaging (MRI), 157
Mahindra & Mahindra, 195
Mail concept test format, 239
Mail-in rebates, 367–368
Male shoppers, 81
Management information systems (MISs), 152–153
Marriott, 199, 200
Market-driven strategy
  aligning organization with market, 414–416

  centralization vs. decentralization, 420, 421
  characteristics of, 8
  classifying capabilities, 8–9
  components, framework of, 11–14
  of corporations, businesses, 10–16
  as cross-functional process, 416–418
  customer-driven, 8–10
  departments for, 418–419
  designing, 404–405
  employee motivation in, 413
  entering new market, 3
  evaluating organization designs, 423
  functions vs. processes, 416
  global issues of, 430–434
  integration vs. diffusion, 420, 421
  logic of, 4
  managing organizational process, 410–411
  market-focused design, 425–426
  matrix design, 426–427
  and networking, 11
  new challenges for, 2, 4
  new era in, 20–26
  new marketing roles, 427–430
  organizational agility, flexibility, 411–413
  organization trends in, 405–413
  organizing, 421–423
  process of, 16–20
  structure for, 414, 415
  structuring resources for, 423–430
  venture marketing organizations (VMO), 428, 429
Marketing decision-support systems (MDSS), 153
Marketing information
  and knowledge resources, 140–153
  and learning processes, 134–140
  and market-sensing processes, 135, 136
  overview of, 132–134
Marketing intelligence, 153–154
Marketing management dashboard, 458–461
Marketing metrics
  advertising, media, web, 469
  brand equity, 469
  competitive, customer, 468
  consumer, 469
  customer profitability, 468
  financial, 469
  innovation, 470
  internal market, 470
  internal process, 470
  pricing issues in, 468
  product, portfolio, 468
  profitability, 468
  promotion, 469
  sales, channel, 468
  using, 455–460
Marketing planning, 441–442

Marketing strategy process
  competitive space, segmentation, 16–17
  and CRM, 17
  designing, 17, 18–19
  implementing, managing, 20
  program development for, 19
Market insights, 141
Market learning processes, barriers to, 138–140
Market opportunity, 56
Market orientation, 4–5
Market potential, 54–55
Markets, and competitive space
  challenges to, 37–39
  competitive forces, 51
  competitor analysis, 48–50, 51–53
  defining, analyzing product-markets, 40–45
  environmental influences on, 46
  estimating size, 54–57
  indentifying, describing buyers, 45–46
  matching needs, benefits, 39–40
  overview, 34–35
  purchase stages, 47
  rapid change in, 37
  strategies for, 35–36
  visions for future, 58–59
Market segmentation
  activities, decisions in, 77–78
  approaches to identifying, 88
  buyers' needs, preferences, 82–83
  and CRM, 83–85, 94
  customer group identification, 89–93
  danger of neglecting, 90
  defining, 77–78
  fine strategies for, 95–97
  forming groups for, 93–95
  illustrations of, 91–93
  levels, types of, 73–74
  and the male shopper, 81
  and market characteristics, 80
  market-driven strategy for, 74–77
  overview, 71–73
  and personal characteristics, 79–80
  and product use situation, 80–82
  selecting strategy for, 97–102
  targeting, positioning, 75–77, 85–88
  value opportunities, new market space, 75
  variables in, 78
Market sensing capabilities, 10
Market-sensing processes, 135
Market share, 56
Market targeting
  in emerging markets, 165–167
  in global markets, 170–172
  in growth markets, 167–168
  in mature markets, 168–170
  overview of, 17, 162–163
  strategies for, 163–165
Market testing, 181–182, 244–247

Marks & Spencer, 310
Marriott, 76, 89, 149
Masterfoods USA, 289
Mattel, 344
Maturiteen, 81
McDonald's, 169, 254, 313, 317
Mechanical Turk, 608, 610, 611–612
Megabus, 129
Metrosexual, 81, 310
Microsoft, 26, 188–189, 257, 274, 290, 310, 434, 461, 464, 465
Millennial Generation, 413
Miller Brewing, 85
Minute Maid, 277
Mitsubishi Heavy Industries, 212
Mobile virtual network operators (MVNOs), 289
Modern man, 81
Monster.com, 279
Morgan Stanley, 141
Mothercare, 307
Motorola, 241, 446
Moxie.com, 142
Multichanneling, 306–307
MySpace, 23, 473

N

Nanjing Automobile, 579–580
Nano, 345–346
Nanophase Technologies Corporation, 613–627
Need recognition, 354
Nespresso, 244, 291, 528
Nestlé, 203, 224, 244, 267, 272–273, 278–279, 312, 528
Neuromarketing, 157
New-product placement, 226–231
Nielsen Buzzmetrics, 152
Nielsen Group, 148
Nike, 262, 266, 277, 310
Nikon, 80
Nissan, 195
Nissan Motor Co., 240
Nokia Corporation, 177–179, 188–189, 224, 241, 257, 313
Novaton, 334, 335
Novet, 334, 335
Numis Network, 163, 164
Nuru, 313–314

O

Objective inquiry, 137–138
Objectives, corporate, 13
Ocado, 194
Office Depot, 337
One Laptop Per Child (OLPC) program, 25, 26

1-800-Flowers, 471
Oneworld, 192
Open Graph, 473
Open Handset Alliance, 188
Oracle, 208, 461
Organizational design, 444
Organizational relationships
  with end-user customers, 199–200
  with intermediate customers, 199
  internal partnerships, 204
  joint ventures in, 203–204
  strategic alliances for, 202–203
  with strategic customers, 200–202
  supplier, 197–199
Organizational stretch, 449–450
Orphan brands, 274
Outliers, 134
Outsourcing, 197–199
Overpositioning, 182

P

Palm Pilot, 262
Pandora, 473
Pantone Color Institute, 141
Patchi, 279
Pay By Touch, 107
Payless ShoeSource, 458
PayPal, 55
PDVSA, 213
Pentax, 168
Pentium, 325–326
PepsiCo, 35–36, 51, 205, 249, 254–255
Perceptual maps, 94–95
Performance, and market orientation, 6
Personal selling, 351
Petrobas, 213
Petronas, 213
Pfizer, 163
Pharmacia, 208
Philips, 313, 406–407
Piggly Wiggly, 107
Placecasting, 399
PlanetTran, 129
Platform products, 249
Poker, 259
Positioning. *See* Strategic positioning
Post-It Notes, 226
PRA (Pacific Rim, Asia) market, 464
Predatory pricing, 338, 339
Price elasticity, 327
Price fixing, discrimination, 337–338
Pricing strategy
  and competitor analysis, 331–332
  cost analysis, 329–331
  customer price sensitivity, 326–329
  determining specific prices, policies, 338, 339–341
  flexibility, cycles of, 342–343

Pricing strategy—*Cont.*
  flexibility in, 333–334, 335
  and global competition, 345–346
  high-active, high-passive, 336–337
  impact of emerging markets, 343–345
  legal, ethical considerations
      of, 337–338
  low-active, low-passive, 337
  objectives of, 324–326, 332
  overview of, 19, 317–318
  and positioning, 320–322
  positioning, visibility, 334, 336
  and the Prisoner's Dilemma, 333
  in the recession, 321
  restriction in global markets, 343, 344
  role of, 318–326
  segmentation of, 341
  selecting, 333–338
  selecting, altering, 323–324, 325
  situations requiring action, 322
  value-chain pricing, 341–342
Prisoner's Dilemma, 333
Private branding, 268
Processes, and structure, 10
Process-intensive products, 249
Procter and Gamble, 133, 139, 189, 194,
      200, 201, 224, 232, 246, 247, 267,
      269, 274, 320, 321, 326–327, 354,
      355, 374–375, 382, 404–405, 431,
      434, 473, 600–608
Product, defined, 255
Product elimination, 271
Product life-cycle (PLC) analysis, 264
Product life cycle (PLC) stages, 165
Product-market, defined, 39
Product-markets
  forming, 42–44
  guidelines for, 41–42
  illustrative structure of, 44
  structure of, 40–41
Product-market structure, 169
Product performance analysis, 264
Product placement, 279, 351
Product Red, 257
Progressive Insurance, 39–40
Promotion strategy
  See also Advertising strategy
  budget for, 356–358
  communication objectives of, 354–356
  component strategies, 358
  vs. conventional advertising, 366, 367
  designing, 353–354
  effectiveness of, 359
  integrating, implementing, 358–359
  nature, scope of, 367–368
  overview of, 19
  purpose of, 349–350
  role of components in, 356
  types of, 350–353
Prototypes, 241

Public relations, 353
Purex, 320

Q

Quaker Oats, 254
Quanta Computer, 26
Quick-build products, 249
Quick Metal, 329
Quintiles Transnational, 10

R

Radio frequency identification (RFID),
      156, 545
Radio Shack, 237
Rainforest Alliance, 256
Ranbaxy Laboratories, 22
Random House, 363
Rapleaf, 152
Ray-Ban, 80
Rebates, 367–368
Reebok, 179
Relationships. *See* Strategic relationships
Remix policy, 544–545
Renault, 195
Rent.com, 55
Reputation, corporate, 118–128
Research, customer and competitor, 181
Research in Motion Ltd. (RIM), 18
Resources, corporate, 13
Retrosexual, 81
Return Exchange, 115
Revenue/cost analysis, 384
Reverse auction pricing, 340
Robinson-Patman Act, 338
Rolex, 296
Rollerblade, 230
Rosneft, 193
Rover Automobile, 576–581
ROW (Rest of World) market, 464
Royal Doulton, 451
Royal Dutch Shell, 213, 408
Russia, 22, 193
Ryanair, 286, 301, 317–318

S

Safeway, 535
Sales and effort response models, 385
Salesforce.com, 24, 384
Sales forecasts, 55–56, 57
Sales promotion
  activities of, 368–370
  advantages, limitations of, 370–371
  overview of, 351
  strategy for, 371

Sales strategy
  See also Digital marketing strategy
  continuing importance of, 373–374
  defining process of, 380–381
  evaluation, control in, 387–389
  managing salespeople for, 385–387
  organizational design for, 382–383
  perspective on, 374–376
  relationships in, 380
  requirements of, 376–377
  role of selling in, 377–378
  sales force deployment, 383–385
  types of jobs in, 378–379
  using channels, 381–382
Sales tax, 339
Salton, 528
Samsung Electronics, 142, 199, 202, 211,
      511–519
Sara Lee, 528
Sears, 268
Segment targeting, 164
Segway, 165
Senseo Coffee Pod System, 528
Sephora, 399
Shanghai Automotive in China (SAIC),
      578–580
Shell, 142, 458
Shopkick, 399
Shopping.com, 55
Siemens, 224, 418, 419
Simple Storage Service, 608, 609, 612
Singapore Airlines, 354
Single-factor model, of salesforce, 384
Skoda, 270, 274
Skype, 55
Skyteam, 192
SlimFast, 277
SmartShop technology, 107
SoBe Beverages, 35–36
Social media, and marketing, 142, 391–392,
      393, 471–475
Society of Competitive Intelligence
      Professionals, 53
Sony, 199, 244, 260–261, 290, 390
Southwest Airlines, 7, 280, 323, 337
Spotify, 24
Standard Chartered Bank, 191–192
Stanley Tools, 230
Staples, 306
Star Alliance, 192
Starbucks, 205, 256, 266, 317, 399, 429,
      519, 524
Starwood, 76
Strategic account management (SAM),
      201–202
Strategic brand management
  analysis of, 262–265
  brand identity, 266–268
  equity measurement, management,
      265–266

leveraging strategy for, 275–281
managing, improving, 268–271
overview of, 254–255
of portfolio, 271–275
Strategic business unit (SBU), 14, 260, 262
Strategic customer management. *See*
    Customer Relationship Management
    (CRM)
Strategic marketing
    audit for, 451–454
    CMO responsibility in, 438–439
    and CRM, 115–118
    evaluation, control of, 450–454
    global issues of, 463–466
    implementation, control of, 437–438
    marketing metrics in, 455–460
    measuring performance, 454–463
    overview of, 15–16
    plan implementation, process, 439–450
Strategic marketing planning
    considerations for, 29–30
    outline for, 30–31
    overview of, 29
    relationships, frequency in, 29
Strategic market segmentation. *See* Market
    segmentation
Strategic positioning
    determining effectiveness of, 180–183
    faulty, 182–183
    overview of, 17
    selecting concept for, 175–176
    strategy for, 172–174
Strategic relationships
    global integrated enterprise, 210–211
    governments' roles in, 211–215
    inter-nation collaborations, 211
    interorganizational, 187–196
    organizational, 196–203
    overview of, 186–187
Structure, and processes, 10
Stubhub, 55
Stumbleupon, 55
Subway, 313
Supply chain strategy, 303–304, 538–541
Suzlon energy, 22
Suzuki Motor, 206–207, 313
Sweet & Sassy, 100

T

Target, 260, 268
Targeting. *See* Market targeting
Tata Steel, 22, 345–346

TCL, 279
Technology, 21, 22, 258
Technology-push products, 249
Telecom, 50
Tesco International, 3, 38, 142, 151, 289, 310,
    311–312, 313, 433, 532–537, 546
Test marketing, 181–182, 244–247
Threat-Tracker, 152
3G mobile phone services, 239
3M, 226, 442
Tide, 355
Timex, 80
TNT, 310
Tobacco industry, 345
Toshiba, 244
Toyota, 51, 141, 257, 304, 366, 367, 409,
    505–511
Toys'R'Us, 306
Trader Joe's, 311
Transformational innovations, 222–223
True Blood series, 259
Tsingtau, 279
Tui, 293–294
TurboTax, 475
Twilight books, 259
Twitter, 23, 142, 152
Tyco Healthcare Group L.P., 221
Tylenol, 271

U

UltraViolet, 412
Unbox, 608
Underpositioning, 182
Unilever, 128, 151, 256, 259, 267, 277,
    364–365
United Parcel Service (UPS), 137
United Spirits, 279
Upjohn, 208
U.S. Automobile Association (USAA), 79
U.Sl Surgical Corporation (USS), 229–230
U.S. Surgical Corporation (USS), 221

V

Value-added chain, 50–51
Value-chain strategy
    channels for. *See* Channel strategy
    and CRM, 114–115
    overview of, 19, 284–285
    strategic role of, 285–290
Van Houtte, 523

Venture marketing organizations (VMO),
    428, 429
Verizon, 461
Vertical marketing system
    (VMS), 292–295
Victoria's Secret, 267, 275, 306, 398
Viral marketing, 363
Virgin Group, 277, 278
Virgin Mobile, 289
Vision, corporate, 12–13
Vodaphone, 139, 224, 313
Voiceover Internet Protocol (VoIP), 167
Volkswagen, 206–207, 230, 270, 276

W

Wahaha, 279
Wal-Mart, 15, 21, 51, 90, 169, 199, 256,
    268, 269, 310, 311, 313, 331–332,
    382, 390, 456, 457, 535, 537,
    539–547
WD-40, 149
Web 2.0, 23
Wentworth Industrial Cleaning Supplies
    (WICS), 475–486
Whole Foods, 162, 311
Williams Sonoma, 306–307
Wisp, 320–321
World Trade Organization, 212
World Wrestling Entertainments
    (WWE), 281
Wyeth, 388

X

Xerox, 25, 202, 203–204
Xtreme! Coolers, 277

Y

Yonghe King, 279
Young & Rubicam, 237, 265, 365
YouTube, 23

Z

Zappos.com, 176, 180
Zara, 174, 286, 293, 412
Zipcar, 129